FIFTY
GREAT WESTERN
ILLUSTRATORS

FIFTY GREAT WESTERN ILLUSTRATORS

A Bibliographic Checklist

by Jeff Dykes

NORTHLAND PRESS

To Martha — sweetheart, wife, partner

TABLE OF CONTENTS

LIST OF ILLUSTRATIONS

ACKNOWLEDGMENTS

MY FIRST AND SPECIAL THANKS go to W. B. (Bill) Thorsen of Chicago until recently the one-man dynamo responsible as publisher and editor for the *American Book Collector*. All fifty of the check lists, then titled "Tentative," appeared in the pages of ABC beginning in 1963. Bill was a critically constructive editor who questioned just about everything. He, along with my daughter Martha Dykes Goldsmith of Clarksville, Tennessee, was responsible for my including Lorence F. Bjorklund in the fifty.

Michael Harrison, noted collector and Western Americana scholar of Fair Oaks, California, checked each of the fifty lists against his own holdings and suggested additions to more than forty of them. My debt to him is big indeed.

Louis P. Merrill, rancher at Midlothian, Texas, was originally scheduled to be the co-compiler. I am not sure now as to which of us first mentioned that the book was needed and that we should tackle it. After the pressure of work on the ranch forced him to bow out, his continued interest helped keep me at it over the years.

John M. Carroll, author-historian of New Brunswick, New Jersey (but fellow native Texan) was very helpful with the lists of Bjorklund, Cisneros, Eggenhofer and Von Schmidt.

Walter E. Latendorf of the Mannados Bookshop in New York was primarily responsible for my including Philip R. Goodwin and Mahonri Young in the fifty. Walter, and after he died Helen (Teri) Card, sold me many of the rarities included in the lists. Both were western illustrator enthusiasts who kept the Mannados shelves well stocked.

Peggy Christian of Los Angeles, J. E. (Jack) Reynolds of Van Nuys, and Preston McMann of Portland, Oregon, were other dealers who contributed information and favored me when books with illustrations by my fifty were available in their stocks. Fred A. Rosenstock of Denver, Byron L. Troyer of Fort Myers, Florida, and James F. Carr of New York City are worthy of special mention among the many other dealers who helped me build the collection.

It was my paisano J. Frank Dobie that first called my attention to Ben Carlton Mead. Frank thought Ben was rather underrated as an illustrator and after studying his illustrations, I agreed.

Carl Hertzog of El Paso, premier designer-printer of Texas, introduced me to the work of Jose Cisneros and made numerous helpful suggestions on both the Cisneros and Tom Lea lists.

Steve Eckhart of Bethesda, Maryland, an ardent Russell collector, found a number of entries for me as he searched for Russell items. In addition, he put in a couple of hard Saturdays in my attic as we sorted and segregated the books of the fifty for easy reference.

Frank B. Beckman of Cincinnati did not bother with written suggestions — he bought books with illustrations by a number of my fifty that had not been included in the ABC tentative lists and mailed them to me with his compliments.

Betsy James (Mrs. Andrew) Wyeth suggested at least thirty additions to the tentative N. C. Wyeth list I had compiled for ABC. Ruth Koerner Oliver of Santa Barbara, California, suggested numerous additions to the tentative list I prepared for her father, W. H. D. Koerner. Vivian Dunton of Taos lent a hand with her father's list, and Katrina Sigsbee Fischer of Woodstock wrote confirming entries in her father's tentative list.

Ross Santee, a dear friend for the last ten years of his life, made many suggestions concerning his list and supplied (with his compliments) rare ephemeral items that I would have otherwise missed. I visited Harvey Dunn at his studio in Tenafly, New Jersey, several times to check my tentative list with him — he added a number of items and told entertaining stories of his experiences as a military illustrator in France during World War I. R. Farington (Bob) Elwell of Phoenix spun many stories of his association with Buffalo Bill on my visits to his home and studio. He put me on the track of, or provided, copies of a good many of the items on my want list. I was fortunate enough to receive an invitation to Frank Schoonover's 95th birthday party at the Delaware Art Museum at Wilmington. Our chat that day was brief as the crowd was large, but there had been others. His grandson Jack opened the Schoonover record book to me after his grandfather died, and it was most helpful in solving some identification problems among his entries. In the early days of the project I had mail contacts with Maynard Dixon, Ed Borein and Anton Otto Fischer on their lists. Harold Bugbee, a college classmate, not only helped with his own list but with that of his friend and advisor, Buck Dunton.

Stanley L. Wood divided his time between his native England and the United States. Biographical and bibliographical information about him was elusive indeed. Arthur Burton-Garbett of Morden, Surrey and England's only full-time professional book scout was my guide and counselor on two buying trips in his country. He was responsible for most of the information on Wood. R. A. Brimmel, bookseller of Hastings, England, found many Wood items for me over a number of years. J. A. Marks of the British Museum, London, arranged for my inspection of the Wood items in the collection there. A. E. Hookham of Shrewsbury and Richard Dalby and Brian Dayle both of London added bits of information. My old friend Vincent Starrett, great Chicago bookman, was an avid admirer of Wood's illustrations and visited with Wood both in London and Chicago. He supplied me with a copy of a part of his manuscript relating to Wood that had been left out of one of his books.

Each of the contemporary artists received a copy of their tentative list for review and revision. All of them responded in one way or another and their participation improved the lists. They are more accurate and more nearly complete as results of the data sent by them or members of their families or friends.

One of the features of each of the tentative lists in ABC was an invitation to the readers to send in additional biographical and bibliographical information. The response was beyond expectations — collectors, dealers and librarians came through with many additions to my lists. I am sure my records are incomplete but I do have notes of contributions by B. W. (Bill) Allred of Tooele, Utah; John F. Apgar, Jr. of Brookside, New Jersey; Charles M. Allmond III of Wilmington, Delaware; Mrs. Edgar Baker of Hamilton, Ohio; James G. Baker of Lubbock, Texas; Thomas B. T. Baldwin, Jr. of Media, Pa.; Les Beitz of Austin, Texas; Colonel Bill Bell of Arlington, Virginia; W. W. Boddie of Freeport, Texas; Abe Brayer of New York City; Velma C. Brown of Elkhorn, Wisconsin; Mr. and Mrs. Fisher A. (Pete and Nancy) Buell, Jr. of Mystic, Connecticut; Mrs. Edward A. Cameron of Chapel Hill, North Carolina; Leland D. Case of Tucson, Arizona; Mrs. Lael C. Coates of Austin, Texas; Harold G. Davidson of Santa Barbara; Bob Dawson of Hazlet, New Jersey; James R. Davis of Dayton, Tennessee; Brian W. Dippie of Victoria, British Columbia, Canada; Dr. E. Lee Worsett of Indianola, Mississippi; Mrs. Eleanor P. Ediger of Calgary, Alberta, Canada; John Edwards of Stratford, Connecticut; Edward F. Ellis of Buffalo, New York; Mrs. Dorothy E. Farmer of Flint, Michigan; Lewis Ferbrache of Berkeley, California; Alvin Fick of Fort Johnson, New York; Mrs. Paul E. Files of Thomaston, Maine; Dick Flood of Mesa, Arizona; Elizabeth Fowler of Houston, Texas; Mrs. Thomas Gallender of Corpus Christi, Texas; Arthur Goldsmith, Jr. of Clarksville, Tennessee; Frederick L. Grillo of Orange, Connecticut; J. Evetts Haley of Canyon, Texas; Richard C. Hamilton of Flagstaff, Arizona; Mrs. J. E. Hampton of Kingsbury, California; William H. Hensler of Aurora, Colorado; Peggy Holchak of Houston, Texas; William H. Holaday of Houston, Texas; M. Hornaday of Treasure Island, Florida; Bob Horvath of Harrisburg, Pennsylvania; Charlotte L. Howard of Bradford, Maine; David Howland of New Canaan, Connecticut; Mrs. M. B. (Doris) Huckle of East Jordan, Michigan; W. H. (Hutch) Hutchinson of Chico, California; Arthur Irwin, Jr. of Latham, Illinois; Frankie Johnson of Granada Hills, California; Phil Kovinick of Los Angeles.

Among other contributors are: Dean Krakel of Oklahoma City; Dick Krieg of Los Altos, California; K. S. Kurtenacker of Warrendale, Pennsylvania; Wright Lewis of Portland, Oregon; John Logan of Chicago; Lisabeth Lovelace of El Paso, Texas; A. W. Lovett of Plymouth, Massachusetts; Al Lowman of San Marcos, Texas; R. B. (Bob) Marsh of Topeka, Kansas; Thomas S. McNeill of Redondo Beach, California; James L. Mendlik of Brecksville, Ohio; Charles J. Meyers of Southfield, Michigan; Marion H. Miley of Greenfield, Ohio; Gertrude H. Muir of Tempe, Arizona; Colonel Tom Munnerlyn of Alexandria, Virginia;

Jack O'Reilly of San Francisco; Arthur P. Pacheco of Iowa City; A. E. Perry of Norman, Oklahoma; T. T. Perry of Charlestown, West Virginia; Donald M. Powell of Tucson, Arizona; Carl J. Pugliese of Yonkers, New York; D. C. Quinn of New Hartford, New York; Henry M. Reed of Bloomfield, New Jersey; Lawrence F. Reeves of New York City; Frederic G. Renner of Washington, D.C.; Hugh Ross of Belmont, California; Don Russell of Elmhurst, Illinois; Mrs. J. W. Rutland of Austin, Texas; Stephen R. Sanderson of Evanston, Illinois; Mabel L. (Mrs. Martin) Schneider of Buck Hill Falls, Pennsylvania; Mrs. Mary Scott of Morrisville, Pennsylvania; Raymond Spinney of Rochester, New Hampshire; Harve Stein of Noank, Connecticut; Brian D. Stilwell of Philadelphia; Patricia A. Sturm of Centerport, Long Island, New York; Mrs. Rose Tisdel of Alhambra, California; F. A. Trevors of Ventura, California; E. A. Tribe of Houston, Texas; Wilfred D. Webb of Austin, Texas; Miss Dolores Williams of Houston, Texas; Tasker H. Williams of Washington, D.C.; Aiken Wright of Houston, Texas; Stimson Wyeth of Needham, Massachusetts; Senator Ralph W. Yarborough of Austin, Texas, and Vivian York of Spruce Head, Massachusetts.

I was fortunate over the years in having two secretaries who could read my penciled manuscript and produce typed versions acceptable to my publishers. Miss Onienell Holliday of Texas and Washington, D.C. (Now Mrs. F. R. Olmsted of Green Valley, Arizona) saw me through the tentative lists for ABC. Mrs. Dale (Bea) Bormuth, my College Park neighbor and friend, has worked with me for nearly ten years in the revision of the lists for Northland. I am most grateful to Nell and Bea for their parts in making this book possible.

Publisher Paul Weaver looked at the bound copy of my tentative lists from ABC for about fifteen minutes before he said he would like to publish this book. I like that kind of decisiveness. Editor Jim Howard and his assistants Elyse Symes and Sandra Mahan were responsible for the finishing touches, and I do appreciate their efforts to eliminate the errors of commission.

INTRODUCTION

ILLUSTRATORS ARE AS TRULY HISTORIANS as writers and in depicting the life, action, character, legends, natural and man-made wonders of the West they have provided particularly worthwhile records. The publishers of Western history, biography, narratives, memoirs, fiction and verse have long recognized the merit of authentic illustrations for their historic value as well as in building sales appeal. These publishers have been most generous in the numbers and the quality of the illustrations provided their customers. A long list of distinguished artists known for their work on the Western subjects have made outstanding contributions to the permanent worth of the books they illustrated. This volume provides bibliographic check lists of the books illustrated by fifty of these artists.

Please note that no claim is made that the fifty artists selected are the best or greatest that ever pictured the West. In fact, one of the greatest of all Western artist-illustrators, Charles Marion Russell — his Northern Plains cowboys, horses and Indians have never been equaled — is not included. There is a logical explanation for the omission — a great bibliography (University of Nebraska Press, Lincoln) of Russell's published works by my close friend and associate, Frederic G. Renner and his compiling partner, Karl Yost, was issued in 1971. That bib records 3500 citations and provides far more information about the Montana cowboy artist's work than could have been included in a check list. Such watered-down duplication was deemed to be wasteful of time and space. However, Russell is included in one of the special features of the various check lists. The names of other artists (including Russell) in parentheses following an entry indicate the presence of illustrations by them. This provides a cross reference to the other check lists and it may lead the Russell collectors to items issued since the Renner-Yost bibliography went to press in 1966.

Why just fifty check lists? My publisher thought fifty was a good round number, and there is a limit to the entries that can be conveniently included between the covers of one book. My collection actually includes the printed works of fifty-six artists, and as a result of our mutual agreement to limit the book to fifty artists, I discarded the check lists of Jerry Bywaters, Dan Muller, Charles H. Owens, W. S. Phillips (El Comancho) and Remington Schuyler — all good but short on entries. My Russell collection of over thirteen hundred items was offered to my customers in my Catalogs Eighteen and Nineteen in 1972. (There was an edition of 100 numbered and signed copies of the two catalogs bound together in cloth with a new title-limitation page covering my Russell gatherings and some duplicates from the tremendous collection of Fred Renner.)

The choosing of the fifty to be included was a personal thing. However, I must acknowledge here that this book in the beginning was a joint project with my long-time friend and fellow conservationist Louis P. Merrill of Midlothian, Texas. We were both relatively new at the collecting game and were neighbors in Fort Worth when Theodore Bolton's *American Book Illustrators* (N.Y., 1938) was issued. It contains bibliographic check lists of 123 artists including just twelve of my *Fifty* plus Russell. Since some of our favorite illustrators were not included, and some of Bolton's check lists were considerably short of the items in our collections at the time, we discussed it on several occasions before dividing our favorites much as the two captains of a pick-up baseball game do in choosing their teams. Merrill took Russell and I took Remington and so on. The morning after that session Merrill's secretary delivered a typed copy of the list to me (I still have it). We added to it from time to time and in the early fifties Merrill decided to devote full-time to his ranching activities. He had so little leisure for collecting that he sent me the check lists he had compiled. As my own collecting interests expanded to include other phases of Western Americana I discovered other worthy illustrators until the total reached fifty-six and was finally reduced to fifty as already explained.

The books, pamphlets, separates and dust wrappers illustrated by each of the fifty are included. However, magazine illustrations are not included although magazine articles of biographical and bibliographical interest (usually illustrated) are included in the sections titled "The Artist and His Art." The reason for eliminating magazines is simple — this book is based on (but not limited to) the personal collection of your compiler, and space, money and time did not permit the addition of thousands of magazines to the some four thousand books in it. I have been asked many times by collectors whether or not they should buy magazines illustrated by their favorite artists, and my answer has always been, "Yes." If the inquirer is collecting the printed illustrated works of only one or two artists the answer is an emphatic, "Yes" — if as many as five the "Yes" is hedged, and I usually end up explaining why I do not collect the illustrated magazines. My failure to collect the magazines does not reflect on the value of the illustrations — many of them were first appearances and therefore desireable. A good many of the items listed were serialized in magazines prior to being issued as books — in a number of cases the magazines used more illustrations than the books. The case for collecting illustrated magazines is strong and if space and funds are adequate by all means include them.

The intent in this book is to provide enough information to the collector, dealer or librarian to identify the first printing of an entry (or the first printing of it to include illustrations by the particular artist). In addition, by noting the number of illustrations and

2

where possible their location, to provide some indication of the value of the entry to an artist collection. To be sure, this falls short of the bibliographic standards in general use — it is a bibliographic check list, not a bibliography. Reprints are not usually included, but new editions with added or changed text or illustrations and foreign editions are listed when known.

It would be too much to expect that any single check list was complete and perfect. There are bound to be errors of omission and commission. It was Bolton's *American Book Illustrators* that taught me to be tolerant — I appreciated the new entries for my want lists, I was disappointed that there were not more, and I was deeply grateful for the tremendous and sustained effort that made it possible. Despite some thousands of hours spent on compiling the fifty lists in the past thirty-five years, I can only claim that they are the best I was able to do even with very considerable help (see the Acknowledgments) from many voluntary helpers. May they prove useful to you!

THE ILLUSTRATORS

SPOOKED by Beeler from *The Joe Beeler Sketch Book*

Catalogues of Art Exhibitions and Galleries

BAKER COLLECTOR GALLERY, LUBBOCK, TEXAS

1 *Joe Beeler*, (March 1968), pic. folder, nine illus. by B. and a photo of him.

THE CURTIS ART GALLERY, SPOKANE, WASHINGTON

2 *Rendezvous of Western Art — 1972* (in cooperation with the Montana Historical Society and edited by Vivian A. Paladin), wraps, illus. including two by B. and with a photo and a biographical sketch of him.

DESERT SOUTHWEST ART GALLERY
PALM DESERT, CALIFORNIA

2a *Spring Roundup of '71*, (Northland Press, Flagstaff), January 30 to February 26, 1971, colored pic. wraps, unpaged, "Foreword" by Dean Krakel, "Preface" by Ginger Schimmel, illus. including two, "Their First Jackpot" and "A Desperate Flight" (in color on back cover), by B. and a biographical sketch of him.

2b *Spring Roundup of '72*, (Northland Press, Flagstaff), colored pic. wraps, unpaged, "Introduction" by Ginger Schimmel, illus. including two, "Catching the Morning Mounts" and "Rye Creek Cowboy" (in color on back cover), by B.

THE FIRST NATIONAL BANK & TRUST CO.
NORMAN, OKLAHOMA

3 *Joe Beeler* (Norman's Observance of its 75th Anniversary), April 16–25, 1964, folder, two illus. by B., a photo of him and lists 18 works by him.

GILCREASE INSTITUTE, TULSA, OKLAHOMA

4 *Joe Beeler*, March 3rd to April 1st (1958), folder, lists 29 paintings by B.

GRAND CENTRAL ART GALLERIES, NEW YORK

5 *1962 Yearbook*, stiff wraps with an illus. in color mounted on the front cover, 74 pp., numerous illus. including one, "Partners," p. 33, by B. (Leigh)

6 *1963 Yearbook*, wraps with illus. in color mounted on the front cover, 74 pp., numerous illus. including one, "Race for the Dinner Bell," p. 43, by B. (Leigh)

7 *1964 Yearbook*, wraps with illus. in color mounted on the front cover, 74 pp., numerous illus. including one, "Preparing the Ambush," p. 49, by B. (Leigh)

THE HEARD MUSEUM, PHOENIX, ARIZONA

8 *Joe Beeler, Noted Western Artist*, April 1967, folder, five illus. by B., a photo and a brief biographical sketch of him.

MISSOURI ATHLETIC CLUB, ST. LOUIS

8a *The West in Paint and Bronze*, March 30 through April 6, 1974, wraps with window, unpaged, numerous illus. including two by B. and a photo of him.

MONGERSON GALLERY LTD., CHICAGO

8b *First Annual Western Art Show*, May 17 through June 9, 1973, stiff wraps, unpaged, numerous illus. including one, "Now or Never," by B. and a brief biographical sketch of him.

MONTANA HISTORICAL SOCIETY, HELENA

9 *Joe Beeler*, July 1 through August 31, 1966, folder, three illus., one drawing, a photo of a bronze and a photo of B. plus a biographical sketch of him.

NATIONAL COWBOY HALL OF FAME
OKLAHOMA CITY

10 *Joe Beeler*, Sept. 4th through Oct. 10th, 1965, folder, three illus. by B., a photo and a biographical sketch of him.

11 *Cowboy Artists of America, First Annual Showing*,

September 9 through October 16, 1966, pic. wraps, unpaged, fifteen illus. including one by B., a photo and a brief biographical sketch of him.

12 Same, *Second Annual Exhibition*, May 27 through September 9, 1967, folder, a photo of B. and a biographical sketch of him.

13 Same, *Third Annual Exhibit*, June 15 through September 2, 1968, pic. wraps, unpaged (16 pp.), numerous illus. including 13 numbered entries — no. 13 is the photo of a bronze, "The Sentinel," by B.

14 ———. Same, *Fourth Annual Exhibit*, 1969, colored pic. wraps, 46 pp., "A Few Words About Myself" by Charles M. Russell, "History of Cowboy Artists of America" by Charlie Dye, numerous illus. including one, photo of a bronze ,"Up the Trail," p. 33, by B. and with a photo and a biographical sketch of him.

15 Same, *Sixth Annual Exhibition*, 1971, Northland Press, Flagstaff, (1971), morocco and cloth, unpaged, "National Cowboy Hall of Fame" by Richard Muno, "The Cowboy Artists of America" by President Gordon Snidow, numerous illus. including one by B. and a photo of him. Limited edition of 100 copies. (Eggenhofer)

16 Same, first trade edition in stiff wraps.

17 Same, *Seventh Annual Exhibition*, 1972, Northland Press, Flagstaff, morocco and cloth, 79 (1) pp., "National Cowboy Hall of Fame" by President Joel McCrea, "The Cowboy Artists of America" by President William Moyers, numerous illus. including two, pp. (20) and 21, by B. and a photo of him. Limited edition of 100 numbered copies signed by twenty-six of the artists. (Eggenhofer)

18 Same, first trade edition in colored pic. wraps.

O S RANCH, POST, TEXAS

19 *Steer Roping and Art Exhibit*, September 30–October 1, 1972, colored pic. wraps, 84 pp., numerous illus including one, p. 18, by B and a photo of him. (Hurd)

20 Same, September 29–30, 1973, colored pic. wraps, oblong with spiral binder, 90 pp., numerous illus. including one, p. 18, by B. and a photo of him.

20a Same, September 28–29, 1974, colored pic. wraps, numerous illus. including one by B. (Hurd)

PHOENIX ART MUSEUM

21 *Eighth Annual Exhibition, Cowboy Artists of America 1973*, September 14–November 4, 1973, Northland Press, Flagstaff, (1973), morocco and decor.

cloth, blue endsheets, 80 pp., "A Statment by the President" by U. Grant Speed, "Foreword" by Senator Barry Goldwater, numerous illus. including one, photo of a bronze, "Calling the Mountain Spirit," p. 22, by B. and a photo of him. One of 100 numbered copies signed by twenty-five members including B.

22 Same, first trade edition in colored pic. wraps.

FRED ROSENSTOCK WITH JAMES PARSONS (GALLERY WEST), DENVER

23 *100 years of Western Art*, November 28 through December 24, 1969, colored pic. wraps, 24 pp., "Introduction" by Parsons, numerous illus. including one, "The Corn Dancer," p. 22, by B. (Borein, Dunton, James, Koerner, Leigh)

C. M. RUSSELL GALLERY
GREAT FALLS, MONTANA

24 *Joe Beeler Shows at the C. M. Russell Gallery*, July 14 through August 30, 1970, colored pic. wraps, unpaged, "Introduction" by Director Terry Melton, "Comments" by Beeler, numerous illus. by B.

SPIVA ART CENTER, JOPLIN, MISSOURI

25 *Joe Beeler Shows at the Spiva Art Center* (Joplin, Missouri Centennial 1873–1973), June 20 to July 31, 1973, colored pic. wraps, 34 pp., "Foreword" by Joe Spiva Cragin and Suzanne Childress Sharp, "Commentary" by Beeler, numerous illus. by B.

TEXAS ART GALLERY, DALLAS (ADOLPHUS HOTEL)

26 *Preview 73*, December 2 and 3, 1972, stiff wraps, unpaged, "Introduction" by William E. Burford, numerous illus. including one in color, "Down to Winter Pasture," by B. and a photo and biographical sketch of him.

26a *Preview 74*, December 7 and 8, 1973, stiff wraps, "Introduction" by William E. Burford, numerous illus. including one in color, "Evening Camp," by B. with several photos and a biographical sketch of him.

TUCSON ART CENTER

27 *The West, Artists and Illustrators*, February 4, 1972–March 5, 1972, colored pic. wraps, unpaged, numerous illustrations, brief biographical sketch of Beeler and lists a bronze and an oil by him included in the exhibit. (Koerner, Russell)

Illustrated by the Artist

28 Adams, Ramon F. *The Rampaging Herd*. Univ. of Okla. Press, Norman, (1959), words "First edition"

on copyright page, cloth, green top, 463 pp., acknowledgments, introduction, index, illus. with facsimiles of title pages and with a drawing on the d/w by B.

29 Ainsworth, Ed. *The Cowboy in Art.* World, N.Y. and Cleveland, (1968), words "First Edition" on copyright page, full leather, orange endsheets, 242 pp., all edges gilt, "Foreword" by John Wayne, index, numerous illus. including one, p. 149, by B. plus a photo and brief biographical sketch of him. Special edition of 1000 copies, slipcase — Ed died before he could sign them. (Borein, Bugbee, De Yong, Dixon, Dunton, Eggenhofer, Ellsworth, Hurd, James, Johnson, Koerner, Mora, Perceval, Remington, Russell, Santee, Schreyvogel, Von Schmidt)

30 ———. Same, first trade edition in gilt lettered and illustrated cloth, orange endsheets.

31 ———. Same, reprint by Bonanza Books, N.Y., in red lettered and illustrated cloth, white endsheets.

32 *The Art of Northland Press 1973.* Calendar, twelve illus. including one, "Stoppin' to Water," under October, by B. (Perceval, Von Schmidt)

33 Bard, Floyd C. (as told to Agnes Wright Spring). *Horse Wrangler, Sixty Years in the Saddle in Wyoming and Montana.* Univ. of Okla. Press, Norman, (1960), words "First edition" on copyright page, cloth, brown top, 296 pp., "Foreword" by Mrs. Spring, index, map, illus. with a frontis. by Eggenhofer and with photos, but the d/w drawing is by B. (Eggenhofer)

34 Beeler, Joe. *Cowboys and Indians.* Univ. of Okla. Press, Norman, (1967, but actually released in 1968), words "First edition" on copyright page, two-tone cloth, (1) xiii pp., 80 plates, xv–xvii, "About Joe Beeler" by Joe De Yong, preface, index, 80 illus. including eight in color by B.

35 ———. Same, a limited special edition of 200 numbered and signed copies, each with an original drawing by the author-artist, bound in full leather and boxed.

35a ———. *The Joe Beeler Sketch Book.* Northland Press, Flagstaff, 1974, cloth, 120 pp., one hundred illus. by B.

35b ———. Same, a limited edition of 50 numbered and signed copies each with an original water color by the artist, bound in full leather, slipcase.

35c ———. *Western Heritage* (appointment calendar). Miller Western Products, 1968, sketches for each month by B. and with brief comments about him.

36 Campa, Arthur L. *Treasure of the Sangre de Cristos, Tales and Traditions of the Spanish Southwest.* Univ. of Okla. Press, Norman, (1963), words "First edition" on copyright page, cloth, red top, 223 pp., preface, bibliography, index, twelve illus. (one repeated on d/w), including a double frontis.-title page, by B.

37 Clay, John. *My Life on the Range.* Univ. of Okla. Press, Norman, (1962), words "First Printing of the New Edition" on copyright page, cloth, tinted top, 372 pp., "Introduction" by Donald R. Ornduff, sources of illustrations, foreword, index, illus. with photos but d/w illus. is by B.

38 *Fifth Annual Last Chance Stampede.* Helena, Montana, August 6-7-8 (1965), colored pic. wraps, 53 (3) pp., numerous illus. including one, p. 6, by B. (Eggenhofer, Russell)

39 *The Franklin Mint Gold Medal Portfolio of Western Art.* Franklin Center, Pa., (1973), wraps, unpaged, eleven illus. in color including one, "Foggy Morning," by B.

40 Gibson, A. M. *The Life and Death of Colonel Albert Jennings Fountain.* Univ. of Okla. Press, Norman, (1965), words "First Edition" on copyright page, cloth, yellow top, 301 pp., acknowledgments, bibliography, index, map, illus. with photos and with a d/w drawing by B.

41 Green, Ben K. *The Last Trail Drive Through Downtown Dallas.* Northland Press, Flagstaff, (1971), leather and cloth, tan endsheets, 73 pp. with six illus., frontis. and pp. (5), 20, (34), (45) and 71, by B, limited edition of 100 numbered copies signed by the author, each with an original drawing by B., slipcase.

42 ———. Same, first trade edition in two-tone cloth.

43 ———. *A Thousand Miles of Mustangin'.* Northland Press, Flagstaff, (1972), words "First Edition" on copyright page, fabricoid and cloth, red endsheets, 145 pp., twelve illus., frontis. and pp. (9), (16–7), (23), (29), 37, (55), 71, (91), (110), (129) and (139), by B., limited, deluxe edition of 150 numbered copies signed by the author and illustrator, slipcase.

44 ———. Same, first trade edition in decor. cloth.

45 ———. *Some More Horse Tradin'.* Knopf, N.Y., 1972, words "First Edition" on copyright page, two-tone decor. cloth, tan endsheets, 255 pp., green top, sixteen illus. by B., one of 350 copies printed on special paper and specially bound, numbered and signed by the author, slipcase.

46 ———. Same, first trade edition in decor. cloth.

47 ———. *Beauty.* Northland Press, Flagstaff, (1974), cloth, 59 pp., illus. by B., one of the four volumes in *Ben Green Tales* inserted in a single slipcase.

48 Hafen, LeRoy R. *Broken Hand.* Old West Publishing Co., Denver, (1973), advs. folder with a drawing on the front cover by B.

48a ———. *Broken Hand* (The Life of Thomas Fitzpatrick — Mountain Man, Guide and Indian Agent). Old West Publishing Co., Denver, (1973), words "First Revised Edition" on copyright page, cloth, black end sheets, preface, introduction, appendices, index, illus. including one, title page (repeated on the d/w), by B.

49 Harmsen, Dorothy. *Harmsen's Western Americana.* Northland Press, Flagstaff, (1971), morocco and cloth, blue endsheets, 213 pp., "Foreword" by Robert Rockwell, Introduction, selected bibliography, numerous illus. including one in color, p. (17), by B. and with a biographical sketch of him. Author's edition of 150 numbered copies signed by the author in slipcase with morocco title label. (Blumenschein, Borein, Dixon, Dunn, Dunton, Eggenhofer, Elwell, Hurd, Johnson, Leigh, Marchand, Miller, Von Schmidt, Wyeth)

50 ———. Same, first trade edition, two-tone cloth with red endsheets.

50a Hassrick, Royal B. *Cowboys* (The real story of Cowboys and Cattlemen). Octopus Books (London but printed in Hong Kong), (1974), words "First published 1974" on copyright page, pic. boards, pic. endsheets, 144 pp., introduction, further reading, index, numerous illus. including one, p. (59), by B. (Borein, Hurd, Johnson, Koerner, Remington, Russell)

51 (Horn.) *Life of Tom Horn, Government Scout and Interpreter* (written by himself). Univ. of Okla. Press, Norman, (1964), words "First printing, 1964" (i.e. in The Western Frontier Library) on the copyright page, boards, 277 pp., "Introduction" by Dean Krakel, "Preface" by John C. Coble, supplementary articles, d/w illus. by B.

51a *Joplin Jaycee Rodeo* (Second Annual). June 7–10, 1961, wraps with front cover illus. by B. and with a biographical sketch of him.

51b Same, (Fourth Annual), June 19–22, 1963, wraps, illus. including one by B. and with a biographical sketch of him.

51c Kennedy, Michael S. (selected and edited by). *Cowboys and Cattlemen.* Hastings House, N.Y., (1964), horsehide with hair out, color pic. endsheets, 364 (2) pp., introduction, index, numerous illustrations. Lim-

ited edition of 199 numbered copies, ten with original watercolors by B., in slipcase. (Borein, Russell)

52 Kennon, Bob, as told to Ramon F. Adams. *From the Pecos to the Powder: A Cowboy's Autobiography.* Univ. of Okla. Press, Norman, (1965), words "First edition" on copyright page, pic. cloth, red top, 251 pp., "Preface" (and edited) by Adams, index, map, illus. with photos and eight drawings, frontis. (repeated on front cover) and pp. 4–5, 30, 55, 91, 109, 183 and 230 (repeated on d/w), by B.

53 Krakel, Dean. *Joe Beeler, Western Artist.* (Northland Press, Flagstaff, Ariz., n.d., pic. wraps, (14) pp., photo of B. on front wrap and 23 illus. by him.

53a McGuire, Jerry. *Elijah.* Northland Press, Flagstaff, 1973, pic. wraps, blue cloth, 112 pp., eight illus. by B.

54 Meigs, John, ed. *The Cowboy in American Prints.* Swallow Press, Chicago, (1972), leather and cloth, pic. endsheets, 184 pp., introduction, numerous illus. including one, p. 89, by B., limited to 300 numbered copies signed by the editor with an added manually signed lithograph by Peter Hurd, slipcase. (Borein, Dixon, Hurd, Remington, Russell, Wood, Zogbaum)

55 ———. Same, trade edition in cloth.

56 (Miller.) Rolle, Andrew F., ed. *The Road to Virginia City: The Diary of James Knox Polk Miller.* Univ. of Okla. Press, Norman, (1960), words "First Edition" on copyright page, two-tone cloth, orange top, 143 pp., editor's acknowledgments and introduction, index, maps (including one double-page), illus. with five drawings, d/w, title page, pp. 3, 33 and 73, by B., and with photos.

57 Murray, Keith A. *The Modocs and Their War.* Oklahoma, Norman, (1959), words "First edition" on copyright page, cloth, 346 pp., black top, foreword, appendices, bibliography, index, map, illus. including one, the double title page, by B. and with a different drawing by him on the d/w. A freight terminal fire destroyed all except 36 copies of the first edition — 29 of the 36 were distributed to libraries of colleges, museums and other institutions selected by lottery from the continuation order file (it is Volume 52 of The Civilization of the American Indian Series) at the Press.

58 ———. Same, with the words "Second printing, March 1959" on copyright page.

58a *1974 Western Art Calendar.* The Leanin' Tree Publishing Co., Boulder, Colo., (1973), colored pic. wraps, fourteen illus. including one, "Enemy Tracks" (over

February), by B. Note: Other Leanin' Tree calendars include illustrations by B.

59 Northland Press. *1970–71 Winter–Spring Book List.* Flagstaff, (1970), pic. wraps, unpaged, numerous illus. including one by B. (Borein, Dixon, Perceval, Remington)

60 ———. *Autumn 1972 Book List.* Flagstaff, (1972), pic. wraps, unpaged, numerous illus. including one by B. (Dixon, Perceval, Remington, Santee, Von Schmidt, Wyeth)

61 ———. *Autumn 1973 Book List.* Flagstaff, (1973), colored pic. wraps, numerous illus. including three by B. Note: Other Northland Press catalogs include illus. by Beeler. (Blumenschein, Dixon, James, Perceval, Remington, Santee, Von Schmidt)

61a ———. *Spring 1974 Book List.* (1974), folder with five illus. including one, front cover, by B.

61b ———. *Ben Green Tales.* Single sheet flyer with four illus. including one by B.

61c ———. Autumn 1974 Book List. (1974), colored pic. wraps, unpaged, numerous illus. including three by B., with an announcement of *The Joe Beeler Sketch Book* for July release and with a biographical sketch of him. (Borein, Dixon, Perceval, Von Schmidt)

62 Parker, Watson. *Gold in the Black Hills.* Oklahoma, Norman, (1966), words "First edition" on copyright page, cloth, 259 pp., preface, appendices, glossary, bibliography, index, maps, illus. with a frontis. by B. and with photos.

63 Pearce, W. M. *The Matador Land and Cattle Company.* Univ. of Okla. Press, Norman, (1963), words "First edition" on copyright page, cloth, brown top, 244 pp., preface, epilogue, appendices, bibliography, index, illus. with photos, d/w illus. by B.

64 Powell, Donald M. *The Peralta Grant, James Addison Reavis and the Barony of Arizona.* Univ. of Okla. Press, Norman, (1960), words "First edition" on copyright page, cloth, grey top, 186 pp., foreword, bibliography, index, maps, eleven illus. including three drawings, pp. (1), (59) and (115), by B.

65 Schiel, Jacob H. *Journey Through the Rocky Mountains and the Humboldt Mountains to the Pacific Ocean.* Univ. of Okla. Press, Norman, (1959), words "First edition" on copyright page, cloth, green top, 114 pp., tr. from the German and edited by Thomas H. Bonner, bibliography, folding map, illus. from the official report of the expedition (1855) and with five

drawings, d/w, title page and pp. (viii), (2) and (62), by B.

66 Schreiner, Charles, III et al. *A Pictorial History of the Texas Rangers* ("That Special Breed of Men"). (Y-O Press, Mountain Home, 1969), words "First Edition" on copyright page, decor. cloth, crash endsheets, 267 pp., preface, "Introduction" by Governor Preston Smith, bibliography, index, numerous illus. including one, a photo of the Texas Ranger bronze, as the frontis. (repeated, reduced size, p. 259), by B.

67 Scott, Dan. *The Mystery of Ghost Canyon.* Grosset & Dunlap, N.Y., (1960), boards, pic. endsheets, 182 pp., 20 drawings by B. (The Bret King Mystery Series.)

68 ———. *The Range Rodeo Mystery.* Grosset & Dunlap, N.Y., (1960), boards, 180 pp., numerous drawings by B. (The Bret King Mystery Series.)

69 ———. *The Secret of Hermit's Peak.* Grosset & Dunlap, N.Y., (1960), boards, pic. endsheets, 181 pp., twenty-one drawings by B. (The Bret King Mystery Series.)

70 ———. *The Secret of Fort Pioneer.* Grosset & Dunlap, N.Y., (1961), boards, pic. endsheets, 181 pp., twenty drawings by B. (The Bret King Mystery Series.)

71 ———. *The Mystery at Blizzard Mesa.* Grosset & Dunlap, N.Y., (1961), boards, pic. endsheets, 182 pp., twenty drawings by B. (The Bret King Mystery Series.)

72 ———. *The Mystery of the Comanche Caves.* Grosset & Dunlap, N.Y., (1962), boards, pic. endsheets, 177 pp., twenty drawings by B. (The Bret King Mystery Series.)

73 ———. *The Phantom of Wolf Creek.* Grosset & Dunlap, N.Y., (1963), boards, pic. endsheets, 178 pp., twenty drawings by B. (The Bret King Mystery Series.)

74 ———. *The Mystery of Bandit Gulch.* Grosset & Dunlap, N.Y., (1964), colored pic. boards and endsheets, 179 pp., twenty drawings by B. (The Bret King Mystery Series.)

75 Shaw, Edward (director). *Fall and Winter Books, 1967–68* (cataogue). Univ. of Okla. Press, Norman, (1967), pic. wraps, 40 pp., describes, p. 1, *Cowboys and Indians* by Beeler, and the cover illus. is by B.

76 ———. *Books Worth Keeping.* Oklahoma, Norman, n.d., advs. folder with a drawing on the front cover by B.

77 *Southwestern Art.* Austin, Texas, n.d., advs. folder with seven illus. including one drawing by B.

78 Steadman, William E. (director). *The West and Walter Bimson.* The University of Arizona Museum of Art, Tucson, (1971), cloth, pic. endsheets, 223 (2) pp., "Foreword" by Dr. Richard A. Harvill, introduction, indices, numerous illus. including photos of six bronzes, pp. 170, 171, 172, 173, 174 and 175, by B. (Johnson, Leigh, Remington, Schoonover, Wyeth)

79 Stone, Will Hale. *Twenty-four Year a Cowboy and Ranchman in Southern Texas and Old Mexico,* by Will Hale (pseud.). Univ. of Okla. Press, Norman, (1959), words "First printing" (i.e. in The Western Frontier Library) on copyright page, boards, 183 pp., "Introduction" by A. M. Gibson, illus. with drawings, by T. O. Donnell, but the d/w illus. is by B.

80 Sunder, John E. *Bill Sublette, Mountain Man.* Univ. of Okla. Press, Norman, (1959), words "First Edition" on copyright page, cloth, brown top, 279 pp., preface, appendices, bibliography, index, maps, illus. including one by Miller, one by Bingham, two by Bodmer and one drawing, title page, by B. (Miller)

81 *Those Early Days* (Oldtimers' Memoirs: Oak Creek-Sedona and the Verde Valley Region of Arizona). Sedona Westerners (Sedona, Arizona), 1968, wraps, 240 pp., back cover illus. by B.

82 Todd, Edgeley Woodman, ed. *A Doctor on the California Trail: The Diary of Dr. John Hudson Wayman,* Old West Publishing Co., (Northland Press), Denver, 1971, cloth, illus. including one, title page (repeated on the front cover) by B.

The Artist and His Art

83 Abrams, Al. "Duane Miller's Steering Committee, an article in *Arizona (The Arizona Republic),* Phoenix, July 11, 1971, a photo essay with captions by Beeler and with several photos of him.

83a Allen, Susan. "Joe Beeler," an article in *The Ranchman,* June 1971 with several illus. by B.

83b "The Art of Banking at Wichita's Fourth National," an article in *Finance* (Magazine of Money), October 1967, with "Ambush at the Spring" in color by B. and with photos in color of three bronzes by him.

84 Beeler, Joe. "An Artist Looks at the American Indian," an article in *Montana, The Magazine of Western History,* vol. 14, no. 2, April, 1964, photo of Beeler and Joe De Yong and eighteen illus. by B.

85 ———. "Cowboy Artists Winners," an article in *The Western Horseman,* December 1969, illus. including one, a photo of a bronze, by B.

85a ———. "Cowboy Artists of America," an article in *American Artist,* April 1970, with two (one in color) illus. by B.

86 ———. "The Cowboy Way," an autobiographical article in *Southwestern Art* 3:2, Autumn 1971, with eleven illus. by B. and a photo of him.

87 ———. "The Great Charlie Dye," an illus. article in *Westerner* 5:3, May–June 1973.

87a Brown, Bing. "The Sculptor's Third Hand," an article about Joe Noggle in *Arizona Days and Ways,* July 11, 1965, with photos of Beeler and Noggle, one with Beeler bronze.

88 Burchardt, Bill, ed. Review of *Cowboys and Indians* in the "Oklahoma Scrapbook" a regular feature of *Oklahoma Today,* vol. 18, no. 2, Spring, 1968, praises Beeler's art and there are two drawings by him.

89 Butler, Ron. "The Big Boom in Western Art," an illus. article in *Arizona Highways* 48:3, March 1972, with a photo of a bronze by B. (Russell)

90 Carlson, Raymond, ed. "Front Cover," a paragraph on the illustration in color by B. in *Arizona Highways* 45:10, October 1969, plus "Barbed Wire," a feature article by Carol Osman Brown with six (one — the double-page center, in color) illus. by B.

91 De Wald, Bud. "Roundup Time," an article in *Arizona (The Arizona Republic),* Phoenix, September 9, 1973, with much on Beeler in the text and with one illus. by him.

91a "First National Bank of Norman to Have Art Exhibit," an article about Beeler in *Oklahoma Banker,* April 1964, with one illus. by B.

92 Forrest, James Taylor. "The Cowman's West of Joe Beeler," an article in *Montana, The Magazine of Western History,* vol. 11, no. 13, Summer of 1961, photos of Beeler and nine illus. by him.

93 Jarrett, Walter. "Joe Beeler, Artist of the American West," in *Mankind* 3:4, December 1971, with eleven (six in color) illus. by B. and a photo of him.

93a "Joe Noggle, A Master at Casting Bronze," an article in *Southern Union News,* December 1967, with a photo of Noggle with the bronze "Sioux Indian" by B.

94 Johnson, Burke. "The Spirit of the Old West," an article in *Arizona Days and Ways,* February 24, 1963, with four illus. in color by B. and four photos of him.

ILLUSTRATION by Beeler from
A Thousand Miles of Mustangin'

95 Krakel, Dean. "Joe Beeler, Cowboy Artist," an article in *Westerner* 1:1, March–April 1969, with ten (two in color) illus. by B. and a photo of him.

95a "La Galeria Presents a Special Invitational Western Show," an article featuring several artists including Beeler in *Arizona Living* 5:4, January 25, 1974, with one illus. by B.

96 Montgomery, Ed. "Cowboy and Indian Artist," an article about Beeler in *Oklahoma's Orbit*, July 14, 1968, with three (two in color) illus. by him and a photo of him.

97 Muno, Richard. "The West in Contemporary Art," an illus. article on the Cowboy Artists of America in *Persimmon Hill* 1:1, Summer 1970, with a photo of the Silver Medal winning sculpture, "Thanks for the Rain," by B.

98 The Old Bookaroos. "Beeler's Best," a review of *Cowboys and Indians* in *Frontier Times* (Magazine), June–July 1968, praises Beeler's art and his book.

99 "Readin' Signs and Trail Notes," a guide to the illus. in this issue of *Arizona Highways* 46:10, October 1970, comments on Beeler's oil in color "Good Neighbors."

100 *A Retrospective Exhibit of Western Art*. The Arizona Bank (Phoenix), October 23–November 3, 1972, pic. wraps, unpaged, lists twenty-five works of art (with a brief biographical sketch of each artist) including no. 22, "The Hostile's Revenge," by B.

100a Rigby, Elizabeth. "La Galeria," an article in *Arizona Living* 5:7, February 15, 1974, with one illus. by B. and with a biographical sketch of him.

100b "School of Old Paint," an article in *Newsweek*, November 8, 1965, with comments on Beeler's art and one illus. by him.

100c Same, reprint on a single sheet.

101 Shirley, Glenn. "Then Came Law," an article in *American Scene*, vol. iv, no. 4, 1962, with a double-page reproduction of an oil, "The Fugitive," by B.

102 Snidow, Gordon (President). "The Cowboy Artists of America," an illus. article in *Persimmon Hill* 1:4, Summer 1971, with two illus. by B. and a photo of him.

102a Snodgrass, Jeanne O. *American Indian Painters, A Biographical Directory*. Museum of the American Indian, Heye Foundation, N.Y., 1968, vol. xxi, part I, Beeler biography pp. 16 and 17.

103 Stacey, Joseph. "Charlie Dye," an illus. article in *Arizona Highways* 47:1, November 1971, Charlie tells Stacey about the organization of the Cowboy Artists of America by Joe Beeler, John Hampton, George Phippen, Fred Harman and himself, photo of the Cowboy Artists on the Trail Ride at Big Sandy, Montana, in 1971.

104 Stewart, Tyrone H. (managing editor). "Joe Beeler, Western Artist," an article in *American Indian Crafts and Culture* 6:1, January 1972, with three (one on front cover) illus. by B. and a photo of him.

105 Weaver, Paul E. "Northland Press and the Fine Art of Bookmaking," an illus. article in *Arizona Highways*, Paul tells about getting Ben Green and Joe Beeler together on *The Last Trail Drive Through Downtown Dallas*, three illus. by B. (Borein, Dixon, Perceval Remington)

106 White, John I. "Badger Clark, Poet of Yesterday's West," an illus. article in *Arizona Highways* 45:2, February 1969, twelve illus. (three in color) by B. and comments on his art.

107 "Why Cowboy Artists of America," an article in *Southwest Art*, October 1972, illus. including a photo of the bronze, "Deneh," by B.

ILLUSTRATION by Bjorklund from *Wild Cow Tales*

LORENCE F. BJORKLUND
Contemporary,

Catalogues of Art Exhibitions and Galleries

THE FORT LEAVENWORTH MUSEUM
LEAVENWORTH, KANSAS

1 *John M. Carroll's Miliary Art Collection* (The Black Military Experience in the American West), December 1973–February 1974, wraps, unpaged, frontis. by B. (especially drawn for this exhibition and it was retired from publication with this printing).

1a Same, thirty presentation copies, each in a four-point slipcase with an original pencil drawing by Bjorklund and each catalog signed by Bjorklund and Carroll.

THE U.S. ARMY MILITARY HISTORY RESEARCH COLLECTION, CARLISLE BARRACKS, PENNSYLVANIA

2 *John M. Carroll's Collection, Illustrations of the Black Soldier in the West*, (1973), pic. wraps, 16 pp., ten illus. including two, front cover and p. 7, by B. (Cisneros)

2a Same, thirty presentation copies, each in a four-point slipcase with an original drawing by Jose Cisneros and each catalog is signed by Colonel George C. Pappas, Carroll, Bjorklund, Grandee, Cisneros and Reusswig.

THE UNITED STATES MILITARY ACADEMY LIBRARY WEST POINT, NEW YORK

3 *Illustrators of the American West*, March 1973, decor. wraps, unpaged, "Program Notes" by John M. Carroll, nine illus. including two by B., limited to 27 Presentation Copies, a four-point slipcase with an original drawing by Jose Cisneros and signed with his initials and each catalog signed by Carroll, Bjorklund, Cisneros, Grandee, Ralston and Rossi.

4 Same, regular edition in decor. wraps.

Illustrated by the Artist

5 (Adams, Mary Scott.) *Jory and the Buckskin Jumper,* by Priscilla D. Willis (pseud.). St. Martin's, N.Y., 1960, cloth, 229 pp., illus. by B.

5a Anderson, Kenneth. *Nine Man Eaters and One Rogue.* Dutton, N.Y., 1955, words "First American Edition" on copyright page, cloth, 251 pp., illus. with photos but d/w drawing by B.

6 Bachmann, Evelyn Trent. *Tressa.* Viking, N.Y., (1966), words "First published in 1966" on copyright page, pic. cloth, red top, 155 pp., sixteen illus. by B.

7 Balch, Glenn. *Spotted Horse.* Thomas Y. Crowell, N.Y., (1961), cloth, 176 pp., twenty-four illus. by B.

8 ———. *Stallion's Foe.* Crowell, N.Y., (1963), cloth, 179 pp., illus. with seventeen drawings by B.

9 ———. *The Flaxy Mare.* Crowell, N.Y., (1967), cloth, 142 (1) pp., twenty-one illus. by B.

10 ———. *Horse of Two Colors.* Crowell, N.Y., (1969), cloth, 170 (2) pp., sixteen illus. by B.

11 Bishop, Curtis. *The First Texas Ranger, Jack Hays.* Messner, N.Y., 1959, decor. cloth, 192 pp., bibliography, index, d/w illus. in color by B.

12 Bjorklund, Karna. *Indians of Northeast America.* Dodd, Mead, N.Y., (1969), cloth, 192 pp., Museums with Woodland Indian Collections, selected readings, index, numerous illus. by B.

13 Bjorklund, Lorence F. *Faces of the Frontier.* Dodd, Mead, N.Y., (1967), cloth, tan endsheets, 119 (3) pp., preface, numerous illus. by the author-artist.

13a ———. *The Bison: The Great American Buffalo.* World, Cleveland and N.Y., 1970, cloth, illus. by B.

14 Boesch, Mark. *The Lawless Land* (A Story of the Vigilantes). Winston, Philadelphia, Toronto, (1953), words "First Edition" on copyright page, boards, pic.

endsheets, 181 pp., "The Wonderful Land," illus. with thirty-five drawings by B.

14a Bolton, Ivy May. *Son of the Land.* Messner, N.Y., (1946), cloth, 211 pp., seventeen illus. by B.

14b ———. *Wayfaring Lad.* Messner, N.Y., (1948), decor. cloth, 192 pp., foreword, fifteen illus. by B.

15 Bowden, Aberdeen Orlando et al. *The Day Before Yesterday in America.* Macmillan, N.Y., (1946), pic. cloth, 283 pp., maps, numerous illus. by B.

16 Brooks, Walted, ed. *Art of Drawing Animals.* Odyssey, N.Y., 1965, wraps or cloth, unpaged, numerous illus. by B. (The Grumbacher Library.)

17 ———. *The Art of Drawing.* Odyssey, N.Y., (1965), wraps or boards, unpaged, numerous illus. including contributions by B. (The Grumbacher Library.)

18 ———. *The Art of Drawing Heads and Hands.* Odyssey, N.Y., (1966), wraps or boards, 48 pp., numerous illus. including contributions by B. (The Grumbacher Library.)

18a ———. *Creative Ways with Drawing Dogs and Cats.* Golden Press, N.Y., 1974, wraps, 32 pp., illus. including contributions by B.

19 Browin, Frances Williams. *Captured Words, the Story of a Great Indian.* Aladdin Books, N.Y., 1954, words "First Edition" on copyright page, pic. cloth and endsheets, yellow top, 192 pp., twenty-four illus. by B.

20 Bruce, William H. *Dragon Prows Westward.* Harcourt, Brace, N.Y., (1946), pic. cloth, map endsheets, 199 pp., introduction, twenty-six illus. by B.

20a Burgess, Alan. *The Small Woman.* Dutton, N.Y., 1957, words "First Edition" on the copyright page, cloth, 256 pp., d/w illus. by B.

21 Burt, Olive W. *Negroes in the Early West.* Messner, N.Y., (1969), cloth, 96 pp., introduction, suggestions for further reading, index, sixteen illus. by B.

22 Carroll, John M., ed. *The Black Military Experience in the American West.* Liveright, N.Y., (1971), words "First edition, first printing" on copyright page, cloth, pic. endsheets, 591 pp., notes, bibliography, index, sixty illus. including nine, pp. (54), (250), (392), (416), (442), (470), (496), (504) and (512), by B., limited to 300 numbered copies signed by Carroll, slipcase. (Bugbee, Cisneros, Eggenhofer, Hurd, Remington, Russell, Schiwetz)

23 ———. Same, first trade edition in cloth, d/w.

24 ———. *Buffalo Soldiers West.* (The Old Army Press, Ft. Collins, Colo., 1971), pic. leather, cloth endsheets, 64 pp., foreword, the artists, 50 illus. including nine, pp. 16, 33, 44, 48, 49, 56, 58, 61 and 62, by B., limited to 50 numbered copies signed by Carroll each with an original drawing by B. and signed by him. (Bugbee, Cisneros, Eggenhofer, Remington)

25 ———. Same, first trade edition in pic. fabricoid.

26 ——— (compiled and introduced by). *The Sand Creek Massacre: A Documentary History.* Sol Lewis, N.Y., 1973, cloth, 456 pp., one double-page foldout plate in color by B. (Edition of 500 copies.)

26a ———, ed. *The Benteen-Goldin Letters on Custer and His Last Battle.* Liveright, N.Y., (1974), cloth, an edition of 1000 copies, signed and numbered by the editor with a full-color plate from an original watercolor by B.

26b ———. Same, limited deluxe edition of 27 copies each with an original pencil drawing by B., slipcase.

26c ———. *The Two Battles of the Little Big Horn.* Liveright, N.Y., (1974), cloth, an edition of 1000 copies, signed and numbered by the editor, with a full-color plate from an original watercolor by B.

26d ———. Same, limited deluxe edition of 27 copies each with an original pencil drawing by B., slipcase.

26e ———. *Limited Editions of Two Valuable Works which are Indispensable to Every Collector of Western Americana.* Liveright, N.Y., (1974), announcement folder for 26a and 26c, with two illus. by B.

27 Cavanah, Frances with Elizabeth Crandall. *Freedom Encyclopedia, American Liberties in the Making.* Rand, McNally, Chicago etc., (1968), words "First printing, September, 1968" on copyright page, pic. cloth, 205 pp., introduction, books for further reading, index, numerous illus. by B.

28 Day, Beth F. *Gene Rhodes, Cowboy.* Messner, N.Y., (1954), cloth, 192 pp., prologue, Rhodes bibliographic check list, index, illus. with twenty-one drawings by B.

29 ———. Same, a 1955 selection of the Weekly Reader, Children's Book Club, Columbus, Ohio.

30 Derleth, August. *The Country of the Hawk.* Aladdin Books, N.Y., 1952, words "First Edition" on copyright page, pic. cloth and pic. map endsheets, yellow top, 192 pp., illus. with twenty-six drawings by B.

31 Dickinson, Alice. *The First Book of Stone Age Man.*

Franklin Watts, N.Y., 1962, cloth, 82 pp., bibliography, illus. by B.

32 Drago, Harry Sinclair. *Outlaws on Horseback*. Dodd, Mead, N.Y., (1964), cloth, red top, pic. endsheets, 320 pp., acknowledgments, introduction, notes, bibliography, index, map, illus. with photos, but endsheet drawings by B.

33 ———. *Great American Cattle Trails*. Dodd, Mead, N.Y., 1965, cloth, pic. endsheets, 274 pp., red top, maps, illus. with photos but endsheet and d/w illus. by B.

34 ———. *Many Beavers*. Dodd, Mead, N.Y., (1967), cloth, 126 (1) pp., a biographical sketch of the author, thirty-four illus. by B.

35 ———. *The Great Range Wars* (Violence on the Grasslands). Dodd, Mead, N.Y., (1970), cloth, tan endsheets, 307 pp., orange top, an introduction and acknowledgment, notes, bibliography, index, illus. with photos but with the d/w illus. in color by B.

36 ———. *Road Agents and Train Robbers*. Dodd, Mead, N.Y., (1973), cloth, 274 pp., blue top, foreword, notes, a selected bibliography, index, illus. with photos but endsheets and d/w (in color) illus. by B.

37 Driggs, Howard R. *Nick Wilson, Pioneer Boy Among the Indians*. Aladdin Books, N.Y., 1951, words "First Edition" on copyright page, pic. cloth, 88 pp., foreword, twelve illus. by B.

38 ———. *Pitch Pine Tales*. Aladdin Books, N.Y., 1951, words "First Edition" on copyright page, decor. cloth, green top, 101 pp., foreword, fifteen illus. by B.

39 Durham, Philip and Jones, Everett L. *The Negro Cowboys*. Dodd, Mead, N.Y., (1965), cloth, 278 pp., preface, prologue, epilogue, notes, bibliography, index, illustrated, d/w drawing by B. (Remington)

40 Eames, Genevieve Torrey. *Flying Roundup*. Messner, N.Y., (1957), pic. cloth, red top, 190 pp., thirteen illus. by B.

40a Ege, Robert. *Curse Not His Curls*. Old Army Press, Ft. Collins, Colo., with illus. by B. (Announced for 1974.)

41 Emery, Anne. *A Spy in Old West Point*. Rand McNally, Chicago etc., (1965), words "First Printing, 1965" on copyright page, pic. cloth, pic. map endsheets, 191 (1) pp., author's note, twenty-two illus. by B.

41a Felton, Harold W. *Ely S. Parker, Spokesman for the Senecas*. Dodd Mead, N.Y., (1973), cloth, 111 pp., illus. by B.

41b Fenner, Phyllis R. (selected by). *Gentle Like a Cyclone* (Stories of Horses and Riders). Morrow, N.Y., 1974, cloth, illus. by B.

42 Fox, Mary Virginia. *Ambush at Fort Dearborn*. St. Martin's, N.Y., (1962), cloth, 173 pp., illus. with thirty-eight drawings by B.

43 Franchere, Ruth. *The Travels of Colin O'Dae*. Crowell, N.Y., 1966, cloth, 261 (1) pp., About the Author, About the Illustrator, eighteen illus. by B.

44 Freeman, Mae Blacher. *Stars and Stripes, The Story of the American Flag*. Random House, N.Y., 1964, cloth, 57 pp., illus. by B.

45 (Furcolo, Foster.) *Marco and the Tiger*, by John Foster (pseud.). Dodd, Mead, N.Y., (1967), cloth, 127 pp., biographical sketch of the author, sixteen illus. by B.

46 ———. *Marco and the Sleuth Hound*. Dodd, Mead, N.Y., (1969), cloth, 153 (1) pp., biographical sketch of the author, sixteen illus. by B.

47 ———. *Marco and that Curious Cat*. Dodd, Mead, N.Y., (1970), cloth, 186 pp., fifteen illus. in text plus d/w (in color) by B.

48 Garst, Shannon. *Cowboy Artist, Charles M. Russell*. Messner, N.Y., (1960), decor. cloth, 192 pp., acknowledgments, bibliography, index, d/w illus. by B.

49 Garthwaite, Marion. *Tomas and the Red Headed Angel*. Messner, N.Y., (1950), decor. cloth, 190 pp., twenty-seven illus. in text plus d/w in color by B.

49a Gault, William Campbell. *Speedway Challenge*. Dutton, N.Y., 1956, words "First Edition" on copyright page, pic. cloth, 189 pp., title page (repeated on front cover) drawing by B.

50 George, Jean Craighead. *The Moon of the Gray Wolves*. Crowell, N.Y., (1969), cloth, 37 (1) pp., twenty-three illus. by B.

51 Grant, Bruce. *American Indians, Yesterday and Today*. Dutton, N.Y., 1958, words "First Edition" on copyright page, pic. cloth, 351 pp., appendices, For Further Reading, profusely illus. with drawings by B.

52 ———. *American Forts — Yesterday and Today*. Dutton, N.Y., 1965, cloth, 381 pp., maps, index, over 100 illus. including the d/w (in color) by B.

52a ———. *Famous American Trails*. Rand McNally, Chicago etc., (1971), words "First Edition" on copyright page, color pic. boards, map endsheets, 95 (1) pp., introduction, numerous illus. including many drawings by B. (Deming, Remington, Russell)

53 Green, Ben K., D.V.M. *Horse Tradin'*. Knopf, N.Y., 1967, words "First Edition" on copyright page, two-tone cloth, 304 (1) pp., preface, a note about the author, illus. with drawings on d/w and twenty-two in the text by B.

54 ——.*Wild Cow Tales*. Knopf, N.Y., 1969, words "First Edition" on copyright page, cloth with morocco title label on spine, tan endsheets, red top, 306 (2) pp., introduction, notes, with over twenty illus. by B. One of 300 copies printed on special paper and specially bound, numbered and signed by the author, in cardboard slipcase. Note: Actually 350 copies of this edition were issued as a result of a late change in the printing order but without a change in the legend in the book.

55 ——. Trade edition, in cloth.

56 ——. Same, paperback edition, Ballantine Books, N.Y., (1974), words "First Printing: February 1974" on copyright page, numerous illus. by B.

57 ——. *The Village Horse Doctor West of the Pecos*. Knopf, N.Y., 1971, words "First Edition" on copyright page, one of 350 copies printed on special paper and specially bound, numbered and signed by the author, 306 (2) pp., red top, map, eighteen illus. in text by B., slipcase.

58 ——. Same, first trade edition in pic. cloth, d/w with an illus. by B.

59 Green, Robert James. *Patriot Silver*. St. Martin's, N.Y., 1961, cloth, 183 pp., illus. by B.

60 ——. *The Whistling Sword*. St. Martin's, N.Y., (1962), decor. cloth, pic. map endsheets, 159 (1) pp., twenty-six illus. by B.

60a Gugliotta, Bobette. *Katzimo, Mysterious Mesa*. Dodd Mead, N.Y., (1974), cloth, illus. by B.

60b Harrison, Mrs. Amelia (Williams). *American Indian Fairy Tales* by Margaret Compton (pseud.). Dodd Mead, N.Y., (1971), cloth, 159 pp., "Introduction" by Lorence F. Bjorklund and with eighteen illus. by him.

61 Hays, Wilma Pitchford. *Pontiac: Lion in the Forest*. Houghton Mifflin, Boston etc., (1965), cloth, 189 (1) pp., (1) of advs., maps, illus. with over forty drawings by B.

62 Heck, Bessie Holland. *The Hopeful Years*. World, Cleveland and N.Y., 1964, words "First Edition" on copyright page, pic. cloth, yellow top, 185 (1) pp., nearly thirty illus. by B.

63 ——. *Cactus Kevin*. World, Cleveland etc., (1965), words "First Edition" on copyright page, pic. cloth, 157 (1) pp., twenty illus. by B.

64 Heckelmann, Charles N. *Hard Man with a Gun*. Little, Brown, Boston, Toronto, (1954), words "First Edition" on copyright page, cloth, 183 pp., d/w illus. in color by B.

64a Hillary, Edmund. *High Adventure*. Dutton, N.Y., 1955, words "First Edition" on copyright page, cloth, 256 pp., illus. with photos but d/w drawing by B.

65 Hirsch, S. Carl. *Famous American Indians of the Plains*. Rand McNally, Chicago, 1973, colored pic. boards, 96 pp., thirteen full-color double-page plates by Remington, Russell et al. plus numerous drawings by B.

65a Hyde, Dayton O. *Cranes in My Corral*. Dial Press, N.Y., (1971), cloth, 85 pp., illus. by B.

65b *Indians* (Quiz Me Series). Junior Golden Books, N.Y., 1963, boards, illus. by B.

66 Ives, Joseph Christmas. *Steamboat up the Colorado*, edited by Alexander L. Crosby. Little, Brown, Boston, Toronto, (1965), words "First Edition" on copyright page, pic. cloth, 112 pp., foreword, index, map, illus. including thirteen drawings by B.

67 Johnson, Enid. *Cochise, Great Apache Chief*. Messner, N.Y., (1953), decor. cloth and endsheets, 180 pp., foreword, bibliography, index, double title page and two chapter head drawings (each repeated several times) by B.

68 ——. *Wyatt Earp, Gunfighting Marshal*, by E. Ned Johnson (pseud.). Messner, N.Y., 1956, decor. cloth and endsheets, 192 pp., illus. with numerous drawings by B.

69 Judson, Clara Ingram. *Theodore Roosevelt, Fighting Patriot*. Wilcox and Follett, Chicago etc., (1953), pic. cloth, 218 (3) pp., author's foreword, numerous illus., including the frontis. in color, by B.

70 ——. *Andrew Jackson, Frontier Statesman*. Follett, Chicago etc., (1954), pic. boards, tinted endsheets, 224 pp., author's foreword, numerous illus. by B.

71 ——. *St. Lawrence Seaway*. Follett, Chicago, (1959), pic. cloth, blue top, 160 pp., author's foreword, illus. with twelve maps, photos, and drawings by B.

ILLUSTRATION by Bjorklund from *Roundup at the Double Diamond*

72 Kane, Harnett T. *Young Mark Twain and the Mississippi*. Random House, N.Y., (1966), colored pic. boards and endsheets, green top, 173 (1) pp., author's note, index, more than thirty drawings by B.

73 Keating, Bern. *Famous American Explorers*. Rand McNally, Chicago, (1972), words "First Printing, 1972" on copyright page, colored pic. boards, pic. map endsheets, ten full-color double-page plates by Remington, Russell et al. plus numerous drawings by B.

74 Kennedy, Marguerite Wallace. *My Home on the Range*. Little, Brown, Boston, 1951, words "First Edition" on copyright page, decor. cloth, pic. endsheets, 341 pp., illus. with twenty-nine drawings by B.

75 Klaperman, Gilbert and Libbey, et al. *The Story of the Jewish People*. Behrman House, N.Y., (1956), 1958, 1961, three volumes, pic. cloth, pp. 189, 221 and 256, "Preface" by Samuel Belkin (I), teacher's bibliography (II, III), index (II, III), maps, numerous illus. by B.

76 Kretchman, Herbert F. *The Story of Gilsonite*. American Gilsonite Co., Salt Lake City, Utah, 1957, decor. morrocco, pic. endsheets, 96 pp., foreword, illus. with numerous maps and drawings by B. and with photos.

77 Kripke, Dorothy K. and Levin, Meyer. *God and the Story of Judaism*. Behrman House, N.Y., (1962), pic. cloth, 191 pp., "Foreword to the Teacher" by Toby K. Kurzband, numerous illus. by B.

78 La Farge, Oliver. *Cochise of Arizona*. Aladdin Books, N.Y., 1953, words "First Edition" on copyright page, cloth, 191 pp., preface, numerous illus. by B.

78a ———. *Indians of the Eastern Woodlands*. S.R.A. Pilot Library, Science Research Associates, Inc., Chicago, 1964, wraps, illus. by B.

79 Lee, Robert Edson. *To the War*. Knopf, N.Y., 1968, words "First Edition" on copyright page, cloth and boards, 179 (1) pp., fifteen illus. by B.

80 Libby, O. G., ed. *Arikara Narrative of the Campaign the Hostile Dakotas, June, 1876*. Sol Lewis, N.Y., 1973, cloth, 256 pp., "Preface" by Dee Brown, "Introduction" by D'Arcy McNickle, illus. including one, the frontis. in color, by B.

81 Lodbell, Helen. *The Fort in the Forest*. Houghton Mifflin, Boston, 1963, pic. cloth, 218 pp., author's note, eighteen drawings by B.

82 McBride, Mary Margaret. *The Growing Up of Mary Elizabeth*. Dodd, Mead, N.Y., (1966), cloth, 175 (1) pp., numerous drawings by B.

83 McGiffin, Lee. *Riders of Enchanted Valley*. Dutton, N.Y., (1966), words "First Edition" on copyright page, pic. cloth, 158 pp., d/w, front cover and frontis. illus. by B.

84 (McGivern, Maureen Daly.) *Rosie, the Dancing Elephant*, by Maureen Daly (pseud.). Dodd, Mead, N.Y., 1967, cloth, 40 (5) pp., biographical sketches of the author and illustrator, 20 illus. by B.

85 McKown, Robin. *Painter of the Wild West: Frederic Remington*. Messner, N.Y., (1959), decor. cloth, 192 pp., acknowledgments, epilogue, selected bibliography, index, d/w illus. by B.

86 Mason, F. Van Wyck. *The Battles for New Orleans*. Houghton Mifflin, Boston, 1962, pic. cloth and endsheets, 183 pp., numerous illus. by B.

87 Matson, Emerson N. *Longhouse Legends*. Nelson, (Camden, N.J., 1968), boards, 127 (1) pp., introduction, illus. with color photos, and twelve drawings by B.

88 May, Julian. *Horses: How They Came To Be*. Holiday House, N.Y., 1968, pic. cloth, unpaged, thirty-four illus. by B.

89 ———. *The First Men*. Holiday, N.Y., 1968, pic. cloth, unpaged, numerous illus. by B.

89a ———. *How the Animals Came to North America*. Holiday House, N.Y., 1974, pic. cloth, illus. by B.

90 Montgomery, Rutherford G. *Crazy Kill Range*. World, Cleveland and N.Y., (1963), pic. cloth, blue top, 192 pp., front cover, d/w, and twenty-one illus. in text by B.

91 ———. *Ghost Town Gold*. World, Cleveland etc., 1965, pic. cloth, orange top, 128 pp., fifteen illus. by B.

92 ———. *A Kinkajou on the Town*. World, Cleveland etc., 1967, cloth, 160 pp., illus. by B.

93 ———. *Thornbush Jungle*. World, Cleveland etc., (1966), words "First Edition" on copyright page, pic. cloth, 159 (1) pp., numerous illus. by B.

94 (Norton, Alice Mary.) *Scarface*, by Andre Norton (pseud.). Harcourt, Brace, N.Y., (1948), cloth, with paper title labels, 263 pp., numerous illus. including six full-page plates, pp. (59), (105), (161), (185), (233) and (257), by B.

95 ———. *Sword in Sheath*. Harcourt, Brace, N.Y.,

(1949), words "First Edition" on copyright page, cloth, 246 pp., eighteen drawings by B.

96 *The Old Army Press.* Catalog no. 5, (Ft. Collins, Colo., 1973), colored pic. wraps, unpaged, numerous illus. including one by B. (Cisneros, Eggenhofer, Von Schmidt)

97 O'Meara, Walter. *The First Northwest Passage.* Houghton Mifflin, Boston, 1960, pic. cloth and endsheets, 183 pp., index, maps, numerous illus. by B.

98 ———. *The Sioux are Coming.* Houghton Mifflin, Boston, 1971, words "First Printing A" on copyright page, pic. cloth, orange endsheets, 105 pp., twenty-one illus. in text plus d/w by B.

99 Powers, Alfred. *True Adventures on Westward Trails.* Little, Brown, Boston, (1954), words "First Edition" on copyright page, decor. cloth, 216 pp., fifteen drawings in text and d/w in color by B.

100 Power-Waters, Alma. *Virginia Giant.* Dodd, Mead, N.Y., 1957, words "First Edition" on copyright page, pic. cloth, 224 pp., bibliography, sixteen drawings by B.

101 Reynolds, Marjorie. *The Cabin on Ghostly Pond.* Harpers, N.Y., (1962), pic. cloth, 216 pp., eleven drawings by B.

102 ———. *Ride the Wild Storm.* Macmillan, N.Y., (1968), words "First Printing" on copyright page, colored pic. cloth, pp. 169, numerous illus. by B.

103 ———. *Sire Unknown.* Macmillan, N.Y., (1968), words "First Printing" on copyright page, colored pic. cloth, 153 (1) pp., fifteen illus. by B.

103a Richard, Adriene. *Pistol.* Little, Brown, Boston, cloth, 245 pp., d/w illus. by B.

103b Ritchie, Rita. *The Golden Hawks of Genghis Khan.* Dutton, N.Y., 1958, words "First Edition" on copyright page, pic. cloth, 191 pp., bibliography, twenty-one illus. by B.

103c ———. *The Year of the Horse.* Dutton, N.Y., words "First Edition" on the copyright page, 1957, cloth, 191 pp., twenty-one illus. by B.

103d Robinson, William P. *Where the Panther Screams.* World, Cleveland and N.Y., (1961), words "First Edition" on copyright page, pic. cloth, 179 pp., thirty-two illus. by B.

104 Schaefer, Jack. *The Plainsmen.* Houghton Mifflin, Boston, 1963, pic. cloth, tan endsheets, 252 pp., publisher's note, thirteen illus. by B.

105 ———. *Stubby Pringle's Christmas.* Houghton Mifflin, Boston, 1964, decor. cloth, green endsheets, 43 pp., numerous drawings by B.

106 ———. *Mavericks.* Houghton Mifflin, Boston, 1967, decor. cloth, 184 pp., d/w, front cover, and eighteen drawings in text by B.

107 ———. Same, London edition by Andre Deutsch, words "First Published 1968" on copyright page, with eighteen drawings by B.

108 Schultz, James Willard. *The Quest of the Fish Dog Skin.* Houghton Mifflin, Boston, (1960), pic. cloth and endsheets, 218 (1) pp., seven illus., front cover, endsheets, d/w, and facing pp. 64, 102, 142 and 186, by B.

109 ———. *The Trail of the Spanish Horse.* Houghton Mifflin, Boston, (1960), pic. cloth and endsheets, 212 (1) pp., publisher's note, seven illus., front cover, endsheet, d/w, and facing pp. 56, 110, 150 and 178, by B.

110 ———. *With the Indians in the Rockies.* Houghton Mifflin, Boston, (1960), pic. cloth and endsheets, 227 (1) pp., publisher's note, preface, seven illus., front cover, endsheet, d/w, and facing pp. 30, 94, 128 and 168, by B.

111 Seibert, Jerry. *Dan Beard, Boy Scout Pioneer.* Houghton Mifflin, Boston, 1963, pic. cloth, 191 pp., (1) of advs., illus. with more than forty drawings by B.

112 Seymour, Alta Halverson. *Erick's Christmas Camera.* Follett, Chicago etc., (1956), pic. boards, 128 pp., twenty-nine drawings by B.

113 Sherman, Jane. *The Real Book about Dogs.* Garden City Books, Garden City, N.Y., (1951), cloth and decor. boards, pic. endsheets, 192 pp., twenty-six drawings by B.

114 Showers, Paul. *Indian Festivals.* Crowell, N.Y., (1969), colored pic. boards, (40) pp., eighteen tinted drawings by B.

115 Silverberg, Robert. *Ghost towns of the American West.* Crowell, N.Y., (1968), cloth, 309 (1) pp., bibliography, index, illus. with twenty drawings by B.

115a Smith, F. S. *"Fremont," Soldier, Explorer, Statesman.* Rand McNally, Chicago, 1966, cloth, maps, illus. including one, the d/w, by B.

115b Smith, Nita Banton, Hart, Hazel C. and Baker, Clare Belle (selected and edited by). *Foolish and Wise.* A volume in the Bobbs-Merrill Best of Children's Literature (Series), Indianapolis, 1960, cloth, illus. pp. 41 through 58 by B.

115c Spies, Victor. *Sun Dance and the Great Spirit*. Follett, Chicago, 1954, pic. boards, 128 pp., fifty drawing by B.

116 Steele, William O. *De Soto, Child of the Sun*. Aladdin Books, N.Y., 1956, words, "First Edition" on copyright page, pic. cloth, pic. map endsheets, 190 pp., thirty drawings by B.

117 Sterne, Emma Gelders. *Let the Moon Go By*. Aladdin Books, N.Y., 1955, pic. cloth and endsheets, 192 pp., thirty-two drawings by B.

117a Surface, Bill. *Roundup at the Double Diamond* (The American Cowboy Today). Houghton Mifflin, Boston, 1974, words "First Printing V" on copyright page, decor. cloth, tan endsheets, 237 pp., preface, eight illus., pp. (xviii), (40), (70), (108), (134), (160), (186) and (210), by B.

118 Taylor, Alice. *Gold Rush of '49*. Nelson Doubleday, n.p., 1960, pic. wraps, 62 pp., maps, numerous drawings by B.

119 Taylor, Don Alonzo. *Old Sam, Thoroughbred Trotter*. Follett, Chicago etc., (1955), pic. boards, 160 pp., twenty-three drawings by B.

120 ———. *Old Sam and the Horse Thieves*. Follett, Chicago, N.Y., (1966), words "First Printing" on copyright page, pic. cloth, fifteen drawings by B.

121 Taylor, Louis. *The Story of America's Horses*. World, Cleveland etc., 1968, cloth, 128 pp., illus. with twenty-five drawings by B.

122 Terrell, John Upton. *Bunkhouse Papers*. Dial, N.Y., 1971, words "First Printing" on copyright page, cloth and boards, tan endsheets, 251 pp., foreword, seventeen illus. in the text plus the d/w illus. by B.

123 (Thompson, George Selden.) *Heinrich Schliemann*, by George Selden (pseud.). Macmillan, N.Y., (1964), words "First Printing" on copyright page, cloth, unpaged, thirty drawings by B.

124 Tinkle, Lon. *The Story of Oklahoma*. Random House, N.Y., (1962), pic. cloth, colored pic. endsheets, index, maps, illus. with more than thirty drawings by B.

125 Vance, Marguerite. *Courage at Sea*. Dutton, N.Y., (1963), words "First Edition" on copyright page, pic. cloth, 86 pp., author's note, fifteen drawings by B.

126 ———. *Esther Wheelright, Indian Captive*. Dutton, N.Y., (1964), words "First Edition" on copyright page, pic. cloth, 96 pp., twelve drawings by B.

127 Violette, Hallie Hall and Ada Claire Darby. *On the Trail to Santa Fe*. Houghton Mifflin, Boston, (1941), pic. cloth, pic. map endsheets, 266 pp., foreword, numerous drawings by B.

128 Watkins, Richard. *Venture West*. Harcourt, Brace, N.Y., (1951), words "First edition" on copyright page, cloth and boards, 238 pp., twenty-two drawings by B.

129 Wellman, Paul I. *Gold in California*. Houghton Mifflin, Boston, 1958, pic. cloth and endsheets, 184 pp., (foreword) by Sterling North, some books to read, index, map, illus. with more than fifty drawings by B.

130 ———. *Indian Wars and Warriors West*. Houghton Mifflin, Boston, 1959, pic. cloth and endsheets, 182 pp., (foreword) by Sterling North, index, maps, illus. with more than forty drawings by B.

131 ———. *Indian Wars and Warriors East*. Houghton Mifflin, Boston, 1959, pic. cloth and endsheets, 184 pp., index, maps, illus. with more than forty drawings by B.

132 ———. *Race for the Golden Spike*. Houghton Mifflin, Cambridge, 1961, pic. cloth and endsheets, 184 pp., some books to read, (foreword) by Sterling North, index, map, thirty-six illus. by B.

133 ———. *A Dynasty of Western Outlaws*. Doubleday, Garden City, N.Y., 1961, words "First Edition" on copyright page, cloth, pic. map endsheets, 384 pp., A Word to the Reader, bibliography (evaluated), index, map (of Outlaw Country), illus. with twenty-five drawings by B.

134 ———. *The Greatest Cattle Drive*. Houghton Mifflin, Boston, 1964, pic. cloth and endsheets, 185 pp., (foreword) by Sterling North, some books to read, index, map, illus. with more than forty drawings by B.

135 ———. *Spawn of Evil*. Doubleday, Garden City, N.Y., 1964, words "First Edition" on copyright page, decor. cloth, pic. map endsheets, 350 pp., bibliography (evaluated), index, illus. with twenty-five drawings by B.

136 White, Dale. *Bat Masterson*. Messner, N.Y., (1960), decor. cloth, 191 pp., bibliography, index, d/w illus. by B.

136a Willis, William. *The Gods Were Kind*. Dutton, N.Y., 1955, cloth, 225 pp., frontis. in color, maps, diagramatic sketches and d/w illus. by B.

137 Witten, Herbert. *Escape from the Shawnees*. Follett, Chicago, 1958, 189 pp., illus. by B.

138 ———. *Desperate Journey*. Follett, Chicago, 1960, cloth, 158 pp., illus. by B.

139 Witty, Paul et al., eds. *Reading Roundup, Book One.* Heath, Boston, (1954), pic. cloth, 502 pp., brief biographies, index of authors and titles, numerous illus. including five, pp. 72, 73, 74, 75 and 77, by B.

139a ———. *Reading Roundup, Book Two.* Heath, Boston, (1955), pic. cloth, 502 pp., brief biographies, index of authors and titles, numerous illus. including four, pp. 100, 103, 105 and 108, by B.

139b *World Book Encyclopedia,* voulme 15. Field Enterprises, Chicago etc., (1973), two-tone fabricoid, the section "Pioneer Life in America" is illus. with fifteen drawings by B. Note: Bjorklund illus. also appear in other volumes.

140 Young, John Richard. *Arabian Cow Horse.* Follett, Chicago, N.Y., (1953), colored pic. boards, 256 pp., illustrated with twenty drawings by B.

The Artist and His Art

141 Bjorklund, Lorence F. "Recollections of an Old West Illustrator," a feature article in *Publishers' Weekly,* Nov. 6, 1967, reminiscences of the artist's early days as an illustrator, photo of him and nine drawings by him.

142 Kingman, Lee et al. (compiled by). *Illustrators of Children's Books: 1957–1966.* The Horn Book, Boston, 1968, pic. cloth, 295 pp., introduction, numerous illustrations, short autobiographical sketch by B., p. 82, and a list of seven books illus. by him, p. 210.

ILLUSTRATION by Bjorklund from *Horse Tradin'*

THE GREAT MYSTERY by Blumenschein from *Indian Boyhood*

ERNEST LEONARD BLUMENSCHEIN
1874–1960

Catalogues of Art Exhibitions and Galleries

ART INSTITUTE OF CHICAGO

1 *Catalogue of the Annual Exhibition of Oil Paintings and Sculpture by American Artists,* 34th, 1921, one illus., "White Son and Star Road," by B.

2 Same, 38th, 1925, one illus., "New Mexico," by B.

3 Same, 42nd, 1929, one illus., "Night Scene," by B.

4 *Catalogue of a Century of Progress Exhibition of Paintings and Sculpture,* June 1 to Nov. 1, 1934, words "First Edition" on title page, 103 pp. plus 95 plates including no. 82 by B.

5 *Half a Century of American Art,* Nov. 16, 1939, to Jan. 7, 1940, 61 pp. plus 78 plates including XXI, "The Chief Speaks," by B. Note on Blumenschein, p. 7. (Remington)

BABCOCK GALLERIES, NEW YORK

6 *Paintings of the West,* 1920, unpaged (16), one illus. by B. (Dunton, Russell)

CARNEGIE INSTITUTE, DEPARTMENT OF FINE ARTS PITTSBURGH

7 *Annual Exhibition of Paintings,* 28th, 1929, one illus., "Landscape with Indian Camp," by B.

8 Same, 29th, 1930, one illus., "Maria," by B.

9 Same, 30th, 1931, one illus., "New Mexican Interior," by B.

10 *Painting in the U.S., 1943,* one illus., "Box Cars and Railroad Tracks," by B. (Hurd)

CINCINNATTI ART MUSEUM

11 *Annual Exhibition of American Art,* 28th, 1921, one illus., "October," by B.

12 Same, 32nd, 1925, one illus., "White Son and Star Road," by B.

CITY ART MUSEUM, ST. LOUIS

13 *Annual Exhibition of Selected Paintings by American Artists,* 15th, 1920, one illus., "Indian Battle," by B.

14 Same, 17th, 1922, one illus., "Superstition," by B.

15 Same, 26th, 1931, one illus., "Adobe Village, Winter," by B.

CORCORAN GALLERY OF ART, WASHINGTON, D.C.

16 *Biennial Exhibition of Contemporary American Oil Paintings,* 1928(–29), one illus., "White Son and Star Road," by B. (Dunton)

17 Same, 1930–31, one illus., "Adobe Village, Winter," by B.

18 Same, 1932–33, one illus., "The City," by B.

EL PASO MUSEUM OF ART

18a *The McKee Collection of Paintings,* (1968), cloth with an illus. in color mounted on the front cover, tan endsheets, 67 pp., "Foreword" by Leonard P. Sipiora (Director), numerous illus. including one in color, p. 30, by B. (Dunton, Hurd, Koerner, Lea)

18b Same, 1000 copies in pic. wraps.

GALLERY OF SCIENCE AND ART, PALACE OF ELECTRICITY AND COMMUNICATION, GOLDEN GATE INTERNATIONAL EXPOSITION, SAN FRANCISCO

18c *Contemporary Art of the United States,* Collection of the IBM Corporation, (1940), morocco, marbled endsheets, unpaged, all edges gilt, numerous illus. including one, "Mountains near Taos," by B. and a photo of him. (Lea)

GALLERY WEST, DENVER

18d *The American Indian and Selected Western Paintings,* January 1974, pic. wraps, 16 pp., eighteen illus. including one, p. 4, by B. (Borein, Deming, Russell)

GRAND CENTRAL ART GALLERIES, NEW YORK

19 *Exhibition of Paintings and Sculpture Contributed by the Founders of the Galleries*, commencing June 27, 1923, wraps, unpaged, numerous illus. including one, "Indian and Red Mountain," by B. and with a brief biographical sketch of him.

20 *Year Book 1930*, stiff boards with illus. in color on front cover, decor. endsheets, 79 (1) pp., numerous illus., including one, "Adobe Village," p. 8, winner of first prize for landscape, by B. (Johnson)

21 *Year Book 1938*, wraps with illus. mounted on front cover, 72 pp., numerous illus. including one, "Moon, Morning Star and Evening Star," p. (18), by B. (Johnson, Leigh)

KENNEDY GALLERIES, NEW YORK

22 *The Things That Were* (19th and 20th century paintings of American West), June, 1968, colored pic. wraps, pp. 52–123, (1), numerous illus. including one, no. 107, "Maurico of Taos Pueblo," by B. (Crawford, Leigh, Miller, Remington, Schoonover, Schreyvogel)

23 *Western Words*, June, 1969, colored pic. wraps, 75 pp. numerous illus. including one by B. (Johnson, Miller, Remington, Russell, Schreyvogel, Zogbaum)

23a *The Great American West*, June 1973, colored pic. wraps, pp. (131)–192, numerous illus. including one in color, p. 170, by B. (Leigh, Miller, Remington, Russell, Schreyvogel)

LOS ANGELES COUNTY MUSEUM OF HISTORY, SCIENCE AND ART, LOS ANGELES

24 *Catalogue of the Mr. and Mrs. William Preston Harrison Galleries of American Art*, 1934, one illus., "Juanita of Taos," by B.

MUSEUM OF MODERN ART, NEW YORK

25 *Paintings and Sculpture from Sixteen American Cities*, 1933, one illus., "Lone Fisherman," by B.

26 *Art in Our Times*, 1939, one illus., "Jury Trial of a Sheepherder for Murder," by B.

MUSEUM OF NEW MEXICO ART GALLERY
SANTA FE

27 *A Retrospect Exhibit of the Life Work of Ernest L. Blumenschein*, May 30 to June 30, 1948, catalogue of paintings (65), six illus. by B. and a brief biographical sketch.

28 *A Retrospective Exhibition, 1902–1958*, at State College, N.M., Dec. 14, 1958, to Jan. 4, 1959, eight illus. by B.

29 *An Exhibition of Paintings from the Santa Fe Railway Collection*, 1966, one illus. by B. (Dunton, Leigh)

NATIONAL ACADEMY OF DESIGN, NEW YORK

30 *Annual Exhibition Catalogue*, 85th, 1910, one illus., "Portrait of a German Tragedian," by B.

31 Same, 90th, 1915, one illus., "Violinist," by B.

32 Same, 92nd, 1917, one illus., "Medicine Man," by B.

33 Same, 98th, 1923, one illus., "The Gift," by B.

34 Same, 99th, 1924, one illus., "Idealist, Dreamer, Idealist," by B.

35 Same, *Centennial Exhibition*, 1925, one illus., by B. (Remington)

36 Same, 104th, 1929, one illus., "Burro," by B.

37 Same, 111th, one illus., "Jury for Trial of a Sheepherder for Murder," by B.

38 Same, 115th, 1941, one illus., "Homeward Bound," by B.

THE NATIONAL ARCHIVES OF THE UNITED STATES
WASHINGTON, D.C.

38a *Indians and the American West*, October 26, 1973–January 21, 1974, colored pic. wraps, unpaged, numerous illus. including no. 5 in color by B. (Dunton, Schreyvogel)

NATIONAL ART SOCIETY, NEW YORK

39 *American Art Today*, World's Fair, 1939-40, one illus., "Red Symphony," by B.

OKLAHOMA ART CENTER, OKLAHOMA CITY

40 *European and American Paintings* (from the collection of Mr. and Mrs. W. E. Davis), Nov. 5–27, 1964, colored pic. wraps, unpaged (16), 25 illus. including one by B. (Hurd, Remington, Russell)

PENNSYLVANIA ACADEMY OF FINE ARTS,
PHILADELPHIA

41 *111th Annual Exhibition*, 1916, one illus., "Chief's Two Sons," by B.

PHOENIX ART MUSEUM

42 *An Exhibition of Paintings of the Southwest from the Santa Fe Railway Collection*, Feb. 1 through April 30, 1966, including one illus., p. 9, by B. (Dunton, Leigh)

THE LAST OF CUSTER by Blumenschein from *Indian Fights and Fighters*

Homer H. Boelter, index, numerous illus., including two pp. 182 and 183 by B., notes on Blumenschein by Don Louis Perceval. Limited to 400 copies. (Borein, Dixon, Johnson, Remington, Russell)

56a Getlein, Frank et al. *The Lure of the Great West.* Country Beautiful, Waukesha, Wisconsin, (1973), boards, 352 pp., introduction, 375 illus. including one, pp. (326)–7, by B. (Koerner, Leigh, Miller, Remington, Russell, Schreyvogel, Wyeth)

57 Harmsen, Dorothy. *Harmsen's Western Americana.* Northland Press, Flagstaff, Arizona, (1971), morocco and cloth, blue endsheets, 213 pp., "Foreword" by Robert Rockwell, introduction, numerous illus. including one in color, p. (29), by B. and with a biographical sketch of him. Author's edition of 150 numbered copies signed by the author in slipcase with morocco title label. (Beeler, Borein, Dixon, Dunn, Dunton, Eggenhofer, Elwell, Hurd, Johnson, Leigh, Marchand, Miller, Russell, Von Schmidt, Wyeth)

58 ———. Same, first trade edition, two-tone cloth with red endsheets.

59 Hewitt, Edgar L. *Representative Art and Artists of New Mexico.* School of American Research, Museum of New Mexico (Santa Fe Press), Santa Fe, 1940, pictorial wraps, 40 pp., biographical notes, numerous illustrations, including one, p. 9, by B. (Dunton, Hurd)

60 Jackman, Rilla Evelyn. *American Arts.* Rand McNally Co., Chicago, New York, San Francisco, (1928), cloth, 561 pp., illustrations, including one, facing p. 272, by B. Biographical sketch, p. 269.

61 Keleher, William A. *Turmoil in New Mexico.* The Rydal Press, Santa Fe, New Mexico, (1952 — released in December, 1951), cloth, map endsheets, 534 pp., foreword, index, illustrated including a frontispiece by B.

62 ———. *Violence in Lincoln County, 1869–1881.* University of New Mexico Press, Albuquerque, (1957), words "First Edition" on copyright page, cloth, map endsheets, 390 pp., foreword, sources, index, illustrated with a frontispiece by B. and with photographs.

63 Kipling, Rudyard. *The Day's Work.* Doubleday & McClure Co., New York, 1898, pic. cloth, 431 pp., gilt top, eight illus. including two, facing pp. 144 and 150, by B.

64 Kloster, Paula R. *The Arizona State College Collec-tion of American Art.* (The Castle Press, Pasadena, California, 1954), wraps, 108 (1) pp., "Foreword" by President Grady Gammage, introduction, acknowledgments, index, 113 illus. including one, p. 34, by B. (Johnson, Remington, Russell)

65 Lanier, Henry W. *The Book of Bravery.* Chas. Scribner's Sons, New York, 1918, words "Published September, 1918" on copyright page, pictorial cloth, 420 pp., preface, illus. including one full-page plate, facing p. 238, by B.

66 Luhan, Mabel Dodge. *Taos and Its Artists.* Duell, Sloan and Pearce, New York, (1947), cloth, red endsheets, 168 pp., acknowledgments, profusely illus. including plate no. 9, "Sheep Herder," by B. Photo and much on Blumenschein in text. (Dunton, Remington)

67 Major, Mabel and Smith, Rebecca W. *The Southwest in Literature.* The Macmillan Co., New York, 1929, cloth, 370 pp., illus. including one, facing p. 121, "The Chief Speaks," by B.

68 Merwin, Samuel. *The Road to Frontenac.* Doubleday, Page & Co., New York, 1901, decorated cloth, 404 pp., four illus., frontis. and facing pp. 36, 64 and 256, by B.

69 Minton, Charles Ethridge (State Supervisor). *New Mexico, A Guide to the Colorful State.* Compiled by Workers of the Writers' Program, W.P.A., Hastings House, New York, 1940. Words "First Published in August 1940," cloth, map on front endsheet, 458 pp., "Foreword" by Clinton P. Anderson, "Preface" by Minton, chronology, Some Books About New Mexico, index, numerous illus. including one, between pp. 394 and 395, by B., maps. (American Guide Series)

70 Neuhaus, Eugen. *The Galleries of the Exposition* (A Critical Review of the Paintings, Statuary and the Graphic Arts in the Palace of Fine Arts at the Panama–Pacific International Exposition). San Francisco, 1915, boards, 98 pp., numerous illus. including one, "The Peacemaker," facing p. 34, by B.

71 ———. *The History and Ideals of American Art.* Stanford University Press, Stanford University, California, etc. 1931, cloth with paper labels, 444 pp., tinted top, preface, bibliography, index, illus. including one, page (310), by B. (Dixon, Remington, and Russell)

72 Pach, Walter et al. *New Mexico Artists.* The University of New Mexico Press, Albuquerque, 1952, pic-

torial boards, 124 (7) pp., "Introduction" by Joaquin Ortega, numerous illus. including eleven by B. (New Mexico Artist Series no. 3) (Hurd)

73 Paine, Ralph D. *The Praying Skipper and Other Stories*. Outing, N.Y., 1906, cloth, 229 pp., six illustrations including one, the frontis. in color, by B.

74 Parrish, Randall. *Molly McDonald*. A. C. McClurg & Co., Chicago, 1912, words "Published April, 1912" on copyright page, 403 (1) pp., four illus. in color, frontis. and facing pp. 108, 220 and 286, by B.

75 Poe, Edgar Allan. *Tales By*. Duffield & Co., New York, 1909 (1908?), words "Centenary Edition" on title page, cloth with small colored illus. mounted on the front cover, 218 (1) pp., gilt top, seven illus. in color, frontis. and facing pp. 36, 48, 74, 92, 110 and 168, by B.

76 Reed, Walt. *The Illustrator in America 1900–1960's*. Reinhold, N.Y., (1966), cloth, pic. green endsheets, 271 (1) pp., "Is Illustration Art?" by Albert Dorne, bibliography, numerous illus. including one, p. 47, by B. and with a brief biographical sketch of him. (Crawford, Dunn, Dunton, Eggenhofer, Fischer, Fogarty, Goodwin, Keller, Koerner, Remington, Russell, Schoonover, Stoops, Wyeth)

77 Rossi, Paul A. and Hunt, David C. *The Art of the Old West* (from the Collection of the Gilcrease Institute). (Knopf, N.Y., but printed in Italy, 1971), words "First Edition" on copyright page, pic. cloth, pic. brown endsheets, 335 (1) pp., preface, listing of artists and works, bibliography, numerous illus. including two in color, pp. (305) and (306–7), by B. (Borein, James, Leigh, Miller, Remington, Russell, Schreyvogel, Wyeth)

78 *The Second Annual of Illustrations for Advertisements in the United States*. The Art Directors Club, N.Y., (1923), cloth and decor. boards, tan endsheets, 171 pp., numerous illus. including one in color, "The Indian Suite," p. (18), by B. It was the First Award Medal winner for Paintings and Drawings in Color. (Dunn, Keller, Wyeth)

79 Taft, Robert. *The End of a Century — The Pictorial Record of the Old West XIII*. Reprinted from The Kansas Historical Quarterly, Topeka, Kansas, August, 1951, pictorial wraps, pp. 225–253, illus. including a photo of B., and one full page plate, between pp. 248–249, by B. (Dixon, Leigh, Lungren, Remington, Russell, Schreyvogel)

80 ———. *Artists and Illustrators of the Old West*,

1850–1900. Charles Scribner's Sons, New York, 1953, code letter "A" follows copyright notice, cloth, map endsheets, 399 pp., preface and acknowledgments, sources and notes, index, 90 numbered illus. including one, no. 89, by B. (Leigh, Remington, Schreyvogel)

81 Watson, Thomas J. et al. *Contemporary Art of the United States*. International Business Machines Corp., N.Y., 1940, wraps, unpaged, foreword, numerous illus. including one, "Mountain Near Taos," by B. (Dixon, Lea)

81a Weaver, Paul E. *Autumn 1973 Book List*. Northland Press, Flagstaff, colored pic. wraps, unpaged, numerous illus. including one by B. (Beeler, Dixon, James, Perceval, Remington, Santee, Von Schmidt)

The Artist and His Art

82 Abousleman, Michael D. (compiler). *Who's Who in New Mexico*. The Abousleman Co., Albuquerque, 1937, fabricoid, 254 pp., preface. Biographical sketch of B. (Dunton, Hurd)

83 Blumenschein, Helen G. *Sangre de Cristo* (A Short Illustrated History of Taos). Privately printed (Taos, 1955), pic. wraps, unpaged, illus. by the author; mentions her father on the page about Taos artists and writers.

83a Dippie, Brian W. "Brush, Palette and the Custer Battle — A Second Look," an article on the art of the Little Big Horn in *Montana* 24:1, Winter 1974, with one illus. by B. (Dunton, Remington, Russell, Schreyvogel, Von Schmidt)

84 Clark, Edna Maria. *Ohio Art and Artists*. Garrett and Massie, Richmond, (1932), cloth, 509 pp., preface, appendices, index, illus. B., pp. 319 and 336-7 and biographical sketch, p. 444. (Deming)

85 Dunton, W. Herbert. "The Painters of Taos," an article in *The American Magazine of Art*, August, 1922, with one illus. by B. (Dunton)

86 Ewing, Robert et al. *50th Anniversary Exhibition, Nov. 12, 1967 to Feb. 18, 1968*. Museum of New Mexico, Fine Arts Bldg., (Santa Fe), colored pic. wraps, unpaged, "Foreword" by Ewing, includes a biographical sketch and a photo of B. and lists his three paintings in the exhibition.

87 Ferbrache, Lewis. *Theodore Wores*. Privately printed, San Francisco, 1968, colored pic. wraps, 63 pp., "Preface" by Joseph A. Baird, Jr., illus. by Wores;

Wores mentions Blumenschein a number of times in his letters (summer 1917) from Taos.

88 Fisher, Reginald (compiled and edited by). *An Art Directory of New Mexico.* Museum of New Mexico and School of American Research (Santa Fe), 1947, words "Edition — 1000" on copyright page, wraps, 78 pp., foreword. The Blumenschein sketch appears on pp. 10 and 11. (Hurd)

89 Forrest, James T. "Ernest L. Blumenschein," an article in *The American Scene* 3:3, Fall 1960, Gilcrease Institute, Tulsa, with four illus. by B. This issue also includes "Tribute to an Artist" by C. L. Packer — reminiscences of an art class at Taos where Blumenschein served as a critic. (Dunton)

90 Hewett, Edgar L. "On the Opening of the Art Galleries," an article in *Art and Archaeology* 7:1–2, Jan.-Feb., 1918, one illus. by B. (Dunton)

91 ———. "Recent Southwestern Art," an article in *Art and Archaeology* 9:1, January, 1920, one illus. by B. (Dunton)

92 Hinshaw, Merton E. (Director). *Painters of the West.* Charles W. Bowers Memorial Museum, Santa Ana, Calif., 1972, includes a biographical sketch of B. (Johnson, Miller, Remington, Russell)

93 Hoeber, Arthur. "Painters of Western Life," an article in *Mentor Magazine,* June 15, 1915, includes one illus. by B. and a photo of him. (Dunton, Leigh, Remington, Russell, Schreyvogel)

94 Ortega, Joaquin, ed. *New Mexico Quarterly Review,* vol. XIX, no. 1. The University of New Mexico, Albuquerque, N.M., Spring, 1949, dec. wraps, 144 pp., five illus. between pp. 24 and 25 by B., contains "Ernest L. Blumenschein — The Artist in His Environment" by Howard Cook, pp. 18–24.

95 Perceval, Don Louis et al. *Art of Western America.* Pomona College Art Gallery, Claremont, Calif., Nov. 1–31, 1949, pic. wraps, unpaged, foreword, very brief biographical sketch of B. and lists his two paintings in the exhibition. (Russell)

96 Ronnebeck, Arnold. "Blumenschein," a biographical sketch in *El Palacio* 24:25, June 23, 1928, Museum of New Mexico, Santa Fe.

97 Russell, Don. *Custer's Last* (The Battle of the Little Big Horn in Picturesque Perspective). (Amon Carter Museum, Ft. Worth, 1968), cloth, 67 pp., notes, bibliography, 17 plates; includes material in text on B. (Deming, Dunton, Russell)

98 *Second Annual Exhibit of the Taos Society of Artists.* Palace of the Governors, Santa Fe, n.d. (1916?), pic. wraps, unpaged, includes a biographical sketch of B. (Dunton)

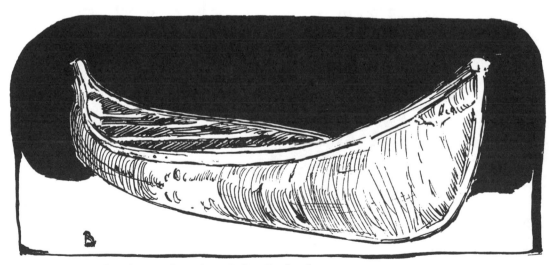

ILLUSTRATION by Blumenschein from *Indian Boyhood*

ILLUSTRATION by Borein from *Edward Borein: Drawings and Paintings of the Old West*

EDWARD BOREIN
1872–1945

Catalogues of Art Exhibitions and Galleries

ART LEAGUE OF SANTA BARBARA

1 *A Loan Exhibition of Etchings of the Far West by Edward Borein* (from the private collection of Francis E. Bliss), May 7 to May 19 inclusive (no year), eight illus. by B. and a photo of him. Lists 115 etchings, one drawing and one watercolor.

BAKER COLLECTOR GALLERY, LUBBOCK, TEXAS

2 *Winter*, 1964, one illus. by B. and lists four etchings and two drawings by him. (Hurd, Wyeth)

BILTMORE GALLERIES, LOS ANGELES

2a *Catalog*, May 1969, colored pic. wraps, 54 pp., numerous illus. including three, pp. 9 and 10 (two), by B. (Dixon, Dunton, Johnson, Koerner, Leigh, Remington, Russell, Young)

BRADFORD BRINTON MEMORIAL,
BIG HORN, WYOMING

3 *A Guide to Quarter Circle A Ranch*, two illus. by B. and lists other B. items in the collection. (Remington, Russell)

CHRISTIE'S (CANADA) WITH
MONTREAL BOOK AUCTIONS

4 *Works of Art and Literature*, The Palliser Hotel, Calgary, September 28, 1970, one illus. by B. and a brief biographical sketch of him.

COLONIAL ART COMPANY, OKLAHOMA CITY
(SENATE ROOM, LINCOLN PLAZA INN)

4a *Western and Traditional American Paintings of the 19th and Early 20th Centuries* (Auction Catalog), June 10, 1973, pic. wraps, unpaged, 76 numbered illus. including nine, nos. 59, 60, 61, 62, 63, 64, 65, 66 and 67, by B. (Deming, Dixon, Eggenhofer, Elwell, Goodwin, Johnson, Koerner, Russell, Schoonover, Wyeth, Young)

EDWARD EBERSTADT AND SONS, NEW YORK

5 *A Distinguished Collection of Western Paintings*, Catalogue 139, 1956, 129 numbered illus. including one, no. 7, by B. (Deming, Dixon, Johnson, Leigh, Miller, Remington, Wyeth, Zogbaum)

6 *American Paintings*, Catalogue 146, 1958 (but issued in December 1957), 191 numbered illus. including two, no. 25 and no. 26, by B. (Deming, Dixon, Dunton, Johnson, Leigh, Miller, Remington, Wyeth)

GALLERY OF WESTERN ART
MONTANA HISTORICAL SOCIETY, HELENA

7 *The True West of Ed Borein* (from the collection of Dr. H. I. Burtness, Santa Barbara), January-February, 1964, ten illus. by B. and a portrait of him by Spencer Bagdatopoulos.

GALLERY WEST, DENVER

8 *Prospectives in Western Art*, 1972, three illus. (one on front cover), by B. and lists a number of other items by him. (Deming, Dixon, Ellsworth, Remington, Russell, Schreyvogel)

GLENBOW-ALBERTA INSTITUTE, CALGARY, ALBERTA

9 *Glenbow Collects an Exhibition*, Art Series No. 1, 1969, one illus. by B.

GREENFIELD GALLERIES, SEATTLE

9a *American Western Art Auction*, October 28 (1972), pic. wraps, 58 pp., numerous illus. including two, pp. 10 and 42, by B. (Deming, Lungren, Remington, Russell, Schreyvogel)

HERITAGE INN, GREAT FALLS, MONTANA
(THE ADVERTISING CLUB OF GREAT FALLS)

9b *C. M. Russell Sixth Annual Auction of Original Western Art*, March 14–15, 1974, pic. wraps, unpaged, lists 165 lots for sale, numerous illus. including three, lots 87, 97 and 122, by B. (Deming)

THE JAMISON GALLERIES, SANTA FE

9c *Edward Borein and Kees Verkade*, August 19 through September 2, 1973, pic. wraps, 4 pp., ten illus. including five, front cover, pp. 3 (two), 4 and back cover, by B.

KENNEDY GALLERIES, NEW YORK

10 *The Western Legend*, April 16 to June 1, 1956, two illus., front cover and p. 5, by B. (Deming, Lungren)

11 *Painters of the Old West*, October 1960, three illus., pp. 111 and 112 (two), by B. (Deming, Leigh, Remington, Russell, Schreyvogel, Zogbaum)

12 *Recent Acquisitions in Important Western Paintings*, October 1961, three illus., pp. 154 (two) and 155, by B. and lists a number of etchings by him. (Deming, Eggenhofer, Johnson, Remington, Russell, Schreyvogel, Zogbaum)

13 *Recent Acquisitions in Important Western and Sporting Paintings and Sculptures*, October 1962, one illus., p. 53, by B. (Johnson, Leigh, Marchand, Miller, Remington, Russell, Schreyvogel)

14 *From Coast to Coast*, June 1967, one illus. in color, p. 134, by B. and a biographical sketch, p. 135. (Johnson, Remington, Russell)

15 *Beyond the Mississippi*, June 1971, two illus., pp. 44 and 51, by B. (Marchand, Remington, Russell, Schreyvogel)

E. WALTER LATENDORF, NEW YORK

16 *C. M. Russell*, Catalogue No. 27 (May, 1957), three illus. by B. (Crawford, De Yong, Goodwin, Leigh, Marchand, Russell)

LOS ADOBES ART GALLERY, SANTA BARBARA

17 *Exciting Western Art by Artist Members of Rancheros Visitadores*, May 4 through May 20, 1962, five illus. by B. and a portrait of him by Spencer Bagdatopoulos. (Johnson)

MAXWELL GALLERIES, SAN FRANCISCO

18 *American Art Since 1850*, August 2 to October 31, 1968, one illus, p. 32, by B. (Dixon, Johnson, Miller, Remington, Russell, Wyeth)

MIDWESTERN GALLERIES, CINCINNATI

19 *Catalogue of Fine Art Number 10* (1972?), two illus. by B. and lists a number of other items by him. (Leigh, Remington)

MUSEUM OF THE PLAINS INDIANS
BROWNING, MONTANA

20 *Forty & Five*, July 1, 1964, one illus., p. 3, by B. (Russell)

PACIFIC NORTHWEST INDIAN CENTER
SPOKANE, WASH.

20a *Third Annual Western Art Show & Auction*, March 2, 3, 4, 1973, pic. wraps, 44 pp., preface, numerous illus. including three, pp. 19 and 27 (two) by B. (Deming, Eggenhofer)

PARKE-BERNET GALLERIES, NEW YORK

21 *Western Americana — Paintings, Prints, Drawings, and Sculpture* (the collection of Dr. Lester E. Bauer, Detroit), Sale No. 3254, Oct. 27, 1971, one illus. by B. (Miller, Russell)

PHOENIX ART MUSEUM

21a *Edward Borein: The Katherine H. Haley Collection*, April 5–May 21, 1974, colored pic. wraps, 23 pp., "Edward Borein, Artist of the West" by Mrs. Haley, fourteen illus. (five in color) by B. plus a photo of him and one of Mrs. Haley with part of her Borein Collection.

RAINBOW HOTEL, GREAT FALLS, MONTANA
(ADVERTISING CLUB OF GREAT FALLS)

21b *Fifth Annual C. M. Russell Auction of Original Western Art*, March 16, 1973, pic. wraps, unpaged, numerous illus. including one, lot 41, by B. (De Yong, Johnson, Koerner, Marchand, Russell, Wyeth)

FRED ROSENSTOCK WITH JAMES PARSONS
(GALLERY WEST), DENVER

22 *100 Years of Western Art*, November 28 through December 24, 1969, five illus. by B. and a brief biographical sketch. (Beeler, Dunton, James, Koerner, Leigh)

SANTA BARBARA MUSEUM OF ART

23 *Edward Borein (1873-1945) Drawings and Watercolors*, July 27 to September 5, 1965, thirteen illus. by B. and a photo and biographical sketch of him.

SOTHEBY PARKE BERNET, NEW YORK

24 *Americana Week*, Sale No. 3467, January 24–27, one illus., p. 43, by B. (Deming, Eggenhofer, Elwell, Koerner)

TRAIL'S END, PASADENA, CALIFORNIA

25 *Announcing a Permanent Exhibition of the Work of*

Charles M. Russell — Paintings and Bronzes (1929), front cover illus. "Trail's End" by B.

WHITNEY GALLERY OF WESTERN ART (BUFFALO BILL HISTORICAL CENTER), CODY, WYOMING

26 *1964 Exhibition of Western Americana Art — "Buffalo Bill Country,"* May 1 to October 1, 1964, one illus., p. (2), by B. and a biographical sketch included in the "Foreword" by Director Harold McCracken. (Russell)

ZEITLIN & VER BRUGGE, LOS ANGELES

27 *Western Art — Etchings, Watercolors, Drawings and Paintings,* February 15 to March 15, 1968, announcement, one illus. by B.

Illustrated by the Artist

28 Acoma Books, Ramona, California. *Americana.* Catalogue 110, February 1969, illus. on front cover by B.

29 ———. *Americana.* Catalogue 112, April 1969, illus. on front cover by B.

30 ———. *Americana.* Catalogue 122, March 1970, illus. on front cover by B.

31 ———. *Americana.* Catalogue 131, February 1971, illus. on front cover by B.

32 Adams, Andy. *The Ranch on the Beaver.* Houghton Mifflin Co., Boston & N.Y., 1927, cloth, 307 pp., 4 illus. — frontis. and opposite pp. 66, 132, and 278 by B. The d/w is also illustrated by B.

33 Ainsworth, Ed. *The Cowboy in Art.* World, N.Y. and Cleveland, (1968), words "First Printing 1968" on copyright page, full leather, orange endsheets, 242 pp., all edges gilt, "Foreword" by John Wayne, index, numerous illus. including three, pp. 62 (two) and 63, by B. and photo of him. Special edition of 1000 numbered copies (Ed died before he had a chance to sign them) in a slip case. (Beeler, Bugbee, De Yong, Dixon, Dunton, Eggenhofer, Ellsworth, Hurd, James, Johnson, Koerner, Mora, Perceval, Remington, Russell, Santee, Schreyvogel, Von Schmidt)

34 ———. Same, first trade edition in gilt lettered and illus. cloth, orange endsheets.

35 ———. Same, reprint by Bonanza Books, N.Y., in red lettered and illus cloth, white endsheets.

36 Alta California Book Store, Berkeley. *California Ephemeral.* Catalogue 5, two illus., front cover and p. (51), by B.

36a Baird, Joseph A., Jr. (compiled by). *The West Remembered.* California Historical Society, San Francisco and San Marino, 1973, colored pic. wraps, 88 pp., "Foreword" by Mitchell A. Wilder, introduction, numerous illus. including four, pp. 32 (color), 49, (55) color, and 57, by B. (Blumenschein, Dixon, James, Lungren, Marchand, Miller, Remington, Russell, Zogbaum)

37 Blitz Books, Los Altos, Calif. *Americana.* Catalogue 22, illus. on front cover by B.

38 (Borein.) *A Merry Xmas and a Happy New Year from the Boreins.* Occasional Papers, no. 7, Santa Barbara Historical Society, 1967, pic. wraps, (24) pp., numerous illus. by B.

39 ———. *Etchings of the Far West by Edward Borein.* El Paseo, Santa Barbara, California, n.d., wraps, 29 (1) pp., 8 illus. from etchings by B. and a photo of B. (A slightly revised edition of the Bliss Exhibition catalogue used by B. as a sales list.)

40 Brayer, Garnet M. and Herbert O. *American Cattle Trails, 1540–1900.* American Pioneer Trails Assn., Bayside, New York, 1952, colored pictorial wraps, 128 pp., "Foreword" by Howard R. Driggs, numerous illus. including seven, pp. 8, 26, (46), 52, 75, (90) and (106), by B. (Stoops)

40a Brookshier, Frank. *The Burro.* Oklahoma, Norman, (1974), words "First edition" on copyright page, cloth, 370 pp., preface, notes, index, numerous illus. including two, pp. 18 and 55, by B. (Remington)

41 Burns, Walter Noble. *The Saga of Billy the Kid.* Garden City, N.Y., Doubleday, Page & Co., 1926, cloth, 322 pp., endsheets are reproductions of a B. drawing.

42 California State Chamber of Commerce, San Francisco. *California Salinas Rodeo, Horse Fair & Stock Show, July 15–18, 1937.* Wraps, 8 pp., two illus. by B. on back wrap and a short article on him.

43 Peggy Christian, Bookseller, Los Angeles, *American Artists and Illustrators.* Catalog no. 4, pic. wraps, 20 pp., one illus., p. 3, by B. (Dixon, Eggenhofer, Ellsworth, Remington, Russell)

44 ———. *American Artists and Illustrators.* Catalog no. 6, pic. wraps, unpaged, seven illus. by B.

45 The Arthur H. Clark Company, Glendale, Calif., *Portrayers of the American West.* List 9400, self-wraps, unpaged, front cover illus. by B. and lists 29 Borein items.

46 Clark, Badger. *Sun and Saddle Leather*. Westerners Foundations, Stockton, California (designed and printed by Lawton Kennedy, San Francisco), 1962, cloth, 201 pp., illus. by B.

47 Cleveland, Agnes Morley. *No Life for a Lady*. Boston, Houghton Mifflin Co., 1941, cloth, 356 pp., 66 illus. by B.

47a Collison, Thomas F. *El Diario del Viajede los Rancheros Visitadores* (The Log of the RV). 1935, privately printed for RV by News-Press Print, Santa Barbara, (1935), decor. stiff wraps, 154 (6) pp., illus. including one, the frontis., by B. and much on him in the text. (De Yong)

48 Conkling, Roscoe P. et al. *The Westerners Brand Book*. The Los Angeles Corral (Los Angeles, Calif.), 1948, dec. cloth, pictorial endsheets, 175 pp., "Preface" by Sheriff Paul W. Galleher, bibliography, index, numerous illustrations including two, pp. 23 and 40, by B. Limited to 400 copies. (Remington, Russell)

48a Cullum, Ridgwell. *The Golden Woman*. Burt, N.Y., 1916), words "Published February, 1916" on copyright page, cloth, 447 pp., frontis. in color (repeated on d/w) by B.

49 Dawson, Glen. *Americana, Catalogue 319*. Dawson's Book Shop, Los Angeles, pictorial wraps, 22 pp., cover illustration by B.

50 Dawson, Muir. *Bibliography, Catalogue 308*. Dawson's Book Shop, Los Angeles, (September, 1959), wraps, (30) pp., illus. including one drawing by B.

51 Dobie, J. Frank. *Guide to Life and Literature of the Southwest*. University of Texas Press, Austin, Texas, 1943, wraps, 111 pages, illus. including two, pp. 50 and 53, by B. (Bugbee, Dunton, Hurd, James, Lea, Leigh, Russell, Santee)

52 Dreyfus, Louis G. (owner's agents). *Beautiful Residential Park Buena-Vista, Santa Barbara, California*. N.p., (1930), parchment with leather tie and illus. in color mounted on front cover, pages unnumbered, illus. with vignettes by B. and with photos.

53 Ellison, William H. and Price, Francis, eds. *The Life and Adventures in California of Don Agustin Janssens, 1834–1856*. The Huntington Library, San Marino, California, 1953, cloth and decorated boards, map endsheets, 165 pp., preface, bibliography, index, four illustrations including one, facing p. 20, by B.

54 Englehardt, Fr. Zephyrin. *San Diego Mission*. The James H. Barry Co., San Francisco, 1920, illus. cloth, 358 (8) pp., preface, appendix, index, illus., cover design by B.

55 ——. *Santa Barbara Mission*. The James H. Barry Co., San Francisco, Calif., 1923, pic. cloth, 470 pp. and (1) p. of advs., preface, index, illus., front cover design by B.

56 ——. *San Francisco or Mission Dolores*. Franciscan Herald Press, Chicago, Ill., 1924, illus. cloth, 432 pp. and (1) p. of advs., preface, appendix, index, illustrated including one etching by B., p. 87, cover design by B.

57 ——. *San Gabriel Mission and the Beginnings of Los Angeles*. Mission San Gabriel, San Gabriel, Calif. (Franciscan Herald Press, Chicago, Ill.), 1927, illus., cloth, 369 pp. and (1) p. of advs., preface, appendix, index, illus., cover design by B.

58 ——. *San Buena Ventura — The Mission by the Sea*. Mission Santa Barbara, Santa Barbara, Calif., (The Schauer Printing Studio, Inc., Santa Barbara, Calif.), 1930, illus., cloth, 166 and (5) pp., and (1) p. of advs., preface, appendix, illus., cover design by B.

59 ——. *Mission Santa Ines*. Mission Santa Barbara, Santa Barbara, Calif. (The Schauer Printing Studio, Inc., Santa Barbara, Calif.), 1932, illus. cloth, 194 (7) pp. and (1) p. of advs., preface, appendix, index, illus. Bound in is *Mission La Concepcion Purisima*, 131 (6) pp. and (1) p. of advs., preface, appendix, index, illus., cover design by B.

60 ——. *Mission San Juan Bautista*. Mission Santa Barbara (The Schauer Printing Studio), Santa Barbara, Calif., 1931, decor. cloth, 148 (6) pp. and (1) p. of advs., preface, appendix, index, illus., cover design by B.

61 Galvin, John. *The Etchings of Edward Borein* (A catalogue of his work). John Howell, San Francisco, 1971, brown linen, 249 pp., compiled with the assistance of Warren R. Howell in collaboration with Harold G. Davidson, over 300 illus. by B.

62 Gann, Dan, ed. *The Branding Iron* (vol. 1, no. 2). The Westerners, Los Angeles Corral, April, 1948, stitched folder, 8 pp., illus. including two etchings, pp. 4 and 5, by B. "Nature Was His Teacher," a note about B., p. 4, by Col. C. B. Benton.

63 ——. *The Branding Iron* (vol. 1, no. 3). The Westerners, Los Angeles Corral, July, 1948, stitched folder, 16 pp., illus. including two etchings, pp. 3 and 16. Photo of B., p. 16.

64 Gann, Dan and Kitchen, Merrell A., eds. *The Westerners Brand Book 1949*. Los Angeles Corral, 1949 (copyrighted 1950), morocco and decorated cloth, pictorial endsheets, 263 pp., "Foreword" by Sheriff Homer H. Boelter, index, numerous illus. including ten, pp. 29, 30, 31 (2), 32 (2), 33, 34 (2) and 35, by B. Article on B. by C. S. Dentzel, pp. 29–30. Limited to 400 copies. (Blumenschein, Dixon, Johnson, Russell, Remington)

65 L. E. Gay, Southwest Books, Lordsburg, N.M. *Catalogue 32*. (1971), wraps, 27 (1) pp., three illus. on front cover by B.

66 George, W. L.; Housman, Laurence; Pound, Ezra et al. *The Apple (of Beauty and Discord)* — a volume devoted to Art and Letters. Stokes, N.Y. (but printed in Great Britain), n.d. (1926?), decor. cloth, unpaged, some 160 illustrations including one, "The Bucking Broncho" by Edward Boscin [*sic*] — from an etching by B.

67 Thomas Gilcrease Institute, Tulsa, Oklahoma. *Gift Shop Catalog*. N.d., pic. wraps, unpaged, numerous illus. including one, "Steer Roping," by B. (Leigh, Remington, Russell)

68 Good, Donnie D. *The Longhorn*. Thomas Gilcrease Institute, Tulsa, 1970, wraps, (20) pp., numerous illus. including six by B. (James, Remington)

69 ———. *Traveling Westward*. Thomas Gilcrease Institute, Tulsa, 1968, colored pic. wraps, 20 pp., numerous illlus. including one by B. (Johnson, Russell)

70 Haines, Francis. *Appaloosa, The Spotted Horses in Art and History*. Published for the Amon Carter Museum of Western Art, Fort Worth, by the University of Texas Press, Austin, (1963), cloth, 103 pp., "Introduction" by Mitchell A. Wilder (Director), numerous illustrations including one, facing p. 68, by B. (Russell)

70a Harding, Frank (compiled by). *A Livestock Heritage: Animals and People in Art*. (Shorthorn World Publication Co., Geneva, Ill., 1971), colored pic. wraps, unpaged, numerous illus. including one by B. (Dunn, Eggenhofer, Koerner, Marchand, Remington, Russell, Wyeth)

71 Harmsen, Dorothy. *Harmsen's Western Americana*. Northland Press, Flagstaff, Arizona, (1971), morocco and cloth, blue endsheets, 213 pp., "Foreword" by Robert Rockwell, introduction, selected bibliography, numerous illus. including one in color, p. (31), by B. and a biographical sketch of him. Limited edition of 150 numbered copies signed by the author, slipcase with morocco title label. (Beeler, Blumenschein, Dixon, Dunn, Dunton, Eggenhofer, Elwell, Hurd, Johnson, Leigh, Marchand, Miller, Russell, Von Schmidt, Wyeth)

72 ———. Same, first trade edition in two-tone cloth and with red endsheets.

73 Hathaway, O. L. (manager). *Joaquin Murieta* (play program). Lobero Theatre, Santa Barbara, California, (1928), pictorial wraps, 18 pp., B. drawing on front cover.

74 Hecht Book Shop, St. Louis, Missouri. *Americana*. Catalogue 97, n.d. (1966?), pic. wraps, unpaged, one illus. by B.

75 Hendryx, James B. *The Texan*. G. P. Putnam's Sons, New York and London, 1918, cloth, pictorial endsheets, 392 pp. The endsheet illus. are by B.

76 Heritage Bookshop, Hollywood, Calif. *Americana*. Catalogue 105, pic. wraps, unpaged, two illus. by B.

77 ———. *Fine Printing and the Illustrated Book*. Catalogue 108, wraps 64 pp., illustrated including three, p. 41, by B.

77a Hill, Stub, ed. *1973 Grand National Souvenir Book*. Cow Palace, San Francisco, colored pic. wraps, 112 pp., "Cow Palace" by Lex Connelly, numerous illus. including one, front cover, by B.

77b Hornung, Clarence P. *Treasury of American Design*. Harry N. Abrams, N.Y., (1967), two volumes, decor. cloth, decor. endsheets, 470 and 846 pp., author's note (I), "Foreword" by J. Carter Brown (I), "Introduction" by Holger Cahill (I), roster of artists (II), index (II), numerous illus. including two pages of sketches, pp. 778 and 779 (II), by B. (Russell)

78 John Howell — Books, San Francisco. Announcement of *The Etchings of Edward Borein* by John Galvin. (1971), folder with one illus., "A Cowman," by B.

79 (Hunley.) *Western Americana, Catalogue 28*. Maxwell Hunley, Beverly Hills, California, 1953, pictorial wraps, (23) pp., B. drawing on front cover.

80 Kennedy, Michael S. (selected and edited by). *Cowboys and Cattlemen*, Hastings House, N.Y., (1964), horsehide with hair out, colored pic. endsheets, 364 (2) pp., introduction, index, numerous illus. including twelve by B. Limited edition of 199 numbered copies, in slipcase. (Russell)

81 ———. Same, first trade edition in cloth, (1964).

82 ———. *The Red Man's West, True Stories of the Frontier Indians.* Hastings House, N.Y., (1965), pic. Indian-tanned deer-skin, colored pic. endsheets, 342 pp., notes, index, numerous illustrations. Limited edition of 199 numbered copies, in slipcase. An unknown number of copies of this limited edition include a Borein print as the extra illustration. (Koerner, Russell, Von Schmidt)

83 Latendorf, E. Walter. *Western Americana, Catalogue No. 24.* Mannados Bookshop, New York, (1954), pictorial wraps, 88 pp., 24 illus. including one, inside front cover, by B. (Dixon, Goodwin, Schreyvogel)

84 Layne, J. Gregg and Robinson, W. W., eds. *The Westerners Brand Book, Book Six.* Los Angeles Corral, 1956, two-tone décor, fabricoid, map endsheets, 163 pp., bibliography, index, numerous illus. including one, the dust jacket, by B. (Ellsworth)

85 Linsenmeyer, Helen Walker. *From Fingers to Finger Bowls.* Union-Tribune Pub. Co., San Diego, 1972, cloth, 142 pp., illustrations including one, p. 41, by B. (Koerner, Remington)

86 Lummis, Charles F. (collected and translated by). *Spanish Songs of Old California.* Privately printed, Los Angeles, 1923, wraps, 4 to 36 pp., "Note" and pianoforte accompaniments by Arthur Farwell, cover design by B.

86a McCracken, Harold. *The American Cowboy.* Doubleday, Garden City, N.Y., 1973, words "Limited Edition" on copyright page, simulated leather, marbled endsheets, 196 pp., all edges gilt, references, index, numerous illus. including twenty-one, including the extra plate, in color (not in the trade edition) by B. 300 numbered and signed copies, slipcase. (Cisneros, Eggenhofer, Koerner, Leigh, Remington, Russell, Wyeth)

86b ———. Same, trade edition with words "First edition after the limited edition of 300 copies" on copyright page, cloth and colored pic. d/w.

86c Meigs, John, ed. *The Cowboy in American Prints.* Swallow Press, Chicago, (1972), leather and cloth, pic. endsheets, 184 pp., introduction, numerous illus. including four, pp. 93, 95, 97 and 99, by B. Limited to 300 numbered copies, signed by the editor with an added manually signed lithograph by Peter Hurd, slipcase. (Beeler, Dixon, Hurd, Remington, Russell, Wood, Zogbaum)

86d ———. Same, trade edition in cloth.

87 Middleton, Charles O. (President). *Western Art.* The Art League of Santa Barbara (Santa Barbara, California), n.d. (1928), introduction, 10 folio mounted prints in cloth and marbled board portfolio, including "San Juan Capistrano" after an etching by B. (Johnson, Russell)

88 *Mission San Buena Ventura* (Celebration Program, One Hundred and Seventy-fifth Anniversary, 1782–1957). Wraps, 20 pp., cover illus. by B.

89 Mohr, Dick. *The Range Country: Catalogue Number 112.* International Bookfinders, Beverly Hills, California, (1963), wraps, (72) pp., (acknowledgments), "Range Life" by J. Frank Dobie, "My Favorite 101 Books about the Cattle Industry" by Loring Campbell, two illustrations including one, "Cowboy," an etching by B.

90 Monaghan, Jay (editor-in-chief). *The Book of the American West.* Julian Messner, New York, (1963), words "First Edition" on copyright page, pictorial cloth, tan endsheets, 608 pp., introduction, suggestions for additional reading, index, about the editor-in-chief and the authors, numerous illustrations including nine, six on front cover, title page and pp. 587 (in color) and 588, by B. An unknown number of copies bound in leather and all edges gilt. (Johnson, Koerner, Leigh, Lungren, Remington, Russell, Schreyvogel)

91 Ord, Angustias de la Guerra. *Occurences in Hispanic California.* Academy of American Franciscan History, Washington, D.C., 1956, cloth, pictorial endsheets, 98 pp., "Foreword" (and translated and edited) by Francis Price and W. H. Ellison, "Introduction" by Thomas Savage, notes, bibliography, index, illustrated. Endsheets illustrations from an etching by B.

92 Osgood, Ernest Staples. *The Day of the Cattle Man.* The University of Minnesota Press, Minneapolis, 1929, decor. cloth, pictorial endsheets, 283 pp., preface, bibliography, index, illus. including one, the frontis., by B., maps.

93 Perkins, Chas. E. *The Phantom Bull.* Boston & New N.Y., Houghton Mifflin Co., 1932, gray cloth, with white chalk lettering on spine and white chalk illus. on front cover, 70 pp., 13 illus. by B.

94 ———. *The Pinto Horse.* Santa Barbara, Calif., Fisher and Skofield, 1927, cloth, 76 pp., 29 illus., d/w (in color), front cover, frontis. (in color), and title page drawing, and 11 others by B. Two bindings noted, red cloth with gilt lettering and draw-

ing; tan cloth with brown lettering and drawing; priority not known — the red seems to be preferred.

95 *Portfolio of Reproductions of Oil Paintings and Etchings by Famous Artists of Santa Barbara.* (Santa Barbara), n.d., 21 full color reproductions by Borein et al. in a blue folder with pic. inset.

96 Renner, Frederick G. (compiled by). *Paper Talk: Illustrated Letter of Charles M. Russell.* Amon Carter Museum of Western Art, Ft. Worth, (1962), pictorial cloth, 120 pp., acknowledgments, introduction, numerous illustrations by Russell and with one, a life mask of Russell, by B. (page 72).

97 Rossi, Paul A. and Hunt, David C. *The Art of the Old West* (From the collection of the Gilcrease Institute). Knopf, N.Y. (but printed in Italy), 1971, words "First Edition" on copyright page, pic. cloth, pic. brown endsheets, 335 pp., preface, bibliography, numerous illus. including two, pp. 162 and 291, by B. (Blumenschein, James, Leigh, Miller, Remington, Russell, Schreyvogel, Wyeth)

98 Salaman, Malcolm C., ed. *Fine Prints of the Year, An Annual Review of Contemporary Etching and Engraving,* vol. 4. Halton & Truscott Smith, London, Minton, Balch, N.Y. (printed in London, November, 1926), cloth, 17 pp., plus 100 plates, XXIV, directory of etchers and engravers, plate no. 70 of an etching, "Bucking Broncho," by B. (Young)

99 Saunders, Charles Francis. *The Wild Gardens of Old California.* Wallace Hebberd, Santa Barbara, 1927, cloth and decorated boards with paper label on front cover, 24 pp., "Foreword" by Ralph Hoffman, frontis. in color by Colin Campbell Cooper and 3 etchings, facing pp. (5), 17, and (19) by B. Contains also "Seeds of Hope for the Dim and Distant Future" (seeds of native California flowers) in a space hollowed out of blank sheets stapled inside the back cover.

100 Shapiro, Irwin. *The Golden Book of California.* Golden Press, New York, (1961), colored pictorial cloth, pictorial endsheets, 97 pp., "Introduction" by Rodman Wilson Paul, numerous illus. including one, pp. 62–63, by B., maps.

101 Smith, Lawrence B. (Lon). *The Sunlight Kid (and Other Western Verses).* N.Y., E. P. Dutton & Co., (1935), words "First Edition" on copyright page, cloth, 120 pp., illus. including d/w, front cover, and frontis. by B.

102 Spaulding, Edward G., ed. *Etchings of the West.* Ed-ward Borein Memorial (Press of The Schauer Printing Studio), Santa Barbara, (1950), pictorial cloth, pictorial endsheets, "Preface" by Dwight Murphy, "foreword," "Life of Ed Borein," by Irving Wills, profusely illus. with 63 etchings, 9 watercolors, and numerous drawings by B. (edition of 1001 numbered copies, boxed).

103 ———. *Borein's West.* (Edward Borein Memorial, Press of the Schauer Printing Studio, Santa Barbara, 1952), pictorial cloth, pictorial endsheets, 10 pp., and (148) pp. of sketches, portrait of B. in color as frontis. Also a Vaquero Edition of 300 numbered copies with 9 vignettes in color added.

104 ———. *Santa Barbara Club* (Schauer Printing Studio, Santa Barbara), 1954, cloth, pic. endsheets, 131 pp., list of members, illustrated including one, the frontispiece in color by B. Caballero Edition of 250 copies.

105 ———. *Adobe Days Along the Channel.* The Schauer Printing Studio, Santa Barbara, 1957, pictorial buckram, pictorial endsheets, 124 (2) pp., "Foreword" by Harold Schauer, sources, numerous illustrations including six, pp. xxi, 28, 37, 47, 87 and facing p. 20 (in color), by B. (Lungren, Mora)

106 ———. *A Brief Story of Santa Barbara.* Santa Barbara Historical Society, 1964, wraps, 78 pp., illus. including one, p. (40), by B. (De Yong, Lungren)

106a *Stetson Hats.* John B. Stetson Co., Philadelphia, n.d., colored pic. wraps, unpaged, numerous illus. including one, front cover in color, by B.

107 Weaver, Paul (publisher). *Autumn 1971 Book List, Northland Press.* Flagstaff, pic. wraps, unpaged, illustrated including one by B. Note: Other Northland Press catalogs also include illus. by B. (Dixon, Perceval, Remington, Santee)

108 Wilson, Neill C. (compiler). *Rancheros Visitadores Twenty-Fifth Anniversary, 1930–1955.* Los Rancheros Visitadores, Santa Barbara, 1955, two-tone fabricoid, pictorial endsheets, 142 (1) pp., acknowledgments, numerous illus. including several drawings by B. and from photos (many in color). Borein was a member. (De Yong, Johnson)

109 Woloshuk, Nicholas, Jr. *Edward Borein Drawings and Paintings of the Old West Volume 1: The Indians.* Northland Press, Flagstaff, 1968, words "First Edition" on copyright page, two-tone pic. cloth, tinted endsheets, 136 pp., "Foreword" by Harold McCracken, profusely illus. by B.

110 ———. *Edward Borein, Stage Coaches.* Institute of Fine Art, Santa Fe, N.M., 1968, pic. wraps, unpaged, seventeen illus. by B.

111 Zeitlin & Ver Brugge: Booksellers, Los Angeles. *Western Americana.* Catalogue no. 204, 1963, pic. wraps, 59 pp., front cover illus. by B.

112 ———. *The Great West.* Catalogue 213, 1966, two illus. by B.

The Artist and His Art

113 Atherton, Lewis. "Cattleman and Cowboy: Fact and Fancy," an illus. article in *Montana* 11:4, Autumn 1961; 3 illus. by B.

114 Bell, William Gardner. "The Cover Artist" (Borein), an illus. article, in *Corral Dust* 11:4, Fall 1966; 2 illus. by B. and a portrait of him.

115 Bingham, Edwin R. *Charles F. Lummis, Editor of the Southwest.* The Huntington Library, San Marino, Calif., 1955, cloth, 218 pp., preface, bibliography, index, illus. Biographical sketch of B.

115a Bolton, Theodore. *American Book Illustrators — Bibliographic Check Lists of 123 Artists.* R. R. Bowker Company, N.Y., 1938, cloth, 290 pp., introduction, index, lists two items illus. by B.

116 Carrillo, Leo. *The California I Love.* Prentice-Hall, Englewood Cliffs, N.J., (1961), words "First printing . . . October 1961" on copyright page, cloth and decor. boards, pic. endsheets, 280 pp., brown top, "Amigos," illustrated; much on Borein in text. (Perceval)

117 The Arthur H. Clark Co., Glendale. *Edward Borein.* Two mimeographed pages listing etchings for sale.

118 Coffen, Herbert, "On the Trail," a brief note in *The Teepee Book* 1:9, September, 1915, on Borein's visits to the Crows with one illus. by him.

119 Dentzel, Carl Schaefer. "Borein's Vanished West," an article in *The Master Key* (Southwest Museum, Los Angeles) 39:1, January–March 1965, cover illus. by B.

120 ———. Invitation to special showings of the Borein exhibit at the Museum, folder with one illus. by B.

121 Ferbrache, Lewis. *The Dr. and Mrs. Bruce Friedman Collection.* California Historical Society, San Francisco, September 30, to November 15, 1969, wraps, unpaged, illustrated; brief biographical sketch of B. (Dixon, Johnson)

122 Finger, Charles J. *Foot-Loose in the West.* Morrow, N.Y., 1932, cloth, 302 pp., index, illus. by Helen Finger; the Fingers visit Borein, pp. 190–192.

123 George Gund Museum of Western Art, N.Y. *American Western Art: A Personal Narrative.* 1970, illustrated; biographical sketch of B. (Johnson, Leigh, Remington, Russell, Schreyvogel)

123a Same, The Gund Collection of Western Art. *A History and Pictorial Description of the American West.* 1973, pic. wraps, numerous illustrations, biographical sketch of Borein and a photo of him. (Johnson, Leigh, Miller, Remington, Russell, Schreyvogel)

124 Hinshaw, Merton E. (Director). *Painters of the West.* Charles W. Bowers Memorial Museum, Santa Ana, March 5–20, 1972, biographical sketch of B. (Johnson, Miller, Remington)

125 Howell, Warren R. "The Etcher of the West," an illus. article in *Bookman, San Francisco* 1:1, October, 1959, John Howell-Books, San Francisco, one illus. by B. and lists 31 items by him for sale.

126 Lummis, Charles F. "A Cowboy's Pencil," an article about Borein in *The Land of Sunshine*, August 1899 with nine illus. by B.

126a Perkins, Edith Forbes. *Letters and Journals, 1908–1925.* Printed at the Riverside Press (Cambridge) for private distribution, 1931, four volumes, edited by Edith Perkins Cunningham (the author's daughter); records contacts with Borein, volume IV, pp. 16, 17, 20, 21, 113, 115 and 220. (The author's son, Charles E. Perkins, was the author of two books illus. by B.)

127 Pomona College Art Dept., Claremont. *Art of Western America.* 1949, "Foreword" by Don Louis Perceval; biographical sketch of B.

128 *Santa Barbara, A Guide to the Channel City and its Environs.* Hastings House, N.Y., 1941, cloth, map endsheets, 106 pp., index, illustrated, Borein credited with the organization of the *Rancheros Visitadores*, pp. 105–106 and mentioned p. 95.

129 Spaulding, Edward Selden, "Ed Borein and His Fellow Artists," an article in *Noticias* 7:3, Autumn, 1961, with three illus. by B. (De Yong)

130 ———. "The Society Dedicates a Bronze Plaque in Memory of Edward Borein," an article in *Noticias* 16:4, Winter 1970, official publication of the Santa Barbara Historical Society.

131 Storke, Thomas M. (in collaboration with Walker A. Tompkins). *California Editor.* Westernlore Press,

Los Angeles, 1958, cloth, pictorial endsheets, 489 pp., "Foreword" by Chief Justice Earl Warren, preface, index, illus. including a photo of B.

132 Tarrant, Irving S. "The Bradford Brinton Memorial Ranch, Wyoming," an article in the Chicago *Westerners Brand Book* 19:1, March 1962, lists Borein

items in the collection — "drawings, personal sketch, a frieze and thirteen etchings."

133 Zietlin & Ver Brugge — Booksellers, Los Angeles. *The Great West.* Catalogue 223, 1970, colored pic. wraps, 86 pp., illustrated; lists four Borein items and quotes Spaulding on his passing, p. 74. (De Yong)

ILLUSTRATIONS by Borein from *No Life For A Lady*

PORTRAIT OF CHARLES GOODNIGHT by Bugbee from *Charles Goodnight: Cowman and Plainsman*

Catalogues of Art Exhibitions and Galleries

BAKER GALLERY OF FINE ART, LUBBOCK, TEXAS

1 *The West in Bronze by Harold Bugbee* (Fall), 1971, photos of seven bronzes by B. and six drawings by him, "About the Artist" by Boone McClure.

THE UNITED STATES MILITARY ACADEMY LIBRARY
WEST POINT, NEW YORK

1a *Illustrators of the American West,* March 1973, decor. wraps, unpaged, "Note" by John M. Carroll, ten illus. including one by B. One of 27 presentation copies signed by Carroll, Bjorklund, Cisneros, Grandee, Ralston and Rossi and laid in a four-point slipcase with an original drawing by Cisneros.

1b Same, first trade edition in decor. wraps.

Illustrated by the Artist

2 Ainsworth, Ed. *The Cowboy in Art.* World, N.Y. and Cleveland, (1968), words "First Printing 1968" on copyright page, full leather, orange endsheets, 242 pp., all edges gilt, "Foreword" by John Wayne, index, numerous illus. including one, p. 40, by B. and a photo of him. Special edition of 1000 numbered copies, slipcase. (Beeler, Borein, De Yong, Dixon, Dunton, Eggenhofer, Ellsworth, Hurd, James, Johnson, Koerner, Mora, Perceval, Remington, Russell, Santee, Schreyvogel, Von Schmidt)

3 ———. Same, first trade edition, in gilt lettered and illustrated cloth, orange endsheets.

4 ———. Same, reprint by Bonanza Books, N.Y., in red lettered and illus. cloth, white endsheets.

5 Allen, John Houghton, *San Juan.* Privately printed (1945), stiff brown wraps, 53 (1) pp., frontis. by the author and eight drawings by B. Edition limited to 420 copies.

6 *Amarillo Fat Stock Show Annual,* 1936, colored pic. wraps, 104 pp., illus. including one, the front cover portrait of Will Rogers, by B. and biographical sketch of him, p. 9.

7 Same, 1946, wraps, 224 pp., numerous illus. including two, pp. 115 and 201, by B.

8 Same, 1947, wraps, 242 pp., numerous illus. including six by B.

9 Same, 1948, wraps, 242 pp., numerous illus. including five by B.

10 Same, 1949, pic. wraps, pp. 208, (30), (18), numerous illus. including six by B.

11 Ashley, Carlos. *That Spotted Sow and Other Hill Country Ballads.* The Steck Co., Austin, 1949, cloth, 63 pp., "Foreword" by Dr. Rebecca W. Smith, seventeen drawings by B.

12 Autry, George. *The Violin.* The Shamrock Oil and Gas Corporation (Standard Printing Co.), Amarillo, Texas, December, 1948, tinted pictorial wraps, (9) pp., five tinted drawings, front cover and four in text, by B.

13 Barker, Omar. *Born To Battle.* (University of New Mexico Press, Albuquerque, 1951), cloth, 187 pp., preface, acknowledgments, frontis. by B. and other illustrations.

14 ———. *Songs of the Saddlemen.* Sage Books, Denver, (1954), cloth, 112 pp., "Foreword" by Fred Gipson, six illustrations, pp. (12), (18), (34), (38), (58), and (70), by B.

15 Beverly, Bob. *Hobo of the Range Land.* Privately printed (Lovington, New Mexico), n.d., (1940?), pictorial wraps, 87 (1) p., illustrations including three, front cover and two full-page drawings, by B.

16 ———. *To All Boys of USA, Greetings, 75 Years with Cowboys on the Range and Cow Trail.* N.p.,

1955, pic. wraps, 11 pp., p. 12 typescript and tipped in, ten illus. including two, pp. 2 and 9, by B.

17 Biederman, Henry, ed. *The Cattleman. Seventh Annual Horse Issue.* The Texas and Southwestern Cattle Raisers' Assn., Ft. Worth, Texas, September, 1945, stiff pictorial wraps, with plastic binder, numerous illustrations including eight drawings by B.

18 ———. *The Cattleman. Eighth Annual Horse Issue.* The Texas and Southwestern Cattle Raisers' Assn., Ft. Worth, Texas, September, 1946, stiff pictorial wraps, with plastic binder, 228 pp., numerous illustrations including three, presentation sheet and pp. 53 and 181, by B. One of 100 special bound presentation copies signed by Biederman. (Russell)

18a Braddy, Haldeen. *Mexico and the Old Southwest: People, Palaver and Places.* National University Publications, Kennikat Press, Port Washington, N.Y., 1971, cloth, includes "Artist Illustrators of the Southwest: H. D. Bugbee, Tom Lea and Jose Cisneros," illus. including one, p. 80, by B. (Cisneros, Lea)

19 Brown, Luron, Lamb, Vic et al. *The XIT Brand.* Annual XIT Cowboy Reunion and Rodeo (Dalhart Publishing Co.), Dalhart, Texas, 1939, pictorial wraps, 99 (1) pp., numerous illustrations including five, pp. (1), 13, 19, 46 and (100) by B. Photo of Bugbee and short biographical sketch, p. 30.

20 Bryson, John. *The Cowboy.* A Picture Press Book (distributed by Garden City Books, Garden City, New York), 1951, pictorial wraps, 78 (2) pp., numerous illustrations including one, p. 4, by B. (Remington)

21 Bugbee, Harold D. *Bill Wharton.* Clarendon Press, Clarendon, Texas, 1960, wraps, (8) pp., one illustration by the author.

22 ———. *The Black Bull.* Clarendon, 1966, pic. wraps, (16) pp., three drawings by the author and a photo of him.

23 Bugbee Portfolio Set no. 1, Clarendon Press, Clarendon, 1959, two 10 x 13 prints, limited to 200 sets.

24 Same, Set no. 2, Clarendon, 1959, two 10 x 13 prints, limited to 200 sets.

25 Same, Set no. 3, Clarendon, 1959, two 10 x 13 prints, limited to 200 sets.

26 Same, Set no. 4, Clarendon, 1959, three 10 x 13 prints, limited to 200 sets.

27 Same, announcement folder, Clarendon, 1959, showing the nine drawings used in the four sets above.

28 Campbell, H. O., ed. *Souvenir, Old Trail Drivers Convention.* San Antonio, Texas, October 14–16, 1948, wraps, (44) pp., numerous illustrations including nine drawings by B.

29 Carroll, H. Bailey. *Texas County Histories, A Bibliography.* The Texas State Historical Assn., Austin, Texas, 1943, cloth. 200 pp., "Foreword" by Dr. Walter Prescott Webb, introduction, index, one drawing by B., folding map.

30 ———. *Texan Santa Fe Trail.* Panhandle-Plains Historical Society, Canyon, Texas, 1951, cloth, map endsheets, 201 pp., brown top, preface, appendix, bibliography, index, illus., boxed. Cover drawing on box by B.

31 ———. *The Junior Historian.* The Texas State Historical Assn., Austin, Texas, 1957, wraps, 32 pp., illustrations including one by B.

32 ———. *Nolan's "Lost Nigger" Expedition of 1877.* Reprinted from *The Southwestern Historical Quarterly* July, 1940, pic. wraps, 23 pp., two illus., front cover and p. (2), by B.

33 ———. (edited, notes and introduction by). *Guadal Pa* (The Journal of Lieut. J. W. Abert from Bent's Fort to St. Louis in 1845). Panhandle-Plains Historical Society, Canyon, 1941, cloth, 121 pp., maps, frontis. by B.

34 Carroll, John M, ed. *The Black Military Experience in the American West.* Liveright, N.Y., (1971), words "first edition, first printing" on copyright page, cloth, pic. endsheets, notes, bibliography, index, sixty illus. including one by B. Limited to 300 copies signed by the editor, slipcase and two extra manually signed prints suitable for framing. (Bjorklund, Cisneros, Eggenhofer, Hurd, Remington, Russell, Schiwetz)

35 ———. Same, first trade edition, d/w.

36 ———. *Buffalo Soldiers West.* (The Old Army Press, Ft. Collins, Colo., 1971), pic. fabricoid, tan endsheets, 64 pp., foreword, the artists, over fifty illus. including two, pp. 30 and 36, by B. (Bjorklund, Cisneros, Eggenhofer, Remington)

37 Clancy, J. J., Cope, Millard et al. *The XIT Brand.* Annual XIT Cowboy Reunion and Rodeo (Dalhart Publishing Co.), Dalhart, Texas, August, 1940, pictorial wraps, 88 pp., numerous illustrations including one, p. 71, by B.

38 Clarendon Press, Clarendon, (1969), folder announc-

ing release of *Rope and Pan* by Martha D. Ellis, front cover by B.

39 Collectors Institute. *Fifth Annual Meeting* (Program), broadside with two folds, one illus. by B.

40 Collier, Edmund, ed. *The Westerners Brand Book, N. Y. Posse, vol. 6.* The Westerners, N.Y., 1959, decor. cloth, 96 pp., illustrations including three, pp. 28, 33 and 34, by B. (Remington)

41 Collinson, Frank. *Life in the Saddle.* University of Oklahoma Press, (1963), words "First Edition" on copyright page, boards, 243 pp., "Introduction" (edited and arranged) by Mary Whatley Clarke, epilogue, 25 illus. by B.

42 Cope, Millard (compiled by). *Christmas in Texas.* Marshall News Messenger, Marshall, n.d., pic. wraps, unpaged, four illus. by B.

43 Daniel, Houston. *Books,* Catalogue Number Two. Liberty, Texas, n.d., pic. wraps, 16 pp., cover drawing by B.

44 Daniel, Price, Jr. *Texas and the West,* Catalogue Number One. Waco, (1960), pic. wraps, 44 pp., cover drawing by B.

45 ———. Same, Catalogue Number Ten, (1961), pic. wraps, 16 pp., cover drawing by B.

46 ———. Same, Catalogue Number Twelve, (1961), pic. wraps, 16 pp., cover drawing by B.

47 ———. Same, Catalogue Number Fourteen, (1962), pic. wraps, 20 pp., cover drawing by B.

48 ———. Same, Catalogue Number Seventeen, (1962), pic. wraps, 14 pp., cover drawing by B.

49 ———. Same, Catalogue Number Nineteen, (1963), decor. wraps, 28 pp., two drawings p. (28), by B. (Cisneros, Lea)

50 ———. Same, Catalogue Number Twenty, (June 1963), pic. wraps, 13 pp., cover drawing by B.

51 ———. Same, Catalogue Number Twenty-two, (1963), pic. wraps, 13 pp., cover drawing by B.

52 ———. Same, *Featuring Books, Pamphlets etc. Illustrated by H. D. Bugbee,* Catalogue Number Twenty-five, 1964, cloth, unpaged (23), "Harold D. Bugbee" by J. C. (Jeff) Dykes, "The Work of H. D. Bugbee" by C. Boone McClure, photo of Bugbee as frontis. and eleven drawings by him, limited to 100 numbered copies signed by Price Jr.

53 ———. Same, regular edition of Catalogue Number Twenty-five in stiff wraps with a title label illus. by B. on front cover.

54 ———. *Texas and the West.* Catalogue Number Twenty-six, (1964), pic. wraps, 13 pp., cover drawing by B.

55 ———. Same, Catalogue Number Twenty-seven, (1964), pic. wraps, 13 pp., cover drawing by B.

56 ———. Same, Catalogue Number Twenty-nine, (1964), pic. wraps, 14 pp., cover drawing by B.

57 ———. Same, Catalogue Number Thirty-one, (1964), pic. wraps, 13 pp., cover drawing by B.

58 ———. Same, Catalogue Number Thirty-three, (1965), pic. wraps, 9 (1) pp., cover drawing by B.

59 ———. Same, Catalogue Number Thirty-four, (1965), pic. wraps, 13 pp., cover drawing by B.

60 ———. Same, Catalogue Number Thirty-five, (1965), pic. wraps, 13 (1) pp., cover drawing by B.

61 ———. Same, Catalogue Number Thirty-six, (1965), pic. wraps, 14 (1) pp., cover illus. by B.

62 ———. Same, Catalogue Number Forty, (1966), pic. wraps, 13 pp., cover illus. by B.

63 Davison, Dr. Stanley R. (Historian). *Nursing in Montana.* Montana Nurses Assn., Helena, 1961, pic. wraps, 99 (1) pp., "Foreword" by Wava Dixon, preface, appendix, numerous illus. including one, p. 22, by B. (Russell)

64 Diamond Shamrock Oil and Gas Company, *Season's Greeting,* Amarillo, 1969, folder with two 8 x 10½ prints by B. laid in.

65 Dobie, J. Frank. *Guide to Life and Literature of the Southwest.* The University of Texas Press, 1943, wraps, 111 pp., illustrations including one, p. 90, by B. (Borein, Dunton, Hurd, James, Lea, Leigh, Russell, Thomason)

66 ———. *Guide to Life and Literature of the Southwest.* Southern Methodist University Press, Dallas, 1952, cloth, tinted endsheets, 222 pp., brown top, "A Preface with Some Revised Ideas," index, 19 illustrations including one, p. 158 by B. (Revised and enlarged edition of no. 65). (Borein, Dunton, Hurd, James, Lea, Leigh, Russell, Thomason)

67 ———. *My Salute to Gene Rhodes.* (Carl Hertzog, El Paso), Christmas, 1947, wraps, 12 pp., tail-piece by B.

68 Dobie, J. Frank; Boatright, Mody C., and Ransom, Harry H., eds. *Mustangs and Cowhorses.* Texas Folklore Society, Austin, 1940, fabricoid, pictorial endsheets, introduction, contributors, index, numer-

ous illustrations including two, endsheets and p. 154 by B. (d/w drawing by B.). (James, Lea, Leigh, Russell, Santee, Thomason)

69 Dykes, Jeff C. *Two of Ten Best Western Books of 1948 Illustrated by H. D. Bugbee.* Clarendon Press, Clarendon, Texas, (1949), illustrated folder, two photos of B. and one drawing by B.

70 Ellis, Martha Downer. *Bell Ranch, Places and People.* Clarendon Press, Clarendon, Texas, 1963, kid finished premoid, 75 pp., foreword, illus. with ten drawings, pp. ix, 24, 37, 41, 45, 48, 54, 60 and 75 by B. and with photos. One of 400 copies.

71 ———. Same, first trade edition bound in Roxite linen.

72 Gregory, A. O. et al. *Souvenir Program, 15th Annual XIT Rodeo — Reunion and Dalhart's Golden Jubilee.* (Bishop Office Supply, Dalhart, Texas), 1951, pictorial wraps, 76 pp., acknowledgments, numerous illustrations including a frontispiece, by B.

73 Haley, J. Evetts. *Pastores Del Palo Duro.* Reprint from *Southwest Review*, Spring, 1934, pic. wraps, 16 pp., five drawings, front cover, and pp. 5, (8), 11 and 16, by B.

74 ———. *Charles Goodnight,* Houghton Mifflin Co., Boston, New York, 1936, cloth, 485 pp., "Cutting for Sign," "A Note on Bibliography," index, numerous drawings by B.

75 ———. *George W. Littlefield, Texan.* University of Oklahoma Press, Norman, 1943, words "First Edition" on copyright page, cloth, 287 pp., green top, "To Whom the Credit," index, numerous drawings by B.

76 ———. *Charles Schreiner, General Merchandise.* Texas State Historical Society (Carl Hertzog, El Paso), Austin, Texas, 1944, cloth, 73 pp., preface, index, drawings by B.

77 ———. *Jeff Milton, A Good Man With a Gun.* University of Oklahoma Press, Norman, 1948, words "First Edition" on copyright page, cloth, 430 pp., red top, "Where Trails Begin," index, numerous drawings by B.

78 ———. *A Bit of Bragging About a Cow.* (George Autry, Amarillo, Texas), March, 1948, wraps, (5) pp., frontis. by B.

79 ———. *The Heraldry of the Range.* Panhandle-Plains Historical Society (Carl Hertzog, El Paso), Canyon, Texas, 1949, decor. cloth, 35 pp., preface, numerous drawings by B.

80 ———. *The Great Comanche War Trail.* Reprinted from *The Panhandle-Plains Historical Review*, Canyon, Texas, 1950, pic. wraps, 11 pp., 2 drawings, front cover and p. 11, by B.

81 ———. *John Bouldin's First Christmas on the Plains.* George Autry, Amarillo, Texas, 1950, pic. wraps, (11) pp., introduction, nine drawings by B.

82 ———. *Then Came Christmas for Mildred Taitt.* George Autry, (Amarillo, Texas, 1951), pic. wraps, (11) pp., Christmas messages by J. Evetts Haley, H. D. Bugbee, and George Autry, seven drawings by B.

83 ———. Same, Shamrock Oil and Gas Corp., Amarillo, 1962, pic. wraps, 15 pp., (Foreword) by Haley, 7 illus., front cover, pp. (1), 6, 7, 8–9, 12 and 15, by B. Typography by Carl Hertzog of El Paso.

84 ———. *Fort Concho and the Texas Frontier.* San Angelo Standard-Times (designed and produced by Carl Hertzog, El Paso, Texas), San Angelo, Texas, 1952, cloth, pictorial endsheets, 352 pp., orange top, preface, index, numerous illustrations by B. San Angelo Edition, limited to 185 numbered, signed copies, boxed. Also trade edition.

85 ———. *And So It Must Be — At Christmas — On the Ranges of Grass!* George Autry, (Amarillo, Texas, 1952), pic. wraps, (8) pp., six drawings, front cover and five in text, by B.

86 ———. *The Heraldry of the Range.* The Shamrock Oil and Gas Corp., Amarillo, Texas, (1952), text on verso of Highway Map, one drawing by B.

87 ———. *Christmas at the Hancock House.* George Autry, (Amarillo, Texas, 1953), pic. wraps, 7 pp., five drawings, front cover and four in text, by B.

88 ———. *Christmas in the Palo Duro* (cover title), *A Repellent World Warmed by the Spirit.* The Shamrock Oil and Gas Corp. (Carl Hertzog, El Paso), Amarillo, (1961), colored pic. wraps, 13 (1) pp., photo as frontis., plus five drawings in text by B.

89 ———. *Those Who Came Before Us — Caught for all time by the Brush of Harold D. Bugbee.* George Autry, (Amarillo), 1955, pic. wraps, (8) pp., "The Indian Murals" in Panhandle-Plains Historical Museum by Harold D. Bugbee, five illus. by B.

90 ———. *A Cowboy's Christmas on the Range.* (Canyon), n.d., folder with one full-page drawing by B. (Nita and Evetts Haley's Christmas Greeting).

91 Haley, J. Evetts, Carroll, H. Bailey et al. *Some Southwestern Trails.* Carl Hertzog, El Paso, Texas, 1948,

decor. cloth, pages unnumbered, "Preface" by Haley, twelve full-page drawings by B. A variant edition of 75 copies has a title page by Tom Lea and eleven drawings by B.

92 Hill, Joseph A. *The Panhandle-Plains Historical Society and Its Museum.* West Texas State College Press, Canyon, 1955, one illus. by B.

93 Howe, Elvon L., ed. *1952 Brand Book.* The Westerners, (Arthur Zeuch Printing), Denver, Colorado, (1953), decor. cloth, pic. endsheets, 297 pp., foreword, acknowledgments, index, numerous illustrations including six by B.

94 Hutchinson, W. H. *A Notebook of the Old West.* Privately printed (Bob Hurst, Chico, California, 1947), pic. wraps, 122 pp., "Introduction" by Vida Hills Shepard, "Con Razon," three drawings, front cover, title page, p. 58, by B.

95 ———. *One Man's West.* Hurst & Yount, Chico, Calif., (1948), pic. wraps, 127 (1) pp., "Introduction" by Robert O'Brien, "Con Razon," illus. by John Pagan but with front cover and title page drawings by B.

96 ———. *Another Notebook of the Old West.* Hurst & Yount, Chico, Calif., (1954), pic. wraps, 88 pp., acknowledgments, front cover and title page drawings by B.

97 ———. *Another Verdict for Oliver Lee.* Clarendon Press, Clarendon, 1965, cloth, tan endsheets, 22 (1) pp., "Con Razon," twelve drawings by B. and four portraits by Olive Vandruff (Mrs. Harold D.) Bugbee.

98 ———, and Mullin, R. N. *Whiskey Jim and a Kid Named Billie.* Clarendon Press, Clarendon, 1967, cloth, pic. endsheets, 41 pp., "Con Razon," brief Baedeker, four drawings, endsheets, frontispiece, title page and p. (xii), by B.

98a *Jefferson Historical Society and Museum.* (Carl Hertzog, El Paso, for the Society, 1949), pic. wraps, unpaged, drawing on front cover by B.

99 Keech, Roy A. *Children Sing in New Mexico.* The Clarendon Press, Clarendon, Texas, 1941, cloth, pages unnumbered, (31) pp., music by J. S. Mackey, drawings by B.

100 King, Frank M. *Longhorn Trail Drivers.* This First Edition Privately Published for His Friends by The Author (Haynes Corp., Los Angeles), 1940, cloth, pictorial front endsheet, map back endsheet, 272

pp., preface, 32 illus. including one, front endsheet, by B.

101 Lewis, Willie Newbury. *Between Sun and Sod.* Clarendon Press, Clarendon, Texas, (1938), pic. cloth, 244 pp., foreword, appendix, numerous illus. by B. The true first printing was withdrawn after about 25 copies were sold due to numerous typographical errors and omissions. "Newberry" for Newbury; minus "Introduction" by John McCarty; "Contents" preceeds "Foreword," minus "List of Illustrations." Bound in crosshatched tan cloth.

102 ———. A second (really the third) printing has words "Second Printing, January, 1939" on the copyright page and differs from the usually accepted first in having a Bugbee drawing on the front cover.

103 Lewis, Mrs. J. W. Jr. et al. *Episcopal Cook Book.* (Compiled by the Women of St. John Episcopal Church), Clarendon Press, Clarendon, 1959, words "Third Edition" on copyright page, pic. wraps with plastic binder, 173 pp., "A History," cover illus. by B. and the first printing with it.

104 Loomis, Noel M. *The Texan-Santa Fe Pioneers.* University of Oklahoma Press, Norman, (1958), words "First Edition" on copyright page, cloth, 329 pp., introduction, appendices, bibliography, index, 12 illus. including one, facing p. 158, by B., maps.

105 McCarty, John L. *Maverick Town, the Story of Old Tascosa.* University of Oklahoma Press, Norman, 1946, words "First Edition" on copyright page, pictorial cloth, map endsheets, 277 pp., red top, foreword, epilogue, bibliography, index, illus. with 17 drawings by B., and with photos.

106 ———. *Adobe Walls Bride.* The Naylor Co., San Antonio, (1955), cloth, pictorial endsheets, 281 pp., introduction, notes, bibliography, index, illus. with 22 drawings by B., and with photos.

107 McClure, Boone (Director). *The Panhandle-Plains Historical Museum,* Canyon, Texas, n.d. (1957?), pic. wraps, 23 pp., illus. including one, p. 22 by B.

108 ———. *The Panhandle-Plains Historical Museum.* The Panhandle-Plains Historical Society (George Autry, Amarillo, 1961), pic. wraps, (12) pp., illus. including one, back cover, by B.

109 ———. *The Panhandle-Plains Historical Museum* (George Autry, Amarillo, 1965), colored pic. wraps, 26 pp., numerous illus including four, pp. 14–15 (in color), 22, 24 and inside book cover by B.

110 Moseley, J. A. R. *The Presbyterian Church in Jefferson*. Texas State Historical Assn. (Carl Hertzog, El Paso), Austin, 1946, pictorial cloth, 52 pp., 7 drawings by B. Edition consisted of 675 copies.

111 (Mosely.) *Greetings from Bob Mosely* (Carl Hertzog, El Paso), Christmas, 1946, folder, one full-page drawing by B.

111a The Naylor Company, San Antonio. *Texana, Western, Southwestern Americana* (Catalog). Fall 1955, pic. wraps, 32 pp., illus. including three, front cover and inside front cover (two), by B. (Mead)

112 Neff, Boss. *Some Experiences of Boss Neff in the Texas and Oklahoma Panhandle*. The Globe-News Publishing Co., Amarillo, 1941, pic. wraps, (30) pp., front cover and 12 full-page drawings by B. Edition limited to 200 copies.

113 Nordyke, Lewis. *Great Roundup*. William Morrow & Co., New York, 1955, cloth and pictorial boards, pictorial endsheets, 316 pp., foreword, acknowledgments, index, appendix, numerous illus. including 19 drawings by B. This is the "Special Edition for the Texas and Southwestern Cattle Raisers Assn." as stated on the title page. The first trade edition does not include the appendix and ends with page 288.

114 ———. *The Angels Sing*. Clarendon Press, Clarendon, 1964, cloth (75 numbered copies) or wraps (100 copies), 21 (1) pp., four illus., frontispiece, facing pp. (1) and pp. 7 and 11, by B.

115 Oden, Bill. *Early Days on the Texas-New Mexico Plains*. Palo Duro Press, Canyon, Texas, 1965, decor. cloth, pic. map endsheets, 69 pp., "Introduction to Bill Oden" and edited by J. Evetts Haley, illus. with five drawings, pp. xi, 10, (24), (34) and (50) by B. and with photos. (750 copies printed by Carl Hertzog at El Paso.) (Cisneros)

116 O'Keefe, Rufe. *Cowboy Life*. The Naylor Co., San Antonio, 1936, cloth, 244 pp., photo of author as frontis. and eleven drawings by B. The first state of the binding has a small drawing by B. on the spine. Copies bound later seem to be first edition of the text but the drawing is missing from the spine. Bugbee drawing on the dust wrapper.

117 Old Trail Drivers Association — 28th Anniversary Program, San Antonio, 1943, pic. wraps, unpaged, illus. including drawings by B.

118 Same, Souvenir Program, San Antonio, 1950, pic. wraps, 30 pp., illus. with four drawings, front cover, pp. 18, 26 and 30, by B. and with photos.

119 *Panhandle-Plains Historical Review*, issued annually by the Panhandle-Plains Historical Society, Canyon, Texas, vol. II, 1929, edited by J. Evetts Haley, wraps, 153 (1) pp., front cover illus. by B.

120 Same, vol. III, 1930, edited by L. F. Sheffy, wraps, 134 pp., five drawings, front cover and pp. 17, 37, 77 and 124, by B., photos.

121 Same, vol. IV, 1931, edited by Sheffy, wraps, 114 (2) pp., two drawings, front cover and facing p. 114, by B.

122 Same, vol. V, 1932, edited by Sheffy, wraps, 102 pp., two illus., front cover and p. 7, by B.

123 Same, vol. VI, 1933, edited by Sheffy, wraps, 99 pp., two-page letter and front cover illus. by B.

124 Same, vol. VII, 1934, edited by Sheffy, wraps, 100 pp., three illus., front cover and pp. 52 and 69, by B.

125 Same, vol. VIII, 1935, edited by Sheffy, wraps, 110 pp., front cover illus. by B.

126 Same, vol. IX, 1936, edited by Sheffy, wraps, 90 pp., front cover illus by B.

127 Same, vol. X, 1937, edited by Sheffy, wraps, 102 pp., five illus., front cover and facing pp. 32, 48, 64 and 80, by B.

128 Same, vol. XI, 1938, edited by Sheffy, wraps, 111 pp., front cover illus. by B.

129 Same, vol. XII, 1939, edited by Sheffy, wraps, 101 pp., front cover illus. by B.

130 Same, vol. XIII, 1930, edited by Sheffy, wraps, 114 pp., front cover illus. by B.

131 Same, vol. XIV, 1941, edited by Sheffy, wraps, 125 pp., front cover illus. by B.

132 Same, vol. XV, 1942, edited by Sheffy, wraps, 96 pp., front cover illus. by B.

133 Same, vol. XVI, 1943, edited by Sheffy, wraps, 106 pp., front cover illus. by B.

134 Same, vol. XVII, 1944, edited by Sheffy, wraps, 136 pp., front cover illus. by B.

135 Same, vol. XVIII, 1945, edited by Sheffy, wraps, 162 pp., front cover illus. by B.

136 Same, vol, XIX, 1946, edited by Sheffy, wraps, 106 pp., nine illus., front cover and pp. 86, 87, 88, 89, 90, 91, 92 and 93, by B.

137 Same, vol. XX, 1947, Hall, Claude V. "The Early History of Floyd County," wraps, 147 pp., bibliography, index, front cover illus. by B. (Also issued in cloth with cover illus. by B.)

138 Same, vol. XXI, 1948, edited by Sheffy, wraps, 112 pp., front cover illus. by B.

139 Same, vol. XXII, 1949, edited by Ima C. Barlow, wraps, 98 pp., front cover illus. by B.

140 Same, vol. XXIII, 1950, edited by Barlow, wraps, 140 pp., front cover illus. by B.

141 Same, vol. XXIV, 1951, edited by Barlow, wraps, 201 pp., front cover illus. by B.

142 Same, vol. XXV, 1952, edited by Barlow, wraps, 120 pp., front cover illus. by B.

143 Same, vol. XXVI, 1953, edited by Seymour V. Connor, wraps, 92 pp., index, two illus., front cover and frontispiece, by B.

144 Same, vol. XXVII, 1954, edited by Connor, wraps, 86 pp., one illus., maps, front cover illus. by B.

145 Same, vol. XXVIII, 1955, Jack T. Hughes (guest editor), wraps, 128 pp. and 32 plates, "Editor's Preface" by Connor, front cover illus. by B.

146 Same, vol. XXIX, 1956, edited by Connor, wraps, 131 pp., index, front cover illus. by B. (Hurd)

147 Same, vol. XXX, 1957, edited by Connor, wraps, 132 pp., front cover illus. by B. (Remington)

148 Same, vol. XXXI, 1958, edited by Ernest R. Archambeau, wraps, 125 pp., index, front cover illus. by B.

149 Same, vol. XXXII, 1959, edited by Archambeau, wraps, 120 pp., front cover illus by B.

150 Same, vol. XXXIII, 1960, edited by Archambeau, wraps, 144 pp., front cover illus. by B.

151 Same, vol. XXXIV, 1961, Taylor, Joe F. "The Indian Campaigns on the Staked Plains, 1874–1875," pictorial wraps, 229 pp., "The Author," acknowledgments, foreword, front cover illus. by B.

152 Same, vol. XXXV, 1962, ———. Same, Part II (continued from Vol. XXXIV), pic. wraps, pp. 216–382, appendix, bibliography, index, folding map, cover drawing by B.

153 Same, vol. XXXVI, 1963, edited by Ernest R. Archambeau, wraps, 136 pp., front cover drawing of Harold Bugbee on horseback by Olive Vandruff Bugbee, tribute to Harold, p. (V).

154 Peterson, Virgil V., ed. *1946 Brand Book*. The Westerners (Artcraft Press), Denver, Colo., 1947, decorated cloth, 242 pp., preface, illus. including one, facing p. 134, by B. Edition limited to 500 numbered copies.

155 Pool, William C. et al. *Texas: Wilderness to Space Age*. Naylor, San Antonio, (1963), words "Second Edition, Revised and Enlarged" on copyright page, pic. cloth, pic. endsheets, 512 pp., preface, appendix, selected bibliography, index, maps, numerous illus. including eight, pp. 18, 79, 227, 287, 388, 409, 412 and 413, by B. (Schiwetz)

156 Porter, Cora Case. *Irving Trail and Other Poems*. Hoffman-Speed Printing Co. Press, Muskogee, Okla., 1946, words "First Printing August 1946" on copyright page, cloth, 70 (1) pp., "Foreword" by Grant Foreman, map, illus. including one drawing, p. (8), by B.

157 Porter, Millie Jones. *Memory Cups of Panhandle Pioneers*. Clarendon Press, Clarendon, Texas, 1945, cloth, 648 pp., illus. including one, p. 532, by B.

158 ———. *Put Up or Shut Up*. (Wilkinson, Dallas, 1950), cloth, 350 pp., preface, index, illustrated. Drawing on d/w by B.

159 Potter, Jack. *Lead Steer and Other Tales*. Leader Press, Clayton, New Mexico, 1939, stiff pictorial wraps, 116 (2) pp., foreword, "Belling the Lead Steer," by J. Frank Dobie, illus. including two, front cover and p. 79, by B.

160 Price, Clyde I. (Bookseller). *Texiana* (Catalog VII). Clarendon, Texas, n.d., pictorial wraps, 32 pp., six illus., front cover, inside front cover, pp. 9, 19, 23 and 32, by B.

161 ———. *A Catalog of Dime Novels and Books Relating to Texas and Southwest* (Catalog VIII). Clarendon, Texas, April 1946, pictorial wraps, 18 pp., (2) of advs., "From the Dust-Bin of Oblivion!" by Jeff C. Dykes, seven illus., front cover, inside front cover, pp. 1, 9, 12, 16 and 17, by B.

162 ———. *A Catalogue of Books, Dime Novels and Pamphlets Relating to Texas and the Southwest, Including a Distinguished List of Western Illustrators* (Catalog IX). Clarendon, Texas, April 1947, pictorial wraps, 38, 2 pp., "Mexican Mescal Mixed Well With Texans," by J. Evetts Haley, "Western Illustrators," by Jeff C. Dykes, six illus., front cover, inside front cover, pp. (1), 38, (39) and (40), by B.

163 ———. *Christmas Card Catalog, 1939*. Clarendon

Press, Clarendon, Texas, pictorial wraps, numerous illus. by B. (Also *Christmas Card Catalogs* for 1940 and 1941.)

164 Rath, Ida Ellen. *The Rath Trail*. McCormick-Armstrong, Wichita, Kans., (1961), words "First Printing" on copyright page, pic. cloth, 204 pp., index, map, drawing on title page and repeated on front cover by B.

164a Rathjen, Frederick W. *The Texas Panhandle Frontier*. Austin and London, (1973), cloth, 286 pp., preface, bibliography, index, maps, illus. including one, between pp. 128 and 129, by B.

165 Reeves, Frank, Sr. *A Century of Texas Cattle Brands*. The Fair Publishing Co., Ft. Worth, 1936, pictorial wraps, 80 pp., "Foreword," by Amon G. Carter, "A Brief Outline of Texas History," by Peter Molyneaux, illus. including two, pp. 13 and 80, by B.

166 ———. Another edition. Russell Stationery Co., Amarillo, Texas, (1945), with a B. illus. on the front cover and with the two drawings pp. 13 and 80.

167 Reynolds, J. E. *Western Americana* (Catalog 55). Van Nuys, California, December, 1959, pictorial wraps, (19) pp., two drawings by B.

168 ———. *Western Americana* (Catalog 62). Van Nuys, California, pictorial wraps, (23) pp., cover drawing by B.

169 Rhodes, Eugene Manlove. *The Little World Waddies*. William H. Hutchinson, Cohasset Stage, Chico, California (designed and printed at The Pass on the Rio Bravo by Carl Hertzog, 1946), pictorial cloth, map endsheets, 234 pp., "Con Razon," "My Salute to Gene Rhodes," by J. Frank Dobie, "Bibliography and Association Items" by Frank V. Dearing, Vincent Starrett and Jeff C. Dykes, photo of Rhodes as frontis. and cover illus. and thirteen drawings in text by B. Edition of 1,000 copies.

169a Rogers, John William, ed. *A Round-Up of the Most Interesting Texas Books of All Time*. The Dallas Times Herald, first separate printing of "Book News" of October 7, 1945, self-wraps, 16 pp., illus. including one, p. 5, by B. (Hurd, Lea, Thomason)

170 Russell, Charles M. *Rawhide Rawlins Rides Again*. Trails End Pub. Co., Pasadena, California, (1948), flexible leather, pictorial endsheets, 61 (3) pp., yellow top, other edges uncut, ten illus. including one, p. (26), by B. Edition limited to 300 numbered copies. (Russell)

171 Russell Stationery Co., Amarillo, Christmas 1950. (Christmas card) folder, illus. in color on front cover by B.

172 Ruth, Kent. *Great Day in the West*, Univ. of Oklahoma Press, Norman, words "First edition" on copyright page, cloth, 308 pp., brown top, preface, index, numerous illus. including one, p. 249, by B. (Miller)

173 Sheffy, L. F. *The Spanish Horse on the Great Plains*. Privately printed, (Canyon, Texas, 1933), pictorial wraps, (22) pp., cover drawing by B.

174 ———. *Opening Program, The Hall of Fine Arts*. Panhandle-Plains Historical Society, Canyon, Texas, May 9, 1952, (4) pp., photo of Bugbee before an easel, tribute to B. and list of 47 B. paintings and drawings on exhibition, wraps.

175 ———. *A Compilation of Articles Published 1909–1936*. Privately printed, (Canyon, Texas, 1961) pictorial wraps, 98 pp., "By Way of Explanation," illus. including two, front cover and facing p. 1, by B.

176 ———. *The Francklyn Land and Cattle Company*. University of Texas Press, Austin, (1963), two-tone brand decor. cloth, brown endsheets, 402 pp., preface, bibliographical note, introduction, appendix, index, illustrated with two drawings, pp. 176 and 177, by B. and with photos.

177 Shuffler, R. Henderson et al. *The Spanish Texans*. Institute of Texas Cultures, San Antonio, 1972, pic. wraps, 32 pp., illustrated including one drawing, p. 5, by B. (Cisneros, Lea, Mead, Remington)

178 Stover, Elizabeth Matchett, ed. *Son-of-a-Gun Stew*. University Press in Dallas, Southern Methodist University, 1945, cloth, 216 pp., "Foreword" by John William Rogers, "The Making of a Son-of-a-Gun Stew," by J. Frank Dobie, (about the contributors), six drawings, title page, pp. 14–15, 46–47, 81, 124–125, 189, by B.

179 Taylor, Joe F. (compiled and edited by). *The Indian Campaign on the Staked Plains, 1874–1875*. (Panhandle-Plains Hist. Society), Canyon, 1962, fabricoid, 368 pp., foreword, appendix, bibliography, index, folding map, one drawing, p. (6), by B. (A combination of volumes 34 and 35 of the Society annuals.)

180 Terry, Cleo Tom and Wilson, Osie. *The Rawhide Tree*. Clarendon Press, (Clarendon, Texas), 1957, words "First Edition" on copyright page, cloth, tinted endsheets, 259 pp., acknowledgment, intro-

duction, illus. with photos and with seven drawings, title page, pp. 118, 178, 203, 213, 240 and 259, by B.

181 Tinkle, Lon and Maxwell, Allen, eds. *The Cowboy Reader.* Longmans, Green & Co., New York, London, Toronto, 1959, words "First Edition" on copyright page, cloth, 307 pp., editors' introduction, numerous illus. including two drawings, pp. 51 and 204, by B. (Lea, Remington, Russell)

182 Towne, Charles Wayland, and Wentworth, Edward N. *Shepherd's Empire.* University of Oklahoma Press, Norman, 1945, words "First Edition" on copyright page, "Foreword" by Archie Gilfillan, bibliography, index, numerous illus. by B., maps.

183 Weadick, Guy. *Clay McGonagil, A Fast Man With a Rope.* Clarendon Press, Clarendon, 1962, wraps, (10) pp., eight drawings by B. Limited to 92 numbered copies.

184 Wentworth, Edward N. *America's Sheep Trails.* The Iowa State College Press, Ames, Iowa, 1948, pictorial cloth, 667 pp., foreword, acknowledgments, appendices, references cited, illus. with photos and numerous drawings by B.

The Artist and His Art

185 Acheson, Sam H. et al. *Texian Who's Who.* vol. I (only one). The Texian Co., Dallas, 1937, cloth, 524 pp. plus index, includes biography of Harold and of his father, Charles H. Bugbee, p. 66.

186 Barnes, Florence E. *Texas Writers of Today.* Tardy, Dallas, (1935), cloth, tan endsheets, 513 (1) pp., preface, "Foreword" by Robert Adger Law, introduction, bibliography, folding literary map of Texas inside book cover. Includes a tribute to Bugbee by J. Evetts Haley, p. 219.

187 Bowen, C. R., ed. *Cowboy-Artist of the Southwest,* an article about B. in *The Shambrock* (Magazine), March, 1950. Photo of B. at work on an oil at his easel with three drawings in background plus one larger drawing on the following page.

188 Braddy, Haldeen. "Artist Illustrators of the Southwest: H. D. Bugbee, Tom Lea and Jose Cisneros," an illus. article in *Western Review* 1:2, Fall 1964, three illus. by B. (Cisneros, Lea)

189 Bywaters, Jerry. *Artist Views Our Picture Makers Found in Books.* An article in *Special Issue of Book News. The Dallas Times Herald,* Dallas, Texas, Oct. 7, 1945, wraps, 16 pp., drawings by B. on p. 5 and bibliographic comments by Bywaters, p. 14.

190 Clarke, Mary Whatley. "Harold Bugbee, Cowboy Artist," an illus. article in *The Cattleman,* May, 1951, illus. by B.

191 Dunton, W. Herbert (Buck). *The "Riggings" of a Texan.* Reprinted from *The Southwestern Historical Quarterly,* vol. XLVII, no. 1, July, 1943, with a frontispiece in color by the author. Quotes a letter from B.

192 Ehly, Jean. "Harold Dow Bugbee and the Texas Panhandle," an illus. article in *Frontier Times,* May 1967, one drawing by B. and two photos of him.

193 Fisk, Frances Battaile. *A History of Texas Artists and Sculptors.* (The Fisk Publishing Co.), Abilene, Texas, 1928, wraps, 228 (3) pp., preface, index, illus. Bugbee pp. 181–183.

194 Forrester-O'Brien, Esse. *Art and Artists of Texas.* Tardy, Dallas, (1935), cloth, blue endsheets, 408 pp., "Preface" by Joseph Sartor, index, illustrated. Biography of Bugbee, pp. 62 and 63.

195 Haley, J. Evetts. "Portraits of the West — Harold Bugbee, Cowboy Artist, Paints the Texas Cow Camp and Trail," an illus. article in *The Alcade,* February 1930, six drawings by B.

196 (Harte). *Announcing — A New Texas Book of Historical Importance* (Fort Concho). Carl Hertzog, El Paso, 1952, folder, tributes to Haley and Bugbee by Houston Harte and six illus. by B.

197 Kirke, C. N. "H. D. Bugbee, Artist on Horseback," an illus. article in *The Western Horseman,* October 1952, photo of Bugbee on horseback.

198 McCarty, John. *The Enchanted West.* Dr. Pepper Co., Dallas, n.d., (1944), decorated wraps, (40) pp. Biographical note on B., p. (24).

199 ——. *Exhibition of Paintings by H. D. Bugbee.* Clarendon, Texas, folder, lists 25 paintings and drawings by B. with the prices. Quotes tribute to Bugbee's art by McCarty from the *Amarillo News.* B. drawing on front cover.

200 ——. "Some Memories of H. D. Bugbee," an illus. article in *South-Western Art* 1:3, 1967, five drawings by B. and a photo of him.

201 Sonnichsen, C. L. *Cowboys and Cattle Kings — Life on the Range Today.* University of Oklahoma Press, Norman, (1950), words "First Edition" on copyright page, cloth, 316 pp., green top, "Two Faces West," "Not From Books," index, illus. including a photo of B. at work in his studio, p. 286. Much on B. in text.

ILLUSTRATION by Cisneros from *The El Paso Salt War of 1877*

Catalogues of Art Exhibitions and Galleries

EL INSTITUTO MEXICANO NORTHEAMERICANO DE
RELACIONES CULTURALES, MEXICO CITY

1 *Exposicion de Dibujos de Jose Cisneros*, (Marzo de 1973), pic. wraps, unpaged, lists 105 works by C. in the exhibition and with seven illus. by him and a photo of him.

2 *Invitation* (to the 1973 exhibition), folder with two illus. by C. and a photo of him.

EL PASO MUSEUM OF ART

3 *Riders of the Border*, June 8–27, 1971, wraps, 64 pp., selected bibliography, thirty illus. by C. (Southwestern Studies, monograph no. 30 with printed orange wraps as the catalog for the exhibition.)

INSTITUTE OF TEXAN CULTURES, THE UNIVERSITY
OF TEXAS, SAN ANTONIO

4 *Jose Cisneros at Paisano, an Exhibit: Riders of the Spanish Borderlands*, June 1969, pic. wraps, unpaged, "Jose Cisneros" by Al Lowman, "The Dobie-Paisano Project" by Bertha McKee Dobie, twenty illus. by C. (Edition of 400 copies.)

5 Same, reissued by Humanities Research Center, University of Texas at Austin in an edition of 100 copies in cloth with a paper title label on front cover and 200 copies in wraps.

ST. EDWARDS UNIVERSITY, AUSTIN, TEXAS

6 *Riders of the Spanish Borderlands*, May 4–June 2, 1969, program folder with illus. on the front and back covers by C.

THE U.S. ARMY MILITARY HISTORY RESEARCH
COLLECTION, CARLISLE BARRACKS, PENNSYLVANIA

7 *John M. Carroll's Collection, Illustrations of the Black Soldier in the West*, (1973), pic. wraps, 16 pp., ten illus. including two, pp. 5 and 13, by C. (Bjorklund)

8 Same, thirty presentation copies, each in a four-point slipcase with an original drawing by Jose Cisneros and each catalog is signed by Colonel George S. Pappas, Carroll, Bjorklund, Grandee, Cisneros and Reusswig.

THE UNITED STATES MILITARY ACADEMY LIBRARY
WEST POINT, NEW YORK

9 *Illustrators of the American West*, March 1973, decor. wraps, unpaged, "Program Notes" by John M. Carroll, nine illus. including one by C., limited to 27 presentation copies, a four-point slipcase with an original drawing by Jose Cisneros and signed with his initials and each catalog signed by Carroll, Bjorklund, Cisneros, Grandee, Ralston and Rossi.

10 Same, regular edition in decor. wraps.

Illustrated by the Artist

11 Alcazar de Velasco, Angel and Calleros, Cleofas. *Historia Del Templode Nuestra Senora de Guadalupe*. Tipografia Internaeional Co., Juarez, Mexico, 1953, gilt decor. leather, silk endsheets, 185 (4) pp., "Introduceion" by Carlos C. Castaneda, *epilogo, razon editorial* (list of subscribers), illus. with ten drawings by C. and with photos and facsimiles, edition limited to 58 numbered copies (I–LVIII) signed by the two authors on "Patapar Parchkin."

12 ———. Same, five lettered copies (A-E) on Pergamino vellum.

13 ———. Same, 200 numbered copies (1–200) "enpapet florentino y couche blanco."

14 Almaraz, Felix D., Jr. *Tragic Cavalier*. Texas, Austin and London, (1971), cloth, slate endsheets, 206 pp., preface, bibliography, index, drawing on title page (enlarged detail on the d/w) by C.

15 *A P One Hundred Years of Service 1849–1949* (The Associated Press Board of Directors Meeting, Jan. 4–7, 1949). Corpus Christi, Texas, (printed by Carl Hertzog for Houston Harte), pic. wraps, unpaged, text by staff of the *Corpus Christi Caller Times*, is on the King Ranch, map of the ranch and portraits of Captain King and Robert J. Kleberg by C. (Lea)

16 Arrott, James W. *Brief History of Fort Union.* Rodgers Library, New Mexico Highlands University, Las Vegas, N.M., (Carl Hertzog, El Paso), 1962, pic. wraps, 20 pp., "Foreword" by W. S. Wallace, map, cover illus. by Cisneros. (Edition of 300 copies.)

17 Barker, Eugene C. *Father of Texas.* Bob Mosely (Jefferson, Texas) but designed and printed by Carl Hertzog, El Paso, Christmas 1950, folder with full-page illus. by C.

18 Beckett, V. B. *Baca's Battle.* Stagecoach Press, Houston, 1962, wraps, 30 pp., illus. on title page (repeated on front cover) by C. (Edition of 800 copies.)

19 Boatright, Mody C. et al., eds. *Texas Folk and Folklore.* SMU Press, Dallas, 1954, decor. Cloth, 356 pp., preface, six illus., pp. 43, 78, 102, 129, 268 and 290, by C.

20 (Boatright, Mody C.) *Forty-third Annual Meeting of the Texas Folklore Society.* Program folder, Austin, March 27–28, 1959, cover illus. by C.

21 (Bode.) *Elroy Bode's Texas Sketchbook.* Texas Western Press, El Paso, 1967, cloth, green endsheets, edited by Milton Leech and S. D. Myres, "Introduction" by Leech, numerous illus. by C.

22 Bolton, Herbert E. *The Mission as a Frontier Institution in the Spanish-American Colonies.* Academic Reprints (Texas Western College Press), El Paso, 1960, pic. wraps, 24 pp., "Introduction" by John A. (Jack) Carroll, cover illus. by C.

23 *Bookplate.* El Paso Public Library (printed by Carl Hertzog, El Paso), 1951, the illus. is by C.

24 *Books from the Texas Folklore Society.* (Austin, 1967), folder with illus. on front cover by C.

25 Bowden, J. J. *Spanish and Mexican Land Grants in the Chihuahuan Acquisition.* Texas Western Press, El Paso, 1971, pic. cloth, pic. endsheets, 231 pp., preface, references, bibliography, index, map, endsheet (repeated on front cover and d/w) illus. by C.

26 Braddy, Haldeen. *Pancho Villa at Columbus, The Raid of 1916.* Texas Western Press, El Paso, 1965, pic. cloth, 43 pp., references, illus. with photos, double-page pic. map, pp. (22–23) by C. (Southwestern Studies, monograph no. 9.)

27 ———. *Pershing's Mission in Mexico.* Texas Western Press, El Paso, 1966, pic. cloth, pic. map endsheets by C., 82 pp., preface, "Introduction" by Richard O'Connor, references, illus. with photos.

28 ———. *Mexico and the Old Southwest: People, Palaver and Places.* National University Publications, Kennikat Press, Port Washington, N.Y., 1971, cloth, 229 pp., preface, introduction, includes "Artists Illustrators of the Southwest: H. D. Bugbee, Tom Lea and Jose Cisneros," illus. including one, p. (83), by C. (Bugbee, Lea)

29 Bratcher, James T. *Analytical Index to Publications of the Texas Folklore Society.* SMU Press, Dallas, 1973, two-tone decor. cloth, pic. map endsheets, 322 pp., "Foreword" by Wilson M. Hudson, preface, "Historical Note on The Texas Folklore Society" by Francis Edward Abernethy, numerous illus. including nine, Frontis. and pp. xviii, (2), (50), (52), 71, 105, 151 and endsheets by C. (James, Leigh, Mead)

30 Calleros, Cleofas. *El Paso's Missions and Indians.* McMath, (El Paso), 1951, pic. wraps, 55 (1) pp., prologue, map, numerous illus. including six, front cover and pp. (6), (10), (12), (14) and (24), by C.

31 ———. *La Antorcha de El Paso del Norte.* American Printing Co., El Paso, 1951, pic. wraps, 47 pp., "Introduccion" by Carlos E. Castaneda, *reconocimiento, bibliografia,* six illus., frontis. and pp. 15, 19, 30, 35 and 43, by C.

32 ———. *Queen of the Missions* (Our Lady of Guadalupe). American Printing Co., El Paso, 1952, pic. wraps, 15 (1) pp., illus. including one, the frontis., by C.

33 ———. *Seventieth Anniversary of Columbianism in Texas.* American Printing Co., El Paso, for the Knights of Columbus, 1973, cloth, advs., nineteen illus. by C.

34 Carroll, John M., ed. *The Black Military Experience in the American West.* Liveright N.Y., (1971), words "First edition, first printing" on copyright page, cloth, pic. endsheets, 591 pp., notes, bibliography, index, sixty illus. including sixteen by C., limited to 300 numbered copies signed by Carroll, and accompanied by two manually signed prints by Grandee and C., slipcase. (Bjorklund, Bugbee, Eggenhofer, Hurd, Remington, Russell, Schiwetz)

35 ———. Same, first trade edition in cloth, d/w.

36 ———. *Buffalo Soldiers West.* (The Old Army Press, Ft. Collins, Colo., 1971), pic. leather, cloth endsheets, 64 pp., foreword, the artists, 50 illus. including eighteen by C., limited to 50 numbered copies signed by Carroll, each with an original drawing by Bjorklund and signed by him. (Bjorklund, Bugbee, Eggenhofer, Remington)

37 ———. Same, first trade edition in pic. fabricoid.

38 Castaneda, Carlos E. *Our Catholic Heritage in Texas, Volume VI, Transition Period, The Fight for Freedom, 1810–1836.* Von Boeckmann-Jones, Austin, 1950, decor. fabricoid, 384 pp., preface, bibliography, index, folding map, illus. including one, the frontis. by C.

39 ———. Same, *Volume VII, The Church in Texas Since Independence, 1836–1950.* Von Boeckmann-Jones, Austin, 1958, decor. fabricoid, 561 pp., preface, bibliography, index, folding map, illus. including two, facing "Preface" and p. 34, by C.

39a (Certificate) *In recognition of distinguished service to the University of Texas.* Designed and printed by Carl Hertzog, El Paso, decorations and calligraphy by C.

40 Chamberlain, C. K. (editor-in-chief). *East Texas Historical Journal.* Stephen F. Austin State College, Nacogdoches, 1963, pic. wraps, 76 pp., pic. map on front cover by C.

41 Charles, Mrs. Tom. *Tales of the Tularosa.* Privately printed (Carl Hertzog, El Paso, Texas), Alamogordo, New Mexico, 1953, wraps, 69 pp., illus. with photos and with a map and drawings by C. (Reprinted in 1954 and 1959.)

42 ———. Same, limited edition of 100 copies bound in cloth.

43 ———. *More Tales of the Tularosa.* Bennett Printing Co., Alamogordo, N.M., 1961, cloth, 58 (1) pp., illus. with photos but with d/w illus. by C. (Limited edition of 300 copies, edited and designed by Hertzog.)

44 ———. Same, first trade edition in pic. wraps.

45 Chavez, Fray Angelico. *Origins of New Mexico Families.* Historical Society of New Mexico, Santa Fe, 1954, pic. wraps, red endsheets, 339 pp., introduction, bibliography, four illus., frontis. (repeated on front cover), title page and pp. (116) and (117), by C.

46 ———. *Coronado's Friars.* Academy of American Franciscan History, Washington, D.C., 1968, decor. cloth, 106 pp., introduction, appendix, bibliography, index, illus. with photos but with a frontis. by C.

47 ———. *Archives of the Archdioces of Santa Fe,* 1678–1900. Academy of American Franciscan History, Washington, D.C., 1957, decor. cloth, pic. map endsheets by C., 283 pp., introduction, appendix, index.

48 Chavez, Armando B. *A Mi Ciudad.* Privately printed, (Juarez, Mexico, 1946), pic. wraps, 26 pp., numerous illus. including fifteen by C. (Lea)

49 ———. *Historia de Ciudad Juarez.* Chihuahua, 1970, colored pic. wraps, 550 (1) pp., *prologo, bibliografia, indice,* numerous illus. from photos and Cisneros plates (as copied from his published works).

50 Christian, Jane M. *The Navajo: A People in Transition.* TWC Press, El Paso, Fall, 1964, pic. wraps, 35 (1) pp., advs., illus. with photos, and with a double-page (pp. 18–19) pic. map, by C. (Southwestern Studies, vol. 2, no. 3)

51 ———. Same, part II, 1965, pic. wraps, pp. (37–67, (2), double-page pic. map pp. (54–55) by C., illus. with photos. (Southwestern Studies, vol. 2, no. 4.)

52 Cisneros, Jose. *Our Spanish Heritage* (Drawings for *The 1951 Flowsheet*). Carl Hertzog, El Paso, 1951, yellow wraps with a plastic binder, twenty-six leaves from the school annual and limited to 35 sets.

53 ———. *Riders of the Border.* Texas Western Press, El Paso, 1971, pic. wraps, 64 pp., "About the Artist" by E. H. Antone, selected bibliography, thirty illus. plus pic. map on front cover by C. (Southwestern Studies, monograph no. 30.)

54 Clossin, Jimmy and Hertzog, Carl. *West Texas Square Dances; Dictionary, Around-the-Ring Dances, Quadrilles, Callers Chatter.* Carl Hertzog, El Paso, 1948, colored pic. wraps, 48 pp., illus. including one, front cover, by C. A revised and enlarged edition of *Honor Your Partner* by Buck Stimson and Hertzog, 1938, but the first with the Cisneros illus. (Lea)

55 Coan, Alphonse. *Prayer Book.* Franciscan Herald Press, Chicago, 1960, wraps, 48 pp., front cover illus. by C.

56 Coe, Wilbur. *Ranch on the Ruidoso.* Knopf, N.Y., 1968, words "First Edition" on copyright page, gilt decor. two-tone cloth, olive endsheets, 279 pp., green top, "Introduction" by Peter Hurd, foreword designed by Carl Hertzog, four pic. maps by C., illus. (Hurd)

57 Cornelius, Fred. *Tambalear the Tumbleweed.* Carl Hertzog, El Paso, 1954, pic. wraps, (16) pp., five illus. including one, p. (16), by C.

58 ———. Same, Carl Hertzog, El Paso, 1959, pic.

wraps, 24 pp., eight illus. including three, pp. 18, 22 and 24, by C. (Second edition of no. 57 with additional stories.)

59 (Daniel.) *Texas and the West.* Catalogue no. 19, Price Daniel, Jr., Bookseller, Waco, (1963), decor. wraps, unpaged, "Printer to the West" (Hertzog) by Dr. Llerena Friend, cataloguer's note, photos of three covers or d/w by C. Also 125 numbered copies in cloth. (Bugbee, Lea)

60 (Dawson.) *American Artists and Illustrators.* Catalogue 21, Bob Dawson, American Books, Hazlet, N.J., n.d., pic. wraps, 31 (1) pp., front cover illus. by C.

61 DeGolyer, Everett. *Across Aboriginal America: The Journey of Three Englishmen across Texas in 1568.* Peripatetic Press (Carl Hertzog, El Paso), 1947, boards, 11 (14) pp., and 6 pp. of Ingraham's narrative in facsimile, frontis. and map by C.

62 Dillon, Myles (collected and translated by). *There was a King in Ireland.* Texas Folklore Society (University of Texas Press), Austin, (1971), cloth, tan endsheets, 114 pp., foreword, six illus., frontis. (repeated on d/w) and pp. (17), (37), (53), (77) and (97), by C.

63 Dobie, J. Frank. *Guide to Life and Literature of the Southwest.* SMU Press, (Dallas, 1952), decor. cloth, tan endsheets, 222 pp., nineteen illus. including one, p. 41, by C. (Bugbee, Lea, Leigh, Russell, Thomason)

64 ———. *The Mezcla Man.* (Carl Hertzog), El Paso Del Norte, 1954, decor. wraps, 11 pp., frontis. by C. (Dobie Christmas booklet for 1954.)

65 ———. *Trans Pecos.* (Carl Hertzog, El Paso, 1955), pic. map on front cover, (2) pp., cover map by C. (Southwest Broadsides of Lawrence Clark Powell, no. 9.)

66 El Paso County Historical Society. Emblem by C. used on the cover of *Password,* quarterly publication of the Society beginning in 1955, also used on the stationery, programs and awards.

67 Farrar, Nancy. *The Chinese in El Paso.* Texas Western Press, El Paso, 1972, pic. wraps, 44 pp., references, illus. with photos, map, p. (23) and pic. map on front cover by C. (Southwestern Studies, monograph no. 33.)

68 Fierman, Floyd S. *Some Early Jewish Settlers on the Southwestern Frontier.* TWC Press, El Paso, 1960, pic. wraps, 58 pp., cover illus. by C. (Edition limited to 250 copies.)

69 ———. Same, thirty copies bound in cloth.

70 ———. *The Impact of the Frontier on a Jewish Family.* TWC Press, El Paso, 1961, pic. wraps, 32 pp., illus. with photos, map on front cover by C.

71 ———. Same, twenty-five copies bound in cloth.

72 ———. *The Spiegelbergs: Pioneer Merchants and Bankers in the Southwest.* Reprinted from *American Jewish Historical Quarterly* 56:4, June 1967, decor. wraps, pp. 371–451, illus. with photos, two maps, frontis. and p. (401), by C.

73 Fitzhugh, Bessie Lee. *Bells Over Texas.* TWC Press, El Paso, 1955, pic. cloth, orange endsheets, 159 pp., foreword, numerous illus. from photos and from drawings by C.

74 ———. Same, announcement folder with front cover illus. by C.

75 *47th Annual Conference, Texas Library Association.* (Carl Hertzog, El Paso), San Antonio, April 6–9, 1960, pic. wraps, 16 pp., illus. including one, front cover, by C. (Lea)

76 Fugate, Francis. *The Spanish Heritage of the Southwest.* TWC Press, El Paso, 1952, cloth and decor. boards, pages unnumbered, fourteen illus. by C. Edition of 525 numbered copies signed by Fugate, Cisneros and Hertzog.

77 ———. Same, trade edition in pictorial wraps, 925 copies.

78 Gambrell, Herbert and Virginia. *A Pictorial History of Texas.* Dutton, N.Y., (1960), words "First Edition" on copyright page, cloth and decor. boards, brand illus. endsheets, 217 pp., numerous illus. including two, pp. 82 and 179, by C. (James, Lea, Remington, Schiwetz)

79 Grisso, W. D. (compiled and edited by). *From Where the Sun Now Stands.* Stagecoach Press, Santa Fe, 1963, words "First Edition" on copyright page, cloth, 73 pp., editor's preface, bibliography, frontis. (repeated on d/w) by C. Cimarron Edition of 99 copies signed by the author and by publisher Jack Rittenhouse.

80 ———. Same, first trade issue of 650 copies with words "First Regular Edition" on copyright page.

81 Haddox, John. *Los Chicanos: An Awakening People.* Texas Western Press, El Paso, 1970, cloth, 44 pp., references, ten illus. facing pp. 6, 10, 11, 18, 19, 26, 27, 34, 35 and 38, by C.

SELF PORTRAIT by Cisneros   *Collection of the author*

82 ———. Same, first edition in wraps. (Southwestern Studies, monograph no. 28.)

83 Haley, J. Evetts. *Fort Concho and the Texas Frontier*. San Angelo Standard Times, San Angelo, Texas, 1952, cloth, pic. endsheets, 352 pp., orange top, illus. by Bugbee, and with four maps, facing pp. 1, (32), (74) and (198), by C. San Angelo edition of 185 numbered and signed copies (in slipcase) designed by Hertzog.

84 ———. Same, first trade edition.

85 ———. *Men of Fiber*. Carl Hertzog, El Paso, 1963, simulated leather, brown endsheets, 39 pp., illus. with five chapter head drawings, pp. 6, 14, 20, 26 and 32, by C., and with photos. Rawhide Edition of 700 copies with a pic. d/w by C.

86 ———. Same, the Shamrock Edition in pic. wraps, illus. by C. (Used by the Shamrock Oil and Gas Corp. of Amarillo as a Christmas greeting to friends and customers in 1963).

87 *Nita Stewart Haley Memorial Library, A Trust Indenture*. Private edition of fourteen copies printed by Carl Hertzog, El Paso, for J. Evetts Haley, cloth, 16 pp., one illus. from the bookplate of the Providence Hospital Library by C.

88 Hallenbeck, Cleve. *The Journey of Fray Marcos de Niza*. University Press in Dallas, 1949, decor. cloth, 115 pp., bibliography, biographical note, decorations and illus. including a double-page pic. map and full-page plates, pp. (8), (14) and (38), by C. Edition of 1065 copies designed and produced by Hertzog.

89 ———. Same, announcement folder, (16) pp., with front cover illus., decor. title page, double-page pic. map, and one decor. chapter heading by C.

90 Hawkins, Walace. *El Sal del Rey*. Texas State Historical Assn., Austin, 1947, decor. cloth, map endsheets, 68 pp., yellow top, maps and illus. by C. Designed and printed by Hertzog.

91 Hertzog, Carl (produced by). *National Music Week*. May 5–12, 1946, printed by Hertzog & Resler for The Music World of El Paso, decor. wraps, unpaged, nine portrait sketches by C.

92 ———. *Signposts of Early El Paso*. State National Bank of El Paso, 1948, decor. wraps, 27 pp., twelve illus. by C.

93 ——— (planned and designed by). *El Paso Public Library*. (Guynes Printing Co., El Paso, 1954), pic. wraps, (16) pp., illus. including a photo of the three plaques on the bookcase ends of the Latin American Collection by C., and the front cover drawing by C. (Lea)

94 ———. *The Making of a Book* (an Exhibition from the Library, The University of Texas at El Paso). Guynes Printing Company, El Paso, folder (to accompany the five-panel exhibit), three illus. including one, front cover reproduction of the d/w for *Morelos of Mexico*, illus. by C. (Also shown at San Antonio, Las Vegas, N.M., and Albuquerque.)

94a *New Courses for Students of Creative Writing, Commercial Art, Advertising, Journalism*. Texas Western College of the University of Texas at El Paso, folder with illus. on cover by C. typography by Carl Hertzog.

95 Hudson, Wilson M., ed. *The Healer of Los Olmos and Other Mexican Lore*. The Texas Folklore Society, Austin, SMU Press, Dallas, 1951, words "First Edition" on copyright page, decor. cloth, 139 pp., "Charm in Mexican Folktales" by J. Frank Dobie, four illus., pp. 48, 75, 82 and 133, by C.

96 Jamieson, Tulitas. *Tulitas of Torreon* (Reminiscences of Life in Mexico). Texas Western Press, El Paso, cloth, 146 pp., d/w illus. and lettering by C.

97 Jarratt, Rie. *Gutierrez de Lara, Mexican-Texan: The Story of a Creole Hero*. Creole Texana, Austin, 1949, cloth, 67 pp., five illus. including one, the frontis., by C., plus a pic. map, p. (6) by C. Designed by Hertzog.

98 Johnson, William. *Captain Cortes Conquers Mexico*. Random, N.Y., (1960), decor. cloth, pic. map endsheets, 186 pp., numerous illus. by C.

99 ———. Same, but first Swedish edition with the title *Corte's Erovrar Mexika*, Stockholm, 1968, colored pic. boards, 157 (1) pp., fourteen illus. by C.

100 Kilgore, D. E. *A Ranger Legacy* (150 Years of Service to Texas). Madrona Press, Austin, (1973), words "First Edition" on copyright page, imitation leather, map endsheets, 104 pp., "Foreword" by Colonel Wilson E. Speir, appendices, bibliography, index, eight illus. including one, the frontis., by C. Edition of 200 numbered copies signed by the author, slipcase.

101 ———. Same, first trade edition in cloth.

102 *La Dona Luz de Taos*. (Carl Hertzog, El Paso, n.d., advs. folder for the La Dona Luz Restaurant and Cantina at Taos), pic. folder, two illus. including one, front cover, by C.

103 Lawrence, F. Lee and Glover, Robert W. *Camp Ford*

C.S.A., The Story of Union Prisoners in Texas. Texas Civil War Centennial Advisory Committee, Austin, 1964, two-tone decor. cloth, map endsheets, 99 pp., illus. with photos, old prints, facsimiles, and drawings, the frontis. and facing p. 1 and a map by C. designed and printed by Hertzog.

104 ———. Same, announcement folder with one illus., back cover, by C.

105 Lea, Tom and Hertzog, Carl (designed by). *Fort Bliss, One Hundred Anniversary, 1848–1948.* (Guynes Printing Co., El Paso, for the Centennial Commission, 1948), pic. wraps, unpaged, map and sketches for a bronze tablet and a commemorative postage stamp by C.

106 ———. Same, private edition of 20 deluxe numbered and signed copies in red leather.

107 ———. Same, 25 copies bound in red cloth.

108 Leach, Joseph. *The Typical Texan: Biography of an American Myth.* SMU Press, Dallas, 1952, cloth, orange endsheets, 178 pp., illus. with old prints, but with a frontis. by C.

109 Lehmann, V. W. *Forgotten Legions; Sheep in the Rio Grande Plain of Texas.* Texas Western Press, El Paso, (1969), sheepskin and pic. hopsacking, tan endsheets, 226 pp., orange top, preface, appendices, bibliography, index, illustrated with photos, maps including one, preceding the frontis., by C. Limited edition of 300 numbered copies signed by the author and by Carl Hertzog, slipcase.

110 ———. Same, first trade edition in cloth.

111 Lowman, Al et al. *The Spanish Texans.* Institute of Texan cultures, The University of Texas, San Antonio, 1972, pic. wraps, 32 pp., numerous illus. including three, pp. (10), 11 and 24, by C. (Bugbee, Lea, Mead, Remington)

112 ———. *First United Methodist Church 125th Anniversary Year, 1847–1972.* San Marcos, (1972), cloth and boards with illus. paper title label on front cover, 29 pp., four illus. including two, pp. 7 and (8), by C. Circuit Rider Edition, limited to 55 numbered copies (50 for sale) signed by Lowman, Cisneros, Schiwetz and William R. Holman (designer), slipcase. (Schiwetz)

113 ———. Same, first trade edition in wraps.

114 ——— (compiled by). *Printer at the Pass: The Work of Carl Hertzog.* Institute of Texas Cultures, The University of Texas, San Antonio, 1972, cloth and boards with paper title label on front cover, brown endsheets, 123 pp., "Carl Hertzog, Printer" by Lowman, "A Hertzog Dozen" by William R. Holman, index, illus. including four, (xii), (32), (33) and (56), by C.

115 ———. Same, limited edition of 200 numbered copies signed by Lowman, Hertzog, Holman and designer William D. Wittliff with five additional photos following the text, leather spine, slipcase.

116 McCracken, Harold. *The American Cowboy.* Doubleday, Garden City, N.Y., 1973, words "Limited Edition" on copyright page, simulated leather, marbled endsheets, 196 pp., all edges gilt, references, index, numerous illus. including two, pp. 29 and 44, by C., 300 numbered copies signed by the author and with the extra color plate by Borein, slipcase. (Borein, Eggenhofer, Johnson, Koerner, Leigh, Remington, Russell, Wyeth)

117 ———. Same, first trade edition, with words "First Edition after the limited edition of 300 copies" on copyright page, cloth, blue endsheets, d/w in color.

118 (McCubbin.) *Western Americana.* Book List no. 1, Bordertown Books, El Paso, n.d., pic. wraps, 9 mimeographed pages, front cover illus. by C.

119 McGaw, William Cochran. *Savage Scene: The Life and Times of James Kirker, Frontier King.* Hastings, N.Y., 1972, cloth, 242 pp., preface, index, illus. including one, the frontis., by C.

120 ———. Same, first Canadian edition by Saunders of Toronto, Ltd., 1972.

121 McKee, Robert E. *The Zia Company in Los Alamos.* Carl Hertzog, El Paso, Texas, 1950, decor. cloth, pic. endsheets, 71 pp., illus. with photos, decor. map by C.

122 Mangan, Frank. *El Paso in Pictures.* The Press, El Paso, 1971, two-tone cloth, pic. endsheets, 174 pp., pictures and art credits, sources, numerous illus. including one, p. 14, by C. (Lea)

122a (Matthews, Watt R.) *Wattisms.* (Collected and reported by Carl Hertzog, El Paso, and printed by him, 1974), broadside, one drawing, decorations and calligraphy by C., signed by Matthews and Hertzog.

123 Metz, Leon C. *John Selman, Texas Gunfighter.* Hastings, N.Y., 1966, cloth, 254 pp., illus. with photos, endpaper map by C.

124 ———. *Pat Garrett, The Story of a Western Lawman.* Oklahoma, Norman, (1974), words "First edition" on copyright page, cloth, grey endsheets, 328 pp., bibliography, index, illus. with a pictorial map, "Pat Gar-

rett's Country" as the frontis. (and repeated p. 276) by C. and with photos.

125 Middagh, John. *Frontier Newspaper: The El Paso Times.* TWC Press, El Paso, Texas, 1958, cloth, facsimiles on endsheets, 333 pp., illus. with photos, d/w illus. by C. Typography by Hertzog.

126 Mountain States Telephone and Telegraph Co. *A City and a Service Grow Up Together.* (Carl Hertzog), El Paso, (1948), wraps, (24) pp., illus. with historical sketches by C. (Lea)

127 Mullin, Robert N. *The Strange Story of Wayne Brazel.* Palo Duro Press, Canyon, Texas, 1969, pic. wraps, 37 pp., "Introduction" by J. Evetts Haley, two illus., front cover and title page plus one map, by C.

128 Myres, S. D. *History of the Permian Basin.* Guynes Printing Co., El Paso, 1973, cloth, illus. including endsheets, chapter heading and three in text by C.

129 Myres, Sandra L. *The Ranch in Spanish Texas 1691– 1800.* Texas Western Press, El Paso, 1969, pic. wraps, 69 pp., introduction, conclusion, references, five illus., front cover and facing pp. 22, 23, 46 and 47, by C.

130 Neville, A. W. *The Red River Valley, Then and Now.* (North Texas Pub. Co.), Paris, Texas, 1946, cloth, pic. map endsheets, 278 pp., illus. with twenty-six drawings, pic. map end sheets and d/w illus. by C. Typography and design by Hertzog.

131 ———. Same, announcement folder with the pic. endsheet map (from no. 130) by C. used as wraps.

131a *The 1951 Flowsheet* (Yearbook, Texas Western College). (El Paso), numerous illus. including twenty-six in text plus front cover by C.

132 Oden, Bill. *Early Days on the Texas-New Mexico Plains.* Palo Duro Press, Canyon, Texas, 1965, pic. cloth, pic. map endsheets, 69 pp., "Introduction" (and edited) by J. Evetts Haley, illus. with drawings by Bugbee and with photos, but pic. endsheets may by C. Edition of 750 copies, designed and produced by Hertzog.

133 *The Old Army Press.* Catalog number 4, (Ft. Collins, Colo., 1972), colored pic. wraps, unpaged, twenty-seven illus. including two by C. (Eggenhofer)

134 *Parent-Educator Leaflet Series of the Confraternity of Christian Doctrine* (translated into Spanish by Sister Mary Eileen). St. Anthony Guild, Patterson, N.J., 1961, twenty-four illus. and two cover designs by C.

135 Pearson, Dr. Jim B. et al. *Texas: The Land and Its People.* Hendrick-Long Pub. Co., Dallas, 1972, colored pic. cloth, tinted endsheets, 600 pp., preface, glossary, index, numerous illus. including eight drawings, pp. 59, 98, 100, 111, 118, 231, 408 and 418, by C.

136 Perez, Al (President). *Fiesta de las Flores Coronation Ball.* L.U.L.A.C., El Paso, Oct. 13, 1962, pic. wraps, unpaged, front cover illus. by C.

137 (Pingenot.) *Southwestern Americana*, Catalogue no. 11, Pen E. Pingenot, Eagle Pass, Texas, (1969), pic. wraps, 20 pp., five illus. including one, front cover, by C.

138 Porter, Eugene O. *San Elizario, A History.* Jenkins Publishing Co., Austin, 1973, cloth with illus. mounted on front cover and with paper title label on spine, brown endsheets, 86 pp., preface, appendices, notes, glossary, bibliography, index, five illus., frontis. map, pp. (xii), (12), (26) (and repeated on front cover) and (40), by C.

139 *Program International Dental Conference.* Third annual, Dec. 5–7, 1965, El Paso, folder with drawing on cover by C.

140 Same, eighth annual, Sept. 16–19, 1970, El Paso, folder with drawing on cover by C.

141 Quinn, The Right Reverend Hugh G. *Anniversary of the Foundation of the Diocese of El Paso.* (Diocese of El Paso, El Paso, 1965), fabricoid with illus. in color mounted on front cover, illus. map on front endsheet, decorated title page and prayer, p. 12, by C.

142 ———. *The Bishop of El Paso and his Diocese.* (Address), El Paso, May 10, 1965, wraps, decor. by C., (5) pp.

143 Ray, Joseph M. *On Becoming a University* (Report on an Octennium). Texas Western Press, El Paso, (1968), fabricoid and decor. boards, tan endsheets, 109 pp., preface, appendices, numerous illus. including one, between pp. 30 and 31, by C. (Lea)

144. (Reynolds.) *Western Americana.* Catalogue 108. J. E. Reynolds, Booksellers, Van Nuys, Calif., February 1969, pic. wraps, unpaged, front cover illus. and calligraphy by C. and with a note on his art inside front cover.

145 Rickards, Colin. *Mysterious Dave Mather.* Press of the Territorian, Santa Fe, 1968, cloth, 42 pp., frontis. by C.

146 Rios, Eduardo Enrique (translated and revised by Benedict Leutenegger, O.F.M.). *Life of Fray Antonio*

Margil. Academy of American Franciscan History, Washington, D.C., 1959, cloth, map endsheets by C., 159 pp., illus. with old prints and facsimiles.

147 Rittenhouse, Jack D. *Cabezon: A New Mexico Ghost Town.* Stagecoach Press, Santa Fe, 1965, words "First Edition" on copyright page, cloth, 95 pp., two maps, illus. with frontis. by C and with photos. Edition of 750 copies.

148 Simmons, Marc. *The Little Lion of the Southwest* (A life of Manuel Antonio Chavez). Swallow Press, Chicago, (1973), words "First Edition, First Printing" on copyright page, cloth, map endsheets, 263 pp., preface, notes, bibliography, index, maps, illus. including the frontis. (repeated on d/w) and calligraphic chapter headings by C.

149 Sinclair, Kenneth L. *Thunder Mountains Mine.* Funk & Wagnalls, N.Y., (1953), two-tone cloth, 264 pp., twenty illus., title page and chapter headings, by C.

150 Slack, John P. *The Expedition of Francisco Vasquez de Coronado.* Southwestern Mounments Association, Gila Pueblo, Globe, 1950.

151 Sonnichsen, C. L. (introduction by) et al. *El Paso County Centennial Celebration.* December 1 to 3, 1950, (Lower Valley Chamber of Commerce, Ysleta, Texas, but printed by McMath, El Paso), pic. wraps, 64 pp., numerous illus. including two, front cover and p. 54, by C.

152 ———. *The El Paso Salt War of 1877.* Carl Hertzog and the Texas Western Press at the Pass of the North, 1961, two-tone cloth, yellow endsheets, 68 pp., foreword, eleven illus. (four repeated on the d/w) by C.

153 ———. Same, pic. wraps with the frontis. repeated on the front cover and with the illus. from pp. (35) and (41) repeated on the back cover.

154 ———, ed. *The Southwest in Life and Literature.* Devin-Adair, N.Y., 1962, decor. cloth, brown endsheets, 554 pp., orange top, introduction, two drawings on d/w by C. (Russell, Santee, Thomason)

155 ———. *I'll Die Before I'll Run.* Devin-Adair, N.Y., 1962, two-tone cloth, 371 pp., twenty-one illus. by C.

156 ———. *Pass of the North: Four Centuries on the Rio Grande.* Texas Western Press, El Paso, 1968, two-tone decor. cloth, olive endsheets, 467 pp., orange top, foreword, sources, references, index, illus. with photos, map (preceding frontis.) and chapter initials by C.

157 ——— and McKinney, M. G. *The State National Since 1881* (The Pioneer Bank of El Paso). Texas Western Press, El Paso, 1971, cloth, pic. map endsheets, 171 pp., brown top, introduction, sources, references, index, illus. with photos, double-page map, between pp. 82 and 83 (center), by C. Limited to 220 especially bound, numbered copies signed by Sonnichsen, McKinney and Carl Hertzog, slipcase.

158 ———. Same, first trade edition.

159 Southwestern Studies, monograph no. 1 — 1963. *The Municipality in Northern Mexico* by Leonard Cardenas, Jr. Texas Western Press, El Paso, pic. map on front cover by C. (Note: all the monographs in the series listed here carry this same map.)

160 Same, no. 2 — 1963. *The Chamizal Settlement* by Gladys Gregory.

161 Same, no. 3 — 1963. *Six Who Came to El Paso: Pioneers of the 1840's* by Rex Strickland.

162 Same, no. 4 — 1964. *The Spiegelbergs of New Mexico* by Floyd S. Fierman.

163 Same, no. 5 — 1964. *The Railways of Mexico* by John H. McNeely.

164 Same, no. 6 — 1964. *"Buckskin Frank" Leslie, Gunman of Tombstone* by Colin Rickards.

165 Same, no. 11 — 1965. *El Paso Merchant and Civic Leader* by Samuel J. Freudenthal.

166 Same, no. 12 — 1965. *The Governors of Mexico* by Marvin Alisky.

167 Same, no. 13 — 1966. *The Theatre in Early El Paso* by Donald V. Brady.

168 Same, no. 14 — 1966. *Early Economic Policies of the Government of Texas* by Lee Van Zant.

169 Same, no. 16 — 1966. *Charles Littlepage Ballard, Southwesterner* by Colin Rickards.

170 Same, no. 17 — 1967. *The Boyhood of Billy the Kid* by Robert Mullin.

171 Same, no. 18 — 1967. *San Antonio During the Texas Republic* by Ray F. Broussard.

172 Same, no. 19 — 1967. *Wings and Saddles* by Stacy C. Hinkle.

173 Same, no. 21 — 1968. *Postwar Readjustment in El Paso* by Patricia Reschenthaler.

174 Same, no. 22 — 1969. *Water Out of the Desert* by Christopher M. Wallace.

175 Same, no. 23 — 1969. *Joseph Wade Hampton* by Ronnie C. Tyler.

176 Same, no. 24 — 1969. *The Ponce de Leon Land Grant* by J. J. Bowden.

177 Same, no. 25 — 1970. *Lord Beresford and Lady Flo* by Eugene O. Porter.

178 Same, no. 26 — 1970. *Wings Over the Border* by Stacy C. Hinkle.

179 Same, no. 27 — 1970. *Music in El Paso, 1919–1939* by Robert M. Stevenson.

180 Same, no. 29 — 1971. *San Antonio Stagelines, 1847–1881* by Robert H. Thonhoff.

181 Same, no. 31 — 1971. *The Yellow Rose of Texas* by Martha Anne Turner.

182 Same, no. 32 — 1972. *The Southwestern International Livestock Show and Rodeo* by Nora Ramirez.

183 Same, no. 35 — 1972. *The Old World Background of the Irrigation System of San Antonio, Texas* by Thomas F. Glick.

184 Same, no. 37 — 1973. *A Geoaphical Survey of Chihuahua* by Robert H. Schmidt, Jr.

185 Same, no. 38 — 1973. *Letters of Ernst Kohlberg, 1875–1877*.

186 Same, no. 39 — 1973. *Juh, An Incredible Indian* by Dan L. Thrapp.

187 *Spring 1972 Booklist*. Texas Western Press, El Paso, 1972, folder with three illus. including one, front cover, by C.

188 Stratton, David H. (edited with annotations by). *The Memoirs of Albert B. Fall*. Texas Western Press, El Paso, 1966, pic. wraps, 63 pp., (1) of advs., introduction, references, illus. with photos but with one small drawing, p. (64) and front cover pic. map by C. (Southwestern Studies, monograph no. 15.)

189 *Texas Western College of the University of Texas, Catalog 1966–67*. (Texas Western Press, El Paso, 1966), wraps, 203 (1) pp., front cover map by C.

190 Thomas of Celano. *St. Francis of Assisi*. Franciscan Herald Press, Chicago, 1962, decor. cloth, pic. endsheets, 245 pp., foreword, introduction, footnotes, bibliography, illus. including four, three chapter headings plus a drawing, p. 64, by C.

191 Timmons, Wilbert H. *Morelos of Mexico, Priest, Soldier, Statesman*. TWC Press, El Paso, 1963, two-tone cloth with a Mexican peso which bears the portrait of Morelos embedded in the front cover, pic. map endsheets, 184 pp., preface, edited by Samuel D. Myres, six illus., endsheets, frontis. and pp. 5, 22, 76

and 120 (three repeated on the d/w), by C. Pesos Edition, signed by the author and the typographer, Carl Hertzog.

191a ———. Same, first trade edition in cloth.

192 ———. Same, announcement folder with one illus. by C.

193 ———. Same, but second edition issued in 1970 with important new material in text.

194 Tinkle, Lon and Maxell, Allen, eds. *The Cowboy Reader*. Longmans, Green, N.Y. etc., 1959, words "First Edition" on copyright page, cloth, 307 pp. twenty-one illus. including one, p. 9, by C. (Bugbee, Lea, Remington, Russell)

195 Turner, Frederick Jackson. *The Significance of the Frontier in American History*. Academic Reprints (TWC Press), El Paso, 1960, pic. wraps, 35 pp., "Introduction" by John A. (Jack) Carroll, front cover illus. by C., typography by Hertzog.

196 ———. Same, issued in cloth and with *The Turner Thesis and the Dry World* by Rex W. Strickland bound in.

197 Vernon, Walter N. *Methodism Moves Across North Texas*. The Historical Society, North Texas Conference, The Methodist, Dallas, (1967), cloth, pic. map endsheets, 416 pp., foreword, appendix, index, numerous illus. including one, p. (21), by C. (Hurd)

198 Whisenhunt, Donald W. *Fort Richardson, Outpost on the Texas Frontier*. Texas Western Press, El Paso, 1968, pic. wraps, 46 pp., (2) of advs., references, illus. with photos but with a small drawing, p. (48) and pic. map on front cover by C. (Southwestern Studies, monograph no. 20.)

199 Williams, Judge O. W. *Pioneer Surveyor, Frontier Lawyer*. TWC Press, 1966, leather and cloth, marbled endsheets, 350 pp., yellow top, "Preface" (and edited and annotated) by S. D. Myres, "Introduction" by C. L. Sonnichsen, illus. with photos, and with three double-page pic. maps, following pp. 39, 111 and 261, by C. Fort Stockton Edition of 150 numbered copies signed by Myres, Sonnichsen, Cisneros, Clayton W. Williams (the Judge's son who did the research) and Hertzog (designer-producer) in a cloth slipcase.

200 ———. Same, first trade edition in cloth.

201 ———. Same, announcement folder with pic. maps by C.

202 ———. *Stories from the Big Bend*. TWC Press, El Paso, 1965, pic. wraps, 44 pp., edited and annotated

by S. D. Myres, illus. with photos, double-page pic. map, pp. (22–23), by C. (Southwestern Studies, monograph no. 10.)

203 Wright, Celia M. *Sketches from Hopkins County History*. The Shining Path Press, Sulphur Springs, Texas, 1959, wraps, 50 pp., pic. map, p. 3, by C. First edition, first impression, carries handwritten corrections pp. 16, 34 and 41 by the author.

The Artist and His Art

204 Anderson, E. Wynn. "Requiem — and Landmarks — An Offer," a brief article in *NOVA* 7:3, June 1972, with a center-fold illus. by C. and a one-page "Requiem for a Mountain," calligraphy by him.

205 Braddy, Haldeen. "Artist Illustrators of the Southwest: H. D. Bugbee, Jose Cisneros, and Tom Lea," an article in *Western Review* 1:2, Fall 1964, with one illus. by C. (Bugbee, Lea)

206 *The Fort Leavenworth Museum presents John H. Carroll's Military Art Collection*. December 1973–February 1974, decor. wraps, unpaged, frontis., short biographical sketch of C. (Bjorklund)

207 Friend, Dr. Llerena. "Thirty-five Years of Hertzog Printing," an article in *The Library Chronicle* of the University of Texas, vol. VI, no. 4, Austin, Winter, 1960. Lists many books illus. by C.

208 Lovelace, Donna. "Jose Cisneros," an article in *Southwestern Art* 2:3, 1969, with one illus. by C. and a photo of his family.

209 Lowman, Al et al. *The Mexican Texans*. Institute of Texan Cultures, The University of Texas, San Antonio, 1971, pic. wraps, 32 pp., introduction, numerous illus., a biographical sketch of Cisneros and a photo of him. (Lea, Remington)

210 ———. Same, but issued in Spanish with the title *Los Mexicano Texanos*.

ILLUSTRATION by Cisneros from *The Ranch In Spanish Texas*

THE CHIEF MEDICINE MAN AT BEAVER CREEK by Crawford from *Indian Fights and Fighters*

WILL CRAWFORD
1869–1944

Catalogues of Art Exhibitions and Galleries

HAMMER GALLERIES, NEW YORK

1 *The works of Charles M. Russell and Other Western Artists.* (1963), pic. wraps, 56 pp., "Charles M. Russell" by Will Rogers, introduction, references, exhibitions, numerous illus. including two, p. 32, by C. (Goodwin, Leigh, Lungren, Miller, Remington, Russell)

KENNEDY GALLERIES, NEW YORK

2 *The Things That Were* (19th and 20th Century Paintings of the American West). June 1968, colored pic. wraps, pp. 53-123, (1), index, numerous illus. including one, p. 109, by C. (Blumenscein, Leigh, Miller, Remington, Schoonover, Schreyvogel)

E. WALTER LATENDORF, NEW YORK

3 *C. M. Russell,* Catalogue No. 27, (May 1957), pic. wraps, unpaged, numerous illus. including six by C. (Borein, De Yong, Goodwin, Leigh, Marchand, Russell)

THE UNIVERSITY OF TEXAS, HUMANITIES RESEARCH CENTER, AUSTIN

4 *Texana at the University of Texas,* an exhibition, March 1962, decor. wraps, 42 (2) pp., illus. including one, p. 37, by C. (Schiwetz)

Illustrated by the Artist

5 Allen, Ethan. *A Narrative of Colonel Ethan Allen's Captivity, Containing His Voyages and Travels.* Ticonderoga Museum, N.Y. (Westport, Conn.), 1930, four illus. by C.

6 Boorstin, Daniel J. *The Landmark History of the American People from Appomattox to the Moon.* Random House, N.Y., (1970), colored pic. boards, pic. endsheets, 192 (1) pp., "A Word to the Reader," index, numerous illus. including one (attributed to Russell), p. 4, by C. (Dunn, Remington)

7 Brady, Cyrus Townsend. *Hohenzollern.* The Century Co., N.Y., 1902, words "Published April 1902" on copyright page, cloth, 288 pp., 8 illus., frontis. and pp. 65, 105, 151, 201, 215, 249 and 269 by C.

8 ———. *Woven with the Ship.* J. B. Lippincott Co., Philadelphia and London, 1902, words "Published October, 1902" on copyright page, cloth, 368 pp., illus. including one, facing p. 342, by C.

9 ———. *Sir Henry Morgan, Buccaneer.* G. W. Dillingham Co., N.Y., (1903), words "Issued October, 1903" on copyright page, pic. cloth, 444 (1) pp., red top, preface, illus. including four full-page plates, pp. 240, 320, 386 and 436 and numerous small drawings in text by C. (Marchand)

10 ———. *Indian Fights and Fighters.* McClure, Phillips & Co., N.Y., 1904, words "Published December 1904N" on copyright page, pic. cloth, 423 pp., preface, bibliography, index, 26 full-page plates including two, facing pp. 98 and 132, by C., 13 maps and plans. (Blumenschein, Deming, Elwell, Remington, Schreyvogel)

11 ———. *Most Politely.* The Crafters, Kansas City, Mo., 1910, limited, signed and numbered edition (number not stated), pic. wraps, colored endsheets, 66 (1) pp., foreword, photo of author, frontis. in color by C.

12 ———. *A Little Book for Christmas.* G. P. Putnam's Sons, N.Y., and London, 1917, cloth, pic. endsheets, 178 pp., four illus., frontis. in color and facing pp. 46, 76 and 96, plus decorations in text, by C.

13 Butler, Ellis Parker. *Pigs is Pigs.* McClure, Phillips & Co., N.Y., 1906, words "Published April 1906"

on copyright page, decorated cloth, 37 pp., five illus., frontis. and facing pp. 18, 20, 30 and 34, by C.

14 ———. *The Great American Pie Company*. McClure, Phillips & Co., N.Y., 1907, pic. cloth, 43 (1) pp., three illus., frontis. and facing pp. 24 and 34, by C.

15 Chapman, Arthur. *The Story of Colorado*. Rand McNally & Co., Chicago, N.Y., (1924), pic. cloth, 270 pp., numerous illus. including frontis. in color and pp. 55 and 89 by C.

16 ———. *The Pony Express*. Burt, N.Y., Chicago, (1932), cloth, map endsheets, 319 pp., yellow top, bibliography, index, illus. with photos and old prints but d/w drawing by C.

17 Collectors' Institute. *Commemorative Brochure*. Inaugural Meeting, Nov. 23, 1968, Austin, Texas, pic. wraps, 19 pp, cover drawing by C.

18 ———. *Transactions*, Second Annual Meeting, Nov. 22, 1969, Austin, pic. wraps, 16 pp., cover drawing by C.

19 ———. *Transactions, Vol. II*, Second Annual Meeting, Nov. 22, 1969, pic. wraps, 16 pp., cover drawing by C.

20 ———. *Transactions*, Third Annual Meeting, Nov. 21, 1970, San Antonio, pic. wraps, 23 pp., cover drawing by C.

21 ———. *Transactions*, Fourth Annual Meeting, Nov. 20, 1971, Austin, pic. wraps, 36 pp., cover drawing by C.

22 ———. *Workshop Report, Restoration and Preservation*, Spring 1969, Austin, pic. wraps, 12 pp., cover drawing by C.

23 ———. *Transactions — Combined Workshop Reports 1971-72*, Austin, pic. wraps, 27 pp., cover drawing by C.

24 Dobie, J. Frank. *Cow People*. Little Brown, Boston, Toronto, (1964), words "First Edition" on copyright page, fabricoid, 305 pp., introduction, a note on sources, index, illus. including one, p. (196), by C. (Lea)

25 ———. Same, Hammond, Hammond & Co., London, (1964), "First Edition" in Great Britain, boards.

26 ———. *Guide to Life and Literature of the Southwest*, Southern Methodist University Press, Dallas, (1969), words "Sixth printing 1969" on copyright page, cloth, 222 pp., "A Preface with Some Revised Ideas," index, illus. including one, title page, by C. and repeated on d/w. (Bugbee, Lea, Leigh, Russell, Thomason)

27 ———. *Forty-four Range Country Books Topped Out by J. Frank Dobie in 1941 and Forty-four More Range Country Books Topped Out by Jeff Dykes in 1971*. Encino Press, Austin, 1972, words "One thousand copies of this book have been produced in March, 1972" on copyright page, cloth with illus. title label on front cover, brown endsheets, 32 pp., "Foreword" by Dykes, Crawford drawing on title page and repeated on title label on front cover.

28 Dunham, Sam C. *Riley Grannan's Last Adventure*. (Packsaddle Press), Austin, Texas (1969 but actually produced in October, 1968), dec. cloth, 33 pp., "Introduction" by Les Beitz (the publisher), map, illus. including one, the frontis., by C. Edition of 500 numbered copies.

29 Elmer, Robert P. and Smart, Charles A. *The Book of the Long Bow*. N.Y., 1929, cloth and boards, illus. by C. Edition limited to 450 copies.

30 Fish, Carl Russell. *History of America*. American Book Co., N.Y. etc., (1925), code letters "E.P.L." on copyright page, cloth, 570, lix pp., preface, 12 colored maps, numerous illus. including five, pp. 149, 184, 319, 393 and 427, by C.

31 Fraser, W. Lewis et al. *The Year's Art, The Quarterly Illustrator for 1894*. Harry C. Jones, N.Y., (1894) decorated cloth, 456 pp., 1400 illus. by 433 artists including one, p. 364, by C. (Deming, Fogarty, Keller, Remington)

32 Gilliam, Franklin. *Texas and the West, List 119*. Brick Row Book Shop, Austin, Texas, (1961), pic. wraps, 23 pp. Front Cover drawing by C.

33 Hardy, Lowell. *Frosty Ferguson, Strategist*. John Lane Co., N.Y., London, Toronto, 1913, cloth, 80 pp., three illus., frontis. and facing pp. 14 and 22, by C.

34 Kantor, MacKinlay. *Long Remember*. Coward-McCann, N.Y., (1934), cloth, pic. endsheets, 411 pp., note, bibliography. Endsheet illustration and decorations by C.

35 ———. *Turkey in the Straw*. Coward-McCann, N.Y., 1935, words "First Trade Edition" on copyright page, decorated two-tone cloth, 90 (1) pp., six illus., pp. (12), (31), (34), (57), (60) and (91), by C.

THE GHOSTLY WHITE THING CAME NEARER AND NEARER — THE GHOST
WAS UPON HIM! by Crawford from *Skunny Wundy and Other Indian Tales*

36 ———. *The Romance of Rosy Ridge.* Coward-McCann, N.Y., (1937), dec. cloth, 96 pp., brown top, thirty illus. by C.

37 Lewis, Alfred Henry. *The Sunset Trail.* A. S. Barnes & Co., N.Y., 1905, words "Published April, 1905" on copyright page, pic. cloth, 393 pp., introduction, illus. including a frontis. by C. (Marchand)

38 Linderman, Frank B. *Bunch-Grass and Blue-Joint.* Charles Scribner's Sons, N.Y., 1921, words "Published August, 1921" on copyright page, cloth, 115 pp., frontis. by C. (Dust wrappers illus. by Russell.)

39 McLaws, Lafayette. *When the Land was Young.* Lothrop, Boston, (1901), words "Published August 13, 1901" on copyright page, cloth, 383 pp., seven illus. including six, frontispiece and facing pp. 16, 124, 136, 288 and 356, by C.

40 Mayer, Charles. *Trapping Wild Animals in Malay Jungles.* Duffield and Co., N.Y., 1921, cloth, 207 pp., eight illus., frontis. and facing pp. 36, 46, 68, 88, 116, 142 and 204, by C.

41 Menken, H. L. *Christmas Story.* Knopf, N.Y., 1946, words "First Edition" on copyright page, cloth with illus. in color mounted on front cover, colored pic. endsheets, 31 pp., twelve illus. by C.

42 Morrow, Honore Willsie. *On to Oregon.* Wm. Morrow & Co., N.Y., 1926, cloth, 247 pp., four illus., frontis. and facing pp. 24, 136 and 232, by C.

43 *Official Program World Series Rodeo for the Championships of 1928, Presented by Tex Rickard, Madison Square Garden.* N.Y., 1928, wraps, 64 pp., numerous illus. including a vignette on the title page by C. (Russell)

44 Parker, Arthur Caswell. *Skunny Wundy and Other Indian Tales.* George H. Doran Co., N.Y., (1926), publisher's device on copyright page, cloth with illus. in color mounted on front cover, pictorial endsheets, 262 pp., fifteen full page illus. including seven in color plus pictorial title page and drawings on chapter headings by C.

45 ———. *Rumbling Wings.* Doubleday, Doran & Co., Garden City, N.Y., 1928, words "First Edition" on copyright page, decorated cloth, pictorial endsheets, 279 pp., red top, six color plates: frontis. and facing pp. 40, 74, 80, 146 and 176 plus three full-page line drawings, facing pp. 6, 90 and 184, plus drawings on title page and thirty-three drawings on chapter headings by C.

46 Parker, Gilbert. *Northern Lights.* Harper & Bros., N.Y. and London, 1909, words "Published September, 1909" on copyright page, pictorial cloth, 351 (1) pp., note, sixteen illus. including one, facing p. 166, by C. (Dunn, Schoonover, Wood)

47 Patten, Gilbert. *The Deadwood Trail.* D. Appleton & Co., N.Y., 1904, code number (1) follows last line of text, pictorial cloth, 261 pp., four illus., frontis. and facing pp. 19, 208 and 250, by C.

48 Phillips, Henry Wallace. *Red Saunders' Pets and Other Critters.* McClure, Phillips & Co., N.Y., 1906, words "Published May, 1906" on copyright page, pictorial cloth, 231 pp., sixteen illus. including five, pp. (44), 47, (52), (69) and 67, by C.

49 Reed, Walt. *The Illustrator in America 1900–1960's.* Reinhold, N.Y., (1966), cloth, pic. green endsheets, 271 (1) pp., "Is Illustration Art?" by Albert Dorne, bibliography, numerous illus. including one, p. (19), by C. (Blumenschein, Dunn, Dunton, Eggenhofer, Fischer, Fogarty, Goodwin, James, Keller, Koerner, Remington, Russell, Schoonover, Stoops, Wyeth)

50 Rickard, Kent. *Highlights of Colorado History for Non-historians.* Privately printed, (Denver, 1971), pic. wraps, 32 pp., numerous illus. including one, p. 3, by C.

51 Rollins, Philip Ashton. *The Cowboy.* Scribner's, N.Y. and London, 1922, words "Published April, 1922" on copyright page, cloth, 353 pp., preface, d/w illus. by C.

52 Roosevelt, Theodore. *The Winning of the West, Vol. V.* Gebbie & Co., Philadelphia, 1903, Edition de Luxe limited to 500 numbered sets, morocco and marbled boards, matching marbled endsheets, 310 pp., all edges gilt, four illus. including three, facing pp. 76, 160 and 277, by C.

53 ———. *The Winning of the West, Vol. VI.* Gebbie & Co., Philadelphia, 1903, Edition de Luxe limited to 500 numbered sets, morocco and marbled boards, matching marbled endsheets, 260 pp., all edges gilt, appendix, index, four illus. including one, facing p. 175, by C.

54 ———. *Hunting Trips of a Ranchman, Vol. I.* Gebbit & Co., Philadelphia, 1903, Edition de Luxe limited to 500 numbered sets, morocco and marbled boards, matching marbled endsheets, 210 pp., all edges gilt, four illus. including a frontis., by C.

55 ———. *Hunting Trips of a Ranchman, Vol. II.* Gebbie &. Co., Philadelphia, 1903, Edition de Luxe limited to 500 numbered sets, morocco and marbled

boards, matching marbled endsheets, 175 pp., all edges gilt, addendum, index, four illus. including a frontispiece by C.

56 Schulman, Max. *Barefoot Boy With Cheek*. Blakiston, Philadelphia, 1944, pictorial boards, 207 pp., note, fourteen illus. by C.

57 Stoddard, William O. *Jack Morgan, a Boy of 1812*. Lothrop, Boston, 1901, four illus. by C.

58 ———. *The Errand Boy of Andrew Jackson*. Lothrop, Boston, (1902), words "Published April, 1902 on copyright page, pictorial cloth, 327 pp., five illus., frontis. and facing pp. 52, 62, 188 and 320, by C.

59 ———. *The Noank's Log*. Lothrop, Boston, (1900), cloth, 337 pp., illus. by C.

60 Sublette, Clifford MacClellan. *Greenhorn's Hunt*. The Bobbs-Merrill Co., Indianapolis, N.Y., (1934), words "First Edition" on copyright page, 241 pp., six illus., frontis. and facing pp. 30, 88, 154, 204 and 238, by C.

61 Van de Water, Frederic F. *Glory Hunter*. The Bobbs-Merrill Co., Indianapolis, N.Y., (1934), words "First Edition" on copyright page, cloth, acknowledgment, bibliography, index, illus. including three full-page drawings, facing pp. 22, 162 and 322, plus three division headings by C.

62 Wadsworth, Wallace C. (retold by). *Paul Bunyan and His Great Blue Ox*. George H. Doran, N.Y., (1926), publisher's device on copyright page, cloth, 238 pp., six illus. in color, frontis. and facing pp. 16, 96, 144, 176 and 208, by C.

63 ———. Another edition of 62, issued by Doubleday & Co., Garden City, n.d., the illus. are in black and white and there is a Crawford drawing on the front cover.

64 Warren, Samuel. *Tittlebat Titmouse*. Funk & Wagnalls, N.Y. and London, 1903, words "Published October, 1903" on copyright page, decorated cloth, 464 pp., introduction, sixty-five illustrations by C. (Abridged by Cyrus Townsend Brady from *Ten Thousand a Year*.)

65 White, Stewart Edward and Adams, Samuel Hopkins. *The Mystery*. McClure, Phillips & Co., N.Y., 1907, words "Published January, 1907" on copyright page, cloth with illus. in color mounted on front cover, 286 pp., sixteen full-page illus. by C.

66 White, Stewart Edward. *Dog Days*. Doubleday, Doran & Co., Garden City, N.Y., 1930, words "First Edition" on copyright page, cloth, colored pictorial endsheets, 285 pp., orange top, other edges uncut, five full-page illus., frontis. and pp. 41, 89, 119 and 249, plus chapter headings by C.

67 Yost, Karl. *Charles M. Russell, The Cowboy Artist, A Bibliography*. (Pasadena, 1948), words "First Edition, 1948" on copyright page, cloth, colored pic. endsheets, 218 pp., (2) of advs., foreword, numerous illustrations including a photo of "Changing Horses at the Pony Express Station," a bronze cast from an original model by Crawford but attributed to Russell with the title "Pony Express." Also issued as Volume II of the Collector's Edition of 600 sets with Adams & Britzman's *Charles M. Russell, The Cowboy Artist: A Biography* bound in morocco and cloth. (Russell)

The Artist and His Art

68 Bolton, Theodore. *American Book Illustrators*. R. R. Bowker Co., N.Y., 1938, cloth, 290 pp., introduction, index. Lists fifteen books illus. by C., p. 34 and 36.

69 Mahony, Bertha E. and Whitney, Elinor. *Contemporary Illustrators of Children's Books*. The Bookshop for Boys and Girls (Women's Educational and Industrial Union), Boston, 1930, decorated cloth with morocco label on spine, 135 pp., introduction, "Contemporary Book Illustration" by Lynd Ward, appendix, numerous illus. (several in color). The Crawford sketch appears on p. 23. (Deming, Hurd, Schoonover, Smith)

70 Russell, Charles M. *Some Incidents of Western Life*. An article, (12) pp., in *Scribners Magazine*, vol. XXXVII, no. 2, February, 1905. Photo of Russell, four full-page plates in color by Russell and two drawings by his friend, Will Crawford.

71 Russell, Charles M. *Good Medicine*. Doubleday, Doran & Co., Garden City, N.Y., 1930, words "First Edition after the printing of 134 DeLuxe copies" on copyright page, decorated cloth, colored pictorial endsheets, 162 pp., "Introduction" by Will Rogers, "Biographical Note" by Nancy C. (Mrs. C. M.) Russell, numerous illus. in color, and black and white, including an illustrated letter, p. 86, to Will Crawford, "considered by Charles M. Russell as one of the best pen artists in America" (p. IX).

72 (Russell.) A Crawford letter to Charlie Russell reproduced in *The Branding Iron*. Los Angeles Corral, the Westerners, September, 1948. Notes by H. E. Britzman and a photo of Crawford.

ILLUSTRATION by Cue from *Cactus Center Poems*

HAROLD JAMES CUE
1887–1961

Illustrated by the Artist

1 "Asterisk" (pseud. of Robert James Fletcher). *Gone Native* (A Tale of the South Seas). Small, Maynard, Boston, (1924), decor. cloth, 332 pp., "To the Wise," frontis. in color by C.

2 Barker, Reginald C. *Wild-Horse Ranch.* L. C. Page, Boston, (1927), words "First Impression, July, 1927" on copyright page, dec. cloth, 314 pp., four illus., frontis. and facing pp. 16, 94 and 172, by C.

3 ———. *The Hair-Trigger Brand.* Page, Boston, (1929), words "First Impression, February, 1929" on copyright page, pic. fabricoid, 311 pp., (8) of advs., five illus., front cover, frontis. and facing pp. 40, 168 and 262, by C.

4 Bartlett, Arthur C. *The Sea Dogs.* W. A. Wilde, Boston, (1927), cloth, 299 pp., foreword, frontis. in color by C.

5 ———. *Game-Legs.* W. A. Wilde, Boston, (1928), cloth, 292 pp., foreword, frontis. in color by C.

6 ———. *The Runaway Dog Team.* W. A. Wilde, Boston, (1929), cloth, 303 pp., foreword, frontis. by C.

7 ———. *Gumpy — Son of Spunk.* W. A. Wilde, Boston, (1930), cloth, 304 pp., foreword, frontis. by C.

8 ———. *General Jim.* W. A. Wilde, Boston, (1931), cloth, 292 pp., d/w design by C. (so noted on title page).

9 ———. *Pal.* Wilde, Boston, (1932), cloth, 301 pp., foreword, frontis. by C.

9a ———. *Skipper, The Guide Dog.* Wilde, Boston, (1933), cloth with illus. mounted on the front cover, 315 pp., foreword, frontis. (repeated on front cover) by C.

9b ———. *A Son of the Wild Pack.* Wilde, Boston, (1934), cloth, 312 pp., foreword, frontis. and d/w illus. by C.

9c ———. *Yankee Doodle.* Wilde, Boston, (1935), cloth, 318 pp., foreword, frontis. by C.

9d ———. *Pilgrim and Pluck.* Wilde, Boston, (1936), cloth, 303 pp., frontis. by C.

10 Chalmers, Margaret Piper. *Pollyanna's Protege.* L. C. Page, Boston, (1944), words "First Impression, July 1944" on copyright page, cloth, 322 pp., frontis. in color by C.

11 Chapman, Arthur. *Cactus Center Poems.* Houghton Mifflin, Boston & New York, 1921, cloth and dec. boards, 122 (1) pp., five drawings, half-title, title page, contents page, page 1 and frontis., by C.

12 Cheley, Frank H. *Boy Riders of the Rockies.* W. A. Wilde, Boston, (1928), cloth, 335 pp., foreword, illus. with photos but d/w illus. in color by C.

13 Child, Richard Washburn. *The Blue Wall.* Houghton Mifflin, Boston and New York, 1912, words "Published June 1912" on copyright page, cloth, 377 (1) pp., (2) pp. of advs., five illus. including four, facing pp. 44, 118, 238 and 372, by C.

14 Clark, Wm. H. *Farms and Farmers.* L. C. Page, Boston, (1945), words "First Impression October, 1945" on copyright page, cloth, 346 pp., foreword, acknowledgments, introduction, appendix, index, illus., d/w illus. in color by C. (Remington, Wyeth)

15 Cowan, John E. *Boy Campaigners of '61.* W. A. Wilde, Boston, (1933), cloth with illus. in color mounted on front cover, 320 pp., foreword, two illus., front cover and frontis., by C.

16 Dudley, A. T. *A Spy of '76.* Lothrop, Lee & Shepard, Boston, (1933), cloth, 323 pp., red top, introduction,

six illus., frontis. and facing pp. 86, 128, 156, 238 and 282, by C.

17 Eaton, Walter P. *Hawkeye's Roommate.* Wilde, Boston, (1927), cloth, 316 pp., foreword, frontis. by C.

18 Fenger, Frederic A. *The Golden Parrot.* Houghton Mifflin, Boston and N.Y., 1921, pic. cloth, 275 pp., charts, maps, numerous illus. by C.

19 Hampden, Mrs. Hobert. *The Secret Valley.* L. C. Page, Boston, (1932), words "First Impression, October, 1932" on copyright page, pic. cloth, 271 pp., 8 pp. of advs., six illus., frontis. and facing pp. 108, 191, 195, 214 and 245, by C.

20 Hart, William S. *"Injun" and Whitey Strike Out for Themselves.* (The Golden West Series.) Houghton Mifflin, Boston and New York, 1921, pic. cloth, 278 (1) pp., preface, four illus., frontis. and facing pp. 64, 136 and 218, by C.

21 ———. *"Injun" and Whitey to the Rescue.* (The Golden West Boys.) Houghton Mifflin, Boston and New York, 1922, dec. cloth, 305 pp., four illus., frontis. and facing pp. 16, 120 and 202, by C.

22 Hartman, Gertrude. *America, Land of Freedom.* Heath, (Boston etc., 1952), decor. cloth, 720 pp., "Foreword" by Allan Nevins, (appendices), index, maps, numerous illus. including eight, pp. (272), 273 (two) and (354) (five), by C.

23 Hauck, Louis Platt. *The Gold Trail.* Lothrop, Lee and Shepard, Boston, (1929), pic. cloth, 256 pp., four illus., frontis. and facing pp. 40, 94 and 200, by C.

24 ———. *Lucky Shot.* Lothrop, Lee and Shepard, Boston, (1931), pic. cloth, 262 pp., four illus., frontis. and facing pp. 48, 90 and 240, by C.

25 Jay, Mae Foster. *The Girl of the Mesa.* Wilde, Boston, (1929), cloth, 300 pp., frontis. by C.

26 ———. *Tad.* Wilde, Boston, (1930), cloth, 294 pp., frontis. by C.

27 ———. *Morning's at Seven.* Wilde, Boston, (1931), cloth, 301 pp., frontis. and d/w illus. by C.

28 ———. *Green Needles.* Wilde, Boston, (1932), cloth, 320 pp., frontis. by C.

29 ———. *The Shell.* Wilde, Boston, (1933), cloth, 314 pp., frontis. by C.

30 ———. *High on a Hill.* Wilde, Boston, (1934), cloth, 313 pp., frontis. by C.

31 ———. *The Sleigh Bell Trail.* Wilde, Boston, (1936), cloth, 314 pp., front cover and d/w illus. by C.

32 Johnston, Annie Fellows. *The Little Colonel Stories — Second Series.* L. C. Page, Boston, (1931), words "First Impression January, 1931" on copyright page, dec. cloth, 276 pp. 6 pp. of advs., foreword, six illus., frontis. and facing pp. 92, 136, 194, 248 and 265, by C.

33 Johnston, William. *The Mystery in the Ritsmore.* Little, Brown, Boston, 1920, words "Published June, 1920" on copyright page, cloth, 293 pp., four illus., frontis. and facing pp. 38, 150 and 236, by C.

34 Kleiser, Clare et al. *The Progressive Road to Reading — Story Steps.* Silver, Burdett & Co., N.Y. etc., (1917), pic. cloth, 96 pp., numerous illus. in color by C.

35 Knibbs, Henry Herbert. *Lost Farm Camp.* Houghton Mifflin, Boston and New York, 1912, pic. cloth, 354 (1) pp., four illus., frontis. and facing pp. 76, 228 and 326, by C.

36 ———. *Songs of the Trail.* Houghton Mifflin, Boston and New York, 1920, pictorial boards with cloth back, 97 (1) pp., drawings on half-title, title, ix, and pp. 1, 2 and 3, by C.

37 ———. *The Sungazers.* Houghton Mifflin, Boston and New York, 1926, cloth, 248 (1) pp., d/w illus. in color by C.

38 Lange, D. *The Silver Cache of the Pawnee.* Lothrop, Lee & Shepard, Boston, (1918), words "Published, August 1918" on copyright page, dec. cloth, 296 pp., six illus., frontis. and facing pp. 50, 72, 134, 216 and 284, by C.

39 ———. *The Iroquois Scout.* Lothrop, Lee & Shepard, Boston, (1923), pic. cloth, 308 pp., six illus., frontis. and facing pp. 62, 108, 192, 222 and 298, by C.

40 ———. *The Boast of the Seminole.* Lothrop, Lee & Shepard, Boston, (1930), pictorial cloth, 271 pp., tinted top, four illus., frontis. and facing pp. 12, 150 and 258, by C.

41 Lloyd, Edward Mostyn. *Tom Anderson, Dare-Devil.* Houghton Mifflin, Boston and New York, n.d., cloth with colored illus. mounted on front cover, 415 pp., four colored illus., frontis. and facing pp. 64, 322 and 372, by C.

42 Maule, Mary K. *A Prairie Schooner Princess.* Lothrop, Lee and Shepard, Boston, (1920), cloth, 283 pp., four illus., frontis. and facing pp. 20, 84 and 222, by C.

43 Mersereau, John and Chambers, E. Whitman. *Gar-*

ber of *Thunder Gorge*. Small Maynard, Boston, 1924, cloth, 305 pp., d/w illus. in color by C.

44 Minot, John Clair. *The Best Bird Stories I Know*. Wilde, Boston, (1930), fabricoid, 316 (1) pp., introduction, frontis. by Bull but d/w illus. in color by C.

45 Moffitt, Virginia May. *Pollyanna at Six Star Ranch*. L. C. Page, Boston, (1947), words "First Impression, March, 1947," on copyright page, cloth, 295 pp., frontis. in color by C.

46 ———. *Pollyanna of Magic Valley*. L. C. Page, Boston, 1949, words "First Impression, September, 1949" on copyright page, cloth, 292 pp., frontis. in color by C.

47 Morgan, Anna Blunt. *Little Folks Tramping and Camping*. Lothrop, Lee & Shepard, Boston, (1920), words "Published August 1920" on copyright page, pic. cloth, 356 pp., six illus. in color, frontis. and facing pp. 78, 102, 154, 246 and 348, by C.

48 Phillips, Ethel Calvers. *Black-eyed Susan*. Houghton Mifflin, Boston and New York, 1921, cloth and dec. boards, 170 pp., frontis. in color and a drawing on the title page by C.

49 Pidgin, Charles Felton and Taylor, J. M. *The Chronicles of Quincy Adams Sawyer, Detective*. Page, Boston, 1912, words "First Impression, October, 1912" on copyright page, pic. cloth, 316 pp., (12) of advs., six illus., frontis. and facing pp. 42, 72, 222, 254 and 304, by C.

50 Raine, Wm. MacLeod. *The Sheriff's Son*. Houghton Mifflin, Boston and New York, 1918, words "Published April, 1918" on copyright page, cloth, 345 (1) pp., four illus., frontis. and facing pp. 32, 70 and 314, by C.

51 Sabatini, Rafael. *The Banner of the Bull*. Houghton Mifflin, Boston & N.Y., 1923, cloth, 254 pp., d/w illus. by C.

52 ———. Same, Grosset & Dunlap, N.Y., n.d., cloth, 258 pp., d/w illus. by C.

53 Schultz, James Willard. *The Dreadful River Cave*. Houghton Mifflin, Boston and New York, 1920, dec. cloth, 243 (1) pp., four line drawings, frontis. and pp. 52, 182 and 240, by C.

54 ———. *In the Great Apache Forest*. Houghton Mifflin, Boston and New York, 1920, pic. cloth, 224 (1) pp., four illus., frontis. and facing pp. 40, 86 and 200, by C.

55 Sharpe, C. *The Lone Star of Carbajal*. Lothrop, Lee

& Shepard, Boston, (1928), pic. cloth, 268 pp., four illus., frontis. and facing pp. 42, 220 and 250, by C.

56 Theiss, Lewis E. *Piloting the U.S. Air Mail*. Wilde, Boston, (1927), cloth with illus. by Cue mounted on front cover, 333 pp.

57 ———. *The Search for the Lost Mail Plane*. Wilde, Boston, (1928), cloth, 304 pp., d/w illus. by C.

58 ———. *Trailing the Air Mail Bandits*. Wilde, Boston, (1929), cloth, 315 pp., frontis. by C.

59 ———. *The Flying Reporter*. Wilde, Boston, (1930), cloth, 312 pp., d/w illus. by C.

60 ———. *The Pursuit of the Flying Smugglers*. Wilde, Boston, (1931), cloth, 320 pp., frontis. by C.

61 ———. *Wings of the Coast*. Wilde, Boston, (1932), cloth, 314 pp., d/w illus. by C.

62 ———. *Flying the U.S. Mail to South America*. Wilde, Boston, (1933), cloth with illus. in color by Cue mounted on front cover, 312 pp.

63 ———. *The Mail Pilot of the Caribbean*. Wilde, Boston, (1934), pic. cloth, 320 pp., d/w illus. by C.

64 ———. *Wings Over the Andes*. Wilde, Boston, (1939), cloth, 327 pp., d/w illus. by C.

65 Tomlinson, Everett T. *The Champion of the Regiment*. Houghton Mifflin, Boston & New York, 1911, cloth, 377 pp., four illus., frontis. and facing pp. 104, 154 and 288, by C.

66 Trevino, Elizabeth (Borton). *Our Little Aztec Cousin of Long Ago*. Page, Boston, (1934), words "First Impression, October, 1934" on copyright page, pic. cloth, 83 pp., six illus., frontis. and facing pp. 14 (repeated on front cover), 30, 38, 54 and 82, by C.

67 ———. *Pollyanna's Castle in Mexico*. Page, Boston, (1934), words "First Impression, October, 1934" on copyright page, cloth, 322 pp., (10) of advs., four illus., frontis. and facing pp. 88, 194 and 270, by C.

68 ———. *Pollyanna's Door to Happiness*. Page, Boston, (1936), words "First Impression, November, 1936" on copyright page, cloth, 359 pp., four illus., frontis. and facing pp. 36, 128 and 278, by C.

69 ———. *Pollyanna and the Secret Mission*. Page, Boston, (1951), cloth, 263 pp., frontis. by C.

70 Wilkinson, Andrews. *Boy Holidays in the Louisiana Wilds*. Little, Brown, Boston, 1918, words "Published, September, 1917" on copyright page, pic. cloth, 259 pp., cover illus. and six plates, frontis. and facing pp. 22, 44, 126, 208 and 256, by C.

ILLUSTRATION by Deming from *Letters From The South-West*

EDWIN WILLARD DEMING
1860–1942

Catalogues of Art Exhibitions and Galleries

HELEN L. CARD, NEW YORK

1 *Salute to the Westerners,* The Latendorfer Number One, (1958), pic. wraps, 48 (2) pp., numerous illus. including one, p. 31, by D. (Remington, Russell)

2 *Hang On, Fellers! We're Out on a Limb,* Catalog No. Five, (1963), pic. wraps, 95 (1) pp., numerous illus. including one, p. 51, by D. (Eggenhefer, Leigh, Remington, Stoops, Varian, Wyeth)

CHAPELLIER GALLERIES, NEW YORK

2a *One Hundred American Selections,* 1966, colored pic. wraps, unpaged but 100 numbered illus. including one, no. 59, by D. (Johnson, Miller, Remington)

COLONIAL ART COMPANY, OKLAHOMA CITY
(SENATE ROOM, LINCOLN PLAZA INN)

2b *Western and Traditional American Paintings of the 19th and Early 20th Centuries* (Auction Catalog), June 10, 1973, pic. wraps, unpaged, 76 numbered illus. including three, nos. 37, 38 and 39, by D. (Borein, Dixon, Eggenhofer, Elwell, Goodwin, Johnson, Koerner, Russell, Schoonover, Wyeth, Young)

EDWARD EBERSTADT AND SONS, NEW YORK

3 *A Distinguished Collection of Western Paintings,* Catalogue 139, (1956), pic. wraps, unpaged, "Introduction" (Western American Art) by Harold McCracken, 129 numbered illus. including one, no. 30, by D. (Borein, Dixon, Dunton, Johnson, Leigh, Remington)

4 *American Painting,* Catalog 146 (December 1957), colored pic. wraps, unpaged, 191 numbered illus. including one, no. 60, by D. (Borein, Dixon, Dunton, Johnson, Leigh, Remington)

GALLERY WEST, DENVER

5 *Prospectives in Western Art,* (1972), pic. wraps, un-paged, "Forward" by James A. Parsons, 21 illus. including one, "True Companions," by D. (Borein, Dixon, Ellsworth, Remington, Russell, Schreyvogel)

5a *The American Indian and Selected Western Paintings,* January 1974, pic. wraps, 16 pp., eighteen illus. including one, photo of the bronze "Hiawatha," p. 7, by D. (Blumenschein, Borein, Russell)

GREENFIELD GALLERIES, SEATTLE

6 *American Western Art Auction,* Oct. 28, 1972, pic. wraps, 58 pp., numerous illus. including one, p. 11, by D. (Borein, Lungren, Remington, Russell, Schreyvogel)

HERITAGE INN, GREAT FALLS, MONTANA
(THE ADVERTISING CLUB OF GREAT FALLS)

6a *C. M. Russell Sixth Annual Auction of Original Western Art,* March 14–15, 1974, pic. wraps, un-paged, lists 165 lots for sale, numerous illus. including one, lot 123, by D. (Borein, Hurd, Russell, Schreyvogel)

KENNEDY GALLERIES, NEW YORK

7 *The Western Legend.* April 16 to June 1, 1956, pic. wraps, 20 pp., "In the History of Our Country" by George Schriever, numerous illus. including one, p. 7, by D. (Borein, Lungren)

8 *Painters of the Old West,* October 1960, wraps with illus. mounted on front cover, pp. 102-147, numerous illus. including one, p. 118, by D. (Borein, Leigh, Remington, Russell, Schreyvogel, Zogbaum)

9 *Recent Acquisitions in Important Western Paintings,* October, 1961, wraps with illus. mounted on front cover, pp. 150-188, numerous illus. including one, p. 160, by D. (Eggenhofer, Johnson, Remington, Russell, Schreyvogel, Zogbaum)

10 *A Plentiful Country*, June 1970, colored pic. wraps, 76 pp., numerous illus. including one, p. 62, by D. (Russell, Varian)

PACIFIC NORTHWEST INDIAN CENTER
SPOKANE, WASH.

10a *Third Annual Western Art Show & Auction*, March 2, 3, 4, 1973, pic. wraps, 44 pp., numerous illus. including three, pp. 20, 23 and 26, by D. (Borein, Eggenhofer, Hurd, Remington, Russell)

THE SCHENECTADY MUSEUM
SCHENECTADY, NEW YORK

11 Collection of Chaylie L. Saxe, March, 1971, wraps, illus. including no. 7, "Attacked by Bears," by D.

SOTHEBY PARKE BERNET, NEW YORK

12 *Traditional & Western American Paintings, Drawings, Watercolors, Sculpture & Illustrations*, Sale Number 3348, April 19-20, 1972, pic. wraps, 147 pp., numerous illus. including one, p. 75, by D. (Johnson, Koerner, Leigh, Remington, Russell)

13 *Americana Week*, Sale Number 3467, January 24-27, 1973, colored pic. wraps, numerous illus. including one, p. 42, by D. (Borein, Eggenhofer, Elwell, Koerner)

13a *18th, 19th and Early 20th Century American Paintings, Drawings, Watercolors and Sculpture*, sale no. 3548, September 28, 1973, pic. wraps, unpaged, numerous numbered illus. including one, no. 110, by D. (Johnson, Koerner, Remington, Russell)

SANDRA WILSON GALLERIES, SANTA FE

14 *Western Legacy*, January 12–February 3, 1973, colored pic. wraps, unpaged, illus. including one, by D. (Leigh, Perceval, Remington, Russell)

Illustrated by the Artist

15 Athearn, Robert G. *Colonial America* (Volume 2, The American Heritage New Illustrated History of the U.S.). Dell, N.Y., (1963), colored pic. cloth, colored pic. endsheets, pp. 94–179 (numerous — many in color) illus. including one double-page plate in color, pp. (112) and (113), by D.

16 Bowker, R. R. (compiled by.) *Christmas Book Shelf*. Powers, Minneapolis, 1902, decor. wraps., 239 pp., numerous illus. including two pp. 112 and 224 by, D. (Remington)

17 Boyesen, Hjalmar Hjorth et al. *The Monthly Illus-trator for the Second Quarter 1895*. Harry C. Jones, N.Y., (1895), decor. cloth, 384 pp., 804 illus. by 114 artists including thirteen by D.

18 Brady, Cyrus Townsend. *Indian Fights and Fighters*. McClure, Phillips, N.Y., 1904, words "Published December, 1904, N" on copyright page, pic. cloth, 423 pp., preface, bibliography, appendices, index, 26 full-page plates including one, facing p. 214, by D., 13 maps and plans. American Fights and Fighters Series. (Blumenschein, Crawford, Elwell, Remington, Schreyvogel)

19 Burdick, Usher L. *The Army Life of Charles "Chip" Creighton*. National Reform Associates, Paris, Md., 1937, wraps, 30 pp., illus. including one, p. 24, by D.

20 Deming, Edwin Willard et al. *Pictures from Forest and Stream*. Forest and Stream Publishing Co., N.Y., 1901, pic. boards, thirty-two proof impressions including five, nos. vii, viii, ix, x and xii, by D.

21 Deming, Therese O. *Indian Child Life*. Frederick A. Stokes, N.Y., 1899, pic. boards and cloth, 11 3/8" x 8 3/8", pages unnumbered and verso of each page of text blank, profusely illus. including sixteen full-page plates in color on heavy calendered paper. (In later editions these plates are on a lighter, glazed paper and the overall size is only 11 1/8" x 8 1/8".)

22 ———. *Little Indian Folk*. Frederick A. Stokes, N.Y., 1899, pic. boards and cloth, pages unnumbered, profusely illus. Contains nine of the stories with the illus. from *Indian Child Life*. (Copyrighted the same day as *Indian Child Life*.)

23 ———. *Indian Pictures*. Frederick A. Stokes, N.Y., 1899, cloth and pic. boards, 12 3/4" x 17 1/4", (7) pp., preface, six full-page illus. in full-color plus drawings in black and white by D.

24 ———. *Little Red People*. Frederick A. Stokes, N.Y., 1899, cloth, 19 pp., numerous illus. including eight in color by D.

25 ———. *Little Brothers of the West*. Frederick A. Stokes, New York, (1902), words "Published in September, 1902" on copyright page, decor. cloth with illus. mounted on front cover, pp. 4, 4, 4, 3, 4, 4, six full-page color plates and numerous black and white drawings by D.

26 ———. *Red Folk and Wild Folk*. Frederick A. Stokes, N.Y., 1902, cloth, 51 pp., numerous illus. in color and black and white by D.

27 ———. *American Animal Life.* Frederick A. Stokes, New York, 1916, pic. cloth, pages unnumbered, twenty-four full-page color plates and numerous black and white drawings by D.

28 ———. *Four-Footed Wilderness People.* Frederick A. Stokes, New York, 1916, decor. cloth with illus. in color mounted on front cover, pages unnumbered, twelve full-page color plates and numerous black and white drawings by D.

29 ———. *Animal Folk of Wood and Plain.* Frederick A. Stokes, New York, 1916, cloth, 38 pp., numerous illus. including twelve in color by D.

30 ———. *Many Snows Ago.* Frederick A. Stokes, New York, 1929, pic. cloth, (100) pp., eighteen full-page color plates and numerous black and white drawings by D.

31 ———. *Wigwam Children.* Frederick A. Stokes, New York, 1929, pic. cloth, pages unnumbered, nine full-page color plates and numerous black and white drawings by D.

32 ———. *The Indians in Winter Camp.* Laidlaw Brothers, Chicago etc., (1931), pic. cloth, 126 pp., introduction, numerous illus. in color by D.

33 ———. *Little Eagle.* Laidlaw Brothers, Chicago etc., (1931), pic. cloth, 96 pp., introduction, ninety-five illus. in color including one on the title page by D. (A book in the "Indian Life Series" edited by Prof. Milo B. Hillegas of Columbia University.)

34 ———. *Red People of the Wooded Country.* Whitman, Chicago, 1932, cloth, 191 pp., numerous illus. by D.

35 ———. *Indians of the Pueblos.* Laidlaw Bros., Chicago etc., (1936), pic. cloth, 224, introduction, thirty-two full-page illus. in color by D. (Fourth book in "Indian Life Series," edited by Prof. Milo B. Hillegas of Columbia University.)

36 ———. *Indians of the Wigwams.* Albert Whitman & Co., Chicago, 1938, pic. cloth, 239 pp., thirty-one full-page color plates by D.

37 ———. *Cosel with Geronimo on His Last Raid.* F. A. Davis, Philadelphia, 1938, cloth, tinted endsheets, 125 pp., preface, "Foreword" by Lt.-General R. L. Bullard, "Copy of a Letter from General James Parker," glossary, eighteen illus. including six in color, facing pp. 10, 18, 34, 54, 92 and 98, by D.

38 ———. *Manabozho — The Indian Story of Hia-watha.* Philadelphia, 1938, cloth, 87 pp., illus. in color by D.

39 Driggs, Howard R. and King, Sarah S. *Rise of the Lone Star.* Frederick A. Stokes, New York, 1936, cloth, 438 pp., eight illus. in color, frontis. and facing pp. 14, 22, 54, 118, 158, 254 and 350, plus line drawings in the text, by D.

40 Eastman, Charles A. and Elaine Goodale. *Wigwam Evenings.* Little, Brown, Boston, (1909), words "Published, September, 1909" on copyright page, pic. cloth, 253 pp., preface, eighteen illus. by D.

41 ———. *Smoky Day's Wigwam Evenings: Indian Stories Retold.* Little, Brown, Boston, 1910, cloth, 149 pp., illus. by D.

42 (Eberstadt.) *Americana,* Catalogue No. 133, Edward Eberstadt & Sons, N.Y., 1954, wraps, illus. including one by D. (Miller)

43 Eickemeyer, Rudolf. *Letters from the South-West.* Privately printed for the author (N.Y., 1894), cloth, decor. endsheets, 111 pp., comments on the illustrations, thirty-three illus. by D.

43a Foreman, Grant (edited and annotated by). *Adventure on Red River* (Report on the Exploration of the Headwaters of the Red River by Captain Randolph B. Marcy and Captain G. B. McClellan). Oklahoma, Norman, 1937, words "First Edition, 1937" on copyright page, cloth with paper title label on spine, 199 (1) pp., editor's introduction, author's introduction, index, folding map, eight illus. including one, facing p. 32, by D.

44 Fraser, W. Lewis et al. *The Year's Art — The Quarterly Illustrator for 1894.* Harry C. Jones, New York, (1894), decor. cloth, 456 pp., 1400 illus. by 433 artists including two, pp. 58 and 240, by D. (Crawford, Fogarty, Keller, Remington)

45 Freeman, Melville. *The Story of Our Republic, or, the Romance of America.* F. A. Davis Co., Philadelphia, (1938), pic. cloth and endsheets, 431 pp., introduction, addenda, index, edited by Eston V. Tubbs, 334 illus. including three, pp. 46, 106 and 123, by D. (Marchand)

46 Gabriel, Ralph Henry. *The Lure of the Frontier.* Yale University Press, New Haven, 1929, The Liberty Bell Edition of "The Pageant of America," vol. 2, limited to 1,500 numbered impressions, morocco and boards, 327 pp., profusely illus. including one, p. 217, by D. (Dixon, Marchand, Remington, Russell)

47 Garland, Hamlin. *Boy Life on the Prairie*. Macmillan, New York, 1899, decor. cloth, 423 pp., gilt top, preface, prologue, eight full-page illus., frontis. and facing pp. 9, 111, 194, 219, 271, 296 and 304, plus line drawings in the text, by D.

48 Gavian, Ruth Wood and Hamm, William A. *The American Story*. D. C. Heath, Boston, 1947, decor. cloth, 695 (1) pp., foreword, appendix, index, numerous illus. including one, p. 182, by D. (Remington)

49 Grant, Bruce. *Famous American Trails*. Rand McNally, Chicago etc., (1971), words "First Printing, August 1971" on copyright page, colored pic. boards map endsheets, 95 (1) pp., introduction, numerous illus. including one in color by D. (Bjorklund, Russell)

50 Grinnell, George Bird. *Jack, the Young Ranchman*. Frederick A. Stokes, New York, (1899), pic. cloth, 304 pp., preface, eight illus., frontis. and facing pp. 84, 130, 142, 178, 200, 232 and 256, by D.

51 ———. *Jack Among the Indians*. Frederick A. Stokes, New York, (1900), pic. cloth, 301 pp., eight illus., frontis. and facing pp. 48, 102, 138, 146, 234, 244 and 280, by D.

52 ———. *The Punishment of Stingy and Other Indian Stories*. Harper, New York and London, 1901, words "September, 1901" on copyright page, decor. cloth and marbled boards, decor. endsheets, 234 (1) pp., gilt top, sixteen illus. by D.

53 ———. *Jack in the Rockies*. Frederick A. Stokes, New York, (1904), words "Published in September, 1904" on copyright page, pic. cloth, 272 pp., eight illus. including four, frontis. and facing pp. 82, 183 and 268, by D.

54 ———. *Jack the Young Canoeman*. Frederick A. Stokes, New York, (1906), words "Published in September 1906" on copyright page, pic. cloth, 286 pp., eight illus. including four, frontis. and facing pp. 58, 82 and 204, by D.

55 ———. *Jack the Young Cowboy*. Frederick A. Stokes, New York, 1913, pic. cloth, 278 pp., illus. with photos but illus. on spine and front cover by D.

56 Haines, Alice Calhoun. *Indian Boys and Girls*. Frederick A. Stokes, New York, (1906), words "Published in September, 1906" on copyright page, decor. cloth with illus. in color mounted on front cover, 47 (1) pp., 8" x 10⅜", four illus. in color by Alice Mar and numerous illus. in black and white by D..

57 Havighurst, Walter, ed. *Land of the Long Horizons*. Coward-McCann, New York, (1960), decor. cloth, red endsheets, 437 pp., introduction, index, numerous illus. including one, p. (23), by D. (Koerner, Remington)

58 Hawthorne, Julian. *United States*. Peter Fenelon Collier, New York, 1898, 3 vols., 1,150 pp., (continuous pagination), introduction (vol. I), illus. including two full-page illus., facing pp. 84 and 204, by D. (vol. I). "Nations of the World," vols. XIII, XIV, and XV.

58a Hordern, Nicholas. et al. *The Conquest of North America*. Aldus, London, (1971), pic. boards, 488 pp., index, illus. including one in color, pp. 240–1, by D. (Miller, Remington)

58b ———. Same, first American edition, Doubleday, Garden City, N.Y., 1973

59 Kelly, Luther S. *Yellowstone Kelly*. Yale University Press, New Haven, 1926, cloth, 268 pp., "Historical Introduction" and edited by M. M. Quaife, "Foreword" by General Nelson A. Miles, index, twenty-one illus. including three, facing pp. 92, 100 and 114, by D. (Russell)

60 King, Charles. *A Daughter of the Sioux*. The Hobart Co., N.Y., 1903, words "Published March 15, 1903" on copyright page, cloth with a colored illus. mounted on the front cover, 306 pp., gilt top, eight illus. including four, facing pp. 135, 141, 246 and 283, by D. (Remington)

61 ———. *An Apache Princess*. The Hobart Co., N.Y., 1903, words "Published Septermber, 1903" on copyright page, cloth with a colored illus. mounted on front cover, 328 pp., gilt top, eight illus. including six, facing pp. 90, 134, 242, 262, 270 and 324, by D. (Remington)

62 ———. *Comrades in Arms*. The Hobart Co., N.Y., 1904, decor. cloth, 350 pp., gilt top, four illus. including one, facing p. 116, by D.

63 ———. *The Medal of Honor*. The Hobart Co., N.Y., 1905, cloth with colored illus. mounted on the front cover, 348 pp., gilt top, illus. including three, facing pp. 30, 46 and 342, by D.

64 King, W. Nephew. *The Story of the Spanish-American War and the Revolt in the Philippines*. Peter Fenelon Collier, N.Y., 1899, morocco and cloth, 248 pp., preface, introduction for the Navy by Captain Robley D. Evans, introduction for the Army by

Major-General O. O. Howard, profusely illus. including one full-page drawing, p. 107, by D. (Leigh)

65 Lawson, Publius V. *Bravest of the Brave: Captain Charles de Langlade.* George Banta Pub. Co., Menasha, Wisconsin, n.d., cloth, 257 (3) pp., index, illus. The frontis. is by D.

66 Leland, Charles Godfrey, and Prince, John Dyneley. *Kuloskap the Master.* Funk & Wagnalls, N.Y. and London, 1902, words "Published November 1902" on copyright page, pic. cloth, 359 pp., illus. The frontis. is by D.

67 Longley, Marjorie et al. (selected by). *America's Taste, 1851-1859.* Simon and Shuster, N.Y., (1960), cloth and boards, red endsheets, 332 pp., editor's note and acknowledgments, picture credits, index, numerous illus. incuding one, p. 108, by D. (Remington)

68 Lounsberry, Col. Clement A. *Early History of North Dakota.* Liberty Press, Washington D.C., 1919, words "Published, 1919" on copyright page, gilt decor. cloth, 7 3/4" x 10 1/2", 645 pp., marbled edges, preface, index, numerous illus. including four, facing pp. 20 (two), 36 and 240, by D.

69 Lumholtz, Carl (Karl Sofus). *Unknown Mexico.* Scribners, N.Y., 1902, 2 vols., cloth, pp. 530 and 496, preface, bibliography, index, numerous illus. including one, p. 58, (I) by D.

70 Lummis, Charles F. *The Land of Poco Tiempo.* Scribner's, N.Y., 1893, decor. cloth, slate endsheets, 310 pp., numerous illus. including one, p. 12, by D.

71 ———. *The Land of Poco Tiempo.* University of N.M., Albuquerque, (1966), words "Illustrated Facsimile Edition" on title page, pic. cloth, orange endsheets, 310 pp., "Foreword to the 1952 Edition" by Paul A. F. Walter, numerous illus. including one, p. 12, by D.

72 Lyons, John J. (State Supervisor). *Wisconsin.* Duell, Sloan and Pearce, New York, (1941), cloth, 651 pp., "Foreword" by Joseph Schafer, preface, appendices, bibliography, index, numerous illus. including one, between pp. 94 and 95, by D., maps.

73 McElrath, Frances. *The Rustler.* Funk & Wagnalls, New York and London, 1902, words "Published April, 1902" on copyright page, pic. cloth, 425 pp., (6) pp. of advs., seven illus., frontis. and facing pp. 74, 138, 214, 236, 318 and 360, by D.

74 McNamara, Emily Steinestet. *History of Virginia in Words of One Syllable.* Belford, Clarke, Chicago

etc., (1888), decor. cloth, 201 pp., preface, the illus. include nine, pp. 11, 84, 103, 104, 106, 125, 128 and 190, by D.

75 Meredith, Roy. *The American Wars.* World, Cleveland and New York, (1955), words "First Edition" on copyright page, pic. cloth, 348 (1) pp., red top, introduction, acknowledgments, numerous illus. including one, p. 23, by D. (Dunn, Fischer, Remington, Thomason)

76 Merriam, C. Hart. *The Dawn of the World.* Arthur H. Clark, Cleveland, 1910, cloth, 273 pp., gilt top and other edges uncut, preface, introduction, note, bibliography, the illus. include ten full-page plates, frontis. (in color) and pp. 41, 51 (in color), 95, 105, 129, 141, 147, 175 (in color) and 233, by D.

77 Myrick, Herbert. *Cache la Poudre.* Orange Judd Co., New York, Chicago, 1905, edition limited to 500 numbered copies, pic. Indian smoke tanned buckskin, marbled endsheets, 202 pp., foreword, acknowledgments, addenda, profusely illus. including four illus. in color, pp. 30, 31, 35, and 145; five tipped-in illus. pp. 40, 68, 117, 134 and 166; and numerous line drawings by D. Trade edition in cloth. (Schreyvogel)

78 Northrop, Henry D. *Indian Horrors.* National Publishing Co., Philadelphia etc., (1891), cloth, 600 pp., numerous illus. including one, facing p. 40, by D. (Reprinted several times.)

79 Osborne, Walter D. and Johnson, Patricia H. *The Treasury of Horses.* A Ridge Press Book, N.Y., (1966), fabricoid, tan endsheets, 251 pp., foreword, index, numerous illus. including one, p. 104, by D. (Russell)

80 Proske, Beatrice Gilman. *Brookgreen Gardens Sculpture.* Printed by order of the Trustees, Brookgreen, S.C., 1943, cloth, 510 pp., foreword, introduction, maps, numerous illus. including a photo of the bronze, "The Fight," p. (166), by D. (Remington)

81 Quick, Herbert. *In the Fairyland of America.* Stokes, N.Y., 1901, cloth, 190 pp., with forty-three illus. by D.

82 Rideout, Henry Milner. *William Jones.* Frederick A. Stokes, N.Y., 1912, words "June, 1912" in box below copyright notice, cloth, 212 (1) pp., illus. The frontis. is by D.

83 Rolt-Wheeler, Francis. *The Boy with the U. S. Indians.* Lothrop, Lee and Shepard, Boston, (1913), words "Published, November, 1913" on copyright

page, pic. cloth with illus. mounted on front cover, 410 pp., preface, thirty-six illus. including one, facing p. 192, by D.

84 Rugg, Harold. *The Conquest of America*. Ginn, Boston, (1937), cloth, 563 pp., numerous illus. including two, pp. 200 and 202, by D. (Marchand)

85 Russell, Don. *Custer's Last; or, The Battle of the Little Big Horn in Picturesque Perspective*. Amon Carter Museum, (Ft. Worth, 1968), cloth, 67 pp., "Preface" by Barbara Tyler, notes, bibliography, seventeen (four in color) plates including one, p. 48, by D. (Dunton, Russell)

86 Russell, Francis. *The French and Indian Wars*. American Heritage, N.Y., 1962, words "First Edition" under frontis., colored pic. cloth, pic. endsheets, 153 pp., "Foreword" by Lawrence Henry Gipson (consultant), numerous illus. including two, front cover and pp. 96–97, by D.

87 Utley, Henry M. and Cutcheon, Byron M. (Burton, Clarence M., advisory editor). *Michigan as a Province, Territory and State, Volume One*. The Publishing Society of Michigan, n.p., 1906, decor. cloth, 361 pp., gilt top, twenty-five illus. including one, facing p. 46, by D.

88 Wallace, Dillon. *The Fur Trail Adventures*. A. C. McClurg, Chicago, 1915, words "Published October, 1915" on copyright page, decor. cloth, 320 (1) pp., seven illus., frontis. and facing pp. 46, 78, 136, 220, 276 and 304, by D.

89 Walsworth, Jeanette H. *History of New York in Words of One Syllable*. Belford, Clarke, Chicago, N.Y., San Francisco, (1888), decor. cloth, 186 pp., introduction to Chapter I, illus. including twenty-four drawings by D. (Remington)

90 Wetmore, Helen Cody. *Last of the Great Scouts*. The Duluth Press Pub. Co., Chicago and Duluth, (1899), cloth, 296 pp., genealogy of Buffalo Bill, preface, seventeen illus. including nine, facing pp. 13, 18, 27, 34, 43, 47, 83, 115 and 217, by D. (Under "Illustrations," "Buffalo Bill on Horseback" p. 266 is listed out of order above "Under the Lime Light," p. 243.)

91 ———. *The Last of the Great Scouts*. The Partington Advertising Co., London, 1903, pic. boards, 296 pp., eleven illus. including five, facing pp. 13, 27, 34, 83 and 217, by D. Sold only at the Wild West shows in Europe. (Remington)

92 ———. *Buffalo Bill*. Verlag Von Engelhorn, Stuttgart, 1902, cloth with illus. in color mounted on front cover, decor. endsheets, 304 pp., twelve illus. including ten by D. First German Edition of no. 90. (Remington)

93 Wheeler, Col. Homer W. *The Frontier Trail*. Times-Mirror Press, Los Angeles, 1923, pic. cloth, 334 pp., preface, "Introduction" by Major-General James G. Harbord, "Introductory Comment" by George Bird Grinnell, "To Whom It May Concern" by Major-Gen. Jesse M. Lee, etc., twenty-one illus. including one, facing p. 72, by D. (Russell)

94 ———. *Buffalo Days*. Bobbs-Merrill, Indianapolis, (1925), cloth, 369 pp., "Introduction" by Gen. J. G. Harbord, "Many Years Ago" by George Bird Grinnell, "A Free-Will Offering" by Gen. Jesse M. Lee, "A True Friend" by Gen. Eben Swift, preface, illus. including one plate, facing p. 12, by D. (Jacket illus. by Remington.)

95 Wisler, Clark et al. *Adventures in the Wilderness*. Yale University Press, New Haven, 1925, The Liberty Bell Edition of "The Pageant of America," vol. 1, limited to 1,500 numbered impressions, morocco and boards, 369 pp., profusely illus. including one, p. 306, by D. (Dixon, Remington, Russell)

96 Woestemeyer, Ina Faye and Gambrill, J. Montgomery. *The Westward Movement*. D. Appleton-Century Co., N.Y., (1939), code number (1) follows last line of text, pic. cloth, map and chart endsheets, preface, introduction, "Notes on the Literature," bibliography, index, 500 pp., illus. including one between pp. 36 and 37 by D. (Remington)

97 Wood, William and Gabriel, Ralph Henry. *The Winning of Freedom*. Yale University Press, New Haven, 1927, The Liberty Bell Edition of "The Pageant of America," vol. 6, limited to 1,500 numbered impressions, morocco and boards, 366 pp., profusely illus. including two, pp. 71 and 77, by D. (Remington)

The Artist and His Art

98 *Art and Archaeology*, April, 1919. One illus., "The Good Luck Arrow," by D.

99 Berg, G. L. *Official Catalogue of the Department of Fine Arts, Alaska-Yukon-Pacific Exposition*. A-Y-P Publishing Co., Seattle, Washington, 1909, wraps., 96 pp., illus. Five items by D. listed in the Catalogue.

100 Clark, Edna Maria. *Ohio Art and Artists*. Garrett and Massie, Richmond, (1932), cloth, 509 pp., pref-

ace, appendices, index, illus., biographical sketch of D. p. 454.

101 Deming, Edwin Willard. "The Indians — A Subject for Art," an article in the *American Museum Journal*, March, 1913, eight illus. by D.

102 Deming, Therese O. (compiled by). *E. W. Deming, His Work* (cover title). (Privately printed by The Riverside Press, N.Y., 1925), wraps., 47 pp., "Indian Mysticism" by Henry Fairfield Osborn, edited by Henry Collins Walsh, fourteen illus. by D. and a photo of him.

103 ———. "A Life-long Painter of the Indians," an illus. article in *Mentor Magazine*, April, 1926, with eight illus. by D. and a photo of him.

104 Frink, Maurice. "Edwin W. Deming: That Man, He Paint," an illus. article in *American Scene* 12:3, 1971, with seventeen illus. by D. and photos of him.

105 Gardner, Albert TenEyck. *American Sculpture.* Metropolitan Museum of Art, (N.Y., 1965), words "First Printing, April 1965, 3,500 copies" follow the text, introduction, index, illustrated; brief biography of D. plus descriptions of two of his bronzes in the Metropolitan.

106 Garneau, F. X. and Ferland, J. B. "Jean Nicolet," an article in *Collections*, State Historical Society of Wisconsin, volume 10, 1909, with one illus. by D.

107 Hinshaw, Merton E. (director). *Painter of the West.* Charles W. Bowers Memorial Museum, Santa Ana, Calif., March 5–30, 1972; short biographical sketch of D. (Borein, Johnson, Miller, Remington)

107a Maxwell, Perriton. "The Illustrations of the Quarter," an illus. article in *The Quarterly Illustrator* 2:5, January, February and March, 1894, with brief comments on Deming's art and one illus. by him.

108 Peterson, William J. "Nicolet and the Winnebagoes," an article in *The Palimpsest*, The State Historical Society of Iowa, July, 1960, with front cover illus. in color, "Nicolet Meeting the Winnebago at Green Bay," by D.

109 Smith, De Cost. "With Gun and Palette Among the Redskins," an illus. article in *Outing Magazine*, February, 1895, with three illus. by D.

110 Stevning, Donald A. "The Western Artist: His Role in History," an article in *The Westerners Brand Book No. 2*, San Diego Corral, 1971, reference to D.

111 Swann, Benjamin (auctioneer). *Indians and the West: The Library of Edwin Willard Deming.* Sale no. 27, Swann Auction Galleries, N.Y., November 5, 1942, pic. wraps., 30 pp., "Deming: An Appreciation" by Henry Fairfield Osborn, front cover illus. by D.

112 Tasse, Joseph. "Memoir of Charles de Langlade," an illus. article in *Collections*, State Historical Society of Wisconsin, volume 7, 1908, with one illus. by D.

EARLY TEXAS TRAIL BOSS by De Yong from *The Cowboy and His Interpreters*

JOE DE YONG
Contemporary, 1894–

Illustrated by the Artist

1 Ainsworth, Ed. *The Cowboy in Art.* World, N.Y., and Cleveland, (1968), words "First Printing 1968" on copyright page, full leather, orange endsheets, 242 pp., all edges gilt, "Foreword" by John Wayne, index, numerous illus. including two, p. 96 and between pp. 114 and 115 in color, by DY and considerable on him in text. Special edition of 1000 numbered copies, slipcase. (Beeler, Borein, Bugbee, Dixon, Dunton, Eggenhofer, Ellsworth, Hurd, James, Johnson, Koerner, Mora, Perceval, Remington, Russell, Santee, Schreyvogel, Von Schmidt)

2 ———. Same, first trade edition in gilt lettered and illus. cloth, orange endsheets.

3 ———. Same, reprint by Bonanza Books, N.Y., in red lettered and illus. cloth, white endsheets.

4 Bauer, E. F. (President) et al. *Your Future.* The Federal School of Commercial Designing, Minneapolis, Minn., 1927, colored pic. wraps, 63 (1) pp., numerous (several in color) illus. including one in color, p. 16, by DY.

5 Benedict, Omar K. *The Roundup.* Privately printed by Joe A. Bartles, Dewey, Oklahoma (The Olds Press, Tulsa, 1916), pic. wraps, (32) pp., six illus., front cover, back cover and four in text, by DY.

5a ———. *"Howdy, Folks!" The Roundup,* Dewey, Okla., (1916), pic. wraps, pp. 16, (32), advertising, seven illus. by DY.

6 Branch, Douglas. *The Cowboy and His Interpreters.* D. Appleton and Co., N.Y., London, 1926, code number "(1)" after last line of text, pic. cloth and endsheets, 277 (1) pp., of advs., bibliography, illus. including 20 by DY. (James, Russell)

7 ———. Same, a facsimile reprint of no. 6 by Cooper Square Publishers, N.Y., (1962), with an introduction by Harry Sinclair Drago and with a Remington illus. on the d/w.

8 (Coburn.) *Walt Coburn's Action Novels* (*The Four Aces, Cartridges Free, Paths to Glory* and *The Maverick Legion*). Fiction House, N.Y., 1931, colored pic. wraps, 160 pp., illus., d/w illus. in color by DY. (James)

9 Collison, Thomas F. *El Diario del Viaje de los Rancheros Visitadores* (The Log of the RV, 1935). Privately printed for the RV by News-Press Print, Santa Barbara, (1935), decor. stiff wraps, 154 (6) pp., numerous illus. including seven, pp. 31 (two), (151) two, 154 and (156) two, by DY., plus dozens of small drawings on the photo panels of the members. Joe's photo appears p. 47. (Borein)

10 Dailey, William B. (prepared by). *The Great West.* Catalog 223, Zeitlin & Ver Brugge, Los Angeles, 1970, colored pic. wraps, 86 pp., nine illus. including one, "The Arrival of the Stagecoach," in color, front cover, by DY.

11 De Yong, Joe. *Friend Will.* The Schauer Printing Studio, Santa Barbara, (1936), wraps, (27) pp., "foreword" by Irwin S. Cobb, "Joe De Yong" by Anne Ellis, two illus., an unpublished photo of Will Rogers as frontis., and a drawing of a branding iron by DY.

11a *History of the Ben Holladay Stage Coach,* invitation folder for a barbecue at Tecolote Ranch, Goleta, Santa Barbara County, California, June 5, 1936 (honoring California Highway Patrol and other law enforcement and peace officers), illus. on front cover by DY.

11b Johnson, Willard. *Western and Traditional American Paintings of the 19th and Early 20th Centuries.* (Auction Catalog). The Colonial Art Co., Oklahoma City, June 9, 1974, pic. wraps, unpaged but 111 numbered lots including one, no. 75, by DY. (Blumenschein,

Borein, Deming, Dixon, Dunton, Ellsworth, Johnson, Leigh, Remington, Schreyvogel, Zogbaum)

12 Lauber, Patricia. *Cowboys and Cattle Ranching, Yesterday and Today.* Thomas Y. Crowell Co., N.Y., (1973), cloth, 148 (1) pp., selected bibliography, photo credits, index, maps, numerous illus. including one, p. 9, by DY. (Remington, Russell)

13 Latendorf, E. Walter. *Catalogue Number 27.* E. W. Latendorf, N.Y., n.d., pic. wraps, 36 pp., 23 illus. including two, pp. 5 and 6, by DY. (Goodwin, Lea, Lungren)

14 ———. *C. M. Russell. Catalogue Number 27* [sic]. E. W. Latendorf, N.Y., n.d., pic. wraps, oblong format, (48) pp., numerous illus. including two by DY. (Borein, Crawford, Goodwin, Leigh, Marchand, Russell)

15 Linderman, Frank B. *Lige Mounts: Free Trapper.* Scribner's, N.Y., 1922, pic. cloth, 330 pp., three illus., frontis. and facing pp. 102 and 164, by DY.

16 McDowell, Bart. *The American Cowboy in Life and Legend.* National Geographic Society, Washington, D.C., (1972), pic. cloth, pic. endsheets, 211 (1) pp., "Foreword" by Joe B. Frantz, index, numerous illus. including one, back endsheet, by DY. (Dunton, Goodwin, James, Remington, Russell)

17 Nichols, Walter H. *Cowboy Hugh.* Macmillan, N.Y., 1927, words "Published April, 1927" on copyright page, cloth, 284 pp., four illus. frontis. and pp. 49, 179 and 233, by DY.

18 Rollins, Phillip A. *Jinglebob.* Scribner's, N.Y., London, 1927, cloth, pic. endsheets, 262 (1) pp., preface, illus. by DY.

19 ———. Same, reprint, Grosset & Dunlap, N.Y., 1928.

20 Russell, Charles M. *Rawhide Rawlins Rides Again.* Trail's End Pub. Co., Pasadena, Calif., (1948), gilt decor. flexible leather, pic. endsheets, 61 (3) pp., orange top, ten illus. including one, p. (54), by DY. One of 300 copies, boxed. (Bugbee, Ellsworth, Perceval, Russell)

21 Shaffer, Ellen (prepared by). *The Charles M. Russell Library.* Catalogue no. 152, Dawson's Book Shop, Los Angeles, February 1941, pic. wraps, 35 pp., "Charles M. Russell" and the front cover drawing, "The Tribal Record," are by DY.

22 Silber, Irwin (compiled and edited by). *Songs of the Great American West.* Macmillan, N.Y., (1967), words "First Printing" on copyright page, two-tone

pic. cloth, tan endsheets, 334 pp., yellow top, music annotated, edited and arranged by Earl Robinson, introduction, bibliography, discography, indices, numerous illus. including one, p. 187, by DY. (Eggenhofer, Remington, Russell)

23 Spaulding, Edward Belden. *A Brief Story of Santa Barbara.* Santa Barbara Historical Society, 1964, wraps, 78 pp., illus. including one, title page, by DY. (Borein, Lungren)

24 Truax, Carol and Barker, S. Omar. *The Cattleman's Steak Book.* Grosset & Dunlap, N.Y., (1967), decor. fabricoid, pic. endsheets, 128 pp., "Foreword" by Larry Ellman, index, numerous illus. including one, p. (9), by DY. (Eggenhofer)

25 ———. Same, A Castle Books, Inc. Edition issued in a small format in 1970, boards and white endsheets.

26 Tucker, Patrick T. *Riding the High Country.* The Caxton Printers, Caldwell, Idaho, 1933, gilt decor. morocco, pic. endsheets, 210 pp., gilt top, edited by Grace Stone Coates, illus. with photos and drawings including one, on each endsheet, by DY. One of the De Luxe Edition of 25 numbered copies signed by Tucker and Coates. (Russell)

27 ———. Same, first trade edition in cloth.

27a (Woodward, Fred B.) *Oklahoma Tales and Jingles.* Parsons, Kansas, 1913, decor. wraps, 40 pp., "Foreword" by Mr. Ratlingourd, "Foreword" by Mr. Sourjohn, with twenty drawings by DY. (Joe's first — he was seventeen.)

28 Wilson, Neill C. (compiled in awe and wonder by). *Rancheros Visitadores, Twenty Fifth Anniversary, 1930-1955.* (Los Rancheros Visitadores, Santa Barbara, 1955), words "Limited Edition" on copyright page, two-tone pic. fabricoid, pic. endsheets, 142 (1) pp., numerous illus. including five, pp. (21) [repeated p. (53)], (59), (89) and (122) two, by DY. (Borein, Johnson)

The Artist and His Art

28a Archer, Ella V. "Cowboy Joe" (Joe De Yong Tells of his Life in Montana) an article in an unknown magazine, n.d. (1924), with three illus. by DY. and a photo of him on horseback.

29 Beeler, Joe. *Cowboys and Indians* (Characters in Oil and Bronze). Oklahoma, Norman, (1967), words "First edition" on copyright page, pic. leather, 80, xvii pp., "About Joe Beeler" by Joe De Yong, preface,

index, numerous illus. by Beeler. Edition of 200 numbered copies signed by Beeler and with an original drawing by him, slipcase.

30 ———. Same, first trade edition in cloth.

31 Cotton, Robert L. "Joe De Yong, Artist from A to Z," an article in *Old West* 9:2, Winter 1972, illus. with four drawings by DY. and several photos of him.

31a Dailey, Arthur A. "Deyong (sic) — Cowboy Artist," an article in an unknown magazine, n.d. (1921), with a photo of a model of a horse by DY. and a photo of him on horseback.

32 De Yong, Joe et al. "The Helpfulness of Charles M. Russell by Friends Who Knew Him Best" in *Federal Illustrator* 9:4, Winter 1926–27.

32a "Joe De Yong," an autobiographical sketch in *The Ranchman* 2:6, October 1942 with a photo of him plus a poem "Jack Pot Slim and Pelican" by him illustrated with one of his drawings.

33 De Yong, Joe. "Modest Son of the Old West, an article about Charlie Russell in *Montana* 8:4, Autumn 1958, illus. including a photo of De Yong with Con Price.

34 ———. "I, Mine and Me," an autobiographical article in *Noticias* 9:3–4, Autumn 1963, four illus. by DY. and a photo of him.

34a Fish, John (Art Director). "Joe De Yong," a brief biographical sketch in *Pacific Pathways* 3:5, Fall 1948, with four illus. in color by DY.

34b Keep, O. D. (Editor and Publisher). "Crayons and Cowboys" (as a part of "People of the Fortnight"), a biographical sketch of De Yong in *Fortnight* (The Magazine of California) 1:5, December 30, 1946, with one drawing (a self portrait) by DY.

35 *Noticias* (Occasional Papers no. 10). Santa Barbara Historical Society, November 1968, a biographical sketch of De Yong by E. S. Spaulding and a photo of DY. (Borein)

36 Price, Con. *Trails I Rode*. Trail's End Pub Co., Pasadena, Calif., (1947), morocco, brand decor. endsheets, 262 pp., illus. with drawings and with photos including one of the author and De Yong. De Yong mentioned in text. De Luxe Edition, 350 numbered and signed copies. (Ellsworth, Russell)

37 ———. Same, first trade edition in cloth.

38 Russell, Austin. *Charles M. Russell, Cowboy Artist*. Twayne Publishers, N.Y., (1957), cloth, 247 pp., foreword, sources, De Yong mentioned in foreword and several pages on him in text, illus. with family photos and drawings by Russell.

39 Russell, Charles M. *Good Medicine*. Doubleday, Doran & Co., Garden City, N.Y., 1929, words "First Edition" on copyright page, three quarters leather and and cloth, pic. endsheets, 162 pp., profusely illus., letters from Russell to his friends including one, p. 76, to De Yong, "Introduction" by Will Rogers, "Biographical Note" by Nancy Russell. One of 134 numbered copies, slipcase.

40 ———. Same, cloth with buffalo skull emblem on front cover, Garden City, N.Y., 1930, words "First Edition after the printing of 134 De Luxe copies" on copyright page. (Reprinted many times.)

41 *RV* (Rancheros Visitadores). No title page, n.p., (compliments of *Horse and Polo*, 1936?) wraps with rawhide tie, 21 pp., illus. with fifteen photos by Carl Obert, "Don Frank Bishop" (author?) in raised gilt on p. (1), Joe De Yong finishes second in calf roping, is a member of the winning potato race team and shows his horse "Bootlegger," a present to him from Mrs. Rogers after Will's death.

42 Spaulding, Edward Selden. "Ed Borein and His Fellow Artist," an article in *Noticias* 7:3, Autumn 1961, illustrated. Joe De Yong is one of the fellow artists. (Borein)

42a Ward, Fay E. (Editor). "Where They Range," a series of brief notes about Westerners including a paragraph on De Yong and one on his father Ade De Yong, the "Puncher Poet," in *The Cow-Country* 1:3, September 1919, with a drawing of "Wm. S. Hart Twenty Years Ago" by DY. with two paragraphs on him plus a poem, "The Mahogany Hand," by his father illus. with a drawing by Joe.

42b Weadick, Guy. "Cowboys I Have Known — Joe De Yong, Noted Artist," a biographical sketch in *West*, June 1937 — also "Any Horse, Any Place — Any Time," an article about John Shipp by De Yong with a drawing of Shipp by him plus a review of De Yong's *Friend Will* by Walt Coburn and the front cover illus. in color is by DY.

43 Yost, Karl and Renner, Frederic G. (compiled by). *A Bibliography of the Published Works of Charles M. Russell*. University of Nebraska Press, Lincoln, (1971), simulated decor. leather, tan endsheets, 317 pp., foreword, index, illus., De Yong in text, pp. 81, 90 and 127. Edition of 600 numbered copies.

44 ———. Same, first trade edition.

PLAINS INDIAN IN WARBONNET by Dixon from *Harmsen's Western Americana*

LAFAYETTE MAYNARD DIXON
1875–1946

Catalogues of Art Exhibitions and Galleries

J. N. BARTFIELD ART GALLERIES, NEW YORK

0 *American Paintings and Sculpture: Historical-Western*, (catalogue no. 120, 1973), wraps with window, unpaged, 82 numbered illus. incuding five, nos. 14, 15, 16, 17 and 18, by D. (Johnson, Leigh, Remington, Russell, Schreyvogel)

BILTMORE GALLERIES, LOS ANGELES

0a *Catalog*, May 1969, colored pic. wraps, 54 pp., numerous illus. including four, pp. 14 (two) and 15 (two), by D. (Borein, Johnson, Koerner, Leigh, Miller, Remington, Russell, Young)

CALIFORNIA PACIFIC INTERNATIONAL EXPOSITION SAN DIEGO

1 *Catalogue*, Frye and Smith, 1935, wraps, one illus., "Earth Knower," by D.

HELEN L. CARD, NEW YORK

2 *Hats Off to the American Illustrator!* Catalog no. 2, (Fall, 1959), pic. wraps, 32 pp., numerous illus. including one, p. 29, by D. (Goodwin, Koerner, Remington, Schoonover, Wyeth)

COLONIAL ART COMPANY, OKLAHOMA CITY
(SENATE ROOM, LINCOLN PLAZA INN)

2a *Western and Traditional American Paintings of the 19th and Early 20th Centuries* (auction catalog), June 10, 1973, pic. wraps, unpaged, 76 numbered illus. including eight, nos. 1, 2, 3, 4, 5, 6, 7 and 8, by D. (Borein, Deming, Eggenhofer, Elwell, Goodwin, Johnson, Koerner, Russell, Schoonover, Wyeth, Young)

CORCORAN GALLERY OF ART, WASHINGTON, D.C.

3 *Exhibition American Painting*, Catalogue, 1935, wraps, one illus., "Earth Knower," by D.

EDWARD EBERSTADT AND SONS, NEW YORK

4 *A Distinguished Catalogue of Western Paintings*, no. 139, 1956, pic. wraps, "Introduction — Western American Art" by Harold McCracken, 129 numbered plates including one, no. 31, by D. (Borein, Deming, Johnson, Leigh, Remington, Wyeth, Zogbaum)

5 *American Paintings*, Catalogue 146, 1958 (but issued in December 1957), colored pic .wraps, 191 numbered plates including one, no. 61, by D. (Borein, Deming, Dunton, Johnson, Leigh, Miller, Remington, Wyeth)

FRESNO ARTS CENTER, FRESNO, CALIFORNIA

6 *Diamond Jubilee Exhibitions*, Oct. 13–Nov. 5, 1961, features work of artists "Around and About Fresno 1900 and Before" and "Maynard Dixon" with one drawing on front cover by D., a list of twenty-seven Dixon items included in the show and a biographical sketch of him.

GALLERY OF SCIENCE AND ART, IBM, NEW YORK

7 *Contemporary Art of the United States*, 1940, wraps, unpaged, numerous illus. including one by D. and a photo of him. (Wyeth)

GALLERY WEST, DENVER

8 *Prospectives in Western Art*, 1972, pic. wraps, twenty-one illus. including one, "Arizona 1900," by D. (Borein, Deming, Ellsworth, Remington, Russell, Schreyvogel)

E. WALTER LATENDORF, NEW YORK

9 *Maynard Dixon, Painter of the West*, n.d., (4) pp., ten illus. by D.

10 *Beware* (broadside notice to the trade describing the

man who got possession of two Dixon paintings with a forged check), n.d., two illus. by D.

Los Angeles County Museum of Art

11 *California Centennial Exhibitions of Art*, 1949, one illus. by D. and a biographical sketch of him.

The Macbeth Galleries, new york

12 *Paintings of the West by Maynard Dixon*, Feb. 13–March 5, 1923, two illus. by D.

Maxwell Galleries, san francisco

13 *One Hundred Years of California Painting from 1849*, March 4–26, 1966, colored pic. wraps, numerous illus. including one, "Roadside," by D.

14 *American Art Since 1850*, Aug. 2–Oct. 31, 1968, pic. wraps, 84 pp., numerous illus. including one, p. 33, by D. (Borein, Johnson, Miller, Remington, Russell, Wyeth)

14a *American Paintings, A Comprehensive Exhibition*, February 23–April 7, 1973, pic. wraps, numerous illus. including one by D.

Montana Historical Society, helena

15 *An Art Perspective of the Historic Pacific Northwest* (from the Collection of Dr. and Mrs. Franz R. Stenzel, Portland, Oregon), August, 1963, wraps, 32 pp., numerous illus. including two, p. 10, by D. (Lungren, Remington, Russell)

Oakland Art Museum

16 *Early Paintings of California in the Robert B. Honeyman, Jr. Collection*, 1956, pic. wraps, 47 pp., numerous illus. including one, p. 46, by D.

The Print Rooms (hill tolerton) san francisco

17 *An Exhibition of Original Drawings by Maynard Dixon*, Nov. 16 to Dec. 1, 1914, wraps, text by Porter Garnett, illus. by D.

The Rotunda Gallery (city of paris) san francisco

18 *Paintings and Drawings by the Late Maynard Dixon*, Jan. 22–Feb. 9, (1954), announcement folder with four drawings by D. and a photo of him.

Sotheby Parke Bernet, los angeles

19 *Important 19th and Early 20th Century American Paintings*, Sale no. 81, May 22–23, 1973, colored pic. wraps, 167 (5) pp., numerous illus. including one, p. 72, by D. (Dunton, Ellsworth, Russell)

The University of Texas, austin

20 *Painting from the C. R. Smith Collection*, Dec. 4, 1969–Jan. 15, 1970, wraps, unpaged, preface by Donald B. Goodall and Marian B. Davis, numerous illus. including three by D. (Eggenhofer, Johnson, Lea, Russell, Schreyvogel, Von Schmidt)

Wells Fargo Bank History Room san francisco

21 *Half an Hour in Eldorado*, (1942), decor. wraps, unpaged, numerous illus. including one by D. (Russell)

22 *A Brief History of Wells Fargo told through the Mementoes in the Wells Fargo Bank History Room*, (1956), pic. wraps, unpaged, numerous illus. including one by D. (Russell)

23 Same, revised September, 1963, pic. wraps, unpaged, numerous illus. including one by D. (Russell)

24 Same, revised (1967), pic. wraps, unpaged, numerous illus. including one by D. (Russell)

Illustrated by the Artist

25 Adams, James Truslow (editor-in-chief). *The March of Democracy* (vol. 3, Album of American History). Scribner's, N.Y., 1948, code letter "A" on copyright page, decor. cloth, decor. endsheets, 385 pp., foreword, acknowledgments, numerous illus. including one, the frontis., by D.

26 Ainsworth, Ed. *Painters of the Desert*. Desert Magazine, Palm Desert, California, 1960, cloth, 111 pp., "Foreword" by Carl Dentzel, numerous illus. including seven, pp. (14) in color, (16), 17, 18 (three) and 19, by D. and two photos of D. (Dunn)

27 ———. *The Cowboy in Art*. World, N.Y. and Cleveland, (1968), words "First Printing 1968" on copyright page, full leather, orange endsheets, 242 pp., all edges gilt, "Foreword" by John Wayne, index, numerous illus. including three, pp. 54 (two) and 55, by D. and a photo of him. Special edition of 1,000 copies, slipcase. (Beeler, Borein, Bugbee, De Yong, Dunton, Eggenhofer, Ellsworth, Hurd, James, Johnson, Koerner, Mora, Perceval, Remington, Russell, Santee, Schreyvogel, Von Schmidt)

28 ———. Same, first trade edition in gilt lettered and illus. cloth, orange endsheets.

29 ———. Same, reprint by Bonanza Books, N.Y., in red lettered and illus. cloth, white endsheets.

30 Armitage, Merle. *Accent on America.* E. Weyhe, N.Y., 1944, decor. cloth, decor. red endsheets, 403 (2) pp., red top, index of eagles, twenty-six illus. including one, p. (330), by D. Edition of 1,675 copies, signed by the author.

31 Atherton, Gertrude, Mary Austin et al. *The Spinners' Book of Fiction.* Paul Elder, San Francisco and N.Y., (1907), cloth, illus. including one in color, "All Their Ways Lead to Death," facing p. 158, by D.

31a Baird, Joseph A., Jr. (compiled by). *The West Remembered.* California Historical Society, San Francisco and San Marino, 1973, colored pic. wraps, 88 pp., "Foreword" by Mitchell A. Wilder, introduction, numerous illus. including three, pp. 29, (33) and 62, by D. (Blumenschein, Borein, James, Lungren, Marchand, Miller, Remington, Russell, Zogbaum)

32 Balch, F. H. *The Bridge of the Gods.* A. C. McClurg, Chicago, 1902, words "Published, August 2, 1902" on copyright page (Seventh Edition — first to have Dixon illustrations), eight illus., frontis. and facing pp. 50, 88, 108, 168, 204, 224 and 264, by D.

33 Beard, Charles A. and Mary R. *A Basic History of the United States.* Doubleday, Doran, N.Y., 1944, cloth, 554 pp., brown top, prefatory note, appendix, reading list, index, illus. including one between pp. 48 and 49, by D. (Lea, Leigh).

34 Bower, Donald E. and Kollings, Patricia, eds. *The Magnificent Rockies, Crest of a Continent.* American West, Palo Alto, (1973), cloth, green endsheets, 285 (2) pp., preface, sources and suggested reading, index, maps, numerous (many in color) illus. including one, p. (126), by D. (Remington)

35 Boyles, Kate and Virgil D. *The Homesteaders.* A. C. McClurg, Chicago, 1909, words "Published September 11, 1909" on copyright page, cloth and pic. boards, 245 (1) pp., four illus. in color, frontis. and facing pp. 62, 154 and 326, by D.

36 ———. *The Spirit Trail.* A. C. McClurg, Chicago, 1910, words "Published October 29, 1910" on copyright page, cloth and pic. boards, 416 pp., four illus. in color, frontis. and facing pp. 144, 388 and 390, by D.

37 Brady, Cyrus Townsend. *The West Wind.* A. C. McClurg, Chicago, 1910, words "Published, September, 1912" on copyright page, cloth, 389 pp., four illus. in color, frontis. and facing pp. 120, 198 and 312, by D.

38 Brininstool, E. A. *Fighting Indian Warriors.* Stackpoole, Harrisburg, Pa., 1953, cloth, 353 pp., numerous illus. including one, p. 142, by D. (Zogbaum)

39 Bronson, Edgar Beecher. *Reminiscences of a Ranchman.* A. C. McClurg, Chicago, (1910), words "Published September 10, 1910" on copyright page (revised edition — the first to have Dixon illustrations), cloth with colored illus. mounted on front cover, 369 (1) pp., seven illus., frontis. and facing pp. 26, 32, 48, 90, 170 and 288, by D.

39a ———. Same, Doran reprint with the title *Cowboy Life on the Western Plains.* (1910).

40 ———. *The Red Blooded.* A. C. McClurg, Chicago, 1910, words "Published September 10, 1910" on copyright page, pic. cloth, 341 (1) pp., nineteen illus. including ten, frontis. and facing pp. 6, 14, 20, 36, 42, 46, 190, 232 and 244, by D. (Johnson, Russell)

41 Buffum, George T. *On Two Frontiers.* Lothrop, Lee & Shepard, Boston, (1918), words "Published, March, 1918" on copyright page, cloth, 375 pp., frontis. by D.

41a Burnside, Wesley M. *Maynard Dixon, Artist of the West.* Brigham Young University Press, Provo, Utah, (1974), words "250 Limited Special Edition" on copyright page, imitation leather and cloth, orange endsheets, 237 pp., preface, introduction, catalog of oil paintings, illustrations in books, illustrations in periodicals, exhibitions, mural decorations, Frederic Remington letters, notes, bibliography, index, numerous (32 in color) illus. by D.

42 Carlson, Ray, ed. *Arizona — Land of Fair Color.* The Arizona Highway Department, Phoenix, Arizona, n d, (1945?), stiff wraps with plastic binding, (86) pp., numerous illus. including eight in color, by D. (Pages from previous issues of *Arizona Highways.*)

43 ———. *Gallery of Western Paintings.* McGraw-Hill, N.Y. etc., (1951), words "First Edition" on copyright page, cloth with illus. in color mounted on front cover, colored endsheets, 85 pp., foreword, 76 illus. including eight in color, pp. 47–54, by D.

44 Carman, Harry J., Kimmell, William G., and Walker, Mabel G. *Historic Currents in Changing America.* John C. Winston, Philadelphia etc., (1938), code number "P-9-38" appears in lower right hand

corner of copyright page, decor. cloth, 854 pp., preface, appendix, index, maps, numerous illus. including one, p. 308, by D. (Remington)

45 Peggy Christian, Bookseller, Los Angeles, *American Artists and Illustrators*, Catalog no. 4, 1965, pic. wraps, 20 pp., numerous illus. including one, p. 7, by D. (Borein, Eggenhofer, Ellsworth, Remington, Russell)

46 Coolidge, Dane. *Hidden Water.* A. C. McClurg, Chicago, 1910, words "Published, October 29, 1910" on copyright page, cloth and pic. boards, 483 pp., four illus. in color, frontis. and facing pp. 177, 287 and 462, by D.

47 ———. *The Texican.* A. C. McClurg, Chicago, 1911, words "Published September, 1911" on copyright page, pic. cloth, 368 (1) pp., five illus. in color, frontis. and facing pp. 56, 188, 250 and 312, by D.

48 Connolly, James B. *Open Water.* Scribners', N.Y., 1910, words "Published October, 1910" on copyright page, pic. cloth, 322 pp., (4) of advs., eight illus. including one, facing p. 134, by D.

49 Dakin, Susanna Bryant. *A Scotch Paisano.* University of California Press, Berkeley, 1939, cloth, 312 pp., preface, note of acknowledgment, appendix, bibliography, index, two illus., pp. (71) and (165), by D., map.

50 Davenport, William and the Sunset Editors. *Art Treasures in the West.* Lane, Menlo Park, Calif., (1966), words "First printing October 1966" on copyright page. Simulated leather and cloth, pic. endsheets, 320 pp., biographical notes, index, profusely illustrated (many in color) including one, p. 197, by D.

51 (Dawson.) *Standard and Exotic Books Relating to the Golden State*, Catalogue 358, Dawson's Book Shop, Los Angeles, 1966, pic. wraps, unpaged, one illus., a mural design, by D.

52 ———. *The Northwest Coast*, Catalogue 361, (1967?), pic. wraps, unpaged, one illus. by D. (Miller)

53 de Garza, Patricia. *Chicanos* (The Story of Mexican Americans). Messner, N.Y., (1973), pic. cloth, 96 pp., index, numerous illus. including one, p. 26, by D.

54 Dillon, Richard H. *The Hatchet Men: The Story of the Tong Wars in San Francisco's Chinatown.* Coward-McCann, N.Y., (1962), decor. cloth, black endsheets, 375 pp., foreword, selective bibliography,

the illus. including one by D. appear between pp. 126 and 127.

55 Dixon, Maynard. *Injun Babies.* Putnam's, N.Y., 1923, cloth with colored illus. mounted on front cover, pic. endsheets, 72 pp., eight illus. in color, frontis. and facing pp. (10), (20), (32), (42), (48), (58) and 66 plus line drawings, by D.

56 ———. *Poems and Seven Drawings.* (Printed by Edwin and Robert Grabhorn and James McDonald, San Francisco), 1923, boards, pages unnumbered, seven drawings by D. Limited to 250 copies.

57 Dykes, J. C. (Jeff) et al., eds. *Great Western Indian Fights.* Doubleday, Garden City, N.Y., 1960, words " First Edition" on copyright page. Decor. cloth, pic. map endsheets, 336 pp., bibliography, index, illus including one, between pp. 216 and 217, by D. (Remington, Russell, Schreyvogel)

58 ———. Same, first Bison Book printing, University of Nebraska Press, Lincoln, 1966, colored pic. wraps.

59 (Eberstadt.) *Americana.* Edward Eberstadt and Sons, N.Y., (1954), pic. wraps, 111 pp., 32 illus. including one, inside back cover, by D. (Johnson)

60 *Fine Art Reproductions of Old and Modern Masters.* New York Graphic Society, Greenwich, Conn. etc., (1961), decor. cloth, 443 pp., introduction, numerous illus. including one in color, p. 312, by D. (Hurd, Remington, Schreyvogel)

61 Ford, Sewell. *Horses Nine.* Scribner's, N.Y., (1931), cloth, 270 pp., nine illus. including three, frontis, and facing pp. 226 and 268, by D.

62 Gabriel, Ralph Henry. *The Toilers of Land and Sea.* Yale University Press, New Haven, Conn., The Liberty Bell Edition of "The Pageant of America," vol. III, limited to 1500 numbered impressions, 1926, morocco and board, 340 pp., numerous illus. including two, pp. 179 and 190, by D. (Remington, Russell)

63 ———. *The Lure of the Frontier.* Yale University Press, New Haven, 1929, The Liberty Bell Edition of "The Pageant of Ameica," vol II, limited to 1500 numbered impressions, morocco and boards, 327 pp., numerous illus. including two, pp. 184 and 297, by D. (Remington, Russell)

64 Gann, Dan and Kitchen, Merrell A., eds. *The Westerners Brand Book 1949.* The Los Angeles Corral, 1949, (copyrighted 1950), morocco and dec. cloth, pic. endsheets, 263 pp., "Foreword" by Sher-

Gemada
Nov - 05

iff Homer H. Boelter, index, numerous illus. including three, pp. 177, 178 and 179, by D. Notes on Dixon by Don Louis Perceval. Limited to 400 copies. (Blumenschein, Borein, Johnson, Remington, Russell)

65 Garnett, Porter, ed. *The Grove Plays of the Bohemian Club*. The H. S. Crocker Co., San Francisco, 1918, 3 vols., full blue crushed morocco or cloth and boards, pp. 219, 274, 282, introduction, illus. with photos and sixteen full-page plates by D. The Collected Edition, limited to 31 sets, printed on handmade paper.

66 Gray, Arthur Amos. *Men Who Built the West*. The Caxton Printers, Caldwell, Idaho, 1945, pic. cloth, 220 pp. foreword, index, maps, illus. including two, facing pp. 20 and 177, by D.

67 Greene, Clay M. (compiled and edited by). *The Annals of the Bohemian Club*, vol. IV. Published by the Club, San Francisco, 1930, decor. cloth, 248 pp., index, numerous illus. including three, facing pp. 162, 176 and (221), by D. Edition of 800 copies.

68 Gregg, Andrew K. *New Mexico in the Nineteenth Century: A Pictorial History*. University of New Mexico Press, Albuquerque, 1968, words, "First Edition" on copyright page, cloth, pic. endsheets, 196 pp., preface, profusely illus. including one, p. 1, by D. (Remington)

69 *Grolier Encyclopedia*, vol. 8, Grolier Society, N.Y. etc., (1952), fabricoid, 579 pp., numerous illus. including one full-page plate in color, facing p. 404, by D.

70 Hanson, Joseph Mills. *Frontier Ballads*. A. C. McClurg, Chicago, 1910, words, "Published October 14, 1910" on copyright page, pic. boards, 92 pp., seven illus. in color, frontis. and facing pp. 21, 31, 40, 52, 71, 77 and other drawings, by D.

71 Harmsen, Dorothy. *Harmsen's Western Americana*. Northland Press, Flagstaff, (1971), morocco and cloth, blue endsheets, 213 pp., "Foreword" by Robert Rockwell, inroduction, numerous illus. including one in color p. (65), by D. and with a biographical sketch of him. Author's edition of 150 numbered and signed copies, slipcase with morocco title label. (Beeler, Blumenschein, Borein, Dunn, Dunton, Eggenhofer, Elwell, Hurd, Johnson, Leigh, Marchand, Miller, Russell, Von Schmidt, Wyeth)

72 ———. Same, first trade edition, two-tone cloth with red endsheets.

73 Heizer, Robert F., ed. *The Indians of Los Angeles County: Hugo Reid's Letters of 1952*. Southwest Museum, Los Angeles, 1968, Museum Papers no. 21, cloth, map endsheets, 142 pp., foreword, notes, illus. including one, the frontis., by D.

73a Hillier, Bevis. *100 Years of Posters*. Harper and Row, N.Y., (1972), words "First U.S. Edition" on copyright page, colored pic. wraps, xvi pp. plus 96 numbered plates including one, no. 29, by D.

74 Hungerford, Edward. *Wells Fargo*. Random House, N.Y., (1949), words, "First Printing" on copyright page, pic. cloth, 274 pp., brown top, acknowledgments, "Introduction" by Elmer Ray Jones, bibliography, index, numerous illus. including one, facing p. 181, by D., maps.

74a Johnson, Paul C. *Pictorial History of California*. Doubleday, 1970, words "First Edition" on copyright page, cloth, numerous illus. including two by D.

74b ———, ed. *The Early Sunset Magazine 1898–1928*. California Historical Society, San Francisco — San Marino, (1973), words "First printing, October 1973" on copyright page, colored pic. wraps, 239 (1) pp., "Preface" by Proctor Mellquist, introduction, notes on contributors, numerous illus. including four, inside front cover and pp. 56, 57 and 58, by D. (James)

75 Kelly, Florence. *The Delafield Affair*. A. C. McClurg, Chicago, 1909, cloth and decor. boards, 422 pp., four illus. in color, frontis. and facing pp. 168, 308 and 404, by D.

76 Klotz, Edwin F. *The Original Constitution of the State of California, 1849*. Telefact Foundation, Sacramento, 1965, illus. including one by D.

77 Kyne, Peter B. *The Three Godfathers*. George H. Doran, N.Y., (1913), cloth, 95 pp., five tinted illus., frontis. and facing pp. 18, (32), 64 and 80, by D.

78 Latendorf, E. Walter. *Western Americana: Catalogue No. 24*. Mannados Bookshop, N.Y., (1954), pic. wraps, 88 pp., numerous illus. including three, p. 9 and 2 on p. 10, by D. (Borein, Schreyvogel)

79 Lillibridge, Will. *Ben Blair*. A. C. McClurg, Chicago, 1905, words "Published October 21, 1905" on copyright page, pic. cloth, 333 pp., frontis. in color, by D.

80 London, Jack. *The Son of the Wolf*. Houghton, Mifflin, Boston & N.Y., 1900, silver decor. cloth, 251 pp., frontis. by D.

81 *Los Angeles Architectural Club Year Book 1913*. Wraps, unpaged, illus. including one, "The Pioneers" (a panel), by D.

82 Lyman, George D. *The Saga of the Comstock Lode.* Scribner's, N.Y., London, 1934, code letter "A" on copyright page, cloth, pic. endsheets, 399 pp., red top, illus. including one, the frontis., by D.

83 Lynde, Francis. *The Taming of Red Butte Western.* Scribner's, N.Y., 1910, words "Published April 1910" on copyright page, pic. cloth, 410 pp., four illus., frontis. and facing pp. 138, 178 and 400, by D.

84 *A. C. McClurg & Co.'s Monthly Bulletin of New Books — No. 439.* December, 1905, numerous illus. including one by D. (Schoonover)

85 McDowell, Jack (supervising editor) et al. *Art Treasures in the West.* Lane, Menlo Park, Calif., (1966), words "First printing October 1966" on copyright page, morocco and cloth, pic. endsheets, 320 pp., introduction, biographical notes, numerous illus. including one, p. 197, by D. and a biographical sketch of him, p. 309.

86 Maule, Mary K. *The Little Knight of the "X Bar B."* Lothrop, Lee and Shepard, Boston, (1910), words "Published, April, 1910" on copyright page, pic. cloth, 461 pp., six illus., frontis. and facing pp. 14, 148, 200, 300 and 352, by D.

87 Meadows, Don, ed. *The Westerners Brand Book, Book Eight.* Los Angeles Corral, (1959), morocco and boards, pic. endsheets, 229 (1) pp., contributors, numerous illus. including many by D.

87a Meigs, John, ed. *The Cowboy in American Prints.* Swallow Press, Chicago, (1972), leather and cloth, pic. endsheets, 184 pp., introduction, numerous illus. including one, p. 22, by D. Limited to 300 numbered copies signed by the editor with an added manually signed lithograph by Peter Hurd, slipcase. (Beeler, Borein, Hurd, Remington, Russell, Wood, Zogbaum)

87b ———. Same, trade edition in cloth.

88 Mitchell, Edmund. *The Call of the Bells.* Menqies Pub. Co., Inc., N.Y., 1916, decor. cloth, 411 pp., frontis. by D.

89 Morrow, W. C. *Lentala of the South Seas.* Frederick A. Stokes, N.Y., (1908), words "September, 1908" on copyright page, decor. cloth with small colored illus. mounted on front cover, 278 pp., six illus. in color, frontis. and facing pp. 12, 18, 232, 252 and 262, by D.

90 Mulford, Clarence E. *Hopalong Cassidy.* A. C. McClurg, Chicago, 1910, words "Published March 12, 1910" on copyright page, cloth and pic. boards, 392 pp., five illus. in color, frontis. and facing pp. 96, 188, 270 and 370, by D.

91 ———. *Bar-20 Days.* A. C. McClurg, Chicago, 1911, words "Published, March 1911" on copyright page, pic. cloth, 412 pp., four illus. in color, frontis. and facing pp. 134, 270 and 346, by D.

92 ——— and John Wood Clay. *Buck Peters, Ranchman.* A. C. McClurg, Chicago, 1912, words "Published, April, 1912" on copyright page, cloth, 367 pp., four illus. in color, frontis. and facing pp. 250, 284 and 340, by D.

93 ———. *The Coming of Cassidy.* A. C. McClurg, Chicago, 1913, words "Published, October, 1913" on copyright page, pic. cloth, 438 pp., five illus. in color, frontis. and facing pp. 39, 133, 249 and 378, by D.

94 Myrtle, Frederick S. (The Music by H. F. Stewart). *Gold — A Forest Play.* Bohemian Club (Taylor and Taylor), San Francisco, 1916, cloth and boards with a colored illus. mounted on the front cover, 60 pp., foreword, cast of characters, reproductions in color of 20 costume designs by D. on 7 plates facing pp. 3, 9, 17, 25, 33, 41 and 49.

95 Neuhas, Eugen. *Painters, Pictures and the People.* Philopolia Press, San Francisco, 1918, plate xxx, "What an Indian Thinks," p. 176, by D.

96 ———. *Appreciation of Art.* Ginn, Boston, 1924, cloth, 250 pp., numerous illus. including one, p. 143, by D.

97 ———. *The History and Ideals of American Art.* Stanford University Press, Stanford University, California etc., 1931, cloth with paper labels, 444 pp., tinted top, preface, bibliography, index, illus. including two, pp. (310) and (368), by D. (Blumenschein, Remington, Russell)

98 ———. *World of Art.* Harcourt Brace, N.Y., 1936, cloth, 292 pp., numerous illus. including one, p. 185, by D.

99 Nicol, Bruce (assembled and edited by). *Nebraska, A Pictorial History.* Nebraska, Lincoln, 1967, cloth, blue endsheets, 231 (1) pp., foreword, numerous illus. including one, p. 97, by D. (Dunn, Miller, Remington, Russell)

100 Pagano, Grace. *The Encyclopaedia Britannica Collection of Contemporary American Painting.* Lakeside Press for Encyclopaedia Britannica, Chicago, (1945), wraps, unpaged, 116 numbered plates including no. 37 in color by D. plus a photo of him.

101 Parkman, Francis. *The Oregon Trail.* Printed for the members of the Limited Editions Club, N.Y., 1943, copies numbered and signed by the illustrator on verso of the last page of text, decor. leather, pic. endsheets, 297 pp., all edges blue, "Introduction" (and edited) by Mason Wade, four full-page illus. in color, facing pp. (1), 158, (211) and 260 and two double-page illus. in color, between pp. 48-49 and 96-97, plus numerous drawings in brown in text, by D.

102 ———. *The Oregon Trail.* The Heritage Press, N.Y., (1943), decor. cloth, 297 pp., maroon edges, "Introduction" (and edited) by Mason Wade, illus. including four full-page illustrations, facing pp. 1, 158, 211 and 260, and 2 double-page illus. between pp. 48–49 and 96–97, plus tinted drawings by D.

103 Penfield, Edward et al. *Posters in Miniature.* R. H. Russell, N.Y., 1897, pic. cloth, pages unnumbered, introduction, numerous illus. including one, by D.

104 Perceval, Don. *Maynard Dixon Sketch Book.* Northland Press, Flagstaff, 1967, cloth, 108 pp., illus. with 164 sketches by D. and with a frontis. portrait of him by Ansel Adams.

105 Porter, Bruce et al. *Art in California.* R. L. Bernier, San Francisco, 1916, full blue morocco, matching silk followed by marbled endsheets, 183 (1) pp., all edges gilt, introduction, index, 332 numbered plates including no. 18, "What an Indian Thinks," by D. Short biographical sketch of Dixon, p. 168. (Lungren)

106 *Quarto-Millenary* (The First 250 Publications and the first 25 years, 1929-1954). The Limited Editions Club, N.Y., 1959, morocco and cloth, 295 pp., note by the publisher, introduction, critique, conspectus, bibliography, indexes, numerous (many in color) illus. including one, p. 61, by D., slipcase, 2,250 numbered copies.

107 Reed, Verner Z. *Lo-To-Kah.* Continental Pub. Co., N.Y. and London, 1897, decor. cloth, 229 pp., illus. including nine full-page drawings, pp. (45), (63), (93), (131), (137), (157), (175), (193) and 217, plus line drawings, by D.

108 ———. *Tales of the Sun-Land.* Continental Pub. Co., N.Y. and London, 1897, pic. cloth, 250 pp., 20 full-page illus. and other drawings, by D.

109 Reed, Walt. *Harold Von Schmidt Draws and Paints the Old West.* Northland Press, Flagstaff, (1972), words "First Edition" on copyright page, morocco and pic. cloth, slate endsheets, 230 pp., "Foreword" by Dean Krakel, "Introduction" by Harold McCracken, bibliography, numerous illus. by Von Schmidt but with one drawing by D., a photo of him and much on him in the text, one of 104 numbered copies signed by Reed and Von Schmidt, slipcase with morocco title label, issued jointly with Von Schmidt's first sculpture, "The Startled Grizzly." (Dunn, James, Russell)

110 ———. Same, first trade edition in pic. cloth.

111 Richards, Irmagarde. *Early California,* Dept. of Education, Sacramento, 1950, cloth, 279 pp., includes photo of part of the Dixon mural in the State Library at Sacramento.

112 Rolt-Wheeler, Francis. *The Book of Cowboys.* Lothrop, Lee and Shepard, Boston, (1921), words "Published, April, 1921" on copyright page, pic. cloth, 394 pp., numerous illus. including "The Marshall!" facing p. 266, by D. (Russell, Stoops)

113 Schmitt, Martin F. and Brown, Dee. *Fighting Indians of the West.* Scribner's N.Y., 1948, code letter "A" on copyright page, pic. cloth, map endsheets, 362 pp., preface, introduction, bibliography, 270 illus. including one, p. 221, by D. (Remington, Schreyvogel)

114 Schutz, Anton, Mimi, and Herbert D. (directors). *Fine Art Reproductions Old and Modern Masters — Supplement.* New York Graphic Society, N.Y., (1948), wraps, (80) pp., foreword, index, profusely illus. including "Home on the Desert" (above foreword) by D.

114a ———. *Fine Art Reproductions Old & Modern Masters, 1925–1950.* N.Y. Graphic Society, (N.Y., 1951), two-tone cloth, 399 pp., foreword, numerous illus. including one, p. 141, by D.

115 Scofield, J. B. (compiled by). *The Land of Living Color.* J. B. Scofield (Sunset Publishing House), San Francisco, (1915), limp leather, 70 pp., numerous illus. in color including one, p. 8, "Spirit Canyon, New Mexico," by D.

116 Service, Robert W. *The Trail of Ninety-Eight.* Dodd, Mead, N.Y., 1911, cloth, 514 pp., four illus., frontis. and facing pp. 116, 316 and 476, by D.

117 Smith, Waddell F. *Pony Express Versus Wells Fargo Express.* (Pony Express History and Art Gallery, San Rafael, Calif.), 1966, decor. wraps, 14 (2) pp., illus. including one, "The Pony Express to California," p. 5, by D.

118 Steele, Rufus. *Mustangs of the Mesas.* Press of Mur-

ray & Gee, Hollywood, California, (1941), cloth, 220 pp., illus. including two, facing pp. 167 and 184, by D. (Stoops)

119 Stilgebauer, F. G. *Nebraska Pioneers.* Wm. B. Erdmans Pub. Co., Grand Rapids, Mich., 1944, cloth, 414 pp., prefaces, foreword, eight illus. including one, "Dull Knife," p. 218, by D.

120 Strate, David K. *Sentinel to the Cimarron.* Cultural Heritage and Arts Center, Dodge City, Kansas, (1970), cloth with illus. by Seltzer mounted on front cover, 147 (1) pp., preface, bibliography, index, maps, illus. including one, between pp. 62 and 63, by D. (Schreyvogel)

121 Strobridge, Idah Meacham. *The Loom of the Desert.* (Artemesia Bindery), (Baumgardt Pub. Co.), Los Angeles, 1907, stiff pic. wraps, 141 pp., illus. including three, frontis. and facing pp. 62 and 78, and other drawings, by D. Limited to 1,000 autographed copies.

122 ————. *The Land of Purple Shadows.* "The Artemesia Bindery," Los Angeles, 1909, autographed edition limited to 1,000 copies, pic. wraps, 133 pp., three illus., frontis. and facing pp. 52 and 104, by D.

123 Truesdell, Amelia Woodward. *Francisca Reina.* The Gorham Press, Boston, 1908, pic. wraps, 44 pp., numerous illus. including eleven by D.

124 Wallace, Andrew. *The Image of Arizona: Pictures from the Past.* New Mexico, Albuquerque, 1971, cloth, 254 pp., numerous illus. including one by D.

125 Watson, Thomas J. (foreword). *Contemporary Art of the Western Hemisphere.* International Business Machines Corp., n.p., (Canada), (1941), pic. wraps, pages unnumbered, 103 numbered plates including no. 55 by D., also photo of Dixon and short sketch. (Remington)

126 Weaver, Paul (publisher). *1970–71 Winter/Spring Book List,* Northland Press, Flagstaff, pic. wraps, unpaged, numerous illus. including one by Dixon. (Beeler, Borein, Perceval, Remington)

127 ————. Same, *Autumn 1971,* one illus. by D. (Borein, Perceval, Remington, Santee)

128 ————. Same, *Autumn 1972,* one illus. by D. (Beeler, Perceval, Remington, Santee, Von Schmidt, Wyeth) Note: Other Northland Press Book Lists include one illustration by Dixon.

128a ————. Same, Autumn 1973, one illus. by D. (Beeler,

Blumenschein, James, Perceval, Remington, Santee, Von Schmidt)

129 Whitaker, Herman, ed. *West Winds.* Paul Elder & Co., San Francisco, (1914), boards with illus. mounted on front cover, 219 pp., illus. including one, facing p. 120, by D. (Crawford)

130 ————. *Over the Border.* Harper, N.Y. and London, (1917), words "Published May, 1917" and code letters "E-R" on copyright page, cloth, 415 (1) pp., tinted frontis., by D.

131 Wissler, Clark, Skinner, Constance Lindsay, and Wood, Wm. *Adventures in the Wilderness.* Yale University Press, New Haven, 1925, The Liberty Bell Edition of "The Pageant of America," vol. 1, limited to 1,500 numbered impressions, morocco and boards, 369 pp., profusely illus. including one, p. 58, by D. (Deming, Remington, Russell)

132 Woehlke, Walter V. et al. *Color Articles Reproduced from Sunset Magazine, 1911.* Flexible leather, brown endsheets, (142) pp., 104 illus. in color including two by D.

133 (Zeitlin.) *Western Americana, Catalogue No. 204.* Zeitlin and Ver Brugge, Los Angeles, 1963, pic. wraps, 59 pp., one illus., facing p. 56, by D. (Borein)

134 ————. *The Great West,* Catalog 213, 1966, wraps, one illus. by D. (Borein)

The Artist and His Art

135 Adams, Ansel. "A Free Man in a Free Country," an illus. article in *The American West* 6:6, November 1969, cover and eight other illus. by D.

135a Ainsworth, Ed. "Maynard Dixon: The Man Who Painted Poems," an article on Dixon in *Palm Springs Villager* 9:5, December 1956, with eight illus. by D. plus photos of him.

136 *American Art Annual,* The American Federation of Arts, Washington, D.C., 1915, includes a biographical sketch of D., p. 361. Note: Other volumes of this Annual include a biographical sketch of D.

137 *American Magazine of Art,* 16:4, April, 1925, includes "Three California Painters," discusses Dixon's easel painting and with an illus. by him.

138 Bingham, Edwin. *Charles F. Lummis, Editor of the Southwest.* The Huntington Library, San Marino, California, 1955, cloth, 218 pp., preface, bibliography, index, illus. Biographical sketch of D.

138a Blanch, Josephine M. "Maynard Dixon, Painter of the West," an article in *The Argonaut*, February 19, 1927.

138b Boeringer, Pierre N. "Some San Francisco Illustrators," an article in *Overland Monthly*, (1895).

138c Bolton, Theodore. *American Book Illustrators — Bibliographic Check Lists of 123 Artists.* R. R. Bowker Co,. N.Y., 1938, cloth, 290 pp., introduction, index, lists eight items illus. by D.

139 California Historical Society, San Francisco. *Collections of California Paintings,* April–May 1958, a catalog of the paintings in the Society collection, short bibliography of Dixon, pp. 10–11.

140 Carlson, Ray, ed. *Arizona Highways,* vol. 18, February, 1942, pp. 16–19. Dixon and others on his art.

141 ———. Same, September, 1945, includes "Maynard Dixon — Artist" with eight illus. by D.

142 Cleaveland, Agnes Morley. *No Life for a Lady.* Houghton Mifflin, Boston, 1941, cloth, map endsheets, 356 pp., red top, illus. Much on Dixon in the chapter, "Gene Rhodes," pp. (278)–287. (Borein)

143 Clouse, Margaret. "Corral Dust," a description of the painting and biography of Dixon in *Fifteen and Fifty* (California Paintings at the 1915 Panama-Pacific International Exposition, San Francisco, on its Fiftieth Anniversary), Art Dept., University of California at Davis, 1965.

144 Dixon, Maynard. "Arizona in 1900," an illus. article in *Arizona Highways*, February 1942, an autobiographical account of his early days in Arizona with fourteen illus. by him.

145 ———. "At Last," a poem in *Arizona Quarterly* 1:1, Spring, 1945.

146 Dobie, J. Frank. *The Longhorns.* Boston, 1941, in "Introductory: Makers of History" praises Dixon's longhorn art as "finished, exact and historical."

146a *Dorothea Lange Looks at the American Country Woman.* Ward Ritchie Press, Los Angeles, for the Amon Carter Museum, Ft. Worth, (1967), pic. cloth, blue endsheets, 72 pp., "Foreword" by Beaumont Newhall with mention of her trips in the Southwest with her husband, Maynard Dixon, and several references to her son, Daniel Dixon, illus. with photos by Dorothea Lange.

147 Gordon, Dudley. "Lummis and Maynard Dixon: Patron and Protege," an article in *The Branding Iron*, no. 102, Los Angeles Westerners Corral, includes an interesting exchange of letters between Lummis and Dixon.

147a Hall, Wilbur. "The Art of Maynard Dixon," an article in *Sunset Magazine*, January 1921.

148 Hilton, John W. "He Wanted to Do Honest Painting," an article in *The Desert Magazine*, July 1940, an evaluation of Dixon's painting by artist Hilton and by Dixon.

149 Hinshaw, Merton E. (director). *Painters of the West.* Charles W. Bowers Memorial Museum, Santa Ana, 1972, includes a biographical sketch of D.

150 *Indians at Work,* July–August 1939, Office of Indian Affairs, USDI, an illus. article, "Unusual Indian Murals Completed by Maynard Dixon," with two illus. by D.

151 Lewis, Oscar. *Bay Window Bohemia.* Doubleday, Garden City, N.Y., 1956, words "First Edition" on copyright page, cloth, 248 pp., yellow top, foreword, index, illus. Much on Dixon in text.

152 Lillard, Richard. "Science and Art in the Southwest," an illus. article in *The American West*, July 1972, with one illus. by D.

153 Lummis, Charles F. "A California Illustrator: L. Maynard Dixon and His Work," an illus. article in *The Land of Sunshine* 10:1, Dec. 1898, with ten illus. by D. This issue includes Mary Foote Hallock's story "The Borrowed Shift" with two illus. by D.

154 *The Masterkey,* July 1940, Southwest Museum, Los Angeles, cover illus., "An Indian of Taos Pueblo, New Mexico," by D., a presentation to the Museum by D.

155 Millier, Arthur (introduction by). *Maynard Dixon, Painter of the West.* Privately printed (Taylor and Taylor, San Francisco), Tucson, Arizona, 1945, decor. wraps, pages unnumbered, photo of Dixon as frontis., lists of exhibitions, mural decorations and works in collections, sixteen, eight in color, full-page illus. plus line drawings by D.

156 ———. "Maynard Dixon" on the editor's page of *Touring Topics*, February 1929, cover illus. by D. and a photo of him.

157 Neuhas, Eugen. *The Art of Treasure Island.* University of California Press, Berkeley, 1939, illustrated, description of Dixon's two murals, "Plowed Land" and "Grass Land" and listing under "Biographical Notes."

158 Perceval, Don Louis et al. *Art of Western America.*

Pomona College Art Gallery, Claremont, Calif., Nov. 1–13, 1949, pic. wraps, unpaged, short biographical sketch of D. and lists seven Dixon items in the exhibition.

159 Pielkovo, Ruth. "Dixon, Painter of the West," an illus. article in *International Studio* 78:no. 322, March 1924, with five illus. by D.

160 Renner, Frederic G. (compiled by). *Paper Talk, Illustrated Letters of Charles M. Russell.* The Amon Carter Museum of Western Art, Fort Worth, (1962), pic. boards or wraps, 120 pp., introduction, numerous illus. by Russell; includes reproduction of two letters and a Christmas card from Russell to Dixon. (Borein)

160a Rollin, LaVerne Bradley. "Maynard Dixon Remembered," an article in *Nevada Highways and Parks.*

161 *Review of Art* 1:8, Christmas, 1903, Mark Hopkins Institute, includes "L. Maynard Dixon's Frontier Studies," with four illus. by D.

162 Roorbach, Eloise J. "The Indigenous Art of California," an article in *The Craftsman* 22:5, August 1912, includes a discussion of Dixon's style.

163 *San Francisco* (American Guide Series). Hastings House, N.Y., 1940, words "First Published in 1940" on copyright page, cloth, 531 pp., appendices, index, maps, numerous illustrations, brief paragraph on Dixon's art and other mentions.

164 Semple, Elizabeth Anna. "Successful Californians in New York," an illus. article in *Overland Monthly,* August 1912, includes Dixon in New York and a photo of him.

165 Stenzel, Dr. Franz. *Early Days in the Northwest.* Portland Art Museum, Portland, Oregon, Sept. 23–Oct. 25, 1959, pic. wraps, 38 pp., illus. biographical sketch of D.

166 ———. *A Catalogue of Art of the Oregon Territory.* Museum of Art, University of Oregon, Eugene, 1959, wraps, unpaged, short biographical sketch of D. and describes his painting in the exhibit.

167 Taft, Robert. *The End of the Century.* (Part XIII, The Pictorial Record of the Old West.) Reprinted from the Kansas Historical Quarterly, Topeka, Kansas, August, 1951, wraps, pp. 225–253, illus., photo of Dixon and comments on his work.

168 ———. *Artists and Illustrators of the Old West.* Scribner's, N.Y., London, 1953, code letter "A" on copyright page, decor. cloth, map endsheets, 400 pp., preface and acknowledgments, sources and notes, index, illus., discusses Dixon's art, pp. 240–241 and 376–378.

168a Tolerton, Hill. "The Art of Maynard Dixon," an article in *International Studio,* May 1915.

169. Wallace, Grant. *Maynard Dixon: Painter and Poet of the Far West.* California Art Research Project, WPA Project 2874, San Francisco, 1937, mimeographed.

169a Wilson, Katherine. "The Murals in the State Library," an article in *California Arts and Architecture,* November 1929.

170 Weitenkampf, F. *American Graphic Art.* Holt, New York, 1912, cloth, 372 pp., gilt top, index, illus., mentions Dixon pp. 237 and 327 and praises a Dixon poster, p. 338. (Keller)

171 *Who's Who in California.* Who's Who Pub. Co., San Francisco, 1929, Dixon biography p. 263.

172 *Who's Who in America* (vol. 24). Chicago, 1946–47, biographical sketch.

173 Wysong, Peggy. "The Mystery of the Missing Maynard Dixons, Three Found . . . Where is the Fourth?" an article in *The Arizonian* 17:39, September 25, 1969, with three illus. in color on front cover by D.

AIN'T THEM GOOD ONES? IT'D BE A SHAME TO LET THEM GO SLICK
by DuFault from *The American Cowboy*

JOSEPH ERNEST NEPHTALI DUFAULT (WILL JAMES)
1892–1942

Catalogues of Art Exhibitions and Galleries

FLATHEAD LAKE GALLERIES, BIGFORK, MONTANA

1 *Mostly Montana* — Western Americana List no. 1, February 1968, pic. wraps, unpaged, lists sixteen originals by James and includes five illus. by J. (Russell)

PETERSEN GALLERIES, BEVERLY HILLS, CALIFORNIA

1a *Americana, Western and Sporting Art / Sculpture,* wraps, 25 pp., numerous illus. including one, p. 11, by J. (Johnson, Leigh, Remington, Russell, Wyeth, Zogbaum)

RAINBOW HOTEL, GREAT FALLS, MONTANA
(ADVERTISING CLUB OF GREAT FALLS)

1b *Fourth Annual C. M. Russell Auction of Original Western Art,* March 17, 1972, pic. wraps, unpaged, lists 145 lots, numerous illus. including lot 131, by J. (Dunton, Johnson, Leigh, Remington, Russell)

FRED ROSENSTOCK WITH JAMES PARSONS
(GALLERY WEST), DENVER

2 *100 Years of Western Art,* November 28th through December 24th, 1969, colored pic. wraps, 24 pp., "Introduction" by Parsons, numerous illus. including two, p. 11, by J. (Beeler, Borein, Dunton, Koerner, Leigh)

SOTHEBY PARKE BERNET, NEW YORK

3 *Important 18th, 19th and Early 20th Century American Paintings, Watercolors and Sculpture,* Sale no. 3498, April 11, 1973, colored pic. wraps, unpaged but with over 70 numbered plates including one, no. 43, by J. (Blumenschein, Eggenhofer, Johnson, Leigh, Miller, Remington, Russell, Varian, Wyeth)

Written and Illustrated by the Artist

4 *Cowboys North and South.* Charles Scribner's Sons,

N.Y. and London, 1924, pic. cloth, 217 pp., numerous illus.

5 *The Drifting Cowboy.* Scribner's, N.Y., London, 1925, cloth and boards, 241 pp., numerous illus.

6 *Smoky.* Scribner's, N.Y., London, 1926, cloth, 310 pp., numerous illus.

7 *Smoky.* Gyldendal, Kobenhavn, (Copenhagen, Denmark), 1928. (A Danish translation of no. 6.)

8 *Smoky.* Scribner's, N.Y., (1929), cloth with illus. in color mounted on the front cover, 263 pp., fourteen illus. including six in color. (Illustrated Classics Edition of no. 6.)

9 *Cow Country.* Scribner's, N.Y., London, 1927, decor. cloth, 242 pp., preface, numerous illus.

10 *Sand.* Scribner's, N.Y., London, 1929, pic. cloth, 328 pp., "A First Word," numerous illus.

11 *Sand.* Scribner's, London, 1929, cloth and pic. boards, 328 pp., "A First Word" numerous illus. (First British edition of no. 10.)

12 *Lone Cowboy.* Scribner's, N.Y., London, 1930, words "Published August, 1930" and code letter "A" on copyright page, two-tone cloth with leather title label, 431 (2) pp., frontis. photo of the author and numerous illus., boxed. Limited to 250 copies, each with an original drawing by the author.

13 *Lone Cowboy.* Scribner's, N.Y., 1930, code letter "A" on copyright page, cloth, 431 pp., numerous illus. (The trade edition of no. 12.)

14 *Lone Cowboy, My Life Story.* Scribner's, London, 1930, code letter "A" on copyright page, blue cloth, 421 (2) pp., numerous illus. (First British edition of no. 12.)

15 *Lone Cowboy.* Scribner's, N.Y., 1932, cloth with illus. in color mounted on the front cover, 431 pp.,

numerous illus. including seven in color. (Illustrated Classics Edition of no. 12.)

16 *Big Enough*. Scribner's, N.Y., London, 1931, code letter "A" on copyright page, decor. cloth, 314 pp., numerous illus.

17 *Sun Up: Tales of the Cow Camps*. Scribner's, N.Y., and London, 1931, code letter "A" on copyright page, cloth, 342 pp., numerous illus. (The Junior Literary Guild edition also was issued in 1931.)

18 *Uncle Bill*. Scribner's, N.Y., London, 1932, code letter "A" on copyright page, cloth, 240 (1) pp., numerous illus.

19 *Uncle Bill*. Scribner's, London, 1933, code letter "A" on copyright page, pic. cloth, 240 (1) pp., preface, numerous illus. (First British edition of no. 18.)

20 *Cowboy*. Gyldendal, Kobenhavn, (Denmark), 1932, pic. wraps, 399 (3) pp., numerous illus. (A Danish translation of no. 12 by H. Marks Jorgensen.)

21 *All in a Day's Riding*. Scribner's, N.Y., London, 1933, code letter "A" on copyright page, cloth, 251 pp., numerous illus.

22 *The Three Mustangeers*. Scribner's, N.Y., London, 1933, code letter "A" on copyright page, cloth, 338 pp., numerous illus.

23 *In the Saddle with Uncle Bill*. Scribner's, N.Y., London, 1935, code letter "A" on copyright page, cloth, 289 (1) pp., yellow top, preface, numerous illus.

24 *Young Cowboy*. Scribner's, N.Y., 1935, code letter "A" on copyright page, cloth, 72 pp., illus. including color plates. (Arranged from nos. 11 and 12.)

25 *Home Ranch*. Scribner's, N.Y., 1935, code letter "A" on copyright page, cloth, 346 pp., tinted top, preface, numerous illus.

26 *Home Ranch*. Bantam Books, N.Y., (1946), words "Bantam Edition Published August, 1946" on copyright page, colored pic. wraps, and endsheets, 279 pp., all edges red, numerous illus. (Bantam Book 47.)

27 *Scorpion*. Scribner's, N.Y., 1936, code letter "A" on copyright page, cloth, 312 pp., numerous illus.

28 *Cowboy in the Making*. Scribner's, N.Y., 1937, code letter "A" on copyright page, pic. cloth, 91 pp., numerous illus. including four in color, frontis. and facing pp. 10, 16 and 46.

29 *Flint Spears*. Scribner's, N.Y., 1938, cloth, 269 pp., numerous illus. (This compiler has, in his copy of this book, a letter from the publisher stating that, in error, the code letter "A" was omitted from the copyright page of the first printing.)

30 *Look-See with Uncle Bill*. Scribner's, N.Y., 1938, code letter "A" on copyright page, 253 pp., numerous illus.

31 *The Will James Cowboy Book*. Scribner's, N.Y. etc., (1938), code letter "A" on copyright page, pic. cloth, yellow pic. endsheets with a letter from Will James inside the front cover and "About Will James" on the back fly, 158 (2) pp., edited by Alice Dalgliesh, numerous illus. including a frontis. in color.

32 *The Dark Horse*. Scribner's, N.Y., 1939, code letter "A" on copyright page, cloth, 280 (1) pp., tinted top, numerous illus. including a frontis. in color.

33 *Horses I've Known*. Scribner's, N.Y., 1940, code letter "A" on copyright page, cloth, 280 (1) pp., tinted top, numerous illus. including a frontis. in color.

34 *My First Horse*. Scribner's, N.Y., 1940, code letter "A" on copyright page, cloth, pages unnumbered, numerous illus.

35 *The American Cowboy*. Scribner's, N.Y., 1942, code letter "A" on copyright page, cloth, 273 pp., numerous illus.

36 *Will James' Book of Cowboy Stories*. Scribner's, N.Y., 1951, code letter "A" on copyright page, pic. cloth, 242 pp., "Will James" by Ross Santee, numerous illus.

37 Same, British edition issued by Phoenix House, London, with words "First Published 1952" on copyright page, cloth, 242 (1) pp., "Will James" by Ross Santee, numerous illus.

Illustrated by the Artist

38 Aakpaer, Jeppe et al., *Juleroser, 1929*. Gyldendalske Boghandel, Nordisk Forlag, Kobenhavn, colored pic. wraps, unpaged, illus., includes "Den Sorte" by James (translated into Danish by H. Marks-Jorgensen), with seventeen drawings by J.

39 Ainsworth, Ed. *The Cowboy in Art*. World, N.Y. and Cleveland, (1968), words "First Printing 1968" on copyright page, full leather, orange endsheets, 242 pp., all edges gilt, "Foreword" by John Wayne, index, numerous illus. including three, pp. 76 (two) and 77, by J., includes a chapter, "Will James, the Lone Cowboy" with two photos of him. Special edition of 1000 copies, slipcase. (Beeler, Borein, Bugbee, De Yong, Dixon, Dunton, Eggenhofer, Ellsworth,

Hurd, Johnson, Koerner, Mora, Perceval, Remington, Russell, Santee, Schreyvogel, Von Schmidt)

40 ———. Same, first trade edition in gilt letter and illus. cloth, orange endsheets.

41 ———. Same, reprint by Bonanza Books, N.Y. in red lettered and illus. cloth, white endsheets.

42 Amaral, Anthony. *Will James, the Gilt Edged Cowboy.* Westernlore, Los Angeles, 1967, cloth, 206 pp., introduction, bibliography, index, numerous illus. by and of J.

42a Baird, Joseph A., Jr. (compiled by). *The West Remembered.* California Historical Society, San Francisco and San Marino, 1973, colored pic. wraps, 88 pp., "Foreword" by Mitchell A. Wilder, introduction, numerous illus. including one, p. 63, by J. (Blumenschein, Borein, Dixon, Lungren, Marchand, Miller, Remington, Russell, Zogbaum)

43 Barton, Fred. *Charles M. Russell,* (An old-time cow-cowman discusses the Life of Charles M. Russell) privately printed, (Los Angeles, 1961), pic. wraps, 15 (1) pp., 26 illus. including three, pp. (2), 9 and 12, by J. (Russell)

44 Branch, Douglas. *The Cowboy and His Interpreters.* D. Appleton and Co., N.Y., London, 1926, code number "(1)" on last page of text, decor. cloth, pic. endsheets, 277 (2) pp., bibliography, twenty-two illus. including one, the frontis. by J. A new edition with an introduction by Harry Sinclair Drago was issued in 1961 by the Cooper Square Publishers of New York — the frontis. by James is retained. (Russell)

44a Bratcher, James T. *Analytical Index to Publications of the Texas Folklore Society.* SMU Press, Dallas, 1973, two-tone decor. cloth, pic. map endsheets, 322 pp., "Foreword" by Wilson M. Hudson, preface, "Historical Note on The Texas Folklore Society" by Francis Edward Abernethy, numerous illus. including one, p. 46, by J. (Cisneros, Leigh, Mead)

45 Briggs, Thomas H. et al. *American Literature.* Houghton Mifflin, Boston etc., 1940, pic. cloth with title label, 748 pp., index, illus. including one, p. (403), by J. (Remington)

46 Burns, Walter Noble. *Tombstone.* Doubleday, Doran & Co., Garden City, N.Y., 1929, cloth, pic. endsheets, 388 pp., sources, illus., drawing on title page and six double-page drawings, each preceded by an illus. title sheet, following pp. 8, 36, 80, 220, 248 and 340, by J.

47 *Chicago Rodeo,* November 16-24, 1929, colored pic. wraps, (48) pp., "Western Writers Praise Rodeo" by Ross Santee, Owen P. White et al., numerous illus. including one, p. (23), by J.

48 Clark, Kenneth S., ed. *Cowboy Sings.* Pioneer Music Corp., N.Y., 1932, pic. wraps, 96 pp., foreword, short statement by James, two illus. including one, verso of the title page, by J.

49 ———. *Buckaroo Ballads.* Paull-Pioneer Music Corp., N.Y., 1940, pic. wraps, 64 pp., numerous illus. including one, p. 64, by J.

50 (Coburn.) *Walt Coburn's Action Novels.* Fiction House, N.Y., (1931), colored pic. wraps, 160 pp., illus. including four, pp. (1), 3, 78 and 79, by J. (De Yong)

51 Coolidge, Dane. *Lorenzo the Magnificent.* Dutton, N.Y., (1925), cloth, 320 pp., d/w illus. in color by J.

52 Cooper, J. Fenimore. *Last of the Mohicans.* Burt, N.Y., Chicago, n.d., cloth, pic. endsheets by James, 412 pp., frontis.

53 Cross, T. P. et al. *Adventure.* Ginn & Co., N.Y. etc., pic. cloth and endsheets, 589 pp., "Dictionary of Names and Phrases," index, numerous illus. including two, pp. 29 and 253, by J. Also contains "Broncho Busting" by James, pp. 251-56 and a short sketch about him, p. 575. (Fischer)

54 Dobie, J. Frank, ed. *Man, Bird, and Beast.* Texas Folk-Lore Society, Austin. 1930, cloth, green endsheets, 185 pp., "Just a Word," proceedings, index, two illus., pp. (9) and 73, by J. (Publication VIII.)

55 ——— et al. *Mustangs and Cowhorses.* Texas Folk-Lore Society, Austin, 1946, fabricoid, pic. endsheets, 429 pp., introduction, contributors, index, numerous illus. including four, pp. (151), 158, 292 and 418, by J. (Publication XVI.) (Bugbee, Lea, Leigh, Russell, Santee, Thomason)

56 ———. *Pitching Horses and Panthers.* Reprinted from no. 55, Austin, Texas, 1940, wraps, 15 pp., one illus., p. 4, by J.

57 ———. *Guide to Life and Literature of the Southwest.* University of Texas Press, Austin, 1943, wraps, 111 pp., "A Declaration," twenty-four illus. including one, p. 94, by J. In the chapter on "Cowboys and Range Life" J. Frank Dobie says, "Will James knew his frijoles, but overboiled them before he died, in 1942." ((Borein, Bugbee, Dunton, Hurd, Lea, Leigh, Russell, Santee, Thomason)

58 Gambrell, Herbert and Virginia. *A Pictorial History of Texas*. Dutton, N.Y., (1960), words "First Edition" on copyright page, cloth and decor. boards, brand illus. endsheets, 217 pp., sources of illustrations, index, numerous illus. including one, p. 187, by J. (Lea, Remington, Schiwetz)

59 Good, Donnie D. *The Longhorn*. Thomas Gilcrease Institute, Tulsa, 1970, wraps, (20) pp., numerous illus. including one, by J. (Borein, Remington)

60 ———. *Mustangs*. Thomas Gilcrease Institute, Tulsa, 1971, wraps, unpaged, numerous illus. including two by J. (Borein, Miller)

61 Gordy, Wilbur Fisk. *Leaders in Making America*. Scribner's, N.Y. etc., 1923, decor. cloth, 478 pp., "To American Boys and Girls," index, maps, numerous illus. including two, pp. 365 and 381, by J.

62 ———. *Stories of Later American History*. Scribner's, N.Y. etc., (1930), pic. cloth, 392 pp., preface, index, illus. including one, p. 292, by J.

63 Greenburg, Dan W. *Sixty Years*. Wyoming Stock Growers Assn. (Pioneer Capitol, Cheyenne, Wyoming, 1932), pic. wraps, 73 pp., "Foreword" by President J. Elmer Brock, preface, illus., James illus. on front cover.

64 *Hamley's Cowboy Catalog, No. 53*. Hamley & Co., Pendleton, Oregon, 1953, colored pic. wraps, 144 pp., "To our Friends and Customers" by L. B. Hamley, index. numerous illus. including four reproductions of James drawings. (Russell, Santee)

65 Harris, Burton et al. *Yellowstone Country*. Gilcrease Institute, Tulsa, 1963, colored pic. wraps, 57 (1) pp., numerous illus. including one, p. (39), by J. (Goodwin, Leigh, Russell)

65a Johnson, Paul C., ed. *The Early Sunset Magazine 1898–1928*. California Historical Society, San Francisco and San Marino, (1973), words "First printing, October 1973" on copyright page, colored pic. wraps, 239 (1) pp., "Preface" by Proctor Mellquist, introduction, notes on contributors, numerous illus. including two, half title and p. (189), by J. (Dixon)

66 Johnston, Harry V. *My Home on the Range*. The Webb Publishing Co., Saint Paul, (1942), decor. cloth, 313 pp., illus. including one, p. 192, by J. (Koerner, Remington)

67 Latendorf, E. Walter. *Frederic Remington, Catalogue No. 17*. Mannados Bookshop, N.Y., (1947), pic. wraps, 72 pp., "An Appreciation" by Harold McCracken, numerous illus. including one, p. 57, by J. (Remington)

68 ———. *Catalogue No. 26*. Mannados Bookshop, N.Y., (1956), pic. wraps, 22 pp., "Fur Trapping in Canada," eight illus. including one, front cover, by J. (Eggenhofer, Schoonover)

69 Linford, Velma. *Wyoming, Frontier State*. Old West Pub. Co., Colorado, 1947, cloth, pic. endsheets, 428 pp., acknowledgments, appendix, bibliography, index, numerous illus. including one, p. 236, by J., maps. (Russell)

70 Lipsey, John J., ed. *The 1962 Brand Book* (18th Annual Volume), Denver Posse of The Westerners, Denver, Colorado, 1963, cloth, 397 pp., introduction, acknowledgments, index, numerous illus. including one, p. 298, by J. (Edition consists of 650 numbered copies in three separate issues.)

71 Logan, Harlan (editor-publisher). *Fiftieth Anniversary, Scribner's Magazine*. Scribner's, N.Y., January, 1937, decor. wraps, 144 pp., numerous illus. including one, p. (66), by J. (Dunn, Remington, Thomason)

72 Macauley, Thurston, ed. *The Great Horse Omnibus: from Homer to Hemingway*. Ziff-Davis Pub. Co., Chicago, N.Y., 1949, cloth, 462 pp., "Introduction" by Bing Crosby, foreword, appendix, acknowledgments, illus. including one, facing p. 320, by J., one James story "Smoky and Old Tom."

73 McCarthy, Don, ed. *Language of the Mosshorn*. (The Gazette Printing, Billings, Montana, 1936), words "First Printing" on page facing the title page, pic. wraps, (20) pp., foreword, numerous illus. including two by J.

74 ———. *Afternoons in Montana*. North Plains Press, Aberdeen, S. D., 1971, fabricoid, 124 pp., foreword, "Language of the Mosshorn," index, illus. including two, p. (4), by J., includes a chapter on James, "Coyotes and Wild Women."

75 McDowell, Bart. *The American Cowboy in Life and Legend*. National Geographic Society, Washington, D.C., (1972), pic. cloth, pic. endsheets, 211 pp., (1) of advs., "Foreword" by Joe B. Frantz, index, additional reading, numerous illus. including one, p. 172, by J. plus a photo of him. (De Yong, Dunton, Goodwin, Remington, Russell)

76 Mills, Enos A. *Watched by Wild Animals*. Doubleday, Page & Co., Garden City, N.Y., and Toronto, 1922, words "First Edition" on copyright page,

cloth, 243 pp., preface, illus. with photos and with four drawings, facing pp. 69, 85, 117 and 197 by J.

77 ———. *Wild Animal Homesteads*. Doubleday, Page, Garden City, N.Y., 1923, words "First Edition" on copyright page, decor. cloth, 259 pp., preface, illus. with photos and with two drawings, frontis. and facing p. 20, by J., issued the same year in London by Eveleigh Nash and Grayson.

78 Montgomery, Vaida Stewart. *Locoed and Other Poems*. The Kaleidoscope Press, Dallas, 1930, pic. two-tone cloth, black endsheets, 59 pp., acknowledgments, three drawings, pp. 2 and 3 (two), by J., drawing on p. 2 also used as front cover illus. and the two drawings from p. 3 repeated on pp. 4 and 5.

79 *Parker County Frontier Days* (Rodeo Livestock Show). Parker County Sheriff's Posse, Weatherford, Texas, July 27-30, 1960, colored pic. wraps, 52 pp., numerous illus. including one, the front cover, by J.

80 Pitz, Henry C., ed. *A Treasury of American Book Illustrations*. American Studio Books and Watson Guptill Publications, N.Y. and London, (1947), decor. cloth, 128 pp., acknowledgments, "The Artists Included in the Book," illus. including one drawing, p. 38, by J. (Remington, Thomason)

81 Porter, Fred, Sr. *Porter's Cowboy Catalog Number 31*. N. Porter Co., Phoenix, Ariz., September 1940, pic. wraps, 104 pp., numerous illus. with most of p. 59 devoted to James' books, photos of six illus., dust wrappers and drawings of six others. (Russell)

82 ———. *Porter's Catalog No. 36*. N. Porter Co., (Prepared by The Cushing Co.), Phoenix, Arizona, (1952), colored pic. wraps, 112 pp., numerous illus. including photos of four James books with illus. dust jackets, p. 93. (Russell)

83 Reed, Walt. *The Illustrator in America 1900-1960's*. Reinhold, N.Y., (1966), cloth, pic. green endsheets, 271 (1) pp., "Is Illustration Art?" by Albert Dorne, bibliography, numerous illus. including two, p. 144, by J. (Blumenschein, Crawford, Dunn, Dunton, Eggenhofer, Fischer, Fogarty, Goodwin, Keller, Koerner, Remington, Russell, Schoonover, Stoops, Wyeth)

84 ———. *Harold Von Schmidt Draws and Paints the Old West*. Northland Press, Flagstaff, (1972), words "First Edition" on copyright page, morocco and pic. cloth, slate endsheets, 230 pp., "Foreword" by Dean Krakel, "Introduction" by Harold McCracken, bibliography, numerous illus. by Von Schmidt but with one, p. 31, by J., a photo of him and comments in

the text. One of 104 numbered copies signed by Reed and Von Schmidt, slipcase with morocco title label, issued jointly with Von Schmidt's first sculpture, "The Startled Grizzly." (Dixon, Dunn, Russell)

85 ———. Same, first trade edition in pic. cloth.

86 Riegel, Robert E. and Hough, Helen. *United States of America*. Scribner's, New York etc., (1949), code letter "A" on copyright page, buckram, 852 pp., preface, index, numerous illus. including three, all on p. 458, by J. (Leigh, Rowe)

87 Ringel, Fred J., ed. *America as Americans See It*. Harcourt, Brace and Co., N.Y., (1932), words "First Edition" on copyright page, cloth, 365 pp., blue top, foreword, illus. including two drawings, pp. 61 and 63, by J. Comments on James' work by Henry Hart and one James story, "Cowboy and Dude Ranches," pp. 61-65. The Literary Guild Edition issued the same year also has the words "First Edition" on the copyright page.

88 Rollins, Philip A. *Jingle Bob*. Scribner's, N.Y., London, 1927, cloth, pic. endsheets, 262 (1) pp., preface, illus. The endsheet illus. are by J. (De Yong)

89 ———. *The Cowboy*. Scribner's, N.Y., 1936, words, "3rd Completely Revised Edition, including revision of illus., published April, 1936" on copyright page, cloth, pic. endsheets, 402 pp., prefaces, appendix index, numerous illus. including one, facing p. 266, by J.

90 Romer, Frank. *The Stetson Hat in Literature*. Stetson Co. (Stetson Press), Philadelphia, 1925, pic. wraps, 32 pp., preface, numerous illus. including one, p. (4), by J. James' work discussed in text, pp. 23-24.

91 Rossi, Paul A. and Hunt, David C. *The Art of the Old West* (from the Collection of the Gilcrease Institute). (Knopf, N.Y., but printed in Italy, 1971), words "First Edition" on copyright page, pic. cloth, pic. brown endsheets, 335 (1) pp., preface, listing of artists and works, bibliography, numerous illus. including one, p. 129, by J. (Blumenschein, Borein, Leigh, Miller, Remington, Russell, Schreyvogel, Wyeth)

92 Simon, Howard. *500 Years of Art and Illustration*, World, Cleveland, (1942), words "First Published August 1942" on copyright page, cloth, 476 pp., brown top, numerous illus. including two, drawings, p. 443, by J. (Remington)

93 Thorp, Jack, as told to Neil McCullough Clark. *Pardner of the Wind*. The Caxton Printers, Cald-

well, Idaho, 1945, cloth, 309 pp., appendices, index, illus. including one drawing, p. 33, by J.

93a Weaver, Paul E. *Autumn 1973 Book List*. Northland Press, Flagstaff, colored pic. wraps, unpaged, numerous illus. including one by J. (Beeler, Blumenschein, Dixon, Perceval, Remington, Santee, Von Schmidt)

94 *World Series Rodeo, Fifth Annual*. Madison Square Garden, N.Y., October 23–November 1, 1930, colored pic. wraps, 56 pp., numerous illus. including two drawings pp. 34 and 35, by J. plus a portrait of him and a short article, "Will James A Cowboy Who 'Couldn't be Throwed.' "

95 Same, *Sixth Annual*, October 17-31, 1931, colored pic. wraps, 56 pp., numerous illus. including two, pp. 8 and 53, by J.

96 Same, *Seventh Annual*, October 14-30, 1932, colored pic. wraps, 48 pp., numerous illus. including one, p. 18, by J. (Crawford, Santee)

97 Same, *Eighth Annual*, October 11-29, 1933, colored pic. wraps, 48 pp., includes "A Rodeo Message from Will James" with three drawings by him. (Santee)

98 Same, *11th Annual*, October 7-25, 1936, colored pic. wraps, 48 pp., numerous illus. including one, p. 30, by J. (Santee)

Written by the Artist

99 Abell, Elizabeth (selected by). *Westward, Westward, Westward*. Franklin Watts, N.Y., (1958), words "First Printing" on copyright page, decor. cloth, orange top, tinted endsheets, 234 pp., acknowledgments, illus. Includes one story, "Going it Alone" from *Lone Cowboy*.

100 Adams, Ramon F. *Western Words, A Dictionary of the Range, Cow Camp and Trail*. University of Oklahoma Press, 1944, words "First Edition" on copyright page, cloth, 182 pp., introduction, "In Appreciation." James quoted pp. 12, 20, 56, 59, 152, 155 and 176.

101 Arbuthnot, May Hill. *Arbuthnot Anthology of Children's Literature*. Scott, N.Y., 1953, includes "Smoky, Range Colt" by J.

102 ———. *Time for True Tales and Almost True*. Scott, N.Y., 1953, includes "Smoky, Range Colt" by J.

103 Braun, P. C., ed. *The Big Book of Favorite Horse Stories*. Platt & Munk, N.Y., (1965), two-tone pic. cloth, 336 pp., "Foreword" and illus. by Sam Savitt, index, includes "The Seeing Eye" by J.

104 Bright, Frank W., ed. and W. W. Wood (general editor). *Looking Ahead* (Reading for Life Series). Lippincott, (1953), cloth, 509 pp., illus., includes "The Squeak of Leather" by J.

105 Brown, Beth, ed. *All Horses go to Heaven*. Grosset & Dunlap, N.Y., 1963, includes "Seeing Eye" by J.

106 Cavanah, Frances and Weir, Ruth Cramer, (collected by). *24 Horses*. Rand McNally & Co., Chicago etc., (1950), words "Edition of 1950" and code letter "A" on copyright page, pic. cloth, 256 pp., acknowledgments, introduction, about the author, illus., includes "Good-by Smoky" from *Smoky*.

107 Clarke, Frances E. (compiled by). *Gallant Horses*. The Macmillan Co., N.Y., 1938, words "Published October, 1938" on copyright page, cloth, 348 pp., brown top, acknowledgments, includes one James story, "The Last Catch at Sand Wash."

108 Coleman, Rufus A., ed. *Western Prose & Poetry*. Harper & Bros., N.Y. and London, 1932, words "First Edition" and code letters "M-F" on copyright page, cloth, 502 pp., notes on the artists, "To the Reader," acknowledgments, appendix, illus. includes "The Last Catch" from *Cow Country*. (Remington, Russell)

109 Cooper, Page, ed. *Great Horse Stories*. Doubleday, Garden City, 1954, includes "Seeing Eye" by J.

110 ———. Same, Berkley, N.Y., 1959, paperback edition.

111 Dennis, Wesley (edited and illustrated by). *Palomino and Other Horses*. World Publishing Co., Cleveland and N.Y., (1950), code number "WPC 7-50" on copyright page, pic. cloth, 249 pp., brown top, introduction, includes "Chapo — the Faker" from *Horses I Have Known*.

112 Fenner, Phyllis R. (selected by). *Horses, Horses, Horses*. Franklin Watts, N.Y., (1949), cloth, pic. endsheets, 285 pp., brown top, acknowledgments, illus., includes "The Squeak of Leather."

113 ———. *Cowboys, Cowboys, Cowboys*. Franklin Watts, N.Y., (1950), decor. cloth, pic. endsheets, 287 pp., orange top, acknowledgments, "Howdy, Stranger" by J.

114 Fielding, Loraine Hornaday. *French Heels to Spurs*. Century Co., N.Y., London, (1930), words "First Edition" on copyright page, two-tone pic. cloth, 203 pp., illus., "Introduction" by J.

115 Gruenberg, Sidonie. *Favorite Stories Old and New.* Doubleday, Garden City, 1955, includes "His First Bronc" by J.

116 Harper, Wilhelmina (selected by). *Flying Hoofs, Stories of Horses.* Houghton, Mifflin Co., Boston, 1939, pic. cloth, 292 pp., foreword, acknowledgments, illus. including three in color, includes "Smoky and the Wolves" from *Smoky.*

117 Hogeboom, Amy (compiled by). *The Boy's Book of the West.* Lothrop, Lee and Shepard Co., N.Y., (1946), pic. cloth, 419 pp., acknowledgments, illus., one James story.

118 Howard, Joseph Kinsey, ed. *Montana Margins.* Yale University Press, New Haven, 1946, cloth, 527 pp., introduction, chronological table, index of authors, includes "I Learned to Ride" from *Lone Cowboy* and "The Starting of Smoky" from *Smoky.* Brief biographical sketch of James, p. 305.

119 Kelley, Robert F., ed. *Junior Sports Anthology.* Howell Soskin, N.Y., 1945, includes "Tom and Jerry" by J.

120 Margulies, Leo, ed. *Selected Western Stories.* Popular Library, N.Y., (1949), colored pic. wraps, all edges green, green endsheets, 192 pp., foreword, includes one James story, "On the Dodge."

121 Matthews, Sallie Reynolds. *Interwoven.* The Anson Jones Press, Houston, Texas, 1936, cloth, brown top, 234 pp., foreword, addenda, includes "A Letter of Introduction" by J.

122 Patten, Will, ed. *The Animal Book* (Junior Classics vol. 7), Collier, N.Y., 1938, includes "A Cowboy and His Pony" by J.

123 Payne, William Howard and Lyons, Jake G. *Folks Say of Will Rogers.* G. P. Putnam's Sons, N.Y., (1936), cloth, green top, 224 pp., preface, "Foreword" by Sallie Rogers McSpadden, frontis., James quoted pp. 199-202.

124 Rice, Grantland and Powell, Harford, eds. *The Omnibus of Sports.* Harper, N.Y., 1950, includes "Bucking Horses and Riders," by J.

125 Self, Margaret (selected and edited by). *A Treasury of Horse Stories.* A. S. Barnes & Co., N.Y., (1945), words "First Printing, September 1945" on copyright page, decor. cloth, tinted top, 368 pp., preface, acknowledgments, indices., one James story.

126 ————. *A World of Horses.* McGraw-Hill, N.Y. etc., (1961), words "First Edition" on copyright page, two-tone cloth, tinted endsheets, 384 (1) pp., acknowledgments, preface, illus., one James story.

127 Seton, Ernest Thompson et al. *Famous Animal Stories.* Coward McCann, N.Y., 1932, includes "Smoky" by J.

128 Targ, William, ed. *The American West.* World Pub. Co., Cleveland and N.Y., (1946), words, "First Published April 1946" on copyright page, pic. cloth, 595 pp., introduction, "A Glossary of Western Words," acknowledgments, includes "Riding Bog" from *Home Ranch.*

129 ————. *Great Western Stories.* Penquin Books, N.Y., (1947), words "First Penguin Books Edition" on copyright page, colored pic. wraps, 183 pp., "About This Book," introduction, includes one James story, "The Seeing Eye."

The Artist and His Art

130 Amaral, Anthony. "Will James and the Horse Called Happy," an article in *Western Horseman,* May 1964.

131 ————. "Will James in Nevada," an illus. article in *Nevada* 26:1, Spring 1966, with eight (five in color) illus. by J. and with photos of him.

132 ————. "Will James, 1892-1942," a dedication in *Arizona and the West,* Autumn 1968.

133 ————. "How Will James got his Start," an illus. article in *Frontier Times* 40:4, June–July 1966, with five illus. by J. and a photo of him.

134 Arbuthnot, May Hill. *Children and Books.* Scott, Foresman, Chicago etc., (1947), cloth, 626 pp., bibliography, index, numerous illus., includes praise of *Smoky* by James, pp. 437-8. (Smith, Wyeth)

135 Bell, William Gardner. "Will James," an article in *Corral Dust,* Potomac Corral, The Westerners, Washington, D.C., Winter 1967, one illus. by J. and a photo of him. .

136 Bennett, Russell H. *The Compleat Rancher.* Rinehart & Co., N.Y., Toronto, (1946), publisher's device on copyright page, cloth, 246 pp., introduction, James, pp. 152-3. (Santee)

137 Bennett, Whitman. *A Practical Guide to American Book Collecting.* Bennett Book Studios, N.Y., (1941), cloth, 254 pp., introduction, index, *Smoky* by James included p. 227.

138 Blanck, Jacob. *Peter Parley to Penrod.* Bowker, N.Y., 1938, cloth, 153 pp., preface, index. Edition limited

to 500 copies. Bibliographical description of *Smoky*, p. 142.

139 Bolton, Theodore. *American Book Illustrators.* R. R. Bowker Co., N.Y., 1938, cloth, 290 pp., introduction, index, James list, pp. 84–86, fourteen items written and illustrated by James and Brand (*sic*), no. 44 this list.

140 Burlingame, Roger. *Of Making Many Books.* Scribner's, N.Y., 1946, code letter "A" on copyright page, cloth, orange top, 347 pp., publisher's note, preface, index, James pp. 105, 139 and 235.

141 Clemo, Margaret E. et al. *The Arch of Experience.* Little Brown, Boston, 1936, decor. cloth, 408 pp., index, illus., lists four books by J., p. 387.

142 Coleman, Dr. Rufus A. (general editor). *Northwest Books.* Binfords and Mort, Portland, Oregon, 1942, cloth, 356 pp., "In Explanation," notes, index, James list pp. 122–27.

143 Corley, George. "Will James as I Knew Him," an article in *Rocky Mountain Empire* Magazine, Jan. 5, 1947.

144 Cormack, Robert B. "A Cowboy for Fifty Years," an article in *Roundup*, Denver Westerners, 1962, one illus. by J. and a photo of him.

145 Crump, Irving. *The Boys' Book of Cowboys.* Dodd Mead, N.Y., 1934, cloth, 232 pp., James mentioned in the "Introduction" by Remington Schuyler.

146 Dykes, Jeff C. *High Spots of Western Illustrating.* The Kansas City Posse, The Westerners, 1954, wraps., 32 pp., High Spot no. 48 is *Cow Country* (no. 6). Also a numbered, signed edition of 250 copies in cloth.

147 Fawcett, Capt. W. H., ed. "A Cowboy in Action," a drawing by James in *Triple X Western*, September 1932, with brief comments by the editor.

148 Flack, M. "Will James at Home," an article in *Wilson Bulletin*, March 38.

149 Frank, Josette. *What Books for Children?* Doubleday, Doran, Garden City, N.Y., 1937, words "First Edition" on copyright page, cloth, blue top, 363 pp., "Introduction" by Sidonia Matsner Gruenberg, book lists, index, James pp. 238–9, 265–6 and 278.

150 *The Gund Collection of Western Art* (a personal narrative). The George Gund Museum of Western Art, (N.Y.), 1970, pic. wraps, 38 pp., biographical sketch of J. and a photo of him, pp. (34) and 35 (Johnson, Leigh, Remington, Russell, Schreyvogel)

151 Same, (A History and Pictorial Description of the American West), (N.Y.), 1973, pic. wraps, 62 pp., biographical sketch of J. and a photo of him, pp. 44 and 45. (Johnson, Leigh, Miller, Remington, Russell, Schreyvogel)

152 Holden, W. C. *Rollie Burns.* The Southwest Press, Dallas, Texas, (1932), pic. cloth, 243 pp., preface, index. Burns differs with James on breaking horses, p. 228.

153 Horan, Jack. *Burnt Leather.* Christopher Publishing House, Boston, (1937), cloth, 105 pp., illus., one poem "To Lone Cowboy" about J.

154 Hubbell, Jay B., ed. *Southwest Review*, vol. 10, no. 4, July, 1925, includes "Filling in the Cracks" with four illus. by J.

155 James, Will. "Winter Months in a Cow Camp," an illus. article in *Scribner's Magazine* 75:2, February 1924, with six illus. by J.

156 "Will James — A Young Old-Timer," an article in *The Rider and Driver*, Feb. 6, 1926.

157 Kerlan, Irwin. *Newbery and Caldecott Awards.* University of Minnesota Press, Minneapolis, (1949), cloth and decor. boards, 51 pp., "Foreword" by Frederic G. Melcher, preface, frontis., includes *Smoky*, the 1926 Newbery Medal winner.

158 Krakel, Dean and Hedgpeth, Don. "Short Grass, Stetsons, and Paint Brushes: A Survey of Cowboy Art," an illus. article in *Persimmon Hill* 1:4, Summer 1971, with one illus. by J.

159 Kunitz, Stanley J. and Haycraft, Howard. *The Junior Book of Authors.* H. W. Wilson Co., N.Y., 1934, pic. cloth, 400 (32) pp., "Introduction" by Effie L. Power, preface, index, illus., James autobiographical sketch, pp. 202–4 and photo of J., p. 203.

160 (Lecky, Peter.) *Peter Lecky by Himself.* Scribner's, N.Y., 1936, code letter "A" on copyright page, cloth, tinted top, 349 pp., apologia, tribute to James, p. 69.

161 McClay, Harriet L. and Judson, Helen. *Story Biographies.* Henry Holt & Co., N.Y., 1936, words "January 1936" on copyright page, decor. cloth, 695 pp., preface, illus., "Lone Cowboy" by J., pp. 151–63.

162 Mahoney, Bertha E. et al. *Illustrators of Children's Books, 1744–1945.* The Horn Book, Boston, 1947, cloth and pic. boards, gilt top, 527 pp., preface, introduction, bibliographies, appendix, index, numerous illus., James list p. 417. (Smith)

163 Merriam, Harold G., ed. *The Frontier*, vol. 10, no. 1,

November, 1929. Includes a review of *Sand* (no. 7) plus one drawing by J.

164 Montague, Doris. "Bucked and Battered to Fame," an illus. article in *American Magazine,* May 1931, one illus. by J. and a photo of him.

165 Olson, Nancy M. "Another Look at Will James," an illus. article in *Montana Arts* 21:3, February–March, 1969, with one photo of a group including J.

166 Perkins, Maxwell E. *Editor to Author.* Scribner's, N.Y., London, 1950, cloth, 315 pp., editor's note, "Introduction" by John Hall Wheelock, index, photo of Perkins as frontis., the Scribner editor to J.

167 Russell, Charles M. *Good Medicine.* Doubleday, Doran, Garden City, N.Y., 1929, leather, 162 pp., numerous illus. by the author. Ltd. to 134 numbered copies. Reproduces two letters from Russell to J.

168 ———. The trade edition of no. 167, 1930, words "First Edition after the printing of 134 De Luxe Copies" on copyright page, decor. cloth.

169 Scully, Frank. *Rogues Gallery.* Murray & Gee, Hollywood, 1943, cloth, 276 pp., preface, includes a chapter on James, pp. 162–78.

170 "Smoky, John Newbery Prize Book," an article in *National Education Association Journal,* Oct. 1927.

171 "Spirit of Will James," an article in *Western Livestock Journal,* February 15, 1943.

172 Wenger, Martin, "Will James . . . Pen and Brush Sketches of the Cowboy and His Horse," an article in *The American Scene* 2:2 , Summer 1959, with one illus. by J. Another J. drawing is used to illustrate "The Art of the Cowboy" by Charles C. Proctor in the same issue.

173 Westermeier, Clifford P. *Man, Beast, Dust.* (World Press, Denver, 1947), decor. cloth, decor. endsheets, 450 pp., bibliography, index, lists a number of books and articles by J. in the bibliography.

174 *Western Horseman.* September, 1952, includes a story about J. plus two small drawings by J.

175 Willard, John, ed. *Hoofprints* 2:3, Yellowstone Corral of the Westerners, Billings, Autumn–Winter 1972, "Will James Issue" with articles by Mrs. Eleanora Snook, Don McCarthy and the editor and with fifteen illus. by J. and several photos of him.

ILLUSTRATION by DuFault from *Lone Cowboy, limited edition*

THE CHUCK WAGON by Dunn from *Harmsen's Western Americana*

HARVEY THOMAS DUNN
1884–1952

Catalogues of Art Exhibitions and Galleries

INTERNATIONAL ART GALLERY, PITTSBURGH

1 *Brandywine Tradition Artists* (featuring the works of Howard Pyle, Frank E. Schoonover, the Wyeth Family, Charles Colombo, David Hanna), October 1971–October 1972, wraps, 54 pp., "Foreword" by Frederick L. Kramer, "Howard Pyle and Late 19th Century American Illustration" by Rowland Elzea, fifty plates including one, no. XXX, p. 28, by D. Note: During the year the same fifty paintings were exhibited at Nashville; Redbank, N.J.; Wichita; New Orleans and Charleston, West Virginia. (Schoonover, Wyeth)

NATIONAL GALLERY OF ART, WASHINGTON, D.C.

2 *American Battle Painting 1776–1918*, July 4 to September 4, 1944, wraps, 59 pp., foreword, "American Battle Painting" by Lincoln Kirstein, forty-one plates including one, no. 38, p. 49, by D. Note: The same paintings were exhibited at The Museum of Modern Art in New York, October 3 to November 18, 1944. (Remington)

Illustrated by the Artist

3 *Advertising Arts and Crafts, Volume 1*, National Edition. Lee and Kirby, N.Y., 1926, cloth and boards, 448 pp., numerous illus. including five, pp. 7, 9, 11, 13 and 69, by D.

4 Ainsworth, Ed. *Painters of the Desert*. Desert Magazine, Palm Desert, Calif., 1960, cloth, 111 pp., "Foreword" by Carl Dentzel, numerous illus. including one, p. 12, by D. (Dixon)

5 *The American Heritage Catalogue 1971–1972*. Marion, Ohio, 1971. Colored pic. wraps., 32, pp., numerous illus. including one in color, p. 22, by D. (Russell, Wyeth)

6 Amory, Cleveland et al. *The American Heritage Cookbook and Illustrated History of American Eating & Drinking*. American Heritage Publishing Co. but distributed by Simon and Schuster, N.Y., (1964), two volumes, pic. endsheets, 629 (11) pp., introduction, index, numerous illus. including one in color, p. (46), by D. (Miller, Remington)

7 *Annual of Illustrations for Advertisements in the U.S. — Second*. The Art Directors Club, N.Y., (1923), cloth and boards, 171 pp., indices, numerous illus. including two, p. 51, by D. (Blumenschein, Keller, Wyeth)

8 Same, *Fifth*, 1926, cloth and boards, 136 pp., (22) of advs., indices, numerous illus. including one, p. 68, by D. (Stoops)

9 Same, *Sixth*, 1927, cloth, colored pic. map endsheets, 152 pp., (24) of advs., (11), indices, numerous illus. including one, p. 35, by D. (Stoops, Von Schmidt, Wyeth)

10 Same, *Seventh*, 1928, cloth, colored pic. endsheets, 136 pp., (32) of advs., (9), indices, numerous illus. including one, p. 48, by D. (Wyeth)

11 Same, *Eighth*, 1929, cloth, decor. endsheets, 134 pp., (36) of advs., (7), indices, numerous illus. including four, pp. 96 (in color), 110 (two) and 111, by D. (Wyeth)

12 Same, *Ninth*, 1930, cloth, green endsheets, 136 (1) pp., (26) of advs., (5), indices, numerous illus. including two, pp. 22 and 62, by D.

13 Athearn, Robert G. The Frontier, Volume 6, *The American Heritage New Illustrated History of the United States*. Dell Publishing Co., N.Y., (1963), pic. boards and endsheets, pp. 454–539, numerous illus. including one, p. 530, by D. (Remington, Russell)

14 ———. *Winning the West, Volume 9*. Dell Pub. Co., N.Y., (1963), pic. boards and endsheets, pp. (723)–809, numerous illus. including one, p. 775, by D. (Leigh, Remington, Russell)

15 Beach, Rex. *The Silver Horde*. Harper, N.Y. and London, 1909, words "Published September, 1909" on copyright page, cloth, with colored illus. mounted on front cover, 389 (1) pp., eight illus., frontis. and facing pp. 48, 96, 126, 169, 206, 236 and 346, by D.

16 Bidwell, John, Bancroft, H. H. and Longmire, James. *First Three Wagon Trains*. Binfords and Mort, Portland, Oregon, (1958), cloth, map endsheets, 104 pp., several illus. including one, between pp. 58 and 59, by D. (Remington)

16a Bourne, Russell (project editor). *200 Years*. U.S. News & World Report, Washington, D.C., 1973, fabricoid and cloth, two vols., numerous illus. including one, p. 247 (I), by D., slipcase. (Miller, Remington, Russell, Wyeth, Zogbaum)

17 Brooks, Noah. *The Boy Emigrants*. Scribner's, N.Y., 1914, words "Published October, 1914" on copyright page, pic. cloth and endsheets, 381 pp., gilt top, ten colored illus., frontis. and facing pp. 30, 100, 140, 182, 200, 226, 292, 336 and 344, by D. (First with Dunn illustrations.)

18 Byrnes, Gene (selected and compiled by — with editorial assistance and text by A. Thornton Bishop). *A Complete Guide to Drawing, Illustration, Cartooning and Painting*. Simon & Schuster, N.Y., (1948), cloth and boards, tinted endsheets, 354 (1) pp., black top, numerous illus. including four, pp. 231, 232, (2), and 233 (in color), by D. Dunn's work discussed, pp. 230–32. (Remington)

19 ———. *Commercial Art*. A Reissue of Item 18 in 1952.

20 Case, Leland G. *The Prairie is My Homeland*. Separate from *Together*, Chicago, September 1960, self-wraps, 8 pp., twelve illus. in color by D. and comments on his art.

20a Caughey, John W. et al. *Land of the Free*. Franklin Publications, Pasadena, Calif., 1965, cloth, 658 pp., glossary, index, maps, numerous illus. including two in color, pp. 432 and 433, by D. (Perceval, Remington, Russell)

21 Department of the Army. *The Executive Corridor of the Secretary of the Army and Chief of Staff, U.S. Army*. Government Printing Office, Washington, 1966, wraps, the illustrations include one by D.

22 Dickens, Charles. *A Tale of Two Cities*. Cosmopolitan Book Corp., N.Y., 1921, pic. cloth, 362 pp., gilt top, preface to the first edition, ten full-page illus. in color, frontis. and facing pp. 22, 34, 152, 176, 214, 246, 280, 334 and 360, and small colored illus. on title page, by D.

23 Dickson, Harris. *Old Reliable*. Bobbs-Merrill, Indianapolis, 1911, cloth, 341 pp., illus. by Emlen McConnell and with one, facing p. 306, by D.

24 Dunn, Harvey T. *An Evening in the Classroom*. (Being notes taken by Miss Taylor in one of the classes in Painting conducted by Harvey Dunn and printed at the instigation of Mario Cooper), (1934), words "This the first edition of *An Evening in the Classroom* consists of one thousand copies" on the copyright page, pic. wraps, 54 pp., (1), foreword, eleven illus., front cover, title page and pp. (5), (8), 9, (16), (18), (27), (44), (49) and (55), by D.

25 Dunn, Harvey T. et al. *The Howard Pyle Brandywine Edition, 1853–1933*. Scribner's, N.Y., 1933, cloth with illus. in color mounted on front cover (sample binding), (25) pp., five illus. in color including one by D. "Howard Pyle," an appreciation by D. (Schoonover)

25a Edmonds, Walter D. *Young Ames*. Little, Brown, Boston, 1942, cloth, 350 pp., red top, d/w illus. by D.

26 Evans, Larry. *His Own Home Town*. The H. K. Fly Co., N.Y., (1917), pic. cloth, 319 pp., frontis. by D.

27 Gallatin, Albert Eugene. *Art and the Great War*. Dutton, N.Y., 1919, cloth and boards, 143 pp., plus 100 plates including one "Kamarad — The Sniper," by D. Also 100 copies in full blue morocco, designed by Goudy and signed by the author.

28 Greene, Harry Irving. *Barbara of the Snows*. Moffat, Yard & Co., N.Y., (1911), words "Published March, 1911" on copyright page, decor. cloth, 358 pp., three illus., frontis. and facing pp. 99 and 224, by D.

29 Grimshaw, Beatrice. *My Lady of the Island*. McClurg, Chicago, 1916, words "Published March, 1916" on copyright page, decor. cloth, 334 pp., five illus., frontis. and four double-page plates between pp. 114 and 115; 138 and 139; 170 and 171; and 294 and 295, by D.

30 Harmsen, Dorothy. *Harmsen's Western Americana*. Northland Press, Flagstaff, (1971), morocco and cloth, blue endsheets, 213 pp., "Foreword" by Robert Rockwell, introduction, numerous illus. including one, p. (67), by D. and with a biographical

BUFFALO BONES ARE PLOWED UNDER by Dunn from *Harold Von Schmidt Draws and Paints the Old West*

sketch of him. (Beeler, Blumenschein, Borein, Dixon, Dunton, Eggenhofer, Elwell, Hurd, Johnson, Leigh, Marchand, Miller, Russell, Von Schmidt, Wyeth)

31 ———. Same, first trade edition, two-tone cloth with red endsheets.

32 *Holiday Books, 1909*. Harper, N.Y., 1909, wraps, numerous illus. including one by D.

33 Hornung, E. W. *Dead Men Tell No Tales*. Scribner's, N.Y., 1906, (copyright 1899), red cloth with gilt lettering, 262 pp., gilt top, three illus., frontis. and facing pp. 120 and 256, by D. (First with Dunn illus.)

34 ———. *The Shadow of the Rope*. Scribner's, N.Y., 1906, (copyright 1902), red cloth with gilt lettering, 377 pp., gilt top, three illus., frontis. and facing pp. 190 and 350, by D. (First with D. illus.)

35 Howell, Edgar M. *Harvey Dunn, Painter of Pioneers*. Montana Historical Society, Helena, n.d., colored pic. wraps, (20) pp., numerous illus. including twelve in color by D. Montana Heritage Series no. 15. (Russell)

36 Irwin, Inez Haynes. *The Happy Years*. Henry Holt, N.Y., 1919, decor. cloth, 310 pp., four illus. including one, facing p. 196, by D.

37 Jennewein, J. Leonard, and Boorman, Jane, eds. *Dakota Panorama*. Dakota Territory Centennial Commission (Midwest-Beach Printing Co., Sioux Falls), 1961, pic. cloth, map endsheets, 468 pp., foreword, appendix, South Dakota reading list, index, numerous illus. Cover illus. is from a woodcut by D. ´

38 Kappalow, Hal. *Laughing Historically*. Bernard Geis Associates, (N.Y., 1961), words "First Printing" on copyright page, stiff pic. boards, 63 (1) pp., "Foreword" by the publisher, numerous illus. including one, p. 31, by D. (Von Schmidt, Wyeth)

39 Karolevitz, Robert F. *The Prairie is My Garden* (The Story of Harvey Dunn, Artist). North Plains Press, Aberdeen, South Dakota, (1969?), colored pic. wraps, 95 pp., foreword, bibliography, index, numerous illus. (four in color) by D. and photos of him.

40 ———. *Where Your Heart Is . . .* (The Story of Harvey Dunn, Artist). North Plains Press, Aberdeen, (1970), cloth, 208 pp., foreword, bibliography, index, numerous illus. (including sixteen in color) by D. and photos of him.

41 Kyne, Peter B. *Cappy Ricks*. The H. K. Fly Co.,

N.Y., (1916), cloth, 349 pp., three illus. by D. (Fischer)

42 Lavender, David. *The American Heritage History of the Great West*. Distributed by Simon & Schuster, 1965, cloth, pic. endsheets, 416 pp., edited by Alvin M. Josephy, Jr., index, numerous illus., De Luxe edition in slipcase with Dunn's "Jedediah Smith" in color mounted on front. (Koerner, Miller, Remington, Russell)

43 ———. Same, first trade edition, cloth and boards and with the Dunn illus. on the d/w.

44 Leckie, Robert. *The Story of World War I*. Random House, N.Y., (1965), pic. cloth, pic. endsheets, 189 pp., prologue, index, numerous illus. including three, pp. (110), (150) in color and (163) in color, by D. (Thomason)

45 Logan, Harlan (editor-publisher). *Fiftieth Anniversary, 1887-1937, Scribner's Magazine*. Scribner's, N.Y., January 1937, decor. wraps, 144 pp., numerous illus. including one, p. (73), by O. (James, Remington, Thomason)

46 London, Jack. *John Barleycorn*. Century Co., N.Y., 1913, words "Published, August 1913" on copyright page, cloth, 343 pp., eight illus., frontis. and pp. 19, 57, 105, 197, 233, 299 and 311, by D.

47 Marshall, General S. L. A. *The American Heritage History of World War I*. American Heritage but trade distribution by Simon and Schuster, N.Y., (1964), cloth, 364 pp., numerous illus. including one by D. (Thomason)

48 ———. *World War I*. American Heritage Press, N.Y., 1971, cloth and boards, map endsheets, 497 (2) pp., numerous illus. including one, p. 371, by D. (Thomason)

49 Meredith, Roy. *The American Wars*. World Publishing Co., Cleveland and N.Y., (1955), words "First Edition" on copyright page, pic. cloth, 348 (1) pp., red top, introduction, acknowledgments, numerous illus. including twenty by D. (Deming, Fischer, Remington, Thomason)

50 Moroso, Owen. *The Stumbling Herd*. Macaulay Co., N.Y., (1923), cloth, 306 pp., frontis. by D.

51 Mugridge, Donald E., and Conover, Helen F. *An Album of American Battle Art, 1755-1918*. Library of Congress, U.S. Government Printing Office, Washington, 1947, decor. cloth, 319 pp., acknowledgments, introduction, graphic index, 150 plates in-

cluding plate no. 150, p. 313, by D. Dunn's work discussed, p. 302. (Remington)

52 Nicoll, Bruce (assembled and edited by). *Nebraska, A Pictorial History*. Nebraska, Lincoln, (1967), cloth, blue endsheets, 231 (1) pp., foreword, picture credits, numerous (many in color) illus. including eight, pp. 69 - two, (70) - two, (71), 72, 73 - two, by D. (Dixon, Miller, Remington, Russell)

53 North Plains Press, *Catalog No. 4*. Aberdeen, S.D., n.d., pic. wraps, unpaged, illus. including three by D.

54 ————. *Harvey Dunn Christmas Cards*, broadside with six (two in color) illus. by D. and a verso *Harvey Dunn Prints* with four illus. in color by D.

55 ————. *Catalog No. 5*, n.d., colored pic. wraps, unpaged, illus. including two by D.

56 *The Outing Magazine for 1909* (advs.). Pic. wraps, (8) pp., illus. including four (two in color) by D.

57 *The Pacific Historian* (advs. folder). Winter 1968, three illus. including one by D.

58 Parker, Gilbert. *Northern Lights*. Harper, N.Y. and London, 1909, words "Published September, 1909" on copyright page, pic. cloth, 351 (1) pp., note, sixteen illus. including three, facing pp. 70, 74 and 198, by D. (Crawford, Schoonover, Wood)

59 Patullo, George. *The Untamed*. Desmond Fitzgerald, Inc., N.Y., (1911), cloth with small illus. mounted on front cover, 288 pp., six illus. including one, facing p. 240, by D. (Russell)

60 Peattie, Donald Culross. *Jedediah Smith — Trailmaker Extraordinary*. Jedediah Smith Society, Stockton, Calif., self wraps, 6 (2) pp., four illus. including two, pp. (1) and (8), by D.

61 Pitz, Henry C. *The Brandywine Tradition*. Houghton Mifflin, Boston, 1969, words "First Printing, W" on copyright page, cloth, tinted endsheets, 252 pp., preface, bibliography, index, numerous illus. including one in color, between pp. 126 and 127, by D. (Hurd, Schoonover, Wyeth)

62 Place, Marian T. *Westward on the Oregon Trail*. American Heritage Publishing Co., N.Y., 1962, words "First Edition" on title page, colored pic. cloth and endsheets, 153 pp., "Foreword" by Earl Pomeroy (consultant), acknowledgments, for further reading, index, numerous illus. including one, p. (38), by D. (Remington)

63 Pyle, Howard. *The Story of Sir Launcelot and His Companions*. Scribner's, N.Y., 1933, cloth, 340 pp., illus. by the author but with a frontis. in color by D. and a note on Pyle by him. (Howard Pyle Brandywine Edition, 1853–1933.)

64 Ray, Frederic (compiled and narrated by). *O! Say Can You See* (The Story of America Through Great Paintings). Stackpole, (Harrisburg, Pa., 1970), cloth, tan endsheets, 189 pp., "An Introduction to the Paintings" by Robt. W. Fowler, numerous illus. including one in color, p. (147), by D. and with a photo and brief biography of him, p. 163. (Koerner, Remington, Russell, Wyeth)

64a *Readers' Digest Illustrated Guide to the Treasures of America*. The Readers' Digest Assn., Pleasantville, N.Y., (1974), fabricoid and decor. cloth, blue endsheets, 624 pp., numerous illus. including one in color, p. 368, by D. (Miller, Remington, Russell)

65 Reed, Walt. *The Illustrator in America 1900–1960's*. Reinhold, N.Y., (1966), cloth, pic. green endsheets, 271 (1) pp., "Is Illustration Art?" by Albert Dorne, numerous illus. including three, pp. 52 (two in color) and 53, by D. and with a brief biographical sketch of him. (Blumenschein, Crawford, Dunton, Eggenhofer, Fischer, Fogarty, Goodwin, Keller, Koerner, Remington, Russell, Schoonover, Stoops, Wyeth)

66 ————. *Harold Von Schmidt Draws and Paints the Old West*. Northland Press, Flagstaff, (1972), words "First Edition" on the copyright page, morocco and pic. cloth, slate endsheets, 230 pp., "Foreword" by Dean Krakel, "Introduction" by Harold McCracken, bibliography, numerous illus. by Von Schmidt but with one, p. 43, by D., a photo of him and much on him in the text. One of 104 numbered copies signed by Reed and Von Schmidt, slipcase with morocco title label, issued jointly with Von Schmidt's first sculpture, "The Startled Grizzly." (Dixon, James, Russell)

67 ————. Same, first trade edition in pic. cloth.

68 Rhodes, Eugene Manlove. *Good Men and True*. Henry Holt, N.Y., 1910, words "Published August, 1910" on copyright page, red cloth, 177 pp., two illus., frontis. and facing p. 166, by D. (Advertisement sheets following text dated "VII '10.")

69 ————. Same, Grosset & Dunlap edition, n.d., but after 1920, with a second story, "Hit the Line Hard," added, pic. cloth, 315 pp., two illus., frontis. and facing p. 164, by D.

70 ———. *Bransford in Arcadia.* Henry Holt, N.Y., 1914, words "Published January, 1914" on copyright page, cloth, 236 pp., frontis. by D. (Advertisement sheets following text dated " '12" and " '13.")

71 ———. *Bransford of Rainbow Range.* Grosset & Dunlap, N.Y., (1920), cloth, 236 pp., (12) pp. of advs., frontis. by D. (A reprint of *Bransford in Arcadia.*)

72 ———. *The Desire of the Moth.* Henry Holt, N.Y., 1916, words "Published April, 1916" on copyright page, pic. cloth, 149 pp., two illus., frontis. and facing p. 38, by D. (Advertisement sheets following text dated "3 '16.")

73 ———. Same, Grosset & Dunlap edition, n.d., but after 1920, with a second story, "The Come On," added, pic. cloth, 282 pp., (2) of advs., two illus., frontis. and facing p. 36, by D.

74 ———. *West is West.* H. K. Fly Co., (1917), pic. cloth, 304 pp., frontis. by D.

75 Stringer, Arthur. *The Prairie Wife.* Bobbs-Merrill, Indianapolis, (1915), decor. cloth, 316 (1) pp., six illus. in color, frontis. and facing pp. 90, 110, 156, 160 and 162, by D.

76 Udall, Stewart L. *The Quiet Crisis.* Holt, Rinehart and Winston, N.Y. etc., (1965), words "First Edition" on copyright page, cloth, 209 pp., foreword, "Introduction" by John F. Kennedy, index, numerous illus. including one, in color, between pp. 82 and 83, by D.

77 Ver Steeg, Clarence L. *The Story of Our Country.* Harper & Row, N.Y., (1965), colored pic. cloth, 416 pp., introduction, glossary, index, maps and diagrams, numerous illus. including two, pp. 6 (in color) and 383, by D. (Miller, Remington, Russell)

78 Watson, Ernest W. *Forty Illustrators and How They Work.* Watson-Guptill Publications, Inc., N.Y., 1946, words "First Edition" on copyright page, cloth with paper title-label, 318 pp., author's preface, profusely illus. including three illus., pp. 116, 118 and 119, by D. A chapter on Dunn's work, pp. 117-120, with a photo of Dunn, p. 117.

79 ———. *Harvey Dunn, A. N. A., Milestone in the Tradition of American Illustration, an Interview.* M. Grumbacher. (A reprint from "American Artist," June, 1942.) N.Y., 1942, folder (stapled), (6) pp., (1) p. advs., four illus. by D., and photo of D.

80 Wister, Owen. *Members of the Family.* MacMillan, N.Y., 1911, words "Published May, 1911" on copy-right page, decor. cloth, 317 pp., preface, twelve full-page illus. by D.

81 Wood, Wm., and Gabriel, Ralph H. *In Defense of Liberty.* Yale University Press, New Haven, 1928, The Liberty Bell Edition of "The Pageant of America," volume 7, limited to 1500 impressions, morocco and boards, 370 pp., numerous illus. including three, pp. 303, 304 and 312, by D.

The Artist and His Art

82 Ainsworth, Ed. *The Cowboy in Art.* World, N.Y. and Cleveland, (1968), words "First Printing 1968" on copyright page, full leather, orange endsheets, 242 pp., all edges gilt, "Foreword" by John Wayne, index, numerous illus., much on Dunn in text— nearly a dozen of his students have illustrations in the book. Special edition of 1000 numbered copies, slipcase.

83 ———. Same, first trade edition in gilt lettered and illus. cloth, orange endsheets.

84 ———. Same, reprint by Bonanza Books, N.Y., in red lettered and illus. cloth, white endsheets.

85 Andres, Charles J. *Notes Taken in the Picture Class of Harvey Dunn, 1938-1941.* (Mimeographed booklet.)

86 "A War Portfolio by American Artists," an article in *American Heritage,* volume X, no. 6, October 1959, twenty illus. including six, pp. (7), 10-11, (12-13), (14), (15) and (16) by D. Dunn was an official artist with the rank of captain in World War I. He served in France.

87 Case, Leland G. "The Prairie is My Homeland," an illus. article in *Together* 4:9, Ssptember 1960, with twelve color plates by D. and with comments on his art.

88 Ferguson, Charles W. "Americans Not Everybody Knows: Harvey Dunn," an illus. article in *The PTA Magazine,* January 1968.

89 Grotta, Gerald, "The Prairie Painter," an illus. article in *The Dakotan,* June 1960.

90 Howell, Edgar, M. "The Look of the Last Frontier," an illus. article in *American Heritage* 12:4, June 1961.

91 ———. "Harvey Dunn: The Searching Artist Who Came Home to His First Horizon," an illus. article in *The Montana Magazine* 16:1, Winter 1966.

92 Hydeman, Sid. *How to Illustrate for Money.* Harper, N.Y. and London, (1936), cloth and boards, 173

pp., "Foreword" by Edwin Balmer, index, illus. with photos, much on Dunn and Von Schmidt in text.

93 Jennewein, J. Leonard (executive secretary). *Middle Border Bulletin*, vol. 4, no. 1. Friends of the Middle Border, Mitchell, South Dakota, Spring, 1956. Contains a "Bibliographic Check List of Books Illustrated by Harvey T. Dunn" by J. C. D. plus a note on "Dakota Woman," an original oil painting by D. owned by the Friends.

94 Lykes, Richard Wayne. "Howard Pyle: Teacher of Illustration," an illus. article in *The Pennsylvania Magazine of History and Biography*, July 1956.

95 Mellquist, Jerome. *The Emergence of an American Art.* Scribner's, N.Y., 1942, code letter "A" on copyright page, cloth, 421 pp., introduction, appendix, index, illustrated; Dunn mentioned in text, p. 152.

96 *1915 Publications of the Bobbs-Merrill Company*, Indianapolis, decor. wraps, 104 pp., lists, pp. 22 and 86, two books, illus. by D.

97 Nissen, S. B. "Magnificent Gift to South Dakota People: Harvey Dunn's Paintings at State College," an article in *SDEA Journal*, December 1950.

98 Pitz, Henry C. "Four Disciples of Howard Pyle," an article in *American Artist*, January 1969.

99 Ray, Frederic (art director). "Our Front Cover," a brief note on "The Prisoner" by D. reproduced on the cover of *American History Illustrated* 1:10, February 1967.

100 Reynolds, Quentin. *The Fiction Factory.* Random House, N.Y., (1958), words "First Printing" on copyright page, fabricoid and decor. cloth, decor. endsheets, 283 pp., tinted top, bibliography, index, illustrated; Dunn in text, p. 209 (Fischer, Wyeth)

101 Sandoz, Mari. "Dakota Country," an article in *American Heritage*, volume XII, no. 4, June, 1961. Tribute to Dunn, photo of Dunn, and eleven illus., nine in color including the front cover, by D.

102 Sherwood, Aubrey H. "Harvey Dunn," an article in *South Dakota Conservation Digest* July-August 1968.

103 ———. "Harvey Dunn: Master Mason," De Smet, S. D., South Dakota Lodge of Masonic Research, 1964.

104 Van Kirk, Elizabeth Daffan. "Harvey Dunn Presents Rare Book Telling of Jedediah Smith," an article in *Middle Border Bulletin* 7:2, Autumn 1947.

CREST OF THE ROCKIES: GRIZZLY by Dunton from *Guide to Life and Literature of the Southwest*

W. HERBERT (BUCK) DUNTON
1878–1936

Catalogues of Art Exhibitions and Galleries

BABCOCK GALLERIES, NEW YORK

1 *Paintings of the West*, 1920, wraps, unpaged, (16), includes one illus. by D. (Blumenschein, Russell)

BILTMORE GALLERIES, LOS ANGELES

1a *Catalog*, May 1969, colored pic. wraps, 54 pp., numerous illus. including one, p. 17, by D. (Borein, Dixon, Johnson, Koerner, Leigh, Miller, Remington, Russell, Young)

CITY ART MUSEUM, ST. LOUIS

2 *23rd Annual Exhibition of Selected Paintings by American Artists*, 1928, includes one illus., "Cattle Buyer" by D.

CORCORAN GALLERY OF ART, WASHINGTON, D.C.

3 *Biennial Exhibition of Contemporary American Oil Paintings*, 1928–(29), includes one illus., "Pastor de Canbras Mexicano" by D. (Blumenschein)

DALLAS MUSEUM OF FINE ARTS

3a *A Century of Art and Life in Texas*, April 9–May 7, 1961, pic. wraps, unpaged, foreword by Jerry Bywaters, numerous illus. including one by D. (Johnson, Lea, Remington, Schiwetz)

EDWARD EBERSTADT AND SONS, NEW YORK

4 *American Paintings*, Catalogue 146, 1958 (but issued in December 1957), 191 numbered illus. including two, no. 63 and no. 64, by D. (Borein, Deming, Dixon, Johnson, Leigh, Miller, Remington, Wyeth)

EL PASO MUSEUM OF ART

4a *The McKee Collection of Paintings*, (1968), cloth with illus. in color mounted on front cover, tan endsheets, 67 pp., designed by Carl Hertzog, "The McKees and Their Art Collection," "Foreword" by Leonard P. Si-

piora, numerous illus. including one in color, p. 39, by D. (Blumenschein, Hurd, Koerner, Lea)

4b Same, 100 copies in pic. wraps.

MUSEUM OF NEW MEXICO, SANTA FE

5 *Paintings of the Southwest* (Santa Fe Railway Collection), 1966, includes two illus, by D. and a short biographical sketch of him. (Blumenschein)

6 *The Changing Image of the Indian*, April 16–June 18, 1967, includes one illus. by D.

THE NATIONAL ARCHIVES OF THE UNITED STATES WASHINGTON, D.C.

6a *Indians and the American West*, October 26, 1973–January 21, 1974, colored pic. wraps, unpaged, numerous illus. including no. 28 by D. (Blumenschein, Schreyvogel)

NATIONAL ACADEMY OF DESIGN, NEW YORK

7 *88th Annual Exhibition*, 1913, includes one illus., "Lonely Vigil," by D.

PENNSYLVANIA ACADEMY OF FINE ARTS, PHILADELPHIA

8 *Catalogue of the Annual Exhibition*, 114th, 1919, includes one illus., "Buffalo Signal," by D.

9 Same, 122nd, 1927, includes one illus., "Pastor de Canbras Mexicano," by D.

PHOENIX ART MUSEUM

10 *An Exhibition of Paintings of the Southwest* (from the Santa Fe Railway Collection), Feb. 1 through April 30, 1966, colored pic. wraps, 26 pp., thirty illus. including two, p. 18, by D. (Blumenschein, Leigh)

11 *Art of the Western Scene, 1880–1940*, 1969, includes one illus. by D. (Koerner, Remington, Russell)

12 *Western Art from the Eugene B. Adkins Collection,* Nov. 1971–Jan. 1972, includes one illus. by D. (Johnson, Leigh, Miller, Remington, Varian)

FRED ROSENSTOCK WITH JAMES PARSONS (GALLERY WEST), DENVER

13 *100 Years of Western Art,* Nov. 28 through Dec. 24, 1969, colored pic. wraps, 24 pp., "Introduction" by Parsons, numerous illus. including one, p. 12, by D. (Beeler, Borein, James, Koerner)

SOTHEBY PARKE BERNET, LOS ANGELES

13a *Western American Paintings, Drawings and Sculpture,* March 4 and 5, 1974, colored pic. wraps, unpaged, 252 lots, numerous illus. including lot 88 by D. (Blumenschein, Johnson, Koerner, Leigh, Remington, Russell)

WHITNEY GALLERY OF WESTERN ART (BUFFALO BILL HISTORICAL CENTER), CODY, WYOMING

14 *Preserving the Heritage of the Old West,* (May, 1961), includes one illus. by D. (Remington, Russell)

WOOLAROC MUSEUM (FRANK PHILLIPS FOUNDATION), BARTLESVILLE, OKLAHOMA

15 *Oklahoma,* 1952, includes one illus. by D. (Johnson, Leigh, Remington, Russell)

Illustrated by the Artist

16 Ainsworth, Ed. *The Cowboy in Art.* World, N.Y. and Cleveland, (1968), words "First Printing 1968" on copyright page, full leather, orange endsheets, 242 pp., all edges gilt, "Foreword" by John Wayne, index, numerous illus. including two, pp. 39 and 84, by D. Special edition of 1000 numbered copies (Ed died before he had a chance to sign them) in a slipcase. (Beeler, Borein, Bugbee, De Yong, Dixon, Eggenhofer, Ellsworth, Hurd, James, Johnson, Koerner, Mora, Perceval, Remington, Russell, Santee, Schreyvogel, Von Schmidt)

17 ———. Same, first trade edition in gilt lettered and illus. cloth, orange endsheets.

18 ———. Same, reprint by Bonanza Books, N.Y. in red lettered and illus. cloth, white endsheets.

19 Bateson, Carlen. The *Man in the Camlet Cloak.* Saalfield, N.Y. and Chicago, 1903, decor. cloth, 320 pp., gilt top, four illus., frontis. and facing pp. 80, 160 and 240, by D.

20 Bickerstaff, Laura M. *Pioneer Artists of Taos.* Sage Books, Denver, (1955), cloth, 93 pp., "Introduction" by Ernest L. Blumenschein, twenty-eight illus. including four, following p. 54, by D. (Blumenschein)

21 Bindloss, Harold. *The Dust of Conflict.* Frederick A. Stokes, N.Y., (1907), words "Published in January 1907" on copyright page, cloth, 320 (1) pp., three illus. in color, frontis. and facing pp. 205 and 282, by D.

22 ———. *Winston on the Prairie.* Frederick A. Stokes, N.Y., (1907), words "Published, September 19707" follow copyright notice, cloth, with illus. in color mounted on front cover, 340 pp., three illus. in color, frontis. and facing pp. 232 and 246, by D.

23 ———. *The Greater Power.* Frederick A. Stokes, N.Y., (1909), words "September, 1909" on copyright page, pic. cloth, 328 pp., frontis. in color by D.

23a ———. Same, first Canadian edition by McLeod & Allen, Toronto, (1909).

24 ———. *Thurston of Orchard Valley.* Frederick A. Stokes, N.Y., (1910), words "Feb. 1910" on copyright page, decor. cloth, 308 pp., frontis. in color by D.

25 ———. *Vane of the Timberlands.* Frederick A. Stokes, N.Y., (1911), words "January, 1912" on copyright page, cloth, 375 pp., frontis. in color by D.

26 ———. *Prescott of Saskatchawan.* Frederick A. Stokes, N.Y., (1913), words "August, 1913" on copyright page, cloth, 346 pp., frontis. in color by D.

27 Braden, James A. *Connecticut Boys in the Western Reserve.* Saalfield, Akron, Ohio, N.Y., Chicago, 1903, pic. cloth, 440 pp., four illus., frontis. and facing pp. 100, 200, 300 by D.

28 ———. *The Cabin in the Clearing.* Saalfield, Akron, Ohio etc., (1904), pic. boards, 233 pp., (11) pp. of advs., frontis. by D. (Title page states "Frontispiece by Fred A. Elliott.")

29 ———. *In the Camp of the Delwares.* Saalfield, Akron, Ohio etc., (1907), pic. boards, 243 pp., frontis. by D.

30 ———. *The Lone Indian.* Saalfield, Akron, Ohio etc., (1908), pic. boards, 249 pp., (3) pp. of advs., frontis. by D. (Reprinted in 1936 as no. 3 in Boy's Indian Series.)

31 Bronson, Edgar Beecher. *Reminiscences of a Ranchman.* A. C. McClurg, Chicago, (1910), words "Published Sept. 10, 1910" on copyright page, (revised edition, first to have a Dunton illustration), cloth with colored illus. mounted on front cover, 369 (1)

pp., illus. including one plate, facing p. 100, by D. (Dixon, Johnson)

31a ———. Same, Doran reprint but with the title *Cowboy Life on the Western Plains,* (1910).

32 Browne, Waldo. *Break O'Day Boys or Ragged Bob's Young Republic* by Victor St. Clair (pseud.). Saalfield, Akron, Ohio, New York, Chicago, 1903, pic. cloth, 275 pp., preface, four illus., frontis. and facing pp. 68, 136 and 204, by D.

33 Burt, Maxwell Struthers. *John O'May.* Scribner's N.Y., 1918, words "Published September, 1918" on copyright page, cloth, 250 pp., illus., including two plates, facing pp. 172 and 180, by D.

34 Capwell, Irene Stoddard. *Mrs. Alderman Casey,* Fenno, N.Y., (1905), decor. cloth, 175 pp., five illus., frontis. and facing pp. 32, 64, 100 and 144 plus cover design by D.

35 Chapman, Katherine Hopkins. *The Fusing Force.* A. C. McClurg, Chicago, 1911, words "Published October, 1911" on copyright page, cloth, 416 pp., frontis. in color, by D.

36 Chipman, Charles P. *Two Boys and a Dog.* Saalfield, N.Y. and Chicago, 1903, pic. cloth, 272 pp., four illus., frontis. and facing pp. 74, 204 and 238, by D.

37 Coke, Van Deren. *Taos and Santa Fe: The Artist's Environment, 1882-1942,* University of New Mexico Press, Albuquerque, (1963), words "First Edition" on copyright page, cloth, 160 pp., "Foreword" by Mitchell A. Wilder, selected bibliography, index, numerous illus. including two, pp. 23 and 114, by D. (Blumenschein)

38 Costello, F. H. *Nelson's Yankee Boy.* Henry Holt, N.Y., 1904, words "Published October 1904" on copyright page, decor. cloth, 293 pp., (3) pp. of advs., six illus., frontis. and facing pp. 14, 62, 180, 230 and 280, by D.

39 Dean, Sara. *Travers.* Frederick A. Stokes, N.Y., (1907), words "Published February, 1908" on copyright page, cloth with colored illus. mounted on front cover, 287 pp., three illus. in color, frontis. and facing pp. 57 and 274, by D.

40 Dobie, J. Frank. *Guide to Life and Literature of the Southwest.* The University of Texas Press, Austin, Texas, 1943, wraps, 111 pp., twenty-four illus. including one, facing p. 92, by D. (Borein, Bugbee, Hurd, James, Lea, Leigh, Russell, Thomason)

41 ———. *The Ben Lilly Legend.* Little, Brown, Boston, 1950, words "First Edition, Published May

1950" on copyright page, pic. cloth, 237 pp., "Esau the Hunter," "Sources: People and Print," index, illus. including one, a full-page plate, "Grizzly," facing p. 158, by D. (Lea)

42 ———. *The Ben Lilly Legend.* Hammond, Hammond & Co., London, (1952), words "First published in Great Britain" on copyright page, cloth, 237 pp., "Esau the Hunter," "Sources: People and Print," index, ten illus. including one, facing p. 158, by D.

43 Dunton, W. Herbert ("Buck"). "The Rigging of a Texan." Reprinted from *The Southwestern Historical Quarterly,* volume XLVII, no. 1, July, 1943, (Austin, Texas), 6 pp., 1943, colored frontis. by D. (First and only separate edition.)

44 Gregory, Jackson. *Judith of Blue Lake Ranch.* Scribner's, N.Y., 1919, words "Published March, 1919" on copyright page, cloth, 393 pp., four illus., frontis. and facing pp. 202, 250 and 392, by D.

45 ———. *Ladyfingers.* Scribner's, N.Y., 1920, words "Published May, 1920" on copyright page, cloth, four illus., frontis. and facing pp. 16, 66 and 270, by D.

46 Grey, Zane. *The Light of the Western Stars.* Harper, N.Y. and London, 1914, words "Published January, 1914," and code letters "M-N" on copyright page, decor. cloth, 388 (1) pp., frontis. in color, by D.

47 ———. *Riders of the Purple Sage.* Harper, N.Y. and London, (1921), code letters, "K-V" on copyright page, cloth with colored illus. mounted on the front cover, 336 pp., (4) pp. of advs., twelve illus. in color by D. (Illustrated Classics Series.)

48 ———. *Wanderer of the Wasteland.* Harper, N.Y. and London, (1923), words "First Edition" and code letters "L-W" on copyright page, pic. cloth, 419 pp., three full-page illus., frontis. and facing pp. 58 and 172, by D.

49 Hains, T. Jenkins. *The Black Barque.* L. C. Page, Boston, 1905, words "Published February, 1905" on copyright page, pic. cloth, 322, 6 pp., and 12 pp. of advs., five illus., frontis. and facing pp. 80, 136, 214 and 280, by D.

50 Harmsen, Dorothy. *Harmsen's Western Americana.* Northland Press, Flagstaff, (1971), morocco and cloth, blue endsheets, 213 pp., "Foreword" by Robert Rockwell, introduction, selected bibliography, numerous illus. including one in color, p. (69), by D. and a biographical sketch of him. Limited edition of 150 numbered copies signed by the author, slipcase with morocco title label. (Beeler, Blumen-

schein, Borein, Dixon, Dunn, Eggenhofer, Elwell, Hurd, Johnson, Leigh, Marchand, Miller, Russell, Von Schmidt, Wyeth)

51 ———. Same, first trade edition in two-tone cloth and with red endsheets.

52 Harvey, A(lbion) K(eith) P. *In the Glow of the Campfire*. The National Sportsmen Press, Boston, Mass., 1903, words "Published August 1903" on copyright page, pic. cloth, 159 pp., illus. with photos and with numerous drawings by D.

53 Hewitt, Edgar L. *Representative Art and Artists of New Mexico*. School of American Research, Museum of New Mexico, (Santa Fe Press), Santa Fe, 1940, pic. wraps, 40 pp., biographical notes, numerous illus. including one, p. 14, by D. (Blumenschein, Hurd)

56 Kellogg, Frank E. *Four Boys on the Mississippi*. Saalfield, Akron, Ohio, 1903, pic. cloth, 319 pp., four illus., frontis. and facing pp. 80, 156 and 234, by D. (Reissued by H. M. Caldwell Co., N.Y., Boston, and later by Dona, Estes & Co., of Boston.)

57 Lewis, Alfred Henry. *Wolfville Folks*. D. Appleton, N.Y., 1908, code number (1) follows last line of text, pic. cloth, 321 (1) pp., frontis. by D.

58 ———. *Faro Nell and Her Friends*. G. W. Dillingham, N.Y., 1913, cloth, 348 pp., illus. including five, facing pp. 18, 42, 138, 222 and 316, by D.

59 Lighton, W. R. *Uncle Mac's Nebraska*. Henry Holt, (N.Y.), 1904, words "Published April, 1904" on copyright page, decor. cloth, 184 pp. frontis. by D.

59a Luhan, Mabel Dodge. *Taos and Its Artists*. Duell, Sloan and Pearce, N.Y., (1947), cloth, red endsheets, 168 pp., numerous illus. including one by D. (Blumenschein)

60 McDowell, Bart. *The American Cowboy in Life and Legend*. National Geographic Society, Washington, D.C., (1972), pic. cloth, pic. endsheets, pp. 2, 11, (1), "Foreword" by Joe B. Frantz, index, additional reading, numerous illus. including one in color, pp. 18-19, by D. (De Yong, Goodwin, James, Remington, Russell)

61 Major, Mabel and Smith, Rebecca W. *The Southwest in Literature*. Macmillan, N.Y., 1929, words "Published April, 1929" on copyright page, cloth, 370 pp., illus. including one, the frontis., by D.

62 Marshall, Edison. *The Voice of the Pack*. Little, Brown, Boston, 1920, words "Published April, 1920" on copyright page, decor. cloth, 305 pp., frontis. by D.

63 ———. *The Strength of the Pines*. Little, Brown, Boston, 1921, words "Published February, 1921" on copyright page, pic. cloth, 308 pp., frontis. by D.

64 ———. *The Land of Forgotten Men*. Little, Brown, Boston, 1923, decor. cloth, 306 pp., frontis. by D.

65 Noyes, Charles Johnson. *Patriot and Tory*. Henry A. Dickerson & Son, Boston and N.Y., (1902), decor. cloth, 315 pp., all edges gilt, frontis. by D.

66 Ogden, G. W. *Tennessee Todd*. A. S. Barnes, N.Y., 1903, word "October" on copyright page, pic. cloth, 344 pp., frontis. by D.

67 ———. *Home Place*. Harper, N. Y. and London, 1912, words "Published October 1912" on copyright page, pic. cloth, 364 (1) pp., frontis. by D.

68 Parrish, Randall. *Keith of the Border*. A. C. McClurg, Chicago, 1910, words "Published, Sept. 24, 1910" on copyright page, pic. cloth, 362 pp., four illus. in color, frontis. and facing pp. 154, 316 and 350 by D.

69 Pearce, Thomas M. and Telfair Hendon. *America in the Southwest*. The University Press, Albuquerque, N. M., 1933, cloth, 346 pp., illus. including one, facing p. 187, by D.

70 Potter, Mary Knight. *Council of Croesus*. L. C. Page, Boston, (1902), words "Published August 1902" on copyright page, cloth, 12 illus. by D.

71 Raine, Wm. McLeod. *A Texas Ranger*. G. W. Dillingham, N.Y., (1911), cloth, 336 pp., frontis. by D.

72 Reed, Walt. *The Illustrator in America 1900-1960's*. Reinhold, N.Y., (1966), cloth, pic. green endsheets, 271 (1) pp., "Is Illustration Art?" by Albert Dorne, bibliography, numerous illus. including one, p. 51, by D. (Blumenschein, Crawford, Dunn, Eggenhofer, Fisher, Fogarty, Goodwin, James, Keller, Koerner, Remington, Russell, Schoonover, Stoops, Wyeth)

73 Russell, Don. *Custer's Last* (The Battle of the Little Big Horn in Picturesque Perspective). (Amon Carter Museum, Ft. Worth, 1968), cloth, 67 pp., "Preface" by Barbara Tyler, notes, bibliography, sixteen illus. including one in color, p. 45, by D. (Deming, Russell)

74 Russell, W. Clark. *The Mate of the Good Ship York*. L. C. Page, Boston, 1902, decor. cloth, 351 pp., frontis. by D.

75 ———. *The Captain's Wife*. L. C. Page, Boston, 1903, words "Published July, 1903" on copyright page, decor. cloth, 480 pp., (7) pp. of advs., gilt top, frontis. by D.

76 Sinclair-Cowan, Bertha M. *Her Prairie Knight* and

Rowdy of the "Cross L" by B. M. Bower (pseud.). G. W. Willingham, N.Y., (1907), pic. cloth, 314 pp., (2) pp. of advs., three illus in color, frontis. and facing pp. 62 and 102, by D. (The second edition has only a frontis. in color by D.)

77 Smith, Wallace. *Garden of the Sun.* Lymanhouse, Los Angeles, (1939), cloth, 558 pp., preface, numerous illus. including one, p. 158, by D.

78 Thwing, Eugene. *The Red-Keggers.* The Book-Lover Press, N.Y., 1903, words "Published, September 1903" on copyright page, decor. cloth, 429 pp., preface, ten illus., frontis. and facing pp. 10, 24, 50, 194, 270, 298, 386, 404 and 426, by D.

79 Tracy, Louis. *The Albert Gate Mystery.* R. F. Fenno, N.Y., 1904, cloth, 309 pp., four illus. including two, frontis. and facing p. 200, by D.

80 Warner, Susan. *The Wide, Wide World.* R. F. Fenno, N.Y., (1904), pic. cloth, 592 pp., six illus., frontis. and facing pp. 100, 254, 350, 410 and 502, by D.

81 Willsie, Honore. *Still Jim.* Frederick A. Stokes, N.Y., (1915), words "April, 1915" on copyright page, cloth, 369 pp., illus. including a frontis. in color by D.

82 ———. *The Heart of the Desert.* Frederick A. Stokes, N.Y., (1913), words "September, 1913" on copyright page, cloth, 313 pp., frontis. in color by D.

83 Wilson, Bingham Thoburn. *The Village of Hide and Seek.* Consolidated Retail Booksellers, N.Y., 1905, words "Published October, 1905" on copyright page, pic. cloth, 190 pp., gilt top, eight illus. in color, frontis. and facing pp. 56, 110, 116, 124, 140, 150 and 176, by D.

84 Wittigschlager, Wilhelmina. *Minna, Wife of the Young Rabbi.* Consolidated Retail Booksellers, N.Y., 1905, words "Published November 1905" on copyright page, dec. cloth, 345 pp., four illus., frontis. and facing pp. 176, 240 and 252, by D.

The Artist and His Art

85 *Art and Archaeology,* January–February, 1918, one illus., "The Buffalo Signal," by D.

86 Same, January, 1920, one illus., "The Scout," by D.

87 *Art and Progress,* June, 1915, one illus., "Navajo Country," by D.

88 Branch, Douglas. "The American Cowboy," an article in *The Mentor,* July, 1927, two illus. by D. (Leigh, Remington, Russell)

88a Dippie, Brian W. "Brush, Palette and the Custer Battle — a Second Look," an article on the art of the Little Big Horn in *Montana* 24:1, Winter 1974, with one illus. by D. (Blumenschein, Remington, Russell, Schreyvogel, Von Schmidt)

89 Dunton, W. Herbert. "The Fair in the Cow Country," an article in *Scribner's Magazine,* April, 1915, eight illus. (one in color), by D.

90 ———. "The West: Today and Yesterday," an article in *Outing,* November, 1920, eight illus., with comments, by D.

91 ———. "The Painters of Taos," an article in *American Magazine of Art,* August, 1922, one illus. by D. (Blumenschein)

92 ———. "Concerning a Custom Sporter," an article in *The American Rifleman* 80:1, January 1932.

93 Hoeber, Arthur. "Painters of Western Life," an article in *Mentor Magazine,* June 15, 1915, one illus. by D. and a photo of him. (Blumenschein, Leigh, Remington, Russell, Schreyvogel)

94 Lord, Alice Frost. "Nationally Famous for Paintings of Western Life was Maine-Born Man," an article in the Magazine Section, *Lewiston Journal,* April 8, 1944.

95 Robinson, F. Warner. "Dunton-Westerner," an article in *The American Magazine of Art,* 15:10, October, 1924, six illus. by D.

95a *Second Annual Exhibit of the Taos Society of Artists,* Palace of the Governors, Santa Fe, n.d. (1916?), pic. wraps, unpaged, includes a biographical sketch of D. (Blumenschein)

96 *Southwestern Art,* March 1968, includes "Custer Exhibit: Amon Carter Museum of Western Art," one illus. by D.

97 Webb, Walter Prescott and Carroll, H. Bailey, eds. *The Southwestern Historical Quarterly,* vol. XLVII, no. 1. The Texas State Historical Association, Austin, Texas, July, 1943, wraps, 90 pp., (7) of advs., one illus. in color, "The Texan," by D., faces p. 2. Contains a long letter from Dunton to Leslie Waggener, dated Oct. 6th, 1929 and titled (by the editors) "The Rigging of a Texan," pp. 1–4. Also quotes a letter, pp. 52–53, from Harold Bugbee praising Dunton's work.

98 Wenger, Martin. "The West Has Passed — W. Herbert Dunton," an article in *The American Scene* 3:3, Fall 1960, one illus. by D. (Blumenschein)

ILLUSTRATION by Eggenhofer from *Western Words*

NICK EGGENHOFER
Contemporary, 1897–

Catalogues of Art Exhibitions and Galleries

HELEN L. CARD, NEW YORK

1 *Hang on, Fellers! We're Out on a Limb*, catalogue no. 5, (1963), pic. wraps, 95 pp., numerous illus. including one, p. 54, by E. (Deming, Leigh, Remington, Schoonover, Varian, Wyeth)

COLONIAL ART COMPANY, OKLAHOMA CITY
(SENATE ROOM, LINCOLN PLAZA INN)

2 *Western and Traditional American Paintings of the 19th and Early 20th Centuries* (auction catalog), June 10, 1973, pic. wraps, unpaged, 76 numbered illus. including one, no. 70, by E. (Borein, Deming, Dixon, Elwell, Goodwin, Johnson, Koerner, Russell, Schoonover, Wycth, Young)

CORNING COMMUNITY COLLEGE
CORNING, NEW YORK

3 *Exhibition of Paintings and Drawings by Nick Eggenhofer*, October 1964, wraps, unpaged, nine illus. by E. and a photo of him.

KENNEDY GALLERIES, NEW YORK

4 *Recent Acquisitions in Important Western Paintings*, October 1961, pic. wraps, pp. 150–188, numerous illus. including three, pp. 164 (two) and 165, by E. (Borein, Deming, Johnson, Remington, Russell, Schreyvogel, Zogbaum)

5 *Nick Eggenhofer, Paintings and Illustrations of the West*, pic. folder with five illus. by him and a list of his art for sale.

THE MAIN TRAIL GALLERIES, SCOTTSDALE, ARIZONA

5a *Nick Eggenhofer*, invitation to the reception opening the Retrospective Exhibition, April 27–May 11, 1974, folder with one illus. by E. and a photo of him.

5b Nick Eggenhofer, Retrospective Exhibition, April 27–May 11, 1974, pic. wraps, illus. by E.

PACIFIC NORTHWEST INDIAN CENTER
SPOKANE, WASH.

6 *Third Annual Western Art Show and Auction*, March 2, 3, 4, 1973, pic. wraps, 44 pp., preface, numerous illus. including one, p. 29, by E. (Borein, Deming, Hurd, Remington, Russell)

6a *Fourth Annual Western Art Show and Auction*, February 15–17, 1974, pic. wraps, 48 pp., numerous illus. incuding one, p. 24, by E. and with a brief biographical sketch of him. (Borein)

THE ROCKWELL GALLERY OF WESTERN ART
ROCKWELL FOUNDATION, CORNING, NEW YORK

7 *The Rockwell Gallery of Western Art*, n.d., folder, ten illus. including one by E. (Remington, Russell)

SHOSHONE FIRST NATIONAL BANK, CODY, WYOMING

8 *Nick Eggenhofer Exhibition, Paintings and Drawings*, March 1967, pic. wraps, folder, "Nick Eggenhofer — the Artist" by Harold McCracken, front cover drawing by E. and lists 49 items by him in the exhibition.

SOTHEBY PARKE BERNET, NEW YORK

9 *Americana Week*, January 24–27, 1973, colored pic. wraps, 257 (3) pp., numerous illus. including one, p. 43, by E. (Borein, Deming, Elwell, Koerner)

UCLA LIBRARY, LOS ANGELES

10 *The West — From Fact to Myth*, September 20–October 24, 1967, decor. wraps, 19 (1) pp., text by Philip Durham and Everett L. Jones, fourteen illus. including two, pp. (15) and (18), by E. (Remington)

THE UNITED STATES MILITARY ACADEMY LIBRARY
WEST POINT, NEW YORK

11 *Illustrators of the American West*, March 1973, decor. wraps, unpaged, "Program Notes" by John M. Car-

roll, nine illus. including one by E. (Bjorklund, Bugbee, Cisneros)

30 Bishop, Curtis. *Shadow Range.* Macmillan, N.Y., 1947, words "First Printing" on copyright page, cloth, 152 pp., d/w illus. by E.

31 ———. *By Way of Wyoming.* Macmillan, N.Y., 1946, words "First printing" on copyright page, cloth, 190 pp., d/w illus. by E.

32 *The Donald E. Boelter Collection of George A. Custer and the West.* Catalogue six, Guidon Books, Scottsdale, Arizona, 1973, colored pic. wraps, unpaged but in the 1134 numbered items two, nos. 828 and 829, are by E. and no. 829 is illustrated opposite nos. 517 and 518.

33 Bowman, Hank Wieand. *Famous Guns from the Smithsonian Collection.* Arco, N.Y., (1967), cloth, 112 pp., introduction, numerous illus. including one, p. 74, by E. (Remington)

34 Brande, Ralph (prepared by). *Workbook for American History for Catholic High School.* Sadlier, N.Y., Chicago, (1957), colored pic. wraps, 159 pp., maps, illus. including one, the complete cover in color by E.

35 Brown, Barron. *Comanche.* Sol Lewis, N.Y., 1973, words "Reprinted 1973 in a one-volume Limited Edition of 500 copies" on copyright page, cloth, blue endsheets, 139 pp., "Foreword" by John M. Carroll, "Preface" by Col. Philip M. Shockley, "Introduction" by Col. Clarence C. Clendenen, "Marching with Custer" by Lt. Col. Elwood P. Nye, twelve illus. including one, facing copyright page, by E.

36 Burnett, W. R. *Mi Amigo.* Knopf, N.Y., 1959, words "First Edition" on copyright page, two-tone cloth, 241 pp., black top, d/w illus. in color by E.

37 Burns, Walter N. *Tombstone.* Penguin Paperback, N.Y., 1942, pic. wraps, 284 pp., front cover by E.

38 Campbell, Walter S. *Mountain Men* by Stanley Vestal (pseud.). Houghton Mifflin, Boston, 1937, cloth, map endsheets, 296 pp., preface, notes, acknowledgments, bibliography, illus. with photos and old prints but d/w illus. in color by E.

39 ———. *Revolt on the Border* by Stanley Vestal (pseud.). Houghton Mifflin, Boston, 1938, cloth, 246 pp., d/w illus. by E.

40 (Carr.) *Historical Americana, Catalog Two.* James F. Carr, N.Y., 1960, pic. wraps, 30 pp., front cover illus. by E.

41 ———. *A Catalog of Books Relating to America and The West, Number Four.* N.Y., (1960), pic. wraps, (30) pp., front cover drawing by E.

42 ———. *Americana Catalog Ten.* James F. Carr, N.Y., 1962, pic. wraps, (32) pp., front cover illus. by E.

43 Carroll, John M., ed. *The Black Military Experience in the American West.* Liveright, N.Y., (1971), words "first edition, first printing" on copyright page, cloth, pic. endsheets, 591 pp., introduction, notes, bibliography, index, numerous illus. including two, endsheets and p. (396), by E. One of 300 (250 for sale) numbered copies signed by Carroll, slipcase, and accompanied by manually signed prints by Cisneros and Grandee.

44 ———. Same, first trade edition in cloth.

45 ———. *Buffalo Soldiers West.* (Old Army Press, Fort Collins, Colo., 1971), pic. leather, cloth endsheets, 63 pp., foreword, the artists, numerous illus. including two, title page and p. 26, by E. and a biographical sketch of him. Limited edition of 50 numbered copies signed by the author, each with an original drawing by Bjorklund. (Bjorklund, Bugbee, Cisneros, Remington)

46 ———. Same, first trade edition in pic. fabricoid.

47 (Christian.) *American Artists and Illustrators* (catalog no. 4). Peggy Christian, Bookseller, Los Angeles, 1965, pic. wraps, 20 pp., twenty-four illus. including one, p. 8, by E. (Borein, Dixon, Ellsworth, Remington, Russell)

48 Clark, Badger. *Sun and Saddle Leather.* Chapman & Grimes, Boston, (1942), words "New Edition 1942" on copyright page, fabricoid, 201 pp., orange top, four illus., front endsheet, back endsheet, title page and d/w, by E.

48a Coffen, Herbert (Editor and Publisher). *The Teepee Book.* Sol Lewis, N.Y., 1974, two volumes, cloth, tan endsheets, 889 pp. (continuous pagination), "Preface" by John M. Carroll, "Introduction" by Gene M. Gressley, index, numerous illus. including one in each volume, copyright pages, by E. Reprints the twenty-one issues. (Borein, Schreyvogel)

49 Collier, Edmund. *The Story of Buffalo Bill.* Grosset & Dunlap, N.Y., (1952), decor. cloth, pic. endsheets, 182 pp., (2) of advs., orange top, numerous drawings in the text and d/w illus. in color, by E.

50 ———. Same, a later printing with the colored illus. from the d/w of the first printed directly on the front cover and plain white endsheets.

51 ———. Same, first Portugese edition, Livraria Civilizacao — Editora, Porto, Portugal, October 1958,

boards, pic. endsheets, 186 (2) pp., numerous illus. by E.

52 ———. *The Story of Kit Carson*. Grosset & Dunlap, 1952, cloth, 180 pp., drawings by E. (Signature Books.)

53 ———. Same, first Portugese edition, Livraria Civilizacao — Editora, Porto, Portugal, May 1958, colored pic. wraps, 191 (1) pp., numerous illus. by E.

54 ———. *The Westerners Brand Book, Volume Five.* New York Posse, 1958, decor. cloth (the four quarterly issues privately bound), 96 pp., numerous illus. including eight, pp. 1, (24), 25, 49, 75, 78, 80 and 96, by E.

55 Collins, Dabney Otis. *Great Western Rides.* Sage Books, Denver, 1961, cloth, 277 pp., illus. by E.

56 Cook, James H. *Fifty Years on the Old Frontier.* Oklahoma, Norman, (1957), words "First printing in the new edition" on copyright page, cloth, 253 pp., brown top, "Captain Cook's Place Among Reminiscencers of the West" by J. Frank Dobie, author's preface, "Introduction" by Gen. Charles King, index, illus. with photos but d/w drawing by E.

57 Cornwell, Dean et al. *Advertising Arts and Crafts, Vol. 11.* Lee & Kirby, N.Y., Chicago, 1924, boards, paper label, 425 pp., numerous illus. including one, p. 122, by E.

58 Cousins, Margaret. *We Were There at the Battle of the Alamo.* Grosset & Dunlap, N.Y., 1958, pic. cloth, pic. map endsheets, 180 (1) pp., numerous drawings by E.

59 ———. Same, later printing with an illus. in color by E. printed directly on the front cover and with plain white endsheets.

60 Cox, Rev. John E. *Five Years in the United States Army.* Sol Lewis, N.Y., 1973, words "Reprinted 1973 in a Limited Edition of 500 copies" on copyright page, cloth, brown endsheets, 169 (2) pp., "Preface" by John M. Carroll, "An Introduction — with some notes" by Don Russell, bibliographical note, illustrated including one, facing copyright page, by E. that did not appear in the rare first issued at Owensville, Indiana, in 1892.

61 Crawford, Thomas Edgar. *The West of the Texas Kid.* University of Oklahoma Press, (1962), words "First Edition" on copyright page, stiff boards, 202 pp., "Introduction" and edited by Jeff C .Dykes, foreword, drawings by E. (The Western Frontier Library, no. 20).

62 ———. Same, first paperback edition, (1973), with front cover illus. by E.

63 Cunningham, Eugene. *Riders of the Night.* Houghton Mifflin, Boston, 1932, cloth, 278 pp., full d/w illus. by E.

64 ———. *Trail of the Macaw.* Houghton Mifflin, Boston and N.Y., 1935, cloth, 276 pp., d/w illus. by E.

65 ———. *The Ranger Way.* Houghton Mifflin, Boston, 1937, cloth, 241 pp., d/w illus. by E.

66 Decker, Peter. *Beyond a Big Mountain.* Hastings, N.Y., (1959), decor. cloth, 278 pp., d/w illus. by E.

67 East, Ben. *Narrow Escapes and Wilderness Adventures.* Outdoor Life and Dutton, N.Y., (1960), cloth, 321 pp., "Foreword" by Bill Rae, introduction, nine drawings, pp. 36, 61, 85, 114, 175, 202, 229, 249 and 261 plus d/w illus. by E.

68 Eggenhofer, Nick. *Wagons, Mules and Men.* Hastings House, (1961), cloth, 184 pp., "Where Thanks Are Due," "The Why and Wherefore," "About Nick Eggenhofer" by Ramon F. Adams, bibliography, index, profusely illus. by the author.

69 ———. Same, limited edition of 215 numbered and signed copies, each with an original watercolor by E., leather and decor. cloth, slipcase.

70 Emmett, Chris. *Shanghai Pierce.* University of Oklahoma Press, (1953), words "First Edition" on copyright page, cloth, 326 pp., drawings by E.

71 Ferris, Robert G. (series editor). *Soldier and Brave.* National Park Service, U.S.D.I., Washington, D.C., 1971, words "New Edition" on title page, cloth, pic. endsheets, 453 pp., "Foreword" by Sec. Rogers C. B. Morton, "Preface" by Director George B. Hartzog, Jr., suggested reading, index, maps, numerous illus. including one, p. 310, by E. (Leigh, Miller, Remington, Russell, Schreyvogel, Zogbaum)

72 Fox, Norman A. *The Valiant Ones.* Dodd Mead, N.Y., 1957, cloth, 241 pp., d/w illus. by E.

73 Frese, Walter (President). *Western Americana Books.* Hastings House, various dates, advertising folders with illustrations by E. on front covers. (This compiler has several, each with a different illustration by E.)

74 Frink, Maurice and Rizzari, Frances B., eds. *The Denver Westerners Brand Book, IX.* Denver, 1954, pic. cloth, 331 pp., appendix, index, illus. by E. (Edition of 500 copies.)

75 ——— et al. *When Grass Was King.* University of

ILLUSTRATION by Eggenhofer from *Wagons, Mules and Men*

Colorado Press, 1956, decor. cloth, map endsheets, 465 pp., green top, preface, bibliographies, index, illus. with photo and with eleven drawings, pp. (2), (4), 92, (134), 269, 297, 321, (331), 344, 378 and 441, by E. (Edition consists of 1500 numbered copies.)

76 Gann, Walter. *The Trail Boss.* Houghton Mifflin, Boston, 1937, cloth, 244 pp., d/w illus. by E.

77 Gard, Wayne. *The Chisholm Trail.* University of Oklahoma Press, (1954), words "First Edition" on copyright page, cloth, 296 pp., bibliography, index, drawings by E.

78 ———. *Fabulous Quarter Horse: Steel Dust.* Duell, Sloan and Pearce, (1958), decor. cloth, 64 pp., "How It Came About," bibliography, index, drawings by E.

79 ———. *The Great Buffalo Hunt.* Alfred A. Knopf, 1959, words "First Edition" on copyright page, pic. cloth, 324, xii, (2) pp., red top, foreword, bibliography, index, drawings by E. (Remington)

80 Gibson, A. M. *The Kickapoos, Lords of the Middle Border.* University of Oklahoma Press, (1963), words "First edition" on copyright page, cloth, 391 pp., brown top, preface, bibliography, index, illus. including two drawings, frontis. and title page, by E.

81 Glass, Major E. L. N. (compiled and edited by). *The History of the Tenth Cavalry 1866–1921.* (The Old Army Press, Ft. Collins, Colo., 1972), gilt decor. cloth, tan endsheets, 141 (4) pp., "Introduction" by John M. Carroll, appendices, maps, numerous illus. including one, the frontis. in color, by E. (First printing with the Eggenhofer frontispiece.)

82 Glidden, Fred. *Ramrod* by Luke Short (pseud.). Macmillan, N.Y., 1943, words "First Printing" on copyright page, cloth, 232 pp., d/w illus. in color by E.

83 ——— et al. *Bad Men and Good.* Dodd Mead, N.Y., 1953, pic. boards, 240 pp., foreword, drawing on title page (repeated on front cover and on the d/w) by E.

84 Greenly, A. H., ed. *The Westerners Brand Book, Volume 4.* New York Posse, The Westerners, N.Y., 1957, decor. cloth (the four quarterly issues privately bound), 95 (1) pp., illus. including one plate in color by E. Includes "Nick Eggenhofer: Today's Remington," an article by James D. Horan plus a photo of Nick in his studio.

85 Grinnell, George Bird. *The Fighting Cheyennes.* Oklahoma, Norman, (1956), new edition, cloth, 453 pp., maps, illustrated including one, d/w, by E. (The Civilization of the American Indian Series, volume 44).

86 *Hail to the Pioneers!* Souvenir program, 78th Convention, Society of Montana Pioneers, in conjunction with 68th Convention, Sons and Daughters of Montana Pioneers, Butte, August 23–25, 1962, colored pic. wraps, 20 pp., numerous illus. including three, front cover in color, inside front cover and back cover, by E. (Russell)

87 Haley, J. Evetts. *The XIT Ranch of Texas.* Oklahoma, Norman, (1953), words "New Edition — October, 1953" on copyright page, cloth, 258 pp., Back of the Story, appendix, bibliography, index, maps, illus. with photos but d/w illus. by E.

88 ———. Same, Western Frontier Library Edition, 1967, in boards and d/w by E.

89 Hamilton, W. T. *My Sixty Years on the Plains.* Oklahoma, Norman, (1960), words "First printing" (i.e. in The Western Frontier Library) on copyright page, "Introduction" by Donald J. Berthrong, "The Western Mountaineer" by Hilma S. Sieber, illus. including one, the d/w by E. (Russell)

90 Harmsen, Dorothy. *Harmsen's Western Americana.* Northland, Flagstaff, (1971), morocco and cloth, blue endsheets, 213 pp., "Foreword" by Robert Rockwell, introduction, selected bibliography, numerous illus. including one in color, p. (73), by E. and a biographical sketch. Limited edition of 150 numbered copies signed by the author, slipcase with morocco title label. (Beeler, Blumenschein, Borein, Dixon, Dunn, Dunton, Elwell, Hurd, Johnson, Leigh, Marchand, Miller, Russell, Von Schmidt, Wyeth)

91 ———. Same, first trade edition in two-tone cloth and with red endsheets.

92 Hastings House, N.Y. *Western Americana Books.* Advs. leaflet listing fifteen items and with front cover and five other illus. by E.

93 ———. Same, advs. leaflet listing twenty-five items and with front cover and two other illus. by E.

94 ———. Same, advs. leaflet listing twenty-nine items and with front cover and three other illus. by E.

95 (Hinkel.) *Southwest Books.* List no. 14, Hinkel's Book Shop, Stillwater, Oklahoma, (1955), pic. wraps, 18 pp., front cover drawing by E.

96 ———. *The Boomer.* No. 36, Hinkel's Book Shop, Stillwater, Oklahoma, August, 1961, pic. wraps, 44 pp., cover drawing by E.

97 ———. *The Boomer.* No. 37, Hinkel's Book Shop, Stillwater, Oklahoma, November, 1961, pic. wraps, 42 pp., one drawing, p. (3), by E.

98 ———. *The Boomer.* No. 53, Hinkel's Book Shop, Stillwater, Oklahoma, (1965), pic. wraps, 32 pp., front cover illus. by E.

99 Hoig, Stanley. *The Humor of the American Cowboy.* Caxton Printers, Caldwell, Idaho, 1958, pic. cloth and endsheets, 193 pp., preface, drawings by E. (Reissued in colored pic. wraps by The New American Library in 1960.)

100 ———. Same, but Signet Book (D1830) edition with the words "First Printing, July, 1960" on copyright page, colored pic. wraps, 157 pp., (3) of advs., all edges red, preface, numerous drawings in text plus the front cover illus. in color by E.

101 Horan, James D. *Across the Cimarron.* Crown, N.Y., (1956), cloth and boards, 301 pp., An Author's Search, epilogue, illus. with photos but the d/w illus. in color by E.

102 ———. *The Great American West.* Crown, N.Y., (1959), cloth and boards, 288 pp., introduction, bibliography, picture credits, index, 650 illus. including one, the d/w in color, by E. (Leigh, Miller, Remington, Russell, Schreyvogel)

103 Howard, Robert West. *This is the West* (The Life, Lore and Legend of the West). The New American Library, (N.Y., 1957), words "First Printing, August, 1957" on copyright page, pic. wraps, 240 pp., all edges red, the authors, two illus. in color, front and back of wraps, by E.

104 Hutchinson, W. H. *A Bar Cross Man.* Oklahoma, Norman, (1956), words "First edition" on copyright page, cloth, blue endsheets, 431 pp., Con Razon, Check List of Eugene Manlove Rhodes' Writing, index, illus. with three drawings, pp. (1), (93) and (229), by E. and with photos.

105 Jahns, Pat. *The Frontier World of Doc Holliday.* Hastings, N.Y., (1957), cloth and boards, 305 pp., prelude, bibliography, index, d/w illus. by E.

106 Jensen, Lee. *The Pony Express.* Grosset & Dunlap, N.Y., (1955), pic. boards, 154 pp., picture credits, "Books on the Period of the Pony Express," numerous illus. including ten double-page drawings, pp. 2–3, 12–13, 28–29, 52–53, 68–69, 74–75, 96–97, 112–113, 122–123 and 138–139, plus the d/w illus. in color, by E. (Lungren, Remington)

107 Kain, Robert C. *In the Valley of the Little Big Horn, the Seventh and the Sioux.* Privately printed for the author, (Newfane, Vermont, 1969), cloth, 128 pp., preface, illus. including one, p. 91, by E. (Leigh)

108 Kappler, Charles J. (compiled and edited by). *Indian Treaties, 1778–1883.* Interland Publishing, N.Y., 1972, decor. cloth, pic. endsheets, 1099 pp., maroon top, "Foreword" by Brantley Blue (Indian Claims Commissioner), "Introduction" by John M. Carroll, index, folding map, foldout double-page frontis. in color by E.

109 ———. Same, advs. folder with one illus. by E.

109a Kennedy, Michael S. (selected and edited by). *Cowboys and Cattlemen.* Hastings House, N.Y., (1964), horsehide with hair out, colored pic. endsheets, 364 (2) pp., introduction, index, numerous illustrations. Limited edition of 199 numbered copies, ten with original watercolors by E., in slipcase. (Borein, Russell)

110 Kilman, Ed and Wright, Theon. *Hugh Roy Cullen.* Prentice-Hall, (1954), cloth, map endsheets, 376 pp., orange top, publisher's note, index, drawings by E. and photos.

111 Knibbs, H. H. and Lummis, Turbese. *Gentlemen, Hush!* Houghton Mifflin, Boston and N.Y., 1933, cloth, 193 pp., d/w illus. in color by E.

112 Koller, Larry. *The Fireside Book of Guns.* Simon and Schuster, (1959), decor. cloth, pic. endsheets, 284 pp., introduction, acknowledgments, index, numerous illus. including one, pp. 136–7, by E. (Remington, Russell)

113 LaFarge, Oliver. *A Pictorial History of the American Indian.* Crown, N.Y., (1956), cloth and boards, 272 pp., index, numerous illus. including one, the d/w, by E. (Miller, Remington)

114 Lake, Stuart N. *Wyatt Earp, Frontier Marshal.* Houghton Mifflin, Boston and N.Y., 1931, cloth, 392 pp., foreword, index, illus. with photos but with d/w illus. by E.

115 ———. Same, special edition, 1955, with complete d/w illus. in color by E.

116 Latham, John H. *The Meskin Hound.* Putnam's, (1958), pic. boards, 191 pp., drawings by E.

117 Latendorf, E. Walter. *Catalogue No. 26.* Mannados Bookshop, N.Y., n.d., pic. wraps, 21 pp., eight illus. including two, on back wraps, by E. (James, Schoonover)

118 ———. *Catalogue No. 27.* Mannados Bookshop, N.Y., n.d., pic. wraps, 36 pp., 22 illus. including three, pp. 9 and 10 (two), by E. Note: Walter issued two catalogues numbered 27 — one upright (here de-

scribed) and one oblong that does not include an Eggenhofer illustration. (Goodwin, Lea, Lungren)

119 Lavender, David. *The Trail to Santa Fe.* Houghton Mifflin, 1958, cloth, 182 pp., illus. by E. (North Star Books.)

120 Leighton, Margaret. *The Story of General Custer.* Grosset & Dunlap, N.Y., (1954), cloth, pic. endsheets, 179 (1) pp., numerous drawings in text and d/w illus. in color by E.

121 ———. Same, a later printing with the colored illus. from the d/w of the first printed directly on the front cover and plain white endsheets.

122 (Lewis.) *A Catalogue of Reprints of Rare, Scholarly and Historical Americana.* Sol Lewis, N.Y., 1973, pic. wraps, 6 pp., nine illus. including one, back wrap, by E.

123 Lucas, Jay. *Boss of the Rafter C.* Green Circle Books, N.Y., 1937, cloth, 313 pp., d/w illus. by E.

124 Lucia, Ellis. *The Saga of Ben Holladay.* Hastings House, 1959, cloth, 374 pp., foreword, bibliography, index, d/w illus. and title page drawing by E.

124a McCracken, Harold. *The American Cowboy.* Double-day, Garden City, N.Y., 1973, de luxe binding, 196 pp., references, index, numerous illus. including five, pp. (89) color, (96), 165, (180) color and 190, by E. Limited edition of 300 numbered copies signed by the author, slipcase. (Borein, Cisneros, Johnson, Koerner, Leigh, Remington, Russell, Wyeth)

124b ———. Same, cloth with words "First edition after the limited edition of 300 copies" on copyright page.

125 MacDonald, William Colt. *The Three Mesquiteers.* Doubleday, Garden City, N.Y., 1944, words "First Edition" on copyright page, cloth, 214 pp., d/w illus. by E.

126 McGee, W. J. et al. *The Sioux Indians.* Sol Lewis, N.Y., 1973, words "Reprinted 1973 in a one-volume Limited Edition of 500 copies" on copyright page, cloth, black endsheets, 138 pp., "Foreword" by John M. Carroll, "Introduction" by Dr. John F. Bryde, numerous (four in color) illus. including one, facing copyright page, by E.

127 McNichols, Charles L. *Crazy Weather.* Macmillan, N.Y., 1944, cloth, 195 pp., d/w in color by E.

128 McPherren, Ida. *Trail's End.* Printed by Prairie Publishing Co., Casper, Wyo., 1938, but with a paste-on label of "Manthorne & Burack, Boston" on title page,

pic. cloth, 322 pp., photo as frontispiece, d/w drawing by E.

129 Meng, John J. et al. *American History for Catholic High School.* Sadlier, N.Y. and Chicago, colored pic. cloth, 682, xlvi pp., appendix, glossary, index, maps, numerous illus. including one, the complete cover, by E.

130 Moody, Ralph. *Geronimo.* Random House, 1958, words "First Printing" on copyright page, decor. cloth and endsheets, 186 pp., yellow top, index, drawings by E.

130a ———. Same, later printing with plain tan endsheets, title page on brown background and with larger illustrations.

131 Murray, Robert A. *Citadel on the Santa Fe Trail.* Old Army Press, Bellevue, Neb., 1970, pic. cloth, 37 (11) pp., illus. including one, front cover in gold and repeated on the title page in black and white, on the half-title and d/w in color, by E.

132 Myers, John Myers. *Maverick Zone.* Hastings House, 1961, pic. cloth, 306 pp., forenote, d/w illus. and three drawings by E.

133 Nye, Nelson. *Cartridge-Case Law.* Macmillan, N.Y., 1944, words "First Printing" on copyright page, cloth, 128 pp., d/w illus. in color by E.

134 ———. *Wild Horse Shorty.* Macmillan, N.Y., 1944, words "First Printing" on copyright page, cloth, 203 pp., d/w illus. by E.

135 ———. *Blood of Kings.* Macmillan, N.Y., 1946, cloth, 203 pp., d/w illus. by E.

136 ———. *Barber of Tubac.* Macmillan, N.Y., 1947, cloth, 208 pp., d/w illus. by E.

137 Nye, Wilbur Sturtevant. *Bad Medicine and Good, Tales of the Kiowas.* University of Oklahoma Press, (1962), words "First Edition" on copyright page, cloth, 291 pp., brown top, illus. by E.

138 The Old Army Press. *American Militaria.* (Fort Collins, Colo.), catalog no. 3, advs. leaflet, numerous illus. including one by E.

139 ———. Same, catalog no. 4, advs. leaflet, numerous illus. including one by E.

140 ———. Same, catalog no. 5, advs. leaflet, numerous illus. including two by E.

141 ———. *No One Illustrates the West Like Eggenhofer!* Advs. flyer with six illus. by E.

142 ———. *Boy, Have We Got a Season for You!* (Christ-

mas Season, That is). Advs. flyer with one illus. by E.

143 Overholser, Wayne D. *Buckaroo's Code*. Macmillan, N.Y., 1947, words "First Printing" on copyright page, cloth, 223 pp., d/w illus. by E.

144 Phares, Ross. *Texas Tradition*. Henry Holt, (1954), words "First Edition" on copyright page, cloth, 231 pp., notes, index, drawings by E.

145 Poe, John W. *The Death of Billy the Kid*. Houghton Mifflin, Boston and N.Y., 1933, cloth, 59 (1) pp., "Introduction" by Maurice Garland Fulton, epilogue, illus. with photos and plans, but d/w drawing by E.

146 Preece, Harold. *The Dalton Gang*. Hastings House, 1963, cloth, 320 pp., notes, bibliography, index, introduction, d/w illus. by E.

147 Raine, William MacLeod. *The Black Tolts*. Houghton Mifflin, Boston, 1932, cloth, 293 pp., d/w illus. by E.

148 ———. Same, Grosset & Dunlap, (N.Y., 1932), reprint with a Russell illus. on the title page and with the d/w illus. by E.

149 ———. *The Broad Arrow*. Houghton Mifflin, Boston, 1933, cloth, 292 pp., d/w illus. by E.

150 ———. *King of the Bush*. Houghton Mifflin, Boston, 1937, cloth, 299 pp., d/w illus. by E.

151 ———. *Run of the Brush*. Houghton Mifflin, Boston, 1937, cloth, 288 pp., d/w illus. by E.

152 ———. *Hell and High Water*. Houghton Mifflin, Boston, 1943, cloth, d/w illus. by E.

153 ———. *Bucky Follows a Cold Trail*. Grosset & Dunlap, N.Y., cloth, 306 pp., d/w illus. by E.

153a Reed, Walt. *The Illustrator in America*. Reinhold, N.Y., (1966), cloth, pic. green endsheets, 217 (1) pp., "Is Illustration Art" by Albert Dorne, bibliography, numerous illus. including one, p. 131, by E. and a biographical sketch of him. (Blumenschein, Crawford, Dunn, Dunton, Fischer, Fogarty, Goodwin, James, Keller, Koerner, Remington, Russell, Schoonover, Stoops, Wyeth)

154 Richthofen, Walter Baron von. *Cattle-Raising on the Plains of North America*. University of Oklahoma Press, (1964), word "First printing of the new edition" on copyright page, stiff boards, 120 pp., "Introduction" by Edward Everett Dale, note, frontis. (and repeated on d/w) by E. (The Western Frontier Library, no. 24.)

155 Sandoz, Mari. *The Cattlemen*. Hastings House, 1958, cloth and boards, map endsheets, 527 pp., green top,

acknowledgments, foreword, notes, bibliography, index, illus. including one double-page drawing in color by E. (Edition limited to 199 copies numbered and signed, boxed.)

156 ———. Same, first trade edition in cloth without the Eggenhofer double-page drawing but the d/w illus. in color by E.

156a Schreiber, Charles D. (editor and publisher). *Old Travois Trails*. Sol Lewis, N.Y., 1974, cloth, green endsheets, 389 pp., "Preface" by John M. Carroll, "Introduction" by Gene M. Gressley, index, numerous illus. including one, copyright page, by E. Reprints the fifteen issues.

157 Sharkey, Don et al. *Before Our Nation Began*. Sadlier, N.Y., Chicago, (1953), colored pic. cloth, 288 pp., glossary, index, numerous illus. including one, the complete cover in color, by E.

158 ———. *How Our Nation Began*. Sadlier, N.Y., Chicago, (1954), colored pic. cloth, 192 pp., index and glossary, numerous illus. including one, the complete cover in color by E.

159 ———. Same, *Teacher's Key*. Sadlier, (1955), pic. wraps, 10 pp., front cover illus. by E.

160 ———. Same, *History Workbook*. By Ralph Brande, Sadlier, Chicago, N.Y., 1956, colored pic. wraps, 96 pp., numerous illus. including one, the complete cover in color by E.

161 ———. *The Making of Our Nation*. Sadlier, N.Y., Chicago, (1955), colored pic. cloth, 376, viii, (1) pp., glossary, index, numerous illus. including twenty-five, twenty-four in the text and complete cover in color, by E.

162 ———. *How Our Nation Grew*. Sadlier, N.Y., Chicago, 1955, colored pic. cloth, 218, x pp., glossary, index, numerous illus. including thirteen, twelve in the text and complete cover in color, by E.

163 Shirley, Glenn. *Buckskin and Spurs*. Hastings House, (1958), two-tone cloth, 191 pp., foreword, bibliography, illus., d/w illus. by E.

164 Shumway, George et al. *Conestoga Wagon, 1750–1850*. Early American Industries Assn. and George Shumway, (York, Pa., 1964), pic. cloth, pic. endsheets, 206 pp., "Foreword" by Lawrence S. Cooke, preface, index, numerous illus. including one, endsheets (repeated on the d/w), by E.

164a ———. Same, second and enlarged edition with added pictures of wagons.

165 Silber, Irwin (compiled and edited by). *Songs of the Great American West.* Macmillan, N.Y., (1967), words "First Printing" on copyright page, two-tone pic cloth, tan endsheets, 334 pp., yellow top, music annotated, edited and arranged by Earl Robinson, introduction, bibliography, discography, indices, numerous illus. including one, p. 183, by E. (De Yong, Remington, Russell)

166 *The Southwest Historical Series.* Porcupine Press, Philadelphia, (1973), pic. advs. folder, five illus. including one, front cover, by E.

167 Springer, Thomas Grant. *The Sagebrush Buckaroo.* Burt, N.Y., Chicago, (1932), cloth, 275 pp., d/w illus. in color by E. (The illus. was a magazine cover and the artist does not know how Burt got the use of it.)

168 *The Story of American Hunting and Firearms.* By the editors of *Outdoor Life,* McGraw-Hill, N.Y. etc., (1959), cloth and decor. boards, 172 pp., index, numerous illus. including more than forty drawings by E., slipcase.

169 Tinker, Edward Larocque. *Los Jinetes de las Americas.* Guillermo Kraft, Buenos Aires, (1949), colored pic. wraps, 147 pp., Un Tributo, El Porqué, "Gaucho" by Fernan Silva Valdes, notes, *bibliografia,* numerous illus., some in color, including four drawings, pp. 95, 96, 102 and 107 and one full-page color plate, facing p. 106, by E. (Edition of 5200 numbered copies.)

170 ———. *The Horsemen of the Americas and the Literature They Inspired.* Hastings House, (Guillermo Kraft, Buenos Aires), 1953, decor. cloth, A Tribute, The Reasons, "Gaucho" by Fernan Silva Valdes, notes, bibliography, numerous illus., some in color, including four drawings, pp. 95, 96, 102 and 107 and one full-page color plate, facing p. 106, by E. (Edition of 1575 numbered copies.)

170a ———. Same, second and revised edition, Texas, Austin and London, (1967), pic. cloth, 147 pp., "Introduction" by Thomas F. McCann, bibliography, index, numerous illus. including three drawings, pp. 102, 108 and 115 and one new plate in color, "Sunfisher," facing p. 102, by E.

170b *Trail Guide to Fort Bowie* (National Historic Site). National Park Service with Southwest Parks and Monuments Assn., revised, third printing, wraps, illus. including one, p. 7, by E.

171 Tuttle, W. C. *Spawn of the Desert.* Doubleday, Garden City, N.Y., 1923, colored pic. wraps, 120 pp., front cover illus. by E.

172 ———. *Rifled Gold.* Houghton Mifflin, Boston, 1934, cloth, 272 pp., d/w illus. by E.

173 ———. *Hashknife of Stormy River.* Houghton Mifflin, Boston, 1935, cloth, 252 pp., d/w illus. by E.

174 ———. *Hashknife of the Double Bar 8.* Houghton Mifflin, Boston and N.Y., 1936, cloth, 244 pp., d/w illus. in color, by E.

175 ———. *Ghost Trails.* Houghton Mifflin, Boston, 1940, cloth, 275 pp., d/w illus. by E.

176 ———. *The Dead-Line.* Grosset & Dunlap, N.Y., (1941), cloth, 261 pp., d/w illus. by E.

177 Ullman, James Ramsey. *Down the Colorado with Major Powell.* Houghton Mifflin, 1960, cloth, 184 pp., illus. by E.

178 Utley, Robert M. *Frontiers Men in Blue.* Macmillan, N.Y., (1967), words "First Printing" on copyright page, cloth, map endsheets, introduction, bibliography, index, maps, illus. including one, between pp. 240 and 241, by E. (Remington)

179 Von Richthofen, Baron Walter. *Cattle-Raising on the Plains of North America.* Oklahoma, Norman, (1964), words "First printing of the new edition" on copyright page, boards, 120 pp., "Introduction" by E. E. Dale, note, frontis. by E.

180 Wagner, Glendolin Damon. *Old Neutriment.* Sol Lewis, N.Y., 1973, words "Reprinted 1973 in a Limited Edition of 500 copies" on copyright page, cloth, black endsheets, 256 pp., "Introduction" by John M. Carroll, notes, illus. including one, facing copyright page, by E.

181 Ward, Don, ed. *Hoof Trails and Wagon Tracks.* Dodd, Mead, N.Y., 1957, cloth, map endsheets, 298 pp., note, introduction, d/w illus. by E.

182 ———. *Bits of Silver.* Hastings House, 1961, cloth, 306 pp., introduction, d/w illus. by E.

183 Ward, Fay E. *The Cowboy at Work.* Hastings, N.Y., (1958), two-tone decor. cloth, decor. endsheets, 289 pp., foreword, index, 600 detail drawings by the author but with an illus. in color on the d/w and with a detail from it in black and white as the frontis., by E.

184 Webb, Walter Prescott. *The Story of the Texas Rangers.* Grosset & Dunlap, N.Y., (1957), pic. cloth, pic. map endsheets, 152 pp., numerous illus. including the d/w, front cover and endsheets, by E.

185 ———. Same, A Bouldin House Book from the Encino Press, Austin, (1971), words "Second Edition"

on copyright page, smaller format with a "Preface" by Terrell (Mrs. W. P.) Webb and with a different Eggenhofer illus. on d/w, front cover and the double title page but the same illus. in the text.

186 Whitman, S. E. *The Troopers.* Hastings House, (1962), pic. cloth, 256 pp., foreword, appendix, bibliography, index, eleven drawings by E.

The Artist and His Art

187 Allred, B. W. (Bill). "Nick Eggenhofer — Western Artist," a biographical sketch in *Corral Dust,* December 1959.

188 Beitz, Lee. "Nick Eggenhofer's West," an article in *True West,* March–April 1968, with four illus. by E.

189 Bell, Col. William Gardner. "Nick Eggenhofer," a biographical sketch in *Corral Dust,* Summer 1964, with one illus. by E.

190 Greenly, A. H., ed. *The Westerners Brand Book, Volume One.* New York Posse, Winter, 1954, decor. cloth, (the four quarterly issues privately bound), pp. 16, 24, 24, 22, illus. Brief biographical sketch of Eggenhofer, new regular member.

191 Krakel, Dean, ed. "Nick Eggenhofer," a brief biographical sketch in *Persimmon Hill* 3:3, (1973), one illus. by E. and a photo of him.

191a ———. "National Academy of Western Art," a report in *Persimmon Hill* 3:4 (1973), Eggenhofer was awarded the Trustees' Gold Medal for outstanding contributions and achievements in the field of Western Art and there is a photo of him (with the medal).

191b Madsen, Brigham D. and Betty M. "The Diamond R Rolls Out," an article in *Montana* 21:2, Spring 1971, with six illus. by E.

192 Muno, Richard. "Nick Eggenhofer: Fifty Years of Painting the West," an article in *Persimmon Hill,* Winter 1971, with seven illus. by E. and five photos of him.

193 Pacific Northwest Indian Center. *Second Annual Art Auction.* Davenport Hotel, Spokane, Wash., February 18–19, 1972, pic. wraps, unpaged, brief biography of E.

194 Richard, Jack. "Eggenhofer, Artist of the Wild West," an article in *In Wyoming* 1:4, Summer 1968, with six illus. by E., a photo of him before his easel and a photo of his scale model of a Concord stagecoach.

THE SILENT PLACES by Ellsworth from *Ellsworth, Artist of the Old West*

CLARENCE ARTHUR ELLSWORTH
1885–1961

Catalogues of Art Exhibitions and Galleries

BAKER COLLECTOR GALLERY, LUBBOCK, TEXAS

1 *Baker Collector Gallery*, n.d., pic. wraps, unpaged, numerous illus. including one, "Iron Eyes Cody," by E. (Hurd, Johnson, Russell, Wyeth)

GALLERY WEST, DENVER

2 *Prospective in Western Art*, 1972, numerous illus. including two by E. (Borein, Deming, Dixon, Remington, Russell, Schreyvogel)

SOTHEBY PARKE BERNET, LOS ANGELES

3 *Important 19th and Early 20th Century American Paintings*, sale no. 81, May 22–23, 1973, colored pic. wraps, 167 (5) pp., numerous illus. including one, p. 74, by E. (Dixon, Dunton, Russell)

Illustrated by the Artist

4 Ainsworth, Ed. *The Cowboy in Art.* World, N.Y. and Cleveland, (1968), words "First Printing 1968" on copyright page, full leather, orange endsheets, 242 pp., all edges gilt, "Foreword" by John Wayne, index, numerous illus. including one, p. 67, by E. and a photo of him with Iron Eyes Cody. Special edition of 1,000 numbered copies, slipcase. (Beeler, Borein, Bugbee, De Yong, Dixon, Dunton, Eggenhofer, Hurd, James, Johnson, Koerner, Mora, Perceval, Remington, Russell, Santee, Schreyvogel, Von Schmidt)

5 ———. Same, first trade edition in gilt lettered and illus. cloth, orange endsheets.

6 ———. Same, reprint by Bonanza Books, N.Y., in red lettered and illus. cloth, white endsheets.

7 Beery, Noah, Jr. et al (Book Committee). *The Westerners Brand Book.* (Book One.) Los Angeles Corral, 1947, morocco and decor. cloth, pic. endsheets, 176 pp., "Preface" by Sheriff H. E. Britzman, appendices,

bibliography, errata, index, numerous illus. including seven, pp. 63 (3), 64, 79 (2) and 136, by E. Edition of 600 copies. (Russell)

8 Boelter, Homer H. et al (Book Committee). *The Westerners Brand Book.* (Book Two.) Los Angeles Corral, 1948, pic. cloth and endsheets, 175 pp., "Preface" by Sheriff Paul W. Galleher, contributors, bibliography, index, numerous illus. including two, pp. 16 and 134, by E. Edition of 400 copies. (Borein, Russell)

9 ——— (Sheriff). *The Westerners Brand Book.* (Book Three.) Los Angeles Corral, (1950), morocco and decor. cloth, pic. endsheets, 263 pp., foreword, contributors, list of Western Artists, index, numerous illus. including seven, pp. 54, 143, 144, 145, 214, 229 and 236, by E. (Blumenschein, Borein, Dixon, Johnson, Perceval, Russell)

10 (Carlisle, Bill.) *Bill Carlisle, Lone Bandit: an Autobiography.* Trail's End Pub. Co., Pasadena, Calif., (1946), morocco, map endsheets by E., 220 pp., illus., deluxe edition, numbered and signed. (Russell)

11 ———. Same, trade edition in cloth.

12 Peggy Christian, Bookseller, Los Angeles. *American Artists and Illustrators.* Catalog no. 4, pic. wraps, 20 pp., two illus., p. 8, by E. (Borein, Dixon, Eggenhofer, Remington, Russell)

13 Cody, Iron Eyes. *How Indians Sign Talk in Pictures.* Homer E. Boelter, Hollywood, (1952), words "First Edition" on copyright page, colored pic. wraps, (Introduction) by F. W. Hodge, numerous illus. by E.

14 Coursey, O. W. *Pioneering in Dakota.* Education Supply Co., Mitchell, S.D., (1937), fabricoid, 160 pp., sixteen illus. including four, pp. (16), (125), (129) and (135), by E.

15 Edwards, Eddie I., ed. *The Westerners Brand Book.*

(Book Ten.) Los Angeles, 1963, two-tone decor. fabricoid, pic. endsheets, 241 pp., foreword, "Brand Book X Tally Sheet" by Don Meadows, index, "Little White Chieftain" (Ellsworth) by Iron Eyes Cody, numerous illus. including forty, one of which is a large folding plate in color, by E. Edition of 525 copies.

16 Ellsworth, Clarence, *Bows and Arrows.* Southwest Museum, Los Angeles, 1950, wraps, 20 pp., illus. by the author. (Southwest Museum leaflets, no. 24.)

17 Hafen, LeRoy R., ed. *The Mountain Men and the Fur Trade of the Far West,* vol. II. Clark, Glendale, Calif., 1965, cloth, 401 pp., (2) of advs., brown top, preface, frontis. by E. and other illus. from photos.

18 Harrington, M. R. *Dickon Among the Lenape Indians.* Winston, Philadelphia etc., (1928), cloth, map endsheets, 353 pp., "The Lenape Language," bibliography, numerous illus. by E.

19 ———. *The Indians of New Jersey (Dickon Among the Lenapes).* Rutgers University Press, New Brunswick, N.J., (1963), cloth, 353 pp., "Introduction" by Mary V. Gaver (Rutgers), author's introduction, "The Lenape Language," numerous illus. by E.

20 Holmes, Roger and Bailey, Paul. *Fabulous Farmer.* Westernlore, Los Angeles, (1956), colored pic. boards, 184 pp., illus. with drawings by Paul von Klieben and E.

21 King, Frank M. *Mavericks.* Trail's End, Pasadena, Calif., (1947), words "First Edition" on copyright page, cloth, pic. endsheets, 275 pp., "Introduction" by Ramon F. Adams, illus. including sixteen section half-title drawings by E. (Russell)

22 Koenig, George, ed. *Brand Book 12.* Los Angeles Corral, The Westerners, (1966), decor. cloth, decor. black endsheets, 211 pp., "The Old West is Gone" (foreword) by the editor, index, numerous illus. including one, p. 75, by E. (Perceval)

23 Layne, J. Gregg and Robinson, W. W., eds. *The Westerners Brand Book.* (Book Five.) Los Angeles Corral, (1953), morocco and decor. cloth, pic. endsheets, 180 pp., "Foreword" by Sheriff Bert H. Olson, contributors, bibliography, index, "We Thank You," numerous illus. including twenty-six, one of which is a double-page plate in color by E. Edition of 400 copies. (Perceval, Russell)

24 ———. *The Westerners Brand Book.* (Book Four.) Los Angeles Corral, (1951), morocco and decor. cloth, pic. endsheets, 232 pp., "foreword" by Sheriff Paul D. Bailey, bibliography, index, "We Thank You," nu-

merous illus. including five, title page and pp. (7), (14), 208 and 209, by E. Edition of 400 copies. (Perceval, Russell)

25 ———. *The Westerners Brand Book.* (Book Six.) Los Angeles Corral, (1956), leatherette and decor. boards, map endsheets, 163 pp., "Foreword" by Sheriff Arthur H. Clark, Jr., contributors, bibliography, index, "Con Mil Gracias," numerous illus. including eight, dedication page and pp. 69, 91, 96, 97, 119, 122 and 123, by E. Edition of 400 copies. (Borein)

26 McCreight, M. I. *Firewater and Forked Tongues.* Trail's End, Pasadena, (1947), words "First Edition" on copyright page, cloth, pic. endsheets, 180 pp., illus. including one drawing, half-title (and repeated on title page), by E. (Russell)

27 Meadows, Don, ed. *The Westerners Brand Book.* (Book Eight.) Los Angeles Corral, (1959), morocco and decor. cloth, 229 (1) pp., foreword, contributors, "Muchas Gracias," numerous illus. including two, title page and p. 36, by E. Edition of 525 copies. (Dixon, Perceval)

28 Nunis, Doyce B., Jr. (introduced and edited by). *The San Francisco Vigilance Committee of 1856 — Three Views:* 1. William T. Coleman, 2. William T. Sherman, 3. James O'Meara. The Silver Anniversary Publication of The Los Angeles Westerners, (1971). Decor. fabricoid, pic. endsheets, 180 pp., preface, appendices, bibliography, index, numerous illus. including one, p. 62, by E. (a charter member of the Corral).

29 O'Neil, Kathryn Fingado. *Retreat of a Frontier.* Westernlore, Los Angeles, 1950, cloth, 276 pp., d/w illus. by E.

30 Price, Con. *Memories of Old Montana.* The Highland Press, Hollywood, (1945), words "Deluxe Edition, 125 copies privately printed, numbered and signed by the author" on copyright page. Pigskin, marbled endsheets, 154 pp., illus.; small drawing of the author on the front flap of the d/w by E. (Russell)

31 ———. Same, first trade edition in cloth.

32 ———. *Trails I Rode.* Trail's End, Pasadena, Calif., (1947), morocco, brand decor. red endsheets by E., illus. Photo of Price and Ellsworth facing p. 161, E. in group picture facing p. 193, tribute to E. p. 50. One of 350 numbered and signed copies. (Russell)

33. ———. Same, trade edition in cloth.

34 Reynolds, J. E. *History of the Westerners.* Reprinted from *The Westerners Brand Book.* (Book Seven.) Los

ILLUSTRATION by Ellsworth from *Cottonwood Yarns*

Angeles Corral, 1957, pic. wraps, one illus. by E. plus photos.

35 ———. *Western Americana*, Catalogue no. 19, Van Nuys, March 1954, pic. wraps, 32 mimeographed pages, four illus., front cover and three inside the front cover, by E. includes a tribute "A Note on Clarence Ellsworth, Artist of the West" and the first check list of Ellsworth illustrated items.

36 ———. *Gunfighters of the Old West.* (Catalogue 40.) J. E. Reynolds, Van Nuys, Calif., April 1957, pic. wraps, (15) pp., front cover illus. by E.

37 Robinson, W. W., ed. *The Westerners Brand Book.* (Book Seven.) Los Angeles Corral, (1957), morocco and decor. cloth, decor. endsheets, publisher's note, contributors, numerous illus. including four, pp. 71, 155, 175, and 213, by E. Edition of 475 copies. (Perceval, Russell)

38 Russell, Charles M. *Rawhide Rawlins Rides Again, or, Behind the Swinging Doors.* Trail's End, Pasadena, Calif., (1948), gilt decor. leather, pic. endsheets, 61 (2) pp., yellow top, fourteen illus. including one, p. (42), by E. One of 300 copies. (Bugbee, Perceval, Russell)

39 Scott, Carroll Dewilton. *Here's Don Coyote.* Westernlore, Los Angeles, (1956), decor. cloth, tan endsheets, 200 pp., ten illus., front cover, title page and facing pp. 32, 48, 80, 96, 128, 144, 160 and 176, by E.

40 Shinn, Charles Howard. *Graphic Description of Pacific Coast Outlaws.* Westernlore Press, Los Angeles, 1958, cloth, 107 pp., pic. endsheets by E., illus. Reprint of very rare 1887 edition but the first with Ellsworth endsheets and introduction and notes by J. E. Reynolds.

41 Stephens, Dan V. *Stephens Family Genealogies.* Privately printed, Fremont, Neb., 1940, cloth, 150 (429) pp., illus. by E. Revised edition but first with E. illus.

42 ———. *Passing of the Buffalo.* Privately printed by the author, Fremont, Neb., (1938), pic. buffalo hide, 35 pp., illus. with drawings by E. and one photo, map.

43 ———. *Cottonwood Yarns.* Hammond & Stephens, Fremont, Neb., 1935, pic. cloth, tinted endsheets, 109 pp., illus. with photos and with over 100 drawings by E.

44 Sutton, Ernest V. *A Life Worth Living.* Trail's End, Pasadena, (1948), words "First Edition" on copyright page, cloth, colored pic. endsheets, 350 pp., red top, illus. with photos and with seventeen chapter head drawings and the endsheets painting in color by E.

45 Walters, Madge Hardin. *Early Days and Indian Ways.* Westernlore, Los Angeles, (1956), decor. cloth, 254 pp., illus., d/w illus. by E.

46 *The Warrior of Midland College* (Midland College Yearbook). Fremont, Nebraska, 1931, fabricoid, 206 pp., numerous illus. including twenty-six by E.

47 Wearin, Otha D. *Wearin's Holiday Life, no. 17,* Christmas 1955, Hastings, Iowa, pic. wraps, unpaged, illus. including a photo of E. with four of his paintings.

48 ———. Same, *no. 18,* Christmas 1956, Hastings, Iowa, pic. wraps, unpaged, cover drawing by E. and a group photo including him.

49 ———. Same, *no. 29,* Christmas 1967, Hastings, Iowa, colored pic. wraps, unpaged, front cover reproduces an oil in color, "Morning Flight," by E.

50 ———. Same, *no. 30,* Christmas 1968, Hastings, Iowa, pic. wraps, unpaged, cover drawing by E.

51 ———. Same, *no. 32,* Christmas 1970, Hastings, Iowa, pic. wraps, unpaged, cover drawing by E.

52 ———. Same, *no. 33,* Christmas 1971, Hastings, Iowa, pic. wraps, unpaged, cover drawing by E.

52a ———. Same, *nos. 34 and 35,* Christmas 1972 and 1973, Hastings, Iowa, pic. wraps, unpaged, illus. including one, front cover, by E.

53 ———. *A Century on an Iowa Farm.* Hastings, Iowa, 1959, wraps, unpaged (84), numerous illus. primarily from photos including one of E. with four of his paintings and with a Russell in the background and E. appears in another photo.

54 ———. *Clarence Arthur Ellsworth, Artist of the Old West.* World Publishing Co., Shenandoah, Iowa, words "This edition is strictly limited to seven-hundred and fifty copies, signed by the author" on p. (7), pic. fabricoid, 171 (4) pp., introduction, bibliography of publications illus. by Ellsworth, appendix, newspaper comment, index, numerous illus. (six in color) by E. and with many photos of him.

55 ———. *Americana, The Story of a Great Western Artist,* advs., folder for *Clarence Arthur Ellsworth* with one illus. by E. and a photo of him.

56 The Westerners, Los Angeles Corral. Broadside invitation to the Annual Rendezvous, Saturday Sept.

20, 1969, 10 3/4 x 17 1/4", four illus. including one by E.

57 Westernlore Press, Los Angeles. *Books of the West from the West.* Spring 1956, decor. wraps, 20 pp., illus. including one, p. 8, by E.

58 White, Michael C. *California All the Way Back to 1828.* G. Dawson, Los Angeles, 1956, cloth, map end-sheets, 93 pp., "Introduction" (and notes) by Glen Dawson, maps, illus. by E. Edition limited to 300 copies. (Written by Thomas Savage for Bencroft Library, 1877.)

The Artist and His Art

59 Bailey, Paul, "Vava Con Dios, Clarence Ellsworth," a tribute in *The Westerners Branding Iron,* publication no. 56, Los Angeles Corral, March 1961 and with a photo of E.

60 Boelter, Homer H. (Roundup Foreman). *The Brand Book,* vol. 1, no. 3. The Los Angeles Corral of the Westerners, (16) pp., numerous illus. including a photo of E. and five drawings by him. Brief biographical sketch of E. and feature article "The Indian as a Seer" by him (partly autobiographical).

61 Bucklin, Clarissa, ed. *Nebraska Art and Artists.* School of Fine Arts, University of Nebraska, Lincoln, (1932), pic. wraps, 82 pp., preface, illus., brief biographical sketch of E., p. 35.

62 Cody, Bertha Parker. "Clarence Arthur Ellsworth," a tribute following his death in *The Masterkey,* Southwest Museum, Los Angeles, April-June 1961 and with a photo of E.

63 Cody, Iron Eyes. His greetings to the members of the Corral with a cartoon by E., *The Westerners Branding Iron,* publication no. 99, December 1970.

64 Dykes, Jeff C. *High Spots in Western Illustrating.* Kansas City Posse, The Westerners, (1964), cloth, 29 pp., two illus. No. 8 above is High Spot 72 and no. 9 is H. S. 75. Limited to 250 numbered and signed copies. (An edition in wraps, was issued to members.)

65 Harrington, M. R. "Ancient Life Among the Southern California Indians," an article in *The Masterkey,* May-September 1955 with nine illus. by E.

66 Hinshaw, Merton E. (Director). *Painters of the West.* Charles W. Bowers Memorial Museum, Santa Ana, 1972, biographical sketch of E.

67 McClintock, Walter. A portrait of "Curley Bear, Blackfoot Chief and Tribal Judge" by Ellsworth presented to the Museum, *The Masterkey,* January 1945 — it is reproduced on the front cover.

68 Wearin, Otha D. *Wearin's Holiday Life, no. 8,* Christmas 1946, Hastings, Iowa, colored pic. wraps, tribute to Ellsworth and two photos of him. (Russell)

69 ———. "California Gold in an Iowa Valley," an article in *The Westerners Branding Iron,* publication no. 33, Los Angeles, March 1956 with one illus. by E.

70 ———. "Clarence Ellsworth, Painter of the Old West," an article in *The Western Collector* 2:4, June 1964, four illus. (one repeated on front cover) by E. and a photo of him.

71 *Who's Who in American Art.* 1959-61, includes a biography of E.

COW HUNTER by Elwell   *Collection of the author*

ROBERT FARRINGTON ELWELL
1874–1962

Catalogues of Art Exhibitions and Galleries

COLONIAL ART COMPANY, OKLAHOMA CITY
(SENATE ROOM, LINCOLN PLAZA INN)

0 *Western and Traditional American Paintings of the 19th and Early 20th Centuries* (auction catalog), June 10, 1973, pic. wraps, unpaged, 76 numbered illus. including one, no. 14, by E. (Borein, Deming, Dixon, Eggenhofer, Goodwin, Johnson, Koerner, Russell, Schoonover, Wyeth, Young)

HERITAGE INN, GREAT FALLS, MONTANA
(THE ADVERTISING CLUB OF GREAT FALLS)

0a *C. M. Russell Sixth Annual Auction of Original Western Art*, March 14–15, 1974, pic. wraps, unpaged, lists 165 lots for sale, numerous illus. including one, lot 117, by E. (Borein, Deming, Hurd, Schreyvogel)

SOTHEBY PARKE BERNET, NEW YORK

1 *Americana Week*, sale no. 3467, January 24–27, 1973, photos of two bronzes, p. 40, by E. (Borein, Deming, Eggenhofer, Koerner)

Illustrated by the Artist

2 Adams, Andy. *Log of a Cowboy*. Houghton Mifflin, 1927, cloth with colored illus. mounted on front cover, pic. endsheets, 324 pp., six illus. in color, frontis. and facing pp. 62, 86, 158, 242 and 304 and drawings on the title page and p. 324, by E.

3 *An Evening with Western Authors*. Presented by Houghton Mifflin Co. (Boston) at the California Library Association meeting, Riverside, April 14, 1928. Brochure, 4 pp., illus. by E. (Among the authors listed inside the front cover: James Willard Schultz, Eugene Manlove Rhodes, William S. Hart, Henry H. Knibbs)

4 Arnold, Oren. *Wildlife in the Southwest*. Banks, Up-shaw, Dallas, Texas, (1935), words "First Printing May, 1935" follow the copyright notice, fabricoid with illus. in color mounted on front cover, pic. end-sheets, 274 pp., preface, glossary, index, profusely illus. including one illus., p. 19, by E.

5 Atwater, Montgomery M. *Flaming Forest*. Little, Brown, 1941, words "First Edition" appear on the copyright page, cloth, pic. endsheets, 211 (1) pp., nine illus., frontis., title page and pp. 7, 53, 79, 89, 117, 143 and 177, by E.

6 Balch, Glen. *Riders of the Rio Grande*. Thomas Y. Crowell, (1937), cloth, 289 pp., tinted top, eight full-page drawings, frontis. and pp. 18, 52, 87, 127, 205, 245 and 279 plus other drawings and pic. endsheets, all by E.

7 Brackett, Dexter (President). *The Banquet, Boston Society of Civil Engineers*. Hotel Brunswick, Boston, March 8, 1898, folder with two drawings by E.

8 Brady, Cyrus Townsend. *Indian Fights and Fighters*. McClure, Phillips, N.Y., 1904, words "Published December 1904 N" follow the copyright notice, pic. cloth, 423 pp., preface, bibliography, appendices, index, 26 full page plates including one illus., facing p. 50, by E., 13 maps and plans. American Fights and Fighters Series. (Blumenschein, Crawford, Deming, Remington, Schreyvogel)

9 Carr, Robert V. *Cowboy Lyrics*. Small, Maynard, (1912), words "Round Up Edition" appear on title page, cloth, 229 pp., gilt top, author's note, frontis. in color by E. (In 1908 the author distributed a gift edition of *Cowboy Lyrics* among his friends. It was printed solely for private distribution. The 1912 Round Up edition is the only authorized edition "published" and is the first to have the Elwell frontispiece.)

10 Chapman, Arthur. *John Crews*. Houghton Mifflin, Boston and N.Y., 1926, cloth, 303 pp., d/w illus. in color by E.

11 Chase, Mary Ellen. *Virginia of Elk Creek Valley*. The Page Co., 1917, words "First Impression, March, 1917" follow copyright notice, cloth with illus. in color mounted on front cover, 297 pp., seven illus., frontis. in color and facing pp. 28, 130, 168, 214, 266 and 282, by E.

12 ———. *The Girl from the Big Horn Country*. The Page Co., 1916, words "First Impression, January, 1916" appear on copyright page, cloth with illus. in color mounted on front cover, 320 pp., (6) pp. of advs., seven illus., frontis. (in color) and facing pp. 4, 32, 133, 170, 304 and 317, by E.

13 Cody, Col. W. F. *True Tales of the Plains* by "Buffalo Bill." Cupples & Leon, N.Y., 1908, cloth with photo mounted on front cover, 259 pp., (6) pp. of advs., numerous illus. including four, facing pp. 150, 154, 180 and 220, by E.

14 Cunningham, Eugene. *Red Range*. Houghton Mifflin, 1939, cloth, 302 pp., d/w illus. in color by E.

14a Dorson, Richard M. *America in Legend*. Pantheon Books (Random), N.Y., (1973), decor. cloth, orange endsheets, 336 pp., foreword, notes, bibliography, index, numerous illus. including one, p. 135, by E. (Smith)

14b (Dykes.) *Texas* (Catalog Thirteen). Jeff Dykes, Western Books, College Park, Md., Spring 1970, pic. wraps, 30 pp., cover illus. by E.

14c ———. *Western Wonderlands* (Catalog Sixteen). Jeff Dykes, Western Books, College Park, Md., Spring 1971, pic. wraps, 30 pp., cover illus. by E.

15 Elwell, R. Farrington. *Wickenburg, Arizona*. Round-Up Club, Wickenburg, Arizona, n.d., pic. wraps, (16) pp., numerous illus. including thirteen by E.

16 ———. *Sporting Prints*. Lyman Gun Sight Corporation, Middlefield, Conn. (printed by the Osborne Co., Newark, N.J. and Toronto), n.d., six prints in color by E., mounted on advs. cards.

17 Fletcher, Robert H. *Free Grass to Fences*. Historical Society of Montana, Helena, (1960), (University Publishers, N.Y.), cloth and brand decor. boards, pic. endsheets, 233 (3) pp., orange top, (acknowledgments), "Speaking of Cow People" by Michael Kennedy, numerous illus. including one, between pp. 108 and 109, by E. (Russell)

18 French, Henry Willard. *Oscar Peterson—Ranchman and Ranger*. D. Lothrop Co., Boston, 1893, pic. cloth, 380 pp., profusely illus. including thirty drawings by E.

19 Grey, Zane. *The U. P. Trail*. Harper, (1918), words "Published January, 1918" and the letters "A-S" follow the copyright notice, pic. cloth, 408 (1) pp., frontis. by E.

20 Harmsen, Dorothy. *Harmsen's Western Americana*. Northland Press, Flagstaff, (1971), morocco and cloth, blue endsheets, 213 pp., "Foreword" by Robert Rockwell, introduction, numerous illus. including one in color, p. (75), by E. and with a biographical sketch of him. Author's edition of 150 numbered copies signed by the author in slipcase with morocco title label. (Beeler, Blumenschein, Borein, Dixon, Dunn, Dunton, Eggenhofer, Hurd, Johnson, Leigh, Marchand, Miller, Russell, Von Schmidt, Wyeth)

21 ———. Same, first trade edition, two-tone cloth with red endsheets.

22 Harte, Bret. *A Niece of Snapshot Harry's and Other Tales*. Houghton Mifflin, 1903, Standard Library Edition, vol. XVII, cloth, 355 pp., gilt top, six illus. including two, engraved title page and facing p. 150, by E. (Keller)

23 ———. *A Treasure of the Redwoods and Other Tales*. Houghton Mifflin, 1903, Standard Library Edition, vol. XVIII, cloth, 363 pp., gilt top, six illus. including one, facing p. 226, by E. (Fogarty, Smith)

24 Johnston, Charles H. L. *Famous Scouts*. L. C. Page, Boston, 1910, words "First Impression, November, 1910" follow copyright notice, pic. cloth, 340 pp., four illus. by E., frontis. and facing pp. 80, 194 and 328. Other illus. from photos, drawings, old prints, etc.

25 Knibbs, Henry Herbert. *Wild Horses*. Houghton Mifflin, 1924, cloth, 271 (1) pp., d/w illus. in color by E.

26 Lamb, Charles and Mary. *Tales from Shakespeare*. Houghton Mifflin, 1925, cloth with illus. in color mounted on front cover, 346 pp., introductory sketch, preface, six illus. in color, frontis. and facing pp. 66, 166, 214, 286 and 336, by E.

27 Lockwood, Frank C. *Pioneer Days in Arizona*. Macmillan, 1932, words "Published October 1932" follow copyright notice, cloth, 387 pp., preface, introduction, index, illus. including one, p. (302), by E. (Remington)

28 Ostrander, Fannie E. *The Boy Who Won.* L. C. Page, 1910, words "First Impression September, 1910" follow copyright notice, pic. cloth and endsheets, 392 pp., eight illus. in color, frontis. and facing pp. 42, 76, 102, 216, 258, 338 and 352, by E.

29 Oxley, J. MacDonald. *Archie of Athabasca.* D. Lothrop, 1893, pic. cloth, 262 pp., (4) pp. of advs., five illus., frontis. and facing pp. 160, 170, 192 and 254, by E.

30 Peplow, Bonnie and Ed (eds.) *Pioneer Stories of Arizona's Verde Valley.* Verde Valley Pioneer's Assn., Camp Verde, Arizona, 1954, pic. wraps, 219 pp., preface, introduction, index, numerous illus. The front cover illus. by E. Photo of Elwell and short biography, pp. 212-13.

31 Phillips, W. S. (El Comancho). *Three Boys in the Indian Hills.* The Page Co., Boston, (1918), words "First Impression, August, 1918" follow copyright notice, pic. cloth and endsheets, 326 pp., seven full-page illus., frontis. in color and facing pp. 34, 72, 126, 189, 250 and 297 and other drawings, by E.

32 Porter, Eleanor H. *Six Star Ranch.* Page, Boston, (1916), words "Third Impression, January, 1916" on copyright page. Cloth, 353 pp., (6) of advs., frontis. in color by Elwell and other illus. by Frank J. Murch from the first impression (1913).

33 Rolt-Wheeler, Francis. *The Boy with the U. S. Mail.* Lothrop, Lee & Shepard, Boston, (1916), words "Published November 1916" on copyright page, cloth, 349 pp., numerous illus. including one, p. 164, by E.

34 Russell, Florence Kimball. *Born to the Blue.* L. C. Page, 1906, words "First Impression, July, 1906" follow copyright notice, pic. cloth, 245 pp., eight illus., frontis. and facing pp. 16, 64, 99, 139, 163, 188 and 217, by E.

35 Sinclair-Cowan, Bertha M. *Five Furies of Leaning Ladder,* by B. M. Bower (pseud.). Little, Brown, 1936, words "Published January, 1936" on copyright page, cloth, 310 (1) pp., d/w illus. in color by E.

36 ———. *Trouble Rides the Wind* by B. M. Bower (pseud.). Little Brown, Boston, 1935, cloth, 299 pp., d/w illus. in color by E.

37 Smith, Leonard K. *Forty Days to Santa Fe.* Little,

Brown, 1938, words "First Edition" follow copyright notice, pic. cloth, 325 pp., sixteen illus. by E.

38 Stein, Ewald A. *Legend of Hassayampa.* Privately printed, (Wickenburg, Arizona, 1947), pic. wraps, (20) pp., numerous illus. including nine by E.

The Artist and His Art

39 Bell, Col. William Gardner. "R. Farrington Elwell," an article in *Corral Dust,* spring 1964, Potomac Corral, The Westerners, Washington, D.C., with one illus. by E.

40 Carlson, Raymond, ed. "R. Farrington Elwell, Painter," an article in *Arizona Highways,* March 1945, with eleven illus. by E. and with a description of each picture by him.

41 Fletcher, Pete (Manager). *Remuda Ranch.* Wickenburg, Arizona, (1949), pic. wraps, (28) pp., profusely illus. Center spread shows location of Elwell's studio.

42 Lee, "Powder River Jack" H. *Cowboy Songs.* Butte, Montana, 1938, fabricoid, 92 pp., intro., index to songs, numerous illus. including a photo of Elwell and the author with the title "Two of Buffalo Bill's Riders." (Russell)

43 Mark, Frederick A. "Last of the Old West Artists," an article in *Montana,* winter, 1957, 6 pp., with seven illus. by E. and two portraits.

44 Russell, Don. *Custer's Last* (The Battle of the Little Big Horn in Picturesque Perspective). (Amon Carter Museum, Ft. Worth, 1968), cloth, 67 pp., "Preface" by Barbara Tyler, notes, bibliography, illus.; Elwell in text. (Deming, Dunton, Russell)

45 Stein, Ewald A. "R. Farrington Elwell," an article in *Arizona Highways,* October 1959, with thirteen illus. by E. and a photo of him.

46 Swan, Oliver G., ed. *Frontier Days.* Macrae-Smith, Philadelphia, (1928), colored pic. wraps, colored pic. endsheets, 512 pp., orange top, intro., illus.; includes "The Story of the Overland Mail" written from data furnished by E. (Schoonover)

47 ———. *Covered Wagon Days.* Grosset & Dunlap, N.Y., (1928), cloth with illus. mounted on front cover, pic. endsheets, 274 pp., includes "The Story of the Overland Mail." A partial reprint of *Frontier Days* (no. 46). (Schoonover)

OVERLAND LIMITED by Fischer from *Overland Red*

ANTON OTTO FISCHER
1882–1962

Illustrated by the Artist

1 Balmer, Edwin. *Resurrection Rock.* Little, Brown, Boston, 1912, words "Published August, 1912" on copyright page, pic. cloth, 383 pp., frontis. by F.

2 Barbour, Ralph Henry. *The New Boy at Hilltop.* Appleton, N.Y. and London, 1910, words "Published September, 1910" on copyright p., cloth with illus. in color mounted on the front cover, 269 (1) pp., (6) pp. of advs., illus. Front cover illus. by F.

3 Bingham, Edfrid A. *The Heart of Thunder Mountain.* Little, Brown, Boston, 1916, cloth, 360 pp., frontis. in color by F.

4 Bullen, Frank Thomas. *The Cruise of the Cachalot.* Appleton, N.Y., 1925, cloth, 379 pp., folding map, four plates in color including three, facing pp. 38, 200 and 238, by F.

5 Colcord, Lincoln. *The Drifting Diamond.* Macmillan, N.Y., 1912, words "Published October, 1912" on copyright p., pic. cloth, 279 pp., frontis. in color by F.

6 Connolly, James D. *Wide Courses.* Scribner's, N.Y., 1912, words "Published April, 1912" on copyright p., pic. cloth, 336 pp., eight illus. including two, facing pp. 22 and 280, by F.

7 ———. *Sonnie-Boy's People.* Scribner's, N.Y., 1913, words "Published September, 1913" on copyright p., pic. cloth, eight illus. including two, facing pp. 156 and 164, by F.

8 Cooper, Courtney Riley. *The White Desert.* Little, Brown, Boston, 1922, cloth, 301 pp., frontis. by F.

9 Cross, T. P. et al. *Adventure.* Ginn, N.Y. etc., (1938), Revised Edition, pic. cloth and endsheets, 589 pp., "Dictionary of Names and Phrases," index, numerous illus. including seven, facing pp. 130 (in color) and pp. 375, 387, 429, 433 (in color), 469 and 487, by F. (James)

10 Cullum, Ridgewell. *The Triumph of John Kars.* George W. Jacobs & Co., Phila., (1917), cloth, 437 pp., three illus. in color, frontis. and facing pp. 133 and 342, by F.

11 ———. *The Law of the Gun.* George W. Jacobs, Phila., (1918), cloth, 420 pp., three illus in color, frontis. and facing pp. 44 and 160, by F.

12 Curwood, James Oliver. *Flower of the North.* Harper, N.Y., 1912, words "Published March, 1912" on copyright p., cloth, 307 (1) pp., frontis. by F.

13 Evans, Larry. *Once to Every Man.* H. K. Fly & Co., N.Y., (1914), pic. cloth, 317 (3) pp., four illus., frontis. and facing pp. 52, 84 and 148, by F.

14 Fischer, Anton Otto. *Focs'le Days.* Scribner's, N.Y., London, 1947, code letter "A" on copyright p., cloth, pic. endsheets, 82 pp., preface, introduction, endsheets and eighteen full page illus. by F.

15 Hawes, Charles Boardman. *The Dark Frigate.* Little, Brown, Boston, 1934, cloth, with illus. in color on front cover, 247 pp., eight illus. in color, cover, endsheets, frontis. and facing pp. 28, 112, 134, 164 and 214, by F. (The Beacon Hill Bookshelf edition.)

16 ———. *The Mutineers.* Little, Brown, Boston, 1941, words "Published August 1941" on copyright p., cloth with illus. in color on front cover, pic. endsheets, 270 pp., yellow top, "To Pay My Shot," eight illus. in color, cover, endsheets, frontis. and facing pp. 32, 180, 136, 212 and 254, by F.

17 Kelty, Mary G. *Life in Modern America.* Ginn, Boston etc., (1941), pic. cloth, 527, xvi (1) pp., index, numerous illus. including one in color, facing p. 200, by F. (Hurd, Lea, Remington, Russell)

18 ———. *The Story of Life in America.* Ginn, Boston etc., (1946), pic. cloth, 607 (1) pp., index, numerous

illus. including one in color, facing p. 518, by F. (Hurd, Lea, Remington)

18a ——— and Sister Blanche Marie. *Modern American Life.* Ginn, Boston etc., (1943), pic. cloth, 444, xvi, (1) pp., index, numerous illus. including one, facing p. 168, by F. (Hurd, Lea, Remington, Wyeth)

19 Kemp, Oliver. *The Outdoor Man.* Outing Publishing Co., N.Y., (1909), portfolio of six mounted plates including one by F.

20 (Knibbs, Henry Herbert.) *Overland Red.* Houghton Mifflin, Boston and N.Y., 1914; words "Published March 1914" on copyright p., cloth, 348 (1) pp., four illus. in color, frontis. and facing pp. 16, 296, and 340, by F. (Smith)

21 ———. *Sundown Slim.* Houghton Mifflin, Boston & N.Y., 1915, words "Published May 1915" on copyright p., cloth, 356 (1) pp., four illus., frontis. (in color) and facing pp. 64, 258, and 328, by F.

22 Kyne, Peter B. *Cappy Ricks.* Fly, N.Y., 1916, cloth, 349 pp., four illus. including one, facing p. 64, by F. (Dunn)

23 London, Jack. *A Son of the Sun.* Doubleday, Page, Garden City, N.Y., 1912, pic. cloth, 333 pp., four illus. including three, frontis. and facing pp. 184 and 308, by F.

24 ———. *South Sea Tales.* Macmillan, N.Y., 1911, cloth, 327 pp., frontis. in color by F.

25 ———. *The Mutiny of the Elsinore.* Macmillan, N.Y., 1914, decor. cloth, 378 pp., frontis. in color by F.

26 McFarland, Raymond. *Skipper John of the Nimbus.* Macmillan, N.Y., 1918, words "Published September, 1918" on copyright p., pic. boards, 294 pp., (4) pp. of advs., frontis. in color by F.

27 McKay, Richard C. *Some Famous Sailing Ships and Their Builder, Donald McKay.* Putnam, N.Y., London, 1928, cloth, 395 pp., index, numerous illus. including one in color, facing p. 258, by F.

28 Melville, Herman. *Moby Dick.* John C. Winston Co., Phila., (1931), illus., cloth, 414 pp., "Introduction" by William McFee, "Notes" by M. Dodge Holmes, nine illus., endsheets and frontis. in color and facing pp. 18, 82, 88, 110 (color), 154 (color), 356 and 390 (color), by F.

29 ———. Same, (The Ten Greatest Novels of the World Series). Winston, Philadelphia and Toronto, (1949), words "First Edition" (of new copyrighted material) on copyright page, cloth, 417 (1) pp., "Introduction" and edited by W. Somerset Maugham, 93 illus. (eight in color) by F.

30 Meredith, Roy. *The American Wars.* The World Pub. Co., Cleveland and N.Y., (1955), words "First Edition" on copyright p., pic. cloth, 348 (1) pp., red top, introduction, acknowledgments, numerous illus. including one, p. 310, by F. (Deming, Dunn, Remington, Thomason)

31 Moore, Frederick F. *The Devil's Admiral.* Doubleday Page, Garden City, N.Y., 1913, cloth, 295 pp., four illus. in color, frontis. and facing pp. 166, 266 and 292, by F.

32 ———. Same, single advs. sheet with one illus. in color by F.

33 Mowery, William Byron. *Resurrection River.* Little, Brown, Boston, 1935, cloth, 306 pp., d/w illus. in color by F.

34 Nordhoff, Charles B. *The Pearl Lagoon.* The Atlantic Monthly Press, Boston, (1924), cloth, 324 pp., preface, four illus., frontis. and facing pp. 12, 90, and 156, by F.

35 Pease, Howard. *Wind in the Rigging.* Doubleday, Doran, N.Y., 1935, words "First Edition" on copyright p., cloth, map endsheets, 333 pp., red top, author's note, frontis. in color by F.

36 ———. *The Ship Without a Crew.* Doubleday, Doran, N.Y., 1936, words "First Edition" on copyright p., cloth, 304 pp., red top, author's note, frontis. by F.

37 ———. *Foghorns.* Doubleday, Doran, Garden City, N.Y., 1937, words "First Edition" on copyright p., cloth, pic. endsheets, 295 pp., green top, endsheet illus. and frontis. in color by F.

38 Reed, Walt. *The Illustrator in America, 1900–1960's.* Reinhold, N.Y., (1966), cloth, pic. green endsheets, 271 (1) pp., "Is Illustration Art?" by Albert Dorne, bibliography, numerous illus. including two, pp. (88) and (89 in color) by F. and with a brief biographical sketch of him. (Blumenschein, Crawford, Dunn, Dunton, Eggenhofer, Fogarty, Goodwin, Keller, Koerner, Remington, Russell, Schoonover, Stoops, Wyeth)

39 Reynolds, Quentin. *The Fiction Factory.* Random House, N.Y., (1955), words "First Printing" on copyright p., morocco and cloth, decor. endsheets, 283 pp., acknowledgments, bibliography, index, numerous illus. including one, p. (201), by F.

40 Sinclair, Bertrand W. *North of Fifty-Three.* Little, Brown, Boston, 1916, cloth, 345 pp., four illus., frontis. and facing pp. 104, 150, and 340, by F.

41 Sinclair-Cowan, Bertha M. *Good Indian,* by B. M. Bower (pseud.). Little, Brown, Boston, 1912, words "Published September, 1912" on copyright p., decor. cloth, 372 pp., four illus. by F.

42 ———. *The Gringos,* by B. M. Bower (pseud.). Little, Brown, Boston, 1913, words "Published October, 1913" on copyright p., cloth, 350 pp., author's note, four illus., frontis. and facing pp. 62, 138, and 246, by F.

43 ———. *The Flying U's Last Stand,* by B. M. Bower (pseud.). Little, Brown, Boston, 1915, cloth, 353 pp., frontis. by F.

44 ———. *Skyrider,* by B. M. Bower (pseud.). Little, Brown, Boston, 1918, cloth, 317 pp., frontis. by F.

45 ———. *The Thunder Bird,* by B. M. Bower (pseud.). Little, Brown, Boston, 1919, cloth, 317 pp., (3) pp. of advs., frontis. by F.

46 ———. *Rim of the World,* by B. M. Bower (pseud.). Little, Brown, Boston, 1919, words "Published November, 1919" on copyright p., pic. cloth, 349 pp., frontis. by F.

47 ———. *The Quirt,* by B. M. Bower (pseud.). Little, Brown, Boston, 1920, words "Published May, 1920" on copyright p., pic. cloth, 298 pp., frontis. by F.

48 Treynor, Albert M. *Rogues of the North.* Chelsea House, N.Y., 1922, cloth, 208 pp., frontis. by F.

49 Verne, Jules. *20,000 Leagues Under the Sea.* John C. Winston, Phila., (1932), pic. cloth and endsheets, 385 pp., "Introduction" by Felix Riesenberg, glossary, numerous illus. including six in color, by F.

50 White, William Patterson. *The Owner of the Lazy D.* Little, Brown, Boston, 1919, words "Published August, 1919" on copyright p., cloth, 324 pp., (3) pp. of advs., frontis. by F.

51 ———. *Lynch Lawyers.* Little, Brown, Boston, 1920, words "Published January, 1920" on copyright p., decor. cloth, 387 pp., frontis. by F.

52 Wilson, John Fleming. *Across the Latitudes.* Little, Brown, Boston, 1911, words "Published October 1911" on copyright page, cloth, 376 pp., (4) of advs., seven illus. including two, facing pp. 76 and 138, by F.

53 Youell, George. *Lower Class.* Privately printed by the author, Seattle, Washington, (Caxton Printers, Caldwell, Idaho), 1938, fabricoid, blue endsheets, 265 pp., foreword, twenty full-page illus. by F.

The Artist and His Art

54 Mahoney, Bertha E. et al. *Illustrators of Children's Books.* The Horn Book, Boston, 1947, cloth and pic. boards, 527 pp., indices, illus. Lists five books illus. by F.

55 Mellquist, Jerome. *The Emergence of an American Art.* Scribner's, N.Y., 1942, code letter "A" on copyright page, cloth, 421 pp., introduction, appendix, index, illustrated; F. mentioned in text, p. 161.

JOHN BASS'S BLACKSMITH SHOP by Fogarty from *Hempfield*

THOMAS FOGARTY
1873–1938

Catalogues of Art Exhibitions and Galleries

THE BROOKLYN MUSEUM

1 *A Century of American Illustration.* (The Brooklyn Museum Press), March 22–May 14, 1972, colored pic. wraps, 155 pp., "Introduction" by Director Duncan F. Cameron, "American Illustration: 1850–1920" by Linda S. Ferber, bibliography, numerous illus. including one, no. 69, by F. (Remington, Schoonover, Wyeth)

Illustrated by the Artist

2 *Annual of Advertising Art in the U.S., Fourth.* The Art Directors Club, N.Y., 1925, cloth and boards, 128 pp., (25) of advs., (11), indices, numerous illus. including one, p. 50 (repeated p. 124), by F. (Stoops)

3 Same, *Fourteenth*, 1935, pic. cloth, 120 pp., (30) of advs., (4) of indices, numerous illus. including two, pp. 45 and 100, by F. (Stoops)

4 Baker, Ray Stannard. *Adventures in Contentment* by David Grayson (pseud.). Doubleday, Page, N.Y., 1907, words "Published, November, 1907" on copyright page, decor. cloth, pic. endsheets, 249 (1) pp., introduction, thirty illus. by F.

Letter from Baker to M. S. Slocum, dated November 13, 1933.

"I have yours of the 4th, together with the photographs of the first two editions of my book 'Adventures in Contentment.' Curiously enough, another collector has also been trying to determine the very point you raise. I cannot be absolutely sure, but I remember distinctly of protesting to my friend Walter H. Page, who was then a partner in the firm of Doubleday, Page & Company, that the first printing of book was poorly done, that the quality of the paper used would not permit a clear imprint of the illustrations. Some of Mr. Fogarty's line drawings were smudgy. I objected also to the binding. Mr. Page was eager to help and another edition of the book was presently issued. Now I think that the book to which I objected was the larger volume in light green cloth, and that the one that was substituted was the dark green edition. I judge this partly from the fact that the smaller, dark green edition is printed on better paper, with clearer definition of the pictures. Still, it was a long time ago, and I am not altogether certain!"

The "First Issue of First Edition" has a picture of cattle grazing on page 110 —Johnson's *High Spot of American Literature.*

5 ———. *Adventures in Friendship* by David Grayson (pseud.). Doubleday, Page, Garden City, N.Y., 1910, words "Published October, 1910" on copyright page, pic. cloth, pic. endsheets, 232 pp., numerous illus. including three in color by F.

6 ———. *The Friendly Road* by David Grayson (pseud.). Doubleday, Page, Garden City, 1913, pic. cloth, pic. endsheets, 342 pp., gilt top, numerous illus. including two in color by F.

7 ———. *Hempfield* by David Grayson (pseud.). Doubleday, Page, Garden City, 1917, pic. cloth, pic. endsheets, numerous illus. including a frontis. by F.

8 ———. *Great Possessions* by David Grayson (pseud.). Doubleday, Page, Garden City, 1917, pic. cloth, pic. endsheets, 208 pp., numerous illus. including a frontis. in color by F.

9 ———. *Adventures in Understanding* by David Grayson (pseud.). Doubleday, Page, Garden City, 1925, words "First Edition" on copyright page, cloth and boards with paper label, pic. endsheets, 273 pp., numerous illus. by F.

10 ———. *A Day of Pleasant Bread* by David Grayson (pseud.). Doubleday, Page, Garden City, 1926, cloth

and pic. boards, 21 pp., six illus., front cover, half title, title and pp. 1, (3) and 21, by F.

11 ———. *The Countryman's Year* by David Grayson (pseud.). Doubleday, Doran, Garden City, 1936, words "First Edition" on copyright page, decor. cloth, tinted endsheets, 270 pp., green top, foreword, numerous illus. by F.

12 ———. *Adventures of David Grayson.* Doubleday, Page, Garden City, 1925, cloth, pp. 249, 232, 342, 208, numerous illus. by F. (Reprints nos. 4, 5, 6 and 8.)

13 ———. *David Grayson Omnibus.* Garden City Pub. Co., Garden City, (1946), cloth, 444 pp., numerous illus. by F. (A reprint of no. 12.)

14 Becker, May Lamberton (arranged by). *Louisa Alcott's People.* Charles Scribner's Sons, N.Y., 1936, code letter "A" on copyright page, cloth with illus. in color mounted on front cover, pic. endsheets, 211 pp., introduction, numerous illus. including four in color by F.

15 Blankenship, Russell et al. *American Literature.* Scribner's, N.Y., (1940), code letter "A" on copyright page, cloth, 1,115 pp., "What is American Literature," acknowledgments, biographical notes, glossary, indices, fifteen illus. in color by F. (Southwestern Edition.)

16 ——— (compiled and edited by). *American Literature — Our Literary Heritage.* Scribner's, N.Y. etc., (1948), cloth, 804 pp., "What is American Literature," biographical notes, glossary, index, illus. (frontis. in color) with fifteen full-page plates by F.

16a Bowman, David W. *Pathway of Progress* (A Short History of Ohio). American, N.Y. etc., (1943), decor. cloth, 546 pp., "Foreword" by Dr. Howard L. Bevis, preface, introduction, appendix, index, numerous illus. including one, p. 414, by F. (Keller)

17 Butler, Ellis Parker. *Hunting the Wow.* McBride, N.Y., 1934, words "First Edition" on copyright page, cloth, 204 pp., foreword, illus. with twenty-six drawings by F.

18 Clemens, Samuel. *Following the Equator, a Journey Around the World* by Mark Twain (pseud.). The American Pub. Co., Hartford, Conn., 1897, cloth, 712 pp., portrait of author as frontis. and numerous illus. including two full page plates, pp. (338) and (342), by F.

19 Comstock, Harriet T. *The Vindication.* Doubleday, Page, Garden City, 1916, cloth, 375 pp., foreword, four illus., frontis. in color and facing pp. 70, 148 and 248, by F.

20 Cook, E. Thornton. *Speaking Dust: Thomas and Jane Carlyle.* Scribner's, N.Y., 1938, code letter "A" on copyright page, cloth, pic. endsheets by F., 398 pp., preface, epilogue.

21 Cortissoz, Royal (introduction by). *Annual of the Society of Illustrators.* Scribner's, N.Y., 1911, words "Published November, 1911" on copyright page, cloth and boards, introduction of pp. xii, (2), list of members, eighty-five full-page plates including one by F. (Blumenschein, Keller, Remington)

22 Crockett, Samuel R. *Cleg Kelly.* Appleton, N.Y., 1896, cloth, 388 pp., eight illus., frontis. and facing pp. 11, 65, 123, 182, 208, 321 and 358, by F.

23 Day, Holman. *The Eagle Badge.* Harper, N.Y. and London, 1908, words "Published October, 1908" on copyright page, pic. cloth, 289 (1) pp., four illus., frontis. and facing pp. 104, 202 and 274, by F.

24 Draper, Andrew S. *The Rescue of Cuba.* Silver, Burdett, Boston etc., Chicago, 1899, pic. cloth, 186 pp., preface, twenty-three plates including three, facing pp. 38, 102 and 108, by F.

25 Durant, John and Alice. *Pictorial History of American Ships.* A. S. Barnes, N.Y., (1953), decor. two-tone cloth, pic. endsheets, 312 pp., yellow top, "Introduction" by Ernest S. Dodge, acknowledgments, credits and references, index, numerous illus. including three, pp. 204 and 206 (two), by F.

26 Dyer, Walter A. *David Grayson, Adventurer.* Doubleday, Page, Garden City, 1926, pic. wraps, 24 pp., ten illus. including eight, front cover, title and pp. 5, 11, between 12 and 13 (two), 13 and 24, by F.

27 ———. *Chronicles of a Countryman.* Ives Washburn, N.Y., 1928, decor. cloth and endsheets, 355 pp., tinted top, foreword, nine full-page illus. on tinted backgrounds plus numerous smaller drawings by F.

28 Eaton, Walter P. *The Idyl of Twin Fires.* Doubleday, Page, Garden City, 1915, pic. cloth and endsheets, 304 pp., four illus., frontis. and facing pp. 124, 174 and 246 plus line drawings, by F.

29 ———. *The Bird House Man.* Doubleday, Page, Garden City, N.Y., 1916, pic. endsheets, 347 pp., five illus., front cover, endsheets, frontis., and facing pp. 78 and 170, by F.

30 Eddy, Arthur Jerome. *Canton & Co.* A. C. McClurg, Chicago, 1908, words "Published Sept. 26, 1908" on

copyright page, cloth, 415 pp., five tinted illus., frontis. and facing pp. 34, 232, 316 and 358, by F.

31 Ferber, Edna. *Buttered Side Down*. Stokes, N.Y., (1912), words "March, 1912" on copyright page, cloth, 230 pp., foreword, five illus. including one, facing p. 110, by F.

32 Ferris, Elmer E. *Jerry of Seven Mile Creek*. Doubleday, Doran, N.Y., 1938, words "First Edition" on copyright page, pic. cloth and endsheets, 280 pp., red top, eight illus., frontis. and pp. (7), (37), (55), (81), (205), (243), and (277), by F.

33 Field, Rachel (arranged by). *People from Dickens*. Scribner's, N.Y., London, 1935, cloth, 208 pp., numerous illus. in color by F.

34 Fraser, W. Lewis et al. *The Year's Art. The Quarterly Illustrator for 1894*. Harry C. Jones, N.Y., (1894), decor. cloth, 456 pp., 1,400 illus. by 433 artists including one, p. 403, by F. (Crawford, Deming, Keller, Remington)

35 Freeland, George Earl, et al. *America's Building, The Makers of Our Flag*. Scribner's, N.Y., (1937), code letter "A" on copyright page, pic. cloth, 425 pp., note, annotated list of readings, index, numerous illus. including four, pp. 85, 189, 191 and 195, by F. (Rowe, Thomason)

36 Furlong, Rev. Philip J. *America*. William H. Sadlier, N.Y., (1928), pic. cloth, 625, xlvii pp., "Foreword" by Rt. Rev. Mgr. Joseph F. Smith, author's note, appendix, index, numerous illus. including six (in color), frontis. and facing pp. 74, 238, 324, 449 and 604, by F. (Deming)

37 ———. *The New History of America*. William H. Sadlier, N.Y., Chicago, 1936, words "February 26, 1936" on copyright page, decor. cloth, 592 (1), lxv pp., preface, appendix, index, numerous illus. including six (in color), frontis. and facing pp. 42, 214, 275, 362 and 439, by F.

38 Guptill, Arthur L. *Drawings with Pen and Ink*. The Pencil Points Press, N.Y., 1928, cloth, 431 pp., "Introduction" by Franklin Booth, numerous illus. including three, pp. 122, 128 and 206, by F. Comments on Fogarty's art in text.

39 Halsey, Forrest. *The Stain*. F. G. Browne & Co., Chicago, 1913, words "Published, March, 1913" on copyright page, cloth, 343 pp., four illus., frontis. and facing pp. 60, 86 and 194, by F.

40 Harte, Bret. *A Treasure of the Redwoods and Other Tales*. Houghton Mifflin, Boston and N.Y., 1903,

cloth, 363 pp., gilt top, six illus. including one, the frontis., by F. (Vol. XVIII, Autograph Edition, limited to 350 sets — later reissued in the Standard Library Edition.) (Elwell, Smith)

41 Jerome, Jerome K. *Tommy & Co*. Dodd Mead, N.Y., 1904, words "Published September, 1904" on copyright page, cloth, 337 pp., eight illus., frontis. and facing pp., 46, 64, 118, 156, 180, 214 and 248, by F.

42 Kauffman, Reginold Wright. *Mat Anthony's Drummer*. Macmillan, N.Y., 1929, words "Published August, 1929" on copyright page, cloth, 211 pp., four illus., frontis. and facing pp. 104, 143 and 200, by F.

43 Kummer, Frederic Arnold. *The First Days of Man*. Doran, N.Y., (1922), publisher's emblem on copyright page, cloth with illus. in color mounted on front cover, 293 pp., preface for parents, illus. including one, the frontis. in color (repeated on front cover), by F.

44 Law, Frederick R., ed. *Modern Short Stories*. The Century Co., N.Y., 1918, cloth, 303 pp., preface, introduction, "Critical Comment," "Suggestive Questions," illus. including one, the frontis., by F.

45 LeGallienne, Richard. *October Vagabonds*. Michael Kennerly, N.Y., London, 1910, cloth, 201 pp., thirty illus., including a frontis. in color, by F.

46 Loomis, Charles Battell. *A Holiday Touch and Other Tales of Undaunted Americans*. Holt, N.Y., 1908, words "Published October 1908" on copyright page, gilt decor. cloth, 327 pp., (10) of advs., eight illus. including two, frontis. and facing p. 136, by F. (Fogarty, spelled with an "e" instead of an "a" in the list of illustrations).

47 MacManus, Seumas. *Yourself and the Neighbours*. Devin-Adair, N.Y., (1914), cloth, 304 pp., five illus., frontis. and facing pp. 50, 148, 164 and 222 by F.

48 Merwin, Samuel. *The Merry Anne*. MacMillan, N.Y., 1904, cloth, 417 pp., illus. and decor. including six plates in color, frontis. and facing pp. 46, 212, 278, 304 and 368, by F.

49 Mitchell and Miller. *Life's Comedy, First Series*. Scribner's, N.Y., 1897, cloth and pic. boards, pp. 32, 32, 32, 34, numerous illus. including three, pp. 31, section three and pp. 25 and 31, section four, by F.

50 Morley, Christopher. *Chimneysmoke*. George H. Doran, N.Y., (1921), publisher's symbol on copyright page, cloth, pic. endsheets, 253 pp., foreword, thirty-four illus. including the frontis. in color by F.

51 Mowry, William A. and Arthur May. *First Steps in the History of Our Country.* Silver, Burdett, N.Y. etc., 1899, pic. cloth, 315 pp., (4) pp. of advs., preface, index, numerous illus. including eleven by F. (Remington)

52 Munger, Dell H. *The Wind Before the Dawn.* Doubleday, Page, Garden City, 1912, decor. cloth, pic. endsheets, 564 pp., illus. including eight (in color), frontis., and facing pp. 8, 92, 184, 228, 386, 460 and 548, by F.

53 O'Higgins, Harvey. *Julie Cane.* Harper, N.Y. and London, (1924), words "Advance copy for private distribution" on copyright page, extra (or facsimile) sheets from *Harper's Magazine* with 41 illus. by F. (Review copy).

54 ———. Same, (1924), cloth, 343 pp., four illus., frontis. and pp. 46, 186 and 254, by F.

55 Oppenheim, James. *Doctor Rast.* Sturgis & Walton, N.Y., 1909, words "Published September, 1909" on copyright page, decor. cloth, 321 pp., five illus. including one, the frontis., by F.

56 Paine, Albert Bigelow. *The Ship Dwellers.* Harper, N.Y., 1910, cloth, 349 pp., illus. with photographs and with a frontis. and twenty-nine drawings by F.

57 ———. *The Lure of the Mediterranean.* Harper, N.Y. and London, 1910, cloth, 394 pp., 33 illus. by F.

58 ———. *Dwellers in Arcadia.* Harper, N.Y., (1919), words "Published March, 1919" on copyright page, cloth and boards with pic. title label on front cover, 242 pp., numerous illus by F.

59 Patten, William, (ed.) *Poems Old and New.* Collier, N.Y., (1912), cloth, 529 pp., illus. including one, facing p. 162, by F. (The Junior Classic, vol. 10.)

60 Payne, Will. *On Fortune's Road.* McClurg, Chicago, 1902, words "Published Sept. 13, 1902" on copyright page, cloth, 290 pp., eight illus., frontis. and facing pp. 28, 50, 126, 164, 172, 206 and 284, by F.

61 Payson, William Farquhar. *Debonnaire.* McClure Phillips, N.Y., 1904, words "Published, October, 1904" on copyright page, decor. cloth, decor. endsheets, 227 (1) pp., six illus., frontis. and facing pp. 10, 74, 18, 176 and 226, by F.

62 Pearson, Edmund Lester. *The Voyage of the Hoppergrass.* Macmillan, N.Y., 1913, words "Published October, 1913" on copyright page, pic. cloth, 348 pp., (5) pp. of advs., illus. with thirty-seven drawings by F.

63 Pier, Arthur Stanwood. *Boys of St. Timothy's.* Scribner's, N.Y., 1904, words "Published September, 1904" on copyright page, cloth, 284 pp., six illus. including one, facing p. 162, by F. (Varian, Wyeth)

64 (Powers.) *The Christmas Book Shelf.* Powers Mercantile, Minneapolis, 1901, decor. wraps, 243 pp., numerous illus. including one, p. 61, by F.

65 Reed, Walt. *The Illustrator in America 1900–1960s.* Reinhold, N.Y., (1966) cloth, pic. green endsheets, 271 (1) pp., "Is Illustration Art?" by Albert Dorne, bibliography, numerous illus. including one, p. 22, by F. and with a brief biographical sketch of him. (Blumenschein, Crawford, Dunn, Dunton, Eggenhofer, Fischer, Goodwin, Keller, Koerner, Remington, Russell, Schoonover, Stoops, Wyeth)

66 Richmond, Grace S. *Brotherly House.* Doubleday Page, Garden City, N.Y., 1912, wraps, 89 pp., frontis. by F.

67 Riis, Jacob A. *The Making of an American.* Macmillan, N.Y., 1901, cloth, 443 pp., illustrated including nineteen of which five are full-page plates facing pp. 2, 173, 225, 287 and 443, by F.

68 ———. *The Battle with the Slum.* Macmillan, N.Y., 1902, cloth, 465 pp., illus. including six, facing pp. 59, 76, 178, 252, 260 and 267, by F. (Facsimile reprint in 1969 by Patterson Smith, Montclair, N.J.)

69 Rinehart, Mary Roberts. *The Breaking Point.* George H. Doran, N.Y., (1922), publisher's symbol on copyright page, cloth, 356 pp., frontis. in color by F.

70 Robertson, Morgan. *Where Angels Fear to Tread.* The Century, N.Y., 1899, pic. cloth, 302 pp., gilt top, frontis. by F.

71 Skinner, Constance Lindsay. "*Good-Morning Rosamond.*" Doubleday, Garden City, N.Y., 1917, cloth, 384 pp., frontis. in color by F.

72 Slocum, Captain Joshua. *Sailing Alone Around the World.* Century, N.Y., 1900, cloth, 294 pp., sixty-five illus. including over thirty drawings by F.

73 Smith, F. Hopkinson et al. *The Year's Art as Recorded in the Quarterly Illustrator.* Harry C. Jones, N.Y., 1893, decor. cloth, 628 illus. by F. (Remington)

74 Smith, F. Hopkinson. *The Under Dog.* Scribner's, N.Y., 1903, words "Published, May, 1903" on copyright page, decor. cloth, 332 pp., "To My Readers," twelve illus. including one, facing p. 92, by F. (Keller)

75 Spearman, Frank H. et al. *Adventures in Field and Forest.* Harper, N.Y. and London, 1909, words "Published March, 1909" on copyright page, colored pic.

cloth, 211 (1) pp., introduction, eight illus. including one, facing p. 38, by F.

76 Stevenson, Burton E. *The Quest for the Rose of Sharon.* Page, Boston, 1909, words "First Impression, April, 1909" on copyright page, pp. 207, 4 and 4 pp. of advs., six illus., frontis. and facing pp. 16, 28, 98, 194 and 198, by F.

77 ———. *The Mystery of the Boule Cabinet.* Dodd, Mead, N.Y., 1912, words "Published, March, 1912" on copyright page, pic. cloth, 362 pp., four illus., frontis. and facing pp. 68, 202 and 236, by F.

78 ———. *The Destroyer.* Dodd, Mead, N.Y., 1913, cloth, 434 pp., frontis. by F.

79 ———. *The Gloved Hand.* Dodd, Mead, N.Y., 1913, cloth, 343 pp., illus by F.

80 Stillman, Albert Lewis. *Drum Beats in Old Carolina.* John C. Winston, Philadelphia etc., (1939), cloth, pic. endsheets, 244 pp., blue top, illus. by Thomas Fogarty and Thomas Fogarty, Jr. The frontis. in color and the full-page drawings, facing pp. 46, 92 and 210 are signed "Thomas Fogarty" in the plates.

81 Stratton-Porter, Gene. *Freckles.* Doubleday, Page, N.Y., 1914, decor. cloth with illus. in color mounted on the front cover, pic. endsheets, 352 pp., twelve illus. (four in color) plus line drawings in text by F.

82 Stuart, Ruth-McEnery. *The Second Wooing of Selina Sue.* Harper, N.Y. and London, 1905, words "Published April, 1905" on copyright page, decor. cloth, 236 (1) pp., illus. including one, the frontis., by F.

83 Tarkington, Booth. *The Gentleman from Indiana.* Grosset & Dunlap, N.Y., (1902), cloth, 504 pp., frontis.; d/w illus. by F. Note: The first edition may have had a d/w illus. by Fogarty but your compiler has never seen a copy in the original d/w.

84 Thanet, Octave (Alice French). *By Inheritance.* Bobbs-Merrill, Indianapolis, (1910), cloth, 394 pp., four illus., frontis. and facing pp. 122, 12 and 318, by F.

85 Towne, Charles Hanson. *Manhattan.* Mitchell, Kennerley, N.Y., 1909, cloth and board, 44 pp., two illus. frontis. and tail piece, by F.

86 ———. *Autumn Loiterers.* Doran, N.Y., 1917, cloth with pic. title label on front cover, pic. endsheets, 129 pp., foreword, 25 illus. by F.

87 ———. *Loafing Down Long Island.* Century N.Y., 1921, pic. cloth, 212 pp., thirty-one full-page drawings by F.

88 Vance, Joseph Louis. *The Black Bag.* Bobbs-Merrill, Indianapolis, (1908), word "January" on copyright page, cloth, 441 pp., ten illus., frontis. and facing pp. 38, 116, 148, 158, 222, 286, 314, 386 and 422, by F.

89 ———. *No Man's Land.* Dodd, Mead, N.Y., 1910, cloth, 356 pp., four illus., frontis. in color, and facing pp. 60, 160 and 352, by F.

90 White, Stewart Edward. *The Blazed Trail.* McClure, Phillips, N.Y., 1902, words "Published, March, 1902" on copyright page, pic. cloth, 412 pp., six plates, frontis. and facing pp. 146, 152, 164, 208 and 308 plus line drawings in text, by F.

91 ———. *The Forest.* Outlook, N.Y., 1903, words "Published October, 1903," pic. cloth, 276 pp., frontis. in color, seventeen other full-page illus. plus line drawings by F.

92 ———. *Blazed Trail Stories.* McClure, Phillips, N.Y., 1904, words "Published September, 1904" on copyright page, pic. cloth, 260 pp., frontis. in color by F.

93 ———. *Gold.* Doubleday, Page, Garden City, N.Y., 1913, pic. yellow cloth, 437 pp., plus acknowledgment "Note," p. (1), plus "Stewart Edward White" by Eugene F. Saxton, pp. 12, (1) without illus., four illus. in color, frontis. and facing pp. 78, 286 and 360 plus line drawings by F.

94 ———. *The Gray Dawn.* Doubleday, Page, Garden City, N.Y., (1915), pic. cloth, pic endsheets, four illus. in color, frontis. and facing pp. 216, 234 and 376 plus line drawings by F. (A continuation of the California story started in *Gold,* no. 93 and continued in *The Rose Dawn,* that was not illus. by Fogarty.)

95 ———. *On Tiptoe.* George H. Doran, N.Y., (1922), publisher's symbol on copyright page, cloth, 264 (1) pp., frontis. in color by F.

The Artist and His Art

96 Baker, Ray Stannard. *American Chronicle — The Autobiography of David Grayson.* Scribner's, N.Y., 1945, code letter "A" on copyright page, cloth, 531 pp., index. Contains a tribute to Fogarty, his illustrator (see entries 4 through 13).

97 *1915 Publications of the Bobbs-Merrill Company* Indianaoplis, decor. wraps, 104 p., lists books illus. by Fogarty, pp. 88 and 92.

98 Skinner, Charles M. "From Many Studios," an illus. article in *The Quarterly Illustrator* 1:4, October, November and December, 1893, with comments on F. as an illustrator and with one drawing by him.

THE BEGINNING OF THE SLAUGHTER by Goodwin from *Musk-Ox, Bison, Sheep, and Goats*

PHILIP R. GOODWIN
1882–1935

Catalogues of Art Exhibitions and Galleries

HELEN L. CARD, NEW YORK

1 *Hats Off to the American Illustrator!* Catalog no. two, (Fall, 1959), pic. wraps, 32 pp., numerous illus. including five, inside front cover and pp. 3, 5 and 6 (two) by G. (Dixon, Koerner, Schoonover, Wyeth)

COLONIAL ART COMPANY, OKLAHOMA CITY
(SENATE ROOM, LINCOLN PLAZA INN)

1a *Western and Traditional American Paintings of the 19th and Early 20th Centuries* (auction catalog), June 10, 1973, pic. wraps, 76 numbered illus. including one, no. 41, by G. (Borein, Deming, Dixon, Eggenhofer, Elwell, Johnson, Koerner, Russell, Schoonover, Wyeth, Young)

HAMMER GALLERIES, NEW YORK

2 *The Works of Charles M. Russell and Other Western Artists* (November, 1962), pic. wraps, 56 pp., introduction, numerous illus. including five, pp. 30 and 31, by G. (Crawford, Lungren, Miller, Remington, Russell)

KENNEDY GALLERIES, NEW YORK

3 *American Sports and Sportsmen*, 1968, colored pic. wraps, 48 pp., 45 illus. including four, pp. 9, 10, 11 and 12, by G. (Lungren, Remington)

E. WALTER LATENDORF, NEW YORK

4 *C. M. Russell*, Catalogue no. 27, (May, 1957), pic. wraps, unpaged, 46 numbered illus. including one, no. 25, by G. (Borein, Crawford, De Yong, Leigh, Marchand, Russell)

Illustrated by the Artist

5 Andrews, Mary Raymond Shipman. *The Eternal Masculine.* Scribner's, N.Y., 1913, words "Published October, 1913" on copyright page, decor. cloth, 430 pp., eight illus. including five, frontis. and facing pp. 46, 98, 126 and 218, by G.

6 Askins, Charles. *Shooting Facts.* Recreation Library by Outdoor Life, N.Y., March 1934, pic. wraps, 96 pp., illus. including one, the front cover, by G.

7 Barnes, Charles Merritt. *Combats and Conquests of Immortal Heroes.* Guessaz and Ferlet Co., San Antonio, Texas, 1910, cloth, 268 pp., numerous illus. including one, p. 205, by G.

8 Chambers, Robert W. *Cardigan* (title in red on title page). Harper, N.Y. and London, 1901, decor. cloth, 512 (1) pp., eight illus. including three, facing pp. 196, 202 and 252, by G. (Schoonover)

9 Christy, Howard Chandler et al. *American Art by American Artists* ("One Hundred Masterpieces representing the best work in pen-and-ink and in color by Twenty-seven Celebrated American Artists"). Collier, N.Y., 1914, cloth with paper label. Five illus., four in color, by G. Goodwin portrait and short sketch on title page. (Keller, Remington)

9a Davidson, Marshall B. et al. *The American Heritage History of the Writers' America.* American Heritage, N.Y., (1973), cloth and boards, blue endsheets, 403 (13) pp., introduction, index, numerous illus. including two, pp. 243 and 259, by G. (Remington, Wyeth)

10 Elman, Robert (selected and text by). *The Great American Shooting Prints.* A Ridge Press Book, Knopf, N.Y., 1972, cloth, tan endsheets, unpaged, "Introduction" by Hermann Warner Williams, Jr., catalogue of the plates, 72 plates in color including one, no. 44, by G. (Leigh, Miller, Remington, Russell)

11 Evans, Joe M. *A Corral Full of Stories.* (The McMath Co., El Paso, Texas, 1939), pic. wraps, tan endsheets, x, 66 pp., illus. including one, facing p. x, by G. (Lea)

12 Grinnell, George Bird. *The Wolf Hunters.* Scribner's, N.Y., 1914, words "Published September, 1914" on copyright page, pic. cloth, 303 pp., (4) pp. of advs., introductory note, four illus., frontis. and facing pp. 60, 154 and 250, by G.

13 Harris, Burton et al. *Yellowstone Country.* (Gilcrease Institute, Tulsa, 1963), colored pic. wraps, 57 (1) pp., numerous illus. including one, p. (53), by G. (James, Leigh, Russell)

14 Hines, Jack. *Seegar and Cigareet.* Doran, N.Y., (1912), pic. boards, 56 (1) pp., four illus., front cover, frontis., and facing pp. 18 and 32, by G.

14a ———. *The Blue Streak.* George H. Doran Co., N.Y., (1917), cloth, 270 pp., five illus., frontis. and facing pp. 50, 102, 148 and 212, by G.

15 Hopkins, Mrs. Herbert Muller. *The Washingtonians* by Pauline Bradford Mackie (pseud.). L. C. Page & Co., Boston, 1902, cloth, 357 pp., frontis. by G.

15a *The Immortal Sportsman's Paradise — Outdoor Masterpieces of Philip R. Goodwin.* Louis F. Dow Co., St. Louis, n.d., seven reproductions in color with a cover in color by G.

16 Latendorf, E. Walter. *Western Americana* (Catalogue no. 24). Mannados Bookshop, N.Y., (1954), pic. wraps., 88 pp., twenty-four illus. including one, p. 19, by G. (Borein, Dixon, Lea, Remington, Russell, Schreyvogel)

17 ———. *Catalogue No. 27.* N.Y., n.d., pic. wraps, 36 pp., several illus. including one, inside front cover, by G. Note: Latendorf, in error, issued two catalogues numbered "27" — the other is item 4 above. (De Yong, Eggenhofer, Lea, Lungren, Young)

18 Laut, Agnes C. *Pathfinders of the West.* Macmillan, N.Y., 1904, words "Published November, 1904" on copyright page, cloth. 380 pp., illus. including two, facing pp. 81 and 196, by G. (Marchand, Remington)

19 London, Jack. *The Call of the Wild.* Macmillan, N.Y., 1903, words "Set up, electrotyped and published July, 1903" on copyright page, green ribbed pic. cloth, pic. endsheets, 231 pp., nineteen illus. including seven in color, pp. (29), (35), (53), 67, (95), (127) and (155), by G.

19a Long, Morden H. *Knights Errant of the Wilderness.* Macmillan, Toronto, 1925, pic. cloth, 223 pp., preface, numerous illus. including two, frontis. and facing p. 128, by G.

20 Lyle, Eugene P., Jr. *The Lone Star.* Doubleday, Page, N.Y., 1907, words, "Published August, 1907" on copyright page, cloth with small oval illus. mounted on front cover, five illus. in color, front cover, frontis. and facing pp. 73, 148 and 246, by G.

21 McDowell, Bart. *The American Cowboy in Life and Legend.* National Geographic Society, Washington, D.C., (1972), pic. cloth, pic. endsheets, 211 pp., (1) of advs., "Foreword" by Joe B. Frantz, index, additional reading, numerous illus. including two in color, pp. (6) and (97), by G. (De Yong, Dunton, James, Remington, Russell)

22 Money, A. W. et al. *Guns, Ammunition and Tackle.* Macmillan, N.Y., 1904, words "Published September, 1904" on copyright page, gilt decor. cloth, 440 pp., (2) pp. of advs., gilt top, index, numerous illus. including one, facing p. 122, by G.

23 Reed, Walt. *The Illustrator in America 1900–1960s.* Reinhold, N.Y., (1966), cloth, pic. green endsheets, 271 (1) pp., "Is Illustration Art?" by Albert Dorne, bibliography, numerous illus. including one, p. (23), by G. (Blumenschein, Crawford, Dunn, Dunton, Eggenhofer, Fischer, Fogarty, James, Keller, Koerner, Remington, Russell, Schoonover, Stoops, Wyeth)

24 Roberts, Charles G. D. *Kings in Exile.* Macmillan, N.Y., 1910, words "Published February, 1910" on copyright page, cloth, 299 pp., twelve illus. including two, facing pp. 72 and 90, by G.

25 Roosevelt, Theodore. *African Game Trails.* Scribner's N.Y., 1910, pic. cloth, 583 pp., gilt top, foreword, appendices, index, illus. with photos and with eight drawings, facing pp. (107), (135), (165), (229), (255), (305), (411) and (455), by G.

26 Roosevelt, Theodore and Heller, Edmund. *Life Histories of African Game Animals.* (2 vols.). Scribner's, N.Y., 1914, cloth with morocco title labels on spines, 798 pp., preface, bibliography, appendix, forty faunal maps, illus. with photos and with eight plates, frontis. (I and II) and facing pp. 176, 310, 522, 648, 710 and 720, by G.

27 Stephens, Robert Neilson. *Captain Ravenshaw.* Page, Boston, 1901, decor. cloth, 369 pp., (8) of advs., gilt top, preface, seven illus. including four, facing pp. 60, 128, 153 and 251, by G.

28 Sunheim, A. M., ed. *Jul i Westerheimen.* Augsburg Publishing House, Minneapolis, 1923, colored pic. wraps, unpaged, numerous illus. including one in color by G. Most of the text is in Norse but minor part in English. (Russell)

29 White, Stewart Edward. *The Silent Places.* McClure,

Phillips, N.Y., 1904, words "Published, April, 1904" on copyright page, decor. cloth, 304 pp., seven illus. in color, frontis. and facing pp. 26, 66, 148, 228, 258 and 294, by G.

30 ——. Same, Hodder & Stoughton, London, 1904, pic. cloth, 304 pp., first British edition of no. 29 with seven illus. in color, frontis. and facing pp. 26, 66, 148, 228, 258 (repeated on front cover) and 294, by G.

31 ——. *The Land of Footprints*. Doubleday, Page, Garden City, N.Y., 1912, pic. cloth, 440 pp., illus. with photos (by the author) and with two plates, frontis. and facing p. 117, by G.

32 ——. Same, Thomas Nelson and Sons, London etc., n.d., decor. cloth, 462 pp., appendices, first British edition of no. 31, eight illus. including two, frontis. and facing p. 128, by G.

33 Whitney, Caspar et al. *Musk-Ox, Bison, Sheep, and Goats*. Macmillan, N.Y., 1904, words "Set-up, electrotyped, and published February, 1904," 100 numbered copies in morocco and marbled boards, 284 pp., gilt top, numerous illus. including one, the frontis., by G. (There was also a trade edition in pictorial cloth.)

34 Winnington, Laura, ed. *The Outlook Story Book for Little People*. The Outlook Co., N.Y., 1902, cloth, 207 pp., numerous illus. including two, frontis. and p. 3, by G.

The Artist and His Art

35 Adams, Ramon F. and Britzman, Homer E. *Charles M. Russell: The Cowboy Artist, a Biography*. Trail's End Pub. Co., Pasadena, Calif., (1948), words "Volume I, Collector's Edition, 1948" on copyright page, morocco and cloth, colored pic. endsheets, 335 pp., preface, acknowledgments, index, numerous illus. Goodwin visits the Russells in Montana — several short incidents. (The Collector's Edition was limited to 600 sets.)

36 *Art of Western America*. Pomona College Art Gallery, Claremont, Calif., November 1 to 31, 1949, pic. wraps, unpaged, "Foreword" by Don Louis Perceval; brief biographical sketch of G. and lists two watercolors by him in the exhibition. (Perceval, Russell)

37 Price, Con. *Trails I Rode*. Trail's End Pub. Co., Pasadena, Calif., (1947), words "De Luxe Edition, Three hundred and fifty copies numbered and signed by the author" on title page, morocco, decor. endsheets, 262 pp., publisher's prologue, index, illus. by Russell and with photos. Con tells of Russell bringing Goodwin to the Lazy KY — a briefer version of the same story was used by Adams (no. 35). There also was a trade edition.

38 Russell, Austin. *Charles M. Russell, Cowboy Artist*. Twayne, N.Y., (1957), cloth, 247 pp., foreword, postscript, sources quoted, illus. with drawings by Russell and with photos. The best source known on the friendship of Russell and Goodwin by Russell's nephew. Austin and Goodwin spent the summer of 1910 with the Russells at Lake McDonald.

39 *Good Medicine, The Illustrated Letters of Charles M. Russell*. Doubleday, Doran, Garden City, N.Y., 1929, leather, 162 pp., numerous illus. by the author. Limited to 134 numbered copies. Reproduces 3 letters from Russell to Goodwin.

40 ——. Same, the trade edition, 1930, words "First Edition after the printing of 134 De Luxe Copies" on copyright page, decor. cloth.

THE WINDMILL CREW by Hurd from *Guide to Life and Literature of the Southwest*

PETER HURD
Contemporary, 1904–

Catalogues of Art Exhibitions and Galleries

 AMON CARTER MUSEUM OF WESTERN ART
FORT WORTH, TEXAS

1 *Sid W. Richardson* (collection), n.d., folder, with six illus. including one, front cover portrait of Richardson in color, by H. (Remington, Russell)

2 *Peter Hurd: The Gate and Beyond.* October 22, 1964 through January 3, 1965, folder with a portrait of Peter by his wife, Henriette Wyeth Hurd and the text by Paul Horgan.

ART INSTITUTE OF CHICAGO

3 *The Sixteenth International Exhibition Water Colors, Pastels, Drawings and Monotypes,* March 18 to May 16, 1937, wraps, unpaged, notes, twelve illus. including one, "El Mocho" (winner of Watson F. Blair Prize), by H.

4 *Catalogue of the 54th Annual Exhibition of Oil Paintings and Sculpture by American Artists,* 1943, wraps, unpaged, numerous illus. including one, "Windmill Crew," by H.

ASSOCIATED AMERICAN ARTISTS, NEW YORK

5 *A Treasury of Fine Art Masterpieces,* (1951), colored pic. wraps, unpaged, numerous illus. including one, "Waterhole," in color and repeated in black and white, by H.

BUSINESS MEN'S ASSURANCE CO. TOWER
KANSAS CITY, MISSOURI

6 *Along the Santa Fe Trail,* (1963), pic. wraps, unpaged, ten illus. including one in color by H. (Remington)

BAKER COLLECTOR GALLERY, LUBBOCK, TEXAS

7 *Winter 1964* (catalog), pic. wraps, unpaged, (preface), numerous illus. including two by H. (Borein, Russell, Wyeth)

8 *Spring 1964* (catalog), pic. wraps, unpaged, (preface), foreword, numerous illus. including two by H. (Remington, Russell, Wyeth)

9 (Catalog), n.d. (1965?), pic. wraps, unpaged, (preface), foreword, numerous illus. including five by H. (Ellsworth, Johnson, Russell, Wyeth)

10 *Exhibition of Paintings by Peter Hurd and Henriette Wyeth,* October 16 through October 31, 1966, wraps, unpaged, "Foreword" by Lennis and James Baker, sixteen illus. including ten by H. and a photo of him.

11 *Original Prints,* n.d., wraps, unpaged, fifteen illus. including two by H.

12 *Great American Realists,* n.d., (1968?), folder, eight illus. by H.

13 *Peter Hurd,* October 1973, folder, seven (three in color) illus. by H. and a photo of him.

CARNEGIE INSTITUTE, DEPT. OF FINE ARTS
PITTSBURGH, PENNSYLVANIA

14 *Survey of American Painting,* 1940, pic. wraps, 135 numbered plates including one, no. 128, by H. (Remington)

15 *Painting in the United States,* 1943, wraps, numerous illus. including one, Anselmo's House," by H. (Blumenschein)

16 Same, 1946, wraps, numerous illus. including one, "Evening in the Sierras," by H.

CITY ART MUSEUM, ST. LOUIS

17 *Annual Exhibition of Selected Paintings by American Artists,* 34th, 1944, wraps, numerous illus. including one, "Made Tank," by H.

18 Same, 35th, 1945, wraps, numerous illus. including one, "Main Street," by H.

THE COLUMBUS GALLERY OF FINE ARTS
COLUMBUS, OHIO

19 *Exhibition of Paintings by Peter Hurd and Henriette Wyeth*, January 12–25, 1967, wraps, unpaged, "Introduction" by Mahonri Sharp Young, numerous illus. including seven by H. and a photo of him with Henriette Wyeth (Mrs. Peter Hurd).

20 *Peter Hurd and Henrietta Wyeth*, folder, (January Calendar) 1971, three illus. including two by H.

M. H. DE YOUNG MEMORIAL MUSEUM
SAN FRANCISCO

21 *Meet the Artist: An Exhibition of Self-Portraits by Living*, 1943, wraps, numerous illus. including one, a self-portrait, by H.

EL PASO MUSEUM OF ART

22 *The McKee Collection of Paintings*, El Paso Museum of Art, (1968), cloth with illus. in color mounted on the front cover, tan endsheets, 67 pp., designed by Carl Hertzog, "The McKees and Their Art Collection," "Foreword" by Leonard P. Sipiora, numerous ous illus. including one, p. 46, by H. (Blumenschein, Dunton, Koerner, Lea)

GOLDEN GATE INTERNATIONAL EXPOSITION
DEPARTMENT OF FINE ARTS, SAN FRANCISCO

23 *Art, Official Catalogue*, 1940, wraps, numerous illus. including one, "River and Canal, San Patricio," by H.

HALLMARK, KANSAS CITY, MISSOURI

24 *Exhibition of Paintings, Fourth International Hallmark Art Award*, 1957, numerous illus. including one, p. 21, by H. Note: Exhibited at Wildenstein Gallery, N.Y., December 3–28, 1957 and at Corcoran, Washington, D.C.; Isaac Delgado Museum, New Orleans; California Palace of the Legion of Honor, San Francisco; Municipal Art Gallery, Los Angeles; William Rockhill Nelson Gallery, Kansas City; and Museum of Fine Art, Boston, in 1958.

HERITAGE INN, GREAT FALLS, MONTANA
(THE ADVERTISING CLUB OF GREAT FALLS)

25 *C. M. Russell Sixth Annual Auction of Original Western Art*, March 14–15, 1974, pic. wraps, unpaged, lists 165 lots for sale, numerous illus. including one, lot 5, by H. (Borein, Deming, Russell, Schreyvogel)

KALAMAZOO INSTITUTE OF ARTS
KALAMAZOO, MICHIGAN

26 *Western Art, Paintings and Sculptures of the West*, February 17–March 19, 1967, pic. wraps, 17 (1) pp.,

(introduction), numerous illus. including one, p. 16, by H. (Johnson, Leigh, Miller, Remington, Russell, Schreyvogel, Wyeth)

MUSEUM OF FINE ARTS, BOSTON

27 *Sport in Art*, November 15–December 15, 1955, wraps, unpaged, numerous illus. including one, "Landscape with Polo Players," by H. Note: This exhibition was a joint presentation of The American Federation of Arts and *Sports Illustrated* and was shown in Washington, D.C., Louisville, Dallas, Denver, Los Angeles, San Francisco and Australia during 1956. (Young)

MUSEUM OF MODERN ART, NEW YORK

28 *La Pintura Contemporanea Norteamericana*, 1941, wraps, numerous illus. including one, "Boy from the Plains," by H.

29 *American Realists and Magic Realists*, 1943, wraps, numerous illus. including one, "Dry River," by H.

MUSEUM OF NEW MEXICO
FINE ARTS BUILDING, SANTA FE

30 *New Mexican National Academicians*, May 24 through June 23, 1964, wraps, unpaged, "Foreword" by James Taylor Forrest, numerous illus. including one by H. and a photo of him.

NATIONAL ACADEMY OF DESIGN, NEW YORK

31 *National Academy 114th Annual Exhibition*, March 15–April 11, 1940, decor. wraps, 97 pp., (6) of advs., numerous illus. including one, "Lady Bronc Rider," p. (50), by H.

NATIONAL COWBOY HALL OF FAME
OKLAHOMA CITY

32 *Inaugural Exhibition*, June 25, 1965, colored pic. wraps, 24 pp., fourteen illus. including one, "Sid W. Richardson," p. 4, by H. (Miller, Remington, Russell)

OKLAHOMA ART CENTER, OKLAHOMA CITY

33 *European and American Paintings* (from the collection of Mr. and Mrs. W. E. Davis, Duncan, Oklahoma), November 5–27, 1964, colored pic. wraps, unpaged, twenty-five illus. including one in color, entry no. 53, by H. Note: Also exhibited at the Philbrook Art Center, Tulsa, December 1–29, 1964. (Blumenschein, Remington, Russell)

O S RANCH, POST, TEXAS

34 *Steer Roping and Art Exhibit.* September 30–October 1, 1972, colored pic. wraps, 84 pp., numerous illus. including one, p. 27, by H. and a photo of him.

PACIFIC NORTHWEST INDIAN CENTER
SPOKANE, WASH.

35 *Third Annual Western Art Show and Auction*, March
2, 3, 4, 1973, pic. wraps, 44 pp., numerous illus. including one, p. 19, by H. (Borein, Deming, Eggenhofer, Remington, Russell)

PARKE-BERNET GALLERIES, NEW YORK

36 *Modern Paintings by French and American Artists*,
1950, wraps, 45 pp., numerous illus. including one,
''My Daughter Carol,'' p. 21, by H.

THE PENNSYLVANIA ACADEMY OF THE FINE ARTS
PHILADELPHIA

36a *Catalogue of the Forty-Third Annual Water Color and
Print Exhibition and the Forty-Fourth Annual Exhibi-
tion of Miniatures*, October 20th–November 25th,
1945, wraps, unpaged, eight illus. including one,
''Evening Star,'' winner of the Dana Water Color
Medal for the best work in Water Color, by H.

PHOENIX ART MUSEUM

37 *Aspects of the Desert* (dedication exhibition), November 14, 1959, wraps, unpaged, (preface) by Director
F. M. Hinkhouse, thirty-one numbered illus. including no. 23 by H. (Remington)

38 *Western Art from the Eugene B. Adkins Collection*,
November 1971–January 1972, colored pic. wraps,
''Preface'' by R. D. A. Puckle, twenty illustrations,
biographical sketch of H. (Dunton, Johnson, Leigh,
Miller, Remington, Varian)

39 *Peter Hurd*, n.d.(1963?), colored pic. wraps, unpaged,
comments by Hurd (dated December 1962), ''Peter
Hurd'' by Director F. M. Hinkhouse, seven illus., including front cover in color, by H.

Illustrated by the Artist

40 *Abert's New Mexico Report, 1846–47*. Horn & Wallace, Albuquerque, 1962, cloth and boards, map endsheets, 182 pp., ''Foreword'' by William A. Keleher,
facsimile of the illus. classic report, frontis. in color
(repeated on d/w) by H.

41 Ainsworth, Ed. *The Cowboy in Art*. World, N.Y. and
Cleveland, (1968), words ''First Printing 1968'' on
copyright page, pic. leather, orange endsheets, all
edges gilt, ''Foreword'' by John Wayne, index, numerous illus. including two, pp. 182 and 183, and a
photo of H. DeLuxe edition of 1000 copies, slipcase.
(Beeler, Borein, Bugbee, De Yong, Dixon, Dunton,
Eggenhofer, Ellsworth, James, Koerner, Leigh, Mora,

Perceval, Remington, Russell, Santee, Schreyvogel,
Von Schmidt)

42 ———. Same, first trade edition in gilt lettered and
illus. cloth, orange endsheets.

43 ———. Same, reprint by Bonanza Books, N.Y., in red
lettered and illus. cloth, white endsheets.

44 *Announcing an Auction of Paintings by Twenty
Noted Artists of the Southwest for the Benefit of the
Dobie-Paisono Project*. Houston, May 11 (1966?),
four-fold flyer with twenty-one illus. including one,
''Border Country,'' by H. (Lea, Schiwetz)

45 (Baker.) *Gift Suggestions*. The Baker Co., Lubbock,
(1973), wraps, unpaged, numerous illus. including
one, ''River Valley in Spring,'' by H.

46 ———. *Christmas Gift Selections*. The Baker Co.,
Lubbock, (1973), decor. wraps, unpaged, numerous
illus. including eight by H. (Remington, Russell)

47 Baldwin, James. *The Story of Roland*. Scribner's,
N.Y., London, (1930), cloth with illus. in color
mounted on front cover, pic. endsheets, 347 pp.,
tinted top. Illus. on front cover, endsheets, title page
and facing pp. 20, 56, 108, 120, 144, 214, 292, 324
and 342, by H. (Scribner Illustrated Classic.)

48 ———. *The Story of Siegfried*. Scribner's, N.Y., London, (1931), cloth with illus. in color mounted on
front cover, pic. endsheets, 279 pp., tinted top. Illus.
on front cover, endsheets, title page and facing pp. 42,
66, 122, 150, 220 and 250, by H. (Scribner Illustrated
Classic.)

49 Baur, John I. H. *Revolution and Tradition in Modern
American Art*. Harvard University Press, Cambridge,
1951, cloth, 170 pp., preface, notes, index, 199 numbered illus. including one, no. 163, ''The Rainy Season,'' by H. (Young)

50 ———. Same, reissued as a Praeger Paperback in
1967, with ''an introduction to the paperback edition''
by the author added.

51 Berger, Josef. *Discoverers of the New World*. American Heritage, N.Y., (1960), colored pic. cloth, colored
map endsheets, 153 pp., ''Foreword'' by Lawrence C.
Wroth (consultant), picture credits, bibliography, index, numerous (many in color) illus. including one,
p. (97), by H.

52 Bonney, Cecil. *Looking Over My Shoulder* (Seventy-
five Years in the Pecos Valley). Hall-Poorbaugh Press,
Roswell, N.M., 1971, pic. cloth, 235 pp., ''Introduction'' by Peter Hurd, foreword, index, illus. including
two, pp. 53 (repeated on the d/w) and 197, by H. plus

a chapter "Peter Hurd: Artist and Conservationist." (Cisneros)

53 Boswell, Jr., Peyton. *Modern American Painting.* Dodd, Mead, N.Y., (1939), cloth, 166 (4) pp., numerous illus. including two in color, pp. 76 and 77, by H.

54 Burglon, Nora. *Deep Silver.* Houghton Miñlin, Boston, 1938, cloth, 215 pp., eleven full-page illus. and a drawing on the title page, by H.

55 Calvin, Ross. *Sky Determines.* University of New Mexico Press, Albuquerque, (1948), decor. cloth and endsheets, 333 pp., foreword, afterthought, bibliography, index, illus. with drawings by H.

56 ———. Same, revised and enlarged in 1965 with sixteen (title page drawing repeated on d/w) drawings by H.

57 Casner, Mabel B. and Gabriel, Ralph H. *The Story of American Democracy.* Harcourt Brace, N.Y., Chicago, 1943, decor. cloth, 632 pp., preface, appendix, index, numerous illus. including one, p. 257, by H. (Russell)

58 Chavez, Fray Angelico. *From an Altar Screen.* Farrar, Straus and Cudahy, N.Y., (1957), words "First Printing 1957" on copyright page, cloth and decor. boards, red endsheets, 119 pp., red top. Author's note, nine illus., title page and pp. (1), (3), (23), (31), (53), (65), (79) and (105), by H.

59 Clemens, Samuel L. *The Adventures of Tom Sawyer* by Mark Twain (pseud.). Winston, Philadelphia, Chicago, Toronto, (1931), cloth with illus. in color mounted on front cover, pic. endsheets, 264 pp., red top. Preface, numerous illus. including five in color, endsheets, frontis., and facing pp. 76, 104 and 232, by H. (Wyeth)

60 Coe, Wilbur. *Ranch on the Ruidoso.* Knopf, N.Y., 1968, words "First Edition" on copyright page, gilt decor. two-tone cloth, olive endsheets, 279 pp., green top, designed by Carl Hertzog, "Introduction" by Peter Hurd, maps, illus. including two in color, frontis. and facing p. 204, by H. (Cisneros)

61 Connor, Seymour V., ed. *Panhandle Plains Historical Review.* Vol. XXIX, Panhandle-plains Historical Society, Canyon, Texas, 1956, pic. wraps, 131 pp., index, photo of Hurd mural. (Bugbee)

62 Cooper, James Fenimore. *The Last of the Mohicans.* David McKay, Philadelphia, (1928), cloth with illus. in color mounted on front cover, 437 pp., pic. endsheets, introduction, nine illus. in color, front cover, frontis. and facing pp. 64, 128, 160, 210, 264, 308 and 420, by H. (The Golden Books.)

63 Crane, Aimee, ed. *Portrait of America.* Hyperion Press (distributed by Duell, Sloan and Pearce), N.Y., (1945), cloth, 101 numbered plates including two, no. 32, "Rio Hondo" (in color) and no. 36, "Sheepherder," by H.

64 Crosby, Thelma and Ball, Eve. *Bob Crosby, World Champion Cowboy.* Clarendon Press, Clarendon, Texas, 1966, pic. fabricoid, 244 pp., "Foreword" by Eve Ball, "Introduction" by S. Omar Barker, illus. by Olive Vandruff Bugbee but frontis. cartoon portrait by H.

65 ———. Same, limited Trophy Edition in Levi denim, signed by the authors.

66 Davis, J. Frank. (State Supervisor.) *Texas: A Guide to the Lone Star State.* Hastings House, N.Y., 1940, words "First Published in 1940" on copyright page, cloth, pic. endsheets, 718 pp., preface, appendices, index, numerous illus. including one, between pp. 340 and 341, by H. (Lea)

67 Dobie, J. Frank. *Guide to Life and Literature of the Southwest.* University of Texas Press, Austin, 1943, wraps, 111 pp. "A Declaration," numerous illus. including one, the frontis., "The Windmill Crew," by H. (Borein, Bugbee, Dunton, James, Lea, Leigh, Russell, Santee, Thomason)

68 Dodge, Mary Mapes. *Hans Brinker of the Silver Skates.* Garden City Pub. Co., (Garden City, N.Y.), 1932, cloth with illus. in color mounted on front cover, 305 pp., tinted top, four illus. in color including three, frontis. and facing pp. 40 and 116, by H.

69 Donauer, Friedrick (tr. from the German by Frederic Tabor Cooper). *The Long Defense.* Longman, Green, Boston, 1931, words "First Edition" on copyright page, decor. cloth, 306 pp., illus. with numerous drawings by H. and four color plates by Karl Muhlmeister. (The Junior Literary Guild edition also is marked "First Edition.")

70 Eliot, Alexander. *Three Hundred Years of American Painting.* Time, Inc., N.Y., 1957, morocco and cloth, 318 pp., acknowledgments, "Introduction" by John Walker, appendices, bibliography, index, numerous illus. including one, p. 211, by H. (Leigh, Remington, Russell)

71 Evans, Joe M. *The Horse.* Privately printed for the author by the Guynes Printing Co., (El Paso, 1962), pic. wraps, 74 pp., illus. with photos but front cover drawing by H.

72 Ferguson, Erna. *Murder and Mystery in New Mexico.* Merle Armitage Editions, Albuquerque, (1948), words

"First Edition" on copyright page, cloth, decor. end-sheets, 192 (1) pp., red top. foreword, illus. including one, the frontis., by H.

73 Ferris, Robet G., ed. *Explorers and Settlers.* National Park Service, Dept. of the Interior, G.P.O., Washington, D.C., 1968, cloth, 506 pp., maps, illus. including one by H.

74 *Fine Art Reproductions of Old and Modern Masters.* New York Graphic Society, Greenwich, Conn., (1960), colored pic. cloth, 420 pp., numerous illus. including two, p. 368, by H. and a biographical sketch of him, p. 410.

75 *Fine Art Reproductions of Old and Modern Masters.* New York Graphic Society, Greenwich, Conn. etc., (1961), decor. cloth, 443 pp., introduction, numerous illus. including two in color, p. 61, by H. (Dixon, Remington, Schreyvogel)

76 Fitzpatrick, George. *This is New Mexico.* Horn & Wallace, Albuquerque, (1962), words "Revised and Enlarged Edition" on copyright page, cloth, map endsheets, 324 pp., illus. including one, "Cow Pasture Polo," by H. (not in the first edition, 1948).

77 Gruskin, Alan D. *Painting in the U. S. A.* Doubleday, Garden City, N.Y., 1946, words "First Edition" on copyright page, cloth, 223 pp., introduction, bibliography, index, numerous illus. including one (in color) by H.

78 (Haddad.) *Reproductions* (A selective, illustrated collection of fine prints). Haddad's Fine Arts, Buena Park, California, 1969, words "First Edition 1969" on title page, colored pic. cloth, 217, xi pp., foreword, index, numerous illus. including one in color, p. 56, by H. (Remington, Russell)

79 Hamilton, Elizabeth. *The P-Zoo.* Coward-McCann, N.Y., (1945), cloth, 32 pp., hand-lettered by Flavia Gag, illustrated by H.

80 Harmsen, Dorothy. *Harmsen's Western Americana.* Northland, Flagstaff, (1971), morocco and cloth, blue endsheets, 213 pp., "Foreword" by Robert Rockwell, introduction, selected bibliography, numerous illus. including one in color, p. (109), by H. Limited edition of 150 copies signed by the author, slipcase with morocco title label. ((Beeler, Blumenschein, Borein, Dixon, Dunn, Dunton, Eggenhofer, Elwell, Johnson, Leigh, Marchand, Miller, Russell, Von Schmidt, Wyeth)

81 ———. Same, first trade edition in two-tone cloth and with red endsheets.

82 Hawley, Zoa Grace. *A Boy Rides with Custer.* Little, Brown, Boston, 1938, words "First Edition" on copyright page, pic. cloth, 295 pp., bibliography, illus. with a frontis. and d/w in color by H. and with photos.

83 Haydon, Harold (text by). *Great Art Treasures in America's Smaller Museums.* Putnam's in association with Country Beautiful, Waukesha, Wis., (1967), words "First Edition" on copyright page, cloth, grey endsheets, 194 pp., introduction, index, numerous illus. including one in color, pp. 144–5, by H. (Miller, Remington, Russell, Wyeth)

84 ———. Same, but title changed to *Great Art Treasures in American Museums* as published by Country Beautiful Corporation, Waukesha, Wisconsin.

85 Heiman, Robert K. (designed and written by). *Nation's Heritage.* Volume 1, no. 1, Heritage Magazine, Inc. (a division of B. C. Forbes & Sons, Publishers), N.Y., 1949, pic. linen, no pagination, acknowledgments, numerous illus. including one by H.

86 ———. Same, volume 1, no. 6, Heritage Magazine, N.Y., 1949, pic. linen, no pagination, acknowledgments, numerous illus. including one by H. (Remington)

87 Henderson, Barbara et al. *Prose and Poetry: The Blue Sky Book.* The L. W. Singer Co., Syracuse, N.Y., (1946), pic. cloth, 472 pp., acknowledgments, dictionary, index, numerous illus. including one, p. (53) in color, by H. Hurd sketch, pp. 52–54.

88 Hewitt, Edgar L. *Representative Art and Artists of New Mexico.* School of American Research, Museum of New Mexico (Santa Fe Press), Santa Fe, 1940, pic. wraps, 40 pp., biographical notes, numerous illus. including one, p. 22, by H. (Blumenschein, Dunton)

89 Holden, Curry. *Hill of the Rooster.* Holt, N.Y., (1956), words "First Edition" on copyright page, two-tone cloth, map endsheets, 319 pp., (preface), d/w illus. in color by H.

90 Horan, James D. *The Great American West.* Crown, N.Y., (1959), cloth and boards, 288 pp., introduction, bibliography, picture credits, index, 650 illus. including one, p. 13, by H. (Eggenhofer, Leigh, Marchand, Remington, Russell, Schreyvogel)

91 Horgan, Paul. *The Return of the Weed.* Harper, N.Y. and London, 1936, words "First Edition" and code letters "H-L" on copyright page, cloth, 97 pp., seven illus., frontis. and facing pp. 5, 15, 29, 43, 67 and 83, by H.

92 ———. *The Habit of Empire.* The Rydal Press, Santa Fe, (1939), cloth, 114 pp., eight double-page landscapes tipped in preceding pp. 17, 22, 27, 39, 47, 69, 103 and 109, by H. (This bibliographer also owns an "Advance Copy" issued by The Rydal Press with 138 pages.)

93 ———. Same, Harper, N.Y. and London, (1939), cloth, 114 pp., eight double-page landscapes following pp. 10, 22, 34, 46, 57, 70, 98 and 110, by H. (The trade edition of no. 92.)

94 ———. *Peter Hurd: A Portrait Sketch from Life.* Amon Carter Museum of Western Art, Ft. Worth (printed by the University of Texas Press, 1965), fabricoid and boards, 68 pp., "Introduction" by Mitchell A. Wilder (director), twenty-two (six in color) illus. by H.

95 Howard, Joseph Kinsey. *Montana: High, Wide and Handsome.* Yale University Press, New Haven, 1959, cloth, 347 pp., "Preface" by A. B. Guthrie, Jr., numerous drawings by H.

96 Hurd, Peter. *Portfolio of Landscapes and Portraits.* University of New Mexico, Albuquerque, 1950, eight color plates in portfolio, New Mexico Artist Series, no. 2.

97 Kelty, Mary G. *The Beginnings of the American People and Nation.* Ginn, Boston etc., (1930), cloth, 567 pp., introduction, appendix, index, maps, numerous illus. including one, frontis. in color, by H.

98 ———. *Life in Modern America.* Ginn & Co., Boston, N.Y. etc., (1941), pic. cloth, 527, xvi, (1) pp., index, numerous illus. including one, pp. 296–97, by H. (Fischer, Lea, Remington, Russell)

99 ———. *The Story of Life in America.* Ginn, Boston etc., (1946), pic. cloth, 607 (1) pp., index, numerous illus. including one, pp. 432–33, by H. (Fischer, Lea, Remington.

100 ——— and Sister Blance Marie. *Modern American Life.* Ginn, Boston etc., (1943), pic. cloth, 444, xvi, (1) pp., index, numerous illus. including one, p. 252–3, by H. (Fischer, Lea, Remington, Wyeth)

101 Lamb, Florence and Noble, Ruth, eds. *Famous Paintings in American Galleries, a 1955 Engagement Calendar.* The Berkshire Pub. Co., Cambridge, Mass., (1954), colored pic. wraps, no pagination, 55 illus. including one, "Jose Herrera," by H.

102 Lipman, Jean et al. (compiled by). *The Collector in America.* A Studio Book, Viking, N.Y., (1971), words "First published in Great Britain in 1971" on copyright page, cloth, 269 pp., "Introduction" by Alan Pryce-Jones, notes about authors, index, numerous illus. including one, p. 153, by H.

103 McCallum, Henry D. and Frances T. *The Wire that Fenced the West.* Oklahoma, Norman, (1965), words "First edition" on copyright page, cloth, 285 pp., preface, bibliography, sixteen illus. including two, facing pp. 16 and 32, by H.

104 McKinzie, Richard D. *The New Deal for Artists.* Princeton University Press, Princeton, N.J., (1973), cloth, 203 pp., preface, numerous illus. including one, p. 177, by H. (Lea)

105 Mackey, Margaret. *Your Country's Story: Pioneers, Builders, Leaders.* Ginn, Boston etc., (1961), colored pic. cloth, 560 pp., appendix, index, numerous illus. including one in color, p. 210, by H. (Lea, Remington, Wyeth)

106 Mann, E. B. and Harvey, Fred E. *New Mexico, Land of Enchantment.* Michigan State University Press, East Lansing (The Lakeside Press, Chicago), (1955), decor. cloth, 295 pp., (Introduction), appendix, numerous illus. including fifteen by H., maps.

107 Mayfield, Frank M. (President). *Missouri, Heart of the Nation.* American Artists Group, N.Y., (1947), cloth, 62 pp., "Missouri" by Mayfield, "An Introduction to Missouri" by Charles Van Ravenswaay, 106 illus. including four, "Missouri Mule Farm," "A Stollen Stallion," "Hackneys at Play," and "Early Morning Exercises," by H. Short statement by, short biography of, and portrait of H.

108 ———. Same, a reprint of no. 107, issued by Scruggs-Vandervoort-Barney, Inc. (St. Louis, Mo., 1948?), in wraps.

109 Meigs, Cornelia. *Swift Rivers.* Little, Brown, Boston, 1937, cloth with illus. in color mounted on front cover, pic. endsheets, 269 (1) pp., six illus. in color, frontis. and facing pp. 36, 76, 80, 142 and 200, by H.

110 Meigs, John, ed. *Peter Hurd, The Lithographs.* Baker Gallery Press, (Lubbock, Texas, 1968), full leather, blue endsheets, 23 pp. plus 58 plates, "Introduction" by Andrew Wyeth, "Foreword" by Meigs, "A Brief Note on the History and Technique of Lithography" by Hurd, index of plates. Limited edition of 325 copies (25 not for sale) numbered and signed by Meigs and Hurd, and each with an original lithograph especially created for this book signed by the artist, pic. slipcase.

111 ———. Same, first trade edition in cloth with pic. d/w.

112 ———. Same, advs. folder with four illus. by H.

113 ———. *Peter Hurd Sketch Book*. Sage Books, Swallow Press, Chicago, 1971, cloth, 121 pp., preface, "Introduction" by Hurd, numerous illus. including forty in color by H.

114 ———, ed. *The Cowboy in American Prints*. Swallow Press, Chicago, 1972, leather and cloth, pic. endsheets, 184 pp., introduction, numerous illus. including three, pp. 109, 111 and 113, by H., limited to 300 numbered copies signed by Meigs, each with an added manually signed lithograph by Peter Hurd, slipcase. (Beeler, Borein, Dixon, Remington, Russell, Zogbaum)

115 ———. Same, first trade edition in cloth.

116 Minton, C. E. (State Supervisor). *New Mexico*. Hastings House, N.Y., 1940, words "First Published in August 1940" on copyright page, cloth, map endsheets, 458 pp., "Foreword" by Clinton P. Anderson, preface, numerous illus. including one, between pp. 394–95, by H. (Blumenschein)

117 Moody, Ralph (Chairman, Program Committee). *Program 1956 Convention of Western Writers of America*. La Fonda Hotel, Santa Fe, June 19–21 (1956), pic. wraps, (4) pp., seven illus. in color by H.

118 Muzzey, David S. *History of the American People*. Ginn, Boston etc., (1938), cloth, 762 pp., maps, facsimiles, numerous illus. including one, frontis. in color, by H.

119 Pach, Walter et al. *New Mexico Artists*. University of New Mexico Press, Albuquerque, 1952, pic. boards, 124 (7) pp., "Introduction" by Joaquin Ortega, numerous illus. including seventeen by H. (New Mexico Artist Series, no. 3). (Blumenschein)

120 Pearson, M. Winston and Bullis, Franklin H. *Injuns Coming!* Scribner's, N.Y., 1935, code letter "A" on copyright page, cloth, 300 pp., tinted top, numerous illus. by H.

121 Pierson, William H., Jr. and Davidson, Martha, eds. *Arts in the United States*. Georgia, Athens, 1966, cloth and boards, 452 pp., "Preface" by Lamar Dodd, Director, introduction, appendices, index, 4156 numbered illus. including one, no. 3180, by H. (Remington, Young)

122 Pleasants, Henry, Jr. *Thomas Mason, Adventurer*. Winston, Philadelphia, (1934), decor. cloth, map endsheets, 366, 12 pp., introduction, appendix, illus. with numerous drawings by H.

123 Pagano, Grace. *The Encyclopaedia Britannica Collection of Contemporary American Painting*. Lakeside Press for Encyclopaedia Britannica, Chicago, (1945), wraps, unpaged, 116 numbered plates including no. 58 by H. (Dixon)

123a ———. Same, words "Second Edition" on copyright page, decor. cloth, decor. endsheets, xxix pp. plus 126 numbered plates including no. 60 by H.

124 (Price.) *The Vincent Price Treasury of American Art*. Country Beautiful, Waukesha, Wis., (1972), cloth, tan endsheets, 320 pp., foreword, biographical index, glossary, more than 300 (150 in color) illus. including two, pp. 238 (in color) and 239, by H. (Miller, Remington, Russell, Schreyvogel, Wyeth)

125 Rhodes, Eugene Manlove. *Pasó Por Aqui*. The Friends of the Alamagordo Public Library (Alamogordo Printing Co.), Alamogordo, New Mexico, 1963, pic. wraps, 68 pp., "Foreword" by Mrs. Tom Charles, bibliography, illus. including two, front cover and frontis., by H.

126 Rollins, Philip Ashton. *Gone Haywire*. Scribner's, N.Y., 1939, code letter "A" on copyright page, pic. cloth, pic. endsheets, 269 pp., brown top, preface; eight illus., d/w, front cover, endsheets, title page, pp. (54–5), (86–7), (160–1) and 234–5), by H.

127 Snort, Annie Laurie and Vineyard, Hazel. *Yucca Land*. American Guild Press, Dallas, 1958, decor. boards, map on front endsheet, 224 (3) pp., Muchas Gracio, foreword, index of names, numerous illus. including one, p. 164, by H.

128 *A Southwestern Portfolio*. Carl Hertzog, El Paso, for the Ex-Student's Association of the Univerity of Texas at El Paso, 1968, comments by S. D. Myres, (4) pp., twelve prints including two by H. (Lea)

129 *Special Book and Record Sale!* Publisher's Central Bureau, Long Island City, N.Y., self wraps, 19 (1) pp., numerous illus. including two in color, p. 4, by H. (Remington, Russell)

130 Tyron, Rolla M. and Lingley, Charles R. *The American People and Nation*. Ginn, Boston etc., (1927), pic. cloth, 654, xxxviii pp., foreword, appendices, index, maps, numerous illus. including one, p. (37), by H. (Wyeth)

131 ——— et al. *The American Nation Yesterday and Today*. Ginn, Boston etc., (1933), pic. cloth, 629, xliii pp., foreword to teachers, appendices, index, maps, numerous illus. including two, p. (19) and facing p. 142 in color, by H. (Wyeth)

132 ———. Same, 1949 edition, 736, xlviii pp., appendix,

index, maps, numerous illus. including two, p. 22 and facing p. 168 in color, by H.

133 Vernon, Walter N. *Methodism Moves Across North Texas*. The Historical Society, North Texas Conference, The Methodist Church, Dallas, (1967), cloth, pic. map endsheets, 416 pp., foreword, appendices, index, numerous illus. including one, p. (12), photo of the Hurd mural in the Dallas Post Office. (Cisneros)

134 Vollintine, Grace. *The American People and their Old World Ancestors*. Ginn, Boston etc., (1930), cloth, 576 pp., preface, numerous illus. including two in color, frontis. and facing p. 318, by H., maps. The Tyron and Lingley history series. (Wyeth)

135 Watson, Forbes (with an essay by). *American Painting Today*. The American Federation of Arts, Washington, 1939, cloth, 179 pp., lists of artists and reproductions, 259 illus. including three, pp. 115 (two) and 172, by H., also one, p. 162, by Henriette Wyeth (Mrs. Peter Hurd). (Lea)

136 *Westvaco Inspirations for Printers: 1946, 1947*. West Virginia Pulp and Paper Co., n.p., decor. cloth, tan endsheets, (3120)–3356 (2) pp., numerous illus. including three in color, pp. 3214 and 3290 plus cover no. 165, by H.

137 Wheeler, Monroe (introduction by). *Painters and Sculptors of Modern America*. Crowell, N.Y., 1942, cloth, 152 pp., publisher's note, introduction, numerous illus. including five, pp. (32-two), (35) and (36-two), by H., article by H., pp. 31–37.

138 Wilder, Howard B. et al. *This is America's Story*. Houghton Mifflin, Boston, (1958), colored pic. cloth, 728 pp., reference section, index, maps, numerous illus. including one, p. 472, by H. (Lea, Remington)

139 ———. Same, reissued in 1960 in a smaller format.

140 Wyeth, N. C. *Marauders of the Sea*. Putnam's, N.Y., (1935), pic. cloth and endsheets, 319 pp., tinted top, introduction, illus. by H.

141 ———. *Great Stories of the Sea and Ships*. McKay, Philadelphia, (1940), pic. cloth and endsheets, 411 pp., green top, foreword, numerous illus. including eighteen full-page plates by H.

The Artist and His Art

142 Ballantine, Bill. *High West*. Rand McNally, Chicago etc., (1969), words "First Printing, September, 1969" on copyright page, cloth, 303 pp., illus. with photos by the author; Bill visits Hurd at San Patricio and hears much about the controversial portrait of President Johnson.

143 Breuning, Margaret. "Peter Hurd Present Impressive Show," an article in *The Art Digest*, vol. 18, no. 12, March 15, 1944, two illus. by H. and "Portrait of Peter Hurd" by Andrew Wyeth.

144 *Catalogue of the 132nd Annual Exhibition*. Pennsylvania Academy of Fine Arts, Phila., 1937, wraps, numerous illus .including one, "Peter Hurd" by Henriette Wyeth (Mrs. Peter Hurd). Her portrait of Pete won the Mary Smith Award for the "best painting by a woman artist of Philadelphia."

145 *Catalogue of the 135th Annual Exhibition*. Pennsylvania Academy of Fine Arts, Phila., 1940, wraps, numerous illus. including one, "Peter in San Patricio," by Henriette Wyeth (Mrs. Peter Hurd).

145a "Cover Story," an article in *Time* 88:23, December 2, 1966, with one illus. in color, front cover, by H.

146 Dykes, Jeff C. *High Spots in Western Illustrating*. (The Kansas City Posse, The Westerners, Kansas City, Missouri, 1964), cloth, 30 pp., introduction, *High Spots* no. 81 and no. 87 have two Hurd illus. Edition limited to 250 autographed copies.

147 Fisher, Reginald (compiled and edited by). *An Art Directory of New Mexico*. Museum of New Mexico and School of American Research, (Santa Fe), 1947, words "Edition - 1000" on copyright page, wraps, 78 pp., foreword, Hurd sketch, p. 30. (Blumenschein)

148 "Fourth of July," a brief article in *The Texas Outlook* 36:7, July 1952, about Hurd and his front cover illus. in color.

149 Gipson, Fred. "A Visit with Peter Hurd," an article in *True West*, October 1966, with three illus. by H. and with a photo of him.

150 Holden, Frances M., ed. "The Peter Hurd Mural," an article in *The Museum Journal*, volume 1, Lubbock, Texas, 1957, pic. wraps, 95 pp., "Planning the Mural" by W. C. Holden, "Dedicatory Remarks" by Paul Horgan, "Some Notes on the Mural" by Peter Hurd, "Fresco Painting" by E. Sasser, numerous illus. including sixteen full-page plates from the mural by H.

151 Horgan, Paul (foreword by). *Peter Hurd, the Permanent Collection*. Roswell Museum, Roswell, New Mexico, (February, 1949), words "First Edition - 1000 copies" on back cover, wraps, (8) pp., foreword, biographical sketch.

152 ———. "The Style of Peter Hurd," an article in *New Mexico Quarterly*, vol. XX, no. 4, Winter 1950–1951, Hurd biographical sketch in "The Editor's Corner." This issue illus. with drawings by H.

153 ———. Same, reprinted by Roswell Museum and Art Center, with six illus. by H.

154 ———. "Peter Hurd: He looks at the gate and sees beyond," an article in *New Mexico* 49:11–12, November–December 1970, with one illus. in color and a photo in color of Hurd, also "Peter Hurd Sketch Book" with seven double-page plates in color by H.

155 ———. "Peter Hurd," an article in *New Mexico*, volume 39, no. 1, January, 1961, photos of Hurd and one double-page illus. by H. This same issue contains an article, "New Mexico," by Peter Hurd.

156 Hurd, Peter. "The Ranch Country as Seen by a New Mexican," an article in *The Art Digest*, volume XI, no. 9, February 1, 1937, illus. with the "Portrait of Peter Hurd" by Henriette Wyeth (Mrs. Peter Hurd), and with one drawing by H.

157 ———. "A Southwestern Heritage," an autobiographical article in *Arizona Highways* 39:11, November 1953, with eighteen (fourteen in color) illus. by H. and a photo of him.

158 ———. "Polo as She's Seldom Seen," an article in *Sports Illustrated* 1:13, November 8, 1954, with one illus. in color by H. and two photos of his ranch polo team.

160 ———. "Countdown at Canaveral," an article in *Art in America*, volume 51, no. 5, October, 1963, a preliminary statement by H. Lester Cooke, Curator of Painting, National Gallery of Art, Washington, D.C., eight illus., four in color, by H.

161 ———. Same, an article in *Southwestern Art* 1:1, Spring 1966, with seven illus. by H.

162 "Peter Hurd, Artist of the Southwest" and "Peter Hurd, A Portrait Sketch from Life," by Paul Horgan, portfolio and article in *Woman's Day* 29:11, August 1966, with ten illus. in color by H. and with a photo in color of him.

163 Jarrell, John. "The Big Swing" (Yesterday, Today and Tomorrow in Southern New Mexico), an illus. article in *New Mexico* 50:9–10, September–October 1972, with a segment on "Hurd and Billy the Kid" and a photo of Hurd on horseback.

164 Kelly, J. R. *A History of New Mexico Military Institute 1891–1941*. (New Mexico, Albuquerque, 1953), cloth with illus. mounted on the front cover, 404 pp., bibliography, index, illus. with photos, Hurd in the text pp. 181, 304 and 314.

165 Magnan, George A. "A Visit with Peter Hurd," an article in *Today's Art* 21:6, June 1973, with five illus. in color by H.

166 Micuda, Jean. "Wherefore Art: Welcome to Peter Hurd and Gerard Delano," an article in *Arizona Living*, Feb. 5, 1971, with one illus. by Hurd and a photo of him.

167 Miller (Mahony), Bertha E. et al. (compiled by). *Illustrators of Children's Books, 1744–1945*. The Horn Book, Boston, 1947, cloth and pic. boards, 527 pp., gilt top, preface, introduction, biographies, bibliographies, appendices, sources, index, numerous illus., Hurd sketches on p. 322 and list on p. 417. (James, Smith)

168 Morre, Dorothy Lefferts. "Painters and Sculptors in Crystal," an illus. article in *Magazine of Art*, January 1940, with a photo of the Steuben Glass vase designed by H.

169 "Native Artist Paints New Mexico," a brief article about Hurd in *The Humble Way* 10:6, March–April 1955, with five illus. in color including the cover by H.

170 "Painters and Sculptors of Modern America," an article in *Magazine of Art* (Thomas Y. Crowell Co.), N.Y., 1942, numerous illus. including four by H.

171 Paylore, Patricia. "The Months of Our Year," an article in *Arizona Highways* 48:11, November 1972, with fifteen illus. in color by H. with comments by him, also "Journey Resumed, Peter Hurd Today" by John Meigs with a color photo of Peter and Henriette Hurd.

172 Sinclair, John L. "Peter Hurd, Artist on Horseback," an article in *El Palacio* 58:6, June 1946, with one illus. by him.

173 "Ten Years of American Art," an illus. article in *Life*, November 25, 1946, with one illus. in color by H. and brief comments on his art.

174 Wertenbaker, Green Peyton. *America's Heartland, The Southwest* by Green Peyton (pseud.). Oklahoma, Norman, 1948, words "First edition" on copyright page, cloth, 285 (1) pp., green top, "A Foreword," index, illus., Hurd in text pp. 228, 244–45, 246 and 248, and a photo of him with Paul Horgan. (Lea)

175 *Western Review* 4:1, Summer 1967, cover illus. and pp. 33–39 by H. and pp. 40–43 by Henriette Wyeth.

176 *Who's Who in America*. Volume 36, Marquis, Chicago, 1970–71, cloth, 2585 pp., the Hurd biography appears p. 1108. Note: the first volume to carry the Hurd biography is not known to the compiler.

177 Young, John V. "The Art of Peter Hurd," an article in *Westways*, July 1972, with three illus. by H. and two photos of him.

INTRODUCING REFORM TO THE WILDERNESS by Hutchison from *Captain Bill McDonald, Texas Ranger*

D. C. HUTCHISON
1869–1954

Illustrated by the Artist

1 Altsheler, Joseph A. *The Young Trailers.* Appleton, N.Y., 1907, code number "(1)" after last line of text, cloth, 331 pp., frontis. in color by H.

2 ————. *The Last of the Chiefs.* Appleton, N.Y. and London, 1909, words "Published September, 1909" on copyright page and code number "(1)" after last line of text, pic. cloth, pp. 336 (1), (6), four illus. in color, frontis. and facing pp. 26, 188 and 246, by H.

3 ————. *The Keepers of the Trail.* Appleton, N.Y. and London, 1916, code number "(1)" after last line of text, cloth, 322 (1) pp., four illus. in color by H. Reprinted in 1922 with only a frontis. by H.

4 ————. *The Hunters of the Hills.* Appleton, N.Y., London, 1916, code no. "(1)" after last line of text, cloth with illus. in color mounted on the front cover, 359 (1) pp., four illus., frontis. and facing pp. 52, 210 and 286, by H.

5 ————. *The Eyes of the Woods.* Appleton, N.Y. and London, 1917, code number "(1)" after last line of text, pic. cloth, 325 (1) pp., four illus. in color, frontis. and facing pp. 78, 204 and 254, by H.

6 Barnes, James. *Rifle and Caravan.* Appleton, N.Y. and London, 1912, words "Published October, 1912" on copyright page and code no. "(1)" after last line of text, pic. cloth, 325 pp., (1), four illus. in color, frontis. and facing pp. 20, 92 and 208, by H.

7 Bindloss, Harold. *The Intriguers.* Frederick A. Stokes, N.Y., (1914), words "February, 1914" on copyright page, cloth, 305 pp., frontis. in color by H.

8 Cheyney, Edward G. *Scott Burton in the Blue Ridge.* Appleton, N.Y. and London, 1924, code number "(1)" after last line of text, decor. cloth, 267 (1) pp., frontis. by H.

9 Coolidge, Dane. *Batwing Bowles.* Stokes, N.Y., (1914), words "March, 1914" on copyright page, cloth, 296 pp., foud illus., frontis. (in color) and facing pp. 76, 180 and 276, by H.

10 Cronin, Bernard. *Timber Wolves.* Macmillan, N.Y., 1921, words "Published, March, 1921" on copyright page, cloth, 358 pp., foreword, frontis. in color by H.

11 Forsyth, Brigadier General George A. *The Soldier.* The Brampton Society, N.Y., (1908), cloth with paper label on spines, two vols., 198 pp.; 199-389, gilt tops, editor's preface, author's preface, index, four illus. in each volume including one, frontis. in color in vol. 1, by H. *Builders of the Nation*, National Edition.

12 Gregor, Elmer Russell. *The White Wolf.* Appleton, N.Y., London, 1921, code number "(1)" after last line of text, decor. cloth, 267 (1) pp., frontis. in color by H.

13 ————. *Three Sioux Scouts.* Appleton, N.Y., London, 1922, code number "(1)" after last line of text, pic. cloth, 252 (1) pp., frontis. by H.

14 ————. *Spotted Deer.* Appleton, N.Y., London, 1922, code number "(1)" after last line of text, cloth, 239 (1) pp., frontis. by H.

15 ————. *Jim Mason, Scout.* Appleton, N.Y., and London, 1923, code number "(1)" after last line of text, cloth, 273 (1) pp., frontis. by H.

16 ————. *Captain Jim Mason.* Appleton, N.Y., London, 1924, code number "(1)" after last line of text, cloth, 252 (1) pp., frontis. by H.

17 ————. *The Medicine Buffalo.* Appleton, N.Y., London, 1925, code number "(1)" after last line of text, cloth, 263 (1) pp., frontis. by H.

18 ————. *Mason and His Rangers.* Appleton, N.Y., London, 1926, code number "(1)" after last line of text, decor. cloth, 244 (1) pp., frontis. by H.

19 ———. *The War Eagle.* Appleton, N.Y., London, 1926, code number "(1)" after last line of text, decor. cloth, 223 (1) pp., frontis. and text drawings by H.

20 ———. *The Mystery Trail.* Appleton, N.Y., London, 1927, code number "(1)" after last line of text, cloth, 224 (1) pp., frontis. by H.

21 ———. *Three Wilderness Scouts.* Appleton, N.Y., London, 1928, code number "(1)" after last line of text, decor. cloth, 238 (1) pp., frontis. by H.

22 ———. *Running Fox.* Appleton, N.Y., London, 1918, code number "(1)" after last line of text, cloth, 317 pp., frontis. by H.

23 ———. *White Otter.* Appleton, N.Y. etc., 1917, code number "(1)" after last line of text, cloth, 312 pp., frontis. by H.

24 Hough, Emerson. *Mother of Gold.* Appleton, N.Y., London, 1924, code number "(1)" after last line of text, cloth, 326 (1) pp., frontis. by H.

25 Laut, Agnes C. *The Trapper.* Brampton Society, N.Y., (1908), cloth with paper labels, two vols., 143 pp.; (144)-284, gilt tops, editor's preface, appendix, six illus. in vol. 1 including one, the frontis., by H. (Four illus. in vol. 2.) *Builders of the Nation,* National Edition. (Johnson)

26 McNeil, Malcolm. *In Texas with Davy Crockett.* Dutton, N.Y., (1908), pic. cloth, 308 pp., tan top, foreword, five illus., frontis. and facing pp. 39, 92, 194 and 298, by H.

27 ———. *With Kit Carson in the Rockies.* Dutton, N.Y., (1909), pic. cloth, 333 pp., (4) of advs., green top, five illus., frontis. and facing pp. 29, 81, 180 and 273, by H.

28 ———. Same, first British edition, W. & R. Chambers, London, Edinburgh, cloth, 333 pp., (5) of advs. foreword, five illus., frontis. and facing pp. 22, 54, 182 and 262, by H.

29 ———. *Fighting with Fremont.* Dutton, N.Y., (1910), pic. cloth, 348 pp., (4) of advs., slate top, foreword, five illus., frontis. and facing pp. 32, 90 118 and 222, by H.

30 Miller, Warren H. *Red Mesa.* Appleton, N.Y., London, 1923, code number "(1)" after last line of text, pic. cloth, 261 (1) pp., (2) of advs., frontis. by H.

31 Moore, Leslie. *The Wiser Folly.* Putnam's, N.Y. and London, 1916, cloth, 354 pp., (4) of advs., frontis. in color by H.

32 Munroe, Kirk. *The Outcast Warrior.* Appleton, N.Y., 1905, code number "(1)" after last line of text, pic. cloth, 279 pp., four tinted illus., frontis. and facing pp. 36, 164 and 196, by H.

33 Paine, Albert Bigelow. *Captain Bill McDonald, Texas Ranger.* J. J. Little & Ives Co., N.Y., 1909, morocco or red cloth with small illus. mounted on front cover, or blue cloth, 448 pp. "Foreword" by Theodore Roosevelt, appendices, illus. including seven, four facing pp. 46, 74, 138 and 172 in color and three facing pp. 210, 282 and 366 tinted only, by H.

34 Pendexter, Hugh. *A Virginia Scout.* Bobbs-Merrill, Indianapolis, (1922), cloth, 353 pp., frontis. by H.

35 Pocock, Roger S. *The Wolf Trail.* Appleton, N.Y., 1923, code number "(1)" after last line of text, cloth, 323 (1) pp., (2) of advs., d/w illus. in color by H.

36 Raine, William MacLeod. *The Vision Splendid.* G. W. Dillingham Co., N.Y., (1913), cloth, 331 pp., three illus., frontis. and facing pp. 56 and 232, by H.

37 ———. *A Daughter of the Dons.* Dillingham, N.Y., (1914), cloth, 320 pp., two illus., frontis. and facing p. 254, by H.

38 ———. *The Pirate of Panama.* Dillingham, N.Y., (1914), cloth, 316 pp., two illus., frontis. and facing p. 240, by H.

39 ———. *The Highgrader.* Dillingham, N.Y., (1915), cloth, 321 pp., illus. by H.

40 ———. *Crooked Trails and Straight.* Dillingham, N.Y., 1913, cloth, 339 pp., illus. by H.

41 Shinn, Charles Howard. *The Mine.* Brampton Society, N.Y., (1908), cloth with paper labels on spines, two vols., 122 pp.; 123-272, gilt tops. "Editor's Preface" by Ripley Hitchcock, author's preface, seven illus. in each vol. including one, the frontis. in vol. 2, by H. *Builders of the Nation,* National Edition. (Johnson)

42 Sinclair, Bertrand W. *The Land of the Frozen Suns.* Dillingham, N.Y., (1910), red cloth with gilt lettering 309 pp., three illus., frontis. (in color) and facing pp. 70 and 288, by H.

43 Sinclair-Cowan, Bertha M. *The Lonesome Trail* by B. M. Bower (pseud.). Dillingham, N.Y., (1909), pic. cloth, 297 pp., (3) of advs., frontis. in color, by H.

44 ———. *The Happy Family.* Dillingham, N.Y., (1910), pic. cloth, 330 pp., frontis. in color, by H.

45 ———. *Flying U Ranch.* Dillingham, N.Y., (1914), red cloth with gilt lettering, 200 pp., three illus., frontis. (in color) and facing pp. 104 and 210, by H.

46 Sullivan, Francis William. *Star of the North*. Putnam's, N.Y. and London, 1916, decor. cloth, 379 pp., frontis. in color, by H.

47 Wheeler, James Cooper. *Captain Pete of Cortesana*. Dutton, N.Y., (1909), pic. cloth, 292 pp., (4) of advs., green top, five illus., frontis. and facing pp. 11, 98, 193 and 269, by H.

48 ———. *Captain Pete of Puget Sound*. Dutton, N.Y., (1909), pic. cloth, 275 pp., green top, five illus., frontis. and facing pp. 64, 117, 210 and 265, by H.

49 Wilson, William R. A. *Comrades Three*. Appleton, N.Y., 1906, code number "(1)" after last line of text, pic. cloth, 248 pp., four illus. in color, frontis. and facing pp. 108, 176 and 236, by H.

50 ———. *The King's Scouts*. Appleton, N.Y., 1907, code number "(1)" after last line of text, decor. cloth, 277 pp., four illus. in color, frontis. and facing pp. 10, 66 and 156, by H.

THE HEAD CAME UP ON THE OTHER SIDE by Hutchison from *The Riflemen Of The Ohio*

THEN CAME THE SECOND MEETING WITH JIM GALLOWAY by Johnson from
The Bells Of San Juan

FRANK TENNEY JOHNSON
1874-1939

Catalogues of Art Exhibitions and Galleries

J. N. BARTFIELD ART GALLERIES, NEW YORK

1 *American Paintings and Sculpture, Historical-Western*, n.d., colored pic. wraps, unpaged but with 64 numbered illus. including three, nos. 26, 27 and 28, by J. (Leigh, Remington, Russell, Schoonover, Wyeth)

1a Same, (catalogue no. 120, 1973), wraps, with window, unpaged, 82 numbered illus. including eight, nos. 19 (color), 20 (color), 21, 22, 23, 24, 25 and 26, by J. (Dixon, Leigh, Remington, Russell, Schreyvogel)

BILTMORE GALLERIES, LOS ANGELES

1b *Catalog*, May 1969, colored pic. wraps, 54 pp., numerous illus. including four, pp. 29, 30 (two) and 31, by J. (Borein, Dixon, Dunton, Koerner, Leigh, Miller, Remington, Russell, Young)

BILTMORE SALON (BILTMORE HOTEL), LOS ANGELES

2 *Under Western Skies*, November 4–30, 1935, French fold pic. wraps, lists ten paintings by J. and the front cover drawing is by him.

3 *Memorial Exhibition of Paintings by F. Tenney Johnson, 1874–1939*, 1939, includes three illus. by J. and a photo of him.

BRADFORD BRINTON MEMORIAL
BIG HORN, WYOMING

4 *The Bradford Brinton Memorial Ranch*, Quarter Circle A Ranch, 1961, folder, fourteen illus. including one by J. (Remington, Russell)

CHARLES W. BOWERS MEMORIAL MUSEUM
SANTA ANA, CALIFORNIA

5 *Painters of the West*, 1972, includes one illus. by J. and a short biographical sketch of him.

CHAPPELLIER GALLERIES, NEW YORK

6 *One Hundred American Selections*, 1966, colored pic.

wraps, unpaged but 100 numbered illus. including one, no. 57, by J. (Deming, Miller, Remington)

CITY ART MUSEUM, ST. LOUIS

7 *23rd Annual Exhibition of Selected Paintings by American Artists*, 1928, wraps, numerous illus. including one, "Haunters of the Silences," by J.

CITY NATIONAL BANK, STUDIO CITY, CALIFORNIA

8 *Western Art Exhibit* (The Art of the Living West), 1965, folder, two illus. by J.

THE COLONIAL ART COMPANY (WILLARD JOHNSON), OKLAHOMA CITY

9 *Western and Traditional American Paintings of the 19th and Early 20th Centuries* (Oil Paintings, Watercolors, and Drawings). Auction, Lincoln Plaza Inn, 4445 Lincoln Blvd., Oklahoma City, June 10, 1973, pic. wraps, unpaged but with seventy-six numbered illus. including two, nos. 32 and 33, by J. (Borein, Deming, Dixon, Eggenhofer, Elwell, Goodwin, Koerner, Russell, Schoonover, Wyeth)

DALLAS MUSEUM OF FINE ARTS

10 *A Century of Arts and Life in Texas*. April 9–May 7, 1961, pic. wraps, unpaged, "Foreword" by Jerry Bywaters, numerous illus. including one by J. (Dunton, Lea, Remington, Schiwetz)

DENVER ART MUSEUM

11 *Colorado Collects Historic Western Art*, January 13 through April 15, 1973, decor. wraps, 72 pp., numerous illus. including one, p. 13, by J. (Miller, Remington, Russell, Schreyvogel)

EDWARD EBERSTADT AND SONS, NEW YORK

12 *A Distinguished Collection of Western Americana* (Catalogue 139), 1956, pic. wraps, "Introduction —

Western Americana Art" by Harold McCracken, 129 numbered illus. including four, nos. 60, 61, 62 and 63, by J. (Borein, Deming, Dixon, Leigh, Remington, Russell)

13 *American Paintings* (Catalogue 146, December 1957), colored pic. wraps, 191 numbered illus. including no. 10 by J. (Borein, Deming, Dixon, Dunton, Leigh, Remington)

GRADY GAMMAGE MEMORIAL AUDITORIUM
TEMPE, ARIZONA

14 *A Nobler Sight* (An Exhibition of Paintings and Prints Selected from the Art Collections of Arizona State University), January 1967, folder with "The Mountain Trail" by J. on the front.

GRAND CENTRAL ART GALLERIES, NEW YORK

15 *Exhibition of Paintings and Sculpture Contributed by Artist Members, Year Book 1930*, boards with illus. in color mounted on front cover, decor. rust endsheets, 79 (1) pp., numerous illus. including one, p. 44, by J. (Blumenschein)

16 Same, *1931*, decor. wraps, green endsheets, 71 (1) pp., numerous illus. including one, p. 47, by J.

17 Same, *1932*, pic. wraps, orange endsheets, 71 (1) pp., numerous illus. including one, p. 51, by J.

18 Same, *1935*, wraps with illus. in color mounted on front cover, tan endsheets, 62 pp., numerous illus. including one, p. 36, by J.

19 Same, *1936*, wraps with illus. in color mounted on front cover, green endsheets, 64 pp., numerous illus. including one, p. 32, by J. (Young)

20 Same, *1937*, wraps with illus. in color mounted on front cover, 80 pp., numerous illus. including one, p. 57, by J.

21 Same, *1938*, wraps, with illus. mounted on front cover, 72 pp., numerous illus. including one, p. 36, by J. (Blumenschein, Leigh)

22 Same, *1939*, wraps with illus. in color mounted on front cover, tan endsheets, 74 pp., numerous illus. including one, p. 44, by J. (Leigh)

23 Same, *1942*, wraps with illus. in color mounted on front cover, 72 pp., numerous illus. including one in color, p. (6), by J.

24 Same, *1943*, wraps with illus. mounted on front cover, 71 (1) pp., numerous illus. including one, p. 39, by J. (Leigh)

25 Same, *1944*, wraps with illus. in color mounted on

front cover, 78 pp., numerous illus. including one in color, p. 6, by J. (Leigh)

26 Same, *1950*, wraps with illus. in color mounted on front cover, 72 pp., numerous illus. including two, pp. (15) and 52, by J. (Leigh)

27 Same, *1951*, wraps with illus. in color mounted on front cover, 72 pp., numerous illus. including one, p. 42, by J. (Leigh)

28 Same, *1955*, wraps with illus. in color mounted on front cover, 76 pp., numerous illus. including one, p. 14, by J. (Leigh, Remington, Schreyvogel)

29 Same, *1970*, wraps with illus. in color mounted on front cover, 68 pp., numerous illus. including one, p. 10, by J. (Leigh, Russell)

THE GEORGE GUND MUSEUM OF WESTERN ART
NEW YORK

30 *The Gund Collection of Western Art, A Personal Narrative*, 1970, colored pic. wraps, 38 pp., nineteen illus. including one in color, p. 21, by J. (Leigh, Remington, Russell, Schreyvogel)

31 Same, *A History and Pictorial Description of the American West*, 1973, pic. wraps, 62 pp., thirty-five illus. including two, pp. 9 and 11 (color), by J. (Leigh, Miller, Remington, Russell, Schreyvogel)

JOSLYN ART MUSEUM, OMAHA, NEBRASKA

32 *Life on the Prairie — A Permanent Exhibition*, 1966, wraps, illus. including one by J. (Leigh, Miller, Remington, Russell)

KALAMAZOO INSTITUTE OF ARTS
KALAMAZOO, MICHIGAN

33 *Western Art* (Paintings and Sculptures of the West), February 17–March 19, 1967, pic. wraps, 17 (1) pp., numerous illus. including one by J. (Hurd, Leigh, Remington, Russell, Schreyvogel, Wyeth)

KENNEDY GALLERIES, NEW YORK

34 *Recent Acquisitions in Important Western Painting*, October 1961, pic. wraps, (40) pp., numerous illus. including three by J. (Borein, Deming, Eggenhofer, Remington, Russell, Schreyvogel)

35 *Kennedy Quarterly* 3:2, October 1962, wraps with illus. in color mounted on front cover, (59) pp., numerous illus. including one by J. (Borein, Leigh, Marchand, Remington, Russell, Schreyvogel)

36 *Western Encounter: The Artists Record*, October 1964, colored pic. wraps, 64 pp., numerous illus. in-

cluding two, p. 53, by J. (Leigh, Marchand, Remington, Russell, Schreyvogel)

37 *From Coast to Coast*, June 1967, colored pic. wraps, pp. 80–152, numerous illus. including one in color, p. 130, by J. and with a brief biographical sketch of him. (Borein, Remington, Russell)

38 *Walking Westward*, March 1972, colored pic. wraps, pp. 196–256, numerous illus. including one, p. 251, by J. (Lungren, Miller, Remington, Russell, Schreyvogel)

LOS ADOBES ART GALLERY, SANTA BARBARA

39 *Exciting Western Art by Artist Members of Rancheros Visitadores*, May 4 through May 20, 1962, pic. wraps, numerous illus. including one by J. (Borein)

THE LOS ANGELES MUNICIPAL ART DEPARTMENT

40 *The C. Bland Jamison Collection of Western Art*, March 29–April 17, 1960, pic. wraps, (8) pp., twelve illus. including five by J. (Remington, Russell)

MAXWELL GALLERIES, SAN FRANCISCO

41 *American Art Since 1850*, August 2–31, 1968, colored pic. wraps, 84 pp., numerous illus. including two by J. (Borein, Dixon, Miller, Remington, Wyeth)

41a *Art of the West*, November 13 through December 1973, colored pic. wraps, 48 pp., numerous illus. including two, pp. 18 and 22, by J. (Leigh, Marchand, Miller)

READ MULLAN GALLERY OF WESTERN ART
PHOENIX, ARIZONA

42 *Read Mullan Gallery of Western Art*, 1964, colored decor. cloth, (41) pp., numerous illus. including three, two in color, by J. (Leigh, Remington)

PETERSEN GALLERIES, BEVERLY HILLS, CALIFORNIA

42a *Americana, Western and Sporting Art / Sculpture*, wraps, 25 pp., numerous illus. including one, p. 7, by J. (James, Leigh, Remington, Russell, Wyeth, Zogbaum)

PHOENIX ART GALLERY

43 *The Discovery of the West*, March 1961, pic. wraps, (12) pp., (Foreword) by Read Mullan, numerous illus. including two by J. (Leigh, Remington, Russell)

PHOENIX ART MUSEUM

44 *Western Art from the Eugene B. Adkins Collection*. November 1971–January 1972, colored pic. wraps, unpaged, numerous illus. including one by J. (Dunton, Leigh, Miller, Remington, Varian)

RAINBOW HOTEL, GREAT FALLS, MONTANA
(ADVERTISING CLUB OF GREAT FALLS)

44a *Fourth Annual C. M. Russell Auction of Original Western Art*, March 17, 1972, pic. wraps, unpaged, lists 145 lots, numerous illus. including lot 70 by J. (Dunton, James, Leigh, Remington, Russell)

44b *Fifth Annual C. M. Russell Auction of Original Western Art*, March 16, 1973, pic. wraps, unpaged, lists 159 lots, numerous illus. including lot 23 by J. (Borein, De Yong, Koerner, Marchand, Russell, Wyeth)

SOTHEBY PARKE BERNET, LOS ANGELES

44c *Western American Paintings, Drawings and Sculpture*, March 4 and 5, 1974, colored pic. wraps, unpaged, 252 lots, numerous illus. including two in color, lots 92 and 103, by J. (Blumenschein, Dunton, Koerner, Leigh, Remington, Russell)

SOTHEBY PARKE BERNET, NEW YORK

45 *Traditional & Western American Paintings, Drawings, Watercolors, Sculpture & Illustrations* (Sale no. 3348), April 19–20, 1972, pic. wraps, 147 pp., numerous illus. including one, p. 83, by J. (Deming, Koerner, Leigh, Remington, Russell)

46 *18th, 19th and Early 20th Century American Paintings, Drawings and Sculpture* (Sale no. 3399), September 13, 1972, pic. wraps, 89 (4) pp., numerous illus. including one, p. 16, by J. (Dixon, Dunton, Koerner, Leigh, Remington, Stoops)

47 *Important 18th, 19th and Early 20th Century American Paintings, Watercolors and Sculpture* (Sale no. 3498), April 11, 1973, colored pic. wraps, unpaged but with over seventy numbered plates including one in color, no. 63, by J. (Blumenschein, James, Leigh, Remington, Russell, Varian, Wyeth)

47a *18th, 19th and Early 20th Century American Painting, Drawings, Watercolors and Sculpture* (sale no. 3548), September 28, 1973, pic. wraps, unpaged, numerous numbered illus. including one, no. 107, by J. (Deming, Koerner, Remington, Russell)

THE UNIVERSITY OF TEXAS, AUSTIN

48 *Paintings from the C. R. Smith Collection*, December 4, 1969–January 15, 1970, wraps, 40 pp., thirty numbered illus. including two, nos. 17 and 18 (color), by J. (Dixon, Eggenhofer, Lea, Russell, Von Schmidt, Schreyvogel)

WHITNEY GALLERY OF WESTERN ART (BUFFALO BILL HISTORICAL CENTER), CODY, WYOMING

49 *Loan Exhibition, Frank Tenney Johnson (1874–1939), Loretta Howard (Contemporary, 1904–)*, May 1 to September 30, 1961, folder with Johnson illus. on front, lists twenty-four paintings by J. and there is an appraisal of his art by Harold McCracken.

50 *Yellowstone Centennial Season*, May 1 to October 1, 1972, pic. wraps, (8) pp., seventeen illus. including four by J. (Remington, Russell)

WOOLAROC MUSEUM (FRANK PHILLIPS FOUNDATION), BARTLESVILLE, OKLAHOMA

51 *Oklahoma*, 1952, pic. wraps, (8) pp., numerous illus. including four, three in color, by J. (Dunton, Leigh, Mora, Remington, Russell)

52 *Woolaroc*, n.d., decor. colored wraps, 31 (1) pp., numerous illus. including three, pp. 15 and 16 (two), by J. (Leigh, Remington, Russell)

53 *Woolaroc Museum*, (1965), decor. colored boards or wraps, 64 (1) pp., numerous illus. in color including eleven by J. (Leigh, Mora, Remington, Russell, Young)

Illustrated by the Artist

54 Ainsworth, Ed. *The Cowboy in Art*. World, N.Y. and Cleveland, (1968), words "First Edition" on copyright page, full leather, orange endsheets, 242 pp., all edges gilt, "Foreword" by John Wayne, index, numerous illus. including one, p. 64, by J. plus a photo of him. Special edition of 1000 numbered copies in a slipcase. (Beeler, Borein, Bugbee, De Yong, Dixon, Dunton, Eggenhofer, Ellsworth, Hurd, James, Koerner, Mora, Perceval, Remington, Russell, Santee, Schreyvogel, Von Schmidt)

55 ———. Same, first trade edition in gilt lettered and illus. cloth, orange endsheets.

56 ———. Same, reprint by Bonanza Books, N.Y., in red lettered and illus. cloth, white endsheets.

57 Boyle, Louis M. *Out West: Growing Cymbidium Orchids: The Story of El Rancho Rinconada*. (Times-Mirror Press, Los Angeles, 1952), words "First Edition" on copyright page, decor. cloth, pic. endsheets, 526 pp., preface, (acknowledgments), index of titles, numerous illus. including one, p. 122, by J.

58 Breeden, Marshall. *The Romantic Southland of California*. Kenmore Publishing Co., Los Angeles, 1928, decor. cloth, colored pic. endsheets, 207 (1) pp., Cali-

fornia Place Names Defined, maps, thirty-two illus. including one, between pp. 136 and 137, by J.

59 Bronson, Edgar Beecher. *Reminiscences of a Ranchman*. McClurg, Chicago, 1910, words "Published September 10, 1910" on copyright page, cloth with illus. in color mounted on front cover, 369 (1) pp., illus. including two, facing pp. 212 and 214, by J. (Dixon, Dunton)

60 ———. *The Red Blooded*. McClurg, Chicago, 1910, words "Published September 10, 1910" on copyright page, pic. cloth, 341 (1) pp., illus. including three facing pp. 324, 330 and 334, by J. (Dixon, Russell)

61 Burroughs, E. R. *The Mad King*. McClurg, Chicago, 1926, cloth, 365 pp., frontis. by J.

62 Callahan, Robert E. *Daughter of Ramona*. Gaines Publishing Co., N.Y. etc., (1930), cloth, 281 pp., foreword, frontis. by J. (Dedicated to Johnson et al.)

63 *Carthay Circle Theatre* (Souvenir Program). Far West Theatres, Inc., Los Angeles, (1926), pic. wraps, unpaged, illustrated; includes "Frank Tenney Johnson, Greatest Living Painter of Western Life" with a photo of him and two full-page plates by him.

64 Catton, Bruce, ed. *American Heritage, vol. VII, no. 6*. American Heritage Pub. Co., N.Y., October, 1956, colored pic. boards, 119 (1) pp., numerous illus. including one in color, p. 8, by J.

65 Chisholm, A. M. *The Boss of Wind River*. Doubleday, Page, Garden City, N.Y., 1911, cloth, 340 (1) pp., four illus. in color, frontis. and facing pp. 32, 188 and 214, by J.

66 ———. *The Land of the Strong Men*. H. K. Fly Co., N.Y., (1919), decor. cloth, 432 pp., four illus., frontis. and facing pp. 138, 212 and 272, by J.

67 Clarke, Laurence. *South of the Rio Grande*. Macaulay, N.Y., (1924), pic. cloth, 319 pp., frontis. by J.

68 Dana, Marvin (from the play by Daniel D. Carter). *The Master Mind*. H. K. Fly Co., N.Y., (1913), decor. cloth, 320 pp., four illus., frontis. and facing pp. 124, 212 and 284, by J.

69 Drago, Harry Sinclair. *Out of the Silent North*. Macaulay, N.Y., (1923), pic. cloth, 304 pp., frontis. by J.

70 ———. *Smoke of the .45*. Macaulay, N.Y., (1923), pic. cloth, 311 pp., frontis. by J.

71 ——— and Joseph Noel. *Whispering Sage*. Century, N.Y., 1922, cloth, 304 pp., frontis. by J.

72 (Eberstadt.) *Americana* (Cat. 134). Edward Eberstadt

& Sons, N.Y., (1954), pic. wraps, 111 pp., thirty-two illus. including one, facing p. 33, by J. (Dixon)

73 ———. *Americana* (Cat. 138). Edward Eberstadt & Sons, N.Y., Dec. 1955, pic. wraps., 128 pp., forty illus. including one, facing p. 64, by J. (Rowe)

74 Frederick, John *Riders of the Silences.* H. K. Fly Co., N.Y., 1920, cloth, 310 pp., frontis. by J.

75 Gann, Dan and Kitchen, Merrell A., eds. *The Westerners.* 1949 (copyrighted 1950), morocco and decor. cloth, pic. endsheets, 263 pp., "Foreword" by Sheriff Homer H. Boelter, index, numerous illus. including two, pp. 180 and 188, by J. Notes on Johnson by Don Luis Perceval, pp. 180–81. Limited to 400 copies. (Blumenschein, Borein, Dixon, Perceval, Remington, Russell)

76 Good, Donnie D. *Traveling Westward.* Thomas Gilcrease Institute, Tulsa, 1968, colored pic. wraps, (20) pp., numerous illus. including three, front cover in color and two in text, by J. (Borein, Russell)

77 Gregory, Jackson. *The Short Cut.* Dodd, Mead, N.Y., 1916, cloth, 383 pp., four illus. in color, frontis. and facing pp. 98, 150, and 338, by J.

78 ———. *Wolf Breed.* Dodd, Mead, N.Y., 1917, cloth, 296 pp., frontis. in color by J.

79 ———. *The Joyous Trouble Maker.* Dodd, Mead, N.Y., 1918, cloth, 330 pp., frontis. in color by J.

80 ———. *Six Feet Four.* Dodd, Mead, N.Y., 1918, cloth, 295 pp., frontis. in color by J.

81 ———. *The Bells of San Juan.* Scribner's, 1919, cloth, 337 pp., four illus., frontis. and facing pp. 140, 214 and 324, by J.

82 ———. *Desert Valley.* Scribner's, N.Y., 1921, words "Published April, 1921" on copyright page, cloth, 318 pp., frontis. by J.

83 Grey, Zane. *The Lone Star Ranger.* Harper, N.Y., Jan. 1915, cloth, 373 pp., frontis. by J.

84 ———. *Wildfire.* Harper, N.Y. and London, (1917), words "Published January, 1917" and code letters "L-Q" on copyright page, cloth, 320 (1) pp., four illus., frontis. and facing pp. 132, 254 and 308, by J.

85 ———. *The Man of the Forest.* Harper, N.Y. and London, (1920), words "Published January, 1920" and code letters "A-U" on copyright page, pic. cloth, 382 (1) pp., four illus., frontis. and facing pp. 118, 264 and 380, by J.

86 ———. *The Mysterious Rider.* Harper, N.Y. and London, (1921), words "Published January 1921"

and code letters "I-U" on copyright page, 335 (1) pp., illus. by Frank B. Hoffman but d/w illus. in color by J.

87 Grinnell, George Bird. *The Indian.* The Brampton Society, N.Y., (1908), two vols., cloth with paper labels on spines, pp. 124 and 125–270, gilt tops, editor's note, introduction, index, eight illus. including a frontis. in each vol. by J. (Builders of the Nation — National Edition.)

88 Harmsen, Dorothy. *Harmsen's Western Americana.* Northland Press, Flagstaff, (1971), morocco and cloth, blue endsheets, 213 pp., "Foreword" by Robert Rockwell, introduction, selected bibliography, numerous illus. including one in color, p. 115, by J. and a biographical sketch of him. Limited edition of 150 numbered copies signed by the author, slipcase with morocco title label. (Beeler, Blumenschein, Borein, Dixon, Dunn, Dunton, Eggenhofer, Elwell, Hurd, Leigh, Marchand, Miller, Russell, Von Schmidt, Wyeth)

89 ———. Same, first trade edition in two-tone cloth and with red endsheets.

90 Hastings, Frank S. *A Ranchman's Recollections.* The Breeder's Gazette, Chicago, 1921, pic. cloth, 235 pp., brown top, "Publisher's Preface" by Alvin H. Sanders, author's preface, illus. with photos and with a frontis. by J.

91 Hauskins, J. E. (Managing Director). *Prescribed Recreation.* All-Year Guest Ranches, Vermejo Park, New Mexico (printed by Young and McCallister, Los Angeles), n.d., wraps, with illus. in color mounted on front cover, 22 (6) pp., "Vermejo Park Ranch" by Stewart Edward White, numerous illus. including two, front cover and frontis., by J.

92 Hinman, Robert B. and Harris, Robert B. *The Story of Meat.* Swift & Co., Chicago, (1950), pic. cloth and endsheets, 291 pp., "Foreword" by Jacob Simonson, acknowledgments, index, numerous illus. including one, p. (14), by J.

93 Holme, Bryan (compiled and edited by). *Pictures to Live With.* N.Y., (1959), "First published in 1959 by The Viking Press" on copyright page, decor. cloth, 152 pp., index to artists, numerous illus. including one, p. 73, by J. (Leigh, Miller, Remington, Schreyvogel)

94 Hough, Emerson. *The Cowboy,* The Brampton Society, N.Y., (1908), two vols., cloth with paper labels on spines, pp. 181 and 182–349, gilt tops, editor's preface, introduction, addenda, six illus. including a

frontis. in each vol. by J. (Builders of the Nation — National Edition.) (Russell)

95 Hughes, Graham (Secretary) et al. *California, 1826–1926* (cover title but really about the Carthay Circle Theatre by the Carthay Center, Historical Committee, Los Angeles, 1926). Pic. wraps, 32 pp., numerous illus. including four, pp. 7 (in color), 16–17 (center spread), 19 and 20, by J. plus photo of Johnson and comments on his art, p. 5.

96 Kyne, Peter B. *The Long Chance*. H. K. Fly Co., N.Y., (1914), cloth with illus. in color mounted on front cover, 313 pp., (4) of advs., four illus. in color, frontis. and facing pp. 24, 72 and 216, by J.

97 Laut, Agnes C. *The Trapper*. The Brampton Society, N.Y., (1908), two vols., cloth with paper labels on spines, pp. 143 and 144–284, gilt tops, editor's preface, six illus. in vol. one and four in vol. two including a frontis. by J. (Builders of the Nation—National Edition.) (Hutchison)

98 MacMinn, George R. *The Theater of the Golden Era in California*. The Caxton Printers, Caldwell, Idaho, 1941, cloth, 530 pp., bibliography, index, illus. including a frontis. sketched from a painting by J.

99 McCraken, Harold. *Frank Tenney Johnson Western Paintings*. Privately printed, The Exchange Bank & Trust Company, Dallas, 1971, colored pic. wraps, unpaged, with 18 (16 in color) illus. by J.

99a ———. *The American Cowboy*. Doubleday, Garden City, N.Y., 1973, words "Limited Edition" on copyright page, simulated leather, marbled endsheets, 196 pp., all edges gilt, references, index, numerous illus. including six, pp. (54) color, (90) color, 159, (161) color, 165 and 190, by J. 300 numbered and signed copies, slipcase. (Borein, Cisneros, Eggenhofer, Koerner, Lea, Leigh, Remington, Russell, Wyeth)

99b ———. Same, trade edition with words "First trade edition after the limited edition of 300 copies" on copyright page, cloth and colored pic. d/w.

100 McCarter, Margaret Hill. *Vanguards of the Plains*. Harper, N.Y. and London, (1917), words "Published October, 1917" and code letters "I-R" on copyright page, cloth, 397 (1) pp., and (4) of advs., foreword, frontis. in color by J.

101 *Master Portfolio of Western Art*. Montana Historical Society, Helena, 1965, limited to 500 sets, one illus. by J. (Lea, Remingon, Russell, Schreyvogel)

102 Middleton, Charles O. (President). *Western Art*. The Art League of Santa Barbara, (California), n.d.,

(1928), portfolio with cloth spine and marbled boards, introduction, ten plates including "An Unexpected Visitor" by J. (Borein, Russell)

103 Monaghan, Jay (editor-in-chief). *The Book of the American West*. Julian Messner, N.Y., (1963), words "First Edition" on copyright page, pic. cloth, tan endsheets, 608 pp., introduction, suggestions for additional reading, index, about the editor-in-chief and the authors, numerous illus. including one in color, p. 587, by J. (Borein, Koerner, Leigh, Remington, Russell, Schreyvogel)

104 Oursler, Fulton. *Behold this Dreamer*. Macaulay, N.Y., (1924), cloth, 320 pp., two illus. including one, facing p. 296, by J.

105 Rachlis, Eugene. *Indians on the Plains*. American Heritage Pub. Co., N.Y., (1960), pic. cloth, pic. endsheets, 132 (1) pp., "Foreword" by John C. Ewers, acknowledgments, picture credits, bibliography, index, numerous illus. including one, p. 115, by J. (Leigh, Remington, Schreyvogel)

106 Reeves, Frank. *The Story of the S.M.S. Ranch*. Swenson Bros., Stamford, Texas, (1922), pic. wraps, 106 pp., numerous illus. including one, p. 40, "The Range Boss" by J.

107 Shinn, Charles Howard. *The Mine*. The Brampton Society, N.Y., (1908), two vols., cloth with labels on spines, pp. 122 and 123-272, gilt tops, "Editor's Preface" by Ripley Hitchcock, author's preface, seven illus. in each vol. including one, the frontis. in vol. one, by J. (Builders of the Nation — National Edition.) (Hutchison)

108 Sinclair-Cowan, Bertha M. (B. M. Bower pseud.). *Cow Country*. Little, Brown, Boston, 1921, words "Published January, 1921" on copyright page, pic. cloth, 249 pp., frontis. by J.

109 ———. *Casey Ryan*. Little, Brown, Boston, 1921, words "Published August, 1921" on copyright page, pic. cloth, 242 pp., (3) of advs., frontis. by J.

110 ———. *The Parowan Bonanza*. Little, Brown, Boston, 1923, words "Published August, 1923" on copyright page, pic. cloth, 305 pp., frontis. by J.

111 ———. *The Eagle's Wing*. Little, Brown, Boston, 1924, words "Published February, 1924" on copyright page, decor. cloth, 296 (1) pp., and (3) of advs., frontis. by J.

112 ———. *The Bellehelen Mine*. Little, Brown, Boston, 1924, words "Published August, 1924" on copyright page, pic. cloth, 308 (1) pp., frontis. by J.

113 ——. *The Trail of the White Mule*. Little, Brown, Boston, 1922, cloth, 298 pp., frontis. by J.

114 Sinclair, Bertrand W. *Poor Man's Rock*. Little, Brown, Boston, 1920, words "Published September, 1920" on copyright page, cloth, 307 pp., (1) of advs., frontis. by J.

115 Steadman, William E. et al. *The West and Walter Bimson*, The University of Arizona Museum of Art, Tucson, (1971), decor. cloth, pic. endsheets, 223 (2) pp., "Foreword" by President Richard A. Harvill, introduction, numerous illus. including four in color, pp. 92, 93, 94 and 95, by J. (Beeler, Leigh, Remington, Russell, Schoonover, Wyeth)

116 Swenson, W. G. *SMS Ranches*. Swenson Land & Cattle Co., Stamford, Texas, (1956), pic. wraps, 47 pp., foreword, numerous illus. including one, p. 12, by J.

117 Warman, Cy. *The Railroad*. The Brampton Society, N.Y., (1908), two vols., cloth with labels on spines, p. 134 and 135-280, gilt tops, "Editor's Preface" by R. H., author's preface, six illus. in vol. one and ten illus. in vol. two including a frontis. by J. (Builders of the Nation — National Edition.)

118 White, Grace Miller. *Storm Country Polly*. Little, Brown, Boston, 1920, words "Published April, 1920" on copyright page, cloth, 309 pp., frontis. by J.

119 Wilson, Neill C. (compiler). *Rancheros Visitadores, Twenty-Five Anniversary, 1930-1955*. Los Rancheros Visitadores, Santa Barabar, 1955, two-tone fabricoid, pic. endsheets, 142 (1) pp., acknowledgments, numerous illus. including one, p. (122), by J. (Borein)

The Artist and His Art

120 Carrillo, Leo. *The California I Love*. Prentice-Hall, Englewood Cliffs, N.Y., (1961), words "First Printing . . . October 1961" on copyright page, cloth and decor. boards, pic. endsheets, 280 pp., brown top, "Amigos"; Johnson in text, pp. 241 and 243.

121 Dykes, Jeff C. *High Spots of Western Illustrating*. (The Kansas City Posse, The Westerners, Kansas City, Missouri, 1964), cloth, 30 pp., two illus. Limited to 250 numbered signed copies. Nos. 75, 119 and 125 in this check list are among the *High Spots*.

122 Ferbrache, Lewis. *The Dr. and Mrs. Bruce Freidman Collection*. California Historical Society, San Francisco, Sept. 30 to Nov. 15, 1969, wraps, unpaged, 11 illus.; brief biographical sketch of J. and lists three of his oils in the exhibition.

123 "Frank Tenney Johnson Holds Art Roundup," an illus. article in *The Art Digest* 9:12, March 15, 1935, with one illus by J. and with a drawing by him in the Grand Central Art Galleries advs.

124 Kelly, Tim J. "He Took Art to the Market Place," an illus. article about Read Mullan in *Arizona Highways* 38:11, November 1962, three illus. by J.

124a Krakel, Dean, ed. "Cover Painting," a brief story about "Rough Riding Rancheros" by J. in *Persimmon Hill* 2:3 (1972).

125 McCracken, Harold. *Portrait of the Old West*. McGraw-Hill, N.Y. etc., (1952), words "First Edition" on copyright page, decor. cloth, 232 pp., special acknowledgment, preface, "Foreword" by R. W. G. Vail, Biographical Check List of Western Artists, index, numerous illus. Brief biography of Johnson, p. 222.

126 McMullen, Phil. *Interesting Data About the Laura A. Clubb Art Collection*. Privately printed, Kaw City, Oklahoma, 1931, wraps., 41 pp., biographical sketch of Johnson, p. 32.

127 Maxwell, Everett Carroll. "Painters of the West: Frank Tenney, Johnson," an illus. article in *Progressive Arizona*, March 1931, with two illus. by J. and a photo of him.

128 ——. "Trailing Artists Through Arizona," an illus. article in *Progressive Arizona*, January 1932, a critique of southwestern Artists with two illus. by J.

129 Perceval, Don Louis et al. *Art of Western America*, Pomona College Art Gallery, Claremont, Calif., Nov. 1 to 31, 1949, wraps, short biographical sketch of J. (Russell)

WHEN YOU CALL ME THAT, SMILE! by Keller from *The Virginian*

ARTHUR IGNATIUS KELLER
1866–1924

Catalogues of Art Exhibitions and Galleries

ASSOCIATED ILLUSTRATORS, NEW YORK

1 *First Annual Exhibition*, 1902, pic. wraps, unpaged, 17 illus. including one, by K. (Remington)

Illustrated by the Artist

2 Andrews, Mary Raymond Shipman. *The Militants.* Scribner's, N.Y., 1907, words "Published May, 1907" on copyright page, decor. cloth, 378 pp., eight illus. including two, facing pp. 346 and 376, by K. (Wyeth)

3 Bacheller, Irving. *Darrell of the Blessed Isles.* Lothrop Pub. Co., Boston, (1903), words "Published April, 1903" on copyright page, decor. cloth, 410 pp., (2) of advs., preface, frontis. by K.

4 ———. *The Light in the Clearing.* Bobbs-Merrill, Indianapolis, (1917), cloth, 414 (1) pp., foreword, preface, epilogue, four illus., frontis, and facing pp. 50, 216 and 220, by K.

5 Bacon, Josephine Daskam. *Open Market.* Appleton, N.Y. and London, 1915, code number "(1)" follows last line of text, cloth, 333 (1) pp., frontis. by K.

6 Baldwin, James. *School Reading by Grades — Fourth Year.* American, N.Y. etc., (1897), decor. cloth, 208 pp., numerous illus. including five, pp. 10, 90, 126, 152 and 161, by K.

7 ———. Same, *Fifth Year.* American, N.Y. etc., (1897), decor. cloth, 208 pp., numerous illus. including one, p. 190, by K.

8 ———. *Barnes's Elementary History of the United States.* American Book Co., N.Y., (1903), cloth, 360 pp., (8) of advs., numerous illus. including two, pp. 78 and 230, by K. (Varian)

9 Barnes, James. *A Loyal Traitor.* Harper, N.Y., 1897, cloth, 306 pp., editor's note, 21 illus. by K.

10 Bland, Mrs. Edith. *The Red House* by E. Nesbit (pseud.). Harper, N.Y. and London, 1902, cloth, 273 (1) pp., illus. by K.

11 Bonner, Geraldine. *Tomorrow's Tangle.* Bobbs-Merrill, Indianapolis, (1903), word "October" on copyright page, decor. cloth, 458 pp., four illus., frontis. and facing pp. 22, 340 and 406, by K.

12 Bowman, David W. *Pathway of Progress* (A Short History of Ohio). American, N.Y. etc., (1943), cloth, 546 pp., numerous illus. including one, p. (122), by K.

13 Calkins, Frank W. *Tales of the West.* Donohue, Chicago, n.d. (1893), pic. cloth, contains "Indian Tales," 150 pp., illus.; "Frontier Sketches," p. 134, illus., and "Hunting Stories," p. 146, illus., including one, p. 101, by K. (Remington)

14 ———. *Hunting Stories.* Donohue, Henneberry, Chicago, (1893), pic. cloth, 146 pp., red top, illus. including one, p. 101, by K. (Part 3 of *Tales of the West*, item 5.) (Remington)

15 Carrington, James B. *Arthur I. Keller, Figure Studies from Life.* H. G. Perleberg, (N.Y., 1920), cloth and boards with illus. mounted on front cover, (4) pp., forty plates, each with several illus. by K.

16 Chambers, Robt. W. *The Hidden Children.* Appleton, N.Y. and London, 1914, code number "(1)" follows last line of text, cloth, 650 (1) pp., four illus., frontis. and facing pp. 276, 572 and 634, by K.

17 ———. *Who Goes There?* Appleton, N.Y., 1915, cloth, 339 (1) pp., illus. by K.

18 ———. Same, A. L. Burt Co., N.Y., (1915), cloth, 339 (1) pp., frontis. by K.

19 ———. *Barbarians.* Appleton, N.Y., 1917, code number "(1)" follows last line of text, cloth, 353 (1) pp., four illus., frontis. and facing pp. 44, 90, and 200, by K.

20 ———. *The Crimson Tide*. Appleton, N.Y., 1919, code number "(1)" follows last line of text, cloth, 366 (1) pp., foreword, preface, argument, four illus., frontis. and facing pp. xxxiv, 230 and 320, by K.

21 ———. *The Moonlit Way*. Appleton, N.Y., London, 1919, code number "(1)" follows last line of text, cloth, 412 (1) pp., four illus., frontis. and facing pp. 8, 100 and 382, by K.

22 Christy, Howard Chandler et al. *Americal Art by American Artists*. P. F. Collier and Sons, N.Y., 1914, cloth with paper label, one hundred illus. including one by K. Keller portrait and short biog. on title page. (Goodwin, Remington)

23 Churchill, Winston. *The Dwelling Place of Light*. Macmillan, N.Y., 1917, words "Published October, 1917" on copyright page, cloth, 462 pp., (5) of advs., frontis. by K.

24 Cooke, Grace Mac Gowan. *The Power and the Glory*. Doubleday, Page, N.Y., 1910, words "Published, August, 1910" on copyright page, cloth with illus. in color mounted on front cover, 373 pp., four illus., frontis. and facing pp. 172, 294 and 346, by K.

25 Cortissoz, Royal (intro by). *Annual of the Society of Illustrators*. Scribner's, N.Y., 1911, words "Published November, 1911" on copyright page, cloth and boards, xii (2) pp., list of members, eighty-five full page plates including one by K. Keller listed as a member of the Committee on Publication. (Blumenschein, Fogarty, Remington)

26 Crawford, F. Marion. *Man Overboard!* Macmillan, N.Y., 1903, cloth, 96 pp., (6) of advs., two illus., pp. 54 and 92, by K.

27 Crockett, S. R. *Kit Kennedy, Country Boy*. Harper, N.Y., 1899, decor. cloth, 408 pp., six illus., frontis. and facing pp. 18, 22, 124, 182 and 280, by K.

27a Davis, Charles Belmont. *The Lodger Overhead and Others*. Scribner's, N.Y., 1909, words "Published April 1909" on copyright page, decor. cloth, 370 pp., (1) of advs., illus. including one by K. (Wyeth)

28 Dejeans, Elizabeth. *The Tiger's Coat*. Bobbs-Merrill, Indianapolis, 1917, decor. cloth, 428 pp., five illus., frontis. and facing pp. 142, 238, 396 and 412, by K.

29 ———. *Nobody's Child*. Bobbs-Merrill, Indianapolis, (1918), cloth, 340 pp., frontis. by K.

30 Dickens, Charles. *Christmas Carol*. McKay, Philadelphia, (1914), cloth, 130 pp., numerous illus. including frontis. in color, title page, and part of plates in color, by K.

31 Dixon, Thomas, Jr. *The Clansman*. Doubleday, Page, N.Y., 1905, cloth, 374 pp., (2) of advs., "To the Reader," eight illus., frontis. and facing pp. 50, 60, 130, 172, 232, 306 and 326, by K.

32 ———. *The Clansman* (A Play). American News Co., N.Y., n.d., pic. wraps, unpaged, illus. with scenes from the play but the front wrap illus. by K.

33 Doyle, Sir Arthur Conan. *The Valley of Fear*. George H. Doran Co., N.Y., (1914), cloth, 320 pp., seven illus. in color, frontis. and facing pp. 94, 126, 196, 220, 262 and 308, by K.

34 (Eberstadt.) *Americana*. Edward Eberstadt & Sons, N.Y., Dec. 1955, pic. wraps, 128 pp., numerous illus. including one by K. (Johnson, Miller, Rowe)

35 Egan, Maurice Francis. *The Wiles of Sexton Maginnis*. Century, N.Y., 1909, words "Published March, 1909" on copyright page, decor. cloth, 380 pp., twenty-one illus. by K.

36 Farnol, Jeffrey. *The Money Moon*. Dodd, Mead, N.Y., 1911, cloth, 385 (1) pp., illus., including frontis., title page and part of the plates in color, by K.

37 ———. Same, first British edition issued by S. Low, Marston & Co., London, 1911, with only a frontis. by K.

38 Fiske, Horace Spencer. *Provincial Types in American Fiction*. The Chautauqua Press, N.Y. etc., 1903, decor. cloth, 264 pp., (3) of advs., preface, illus. including one, facing p. 235, by K.

39 Ford, Sewell. *Truegate of Mogador and Cedarton Folks*. Scribner's, N.Y., 1906, words "Published October, 1906" on copyright page, cloth, 324 pp., eight illus. including three, facing pp. 112, 116 and 118, by K.

40 Fox, John, Jr. *Christmas Eve on Lonesome*. Scribner's, N.Y., 1904, words "Published, September, 1904" on copyright page, decor. cloth, 234 pp., eight illus. in color including one, facing p. 230, by K. (Schoonover)

41 Fraser, W. Lewis et al. *The Year's Art — The Quarterly Illustrator for 1894*. Harry C. Jones, N.Y., (1894), decor. cloth, 456 pp., 1,400 illus. by 433 artists including one, p. 46, by K. (Crawford, Deming, Fogarty, Remington)

42 Goodwin, Maul Wilder. *Four Roads to Paradise*. Century, N.Y., 1904, words "Published April 1904" on copyright page, decor. cloth, 347 pp., six illus., frontis. and pp. 39, 77, 173, 211 and 333, by K.

43 Grand, Sarah. *Babs the Impossible*. Harper, N.Y. and

London, 1901, decor. cloth, 461 (1) pp., nineteen illus. by K.

44 Guerber, H. A. *The Story of the Thirteen Colonies* (Eclectic School Readings). American, N.Y. etc., (1898), decor. cloth, 342 pp., maps, numerous illus. including four, pp. 69, 93, 99 and 221, by K. (Varian)

45 *Harpers Encyclopedia of United States History.* Harper, N.Y., (1912), (New edition, entirely revised and enlarged), ten vol., cloth, unpaged, vol. V, numerous illus. including one by K. (Remington)

46 Hart, Albert Bushnell. *School History of the United States.* American, N.Y., (1918), cloth, 505 pp., numerous illus. including one, p. 47, by K. (Rowe, Varian)

37 Harte, Bret. *Three Partners and Other Tales.* Houghton, Mifflin, Boston and N.Y., 1900, cloth, 382 pp., gilt top, six illus., frontis., engraved title page, and facing pp. 200, 234, 302 and 332, by K. (Standard Library Edition.)

48 ———. *A Niece of Snapshot Harry's and Other Tales.* Houghton, Mifflin, Boston and N.Y., 1903, cloth, 355 pp., gilt top, six illus. including one, the frontis., by K. (Elwell)

49 ———. *Her Letter.* Houghton, Mifflin, Boston and N.Y., 1905, dec. cloth with illus. in color mounted on front cover, decor. endsheets, 98 (1) pp., profusely illus. and decorated by K.

50 ———. *Salomy Jane.* Houghton, Mifflin, Boston and N.Y., 1910, words "Published October 1910" on copyright page, decor. cloth, illus. including one plate in color, facing p. 10, by K.

51 ———. *A Portage of Jack Hamlin's and Other Stories.* The Regent Press, N.Y., (1894), decor. cloth, 292 pp., frontis. by K.

52 ———. *Stories in Light and Shadow, The Argonauts of North Liberty.* Collier, N.Y., n.d., Argonaut Edition, cloth, 484 pp., frontis. by K.

53 Hill, Frederick Trevor. *The Web.* Doubleday, Page, N.Y., 1904, words "Published, October, 1903" on copyright page, decor. cloth, 344 pp., four illus., frontis. and facing pp. 14, 92 and 138, by K.

54 Hough, Emerson. *The Law of the Land.* Bobbs-Merrill, Indianapolis, (1904), word "October" on copyright page, decor. cloth, 416 pp., five illus., frontis. and facing pp. 58, 140, 358 and 410, by K.

55 ———. *54–40 or Fight.* Bobbs-Merrill, Indianapolis, (1909), word "January" on copyright page, cloth, 402 pp., four illus., frontis. and facing pp. 48, 181 and 202, by K.

56 ———. *The Magnificent Adventure.* Appleton, N.Y, London, 1916, code number "(1)" follows last line of text, cloth, 355 (41) pp., four illus., frontis. and facing pp. 50, 162 and 252, by K.

57 Howells, W. D. *Ragged Lady.* Harper, N.Y., 1899, cloth, 357 pp., illus. by K.

58 ———. *Heroines of Fiction.* Harper, N.Y., 1901, 2 vols., cloth, 238 (1) and 273 (11) pp., numerous illus. including seven, facing pp. 42, 44, 46 and 224 (vol. 1), and 8, 76 and 116 (vol. 2), by K.

59 Irving, Washington. *The Legend of Sleepy Hollow.* Bobbs-Merrill, Indianapolis, (1906), cloth, 91 (1) pp., illus. including thirteen plates in color, by K.

60 Johnston, Mary. *The Fortunes of Garin.* Houghton Mifflin, Boston and N.Y., 1915, words "Published October 1915" on copyright page, cloth, 375 (1) pp., frontis. in color by K.

61 Judson, Harry Pratt and Bender, Ida C. *Graded Literature Readers, Fourth Book.* Maynard, Merrill & Co., N.Y., (1900), decor. cloth, 262 pp., numerous illus. including six, pp. 32, 125, 128, (136) color, 144 and 162, by K.

62 ———. Same, *Fifth Book.* Maynard, Merrill & Co., N.Y., (1900), decor. cloth, 259 pp., numerous illus. including three, frontis. in color, pp. 65 and (103) color, by K.

63 ———. Same, *Sixth Book.* Maynard, Merrill & Co., N.Y., (1901), decor. cloth, 256 pp., numerous illus. including three, frontis. in color, pp. 58 and 140, by K.

64 Laughlin, Clara E. *Everybody's Lonesome.* Revell, N.Y,. (1910), cloth and decor. boards, 121 pp., (4) of advs., two illus., frontis. and facing p. 102, by K.

65 Lighton, W. R. *The Ultimate Moment.* Harper, N.Y. and London, 1903, words "Published October, 1903" on copyright page, decor. cloth, 310 (1) pp., eight illus., frontis. and facing pp. 114, 126, 154, 204, 220, 262 and 270, by K.

66 Lindsey, William. *The Severed Mantle.* Houghton Mifflin, Boston and N.Y., 1909, words "Published October 1909" on copyright page, decor. cloth, 452 (1) pp., (4) of advs., foreword, seven illus. in color, frontis. and facing pp. 74, 190, 286, 318, 350 and 450, by K.

67 Locke, William J. *The Glory of Clementina.* John Lane, N.Y., 1911, cloth, 367 pp., (8) of advs., eight

illus., frontis. and facing pp. 19, 50, 108, 128, 202, 249 and 317, by K.

68 ———. *The Fortunate Youth.* John Lane Co., N.Y., London, 1914, cloth, 352 pp., eight illus., frontis. and facing pp. 44, 60, 122, 194, 210, 234 and 346, by K.

69 Longfellow, H. W. *The Hanging of the Crane.* Houghton Mifflin, Boston & N.Y., 1907, decor. cloth, 30 pp., with title in red and black and initials in color, thirteen plates in color by K. Centennial Edition, limited to 1000 numbered copies.

70 Lowell, James Russell. *The Courtin'.* Houghton Mifflin, Boston, (1909), decor. cloth and boards, pic. endsheets, pages unnumbered, publisher's note, profusely illus. in color by K.

71 Lynde, Francis. *The Grafters.* Bobbs-Merrill, Indianapolis, (1904), word "April" on copyright page, decor. cloth, 408 pp., six illus., frontis. and facing pp. 144, 200, 278, 304 and 376, by K.

72 McCutcheon, George Barr. *The Rose in the Ring.* Dodd, Mead, N.Y., 1910, words "Published September, 1910" on copyright page, cloth, 425 pp., four illus. in color, frontis. and facing pp. 44, 318 and 362, by K.

73 ———. *The Hollow of Her Hand.* Dodd, Mead, N.Y., 1912, cloth, 422 pp., five illus. in color by K.

74 ———. *A Fool and His Money.* Dodd, Mead, N.Y., 1913, cloth, 373 pp., ten illus., frontis. in color and facing pp. 18 (color), 34, 72 (color), 84, 168 (color), 246, 266, 306 (color) and 346, by K. One of 40 copies on French hand-made paper for private circulation.

75 ———. Same, first trade edition, 1913.

76 ———. *The Prince of Graustark.* Dodd, Mead, N.Y., 1914, words "Published, September, 1914" on copyright page, cloth with illus. in color mounted on the front cover, 394 pp., five illus. in color, frontis. and facing pp. 90, 156, 200 and 300, by K. One of 40 copies for private circulation.

77 ———. Same, first trade edition, 1914.

78 ———. *Black is White.* Dodd, Mead, N.Y., 1914, cloth, 389 pp., five illus. in color by K.

79 MacGrath, Harold. *The Place of Honeymoons.* Bobbs-Merrill, Indianapolis, (1912), cloth, 378 pp., four illus., frontis. and facing pp. 256, 324 and 342, by K.

80 Mather, Frank Jewett, Jr. et al. *The American Spirit in Art.* Yale, New Haven, 1927, leather and boards, 354 pp., numerous illus. including one, p. 298, by K. Vol. 12, The Liberty Bell Edition of *The Pageant of America*, limited to 1500 sets. (Remington)

81 Mertins, Gustave Frederick. *The Storm Signal.* Bobbs-Merrill, Indianapolis, (1905), cloth, 425 pp., five illus. by K.

82 Mitchell, John A. *Amos Judd.* Scribner's, N.Y., 1901, decor. cloth, 251 (1) pp., gilt top, eight illus. in color, frontis. and facing pp. 18, 48, 136, 168, 182, 204 and 250, by K.

83 Mitchell, S. Weir. *The Red City.* Century, N.Y., 1908, words "Published October, 1908" on copyright page, cloth with illus. in color mounted on front cover, 421 pp., ten illus. by K.

84 ———. *The Autobiography of a Quack and Other Stories.* Century, N.Y., 1905, cloth, 311 pp., introduction, three illus., frontis. and facing pp. 40 and 64, by K.

85 Montgomery, James. *A Study in Pictures.* International Printing Co., Phila., 1954, pic. wraps, 64 pp., foreword, addenda, index, thirty-two illus., including one, no. 27, by K.

85a Motley, John Lothrop. *The Rise of the Dutch Republic.* Volume 3, Harper, N.Y. and London, 1900, pic. cloth, 422 pp., gilt top and other edges uncut, six illus. including one, the frontispiece, by K. and signed by him. Netherlands Edition of 500 numbered sets.

86 Muir, John, ed. *Picturesque California.* The J. Deming Co., San F. and N.Y., 1888, 2 vols., morocco and cloth, marbled endsheets, 478 pp., gilt tops, numerous illus. including 120 tinted plates — five by K. plus thirteen drawings by K.

87 Nesbit, Wilbur. *The Land of Make Believe — and Other Christmas Poems.* Harper, N.Y. and London, 1907, words "Published October 1907" on copyright page, decor. cloth, 98 (1) pp., five illus. including one, the frontis. (tinted), by K.

88 Nicholson, Meredith. *Rosalind at Red Gate.* Bobbs-Merrill, Indianapolis, (1907), word "November" on copyright page, cloth with illus. in color mounted on front cover, 387 pp., ten illus. by K.

89 ———. *The Lords of High Decision.* Doubleday, Page, N.Y., 1909, words "Published October 1909" on copyright page, cloth, 503 pp., four illus. in color by K.

90 ———. *The Port of Missing Men.* Bobbs-Merrill, Indianapolis, 1915, special de luxe edition, cloth, 399 pp., illus. by K. (The trade edition, first issued in 1907, was illus. by Clarence Underwood.)

91 Norris, Kathleen. *Lucretia Lombard.* Doubleday, Page, Garden City, N.Y. and Toronto, 1922, words

"First Edition" on copyright page, decor. cloth, 316 pp., four illus., frontis. (in color) and facing pp. 140, 260 and 284, by K.

92 Overton, Gwendolen. *Anne Carmel.* Macmillan, N.Y., London, 1903, words "Published June 1903" on copyright page, cloth, 335 pp., (4) of advs., gilt top, six illus., frontis. and facing pp. 31, 76, 132, 283 and 317, by K.

93 Parker, Gilbert. *The Right of Way.* Harper, N.Y. and London, 1901, decor. cloth, 419 pp., sixteen full-page illus. by K.

94 ———. *The World for Sale.* Harper, N.Y., (1916), words "Published Sept. 1916" and code letters "H-Q" on copyright page, cloth, 405 (1) pp., eight illus., frontis. and facing pp. 24, 96, 158, 260, 284, 346 and 400, by K.

95 Parrish, Maxfield et al. *Thirty Favorite Paintings by Leading American Artists.* (P. F. Collier & Son, N.Y., 1908), cloth and boards with paper label, pages unnumbered, thirty illus. including one, "Washington's Birthday" by K. (Remington)

96 Parrish, Randall. *Bob Hampton of Placer.* McClurg, Chicago, 1906, words "Published September 22, 1906" on copyright page, pic. cloth, 383 (1) pp., four illus. in color, frontis. and facing pp. 54, 110 and 264, by K.

97 Potter, Margaret Horton. *The House of de Mailly.* Harper, N.Y. and London, 1901, decor. cloth, 468 (1) pp., and (2) of advs., twelve full-page illus. by K.

98 Putnam, Nina Wilcox. *The Impossible Boy.* Bobbs-Merrill, Indianapolis, (1913), cloth, 395 pp., four illus., frontis. and facing pp. 54, 110 and 264, by K.

99 Reed, Walt. *The Illustrator in America 1900–1960s.* Reinhold, N.Y., (1966), cloth, pic. green endsheets, 271 (1) pp., "Is Illustration Art?" by Albert Dorne, bibliography, numerous illus. including three, p. (58), by K. and comments on his art. (Blumenschein, Crawford, Dunn, Dunton, Eggenhofer, Fischer, Fogarty, Goodwin, Koerner, Remington, Russell, Schoonover, Stoops, Wyeth)

100 Rinehart, Mary Roberts. *The Windows at the White Cat.* Bobbs-Merrill, Indianapolis, (1910), decor. cloth, 378 (1) pp., four illus., frontis. and facing pp. 78, 126 and 330, by K.

101 Rohlfs, Mrs. Charles. *The Millionaire Baby* by Anna Katherine Green (pseud.). Bobbs-Merrill, Indianapolis, (1905), word "January" on copyright page, cloth,

358 pp., five illus., frontis. and facing pp. 90, 168, 193 and 320, by K.

102 ———. *The Woman in the Alcove.* Bobbs-Merrill, Indianapolis, (1906), word "April" on copyright page, decor. cloth, 371 (1) pp., five illus., frontis. and facing pp. 90, 290, 322 and 368, by K.

103 ———. *The House of the Whispering Pines.* Putnam's, N.Y. and London, (1910), cloth, 425 pp., frontis. in color by K.

104 ———. *Initials Only.* Dodd, Mead, N.Y., 1911, words "Published September, 1911" on copyright page, cloth, 356 pp., frontis. in color by K.

105 ———. *The Golden Slipper.* Putnam's, N.Y. etc., 1915, cloth, 425 pp., frontis. in color by K.

106 *The Second Annual of Illustrations for Advertisements in the United States.* The Art Directors Club, N.Y., (1923), cloth and decor. boards, 171 pp., numerous illus. including one, p. 45 (and repeated p. 153) by K. (Blumenschein, Dunn, Wyeth)

107 Sheldon, George William. *Recent Ideals of American Art.* Appleton, N.Y., 1888, three-quarters morocco, 8 vols., 184 illus. including one, "See Him Squirm," by K. Edition limited to 500 sets. (Remington)

108 Sinclair, May. *The Creators.* Century, N.Y., 1910, words "Published, October, 1910" on copyright page, cloth, 517 pp., eleven illus. by K.

109 Smith, F. Hopkinson. *Caleb West, Master Driver.* Houghton Mifflin, Boston and N.Y., 1898, pic. cloth, 378 pp., ten illus. including six, facing pp. 70, 154, 198, 294, 372 and 375, by K.

110 ———. *The Romance of an Old-Fashioned Gentleman.* Scribner's, N.Y., 1907, words "Published, October, 1907" on copyright page, cloth with illus. in color mounted on front cover, 213 pp., gilt top, five illus in color, frontis. and facing pp. 28, 80, 96 and 150, by K.

111 ———. *Peter.* Scribner's, N.Y., 1908, words "Published August, 1908" on copyright page, decor. cloth, 482 pp., four illus., frontis. and facing pp. 154, 424 and 480, by K.

112 ———. *Kennedy Square.* Scribner's, N.Y., 1911, words "Published August, 1911" on copyright page, decor. cloth, 504 pp., preface, six illus., frontis. and facing pp. 26, 54, 222, 408 and 500, by K.

113 ———. *The Arm-Chair at the Inn.* Scribner's, N.Y., 1912, words "Published August, 1912" on copyright page, decor. cloth, 351 pp., preface, eight illus. in-

cluding four, frontis. and facing pp. 30, 132 and 350, by K.

114 Stockton, Frank R. *Stories of New Jersey*. American, N.Y. etc., 1896, decor. cloth, decor. endsheets, 254 pp., preface, maps, numerous illus. including five, pp. 89, 108, 118, 127 and 198, by K. (Varian)

115 ——. *Kate Bonnet, the Romance of a Pirate's Daughter*. Appleton, N.Y., 1902, words "February, 1902" on copyright page, decor. cloth, 420 pp., illus. including eight full-page plates, frontis. and facing pp. 46, 124, 155, 241, 260, 337 and 403, by K.

116 ——. Same, first British edition by Cassell, London, 1902.

117 Tappan, Eva March. *An Old, Old Story Book*. Houghton Mifflin, Boston and N.Y., 1910, cloth with illus. mounted on front cover, 294 (1) pp., illus. including one, the frontis., by K.

118 —— (selected and arranged by). *Folk Stories and Fables*. Houghton Mifflin, (Boston), 1907, decor. cloth, decor. endsheets, 519 (1) pp., gilt top, introduction, sixteen illus. including one, the frontis. in color, by K. Vol. 1, *The Children's Hour*. (Smith)

119 Vance, Louis Joseph. *Cynthia-of-the-Minute*. Dodd, Mead, N.Y., 1911, decor. cloth, 349 pp., four illus., frontis. and facing pp. 72, 182, and 280, by K.

120 ——. *The Destroying Angel*. Little, Brown, Boston, 1912, words "Published, October, 1912" on copyright page, cloth, 325 pp., four illus., frontis. and facing pp. 82, 214 and 308, by K.

121 ——. *The Bandbox*. Little, Brown, Boston, 1912, cloth, 319 pp., five illus. by K.

122 Van de Water, Virginia Terhune. *The Two Sisters*. Hearst's, N.Y., 1914, decor. cloth, 332 pp., four illus. including one, facing p. 48, by K.

123 Van Zile, Edward S. *With Sword and Crucifix*. Harper, N.Y. and London, 1900, decor. cloth, 298 (1) pp., six illus., frontis. and facing pp. 46, 112, 176, 238 and 296, by K.

124 Waller, Mary E. *A Cry in the Wilderness*. Little, Brown, Boston, 1912, words "Published October, 1912" on copyright page, cloth, 428 pp., frontis. in color, by K.

125 Weitenkampf, Frank. *American Graphic Art*. Holt, N.Y., 1912, words "Published October, 1912" on copyright page, cloth, 372 pp., gilt top, "A Word of Explanation," index, thirty-seven illus. including one, facing p. 238, by K. (Remington)

126 ——. *The Illustrated Book*. Harvard University Press, Cambridge, 1938, cloth, 314 pp., "A List of Books," index, illus. including one, a drawing, p. 201, by K. (Remington)

127 White, William Allen. *Stratagems and Spoils*. Scribner's, N.Y., 1901, cloth, 289 pp., preface, six illus. including three, frontis. and facing pp. 30 and 38, by K. (Leigh)

128 Wilkins, Mary E. Jerome. *A Poor Man*. Harper, N.Y. and London, 1897, cloth, 506 pp., (4) of advs., twenty-six full-page plates by K.

129 Williams, Churchill. *The Captain*. Lothrop Pub. Co., Boston, (1903), words "Published January, 1903" on copyright page, cloth, 439 pp., (4) of advs., "To the Reader," four illus., frontis. and facing pp. 16, 152 and 436, by K.

130 Williams, Jesse Lynch. *The Stolen Story & Other Newspaper Stories*. Scribner's, N.Y., 1899, cloth, 291 pp., gilt top, frontis. by K.

131 Wister, Owen. *The Virginian*. Macmillan, N.Y., 1902, words "Set up and electrotyped April, 1902" on copyright page, decor. cloth, 504 pp., (4) of advs., "To the Reader," eight illus., frontis. and facing pp. 29, 101, 122, 200, 356, 421 and 476, by K.

132 Wood, William and Gabriel, Ralph Henry. *In Defense of Liberty*. Yale, New Haven, 1928, morocco and boards, decor. endsheets, 370 pp., gilt top, "The Military Folkways of Recent America" by Gabriel, notes on the pictures, index, numerous illus. including one, p. 121, by K. *The Pageant of America*, vol. 7, The Liberty Bell Edition, limited to 1,500 sets. (Thomason, Wyeth)

133 Wright, Harold Bell. *The Calling of Dan Matthews*. The Book Supply Co., Chicago, 1909, words "Published August 1909" on copyright page, cloth, 363 (1) pp., illus. by K.

The Artist and His Art

134 De Kay, Charles. "A Half-hour with Studio Bores," an illus. article in *The Quarterly Illustrator* 2:5, January, February and March 1894, with one illus., p. 46, by K.

135 Dykes, Jeff C. *High Spots of Western Illustrating*. (The Kansas City Posse, The Westerners, 1964), cloth, 30 pp., introduction, two illus. High Spot 31 was illustrated by K. Edition limited to 250 numbered, signed copies. (An issue in wraps was distributed to members.)

136 Isham, Samuel. *The History of American Painting.* Macmillan, N.Y., 1905, words "Published November, 1905" on copyright page, calf and cloth, decor. endsheets, 573 pp., "Editor's Note" by John C. Van Dyke, introduction, general bibliography, index of painters' names, illus. Brief comment on K. as a painter, p. 510.

137 Keller, Arthur I. *Figure Studies from Life.* Phila., n.d., folio, eighty plates loose in two portfolios.

138 McCracken, Harold. *Portrait of the Old West.* Mc-Graw-Hill, N.Y. etc., (1952), words "First Edition" on copyright page, decor. cloth, 232 pp., special acknowledgment, preface, "Foreword" by R. W. G. Vail, Biographical Check List of Western Artists, index, numerous illus., Keller mentioned in text, p. 172 and biographical sketch, p. 223, (Remington, Russell, Schreyvogel)

139 *1915 Publications of the Bobbs-Merrill Company.* Indianapolis, decor. wraps, 104 pp., lists fourteen books illus. by K.

THAT MY HEART'S SOMEWHERE THERE IN THE DITCHES, AND YOU'VE STRUCK IT, — ON POVERTY FLAT by Keller from *A Protégée of Jack Hamlins*

MADONNA OF THE PRAIRIE by Koerner from *The Covered Wagon*

WILLIAM HENRY DETHLEP KOERNER
1878–1938

Catalogues of Art Exhibitions and Galleries

ANDERSON GALLERIES (AMERICAN ART ASSOCIATION), NEW YORK

1 *Oil Paintings,* Sale no. 4413, 1938, wraps, 33 pp., illustrations including one, p. 14, 'Holding Up the Western Mail,'' by K. (Russell)

BILTMORE GALLERIES, LOS ANGELES

1a *Catalog,* May 1969, colored pic. wraps, 54 pp., numerous illus. including one, p. 32, by K. (Borein, Dixon, Dunton, Johnson, Leigh, Miller, Remington, Russell, Young)

CHARLES W. BOWERS MEMORIAL MUSEUM SANTA ANA, CALIFORNIA

1b *Painters of the West,* March 5–30, 1972, pic. wraps, unpaged, fifteen illus. including one, front cover, by K. (Johnson, Miller, Remington, Russell)

BUFFALO BILL HISTORICAL CENTER CODY, WYOMING

1c *Special Exhibitions, Loans and New Acquisitions,* 1973 season, pic. wraps, unpaged, numerous illus. including six by K. (Remington, Russell)

HELEN L. CARD, NEW YORK

2 Hats Off to the American Illustrator! Catalog no. 2, (Fall, 1959), pic. wraps, 32 pp., numerous illus. including one, p. 7, by K. (Dixon, Goodwin, Schoonover, Wyeth)

AMON CARTER MUSEUM OF WESTERN ART FORT WORTH

3 *W. H. D. Koerner: Illustrating the Western Myth,* beginning January 23, 1969, wraps, ten illus. by K.

THE COLONIAL ART COMPANY (WILLARD JOHNSON), OKLAHOMA CITY

4 *Western and Traditional American Painting of the 19th and Early 20th Centuries* (Oil Paintings, Water-colors, and Drawings), auction, Lincoln Plaza Inn, Oklahoma City, June 10, 1973, pic. wraps, unpaged but with 76 numbered illus. including one, no. 73, by K. (Borein, Deming, Dixon, Eggenhofer, Elwell, Goodwin, Johnson, Russell, Schoonover, Wyeth)

EL PASO MUSEUM OF ART

4a *The McKee Collection of Paintings,* (1968), cloth with an illus. in color mounted on the front cover, tan endsheets, 67 pp., "Foreword" by Leonard P. Sipiora (Director), numerous illus. including one, p. 47, by K. (Blumenschein, Dunton, Hurd, Lea)

4b Same, 1000 copies in pic. wraps.

FAULKNER MEMORIAL ART GALLERY (SANTA BARBARA PUBLIC LIBRARY), SANTA BARBARA

5 *Riders and Indians of the Old West* (An Exhibition of Selected Oil Paintings by the late W. H. D. Koerner), the month of October 1962, folder (invitation) with two illus. by K.

FESTIVAL OF ARTS AND PAGEANT OF THE MASTERS LAGUNA BEACH, CALIFORNIA

5a *Catalog,* July 14 through August 27, 1972, wraps, 65 pp., illus. including two, p. 8, by K.

HIBBITTS ART GALLERY, DALLAS

5b *Old Western, American and European Paintings* (auction catalog), November 20, 1972, pic. wraps, illus. including lot 20 by K.

KENNEDY GALLERIES, NEW YORK

6 *Tradition and Change,* December 1963, colored pic. wraps, (45) pp., introduction, numerous illus. including six, pp. (90), 91, 92 (two) and 93 (two), by K. (Leigh, Lungren, Remington, Russell, Schreyvogel)

7 *W. H. D. Koerner — First New York Exhibition,* March 1964, invitation card with one illus. by K.

8 Same, catalog of the exhibition, March 1964, pic. wraps, (8) pp., twelve illus. by K.

LOS ANGELES COUNTY MUSEUM OF
NATURAL HISTORY

9 *W. H. D. Koerner, Illustrator of the West*, invitation folder to reception on February 20 (1968) with one illus. by K.

10 Same, catalog of the exhibition, colored pic. wraps, 64 pp., "Introduction" by Ruth I. Mahood, "Illustrator, Iconographer and More" by W. H. Hutchinson, "My Father — The Artist" by Ruth Koerner Oliver, 58 illus. including nine in color by K. and a photo of him.

10a *America's Black Heritage*, December 3, 1969, through March 15, 1970, wraps, 64 pp., illus. including one, p. 34, by K.

LOS ROBLES GALLERY, PALO ALTO, CALIFORNIA

10b Invitation to exhibition, February and March 1967, with one illus. by K.

MONTANA HISTORICAL SOCIETY, HELENA

11 *W. H. D. Koerner and Montana*, July–September 1971, pic. wraps, 28 pp., "Introduction" by Vivian A. Paladin, 56 illus. including fourteen in color by K.

MILLER SCHOOL (CHEYENNE CENTENNIAL COMMITTEE), CHEYENNE, WYOMING

12 *150 Years in Western Art*, July 1–August 15, 1967, colored pic. wraps, 30 (2), pp., numerous illus. including one, p. 14, by K. (Remington, Russell, Schreyvogel)

PHOENIX ART MUSEUM

13 *Art of the Western Scene, 1880–1940*, November 15, 1969, through March 15, 1970, wraps, numerous illus. including four, front cover in color and three in text, by K. (Dunton, Remington, Russell)

14 *Annual Report* 1969, pic. wraps, unpaged, "President's Report" by Harry Montgomery, numerous illus. including a photo of Mrs. Ruth Koerner Oliver and George F. Getz of the Western Art Associates standing before a western painting.

RAINBOW HOTEL, GREAT FALLS, MONTANA
(ADVERTISING CLUB OF GREAT FALLS)

14a *Fifth Annual C. M. Russell Auction of Original Western Art*, March 16, 1973, pic. wraps, unpaged, lists 145 lots, numerous illus. including one, lot 85,

by K. (Borein, De Yong, Johnson, Marchand, Russell, Wyeth)

FRED ROSENSTOCK WITH JAMES PARSONS
(GALLERY WEST), DENVER

15 *100 Years of Western Art*, November 28 through December 24, 1969, pic. wraps, 24 pp., numerous illus. including one, p. 10, by K. (Beeler, Borein, Dunton, James, Leigh)

C. M. RUSSELL MUSEUM, GREAT FALLS, MONTANA

15a *C. M. Russell Musuem Presents W. H. D. Koerner*, July through Sept. 15, 1972, brochure with three illus. by K.

SOTHEBY PARKE BERNET, NEW YORK

16 *Traditional & Western American Paintings, Drawings, Watercolors, Sculpture & Illustrations*, Sale Number 3348, April 19–20, 1972, pic. wraps, 147 pp., numerous illus. including one, p. 111, by K. (Deming, Johnson, Leigh, Remington, Russell)

17 *18th, 19th and Early 20th Century American Painting, Drawings and Sculpture*, Sale Number 3399, Sept. 13, 1972, pic. wraps, 89 (3) pp., numerous illus. including one, p. 21, by K. (Dunton, Johnson, Stoops)

18 *Highly Important 18th, 19th and Early 20th Century American Paintings, Drawings, Watercolors and Sculpture*, Sale Number 3419, October 19, 1972, pic. wraps, unpaged, numerous illus. including two in color by K. (Remington)

19 *Americana Week*, Sale Number 3467, January 24–27, 1973, colored pic. wraps, 257 (3) pp., numerous illus. including one, p. 38, by K. (Borein, Deming, Eggenhofer, Elwell)

19a *18th, 19th and Early 20th Century American Painting, Drawings, Watercolors and Sculpture*, sale no. 3548, September 28, 1973, pic. wraps, unpaged, numerous numbered illus. including two, nos. 114 and 115, by K. (Deming, Johnson, Remington, Russell)

TUCSON ART CENTER

20 *The West, Artists and Illustrators*, February 4, 1972–March 5, 1972, colored pic. wraps, unpaged, seven illus. including one, "The Homesteaders," by K. (Russell)

WHITNEY GALLERY OF WESTERN ART
(BUFFALO BILL HISTORICAL CENTER)
CODY, WYOMING

21 *Special Exhibition Opening Season*, June 1 to October 1, 1969, pic. wraps, unpaged, ten illus. including one by K. (Leigh, Wyeth)

21a *W. H. D. Koerner*, June 1–July 21, 1974, wraps, unpaged, "Introduction" by Director John A. Armstrong, thirteen illus. by K. and a photo of him in his studio.

Illustrated by the Artist

22 Ainsworth, Ed. *The Cowboy in Art*. World, N.Y. and Cleveland, (1968), words "First Printing 1968" on copyright page, full leather, orange endsheets, 242 pp., all edges gilt, "Foreword" by John Wayne, index, numerous illus. including six, pp. 20, 21, 24 (two), 25 and 57, by K. and a photo of him. Special edition of 1000 numbered copies, slipcase. (Beeler, Borein, Bugbee, De Yong, Dixon, Dunton, Eggenhofer, Ellsworth, Hurd, James, Johnson, Mora, Perceval, Remington, Russell, Santee, Schreyvogel, Von Schmidt)

23 ———. Same, first trade edition in gilt lettered and illus. cloth, orange endsheets.

24 ———. Same, reprint by Bonanza Books, N.Y. in red lettered and illus. cloth, white endsheets.

24a Ashton, William F. *Survival in the American Desert* (The Mormons' Contribution to Western History). Buena Park, Calif., 1969, cloth, 100 pp., illus. including one in color, p. 51, by K.

25 Bacheller, Irving. *Keeping Up with Lizzie*. Harper, N.Y. and London, 1911, words "Published March 1911" on copyright page, pic. cloth, 157 (1) pp., twelve full-page plates by K.

26 ———. *"Charge It."* Harper, N.Y. and London, 1912, words "Published September 1912" on copyright page, cloth with illus. mounted on front cover, 191 (1) pp., foreword, six illus., frontis. and facing pp. 60, 86, 94, 148 and 188, by K.

27 Beach, Rex. *Flowing Gold*. Harper, N.Y. and London, (1922), words "First Edition" on copyright page, cloth, 377 pp., four illus., frontis. and facing pp. 44, 224 and 284, by K.

27a ———. Same, first Canadian edition by Musson Book Co., Toronto, (1922), with the frontis. by K.

28 Biggers, Earl Derr. *The Chinese Parrot*. Bobbs-Merrill, Indianapolis, 1926, cloth, 316 pp., d/w illus. by K.

29 Bowman, Earl Wayland. *The Ramblin' Kid*. Bobbs-Merrill, Indianapolis, (1920), cloth, 323 pp., six illus. including one, facing p. 106, by K. (Words "With frontispiece by W. H. D. Koerner" on title page.)

30 ———. Same, photo-play edition by Grosset & Dunlap, N.Y., (1920), cloth, 323 pp., (5) of advs., illus. with photos from the movie starring Hoot Gibson but with the d/w in color by K.

31 Boyle, Jack. *Boston Blackie*. The H. K. Fly Co., N.Y., (1919), pic. cloth, 318 pp., four illus., frontis. and facing pp. 66, 242 and 288, by K.

32 Chamberlain, George Agnew. *White Man*. Bobbs-Merrill, Indianapolis, (1919), cloth, 299 (1) pp., seven illus., facing pp. 35, 94, 111, 134, 164, 209 and 230 plus d/w, by K.

32a *Cheyenne Frontier Days, Souvenir Program 1973*. Pic. wraps, 64 pp., front cover in color, one illus. and 40 small drawings by K. and with an article, "Koerner Painted the West as He Saw It."

33 (Crockett.) *The Life of Colonel David Crockett* (An Autobiography). Burt, N.Y., 1928, cloth, 415 pp., frontis. and d/w illus. by K.

34 Dejeans, Elizabeth. *The Moreton Mystery*. Bobbs-Merrill, Indianapolis, 1920, cloth, d/w illus. by K.

35 Deland, Margaret. *The Voice*. Harper, N.Y. and London, 1912, words "Published Sept. 1912" on copyright page, pic. cloth, 84 (1) pp., three illus., frontis. and facing pp. 28 and 66, by K.

36 ———. *Around Old Chester*. Harper, N.Y. and London, (1915), words "Published September, 1915" on copyright page, cloth, 377 (1) pp., seven illus. including two, facing pp. 120 and 156, by K.

37 Evarts, Hal G. *Tumbleweeds*. Little, Brown, Boston, 1923, words "Published January 1923" on copyright page, pic. cloth, 297 pp., frontis. by K.

38 ———. *The Painted Stallion*. Little, Brown, Boston, 1926, words "Published May, 1926" on copyright page, pic. cloth, 266 (1) pp., orange top, front cover and d/w illus. by K.

39 ———. *Fur Brigade*. Little, Brown, Boston, 1928, cloth, 279 pp., d/w illus. by K.

39a ———. *Shortgrass*. Little, Brown, Boston, 1929, cloth, 319 pp., d/w illus. by K.

40 ———. *Shortgrass*. Little, Brown, Boston, 1932, cloth, 309 pp., d/w illus. by K.

40a Foote, John Taintor. *The Number One Boy*. Appleton, N.Y., 1926, cloth, d/w illus. by K.

40b Forbis, William H. (text by). *The Cowboy*. Time-Life Books, N.Y., (1973), decor. fabricoid with illus. in color mounted on front cover, decor. endsheets, 240 pp., credits, bibliography, index, 250 illus. including two in color, pp. 148–9 and 158–9, by K. (Remington, Russell)

41 Fronval, George. *La Fantastique Epopee du Far West.* Dargaud, Nevilly/s/Seine, France, (1969), two volumes, colored pic. boards, pp. 126, (2), and 127, (1), numerous illus. including one, p. 6 (II), by K. (Miller, Remington, Russell, Schreyvogel, Zogbaum)

41a ———. *La Veritable Histoire Des Indians Peaux-Rouges.* Fernand Nathan, Paris, France, 1973, cloth, pic. front endsheet, map back endsheet, 125 pp., numerous illus. including eight in color, pp. 27, 31, 33, 51 (two), 63, 77 and 96, by K. (Leigh, Miller, Remington, Schreyvogel, Von Schmidt, Zogbaum)

41b Getlein, Frank et al. *The Lure of the Great West.* Country Beautiful, Waukesha, Wisconsin, (1973), boards, 352 pp., introduction, 375 illus. including one, pp. 328–29, by K. (Blumenschein, Leigh, Miller, Remington, Russell, Schreyvogel, Wyeth)

42 Grey, Zane. *The Desert of Wheat.* Harper, N.Y. and London, (1919), words "Published January, 1919" on copyright page, cloth, 376 (1) pp., four illus., frontis. and facing pp. 111, 118 and 218, by K.

43 ———. *The Drift Fence.* Harper, N.Y., 1933, cloth, 314 pp., d/w illus. by K.

44 ———. *Sunset Pass.* Harper, N.Y., 1931, cloth, 349 pp., d/w illus. by K.

SOTHEBY PARKE BERNET, LOS ANGELES

44a *Western American Paintings, Drawings and Sculpture,* March 4 and 5, 1974, colored pic. wraps, unpaged, 252 lots, numerous illus. including lot 111, by K. (Blumenschein, Dunton, Johnson, Leigh, Remington, Russell)

45 Hallet, Richard Matthews. *The Canyon of Fools.* Harper, N.Y. and London, 1922, code letters "C-W" on copyright page, cloth, 409 pp., four illus., frontis. and facing pp. 104, 168 and 232, by K.

45a Harding, Frank (compiled by). *A Livestock Heritage: Animals and People in Art.* (Shorthorn World Publication Co., Geneva, Ill., 1971), colored pic. wraps, unpaged, numerous illus. including one in color by K. (Borein, Dunn, Eggenhofer, Marchand, Remington, Russell, Wyeth)

46 Harriman, Karl Edwin. *The Girl and the Deal.* Jacobs, Philadelphia, (1905), words "Published June, 1905" on copyright page, cloth with illus. mounted on front cover, 349 pp. twelve full-page plates and a detail from the frontis. on the front cover by K.

47 Harris, Kennett. *Meet Mr. Stegg.* Holt, N.Y., 1920, cloth, 320 pp., introduction, frontis. d/w illus. in color by K.

48 Havighurst, Walter, ed. *Land of the Long Horizons.* Coward-McCann, N.Y., (1960), decor. cloth, red endsheets, 437 pp., introduction, index, numerous illus. including one, p. (31), by K. (Deming, Remington)

48a Hine, Robert V. *The American West: an Interpretive History.* Little, Brown, Boston, (1973), words "First Printing" on copyright page, cloth, orange endsheets, 371 pp., preface, bibliography, index, numerous illus. including one, p. 319, by K. (Miller, Remington, Russell)

49 Hough, Emerson. *The Covered Wagon.* Appleton, N.Y., London, 1922, code No. "(1)" follows last line of text, cloth, 378 (1) pp., frontis. by K.

50 ———. *North of 36.* Appleton, N.Y., London, 1923, code No. "(1)" follows last line of text, cloth, 429 pp., four illus., frontis. and facing pp. 53, 145 and 277, by K.

51 ———. *The Ship of Souls.* Appleton, N.Y., London, 1925, code No. "(1)" follows last line of text, cloth, 291 (1) pp., frontis. by K.

52 Hutchinson, W. H. *A Bar Cross Man* (The Life and Personal Writings of Eugene Manlove Rhodes). Oklahoma, Norman, (1956), words "First Edition" on copyright page, cloth, blue endsheets, 432 pp., "Con Razon," check list of Eugene Manlove Rhodes' writings, index, map, illus. with photos but d/w illus. by K.

53 Johnston, Harry V. *My Home on the Range.* Webb Pub. Co., St. Paul, Minn., (1942), decor. cloth, 313 pp., illus. including one, p. 292, by K. (James, Remington)

54 Kennedy, Michael S. (selected and edited by). *The Red Man's West* (True Stories of the Frontier Indians). Hastings, N.Y., (1965), cloth, 342 pp., introduction, index, numerous illus. including ten, pp. (1), (21), (107), (155), (191), (236) (two), (261), (269) and (311), by K. (Russell, Von Schmidt)

55 Kimball, George Selwyn. *The Lackawannas at Moosehead.* The Ball Pub. Co., Boston, 1908, pic. cloth, 320 pp., eight illus. including three, frontis. and facing pp. 169 and 294, by K.

56 King, Basil. *The Way Home.* Harper, N.Y. and London, 1913, cloth, 546 (1) pp., four illus. by K.

57 Lavender, David. *The American Heritage History of The Great West.* American Heritage, N.Y., 1965, decor. cloth, tan pic. endsheets, 416 pp., foreword,

index, maps, numerous illus. including one in color, pp. 406–7, by K. De Luxe Edition, slipcase. (Miller, Remington, Russell)

58 ———. Same, first trade edition, cloth and boards, 1965.

59 Linsenmeyer, Helen Walker. *From Fingers to Finger Bowls*. Copley, (San Diego, 1972), decor. cloth, brown endsheets, 142 pp., "About the Illustrations" by Richard F. Pourade, foreword, bibliography, index, numerous illus. including ten in color, pp. 31 (two), 34 (two), 35 (two), 38 (two) and d/w (front and back), by K. (Borein, Remington)

59a McCracken, Harold. *The American Cowboy*. Double-day, Garden City, N.Y., 1973, words "Limited Edition" on copyright page, simulated leather, marbled endsheets, 196 pp., all edges gilt, references, index, numerous illus. including seven, pp. (16), (49), 62, 122, (157), (162) color and (179) color, by K. 300 numbered and signed copies, slipcase. (Borein, Cisneros, Eggenhofer, Johnson, Lea, Leigh, Remington, Russell, Wyeth)

59b ———. Same, trade edition with words "First edition after the limited edition of 300 copies" on copyright page, cloth and colored pic. d/w.

60 McGrath, Harold. *The Luck of the Irish*. Harper, N.Y. and London, 1917, words "Published September, 1917" on copyright page, cloth, 335 (1) pp., (4) of advs., tinted frontis. by K.

61 ———. *The Pagan Madonna*. Doubleday, Page, Garden City, N.Y. and Toronto, 1921, cloth, 287 pp., frontis. in color by K.

62 Manning, Marie. *Judith of the Plains*. Harper, N.Y. and London, 1903, cloth, 301 (1) pp., frontis. by K.

63 Monaghan, Jay (editor-in-chief). *The Book of the American West*. Messner, N.Y., (1963), words "First Edition" on copyright page, pic. cloth, tan endsheets, 608 pp., introduction, suggestions for additional reading, index, about the editor-in-chief and the authors, numerous illus. including seven, pp. 15, 18, (36), (39), 51, 63 and 67, by K. (Borein, Johnson, Leigh, Lungren, Remington, Russell, Schreyvogel)

64 Ostenso, Martha. *Wild Geese*. Dodd Mead, N.Y., 1925, cloth, 356 pp., frontis. and d/w illus. by K.

65 Patten, William. (selected and arranged by). *Stories of Today*. P. F. Collier & Son, N.Y., (1918), vol. 9 (of 10), illus. by K. (The Junior Classics.)

66 The Potomac Corral of the Westerners, Washington, D.C., Ladies Night, May 20, 1971, program folder with one illus. on cover by K. (The guest speakers were W. H. D. Koerner, Jr. and Mrs. Diane Koerner Schwartz, son and granddaughter of the artist).

67 Ray, Frederic (selections and commentary by). *O! Say Can You See*. Stackpole, Harrisburg, Pa., (1970), cloth, tan endsheets, numerous illus. including three in color, pp. (81), 96 and 97 by K. and with a photo of him and biographical sketch, p. 165.

68 Reed Walt. *The Illustrator in America 1900–1960s*. Reinhold, N.Y., (1966), cloth, pic. green endsheets, 271 (1) pp., "Is Illustration Art" by Albert Dorne, bibliography, numerous illus. including one, p. (97), by K. and with a brief biographical sketch of him. (Blumenschein, Crawford, Dunn, Dunton, Eggenhofer, Fischer, Fogarty, Goodwin, Keller, Remington, Russell, Schoonover, Stoops, Wyeth)

69 Rhodes, Eugene Manlove. *The Proud Sheriff*. Houghton, Mifflin, Boston & N.Y., 1935, cloth, 177 pp., "Gene Rhodes" by Henry Herbert Knibbs, d/w in color by K.

70 ———. Same, Oklahoma, Norman, (1968), words "First printing in new edition" on copyright page, boards, 177 pp., d/w illus. by K. (A Western Frontier Library Novel.)

71 ———. *Stepsons of Light*. Houghton Mifflin, Boston and N.Y., 1921, pic. cloth, 317 pp., d/w illus. by K.

72 ———. Same, Oklahoma, Norman, (1969), words "First printing of the new edition" on copyright page, boards, 317 pp., "Introduction" by W. H. Hutchinson, eight illus., facing pp. 28, 42, 134, 168, 180, 258, 268 and d/w, by K. (A Western Frontier Library Novel.)

73 ———. *The Trusty Knaves*. Boston and N.Y., 1933, cloth, 238 pp., "Dear Reader," d/w illus. by K.

74 ———. Same, Oklahoma, Norman, (1971), words "First printing of the new edition" on copyright page, 189 pp., "Con Razon" by W. H. Hutchinson, six illus. pp. (607), (48), (54), (69), (136–7) and (182–3) two repeated on d/w by K. (A Western Frontier Library Novel.)

75 ———. *Beyond the Desert*. Houghton Mifflin, Boston and New York, 1934, cloth, 237 pp., d/w illus. in color by K.

76 ———. Same, Nebraska, Lincoln, (1967), words "First Bison Book printing October, 1967" on copyright page, colored pic. wraps, 237 pp., "Con Razon"

by W. H. Hutchinson, two illus., frontis. and front cover in color, by K.

77 ———. *Copper Streak Trail.* Oklahoma, Norman, (1970), words "First printing of new edition" on copyright page, boards, 318 pp., "Con Razon" by W. H. Hutchinson, frontis. in color (repeated on d/w) by K. (A Western Frontier Library Novel.)

77a ———. *Paso Por Aqui.* Oklahoma, Norman, (1973), words "First printing of the new edition," boards, 128 pp., "Con Razon' by W. H. Hutchinson, four double-page illus., pp. (40–41) in color, (78–79), (86–87) and (104–105) in color (repeated on d/w), by K.

78 Richmond, Grace S. *Mrs. Red Pepper.* Burt, N.Y., 1913, cloth, 339 pp., illus. and d/w by K.

79 Rinehart, Mary Roberts. *Lost Ecstacy.* George H. Doran Co., N.Y., (1927), cloth, 372 pp., illus. by K.

79a Sadlier, Anna Theresa. *Gerald Delacey's Daughter* (alias The Fortune of Evelyn). Kennedy & Co., N.Y., 1916, cloth, one illus. by K.

80 Scoggins, C. E. *The Proud Old Name.* Bobbs-Merrill, Indianapolis, (1925), cloth, 137 (1) pp., frontis. by K.

81 ———. *Pampa Joe.* Appleton-Century, N.Y., London, 1936, code number "(1)" after last line of text, cloth, 280 pp., d/w illus. in color by K.

82 Stevenson, Burton E. *King in Babylon.* Small, Maynard, N.Y., (1917), cloth, 391 pp., five illus., frontis. in color and facing pp. 58, 76, 186 and 314, by K.

83 Stringer, Arthur. *The Prairie Child.* Bobbs-Merrill, Indianapolis, 1922, cloth, d/w illus. by K.

84 ———. *A Lady Quite Lost.* Bobbs-Merrill, Indianapolis, 1931, cloth, 303 pp., d/w illus. by K.

84a Turner, George Kibbe. *The Last Christian.* Hearsts, N.Y., 1914, cloth, frontis. in color by K.

85 Van Schaick, George. *The Peace of Roaring River.* Small, Maynard & Co., N.Y., (1918), cloth, 313 pp., four illus., frontis. and facing pp. 98, 120 and 270, by K.

86 White, Stewart Edward. *The Leopard Woman.* Doubleday, Page, Garden City, N.Y., 1916, pic. cloth, 313 pp., eight illus., frontis. and facing pp. 40, 66, 122, 180, 282, 300 and 308, by K.

87 ———. *Ranchero.* Doubleday, Doran, Garden City, N.Y., 1933, words "First Edition" on copyright page, red and black pic. cloth, 302 pp., illus. on endsheets and title page by K.

87a Williams, Ben Ames. *The Silver Forest.* Dutton, N.Y., 1926, cloth, d/w illus. by K.

87b Wilson, Philip et al. *Art at Auction* (The Year at Sotheby & Parke-Bernet 1971–72). Viking, N.Y., (1972), cloth, 448 pp., index, numerous illus. including one, p. 117, by K.

The Artist and His Art

87c "An Act of Devotion," reminiscences of Ruth Koerner Oliver in the *New York Posse Brand Book, The Westerners* 17:4, 1970, with two illus. plus the front cover by K. and a photo of him.

87d *An Exhibit of Paintings by W. H. D. Koerner.* The Wyoming State Art Gallery, Cheyenne, July 2–August 31, 1973, folder, biographical sketch and lists works of art in exhibit.

87e Birmingham, Frederic and Oliver, Ruth Koerner. "The Koerner Treasury of Western Art," an article in *Saturday Evening Post* 244:2, Summer 1972, with nine illus. in color by K.

88 Hedgpeth, Don. "W. H. D. Koerner and the West," an illus. article in *Persimmon Hill* 2:2, 1971, with six illus. by K. and a photo of him.

89 Hinshaw, Merton E. *Painters of the West,* catalog of an exhibition at the Charles W. Bowers Memorial Museum, Santa Anna, 1972, with a short biographical sketch of K.

90 Hutchinson, W. H. "The Mystic of W. H. D. Koerner," an illus. article in *The American West,* May 1967, with seven illus. by K.

91 ———. "Who Put Marx in the Saddle?," an illus. article about Gene Rhodes in *Westways* 63:3, March 1971, with five drawings by K.

92 Kennedy, Michael S. "W. H. D. Koerner, Portrayer of Pioneers," an illus. article in *Montana* XV:1, Winter 1965, with nine illus. by K. and a photo of him.

92a "W. H. D. Koerner — A True Western Master — Rediscovered," an article in *Westerner,* July–August, 1969, with front cover in color and eight (two in color) by K. and a photo of him.

92b "W. H. D. Koerner — A Cowboy Master," an article in *Westerner,* September–October 1969, with front cover in color and nine (two in color) by K. and a photo of him.

93 *Los Angeles Museum Quarterly* 6:4, Spring 1968, a brief biographical sketch of K. and with one illus, by him.

94 McCracken, Harold. *Catalogue of the Whitney Gal-*

lery of Western Art, Cody, Wyoming, Summer 1963, praise of Koerner's art.

94a "Memorabilia of Spear and Koerner Families Welcomed by Society," an article in *Montana Post,* May 1965, with a photo of Lillian and W. H. D. Koerner.

95 Oliver, Ruth Koerner. "An Act of Devotion," an illus. article in *The Westerners Brand Book,* New York, 17:4, 1970, with three illus. by K. and a photo of him.

96 ———. "The Koerner Treasury of Western Art," an illus. article in *The Saturday Evening Post* 244:2, Summer 1972, with nine illus. in color by K.

97 Randle, Mallory B. "Rediscovery of a Western Illustrator: W. H. D. Koerner," an illus. article in the *Southwestern Art* 2:2, March 1968, with eight illus. by K. and two photos of him.

98 The Westerners. *New York Posse Brand Book* 14:4,

1967, review of Hutchinson's article in *The American West,* see no. 90.

99 "Western Oils by W. H. D. Koerner in Centennial Showing," an article in *Montana Post,* May 1964, with one illus. by K. and a photo of him.

100 "W. H. D. Koerner — Illustrator of the West," an article in *Museum Alliance Quarterly,* Spring 1968, with one illus. in color by K.

101 Whitney Gallery of Western Art and Buffalo Bill Historical Center, Cody, Wyoming. *Exhibit of Western Americana Art.* May 1 to October 1, 1963, pic. wraps, 16 pp., five illustrations; includes text on the "Indian Wing — W. H. D. Koerner 1878–1938" and lists twelve paintings by K.

102 Same, *Buffalo Bill Country.* Pic. wraps, 16 pp., four illus.; includes text on the "Indian Wing — Edward Borein and W. H. D. Koerner" and lists eleven paintings by K.

STOLEN PONIES by Koerner from *Fur Brigade*

ILLUSTRATION by Lea from *John C. Duval: First Texas Man of Letters*

TOM LEA
Contemporary, 1907–

Catalogues of Art Exhibitions and Galleries

CENTENNIAL MUSEUM GALLERY, EL PASO, TEXAS

1 *Exhibition of the Fifty Original Drawings by Tom Lea Illustrating J. Frank Dobie's Apache Gold and Yaqui Silver*, April 10–14, 1939, catalog, unpaged, listing fifty illus. with comments by J. Frank Dobie, illus. by L.

COLORADO SPRINGS FINE ART CENTER

2 *Paintings by Artists West of the Mississippi*, July 15– August 31, 1938, catalog, illus. including one, "Lonely Town," by L.

DALLAS MUSEUM OF FINE ARTS

3 *Western Beef Cattle*, October, 1950, pic. wraps, unpaged, eleven illus. by L.

4 *Texas Paintings and Sculpture in the Collection of the Dallas Museum of Fine Arts*, 1951, wraps, numerous illus. including three by L.

5 *A Century of Art and Life in Texas*, April 9–May 7, 1961, wraps, numerous illus. including two, "Wild Cattle of South Texas" and "Branding a Calf," by L.

EL PASO MUSEUM OF ART

6 *One Hundred Paintings and Drawings by Tom Lea*, May and June 1963, decor. cloth, pic. endsheets, unpaged, "Tom Lea — Artist" by Reginald Fisher (Director), thirty illus. plus the endsheets by L.

7 ———. Same, in pic. wraps using the endsheets of no. 6 as the cover.

8 *An Exhibition of Watercolors by Pablo Fischer*, September–October 1963, wraps, "Introduction" by Tom Lea, illus. by Fischer but cover design and Fischer's monogram by L.

9 *The McKee Collection of Paintings*, (1968), cloth with an illus. in color mounted on the front cover, tan endsheets, 67 pp., "Foreword" by Leonard P. Sipiora (Director), numerous illus. including one, p. 48, by L. (Blumenschein, Dunton, Hurd, Koerner)

10 Same, 1000 copies in pic. wraps.

11 *87 Paintings and Drawings by Tom Lea*, November 5–28, 1971, cloth and pic. boards, black endsheets, unpaged, "The Universality of Tom Lea" by Leonard P. Sipiora (Director). Edition of 300 copies signed by Lea, slipcase.

12 Same, first trade edition in pic. wraps.

EL PASO PUBLIC LIBRARY

13 *Exhibition of Preliminary Drawings for a Mural in the Lobby of the United States Court House, El Paso, Texas*, November 15–21, 1937, folder with drawing on front cover by L.

14 *The People of El Paso Honor Tom Lea: Native Son* (catalog of exhibitions in the Maud Sullivan Room), September 16–30, 1957, folder with illus. on front cover by L.

15 *A Bibliography of Writings and Illustrations by Tom Lea* (an illustrated catalog of the exhibit), December 1971–January 1972, two-tone cloth, green endsheets, 54 pp., compiled and preface by Glennis Hinshaw and Lisabeth Lovelace, "Introduction" by Dr. Frank Connally, index, twenty-two illus. plus the d/w drawing by L. Limited edition of 280 numbered copies signed by Tom Lea.

16 Same, first trade edition in wraps.

FORT WORTH ART CENTER

17 *Tom Lea*, January 12–February 5, 1961, pic. wraps, 19 (1) pp., twelve illus. by L.

GALLERY OF SCIENCE AND ART, PALACE OF
ELECTRICITY AND COMMUNICATION, GOLDEN GATE
INTERNATIONAL EXPOSITION, SAN FRANCISCO

18 *Contemporary Art of the United States,* collection of
the IBM Corporation, (1940), morocco, marbled endsheets, unpaged, all edges gilt, numerous illus. including one, "Portrait of Artist's Wife," by L. and a photo
of him. (Blumenschein)

INSTITUTE OF TEXAN CULTURES, THE UNIVERSITY
OF TEXAS, SAN ANTONIO

19 *Tom Lea, A Selection of Paintings and Drawings
from the Nineteen-Sixties,* December 6, 1969–January
17, 1970, cloth and decor. boards, brown endsheets,
unpaged, "Tom Lea, An Appreciation" by Harry H.
Ransom, "Tom Lea, Man of Mount Franklin" by Al
Lowman, Rio Bravo Edition of 200 numbered copies
signed by Lea, Ransome, Lowman and designer William D. Wittliff, slipcase.

20 Same, first trade edition with plain wraps and a decor.
d/w.

LAGUNA GLORIA MUSEUM, AUSTIN

21 *Our Southwestern Heritage,* February 5–March 3
(1963), pic. wraps, 14 pp., front cover illus. by L.

LOS ANGELES COUNTY FAIR GALLERY, POMONA

22 *The Theodore B. Modra Memorial Exhibition of Art,*
September 17–October 2, 1937, catalog, illus. including one, "Lonely Town," by L.

MUSEUM OF FINE ARTS, LITTLE ROCK

23 *Paintings from the Collection of Count Ivan N. Pod-
goursky,* December 1958, wraps, six illus. including
one, "Aurora," by L.

NATIONAL GALLERY OF ART, WASHINGTON, D.C.

24 *War Art: A Catalogue of Paintings Done on the War
Fronts by American Artists for Life,* wraps, numerous
illus. including four in color by L. (Catalog printed
by *Life* — also exhibited at the Metropolitan in N.Y.,
etc.)

THE UNIVERSITY OF TEXAS AT AUSTIN

25 *Paintings from the C. R. Smith Collection,* December
4, 1969–January 15, 1970, wraps, unpaged, preface
by Donald B. Goodall and Marian B. Davis, numerous
illus. including two by L. (Dixon, Eggenhofer, Johnson, Russell, Schreyvogel, Von Schmidt)

VILLITA GALLERY, SAN ANTONIO, TEXAS

26 *Pictures by Tom Lea,* January 1–31, 1948, catalog of
Lea's first one-man exhibition outside El Paso.

WHITNEY MUSEUM OF AMERICAN ART, NEW YORK

27 *Regional Exhibition: Paintings by Artists West of the
Mississippi,* 1938, wraps, numerous illus. including
one, "Lonely Town," by L.

Written and Illustrated by the Artist

28 *Randado.* (Carl Hertzog, El Paso, Texas, 1941), wraps,
with illus. mounted on front cover, (13) pp., note,
illus., limited to 100 copies, numbered and signed.
Randado was reprinted without illus. in the program
for the 58th Annual Meeting of the Texas State Historical Association, Austin, 1954.

29 *A Grizzly from the Coral Sea.* (Carl Hertzog, El Paso,
Texas, 1944), gilt starred blue cloth with vellum back,
pic. endsheets, iv, 32 pp., illus., limited to 10 copies.
An edition of 295 copies bound in green cloth on a
lighter weight paper also was issued in 1944.

30 *Peleliu Landing.* Carl Hertzog, El Paso, 1945, U. S.
Regulation Marine Herringbone Twill (combat dun-
garee cloth), pic. endsheets, 34 pp., ten illus. by L. and
the endsheets from a photo made by him from a fox-
hole on Peleliu. Limited to 500 numbered and signed
copies with the first ten copies each having one original drawing made at Peleliu, two copies bound in
morocco with the Marine seal stamped in gold on the
cover.

31 Same, first trade edition bound in boards covered with
paper printed to imitate Marine twill, 1945.

32 Same, announcement folder with one drawing by L.

33 *Calendar of Twelve Travelers Through the Pass of the
North.* At the Pass (Carl Hertzog, El Paso, Texas),
1946, cloth, (38) pp., illus., limited to 365 numbered
copies.

34 A reprint of no. 33 in approximately half size facsimile, 1947, 150 copies bound in cloth: 100 copies on
all-rag paper and 50 copies on hand-made paper —
and 25,000 copies in wraps, sponsored by the El Paso
Electric Co. and presented to the El Paso Public
Schools.

35 *Fort Bliss, One Hundredth Anniversary, 1848–1948.*
(Guynes Printing Co., El Paso, 1948), pic. wraps, 24
pp., illus., map, front cover drawing by L. Designed
by Carl Hertzog and Tom Lea.

36 *The Brave Bulls.* Little, Brown, Boston, 1949, words
"First Edition" on copyright page, decor. cloth, pic.
endsheets, 270 pp., preface, illus. There is a rare "first
issue" of the First Edition with a misplaced linotype

slug making a bad typographical error, lines 4, 5, 6, p. 147.

37 Same, *Omnibook*. October, 1949. Post-publication abridgment of no. 36, front cover illus. by L.

38 Same, *Tyrefekteren fra Guerreras*. Dreyer, (Oslo, Norway, 1949), cloth and boards, 278 pp., opptakten. First Norwegian edition of no. 36.

39 Same, *The Brave Bulls*. William Heinemann, (London, 1950), words "First Published 1950" on copyright page, cloth, 256 pp., illus. First British edition of no. 36.

40 Same, *Blood and Sand*. L. Carmi, Israel, 1950, wraps. First Hebrew edition of no. 36.

41 Same, *Toros Bravos*. Editorial Constancia, Mexico (City), (1951), words "1st Edicion en Espanol, Julio de 1951" on copyright page, decor. cloth, pic. endsheets, 299 pp., *prefacio*, illus. First edition in Spanish of no. 36.

42 Same, *Der Torero*. Hans E. Gunther Verlag, Stuttgart (Germany), (September, 1951), pic. cloth and endsheets, 266 pp., blue top, illus. First German printing of no. 36.

43 Same, *The Brave Bulls*. Pocket Books, N.Y., 1951, First American paperback edition of no. 36

44 Same, *I Tori*. Garzanti, Milan, 1952. First Italian edition of no. 36.

45 Same, *Toros Bravos*. Luis de Caralt, Barcelona, Spain, 1952. First edition in Spain of no. 36 and according to Tom Lea, the best translation into Spanish.

46 Same, *Corrida de la Peur*. Les Editions du Scorpion, Paris, 1952. First French edition of no. 36.

47 Same, *Een Man Vecht Voor Zickzelf*. Unicum-Reeks, 's-Gravenhage, Nederland, 1953. First Dutch edition of no. 36.

48 Same, *The Brave Bulls*. Penguin Books, London, 1953. First British paperback edition of no. 36.

49 Same, *The Brave Bulls*. Horwitz Publications, Sydney etc., Australia, 1960. First Australian edition of no. 36. (Paperback.)

50 Same, *The Brave Bulls*. Little, Brown reprint, (1964), from the original plates without colored illustrations.

51 *Personal File Selected from the Letters of Tom Lea to His Publisher*. Little, Brown, Boston, (1949), pic. wraps, (18) pp., illus.

52 *Bullfight Manual for Spectators*. Plaza de Toros of Ciudad Juarez, Chihuahua, Mexico (Carl Hertzog, El Paso), (1949), colored pic. wraps, 24 pp., foreword, illus. Reprinted in 1952, 1954 and 1957.

52a Same, reprinted for Del Camino Motel, El Paso, 1973, includes "Bullfight Museum."

53 *The Wonderful Country*. Little, Brown, Boston, (1952), words "First Edition" on copyright notice, pic. cloth and endsheets, 387 pp., red top, illus.

54 Same, *Omnibook*. May 1953, post-publication abridgment of no. 53.

55 Same, Bantam Books, N.Y., 1953. First American paperback edition of no. 53. Reprinted by Bantam Books in 1959 with a different illus. on the front wrap — neither by Lea.

56 Same, *Martin Brady*. Heinemann, Nederland, 's-Gravenhage, 1954. First Dutch edition of no. 53.

57 Same, *La Frontera*. Luis de Caralt, Barcelona, Spain, 1955. First Spanish edition of no. 53.

58 Same, *The Wonderful Country*. William Heinemann, London etc., (1955), words "First Published 1955" on copyright page, pic. cloth and endsheets, 362 pp., illus. First British edition of no. 53.

59 Same, Transworld Publishers, (London, 1956), words "Corgi Edition, 1956" on copyright page, colored pic. wraps, 384 pp., illus. First British paper cover edition of no. 53.

60 Same, words "Ten copies of the first edition of *The Wonderful Country* have been especially boxed with a print of the painting by Tom Lea 'Recuerdo de Lagrimas' now owned by H. Frank Connally of Waco" inside the box, the print in color is signed by Lea and the box was designed by Carl Hertzog.

61 *Sunland: The Story of the El Paso Southwest*. El Paso Sunland Club, El Paso, 1952, pic. wraps, 31 pp., numerous illus. including two, pp. (22) and (23), by L. An article, "415 years of History" by Tom Lea.

62 *The Stained Glass Designs in the McKee Chapel*. Church of Saint Clement (typography by Carl Hertzog, printed by Guynes Printing Co.), El Paso, 1953, wraps, (24) pp., illus. (Also 100 copies bound in cloth, signed, and numbered.)

63 *Eyewitnesses at Early El Paso: 1598–1923* (a bibliography compiled by Lea). Carl Hertzog for the El Paso Public Library, 1956, wraps with "Southwest" from the mural in the Library by L. on the cover.

64 *Captain King of Texas: The Man Who Made the King Ranch*. Reprinted from *The Atlantic Monthly*, Boston,

April 1957, colored pic. wraps, (7) pp., illus. on front cover.

65 *The King Ranch.* Printed for the King Ranch, Kingsville, Texas (Carl Hertzog, El Paso), 1957, 2 vols., cloth in a replica of the King Ranch saddle blanket with the Running "W" brand, 838 pp. (paged continuously), "Research" by Holland McCombs, "Annotations" by Francis L. Fugate, index, illus., slipcase to match binding with leather label on spine.

66 Same, trade edition of no. 66, Little, Brown, Boston, 1957, 2 vols., two-tone buckram in cardboard slipcase.

67 *Response.* (Carl Hertzog, El Paso, October 24, 1957), wraps, (3) pp., edition of 210 copies. (From a tape recording of Lea's remarks at a dinner given in his honor on the occasion of the publication of *The King Ranch.*)

68 Lea et al. *Reading for Men.* Nelson-Doubleday, Garden City, N.Y., (1958), boards, green top, 326 pp., editor's note, excerpts from *The King Ranch*, pp. 33–71, nine illus. by L.

69 *The Primal Yoke.* Little, Brown, Boston, Toronto, (1960), words "First Edition" on copyright page, gilt decor. cloth, tinted endsheets, 336 pp., illus.

70 Same, first paperback edition by Bantam Books, N.Y., 1965.

71 Same, Macmillan, London, 1961, First British edition of no. 69.

72 *The Hands of Cantu.* Little, Brown, Boston, Toronto, (1964), words "First Edition" on copyright page, cloth, brown top, 244 pp., frontis. in color, eight double-page and sixteen single-page plates.

73 Same, autographed edition of no. 72, limited to one hundred copies numbered and signed by Lea, bound in full leather, gilt top, in slipcase.

74 Same, first British edition issued by Hammond, Hammond and Co., London, (printed in U.S., 1964) with the words "First Edition" on the copyright page.

75 Same, Talking Book edition recorded by Luis van Rooten and published by the Library of Congress, Washington, D.C.

76 *The Graduate Journal* 6:1 (Winter, 1964). The University of Texas, Austin, decor. wraps, 212 pp., frontis. by L. Tributes to Walter Prescott Webb by Tom Lea, J. Frank Dobie, et al.

77 *Toward the Morning Sun* reprinted from *The Graduate Journal* 6:1 (Winter 1964) and 7:2 (Spring 1967).

Tributes to Walter Prescott Webb with eight illus. in color by L.

78 "The Land of the Mustang," an article in *The Graduate Journal* 7:2, Spring 1967, The University of Texas, Austin, tribute to Lea's art by W. Gordon Whaley, with eight mounted illus. in color by L. and with comments by him.

79 *The Land of the Mustang.* First separate printing of no. 78, bound in fabricoid.

79a Same, 25 numbered copies bound in limp leather for W. Gordon Whaley.

80 *Western Beef Cattle.* Encino Press, Dallas, 1967, cloth, brown endsheets, 34 pp., foreword, eleven plates in black and white with one (no. III) repeated in color on the title page plus four drawings. Edition of 850 copies, slipcase.

81 *Old Mount Franklin.* (Carl Hertzog, El Paso, 1968), cloth, decor. endsheets, unpaged, six illus. by L., printing of 450 copies — first 300 copies printed especially for Tom Lea and not for sale and the Sand and Rock edition of 150 copies numbered 301–450.

82 *A Picture Gallery.* Little, Brown, Boston, Toronto, (1968), words "First Edition" on copyright page, two-tone cloth, 160 (1) pp., prefatory note, numerous illus. by the author plus a matching two-tone cloth portfolio with 35 (12 in color) plates — the two volumes in one slipcase.

Written by the Artist

83 *Flowsheet* (yearbook). Texas Western College, El Paso, 1951, "Dedication" to Carl Hertzog was worded by L.

84 Johnson, William Weber. *Kelly Blue.* Doubleday, Garden City, N.Y., 1960, words "First Edition" on copyright page, cloth, colored pic. endsheets, 263 pp., "Foreword" by Tom Lea, acknowledgments, illus. by Kelly.

85 Lasswell, Mary. *I'll Take Texas.* Houghton Mifflin, Boston, 1958, words "First Printing" on copyright page, cloth and boards, 376 pp., purple top, illus., reprints "Randado" by L. without illustrations.

86 *The Notebook of Nancy Lea, 1932–1935.* Carl Hertzog, El Paso, 1937, cloth, 266 pp., "Introduction" and edited by Tom Lea. Private edition of 25 copies, slipcase.

87 *John W. Norton, American Painter, 1876–1934.* Privately printed for the Friends of the Artist by The

Lakeside Press, Chicago, 1935. Lea's contribution was an essay titled "John W. Norton: An Appreciation of His Work." This tribute to his Maestro was Lea's first published writing.

88 Saber, Cliff. *Desert Rat Sketch Book*. Sketchbook Press, N.Y., 1959, "Foreword" by L. with an accompanying portrait drawing.

89 Schwartz, Irving and Lea, Tom (text by). *Memorial to Maud Durlin Sullivan*. (Carl Hertzog, El Paso), Dec. 28, 1943, one sheet, print on one side.

90 *Horst Schreck*. El Paso Museum of Art, June 4, 1967, exhibition catalog with the "Introduction" by L.

91 Shockley, Martin, ed. *Southwest Writers Anthology*. Steck-Vaughn Co., Austin, (1967), stiff wraps, 328 pp., preface, introduction, includes "Paso del Aguila" (from *The Wonderful Country*) by L.

92 Smith, Stanley E. (compiled and edited by). *The United States Marine Corps in World War II*. Random, N.Y., 1969, cloth, "Introduction" by Julian C. Smith, reprints about half of *Peleliu Landing*, pp. 632–43.

93 Stone, Marvin. *The Spanish Southwest* (an exhibit at the Dallas Public Library, June 15–July 2, 1971). (Encino Press, Austin), wraps with title label mounted on the front cover, unpaged "Preface" by Tom Lea, introduction, illus. with old prints.

94 *Maud Durlin Sullivan, 1872–1944, Pioneer Southwestern Librarian*. Carl Hertzog (for the Class of 1962, School of Library Service, University of California, Los Angeles), El Paso, Texas, 1962, wraps, (16) pp., "Foreword" by Lawrence Clark Powell, photo of Mrs. Sullivan as frontis.

95 *The Texas State Historical Association, Fifty-Eighth Annual Meeting, April 30 and May 1, 1954*. Driskill Hotel, Austin, (program), reprints *Randado* without illustrations.

96 *Weather in Art*. Pomona College, Claremont, California, March, 1946. An essay, "Painting the Weather," by L. discusses the theme of the exhibition.

Illustrated by the Artist

97 Abernethy, Francis Edward, ed. *Observations and Reflections on Texas Folklore*. Encino Press (Austin) for the Texas Folklore Society, 1972, words "First Edition" on copyright page, cloth, tan endsheets, 151 pp., preface, index, illus. including one, p. (74), by L. (Mead)

98 Adams, Frank Carter, ed. *State of Texas Building* (Central Exposition, Texas Centennial Celebrations, Dallas). The Steck Co., Austin, 1937, decor. fabricoid, 48 p., numerous illus. including two, p. 28, by L.

99 Amsden, Charles Avery. *Navajo Weaving*. The Fine Arts Press, Santa Ana, Calif., in cooperation with The Southwest Museum, 1934, colored pic. cloth, map endsheets, 261 (1) pp., "Foreword" by F. W. Hodge, work cited, index, numerous illus. including a folding plate, no. 1, colored, by L.

100 ———. Same, reprinted by The Rio Grande Press, Chicago, 1964.

101 *Announcing An Auction of Paintings by Twenty Noted Artists of the Southwest for the Benefit of The Dobie-Paisana Project*. Houston, May 11 (1966?), four-fold flyer with Lea's portrait of Dobie on the front cover plus his working drawing of "Ranger Captain George W. Baylor." (Hurd, Schiwetz)

102 *Art Guides: No. Two, A Guide to the Paintings and Sculpture in the Post Office Department Buildings, Washington, D.C.* Art in Federal Buildings Incorporated, Washington, D.C., 1938, cloth, illus. including one, "The Nester," by L.

103 Atkins, Lloyd (glass design by). *Trail Driver*. Steuben Glass, N.Y., n.d., crystal bowl, diameter 10″, with the engraving design (mounted trail driver with Long horn steers) by L.

104 (Bandelier.) *The Unpublished Letters of Adolphe F. Bandelier*. Carl Hertzog, El Paso, Texas, 1942, cloth, red top, 33 pp., "Introduction" by Paul Radin, frontis. by L. Edition limited to 295 numbered copies.

105 Beard, Charles A. and Mary R. *A Basic History of the United States*. Doubleday, Doran, N.Y., 1944, cloth, brown top, 554 pp., prefatory note, appendix, reading list, index, sixty-four illus. including three, between pp. 176–7, 304–5 and 464–5, by L. (Dixon, Leigh, Wyeth)

106 Bloomgarden, Henry S. *American History Through Commemorative Stamps*. Arco Publishing Co., N.Y., (1969), cloth, 141 pp., "Introduction" by Carl Scheele (Smithsonian), numerous illus. including one, p. 62, by L. (Russell, Von Schmidt)

107 Bode, Winston. *A Portrait of Pancho*. The Pemberton Press, Austin, 1965, words "First Printing" on copyright page, full leather, Paisano decor. endsheets, 164 pp. "Introduction" by Harry Ransom, preface, numerous illus. including the Lea portrait on the title page and repeated on pp. (148) and (155) and a photo

of Lea and Dobie, p. (149). Limited edition of 150 numbered copies signed by author, slipcase.

108 ———. Same, first trade edition in cloth with the Lea portrait of Dobie on the d/w.

109 *Book in Prints, 1967*. The Pemberton Press, Austin, wraps, 34 (2) pp., illus. including one, p. 20, by L.

110 Braddy, Haldeen. *Mexico and the Old Southwest: People, Palaver and Places*. National University Publications, Kennikat Press, Port Washington, N.Y., 1971, cloth, 229 pp., preface, introduction, includes 'Artist Illustrators of the Southwest: H. D. Bugbee, Tom Lea and Jose Cisneros," illus. including three, pp. (81) two and (82), by L. (Bugbee, Cisneros)

111 Brotze, Emma Mae and Lehmberg, A. E. *The History of Texas*. Noble and Noble, Dallas (1954), pic. cloth, 199 pp., appendix, index, numerous illus. including one, p. 137, by L. (Wyeth)

112 Bruce, Edward and Watson, Forbes. *Art in Federal Buildings: An Illustrated Record of the Treasury Department's New Program in Painting and Sculpture* (volume 1). Art in Federal Buildings Incorporated, 1936, cloth, illus. including a study for Lea's mural in the Benjamin Franklin Postal Station, P. O. Dept. Bldg., Wash., D.C.

113 Calvin, Ross. *River of the Sun*. New Mexico, Albuquerque, 1946, cloth, decor. endsheets, 153 pp., designed by Carl Hertzog, hand-lettered chapter headings by L. and his suggestion led to the use of the design from Gila polychrome pottery on the d/w and the endsheets.

114 Carroll, H. Bailey et al. *The Story of Texas*. Noble & Noble, New York, (1963), colored pic. cloth, 360 pp., preface, acknowledgments, (appendix), index, numerous illus. including one, p. (214), by L. (Schiwetz, Wyeth)

115 (Catlin.) *George Catlin, Westward Bound a Hundred Years Ago*. The Pass of the North (Carl Hertzog, El Paso, Texas), 1939, two-tone boards, 14 pp., preface and illus. by L., limited to 115 numbered, signed copies.

116 Catlin, Ralph. *Goodby to Gunsmoke*. Little, Brown, Boston, Toronto, (1955), words "First Edition" on copyright page, cloth, 428 (1) pp., d/w illus. by L.

117 Cervenka, R. W. *John Kohut and His Son Josef, Czechoslovak Countrymen in Early Texas*. Privately printed for the author (Texian Press, Waco), pic. wraps, 40 (1) pp., foreword, appendix, 32 illus. in-

cluding one, "The Stampede," between pp. 24 and 25, by L.

118 Chavez, M. Prof. Armando B. *A Mi Ciudad*. Privately printed, (Juarez, Mexico, Dec. 1946), pic. wraps, 26 pp., numerous illus. including three, pp. 9, 12 and 17, by L.

119 Commager, Henry Steele and Nevins, Allan. *The Heritage of America*. Little, Brown, Boston, 1939, cloth, 1152 pp., introduction, bibliography, index, thirty-seven illus. including one, the frontis., by L.

120 Craven, Avery and Johnson, Walter. *The United States — Experiment in Democracy*. Ginn, Boston etc., (1957), cloth, numerous illus. including one, p. 333, by L. (Remington)

121 (Daniel.) *Texas and the West. Featuring the Writings of J. Frank Dobie* (catalogue no. 24). Price Daniel, Jr., Waco, Texas (Carl Hertzog, El Paso, 1963), decor. cloth, (32) pp., "J. Frank Dobie and His Books" by Jeff C. Dykes, "Mr. Southwest" by Lawrence Clark Powell, Lea portrait of Dobie on title page. Edition limited to 210 numbered copies signed by Daniel.

122 Same, catalogue no. 24, as distributed to customers, wraps with Lea portrait of Dobie on front cover.

123 Daniels, A. Pat. *Texas Avenue at Main Street*. Allen Press, Houston, (1964), pic. wraps, 88 pp., illus. including the drawing of Sam Houston for the 5¢ stamp by L. on the back cover, also p. 58 and a reproduction of a First Day Cover with the stamp, p. 84.

124 Davis, J. Frank (State Supervisor). *Texas: A Guide to the Lone Star State*. Hastings, N.Y., words 'First Published in 1940" on copyright page, cloth, pic. endsheets, 718 pp., preface, appendices, index, numerous illus. including two, between pp. 28 and 29, by L. (Hurd)

125 Dobie, J. Frank. *Apache Gold and Yaqui Silver*. A salesman's dummy with 28 pages of text and illus. both in color and black and white, bound in brown linen as is the first trade edition. The only known copy in Lea's Dobie collection.

126 Dobie, J. Frank. *Apache Gold and Yaqui Silver*. Little, Brown, Boston, 1939, words "First Edition" and "Published March, 1939" on copyright page, buckram and boards with paper label, 366 pp., "The Trail of a Story Hunter," appendix, illus. including five full-page plates in color by L., slipcase. Edition limited to 265 numbered copies signed by Dobie and Lea.

127 ———. Same, first trade edition of no. 126 in pic.

ILLUSTRATION by Lea from *The Hands Of Cantú*

cloth with words "Published March 1939" on copyright page.

128 ———. Same, Bantam Books, N.Y., (1951), words "1st Printing, October, 1951" on copyright page, colored pic. wraps, 212 pp., all edges red, drawing of Dobie by L. on back cover.

129 ———. Same, issued by Hammond, Hammond & Co., London, with the words "First published in Great Britain 1956" on copyright page.

130 ———. Same, first British paperback edition issued by Transworld Publishers, 1957.

131 ———. *John C. Duval: First Texas Man of Letters.* Southwest Review, Dallas, 1939, two-tone cloth, 105 pp., preface, nine illus., frontis., title page and pp. 52, 58, 64, 70, 76, 80 and 86, by L. Edition limited to 1000 copies of which 950 were for sale.

132 ———. Same, second edition issued by Southern Methodist University Press, 1964.

133 ———. *The Longhorns* (advertising booklet). (Little, Brown, Boston, 1941), pic. wraps, (16) pp., five illus. by L.

134 ———. Same (salesman's dummy). Little, Brown, Boston, 1941, rawhide, (3) pp., all the illus. by L. plus many blank sheets.

135 ———. Same, Little, Brown, Boston, 1941, words "First Edition" and "Published March 1941" on copyright page, rawhide, 388 pp., "Makers of History," notes, index, numerous illus. including a frontis. in color and drawings by L. and photos, slipcase. Rawhide Edition limited to 265 numbered copies signed by Dobie and Lea.

136 ———. Same, first trade edition in colored pic. cloth with words "Published March 1941" on copyright page.

137 ———. Same, Nicholson & Watson, London, (1943), cloth, 292 (31) pp., introduction, illus. with a frontis. in color by L. and with photos. First British edition of no. 135.

138 ———. Same, Grosset & Dunlap, N.Y., (1957), decor. wraps, 387 pp., illus. by L.

139 ———. Same, Bramhall House, N.Y., n.d., (1964), a facsimile reprint of the first trade edition, no. 136.

140 ———. *Guide to Life and Literature of the Southwest.* University of Texas Press, Austin, Texas, 1943, wraps, 111 pp., numerous illus. including two, pp. 36 and 63, by L. (Borein, Bugbee, Dunton, Hurd, James, Leigh, Russell, Santee)

141 ———. Same, Southern Methodist University Press, Dallas, 1952, cloth, tinted endsheets, brown top, 222 pp., preface, index, nineteen illus. including five, pp. 31, 37, 91, 103 and 138, by L. A reprint of no. 140, "Revised and Enlarged in both Knowledge and Wisdom." (Bugbee, Leigh, Russell, Thomason)

142 ———. *A Texan in England.* Little, Brown, Boston, 1945, words "First Edition" on copyright page, decor. cloth, 285 pp., "P for Preface," index, Lea's portrait of Dobie on back of d/w.

143 ———. *The Ben Lilly Legend.* Little, Brown, Boston, 1950, words "First Edition, Published May, 1950" on copyright page, pic. cloth, 237 pp., "Esau, the Hunter," "Sources — People and Print," index, illus. including three, front cover design, frontis. in color, and one drawing, by L. (Dunton)

144 ———. *Cow People.* Little, Brown, Boston, Toronto, (1964), words "First Edition" on copyright page, fabricoid, 305 pp., introduction, "A Note on Sources," index, illus., portrait of Dobie by L. on back d/w. (Crawford)

145 ——— et al. *Mustangs and Cowhorses.* Texas Folk-Lore Society, Austin, 1940, fabricoid, pic. endsheets, 429 pp., introduction, contributors, index, numerous illus. including two, pp. (185) and 199, by L. (Bugbee, James, Leigh, Russell, Santee, Thomason)

146 ——— et al. *Statewide Texas Salute to U. S. Senator Ralph W. Yarborough.* Municipal Auditorium, Austin, Texas, Oct. 19, 1963, pic. wraps, (16) pp., "Salute to Senator Ralph Yarborough" by Dobie, illus. including one, a portrait of Dobie, by L.

147 ———. *Out of the Old Rock.* Little, Brown, Boston, Toronto, (1972), words "First Edition" on copyright page, boards, maroon endsheets, 237 pp., "Preface" by Bertha McKee Dobie, d/w illus. with the Lea portrait of Dobie, and a chapter on "Tom Lea," from no. 246.

148 *The Dobie-Paisana Project.* Folder with Lea's portrait of Dobie on the front cover, Austin, July 16, 1965.

149 Elms, Ray (wagon boss). *Snack List.* Murray Hotel Coffee Shop, Silver City, New Mexico, (Carl Hertzog, El Paso, 1939), folder (menu), seven illus. by L. Only known copy in possession of Carl Hertzog, El Paso, Texas. (Same illus. used on a menu, Knox Hotel Coffee Shop, El Paso, Texas.)

150 *Enjoy All the Scenic Historic Southwest.* Guynes Printing Co., El Paso, (1942), brochure with front cover illus. in color by L.

151 Escobar, Jose U. *Siete Viajeros y Unas Apostillas de Passo del Norte.* Ciudad Juarez, Chihuahua, Marzode, 1943, seven illus. by L. The author pirated the illus. from the hotel menus (see no. 149) and wrote his own version of the *Travelers.*

152 *Estampas de una Democracia los Estados Unidos de America.* G.P.O., Washington, D.C., n.d., cloth, illus. including one, reproduction of a detail from the mural "Pass of the North," p. 112, by L.

153 Evans, Joe M. *A Corral Full of Stories.* Privately printed (The McMath Co., El Paso, 1939), pic. wraps, tan endsheets, x, 66 p., illus. including one, p. (24), by L. (Goodwin)

154 *Fifty-second Annual Meeting of the Texas Folklore Society.* Sul Ross State College, Alpine, April 12 and 13, 1968, program folder with L. illus. on front cover.

155 Forester, C. S. *The Ship.* Little, Brown, Boston, 1943, cloth, d/w illus. by L.

156 *Friends of Columbia Libraries* (program). February 4, 1970, pic. wraps with front cover illus. by L.

157 Gambrell, Herbert and Virginia. *A Pictorial History of Texas.* Dutton, N.Y., (1960), words "First Edition" on copyright page, cloth and decor. boards, brand illus. endsheets, 217 pp., acknowledgments, sources of illus., index, illus. including six, pp. 15, 28, 31, 178, 185 and 186, by L. (James, Remington, Schiwetz)

158 Gard, Wayne. *Rawhide Texas.* Oklahoma, Norman, (1965), words "First edition" on copyright page, cloth, 236 pp., foreword, selected bibliography, index, illus. with old prints and photos but d/w drawing by L.

159 Gilliam, Franklin. *Texas and the West.* List 113. The Brick Row Book Shop, Austin, Texas, (1959), pic. wraps, no pagination, drawing on front cover by L.

160 Grey, Katharine. *Hills of Gold.* Little, Brown, Boston, 1949, words "First Edition" on copyright page, cloth, 298 pp., frontis. and d/w illus. in color by L.

161 Hafen, LeRoy and Ann. *The Colorado Story.* The Old West Publishing Co., Denver, Colo., (1953), pic. cloth and endsheets, 536 (1) pp., "To the Reader," acknowledgments, appendix, index, numerous illus. including three, pp. (81), (85) and (87), by L. (Remington)

162 Hail, Marshall. *Knight in the Sun.* Little, Brown, Boston, Toronto, (1962), words "First Edition" on copyright page, decor. cloth, yellow top, 234 pp., foreword, appendix, bibliography, acknowledgments and sources, eighteen illus. by L.

163 Haley, J. Evetts et al. *Some Southwestern Trails.* Carl Hertzog, El Paso, 1948, decor. cloth, unpaged, twelve illus. by Bugbee but cover decorations by L.

164 ———. Same, variant with title page drawings by L. and eleven illus. by Bugbee, limited to 75 copies.

165 Haycox, Ernest. *Trail Town.* Little, Brown, Boston, 1941, words "First Edition" on copyright page, pic. cloth, 298 pp., design on front cover and illus. in color on d/w by L.

166 ———. *Rim of the Desert.* Little, Brown, Boston, 1941, words "First Edition" on copyright page, pic. cloth, 305 pp., design on front cover and illus. in color on d/w by L.

167 ———. *Alder Gulch.* Little, Brown, Boston, 1942, words "First Edition" on copyright page, pic. cloth, 302 (1) pp., design on front cover and illus. on d/w spine by L.

168 ———. *The Wild Bunch.* Little, Brown, Boston, 1943, words "First Edition" on copyright page, pic. cloth, 245 pp., design on front cover and illus. in color on d/w by L.

169 Hertzog, Carl (planned and designed by). *El Paso Public Library.* (Guynes Printing Co., El Paso, 1954), pic. wraps, (16) pp., illus., front cover illus. by Jose Cisneros of the owl designed by L. and which is carved in stone on the Library facade.

170 ———. *Hotel Paso de Norte Bill of Fare.* (Carl Hertzog, El Paso, 1938), folder with L. illus. on front cover. Seven each with a different L. illus.

171 *History below the Jet Trails* (Historical Series, Booklet no. 2). American Airlines, 1953, wraps with front cover illus. by L.

172 Household, Geoffrey. *The Salvation of Pisco Gabar and Other Stories.* Little, Brown, Boston, 1940, with illus. in color on d/w by L.

173 Jackson, Joseph Henry. *The Christmas Flower.* Harcourt, Brace, N.Y., (1951), words "first edition" on copyright page, pic. boards, decor. endsheets, 31 pp., illus. by L.

174 Kelty, Mary G. *Life in Modern America.* Ginn & Co., Boston etc., (1941), pic. cloth, 527, xvi, (1) pp., index, numerous illus. including one, p. 258, by L. (Fischer, Hurd, Remington, Russell)

175 ———. *The Story of Life in America.* Ginn, Boston, etc., (1945), pic. cloth, 407 (1) pp., index, numerous illus. including one, p. 423, by L. (Fischer, Hurd, Remington)

176 Kennedy, John F. *Sam Houston and the Senate*. The Pemberton Press, Austin and N.Y., (1970), morocco and marbled boards, brown endsheets, 33 pp., six illus. including one by L. Limited edition of 67 copies each containing an original document signed by Sam Houston, slipcase.

177 ———. Same, first trade edition in decor. two-tone cloth.

178 Klitgaard, Maj. (Georgina B.). *Through the American Landscape*. University of North Carolina Press, Chapel Hill, N.C., (1941), cloth, xi, 323 pp., numerous illus. including one, "Nesters," by L.

179 *Know El Paso: An Authoritative Guide to the City and Its Environs*. Woman's Club of El Paso (printed by Carl Hertzog), 1939, pic. wraps, 80 pp., numerous illus. including four by L.

180 *Life's Picture History of World War II. Life*, Chicago, n.d., numerous illus. including one in color, p. 325, a Peleliu combat painting, by L.

181 Lowman, Al et al. *The Mexican Texans*. Institute of Texan Cultures, the University of Texas, San Antonio, 1971, pic. wraps, 32 pp., numerous illus. including one, p. 21, by L. (Cisneros, Remington)

182 ———. Same, but in Spanish with the title *Los Mexicano Texanos*.

183 ———. *The Indian Texans*. Institute of Texan Cultures, The University of Texas, San Antonio, 1972, pic. wraps, 32 pp., numerous illus. including one by L.

184 ———. *The Spanish Texans*. Institute of Texan Cultures, The University of Texas, San Antonio, 1972, pic. wraps, 32 pp., numerous illus. including four, front cover and pp. 1, 3 and 9, by L. (Bugbee, Cisneros, Mead, Remington)

185 Lowman, Al (compiled by). *Printer at the Pass: The Work of Carl Hertzog*. Institute of Texan Cultures, The University of Texas, San Antonio, 1972, morocco and boards with paper title label on front cover, orange endsheets, 123 (6) pp., "Carl Hertzog, Printer," "A Hertzog Dozen" by William R. Holman, index, illus. including photos of covers and title pages including six, pp. (12), (32), (40), (51), (94) and 95, by L. Edition limited to 200 numbered copies signed by Carl Hertzog, Al Lowman, William R. Holman and designer William D. Wittliff, with five added pages of photos, two including Lea, slipcase.

186 ———. Same, first trade edition in cloth and boards, 123 pp.

187 McCauley, James Emmit. *A Stove-up Cowboy's Story*. Texas Folklore Society, Austin, Texas, and the University Press in Dallas (Carl Hertzog, El Paso), 1943, pic. cloth and endsheets, 73 pp., "introduction" by John A. Lomax, five illus., front cover, endsheets, frontis., facing p. 1 and p. 73, by L.

188 ———. Same, announcement flyer with one illus. by L.

189 ———. Same, second printing by Southern Methodist University Press, Dallas, 1965, with an added "Afterword" by Carl Hertzog.

190 McCracken, Harold. *The American Cowboy*. Doubleday, Garden City, N.Y., 1973, words "Limited Edition" on copyright page, simulated leather, marbled endsheets, 196 pp., all edges gilt, references, index, numerous illus. including one, p. 27, by L. 300 numbered and signed copies, slipcase. (Borein, Cisneros, Eggenhofer, Johnson, Koerner, Leigh, Remington, Russell, Wyeth)

191 ———. Same, trade edition with words "First edition after the limited edition of 300 copies" on copyright page, cloth and colored pic. d/w.

192 McKinzie, Richard D. *The New Deal for Artists*. Princeton University Press, Princeton, N.J., (1973), cloth, 203 pp., preface, notes, index, numerous illus. including one, p. 71 (detail repeated on d/w), by L. (Hurd)

193 McMillan, George. *The Old Breed*. Infantry Journal Press, Washington, D.C., (1949), words "First Edition" on copyright page, decor. cloth, map endsheets, 483 pp., "Foreword" by General A. A. Vandergrift, appendices, numerous illus. including two, pp. (443) and (444), by L.

194 McVicker, Mary Louise. *The Writings of J. Frank Dobie: A Bibliography*. Museum of the Great Plains, Lawton, (Oklahoma), (1968), words "First Edition" on copyright page, Gane Imitation Leather and cloth, 268 pp., preface, "Introduction" by Chancellor Harry E. Ransom, index, illus. with photos and facsimiles of title pages including two, pp. (17) and (22) by L. and his portrait of Dobie, p. (163). Edition of 500 numbered copies signed by the author, slipcase. (Mead)

195 ———. Same, first trade edition in cloth.

196 Mackey, Margaret G. et al. *Your Country's Story: Pioneers, Builders, Leaders*. Ginn, Boston etc,, (1961), colored pic. cloth, 560 pp., appendix, index, maps, numerous illus. including two, pp. 292 and 310, by L. (Hurd, Remington, Wyeth)

197 Mangan, Frank. *El Paso in Pictures*. The Press, El Paso, 1971, two-tone cloth, pic. endsheets, 173 pp., picture and art credits, sources, index, numerous illus. including one, p. 15, by L. (Cisneros)

198 Marzulla, Elena, ed. et al. *United States and Stories* (The Exciting Saga of U.S. History Told in Stamps). Printed for the United States Postal Service by Scott Publishing Co., Omaha, 1972, words "First Edition" front cover, colored pic. wraps, 224 pp., numerous illus. including the Sam Houston 5¢ stamp, p. 97, by L.

199 *Master Portfolio of Western Art*. Montana Historical Society, Helena, 1965, limited to 500 sets, one illus. by L. (Johnson, Remington, Russell, Schreyvogel)

200 Mera, H. P. *The "Rain Bird," A Study in Pueblo Design*. Laboratory of Anthropology, Santa Fe, N.M., (Press of W. F. Roberts Co., Washington, D.C.), 1937, stiff wraps, 113 pp., foreword, all illus. from Indian pottery designs, by L.

201 ———. Same, reprint by Dover, N.Y., 1971, in wraps.

202 Miller, Townsend. *A Letter from Texas*. Carl Hertzog, El Paso, 1939, boards, unpaged, cover design and typographical ornaments by L. Edition of 415 copies — 100 for the author, 300 for Nieman-Marcus, Dallas, and 15 for Hertzog.

203 ———. Same, second edition in a smaller format for Nieman-Marcus in 1944.

204 Mills, W. W. *Forty Years at El Paso*. Carl Hertzog, El Paso, Texas, 1962, two-tone cloth, mesquite decor. endsheets, 212 (1) pp., "Introduction" (and notes) by Rex W. Strickland, appendices, index, illus. with twenty-four drawings by L. and with one photo, slipcase. Edition limited to 100 numbered copies signed by Strickland, Lea and Hertzog and with a Lea print, 24" x 18", suitable for framing.

205 ———. Same, trade edition of no. 204, decor. cloth.

206 ———. Same, announcement folder with two illus. by L., with an "an advance showing" of 24" x 18" print to accompany the limited edition of 100 copies.

207 ———. Same, Colophon Edition of 100 copies for Texas Western College in cloth with the mesquite leaf design on endsheets.

208 Murray, Lois Smith. *Baylor at Independence*. Baylor University Press, Waco, 1972, two-tone cloth with Baylor seal in gold on front cover, 421 pp., "Introduction" by Robert Crawford Cotner, bibliography, appendix, index, numerous illus. including one, the frontis., by L. (Schiwetz)

209 *100 Years of Ranching — King Ranch* sponsored and published by the *Corpus Christi Caller-Times*, (1953), pic. cloth, 143 pp., maps, illus. with photos but front cover design by L.

210 *The People of the Southwest Invite Your Interest and Solicit Your Presence at their First Book Fair of the Southwest*. (Carl Hertzog), El Paso, November 12–13, 1949, folder with front cover illus. by L.

211 *Plaza de Toros, Ciudad Juarez, Chih.* (Mexico). Domingo 6 de Noviembre de 1949, cartel of a corrida dedicated to Tom Lea with one illus. by him and a photo of him.

212 *A Portion of the Pack Trip Country in the Wind River Mountains, Sublette County, Wyoming* (a map drawn by L.). Carl Hertzog, El Paso, for Skinner Brothers, Guides and Outfitters, Pinedale, Wyoming, 1957.

213 Powell, Lawrence Clark. *A Southwestern Century*. J. E. Reynolds, Bookseller, Van Nuys, Calif. (Carl Hertzog, El Paso, Texas, 1958), cloth and boards, 29 pp., preface, illus. by L. Edition limited to 500 copies.

213a ———. *Southwest Classics* (The Creative Literature of the Arid Lands — Essays on the Books and Their Writers). Ward Ritchie, Los Angeles, 1974, cloth (or decor. wraps), 370 pp., index, illus. including one, portrait of Dobie, p. (342), by L.

214 *Presentation of the Isabel Gaddis Collection of J. Frank Dobie by Dr. and Mrs. Charles N. Prothro*. Rare Book Room, Cody Memorial Library (Southwestern University, Georgetown, Texas), October 27, 1970, decor. wraps, unpaged, illus. including three by L. (Mead)

215 Ray, Joseph M. *On Becoming a University* (Report on an Octennium). Texas Western Press, El Paso, (1968), fabricoid and boards, 109 pp., illus. including one in color, the frontis., by L. (Cisneros)

216 Richardson, Rupert N. *Texas, The Lone Star State*. Prentice-Hall, Englewood Cliffs, N.J., (1958), decor. cloth, 460 pp., preface, index, folding map in color as frontis., illus. including one, between pp. 240 and 241, by L.

217 Rogers, John William, ed. *A Round-Up of the Most Interesting Texas Books of All Time*. The *Dallas Times Herald*, first separate printing of "Book News" of October 7, 1945, self-wraps, 16 pp., illus. including one, p. 7, by L. (Bugbee, Hurd, Thomason)

218 *Rotary International, Thirteenth Conference Forty-second District* (program). El Paso, April 23–24, 1937, wraps, unpaged, frontis. by L. plus the first appearance of Hertzog's "brand" (printer's device) drawn for him by L.

219 (Russell.) *Seven Drawings by Charles M. Russell* (with an additional drawing by Tom Lea). Portfolio, 8 plates, with an essay, "The Conservatism of Charles M. Russell," by J. Frank Dobie. Printed for C. R. Smith by Carl Hertzog, El Paso, Texas, (1950), limited to 675 sets.

220 ———. *History of Transportation in the Early West* (announcement folder). Four illus. incuding one by L. (Russell)

221 *Santa Gertrudis.* S. G. B. I., Kingsville, Texas, 1956, pic. folder with one illus. by L.

222 *Santa Gertrudis.* S. G. B. I., Kingsville, Texas, (1958), pic. folder with one illus. by L.

223 *Santa Gertrudis para la Produccion de Mas y Mejor Carne.* Carl Hertzog for the Santa Gertrudis Breeders International, Kingsville, 1958, folded to 12 unnumbered pages with the front cover illus. by L.

224 *Santa Gertrudis Proven Performance.* Santa Gertrudis Breeders International, Kingsville, Texas, n.d., (1973), decor. wraps, unpaged, (12), cover design by L.

225 Schwettmann, Martin W. *Santa Rita.* The Texas State Historical Assn., Austin (Carl Hertzog, El Paso), 1943, cloth, 43 pp., preface, illus. by L. Edition limited to 440 numbered copies.

226 ———. Same, facsimile reprint in 1958 of no. 225.

227 ———. Same, announcement folder with one illus. by L.

228 ———. Same, facsimile reprint of 100 numbered copies by Carl Hertzog, 1969, for the University of Texas System Development Board for use by the Santa Rita Award Committee, embossed red calf binding — design based on Lea's frontispiece.

229 *The Sheriff's Posse Championship* (rodeo). March 28–31, 1941, pic. wraps, unpaged, numerous illus. including one full-page drawing by Tom Lea.

230 Sinclair-Crown, Bertha M. *The Family Failing* by B. M. Bower (pseud.). Little, Brown, Boston, 1941, cloth, illus. on back of d/w by L.

231 Siringo, Charles A. *A Texas Cowboy.* William Sloane Associates, N.Y., (1950), cloth, 198 pp., "Charlie Siringo, Writer and Man" and "Bibliography of Siringo's Writings" by J. Frank Dobie, illus. by L. Designed by Carl Hertzog, El Paso, Texas.

232 ———. Same, The New American Library, N.Y., (1951), words "First Printing, Sept. 1951" on copyright page, colored pic. wraps, 176 pp., all edges red. First paperback printing of no. 231.

233 Smith, Rex, ed. *Biography of the Bulls.* Rinehart & Co., N.Y., Toronto, (1957), publisher's symbol on copyright page, pic. boards and endsheets, 384 pp., preface, numerous illus. including two, pp. 342 and 351, by L. Front cover and d/w illus. by L., and reprints chapters seven and eight from no. 36.

234 *A Southwestern Portfolio.* Carl Hertzog, El Paso, for the Ex-Student's Association of the University of Texas at El Paso, 1968, comments by S. D. Myres, (4) pp., twelve prints including two, "Toro" and "Toribio," by L. (Hurd)

235 Sparkman, Dr. Robert S., ed. *The Texas Surgical Society, The First Fifty Years.* (The Texas Surgical Society), Dallas, (but designed and printed by Carl Hertzog, El Paso), 1965, decor. cloth, tan endsheets, 152 pp., preface, appendices, illus. with photos but with one double-page plate "The First Recorded Surgical Operation in North America," following p. 5, and Cabeza de Vaca insignia as frontis. (repeated on front cover), by L. Edition of 1050 numbered copies, slipcase.

236 *A Special Subject Bulletin.* El Paso Public Library, n.d., wraps with "Southwest" from the mural in the library by L. on the cover.

237 *The Spur* (yearbook of El Paso High School). 1921, includes art work by L.

238 Same, 1922, includes art work by L.

239 Same, 1923, includes art work by L.

240 Same, 1924, edited, cover design, section illustrations and the poem "Ambition" by L.

241 Staff of the Corpus Christi *Caller Times. Associated Press Centennial Meeting of the Board of Directors at the King Ranch* (program). January 4–7, 1949. Carl Hertzog (El Paso, Texas) for Houston Harte, pic. wraps, 16 pp., illus., map, front cover illus. by L.

242 Staff of M. S. T. & T. C., Larry Effinger et al. *A City and a Service Grow Up Together.* Mountain States Telephone and Telegraph Co., El Paso, (Carl Hertzog, El Paso, Texas, 1948), pic. wraps, (24) pp., (preface) by E. G. Phillips, illus. front cover illus. by L.

243 Stinson, Buck and Hertzog, Carl. *Honor Your Partner.*

Carl Hertzog, El Paso, 1938, pic. wraps, 32 pp., illus. including one, front cover, by L.

244 *Texas Library Assn.–New Mexico Library Assn.: Library Conference at El Paso, Texas.* (Carl Hertzog, El Paso, 1961), pic. wraps, 15 (1) pp., two illus. by L.

245 *Timelessness: The Fourth Dimensions in Books.* 47th Annual Conference, Texas Library Association, San Antonio, April 6-9, 1960, pic. wraps, 16 pp. designed by Carl Hertzog, illus. from *The King Ranch* by L. (Cisneros)

246 Tinkle, Lon and Maxwell, Allen, eds. *The Cowboy Reader.* Longmans, Green, N.Y. etc., 1959, words "First Edition" on copyright page, cloth, 307 pp., introduction, twenty-three illus. including six, between pp. 68 and 69, by L. (Bugbee, Remington, Russell)

247 *Tom Lea. A Portfolio of Six Paintings.* University of Texas Press, Austin, Texas, 1953, biographical introduction by J. Frank Dobie, six full-color plates, 16½" x 20", in a portfolio with lettering and the printing mark of the University of Texas Press by L.

248 Same, announcement folder for the reprint with four illus. by L.

249 Same, second issue in a blue cardboard portfolio.

250 Vann, William H. *The Texas Institute of Letters, 1936–1966.* Encino Press, Austin, (1967), cloth and boards with paper title label on front cover, green endsheets, 101 pp., "A Prefatory Note" by Lon Tinkle, appendix (members, awards), illus. including Lea's portrait of Carl Hertzog, p. 35 and Lea appears in photos, pp. 36 and 40; his *The Brave Bulls* won the outstanding Texas book award in 1949.

251 Wardlaw, Frank H. *I Have that Honor* (Tributes to J. Frank Dobie). The Congressional Press, Paisano, Texas and Biddeford Pool, Maine, 1965, wraps, unpaged, "Foreword" by Walter Muir Whitehill, illus. with photos but the Lea portrait of Dobie appears on the title page.

252 Watson, Forbes (with an essay by). *American Painting Today.* The American Federation of Arts, Washington, D.C., 1939, cloth, 179 pp., list of artists and reproductions, 259 illus. including two, pp. 70 and 168, by L. (Hurd)

253 Watson, Thomas J. (foreword by). *Contemporary Art of the United States.* IBM Corporation, N.Y., 1940, wraps, unpaged, numerous illus. including one, "Portrait of Artist's Wife," by L. (Blumenschein, Dixon)

254 Webb, Walter Prescott. *The Texas Rangers: A Cen-*

tury of Frontier Defense. Texas, Austin, 1965, words "Second Edition" on copyright page, cloth, 583 (1) pp., "Foreword" by Lyndon B. Johnson, illus. with drawings by Lonnie Rees and with photos but double title page (repeated on d/w in color), "Ranger Escort West of the Pecos," by L.

255 Welch, June Rayfield. *Historic Sites of Texas.* (G.L.A. Press, Dallas, 1972), words "First Printing 1972" on copyright page, cloth, 196 pp., introduction, bibliography, index, numerous illus. including one, p. 15, by L.

256 Wertenbaker, Green Peyton. *America's Heartland, The Southwest* by Green Peyton (pseud.). Oklahoma, Norman, 1948, words "First Edition" on copyright page, cloth, 285 (1) pp., green top, "A Foreword," index, illus. including one, facing p. 6, by L. and a photo of him.

257 West, John O. *Tom Lea, Artist in Two Mediums.* Steck-Vaughn Co., Austin, (1967), wraps, 44 pp., selected bibliography, eight illus., pp. 34, 35, 36, 37, 38, 39, 40–1 and 42, by L.

258 *Western Americana.* Texas, Austin, n.d., pic. wraps, 16 pp., front cover illus. by L.

258a *Western Americana.* Texas, Austin, (1974), pic. wraps, 37 (2) pp., order form, numerous illus. including one, p. 25, by L. (Schiwetz, Thomason)

259 *Westward High* (Historical Series, booklet no. 3). American Airlines, 1953, wraps, with one illus. inside back cover by L.

260 White, Anne Terry. *Indians and the Old West.* Simon and Shuster, N.Y., (1958), pic. boards, 56 pp., all edges red, numerous illus. including one, p. 42, by L. (Leigh, Remington, Russell, Schreyvogel)

261 Wierzbinski, Fryderyk. *Indianski Pirorpusz.* Biuro Wydawnicze, Warszawa, Poland, 1971, wraps, 82 (1) pp., numerous illus. including the Sam Houston stamp, p. 47, by L. (Remington, Russell, Von Schmidt)

262 Wilder, Howard B. et al. *This is America's Story.* Houghton, Mifflin, Boston, (1958), pic. cloth, 728 pp., appendix, indices, numerous illus. including two, pp. 340 and 422, by L. (Remington)

263 ———. Same, reissued in 1960 in a smaller format.

264 Wingfield, Clyde J., ed. *Urbanization in the Southwest, a Symposium.* Texas Western Press, El Paso, 1968, pic. wraps, 87 pp., front cover illus. by L.

265 Wright, Reverend William G. *Excerpts from the First Sermon Preached at the Church of Saint Clement, El Paso.* (Carl Hertzog, El Paso, 1953), decor. wraps, (8) pp., decor. by L.

266 Yarborough, Ralph and Opal. *Christmas in El Paso.* (Carl Hertzog, El Paso, December, 1973), Christmas folder with cover illus. by L.

The Artist and His Art

267 Braddy, Haldeen. "Artist Illustrators of the Southwest: H. D. Bugbee, Jose Cisneros, and Tom Lea," an article in *Western Review* 1:2, Fall 1964, with three illus. plus the front cover by L. (Bugbee, Cisneros)

268 Bromfield, Louis. "Triumph in the Arena," a review of *The Brave Bulls* in the *Saturday Review of Literature*, April 23, 1949, with one illus. by L. and a portrait of him on the front cover.

269 (Daniel.) *Texas and the West Featuring Books Printed and/or designed by Carl Hertzog* (a bibliography). Catalogue no. 19, Price Daniel, Jr., Waco, Texas, (1963), cloth, 32 pp., "Printer to the West" by Dr. Llerena Friend, cataloguer's note, illus., catalogs many of the items included in this check list. Edition limited to 115 numbered copies. (Also an issue in wraps was mailed to his customers.)

270 Dobie, J. Frank. "He Paints Texas," an article in *The American Weekly*, Dec. 5, 1954, praise of Lea's work with five illus. in color by L.

271 Dykes, Jeff C. *High Spots of Western Illustrating.* The Kansas City Posse, The Westerners, (1964), cloth, 30 pp., introduction, two illus., Highspots nos. 59, 62 and 68 were illus. by Lea. Edition limited to 250 numbered, signed copies. (An issue in wraps was distributed to members.)

272 Faries, Belmont. "Tom Lea. A Texas Artist Designs a Stamp in Honor of the Greatest Texan (Sam Houston)," an article in *S. P. A. Journal* (Society of Philatelic Americans), vol. 26, no. 4, Dec. 1963 with illus. on front cover by L.

273 ———. "The Houston Stamp Record," an article in *S. P. A. Journal*, vol. 26, no. 8, April, 1964, with illus. on front cover by L.

274 Frederick, John T. "Speaking of Books," a review of recent books about Texas in *The Rotarian*, February 1958, includes a review of *The King Ranch* by L. with three illus. by him and a photo of him.

275 Glasscock, James W. "Tom Lea of Texas," an article

in *Texas Parade*, vol. XII, no. 1, June, 1951, two photos of Lea, one illus. by L.

276 Hazard, Eloise. "Notes on a Baker's Dozen," biographies of thirteen artists in *Saturday Review of Literature* 33:5, February 11, 1950, biography of L. and a photo of him.

277 Hertzog, Carl. "A Tribute to Tom Lea," an article in *Saturday Review of Literature* 32:17, April 23, 1949, with six drawings by L.

278 Latendorf, E. Walter. *Western Americana.* Catalogue no. 24, Mannados Bookshop, N.Y., (1954), pic. wraps, 88 pp., catalogs many items included in this check list. (Borein, Dixon, Goodwin, Schreyvogel)

279 ———. Same, catalogue no. 27, Mannados Bookshop, N.Y., n.d., pic. wrapjs, 36 pp., catalogs many items included in this check list, also five illus. by L. (Eggenhofer, Goodwin, Lungren)

280 Lea, Tom. "Quite a Beach," a short story in *The Atlantic Monthly*, September 1949. So far as known, Lea's only published short story.

281 ———. "Brave Bulls and Brave Men," an article in *Saturday Review of Literature*, Sept. 15, 1951.

282 ———. "The Affair of the Fifteen Aprils," a translation from *Vida y Hazanasde Pancho Villa* by Elias L. Torres in *The Southwest Review*, Winter, 1951, with drawing of Pancho Villa by L.

283 ———. Short article in *Wings*, the Literary Guild, December, 1952, about the writing of *The Wonderful Country*.

284 ———. "Journeying Vicariously," a short article in *Book News*, October, 1964, about the writing of *The Hands of Cantu*.

285 "Tom Lea and His Brave Bulls," an illus. article in *Life Magazine*, 1949.

286 Liggett, Lyle. "The King Ranch," a review in *American Cattle Producer* 39:4, September 1957, with four drawings by L.

287 Lowman, Al. "Tom Lea," an article in *Southwestern Art* 2:4, Austin, 1970, with ten illus. by L.

288 Morris, Willie. "El Paso's Tom Lea, A Desert and Ranch Man," a feature article in *The Texas Observer*, January 13, 1962, with a photo of L. and one illus. by him.

289 Morrison, W. M. (Books). *List 277.* Waco, 1971, pic. wraps, 11 pp., photo of Tom Lea and Carl Hertzog on the front cover on the occasion of each receiving an

honorary doctor of letters degree from Baylor University.

290 Powell, Lawrence Clark. "Return to the Heartland," an article in *ALA Bulletin,* vol. 53, no. 6, June, 1959, photos of Dobie and Clark and one drawing by L.

291 "Presenting Tom Lea," an unsigned article in *The Cattleman,* January, 1961, with illus. by L.

292 Reynolds, J. E. "A Fiesta for Tom Lea," a report on a testimonial dinner and a running of Six Brave Bulls to honor Tom Lea (El Paso, September 14th and Juarez, September 15th) in *Antiquarian Bookman* 20:14, September 30, 1957, with a photo of Lea and Carl Hertzog and J. Frank Dobie on the front cover.

293 Short, Clarice. "Tom Lea's Symbolism," a critical essay in *The Western Humanities Review,* Winter, 1954. Discusses Lea's first two novels.

294 Tinkle, Lon. A review of Lea's *The Wonderful Country* in *Saturday Review,* Nov. 15, 1952. Also a profile of Lea by Bernard Kalb and illus. by L.

295 ———. *J. Frank Dobie — The Makings of an Ample Mind.* Encino Press, Austin, 1968, cloth and decor. boards, matching grey endsheets, 57 pp., illus. with photos, Lea in the text pp. 35, 45, 48–51, 53, and he is in the photo of "The Texas Institute of the Unlettered," p. 52.

296 ———. *Mr. De* (A Biography of Everette Lee De Golyer). Little, Brown, Boston, Toronto, (1970), words "First Edition" on copyright page, two-tone cloth, brown endsheets, 393 pp., "Foreword" by Norman Cousins, appendix, a bibliographical note, index, illus. with photos, Lea in text, pp. 307, 310–14, 328, 341 and 347.

297 *Who's Who in America* (volume 32). Marquis, Chicago, 1962–63, biography of L. Note: The Lea biography appears in all volumes issued after no. 32.

297a *Who's Who in the World.* Marquis, Chicago, 1971–72, biography of L. Note: The Lea biography also appears in the 1973 edition.

298 "World War II — As the Soldier Artist Saw It," an illus. article in *Army Digest* 20:6, June 1965, with one illus. in color by L.

ILLUSTRATION by Lea from *The Wonderful Country*

MUSTANGS OF THE STAKED PLAINS by Leigh from *Mustangs And Cow Horses*

WILLIAM ROBINSON LEIGH
1866–1955

Catalogues of Art Exhibitions and Galleries

ADDISON GALLERY OF AMERICAN ART
(PHILLIPS ACADEMY), ANDOVER, MASSACHUSETTS

1 *The American Line — 100 Years of American Draw-ing*, (1959), oblong cloth, index, 100 numbered illus. including no. 67 by L.

ART INSTITUTE OF CHICAGO

2 *Catalogue of the 29th Annual Exhibition of Oil Paintings and Sculpture by American Artists*, 1916, wraps, numerous illus. including one, "Land of His Fathers," by L.

J. N. BARTFIELD ART GALLERIES, NEW YORK

3 *American Painting and Sculpture, Historical — Western*, n.d., colored pic. wraps, unpaged but with 64 numbered illus. including two in color, nos. 31 and 32, by L. (Johnson, Remington, Russell, Schoon-over, Wyeth)

3a Same, (catalogue no. 120, 1973), wraps with window, unpaged, 82 numbered illus. including one, no. 29 (color), by L. (Dixon, Johnson, Remington, Russell, Schreyvogel)

BILTMORE GALLERIES, LOS ANGELES

3b *Catalog*, May 1969, colored pic. wraps, 54 pp., nu-merous illus. including one, p. 33, by L. (Borein, Dixon, Dunton, Johnson, Koerner, Miller, Reming-ton, Russell, Young)

HELEN L. CARD, NEW YORK

4 *Hang On, Fellers! We're Out on a Limb*, Catalog No. Five, (1963), pic. wraps, 95 pp., numerous illus. in-cluding one, p. 55, by L. (Deming, Eggenhofer, Rem-ington, Schoonover, Stoops, Wyeth)

EDWARD EBERSTADT AND SONS, NEW YORK

5 *A Distinguished Collection of Western Paintings*, Catalog 139, 1956, pic. wraps, "Introduction: West-ern American Art" by Harold McCracken, 129 num-bered illus. including seven, nos. 66, 67, 68, 69, 70, 71 and 72, by L. (Borein, Deming, Dixon, Johnson, Remington, Russell)

6 *American Paintings*, Catalog 146 (December 1957), colored pic. wraps, 191 numbered plates including four, nos. 115, 116, 117 and 118, by L. (Borein, Dem-ing, Dixon, Dunton, Johnson, Remington)

HAMMER GALLERIES, NEW YORK

7 *The Works of Charles M. Russell and Other Western Artists*, (November, 1962), pic. wraps, 56 pp., intro-duction, numerous illus. including five, pp. 47 (three), 51 and 55, by L. (Crawford, Goodwin, Lungren, Rem-ington, Russell)

GRAND CENTRAL ART GALLERIES, NEW YORK

8 *Americana — Paintings by W. R. Leigh*, March 4–22, 1941, broadside (folded), 24 illus. by L. and a photo of him.

9 *"Our Fabulous West" — A Restrospective Exhibition 1906–1953*, April 14–May 2, 1953, folder, three illus. by L. and a photo of him.

10 *Eight Decades in Review 1870–1955 by W. R. Leigh*, Jan. 11–29, 1955, broadside (folded), five illus. by L. and a photo of him.

11 *90th Anniversary Roundup of Paintings by W. R. Leigh*, Sept. 25–Oct. 12, 1956, broadside (folded), five (two in color) illus. by L. and a photo of him.

12 *Exhibition Sports in Art*, March 16–April 3, 1965, pic. wraps, (12) pp., "Foreword" by Director Erwin S. Barrie, seven illus. including one, "The Master Hand," by L.

13 *A Salute to the Old West*, April 17–May 12, 1973, wraps with illus. in color mounted on the front cover, unpaged, "Introduction" by Harold McCracken, "In-

troduction" by Dean Krakel, "Foreword" by Erwin S. Barrie, two illus. by L.

14 *Exhibition of Painting and Sculpture Contributed by Artist Members 1938*, wraps with illus. mounted on front cover, 72 pp., numerous illus. including one, p. 47, by L. (Blumenschein, Johnson)

15 Same, *1939*, wraps with illus. in color mounted on front cover, tan endsheets, 74 pp., numerous illus. including five, pp. 37 and 57 (four), by L. and a photo of him. (Johnson)

16 Same, *1940*, wraps with illus. in color mounted on front cover, green endsheets, 74 pp., numerous illus. including four, pp. 24 (color) and 59 (three), by L. and a photo of him.

17 Same, *1943*, wraps with illus. mounted on front cover, 71 (1) pp., numerous illus. including one, p. 38, by L. (Johnson)

18 Same, *1944*, wraps with illus. in color mounted on front cover, 78 pp., numerous illus. including one, p. 41, by L. (Johnson)

19 Same, *1945*, wraps with illus. in color mounted on front cover, 75 pp., numerous illus. including two, pp. 7 (color) and 37, by L. (Young)

20 Same, *1946*, wraps with illus. in color mounted on front cover, 65 pp., numerous illus. including one, p. 45, by L.

21 Same, *25th Anniversary 1947*, wraps with illus. in color mounted on front cover, 69 pp., numerous illus. including one, p. 45, by L.

22 Same, *1948*, wraps with illus. in color mounted on front cover, 70 pp., numerous illus. including two, front cover and p. 38, by L.

23 Same, *1949*, wraps with illus. in color mounted on front cover, 70 pp., numerous illus. including one, p. 48, by L.

24 Same, *1950*, wraps with illus. in color mounted on front cover, 72 pp., numerous illus. including one, p. 50, by L. (Johnson)

25 Same, *1951*, wraps with illus. in color mounted on front cover, 72 pp., numerous illus. including three, pp. 11 (color), 23 and 46, by L. (Johnson)

26 Same, *1952, Thirtieth Anniversary*, wraps with illus. in color mounted on front cover, 72 pp., numerous illus. including one, p. 50, by L.

27 Same, *1953*, wraps with illus. in color mounted on front cover, 74 pp., numerous illus. including four,

front cover in color, pp. 17, 31 and 51, by L. and a photo of him.

28 Same, *1955 Yearbook*, wraps with illus in color mounted on front cover, 76 pp., numerous illus. including two, pp. 20 and 59, by L. and a photo of him. (Johnson, Remington, Schreyvogel)

29 Same, *1956*, wraps with illus. in color mounted on front cover, 74 pp., numerous illus. including three, pp. 29 (color), 47 and 57, by L.

30 Same, *1958*, wraps with illus. in color mounted on front cover, 74 pp., numerous illus. including four, pp. 56 (two in color) and 57 (two in color), by L. and two photos of him. (Remington)

31 Same, *1961 Yearbook*, wraps with illus. in color mounted on front cover, 74 pp., numerous illus. including one, p. 39, by L.

32 Same, *1962 Yearbook*, wraps with illus. in color mounted on front cover, 74 pp., numerous illus. including two, pp. 6 and 33, by L. and a photo of him. (Beeler)

33 Same, *1963 Yearbook*, wraps with illus. in color mounted on front cover, 74 pp., numerous illus. including one, p. 28, by L.

34 Same, *1964 Yearbook*, wraps with illus. in color mounted on the front cover, 74 pp., numerous illus. including one, p. 48, by L. (Beeler)

35 Same, *1965 Yearbook*, wraps with illus. in color mounted on the front cover, 74 pp., numerous illus. including one, p. 34, by L.

36 Same, *1966 Yearbook*, wraps with illus. in color mounted on the front cover, 74 pp., numerous illus. including two, pp. 28 and 32, by L.

37 Same, *1970 Yearbook*, wraps with illus. in color mounted on the front cover, 68 pp., numerous illus. including one, p. 10, by L. (Johnson, Russell)

THE GEORGE GUND MUSEUM OF WESTERN ART NEW YORK

38 *The Gund Collection of Western Art, A Personal Narrative*, 1970, colored pic. wraps, 38 pp., nineteen illus. including one in color, p. 11, by L. (Johnson, Remington, Russell, Schreyvogel)

39 Same, *A History and Political Description of the American West*, 1973, pic. wraps, 62 pp., thirty-five illus. including one, p. 13, by L. (Johnson, Miller, Remington, Russell, Schreyvogel)

INDIANAPOLIS MUSEUM OF ART

40 *West America* (A Selection of Paintings, Bronzes, and

Artifacts from the Harrison Eiteljorg Collection), Summer 1971, colored pic. wraps, unpaged, illus. including one by L. (Remington, Russell)

JOSLYN ART MUSEUM, OMAHA, NEBRASKA

41 *Life on the Prairie — A Permanent Exhibition*, 1966, wraps, illus. including one by L. (Johnson, Miller, Remington, Russell)

KALAMAZOO INSTITUTE OF ARTS KALAMAZOO, MICHIGAN

42 *Western Art* (Paintings and Sculptures of the West), February 17–March 19, 1967, pic. wraps, 17 (1) pp., numerous illus. including one by L. (Hurd, Johnson, Remington, Russell, Schreyvogel, Wyeth)

KENNEDY GALLERIES, NEW YORK

43 *Painters of the Old West*, October 1960, wraps with illus. mounted on front cover pp. (101)-147, introduction, numerous illus. including one, p. 122, by L. (Borein, Deming, Remington, Russell, Schreyvogel, Zogbaum)

44 *Recent Acquisitions in Important Western and Sporting Paintings and Sculptures*, October 1962, wraps with illus. in color mounted on the front cover, pp. (49)-108, introduction, numerous illus. including three, pp. 68 and 69 (two), by L. (Borein, Johnson, Marchand, Miller, Remington, Russell, Schreyvogel)

45 *Tradition and Change*, December 1963, colored pic. wraps, pp. 68-112, introduction, numerous illus. including two, pp. 82 and 83, by L. (Koerner, Lungren, Remington, Russell, Schreyvogel)

46 *Exhibition of Western Paintings*, October 1964, colored pic. wraps, 64 pp., introduction, numerous illus. including one, p. 52, by L. (Johnson, Marchand, Remington, Russell, Schreyvogel)

47 *"The Wild Riders and the Vacant Land,"* June 1966, colored pic. wraps, pp. (67)-128, introduction, numerous illus. including two, p. 124, by L. (Miller, Remington, Russell)

48 *The Things that Were*, June 1968, colored pic. wraps, pp. (51)-(124), introduction, index, numerous illus. including one, p. 92, by L. (Blumenschein, Crawford, Miller, Remington, Schoonover, Schreyvogel)

49 *The Great American West*, June 1973, colored pic. wraps, pp. (131)-192, introduction, notes, numerous illus. including two, pp. 178-179, by L. (Blumenschein, Miller, Remington, Russell, Schreyvogel)

E. WALTER LATENDORF, NEW YORK

50 *C. M. Russell*, Catalogue No. 27, pic. wraps, (48) pp., forty-six illus. including three by L. (Borein, Crawford, Goodwin, Marchand, Russell)

MAXWELL GALLERIES, SAN FRANCISCO

50a *Art of the West*, November 13 through December 1973, colored pic. wraps, 48 pp., numerous illus. including one, p. 9, by L. (Johnson, Marchand, Miller)

MIDWESTERN GALLERIES, CINCINNATI

51 *Catalogue of Fine Art*, Number 10 (1972?), folder, eleven illus. including one by L. (Borein, Remington)

READ MULLAN GALLERY OF WESTERN ART PHOENIX, ARIZONA

52 Read Mullan Gallery of Western Art, 1964, pic. wraps, (12) pp., (Foreword) by Read Mullan, numerous illus. including one by L. (Johnson, Remington)

MUSEUM OF ART, SMITH COLLEGE NORTHAMPTON, MASSACHUSETTS

53 *Supplement to the Catalog of 1937*, 1941, wraps, numerous illus. including one, "Landscape," by L.

MUSEUM OF NEW MEXICO ART GALLERY SANTA FE

54 *An Exhibition of Paintings from the Santa Fe Railway Collection*, 1966, wraps, three illus. by L. (Blumenschein, Dunton)

NATIONAL ACADEMY OF DESIGN, NEW YORK

55 *69th Annual Exhibition*, 1894, numerous illus. including one, "End of the Play," by L.

56 *70th Annual Exhibition*, 1895, numerous illus. including one, "New Acquaintances," by L.

OESTREICHER'S, NEW YORK

57 *The World's Largest Collection of Fine Color Art Reproductions*, (1954), pic. wraps, 95 (1) pp., introduction, numerous illus. including two, p. 91, by L.

PARKE-BERNET GALLERIES, NEW YORK

58 *French and English Furniture and Decorations*, Sale No. 726, 1946, wraps, 126 pp., numerous illus. including one, p. 29, by L.

59 *American Paintings and Drawings*, Sale No. 2276, April 23, 1964, wraps, 54 (2) pp., numerous illus. including one, p. 37, by L. (Remington, Russell, Schreyvogel)

PETERSEN GALLERIES, BEVERLY HILLS, CALIFORNIA

59a *Americana, Western and Sporting Art / Sculpture*, wraps, 25 pp., numerous illus. including one, p. 6, by L. (James, Johnson, Remington, Russell, Wyeth, Zogbaum)

60 *The Discovery of the West*, March 1961, pic. wraps, (12) pp., (Foreword) by Read Mullan, preface, numerous illus. including two by L. (Johnson, Remington, Russell)

61 *An Exhibition of Paintings of the Southwest from the Santa Re Railway Collection*, Feb. 1 through April 30, 1966, including one by L. (Blumenschein, Dunton) .

62 *Western Art from the Eugene B. Adkins Collection*, November 1971–January 1972, colored pic. wraps, unpaged, "Preface" by R. D. A. Puckle (Associate Director), numerous illus. including one in color by L. (Dunton, Johnson, Miller, Remington, Varian)

FRED ROSENSTOCK WITH JAMES PARSONS (GALLERY WEST), DENVER

63 *100 Years of Western Art*, Nov. 28, through Dec. 24, 1969, colored pic. wraps, 24 pp., numerous illus. including two, p. 7, by L. (Beeler, Borein, Dunton, James, Koerner)

SOTHEBY PARKE BERNET, LOS ANGELES

63a *Western American Paintings, Drawings and Sculpture*, March 4 and 5, 1974, colored pic. wraps, unpaged, 252 lots, numerous illus. including lot 108 by L. (Blumenschein, Dunton, Koerner, Remington, Russell)

SOTHEBY PARKE BERNET, NEW YORK

64 *Traditional & Western American Paintings, Drawings, Watercolors, Sculpture & Illustrations*, Sale Number 3348, April 19–20, 1972, pic. wraps, 147 pp., numerous illus. including two, pp. 89 and 113, by L. (Deming, Johnson, Koerner, Remington, Russell)

65 *Important 18th, 19th, and Early 20th Century American Paintings, Watercolors and Sculpture*, Sale Number 3498, April 11, 1973, colored pic. wraps, unpaged but with over 70 numbered plates including two, nos. 59 and 62, by L. (Blumenschein, Eggenhofer, James, Johnson, Remington, Russell, Varian, Wyeth)

WHITNEY GALLERY OF WESTERN ART (BUFFALO BILL HISTORICAL CENTER) CODY, WYOMING

66 *Special Exhibition Opening Season*, June 1 to October 1, 1969, pic. wraps, (8) pp., ten illus. including one by L. (Koerner, Wyeth)

SANDRA WILSON GALLERIES, SANTA FE

67 *Western Legacy*, Jan. 12–Feb. 3, 1973, colored pic. wraps, unpaged, numerous illus. including one (repeated on front cover) by L. (Deming, Perceval, Remington, Russell)

WOOLAROC MUSEUM (FRANK PHILLIPS FOUNDATION), BARTLESVILLE, OKLAHOMA

68 *Oklahoma*, 1952, pic. wraps, (8) pp., numerous illus. including one by L. (Dunton, Johnson, Remington, Russell)

69 *Indians*, (1965), colored pic. wraps, (12) pp., numerous illus. including five by L. (Remington, Russell)

70 *Woolaroc*, n.d., colored decor. wraps, 31 (2) pp., numerous illus. including four, pp. 13, (18), 19 and (21) by L. (Johnson, Remington, Russell)

71 *Woolaroc Museum, Frank Phillips Ranch*, Bartlesville Chamber of Commerce, n.d., pic. folder, 13 illus. including one by L., map. (Remington)

72 *Woolaroc Museum* by Ke Mo Ha (Patrick Patterson, Museum Director, 1965), colored decor. boards (or wraps), 64 (1) pp., numerous illus in color including seven, pp. 18, 22, 23, (46), 47 53 and 57, by L. (Johnson, Mora, Remington, Russell, Young)

Illustrated by the Artist

73 Ainsworth, Ed. *The Cowboy in Art*, World, N.Y. and Cleveland, (1968), words "First Printing 1968" on copyright page, full leather, orange endsheets, 242 pp., all edges gilt, "Foreword" by John Wayne, index, numerous illus. including two, p. 68 and between pp. 114 and 115 (color) by L. Special edition of 1000 copies, slipcase. (Beeler, Borein, Bugbee, De Yong, Dixon, Dunton, Eggenhofer, Hurd, James, Johnson, Koerner, Mora, Perceval, Remington, Russell, Santee, Schreyvogel, Von Schmidt)

74 ———. Same, first trade edition in gilt lettered and illus. cloth, orange endsheets.

75 ———. Same, reprint by Bonanza Books, N.Y., in red lettered and illus. cloth, white endsheets.

75a Allen, Durward L. *The Life of Prairies and Plains*. McGraw Hill, N.Y. etc., (1969), colored pic. cloth, 233 pp., glossary, bibliography, index, numerous illus. including one in color, pp. (174–5), by L.

76 Andrews, E. Benjamin. *The History of the Last Quarter-Century in the U.S., 1870–1895*. Scribner's, N.Y., 1896, 2 vols., decor. cloth, pp. 390 and 409, gilt tops, preface (I), index (II), more than 350 illus. including eleven in vol. I and three in vol. II, by L. (Lungren)

77 ———. *The United States in Our Own Times*. Scribner's, 1903, decor. cloth, 961 pp., gilt top, index, nu-

merous illus. including seventeen by L. (Lungren)

78 Athearn, Robert G. *Winning the West*. Dell Pub. Co., N.Y., (1963), pic. boards and endsheets, pp. (723)-809, numerous illus. including one, pp. 786-787, by L. (Dunn, Remington, Russell)

79 Beard, Charles A. and Mary R. *A Basic History of the United States*. Doubleday, Doran, N.Y., 1944, cloth, 554 pp., brown top, prefatory note, appendix, reading list, index, sixty-four illus. including three, between pp. 304 and 305, by L. (Dixon, Lea, Wyeth)

80 Beebe, Lucius and Clegg, Charles. *Hear the Train Blow*. Dutton, N.Y., 1952, words "First Edition" on copyright page, decor. cloth, pic. endsheets, 407 (9) pp., foreword, 870 illus. including one, p. (129) by L. (Remington)

81 Benedict. H. Y. and Lomax, John A. *The Book of Texas*. Doubleday, Page, Garden City, N.Y., 1916, decor. cloth, 448 pp., gilt top, numerous illus. including one, "And woe to the Rider, and woe to the Steed, who Falls in Front of the Mad Stampede," facing p. 168, by L.

82 Bradley, Lt. James H. *The March of the Montana Column — A Prelude to the Custer Campaign*. Oklahoma, Norman, 1961, words "First printing" on copyright page, cloth, 182 pp., "Introduction" and edited by Edgar I. Stewart, "A Brief Biography of Lieutenant Bradley," index, illus., including one, the d/w, by L.

83 Brown, Dee and Schmitt, Martin F. *Trail Driving Days*. Scribner's, N.Y., London, 1952, code letter "A" on copyright page, decor. cloth, 264 pp., foreword, bibliography, profusely illus. including one, p. 61, by L. (Remington, Russell, Zogbaum)

84 Bryant, (Mrs.) Lorinda Munson. *American Pictures and Their Painters*. John Lane Co., N.Y., 1917, decor. cloth, 307 pp., (2) of advs., introduction, index, 229 illus. including one, facing p. 250, by L.

85 ———. *The Children's Book of Animal Pictures*. Century, N.Y. and London, (1931), words "First Printing" on copyright page, cloth, 105 pp., "Dear Children," index, 51 illus. including one, p. (89), by L.

86 Camp, Walter (editor-in-chief). *Authors and Inventors* (Library for Young People). Collier, N.Y., 1903, cloth, decor. endsheets, 630 pp., "Introduction" by Henry S. Pritchett, two illus. in color, frontis. and facing p. 108, by L.

87 ———. *Travellers and Explorers*. (Library for Young People). Collier, N.Y., 1903, cloth, decor. cloth, 607 pp., "Introduction" by Lieut. Robert E. Peary, two illus. in color, frontis. and facing p. 574, by L.

88 Carlson, Raymond, ed. *Gallery of Western Painting*. McGraw-Hill, N.Y. etc., (1951), words "First Edition" on copyright page, cloth with illus. in color mounted on the front cover, colored endsheets, 85 pp., foreword, 76 illus. including seven in color by L. (Dixon, Remington, Russell, Santee)

89 Clark, Thomas D. *Frontier America: The Story of the Westward Movement*. Scribner's, N.Y., 1959, code letter "A" on copyright page, cloth, d/w illus. by L.

90 (Collier.) *The Lion's Mouth, 1903*. P. F. Collier & Son, N.Y., 1902, decor. wraps, 48 pp., numerous illus. including one, p. 38, by L. (Remington)

91 Dobie, J. Frank. *Guide to Life and Literature of the Southwest*. The University of Texas Press, Austin, Texas, 1943, wraps, 111 pp., numerous illus. including one, p. 73, by L. (Borein, Bugbee, Dunton, Hurd, James, Lea, Russell, Santee)

92 ———. Same, Southern Methodist University Press, Dallas, 1952, cloth, tinted end sheets, 222 pp., brown top, preface, index, nineteen illus. including one, p. 81, by L. (Bugbee, Lea, Russell, Thomason)

93 ——— et al. *Mustangs and Cow Horses*. Texas Folklore Society, Austin, 1940, fabricoid, 429 pp., numerous illus. including two, pp. (67) and 374, by L. (Bugbee, James, Lea, Russell, Santee, Thomason)

94 Downey, Fairfax. *Indian Fighting Army*. Scribner's, 1941, code letter "A" on copyright page, cloth, 329 pp., 43 illus. including one, facing p. 210, by L. (Remington, Schreyvogel)

95 (Eberstadt.) *Americana* (Catalogue 132). Edward Eberstadt & Sons, N.Y., (1953), pic. wraps, 128 pp., 25 illus. including one, front cover, by L. (Remington)

96 ———. *Americana* (Catalogue 135). Edward Eberstadt & Sons, N.Y., (1954), pic. wraps, 160 pp., 42 illus. including one, facing p. 96, by L. (Remington)

97 Eliot, Alexander. *Three Hundred Years of American Painting*. Time, Inc., N.Y., 1957, morocco and cloth, 318 pp., acknowledgments, "Introduction" by John Walker, appendices, bibliography, index, numerous illus. including one, p. 104, by L. (Hurd, Remington, Russell)

98 Elman, Robert (selected and text by). *The Great American Shooting Prints*. A Ridge Press Book, Knopf, N.Y., 1972, cloth, tan endsheets, unpaged, "Introduction" by Hermann Warner Williams, Jr.,

catalogue of the plates, 72 numbered plates in color including no. 34, "Hunting Mountain Sheep," by L. (Goodwin, Miller, Remington, Russell)

99 Ferris, Robert G. (series editor). *Soldier and Brave* (The National Survey of Historic Sites and Buildings, vol. XII, new edition). National Park Service, Washington, D.C., 1971, cloth, pic. endsheets, 453 pp., "Foreword" by Secretary Rogers C. B. Morton, "Preface" by George B. Hartzog, Jr. (Director), suggested reading, index, numerous illus. including one, p. 188, by L. (Eggenhofer, Miller, Remington, Russell, Schreyvogel)

99a Fronval, George. *La Veritable Histoire Des Indiens Peaux-Rouges.* Fernand Nathan, Paris, France, (1973), cloth, pic. front endsheet, map back endsheet, 125 pp., numerous illus. including two in color, pp. 43 and 54, by L. (Koerner, Miller, Remington, Schreyvogel, Von Schmidt, Zogbaum)

100 Frost, Lawrence A. *The Custer Album: A Pictorial Biography of General George A. Custer.* Superior, Seattle, 1964, words "First Edition" on copyright page, cloth, 192 pp., numerous illus. including one, p. (12), by L. (Remington, Schreyvogel)

100a Getlein, Frank et al. *The Lure of the Great West.* Country Beautiful, Waukesha, Wisconsin, (1973), boards, 352 pp., introduction, 375 illus. including three in color, pp. 288, 289 and 290, by L. (Blumenschein, Koerner, Miller, Remington, Russell, Schreyvogel, Wyeth)

101 *Gilcrease Institute of American History and Art: A National Treasury.* Gilcrease, Tulsa, wraps, illus. including one by L. (Remington, Russell)

102 (Gilcrease.) *Gift Shop Catalog.* Tulsa, n.d., pic. wraps, unpaged, numerous illus. including two by L. (Borein, Remington, Russell)

103 ————. *Gift Shop Catalog.* Tulsa, (1973), pic. wraps, unpaged, numerous illus. including two by L. (Remington, Russell)

104 Good, Donnie D. and Traphagen, John C. *W. R. Leigh: The Artist's Studio Collection.* Gilcrease, Tulsa, 1968, pic. wraps, unpaged, numerous illus. by L.

105 Grey, Zane. *The Vanishing American.* Harper, N.Y., 1925, decor. cloth, 308 pp., (4) of advs., illus., d/w illus. in color by L.

106 Harmsen, Dorothy. *Harmsen's Western Americana.* Northland Press, Flagstaff, (1971), morocco and cloth, blue endsheets, 213 pp., "Foreword" by Robert Rockwell, introduction, selected bibliography, num-

erous illus. including one in color, p. (123), by L. and a biographical sketch of him. Limited edition of 150 numbered copies signed by the author, slipcase with morocco title label. (Beeler, Blumenschein, Borein, Dixon, Dunn, Dunton, Eggenhofer, Elwell, Hurd, Johnson, Marchand, Miller, Russell, Von Schmidt, Wyeth)

107 ————. Same, first trade edition in two-tone cloth and with red endsheets.

108 Harris, Burton et al. *Yellowstone Country.* Gilcrease, Tulsa, (1963), pic. wraps, 57 (1) pp., numerous illus. including one in color, p. (46), by L. (Goodwin, James, Russell)

109 Herr, Major General John K. and Wallace, Edward S. *The Story of the U. S. Cavalry.* Little, Brown, Boston, (1953), words "First Edition" on copyright page, cloth, yellow endsheets, 275 pp., author's note, "Foreword" by General Jonathan M. Wainwright, bibliography, numerous illus. including one, the d/w in color, by L. (Remington, Schreyvogel, Zogbaum)

110 Holme, Bryan (compiled and edited by). *Pictures to Live With.* N.Y., (1959), words "First published in 1959 by The Viking Press" on copyright page, decor. cloth, 152 pp., index to artists, numerous illus. including two, pp. 76 and 77, by L. (Johnson, Miller, Remington, Schreyvogel)

110a Holloway, David. *Lewis and Clark and the Crossing of North America.* Saturday Review Press, N.Y., 1974, cloth, pic. endsheets, 224 pp., "Introduction" by V. E. Fuchs, author's note, selected bibliography, index, maps, numerous illus. including two, pp. 98 and (148), by L. (Miller, Remington, Russell)

111 Horan, James D. *The Great American West.* Crown Pub., N.Y., (1959), cloth and boards, 288 pp., introduction, bibliography, picture credits, index, 650 illus. including one, after p. 16, by L. (Marchand, Remington, Russell, Schreyvogel)

112 Horne, Chas. F. *The Story of the American People.* National Alumni, N.Y., n.d., decor. fabricoid, 2 vols. vol. 1, 465 pp., introduction, appendix, index, numerous illus. including one, facing p. 365, by L., maps. (Remington, Schoonover)

113 Hunt, David C. *W. R. Leigh, Portfolio of an American Artist.* Gilcrease, Tulsa, (1966), pic. wraps, unpaged, numerous illus. by L.

114 Kain, Robert C. *In the Valley of the Little Big Horn, the 7th and the Sioux.* Privately printed for the author (Newfane, Vt., 1969), cloth, 128 pp., preface, illus. including one, p. 91, by L.

115 King, William Nephew. *The Story of the Spanish American War and the Revolt in the Philippines.* P. F. Collier, 1899, oblong morocco and decor. cloth. 248 pp., preface. "Introduction for the Navy" by Capt. Robley D. Evans, "Introduction for the Army" by Major General O. O. Howard, numerous illus. including one, p. 123, by L. (Deming)

116 Leckie, William H. *The Military Conquest of the Southern Plains.* Oklahoma, Norman, (1963), words "First edition" on copyright page, cloth, 269 pp., red top, preface, bibliography, index, maps, 21 illus. including one, between pp. 84 and 85, by L. (Remington)

117 Lefevre, Edwin. *The Golden Flood.* McClure, Phillips & Co., N.Y., 1905, words "Published, April, 1905" on copyright page, decor. cloth, 198 (1) pp., four illus., frontis. and facing pp. 34, 74 and 192, by L.

118 Leigh, W. R. *Painting the Backgrounds for the African Hall Groups.* Reprinted from *Natural History* 27:6, 1927, wraps, pp. 575-582, frontis. in color by L. and a group photo including him.

119 ———. *A Night with an African Herder.* Reprinted from *Natural History* 29:4, 1929, wraps, pp. (380)-391, eight illus. pp. 381, 383, 384, 385, 387, 388, 389 and 390, by L.

120 ———. *The Western Pony.* Huntington Press, N.Y., (1933), words "First Edition" on copyright page, cloth, with gilt horsehead on morocco mounted on front cover, 116 pp., gilt top, "Foreword" by James L. Clark, introduction, author's note, publisher's note, 24 illus. incuding six in color by L. (Reprinted by another publisher in 1935 but the color plates did not equal those in the first edition.)

121 ———. *Frontiers of Enchantment.* Simon & Schuster, N.Y., 1938, cloth, map on endsheets, 299 pp., "Note about the Author," tinted top, drawings by L.

122 Logue, Roscoe. *Under Texas and Border Skies.* Russell Stationery Co., Amarillo, Texas, 1935, pic. wraps, 111 pp., "By Way of Explanation" by Horace M. Russell, introduction, numerous illus. including one, facing p. 44, by L.

123 London, Jack. *When God Laughs and Other Stories.* Macmillan, N.Y., 1911, words "Published January, 1911" on copyright page, decor. cloth, 319 pp., (4) of advs., six illus. including two, facing pp. 32 and 38, by L.

124 (Macmillan.) *The Monthly List of New Macmillian Books.* No. 137. N.Y., 1911, numerous illus. including one by L.

124a McCracken, Harold. *The American Cowboy.* Doubleday, Garden City, N.Y., 1973, words "Limited Edition" on copyright page, simulated leather, marbled endsheets, 196 pp., all edges gilt, references, index, numerous illus. including one, the frontis., in color, by L. 300 numbered and signed copies, slipcase. (Borein, Cisneros, Eggenhofer, Johnson, Koerner, Lea, Remington, Russell, Wyeth)

124b ———.Same, trade edition with words "First edition after the limited edition of 300 copies" on copyright page, cloth and pic. colored d/w by L.

125 McMurray, Floyd I. *West Bound.* Scribner's, (1943), code letter "A" on copyright page, decor. cloth, decor. endsheets, 394 pp., index, illus. including one, p. (257), by L.

126 Monaghan, Jay. (editor-in-chief). *The Book of the American West.* Julian Messner, N.Y., (1963), words "First Edition" on copyright page, pic. cloth, tan endsheets, 608 pp., introduction, suggestions for additional reading, index, about the editor-in-chief and authors, numerous illus. including three, pp. (82), (434-5) and 592, by L. (Borein, Johnson, Koerner, Lungren, Remington, Russell, Schreyvogel)

127 Nolan, Frederick W., ed. *The English Westerners Brand Book,* vol. III. The English Westerners, New Brighton, Cheshire, England, Nov. 1956–Oct. 1957, mimeographed p. (247), illus. including poor reproductions of Leigh drawings. (Remington, Russell)

127a *100 of the World's Most Beautiful Paintings.* N.Y., (1966), cloth or pic. boards, unpaged, no. 35 by L. (Remington)

128 Pomeroy, Daniel E. *The Complete Book of African Hall.* The American Museum of Natural History, N.Y., 1936, boards with decor. title label on the front cover, grey endsheets, 99 pp., numerous illus. including ten backgrounds of exhibit groups, pp. (12-13), (14), (15), 16, (36), (38), (40), (44), 82-83) and (84-85) by L. and photos of him.

129 Quick, Herbert. *Virginia of the Air Lanes.* Bobbs-Merrill, Indianapolis, (1909), word "October" on copyright page, cloth, 424 pp., five illus., frontis. and facing pp. 14, 18, 74 and 266, by L.

130 Rachlis, Eugene. *Indians on the Plains.* American Heritage Pub. Co., N.Y., (1960), pic. cloth and endsheets, 132 (1) pp., "Foreword" by John C. Ewers, acknowledgments, picture credits, bibliography, index, numerous illus. including one in color, p. 126, by L.

131 Riegel, Robert E. and Haugh, Helen. *United States of America.* Scribner's, (1949), code letter "A" on copyright page, buckram, 852 pp., preface, index, numerous illus. including one, p. 458, by L. (James, Rowe)

132 Roe, Frank Gilbert. *The Indian and the Horse.* University of Okla. Press, Norman, 1955, words "First Edition" on copyright page, cloth, 434 pp., preface, introduction, appendices, bibliography, index, 31 illus. including one, between pp. 302 and 303, by L.

133 Rossi, Paul A. and Hunt, David C. *The Art of the Old West* (from the Collection of the Gilcrease Institute). (Knopf, N.Y., but printed in Italy, 1971), words "First Edition" on copyright page, pic. cloth, pic. brown endsheets, 335 (1) pp., preface, listing of artists and works, bibliography, numerous illus. including twenty-three by L. (Blumenschein, Borein, James, Miller, Remington, Russell, Schreyvogel, Wyeth)

134 *The Rugged Spirit of the Golden West* (as seen through the eyes of an artist-descendent of Pocohontas). Reprinted from *Think Magazine,* February 1951, folder, eleven illus. by L.

135 (Santa Fe Railway.) *Dinner Aboard the Super Chief,* n.d., folder (menu) with illus. in color on front cover by L.

136 Schmedding, Joseph. *Cowboy and Indian Trader.* Caxton Printers, Caldwell, Idaho, 1951, pic. cloth, map endsheets, 364 pp., acknowledgment, foreword, illus., one, facing p. 225, by L.

137 Severy, Merle, ed. et al. *America's History Lands.* National Geographic Society, Wash., D.C., (Lakeside Press, Chicago, 1962), words "First Printing" on copyright page, two-tone decor. cloth, pic. front endsheets, 576 pp., "Foreword" by Melville Bell Grosvenor, "Introduction" by Conrad L. Wirth, index for reference, 676 illus. (463 in full color) including one, pp. 510-11, by L. (Remington, Russell, Schreyvogel)

137a Seymour, Peter, ed. *The West That Was.* Hallmark Crown Editions, (Kansas City, Mo., 1973), fabricoid, pic. endsheets, 76 (1) pp., introduction, numerous illus. including one in color, p. 69, by L. (Remington, Russell, Wyeth)

137b Steadman, William E. et al. *The West and Walter Bimson.* The University of Arizona Museum of Art, Tucson, (1971), decor. cloth, pic. endsheets, 223 (2) pp., "Foreword" by President Richard A. Harvill, introduction, numerous illus. including one in color, p.

109, by L. (Beeler, Johnson, Remington, Russell, Schoonover, Wyeth)

138 Stewart, Edgar I. *Custer's Luck.* Oklahoma, Norman, (1955), words "First Edition" on copyright page, cloth, 506 pp., maps, illus. including one, facing p. 433, by L.

139 Taft, Robert. *The Pictorial Record of the Old West, XIII: The End of a Century.* Reprinted from *The Kansas Historical Quarterly,* August, 1951, pic wraps, pp. 225-253, illus. including one between pp. 240 and 241, by L., photo of Leigh between pp. 248 and 249. (Blumenschein, Schreyvogel)

140 ———.*Artists and Illustrators of the Old West.* Scribner's, 1953, code letter "A" on copyright page, cloth, map endsheets, 399 pp., preface and acknowledgments, sources and notes, index, 90 numbered illus. including one, no. 90, by L. (Blumenschein, Remington, Schreyvogel)

141 Thompson, Holland, ed. *The Book of Texas.* The Grolier Society, Dallas, (1929), decor. blue-fabricoid, blue endsheets, 384 pp., gilt top, numerous illus. including one, p. 77, by L. The Book of Knowledge, vol. xxi, The Lone Star Edition.

142 Ward, Baldwin G., ed. *Year's Pictorial History of America.* (Year, Inc., Los Angeles, 1954), cloth and boards, 417 (17) pp., "Foreword" by Allan Nevins, publisher's note, index, 2500 illus. including one, p. 15, by L., fifty-five historical maps in color. (Marchand, Remington, Russell)

143 Wellman, Paul I. *Death on the Prairie.* Pyramid Books, N.Y., 1963, colored pic. wraps, with a detail from "Custer's Last Fight" by L. on the front cover.

144 White, Anne Terry. *Indians and the Old West.* Simon and Schuster, (1958), pic. boards, 56 pp., all edges red, numerous illus. including two, pp. 24-5 and 38-9, by L. (Lea, Remington, Russell, Schreyvogel)

145 White, William Allen. *Stratagems and Spoils.* Scribner's, 1901, cloth, 289 pp., preface, six illus. including two, facing pp. 54 and 74, by L. (Keller)

146 Willetts, Gibson et al. *Workers of the Nation.* P. F. Collier and Son, 1903, 2 vols., cloth with paper labels, 1104 pp. (continuous pagination), preface, appendix, index, 66 illus. including two, frontis. in vol. II and facing p. 530, by L. (Remington)

147 Williams, Jesse Lynch. *New York Sketches.* Scribner's, 1902, words "Published, November, 1902" on copyright page, cloth, 133 pp., numerous illus. including four, pp. (11), (17), (91) and 93, by L.

148 Wyckoff, Walter A. *The Workers: An Experiment in Reality (The West)*. Scribner's, 1898, cloth, 378 pp., thirty-two full-page plates, not included in pagination, by L.

The Artist and His Art

149 "America's 'Sagebrush' Rembrandt," an article in *Today's Art*, vol. 3, no. 2, February, 1955, Bader's, St. Louis, Mo., with four illus. by L.

150 Branch, Douglas. "The American Cowboy," an illus. article in *The Mentor*, July, 1927, with one illus. by L. (Dunton, Remington, Russell)

151 "Crazy Over Horses," an illus. article in *Time*, April 20, 1953 with two illus. in color by L.

152 Dykes, Jeff C. *High Spots in Western Illustrating*. (The Kansas City Posse, The Westerners, 1964), cloth, 30 pp., introduction, two illus. High Spots nos. 53, 63 and 83 are included in the entries above. Edition ltd. to 250 numbered, signed copies. (An edition in wraps was distributed to the members of The Posse.)

153 *The Farm*, Winter 1964–65 includes a biographical sketch of Leigh and seven illus. in color by him.

154 *Fashion Digest*, Spring–Summer 1962 includes three illus. by L. and a group photo including him.

155 *The Gund Collection of Western Art*, Squibb Gallery, Princeton, N.J., March 9–16, 1973, pic. wraps, unpaged, describes two paintings in the Collection by L. (Remington)

156 Same, an illus. article in *Squibbline* 8:2, March 1973, with one illus. by L. (Remington)

157 Hinshaw, Merton E. *Painters of the West*. Charles W. Bowers Memorial Museum, Santa Ana, Calif., 1972, includes brief biography of L.

158 Hoeber, Arthur. "Painters of Western Life," an illus. article in *The Mentor* 3:9, June 15, 1915, with one illus. by L. and with a Mentor Gravure of his "An Argument with the Sheriff" laid in. (Blumenschein, Dunton, Remington, Russell, Schreyvogel)

159 "Isochromatic Exhibit to be Uniform in Sizes, Frames, Pigments," an article in *The Art Digest* 10:5, Dec. 1, 1935 with one illus. by L.

160 Kelly, Tim J. "He Took Art to the Market Place," an illus. article about Read Mullan in *Arizona Highways*, November 1962, with one illus. by L. (Dixon, Johnson, Remington)

161 Kennedy, Michael. "W. R. Leigh, Sagebrush Rembrandt," an illus. article in *Montana* 6:1, Winter 1956, with fourteen illus. by L. and a photo of him.

162 Krakel, Dean. *W. R. Leigh*. Thomas Gilcrease Institute of American History and Art, (Tulsa, Oklahoma), 1964, folder with Leigh drawing on front cover.

163 ———. "Mr. Leigh and His Work," an illus. article on the acquisition of the Leigh Studio Collection by Gilcrease in *Montana*, Summer 1967, with numerous illus. by L. and photos of him.

164 *La Revue Moderne Des Arts et de La Vie*, Paris, October 1954, biographical sketch of L. and front cover plus three illus. in text by him.

165 Same, Janvier 1957, biographical sketch of L., a photo of him and the cover plus one illus. in text by him.

166 Leigh, W. R. *Clipt Wings*. Thorton W. Allen Co., N.Y., 1930, cloth with paper labels, 159 pp., "Shakespeare, Man-Mask-Myth" by Henry W. Wack, portrait of Leigh as frontispiece.

167 McCraken, Harold. *Portrait of the Old West*. McGraw-Hill, (1952), words "First Edition" on copyright page, decor. cloth, 232 pp., special acknowledgment, preface, "Foreword" by R. W. G. Vail, Biographical Check List of Western Artists, index, numerous illustrations. Leigh mentioned in text, p. 170, and biographical sketch, p. 223 (Remington, Russell, Schreyvogel)

168 "Master of the Old West," an illus. article about Leigh in *True*, September 1956, with six illus. in color by him.

169 "Paintings by Leigh," an illus. article in *Arizona Highways*, February 1948 with an autobiographical sketch by L., a photo of him and eleven illus. by him.

170 *Representational Art by Contemporary American Artists*, Gilcrease, Tulsa, No. 14–Dec. 16, 1957, folder, includes a brief biographical sketch of L.

171 Richardson, T. C. "Texas Cattle," an illus. article in *American Heritage* 4:1, Fall 1952, with a double-page plate in color by L.

172 Ryan, Marie B. *The Sketch Book of Kappa Pi*, Spring 1956, Kearney, Nebraska, includes a biographical sketch of L., a photo of him and seven illus. by him.

173 *The West Virginia Hillbilly* 8:25, June 24, 1967, Richwood, West Virginia, includes "W. R. Leigh," a brief article about the artist and reproduces on the front cover a painting by him.

174 *Who's Who, The Monthly Supplement*, December 1955, wraps, pp. (1761)-1785, cumulative index, includes biography of Leigh, pp. 1783-1784.

ON THE WAY TO FORT WINGATE by Lungren from *Stories Retold from St. Nicholas*

FERNAND HARVEY LUNGREN
1859–1932

Catalogues of Art Exhibitions and Galleries

AMERICAN WATERCOLOR SOCIETY, NEW YORK

1 *Illustrated Catalogue of 29th Annual Exhibition,* 1895, pic. wraps, 42 pp., (4) of advs., numerous illus. including one, facing p. 28, by L.

COUNTY NATIONAL BANK AND TRUST COMPANY
SANTA BARBARA

2 *Exhibit of Painting by Fernand Lungren, 1857–1932,* n.d., wraps, photo of Lungren before his large oil, "In the Abyss" and lists 26 of his pictures exhibited in the Bank.

GREENFIELD GALLERIES, SEATTLE

3 *American Western Art Auction,* Oct. 28, 1972, pic. wraps, 58 pp., numerous illus. including one, p. 20, by L. (Borein, Deming, Remington, Russell, Schreyvogel)

HAMMER GALLERIES, NEW YORK

4 *The Works of Charles M. Russell and Other Western Artists,* November 1962, pic. wraps, 56 pp., introduction, numerous illus. including one, p. 49, by L. (Crawford, Goodwin, Leigh, Miller, Remington, Russell)

KENNEDY GALLERIES, NEW YORK

5 *The Western Legend,* 1965, pic. wraps, 20 pp., "In the History of our History," numerous illus. including one, p. 7, by L. (Borein, Deming, Remington, Russell)

6 *Tradition and Change,* December 1963, colored pic. wraps, pp. 68-112, introduction, numerous illus. including one, p. 69, by L. (Koerner, Leigh, Remington, Russell, Schreyvogel)

7 *American Sports and Sportsmen,* 1968, colored pic. wraps, 48 pp., forty-five illus. including one, p. 6, by L. (Goodwin, Remington)

8 *Walking Westward,* March 1972, colored pic. wraps, pp. 196-256, introduction, numerous illus. including one, p. 200, by L. (Johnson, Miller, Remington, Russell, Schreyvogel)

MONTANA HISTORICAL SOCIETY, HELENA

9 *An Art Perspecitve of the Historical Pacific Northwest* (from the Collection of Dr. and Mrs. Franz R. Stenzel, Portland, Oregon), August 1963, wraps, 32 pp., numerous illus. including one, p. 14, by L. (Dixon, Remington, Russell)

MUSEUM OF ART, SMITH COLLEGE
NORTHAMPTON, MASSACHUSETTS

10 *Catalog Supplement,* 1941, wraps, includes one illus., "Landscape," by L.

NATIONAL ACADEMY OF DESIGN, NEW YORK

11 *Illustrated Catalogue Seventy-First Annual Exhibition,* 1896, pic. wraps, 104 pp., (4) of advs., numerous illus. including one, p. (84). "The Snake Dance," by L. and he is listed as a member, p. 92. (Remington)

PENNSYLVANIA ACADEMY OF FINE ARTS,
PHILADELPHIA

12 *Catalogue of the 106th Annual Exhibition,* 1911, numerous illus. including one, "Above Timber Line: A Snow Squall," by L.

Illustrated by the Artist

13 Andrews, E. Benjamin. *The History of the Last Quarter-Century in the United States, 1870–1895.* Scribner's, N.Y., 1896, 2 vols., decor. cloth, pp. 390 and 409, gilt tops, preface (I), index (II), with over 350 illus. including one, p. 365 (I), by L. (Leigh)

14 ———. *The United States in Our Times.* Scribner's,

1903, decor. cloth, 961 pp., gilt top, index, numerous illus. including one, p. 365, by L. (Leigh)

14a Baird, Joseph A., Jr. (compiled by). *The West Remembered.* California Historical Society, San Francisco and San Marino, 1973, colored pic. wraps, 88 pp., "Foreword" by Mitchell A. Wilder, introduction, numerous illus. including one in color, p. (51), by L. (Blumenschein, Borein, Dixon, James, Marchand, Miller, Remington, Russell, Zogbaum)

15 Barstow, Charles L., ed. *The Westward Movement.* Century, N.Y., 1912, words "Published April, 1912" on copyright page, decor. cloth, 231 pp., index, numerous illus. including two, pp. 47 and (53), by L. (Remington)

16 Berger, John A. *Announcing the Publication of Fernand Lungren: A Biography.* (The Schauer Press, Santa Barbara, Calif., 1936), leaflet, photos of Lungren, with a color print "Desert Dawn," by L. and an order blank laid in.

17 ———. *Fernand Lungren.* The Schauer Press, Santa Barbara, California, 1936, cloth with paper label, 347 pp., "Foreword," by Stewart Edward White, nineteen (three in color) illus. by L.

18 Brooks, Elbridge S. *The Century Book for Young Americans.* Century, N.Y., (1894), pic. cloth with lettering on spine in red, 249 pp., "Introduction," by Horace Porter, numerous illus. including one, p. 6, by L. (Remington)

19 ———. *The Century Book of the Colonies.* Century, (1900), pic. cloth, 233 pp., "Introduction" by Frederic J. De Peyster, index, numerous illus. including two, pp. 120 and 225, by L.

20 Browning, Mrs. E. B. et al. *Heroines of the Poets.* D. Lothrop and Co., Boston, (1886 but received by the L. C. on Dec. 14, 1885), decor. leather, floral endsheets, 182 (1) pp., all edges gilt, fifteen full-page plates by L.

21 Dimitry, John et al. *Stories Retold from St. Nicholas.* Century, 1905, pic. cloth, 179 pp., publisher's note, numerous illus. including two, pp. 104 and 109, by L. (Remington)

22 Embree, Charles Fleming. *For the Love of Tonita.* Herbert S. Stone & Co., Chicago and N.Y., 1897, pic. cloth, 265 pp., (15) of advs., gilt top, front cover illus. by L.

23 Harland, Marion, ed. *Character Sketches of Romance, Fiction and the Drama.* Selmar Hess, N.Y., 1892, ¾ morocco and cloth, marbled endsheets, (vol. 1), 408 pp., all edges red, preface, numerous illus. including one, facing p. 90, by L.

24 (Harvey.) *The Great Southwest.* Fred Harvey, Kansas City, Mo., (1914), oblong wraps, with illus in color mounted on front cover, no pagination, numerous illus. including one in color, "Arizona Afterglow," by L.

25 Higgins, C. A. *Grand Canyon of the Colorado River, Arizona.* Chicago, 1893, oblong wraps, 31 pp., numerous illus. including one by L.

26 Hornung, Clarence P. *Wheels Across America.* A. S. Barnes & Co., N.Y., (1959), decor. cloth, pic. endsheets, 341 pp., foreword, over 1100 illus. including one, p. 20, by L. (Remington)

27 Irving, Washington et al. *The Discovery and Conquest of the New World.* Conquest Pub. Co., Cincinnati, 1899, pic. cloth, colored map endsheets, 923 pp., "Preface and Introduction" by Murat Halstead, maps, nearly 600 illus. including five, pp. 135, 213, 255, 287 and 385, by L.

28 Jensen, Lee. *The Pony Express.* Grossett and Dunlap, N.Y., (1955), boards, 154 pp., brown top, acknowledgments, picture credits, numorus illus. including one, p. 110, by L. (Remington)

29 Ladd, Horatio O. *The Story of New Mexico.* Lothrop, Boston, 1891, cloth, illustrated including one by L.

30 Latendorf, E. Walter. *Catalogue No. 27.* Mannados Bookshop, N.Y., n.d., pic. wraps, 36 (2) pp., numerous illus. including one, p. 22, by L. (Eggenhofer, Goodwin, Lea)

31 Mabie, Hamilton Wright et al. *Book of Nature and Outdoor Life* (part 2). The University Society, N.Y., (1912), decor. cloth and endsheets, 416 pp., numerous illus. including two, pp. 65 and 69, by L. (Remington, Rowe)

32 Miller, Joaquin et al. *Western Frontier Stories Retold from St. Nicholas.* Century, 1907, pic. cloth, 198 pp., illus. including one, p. 152, by L. (Remington)

33 Monaghan, Jay (editor-in-chief). *The Book of The American West.* Julian Messner, N.Y., (1963), words "First Edition" on copyright page, pic. cloth, tan endsheets, 608 pp., introduction, suggestions for additional reading, index; about the editor-in-chief and the authors, numerous illus. including one, p. (93), by L. (Borein, Johnson, Koerner, Leigh, Remington, Russell, Schreyvogel)

34 Munroe, Kirk. *The Painted Desert.* Harper, N.Y. and London, 1897, pic. cloth, 274 pp., twenty illus. by L.

ILLUSTRATION by Lungren from *The Pass*

35 Parrish, Randall. *The Great Plains*. McClurg, Chicago, 1907, words "Published September 14, 1907" on copyright page, pic. cloth, 399 pp., preface, note of acknowledgment, index, illus. including five drawings on two plates, facing pp. 136 and 220, by L. (Remington)

36 Pennell, Joseph. *Pen Drawings and Pen Draughtsmen* (Their Work and Their Methods, A Story of the Art To-day with Technical Suggestions). Macmillan, London and N.Y., 1889, boards, 318 pp., preface, index, 158 illus. including one, p. (225), by L. and with comments on his art, p. 224. (Remington)

37 Porter, Bruce et al. *Art in California*. R. L. Bernier, San Francisco, 1916, cloth and boards, tan endsheets, 183 (1) pp., gilt top, introduction, indices, 332 numbered plates including no. 10 by L. (Dixon)

38 *Portfolio of Reproductions of Oil Paintings and Etchings by Famous Artists of Santa Barbara*. N.d., twenty-one full color reproductions including one, "A Santa Ynez River Wash," by L. (Borein)

39 Spaulding, Edward Selden (compiled by). *Adobe Days Along the Channel*. (The Schauer Printing Studio, Santa Barbara), 1957, pic. buckram, pic. endsheets, 124 (2) pp., "Foreword," by Harold Schauer, sources, numerous illus. incuding one, in color, facing p. 108, by L. (Borein)

40 ———. *A Brief Story of Santa Barbara*. Santa Barbara Historical Society, Santa Barbara, 1964, illus. including one by L. (De Yong, Borein)

41 ———. *Santa Barbara, 1895–1925, As Seen by a Boy*. Santa Barbara, 1966, illus. including one by L. (Borein)

42 Thackeray, William Makepeace. *The Chronicle of the Drum*. Scribner's, 1882, decor. cloth, 70 pp., all edges gilt, thirty-two illus. including three, pp. 6, 17 and 19, by L.

43 Wallace, Andrew. *The Image of Arizona: Pictures from the Past*. New Mexico, Albuquerque, 1971, cloth, pic. endsheets, 254 p., bibliography, index, numerous illus. including one by L. (Dixon, Remington, Zogbaum)

44 Welch, Charles et al. *Historic Tales and Golden Deeds* (vol. I). The University Society, N.Y. and The After School Club of America, Philadelphia, (1912), decor. cloth and endsheets, 208 pp., numerous illus. including three, pp. 160, 161 and 162, by L.

45 Westermeier, Clifford P. *Colorado's First Portrait: Scenes by Early Artists*. New Mexico, Albuquerque, 1970, words "First Edition" on copyright page, cloth, pic. endsheets, 206 pp., preface, numerous illus. including one by L. (Remington, Zogbaum)

46 White, Stewart Edward. *The Mountains*. McClure, Phillips & Co., N.Y., 1904, words "Published October, 1904" on copyright page, pic. cloth, 282 pp., frontis. in color and fifteen other full-page illus. by L.

47 ———. Same, first British edition, issued by Hodder and Stoughton, London, 1904.

48 ———. *The Pass*. The Outing Publishing Co., N.Y., 1906, pic. cloth, 198 pp., illus. with a frontis. in color by L. and with photos.

49 ———. *Camp and Trail*. The Outing Publishing Co., 1907, pic. cloth, 236 pp., illus. with a frontis. in color by L. and with photos.

The Artist and His Art

50 Bolton, Theodore. *American Book Illustrators: Bibliographic Check List of 123 Artists*. R. R. Bowker Co., 1938, cloth, 290 pp., introduction, index. Bolton lists four Lungren items, p. 106.

51 *Catalogue of the Art Collection of the St. Louis Exposition and Music Hall Association Tenth Annual Exhibition*. St. Louis, 1893, wraps, lists 38 paintings by L.

52 Darling, Jim, ed. *Brand Book II, The San Diego Corral, The Westerners*. (1971), brand decor, fabricoid, tan endsheets, 195 pp., includes "The Western Artist, His Role in History" by Donald A. Stevning with a mention of Lungren. (Miller, Remington, Russell)

53 Dykes, Jeff C. *High Spots in Western Illustrating*. (The Kansas City Posse, The Westerners, 1964), cloth, 30 pp., introduction, two illus. High spots 35 and 55 are illus. by L. Edition limited to 250 numbered, signed copies. (The Posse issued an edition in wraps to the members.)

54 Gidney, C. M. et al. *History of Santa Barbara, San Luis Obispo, and Ventura Counties*. The Lewis Publishing Co., Chicago, 1917, morocco and cloth, decor. endsheets, 873 pp., decor. edges, illus., contains a biographical sketch of L.

54a Perkins, Edith Forbes. *Letters and Journals, 1908–1925*. Printed at The Riverside Press (Cambridge) for private distribution, 1931, four volumes, edited by Edith Perkins Cunningham (the author's daughter), records contacts with Lungren, vol. I, pp. 29 and 72.

55 Taft, Robert. *The End of the Century: The Pictorial

Record of the Old West (XIII). Reprinted from *The Kansas Historical Quarterly*, Topeka, August, 1951, pic. wraps, pp. 225–53, illus. including a photo of Lungren working on his painting, "In the Abyss," between pp. 240 and 241. (Blumenschein, Dixon, Leigh, Remington, Russell, Schreyvogel)

56 ———. *Artists and Illustrators of the Old West: 1850–1900*. Scribner's, N.Y., London, 1953, code letter "A" on copyright page, decor. cloth, map endsheets, 400 pp., preface and acknowledgments, sources and notes, index, 72 pp. of illus., Lungren's art discussed in text.

SEATS OF THE MIGHTY by Lungren from *Fernand Lungren: A Biography*

RIDIN' HARD by Marchand from *Harmsen's Western Americana*

JOHN N. MARCHAND
1875–1921

Catalogues of Art Exhibitions and Galleries

KENNEDY GALLERIES, NEW YORK

1 *Recent Acquisitions in Important Western and Sporting Paintings and Sculptures,* October 1962, wraps with illus. in color mounted on front cover, pp. 51–108, introduction, numerous illus. including one, p. 75, by M. (Borein, Johnson, Leigh, Miller, Remington, Russell, Schreyvogel)

2 *Exhibition of Western Paintings,* October 1964, colored pic. wraps, 64 pp., introduction, numerous illus. including one, p. 39, by M. (Johnson, Leigh, Remington, Russell, Schreyvogel)

3 *An Artist's Gazetteer: Beyond the Mississippi,* June 1971, colored pic. wraps, 64 pp., numerous illus. including two, pp. 48 and 50, by M. (Borein, Remington, Russell, Schreyvogel)

E. WALTER LATENDORF, NEW YORK

4 *C. M. Russell,* Catalogue No. 27, (May 1957), pic. wraps, unpaged, numerous illus. including five by M. (Borein, Crawford, De Yong, Goodwin, Leigh)

MAXWELL GALLERIES, SAN FRANCISCO

4a *Art of the West,* November 14 through December 1973, colored pic. wraps, 48 pp., numerous illus. including one by M. (Johnson, Leigh, Miller)

RAINBOW HOTEL, GREAT FALLS, MONTANA
(ADVERTISING CLUB OF GREAT FALLS)

4b *Fifth Annual C. M. Russell Auction of Original Western Art,* March 16, 1973, pic. wraps, unpaged, lists 159 lots, numerous illus. including one, lot 61, by M. (Borein, De Yong, Johnson, Koerner, Russell, Wyeth)

Illustrated by the Artist

5 Ames, Merlin M. and Jesse H. *Homelands, America's Old World Backgrounds.* Webster Pub. Co., N.Y. etc., (1939), cloth, numerous illus. including one, p. 378, by M.

5a Baird, Joseph A., Jr. (compiled by). *The West Remembered.* California Historical Society, San Francisco and San Marino, 1973, colored pic. wraps, 88 pp., "Foreword" by Mitchell A. Wilder, introduction, numerous illus. including one, p. (34), by M. (Blumenschein, Borein, Dixon, James, Lungren, Miller, Remington, Russell, Zogbaum)

6 Barbour, A. Maynard. *At the Time Appointed.* Lippincott, Philadelphia and London, 1903, cloth, 371 pp., frontis. in color by Marchand.

7 Barker, Eugene C. et al. *The Growth of a Nation.* Row, Peterson and Co., Evanston, Ill. etc., (1928), decor. fabricoid, 287, xxxvi pp., preface, appendix, index, numerous illus. including one, p. 126, after a painting by M., maps.

8 Beach, Rex. *Pardners.* McClure, Phillips & Co., N.Y., 1905, cloth, 278 pp., frontis., 7 plates.

9 Belasco, David. *The Girl of the Golden West.* Dodd, Mead, N.Y., 1911, words "Published, Oct. 1911" on copyright page, cloth with illus. in color mounted on front cover, 346 pp., four illus. in color, frontis. and facing pp. 126, 254 and 334, by M.

10 Brady, Cyrus Townsend. *Border Fights and Fighters.* McClure, Phillips & Co., N.Y., 1902, words "Published October, 1902, N" on copyright page, pic. cloth, 382 pp., prefatory note, index, sixteen full-page illus. including three, frontispiece and facing pp. 250 and 300, by M., nine maps and plans.

11 ———. *Sir Henry Morgan, Buccaneer.* Dillingham, N.Y., (1903), words "Issued October 1903" on copyright page, pic. cloth, 444 (1) pp., red top, illus. including nine, frontis. (in color), and facing pp.

40, 89, 139, 215, 269, 333, 413 and 441, by M. (Crawford)

12 ———. *Three Daughters of the Confederacy.* Dillingham, N.Y., (1905), words "Issued September, 1905" on copyright page, decor. cloth, 440 pp., (8) of advs., preface, six illus. in color, frontis. and facing pp. 78, 114, 260, 306 and 372, by M. (A reprint by Dillingham retains only the frontis. by M.)

13 ———. *Northwestern Fights and Fighters.* The McClure Co., N.Y., 1907, pic. cloth, 373 pp., preface, acknowledgment, appendix, index, illus. including three, facing pp. 39, 230 and 247, by M., maps and plans.

14 ———. *South American Fights and Fighters.* Doubleday, Page, N.Y., 1910, words "Published, April, 1910" on copyright page, pic. cloth, 342 pp., preface, index, sixteen illus. including one, facing p. 248, by M.

15 ———. *As Sparks Fly Upward.* McClurg, Chicago, 1911, words "Published October, 1911" on copyright page, cloth, 386 pp., four illus. in color, frontis. and facing pp. 140, 182 and 348, by M.

16 ———. *Chalice of Courage.* Dodd, Mead, N.Y., 1912, words "Published February, 1912" on copyright page, cloth, 382 pp., preface, four illus. in color, frontis. and facing pp. 71, 157 and 354, by M.

17 Coolidge, Herbert. *Pancho McClish.* McClurg, Chicago, 1912, words "Published, October, 1912" on copyright page, cloth, 341 pp., four illus. in color, frontis. and facing pp. 6, 28 and 312, by M.

18 Coulomb, Charles A. *American History for Pennsylvania.* Macmillan, N.Y., 1933, words "Published August 1933" on copyright page, pic. cloth, 402, xxviii pp., preface, appendices, index, numerous illus. including one, p. (55), by M.

19 Dixon, Thomas. *The Southerner* (A Romance of the Real Lincoln). Grosset & Dunlap, N.Y., (1913), decor. cloth, 543 (1) pp., To the Reader, four illus., frontis. and facing pp. 252, 316 and 400, by M.

20 ———. *The Victim.* Appleton, N.Y. and London, 1914, code no. "(1)" follows last line of text, decor. cloth, 510 (1) pp., six illus., frontis. and facing pp. 48, 216, 310, 388 and 490, by M.

21 Freeman, Melville. *The Story of Our Republic.* F. A. Davis Co., Philadelphia, (1938), pic. cloth and endsheets, 431 pp., introduction, addenda, index, edited by Eston V. Tubbs, 334 illus. including one, p. 110, by M. (Deming)

22 Gabriel, Ralph Henry. *The Lure of the Frontier.* Yale University Press, New Haven, 1929, morocco and boards, decor. endsheets, 327 pp., gilt top, numerous illus. including one, p. 287, by M. The Liberty Bell Edition of *The Pageant of America*, vol. 2, limited to 1,500 numbered sets. (Deming, Dixon, Remington, Russell)

23 Garland, Hamlin. *Money Magic.* Harper, N.Y. and London, 1907, words "Published October, 1907" on copyright page, decor. cloth, 354 (1) pp., eight illus., frontis. and facing pp. 36, 108, 170, 222, 252, 332 and 352, by M.

24 ———. *Hesper.* Harper, N.Y. and London, (1912), words "Sunset Edition" on title page and code letters "L-M" on copyright page, cloth, 444 (1) pp., frontis. by M.

25 ———. *They of the High Trails.* Harper, N.Y. and London, (1916), words "Published April, 1916" and code letters "D-Q" on copyright page, cloth, 381 pp., illus. including one, facing p. 254, by M.

26 Gregory, Jackson. *The Outlaw.* Dodd, Mead, N.Y., 1916, cloth, 328 pp., four illus., frontis. and facing pp. 68, 150 and 300, by M. (Reprint by Burt in 1918 and 1922 with only a frontis. by M.)

27 Guillet, Edwin and Mary. *The Pathfinders of North America.* Macmillan of Canada, Toronto, 1939, pic. silver cloth, map endsheets, 304 pp., preface, index, 73 illus. including one, p. 126, by M. Reprinted in 1946, as above except in pic. cloth. (Remington)

28 Harding, Frank (compiled by). *A Livestock Heritage: Animals and People in Art.* (Shorthorn World Publication Co., Geneva, Ill., 1971), colored pic. wraps, unpaged, numerous illus. including one in color by M. (Borein, Dunn, Eggenhofer, Koerner, Remington, Russell, Wyeth)

29 Harmsen, Dorothy. *Harmsen's Western Americana.* Northland, Flagstaff, (1971), morocco and cloth, blue endsheets, 213 pp., "Foreword" by Robert Rockwell, introduction, selected bibliography, numerous illus. in color including one, p. (137), by M. and a biographical sketch of him. Limited edition of 150 numbered copies signed by the author, slipcase with morocco title label. (Borein, Blumenschein, Dixon, Dunn, Dunton, Eggenhofer, Elwell, Hurd, Johnson, Leigh, Miller, Russell, Von Schmidt, Wyeth)

30 ———. Same, first trade edition in two-tone cloth and with red endsheets.

31 Horan, James D. and Sann, Paul. *Pictorial History of the Wild West.* Crown, N.Y., (1954), cloth and

THE DISCOVERY OF THE GREAT FALLS by Marchand from *Pathfinders of the West*

boards, 254 pp., introduction, picture credits, bibliography, numerous illus. including one, p. 63, by M. (Remington)

32 ———. Same, first British edition issued by Spring Books, London, in 1954.

33 Horan, James D. *The Great American West.* Crown, N.Y., (1959), cloth and boards, 288 pp., introduction, bibliography, picture credits, index, 650 illus. including one, p. 249, by M. (Leigh, Remington, Russell, Schreyvogel)

34 Keir, Malcolm. *The Epic of Industry.* Yale University Press, New Haven, 1926, morocco and boards, decor. endsheets, 329 pp., gilt top, numerous illus. including one, p. 175, by M. The Liberty Bell Edition of *The Pageant of America,* vol. 5, limited to 1,500 numbered sets.

35 Laut, Agnes C. *Pathfinders of the West.* Macmillan, N.Y., 1904, words "Published November, 1904" on copyright page, decor. cloth, 380 pp., illus. including one, p. 317, by M. (Goodwin, Remington)

36 Lewis, Alfred Henry. *The Sunset Trail.* A. S. Barnes & Co., N.Y., 1905, words "Published April 1905" on copyright page, pic. cloth, 393 pp., (6) of advs., illus. including three, facing pp. 299, 307 and 345, by M.

37 ———. *Faro Nell and Her Friends.* Dillingham, N.Y., (1913), cloth, 348 pp., twelve illus. including seven, frontis. and facing pp. 29, 90, 118, 238, 281 and 336, by M. (Dunton)

38 Lillibridge, Will. *A Breath of Prairie.* McClurg, Chicago, 1911, words "Published April, 1911" on copyright page, cloth, 417 pp., five illus. in color, frontis. and facing pp. 74, 190, 326 and 388, by M.

39 Lincoln, Joseph C. *Kent Knowles: "Quahaug."* Appleton, N.Y. and London, 1914, code no. "(1)" after last line of text, cloth with illus. in color mounted on the front cover, 450 (1) pp., four illus., frontis. and facing pp. 152, 250 and 274, by M.

40 Lockridge, Ross F. *La Salle.* World Book Co., Yonkers-on-Hudson, N.Y., 1931, code no. "LL-1" on copyright page, pic. cloth, 312 pp., preface, "Introduction" by James Albert Woodburn, index, numerous illus. including two, pp. 211 and 285, by M., maps.

41 McCarter, Margaret Hill. *The Price of the Prairie.* McClurg, Chicago, 1910, words "Published October 8, 1910" on copyright page, cloth, 489 pp., five illus. in color, frontis. and facing pp. 158, 244, 288 and 394, by M.

42 ———. *A Wall of Men.* McClurg, Chicago, 1912,

words "Published October, 1912" on copyright page, cloth, 494 pp., four illus. in color, frontis. and facing pp. 20, 252 and 430, by M.

43 ———. *Winning the Wilderness.* McClurg, Chicago, 1914, words "Published September, 1914" on copyright page, cloth, 404 pp., four illus., frontis. (in color) and facing pp. 166, 180 and 274, by M.

44 McKishnie, Archie P. *Love of the Wild.* Desmond Fitzgerald, N.Y., (1910), cloth, 327 pp., frontis. in color by M.

45 ———. Same, first Canadian edition, issued by McLeod & Allen, Toronto, in 1910, frontis. in color by M.

46 Mighels, Philip Verrill. *The Furnace of Gold.* Desmond Fitzgerald, N.Y., (1909), cloth with illus. in color mounted on front cover, 402 pp., twelve illus. by M.

47 Page, Thomas Nelson. *Under the Crust.* Scribner's, N.Y., 1907, words "Published, November, 1907" on copyright page, decor. cloth, 307 pp., gilt top, eight illus. including one, the frontis., by M. (Schoonover, Wyeth)

48 (Parkman, Francis, text after.) *Singer Souvenir of the Louisiana Purchase Exposition, AD 1904.* The Singer Mfg. Co., (St. Louis), 1904, decor. wraps, (14) pp., illus. including three by M.

48a Rennert, Vincent Paul. *Western Outlaws.* Crowell-Collier Press, N.Y., (1968), words "First Printing" on copyright page, colored pic. cloth, 152 pp., introduction, bibliography, index, numerous illus. including one, p. (77), by M. (Remington)

49 Rugg, Harold. *The Conquest of America.* Ginn and Co., Boston etc., (1937), cloth, 563 pp., preface, acknowledgment, index, numerous illus. including two, pp. 118 and 119, by M., maps including one double in color. (Deming)

50 Shirley, Glenn. *Buckskin & Spurs.* Hastings, N.Y., 1958, two-tone cloth, 191 pp., foreword, bibliography, numerous illus. including three, pp. (71), (72) and (76), by M. (Eggenhofer)

51 Thomas, Augustus. *Arizona.* Dodd, Mead, N.Y., 1914, decor. cloth, 326 pp., two illus. in color, frontis. and facing p. 150, by M.

52 Thompson, Charles Manfred. *History of the United States.* Sanborn & Co., N.Y., (1917), cloth, numerous illus. including one, p. 29, by M.

53 Walton, Ray S. *Texas and the West.* Catalogue Five,

Summer 1970, Austin, Texas, pic. wraps, 30 pp., front cover illus. by M.

54 Ward, Baldwin H., ed. *Year's Pictorial History of America.* (Year, Inc., Los Angeles, 1954), cloth and boards, 415 (17) pp., "Foreword" by Allan Nevins, publisher's note, index, 2,500 illus. including one, p. 17, by M., 55 historical maps in color. (Leigh, Remington, Russell)

55 *The West in a Bookshelf.* Comstock Editions, Ballantine, N.Y., Spring 1972, folder, numerous illus. including one by M. (Remington)

56 West, Willie Mason. *The Story of Man's Early Progress* (cover title: *Early Progress*). Allyn & Bacon, N.Y. etc., (1920), cloth, numerous illus. including one, p. 671, by M.

57 Wissler, Clark et al. *Adventures in the Wilderness.* Yale University Press, New Haven, 1925, morocco and boards, pic. endsheets, 369 pp., gilt top, "The American Indian" by Ralph H. Gabriel, notes on the pictures, index, numerous illus. including two, pp. 320 and 321, by M. The Liberty Bell Edition of *The Pageant of America,* vol. 1, limited to 1,500 numbered sets. (Deming, Dixon, Remington, Russell)

The Artist and His Art

58 Adams, Ramon F. and Britzman, Homer E. *Charles M. Russell, The Cowboy Artist, A Biography.* Trail's End Publishing Co., Pasadena, Calif., (1948), words "Collector's Edition, Volume I, 1948" on copyright page, morocco and cloth, pic. endsheets, 335 pp., "Preface" by Britzman, "Prologue" by Irwin S. Cobb, acknowledgments, index, numerous illus. by Russell and photos of him. Marchand as a friend; with the help of Will Crawford, persuades Russell to visit New York, shares studio with Russell.

59 Holsinger, M. Paul. "Hamlin Garland's Colorado," an illus. article in *The Colorado Magazine,* Winter 1967, with one illus. by M.

60 Manzo, Flournoy D. "Alfred Henry Lewis: Western Story Teller," an illus. article in *Arizona and the West,* Spring 1968, with one illus. by M.

61 Russell, Austin. *Charles M. Russell, Cowboy Artist.* Twayne Publishers, N.Y., (1957), cloth, 247 pp., postscript, sources quoted, illus. with photos and with drawings by Russell. Austin, Charlie's nephew, lived with the Russells at Great Falls and visited them at Lake McDonald whenever he could get away from his job. He tells some interesting things about Marchand.

62 Shelton, Lola. *Charles Marion Russell: Cowboy, Artist, Friend.* Dodd, Mead, N.Y., 1962, cloth, 230 (1) pp., acknowledgments, "Introduction" by Mike Kennedy, bibliography, index, numerous illus. including four in color. Comments on the Russell-Marchand friendship in the text.

"MÁS ALLÁ (FARTHER ON)," THE APACHE TOLD DON MIRANDA, "ARE
MORE AND RICHER MINES" by Mead from *Coronado's Children*

BEN CARLTON MEAD
Contemporary, 1902–

Illustrated by the Artist

1 Abernethy, Francis Edward, ed. *Observations and Reflections on Texas Folklore.* Encino Press, Austin, 1972, words "First Edition" on copyright page, tan endsheets, 151 pp., preface, index, illus. including one, Texas Folklore Society trademark "Paisano," p. 15 (and repeated several times), by M.

2 *Amarillo Fat Stock Show* (catalog). 1934, colored pic. wraps, 72 pp., numerous illus. including two, p. 34 and inside back wrap, by M.

3 Same, 1937, colored pic. wraps, 108 (24) pp., numerous illus. including two, pp. 17 and 108, by M.

4 Same, 1938, colored pic. wraps by M., the first of a series of sixteen consecutive covers from an original oil painting commissioned by the show committee and sold at auction during the show to help meet the cost of the catalog.

5 Same, 1939, colored pic. wraps by M.

6 Same, 1940, colored pic. wraps by M.

7 Same, 1941, colored pic. wraps by M.

8 Same, 1942, colored pic. wraps by M.

9 Same, 1943, colored pic. wraps by M.

10 Same, 1944, colored pic. wraps by M.

11 Same, 1945, colored pic. wraps by M.

12 Same, 1946, colored pic. wraps by M.

13 Same, 1947, colored pic. wraps by M.

14 Same, 1948, colored pic. wraps by M.

15 Same, 1949, colored pic. wraps by M.

16 Same, 1950, colored pic. wraps by M.

17 Same, 1951, colored pic. wraps by M.

18 Same, 1952, colored pic. wraps by M.

19 Same, 1953, colored pic. wraps by M. Note: Each catalog carries a brief article about the cover illustration by M. and a number of the catalogs include additional small black and white drawings by him.

20 Burkhalter, Lois Wood. *Marion Koogler McNay, A Biography, 1883–1950.* The Marion Koogler McNay Art Institute, A Museum of Modern Art, San Antonio (but printed by Steck Co., Austin), 1968, cloth, 97 pp., illus., Mead was the art director for the book, designed the binding and the endsheets and prepared the d/w.

21 Cross, Ruth. *Soldier of Good Fortune.* Banks Upshaw and Co., Dallas, (1936), cloth, decor. map endsheets by M., 347 pp., historical foreword, map, illustrated.

22 Dobie, J. Frank. *Coronado's Children.* The Southwest Press, Dallas, (1930), pic. cloth, pic. map endsheets, 367 pp., red top, illus. including six full-page plates on glazed paper, frontis. and facing pp. 114, 170, 194, 260 and 330, by Mead, maps and charts. The first printing does not include the word "clean" in the dedication, added in later printings — and there were several.

23 ———. *On the Open Range.* Southwest Press, Dallas, (1931), pic. cloth, small illus. on endsheets, 312 pp., illus. including four in color, frontis. and facing pp. 22, 98 and 292, by M. One of 750 copies. Reprinted in a school edition of 15,000-plus copies.

24 ———. Same, Sir Isaac Pitman & Sons, London, 1946, words "First published in Great Britain . . . 1946" on copyright page, decor. boards, 214 pp. twelve illus. by M. Some of the stories in the American edition (no. 23) were omitted.

25 ———. Same, reprint bound in dark blue cloth and lighter weight paper but without the textbook stamp.

26 ———. Same, fifth printing, March 1940, by Banks Upshaw and Company, Dallas, with the last paragraph of the preface (of previous printings) deleted.

27 ———. *I'll Tell You a Tale*. Little, Brown, Boston, Toronto, (1960), words "First Edition" on copyright page, decor. cloth, 362 pp., glossary of Spanish-Mexican words, illus. with drawings by M.

28 ———. *Lost Mines of the Old West, Coronado's Children*. Hammond, Hammond, London, (1960), words "First published in Great Britain 1960," cloth, 367 pp., illus. with drawings by M. (A reprint of no. 22 but without the six full-page Mead plates.)

29 ———. *Cow People*. Little, Brown, Boston, Toronto, (1964), words "First Edition" on copyright page, fabricoid, 305 pp., introduction, a note on sources, numerous illus. including two drawings and the facsimile of a handwritten note, p. (253), by M. (Crawford)

30 ———. Same, first British edition, Hammond, Hammond & Co., London, (1964).

31 ———, ed. *Tone the Bell Easy*. Printed by the University of Texas Press for the Texas Folklore Society (publication number X), 1932, cloth, 199 pp., introduction, index, illus. including the first use of the Mead paisano drawing as official emblem of the Society. Note: It was used in a number of other Society publications.

32 ——— et al., eds. *Coyote Wisdom*. Texas Folklore Society, Austin, 1938, two-tone cloth, 300 pp., illus. including one, p. 262, by M.

33 ——— (general editor). *Backwoods to Border*. Texas Folklore Society, Austin, 1943, cloth, 235 pp., "Twenty Years an Editor" etc. by Dobie, illus. including one, p. 140, by Mead. Publication XVIII, edited by Mody C. Boatright and Donald Day.

34 Eisen, Edna E. *Our Country from the Air*. Wheeler Publishing Co., Chicago, 1937, pic. cloth, pic. map endsheets, 212 pp., foreword, numerous illus. from photos but front cover, perspective map, and endsheets by M.

35 Gough, Lysius. *Spur Jingles and Saddle Songs*. Russell Stationery, Amarillo, Texas, 1935, pic. wraps, 110 pp., "Foreword" by L. F. Sheffy, illus. with photos and with four plates, "Fire," "Wind," "Sunshine" and "Snow," facing pp. 16, 48, 80 and 104, by M.

36 Green, Paul. *Texas* (A Musical Romance of Panhandle History — souvenir program). Palo Duro Canyon State Park, (Canyon, Texas), 1970, colored pic. wraps, unpaged, thirty illus. (both d/w illus. in color) by M. and "About the Drawings" by him.

37 Greer, Margaret R. et al., eds. *Prose and Poetry Adventures*. L. W. Singer Co., Syracuse, N.Y., (1935), decor. cloth, 784 pp., preface, index, numerous illus. by M. (New Prose and Poetry Series.)

38 ———. *Prose and Poetry Journeys*. L. W. Singer Co., Syracuse, N.Y., (1935), decor. cloth, pic. map endsheets, 750 pp., preface, index, numerous illus. by M.

39 Hamner, Laura V. *The No-Gun Man of Texas*. Privately printed, (Amarillo), August, 1935, pic. cloth, map on front fly, 256 pp., "Introduction" by Judge R. W. Hall, appendix, glossary, six illus. including four, pp. 2, 95, 209 and 234, by M.

40 Holmes, Burton, ed. *Mexico*. Wheeler Publishing Co., Chicago, (1939), colored pic. cloth, pic. endsheets, 440 pp., text by Carlos Castillo, foreword, glossary, index, numerous illus. including two, front cover and endsheets by M. (The Burton Holmes Travel Stories.)

41 ———. *Egypt and the Suez Canal*. Wheeler, Chicago, (1939), pic. cloth, pic. endsheets, foreword, glossary, index, numerous illus. including two, front cover and endsheets, by M.

42 ———. *China*. Wheeler, Chicago, (1940), pic. cloth, pic. map endsheets, 420 pp., text by Eunice Tietjens and Louise Strong Hammond, foreword, glossary, index, numerous illus. including two, front cover and endsheets, by M.

43 Jones, Paul A. *Coronado and Quivira*. (Lyons Pub. Co., Lyons, Kansas, 1937), decor. cloth, colored pic. map endsheets, 242 pp., bibliography, numerous illus. incuding one, facing p. 49, by M. (Remington)

44 Lloyd, Everett. *Law West of the Pecos*. Naylor, San Antonio, 1936, cloth, or pic. wraps, 124 pp., illus. with photos and with five sketches, pp. 30, 44, 56, 105 and 122, by M. Centennial Edition (or third edition) but the first printing illus. by M.

45 Logue, Roscoe. *Under Texas and Border Skies*. Russell, Amarillo, 1935, pic. wraps, 111 pp., illus. with photos, and with nine drawings, pp. (2), 13, 20, 23, 36, 59, 69, 96 and 111, by M. (Leigh)

46 Lowman, Al et al. *The Spanish Texans*. Institute of Texan Cultures, University of Texas, San Antonio, (1972), pic. wraps, 32 pp., numerous illus. including one, double-page plate inside the wraps, by M. (Bugbee, Cisneros, Lea, Remington)

ONE OF THE PROSPECTORS WAS KNOWN AS OLD MISSOURI by Mead
from *Coronado's Children*

47 McCarty, John. *Literature of the Plains.* Russell, Amarillo, October, 1940, pic. wraps, 16 pp., cover illus. by M. (Reprinted from Panhandle-Plains Hist. Review.)

48 McClure, C. H. and Yarborough, W. H. *The United States of America.* Laidlaw Bros., Chicago, (1937), decor. cloth, 672 pp., maps, numerous illus. by M.

49 ———— et al. *A World Background for the United States.* Laidlaw Bros., Chicago etc., (1941), decor. cloth, 512 pp., introduction, pronouncing index, numerous illus. by Frederick Seyfarth and by M.

50 McGraw, H. Ward, ed. *Prose and Poetry of America.* L. W. Singer Co., Syracuse, N.Y., (1934), decor. cloth, 1198 pp., preface, index, numerous illus. including thirty-four by M. (New Prose and Poetry Series — Southwestern Edition.)

51 ————. *Prose and Poetry of England.* L. W. Singer Co., Syracuse, N.Y., (1934), decor. cloth, 1196 pp., preface, index, numerous illus. including one, p. 85, by M.

52 McVickar, Mary Louise. *The Writings of J. Frank Dobie: A Bibliography.* Museum of the Great Plains, Lawton, (Oklahoma, 1968), words "First Edition" on copyright page, Gane Imitation Leather and cloth, 258 pp., preface, "Introduction — The Work of J. Frank Dobie" by Chancellor Harry E. Ransom, index, illus. including one, p. (42), by M. Edition of 500 numbered copies signed by the author, slipcase. (Lea)

53 ————. Same, first trade edition in cloth.

54 Mead, Ben Carlton. *Buy War Bonds* (poster). War Activities Committee of the Motion Picture Industry, lithographed in Washington, D.C., 1945, and shown in the display frames in the lobbies of 17,000 theatres in the U.S.

54a The Naylor Company, San Antonio. *Texana, Western, Southwestern Americana* (catalog). Fall 1955, pic. wraps, 32 pp., illus. including one, p. 16, by M. (Bugbee)

55 *The Palo Duro.* (Russell, Amarillo, 1934), colored pic. wraps, 16 pp., numerous illus. including one, the front cover illus. plus a double-page map by M.

56 Perkins, Marion McDermott. *Philip Andre.* Wetzel Publishing Co., Los Angeles, 1930, cloth, 278 pp., frontis. by M.

57 Quillin, Ellen Schulz. *Nature Science Series,* two vols., Southwest Press, Dallas, (1931), cloth, twenty-five illus. by M.

58 ————. *Cactus Culture.* Orange-Judd Co., N.Y., 1932, cloth, 137 pp., introduction, index, illus. with drawings by M. and with photos.

59 ————. Same, enlarged edition of 180 pages issued by Orange-Judd in 1942.

60 ————. *Thin Wings.* Turner Co., Dallas, (1963), pic. wraps, 28 pp., six illus. by M.

61 ———— and Gable, Charles H. *The Book of Little Creatures with Many Legs.* Albert Whitman & Co., Chicago, 1944, cloth, 48 pp., illus. including three, pp. 11, 19 and 35, by M. (The Nature Science Books — Outdoor Adventures.)

62 ————. *The Book of Along the Creek.* Whitman, Chicago, 1944, cloth, 46 pp., illus. including four, pp. 15, 18, 22 and 27, by M.

63 ————. *The Book of Seed to Tree.* Whitman, Chicago, 1944, cloth, 48 pp., illus. including three, pp. 11, 23 and 27, by M.

64 ————. *The Book of Queer Animals.* Whitman, Chicago, 1944, cloth, 47 pp., illus. including six, pp. 11, 18, 27, 35, 38 and 43, by M.

65 ————. *The Book of Thin Wings.* Whitman, Chicago, 1944, cloth, 46 pp., illus. including six, d/w, frontis. and pp. 27, 34, 38 and 39, by M.

66 ————. *The Book of Feathered Flights.* Whitman, Chicago, 1944, cloth, 47, pp., illus. including six, d/w, frontis. and pp. 11, 18, 38 and 43, by M.

67 ————. *The Book of Finding Nature's Treasures.* Whitman, Chicago, 1944, cloth, 48 pp., illus. including two, pp. 42 and 46, by M.

68 Scarborough, W. Frances (compiled by). *Stories from the History of Texas.* Southwest Press, Dallas, 1928, cloth, 100 pp., d/w illus. by M.

69 ————. Same, enlarged edition of 138 pages, 1929.

70 Sheffy, L. F., ed. *Panhandle–Plains Historical Review* volume VII). Panhandle–Plains Historical Society, Canyon, Texas, 1934, pic. wraps, 100 pp., includes an article, "Netz-A-Huatl's Legend of the Origin of the Pueblo Tribes," by M. and with one illus. by him. (Bugbee)

71 Spencer, Elma Dill Russell. *Green Russell and Gold.* Texas, Austin and London, (1966), cloth, green endsheets, 239 pp., orange top, publisher's preface,

"Grandma Said," appendix, bibliography, index, maps, five illus., frontis. and pp. 26–7, 44–5 (details repeated on the d/w), 80–1 and 152–3, by M.

72 Taylor, H. C. *Private Doakes and Me!* Taylor Engraving Corporation, Dallas, 1942, cloth, numerous cartoon type drawings by M.

73 Turner, Mary Honeyman Ten Eyck (Mrs. Avery). *Into the West.* Privately printed, Amarillo, Texas, 1938, fabricoid with illus. in color mounted on front cover, 61 pp., illus. with photos, but cover illus. by M. Edition limited to 125 copies.

74 ———. *These High Plains.* Privately printed, Amarillo, Texas, 1941, fabricoid with illus. in color mounted on front cover, 94 pp., illus. with photos, but the cover illus. by M. Edition limited to 150 copies.

75 Williams, Harry. *Legends of the Great Southwest.* Naylor, San Antonio, (1932), words "First Edition" on title page, pic. cloth and endsheets, 269 pp., "Foreword" by Joe O. Naylor, index, illus. including two, cover and endsheets, by M.

76 Woolford, Bess Carroll and Quillin, Ellen Schulz. *The Story of the Witte Memorial Musuem 1922–1960.* San Antonio Museum Assn., (1966), two-tone cloth, 374 pp., "Foreword" by Mrs. Quillin, appendix, index, numerous illus. including two, p. 5 and d/w, by M. who served as art director of the book. Mead was the staff artist at the Museum 1930–32 and he is in the text, pp. vii–viii, 107, 108, 111, 113, 201, 208 and 210.

The Artist and His Art

77 Cook, Spruill (compiled by). *J. Frank Dobie Bibliography.* Printed for the author by Texian Press, Waco, Texas, (January 1968), pic. cloth, 64 pp., "Foreword" by Mrs. J. Frank Dobie, preface, index, illus. with title pages, Mead in text, p. 2 and 13 plus the title page of *Coronado's Children.* Edition of 500 numbered copies signed by the author.

78 Dykes, Jeff. *My Dobie Collection.* Keepsake Number One, Friends of the Texas A&M University Library, (College Station, 1971), pic. cloth, 43 pp., preface, "Foreword" by Dudley R. Dobie, frontis., Mead's paisano drawing adopted as offcial emblem of the Texas Folklore Society in 1932, p. 4. Limited edition of 300 numbered copies signed by the author.

79 ———. Same, first trade edition in wraps.

80 Forrester-O'Brien, Esse. *Art and Artists of Texas.* Tardy, Dallas, (1935), cloth, 408 pp., illus., includes a biographical sketch, pp. 156–7, of M.

81 Mead, Ben Carlton. "Ben Mead and Matt Dillon," a letter to the editor, *True West* 21:1, September–October 1973, with a photo of M.

THE SCALP LOCK by Miller from *Harmsen's Western Americana*

ALFRED JACOB MILLER
1810–1874

Catalogues of Art Exhibitions and Galleries

BILTMORE GALLERIES, LOS ANGELES

0 *Catalog*, May 1969, colored pic. wraps, 54 pp., numerous illus. including one, p. 38, by M. (Borein, Dixon, Dunton, Johnson, Koerner, Leigh, Remington, Russell, Young)

BOATMEN'S NATIONAL BANK OF ST. LOUIS

1 *Exhibit of Boatmen's Art Collection*, Special Bicentennial Showing, May 4–29, 1964, colored pic. wraps, unpaged, 15 illus. including one, "Departure of Caravan at Sunrise," by M. (Remington, Russell)

CHARLES W. BOWERS MEMORIAL MUSEUM
SANTA ANA, CALIFORNIA

2 *Painters of the West*, 1972, wraps, illus. including one by M. (Johnson, Koerner, Remington, Russell)

CHAPPELLIER GALLERIES, NEW YORK

3 *One Hundred American Selections*, (1966), colored pic. wraps, unpaged, 100 numbered illus. including one, no. 60, by M. (Deming, Johnson, Remington)

CORCORAN GALLERY OF ART, WASHINGTON, D.C.

4 *American Processional: The Story of Our Country*, June 8 through December 17, 1950, colored pic. wraps, 270 pp., index, numerous illus. including two, p. 129, by M. (Remington, Zogbaum)

DENVER ART MUSEUM

5 *Building the West*, October 1955, wraps, 32 pp., (introduction), numerous illus. including one by M. (Remington, Russell, Schreyvogel)

6 *Colorado Collects Historic Western Art*, January 13 through April 15, 1973, decor. wraps, 72 pp., numerous illus. including one by M. (Johnson, Remington, Russell, Schreyvogel)

EDWARD EBERSTADT & SONS, NEW YORK

7 *A Distinguished Collection of Western Paintings*, Catalogue 139, (1956), pic. wraps, 129 numbered illus. including thirteen, front cover and nos. 77–88, by M. (Borein, Deming, Dixon, Johnson, Leigh, Remington, Wyeth, Zogbaum)

8 *American Paintings*, Catalogue 146 (December, 1957), pic. wraps, 191 numbered illus. including twenty-one by M. (Borein, Deming, Dixon, Dunton, Johnson, Leigh, Remington, Wyeth)

FINE ARTS MUSEUM OF NEW MEXICO, SANTA FE

9 *The Artist in the American West, 1800–1900*, Oct. 8 through Nov. 22, 1961, pic. wraps, unpaged, introduction, numerous illus. including two, nos. 43 and 47, by M. (Remington, Russell, Zogbaum)

FLINT INSTITUTE OF ARTS
(DE WATERS ART CENTER), FLINT, MICHIGAN

10 *Artists of the Old West*, Nov. 15 through Dec. 6, 1964, pic. wraps, unpaged, nine illus. including two by M. (Remington, Russell)

THE GEORGE GUND MUSEUM OF WESTERN ART
NEW YORK

11 *The Gund Collection of Western Art, A History and Pictorial Description of the American West*, 1973, pic. wraps, 62 pp., thirty-five illus. including one in color, p. 15, by Miller, and a biographical sketch of him, p. 48. (Johnson, Leigh, Remington, Russell, Schreyvogel)

HAMMER GALLERIES, NEW YORK

12 *The Works of Charles M. Russell and Other Western Artists*, (1963), pic. wraps, 56 pp., "Charles M. Russell" by Will Rogers, introduction, numerous illustrations including five, pp. 41, 42 and 43, by M. (Crawford, Goodwin, Leigh, Lungren, Remington, Russell)

JOSLYN ART MUSEUM, OMAHA, NEBRASKA

13 *Catlin, Bodmer, Miller* (Artist Explorers of the 1830's), May 1–Sept. 2, 1963, colored pic. wraps, 35 pp., "The Miller Collection" by Mae Reed Porter, twelve illus. by M.

14 Same, reprinted in 1967, colored pic. wraps, 38 pp., twelve illus. by M.

15 *The Stewart-Miller Collection* (permanent exhibition — owned by the Northern Natural Gas Company), folder with five illus. by M.

16 *Life on the Prairie — A Permanent Exhibition*, 1966, wraps, illus. including four by M. (Johnson, Leigh, Remington, Russell)

KALAMAZOO INSTITUTE OF ARTS
KALAMAZOO, MICHIGAN

17 *Western Art*, February 17–March 19, 1967, pic. wraps, 17 (1) pp., numerous illus. including one, p. 5, by M. (Hurd, Johnson, Remington, Russell, Schreyvogel, Wyeth)

KENDE GALLERIES (AT GIMBEL BROTHERS)
NEW YORK

18 *Paintings and Bronzes, The Collection of the late Charles H. Linville, Baltimore,* January 24, 1942, wraps, 29 pp., illus. including two, pp. 9 and 10, by M. (Remington)

KENNEDY GALLERIES, NEW YORK

19 *Recent Acquisitions in Important Western and Sporting Paintings and Sculptures*, October 1962, wraps with illus. in color mounted on the front cover, pp. 50–108, introduction, numerous illus. including one, p. 71, by M. (Borein, Johnson, Leigh, Marchand, Remington, Russell, Schreyvogel)

20 *The Wild Riders and the Vacant Land*, June 1966, colored pic. wraps, pp. 68–128, introduction, numerous illus. including seven, pp. 72, 73, 74 and 75, by M. (Leigh, Remington, Russell)

21 *The Things that Were*, June 1968, colored pic. wraps, pp. 52–123, (1), numerous illus. including nine, pp. 56, 72 (two), 104, 105 (two), and 112 (two in color), by M. (Blumenschein, Crawford, Leigh, Remington, Schoonover, Schreyvogel)

22 *Paintings, Watercolors, Bronzes of the American West*, announcement (large post card) of an exhibition of The Old West in Art: June 3 through 31, 1971, one illus. in color by M.

23 *An Artist's Gazetteer: Beyond the Mississippi*, June 1971, colored pic. wraps, 64 pp., introduction, numerous illus. including one, front cover in color, by M. (Borein, Marchand, Remington, Russell, Schreyvogel)

24 *Walking Westward*, March 1972, colored pic. wraps, pp. 196–256, introduction, numerous illus. including three, pp. 208 (color), 224 and 225, by M. (Johnson, Lungren, Remington, Russell, Schreyvogel)

25 *The Great American West*, June 1973, colored pic. wraps, pp. 132–92, introduction, numerous illus. including one, p. 164, by M. (Blumenschein, Leigh, Remington, Russell, Schreyvogel)

LOS ANGELES COUNTY MUSEUM OF ART

26 *The American West*, March 21–May 27, 1972, words "First Published in 1972" on copyright page, cloth or colored pic. wraps, 192 pp., "Foreword" by Archibald Hanna, "Painters from Catlin to Russell" by Larry Curry, 133 numbered plates including twelve, nos. 2 (color), 3 (color) and 25–34, by M. Also shown at M. H. de Young Memorial Museum, June 9–September 17, 1972 and the St. Louis Art Museum, November 2–December 31, 1972. (Remington, Russell)

MAXWELL GALLERIES, SAN FRANCISCO

27 *American Art Since 1850*, August 2–October 2, 1968, pic. wraps, 84 pp., comments by Dr. F. M. Hinkhouse, numerous illus. including one in color, p. 28, by M. (Borein, Dixon, Johnson, Remington, Russell, Wyeth)

27a *Art of the West*, November 13 through December, 1973, colored pic. wraps, 48 pp., numerous illus. including one, p. 7, by M. (Johnson, Leigh, Marchand)

MILLER SCHOOL (CHEYENNE CENTENNIAL COMMITTEE), CHEYENNE, WYOMING

28 *150 Years in Western Art*, July 1–August 15, 1967, colored pic. wraps, 30 (2) pp., numerous illus. including three by M. (Koerner, Remington, Russell, Schreyvogel)

MUSEUM OF FINE ARTS, BOSTON

28a *American Paintings 1815–1865*, 1957–59, wraps, 112 pp., numerous illus. including one, p. 83, by M.

NATIONAL COWBOY HALL OF FAME
OKLAHOMA CITY

29 *Inaugural Exhibition*, June 25, 1965, colored pic. wraps, 24 pp., numerous illus. including two, p. 16, by M. (Hurd, Remington, Russell)

PARKE-BERNET GALLERIES, NEW YORK

30 *Western Americana — Paintings, Prints, Drawings and Sculpture* (the collection of Dr. Lester E. Bauer, Detroit), Sale no. 3254, October 27, 1971, one illus. by M. (Borein, Russell)

PEALE MUSEUM, BALTIMORE

31 *Alfred Jacob Miller, Artist of Baltimore and the West,* January 8 to February 12, 1950, wraps, unpaged, "Foreword" by Mae Reed Porter, thirteen illus. by M.

PHOENIX ART MUSEUM

32 *Western Art from the Eugene B. Adkins Collection,* November 1971–January 1972, colored pic. wraps, unpaged, numerous illus. including one in color by M. (Dunton, Johnson, Leigh, Remington, Varian)

SOTHEBY PARKE BERNET, NEW YORK

33 *Important 18th, 19th, and Early 20th Century American Paintings, Watercolors and Sculpture,* Sale no. 3498, April 11, 1973, colored pic. wraps, unpaged, numerous illus. including one by M. (Blumenschein, Eggenhofer, James, Johnson, Leigh, Remington, Russell, Varian, Wyeth)

Illustrated by the Artist

34 Alter, J. Cecil. *Jim Bridger.* Oklahoma, Norman, 1962, cloth, illus. including three in text plus one on title page (reproduced on d/w) by M.

35 Anderson, Wm. Marshall. *Adventures in the Rocky Mountains in 1834.* (Eberstadt, N.Y., 1951, reprinted from *The American Turf Register and Sporting Magazine,* May, July and November, 1837), wraps, 21 pp., two illus. in color by M. (Remington)

36 Athearn, Robert G. *The Frontier* (volume 6, The American Heritage New Illustrated History of the United States). N.Y., (1963), colored pic. cloth and endsheets, pp. 435 through 539, for further reading, numerous illus. including two in color, pp. 526, and 532–33, by M. (Dunn, Remington, Russell)

37 Babian, Haig. *The Permanent Frontier.* Institute of Economic Affairs, N.Y. University, (1961), colored pic. boards, 120 (1) pp., foreword, numerous illus. including one in color, p. (iv), by M.

37a Baird, Joseph A., Jr. (compiled by). *The West Remembered.* California Historical Society, San Francisco and San Marino, 1973, colored pic. wraps, 88 pp., "Foreword" by Mitchell A. Wilder, introduction, numerous illus. including three, pp. 17 (color) and 19 (two), by M. (Blumenschein, Borein, Dixon, James, Lungren, Marchand, Remington, Russell, Zogbaum)

38 Baur, John I. H. *American Painting in the Nineteenth Century.* Praeger, N.Y., (printed in Germany, 1953), cloth, 59 (1) pp., foreword, numerous illus. including one, p. (47), by M.

39 Beebe, Lucius and Clegg, Charles. *The American West: The Pictorial Epic of a Continent.* Dutton, N.Y., 1955, cloth, numerous illus. including one by M. (Remington, Zogbaum)

40 Bell, Colonel William Gardner. *The Snake: A Noble and Various River.* Potomac Corral, The Westerners, Washington, D.C., March, 1969, pic. boards, 20 pp., map, ten illus. including one, p. 6, by Miller. Limited to 250 numbered and signed copies. (Remington)

41 ———. Same, a trade edition in wraps.

41a Bennett, Ian. *A History of American Painting.* Hamlyn, London etc., (printed in Italy, 1973), cloth, black endsheets, 239 (1) pp., index, numerous illus. including two in color, p. 123, by M. (Remington, Russell, Schreyvogel)

42 Berry, Don. *A Majority of Scoundrels.* Harper, N.Y., (1961), words "First Edition" on copyright page, cloth, 432 pp., author's preface, appendices, notes, index, two folding maps, sixteen illus. including ten, between pp. 242–43, by M.

43 Billington, Ray Allen. *The Far Western Frontier, 1830–1860.* Harper, N.Y., (1956), words "First Edition" on copyright page, cloth, 324 pp., "Editor's Introduction" by Henry Steele Commager and Richard Brandon Morris, preface, bibliography, index, 14 maps, 32 illus. including one, between pp. 138 and 139, by M.

43a Bourne, Russell (project editor). *200 Years.* U.S. News and World Report, Washington, D.C., 1973, fabricoid and cloth, two volumes, numerous illus. including two in color, pp. 249 and 250 (I), slipcase. (Dunn, Remington, Russell, Wyeth, Zogbaum)

44 Bragdon, Henry W. and McCutchen, Samuel P. *History of a Free People.* Macmillan, (N.Y., 1954), decor. cloth, blue endsheets, 724 pp., prologue, appendix, index, maps, charts, numerous illus. including one, p. (282), by M. (Remington)

45 Branch, E. Douglas (narrated by). *The Story of America in Pictures.* Spencer Press, Chicago, 1954, wraps, unpaged, edited by Franklin J. Meine, introduction, numerous illus. including one, "Fort Laramie," by M. (Remington)

46 Brandon, William. *The American Heritage Book of Indians.* American Heritage Pub. Co., N.Y., (1961), cloth with slipcase, 424 pp., Alvin M. Josephy, Jr. (editor-in-charge), "Introduction" by President John F. Kennedy, acknowledgments and index, numerous illus. including three, pp. 350 in color and 351 (two), by M. (Remington, Russell)

47 ———. Same, trade edition, cloth and decor. boards.

48 Brion, Marcel. *Romantic Art.* N.Y. etc., (1960), cloth, grey endsheets, 240 pp., introduction, index, 230 (64 in color) illus. including one, p. (218), by M.

49 Brown, David L. *Three Years in the Rocky Mountains.* (Eberstadt, N.Y., 1950, from *The Cincinnati Atlas,* 1845), wraps, 20 pp., two illus. preceding p. 5, by M.

50 Butterfield, Roger (text by). *America's Arts and Skill.* Dutton, N.Y., 1957, cloth, and decor. boards, 172 pp., edited by Margit Varga, "Introduction" by Charles F. Montgomery (Winterthur Museum), picture sources, index, numerous illus. including one in color, p. 100, by M. (Russell)

51 Capps, Benjamin (text by). *The Indians* (a volume in The Old West series). Time-Life Books, N.Y., (1973), fabricoid with illus. in color mounted on the front cover, marbled endsheets, 240 pp., index, numerous illus. including one in color, pp. 62–63, by M.

52 Clark, Ella E. *Indian Legends from the Northern Rockies.* University of Oklahoma Press, Norman, (1966), words "First edition" on copyright page, cloth, stippled top, 350 pp., introduction, source notes, bibliography, index, map, 24 illus. including four, between pp. 294–95, by M. (Russell)

53 Clark, Thomas D. *Frontier America: The Story of the Westward Movement.* Scribner's, N.Y., 1959, code letter "A" on copyright page, cloth, numerous illus. including two by M. (Leigh)

54 Cline, Gloria Griffin. *Exploring the Great Basin.* Oklahoma, Norman, 1963, words "First edition" on copyright page, cloth, illus. including one by M.

55 Conner, Daniel Ellis. *Joseph Reddeford Walker and the Arizona Adventure.* Oklahoma, Norman, (1956), words "First edition" on copyright page, 364 pp., "Introduction" and edited by Donald J. Berthrong and Odessa Davenport, bibliography, index, maps, eight illus. including one, facing p. 10 (repeated on d/w), by M.

55a (Cooke.) *Alistair Cooke's America.* Knopf, N.Y., 1973, words "First Edition" on copyright page, two-tone cloth, map endsheets, 400 pp., numerous illus. including two in color, pp. (154) and (172–73), by M.

56 Crosby, Alexander L. *Old Greenwood, Pathfinder of the West.* The Talisman Press, Georgetown, Calif., 1967, cloth, pic. endsheets, 144 pp., acknowledgment, index, maps, illus. including one, front endsheet, by M. (Remington)

57 Cutright, Paul Russell et al. *The American Heritage Book of Great Adventures of the Old West.* N.Y., (1969), cloth, 384 pp., "Introduction" by Archibald Hanna, Jr., numerous illus. including five by M. (Russell, Zogbaum)

58 Darling, Jim, ed. *Brand Book II, The San Diego Corral, The Westerners.* (1971), brand decor. fabricoid, tan endsheets, 197 pp., numerous illus. including one, p. 56, by M. (Remington, Russell)

59 Davidson, Marshall B. *Life in America.* Houghton Mifflin, Boston, 1951, two volumes in cardboard slipcase, decor. cloth, 575 and 503 pp., "Foreword" by Francis Henry Taylor, Director, the Metropolitan Museum of Art (1), introduction (1), notes (2), acknowledgments (2), bibliography (2), list of artists (2), index (2), over 1,200 illus. including seven (all in vol. 1), pp. 197, 198, 199, (222–23), 226, 228, by M. (Remington, Zogbaum)

59a ——— et al. *The American Heritage History of the Artist's America.* American Heritage, N.Y., (1973), cloth and boards, blue endsheets, 402 (14) pp., introduction, index, numerous illus. including one in color, p. 139, by M. (Remington, Russell, Schreyvogel)

60 (Dawson.) *The Northwest Coast,* Catalogue 361. Dawson's Book Shop, Los Angeles, n.d., pic. wraps, (31) pp., four illus. including one by M. (Dixon)

61 Debo, Angie. *A History of the Indians of the United States.* Oklahoma, Norman, 1970, words "First edition" on copyright page, cloth, illus. including one by M.

62 DeVoto, Bernard. *Across the Wide Missouri.* Houghton Mifflin, Boston, 1947, decor. cloth, map endsheets, 483 pp., acknowledgments, preface, "Foreword" by Mae Reed Porter, appendices, bibliography, index, 81 illus. including sixty-eight (thirteen in color) by M.

63 Dorra, Henri. *The American Muse.* Viking, N.Y. (but printed in Italy), (1961), words "First Published in 1961" on copyright page, cloth and pic. boards, 163 pp., "Foreword" by Hermann Warner Williams, Jr. (Director, The Corcoran Gallery of Art), index, numerous illus. including one, p. 63, by M. (Remington)

64 Drago, Harry Sinclair. *Roads to Empire.* Dodd, Mead, N.Y., 1968, cloth, 270 pp., notes, bibliography, index, illus. including one, between pp. 46 and 47, by M.

65 Edward Eberstadt & Sons. *Americana — Books, Manuscripts & Paintings, Catalogue 126.* N.Y., 1950, pic. wraps, 75 pp., illus. including one, facing p. 48, by M.

66 ———. Same, *Catalogue 127.* N.Y., 1950, pic. wraps, 76 pp., illus. including three, front cover and facing pp. 48 and 49, by M.

67 ———. Same, *Catalogue 128.* N.Y., 1951, pic. wraps, 80 pp., illus. including two, facing p. 33, by M.

68 ———. Same, *Catalogue 130.* N.Y., 1952, pic. wraps, 111 pp., illus. including one in color inside front cover by M.

69 ———. Same, *Catalogue 131.* N.Y., 1953, pic. wraps, 127 pp., illus. including two, inside back cover, by M.

70 ———. Same, *Catalogue 132.* N.Y., 1953, pic. wraps, 128 pp., illus. including two, facing p. 97, by M. (Leigh, Remington)

71 ———. Same, *Catalogue 133.* N.Y., 1954, pic. wraps, 144 pp., illus. including four, facing p. 120, by M. (Deming)

72 ———. Same, *Catalogue 134.* N.Y., 1954, pic. wraps, 111 pp., illus. including one, facing p. 64, by M. (Dixon, Johnson, Wyeth)

73 ———. Same, *Catalogue 136.* N.Y., 1955, pic. wraps, illus. including one by M. (Schreyvogel, Zogbaum)

74 ———. Same, *Catalogue 138.* N.Y., 1956, pic. wraps, illus. including two by M.

75 Eliot, Alexander. *Three Hundred Years of American Painting.* Time, Inc., N.Y., 1957, fabricoid and buckram, 318 pp., "Introduction" by John Walker (National Gallery), bibliography, index, 250 illus. in color including two, pp. 90–91 and 92, by M. (Hurd, Leigh, Remington, Russell)

76 Elman, Robert (selected and text by). *The Great American Shooting Prints.* A Ridge Press Book, Knopf, N.Y., 1972, cloth, tan endsheets, unpaged, "Introduction" by Hermann Warner Williams, Jr., catalogue of the plates, 72 numbered plates in color including one, no. 5, by M. (Goodwin, Leigh, Remington, Russell)

77 Ewers, John C. *Artists of the Old West.* Chanticleer Press, Doubleday, Garden City, N.Y. (but printed in Milan, Italy), (1965), cloth, 240 pp., "The Artist as Explorer and Historian," acknowledgments, bibliography, numerous illus. including fourteen, four in color, by M. (Remington, Russell)

78 Favour, Alpheus H. *Old Bill Williams, Mountain Man.* Oklahoma University Press, Norman, (1962), cloth, green top, 234 pp., bibliography, index, 12 illus. including three, facing pp. 65, 81 and 128, by M. (Remington)

79 Felton, Harold W. *Jim Beckwourth, Negro Mountain Man.* Dodd, Mead, N.Y., (1966), cloth, 173 pp., selected bibliography, index, 21 illus. including three, between pp. 46 and 47, by M.

80 ———. *Edward Rose: Negro Trail Blazer.* Dodd, Mead, N.Y., 1967, cloth, twelve illus. by M.

81 Ferris, Robert G. (series editor). *Soldier and Brave.* U. S. Department of the Interior, Washington, D. C., 1971, words "New Edition" on title page, cloth, pic. endsheets, 453 pp., "Foreword" by Secretary Rogers C. B. Morton, "Preface" by George B. Hertzog, Jr., suggested reading, index, numerous illus. including one, p. 6, by M. (Eggenhofer, Leigh, Remington, Russell, Schreyvogel)

82 Field, Matthew C. *Prairie & Mountain Sketches.* Oklahoma University Press, Norman, (1957), words "First Edition" on copyright page, cloth, green top, 239 pp., collected by Clyde and Mae Reed Porter, edited by Kate L. Gregg and John Francis McDermott, "Foreword" by Mrs. Porter, "Preface" and "Introduction" by Dr. McDermott, appendix, index, map, 25 illus. including eight, frontis. in color and facing pp. 58, 74, 122, 123, 170, 186, 187 plus d/w by M.

83 *50 American Masterpieces: 200 Years of Great Paintings.* Shorewood Publishers, (N.Y., 1968), colored pic. wraps, 50 illus. including one, no. 20, by M. (Remington)

84 Flexner, James Thomas. *That Wilder Image: The Painting of America's Native School from Thomas Cole to Winslow Homer.* Little, Brown, Boston, 1962, cloth, illustrated including two by M.

85 Fontana, Bernard L. et al. *Look to the Mountain Top.* Gousha Publications, San Jose, 1972, cloth, illus. including two by M. (Russell)

86 Franzwa, Gregory M. *The Oregon Trail Revisited.* Patrice Press, (St. Louis, 1972), colored pic. wraps, 417 pp., preface, "Foreword" by George B. Hertzog, Jr., bibliography, index, maps, numerous illus. including two, pp. 230 and 231, by M.

87 Fronval, George. *La Fantastique Epopee du Far West.* Dargaud, Nevilly/s/Seine, France, (1969), two volumes, colored pic. boards, pp. 126, (2) and 127, (1), numerous illus. including three, (I), pp. 17, 98 and 99 by M. (Koerner, Remington, Russell, Schreyvogel, Zogbaum)

87a ———. *La Veritable Histoire Des Indians Peaux-Rouges.* Fernand Nathan, Paris, France, (1973), cloth, pic. front endsheet, map back endsheet, 125 pp., numerous illus. including three in color, pp. 30, 35 and

56, by M. (Koerner, Leigh, Remington, Schreyvogel, Von Schmidt, Zogbaum)

88 Garraty, John A. *The American Nation Since 1865.* Harper & Row, N.Y. etc., (1966), cloth, colored map endsheets, 498 pp., preface, appendix, index, maps and charts, numerous illus. including three, pp. 38-9, (40) in color and 51 in color, by M. (Remington, Russell)

89 ———. *The American Nation — A History of the United States.* Harper & Row and American Heritage Pub. Co., (1966), cloth, map endsheets, 920 pp., preface, appendix, index, over 60 maps and charts, over 400 (100 in color) illus. including three, pp. 454-5, (456) in color and 467 in color, by M. (Remington, Russell)

89a Getlein, Frank et al. *The Lure of the Great West.* Country Beautiful, Waukesha, Wisconsin, (1973), boards, 352 pp., introduction, 375 illus. including thirty-four (sixteen in color), by M. (Blumenschein, Koerner, Leigh, Remington, Russell, Schreyvogel, Wyeth)

90 Ghent, W. J. *The Early Far West.* Longmans, Green, N.Y., 1931, cloth, 411 pp., preface, index, maps, five illus. including one, facing p. 262, by M.

91 Glubok, Shirley. *The Art of the Old West.* Macmillan, N.Y., 1971, cloth and colored pic. boards, pic. endsheets, 48 pp., numerous illus. including four, front cover and pp. 11, 12 and 13, by M., with comments on his art. (Remington, Russell)

92 Goetzmann, William H. *Exploration and Empire: The Explorer and the Scientist in the Winning of the American West.* Knopf, N.Y., 1966, words "First Edition" on copyright page, two-tone cloth, 656, xviii (12) pp., orange top, introduction, a note on the sources, index, numerous illus. including eight by M.

93 Good, Donnie D. *Mustangs.* Gilcrease, Tulsa, 1971, wraps, unpaged, numerous illus. incuding one by M. (Borein, James)

94 Goodrich, Lloyd et al. *The Artist in America.* Norton, N.Y., (1967), words "First Edition" on copyright page, cloth, grey endsheets, 256 pp., introduction, "Foreword" by Russell Lynes, contributors, acknowledgments, index, numerous illus. including four, pp. 53, 55 (two) and 62 (in color), by M. (Remington, Russell)

95 Greenbie, Sidney. *Furs to Furrows.* Caxton, Caldwell, Idaho, 1939, decor. fabricoid, 413 pp., preface, appendix, bibliography, index, numerous illus. including one, the frontis., by M.

96 Hafen, LeRoy R. and Young, Francis M. *Fort Laramie and the Pageant of the West, 1834–1890.* Clark, Glendale, Calif., 1938, cloth, 429 pp., index, maps, illus. including two, frontis. and p. (47), by M.

97 Hafen, LeRoy R., ed. *Ruxton of the Rockies.* Oklahoma University Press, Norman, (1950), words "First Edition" on copyright page, cloth, 325 pp., collected by Clyde and Mae Reed Porter, foreword, "Introduction" by Mrs. Porter, index, sixteen illus. including ten, facing pp. 138, 154, 179, 202, 218, 234, 250, 266, 282 and 298, by M.

98 Hafen, LeRoy R. (editorial supervision). *The Mountain Men and the Fur Trade of the Far West, Volume I.* Clark, Glendale, 1965, cloth, 397 pp., brown top, introduction, map, 23 illus. including one, p. (153), by M.

99 ———. Same, *Volume IV.* Clark, Glendale, 1966, cloth, 397 pp., brown top, preface, 14 illus. including one, the frontis., by M.

100 ———. Same, *Volume V.* Clark, Glendale, 1968, cloth, 401 pp., brown top, preface, 16 illus. including two, the frontis. and p. (20), by M.

101 ———. Same, *Volume VI.* Clark, Glendale, 1968, cloth, 407 pp., brown top, preface, 18 illus. including one, the frontis., by M.

102 ——— Same, *Volume IX.* Clark, Glendale, 1972, cloth, 420 pp., brown top, editor's note and acknowledgment, publisher's preface, 18 illus. including one, the frontis., by M.

103 ——— and Rister, Carl Coke. *Western America: The Exploration, Settlement and Development of the Region Beyond the Mississippi.* Prentice-Hall, N.Y., 1947, cloth, numerous illus. including one by M.

104 Haines, Francis. *Appaloosa, the Spotted Horse in Art and History.* University of Texas Press for the Amon Carter Museum of Western Art, Fort Worth, (1963), cloth, tinted endsheets, 103 pp., "Introduction" by Mitchell A. Wilder, (Director), bibliography, numerous illus. including one, p. 72, by M. (Borein, Russell)

105 ———. *The Buffalo.* Crowell, N.Y., (1970), cloth, grey endsheets, 242 pp., appendix, selected bibliography, index, map, illus. including five, pp. (35), (58), (88) two and (107), by M.

106 Harmsen, Dorothy. *Harmsen's Western Americana.* Northland Press, Flagstaff, (1971), morocco and cloth, blue endsheets, 213 pp., "Foreword" by Robert Rockwell, introduction, selected bibliography, numerous illus. including one in color, p. (143), by M. and a

FORT LARAMIE by Miller from *The West of Alfred Jacob Miller*

biographical sketch of him. Limited edition of 150 numbered copies signed by the author, slipcase with morocco title label. (Beeler, Blumenschein, Borein, Dixon, Dunn, Dunton, Eggenhofer, Elwell, Hurd, Johnson, Leigh, Marchand, Russell, Von Schmidt, Wyeth)

107 ———. Same, first trade edition in two-tone cloth and with red endsheets.

108 Hartman, Gertrude. *America.* Heath, Boston, 1946, cloth, 664 pp., "Foreword" by Allan Nevins, appendix, index, numeorus illus. including one, p. 330, by M. (Remington)

109 ———. *America, Land of Freedom.* Heath, (Boston etc., 1952), decor. cloth, 720 pp., "Foreword" by Allan Nevins, (appendices), index, maps, numerous illus. including one, p. 350, by M. (Cue)

110 Hassrick, Royal B. *The Sioux* (Life and Customs of a Warrior Society). Oklahoma University Press, Norman, (1964), words "First Edition" on copyright page, cloth, tan top, 337 pp., introduction, in collaboration with Dorothy Maxwell and Cile M. Bach, appendices, bibliography, index, 8 plates of drawings and sixteen illus. including one, between pp. 100-101, by M.

111 Hawgood, John A. *The American West.* Eyre and Spottiswoode, London, (1967), words "First published in Great Britain 1967" on copyright page, cloth, map endsheets, 399 pp., preface, introduction, bibliographical note, index, maps, numerous illus. including five, one, between pp. 112 and 113 and four between 128 and 129, by M. (Remington, Russell)

112 ———. *America's Western Frontiers.* The U.S. edition of no. 111.

113 Haydon, Harold (text by). *Great Art Treasures in America's Smaller Museums.* Putnam, N.Y., and Country Beautiful, Waukesha, Wis., (1967), words "First Edition" on copyright page, cloth, grey endsheets, 194 pp., edited by Robert L. Polley, introduction, index of reproductions, over 200 illus. including one in color, p. 164, by M. (Hurd, Remington, Russell, Wyeth)

114 ——— (text by). *Great Art Treasures in American Museums.* Country Beautiful, Waukesha, Wis., (1967), words "First Edition" on copyright page, cloth, 194 pp., edited by Robt. L. Polley, introduction, index of reproductions, over 200 illus. including one in color, p. 164, by M. Note: text and plates same as no. 113 above. (Hurd, Remington, Russell, Wyeth)

115 Heiderstadt, Dorothy. *Painters in America.* N.Y., (1970), cloth, red endsheets, 180 pp., introduction, index, illus. including one, p. (56), by M. and a chapter on him. (Remington, Russell, Schreyvogel)

116 Hieb, David L. *Fort Laramie National Monument, Wyoming.* Washington, D.C., 1954, pic. wraps, 43 pp., maps, numerous illus. including one, facing p. 1, by M.

117 Hillman, Martin. *Bridging a Continent* (Encyclopedia of Discovery and Exploration, volume 8). Aldus Books, London, (1971), cloth and colored pic. boards, 191 pp., glossary, index, picture credits, numerous illus. including ten, pp. 41 (color), 42 (color), 44 (color), 48 (color), 79 (color), 100 (color), 101 (color), 106 (color), 109 and 134–5 (color) by M. (Remington)

118 Hine, Robert V. and Lottinville, Savoie, eds. *Soldier in the West: Letters of Theodore Talbot During His Service in California, Mexico and Oregon, 1845-1853.* Oklahoma, Norman, (1972), words "First edition" on copyright page, cloth, illus. including one by M.

118a ———. *The American West — An Interpretive History.* Little, Brown, Boston, (1973), words "First Printing" on copyright page, cloth, 371 pp., preface, bibliography, index, numerous illus. including five, pp. 46, 49, 53, 55 and 102, by M. (Koerner, Remington, Russell)

119 Hollmann, Clide. *Five Artists of the Old West.* Hastings, N.Y., (1965), cloth, 128 pp., introduction, conclusion, index, chapter on Miller and four illus., pp. (69), (71), (72-3) and 75, by him. (Remington, Russell)

119a Holloway, David. *Lewis and Clark and the Crossing of North America.* Saturday Review Press, N.Y., (1974), cloth, pic. endsheets, 224 pp., "Introduction" by V. E. Fuchs, author's note, selected bibliography, index, maps, numerous illus. including four, d/w and pp. 50, (122–3) and 192–3, by M. (Leigh, Remington, Russell)

120 Holme, Bryan (compiled and edited by). *Pictures to Live With.* N.Y., (1959), words "First published in 1959 by The Viking Press" on copyright page, decor. cloth, 152 pp., index to artists, numerous illus. including one, p. 68, by M. (Johnson, Leigh, Remington, Schreyvogel)

121 Horan, James D. *The Great American West.* Crown, N.Y., (1959), cloth and boards, 288 pp., introduction, bibliography, picture credits, index, 650 illus. including two, pp. 29 and (74) in color, by M. (Eggenhofer, Hurd, Remington, Russell)

122 Hyde, George E. *A Life of George Bent, Written from His Letters.* Oklahoma University Press, Norman, (1968), words "First edition" on copyright page, two-toned cloth, orange top, 389 pp., introduction, "Preface" and edited by Savoie Lottinville, works cited, index, illus. including one, between pp. 198 and 199, by M.

123 Irving, Washington. *The Adventures of Captain Bonneville, U. S. A. in the Rocky Mountains and the Far West.* Oklahoma University Press, Norman, (1961), words "First Printing" (i.e. of the new edition) on copyright page, cloth, green top, 424 pp., "Foreword," "Introduction," (and edited) by Edgeley W. Todd, introductory notice, appendices, editor's bibliography, index, sixteen illus. including one, facing p. 11 plus d/w, by M.

124 Jensen, Oliver, ed. *A Treasury of American Heritage.* Simon & Schuster, N.Y., 1960, cloth, illus. including two by M.

125 Jones Evan, in consultation with Dale L. Morgan. *Trappers and Mountain Men.* American Heritage, N.Y., (1961), words "First Edition" on copyright page, colored pic. cloth and endsheets, 153 pp., "Foreword" by Morgan, picture credits, bibliography, index, numerous illus. including nine in color, pp. 94-5, (97), 100-1, 104, 105, 110, 110-1, 122-3 and 131, by M. (Remington, Russell, Schoonover)

126 Josephy, Alvin M., Jr. (editor in charge). *The American Heritage Book of Natural Wonders.* American Heritage, (N.Y., 1963), cloth, 384 pp., introduction, acknowledgments, index, profusely illus. including three in color, pp. (192) two and 225, by M. *De luxe* edition in slipcase. (Russell)

126a Horden, Nicholas et al. *The Conquest of North America.* Aldus, London, (1971), pic. boards, 488 pp., index, illus. including four in color, pp. 361, 362, 398-9 and 421, by M. (Deming, Remington)

126b ———. Same, first American edition by Doubleday, Garden City, N.Y., 1973.

127 ———. Same, first trade edition in cloth and boards.

128 *The M. and M. Karolik Collection of American Paintings, 1815–1865.* Harvard, Cambridge, 1949 (i.e. 1951), cloth, 554 pp., appendices, numerous illus., biographical sketch of and one plate by M.

129 *The M. and M. Karolik Collection of American Watercolours and Drawings,* vol. 1. Boston, 1962.

130 Kelly, Charles and Morgan, Dale L. *Old Greenwood* (The Story of Caleb Greenwood: Trapper, Pathfinder, and Early Pioneer). The Talisman Press, Georgetown, Calif., 1965, buckram, gilt top, pic. endsheets, 361 (19) pp., "Preface" by Kelly, appendix, bibliography, index, folding map, illus. including one, front endsheets, by M. (Limited edition of 100 numbered and signed copies, boxed.)

131 Kennerly, Wm. Clark. *Persimmon Hill.* Oklahoma University Press, Norman, 1948, words "First Edition" on copyright page, cloth, 273 pp., "Introduction" and "as told to" Elizabeth Russell, sources, index, illus. including two, facing pp. 149 and 196, by M.

132 Ketchum, Richard M. *The American Heritage Book of Great Historic Places.* American Heritage, N.Y., (1957), cloth with slipcase, 376 pp., "Introduction" by Bruce Catton, acknowledgments, index, numerous illus. including two in color, pp. 278-9 and 342, by M.

133 ———. Same, first trade edition, cloth and boards.

134 ——— (editor in charge). *The American Heritage Book of The Pioneer Spirit.* American Heritage, N.Y., (1959), cloth, 394 (6), pp., introduction, acknowldgments and index, profusely illus. including seven in color, double title page, pp. (5), (144), 162-3), 164, (165), and 344, by M. *De luxe* edition in slipcase. (Remington, Russell)

135 ———. Same, first trade edition, cloth and boards.

136 ——— (editor in charge). *The American Heritage Cookbook and Illustrated History of American Eating and Drinking.* American Heritage, N.Y., (1964), two vols. (in slipcase), cloth, pic. endsheets, 629 (11) pp., [continuous pagination], introduction, index, numerous illus. including two in color, pp. 40-41 and (67), by M. *De luxe* edition. (Dunn, Remington)

137 ———. Same, one volume trade edition, cloth and boards, with same illustrations.

138 LaFarge, Oliver. *A Pictorial History of the American Indian.* Crown, N.Y., (1956), cloth and boards, 272 pp., index, numerous illus. including one, p. 177, by M. (Eggenhofer, Remington)

139 ———. *The American Indian.* (Special Edition for Young Readers.) Golden Press, N.Y., (1960), colored pic. cloth, pic. map endsheets, 213 pp., index, profusely illus. including three in color, pp. 142 (two) and (164), by M. A *de luxe* Golden Book. (Remington, Russell)

140 Lavender, David. *The American Heritage History of the Great West.* American Heritage, N.Y., 1965,

decor. cloth, tan pic. endsheets, 416 pp., foreword, index, numerous illus. including three in color, pp. 204 and 205 (two), by M. (Koerner, Remington, Russell)

141 Leonard, Zenas. *Adventures of Zenas Leonard.* Oklahoma University Press, Norman, 1959, cloth, green top, 172 pp., edited by John C. Ewers, "Editor's Introduction" bibliography, index, map, 16 illus. including five, facing pp. 13, 28, 29, 60 and 61, by M. (Remington)

142 McCraken, Harold. *Portrait of the Old West.* McGraw-Hill, N.Y. etc., (1952), words "First Edition" on copyright page, decor. cloth, 232 pp., preface, "Foreword" by R. W. G. Vail, biographical check list of Western artists, index, numerous illus. including two, pp. (62) and (63) in color, by M. (Remington, Russell, Schreyvogel)

143 Mattes, Merrill J. *Fur Traders and Trappers of the Old West.* Yellowstone Library and Museum Assn., n.p., n.d., pic. wraps, 15 pp., eleven illus. including one, p. 8, by M.

144 ————. *Scotts Bluff National Monument, Nebraska* (Historical Handbook Series no. 28). National Park Service, Washington, D.C., 1961, decor. wraps, illus. including one by M.

144a Mendelowitz, Daniel M. *A History of American Art.* Holt, Rinehart & Winston, N.Y., 1960, cloth, 662 pp., bibliography, index, numerous illus. including one, p. (318), by M. (Remington, Young)

145 (Miller.) *A Series of Watercolour Drawings by Alfred Jacob Miller* (the Property of Major G. H. Power of Great Yarmouth, England). Parke-Bernet, N.Y., 1966, wraps, 51 pp., lists 83 drawings to be sold at auction, 48 illus. (six in color), by M.

146 Morgan, Dale L. and Harris, Eleanor Towles, eds. *Rocky Mountain Journals of Wm. Marshall Anderson.* (The West in 1834), Huntington Library, San Marino, Calif., 1967, cloth, 430 pp., map endsheets, illus. including two by M.

147 Nadeau, Remi. *Fort Laramie and the Sioux Indians.* Prentice-Hall, Englewood, N.J., 1967, cloth, illus. including one by M.

148 Neider, Charles, ed. *The Great West.* Coward-McCann, N.Y., (1958), decor. cloth, brown top, map endsheets, 457 pp., introduction, notes, maps, numerous illus. including six, pp. 37, 78, (100), 109, 165 and 204, by M. (Remington, Schreyvogel)

149 Nicoll, Bruce (assembled and edited by). *Nebraska,*

A Pictorial History. Lincoln, Neb., (1967), cloth, blue endsheets, 231 (1) pp., foreword, picture credits, numerous illus. (many in color) including three, pp. 21, 22 and 22-3, by M. (Dixon, Dunn, Remington, Russell)

150 Nieman, Egvert W. and O'Daly, Elizabeth C. *Adventures for Readers* (Book Two). Harcourt, Brace, N.Y. etc., (1963), words "Laureate Edition" on title page, cloth, 626 pp., glossary, index of authors and titles, numerous illus. including one, p. (200), by M. (Russell)

151 Nunis, Doyce Blackman, Jr. *Andrew Sublette, Rocky Mountain Prince, 1808–1853.* Dawsons, Los Angeles, 1960, cloth, 123 pp., foreword, two illus. including one, facing p. 1, by M. (A Plantin Press book, one of 330 copies.)

152 O'Meara, Walter. *Daughters of the Country: The Women of the Fur Traders and Mountain Men.* Harcourt, Brace & World, N.Y., (1968), words "First Edition" on copyright page, cloth, green endsheets, 368 pp., foreword, introduction, glossary, "Tribal Distribution," notes and references, bibliography, index, 16 illus. including one, between pp. 178 and 179, by M. (Russell)

153 Phillips, Paul Chrisler and Smurr, J. W. *The Fur Trade.* Oklahoma University Press, Norman, (1961), words "First edition" on copyright page, two volumes, (slipcase), cloth, brown top, 686 and 696 pp., "Foreword" (I) by Alice M. Phillips and Smurr, preface (I), bibliography (II), index (I, II), maps, numerous illus. including four, facing pp. 455 (I), 89 (II), 120 (II), and 1210 (II), by M.

154 Place, Marian T. *Westward on the Oregon Trail.* American Heritage, N.Y., 1962, words "First Edition" on title page, colored pic. cloth and endsheets, 153 pp., "Foreword" by Earl Pomeroy (Consultant), for further reading, index, numerous illus. including twelve, most in color, by M. (Dunn, Remington)

155 Platt, Rutherford. *Adventures in the Wilderness.* American Heritage, N.Y., 1963, words "First Edition" under frontis., colored pic. wraps and endsheets, 153 pp., foreword, Horace M. Albright, consultant, for further reading, index, numerous illus. including one in color, pp. 56–57, by M. (Remington)

156 Polley, Robert L., ed. *The Beauty of America in Great American Art.* Country Beautiful Foundation, Waukesha, Wis., (1965), decor. cloth, grey endsheets, 162 pp., "Preface" by Eric F. Goldman, "Introduction" by Tracy Atkinson (Director, Milwaukee Art Center),

indices, numerous illus. including one in color, p. 76, by M. (Remington, Russell)

157 Porter, Clyde and Mae Reed. *Matt Field on the Santa Fe Trail*. Oklahoma, Norman, (1960), words "First edition" on copyright page, cloth, illus. including one (and repeated on d/w) by M.

158 Porter, Mae Reed and Davenport, Odessa. *Scotsman in Buckskin* (Sir William Drummond Stewart and the Rocky Mountain Fur Trade). Hastings, N.Y., (1963), cloth, 306 pp., "Preface" by Odessa Davenport, bibliography, index, thirteen illus. including nine, between pp. 148 and 149, plus the d/w, by M.

159 (Price.) *The Vincent Price Treasury of American Art*. Country Beautiful, Waukeska, Wis., (1972), cloth, tan endsheets, 320 pp., foreword, biographical index, glossary, numerous illus. including one in color, p. 79, by M. and comments on his art, p. 78. (Hurd, Remington, Russell, Schreyvogel, Wyeth)

160 Rachlis, Eugene, in consultation with John C. Ewers. *Indians of the Plains*. American Heritage, N.Y., (1960), colored pic. wraps, 152 (1) pp., "Foreword" by Ewers, picture credits, bibliography, index, numerous illus. including five, pp. (24) in color, 26–27 in color, 43 in color, 86 in color and (87), by M. (Leigh, Remington, Schreyvogel)

161 Rasky, Frank. *The Taming of the Canadian West*. McClelland and Stewart, Ltd., (Toronto, 1967), decor. two-tone cloth, pic. endsheets, 270 (1) pp., epilogue, bibliography, index, numerous illus. including eight in color, pp. 25, 49, 52–53, 117, 118–19, 120 (two) and 125, by M. (Remington)

162 Rathbone, Perry T., ed. *Westward the Way*. City Art Museum of St. Louis, Walker Art Center, Minneapolis, (1954), pic. cloth, 280 pp., introduction, biographies of the artists (Miller, pp. 276–77), numerous illus. including fourteen by M. (Remington)

163 Roe, Frank Gilbert. *The Indian and the Horse*. Oklahoma University Press, Norman, (1955), words "First Edition" on copyright page, cloth, brown top, 434 pp., preface, introduction, appendices, bibliography, index, map, 31 illus. including five, four between pp. 110 and 111 and one between pp. 206 and 207, by M. (Leigh, Remington, Russell)

163a Rorabacker, J. Albert. *The American Buffalo in Transition*. North Star Press, Saint Cloud, Minn., (1970), decor. fabricoid, pic. endsheets, 141 (5) pp., preface, appendices, bibliography, index, maps, numerous illus. including one, p. 22, by M. (Remington, Russell)

164 Ross, Alexander. *The Fur Hunters of the Far West*. Oklahoma University Press, Norman, (1956), words "First edition" (i.e. in The American Exploration and Travel Series) on copyright page, decor. cloth, orange top, 304 pp., "Editor's Introduction" by Kenneth A. Spaulding, index, map, 19 illus. including eight, facing pp. 24, 25, 72, 137, 152, 153, 184 and 200, by M.

165 Ross, Marvin C. *The West of Alfred Jacob Miller*. Oklahoma University Press, Norman, (1951), words "First Edition" on copyright page, cloth, 200 pp., acknowledgments, appendix, bibliography, index, two hundred plates by M.

166 ———. Same, revised and enlarged edition, Oklahoma University Press, Norman, (1968), words "First printing of the revised and enlarged edition" on copyright page, cloth, lxxxiii pp., 208 numbered plates plus nine plates in color by M., other additions include "Bibliography since 1950," list of "Museums where Miller's Work may be Seen," "Recent Exhibitions," etc.

167 Rossi, Paul A. and Hunt, David C. *The Art of the Old West* (from the Collection of the Gilcrease Institute). (Knopf, N.Y., but printed in Italy, 1971), words "First Edition" on copyright page, pic. cloth, pic. brown endsheets, 335 (1) pp., preface, listing of artists and works, bibliography, numerous illus. including eleven by M. (Blumenschein, Borein, James, Leigh, Remington, Russell, Schreyvogel, Wyeth)

168 Russell, Osborne. *Journal of a Trapper*. Nebraska, Lincoln, (1965), first Bison Book printing, colored pic. wraps, 191 (1) pp., "Preface," "Introduction" and edited by Aubrey L. Haines, notes, sources, "Osborne Russell's Letters," index, maps, illustrated including two by M. (Remington, Russell)

169 Ruth, Kent. *Great Day in the West*. Oklahoma University Press, Norman, (1963), words "First edition" on copyright page, cloth, brown top, 308 pp., preface, index, numerous illus. including six, pp. (135), (137), (279), (281), (287) and (289), by M.

170 Ruxton, George Frederick. *Life in the Far West*. Oklahoma University Press, Norman, (1964), cloth, 252 pp., edited and notes by LeRoy Hafen, illus. by M.

171 Savelle, Max, with the assistance of Tremaine McDowell. *A Short History of American Civilization*. The Dryden Press, (N.Y., 1957), decor. cloth, green top, tan endsheets, 665 pp., preface, acknowledgments, postscript, appendix, index, maps and charts, numerous illus. including one, p. 283, by M. (Remington)

172 Schmitt, Martin F. and Brown, Dee. *Fighting Indians of the West*. Scribner's, N.Y., London, 1948, code letter "A" on copyright page, pic. cloth, map endsheets, 362 pp., preface, bibliography, 270 illus. including one, p. 27, by M. (Dixon, Remington, Schreyvogel)

173 Schomaekers, Von G. *Der Wilde Westen*. L. R. Ahnert Verlag, West Germany, 1972, cloth, map endsheets, 217 (1) pp., *Ein Wort Zuvor*, profusely illus. including fourteen (seven in color) by M. (Remington, Russell, Schreyvogel)

174 Shapiro, Irwin (adapted for young readers by). *The Golden Book of America*. Simon and Shuster, N.Y., (1957), words "First Printing" on copyright page, cloth and pic. boards and endsheets, "Foreword" by Bruce Catton, index, numerous illus. including four in color, pp. 18, 99 and 118–19 (two), by M. (Remington, Russell, Schreyvogel)

175 ———. *America on Parade*. Guild Press, Poughkeepsie and N.Y., (1964), colored pic. boards and endsheets, 91 pp., "Foreword" by Bruce Catton, numerous illus. incuding two in color, front endsheet and p. 57, by M.

176 Soby, James Thrall and Miller, Dorothy C. *Romantic Painting in America*. Museum of Modern Art, N.Y., (1943), cloth, 143 pp., foreword and acknowledgment, "Preface" by Alfred H. Barr, Jr., biographies of the artists (Miller, p. 139), numerous illus. including one, p. 60, by M. (Remington)

177 Speck, Gordon. *Breeds and Half-Breeds*. Potter, N.Y., (1969), words "First Edition" on copyright page, cloth, 361 pp., sources, notes, a selected bibliography, index, maps, numerous illus. including one, p. (264), by M.

178 Sprague, Marshall. *A Gallery of Dudes*. Little, Brown, Boston, Toronto, (1967), words "First Edition" on copyright page, two-tone decor. cloth, green endsheets, index, maps, numerous illus. including one, a self-sketch, by M. Information on Miller in text.

179 Stuart, Robert. *On the Oregon Trail: Robert Stuart's Journey of Discovery, 1812–13*. Oklahoma, Norman, 1953, cloth, edited by Kenneth A. Spaulding, illus. including one by M.

180 Sunder, John E. *Bill Sublette, Mountain Man*. Oklahoma University Press, Norman, (1959), words "First Edition" on copyright page, cloth, maroon top, 279 pp., preface, appendices, bibliography, index, maps, 14 illus. including one, facing p. 96, by M. (Beeler)

181 Swingle, John (compiled by). *Rare Books & Manuscripts*. John Howell, San Francisco, 1961, decor. wraps, unpaged, "Introduction" by Rebecca Richardson (Mrs. John) Howell, illus. with photos, facsimiles and with one plate by M. (A Lawton Kennedy book.)

182 Tebbel, John and Jennison, Keith. *The American Indian Wars*. Harper, N.Y., (1960), cloth, map endsheets, 312 pp., epilogue, bibliographical notes, index, maps, numerous illustrations including one, d/w in color, by M. (Remington, Schreyvogel, Zogbaum)

183 Thompson, Erwin N. *Whitman Mission National Historic Site* (National Park Service Handbook Series no. 37), Government Printing Office, Washington, D.C., 1964, wraps, illus. including one by M.

184 Todd, Lewis Paul et al. *Rise of the American Nation*. Harcourt, Brace, N.Y., Burlingame, (1961), pic. cloth, 880 pp., index, acknowledgments, maps in color, numerous illus. including one, p. 321, by M. John Carroll Edition. (Remington)

185 Toole, K. Ross. *Montana, an Uncommon Land*. Oklahoma University Press, Norman, (1959), words "First edition" on copyright page, cloth, blue top, 278 pp., bibliography, index, maps, illustrated primarily with photos but d/w illus. by M. (Russell)

186 Trenholm, Virginia and Carley, Maurine. *The Shoshonis, Sentinels of the Rockies*. Oklahoma University Press, Norman, (1964), words "First edition" on copyright page, cloth, green top, 367 pp., preface, bibliography, index, maps, 24 illus. including one, between pp. 66–67, by M.

187 Truettner, William H. et al. *National Parks and the American Landscape*. National Collection of Fine Arts, Smithsonian Institution, Washington, D.C., 1972, wraps, illus. including one by M.

188 Tyler, Ronnie C. *Alfred Jacob Miller*. (Amon Carter Museum, Fort Worth, 1972), pic. wraps, unpaged, eleven illus. by M.

189 Ver Steeg, Clarence L. *The Story of Our Country*. Harper & Row, N.Y., (1965), colored pic. cloth, 416 pp., introduction, glosary, index, maps and diagrams, numerous illus. including one in color, p. 226, by M. (Dunn, Remington, Russell)

190 Webber, C. W. *The Hunter-Naturalist. Romance of Sporting; or, Wild Scenes and Wild Hunters*. J. W. Bradley, Philadelphia, (1851), cloth, 610 pp., introduction, numerous illus. including five lithographed plates in full color, frontis. and facing pp. 292, 359, 399 and 469, by M.

191 ———. *The Hunter Naturalist: Wild Scenes and*

Song Birds. Putnam, N.Y., 1854, decor. cloth, 347 pp., illus. with 25 colored lithographs including five by M.

192 *West to the Rendezvous* (America and the Future no. 3). Reprint from *Fortune*, January, 1944, wraps, pp. 111–21, map, nineteen illus., seventeen in color, by M.

193 White, Anne Terry. *Indians and the Old West.* Simon and Schuster, N.Y., 1954, colored pic. boards, decor. endsheets, 56 pp., picture credits, numerous illus. including one, p. 31, by M. (Lea, Leigh, Remington, Russell, Schreyvogel)

194 Willard, John. *Adventure Trails in Montana.* Montana Historical Society (sponsored by), (Helena, 1964), cloth with illus. in color mounted on front cover, or colored pic. wraps, 243 (7) pp., "Foreword" by Director Michael Kennedy, "Introduction" by Harold McCracken, index, numerous illus. including one, p. 147, by M. (Remington, Russell, Von Schmidt)

195 Wirth, Conrad L. (Director, National Park Service) et al. *Soldier and Brave.* Vol. XII, The National Survey of Historic Sites and Buildings, National Park Service, Harper & Row, N.Y. etc., 1963, words "First Edition" on copyright page, cloth, map endsheets, 279 pp., "Introduction" by Ray Allen Billington, "Foreword" by Wirth, suggested reading, notes, index, maps, numerous illus. including one, p. (18), by M. (Remington)

The Artist and His Art

196 "America and the Future: West to the Rendezvous, an Artist Travels the Oregon Trail," an article in *Fortune*, vol. XXIX, no. 1, January, 1944.

197 *The American Indian and the West.* Washington County Museum of Fine Arts, Hagerstown, Maryland, 1947, wraps, entries nos. 56–76 by M.

198 Brandon, William. "The Wild Freedom of the Mountain Men," an illus. article in *American Heritage*, August 1955, with two illus. by M.

199 Brown, D. Alexander. "Jim Bridger," an illus. article in *American History Illustrated*, July 1968, with three illus. by M. (Koerner, Russell)

200 Brown, Mark H. *The Plainsmen of the Yellowstone.* Putnam's, N.Y., (1961), cloth, black top, map endsheets, 480 pp., "Some Interesting Books," index, maps; Miller with Stewart on the expedition, pp. 96–97.

201 Brunet, Pierre. *A Descriptive Catalogue of a Collection of Watercolour Drawings by Alfred Jacob Miller in the Public Archives of Canada.* E. Cloutier, King's Printer, Ottawa, 1951, wraps, 39 pp., with notes by Miller written in 1867.

202 *Catalogue of Exhibition, 1848,* Maryland Historical Society, Baltimore, includes entries by M.

203 Same, *1849,* Maryland Historical Society, Baltimore, includes entries by M.

204 Same, *1850,* Maryland Historical Society, Baltimore, includes entries by M.

205 Cowdrey, Bartlett and Comstock, Helen. "Alfred Jacob Miller and the Farthest West," an article in *Panorama*, Henry Shaw Newman Gallery, N.Y., August–September 1947.

206 Dawson's Book Shop, Los Angeles. *An Exhibition of Original Western Paintings, Watercolors & Prints,* beginning October 15, 1952, folder, describes two watercolors and one oil by M.

207 Decatur, Stephen. "Alfred Jacob Miller: His Early Indian Scenes and Portraits," an article in *The American Collector*, vol. VIII, no. 11, December, 1939.

208 Early, Mrs. John D. *Alfred J. Miller, Artist.* Baltimore, (1894), the only known copy is in the library of the Maryland Historical Society.

209 Fielding, Mantle. *Dictionary of American Painters, Sculptors and Engravers.* Philadelphia, 1926, cloth, 433 pp., preface, bibliography, brief biographical sketch of M., p. 241.

210 ———. Same, with addendum by James F. Carr and issued by him, N.Y., 1965, cloth, 529 pp., with a few additional notes on M., p. 496.

211 Forrest, James T. "Fort William, the First Fort on the Laramie," an illus. article in *The American Scene*, Winter 1959–60, with two illus. by M.

212 ———. "Capturing the American Scene," an article in *El Palacio*, Autumn 1961, mentions M.

213 Gold, Barbara. "Alfred Jacob Miller, 19th Century Artist," an illus. article in *Maryland*, Spring 1973, with eleven (four in color) illus. by M.

214 Goosman, Mildred. "Collector's Choice: Old Gabe of Her Majesty's English Life Guards," an illus. article in *The American West*, November 1969, with one illus. by M.

215 Hafen, LeRoy R. "Etienne Provost, Mountain Man and Utah Pioneer," an illus. article in *Utah Historical Quarterly*, Spring 1968, with two illus. by M.

216 Hill, Don. "Notes on Some Artists in the Early West," an article in *The Westerners Brand Book, Los Angeles Corral, Volume I, 1948,* reference to M.

217 Huth, Hans. *Nature and the American.* California, Berkeley, 1957, cloth, 250 pp., preface, index, illus., Miller in text.

218 Josephy, Alvin M., Jr. "First Dude Ranch Trip to the Untamed West," an illus. article in *American Heritage,* 1956, with seven illus. by M.

219 King, Edward S. "A. J. Miller's Expedition to the Far West," an article in *The Bulletin,* Walters Art Gallery, Baltimore, April 1950.

220 ———. "Miller on Tour," an article in *The Bulletin,* April 1951.

221 ———. "The Old West of A. J. Miller," an article in *The Bulletin,* May 1964.

222 Kingman, Eugene. "Painters of the Plains," an illus. article in *American Heritage,* December 1954, with one illus. by M.

223 La Farge, Oliver. "Myths that Hide the American Indian," an illus. article in *American Heritage,* October 1956, with five illus. by M.

224 Laubin, Reginald and Gladys. *The Indian Tipi.* Oklahoma University Press, Norman, 1957, words "First edition" on copyright page, cloth, 208 pp., "Foreword" and "The History of the Tipi" by Stanley Vestal, bibliography, index, illus. Comments on Miller's Tipis, p. 11.

225 McDermott, John Francis. *Seth Eastman, Pictorial Historian of the Indian.* Oklahoma University Press, Norman, (1961), words "First edition" on copyright page, cloth, tan top, 270 pp., preface, chronology, check list of works, source consulted, index, illus., comments on Miller's art in the chapter "The Homely Truth of Indian Life," pp. 103–12.

226 ———. "Miller," a feature article in *American Scene* (the Gilcrease Magazine, Tulsa, Okla.), vol. IV, no. 3, 1962, with 24 illus., including the front cover in color, by M.

227 MacGill, James. *Alfred Jacob Miller, 1810–1874.* Peale Museum, Baltimore, 1933, wraps, issued on the occasion of Miller's first one-man exhibition in this century.

228 "Alfred Jacob Miller," an article in *Maryland Historical Magazine,* March 1953.

229 "Alfred Jacob Miller — Indian Painter, 1810–1874,"
an article in *The Portfolio,* vol. VIII, no. 3, November, 1943.

230 Monaghan, Jay. "The Hunter and the Artist," an illus. article in *The American West,* November 1969, with ten illus. by M.

231 Nunis, Doyce B., Jr. "Milton Sublette: Thunderbolt of the Rockies," an illus. article in *Montana,* Summer 1963, with eight illus. by M.

231a *Readers' Digest Illustrated Guide to the Treasures of America.* The Readers' Digest Assn., Pleasantville, N.Y., (1974), fabricoid and decor. cloth, blue endsheets, 624 pp., index, numerous illus. including two in color, pp. 370 and 423, by M. (Dunn, Remington, Russell)

232 Richardson, E. P. *Painting in America, the Story of 450 Years.* Crowell, N.Y., (1956), cloth, 447 pp., selected bibliography, index, 189 illustrations, brief biographical sketch, p. 178, of M.

233 Ross, Marvin C., ed. *Artists' Letters to Alfred Jacob Miller.* Walters Art Gallery, Baltimore, 1951, wraps, 15 mimeo. pages, note, footnotes.

234 ———. "A List of Portraits and Paintings from Alfred Jacob Miller's Account Book," an article in *Maryland History Society Magazine,* 1953, pp. 27–36.

235 Rutledge, Anne Wells. *Cumulative Record of Exhibition Catalogues, The Pennsylvania Academy of Fine Arts, 1807–1870.* A.P.S., Philadelphia, 1955, cloth, 450 pp., lists Miller items.

236 *Sale Catalogue — Choice Oil Painting,* Dec. 17, 1863, Bennet and Co., Baltimore, entries nos. 104–07, by M.

237 *Sale Catalogue,* April 22, 1903, Crim, Baltimore, entries nos. 1380 and 1685 by M.

238 *Sale Catalogue — Paintings, the Property of the Late Wm. C. Wait,* April 23, 1861, Gibson and Co., Baltimore.

239 *Sale Catalogue,* May 31, 1910, Latimer J. Hoffman, Baltimore, entries nos. 714 and 721 by M.

240 *Sale Catalogue of Baltimoreana — Paintings, the Property of Two Gentlemen of Baltimore,* Jan. 30, 1935, Sam W. Pattison, Baltimore, entry no. 127 by M.

241 *A Sale of Paintings Comprising the XVIII Century English School — Six Ultra Important Paintings by Alfred J. Miller of Baltimore,* Feb. 6, 1933, Perry W. Fuller Galleries, Baltimore.

242 Saum, Lewis O. "Frenchmen, Englishmen and the Indian," an illus. article in *The American West*, Fall 1964, with one illus. by M.

243 Seldis, Henry J. "Boom Interest in Western Art," an illus. article in *Art in America* 47:3, Fall 1959, with one illus. by M. and comments on his art.

244 (Stewart, Sir William George Drummond.) *Altowan; or Incidents of Life and Adventure in the Rocky Mountains*, by an Amateur Traveller, edited by J. Watson Webb. Harper, N.Y., 1846, 2 vols., cloth, "written for the amusement of some young friends . . ." as fiction but based on Sir William's expedition.

245 Taggart, Ross E. *The Last Frontier*. William Rockhill Nelson Gallery of Art, Kansas City, Mo., October 5 to November 17, 1957, pic. wraps, 28 pp., introduction, illustrated, entries 31 through 43 by M. and a brief biographical sketch of him. (Remington, Russell)

246 Thomas, Phillip Drennon. "Artists Among the Indians, 1493–1850," an article in *Kansas Quarterly*, Fall 1971, mentions M.

247 *Two Hundred and Fifty Years of Painting in Maryland*. Baltimore Museum of Art, 1946, wraps, entries 126–31 by M.

248 Vail, R. W. G. "The First Artist of the Oregon Trail," an article on Miller in *The New York Historical Society Quarterly*, vol. XXXIV, no. 1, Jan. 1950, one illus. by M.

249 Wasserman, Emily. "The Artist Explorers," an illus. article in *Art in America*, July–August 1972, with two illus. by M.

250 *The Land of Buffalo Bill*, Whitney Gallery of Western Art, Cody, 1959, catalogue of exhibition at opening of the Center, includes biographical sketch of M.

251 Woodward, Arthur. "Indian Sketches in the Archives of Canada," an article in *Masterkey*, September 1948, a description of the Miller portfolio now in the archives in Ottawa.

WONGO, THE LITTLE BROWN BEAR, CHO-GAY, THE INDIAN BOY-RULER
AND KAW, THE WISE OLD CROW by Moon from *Wongo, and the Wise Old Crow*

CARL MOON
1879–1948

Illustrated by the Artist

1 Moon, Carl. *Photographic Studies of Indians.* Fred Harvey, Grand Canyon, Arizona, 1910, wraps, 15 pp., decor. by the artist-photographer.

2 ———. *The Flaming Arrow.* Frederick A. Stokes Co., N.Y., 1927, cloth with illus. in color mounted on front cover, four illus., front cover, endsheets, frontis. in color and title page, by the author.

3 ———. *Painted Moccasin.* Stokes, N.Y., 1931, cloth, pic. endsheets, 318 pp., three illus., endsheets, frontis. in color and title page, by the author.

4 ———. *Tah-Kee.* Stokes, N.Y., 1932, cloth, 282 pp., illus. including five full-page plates, frontis. (in color) by the author.

5 ———. *Indians of the Southwest.* C. Moon., Pasadena, Calif., 1936, 4 volumes each containing twenty-five photos of Indians (of Oklahoma, New Mexico and Arizona), bound in boards with laced leather back and leather hinges and corners, painted colored borders and title on mounted label, title in color within ornamental borders, foreword (I) by F. W. Hodge. Limited to 50 sets.

6 Moon, Grace and Carl. *Lost Indian Magic.* Stokes, N.Y., (1918), cloth, pic. endsheets, 301 pp., illus., including frontis. in color, by M.

7 ———. *Wongo and the Wise Old Crow.* Reilly & Lee, Chicago, (1923), cloth, pic. endsheets, illus. with numerous drawings and a frontis. in color by M.

8 ———. *The Book of Nah-Wee.* Doubleday, Doran, Garden City, N.Y., 1932, words "First Edition" on copyright page, colored pic. boards, pic. endsheets, 59 pp., illus. including 22 in color by M.

9 ———. *One Little Indian.* Whitman, Chicago, 1950, cloth, with illus. in color mounted on front cover, pic. endsheets, 82 pp., illus. including four in color by M.

10 Moon, Grace. *Indian Legends in Rhyme.* Stokes, N.Y., (1917), cloth, with illus. in color mounted on front cover, 54 pp., illus. including five in color by M.

11 ———. *Chi-Wee'.* Doubleday, Page, Garden City, N.Y., 1925, words "First Edition" on copyright page, decor. cloth, pic. endsheets, 239 pp., illus. including eleven full-page plates, frontis. in color, by M.

12 ———. *Chi-Wee' and Loki of the Desert.* Doubleday, Page, Garden City, N.Y., 1926, words "First Edition" on copyright page, decor. cloth, tan endsheets, 208 pp., illus. including eleven full-page plates, frontis. in color, by M.

13 ———. *Nadita.* Doubleday, Page, Garden City, N.Y., 1927, words "First Edition" on copyright page, decor. cloth, 274 pp., illus. including seventeen full-page plates, by M.

14 ———. Same, Young Moderns Books, Doubleday, Doran, Garden City, N.Y., 1936.

15 ———. *The Runaway Papoose.* Doubleday, Doran, Garden City, N.Y., 1928, words "First Edition" on copyright page, decor. cloth, pic. endsheets, 264 pp., illus. including fourteen full-page plates, frontis. in color, by M.

16 ———. *The Magic Trail.* Doubleday, Doran, Garden City, N.Y., 1929, words "First Edition" on copyright page, cloth, map endsheets, 234 pp., illus. including frontis. in color by M.

17 ———. *The Missing Katchina.* Doubleday, Doran, Garden City, N.Y., 1930, words "First Edition" on copyright page, cloth, pic. endsheets, 286 pp., red top, illus. including frontis. in color by M.

18 ———. *The Arrow of Tee-May.* Doubleday, Doran, Garden City, N.Y., 1931, words "First Edition" on copyright page, decor. cloth, pic. endsheets, 284 pp.,

SHE WAS GATHERING STICKS TO MAKE A FIRE by Moon from *The Missing Katchina*

black top, illus. including eleven full-page plates, frontis. in color, by M.

19 ————. *Far-Away Desert.* Doubleday, Doran, Garden City, N.Y., 1932, words "First Edition" on copyright page, decor. cloth, pic. endsheets, 261 pp., illus. including frontis. in color by M.

20 ————. *Tita of Mexico.* Stokes, N.Y., 1934, decor. cloth, pic. endsheets, 213 pp., illus. including a frontis. in color by M.

21 ————. *Shanty Ann.* Stokes, N.Y., 1935, cloth, pic. endsheets, 200 pp., illus. including frontis. in color by M.

22 ————. *Singing Sands.* Doubleday, Doran, Garden City, 1936, words "First Edition" on copyright page, decor. cloth, pic. endsheets, 245 pp., six illus., frontis. in color, and facing pp. 118, 128, 140, 230 and 240, by M.

23 ————. Same, Junior Literary Edition in decor. fabricoid, (1936).

24 ————. *White Indian.* Doubleday, Doran, Garden City, N.Y., 1937, words "First Edition" on copyright page, pic. cloth, pic. endsheets, 221 pp., illus. including a frontis. in color by M.

25 ————. *Solita.* Doubleday, Doran, Garden City, N.Y., 1938, words "First Edition" on copyright page, cloth, pic. endsheets, illus. including frontis. in color by M.

26 ————. *Daughter of Thunder.* Macmillan, N.Y., 1942, cloth, pic. endsheets, 184 pp., frontis. in color by M.

27 Moore, Anne Carroll. *The Three Owls, A Book About Children's Books.* Macmillan, N.Y., 1925, words "Published, November, 1925" on copyright page, cloth, 376 pp., foreword, appendix, index, numerous illus. including one, p. 320, by M.

The Artist and His Art

28 Arbuthnot, May Hill. *Children and Books.* Scott, Foresman & Co., Chicago etc., (1947), cloth, 626 pp., notes, index, numerous illus. "Grace and Carl Moon," pp. 384–85. (Smith, Wyeth)

29 Burke, W. J. and Howe, Will D. *American Authors and Books, 1640–1940.* Gramercy Pub. Co., N.Y., (1943), cloth, 858 pp., preface, brief biographical sketch of M., p. 497.

30 Mahoney, Bertha E. and Whitney, Elinor. *Contemporary Illustrators of Children's Books.* Bookshop for Boys and Girls, Boston, 1930, decor. cloth, 135 pp., introduction, numerous illustrations, includes a brief biographical sketch of Moon, p. 49. (Wyeth)

31 Mahoney, Bertha E. et al. (compiled by). *Illustrators of Children's Books, 1744–1945.* The Horn Book, Boston, 1947, cloth and pic. boards, 527 pp., gilt top, preface, introduction, appendix, index, illustrated, includes a biographical sketch of Moon, p. 340 and lists four items illus. by him, p. 423. (Smith)

32 Rankin, Antoinette. "He Knows the Red-man," an article about Moon in *Sunset Magazine* 54:2, February 1925, with a photo of him.

33 Schmitt, Martin F. and Brown, Dee. *Fighting Indians of the West.* Scribner's, N.Y., 1948, code letter "A" on copyright page, pic. cloth, map endsheets, 362 pp., preface, introduction, bibliography, numerous illus. including one, "Indian Runner," p. 6, from a photo by M.

NEOPHYTE MISSION VAQUEROS by Mora from *Californios: The Saga of the Hard-riding Vaqueros, America's First Cowboys*

JO MORA

JOSEPH JACINTO (JO) MORA
1876–1947

Catalogues of Art Exhibitions and Galleries

WOOLAROC MUSEUM (FRANK PHILLIPS FOUNDATION), BARTLESVILLE, OKLAHOMA

1 *Oklahoma*, (1952), colored pic. wraps, (8) pp., numerous illus. including a photo of the bronze, "The Cowboy," by M. (Dunton, Johnson, Leigh, Remington, Russell)

2 *Indians*, (1952), colored pic. wraps, (12) pp., numerous illus. including a photo of the bronze, "The Squaw," by M. (Leigh, Remington, Russell)

3 *Woolaroc*, (n.d.), colored decor. wraps, 31 (1) pp., numerous illus. including a photo of the bronze, "The Cowboy," p. 23, by M. (Johnson, Leigh, Remington, Russell)

4 *Woolaroc Museum*, (1965), colored decor. boards (or wraps), 64 pp., "Welcome to Woolaroc," numerous illus. including photos of two bronzes, pp. 40 (Belle Starr) and 41 (The Cowboy), repeated in double-page spread pp. 44-5, by M. (Johnson, Leigh, Remington, Russell, Young)

Illustrated by the Artist

5 Ainsworth, Ed *The Cowoby in Art*. World, N.Y. and Cleveland, (1968), words "First Edition" on copyright page, full leather, orange endsheets, 242 pp., all edges gilt, "Foreword" by John Wayne, index, numerous illus. including one, p. 10, by M. Special edition of 1000 numbered copies in slipcase. (Beeler, Borein, Bugbee, De Yong, Dixon, Dunton, Eggenhofer, Ellsworth, Hurd, James, Johnson, Koerner, Perceval, Remington, Russell, Santee, Schreyvogel, Von Schmidt)

6 ———. Same, first trade edition in gilt lettered and illus. cloth, orange endsheets.

7 ———. Same, reprint by Bonanza Books, N.Y., in red lettered and illus. cloth, white endsheets.

8 Davenport, William. *The Monterey Peninsula*. Lane Books, Menlo Park, Calif., (1965), colored pic. wraps, 80 pp., foreword, index, numerous illus. from photos plus twenty drawings in margins by M.

9 Ford, Tiery L. *Dawn and the Dons*. A. M. Robertson, San Francisco, 1926, cloth and pic. boards, pic. map endsheets, 236 pp., illus. with numerous vignettes and sketches by M.

9a Gridley, Marion. *America's Indian Statues*. The Amerindian, Chicago, (1966), pic. wraps, 104 pp., illus. including one, photo of the bronze "The Indian," p. 101, by M.

10 Leeth, Dorothy Lyman. *Benito and Loreta Delfin* (Children of Alta California). Lothrop, Boston, (1932), colored pic. cloth, 267 pp., twenty-two illus., front cover and d/w, by M.

11 McCarty, Don, ed. *Language of the Mosshorn*. The Gazette Printing Co., Billings, Montana, 1936, words "First Printing" opposite the title page, pic. wraps, unpaged, foreword, illus. including a double-page pic. map, "The Birth of the Rodeo," by M. (James)

12 Monaghan, Jay (editor-in-chief). *The Book of the American West*. Messner, N.Y., (1963), words "First Edition" on copyright page, pic. cloth, tan endsheets, 608 pp., introduction, suggestions for additional reading, index, about the editor-in-chief, and the authors, numerous illus. including four groups of drawings, pp. 334, (339), 342 and (345), by M. (Borein, Johnson, Koerner, Leigh, Lungren, Remington, Russell, Schreyvogel, Zogbaum)

13 Mora, Jo. *A Log of the Spanish Main*. Privately printed by the author, San Francisco, 1934, colored pic. cloth, endsheets, pages unnumbered, profusely illus. by M.

14 ———. *Trail Dust and Saddle Leather*. Scribner's,

N.Y., 1946, code letter "A" on copyright page, cloth, colored pic. endsheets, 246 pp., numerous illus. by M.

15 ———. *Californios: The Saga of the Hard-riding Vaqueros, America's First Cowboys.* Doubleday, Garden City, N.Y., 1949, words "First Edition" on copyright page, decor. cloth, pic. endsheets, 175 pp., numerous illus. by M.

16 ———. *The Historical Pageant of the Monterey Peninsula, in Twelve Episodes Pictorially Rendered by Jo Mora.* Del Monte Properties Co., Del Monte, Calif., (1933).

17 ———. *Andersen's Fairy Tales* (edited and illustrated by).

18 ———. *Animals of Aesop* (edited and illustrated by).

19 ———. *Hotel Del Monte Menus.* Monterey, 1938, 10 different historical illustrations, 4¾" x 10", by M.

20 ———. *Horsemen of the West.* Reprinted from *Arizona Highways,* September 1952 for Carl A. Bimson, President, Valley National Bank, Phoenix, portfolio with eight illus. in color by M.

21 Porter, Bruce et al. *Art in California.* R. L. Bernier, San Francisco, 1916, cloth and boards, tan endsheets, 183 (1) pp., plus 332 numbered plates, including one, no. 205, "Poppy Nymph," by M. Biographical sketch, p. 173, of M. (Dixon, Lungren)

22 Reinke, de Vos. *Reynard the Fox.* D. Estes & Co., Boston, 1901, colored pic. cloth, 186 pp., profusely illus. by M. (Translated from the German.)

23 ———. *King Lion and Reynard the Fox,* as retold by John L. Forrest. A. Whitman Co., Chicago, 1920, cloth, pic. endsheets, 186 pp., illus. including frontis. in color by M.

24 (Reynolds.) *The West and Florencio Molina Campos* (Artista del Gaucho y de la Pampa), Catalogue 102, J. E. Reynolds, Bookseller, Van Nuys, Calif., Winter 1968, pic. wraps, unpaged, introduction, "Florencio Molina Campos, Artist" by Lynton Kistler, "Recollections of a Friendship" by Herbert Ryman, five illus. including one, a photo of the bronze, "Bronco Buster," by M.

25 Spaulding, Edward S. *Adobe Days Along the Channel.* The Schauer Printing Studio, Santa Barbara, 1957, pic. buckram, pic. endsheets, 124 (2) pp., "Foreword" by Harold Schauer, sources, numerous illus. including one, p. 52, by M. (boxed). (Borein, Lungren)

26 Stratemeyer, Edward. *Under Scott in Mexico* by Captain Ralph Bonehill (pseud.). Dana Estes & Co., Boston, (1902), words "Published, September 1902" on copyright page, pic. cloth, 287 pp., preface, eight illus., frontis. and facing pp. 68, 86, 134, 136, 180, 212 and 282, by M. (Volume 3, Mexican War Series.)

26a Trask, John E. D. and Laurik, J. Nilsen, eds. *Catalogue De Luxe of the Department of Fine Arts, Panama-Pacific Exposition.* Paul Elder and Co., San Francisco, 1915, two volumes, vellum and boards, brown endsheets, 482 (2) pp. gilt tops, introduction, numerous illus. including one, facing p. 424, by M. (Edition of 1100 copies.) (Young)

The Artist and His Art

27 Blumann, Ethel and Thomas, Mabel W. *California Local History,* A Centennial Bibliography. Stanford University Press, Stanford, Calif., 1950, fabricoid, printed endsheets, 576 pp., "Preface" by Lawrence Clark Powell. No. 16 above is no. 2050 in Blumann and Thomas.

28 Fielding, Mantle. *Dictionary of American Painters, Sculptors and Engineers.* N.Y., 1926, cloth, 443 pp., very brief biographical sketch, p. 246, of M.

29 ———. Same, but with addendum and published by James F. Carr, N.Y., 1965, cloth, 529 pp., but no new material on M.

30 Gridley, Marion E. "America's Indian Statues," an illus. article in *The Amerindian,* 1966, includes photo of one bronze by M. (Young)

31 "Jo Mora's Horsemen of the West," an article in *Arizona Highways,* September 1952, with nine illus. by M. and a photo of him.

32 Perceval, Don Louis (foreword). *Art of Western America* (Catalog of Exhibition at Pomona College Art Gallery). Claremont, Calif., Nov. 1 to 31, 1949, pic. wraps, pages unnumbered, illus., biographical sketch of M.

33 *San Francisco* (A Guide to the Bay and its Cities). Hastings, N.Y., 1940, words "First Published in 1940" on copyright page, cloth, 531 pp., "Preface" by State Supervisor Walter McElroy, appendices, index, illustrated, Mora's art mentioned, pp. 183, 184 and 338.

33a Tid, Lowell (of Ukiah, California). "Mora Plaque at Rainbow Bridge," a letter to *Arizona Highways* 44:4, April 1968, with a photo of the plaque.

The Rep

JO MORA

THE REP by Mora from *Trail Dust and Saddle Leather*

DON PERCEVAL.

ILLUSTRATION by Perceval from *A Navajo Sketch Book*

DON LOUIS PERCEVAL
Contemporary, 1908–

Catalogues of Art Exhibitions and Galleries

COWIE GALLERIES (BILTMORE HOTEL), LOS ANGELES

0 *Don Perceval*, a catalog of paintings, February 1961, "Foreword" by Alexander S. Cowie, one illus. by P.

Illustrated by the Artist

1 Adams, Earl C. (Sheriff). *Membership Directory — 1972*. Los Angeles Corral, The Westerners, 1972, wraps, 32 pp., illus. with four drawings, pp. (1), 7, 29 and 32, by P.

2 Ainsworth, Ed. *Painters of the Desert*. Desert Magazine, Palm Desert, California, 1960, gold stamped cloth, 111 pp., "Foreword" by Carl Schaefer Dentzel, numerous illus. Don Louis Perceval, pp. 70–75, illus. with reproductions of oil, watercolor and book illus. by P. (Dixon)

3 ———. *The Cowboy in Art*. World, N.Y. and Cleveland, (1968), words "First Printing 1968" on copyright page, full leather, orange endsheets, 242 pp., all edges gilt, "Foreword" by John Wayne, index, numerous illus. including one, p. 192, by P. and a photo of him, plus the title page and eighteen chapter head drawings. Special edition of 1000 copies, slipcase. (Beeler, Borein, Bugbee, De Yong, Dixon, Dunton, Eggenhofer, Ellsworth, Hurd, James, Johnson, Koerner, Leigh, Mora, Remington, Russell, Santee, Schreyvogel, Von Schmidt)

4 ———. Same, first trade edition in gilt lettered and illus. cloth, orange endsheets.

5 ———. Same, reprint by Bonanza Books, N.Y., in red lettered and illus. cloth, white endsheets.

6 *The Art of Northland Press, 1973* (calendar). Flagstaff, (1972), wraps, twelve illus. in color including one, "Navajo Riders," under December, by P. (Beeler, Von Schmidt)

7 Bailey, Paul. *Grandpa Was a Polygamist*. Westernlore Press, Los Angeles, 1960, gilt stamped, cloth, illus. including the d/w in color by P.

8 ———. *Polygamy was Better than Monotony*. Westernlore Press, Los Angeles, 1972, cloth, pic. endsheets, 200 pp., numerous illus. including endsheets and d/w by P.

9 Boelter, Homer H. (Sheriff). *The Westerners Brand Book* (Book Three). Los Angeles Corral, (1950), morocco and decor. cloth, pic. endsheets, 263 pp., foreword, contributors, list of western artists, index, numerous illus. including sixteen by P. plus three pp. of brands and two articles, "The Art of Western America" and "Forty-Nine A's" (brands) by him. Edition limited to 400 copies. (Blumenschein, Borein, Dixon, Johnson, Russell)

10 Bynum, Lindley. *An Early California Christmas in the Year 1775*. A Christmas booklet for Homer H. Boelter Lithography, Hollywood, Calif., (1955), decor. wraps, 33 pp., designed by Don Perceval and Homer H. Boelter, illus. by P.

11 ——— (foreword by). *Los Pastores: An Old California Christmas Play*. A Christmas booklet for Homer H. Boelter Lithography, Hollywood, Calif., (1954), decor. wraps and endsheets, 60 pp., tr. from original ms. in the Bancroft Library by Maria Lopez de Lowther, illus. by P.

12 Carillo, Leo. *The California I Love*. Prentice-Hall, Englewood, N.J., 1961, words "First printing, October, 1961" on copyright page, cloth and decor. boards and endsheets, 280 pp., art of Borein and Johnson discussed in text, drawings and decor. by P.

13 Caughey, John W. et al. *Land of the Free*. Franklin Publications, Pasadena, Calif., 1965, cloth, 658 pp.,

glossary, index, maps, numerous illus. including one, p. 479, by P. (Dunn, Remington, Russell)

13a ———. Same, maps in later editions by P.

14 Caughey, Lauee. *The Wilderness is a Book* (A Story of Young 49'ers on the Trail). Ward Ritchie Press, (Los Angeles), 1966, pic. cloth, 110 pp., numerous illus. including the d/w by P.

15 *Christmas Week with the Clampers at Mokulumne Hill, 1856.* E. Clampus Vitus, Platrix Chapter, (Westernlore Press, Los Angeles), Christmas 1960, wraps, two illus. by P.

16 Clark, Ann Nolan. *The Little Indian Pottery Maker.* Melmont Publishers, Los Angeles, (1955), cloth, 31 pp., illus. by P.

17 Corle, Edwin. *Fig Tree John.* The Ward Ritchie Press, Los Angeles, 1955, cloth and decor. boards, 318 pp., "Foreword" by Lawrence Clark Powell, designed by Ward Ritchie, illus. by P. Edition limited to 550 numbered copies, boxed.

18 Craig, Reginald S. *The Fighting Parson: Biography of Col. John M. Chivington.* Westernlore Press, 1959, stamped fabricoid, appendix, index, illus. with photos and maps, endsheets and chapter decorations by P.

19 Cunningham, Capt. William H. *Log of the Courier, 1826–1827–1828.* Glen Dawson, Los Angeles, 1958, cloth and decor. boards, 78 pp., print of the *Courier* tipped in as frontis. boards and marginal decor. by P. (From an original ms. in the Peabody Museum, Salem, Mass.)

20 (Dawson.) *Selections from the Library of Stuart N. Lake.* Catalogue 350, Dawson's Book Shop, Los Angeles, n.d., pic. wraps, 31 pp., illus. including one, front cover, by P.

21 DeWitt, Ward G. and Florence S. *Prairie Schooner Lady: The Journal of Harriet Sherrill Ward, 1853.* Westernlore Press, 1959, gilt stamped cloth, 180 pp., illus. with photos and maps, map endsheets and title page decorations by P.

21a Di Peso, Charles C. *The Amerind Foundation.* Northland Press, Flagstaff, 1967.

21b ———. *Casa Grandes and the Gran Chichimeca.* Museum of New Mexico Press, Santa Fe, 1968, wraps, unpaged, illus. by P.

22 Dobyns, Henry F. and Euler, Robert C. *The Ghost Dance of 1889 Among the Pai Indians of Northwestern Arizona.* Prescott College Press, Prescott, 1967,

decor. two-tone cloth, 67 pp., "Foreword" by Edward H. Spicer, preface, references, index, map, d/w illus. by P.

23 Doctor, Joseph E. *Shotguns on Sunday.* Westernlore Press, (1958), cloth, 230 pp., endsheets, chapter heading and blind stamps by P.

24 Evans, Max. *Long John Dunn of Taos.* Westernlore Press, (1959), cloth, 174 pp., foreword, d/w design by P.

25 Forrest, Earle R. *The Snake Dance of the Hopi Indians.* Westernlore Press, 1961, pic. cloth, map endsheets, 172 pp., bibliography, index, illus. by P.

25a Fraser, James. *Cattle Brands in Arizona.* Northland, Flagstaff, 1968, boards with brand decorated title label on front cover, 45 pp., "Introduction" by P. who also drew, researched and described the brands used on the title label and in the text.

26 Harrington, M. R. *The Iroquois Trail: Dickon Among the Onondagas and Senecas.* Rutgers University Press, New Brunswick, New Jersey, 1965, illus. by P.

26a ———. Same, first paperback edition.

27 Hayes, Will. *The Biggest Pine Tree.* Melmont Publishers, (1957), cloth, 31 pp., illus. by P.

28 Henderson, Randall. *On Desert Trails.* Westernlore Press, (1961), cloth, appreciation, preface, index, illus. with chapter headings by P. and with photos, maps.

29 Henson, Pauline. *Founding a Wilderness Capital: Prescott, A. T., 1864.* Northland Press, Flagstaff, Arizona, 1965, cloth, 224 pp., foreword, illus. with photos and with title page and twenty-five chapter head illus. by P.

30 Hood, Mary V. *Outdoor Hazards: Real and Fancied.* Macmillan, N.Y., 1955, decor. cloth, 242 pp., foreword, bibliography, index, illus. by P.

30a ——— and Williams, A. *Nature and the Camper* (A guide to safety and enjoyment for hunters, fishermen, campers and hikers on the Pacific slope and Southwestern Deserts). Ward Ritchie Press, Los Angeles, 1966, wraps, 157 pp., illus. by P. (A revised and rewritten edition of no. 30.)

31 James, Harry C. *The Treasure of the Hopitu: A Story of the Arizona Desert of Today.* (Los Angeles, 1927), cloth, 99 (1) pp., illus. by P.

32 ———. *The Hopi Indians.* The Caxton Printers, Cald-

well, Idaho, 1956, cloth, map endsheets, 236 pp., acknowledgments, "Foreword" by F. W. Hodge, illus. with drawings by P. and with photos.

33 ———. *A Day with Honau, a Hopi Indian Boy*. Melmont Publishers, (1957), cloth, 31 pp., illus. by P.

34 ———. *A Day with Poli, a Hopi Indian Girl*. Melmont Publishers, (1957), cloth, 31 pp., illus. by P.

35 ———. *Red Man, White Man*. The Naylor Co., San Antonio, 1958, words "First Edition" on copyright page, decor. cloth, map endsheets, 286 pp., designed and decor. by P.

36 ———. *A Day in Oraibi: a Hopi Indian Village*. Melmont Publishers, (1959), cloth, 31 pp., illus. by P.

37 ———. *The Hopi Indian Butterfly Dance*. Melmont Publishers, (1959), cloth, 31 pp., illus. by P.

38 ———. *The Cahuilla: California's Master Tribe*. Westernlore Press, (1960), decor. cloth and endsheets, 185 pp., acknowledgments, appendix, bibliography, illus. by P.

39 ———. *Ovada: An Indian Boy of the Grand Canyon*. Ward Ritchie Press, Los Angeles, 1969, cloth, 46 pp., numerous illus. by P.

40 Kimes, William F., ed. *The Westerners Brand Book Number 13*. Los Angeles Corral, (1969), decor. cloth, pic. endsheets, contributors, index, numerous illus. including endsheets and d/w by P. and with a biographical sketch and photo of him. (Remington)

41 Koenig, George, ed. *Brand Book XII*. The Westerners, Los Angeles Corral, (1966), decor. cloth, decor. endsheets, 211 pp., "The Old West is Gone" by the editor, index, numerous illus. including one, pp. 16–17, by P. (Ellsworth)

42 Lawton, Harry. *Willie Boy*. Paisano Press, Balboa Island, California, 1960, cloth, 240 pp., art and designs by P.

43 Layne, J. Gregg and Robinson, W. W., eds. *The Westerners Brand Book* (Book Four). Los Angeles Corral, (1951), morocco and decor. cloth, pic. endsheets, 231 pp., "Foreword" by Sheriff Paul D. Bailey, bibliography, index, "We Thank You," numerous illus. Contains an illus. article, "Names on Cows," by P. Edition limited to 400 copies. (Russell)

44 ———. *The Westerners Brand Book* (Book Five). Los Angeles Corral, (1953), morocco and decor. cloth, pic. endsheets, 180 pp., "Foreword" by Bert H. Olson, contributors, bibliography, index, "We Thank You,"

numerous illus. including two, dedication page and p. 53, by P. Edition limited to 400 copies.

45 Leadabrand, Russ, ed. *The California Deserts: The Westerners Brand Book* (Book Eleven). Los Angeles Corral, 1964, decor. cloth, pic. endsheets, 250 pp., preface, bibliography, index, illus. with drawings by P. and with photos. Edition limited to 525 copies.

46 ———. *The Secret of Drake's Bay*. Ward Ritchie, Los Angeles, 1969, pic. cloth, 45 (1) pp., numerous illus. by P.

47 Lee, Weston and Jeanne. *Torrent in the Desert*. Northland Press, Flagstaff, Arizona, 1962, 117 pages of natural-color photos, endpaper and other maps by P.

48 Lummis, Charles F. *General Crook and the Apache Wars*. Northland Press, 1965, cloth, 224 pp., "Foreword" by Dudley Gordon, illus. by P.

49 ———. Same, special Northland Press–Southwest Museum edition of 250 numbered and signed copies in a different binding, slipcase.

50 Momaday, Natachee Scott. *Owl in the Cedar Tree*. Ginn, Boston, 1965, cloth, 116 pp., illus. by P.

51 Moore, Adam Lee et al. *No More Gold Slugs on Bare Bed Rock*. E Clampus Vitus, Platrix chapter (Westernlore Press, Los Angeles), Christmas 1961, wraps, illus. by P.

52 Perceval, Don. *A Navajo Sketch Book* with descriptive text by Clay Lockett. Northland Press, 1962, cloth, 98 pp., "Preface" by Paul Jones, "Introduction" by Lockett, numerous illus. including thirteen in color by P. Trailfinders Edition, limited to 55 numbered copies each with an original watercolor by P., boxed.

53 ———. Same, trade edition of no. 52.

54 ———. *Bucking Horse Portfolio*. Westernlore Press, 1960, pic. folder, thirteen plates (loose in folder) by P.

54a ———. *Meet Arizona's Indians*. Northland for the Arizona Development Board, State of Arizona, Phoenix, wraps, designed and illus. by P.

55 ———. *Elements of Drawing: Folder No. 54: Domestic Animals*. Stehli Bros., Zurich, Switzerland, 1930, decor. paper folder, 2 pp., twelve lithographed plates by P.

55a ———. *How to Draw Horses*. Walter Foster Publications, Palm Springs, Calif., 1930, decor. wraps, unpaged.

56 ———. *The Only True and Authentic ECV Coat of Arms*. E Clampus Vitus, Yerba Buena Chapter, San Francisco, 1968, wraps, text and illus. by P.

57 ———. *The Coronado Expedition Route Map.* South-western Monuments Assn., Globe, Arizona, 1961, parchment paper, 14" x 25", decorated with figures of men, beasts and plants (from a mural by P. for the Coronado National Memorial in southern Arizona, National Park Service). Issued with a two-fold informational leaflet by John P. Slack.

57a ———. *The Street Fight.* Wyatt Earp's West, (Tombstone), 1966, a color print 12" x 22" (from a mural by P. in the Wyatt Earp Museum, Tombstone). Issued with a descriptive text by John D. Gilchriese.

57b Powell, Lawrence Clark. *California Classics.* Ward Ritchie Press, Los Angeles, 1971, cloth, 393 pp., index, one illus., title page (repeated on cover and d/w), by P.

57c ———. *The Desert as Dwelled On.* Dawson's Book Shop, Los Angeles, 1973, cloth, 30 pp., illus. by P., boxed. Limited edition of 250 copies.

58 Price, Doughbelly. *Short Stirrups.* Westernlore Press, 1960, decor. fabricoid, blue endsheets, 205 pp., "An Introduction" by Richard G. Hubler, illus. with drawings by P.

59 Reynolds, J. E. (Bookseller). *The West.* Fall 1960, Van Nuys, California, pic. wraps, unpaged, front cover illus. by P.

60 ———. *The West* (catalogue 117). Summer 1970, Van Nuys, California, pic. wraps, unpaged, front wrap illus. by P.

61 Robinson, W. W., ed. *The Westerners Brand Book* (Book Seven). Los Angeles Corral, (1957), morocco, decor. cloth and endsheets, 293 pp., contributors, publisher's note, numerous illus. including two, title page and p. 14, plus endsheet designs by P. Edition limited to 475 copies. (Russell)

62 Rowntree, Lester. *Ronnie.* Viking Press, N.Y., 1952, cloth, 188 pp., illus. by P.

63 ———. *Ronnie and Don.* Viking Press, N.Y., 1953, cloth, 100 pp., illus. by P.

64 Russell, Charles M. *Rawhide Rawlins Rides Again.* Trail's End Publishing Co., Pasadena, Calif., 1948, gold stamped leather, pic. endsheets, 62 pp., ten illus. including one by P. Edition limited to 300 numbered copies, boxed. (Bugbee, Russell)

65 Springer, "Panchito," ed. *Fool's Gold.* Platrix Chapter of E Clampus Vitis, Los Angeles, 1957, cloth and boards, 75 pp., articles by Ed Ainsworth et al., illus. by P. Edition limited to 300 copies.

66 *The Story of Christmas: The Gospel According to St. Matthew and St. Luke.* Christmas booklet for Homer H. Boelter Lithography, Hollywood, Calif., 1956–57, decor. wraps and endsheets, 32 pp., typography by Homer H. Boelter, designed and illus. by P.

67 Toole, K. Ross, ed. *Probing the American West.* Museum of New Mexico Press, Santa Fe, (1962), 216 (7) pp., preface, "Introduction" by Ray A. Billington, notes, index, program of Western History Assn. Conference with one illus. by P.

68 Van Dyke, Henry. *The First Christmas Tree.* A Christmas booklet for Homer H. Boelter Lithography, Hollywood, Calif., n.d., decor. wraps and endsheets, 24 pp., designed by Homer H. Boelter, illus. by P.

69 Waters, Frank. *The Man Who Killed the Deer.* Northland Press, 1965, cloth and decor. boards, 328 pp., illus. by P. Limited, numbered and signed edition, in slipcase.

70 Weaver, Paul E., Jr. *Northland Press, Winter/Spring Book List, 1970–71.* Pic. wraps, unpaged, numerous illus. including two by P. (Beeler, Borein, Dixon, Remington)

71 ———. Same, *Autumn Book List, 1971.* Pic. wraps, unpaged, numerous illus. including two by P. (Borein, Dixon, Remington, Santee)

72 ———. Same, *Autumn Book List, 1973.* Colored pic. wraps, unpaged, numerous illus. including one by P. (Beeler, Blumenschein, Dixon, James, Remington, Von Schmidt) (Note: Other Northland Press catalogs also include illus. by P.)

72a ———. Same, *Autumn 1974 Book List.* Colored pic. wraps, unpaged, numerous illus. including two by P. (Beeler, Borein, Dixon, Von Schmidt)

73 (Westerners.) *Articles of Incorporation and Range Rules.* Los Angeles Corral, The Westerners, 1960, wraps, 24 pp., illus. by P.

74 ———. *Range Rules (By-Laws) and Articles of Incorporation.* The Westerners, Los Angeles Corral, (1966), wraps, 24 pp., foreword, illus. with seventeen cartoon-type drawings by P.

75 ———. Same, reprint with slight revised foreword and small drawings on front of self-wrap, 1972.

76 Woodward, Arthur. *Trapper Jim Waters.* Publication no. 23, Los Angeles Corral, The Westerners, (1954), pic. wraps, 15 pp., bibliographical notes, illus. including one, front cover, by P.

Written by the Artist

77 *Art of Western America.* Pomona College Art Gallery, Claremont, Calif., Nov., 1949, (catalogue of exhibition), pic. wraps, (12) pp., illus. (Russell)

78 Belknap, William Jr. and Frances S. *Gunnar Widforss: Painter of the Grand Canyon.* Northland Press for the Museum of Northern Arizona, Flagstaff, 1969, cloth, 86 pp., "Preface" by Perceval, numerous illus. by Widforss.

79 ———. Same, limited edition in deluxe binding, numbered and signed by the authors, slipcase.

80 "A Maynard Dixon Sketch Book," an article in *The Westerners Brand Book* (Book Eight). Los Angeles Corral, (1959), morocco and decor. cloth, pic. end-sheets, 229 (1) pp., foreword, contributors, "Muchas Gracias," illus. Edition limited to 525 copies. (Dixon)

81 *Maynard Dixon Sketch Book.* Northland Press, Flagstaff, Arizona, 1967, cloth and decor. boards, unpaged, introduction and descriptive text by P., numerous illus. by Dixon.

The Artist and His Art

82 Ainsworth, Ed. "The Painter Who Captures History in the Desert: Don Louis Perceval," a magazine article in *The Villager,* Palm Springs, Calif., Jan. 1958, pp. 15–21, illus. with reproductions of oils, watercolors and book illus. by P.

83 Dykes, Jeff C. *High Spots in Western Illustrating.* (The Kansas City Posse, The Westerners, 1964), cloth, 30 pp., introduction, two illus., no. 52 above is

High Spot 100. (An edition in wraps was issued to the members.)

84 Edwards, E. I. *Twelve Great Books* (A Guide to the Subject Matter and Authors of the First Twelve Brand Books). The Westerners, Los Angeles Corral, (Westerners Keepsake — Publication no. 80, 1966), wraps, 46 pp., "Foreword" by Paul Bailey, Perceval in text, pp. 9, 10, 17, 18, 22 and 35.

85 Leadabrand, Russ. "An Artist with an Idea," an article about Perceval in *Pasadena Independent — Scene,* August 2, 1953, illus. by P. and with a photo of him.

86 Powell, Lawrence Clark. *The Little Package.* The World Pub. Co., Cleveland and N.Y., (1964), words "First Edition" on copyright page, cloth, 316 (3) pp., green top, preface, index. Contains high praise for *A Navajo Sketch Book* (no. 52 above) ". . . the most beautiful book ever produced in Arizona."

87 ———. *Southwestern Book Trails: A Reader's Guide to the Heartland of New Mexico and Arizona.* Horn and Wallace, Albuquerque, 1963, cloth, 92 pp., preface, index. Mentions the Dixon article (no. 80) and praises nos. 47 and 52 as being "at the peak of fine book work in the Southwest."

88 ———. "Northland Press," a magazine article in *Arizona Highways,* Sept. 1963, pp. 2–13, with illus. from nos. 47 and 52 by P.

89 Weaver, Paul E. "Northland Press and the Fine Art of Bookmaking," an article in *Arizona Highways* 47:10, October 1971, includes the story of his first book *A Navajo Sketch Book* by Perceval (no. 52) with one illus. from the book.

ILLUSTRATION by Perceval from *General Crook And The Apache Wars*

HUNTERS' CAMP IN THE BIG HORN by Remington   *Collection of the*
National Cowboy Hall of Fame

FREDERIC SACKRIDER REMINGTON
1861–1909

Catalogues of Art Exhibitions and Galleries

AMERICAN WATERCOLOR SOCIETY, NEW YORK

1 *Twentieth Annual Exhibition,* 1887, pic. wraps, 44 pp., thirty plates including one, facing p. 36, by R.

2 *Twenty-First Annual Exhibition,* 1888, wraps, numerous illus. including one by R.

3 *Twenty-Fourth Annual Exhibition,* 1891, pic. wraps, 45 (1) pp., illus. including one, p. 18, by R.

ARGOSY GALLERY, NEW YORK

4 *101 American Paintings,* (1960), pic. wraps, 48 pp., 102 illus. including one, front cover, by R.

ART INSTITUTE OF CHICAGO

5 *Half a Century of American Art,* Nov. 16, 1939 to Jan. 7, 1940, wraps, 61 pp., plus 78 plates including one by R. (Blumenschein)

ASSOCIATED ILLUSTRATORS, NEW YORK

6 *First Annual Exhibition,* 1902, pic. wraps, unpaged, seventeen illus. including one by R. (Keller)

BAKER COLLECTOR GALLERY, LUBBOCK, TEXAS

6a *Spring 1964* (catalog), pic. wraps, unpaged, (preface), foreword, numerous illus. including one by R. (Hurd, Russell, Wyeth)

J. N. BARTFIELD ART GALLERIES, NEW YORK

7 *American Paintings and Sculpture: Historical–Western,* n.d., colored pic. wraps, unpaged but with 64 numbered illus. including five, nos. 1, 40, 41, 42 and 43, by R. (Johnson, Leigh, Russell, Schoonover, Wyeth)

8 *American Paintings and Sculpture: Historical–Western,* catalogue no. 120, colored pic. wraps, unpaged but with 82 numbered illus. including six, nos. 41, 42, 73, 74, 75 and 76, by R. (Dixon, Johnson, Leigh, Russell, Schreyvogel)

BILTMORE GALLERIES, LOS ANGELES

8a *Catalog,* May 1969, colored pic. wraps, 54 pp., numerous illus. including one, p. 41, by R. (Borein, Dixon, Dunton, Johnson, Koerner, Leigh, Miller, Young)

BIRMINGHAM MUSEUM OF ART

8b *Twentieth Anniversary Bulletin* (1971), pic. wraps, unpaged, foreword, "Introduction" by William M. Spencer, twenty-two illus. including one, photo of the bronze "Trooper of the Plains," by R.

BOATMEN'S NATIONAL BANK OF ST. LOUIS

9 *Exhibit of Boatmen's Art Collection,* May 4 through May 29, 1964, pic. wraps, unpaged, fifteen illus. including one by R. (Russell)

BOWDOIN COLLEGE MUSEUM OF ART
BRUNSWICK, MAINE

10 *The Portrayal of the Negro in American Painting,* 1964, pic. wraps, unpaged but with 80 numbered plates including one, no. 66, by R.

CHARLES W. BOWERS MEMORIAL MUSEUM
SANTA ANA, CALIFORNIA

11 *Painters of the West,* March 5–30, 1972, pic. wraps, unpaged, fifteen illus. including one by R. (Johnson, Koerner, Miller, Russell)

BRADFORD BRINTON MEMORIAL
BIG HORN, WYOMING

12 *Quarter Circle A Ranch,* (1961), folder, fourteen illus. including one by R. (Johnson, Russell)

13 *A Guide to Quarter Circle A Ranch,* (1968), pic.

wraps, 20 pp., numerous illus. including four, front cover and pp. 7, 11 and 15, by R. (Borein, Russell)

THE BROOKLYN MUSEUM

14 *A Century of American Illustration*, March 22–May 14, 1972, colored pic. wraps, 155 pp., numerous illus. including no. 23 by R. (Fogarty, Schoonover, Wyeth)

BUFFALO BILL HISTORICAL CENTER
CODY, WYOMING

15 *See the Old West as it Really Was*, (1969), folder, five illus. including one by R.

16 *The Story of the Buffalo Bill Historical Center*, (1969), colored pic. wraps, unpaged, eight illus. including a photo showing some of the bronzes by R.

17 *Yellowstone Centennial Season, Special Exhibitions, Loans and New Acquisitions*, May 1 to October 1, 1972, pic. wraps, unpaged, 17 illus. including three, front cover and two inside back cover, by R. (Johnson, Russell)

18 *Special Exhibitions, Loans and New Acquisitions*, 1973 season, pic. wraps, unpaged, 21 illus. including two by R. (Koerner, Russell)

BUSINESS MEN'S ASSURANCE CO. COLLECTION
KANSAS CITY, MISSOURI

19 *Along the Santa Fe Trail*, (1963), pic. wraps, unpaged, ten illus. including one in color by R. (Hurd)

HELEN L. CARD, NEW YORK

20 Number 1, *Salute to the Westerners*, 1958, pic. wraps, 48 (2) pp., numerous illus. including two photos of a bronze, front cover and p. 47, by R. (Deming, Russell)

21 Number 2, *Hats Off to the American Illustrator*, (1959), pic. wraps, 32 pp., illus. including one, p. 26, by R. (Dixon, Goodwin, Schoonover)

22 Number 3, *Gentlemen, What'll You Have?* (1960), pic. wraps, 80 (2) pp., numerous illus. by R.

23 Number 5, *Hang on, Fellers! We're Out on a Limb*, (1963), pic. wraps, 95 pp., numerous illus. including five, pp. 90, 91, 92, 93 and 94, by R. (Deming, Eggenhofer, Leigh, Schoonover, Stoops, Wyeth)

CARNEGIE INSTITUTE, DEPARTMENT OF FINE ARTS
PITTSBURGH

24 *Survey of American Painting*, (1940), pic .wraps, unpaged but with 135 numbered plates including no. 78 by R. (Hurd)

AMON CARTER MUSEUM OF WESTERN ART
FORT WORTH

25 *Inaugural Exhibition, Selected Works of Frederic Remington and Charles Marion Russell*, January 1961, wraps, tinted endsheets, unpaged, sixteen illus. by R. (Russell)

26 *Frederic Remington*, an essay and catalogue by Peter H. Hassrick to accompany a retrospective exhibition, (1973), colored pic. wraps, 48 pp., numerous illus. by R.

26a *Catalogue of the Collection 1972* (1974), wraps, 602 pp., "Preface" by Director Mitchell A. Wilder, general index, numerous illus. including forty by R. plus photos of seventeen bronzes by him. (Borein, Crawford, Deming, Dixon, Dunton, James, Johnson, Miller, Russell)

CHAPPELLIER GALLERIES, NEW YORK

27 *One Hundred American Selections*, (1966), colored pic. wraps, unpaged but with 100 numbered illus. including one, no. 58, by R. (Deming, Johnson, Miller)

CHILDS GALLERY, BOSTON

28 *Bulletin for March 1950*, folder, two illus. by R.

STERLING AND FRANCINE CLARK ART
INSTITUTE, WILLIAMSTOWN, MASS.

29 *Exhibit Four and Exhibit Seven*, n.d., wraps, unpaged but 75 numbered plates including three, nos. 50, 51 and 52, by R.

CORCORAN GALLERY OF ART, WASHINGTON, D.C.

30 *American Processional, 1492–1900*, July 8–December, 17, 1950, pic. wraps, 270 pp., index, numerous illus. including one, p. 225, by R.

DALLAS MUSEUM OF FINE ARTS

31 *200 Years of American Painting*, October 5 to November 4, 1946, pic. wraps, unpaged, numerous illus. including one by R.

32 *A Century of Art and Life in Texas*, April 9–May 7, 1961, pic. wraps, unpaged, "Foreword" by Jerry Bywaters, numerous illus. including one by R. (Dunton, Johnson, Lea, Schiwetz)

DELAWARE ART MUSEUM, WILMINGTON

33 *The Golden Age of American Illustration, 1880-1914*, September 14–October 15, 1972, pic. wraps, 67 pp., numerous illus. including one, p. 46, by R.

DENVER ART MUSEUM

34 *Building the West*, October 1955, wraps, 32 pp., numerous illus. including one, p. 24, by R. (Schreyvogel)

35 *Colorado Collects Historic Western Art*, January 13 through April 15, 1973, brand decor. wraps, 72 pp., numerous illus. including four, pp. 15, 29 (two) and 31, by R. (Johnson, Miller, Russell, Schreyvogel)

EDWARD EBERSTADT & SONS, NEW YORK

36 *A Distinguished Collection of Western Painting*, catalogue 139, (1956), pic. wraps, unpaged but with 129 numbered illus. including no. 99 by R. (Borein, Deming, Dixon, Johnson, Leigh, Russell)

37 *American Paintings*, catalog 146, colored pic. wraps, unpaged but with 191 numbered illus. including two, nos. 145 and 191, by R. (Borein, Deming, Dixon, Dunton, Johnson, Leigh, Miller, Wyeth)

FINE ARTS GALLERY OF SAN DIEGO

38 *Catalogue*, 1960, words "First Edition" on copyright page, cloth, 141 pp., preface, numerous illus. including a photo of a bronze, p. 18, by R.

FINE ARTS MUSEUM OF NEW MEXICO, SANTA FE

39 *The Artist in the American West*, 1800–1900, October 8 through November 22, 1961, pic. wraps, unpaged, numerous illus. including four by R. (Miller, Russell, Zogbaum)

FLINT INSTITUTE OF ARTS, FLINT, MICHIGAN

40 *Artists of the Old West*, November 15–December 6, 1964, pic. wraps, unpaged, nine illus. including one, front cover, by R.

GALLERY WEST, DENVER

41 *Prospectives in Western Art*, 1972, pic. wraps, unpaged, numerous illus. including one by R. (Borein, Deming, Dixon, Ellsworth, Russell, Schreyvogel)

THOMAS GILCREASE INSTITUTE, TULSA

42 *Opening Exhibition of Pictures*, 1949, wraps, 17 pp., frontis., lists six illus., nos. 71-76, by R.

43 *An Exhibition of Paintings and Bronzes by Frederic Remington, Charles M. Russell*, May to October, 1950, wraps, unpaged, seven illus. by R. and a photo of him. (Russell)

44 *Frederic Remington Exhibition*, Summer 1961, stiff wraps, 35 (1) pp., "Frederic Remington, Western Historian" by Jeff C. Dykes, thirty-one illus. by R.

45 *Frederic Remington, Charles Russell, Titans of West-ern Art*, 1964, stiff wraps, 64 (4) pp., numerous illus. in color by R. (Russell)

GLENBOW-ALBERTA INSTITUTE, CALGARY, ALBERTA

46 *Glenbow Collects an Exhibition*, 1969, wraps, illus. including one by R. (Borein, Russell, Schoonover)

GRAND CENTRAL ART GALLERIES, NEW YORK

47 *Remington to Today*, April 5 through April 30, 1955, pic. wraps, (8) pp., two illus. by R.

48 *1955 Yearbook*, wraps with illus. in color mounted on front cover, 76 pp., numerous illus. including eight, pp. 10, (11) color, 12, 14 (four) and (15) color, by R. (Johnson, Leigh, Schreyvogel)

49 *1958 Yearbook*, wraps with illus. in color mounted on front cover, 74 pp., numerous illus. including two in color, front cover and p. (31), by R. (Leigh)

THE GEORGE GUND MUSEUM OF WESTERN ART NEW YORK

50 *The Gund Collection of Western Art, A Personal Narrative*, 1970, colored pic. wraps, 38 pp., nineteen illus. in color including three, pp. 9, 15 and 23 (a detail repeated on front cover), by R. and a photo of him. (Johnson, Leigh, Russell, Schreyvogel)

51 Same, *A History and Pictorial Description of the American West*, 1973, pic. wraps, numerous illus. including nine, front cover and pp. 16, 17, 18, 19, 20, 21, 22 and 23, by R. and a photo of him. (Johnson, Leigh, Miller, Russell, Schreyvogel)

HAMMER GALLERIES, NEW YORK

52 *The Works of Charles M. Russell and Other Western Artists*, (November, 1962), pic. wraps, 56 pp., numerous illus. including six, pp. 36, 39 and 40 (four), by R. (Crawford, Goodwin, Lungren, Miller, Russell)

HETZEL UNION GALLERY, UNIVERSITY PARK, PA. (THE PENNSLYVANIA COLLEGE OF ART AND ARCHITECTURE)

53 *Artists of the American Frontier*, February 21–March 31, 1965, pic. wraps, unpaged, twelve illus. including eight by R. (Russell)

ARTHUR A. HOUGHTON, JR. LIBRARY CORNING, NEW YORK

54 *The Rockwell Collection of Western Americana, Frederic Remington*, pic. wraps, 8 pp., eight illus. by R.

HOUSTON CLUB

55 *Catalogue of the Works of Frederic Remington and Charles M. Russell Loaned Through Courtesy of Wyatt C. Hedrick*, (J. W. Young, Chicago, 1947), pic.

wraps, 20 pp., fifteen illus. including four by R. (Russell)

IBM Gallery, New York

56 *Art of the Western Frontier*, March 23 through April 18, (?), pic. wraps, unpaged, nine illus. including two by R. (Russell)

57 *Portrait of America; 1865–1915*, January 16 to February 25, (?), colored pic. cover, double folder, four illus. including one by R.

Indianapolis Museum of Art

58 *West America*, Summer 1971, colored pic. wraps, unpaged, fourteen illus. including one by R. (Leigh, Russell)

Joslyn Art Museum, Omaha, Nebraska

59 *Artists of the Western Frontier*, permanent exhibition, folder, eight illus. including one on front cover by R. (Russell)

60 *Life on the Prairie*, permanent exhibit, pic. wraps, 40 pp., numerous illus. including two, pp. 26 and 35, by R. (Johnson, Leigh, Miller, Russell)

61 *An Introduction to the Museum*, 1965, folder, one illus. by R. (Miller)

Kalamazoo Institute of Arts Kalamazoo, Michigan

62 *Western Art*, February 17–March 19, 1967, pic. wraps, 17 (1) pp., numerous illus. including seven, pp. 9 (two), 10 (three) and 11 (two), by R. (Hurd, Johnson, Leigh, Miller, Russell, Schreyvogel)

Kennedy Galleries, New York

63 *Painters of the Old West*, October 1960, wraps with illus. mounted on front cover, pp. 102-147, numerous illus. including nine, pp. 126, 128 (two), 129 (two), 130 (two) and 131 (two), by R. (Borein, Deming, Leigh, Russell, Schreyvogel, Zogbaum)

64 *Recent Acquisitions in Important Western Paintings*, October 1961, pic. wraps, numerous illus. including six by R. (Borein, Deming, Eggenhofer, Johnson, Russell, Schreyvogel)

65 *Recent Acquisitions in Important Western and Sporting Paintings and Sculptures*, October, 1962, wraps with illus. in color mounted on front cover, pp. 50-108, numerous illus. including fifteen, front cover in color and fourteen, pp. 80-89, by R. (Borein, Johnson, Leigh, Marchand, Miller, Russell, Schreyvogel)

66 *Tradition and Change*, December 1963, colored pic.

wraps, numerous illus. including two by R. (Koerner, Leigh, Lungren, Russell, Schreyvogel)

67 *Western Encounter: The Artists' Record*, October 1964, colored pic. wraps, 64 pp., numerous illus. including five, pp. 36, 37 and 38 (three), by R. (Johnson, Leigh, Marchand, Russell, Schreyvogel)

68 *Farewell to Adventure*, May 1965, colored pic. wraps, pp. 196-256, numerous illus. including fourteen by R. (Russell, Schreyvogel)

69 *The Wild Riders and the Vacant Land*, June 1966, colored pic. wraps, pp. 68-128, numerous illus. including five, pp. 102, 104 (two) and 105 (two), by R. (Leigh, Miller, Russell)

70 *From Coast to Coast*, June 1967, colored pic. wraps, pp. 80-152, numerous illus. including one, p. 132, by R. (Borein, Johnson, Russell)

71 *The Things That Were*, June 1968, colored pic. wraps, pp. 52-123, (1), numerous illus. including two, pp. 88 and 100, by R. (Blumenschein, Crawford, Leigh, Miller, Schoonover, Schreyvogel)

72 *American Sports and Sportsmen*, (1968), colored pic. wraps, 48 pp., numerous illus. including one, p. 7, by R. (Goodwin, Lungren)

73 *The West in Bronze*, (1968), pic. wraps, 28 pp., illus. with photos of 25 bronzes including two views of "The Bronco Buster," front cover and p. 27, by R.

74 *Frederic Remington 1861–1909, Drawings in Pen and Ink for Hiawatha*, Summer 1970, double folder, two illus. by R.

75 *American Masters 18th to 20th Centuries*, March 10 through April 3, 1971, wraps, 47 pp., numerous illus. including one, p. 37, by R.

76 *An Artist's Gazetteer: Beyond the Mississippi*, June 1971, colored pic. wraps, 64 pp., numerous illus. including four, pp. 32, 47 (two) and 49 (color), by R. (Borein, Marchand, Russell, Schreyvogel)

77 *A Selection of Works of Art from Kennedy Galleries*, December 1971, double folder, six illus. including one by R. (Russell)

78 *Walking Westward: An American Journey*, March 1972, colored pic. wraps, pp. 196-256, numerous illus. including five, pp. 226, 228, 238, 240 and 241, by R. (Johnson, Lungren, Miller, Russell, Schreyvogel)

79 *The Great American West*, June 1973, colored pic. wraps, pp. 132-192, numerous illus. including p. 177

by R. (Blumenschein, Leigh, Miller, Russell, Schrey-vogel)

79a *The Northern Lands*, December 1973, colored pic. wraps, pp. (195)–256, numerous illus. including one, p. 230, by R.

LA JOLLA MUSEUM OF ART, LA JOLLA, CALIF.

80 *Two Giants of the American West: Frederic Remington and Charles M. Russell*, October 23–November 20, 1966, decor. wraps, unpaged, twelve illus. including three by R. Note: also exhibited at Phoenix Art Museum, Dec. 1, 1966–Feb. 19, 1967 and at Palm Springs Desert Museum, March 3–April 2, 1967. (Russell)

E. WALTER LATENDORF, NEW YORK

81 *A Brochure of Paintings, Drawings and Bronzes*, (1948), pic. wraps, unpaged, "Foreword" and designed by E. Douglas Allen, twenty-one illus. by R.

82 *I'd Like to Have it Over*, 1951, folder with three illus. by R.

83 *Young Spanish Officer*, 1952, folder, one illus. by R. (Lea, Schreyvogel, Young)

LOS ANGELES COUNTY FAIR, POMONA

84 *Painting in the USA, 1721 to 1933*, Sept. 18–Oct. 4, 1953, pic. wraps, 60 (3) pp., "Introduction" by Arthur Miller, 151 illus. including one, p. 26, by R.

LOS ANGELES COUNTY MUSEUM OF ART

85 *The American West* by Larry Curry, The Viking Press, N.Y., (1972), March 21–May 28, 1972, cloth or colored pic. wraps, 198 pp., "Foreword" by Archibald Hanna, bibliography, artist bibliographies, 133 numbered plates including seven, nos. 20 (color) and 128-133, by R. Note: also exhibited at M. H. de Young Memorial, June 9–September 17, 1972 and The St. Louis Art Museum, Nov. 1–Dec. 31, 1972. (Miller, Russell)

LOS ANGELES MUNICIPAL ART DEPARTMENT

86 *The C. Bland Jamison Collection of Western Art*, March 22–April 17, 1960, pic. wraps, unpaged, twelve illus. including two by R. (Johnson, Russell)

MAXWELL GALLERIES, SAN FRANCISCO

87 *American Art Since 1850*, August 2–October 31, 1968, pic. wraps, 84 pp., (Foreword) by Dr. F. M. Hinkhouse, numerous illus. including one, p. 34, by R. (Borein, Dixon, Johnson, Miller, Russell, Wyeth)

METROPOLITAN MUSEUM OF ART, NEW YORK

88 *100 American Painters of the 20th Century*, 1950, colored pic. wraps, 111 pp., introduction, 101 illus. including one, p. 6, by R.

89 *The 75th Anniversary Exhibition of Painting and Sculpture by 75 Artists Associated with the Art Students League of New York*, 1951, wraps, xx pp., 75 full-page illus. including one by R.

90 *19th Century America, Paintings and Sculpture*, April 16 through September 7, 1970, colored pic. wraps, unpaged, 201 numbered illus. including two, nos. 197 and 198, by R.

MIDWESTERN GALLERIES, CINCINNATI

91 *Catalogue of Fine Art Number 10*, (1972?), folder, eleven illus. including one by R. (Borein, Leigh)

MILLER SCHOOL (CHEYENNE CENTENNIAL COMMITTEE), CHEYENNE, WYOMING

92 *150 Years in Western Art*, July 1 through August 15, 1967, colored pic. wraps, 30 (2) pp., numerous illus. including four, pp. 6, 14, 27 and (31), by R. (Koerner, Miller, Russell, Schreyvogel)

THE MINNEAPOLIS INSTITUTE OF ARTS

93 *Four Centuries of American Art*, November 27, 1963–January 19, 1964, colored pic. wraps, unpaged, numerous illus. including a photo of one bronze by R.

MONTANA HISTORICAL SOCIETY, HELENA

94 *An Art Perspective of the Historical Pacific Northwest*, August 1963, wraps, 32 (2) pp., numerous illus. including one, p. 19, by R. Note: Also exhibited at Eastern Washington State Historical Society, September 1963. (Dixon, Lungren, Russell)

MONTCLAIR ART MUSEUM, MONTCLAIR, N. J.

95 *Charles Parsons and His Domain*, April 6–27, 1958, pic. wraps, 47 pp., numerous illus. including one, p. 46, by R.

READ MULLAN GALLERY OF WESTERN ART PHOENIX, ARIZONA

96 *Catalogue 1964*, colored decor. cloth (or wraps), unpaged, numerous illus. including one by R. (Johnson, Leigh)

MUSEUM OF FINE ARTS OF HOUSTON

97 *Bulletin*, Spring 1944, pic. wraps, unpaged, lists the 66 Remington items presented to the Museum by the Hogg brothers of Houston and includes one illus. by R.

NATIONAL ACADEMY OF DESIGN, NEW YORK

98 *Seventieth Annual Exhibition*, 1895, wraps, numerous illus. including one by R.

99 *Seventy-Fourth Annual Exhibition*, 1899, wraps, numerous illus. including one by R.

THE NATIONAL ART MUSEUM OF SPORT
NEW YORK (MADISON SQUARE GARDEN CENTER)

100 *The Artist and the Sportsman*, April 18–June 16, 1968, cloth, 95 pp., compiled by Martha B. Scott, numerous illus. including two, pp. 59 and 60, by R. (Young)

NATIONAL COWBOY HALL OF FAME
OKLAHOMA CITY

101 *Inaugural Exhibition*, June 25, 1965, colored pic. wraps, 24 pp., numerous illus. including four, front cover and pp. 12, 13 and 17, by R. (Hurd, Russell)

NATIONAL GALLERY OF ART, WASHINGTON, D.C.

102 *American Battle Painting, 1776–1918*, 1944, decor. wraps, 59 (1) pp., "Foreword" by Lincoln Kirsten, 41 plates including one by R. and comments on his art, pp. 10-11.

WILLIAM ROCKHILL NELSON GALLERY OF ART
KANSAS CITY, MISSOURI

103 *The Last Frontier*, October 5–November 17, 1957, pic. wraps, 28 pp., numerous illus. including five, front cover, title page, p. 27 (two) and back cover, by R. (Russell)

HARRY SHAW NEWMAN GALLERY, NEW YORK

104 *Panorama*, 1:9, June–July 1946, pic. wraps, (8) pp., "Remington's Panorama of the West" by Helen Comstock, twelve illus. including nine by R.

105 *Panorama*, 2:8, April 1947, pic. wraps, (8) pp., twelve illus. including one by R.

106 *Panorama*, 4:9, May–June 1949, pic. wraps, (8) pp., sixteen illus. including one, front cover, by R.

OKLAHOMA ART CENTER, OKLAHOMA CITY

107 *European and American Painting from the Collection of Mr. and Mrs. W. B. Davis* (of Duncan, Okla.), 1964, colored pic. wraps, 16 pp., illus. including one by R. Note: also exhibited at Philbrook Art Center, Tulsa, Dec. 1–29, 1964. (Blumenschein, Hurd, Russell)

PACIFIC NORTHWEST INDIAN CENTER
SPOKANE, WASH.

107a *Third Annual Western Art Show & Auction*, March 2, 3, 4, 1973, pic. wraps, 44 pp., numerous illus including one, p. 11, by R. (Borein, Deming, Eggenhofer, Hurd, Russell)

THE PAINE ART CENTER AND ARBORETUM
OSHKOSH, WISCONSIN

108 *Frederic Remington, A Retrospective Exhibition of Painting and Sculpture*, August 1–September 24, 1967, pic. wraps, (11) pp., plus 72 illus. with descriptions, by R.

PETERSEN GALLERIES, BEVERLY HILLS, CALIFORNIA

108a *Americana, Western and Sporting Art / Sculpture*, wraps, 25 pp., numerous illus. including three, pp. 2, 4 and 5, by R. (James, Johnson, Leigh, Russell, Wyeth, Zogbaum)

PHOENIX ART GALLERY

109 *Aspects of the Desert* (The Dedication Exhibition), Nov. 14, 1959, wraps, unpaged, 31 numbered illus. including one, no. 31, by R. (Hurd)

110 *The Discovery of the West*, March 1961, pic. wraps, unpaged, numerous illus. including five by R. (Johnson, Leigh, Russell)

111 *Art of the Western Scene, 1880–1940*, Phoeniz, Arizona, Nov. 15, 1969–March 15, 1970, colored pic. wraps, unpaged, "Preface" by R. D. A. Puckle, Acting Director, 23 illustrations including three by R. (Dunton, Koerner, Russell)

112 *The West in Bronze*, May–July 1971, pic. wraps, unpaged, numbered plates including one, no. 28, by R. (Beeler, Russell, Schreyvogel)

113 *Western Art from the Eugene B. Adkins Collection*, November 1971–January 1972, colored pic. wraps, unpaged, numerous illus. including one in color by R. (Dunton, Johnson, Leigh, Miller, Varian)

REMINGTON ART MEMORIAL
OGDENSBURG, NEW YORK

114 *The Frederic Remington Memorial*, pic. wraps, (5) pp., drawing on front cover by R.

115 *A Catalogue of the Frederic Remington Memorial Collection*, privately printed for the Memorial by Knoedler's, N.Y., 1954, pic. boards, 73 pp., numerous illus. by R.

C. M. RUSSELL GALLERY
GREAT FALLS, MONTANA

116 *The Russell Years, 1864–1926*, May 4–June 1, 1969, pic. wraps, unpaged, numerous illus. including one by R. (Russell)

THE SCHENECTADY MUSEUM
SCHENECTADY, NEW YORK

117 *Collection of Chaylie L. Saxe*, March 7, 1971, pic.

wraps, unpaged, including five, nos. 16-20, by R. (Deming)

St. Louis City Art Museum

118 *Catalogue of Paintings*, 1915, wraps, 229 (2) pp., numerous illus. including one by R.

Squibb Gallery, princeton, n. j.

119 *The Gund Collection of Western Art*, March 9–16, 1973, pic. wraps, unpaged, front cover illus. by R.

Tucson Art Center

120 *Western Art in Arizona Collections*, February 18–March 18, 1973, pic. portfolio with ten prints including one by R. (Russell, Wyeth)

Union League Club, brooklyn, new york

121 *Exhibition of Bronzes*, May 4–6, 1905, decor. wraps, unpaged, photos of six bronzes incuding four by R.

UCLA Library, los angeles

122 *The West — From Fact to Myth*, September 20–October 24, 1967, decor. wraps, 19 (1) pp., "Preface" by Philip Durham and Everett L. Jones, illus. including one, p. (5), by R.

University of Arizona Art Gallery, tucson

123 *Our Western Heritage*, February 1–26, 1962, colored pic. wraps, unpaged, five illus. including one, front cover, by R. (Russell)

Whitney Gallery of Western Art
cody, wyoming

124 *The Frederic Remington Studio Collection*, (1959), wraps, 12 pp., numerous illus. by R.

125 *Frederic Remington (1861–1961) Centennial Exhibition*, 1961, pic. wraps, 16 pp., "Frederic Remington" by Harold McCracken, five illus. including two, pp. 4 and 15, by R. and a photo of him. (Russell)

126 *Exhibition of Western American Art*, 1962, pic. wraps, 16 pp., five illus. including two, inside front cover and p. 2, by R. (Russell)

127 *Exhibition of Western American Art*, 1963, pic. wraps, 16 pp., five illus. including one, inside front cover, by R. (Russell)

128 *Exhibition Catalog, Wyoming's 75th Anniversary*, 1965, pic. wraps, 16 pp., illus. including one, inside front cover, by R. (Russell)

128a *The Art of Frederic Remington* (An Exhibition Honoring Harold McCracken), wraps with window, 96 pp., "Harold McCracken, Puro Hombre" by Don Hedgpeth, "Frederic Remington, Pictorial Historian" by Harold McCracken, numerous illus. (some in color) by R.

128b *A Weekend with Frederic Remington*, June 15, 1974, folder with program and menu, front cover illus. by R.

128c *A Special Exhibition of Paintings and Sculpture by Frederic Remington* (1974), folder, lists 156 Remington items with one illus. on the front cover by him.

Wildenstein, new york

129 *How the West Was Won*, May 22–June 22, (1968), pic. wraps, unpaged, "Remington and Russell" by Harold McCracken, numerous illus. including forty-three by R. (Russell)

Woolaroc Museum (frank phillips foundation), bartlesville, oklahoma

130 *Woolaroc*, n.d., colored decor. wraps, 31 (1) pp., illus. including two, pp. 17 and 21, by R. (Johnson, Leigh, Mora, Russell)

131 *Oklahoma*, (1952), pic. wraps, unpaged, numerous illus. including one by R. (Dunton, Leigh, Mora, Russell)

132 *Indians*, (1956), pic. wraps, unpaged, numerous illus. including one by R. (Leigh, Mora, Russell)

133 *Woolaroc Museum, Frank Phillips Ranch*, Bartlesville Chamber of Commerce, n.d., pic. folder, 13 illus. including one by R. (Leigh)

134 *Woolaroc Museum* by Ke Mo IIa (Patrick Patterson, Museum Director, 1965), colored decor. boards (or wraps), 64 (1) pp., numerous illus. in color including four, pp. 40 (two), 51 and 52, by R. (Johnson, Leigh, Mora, Russell, Young)

J. W. Young Galleries, chicago

135 *Catalog of Selected Paintings*, (1946), wraps, unpaged, foreword, 28 illus. including three by R. (Russell)

136 *Art Notes*, February 1946, pic. wraps, unpaged, illus. including one by R.

137 *Exhibition and Sale of the Works of Frederic Remington and Charles M. Russell and Sculptures by Curt Dennis*, n.d., pic. wraps, unpaged, numerous illus. including five by R. (Russell)

138 *Catalog of 62 Paintings and Bronzes*, n.d., wraps, unpaged but with 62 numbered illustrations included, nos. 41 and 42 by R. (Russell)

Catalogues of Auction Sales

AMERICAN ART ASSOCIATION
ANDERSON GALLERIES, NEW YORK

139 *Works of Frederic Remington*, 1983, wraps, pages unnumbered, five illus. by R.

140 *Paintings by Eighteenth and Nineteenth Century Portraitists, Marine and Landscape Artists*, 1927, "An Indian on the Warpath," by R.

141 Number 2098, *Paintings of the American and European Schools*, 1926, wraps, 79 pp., numerous illus. including one, p. 70, by R.

142 Number 3791, *American and English Furniture and Decorations*, 1929, wraps, 178 (1) pp., numerous illus., including a photo of the bronze, "The Broncho Buster," p. 132, by R.

143 Number 4153, *Oil Paintings*, 1935, wraps, 37 pp., numerous illus., including one, p. 9, by R.

144 Number 4156, *Etchings and Drawings*, 1935, wraps, 34 pp., illus. including one, p. 27, by R.

145 Number 4227, *Paintings*, 1936, wraps, 57 (7) pp., illus. including two, p. (5), by R.

146 Number 4243, *American and European Paintings*, 1936, wraps, 59 (3) pp., illus. including one, p. 34, by R.

147 Number 4329, *Antique Furniture, Tapestries, Rugs, Other Art Property* (Collection of Genevieve Garvan Brady), 1937, cloth and boards, 555 pp., "Foreword" by Leslie A. Hyam, numerous illus. including two, pp. 344 and 345, by R. (Russell)

148 Number 4368, *American Historical Painting*, 1938, wraps, 58 pp., numerous illus. including two, p. (37), by R. and lists six other items by him.

149 Number 4415, *English and American Furniture and Decorations — Remington and Bayre Bronzes*, 1938, wraps, 32 pp., illus. including photos of two bronzes, p. (11), by R.

ASTOR GALLERIES, NEW YORK

150 *Western Bronzes and Painting*, Oct. 14, 1970, pic. wraps, 40 pp., six illus. by R. (Russell)

G. A. BAKER & CO., GALLERY, NEW YORK

151 Sale Number 69, *A Very Fine Collection of Ornithol-*ogical Books, Audubon Books and Prints, First Editions etc.*, May 13, 1941, wraps, 62 pp., five illus. including one, between pp. 32 and 33, by R.

CHICAGO ART GALLERIES
(M. KALLIS & CO.), CHICAGO

152 *Sale by Auction*, 1953, wraps, 39 pp., illus. including one, "The Charge," p. 35, by R.

COLEMAN AUCTION GALLERIES, NEW YORK

153 *American, English and French Provincial Furniture*, Oct. 20–22, 1949, wraps, pages unnumbered, one illus., "The Grass Fire," by R.

CHRISTIE'S, LONDON

153a *Christie's Review of the Year 1967/1968*, Newman Neame, (London, 1968), cloth, pic. endsheets, 303 pp., "Foreword" by John Russell, index, numerous illus. including one, p. (99), by R. (Russell)

SAMUEL T. FREEMAN & CO., PHILADELPHIA

154 *The Hinkle Smith Collection*, 1971, pic. wraps, unpaged, numerous illus. including one by R. (Russell, Schreyvogel)

GREENFIELD GALLERIES, SEATTLE

155 *American Western Art Auction*, October 28, 1972, pic. wraps, 58 pp., numerous illus. including two, pp. 18 and 28, by R. (Borein, Deming, Lungren, Russell, Schreyvogel)

KENDE GALLERIES
(OF GIMBEL BROS.), NEW YORK

156 Number 42, *Paintings and Bronzes from the Collections of Charles H. Linville and Mrs. William B. Dickson*, 1942, wraps, 29 pp., illus. including a photo of the bronze, "The Scalp," p. 12, by R.

157 Number 81, *Paintings*, 1943, wraps, 53 (1) pp., numerous illus., including five, pp. 11, 14, 19, 23 and 24, by R.

158 Number 85, *Paintings, Bronzes*, 1943, wraps, 31 pp., numerous illus., including one, p. 22, and a photo of a bronze, p. 19, by R. (Schreyvogel)

159 Number 89, *Nineteenth Century Paintings*, 1943, wraps, 35 pp., numerous illus., including a photo of a bronze, by R.

160 Number 201, *Representative Paintings by Famous Nineteenth Century Artists*, 1945, wraps, 143 pp., illus. including one, "A Dash for Timber," p. 121, by R.

161 Number 229, *American Painting*, February, 1946, wraps, 45 pp., illus. including one, p. 28, by R.

162 Number 264, *Fine Paintings, Bronzes by Remington*, Dec. 12, 1946, wraps, 75 pp., numerous illus. including one, p. 28, by R.

162 Number 264, *Fine Paintings, Bronzes by Remington*, Dec. 12, 1946, wraps, 75 pp., numerous illus. including photos of three bronzes, pp. 15, 17 and 18, by R.

163 Number 268, *Modern and Other Paintings*, 1947, wraps, 72 pp., numerous illus. including two, p. 35, and photos of three bronzes, pp. 10, 13 and 14, by R.

PARKE-BERNET GALLERIES, NEW YORK

164 Number 4, *American Paintings*, 1938, wraps, 481 (2) pp., numerous illus. including two, p. (3), by R.

165 Number 5, *French Period Furniture*, 1938, wraps, 83 pp., illus. including a photo of the bronze, "The Broncho Buster," p. 34, by R.

166 Number 81, *Early American Furniture and Decorations*, 1939, wraps, 61 (1) pp., numerous illus. including photos of three bronzes, pp. 8, 9 and 10, by R. (Russell)

167 Number 314, *The Arthur Curtiss James Art Collection*, 1941, wraps, 161 pp., illus. including a photo of the bronze, "The Wounded Bunkie," p. 67, by R.

168 Number 439, *American and English Furniture*, 1943, wraps, 76 (1) pp., illus. including photos of three bronzes, pp. 42, 43 and 44, by R.

169 Number 573, *Paintings by Old and Modern Masters*, 1944, wraps, 79 pp., illus. including one, p. 3, by R.

170 Number 574, *Georgian and Continental Silver of the Seventh–Eighth Century*, 1944, wraps, 103 pp., numerous illus. including one, a photo of the bronze, "Bronco Buster," p. 89, by R.

171 Number 617, *Furniture and Decorations*, 1944, wraps, 239 pp., illus. including one, p. 136, and a photo of a bronze, p. 190, by R.

172 *English and Other Furniture and Decorations — Oriental Rugs*, 1945, wraps, 178 pp., numerous illus. including photos of two bronzes, pp. 44 and 45, by R.

173 Number 795, *Georgian Silver, Paintings and Drawings*, 1946, wraps, 96 pp., numerous illus. including one, a photo of the bronze, "The Outlaw," p. 15, by R.

174 Number 823, *Fine Prints and Drawings*, 1947, wraps, 49 pp., illus. Lists an unusual wash drawing, "Trained Moose Drawing a Sleigh," p. 34, by R.

175 Number 848, *Notable American and English Furniture and Decorations*, 1947, pic. wraps, 167 pp., illus. including one, a photo of a bronze, p. 61, by R.

176 Number 888, *English Furniture*, 1947, wraps, 102 pp., numerous illus. including one, a photo of the bronze, "Cheyenne," p. 25, by R.

177 Number 941, *American and Other Paintings, Tapestries and Oriental Rugs*, 1948, wraps, 62 pp., illus. including one, "A Revolver Charge," p. (27), by R.

178 Number 1033, *Nineteenth Century Genre and Barbizon Paintings*, 1949, wraps, 40 pp., long note on Remington, p. 20, numerous illus. including one, p. (21), by R.

179 Number 1115, *Early American Furniture and Paintings*, 1950, wraps, 96 pp., numerous illus. including one, a photo of the bronze, "The Mountain Man," p. 25, by R.

180 Number 1123, *Barbizon and Other Nineteenth Century Paintings*, 1950, wraps, 36 pp., illus. including including one, "The Drum Corps," p. (27), by R.

181 Number 1172, *Garden and Other Furniture and Sculptures*, 1950, wraps, 49 pp., numerous illus. including two, photos of the bronzes, "The Rattlesnake" and "The Bronco Buster," pp. 25 and 26, by R.

182 Number 1240, *English, American and French Furniture and Decorations*, 1951, wraps, 93 pp., long note on Remington, p. 55, numerous illus. including two, pp. 55 and 56, by R.

183 Number 1290, *Cabinet Objects of Art*, 1951, wraps, 64 pp., numerous illus. including one, a photo of the bronze, "The Bronco Buster," p. 60, by R.

184 Number 1383, *American and English Furniture and Decorations*, 1952, wraps, 45 pp., numerous illus. including one, p. 7, by R.

185 Number 1409, *American and English Furniture and Decorative Objects*, 1953, wraps, 73 pp., numerous illus. including photos of two bronzes, pp. 45 and 46, by R.

186 Number 1443, *Superb Chippendale and Other English Eighteenth Century Furniture*, 1953, wraps, 98 pp., numerous illus. including one, a photo of the bronze, "The Fallen Rider," by R.

187 Number 1572, *Primitive and Old Master Paintings and Nineteenth Century Works*, 1955, wraps, 52 pp., 38 illus. including one, "Night Call," p. 8, by R.

188 Number 1613, *Early American Furniture, Important Miniatures and Prints*, 1955, wraps, 104 pp., 63 illus. including one, a photo of the bronze, "The Snake in the Path," p. 80, by R.

189 Number 1646, *American and English Furniture*, 1956, wraps, 93 pp., numerous illus. including one, a photo of the bronze, "The Sergeant," p. 3, by R.

190 Number 1654, *Valuable and Important Old Masters and Nineteenth Century Paintings*, 1956, wraps, 50 (1) pp., numerous illus. including one, p. 50, by R.

191 *American and English Furniture*, 1956, wraps, 93 pp., illus. including one, a photo of a bronze, by R.

192 Number 1918, *Old Masters*, 1959, wraps, 47 pp., numerous illus. including one, p. 35, by R.

193 Number 2272, *Important Graphics*, 1964, decor. wraps, 44 (2) pp., eighteen illus. including two, p. (29), by R.

194 Number 2276, *American Paintings and Drawings*, 1964, decor. wraps, 54 (2) pp., numerous illus. including one, p. 34, by R. (Leigh, Russell, Schreyvogel)

195 Number 2822, *18th–20th Century American Paintings, Drawings, Sculpture*, 1969, wraps, 158 pp., numerous illus. including four, pp. 14, 15, (19) and (37), by R. (Johnson, Leigh, Russell)

196 Number 2977, *American Paintings and Sculpture*, 1970, pic. wraps, 153 pp., numerous illus. including five, pp. 98, (101), (103), 104 and 105, by R. (Russell)

197 Number 3133, *Important American Painting, Sculpture and Drawings*, 1970, pic. wraps, 97 pp., numerous illus. including four, pp. 10, 11, (13) color and 73, by R.

RAINS GALLERY, NEW YORK

198 Number 553, includes "The Famous Frederic Remington Collection Formed by the Late Merle Johnson," items no. 406 to 451.

C. M. RUSSELL ART AUCTION
GREAT FALLS, MONTANA

199 *Fourth Annual C. M. Russell Auction of Original Western Art*, 1972, pic. wraps, unpaged, numerous illus. including one, "Ganderpull," by R. (Dunton, James, Johnson, Leigh, Russell)

SOTHEBY AND CO., LONDON

200 *The Valuable Library . . . of the Late Harry T. Peters of New York City*, 1961, wraps, 70 pp., seven illus. including one, facing p. 53, by R.

SOTHEBY PARKE BERNET, LOS ANGELES

200a *Western American Paintings, Drawings and Sculpture*, March 4 and 5, 1974, colored pic. wraps, unpaged, 252 lots, numerous illus. including lots 95, 106A and 114, by R. (Blumenschein, Dunton, Johnson, Koerner, Leigh, Russell)

SOTHEBY PARKE BERNET, NEW YORK

201 Number 3348, *Traditional and Western American Paintings, Drawings, Watercolors, Sculpture and Illustrations*, April 19–20, 1972, pic. wraps, 147 pp., numerous illus. including two, pp. 100 and 101, by R. (Deming, Johnson, Koerner, Leigh, Russell)

202 Number 3419, *Highly Important 18th, 19th and Early 20th Century American Paintings, Drawings, Watercolors and Sculpture*, October 19, 1972, pic. wraps, unpaged, numerous illus. including photos of three bronzes by R. (Koerner)

203 Number 3498, *Important 18th, 19th and Early 20th Century American Paintings, Watercolors and Sculpture*, April 11, 1973, colored pic. wraps, unpaged but with over 70 numbered plates including four, nos. 53, 65, 66 and 70, by R. (Blumenschein, Eggenhofer, James, Johnson, Leigh, Russell, Varian, Wyeth)

204 Number 3548, *18th, 19th and Early 20th Century American Paintings, Drawings, Watercolors and Sculpture*, September 28, 1973, pic. wraps, unpaged, numerous illus. including four, nos. 101, 102, 121, and 122, by R. (Deming, Johnson, Koerner, Russell)

TOBIAS, FISHER & CO., NEW YORK

205 *The Campbell Collection of Persian Silk Rugs, Remington and Russell Bronzes, etc.*, Sept. 21–23, 1944, wraps, 68 pp., illus. including photos of five bronzes, pp. 16, 19, 25, 28 and 40, by R. (Russell)

ADAM A. WESCHLER & SON, WASHINGTON, D.C.

206 *Important Three-Day Estate Sale by Auction*, Oct. 30–Nov. 1, 1970, wraps, 214 (1) pp., numerous illus. including one by R. (Russell)

Catalogues of Book and Print Publishers and Dealers

RICHARD ABEL, BOOKSELLER, BEAVERTON, OREGON

207 *Catalog of Books for Collectors 1973*, pic. wraps, 24 pp., numerous illus. including one, p. 6. by R.

ACOMA BOOKS, RAMONA, CALIFORNIA

208 *Americana*, Catalog 134, May–June 1971, pic. wraps, unpaged, front cover illus. by R.

209 *Americana*, Catalog 140, April 1972, pic. wraps, un-paged, front illus. by R.

210 *Americana*, Catalogue 141, May 1972, pic. wraps, unpaged, front cover illus. by R.

210a *Americana*, Catalogue 149, February–March 1974, wraps, unpaged, illus. inside the front cover by R.

210b *Americana*, Catalogue 150, March–April 1974, wraps, unpaged, front cover illus. by R.

ALTA CALIFORNIA BOOKSTORE
ALBANY, CALIFORNIA

211 *Omnium Catherum*, Catalogue 53, n.d., pic wraps, unpaged, illus. including one by R.

ARGONAUT BOOK SHOP (HAINES AND ROSE)
SAN FRANCISCO

212 Number 14, *Frederic Remington*, (1950), pic. wraps, 36 (1) pp., front cover illus. attributed to R.

DAVID ASHLEY, INC., NEW YORK

213 *Fine Color Reproductions*, January, 1946, wraps, 32 pp., index, 200 illus. including two, p. 32, by R. (Russell)

AUTHENTIC REPRODUCTIONS, LOVELAND, COLORADO

214 *Fine Art Reproductions on Canvas*, n.d., wraps, 24 pp., numerous ilus. including three, p. 20, by R. (Russell)

BOBBS-MERRILL COMPANY, INDIANAPOLIS

215 *1915 Publications*, decor. wraps, 104 pp., one item illus. by R., described p. 35.

JAMES F. CARR, NEW YORK

216 Number 11, *Americana*, (1962), pic. wraps, 48 pp., front cover illus. by R.

CATALDA FINE ARTS, INC., NEW YORK

217 *Color Reproductions of U. S. Prints*, (1948), wraps, 81 (1) pp., index, 164 illus. including two, p. 25, by R.

PEGGY CHRISTIAN, LOS ANGELES

218 *American Artists and Illustrators*, Catalog Four, 1965, pic. wraps, 20 pp., 24 illus. including one, p. 13, by R. (Borein, Dixon, Eggenhofer, Ellsworth, Russell)

P. F. COLLIER AND SON, NEW YORK

219 "*The Lion's Mouth*," 1903, decor, wraps, 48 pp., numerous illus. including two, pp. 33 and 38, by R. (Leigh)

220 *Prints and Calendars*, (1907), cloth with morocco label or decor. wraps, pages unnumbered, numerous illus. including eighteen (one in color), by R.

221 *Art Prints*, 1910, wraps, numerous illus. with seven pages of reproductions, by R.

THE CURRENT COMPANY, BRISTAL, RHODE ISLAND

222 *Chapter and Verse*, Catalogue Four, n.d., pic. wraps, 59 (1) pp., illus. including one, p. 21, by R.

223 *Chapter and Verse*, Catalogue Five, n.d., pic. wraps, 60 pp., illus. including one, p. 30, by R.

CURTIS AND CAMERON, BOSTON

224 *The Copley Prints*, (1909), wraps, 146 pp., numerous illus. including one, p. 103, by R.

225 *The Copley Prints*, 1916, wraps, 104 pp., (8) of advs., numerous illus. including two, p. 70, by R. (Schoonover)

HOUSTON DANIEL, AUSTIN, TEXAS

226 Number 6, *Texas and the West*, n.d., pic. wraps, 21 pp., front cover illus. by R.

PRICE DANIEL, JR., WACO, TEXAS

227 Number 21, *Texas and the West* (Featuring Books Written and Illustrated by Frederic Remington) with a facsimile of Remington's signature on the front cover, 13 (1) pp.

228 Number 22, *Texas and the West*, (1963), pic. wraps, 13 (1) p., illus., p. 11, attributed to R. (Bugbee)

DAWSON'S BOOK SHOP, LOS ANGELES

229 *Frontier America*, 1950, two-tone fabricoid, 184 pp., index, illus. incuding one by R.

229a Number 232, *Americana*, 1949, wraps, illus. including one, p. 18, by R.

230 Number 307, *Western Americana*, (1959), colored pic. wraps, 31 pp., front cover illus. by R.

DODGE PUBLISHING CO., NEW YORK

231 *Fine Art Prints*, 1922, colored pic. wraps, (32) pp., numerous illus. including thirty-two by R. Photo and short biographical sketch of R.

232 *Framed Pictures and Framed Mottos*, 1922, pic, wraps, numerous illus. including three by R.

EDWARD EBERSTADT & SONS, NEW YORK

233 Number 132, *Americana*, (1953), pic. wraps, 128 pp., 25 illus. including one, facing p. 96, by R. (Leigh)

HARPER & BROTHERS, NEW YORK

234 *Descriptive List of Their Publications*, 1894, wraps, illus. including one by R.

235 *Holiday Books*, (1895), pic. wraps, numerous illus. including one, p. 5, by R.

236 *Holiday Books for 1896*, pic. wraps, illus. by R. and others.

237 *Holiday Books*, (1896), pic. wraps, numerous illus. including two by R.

238 *Descriptive List of Their Publications*, 1896, wraps, illus. by, and portrait of, R.

239 *Holiday Books*, 1897, wraps, illus. including one by R.

THE HOLMES BOOK CO.
(HAROLD C. HOLMES), OAKLAND, CALIF.

240 *A Descriptive and Priced Catalogue of Books, Pamphlets and Maps Relating Directly or Indirectly to the History, Literature, and Printing of California and the Far West, Formerly the Collection of Thomas Wayne Norris, Livermore, California*, Grabhorn Press, S.F., October, 1948, cloth and boards, 217 pp., introduction, frontis. by R. Lists many books illus. by R.

HOUGHTON MIFFLIN CO., BOSTON

241 *Holiday Bulletin*, 1895, decor. wraps, 65 (1) pp., illus. including one, p. 6, by R.

242 *The Private Library Department*, n.d., wraps, 111 pp., illus. including two, pp. 22 and 25, by R.

J & S GRAPHICS, CHICAGO

243 *J & S Catalogue Number Five*, n.d., pic. wraps, unpaged, lists nearly sixty items illus. by R. and with one illus. inside back cover by him.

244 *J & S Catalogue Number Eight, Sixteen Collections of American Authors*, wraps, unpaged and includes as Collection 18 "A remarkable collection of Remington prints, paintings and proofs" — describes approximately 100 items priced at $3850.00.

245 *J & S Catalogue Number Eight and One Half*, 1971, a folder (laid in Catalogue Nine) with 2 drawings on front by R.

246 *J & S Catalogue Number Ten*, n.d., colored pic. wraps, 112 pp., illus. including one in color on back cover by R.

KANSAS HERITAGE CENTER, DODGE CITY, KANSAS

247 *Reference Materials and Resources*, January 1973, decor. wraps, 63 pp., numerous illus. including one, p. 54, by R. (Russell)

LATENDORF BOOK SHOP
(HELEN L. CARD), NEW YORK

248 Number 1, *Salute to the Westerners*, 1958, pic. wraps, 48 (2) pp., "The Art of Carl Kauba," numerous illus. including one, the photo of a bronze, by R. (Deming, Russell)

249 Number 2, *Hats Off to the American Illustrator*, (1959), pic. wraps, 32 pp., numerous illus. including one, p. (26), by R. (Dixon, Goodwin, Schoonover)

250 Number 3, *Gentlemen, What'll You Have?* 1960, pic. wraps, 80 (2) pp., numerous illus. by R.

251 Number 5, *Hang on, Fellers! We're Out on a Limb*, (1963), pic. wraps, 95 pp., numerous illus. including five, pp. 90, 91, 92, 93 and 94, by R. (Deming, Eggenhofer, Leigh, Schoonover, Stoops, Wyeth)

LEEKLEY RARE & SCHOLARLY BOOKS
WINTHROP HARBOR, ILLINOIS

252 *A Flourish for Wright Howes: Americana*, Catalogue 100, (1971), pic. wraps, 80 pp., illus. including one, p. 1 (title page), by R.

LONG'S COLLEGE BOOK CO.
COLUMBUS, OHIO

253 Number 22, *America*, Oct. 1951, pic. wraps, 28 pp., front cover illus. by R.

THE MACMILLAN CO., NEW YORK

254 *A Selected List of Illustrated Books*, Christmas, 1897, wraps, illus. including one, "An Old-time Hunter," by R.

MANNADOS BOOKSHOP
(E. WALTER LATENDORF), NEW YORK

255 Number 15, *Fact and Fiction of The Old West and the Wild West*, n.d., pic. wraps, 43 pp., eight illus. including seven, front cover and pp. 19, 23, 25, 27, 31 and 33, by R.

256 Number 17, *Frederic Remington* (Bibliographical Check List etc.), (1947), pic. wraps, 72 pp., "Frederic Remington, An Appreciation" by Harold McCracken, illus. including twenty-five by R. (James)

257 Number 23, *First Editions, Rare Books Association Items*, (1952), wraps, 36 pp., one illus., inside back wrap, by R.

258 Number 25, *The West*, (1955), pic. wraps, 40 pp., illus. including five, inside front cover and pp. 19, 20, 21 and 22, by R. Several letters by R. quoted. (Russell)

JULIAN MESSNER, INC., NEW YORK

259 *Advance Announcement and Prospectus for "The Book of the American West,"* self-wraps, 15 (1) pp., fifteen illus. by R.

W. M. MORRISON, WACO, TEXAS

260 *List Number 173,* (1962), pic. wraps, with front cover illus. by R.

KENNETH NEBENZAHL, INC.
CHICAGO, ILLINOIS

261 Number 5, *The American West in the Nineteenth Century,* (1960), pic. wraps, 64 pp., references, front cover illus. by R.

262 Number 11, *Western Americana,* (1963), pic. wraps, 87 pp., references, front cover illus. by R.

263 Number 19, *Old and Rare Books About the American West,* (1967), pic. wraps, 44 pp., two illus., front cover and back cover, by R.

NEW YORK ENGRAVING & PRINTING CO.
NEW YORK

264 *Artistic Illustrations,* n.d., wraps, specimens of book magazine illus. including one by R.

NEW YORK GRAPHIC SOCIETY
GREENWICH, CONN.

265 *Fine Art Reproductions of Old and Modern Masters,* (1961), decor. cloth, 443 pp., introduction, numerous illus. including seven in color by R. (Dixon, Hurd, Schreyvogel)

NORTHLAND PRESS, FLAGSTAFF, ARIZONA

266 *Autumn 1972 Book List,* pic. wraps, unpaged, numerous illus. including one by R. Note: Other Northland Press catalogs also include a Remington illustration. (Beeler, Dixon, Perceval, Santee, Von Schmidt, Wyeth)

OESTREICHER'S, NEW YORK

267 *The World's Largest Collection of Fine Color Art Reproductions,* (1954), pic. wraps, 95 (1) pp., introduction, numerous illus. including two, p. 45, by R. (Leigh)

THE OLD PRINT SHOP, NEW YORK

268 *Remington and the West,* portfolio, January 1943, one illus. by R.

LEWIS OSBORNE BOOKS, ASHLAND, OREGON

269 Catalog Number 1. *Western Americana,* 1969, pic.

wraps, (14) pp., thirteen illus. including one, "Opening Fire on the Apache," by R.

PACK-SADDLE BOOKS, EAGLE PASS, TEXAS

270 *An Offering of Collectors Books on Texas, Mexico, Military and the West,* November 1971, pic. wraps, 12 pp., front cover illus. by R.

271 Same, Catalogue Number 2, November 1972, pic. wraps, 29 (1) pp., front cover illus. by R.

271a *An Offering of Collectors Books on Western Americana, plus Mexico,* Catalogue Number 3, November 1973, pic. wraps, 27 pp., cover drawing by R.

PAYOT, UPHAM & CO., SAN FRANCISCO

272 *A Selected List of Illustrated Books,* Christmas 1897, decor. wraps, 32 pp., numerous illus. including one by R.

POWERS MERCANTILE CO., MINNEAPOLIS

273 *Summer Reading,* (1902), decor. wraps, 98 pp., numerous illus. including two, pp. 9 and 26, by R.

274 *Christmas Book Shelf,* 1902, decor. wraps, 239 pp., numerous illus. including one, p. 48, by R. (Deming)

PUBLISHERS CENTRAL BUREAU
LONG ISLAND CITY, NEW YORK

275 *Print, Book and Record Sale!,* n.d., self-wraps, 19 pp., numerous illus. in color including eleven by R. (Hurd, Russell)

J. E. REYNOLDS, BOOKSELLER, VAN NUYS, CALIF.

276 Number 110, *Western Americana,* May, 1969, pic. wraps, (27) pp., cover illus. by R.

277 Number 112, *Western Americana,* Fall 1969, pic. wraps, unpaged, cover illus. by R.

278 Number 113, *Americana,* December 1969, pic. wraps, unpaged, front cover illus. by R.

279 Number 114, *Western Americana,* Winter 1970, pic. wraps, unpaged, front cover illus. by R.

280 Number 122, *The West,* Summer 1971, pic. wraps, unpaged, front cover illus. by R.

FRANKLIN M. RUSHON, PHOENIXVILLE, PA.

281 *Sporting Books and Prints,* Summer 1951, wraps, 28 pp., eight illus. including two, pp. 26 and 27, by R. (Russell)

R. H. RUSSELL, NEW YORK

282 *Illustrated and Descriptive List,* 1897, wraps, illus. by R. and others.

283 *Illustrated and Descriptive List,* 1898, wraps, illus. by R. and others.

284 *The Holiday List, 1898–1899,* decor. wraps, (32) pp., numerous illus. including four by R.

285 *Illustrated and Descriptive List,* 1899, pic. wraps, illus. by R. and others.

286 *The Holiday List, 1899–1900,* pic. wraps, (48) pp., numerous illus. including five by R.

287 *Illustrated and Descriptive List,* 1901, pic. wraps, illus. by R. and others.

CHARLES SCRIBNER'S SONS, NEW YORK

288 *The Book Buyer,* Christmas 1897, colored pic. wraps, pp. 401-628, numerous illus. including eight, pp. (459), 460 (two), 461, 462, 463 (two) and (465), by R.

SHOREY'S BOOK STORE, SEATTLE

289 *American Indian Catalog Number 6,* June 1972, pic. wraps, 46 pp., illus. including one, p. 17, by R.

SMITH BOOK STORE, BALTIMORE, MD.

290 *Catalogue Number 12,* February, 1960, pic. wraps, 19 pp., front cover illus. by R.

TILTON INDIAN RELICS, TOPEKA, KANSAS

291 Number 19, *Rare Out-of-Print Books,* (1958), pic. wraps, 97 pp., illus. including one, p. 55, by R.

292 Number 15, *Rare Out-of-Print Books,* 1959, pic. wraps, 97 pp., illus. including one, p. 56, by R.

JOHN ALAN WALKER, PANORAMA CITY, CALIF.

293 *Exploring New Frontiers in Art,* Catalogue Two, 1973, pic. wraps, illus. including one by R.

RAY S. WALTON – BOOKSELLER
AUSTIN, TEXAS

294 *Texas and the West,* Catalogue One, Fall 1969, pic. wraps, 37 pp., front cover illus. by R.

295 Same, Catalogue Three, Winter 1970, pic. wraps, 22 pp., front cover illus. by R.

296 Same, Catalogue Six, Fall 1970, pic. wraps, 46 pp., front cover illus. by R.

297 Same, Catalogue Eight, Winter 1971, pic. wraps, 46 pp., front cover illus. by R.

298 Same, Catalogue Eleven, Feb. 1971, pic. wraps, 21 pp., front cover illus. by R.

CHARLES L. WEBSTER & CO., NEW YORK

299 *Illustrated Catalogue of Publications,* 1892, wraps, 40 pp., testimonials by Clemens (Twain), Howell, Whittier, et al., illus. including one by R.

WESTERN HEMISPHERE, SHARON, MASS.

300 Catalogue Two, *Western Americana,* Fall 1967, pic. wraps, 65 pp., cover illus. by R.

301 Catalogue Ten, *Western Americana,* Winter 1969, pic. wraps, 65 pp., cover illus. by R.

WESTERNLORE PRESS, LOS ANGELES

302 *Books of the West — from the West,* Spring and Summer, 1968, pic. wraps, 29 (1) pp., cover illus. by R.

THE WILSON BOOKSHOP, DALLAS

303 Number 4, *Texas and the American West,* July 1970, pic. wraps, 40 pp., cover illus. by R.

304 Number 5, *Texas and the American West,* September 1970, pic. wraps, 40 pp., cover illus. by R.

Written and Illustrated by the Artist

305 *Pony Tracks.* Harper, N.Y., 1895, pic. cloth, 269 pp., seventy illus. (An issue in full leather is reported.)

306 Same, Long's College Book Co., Columbus, Ohio, 1951, pic. cloth, 269 pp., "Introduction" by Harold McCracken, "Books by Remington," seventy illus. The Harold McCracken Edition.

307 Same, University of Oklahoma Press, Norman, (1961), words "First Printing" on copyright page, hard boards, 176 pp., "A Summary Introduction to Frederic Remington," by J. Frank Dobie, numerous illus. The Western Frontier Library. (Russell)

308 *A Rogers Ranger in the French and Indian War, 1757–1759.* Reprinted from *Harper's Magazine,* Nov. 1897, wraps, 12 pp., five illus., pp. 4, 6, 8, 10 and 11.

309 *Crooked Trails.* Harper, N.Y. and London, 1898, pic. cloth, 150 (1) pp., numerous illus.

310 Same, Harper, London and N.Y., 1898, gilt lettering on slate colored pic. cloth with design on front cover taken from "On the Moose Trail," *(Harper's Monthly,* Oct. 1890), 150 (1) pp., gilt top, numerous illus. First British edition.

311 Same, Grosset & Dunlap, N.Y., (1914?), decor. cloth, 150 (1) pp., "To the Public" by Chief Scout Executive James E. West, numerous illus. Boy Scout Edition.

312 Same, Harper, N.Y. and London, (1923), pic. cloth, 150 (1) pp., (2) of advs., "Foreword" by Zane Grey, numerous illus.

313 *Sundown Leflare.* Harper, N.Y. and London, 1899, decor. cloth, 114 (1) pp., twelve illus.

314 *Stories of Peace and War.* Harper, N.Y. and London, 1899, decor. cloth, 98 pp., (1) of advs., blue top, two illus. (Author's first name misspelled with added "K" on front cover.)

315 *Men with the Bark On.* Harper, N.Y. and London, 1900, pic. cloth, 208 (1) pp., thirty-two illus. The first issue measures less than one inch across the top of the covers.

316 *John Ermine of the Yellowstone.* Macmillan, N.Y., 1902, words "Set up and electrotyped November, 1902" follow copyright notice, pic. cloth, 271 pp., gilt top, illus. including eight full-page plates. Author's last name misspelled "Reminigton" on spine of first issue.

317 (Remington.) Program for the play *John Ermine of the Yellowstone.* Manhattan Theatre, N.Y., ninth week of the season, Nov. 2–7, 1903, pic. wraps, unpaged, frontis. by R.

318 *The Way of an Indian.* Fox, Duffield & Co., N.Y., 1906, words "Published, February, 1906" on copyright page, decor. cloth with illus. in color mounted on front cover, 251 (1) pp., fourteen full-page illus. including the frontis. in color. The first issue has p. 9 so numbered, "Fox Duffield & Company" on spine and yellow lettering on cover.

319 *Frederic Remington's Own West.* Dial Press, N.Y., 1960, full leather, tinted endsheets, 254 pp., gilt top, "Introduction" (and edited) by Harold McCracken, numerous illus. including two in color. Edition limited to 167 copies, signed by McCracken, in slipcase.

320 Same, first trade edition of no. 319, bound in cloth with words "First Edition after Limited Edition of 167 copies," numerous illus. including one, the frontis., in color.

321 Same, F. Foulsham & Co., London, (1960). First British edition of no. 319.

322 *Frederic Remington's Own Outdoors.* Dial Press, N.Y., (1964), cloth, yellow endsheets, 180 pp., "Introduction" by Harold McCracken, "Preface" (and edited) by Douglas Allen, numerous illus.

323 *Horses of the Plains* and *A Scout with the Buffalo Soldiers* (excerpts from *The Century Magazine*, 1888–1889). W. T. Genns, Santa Barbara, n.d., pic. wraps, pp. 332–343 and 899–912, twenty-three illustrations.

Books and Portfolios of Pictures Frederic Remington

324 (Miles.) *Rotogravures.* N.p., n.d., fourteen 23" x 16" black and white prints — the subjects first appeared as the full-page illus. in General Miles' *Personal Recollections*, no. 848.

325 *Drawings.* R. H. Russell, N.Y., 1897, full suede, sixty plates, "Foreword" by Owen Wister. De Luxe Edition, publication notice signed by Remington and Russell, in a cardboard box, with one artist's proof print signed by Remington laid in.

326 Same, bound in pictorial boards. First Trade edition of no. 325.

327 *Frontier Sketches.* The Werner Co., Akron, Ohio etc., 1898, cloth or pic. boards, (3) pp., "Introduction" by Geo. S. Rowe, fifteen plates with protective parchment title tissues.

328 *A Bunch of Buckskins.* R. H. Russell, N.Y., 1901, portfolio with paper title labels, 15" x 20", "Introductory Note" by Owen Wister, eight drawings in pastel.

329 *Indians.* The four Indian drawings from no. 328, probably issued in 1901.

330 *Rough Riders.* The four "rough riders" from no. 328, probably issued in 1901.

331 *Western Types.* Scribner's, N.Y., 1902, set of four color prints, 12" x 16".

332 Same, but prints are 5" x 7¼".

333 *Done in the Open.* R. H. Russell, N.Y., 1902, cloth and pic. boards, "Introduction" (and verses) by Owen Wister, seventy-seven drawings including one, "Caught in the Circle" (double-page), in color. Artist's first name misspelled with an added "k" on front cover, and with lettering under color plate in *blue and red.*

334 Same, P. F. Collier & Son, N.Y., 1902, with the misspelled first name on the front cover — recalled as was the Russell imprint. (Evidently printed for Collier by Russell and while the Russell issue has long been considered the first printing there seems to be no real doubt that both were printed and bound at the same time.)

335 Same, Russell and Collier imprints with the correct spelling of "Frederic" on the front cover, both released in 1902 to replace the issues recalled.

336 Same, De Luxe edition of no. 333, limited to 250 copies bound in full suede, boxed, inserted publication notice signed by Russell and Remington.

337 *Portfolio of Drawings.* Collier, N.Y., 1904, decor. boards, tied, three full-color prints, 5" x 7½" with letter-press advertising a set of twelve.

338 *Six Remington Prints in Color.* Collier, N.Y., 1904–1908, cloth and gray boards portfolio with paper title label, six prints, 11″ x 17″, in color.

339 *Remington's Four Best Paintings.* Collier, N.Y., 1908, large envelope with paper title label, four prints, 11″ x 15″.

340 *Seven Remington Prints* (issued as a supplement to *Chicago Examiner*). The McConnell Printing Co., N.Y., n.d., (1908?), seven prints in color, 14″ x 9¼″. The subjects appeared in *The Way of an Indian* (no. 318), facing pp. 42, 80, 92, 150, 172, 216 and 238.

341 *Eight New Remington Paintings.* Collier, N.Y., 1908–1909, cloth and red boards with decor. title label, eight full-color prints varying in size from 10⅜″ x 6¾″ to 13″ x 8¾″.

342 *Frederic Remington's Paintings.* 1912, portfolio with paper title label, four prints in full color.

343 *Frederic Remington Reproductions.* Museum of Fine Arts of Houston, (Texas), n.d., large envelope with title label, twelve prints in color, approximately 12″ x 8½″.

344 *Frederic Remington, A Painter of American Life.* Robert Isaacson, Brooklyn, N.Y., 1943, stiff wraps with spiral spine, (2) pp., portrait of Remington and brief appraisal of his art, twenty-six plates, in slipcase, edition limited to 500 copies.

345 *Frederic Remington's Buckskins.* Eight prints from no. 328, in a portfolio by Penn Prints for the Remington Art Memorial, Ogdensburg, N.Y., 1956.

346 *Bronco Busters.* Two prints by Penn Prints for the Remington Art Memorial, n.d.

347 *Painting and Drawing of the Old West.* (C. F. Braun & Co., Alhambra, California), 1963, morocco and marbled boards, "Foreword" by John G. Braun, sixty-one plates.

348 *101 Frederic Remington Drawings of the Old West.* (Text by Irvin W. Hansen), Color Press, Willmar, Minn., 1968, decor. cloth, tan endsheets, 203 (1) pp., foreword.

349 *The Illustrations of Frederic Remington.* (Edited by Marta Jackson), Bounty Books, N.Y., (1970), fabricoid, decor. endsheets, 192 pp., "Commentary" by Owen Wister, over 200 illus. by R.

350 *Frederic Remington* — (12 slides). Amon Carter Museum, Fort Worth, (but printed in Italy), 1972, colored pic. wraps, unpaged, three illus. by R. and two photos plus twelve slides in color.

Frederic Remington et al.

351 *Sport: or Shooting and Fishing.* Bradless, Whidden Publishing Co., Boston, 1889, edited by A. C. Gould, cloth bound portfolio containing the five separate parts, each in printed tan wraps, fifteen color plates including two, "Antelope Hunting" and "Canada Goose Shooting," by R., 18″ x 24″. (Zogbaum)

352 *The Century Gallery — Selected Proofs from the Century and St. Nicholas Magazine.* The Century Co., N.Y., 1893, folio folder, with letter press, containing sixty-four proof plates including two, "Moving the Led Horses" and "Sioux Indian Charging the Sun-Pole," by R.

353 *Six Modern Masters.* N.Y., 1903–1906, portfolio with cloth back, six artist proof impressions including one, "Evening on a Canadian Lake," by R.

354 *Frederic Remington—Four Pictures in Color: Charles Dana Gibson — Four Pictures in Color.* Collier, N.Y., 1903–1907, black boards with cloth back and pic. Remington title label, the eight prints are approximately 14″ x 19¾″.

355 *Eight Pictures in Color.* Collier, N.Y., 1907, cloth backed portfolio, 14″ x 20″, one, "The Cowpuncher," by R.

356 *Thirty Favorite Paintings by Leading American Artists.* Collier, N.Y., (1908), cloth and boards, paper label, two illus. in color, "The Shadow at the Water Hole" and "A Spanish Escort," by R.

357 *American Art by American Artists.* Collier, N.Y., 1914, cloth with paper label, "100 masterpieces representing the best work in pen-and-ink and in color of twenty-seven Celebrated American Artists," including twelve, eight in color, approximately 16½″ x 12¼″, by R.

358 *Twenty-five Art Pictures Representing the Best Work in Color and Pen and Ink of America's Greatest Artists.* Collier, N.Y., n.d., portfolio approximately 12″ x 16½″, includes two, "The Buffalo Runner" and "The Squall," by R.

359 *Master Portfolio of Western Art.* Montana Historical Society, Helena, 1965, two prints by R., limited to 500 sets. (Johnson, Lea, Russell, Schreyvogel)

360 *100 of the World's Most Beautiful Paintings.* N.Y., (1966), cloth or pic. boards, unpaged, no. 38 by R. (Leigh)

361 *The Great American Shooting Prints.* (Selections and text by Robert Elman Knopf), N.Y., 1972, cloth, tinted endsheets, unpaged but with 72 numbered plates in-

cluding no. 22 with two illus., one in color, by R. (Goodwin, Leigh, Miller, Russell)

362 *50 American Masterpieces — 200 Years of Great Paintings.* Shorewood Publishers, (N.Y., 1968), colored pic. wraps, 50 numbered illus. including one, no. 36, by R. (Miller)

362a (Haddad.) *Reproductions.* Haddad's Fine Arts, Buena Park, California, 1969, words "First Edition 1969" on title page, colored pic. cloth, 217, xi pp., index, numerous illus. including nine in color, pp. 45 (three), 46 (three) and 47 (three), by R. (Hurd, Russell)

Illustrated by Remington

363 Adams, James Truslow (editor-in-chief). *End of an Era.* Scribner's, N.Y., 1948, code letter "A" on copyright page, decor. cloth and endshets, 385 pp., foreword, acknowledgments, numerous illus. including two, pp. 34 and 35, by R. *Album of American History,* vol 4.

364 Adams, Kenneth C., ed. *From Trails to Freeways.* (California State Printing Office, Sacramento), 1950, pic. wraps, 161 (1) pp., ("Foreword") by Governor Earl Warren, numerous illus. including two, pp. (28) and 30, by R.

365 Adams, Ramon F. *Cowboy.* Feltrinelli Editore, Milano, (1958), words "Prima edizione italiana; decembre, 1958," *introduzione,* indices, twenty-seven illus. including one in color, facing p. 240, by R., slipcase.

366 ———. *The Cowboy and His Humor.* The Encino Press, Austin, 1968, pic. boards, 71 pp., four illus., front cover, double-title page and pp. 3 and 45, by R. Edition of 850 copies numbered and signed by the author.

367 ———. *The Cowman and His Code of Ethics.* The Encino Press, Austin, 1969, pic. boards, 33 pp., a Note to the Reader, three illus., double-title page (repeated on the covers), pp. 3 and 15, by R. Edition of 850 copies numbered and signed by the author.

368 Ainsworth, Ed. *The Cowboy in Art.* World, N.Y. and Cleveland, (1968), words "First Printing 1968" on copyright page, pic. leather, orange endsheets, all edges gilt, "Foreword" by John Wayne, index, numerous illustrations (twenty-four in color) including four, pp. 47 and 48 (two) and one in color between pp. 114 and 115, by Remington plus "He (Remington) Gave Us the Wild Old West for Keeps," a painting, p. 47, by Harold Von Schmidt and much on him in the text. DeLuxe Edition in slipcase. (Beeler,

Borein, Bugbee, De Yong, Dixon, Dunton, Eggenhofer, Ellsworth, Hurd, James, Johnson, Koerner, Mora, Perceval, Russell, Santee, Schreyvogel, Von Schmidt)

369 ———. Same, first trade edition in pic. cloth.

370 Akehurst, Richard *The World of Guns,* Hamlyn, London etc. (but printed in Italy, 1972), cloth, pic. endsheets, 127 pp., index, numerous (32 in color) illus. including four, pp. 70-1, 73, 80 and 81 (color), by R.

371 Alexander, David. *The History and the Romance of the Horse* (told with pictures). Cooper Square Publishers, N.Y., 1962, colored pic. wraps, 127 (1) pp., numerous illus. including seven, pp. 15, (19), 20, 46, 48, 49 and 94, by R.

372 Allen, Douglas. *Frederic Remington and the Spanish-American War.* Crown, N.Y., (1971), cloth, tan endsheets, 178 pp., preface, notes, bibliography, index, map, 100 illus. (frontis. in color) by R. plus photos of him.

373 Allen, Frederic L. (editor-in-chief). *Centennial of Harper's Magazine 1850–1950.* Harper, N.Y., 1950, pic. wraps, 288 pp., (8) of advs., numerous illus. including two, pp. 121 and 134, by R.

374 Allred, B. W. *Practical Grassland Management.* Sheep and Goat Raiser Magazine, San Angelo, Texas, (1950), cloth, 307 pp., "Editor's Introduction" by H. M. Phillips, "Foreword" by F. G. Renner, index, numerous illus. including three, facing pp. 16 (in color) and 48 (in color) and p. 145, by R. (Russell)

375 Altman, Seymour and Violet. *The Book of Buffalo Pottery.* Crown, N.Y., 1969, cloth and boards, 192 pp., "Foreword" by Harold M. Esty, Jr. and Harry H. Larkin, Jr., introduction, glossary, index, 400 illus. including "The Buffalo Hunt Jug" (1906) and "Oval Platter" (1897) with scenes adapted from "Her Calf," pp. 50 and 56, by R.

376 *American Peoples Encyclopedia* (20 volumes). Grolier Inc., N.Y., (1968), vol. 16 includes "A Dash for Timber," p. 2, by Remington and a brief biography of him, pp. 1 and 2.

377 Asch, Moses and Lomax, Alan, eds. *The Leadbelly Song Book.* Oak Publications, N.Y., (1962), pic. wraps, 96 (1) pp., "Foreword" by Asch, "Leadbelly" by Pete Seeger, "Leadbelly's Legacy" by Frederic Ramsey, Jr., discography and song index, numerous illus. including one, p. 47, by R.

378 Athearn, Robert G. *The New World.* Dell Pub. Co.,

N.Y., (1963), colored pic. boards and endsheets, 87 (2) pp., "Foreword" by President John F. Kennedy, "Introduction" by Allan Nevins, "For Further Reading," numerous illus. in color including two, pp. (82) and (88), by R. Vol. 1 of the *American Heritage New Illustrated History of the U. S.*

379 ——. *The Frontier.* Dell Pub. Co., N.Y., (1963), colored pic. boards and endsheets, pp. 454–539, numerous illus. including five, frontis., pp. (523) and 537, back endsheet and back cover, by R. Vol. 6 of series with continuous pagination started with no. 378. (Dunn, Russell)

380 ——. *Winning the West.* Dell Pub. Co., N.Y., (1963), color pic. boards and endsheets, pp. (723)–809, numerous illus. including ten, front cover, pp. 727, 745 (four), (752–53), 760–61, 762–63, and back cover, by R. (Dunn, Leigh, Russell)

381 —— and Carl Ubbelohde. *Centennial Colorado.* E. L. Chambers, Denver, (1959), words "First Edition" on copyright page, pic. boards, map endsheets, 93 (3) pp., numerous illus. including one, p. 13, by R.

382 Bacheller, Irving, ed. *Best Things from American Literature.* The Christian Herald, N.Y., 1899, decor. cloth, 416 pp., preface, index to the selections, index to the authors, index to the illustrations, numerous illus. including one, p. 21, by R.

383 Baird, Major G. W. *A Report to the Citizens Concerning Late Disturbances on the Western Frontier* etc. Lewis Osborne, Ashland, Oregon, 1972, cloth, 70 pp., "Introduction" by W. H. Hutchinson, numerous illus. by R.

383a Baird, Joseph A., Jr. (compiled by). *The West Remembered.* California Historical Society, San Francisco and San Marino, 1973, colored pic. wraps, 88 pp., "Foreword" by Mitchell A. Wilder, introduction, numerous illus. including one, p. (53), by R. (Blumenschein, Borein, Dixon, James, Lungren, Marchand, Miller, Russell, Zogbaum)

383b (Baker.) *Christmas Gift Selections.* The Baker Co., Lubbock, (1973), decor. wraps, unpaged, numerous illus. including one by R. (Hurd, Russell)

384 Bakker, Elna and Lillard, Richard G. *The Great Southwest.* American West, Palo Alto, (1972), cloth, tan endsheets, 283 (4) pp., introduction, sources and suggested reading, index, reference maps, numerous illus. including one, p. 139, by R.

385 Bancroft, Caroline. *Glenwood's Early Glamour.* (Johnson Pub. Co., Boulder, Colo., 1958), pic. wraps,

24 pp., "The Author" by Governor Stephen L. R. McNichols, acknowledgments, illus. including one, front cover, by R.

386 ——. *Colorful Colorado.* Sage Books, Denver, (1959), cloth, map endsheets, 127 pp., "The Author" by Governor Stephen L. R. McNichols, acknowledgments, "For Further Reading," index, numerous illus. including two, pp. 9 and 110, by R. (Schreyvogel)

387 Bang, Roy T. *Heroes Without Medals: A Pioneer History of Kearney County, Nebraska.* Warp Pub. Co., Minden, Neb., (1952), words "First Edition" on copyright page, fabricoid, 286 pp., foreword, references, index, numerous illus. including one, p. 6, by R., maps.

388 Barnum, Frances Courtenay (Baylor). *Juan and Juanita.* Tichnor & Co., Boston, 1888, pic. cloth, decor. endsheets, 276, xvi pp., all edges red, preface, title page statement "With Illustrations by Henry Sandham" but with two, pp. 15 and 22, by R.

389 Barry, Herbert et al. *Squadron A: A History of Its First Fifty-Years, 1889–1939.* Assn. of Ex-Members of Squadron A, N.Y., 1939, cloth, preliminary statements, lists, illus. including one, facing p. 18. by R.

390 Barstow, Charles L., ed. *The Westward Movement.* The Century Co., N.Y., 1918, decor. cloth, 231 pp., numerous illus. including twelve by R. (Lungren)

391 ——. *The Progress of a United People.* The Century Co., N.Y., (1912), words "Published May, 1912" on copyright page, decor. cloth, 220 pp., index, numerous illus. including three, pp. 54, 56 and 69, by R.

392 Bauer, John E. *Dogs on the Frontier.* Naylor, San Antonio, 1964, cloth, 238 pp., illus. including one, p. 33, by R.

393 Baxter, Elizabeth. *Historic Ogdenburg, Centennial 1968.* (Ryan Press, Ogdensburg, N.Y.), pic. wraps, 28 pp., numerous illus. including a photo of the Remington Art Memorial and three illus., pp. 23 and 24 (two), by R.

394 Bechdolt, Rrederick R. *When the West was Young.* The Century Co., N.Y., 1922, decor. cloth, 309 pp., acknowledgments, frontis. by R.

395 ——. *Tales of the Old Timers.* The Century Co., N.Y. and London, (1924), decor. cloth, 367 pp., acknowledgments, frontis. by R.

396 Beebe, Lucius and Clegg, Charles. *The American West.* Dutton, N.Y., 1955, words "First Edition" on copyright page, decor. cloth, pic. endsheets, 511 (1)

pp., acknowledgments, foreword, bibliography, over 1000 illus. including twenty-five by R.

397 ———. *Hear the Train Blow*. Dutton, N.Y., 1952, words "First Edition" on copyright page, decor. cloth, pic. endsheets, 407 (9) pp., foreword, 870 illus. including one, p. (263), by R. (Leigh)

398 Beitz, Les. *Treasury of Frontier Relics* (A Collector's Guide). Edwin House, N.Y., (1966), decor. cloth, 246 pp., "Foreword" by Fred Gipson, introduction, appendix, picture credits, index, numerous illus. including three, pp. (141), 142 and 189, by R. (Wyeth)

399 Bell, Colonel William Gardner. *The Snake, A Noble and Various River*. Potomac Corral, The Westerners, Washington, D.C., March 1969, pic. boards, 20 pp., map, ten illus. including two, pp. 13 and 15, by R. Limited to 250 numbered and signed copies. (Miller)

400 ———. Same, first trade edition in wraps.

400a Bennett, Ian. *A History of American Painting*. Hamlyn, London etc., (printed in Italy, 1973), cloth, black endsheets, 239 (1) pp., index, numerous illus. including two, pp. 114–5 and 124, by R. (Miller, Russell, Schreyvogel)

401 Bentel, Dwight and Freitas, Dolores. *Stories of the Santa Clara Valley*. The Rosicrucian Press, San Jose, Calif., (1942), pic. cloth and endsheets, 144 pp., introduction, acknowledgments, bibliography, numerous illus. including two, pp. 82 and 95, by R.

402 Berger, Josef in consultation with Lawrence C. Wroth. *Discoverers of the New World*. American Heritage Pub. Co., N.Y., (1960), colored pic. cloth, map endsheets, 153 pp., "Foreword" by Wroth, appendix, bibliography, index, numerous illus. in color including two, pp. 94 and 110–11, by R. (Hurd)

403 Bidwell, John et al. *First Three Wagon Trains*. Binfords & Mort, Portland, Ore., (1958), cloth, map endsheets, 104 pp., "Earliest Settler Caravans," illus. including four, two between pp. 26 and 27 and two between pp. 58 and 59, by R. (Dunn)

404 ———. *Life in California Before the Gold Discovery*. Lewis Osborne, Palo Alto, 1966, pic. cloth, map endsheets, 76 pp., "Foreword" (and edited) by Oscar Lewis, illus. including four, pp. 32, 33, 35 and 39, by R. Edition of 1950 copies.

405 ———. *The First Emigrant Train to California*. Penlitho Press, Palo Alto, 1966, collectors edition of 400 copies, cloth, 56 pp., "Foreword" by Oscar Lewis, seven illus., pp. 20, 24, 27, 29, 32, 35 and 41, by R.

406 Bigelow, Lt. John, Jr. *On the Bloody Trail of Geronimo*. Westernlore Press, Los Angeles, 1958, decor. cloth, map endsheets, 237 pp., "Foreword" and "Introduction" (and notes) by Arthur Woodward, index, numerous illus. by R.

407 ———. Same, but "A facsimile reissue" (of the 1958 edition) with a different drawing on the d/w by R.

408 Bigelow, Poultney. *The Borderland of Czar and Kaiser*. Harper, N.Y., 1895, decor. cloth, 343 pp., numerous illus. by R.

409 ———. *White Man's Africa*. Harper, N.Y. and London, 1900, pic. cloth, 271 pp., preface, numerous illus. including three, facing pp. 88, 96 and 104, by R.

410 Blake, Nelson Manfred. *A Short History of American Life*. McGraw-Hill, N.Y. etc., 1952, cloth, 732 pp., preface, "Suggestions for Further Reading," index, 54 illus. including one, p. 392, by R. Mentioned in text, p. 544.

411 *Blätter and Blüten*. Louis Lange Pub. Co., St. Louis, Mo., (1907), decor. cloth, 388 pp., (4) of advs., numerous illus. including four, pp. 67, 70, 73 and 77, by R. (Text in German.)

412 Same, Band 29, n.d., wraps, 154 pp., illus. by R.

413 Bloss, Roy S. *Pony Express — The Great Gamble*. Howell-North, Berkeley, Calif., 1959, cloth, pic. endsheets, 159 pp., preface, acknowledgments, bibliography, index, numerous illus. including one, the frontis., by R.

414 Boniface, First Lt. Jno. J(acob). *The Cavalry Horse and His Pack*. Hudson Kimberly Pub. Co., Kansas City, Mo., 1903, pic. cloth, 538 pp., preface, "Books Consulted," appendices, numerous illus. including one, the frontis., by R.

415 Boorstin, Daniel J. *The Landmark History of the American People from Appomattox to the Moon*. Random House, N.Y., (1970), colored pic. boards, pic. endsheets, 192 (1) pp., index, numerous illus. including three, front cover, and pp. (3) and 146, by R. (Russell)

416 Bostwick, Arthur Elmore, ed. *Doubleday's Encyclopedia*. Doubleday, N.Y., 1931, eleven volumes — vol. IX includes one illus., p. 24, by R. plus a brief biography of him.

417 Botkin, Ben A., ed. *A Treasury of Western Folklore*. Crown Pub., N.Y., 1951, words "Southwest Edition" on front cover, cloth, 806 pp., "The Southwest" by

J. Frank Dobie, "Foreword" by Bernard De Voto, indices, illus. on title page by R.

418 Bourke, Captain John G. *An Apache Campaign.* Scribner's, N.Y., (1958), cloth and decor. boards, 128 pp., "Captain John G. Burke as Soldier, Writer and Man" by J. Frank Dobie, one drawing on the double title page by R.

419 ———. *With General Crook in the Indian Wars.* Lewis Osborne, Palo Alto, 1968, decor. cloth, pic. endsheets, 59 (2) pp., "Foreword" by W. H. Hutchinson, two folding maps in color, photos of Burke and Crook and eleven illus. by R.

420 ———. *Mackenzie's Last Fight with the Cheyennes.* Argonaut Press, N.Y., for University Microfilms, Ann Arbor, 1966, decor. two-tone cloth, 56 (2) pp., note, "A Battle, A Book and A Man — An Introduction" by Joseph P. Peters, four maps, seven illus. including one, p. (27), by R.

420a Bourne, Russell (project editor). *200 Years.* U.S. News and World Report, Washington, D.C., 1973, two volumes, fabricoid and cloth, numerous illus. including two, pp. (206) and 208 (I), by R. (Dunn, Miller, Russell, Wyeth, Zogbaum)

420b Bowman, Hank Wieand. *Famous Guns from the Smithsonian Collection.* Arco, N.Y., (1967), cloth, 112 pp., introduction, numerous illus. including one, p. 98, by R. (Eggenhofer)

421 Brady, Buckskin. *Stories and Sermons.* William Briggs, Toronto, 1905, cloth with photo of author mounted on front cover, 135 pp., fifteen illus. including one, "Broncho Breaking," facing p. 64, by R.

422 Brady, Cyrus Townsend. *Indian Fights and Fighters.* McClure, Phillips & Co., N.Y., 1904, words "Published December, 1904, N" on copyright page, 423 pp., preface, bibliography, appendices, index, illus. including three, facing pp. 60, 194 and 316, by R. (Blumenschein, Crawford, Deming, Elwell, Schreyvogel, Zogbaum)

423 ———. *Indian Fights and Fighters.* Nebraska, Lincoln, (1971), words "First Bison Book printing: November 1971" on copyright page, colored pic. wraps, 423 pp., "Introduction" by James T. King, index, illus. including three, pp. 60, 194 and 316, by R. (Blumenschein, Crawford, Deming, Elwell, Schreyvogel, Zogbaum)

424 Bragdon, Henry W. and McCutcheon, Samuel P. *History of a Free People.* Macmillan, N.Y., (1954), cloth, blue endsheets, 724 pp., numerous illus. including one, p. 383, by R., charts, maps.

425 ———. Same, teachers annotated edition, Macmillan, N.Y., (1961), decor. cloth, 11, xiii, 768 pp., appendix, index, maps, charts, graphs and tables, numerous illus. including one, p. 404, by R. (Miller)

426 Braider, Donald. *The Life, History and Magic of the Horse.* Madison Square Press (Grosset & Dunlap), N.Y., (1973), cloth, pic. endsheets, 247 pp., index, numerous illus. including one, p. 94, by R. (Russell)

427 Branch, E. Douglas (narrated by). *The Story of America in Pictures.* The American Peoples Encyclopedia, Spencer Press, (Chicago, 1954), wraps, 64 pp., (2) of advs., introduction, edited by Franklin J. Meine, numerous illus. including one, "A Dash for Timber," by R.

428 Briggs, Harold E. *Frontiers of the Northwest.* Appleton-Century, N.Y., London, 1940, code number "(1)" after last line of text, cloth, map endsheets, 629 pp., preface, bibliography, index, 38 illus. including one, facing p. 288, by R., seven maps.

429 Briggs, Thomas H. et al. *American Literature.* Houghton Mifflin, Boston etc., 1933, cloth, 764 pp., preface, acknowledgments, index, illus. including one, the frontis., "The Emigrants," in color, by R. (Reprinted in 1940 with same Remington plate as frontispiece and with illus. by James added.)

430 Britt, Albert. *Toward the Western Ocean* (The Story of the Men Who Bridged the Continent, 1803–1869). Barre Publishing Co., Barre, Mass., 1963, cloth, 164 pp., illus. including one, between pp. 54 and 55, by R.

431 Brooks, Elbridge S. *The Century Book for Young Americans.* The Century Co., N.Y., 1894, cloth with lettering on spine in red and lettering and illus. stamped on front cover, 249 pp., "Introduction" by Horace Porter, numerous illus. including two, pp. 113 and 114, by R. (Lungren)

432 Brooks, Van Wyck and Bettman, Otto L. *Our Literary Heritage, A Pictorial History of the Writer in America.* Dutton, N.Y., (1956), cloth and decor. boards, grey endsheets, 241 (5) pp., introduction, index, numerous illus. including five, pp. 23, 127 (two), 129 and 190, by R. (Keller, Smith)

432a Brookshier, Frank. *The Burro.* Oklahoma, Norman, (1974), words "First edition" on copyright page, cloth, 370 pp., preface, notes, index, numerous illus. including one, p. 240, by R. (Borein)

433 Brophy, Frank Cullen. *Arizona Sketch Book.* Privately printed (Arizona-Messenger Printing Co., Phoenix, 1952), fabricoid, map endsheets, 310 pp., foreword,

RAY'S TROOP by Remington from *A Daughter Of The Sioux*

bibliography, index, numerous illus. including two, facing pp. 23 and 257, by R.

434 Brown, Charles H. *The Correspondents' War, Journalists in the Spanish-American War.* Scribner's, N.Y., 1967, code letter "A" on copyright page, cloth, map endsheets, 478 (1) pp., foreword, sources, bibliography, index, maps, twenty-six illus. including two, between pp. 368 and 369, by R.

435 Brown, D. Alexander. *The Galvanized Yankees.* (Urbana, Illinois, 1963), cloth, map endsheets, 243 pp., introduction, notes, sources, index, illustrated including one, facing pp. 86 (and repeated on d/w), by R.

436 Brown, Dee (text by) and Schmitt, Martin F. (picture research by). *Trail Driving Days.* Scribner's, N.Y., 1952, code letter "A" on copyright page, decor. cloth, 264 pp., foreword, bibliography, 229 illus. including three, pp. 60, 80 and 104, by R. (Russell)

437 Brown, Henry Collins, ed. *Valentine's Manual of Old New York, 1926.* Valentine's Manual, Inc., N.Y., (1925), decor. cloth, 404 pp., gilt top, foreword, index, numerous illus. including one, p. 287, by R.

438 ———. *In the Golden Nineties.* Valentine's Manual, Hastings-on-Hudson, N.Y., 1928, cloth, pic. endsheets, 422 pp., foreword, acknowledgments, "Valentine's Manual," index, numerous illus. including one, drawing after a photo, by R.

439 Brown, Jennie Broughton. *Fort Hall on the Oregon Trail.* The Caxton Printers, Caldwell, Idaho, 1932, full morocco, pic. endsheets, 466 (1) pp., gilt top, preface, notes and additions, an appreciation, "Ferry Butte" by Susie Boice Trego, index, numerous illus. including three, pp. (94), (172) and (280), by R. Limited to 25 numbered and signed copies.

440 ———. Same, trade edition of no. 439 issued in cloth.

441 Bryson, John. *The Cowboy.* A Picture Press Book (distributed by Garden City Books, Garden City, N.Y.), 1951, pic. wraps, 78 (2) pp., numerous illus. including one, p. 4, by R. (Bugbee)

442 Burckhardt, Herausgegeben von Titus. *Der Wilde Westen.* Urs Graf-Verlag, Olten and Lausanne, Switzerland, (1966), colored pic. boards, 59 (1) pp., record in pocket inside back cover, illus. including two, pp. 31 and 43, by R. (German text.)

443 Burke, John M. *Buffalo Bill's Wild West and Congress of Rough Riders of the World.* Cody and Salsbury, N.Y., (1900), colored pic. wraps, 64 pp., (8) of advs., "Introductory" by Nate Salsbury, illus. including one, the front cover in color, by R.

444 Butterfield, Roger. *The American Past.* Simon and Shuster, N.Y., (1947), decor. cloth, plate endsheets, 476 pp., foreword, bibliography, index, numerous illus. including one, p. 266, by R.

445 Calkins, Frank W. *Indian Tales.* Donohue, Henneberry & Co., Chicago, (1893), pic. cloth, decor. endsheets, 150 pp., red top, illus. including one, p. 90, by R.

446 ———. *Hunting Stories.* Donohue, Henneberry & Co., Chicago, (1893), pic. cloth, decor. endsheets, 146 pp., red top, illus. including one, p. 18, by R. (Keller)

447 ———. *Boy's Life on the Frontier.* Donohue, Henneberry & Co., Chicago, (1893), pic. cloth, bound together *Frontier Sketches*, 134 pp., illus.; *Indian Tales*, as in no. 445 above, and *Hunting Stories* as in no. 446 above. (Keller)

448 ———. *Old Stumpy or, Indian Tales of the West.* Donohue & Co., Chicago, n.d., illus. including one, p. 90, by R. (Flashlight Detective Series, no. 78.)

449 Carey, Fred. *Mayor Jim, An Epic of the West.* Omaha Printing Co., Omaha, Neb., 1930, pic. cloth, 175 (1) pp., illus. including two, pp. 37 and 44, after R. originals in *Drawings*, no. 325.

450 Carlson, G. Robert (general editor) et al. *Encounters, Themes in Literature.* Webster Division, McGraw-Hill, St. Louis etc., 1967, decor. cloth, 758 pp., biographical notes, glossary, indices, numerous illus. including two in color, title page and p. 14, by R. (Schoonover)

451 ———. *Perception, Themes in Literature.* Webster Division, McGraw-Hill, St. Louis etc., 1969, decor. cloth, 630 pp., biographical notes, indices, numerous illus. including one in color, p. 281, by R.

452 Carlson, Raymond, ed. *Gallery of Western Paintings.* McGraw-Hill, N.Y. etc., (1951), words "First Edition" on copyright page, cloth with illus. in color mounted on front cover, colored endsheets, 85 pp., foreword, 76 illus. including seven in color by R. (Dixon, Leigh, Russell, Santee)

453 Carman, Harry J. et al. *Historic Currents in Changing America.* Winston, Philadelphia etc., 1938, code number "P-9-38" on copyright page, decor. cloth, 854 pp., preface, appendix, index, maps, numerous

illus. including one, p. (605), by R. Reprinted in 1942 with the same R. illus. (Dixon)

454 Carmer, Carl, ed. *Cavalcade of America.* Crown Publishers — Lothrop, Lee & Shepard, N.Y., (1956), cloth and boards, 382 pp., acknowledgments, introduction, appendix, index, 200 illus. (50 in color) including four, three in color, by R. The chapter "Recorder of the Last Frontier" is about R. with a photo of him.

455 Carpenter, Frances. *Canada and Her Northern Neighbors.* American Book Co., N.Y. etc., 1953, decor. cloth, map endsheets, 438 pp., preface, index, numerous illus. including one, p. 83, by R.

456 Carroll, John M., ed. *The Black Military Experience in the American West.* Liveright, N.Y., (1971), words "first edition, first printing," on copyright page, cloth, pic. endsheets, 591 pp., notes, bibliography, index, sixty illus. including seventeen by R. Limited to 300 numbered copies signed by the editor, slipcase and with two extra manually signed prints. (Bjorklund, Bugbee, Cisneros, Eggenhofer, Hurd, Russell, Schiwetz)

457 ———. Same, first trade edition, d/w.

458 ———. *Buffalo Soldiers West.* (The Old Army Press, Ft. Collins, Colo., 1971), pic. leather, cloth endsheets, 64 pp., foreword, the artists, 50 illus. including three, pp. 39, 40 and 41, by R. One of 50 numbered copies signed by the editor, each with an original drawing by Bjorklund.

459 ———. Same, first trade edition in pic. fabricoid.

460 Carter, M. H., ed. *Panther Stories Retold from St. Nicholas.* The Century Co., N.Y., 1904, pic. cloth, 189 pp., preface, illus. inclding two, facing pp. 24 and 28, by R.

461 Carter, Lt. Col. W. H. *From Yorktown to Santiago with the Sixth U. S. Cavalry.* The Lord Baltimore Press, Baltimore, Md., 1900, pic. cloth, 317 pp., gilt top, other edges uncut, preface, thirteen illus. including three, facing pp. 146, 258 and 260, by R.

462 ———. *Old Army Sketches.* The Lord Baltimore Press, Baltimore, Md., 1906, cloth, 203 pp., gilt top, foreword, illus. including one, facing pp. 177, by R., and three, pp. 51, 83 and 123, by C. H. Ourand after R. (In the six years between 1900 and 1906 the Lt. Colonel became a Brigadier-General.)

463 Catton, Bruce et al. *The American Heritage Reader.* (Dell Pub. Co., N.Y., 1956), words "A Dell First Edition" on title page, colored pic. wraps, 253 pp., (2) of

advs., all edges yellow, illus. including seven, two in color, by R. (Russell)

463a Caughey, John W. et al. *Land of the Free.* Franklin Publications, Pasadena, Calif., 1965, cloth, 658 pp., glossary, index, maps, numerous illus. including one, p. 519, by R. (Dunn, Perceval, Russell)

464 Chapel, Charles Edward. *Guns of the Old West.* Coward-McCann, N.Y., (1961), decor. cloth, brown endsheets, 306 pp., foreword, bibliography, index, numerous illus. including two, pp. 1 and 133, by R.

465 Chappell, Gordon. *The Search for the Well-Dressed Soldier, 1865–1890* (Museum Monograph no. 5). Arizona Historical Society, Tucson, 1972, wraps, 51 pp., illus. on title page (repeated on cover) by R.

466 Chenevix-Trench, Clarles. *A History of Horsemanship.* Doubleday, Garden City (printed in England, 1970), words "First published 1970" on copyright page, decor. cloth, 320 pp., bibliography, index, numerous illus. including three, pp. 238, 240 and 242, by R.

467 Chew, Samuel C., ed. *Fruit Among the Leaves.* Appleton-Century-Croft, N.Y., 1950, code number "(1)" after last line of text, cloth, 535 pp., preface, numerous illus. including one, p. (280), by R. and the text includes part of "A Scout with the Buffalo Soldiers" by him. (Varian)

468 Child, Theodore. *The Spanish-American Republics.* Harper, N.Y., 1891, decor. cloth, 444 pp., preface, numerous illus. including three, pp. 35, 73 and 93, by R.

469 ———. Same, first British edition, James R. Osgood, McIlvaine & Co., 1892.

470 *The Story of Evangelina Cisneros,* told by herself. Continental Pub. Co., N.Y., 1898, cloth 257 pp., map, "Introduction" by Julian Hawthorne, Karl Decker's "Story of the Rescue," illus. including four, pp. 21, 109, 161 and 181, by R.

471 Clark, Joseph L. *A History of Texas, Land of Promise.* D. C. Heath and Co., Boston etc., (1939), decor. cloth, 534, xxiii pp., preface, "Foreword" by H. F. Estill, index, maps, numerous illus. including one, p. 7, by R. (Marchand)

472 ——— Same, (1940), decor. cloth, 534, lvi pp., (appendix and glossary added).

473 ——— and Garrott, Julia Kathryn. Same, (1945), decor. cloth, 626 pp., illus. including one, p. 54, by R. (Marchand)

474 ———. Same, (1949), decor. cloth, 692 pp.

475 Clark, William H. *Farms and Farmers*. Page, Boston, (1945), words "First Impression, Oct. 1945" on copyright page, cloth, 346 pp., foreword, acknowledgment, appendix, bibliography, index, illus. including one, facing p. 134, by R.

476 Clendenen, Clarence C. *Blood on the Border* (The United States Army and the Mexican Irregulars). Macmillan, N.Y., (1969), words "First Printing" on copyright page, cloth, 390 pp., bibliography, maps, illus. including two (one repeated on title page) by R.

477 Cody, Hon. W. F. *Story of the Wild West and Camp-Fire Chats* by Buffalo Bill (pseud.). Historical Pub. Co., Phila., (1888), pic. stamped cloth, 766 pp., preface, 250 illus. including two, facing p. 285 and p. 732, after originals by R. Reprinted by John H. Stanton Co. of Chicago in 1901 with one of the redrawn illus. after R.

478 Coleman, Rufus A., ed. *Western Prose and Poetry*. Harper, N.Y. and London, 1932, words "First Edition" on copyright page, cloth, 502 pp., "Notes on the Artists," "To the Reader," acknowledgments, "Aids to Interpretation," ten illus. including eight, facing pp. 1, 34, 252, 274, 306, 334, 386 and 422, by R. (Russell)

479 Collier, Edmund, ed. *The Westerners Brand Book* (vol. 6). The Westerners, N.Y., 1959, decor. cloth, 96 pp., illus. including three, pp. 5, 6 and 16, by R. (Bugbee)

480 (Collier.) *A Dinner on the Occasion of the Tenth Anniversary of Collier's under the Guidance of Mr. Robert F. Collier.* P. F. Collier & Sons, N.Y., Jan. 27, 1908, gilt stamped vellum, 30 pp. Reproduces *Collier's Weekly* for Jan. 27, 1898 with one illus., "The Curse of the Wolves," by R. Limited to 25 copies, slipcase, and signed by the guests at the dinner including R.

481 Collins, Alan C. (compiled by). *The Story of America in Pictures*. Doubleday, Doran, Garden City, N.Y., 1935, words "First Edition" on copyright page, gilt decor. red cloth, 447 pp., red top, "Introduction" by Claude C. Bowers, numerous illus. including two, pp. 30 and 79, by R. The Literary Guild edition also has the words "First Edition" on copyright page.

482 Collins, Dabney Otis, ed. *1948 Brand Book*. The Westerners, Denver, Colo., (1949), decor. cloth and endsheets, 271 pp., "Preface" by Thomas Hornsby Ferril, acknowledgments, index, thirteen illus. including one, p. 179, by R. Edition limited to 500 numbered copies.

483 Commanger, Henry Steele, ed. *The St. Nicholas Anthology*. Random House, N.Y., (1948), words "First printing" on copyright page, decor. cloth, tinted endsheets, 542 pp., green top, "Introduction" by May Lamberton Becker, preface, illus. including seven, pp. 57 (two), 62, 63, 64 and 65 (two), by R.

483a Comstock, Helen, ed. *The Concise Encyclopedia of American Antiques*. Hawthorn Books, N.Y., (1958), words "First Edition" on copyright page, two volumes (slipcase), decor. cloth, decor. red endsheets, pp. 269, 277–542, grey tops, foreword (I), index (I and II), numerous illus. including two, between pp. 368 and 369, by R. (Russell)

484 Conkling, Roscoe P. et al. *The Westerners Brand Book*. Los Angeles Corral, (1948), decor. cloth, pic. endsheets, 175 pp., "Preface" by Sheriff Paul W. Galleher, bibliography, index, numerous illus. including one, p. 134, by R. (Borein, Russell)

485 Connelly, William Elsey. *Doniphan's Expedition and the Conquest of Mexico and California*. Bryant and Douglas, Kansas City, Mo., 1907, cloth with R. illus. mounted on front cover, 670 pp., illus., two folding maps.

486 Connor, Seymour V., ed. *Panhandle-Plains Historical Review*, vol. XXX. P-P Historical Society, Canyon, Texas, 1957, pic. wraps, 132 pp., frontis. by R. (Bugbee)

487 Cortissoz, Royal et al. *Annual of the Society of Illustrators*. Scribner's, N.Y., 1911, words "Published, November, 1911" on copyright page, cloth and boards, tan endsheets, (97) pp., gilt top, introduction, list of members, 85 illus. including one by R. (Blumenschein, Fogarty, Keller)

488 Coy, Owen C. (compiled and edited by). *Pictorial History of California*. University of Calif., Berkeley, (1925), cloth, tinted endsheets, 261 pp., foreword, 261 numbered plates including five, nos. 96, 110, 134, 198 and 205, by R.

489 *Dr. J. B. Cranfill's Chronicle, A Story of Life in Texas*. Fleming H. Revell Co., N.Y. etc., (1916), cloth, 456 pp., foreword, 39 illus. including three, facing pp. 37, 66 and 148, by R.

489a Craven, Avery and Johnson, Walter. *The United States — Experiment in Democracy*. Ginn, Boston etc., (1957), cloth, numerous illus. including one, p. 477, by R. (Lea)

490 Creelman, James. *On the Great Highway*. Lathrop Pub. Co., Boston, (1901), words "Published in Octo-

ber'' on copyright page, decor. cloth, 418 pp., preface, nine illus. including one, facing p. 198, by R.

491 Crosby, Alexander L. *Old Greenwood, Pathfinder of the West.* The Talisman Press, Georgetown, Calif., 1967, cloth, pic. endsheets, maps, numerous illus. including one, title page (repeated on d/w), by R. (Miller)

492 Cross, Major Osborne. *March of the Regiment of Mounted Riflemen to Oregon in 1849.* Ye Galleon Press, Fairfield, Wash., 1967, pic. cloth, pic. endsheets, 218 pp., illustrated with photos and 35 drawings by Wm. H. Tappan but front cover illus. (in gilt) and endsheets illus. by or after R.

493 Currey, J. Seymour. *Chicago: Its History and Its Builders.* S. J. Clarke Pub. Co., Chicago, 1912, cloth, five volumes with one illus., "A French Voyageur," facing p. 64, vol. 1, by R.

494 Custer, Elizabeth B. *Tenting on the Plains.* Charles L. Webster Co., N.Y., 1887, decor. cloth and endsheets, 702 pp., 29 illus. including eleven by R.

495 ———. *Tenting on the Plains.* Three vol. reprint, Oklahoma, Norman, (1971), words "First printing of the new edition" on copyright page, boards, 706 pp., "Introduction" by Jane R. Stewart, maps, illus. including eleven by R., slipcase.

496 ———. Same, reprint by Oklahoma, Norman, (1966), boards, 341 pp., "Introduction" by Jane R. Stewart. (Western Frontier Library no. 33.)

497 ———. *Following the Guidon.* Harper, N.Y., 1890, decor. cloth, brown endsheets, 341 pp., preface, sixteen illus. including two, facing pp. 6 and 18, by R.

498 Custer, Gen. George A. et al. *Wild Life on Plains and Horrors of Indian Warfare.* Royal Pub. Co., St. Louis, Mo., (1891), gilt decor. pic. cloth, 592 pp., numerous illus. including one, p. 552, by R. Reprinted by various other publishers.

499 ———. Same, reprint by Arno Press, N.Y., 1969.

500 ———. *My Life on the Plains.* Nebraska, Lincoln, n.d. (1966), pic. wraps, 626 pp., index, "Historical Introduction" and edited by Milo Milton Quaife, map, illus. including one, front cover, by R.

501 Darling, Jim, ed. *Brand Book II, the San Diego Corral, The Westerners.* (1971), brand decor. fabricoid, tan endsheets, 197 pp., numerous illus. including one, p. 59, by R. (Miller, Russell)

501a Dary, David A. *The Buffalo Book.* Swallow, Chicago, (1974), words "First Edition, First Printing" on copy-

right page, cloth, 374 pp., introduction, appendices, notes, bibliography, index, tables, numerous illus. including three, pp. 120, 179 and 221, by R. (Russell)

502 Davidson, Marshall B. *Life in America.* Houghton Mifflin, Boston, 1951, 2 vols., decor. cloth, 573 and 503 pp., "Foreword" by F. H. Taylor, introduction, notes, acknowledgments, bibliography, list of artists, index, over 1200 illus. including five by R.

503 ——— et al. *The American Heritage History of the Artists' America.* American Heritage, N.Y., (1973), cloth and boards, blue endsheets, 402 (14) pp., introduction, index, numerous illus. including seven, pp. (167), (274) in color, 275 four — one in color and 276, by R. (Miller, Russell, Schreyvogel)

504 ——— et al. *The American Heritage History of the Writers' America.* American Heritage, N.Y., (1973), cloth and boards, 403 (13) pp., introduction, index, numerous illus. including three, pp. 164, 239 and 250, by R. The two volumes in de luxe bindings also issued as a set in a slipcase. (Goodwin, Wyeth)

505 Davie, Emily, ed. *Profile of America.* A Studio Book, Crowell, N.Y., (1954), words "First Printing, September 1954" on copyright page, cloth, 415 pp., acknowledgments, "Foreword" by Charles A. Lindbergh, "Introduction" by Louis Bromfield, editor's note, index, numerous illus. including one, p. 163, by R.

506 Davis, Deering. *The American Cow Pony.* D. Van Nostrand Co., Princeton, N.J., (1962), words "First Edition" on copyright page, cloth, 166 pp., acknowledgments, bibliography, numerous illus. including four, frontis. and pp. 8, 34 and 38, by R. (Russell)

507 Davis, Richard Harding. *The West From a Car Window.* Harper, N.Y., 1892, pic. cloth, 242 (1) pp., numerous illus. including twenty by R.

508 ———. *A Year from a Reporter's Note Book.* Harper, N.Y., 1898, boards, 304 (1) pp., author's note, illus. including four, facing pp. 100, 108, 116 and 118, by R.

509 ———. *Cuba in War Time.* R. H. Russell, N.Y., 1899, boards, 143 pp., gilt top, author's note, illus. by R.

510 ———. Same, but issued in wraps with a folding map inside back cover added.

511 ———. *Ransom's Folly.* Scribner's, N.Y., 1902, words "Published July, 1902" on copyright page, pic. cloth, 345 pp., gilt top, other edges uncut, illus. including three, frontis. and facing pp. 8 and 88, by R.

First issue advertises *Captain Macklin* as being "In Press" in list following text.

512 ——. *In the Fog.* Grosset & Dunlap, N.Y., 1903, words "Special Edition" on title page, decor. cloth, 189 pp., with a second story, "The Death of Rodriguez" added and with six illus., pp. (161), (165), (169), (175), (181) and (187), by R. (This second story and the R. illus. did not appear in the first or Russell ed. of 1901.)

513 ——. *Notes of a War Correspondent.* Scribner's N.Y., 1910, cloth with publisher's symbol in gilt on front cover, 263 pp., gilt top, fourteen illus. including one, facing p. 10, by R.

514 Deatherage, Charles P. *Early History of Greater Kansas City, Missouri and Kansas.* (Interstate Publishing Co.), Kansas City, 1927, decor. fabricoid, grey endsheets, 701 pp., numerous illus. including one, p. (27), by R., folding map

515 *De Hem vi Lemnade och de Hem vi Funno.* Salesman's subscription book, L. M. Ayer Publishing Co., Minneapolis, Minn., 1893, pic. cloth, floral endsheets, sample pages of text with numerous illus. including four by R. Also *De Hjem vi Forlod og de Hjem vi Fandt,* sample pages of text with numerous illus. including three by R. Blanks to record orders inside back cover. The subscription book was also issued with the Danish-Norwegian sample pages preceding those in Swedish. It bears the imprint of the International Pub. Co., Chicago, Ill. and also is dated 1893. My Scandinavian expert informs me that Danish-Norwegian was the common language of the two countries for many years until in 1937 the Norwegian Parliament adopted a new orthographic reform, still easily understood by the Danes.

516 Delacorte, George T. (President). *Indian Chief.* Dell Pub. Co., N.Y., (1951), colored pic. wraps, pages unnumb., numerous illus. including one, "Indian Method of Breaking a Pony," back cover, by R.

517 Dempsey, Hugh A. *Crowfoot, Chief of the Blackfeet.* Oklahoma, Norman, (1972), words "First edition" on copyright page, cloth, 226 pp., bibliography, illus. including one by R.

518 Dept. of the Army. *American Military History, 1607–1953* (R.O.T.C. Manual 145–20). G.P.O., Washington, D.C., 1954, cloth, 307 pp., bibliography, illus. including one, p. 288, by R.

519 ——. Same, *1607–1958* (R.O.T.C. Manual 145–20). G.P.O., Washington, D.C., 1959, cloth, 558 pp., bibliography, illus. including one, p. 288, by R.

520 Dickman, Major General J. T., ed. *The Santiago Campaign.* Williams Printing Co., Richmond, Va., 1927, cloth, 442 pp., "Foreword" by Brig. Gen. C. D. Rhodes, intro., appendices, index, illus. including one, facing p. 232, by R. Remington in text, p. 323.

521 Dillon, Richard H. *Fool's Gold* (The Decline and Fall of Captain Sutter of California). Coward-McCann, N.Y., (1967), cloth, 380 pp., bibliographical reprise, maps, illus. including one, between pp. 128 and 129, by R.

522 Dimitry, John et al. *Indian Stories Retold from St. Nicholas.* Century Co., N.Y., 1905, pic. cloth, 179 pp., publisher's note, illus. including two, frontis. and title page, by R. (Lungren)

523 Dinsmore, Wayne. *Our Equine Friends.* Horse and Mule Assn. of America, (Drovers Journal Press), Chicago, (1944), self-wraps, 32 pp., illus. including one drawing, "Indian Pony," p. 7, by R.

524 *Diving and Digging for Gold.* (Pages of History, Sausalito, Calif., 1960), decor. wraps, 23 (1) pp., illus. including one, p. 9, by R.

525 Doble, John. *Journals and Letters from the Mines.* Old West Publishing Co., Denver, Colo., (1962), pic. cloth, 304 (3) pp., "Publisher's Preface" by Fred A. Rosenstock, "Introduction to John Doble's Journal" (and edited) by Charles L. Camp, map, acknowledgments, notes, index, illus. including three small drawings, p. IX, by R. Edition of 1000 copies designed and printed by Lawton Kennedy.

526 Dodge, Mary Mapes (conducted by). *A Year of St. Nicholas.* Century Co., N.Y., Nov. 1887–Oct. 1888, decor. cloth, pic. endsheets, 960 pp., numerous illus. including three by R.

527 Dodge, Theodore Ayrault. *Riders of Many Lands.* Harper, N.Y., 1894, decor. cloth, 406 pp., gilt top, preface, numerous illus. including eighteen by R. A British edition was issued by Osgood, McIlvaine & Co., London, 1894.

528 Dolan, J. R. *The Yankee Peddlers of Early America.* Clarkson N. Potter, N.Y., (1964), words "First Edition" on copyright page, cloth, decor. endsheets, 270 pp., introduction, bibliography, numerous illus. including two, pp. 75 and 78, by R. (Eggenhofer)

529 Downey, Fairfax. *Indian Fighting Army.* Scribner's, N.Y., 1941, code letter "A" on copyright page, cloth, 329 pp., illus. including forty by R. (Leigh, Schreyvogel, Zogbaum)

530 ——. Same, but Bantam Pathfinder Edition, N.Y.,

May, 1963, words "Especially Revised by the Author" on the title page, colored pic. wraps, 275 (2) pp., acknowledgments, sixteen illus. including fourteen (eight of which were not used in the Scribner edition), by R. (Zogbaum)

530a Drake, F. S. *Indian History for Young Folks*. Harpers, N.Y., (1919), cloth, 454 pp., "Introduction" by F. J. Dowd, preface, index, maps, numerous illus. including five, facing pp. 140, 486, 498, 500 and (504), by R. (Zogbaum)

531 Duewall, L .A. *The Story of Monument Hill*. La Grange Journal, La Grange, Texas, 1955, pic. wraps, 34 pp., acknowledgments, foreword, bibliography, rosters, seven illus. including one, p. 16, by R.

532 Durant, John and Bettman, Otto. *Pictorial History of American Sports*. A. S. Barnes and Co., (N.Y., 1952), decor. two-tone cloth, pic. endsheets, 280 pp., "Introduction" by John K. Hutchens, picture credits and acknowledgments, numerous illus. including three, pp. 63, 65 and 68, by R.

533 ——— and Durant, Alice. *Pictorial History of American Ships*. Barnes, N.Y., (1953), decor. two-tone cloth, pic. endsheets, 312 pp., yellow top, "Introduction" by Ernest S. Dodge, acknowledgments, credits and references, index, numerous illus. including one, p. 38, by R. (Fogarty)

534 ———, ed. *Yesterday in Sports*. Barnes, N.Y., 1956, two-tone cloth, 136 pp., "Introduction" by Sidney L. James, picture credits, numerous illus. including seven, pp. 36 and 37, by R., plus a photo of 1879 Yale football team of which Remington was a member.

535 Durham, Philip and Jones, Everett L. *The Negro Cowboys*. Dodd, Mead, N.Y., 1965, cloth, 378 pp., preface, notes, bibliography, index, illus. including two, between pp. 86 and 87, by R.

536 ———. *The Adventures of the Negro Cowboys*. Dodd, Mead, N.Y., (1968), cloth, 143 pp., preface, index, map, 21 illus. including two, between pp. 48 and 49, by R.

537 ———. Same, but Bantam Pathfinder Edition, N.Y., April 1969, colored pic. wraps, 120 pp., with the same two illus. between pp. 56 and 57, by R.

538 Dutton, Davis. *A California Portfolio: The Golden State in Words and Pictures*. Automobile Club of Southern California, Los Angeles, 1970, wraps, 70 pp., illus. including two, p. 27, by R.

539 Dykes, Jeff C., Allred, B. W. et al., eds. *Great Western Indian Fights*. Doubleday, Garden City, N.Y.,

1960, words "First Edition" on copyright page, decor. cloth, pic. map endsheets, 336 pp., "The Writers" (Members of the Potomac Corral of The Westerners), numerous illus. including four, two between pp. 120 and 121, and two between pp. 216 and 217, by R. (Dixon, Russell, Schreyvogel)

540 ———. Same, Bison Book 339, reprint in colored pic. wraps, Lincoln, 1966.

541 ———. *Law on a Wild Frontier, Four Sheriffs of Lincoln County*. Potomac Corral, The Westerners, Washington, D.C., 1969, decor. boards, 25 pp., map, eight illus. including one, p. 13, by R. (Russell)

542 ———. Same, but issued in decor. wraps.

543 Editors of *Army Times*. *Great American Cavalrymen*. Dodd, Mead, N.Y., (1964), cloth, 156 pp., illus. including one, between pp. 64 and 65, by R.

544 Eggleston, Edward. *A History of the United States and its People*. Appleton, N.Y., 1888, decor. cloth, map endsheets, 398 pp., all edges tinted, preface, index, numerous illus. including three, pp. 75, 96 and (369), by R.

545 ———. *The Household History of the United States and its People for Young Americans*. Appleton, N.Y., 1889, decor. cloth, map endsheets, 396 pp., preface, index, numerous illus. including three, pp. 75, 95 and (363), by R., colored maps.

546 Eliot, Alexander. *Three Hundred Years of American Painting*. Time, Inc., N.Y., 1957, morocco and cloth, 318 pp., acknowledgments, "Introduction" by John Walker, appendices, bibliography, index, numerous illus. including three, pp. 97, 98 and 100, by R. (Hurd, Leigh, Russell)

547 Ellis, Amanda M. *The Strange, Uncertain Years*. Shoe String Press, Hamden, Conn., cloth, 423 pp., "Preface" by Governor Steve McNichols, introduction, bibliography, 127 illus. including three, pp. (31), (83) and (85), by R. (Russell)

548 Ellis, Edward S. *Up the Forked River*. John C. Winston Co., Phila. etc., (1904), pic. cloth, 304 pp., front cover illus. by R.

549 ———. *Thrilling Adventures among the American Indians*. Winston, Phila. etc., (1905), cloth with illus. in color mounted on front cover, 244 pp., numerous illus. including one, p. 237, by R.

550 ———. *True Stories of the American Indians*. (W. E. Scull, Chicago, 1905), colored pic. cloth, decor. endsheets, 240 pp., numerous illus. (several in color), including two drawings, pp. 9 and 213, by R.

551 ———. *The Round Up.* Winston, Phila. etc., (1908), pic. cloth, 347 pp., (5) of advs., illus. including one, front cover, by R.

552 ———. *Outdoor Life and Indian Stories.* L. T. Myers, (Chicago, 1912), cloth with illus. mounted on front cover, 244 pp., numerous illus. including one, p. 237, by R.

553 ———. *Trailing Geronimo.* Winston, Phila. etc., (1908), pic. cloth, 353 pp., (7) of advs., illus. including one, front cover, by R.

554 ———. *Off the Reservation.* Winston, Phila. etc., (1908), pic. cloth, 331 pp., two illus. including one, front cover, by R.

555 ———. *Limber Lew: The Circus Boy.* Winston, Phila. etc., n.d., pic. cloth, 439 pp., two illus. including one, front cover, by R.

556 ———. *Wyoming.* Winston, Phila. etc., n.d., pic. cloth, 371 pp., front cover illus. by R.

557 ———. *Brave Billy.* Winston, Phila. etc., (1907), pic. cloth, 360 pp., illus. including one, front cover, by R.

558 ———. *Tam, or, Holding the Fort.* Winston, Phila. etc., (1907), pic. cloth, 351 pp., illus. including one, front cover, by R.

559 ———. *The Young Ranchers.* Winston, Phila. etc., n.d., colored pic. cloth, pic. endsheets, 284 pp., frontispiece, front cover illus. by R.

560 Ellis, Richard Williamson. *Book Illustration, A Survey of Its History and Development.* The Kingsport Press, Kingsport, Tenn., 1952, cloth, 76 pp., publisher's note, an introduction, numerous illus. including one, p. 30, by R. plus a biographical sketch of him.

561 Emerson, Edwin, Jr. *A History of the Nineteenth Century Year by Year.* Collier, N.Y., 1901, 3 vols., cloth, 1924 pp. (continuous pagination), preface, "An Introduction" by Georg Gottfried Gervinus, 48 illus., of which 16 are in color, including one, facing p. 1782, by R.

562 ———. Same, but salesman's dummy with a number of plates in color including one, "Rough Riders Charge up San Juan Hill," by R.

563 Ewers, John C. *Artists of the Old West.* Doubleday, Garden City, N.Y., (1965), cloth, 240 pp., acknowledgments, bibliography, numerous illus. including eight, pp. 208, 209, 210, 211, 212, (213) and 215 (two in color), by R. (Russell)

563a ———. Same, enlarged edition 1973, with 194 (44 color) illus. including nine, pp. (198), (199), 200, 201, (202–3), (210) color, (211) two in color and 218, by R.

564 Exman, Eugene. *The House of Harper* (One Hundred and Fifty Years of Publishing). Harper, N.Y. etc., (1967), words "First Edition" on copyright page, cloth, pic. endsheets, 326 pp., foreword, acknowledgments and credits, index, numerous illus. including one, p. (115), by R. and much on him in the text.

565 Faison, S. Lane, Jr. *Art Tours and Detours in New York State.* Random House, (N.Y., 1964), words "First Printing" on copyright page, cloth (or wraps), 303 pp., preface, "Introduction" by Louis C. Jones, index, numerous illus. including seven, pp. 87 (four), 88, 161 and 272, by R.

566 Fehrenbacher, Don E. and Tutorow, Norman E. *California, An Illustrated History.* Van Nostrand, (N.Y. etc., 1968), cloth, maroon endsheets, 184 pp., preface, index, numerous illus. including one, p. 31, by R.

567 Ferris, Robt. G., ed. *Explorers and Settlers.* National Park Service, G.P.O., Washington, 1968, cloth, 506 pp., numerous illus. including two, pp. 24 and 55, by R. (The National Survey of Historic Sites and Buildings, vol. 5.)

568 Field, Eugene. *Field Flowers.* Monument Fund Committee (A. L. Swift & Co., Chicago, 1896), decor. white cloth, pages unnumb., all edges gilt, numerous illus. including two by R. Also an issue in decor. green cloth that may be a trade edition of no. 568.

569 Finerty, John F. *War-Path and Bivouac* (The Big Horn and Yellowstone Expedition). Nebraska, Lincoln, n.d., pic. wraps, 375 pp., "Historical Introduction" and edited by Milo Milton Quaife, appendix, index, illus. including one, front cover, by R.

570 Fitzgerald, James (President). *Proceedings at the 121st Anniversary Dinner of the Society of the Friendly Sons of St. Patrick.* Dempsey & Carroll, N.Y., 1905, decor. cloth, 71 (1) pp., intro., six illus. including one, facing p. 16, by R.

571 Fitzhugh, Percy Keese. *The Boys' Book of Scouts.* Thomas Y. Crowell Co., N.Y., (1917), pic. cloth, 317 pp., preface, sixteen illus. including three, facing pp. 82, 100 and 182, by R.

572 ———. *From Appomatox to Germany.* Harper, N.Y. and London, (1919), words "Published April 1919" on copyright page, pic. cloth, 409 (1) pp., publisher's note, numerous illus. including four, pp. (89), (91), (97) and (318), by R.

573 Flandrau, Grace. *Historic Northwest Adventure Land.*

Great Northern Railway, (St. Paul), n.d., wraps, 32 pp., illus. including one by R.

574 ———. *Historic Adventure Land of the Northwest.* Compliments of the Great Northern Railway, n.p., n.d., wraps, 40 pp., illus. including one, p. 38, by R. (A revised and enlarged edition of no. 573.)

575 Fleming, Chaplain David L. *From Everglade to Canon with the Second Dragoons.* Reprinted from the *Journal*, Military Service Institution, Governor's Island, N.Y., (1911), decor. wraps, 32 pp., numerous illus. including two, pp. (30) and (32), by R., folding map inside back wrap.

576 Flexner, James Thomas. *Nineteenth Century American Painting.* Putnam, N.Y., (1970), words "First Edition" on copyright page, cloth, 256 pp., numerous illus. including one, p. 135, by R. (Miller, Russell)

577 Forbes, Mrs. A. C. (edited by Edgar Lloyd Hampton). *Then and Now, 100 Landmarks within 50 Miles of Los Angeles Civic Center.* Board of Supervisors, Los Angeles County, L.A., 1939, pic. wraps, pages unnumb., numerous illus. including one by R.

578 Forbis, William H. (text by). *The Cowboy.* Time-Life Books, N.Y., (1973), decor. fabricoid with illus. in color mounted on front cover, decor. endsheets, 240 pp., credits, bibliography, index, 250 illus. including five, front cover, frontis., pp. (6–7) in color, (146–47) in color and (152–53) in color, by R. (Koerner, Russell)

579 Fowler, Albert, ed. *Cranberry Lake from Wilderness to Adirondack Park.* Syracuse University Press, Syracuse, N.Y., (1968), words "First Edition" on copyright page, cloth, blue endsheets, 207 pp., preface, index, folding map, numerous illus. including five, pp. 66, 72, 74, 75 and 78, by Remington, two photos of him and a chapter about him. An Adirondack Museum book.

580 Fraser, W. Lewis et al. *The Year's Art.* Harry C. Jones, N.Y., 1894, decor. cloth, 458 pp., index, 1400 illus. including four, pp. 59, 83, 311 and 436, by R. (Crawford, Deming, Fogarty, Keller)

581 Freeman, James W. (President). *Prose and Poetry of the Livestock Industry of the United States.* National Livestock Historical Assn., Denver and Kansas City, (1905), decor. morocco, gray endsheets, 757 pp., numerous illus. including two, pp. 407 and 553, by R.

582 ———. Same, a reprint of no. 581, N.Y., 1959, with a new introduction by Ramon F. Adams, bound in cowhide and buckram, boxed. Edition consists of 550 numbered copies.

583 Friedel, Frank. *The Splendid Little War.* Little, Brown, Boston, and Toronto, (1958), words "First Edition" on copyright page, decor. cloth, 314 pp., acknowledgments, picture credits, "For Further Reading," numerous illus. including seven, pp. 127, 130 (two), 145, 156, 168-9 and 172, by R.

584 French, Dr. L. H. *The Desertion of Sergeant Cobb.* (The Knickerbocker Press, N.Y.), n.d., vellum and boards, marbled endsheets, 18 pp., gilt top and other edges uncut, frontis. dated 1901, by R.

585 Frink, Maurice, ed. *The Denver Brand Book.* The Westerners, Denver, Colo., 1954, decor. cloth, pic. endsheets, 331 pp., acknowledgment, appendices, index, illus. including one drawing, p. 237, by R. (Eggenhofer)

586 ———. *Fort Defiance and the Navajos.* Pruett Press, Boulder, Colo., (1968), cloth, green endsheets, 124 pp., source notes, index, numerous illus. including seven, pp. vii, 9, 18, 32, 50, 84 and 114, by R.

587 ———. Same, but issued in colored pic. wraps.

588 Fronval, George. *La Fantastique Epopee du Far West.* Dargaud, Nevilly/s/Seine, France, (1969), two volumes, colored pic. boards, pp. 126, (2) and 127, (1), numerous illus. including seventeen, seven (I) and ten (II), by R. (Koerner, Miller, Russell, Schreyvogel, Zogbaum)

588a ———. *La Veritable Histoire Des Indians Peaux-Rouges.* Fernand Nathan, Paris, France, (1973), cloth, pic. front endsheet, map back endsheets, 125 pp., numerous illus. including eight, pp. 22, 49 (color), 54 (color), 84 (color), 87 (color), (95), 103 (color) and 124, by R. (Koerner, Leigh, Miller, Schreyvogel, Von Schmidt, Zogbaum)

589 Frost, Dr. Lawrence A. *The Custer Album.* Superior Pub. Co., Seattle, (1964), words "First Edition" on copyright page, cloth, pic. endsheets, 192 pp., author's preface, acknowledgments, bibliography, index, numerous illus. including four, pp. 78, 86, (105) and (117), by R. (Leigh, Schreyvogel)

590 Fry, James B. *Army Sacrifices* but with cover title *Indian Fights, Illustrated, 1887.* D. Van Nostrand, N.Y., 1879, cloth, 254 pp., preface, twelve illus. inclding four, facing pp. 17, 135, 162 and 181, by R. (Evidently unbound sheets from the first printing of 1879 with illus. and a new cover title added and dated.)

591 Furlong, Rev. Philip J. *Pioneers and Patroits of America.* William H. Sadlier, N.Y., (1926), pic. cloth,

425 (8) pp., acknowledgments, "Foreword" by Rt. Rev. Msgr. Joseph F. Smith, author's note, index, illus. including one, p. 40, by R.

592 Gable, Thomas P. *First Report of Game and Fish Warden for New Mexico, 1909–1910–1911.* New Mexican Printing Co., Santa Fe, 1912, 88 pp., introduction, index, numerous illus. including one, by R.

593 Gabriel, Ralph Henry. *The Lure of the Frontier.* Yale, New Haven, 1929, morocco and boards, decor. endsheets, 327 pp., numerous illus. including twenty-seven by R. The Liberty Bell Edition of "The Pageant of America," vol. 2, 1500 copies. (Deming, Dixon, Marchand, Russell)

594 ———. *Toilers of Land and Sea.* Yale, New Haven, 1929, morocco and boards, decor. endsheets, 340 pp., numerous illus. including three, pp. 176, 180 and 184, by R. The Liberty Bell Edition of "The Pageant of America," vol. 3, 1500 copies. (Dixon, Russell)

595 Gambrell, Herbert and Virginia. *A Pictorial History of Texas.* Dutton, N.Y., (1960), words "First Edition" on copyright page, cloth and decor. boards, brand illus. endsheets, 217 pp., acknowledgments, sources of illus., index, numerous illus. including three, pp. 129, 190 and 191, by R. (James, Lea, Schiwetz)

596 Gard, Wayne. *The Great Buffalo Hunt.* Knopf, N.Y., 1959, words "First Edition" on copyright page, pic. cloth, 324, xii (2) pp., red top, foreword, bibliography, index, seventeen illus. including one, facing p. 114, by R. (Eggenhofer)

597 ———. Same, first Bison Book printing, Oct. 1968, University of Nebraska Press, Lincoln, colored pic. wraps. (Eggenhofer)

598 Gardner, Pliny. *Random Notes on Early American History and Hannah Dustin.* (Hungerford-Holbrook Co., Watertown, N.Y.), 1946, cloth and boards, pic. endsheets, 164 pp., foreword, illus. including two, endsheets and d/w., by R.

599 Garland, Hamlin. *The Book of the American Indian.* Harper, N.Y. and London, 1923, words "First Edition" on copyright page, cloth and boards with illus. mounted on front cover, 274 pp., thirty-seven illus., four in color, by R.

600 Garraty, John A. *Theodore Roosevelt, The Strenuous Life.* American Heritage Pub. Co., N.Y., 1967, words "First Edition" on title page, pic. cloth, pic. endsheets, "Foreword" by the editors, further reference, index, numerous illus. including one double-page plate in color, pp. 52-53, by R.

601 ———. *The American Nation* (A History of the United States). Harper & Row, N.Y. and London, (1966), cloth, map endsheets, 920 pp., preface, appendix, index, maps and charts, numerous illus. including one, pp. 564–65, by R. (Miller, Russell)

601a ———. *The American Nation Since 1865.* Harper & Row, N.Y. etc., (1966), cloth, colored map endsheets, 498 pp., preface, appendix, index, maps and charts, numerous illus. including one by R. (Miller, Russell)

602 Gavin, Ruth Wood and Hamm, William A. *The American Story.* Heath, Boston, 1947, decor. cloth, foreword, appendix, index, numerous illus. including one, p. 245, by R. (Deming)

602a Getlein, Frank et al. *The Lure of the Great West.* Country Beautiful, Waukesha, Wisconsin, (1973), boards, 352 pp., introduction, 375 illus. including forty-eight (twelve in color) by R. (Blumenschein, Koerner, Leigh, Miller, Russell, Schreyvogel, Wyeth)

603 Gibson, Joe A. *Forts and Treasure Trails of West Texas.* Educator Books, San Angelo, Texas, 1969, words "First Edition" on copyright page, pic. wraps, 119 pp., preface, location maps, numerous illus. including one, title page, (enlarged and repeated on front cover), by R.

604 Glubok, Shirley. *The Art of the Old West.* Macmillan, N.Y., London, (1971), cloth and colored pic. boards, pic. endsheets, 48 pp., numerous illus. including seven, endsheets, pp. 26, 27 (two), 28, (29) and 34, by R. (Miller, Russell)

605 Godfrey, General Edward S. *General George A. Custer and the Battle of Little Big Horn.* Century Co., N.Y., n.d. (1908), wraps, 38 pp., illus. including five, pp. 6, 11, (24), 31 and 35, by R. First separate edition.

606 ———. Same, a 1921 reprint of no. 605 with a Preface by Elizabeth B. Custer and with a printed slip signed by her on the title page.

607 *The Field Diary of Lt. Edward Settle Godfrey.* Champoeg Press, (Portland, Ore.), pic. cloth, 74 pp., "Introduction" (and edited with notes) by Edgar I. and Jane R. Stewart, "Kicking Bear Pictographs" by Carl S. Dentzel, notes, eight illus. including five, front cover and facing pp. 10, 30, 42 and 56, by R., two folding maps.

608 Godfrey, Edward S. and McAuliffe, Eugene. *Custer's Last Battle.* Omaha, 1955, wraps, 39 pp., six illus., pp. 7, 18, 21, 25, 27 and 33, by R.

609 Godfrey, Captain Edward S. *An Account of Custer's*

Last Campaign and the Battle of the Little Big Horn. Lewis Osborne, Ashland, Oregon, 1968, cloth, 88 pp., six illus., pp. 22-3, 43, 47, 56-7, 73 and 83, by R.

610 Goff, Richard and McCaffree, Robert H. *Century in the Saddle 1867–1967* (The 100 Year Story of the Colorado Cattlemen's Association). (Colorado Cattlemen's Centennial Commission, Denver, Colo., but printed by Johnson Publishing Co., Boulder, 1967), brand decor. cloth, 365 pp., "Foreword" by President W. P. "Wad" Hinman, preface, appendices, bibliography, index, numerous illus. including three, pp. 12, 38 and 48, by R.

611 ——— et al. *Centennial Brand Book.* (Colorado Cattlemen's Centennial Commission, Denver, Colo., but printed by Johnson Publishing Co., Boulder, 1967), decor. cloth, 196 pp., foreword, index, memorials, profusely illus. with photos and brands and with two drawings, pp. 122 and 137, by R. The first (1886) Brand Book is reproduced in facsimile.

612 Good, Donnie D. *The Buffalo Soldier.* Thomas Gilcrease Institute, Tulsa, 1970, colored pic. wraps, unpaged, bibliography, numerous illus. including two drawings by R.

613 Goodman, David M. *Arizona Odyssey: Bibliographic Adventures in Nineteenth Century Magazines.* Arizona Historical Foundation, Tempe, 1969, words "First Edition" on copyright page, pic. cloth, orange endsheets, 360 pp., "Foreword" by Senator Barry M. Goldwater, preface, illus. including one, p. 214, by R. (Zogbaum)

614 Gordon, Charles W. *The Patrol of the Sundance Trail,* by Ralph Connor (pseud.). Hodder and Stoughton, London etc., (1914), words "Printed in 1914" on copyright page, pic. cloth, 304 pp., (6) of advs., front cover design by R.

615 Green, Samuel M. *American Art* (A Historical Survey). Ronald Press, N.Y., (1966), cloth, 706 pp., index, numerous illus. including one, p. 378, by R.

616 Gregg, Andy. *Drums of Yesterday: The Forts of New Mexico.* Press of the Territorian, Santa Fe, (1968), wraps, 40 pp., directions, illus. including one, the frontis., by R.

617 Gregg, Andrew K. *New Mexico in the 19th Century, A Pictorial History.* University of New Mexico Press, Albuquerque, (1968), words "First Edition" on copyright page, cloth, 196 pp., preface, sources, index, numerous illus. including six, pp. 3, 142, 148, 149, 154 and 185, by R. (Dixon)

618 Griffin, Solomon Bulkley. *Mexico of Today.* Harper, N.Y., 1886, silver and black decor. brown cloth, brown endsheets, 267 pp., (4) of advs., preface, index, 24 maps and illus. including two drawings, pp. 11 and 101, by R.

619 *Grolier Encyclopedia.* Grolier Society, N.Y. etc., (1952), ten volumes — volume 9 includes "Hunting Geronimo," p. 24, by Remington plus a brief biography of him.

620 *Grundiss der Geschichte der Vereinigten Staaten von Amerika.* Bad Godesberg, (Germany), 1954, pic. boards, 159 pp., illustrated (some in color) including one full-page in color by R.

621 Guillet, Edwin and Mary. *The Path Finders of North America.* Macmillan, Toronto, 1939, pic. silver cloth, map endsheets, 304 pp., preface, index, 73 illus. including two, pp. 45 and 89, by R. (Marchand)

622 Gunnison, Almon. *Wayside and Fireside Rambles.* Universalist Pub. House, Boston, 1894, cloth, 241 pp., preface, illus. including nine, pp. 11, 57, 87, 102, 123, 186, 207, 222 and 232, by R. Remington's first name misspelled with an added "K" on the title page.

623 Guthrie, A. B., Jr. *The Big Sky.* Eyre and Spottiswoode, (London, 1965), cloth, map endsheets, 415 (1) pp., blue top, illus. with six drawings, title page and pp. (9), (75), (183), (277) and 369, by R., and with a photo of the bronze, "The Mountain Man," on back of d/w., by R.

624 Hafen, LeRoy R., ed. *Colorado and Its People.* Lewis Historical Pub. Co., N.Y., 1948, 4 vols., cloth, map endsheets, pp. 644, 784, 804 and 810, foreword, index, numerous illus. including two in vol. 1, pp. 10 and 19, by R.

625 ——— and Ann. *The Colorado Story.* Old West Publishing Co., Denver, (1953), pic. cloth and endsheets, 536 (1) pp., "To the Reader," acknowledgments, appendix, index, numerous illus. including three, pp. 82, 140 and 211, by R. (Lea)

626 ———, eds. *Fremont's Fourth Expedition.* Arthur H. Clark Co., Glendale, Calif., 1960, cloth, 319 pp., brown top, introduction and summary, appendices, index, illus. including four drawings, pp. (179) two, and (180) two, by R., maps.

627 Hall, Bert L. *Roundup Years.* Privately Printed, Kennebec, S. D., 1956, pic. boards, map endsheets, 605 (11) pp., index, numerous illus. including one, p. 598, by R. Second edition but the first issue with the Remington and Russell illustrations. (Russell)

628 Hamm, William A. *From Colony to World Power.* D. C. Heath & Co., Boston, (1947), decor. cloth, 854 pp., preface, appendix, index, numerous illus. including one, p. (375), by R., maps.

629 Hans, Fred M. *The Great Sioux Nation.* Donohue, Chicago, (1907), cloth with illus. mounted on front cover, 575 pp., preface, numerous illus. including six composites, pp. 61, 89, 508, 525, 542 and 562, from illus., by R.

630 ———. Same, reprinted by Ross and Haines, Minneapolis, (1964), cloth, 586 pp., The reissue was 2000 copies.

631 Harding, Frank (compiled by). *A Livestock Heritage: Animals and People in Art.* (Shorthorn World Publication Co., Geneva, Ill., 1971), colored pic. wraps, unpaged, numerous illus. including two in color by R. (Borein, Dunn, Eggenhofer, Koerner, Marchand, Russell, Wyeth)

632 Harger, Charles Moreau. *Cattle Trails of the Prairies.* Highlands Historical Press, (Dallas, Texas, 1961), pic. wraps, (12) pp., six illus. including one, p. (12), by R. The issue was 1000 copies. This is the first separate printing of an article from *Scribner's Magazine,* 1892.

633 *Harpers Encyclopedia of United States History.* N.Y., 1901, ten volumes, cloth, no pagination, volumes III, IV, VII and IX each has one illus. by R. and volume V has two. (Keller, Zogbaum)

634 Harrower, James et al. *30 Years a Historical Society, 1935–1965* (cover title: "Museum of the Mountain Men"). Sublette County Historical Society, Pinedale, Wyo., pic. wraps, unpaged, map, illus. including one, front cover, by R.

635 Hart, R. A. (President). *Artistic Illustration.* New York Engraving & Printing Co., N.Y., n.d., wraps, nineteen "Specimens of Magazine and Book Illustrations Engraved on Copper by our Enamel Half-Tone Process" including one by R.

636 Harte, Bret. *Agents Prospectus for the Complete Writings of Bret Harte.* Houghton Mifflin, Boston, n.d. (1896?), leather, seventeen plates including four by R.

637 ———. *The Luck of Roaring Camp.* Houghton Mifflin, Boston and N.Y., (1896), cloth with paper label on spine, 444 pp., publisher's note, general introduction, seven illus. including one, facing p. 6, by R. Autographed edition, vol. I, limited to 350 sets. (Some sets of this edition were bound in morocco and boards.)

638 ———. Same, Houghton Mifflin, Boston and N.Y., n.d., decor. cloth, 256 pp., black top, preface, frontis. by R. The Riverside Library edition.

639 ———. *Tales of the Argonauts.* Houghton Mifflin, Boston and N.Y., (1896), cloth with paper label on spine, 440 pp., introduction, eight illus. including one, facing p. 4, by R. Autographed edition, vol. II, limited to 350 sets. (Smith)

640 ———. Same, special edition made for *Review of Reviews.* Houghton Mifflin, Cambridge, Mass., n.d., cloth, 283 pp., frontis. by R.

641 ———. *Maruja and Other Tales.* Houghton Mifflin, Boston and N.Y., (1896), cloth with paper label on spine, 482 pp., six illus. including one, frontis., by R. Autographed edition, vol. V, limited to 350 sets.

642 ———. *Poems and Two Men of Sandy Bar.* Houghton Mifflin, Boston and N.Y., (1896), cloth with paper label on spine, 443 pp., publisher's note, seven illus. including one, facing pp. 132, by R. Autographed edition, vol. XII, limited to 350 sets.

643 Hartman, Gertrude. *America, Land of Freedom.* D. C. Heath & Co., Boston, (1946), pic. cloth, 644 pp., "Foreword" by Allan Nevins, acknowledgments, appendix, index, map endsheets, numerous illus. including one, p. 343, by R.

644 Hassrick, Peter H. *Frederic Remington.* (Amon Carter Museum, Fort Worth, 1972), pic. wraps, unpaged, suggested readings, fifteen illus. by R.

645 ———. *Frederic Remington.* Abrams, N.Y., 1973, cloth, 192 pp., 94 illus. including 60 in color by R. (From the Amon Carter and Sid Richardson Collections.)

646 Hatcher, J. F. and Montgomery, T. T. *Elementary History of Oklahoma.* Warden Co., Oklahoma City, 1924, cloth, 314 pp., preface, introduction, appendix, index, illus. including one drawing, p. 2, by R., maps.

647 Haven, Charles T. and Belden, Frank A. *A History of the Colt Revolver.* Wm. Morrow & Co., N.Y., 1940, fabricoid, green endsheets, 711 pp., "Foreword" by Stephen V. Grancsay, "Introduction" by Stephen W. Dimick, preface, glossary, index, numerous illus. including one, p, 432, by R.

648 ———. Same, a reprint by Bonanza Books, N.Y.

649 Havighurst, Walter, ed. *Land of the Long Horizons.* Coward-McCann, N.Y., (1960), decor. cloth, red endsheets, 437 pp., introduction, index, numerous illus. including one, p. (51), by R., maps. (Deming, Koerner)

650 Hawgood, John A. *America's Western Frontiers.* Knopf, N.Y., 1967, words "First American Edition" on copyright page, two-tone cloth, black endsheets, 440, X (2) pp., yellow top, preface, bibliographic note, index, maps, 98 illus. including six, pp. 107, 315, 319, 321, 327 and 333, by R. (Miller, Russell)

651 ———. Same, "First published in Great Britain 1967" by Eyre and Spottiswoode, London, under the title *The American West.*

652 Hawthorne, Julian. *The History of the United States from 1492 to 1910.* Collier, N.Y., (1910), 3 vols., cloth, 1215 pp., (continuous pagination), index, illus. including two, frontis. in color in vol. 1 and 2, by R.

653 Haydon, Harold (text by). *Great Art Treasures in America's Smaller Musuems.* Putnam's in association with Country Beautiful Foundation, Waukesha, Wisconsin, (1967), words "First Edition" on copyright page, cloth, grey endsheets, 194 pp., introduction, index, numerous illus. including three, pp. 118, 122, and 159, by R. (Hurd, Miller, Russell)

654 ———. Same, but with title changed to *Great Art Treasures in American Museums* as published by Country Beautiful Corporation, Waukesha, Wisconsin.

655 Hayes, Bartlett H., Jr. *American Drawings* (a volume in the series "Drawings of the Masters"). Shorewood Publishers, N.Y., (1965), cloth or colored pic. wraps, 141 pp., biographies, bibliography, 110 (102 in color) illus. including one, p. 61, by R.

656 Heiderstadt, Dorothy. *Painters of America.* McKay, N.Y., (1970), cloth, red endsheets, 180 pp., introduction, bibliography, index, numerous illus. including one, p. (120), by R. and with a chapter "Frederic Remington, Painter of Cowboys." (Miller, Russell, Schreyvogel)

657 Heilbron, Bertha L. *The Thirty-Second State: A Pictroial History of Minnesota.* The Minn. Historical Society, St. Paul, 1958, cloth, green endsheets, 306 pp., preface, picture sources, index, numerous illus. including two, pp. 5 and 9, by R.

658 Heiman, Robert K. (designed and written by). *Nation's Heritage, No. 5.* B. C. Forbes & Sons Pub. Co., N.Y., 1949, pic. linen, bronze endsheets, 284 (3) pp., acknowledgments, numerous illus. including twenty-six by R.

659 ———. *Nation's Heritage, No. 6.* B. C. Forbes & Sons Pub. Co., N.Y., 1949, pic. linen, pages unnumbered, acknowledgments, numerous illus. including one by R. (Hurd)

660 Hermann, Richard. *Julien Dubuque, His Life and Adventures.* (Times-Journal Co., Dubuque, Iowa, 1922), wraps, 91 pp., addendum, illus. including one, facing p. 35, by R.

661 Herr, Major Gen. John K. and Wallace, Edward S. *The Story of the U. S. Cavalry, 1775–1942.* Little, Brown, Boston, (1953), words "First Edition" on copyright page, cloth, tinted endsheets, 275 pp., author's note and acknowledgments, "Foreword" by General Jonathan M. Wainwright, bibliography, numerous illus. including eleven, pp. (180), 184, 195, (197), 205 and (215, six), by R. (Schreyvogel)

662 Hester, George C. et al. *Texas, The Story of the Lone Star State.* Holt, (N.Y., 1948), decor. cloth, 472 pp., preface, appendices, proper names, index, acknowledgments, references, maps, numerous illus. including one, p. 185, by R. (Schreyvogel)

663 Hill, Dean. *Football thru the Years.* Gridiron Pub. Co., N.Y., 1940, fabricoid, pic. endsheets, 114 pp., foreword, numerous illus. including seventeen by R.

664 Hillman, Martin. *Bridging a Continent* (Encyclopedia of Discovery and Exploration, volume 8). Aldus Books, London, (1971), cloth and colored pic. boards, 191 pp., glossary, index, picture credits, numerous illus. including two in color, pp. 70-1 and 94-5, by R. (Miller)

665 Hillyer, V. M. and Huey, E. G. *A Child's History of Art.* Appleton-Century, N.Y. and London, 1933, words "First Printing" on copyright page, cloth, 443 pp., numerous illus. including one, p. 152, by R. There is much on Remington in the chapter "Real-Men Artists."

665a Hine, Robert V. *The American West: An Interpretive History.* Little, Brown, Boston, (1973), words "First Printing" on copyright page, cloth, orange endsheets, 371 pp., preface, notes, bibliography, index, numerous illus. including seven, pp. 3, 22, 57, 102, 205, 207 and 295, by R. (Koerner, Miller, Russell)

666 *Historical Sketch Troop A First Cavalry, Wisconsin National Guard* (Light Horse Squadron) *Commemorating its 20th Anniversary.* Milwaukee, Wis., 1899, oblong folio with a frontis. by R.

667 Hitchcock, Ripley, ed. *Decisive Battles of America.* Harper, N.Y. and London, 1909, words "Published October, 1909" on copyright page, cloth, 396 (1) pp., introduction, index, sixteen illus. including one, facing p. 70, by R.

668 Hollmann, Clide. *Five Artists of the Old West.* Hast-

ings House, N.Y., (1965), cloth, 128 pp., introduction, bibliography, index, 28 illus. including five, pp. (80), 81, (85), (91) and (92), by R. Much on Remington in the text. (Russell)

668a Holloway, David. *Lewis and Clark and the Crossing of North America.* Weidenfeld and Nicolson, London, (1974), cloth, pic. endsheets, 224 pp., "Introduction" by V. E. Fuchs, author's note, selected bibliography, index, maps, numerous illus. including two, pp. 160 and 165, by R. (Leigh, Miller, Russell)

668b ———. Same, Saturday Review Press, N.Y. (but printed in England, 1974), first American edition of 668a.

669 Holme, Bryan, ed. *Horses.* Studio Publications, N.Y. and London, (1951), boards, 98 pp., foreword, Introduction" by Alleine E. Dodge, numerous illus. including one, p. 92, by R.

670 ——— (compiled and edited by). *Pictures to Live With.* The Viking Press, N.Y., (1959), words "First published in 1959" on copyright page, pic. cloth, 152 pp., index, numerous illus. including four, title page, pp. 71 and 72 (two), by R. (Johnson, Leigh, Miller)

671 Holmes, Kenneth L. *Ewing Young, Master Trapper.* Binfords & Mort, Portland, Oregon, (1967), words "First Edition" on copyright page, cloth, map endsheets, 180 pp., preface, bibliography and notes, index, illustrated including seven, d/w in color, three between pp. 38 and 39, and three between pp. 102 and 103, by R. (Russell)

672 Holmes, Louis A. *Fort McPherson, Nebraska.* Johnsen Pub. Co., Lincoln, (1963), pic. cloth, 108 pp., preface, acknowledgments, appendix, bibliography, index, illus. including two, front cover and facing p. 97, by R. Designed and printed by Lawton Kennedy, S. F.

673 Holmes, Oliver W. *The Arkansas, Lifeline of Empire.* Potomas Corral, The Westerners, Washington, D.C., November 1969, pic. boards, 28 pp., the author, map, illus. including five, pp. 4, 5, 8, 9 and 17, by R. Limited edition of 250 numbered copies signed by the author.

674 ———. Same, first trade edition in pic. wraps.

675 Honig, Donald. *In the Days of the Cowboy.* Random House, N.Y., (1970), pic. cloth, pic. endsheets, 74 (4) pp., index, numerous illus. including five, front cover in color, facing half-title, pp. 4, (9) and 56, by R. (Russell)

676 Horan, James D. and Sann, Paul. *Pictorial History of the Wild West.* Crown Publishers, N.Y., (1954), cloth

and boards, 254 pp., acknowledgments, introduction, picture credits, bibliography, index, numerous illus. including eleven by R.

677 ———. Same. first British Edition of no. 676 issued by Spring Books, London, (1954).

678 ———. *The Great American West.* Crown, N.Y., (1959), cloth and boards, 288 pp., introduction, bibliography, index, picture credits, 650 illus. including eight, title page and pp. 97, 178, (185), (186), (187, two) and 188, by R. (Leigh, Marchand, Russell, Schreyvogel)

678a Hordern, Nicholas et al. *The Conquest of North America.* Aldus, London, (1971), pic. boards, 488 pp., index, illus. including three in color, pp. 293, 390–1 and 414–5, by R. (Deming, Miller)

678b ———. Same, first American edition by Doubleday, Garden City, N.Y., 1973.

679 Hornung, Clarence P. *Wheels across America.* A. S. Barnes & Co., N.Y., (1959), decor. cloth, pic. endsheets, 341 pp., foreword, over 1100 illus. including three, pp. 39, 60 and (64), by R. (Lungren)

679a Horrall, S. W. *The Pictorial History of the Royal Canadian Mounted Police.* McGraw-Hill, Ryerson, Toronto etc., (1973), decor. cloth, red endsheets, 256 pp., "Foreword" by Commissioner W. L. Higgitt, index, numerous illus. including double title page and repeated on p. 159 by R. (Russell)

680 Hough, Emerson. *The Way to the West.* Bobbs-Merrill, Indianapolis, (1903), word "October" on copyright page, decor. cloth, 446 pp., five full-page illus., frontis. and facing pp. 66, 150, 290 and 384, by R.

681 Howard, Helen Addison and McGrath, Dan L. *War Chief Joseph.* University of Neb. Press, Lincoln, (1964), pic. wraps, 368 pp., acknowledgments, "Foreword" by Clifford M. Drury, appendices, notes, bibliography, index, maps, illus. including one, front wrap, by R.

682 Howard, Major Gen. O. O. *My Life and Experiences among our Hostile Indians.* A. D. Worthington & Co., Hartford, Conn., (1907), cloth, decor. endsheets, 570 pp., introduction, preface, numerous illus. including twelve on nine plates, facing pp. 106, 132, 240, 280, 328 (two), 384 (two), 460, 534 (two) and 564, by R.

683 ———. Same, reprint by Da Capo Press, N.Y., 1972, with a new introduction by Robert M. Utley.

684 ———. *Famous Indian Chiefs I Have Known.* Cen-

tury Co., N.Y., 1908, words "Published September, 1908" on copyright page, pic. cloth, 364 pp., numerous illus. including one, p. 345, by R.

685 Howard, Robert W., ed. *This is the West.* Rand McNally, N.Y. etc., (1957), words "First Printing, August, 1957" on copyright page, cloth, 248 pp., acknowledgments, appendix, map, over fifty illus. including twelve by R. The text appeared prior to this issue in wraps, the note on the copyright page should read "First Illustrated Printing, August, 1957." (Russell)

686 Howard, Robert West. *The Horse in America.* Follett, Chicago, N.Y., (1965), words "First Printing" on copyright page, cloth and boards, 298 (1) pp., chronology, glossary, notes, acknowledgments, index, numerous illus. including one, between pp. 52 and 53, by R.

687 Hughes, W. J. *Rebellious Ranger: Rip Ford and the Old Southwest.* Univ. of Oklahoma Press, Norman, (1964), words "First Edition" on copyright page, decor. cloth, 300 pp., yellow top, "By Way of Explanation," bibliography, index, twelve illus. including two, facing pp. 52 and 149, by R.

688 Hulbert, Archer Butler, ed. *Southwest on the Turquoise Trail.* The Stewart Commission of Colorado College and the Denver Public Library (Smith-Brooks Press, Denver, 1933), words "First Printing May 1933" on copyright page, cloth, 301 pp., note, index, three illus. including one, the frontis., by R.

689 Humble Oil & Refining Co. *Western Sketchbook.* Houston, 1967, wraps, 40 pp., illus. including one, p. 17, by R.

690 Humfreville, J. Lee. *Twenty Years Among Our Savage Indians.* The Hartford Pub. Co., Hartford, Conn., 1897, cloth, 674 pp., author's preface, nearly 250 illus. including forty-six by R.

691 Humphries, Rolph and John (selected and edited by). *Wolfville Yarns of Alfred Henry Lewis.* The Kent State University Press, (Kent, Ohio, 1968), pic. wraps, 501 pp., introduction, fifteen illus. by R.

692 Hunt, Frazier and Robert. *I Fought with Custer.* Scribner's, N.Y., 1947, code letter "A" on copyright page, cloth, 236 pp., preface, acknowledgments, bibliography, index, 29 illus. including two, facing pp. 92 and 93, by R. (Thomason)

693 Huntington, Francis C. et al. (Programme Committee). *Programme of the Tenth Annual Mounted Games of Squadron "A."* Knickerbocker Press, N.Y.,

March 9, 1900, colored pic. wraps, 42 pp., numerous illus. including one, p. (20), by R.

694 Hutchins, James S. *Horse Equipments and Cavalry Accoutrements,* Ordnance Memorandum 29. Socio-Technical Publications, Pasadena, 1970, wraps with cover illus. by R., 59 pp.

695 Inman, Col Henry. *The Old Santa Fe Trail.* Macmillan, N.Y., 1897, pic. cloth, 493 pp., gilt top, "Preface" by W. F. (Buffalo Bill) Cody, illus. including eight full-page plates, facing pp. 5, 57, 109, 209, 263, 367, 413 and 485, plus small drawings on title page, by R.

696 ———. Same, Macmillan, N.Y., 1898, cloth, prospectus for the January 1898 edition with sample pages and illus. including two full-page plates and several drawings, by R.

697 Irving, Washington. *Astoria.* Century Co., N.Y., 1910, cloth, 488 pp., gilt top, introduction, appendix, four illus. including three, facing pp. 32, 230 and 360, by R.

698 Isely, Bliss. *Early Days in Kansas.* The Wichita Eagle Press, Wichita, Kansas, 1927, pic. wraps, 152 pp., illus. including six, pp. 12, 15, 20, 38, 105 and 124, by R.

699 ——— and Richards, W. M. *Four Centuries in Kansas.* State of Kansas, W. C. Austin, State Printer, Topeka, 1937, decor. cloth, pic. endsheets, 344 pp., "An Eye-Witness Report," bibliography, index, nearly 100 illus. including three, pp. 64, 102 and 192, by R.

700 ———. *The Story of Kansas.* State of Kansas (Ferd Voiland, Jr., State Printer, Topeka, 1953), decor. cloth, 216 pp., "Handy Reference," index, numerous illus. including three, pp. 24, 25 and 28, by R.

701 Ivins, Wm. M. (Acting Director). *Life in America.* Metropolitan Museum of Arts, N.Y., 1939, wraps, 230 pp., "Introduction" by Harry B. Wehle, index, numerous illus. including one, p. 177, by R. (Schreyvogel)

702 Jackson, Donald D., ed. *The Journals of Zebulon Montgomery Pike, with Letters and Related Documents.* Oklahoma, Norman, (1966), 2 vols., cloth, 397 and 409 pp., bibliography (2), maps, illus. including one (1) by R.

703 Jacobs, Wilbur R., ed. *Letters of Francis Parkman.* Oklahoma, Norman, (1960), words "First Edition" on copyright page, two vols., cloth, 204 and 286 pp., preface, introduction, indices, illus. including two, facing pp. 46 and 47, vol. 1, by R. and facsimile of

p. two of a letter by him to Parkman, facing p. 265, vol. 2.

704 Janvier, Thomas A. *The Aztec Treasure House.* Harper, N.Y., 1890, decor. cloth, 446 pp., gilt top, nineteen illus. by R.

705 ———. Same, first British edition of no. 704, issued by Sampson, Low, Marston, Searle & Rivington, London, 1890.

706 ———. Same, but a "New and Cheaper Edition," London, n.d. (1897), R. illus. on the spine and front cover.

707 Jenks, Tudor. *The Century World's Fair Book for Boys and Girls.* Century Co., N.Y., (1893), pic. boards, map on front endsheet, 246 pp., numerous illus. including one, facing p. 151, by R.

708 Jensen, Lee. *The Pony Express.* Grosset & Dunlap, N.Y., (1955), boards, 154 pp., brown top, acknowledgments, picture credits, numerous illus. including three, pp. 7, 63 and 98, by R. (Eggenhofer, Lungren)

709 Jernigan, Rev. C. B. *From the Prairie Schooner to a City Flat.* Privately printed, (Brooklyn, 1926), cloth with illus. mounted on front cover, 140 pp., "Introduction" by Chas. A. McConnell, illus. including one, facing p. 71, by R.

710 Johnson, Lieutenant Colonel Jesse J., AUS (Ret.). *A Pictorial History of Black Soldiers in the United States in Peace and War (1619–1969).* Hampton Institute, Hampton, Virginia, (1970), cloth, 125 (3) pp., about the author, bibliography, numerous illus. including one, p. 34, by R.

711 Johnson, Virginia W. *The Unregimented General.* Houghton Mifflin, Boston, 1962, words "First Printing" on copyright page, cloth, 401 pp., acknowledgments, preface by Major Gen. Sherman Miles, notes, bibliography, index, map, illus. including four, between pp. 178 and 179, by R.

712 Johnston, Harry V. *My Home on the Range.* Webb Pub. Co., St. Paul, (1942), pic. cloth, 313 pp., tinted top, author's note, numerous illus. including one, p. 309, by R. (James, Koerner)

713 Jones, Billy M. *Health-Seekers in the Southwest, 1817–1900.* Oklahoma, Norman, (1967), words "First edition" on copyright page, cloth, 254 pp., preface, bibliography, index, map, 18 illustrations including one, between pp. 82 and 83, by R.

714 Jones, Evan, in consultation with Dale L. Morgan. *Trappers and Mountain Men.* American Heritage Pub. Co., N.Y., (1961), words "First Edition" on copyright page, pic. cloth and endsheets, 153 pp., "Foreword" by Dale L. Morgan, picture credits, bibliography, index, numerous illus. including four in color, pp. (18–19), 59, (79) and (119), by R. (Russell)

715 Jones, Horace. *Up From the Sod* (The Life Story of a Kansas Prairie County). Coronado Publishers, Lyons, Kansas, (1968), pic. cloth, map endsheets, 207 pp., foreword, selected bibliography, map, illus. including one, p. 82, by R. (Wyeth)

716 Jones, Paul A. *Quivira.* McCormick-Armstrong Co., Wichita, Kansas, (1929), words "First Edition" on title page, 182 pp., foreword, numerous illus. including three, pp. (74), (112) and (154), by R.

717 ———. *Coronado and Quivira.* (Lyons Pub. Co., Lyons, Kansas, 1937), cloth, 242 pp., illus. including two, pp. (50) and (109), by R.

718 Josephy, Alvin M., Jr., ed. *The American Heritage Book of Indians.* American Heritage Pub. Co., (N.Y., 1961), cloth, 424 pp., "Introduction" by John F. Kennedy, acknowledgments, index, maps, numerous illus. including one, p. 366, by R. (Russell)

719 Judd, Mary Catherine. *The Story of Fremont and Kit Carson.* Published jointly by F. A. Owen Pub. Co., Dansville, N.Y., and Hall & McCreary, Chicago, 1906, decor. wraps, 32 pp., four illus. including one, p. 11, by R.

720 *Jul i Vesterheimen 1919.* Augsburg Publishing House, Minneapolis, 1919, colored pic. wraps, unpaged, numerous illus. including one in color, "The Stampede," by R. Text part English and part Norse — a Christmas Annual.

721 Karolevitz, Robert F. *Doctors of the Old West.* Superior, Seattle, 1967, words "First Edition" on copyright page, cloth, 192 pp., bibliography, numerous illus. including one, p. 14, by R.

722. Katz, William Loren. *The Black West* (A Documentary and Pictorial History). Doubleday, Garden City, N.Y., (1971), words "First Edition" on copyright page, cloth, 336 pp., introduction, appendices, bibliography, index, numerous illus. including sixteen by R.

723 Keir, Malcolm. *The March of Commerce.* Yale, New Haven, 1927, leather and boards, 361 pp., numerous illus. including one, p. 223, by R. The Liberty Bell Edition of "The Pageant of America," 1500 numbered impressions.

724 Kelsey, D. M. *History of Our Wild West and Stories of Pioneer Life.* Thompson & Thomas, Chicago, 1902,

cloth, 542 pp., numerous illus. including two, p. 509 and facing p. 523, by R.

725 Kelty, Mary G. *The Story of the American People.* Ginn, Boston etc., (1931), pic. cloth, 663 pp., introduction for teachers, appendix, index, numerous illus. including one, p. 597, by R.

726 ———. *Life in Modern America.* Ginn, Boston etc., (1941), pic. cloth, 527, xvi (1) pp., index, numerous illus. including one, p. (289), by R. (Fischer, Lea, Hurd, Russell)

727 ———. *The Story of Life in America.* Ginn, Boston etc., (1946), pic. cloth, 607 (1) pp., index, numerous illus. including one, p. 422, by R. (Fischer, Hurd, Lea)

727a ——— and Sister Blanche Marie. *Modern American Life.* Ginn, Boston etc., (1943), pic. cloth, 444, xvi, (1) pp., index, numerous illus. including one, p. (245), by R.

728 Kemble, Edward et al. (Programme Committee). *Lambs All Star Gambol.* (Tribune Printing Co., N.Y.), week of May 24, 1909, colored pic. wraps, pages unnumb., illus. including one, "Prepared to Elevate the Stage," by R.

729 Kennedy, H. A. *The Book of the West.* Ryerson Press, Toronto, (1925), cloth (or pic. wraps), 205 pp., index, numerous illus. including two, p. 52, by R.

730 Kennefeck, Margaret Mary. *California History.* W. H. Sadlier, n.p., (1937), decor. cloth, 241 pp., preface, "Foreword" by Herbert E. Bolton, index, numerous illus. including four, pp. 42, 139, 167 and 180, by R.

731 Ketchum, Richard M. et al., eds. *The American Heritage Book of the Pioneer Spirit.* American Heritage Pub. Co., N.Y., (1959), cloth, 394 (6) pp., introduction, acknowledgments, index, numerous illus. including seven, pp. 84, (166), 286, 325 and (338, three), by R. (Miller, Russell)

732 Keyes, Nelson Beecher and Gallagher, Edward Felix. *Hope of the Nation, Our American Heritage.* Good Will Publishers, Gastonia, N.C., (1952), simulated leather, red endsheets, 401 (2) pp., all edges lightly stipled, numerous illustrations, many in color including one, p. (387), by R.

733 Kimball, Ward. *Art after Pieces.* Pocket Books, N.Y., 1964, stiff pic. wraps, (4) pp., "Foreword" by Walt Kelly, 61 comically retouched color plates, including one, "The Fight for the Water Hole," by R.

733a Kimes, William F., ed. *The Westerners Brand Book Number 13.* Los Angeles Corral, (1969), decor. cloth,

pic. endsheets, contributors, index, numerous illus. including one, p. 19, by R. (Russell)

734 King, General Charles. *A Daughter of the Sioux.* Hobart Co., N.Y., 1903, words "Published March 15, 1903" on copyright page, cloth with illus. in color mounted on front cover (or red cloth with red and black decorations), 306 pp., gilt top, eight illus. including four, frontis. and facing pp. 21, 72 and 94, by R. (Deming)

735 ———. *An Apache Princess.* Hobart Co., N.Y., 1903, words "Published September, 1903" on copyright page, cloth and small round colored illus. mounted on front cover (or red cloth with red and black decorations), 328 pp., gilt top, eight illus. including "The Fight in the Canyon," by R., used both as the frontis. and facing p. 220. (Deming)

736 ———. *To the Front.* Harper, N.Y. and London, 1908, words "Published March, 1908," on copyright page, decor. cloth (or pic. boards), 260 (1) pp., eight illus. including four, frontis. and facing pp. 236, 242 and 248, by R.

737 ———. *A Soldier's Trial: an Episode of the Canteen Crusade.* Grosset & Dunlap, N.Y., n.d. (1905), cloth, 333 pp., with a frontis. by R. (In the first edition issued by Hobart in 1905, the frontis. is a photo of the author.)

738 King, James T. A. *War Eagle: A Life of General Eugene A. Carr.* Nebraska, Lincoln, (1963), cloth, map endsheets, 323 pp., bibliography, illus. including one, facing p. 241, by R.

739 Kloster, Paula R. *The Arizona State College Collection of American Art.* (The Castle Press, Pasadena, Calif., 1954), wraps, 108 (1) pp., "Foreword" by President Grady Grammage, introduction, index, 113 illus. including one, p. 31, by R. (Blumenschein, Johnson)

740 Knox, Thomas W. *The Boy Travellers in Mexico.* Harper, N.Y., 1890, decor. cloth, map endsheets, 552 pp., (4) of advs., preface, numerous illus. including two, pp. 120 and 121, by R.

741 Kohn, Bernice. *The Look-it-up Book of Transportation.* Random House, (1968), colored pic. boards, pic. endsheets, 132 pp., index, numerous illustrations from photos and by George Tuckwell but with two, pp. 76 (color) and 119, by R.

742 Koller, Larry. *The Fireside Book of Guns.* Simon and Schuster, N.Y., (1959), decor. cloth, colored pic. endsheets, 284 pp., introduction, acknowledgments,

bibliography, index, numerous illus. including eight, pp. 93, 94–95, (102), 104–05, 106–07, 108–09, 139 and 140–41, by R. (Eggenhofer, Russell)

743 Kouwenhoven, John A. *Adventures of America 1857–1900*. Harper, N.Y. and London, 1938, words "First Edition" on copyright page, cloth with paper labels (or illus. boards), 255 numb. illus. including four, nos. 223, 233, 243 and 244, by R.

744 Krout, John Allen. *Annals of American Sport*. Yale, New Haven, 1929, leather and boards, 352 pp., numerous illus. including three, pp. 37 and 108 (two), by R. The Liberty Bell Edition of "The Pageant of America," 1500 numb. impressions.

745 Kuhlman, Charles. *Legend into History, the Custer Mystery*. The Stackpole Co., Harrisburg, Pa., (1951), pic. cloth, 250 pp., foreword, acknowledgments, bibliography, index, maps, illus. including one, front cover, by R.

746 Kurtz, Kenneth. *Literature of the American Southwest*. Occidental College. L.A., 1956, wraps, 63 pp., preface, drawing on title page by R.

747 La Farge, Oliver. *A Pictorial History of the American Indian*. Crown Pub., N.Y., (1956), cloth and boards, 272 pp., publisher's acknowledgment, index, 350 (many in color) illus. including one, p. 223, by R.

748 ———. *The American Indian*. Golden Press, N.Y., (1960), colored pic. boards and endsheets, 213 pp., picture credits, numerous illus. including two, pp. (194) and 196, by R. Special edition of item no. 747 for young readers. (Russell)

749 Lamb, Arthur H. *The Osage People*. Osage Printery, Pawhuska, Okla., (1930), pic. wraps, 31 (1) pp., (1) of advs., preface, numerous illus. including one, p. 22, after R.

750 Lang, Mrs. Wayne F., ed. et al. *Faith Country 1910–1960*. 50th Anniversary Golden Jubilee of Faith Committee, Faith, S.D., (1960), pic. fabricoid, pic. endsheets, 302 pp., "Introduction" by True Joyce, advs., numerous illus. including one, "Stampede," p. 75 (Sunny Brook adv.), by R.

751 Lanier, Henry Wysham (collected and recounted by). *The Book of Bravery — Second Series*. Scribner's, N.Y., 1919, words "Published September, 1919" follow copyright notice, pic. cloth, 430 pp., sixteen illus. including one, facing p. 112, by R.

752 Larkin, Margaret (collected and edited by). *Singing Cowboy*. Oak Publication, N.Y., (1963), decor. wraps, 176 pp., (acknowledgment), introduction, glossary,

index of first lines, numerous illus. including six, pp. (8), 52, 85, 139, 147 and 170, by R. (Russell)

753 Larkin, Oliver W. *Art and Life in America*. Rinehart & Co,. N.Y., (1949), publisher's device on copyright page, cloth, 547 pp., author's foreword, acknowledgments, bibliographical notes, index, numerous illus. including one, p. 257, by R. Some material on Remington in text. (Young)

754 ———. Same, but revised and enlarged edition, Holt, Rinehart and Winston, N.Y. etc., (1960), cloth, 559 pp., "author's foreword to revised edition," numerous illus. including one, p. 257, by R. (Young)

755 Laut, Agnes C. *Lords of the North*. J. F. Taylor & Co., N.Y., 1900, pic. cloth, 442 pp., (8) of advs., acknowledgment, introduction, cover design by R.

756 ———. *Pathfinders of the West*. Macmillan, N.Y., 1904, words "Published November, 1904" on copyright page, decor. cloth, 380 pp., gilt top, foreword, appendix, index, numerous illus. including four, frontis. and facing pp. 120, 194 and 328, by R. Slight variation noted in size of type in which "The Macmillan Company" is printed at the base of the spine — no known priority. (Goodwin, Marchand)

757 Lavender, David (author) and Josephy, Alvin M., Jr. (editor-in-charge). *The Great West*. American Heritage, N.Y., 1965, cloth, pic. endsheets, 416 pp., foreword, acknowledgments, index, numerous illus. including one in color, p. 406, by R., slipcase. (Dunn, Koerner, Russell)

758 ———. *The Rockies*. Harper, N.Y. etc., 1968, words "First Edition" on copyright page, cloth, pic. endsheets, 404 pp., "With Thanks," bibliography, index, maps, one illus. on front endsheet, by R. "Regions of America" book.

759 Leach, Douglas Edward. *Arms for Empire* (A Military History of the British Colonies in North America, 1607–1763). Macmillan, N.Y., (1973), words "First Printing" on copyright page, two-tone cloth, map endsheets, 566 pp., brown top, preface, bibliography, index, maps, illus. including one, between pp. 376 and 377, by R. (Deming)

760 Leckie, Robert. *Great American Battles*. Random House, N.Y., 1968, colored pic. boards, pic. endsheets, 177 pp., index, numerous illus. including the double-title page by R. (Zogbaum)

761 Leckie, Wm. H. *The Military Conquest of the Southern Plains*. Univ. of Okla. Press, Norman, (1963), words "First edition" on copyright page, cloth, 269

pp., red top, preface, bibliography, index, maps, twenty-one illus. including one, between pp. 84 and 85, by R. (Leigh)

762 ———. *The Buffalo Soldiers* (A Narrative of the Negro Cavalry in the West). Oklahoma, Norman, (1967), words "First edition" on copyright page, cloth, 290 pp., bibliography, maps, illus. including one, p. 94, by R.

763 Leifur, Conrad W. *Our State North Dakota*. American Book Co., N.Y. etc., (1942), decor. cloth, 621 pp., numerous illus. including two, pp. 172 and 229, by R., maps.

764 Lewis, Alfred Henry. *Wolfville*. Stokes, N.Y., (1897), pic. cloth, 337 pp., preface, nineteen illus. by R.

765 ———. Same, n.d., words "Special Limited Edition" and "Tenth Edition" on title page, cloth, 337 pp., (5) of advs., preface, seven illus., title page and pp. 120, 172, 227, 278, 328 and 337, by R.

766 ———. Same, first British edition, Lawrence and Bullen, Ltd., London, 1897.

767 ———. *Wolfville Days*. Stokes, N.Y., (1902), pic. cloth, 311 pp., frontis. by R.

768 ———. *The Black Lion Inn*. R. H. Russell, N.Y., 1903, words "Published May, 1903" on copyright page, pic. cloth, 380 (1) pp., sixteen illus. including fifteen by R.

769 ———. *Old Wolfville, Chapters from the Fiction of Alfred Henry Lewis*. Antioch Press, (Yellow Springs, Ohio), 1968, cloth, 260 pp., "Introduction" (selected, edited and commentary) by Louis Filler, illustrated including the frontis. in color by R.

770 Lewis, John. *The Twentieth Century Book* (Its Illustration and Design). Reinhold, N.Y. (but printed in Great Britain), (1967), red balacron, 272 pp., preface, index, numerous illus. including three, p. 130, by R. (Wyeth)

771 Lewis, Wm. Dodge and Rowland, Albert Lindsay. *The Round-Up*. Winston, Phila. etc., (1931), code number "P-10-31" on copyright page, pic. cloth and endsheets, "Reading and Learning," copyright acknowledgments, index, illus. including one, front cover, by R.

772 Liebman, Rebekah R. and Young, Gertrude. *The Growth of America*. Prentice-Hall, Englewood Cliffs, N.J., (1964), pic. cloth, 482 pp., index, numerous illus. including two, pp. 23 and 337, by R.

773 Lindsey, Almont. *The Pullman Strike*. Univ. of Chi-

cago Press, Chicago, (1942), words "Published December 1942" on copyright page, cloth, 385 pp., preface, bibliography, eight illus. including one, facing p. 214, by R.

774 Linsenmeyer, Helen Walker. *From Fingers to Finger Bowls* (A Sprightly History of California Cooking). A Copley Book, (Union Tribune Pub. Co., San Diego, 1972), decor. cloth, brown endsheets, 142 pp., about the illustrations, foreword, bibliography, index, numerous illus. including two, pp. 30 and 32, by R. (Borein, Koerner)

775 Lipman, Jean, ed. *Art in America*, vol. 47, no. 3, 1959, pic. boards, 132 pp., numerous illus. including two, pp. 12 and 60, by R. (Russell)

776 Locke, Raymond Friday (compiled, edited and with an introduction by). *The American West*. Hawthorn Books, N.Y., (1971), boards, contributors, index; includes "Frederic Remington: The Man Who Invented John Wayne" by Robert Hardy Andrews, numerous illus. including fourteen by R. (Russell)

777 ———. *The American Indian*. Hawthorn Books, N.Y., (1970), boards, 256 pp., contributors, index, numerous illus. including five, pp. (128–29), (132–33), (138–39), (164–65) and (243), by R.

778 Lockwood, Frank C. *Arizona Characters*. Times-Mirror Press, L.A., 1928, cloth, 230 pp., preface, 34 illus. including two, facing pp. 16 and 24, by R.

779 ———. *Pioneer Days in Arizona*. Macmillan, N.Y., 1932, words "Published October, 1932" on copyright page, cloth, 387 pp., preface, introduction, index, illus. including three, pp. (18), 64 and 66, by R. (Elwell)

780 ———. *The Apache Indians*. Macmillan, N.Y., 1938, words "Published March 1938" on copyright page, decor. cloth, 348 pp., preface, index, illus. including four, facing pp. 175 (two), 263 and 306, plus one full page of small drawings, facing p. 174, by R. The note below the plate facing p. 295 states "Drawing by Frederick (*sic*) Remington" but the plate is signed by F. Holroyd Lambert. Remington's first name is misspelled with the added "k" in each of the notes below his illustrations.

781 ——— and Page, Capt. Donald W. *The Old Pueblo*. Manufacturing Stationers, Phoenix, Arizona, n.d. (1930?), fabricoid, 94 pp., illus. including one, facing p. 10, by R.

782 Loftus, Charles, ed. *Official Football Program, Harvard vs. Yale, Saturday, November 22, 1947*. Yale

Univ. Athletic Assn., New Haven, colored pic. wraps, 69 (1) pp., numerous illus. including one, p. 15, by R. "Frederic Remington" by Lou Black in text.

783 Logan, Harlan (editor-publisher). *Fiftieth Anniversary Scribner's Magazine, 1887–1937.* Scribner's, N.Y., Jan., 1937, decor. wraps, 144 pp., numerous illus. including one in color, p. 66, by R. (Dunn, James, Thomason)

784 Lomax, John A. *Songs of the Cattle Trail and Cow Camp.* Duell, Sloan and Pearce, N.Y., (1950), cloth, pic. endsheets, 189 pp., red top, "Foreword" by Wm. Lyon Phelps, introduction, 78 illus. including twenty-one by R. (Russell, Santee)

785 Long, Margaret. *The Smoky Hill Trail.* W. H. Kistler Co., Denver, 1943, cloth, 336, 38 pp., folding maps, illus. including one, p. 20, by R.

786 Longfellow, Henry Wadsworth. *The Song of Hiawatha.* Houghton Mifflin, Boston and N.Y., 1891, suede, 224 pp., gilt top, "Introductory Note" includes discussion of Remington's illus., pp. x–xiii, portrait frontis. of author, illus. with numerous drawings and twenty-two full-page photogravures, by R.

787 ———. Same, but limited to 250 numbered copies in vellum, boxed.

788 ———. Same, (1898), cloth, 193 pp., "Mr. Remington's Illustrations," introductory note, "Books Relating to the Indians," pronouncing vocabulary, numerous drawings and nine full-page plates by R. Riverside Literature Series.

789 ———. Same, but issued in cloth in 1908 with a frontis. in color by Wyeth.

790 ———. Same, first British edition, George C. Harrap & Co., London, 1911, full leather with embossed cover design by Maxfield Parrish and the frontis. by Wyeth.

791 Longley, Marjorie et al. *America's Taste.* Simon and Schuster, N.Y., (1960), cloth and boards, red endsheets, 332 pp., editor's note and acknowledgments, picture credits, index, numerous illus. including one, the same illus. on the contents page and p. 148, by R.

792 Loofbourow, Leon L. *Have a Western! Meet Alexander Majors.* Lexicon Press, S.F., (1960), pic. wraps, 14 pp., six illus. including one, p. 3, by R.

793 Lorant, Stefan. *The Life and Times of Theodore Roosevelt.* Doubleday, Garden City, N.Y., (1959), words "First Edition" on copyright page, two-tone cloth, 640 pp., foreword, bibliography, index, 750

illus. including two, pp. 206 and 315, by R. The illus. on p. 328 is a photo of the presentation of a Remington bronze to Teddy by his Rough Riders, Sept. 15, 1898.

794 Lovett, Richard. *United States Pictures drawn with Pen and Pencil.* Religious Tract Society, (London), 1891, gilt decor. pic. cloth, decor. endsheets, 223 (1) pp., 8 of advs., all edges gilt, introduction, index, numerous illus. including one, p. 209, by R.

794a Lowman, Al et al. *The Mexican Texans.* Institute of Texan Cultures, The University of Texas, San Antonio, 1971, pic. wraps, 32 pp., numerous illus. including one, p. 26, by R. (Cisneros, Lea)

794b ———. Same, but in Spanish with the title *Los Mexicano Texanos.*

794c ———. *The Spanish Texans.* Institute of Texan Cultures, The University of Texas, San Antonio, 1972, pic. wraps, 32 pp., numerous illus. including two, pp. 4 and 15, by R. (Bugbee, Cisneros, Lea, Mead)

795 Lucia, Ellis. *Tough Men, Tough Country.* Prentice-Hall, Englewood Cliffs, N.J., (1963), two-tone cloth, black endsheets, 336 pp., foreword, bibliography, numerous illus. including one, p. (93), by R.

796 *The Lucky Bag, 1904, Vol. 11.* U.S. Naval Academy, Annapolis, 1904, sail canvas, oblong quarto, numerous illus. including one by R. (Class Annual.)

797 Lyon, Peter. *The Wild, Wild West.* Funk and Wagnalls, N.Y., (1969), cloth and fabricoid, colored pic. cloth, 156 pp., an introductory note, selected bibliography, index, numerous illus. including ten, pp. 21, (22), 23, (26–27), (64–65), (136–37), 138 and (142–43), by R.

798 McAuliffe, Eugene and Godfrey, General E. S. *Eighty Years After and Custer's Last Battle.* Omaha, n.d., wraps, 40 pp., six illus., pp. 7, 18, 21, 25, 27 and 33, by R.

799 McConathy, Osbourne; Beattie, John W. and Morgan, Russell V. *Music, Highways and Byways.* Silver Burdett Co., N.Y., 1936, cloth, 252 pp., illustrated including one in color, "The Blanket Signal," p. 77, by R. (Wyeth)

800 McCracken, Harold. *Pershing.* Brewer & Warren, N.Y., 1931, decor. cloth, pic. endsheets, 193 pp., twenty-three illus. including four, facing pp. 45, 68, 69 and 76, by R.

801 ———. *Frederic Remington, Artist of the Old West.* Lippincott, Phila., and N.Y., (1947), words "First Edi-

tion" on copyright page, cloth, 157 pp., forty-eight plates, "Introduction" by James Chillman, Jr., foreword, bibliographical check list, numerous illus. including thirty-two in color by R.

802 ———. *Portrait of the Old West.* McGraw-Hill, N.Y. etc., (1952), words "First Edition" on copyirght page, decor. cloth, 232 pp., special acknowledgment, preface, "Foreword" by R. W. G. Vail, "Biographical Check List of Western Artists," index, numerous illus. including sixteen by R. (Russell, Schreyvogel)

803 ———. *The Beast that Walks like a Man.* Hanover House, Garden City, N.Y., (1955), words "First Edition" on copyright page, cloth, 319 pp., foreword, appendix, index, sixteen illus. including one, p. 94, by R. Remington in text, p. 185.

804 ———. *Preserving the Heritage of the Old West.* Buffalo Bill Historical Center, (Cody, Wyo., 1961), pic. wraps, 29 (1) pp., numerous illus. including seven, pp. 8 (two), 9, 13 and 20 (three), by R. (Dunton, Russell)

805 ———. *The Frederic Remington Book.* Doubleday, Garden City, N.Y., 1966, words "First Edition" on copyright page, de luxe edition of 500 numbered and signed copies in gilt decor. leather, green endsheets, 284 (1) pp., all edges gilt, numerous illustrations, many in color, by R., slipcase.

806 ———. Same, but first trade edition in cloth.

807 ———. *I Knew the Wild Riders and Vacant Land.* Produced for Marlboro customers, Westbury, Conn., 1968, a short biography of Remington plus four prints by him.

808 ———. *The American Cowboy.* Doubleday, Garden City, N.Y., 1973, de luxe binding, 196 pp., references, index, numerous illus. including thirty-eight (six in color) by R. Limited edition of 300 numbered copies signed by the author, slipcase. (Borein, Cisneros, Eggenhofer, Johnson, Koerner, Leigh, Russell, Wyeth)

809 ———. Same, cloth with words "First edition after the limited edition of 300 copies" on copyright page.

810 McDowell, Bart. *The American Cowboy in Life and Legend.* National Geographic Society, Washington, D.C., (1972), pic. cloth, pic. endsheets, 211 (1) pp., "Foreword" by Joe B. Frantz, additional reading, index, numerous illus. including seven, title page and pp. 34 (two), 35, 166 (two), and 207, by R. and a photo of him. (DeYong, Dunton, Goodwin, James, Russell)

811 McGee, Gentry R. and Ijams, C. B. (revised and en-larged by). *A History of Tennessee.* American Book Co., N.Y. etc., (1924), cloth, 337, xl pp., preface, preface to revised edition, appendix, index, illus. including one, p. 48, by R.

812 McLanathan, Richard. *Art in America, A Brief History.* Harcourt Brace, N.Y., (1973), words "First American Edition" on copyright page, pic. wraps, 216 pp., 189 illus. including one, p. (167), by R.

813 McLennan, William. *In Old France and New.* Harper, N.Y. and London, 1900, decor. cloth, 319 (1) pp., preface, numerous illus. including one, facing p. 138, by R.

814 McReynolds, Edwin. *Missouri, A History of the Crossroads State.* Oklahoma, Norman, (1962), words "First edition" on copyright page, cloth, 483 pp., preface, bibliography, index, maps, illus. including one, between pp. 210–11, by R.

815 McSpadden, J. Walker. *Indian Heroes.* Crowell, N.Y., (1928), pic. cloth, 305 pp., introduction, title page states "Illustrated in color by Howard L. Hastings" but there is one plate, facing p. 252, by R.

816 MacVicar, Nell and Craig, Irene. *Tales and Trails of Western Canada.* School Aids and Text Book Pub. Co., Regina and Toronto, (1947), pic. cloth, 144 (1) pp., "Foreword" by R. O. MacFarlane, bibliography, numerous illus. including one, p. (7), after R.

817 Mabie, Hamilton W. and Bright, Marshal H. *The Memorial Story of America.* Winston, Phila etc., 1893, decor. cloth and endsheets, 851 pp., introduction, over 350 illus. including seven, pp. 247, 269, 270, 417, 697, 700 and 703, by R.

818 ———. Same, but with title *Footprints of Four Centuries.* International Pub. Co., Phila. etc., 1894.

819 ———. *Our Own Country.* Monarch Book Co., Phila. etc., 1895, decor. cloth, 560 pp., numerous illus. including four, pp. 249, 269, 270 and 471, by R. Reprinted in 1898 with the title *Our Country in Peace and War.*

820 ———. Same, but salesman's dummy, 1895, with five illus. by R.

821 Mabie, Dr. Hamilton W., Parton, James et al. *Giants of the Republic.* Winston, Philadelphia etc., 1895, cloth, numerous illus. including two, pp. 218 and 224, by R.

822 ———et al. *Book of Nature and Outdoor Life* (part 2). University Society, N.Y., (1912), decor. cloth and endsheets, 416 pp., numerous illus. including two, pp. 245 and 246, by R. (Lungren, Rowe)

823 Mackey, Margaret G. et al. *Your Country's Story: Pioneers, Builders, Leaders.* Ginn, Boston etc., (1961), colored pic. cloth, 560 pp., appendix, index, numerous illus. including two, pp. 315 and 348, by R. (Hurd, Lea, Wyeth)

824 Mahan, Capt. A. T. *The War in South Africa.* Peter Fenelon Collier & Son, N.Y., 1900, cloth, 208 pp., "Introduction" by Sir John G. Bourinot, numerous illus. including one in color, facing p. 144, by R.

825 Manach, Jorge. *Marti, Apostle of Freedom.* Devin-Adair Co., N.Y., 1950, cloth, 363 pp., acknowledgments, "On Jorge Manach" by Gabriela Mistral, twenty-three illus. including six, pp. (59), (181), (205), (233), (245) and (283), by R. Tr. from the Spanish by Coley Taylor.

826 Manley, Atwood. *Frederic Remington in the Land of his Youth.* Canton's Remington Centennial Observance, (Canton, N.Y., 1961), colored pic. wraps, 47 pp., acknowledgments, numerous illus. of and by R.

827 ———— with the assistance of Paul F. Jamieson. *Rushton and His Times in American Canoeing.* Syracuse University Press, Syracuse, N.Y., (1968), words "First Edition" on copyright page, cloth, gold endsheets, 203 pp., "Foreword" by Homer L. Dodge, appendices, index, numerous illus. including first book appearances of two drawings, between pp. 60 and 61, by R.

828 Markham, Edwin, ed. *The Eagle's Wings, The Age of Expansion, 1868–1910.* William H. Wise & Co., N.Y. and Chicago, (Lakeside Press, Chicago), 1914, morocco, marbled endsheets, 524 pp., all edges gilt, foreword, index, numerous illus. including one, p. 247, by R.

829 *Marlin Sporting Firearms 1964.* N.p. (New Haven), 1964, colored pic. wraps, 20 pp., numerous illus. including one, front cover, by R.

830 *Marlin Sporting Firearms 1965.* Marlin Firearms Co., New Haven, Conn., (1965), pic. wraps, 19 pp., numerous illus. including one in color, back cover, by R.

831 (Martin, John Stuart.) *American Heritage,* vol. XII, no. 6, Oct., 1961, one illus. by R. for John Stuart Martin's "Walter Camp and His Gridiron Game."

832 Mather, Frank Jewett, Jr. et al. *The American Spirit in Art.* Yale, New Haven, 1927, leather and boards, 354 pp., numerous illus. including one, p. 299, by R. The Liberty Bell Edition of "The Pageant of America," vol. 12, 1500 numb. impressions.

833 Mathieson, Theodore. *The Nez Perce Indian War.* Monarch, Derby, Conn., Dec. 1964, pic. wraps, 156 pp., (4) of advs., all edges red, front cover illus. by R.

834 Matloff, Maurice (general editor). *American Military History.* Office of the Chief of Military History, U.S. Army, G.P.O., Washington, D.C., 1969, cloth, 701 pp., "Foreword" by Brigadier General Hal C. Pattison, "Preface" by Stetson Conn, introduction, index, illus. including one, p. 312, by R.

835 Matthews, E. C. *Sketches of the Old West.* New Era Studio, St. Louis, (1962), fabricoid, 162 pp., introduction, numerous illus. including two, pp. 52 and 126, by R.

836 Mazzanovich, Anton. *Trailing Geronimo.* A. Mazzanovich, Hollywood, Calif., 1931, words "Third Edition" on the title page, cloth, 322 pp., preface, "Foreword" by Col. Chas. B. Gatewood, Retired, numerous illus. including one, p. 90, by R. (First printing with the Remington illustration.)

837 Meadon, Joseph, ed. *The Graphic Arts and Crafts Yearbook, 1908.* Republican Pub. Co., Hamilton, Ohio, (1908), leather, tinted endsheets, 355 pp., lviii of advs., preface, numerous illus. including one in color, facing p. 114, by R.

838 Meigs, John, ed. *The Cowboy in American Prints.* Swallow Press, Chicago, (1972), leather and cloth, pic. endsheets, 184 pp., introduction, numerous illus. including twenty-nine by R., limited to 300 numbered copies signed by the editor with an added manually signed lithograph by Peter Hurd, slipcase. (Beeler, Borein, Dixon, Hurd, Russell, Wood, Zogbaum)

839 ————. Same, trade edition in cloth.

840 Meltzer, Milton. *Milestones to American Liberty: the Foundations of the Republic.* Crowell, N.Y., (1961), decor., handcrafted Mission Leather, pic. endsheets, 237 pp., all edges lightly stippled, preface, picture credits, index, numerous illus. including one, p. 168, by R. (Russell)

840a Mendelowitz, Daniel M. *A History of American Art.* Holt, Rinehart & Winston, N.Y., 1960, cloth, 662 pp., bibliography, index, numerous illus. including two, pp. (447) and 480, by R. (Miller, Young)

841 Meredith, Roy. *The American Wars.* World Pub. Co., Cleveland and N.Y., (1955), words "First Edition" on copyright page, pic. cloth, 348 (1) pp., red top, introduction, acknowledgments, numerous illus. including thirty-eight by R. (Deming, Dunn, Fischer, Thomason)

842 Merillat, Louis A. and Campbell, Delwin M. *Veteri-*

nary Military History of the United States. Veterinary Magazine Corp., Chicago, 1935, 2 vols., cloth, 1172 pp., numerous illus. including one (I), p. 83, by R.

843 Merrill, James M. *Spurs to Glory.* Rand McNally, Chicago etc., (1966), words "First Printing, August, 1966" on copyright page, decor. cloth, 302 (1) pp., "Prepare to Mount," bibliography, index, numerous illus. including four, double title-page and pp. (63) two and (239), by R. (Zogbaum)

844 Merritt, Brig. Gen. Wesley et al. *The Armies of To-day.* Harper, N.Y., 1893, decor. cloth, 438 pp., gilt top, illus. including eight full-page plates, facing pp. 362, 366, 370, 374, 378, 382, 388 and 392, plus six drawings in text, by R.

845 Merwin, Henry Childs. *The Life of Bret Harte.* Houghton Mifflin, Boston and N.Y., 1911, words "Published September 1911" on copyright page, cloth, 362 pp., gilt top, preface, index, seventeen illus. including one, facing p. 114, by R. (Smith)

846 ———. Same, first British edition. Chatto and Windus, London, 1912.

847 Mich, Daniel D. (executive editor). *The Santa Fe Trail,* by the editors of *Look.* Random House, N.Y., (1946), pic. cloth, 271 pp., introduction, acknowledgments, picture credits, numerous illus. including two, pp. 69 and 85, by R.

848 Miles, General Nelson A. *Personal Recollections and Observations of.* Werner Co., Chicago and N.Y., 1896. The sample book of a subscription taker, the three bindings are cleverly combined, sample pages from text, illus. including fifteen by R., subscription blanks.

849 ———. Same, Werner Co., Chicago and N.Y., 1896, pic. cloth with plain edges (or morocco with gold edges), 550 pp., preface, numerous illus. including fifteen, by R. "Major General" under frontis. in second edition.

850 ——— (introduction by). *Harper's Pictorial History of the War with Spain.* Harper, N.Y. and London, 1899, pic. cloth in 2 vols. (or in 32 parts in pic. wraps), 507 (1) pp., introduction, index, numerous illus. including twenty-two by R. Also articles by Remington. (Zogbaum)

851 ———. *Serving the Republic.* Harper, N.Y .and London, 1911, words "Published October 1911" on copyright page, decor. cloth, 339 (1) pp., gilt top, introduction, appendix, index, illus. including one, facing p. 124, by R.

852 Millbrook, Minnie Dubbs. *Ness, Western County, Kansas.* Millbrook Printing Co., Detroit, (1955), cloth, 319 (10) pp., preface, bibliography and notes, appendix, index, numerous illus. including one, p. 29, by R., maps.

853 Miller, Joaquin et al. *Western Frontier Stories retold from St. Nicholas.* Century N.Y., 1907, pic. cloth, 198 pp., illus. including six, title page and pp. (7), (14), 17, 37 and 40, by R. (Lungren)

854 Miller, Lewis B. *Saddles and Lariats.* Dana Estes & Co., Boston, (1912), pic. cloth, 285 pp., (2) of advs., author's note, illus. including four composites, facing pp. 34, 38, 106 and 114, from illus., by R.

855 Miller, Nyle II et al. *Kansas, A Pictorial History.* Kansas Centennial Commission and State Historical Society, Topeka, 1961, cloth, map, pic. endsheets, 319 pp., foreword, picture credits, index, numerous illus. including four, pp. 10, (12), 129 and 255, by R. (Schreyvogel)

856 Millis, Walter. *The Martial Spirit.* Houghton Mifflin, Boston and N.Y., 1931, cloth, map endsheets, 427 pp., tinted top, bibliographical acknowledgments, index, numerous illus. including one, facing p. 68, by R. Remington in text.

857 Monaghan, Jay (editor-in-chief). *The Book of the American West.* Julian Messner, N.Y., (1963), words "First Edition" on copyright page, pic. cloth, tan endsheets, 608 pp., introduction, index, numerous illus. including forty-four (three in color), by R. (Borein, Koerner, Leigh, Lungren, Russell, Schreyvogel)

857a ———. Same, deluxe edition in full leather, decor. endsheets, all edges gilt, slipcase. (Number of copies not stated.)

858 Moore, Charles. *The Northwest under Three Flags.* Harper, N.Y. and London, 1900, cloth, 401 (1) pp., introduction, index, numerous illus. including ten, facing pp. 4, 42, 60, 118, 120, 124, 132, 164, 292 and 296, by R., maps.

858a Morgan, Dale L. *Life in America — The West.* The Fideler Co., Grand Rapids, Michigan, (1952), cloth, pic. map endsheets, 160 pp., index, numerous illus. including two, pp. 13 and (14), by R.

859 Morris, Charles. *The Greater Republic.* Winston, Phila. etc., 1899, decor. morocco and endsheets, 711 pp., all edges gilt, publisher's and author's introductions, over 300 illus. including two, pp. 484 and 513, by R., map frontis. in color.

860 ———. *The Child's History of the United States.*

(W. E. Scull, 1900), cloth, 237 pp., plus a page numb. 254, preface, illus. including one, p. 177, by R.

861 ———. *This Country of Ours.* International Pub. Cu., Phila., (1901), decor. cloth with illus. mounted on front cover, decor. endsheets, 600 (2) pp., publisher's and author's introductions, over 300 illus. including two, pp. 484 and 513, by R. (Slightly expanded edition of no. 859.)

862 Mowry, William A. and Arthur M. *A History of the United States for Schools.* Silver, Burdett & Co., N.Y., 1896, decor. cloth, map endsheets, 437 pp., preface, appendices, bibliography, index, illus. including one, p. 236, by R., maps.

863 ———. *First Steps in the History of Our Country.* Silver, Burdett and Co., N.Y. etc., 1899, pic. cloth, 315 pp., (4) of advs., preface, index, numerous illus. including one, p. 165, by R., maps. (Fogarty)

864 ——— and Blanche S. *American Pioneers.* Silver, Burdett and Co., N.Y. etc., (1905), pic. cloth, 363 pp., preface, index, numerous illus. including two, pp. 104 and 182, by R.

865 Mugridge, Donald E. and Conover, Helen F. *An Album of American Battle Art 1755–1918.* Library of Congress, (G.P.O.), Washington, D.C., 1947, decor. cloth, 319 pp., acknowledgments, introduction, graphic index, 150 plates, including one, no. 127, p. 273, by R. (Dunn)

866 Muir, John ed. *Picturesque California.* J. Dewing Co., S. F. and N.Y., 1888, morocco and cloth, marbled endsheets, 2 vols., 478 pp. (continuous pagination), gilt tops and other edges uncut, numerous (120 tintplates) illus. including four, facing pp. 28, 184, 236 and 323, plus drawings. p. 238, by R. Also issued in ten parts and in a single volume in cloth. No priority known. (Keller)

867 (Mulford.) *Prentice Mulford's Story.* Biobooks, Oakland, Calif., 1953, linen with paper title label on front cover, 145 pp., "Aftword" by Joseph A. Sullivan, (publisher), four illus., facing pp. 28, 61, 88 and 121, by R. First California edition, limited to 500 copies.

868 Mumie, Nolie. *Hoofs to Wings: The Pony Express.* Johnson Pub. Co., Boulder, Colo., 1960, cloth and decor. boards with paper label on front cover, 116 pp., preface, index, numerous illus. including one, following p. 75, by R. Issued in a limited, signed edition of 200 copies. (Russell)

869 Mundell, Frank. *Stories of the Far West.* Sunday School Union, London, (1896), pic. cloth, 159 (1) pp.,

16 of advs., prefatory note, illus. including one, front cover, after R.

870 Murphy, Virginia Reed. *Across the Plains in the Donner Party.* Lewis Osborne, Palo Alto, Calif., n.d., decor. cloth, 55 (1) pp., "Foreword" by George R. Stewart, bibliography, sixteen illus. including four, pp. 17, 21, 24 and 29, by R. Folding map and an enlarged set of the four Remington illustrations (in an envelope) laid in.

871 Myers, Lee. *New Mexico Military Installations.* Southwestern Monuments Assn., Globe, Arizona, (1966), pic. wraps, 10 (1) pp., one illus. (repeated, greatly enlarged, on front cover) by R.

872 Nail, Rev. Olin W. et al., eds. *Texas Methodist Centennial Yearbook 1834–1934.* Published by Rev. Nail, Elgin, Texas, (1935). Pic. fabricoid, pic. endsheets, 801 pp., (13) of advs., preface, letter from President Franklin D. Roosevelt, indices, errata, profusely illustrated with photos and prints and including two drawings, p. 39, by R.

873 Neider, Charles, ed. *The Great West.* Coward-McCann, N.Y., (1958), cloth, map endsheets, 457 pp., brown top, introduction, "A Note on the Selections," numerous illus. including twelve by R.

874 Neihardt, John G. *The Mountain Men.* Nebraska, Lincoln, (1971), words "First Bison Book printing: June 1971" on copyright page, pic. wraps, pp. 254 and 111, introduction, front cover illus. by R.

875 Nelson, William H. and Vandiver, Frank E. *Fields of Glory.* Dutton, N.Y., (1960), words "First Edition" on copyright page, cloth, 316 pp., preface, index, numerous illus. including seven, pp. 106, 107, 114, 119, 125 (two) and 129, by R.

876 Nickel, Helmut. *Warriors and Worthies.* (Arm and Armor Through the Ages). Atheneum, N.Y., 1969, words "First Edition on copyright page, decor. cloth, 122 pp., introduction, glossary, numerous illus. including three, pp. 108, (109) and 111, by R.

877 Nicoll, Bruce (assembled and edited by). *Nebraska, A Pictorial History.* Nebraska, Lincoln, (1967), cloth, blue endsheets, 281 (1) pp., numerous illus. including four, pp. 27 (color), 34-35 (color), 47 (color) and 95, by R. (Dixon, Dunn, Miller, Russell)

878 Nolan, Frederick W., ed. *The English Westerners Brand Book,* vol. III. English Westerners, New Brighton, Cheshire, England, Nov. 1956–Oct. 1957, decor. cloth, (247) mimeographed pp., illus. including poor copies of drawings by R. (Leigh, Russell)

879 Norris, Frank. *A Deal in Wheat.* Doubleday, Page, N.Y., 1903, decor. cloth, 272 pp., gilt top and other edges uncut, four illus. including one, facing p. 120, by R.

880 Nye, Elwood L. *Marching with Custer.* Arthur H. Clark Co., Glendale, Calif., 1964, two-tone decor. fabriciod, 53 pp., publisher's preface, "Introduction" and "The Equestrian Custer" by Carroll Freswold, illus. including two, title page and p. (35), by R. Edition limited to 300 copies.

881 O'Day, Edward F. *Old San Francisco.* News, S. F., n.d., pic. wraps, (7) pp., seven illus. including one, front cover, by R.

882 (O'Brien et al.) *How the West was Won.* Metro-Goldwyn-Mayer and Cinerama (Random House, N.Y.), 1963, colored pic. boards, unpaged, "An Introduction to a New Era in Entertainment" by Robert H. O'Brien and Nicolas Reisini, numerous illustrations from the movie but with one in black and white, "Attack on the Sun Pole," by R.

883 Page, Thomas Nelson et al. *Stories of the South.* Scribner's, N.Y., 1893, cloth, 222 pp., gilt top, illus. including six, pp. (54), (97), (104), (119), (122) and 127, by R.

884 Paine, Lauran. *Conquest of the Great Northwest.* McBride, N.Y., 1959, words, "First Edition 1959" on copyright page, cloth, 194 pp., index, illus. including seven, four between pp. 34 and 35 and three between pp. 66 and 67, by R., d/w by R.

885 Pare, Madeline Ferrin (with the collaboation of Bert M. Fireman). *Arizona Pageant* (A Short History of the 48th State). Arizona Historical Foundation, Phoenix, 1965, pic. cloth, 336 pp., "Introduction" by Barry M. Goldwater, maps, appendix, index, illus. including one, p. 36, by R.

886 Parker, Horace. *Anza Borrego, Desert Guide Book.* Paisano Press, Balboa Island, Calif., (1958), pic. boards with plastic binder, 108 pp., acknowledgments, numerous illus. including one, p. 61, by R., maps.

887 ———. *Anza-Borrego Guide Book.* Paisano Press, Balboa Island, Calif., 1963, colored pic. wraps, 139 pp., (2) of advs., acknowledgments, introduction to second ed., index, numerous illus. including one, p. 61, by R. Revised and enlarged edition of no. 886.

888 Parkman, Francis. *The Oregon Trail.* Little, Brown, Boston, 1892, decor. natural colored linen (or decor. leather), 411 pp., gilt top, "Preface to the Illustrated Edition," numerous illus. by R., including ten tinted plates on special coated paper, frontis. and facing pp. (104), 108, 141, 161, 209, 236, (269), 293 and 364.

889 ———. Same, Macmillan, London, 1892. First British printing of no. 888.

890 ———. Same, Little, Brown and J. F. Taylor and Co., N.Y., 1898, morocco and cloth, 2 vols., 231 and 249 pp., gilt tops, seven illus. by R. Vols. xix and xx of the edition *de luxe* of Parkman's Works, limited to 300 sets.

891 ———. Same, Little, Brown, Boston, 1925, cloth and pic. boards, 364 pp., gilt top, publisher's preface, ten tipped in illus. including five photogravures, facing pp. 96, 124, 184, 208 and 318, by R. The Wyeth-Remington Edition, limited to 975 numb. copies, boxed. The trade edition does not have the Remington illus. (Wyeth)

892 ———. Same, University of Wisconsin Press, Madison etc., 1969, cloth, 758 pp., edited by E. N. Feltskog, Editor's Preface, Editor's Introduction, notes, bibliography, index, maps, numerous illus. plus d/w illus. by R.

893 (Parkman.) *The Works of Francis Parkman* (Frontenac Edition). Scribner's, N.Y., 1916, salesman's dummy, decor. cloth, binding samples mounted inside front cover, sample pages, sample illus. including two by R.

894 Parrish, Randall. *The Great Plains.* McClurg, Chicago, 1907, words "Published September 14, 1907" on copyright page, pic. cloth, 399 pp., preface, note of acknowledgment, index, illus. including one (of three), on the plate facing p. 228, by R. (Lungren)

895 Parsons, John E. *The Peace-Maker and Its Rivals.* Morrow, N.Y., 1950, cloth, pic. endsheets, 184 pp., foreword, notes, index, numerous illus. including one, p. 138, by R. Remington in text, pp. 139 and 164.

896 ———. *The First Winchester.* Morrow, N.Y., 1955, decor. cloth and endsheets, 207 pp., foreword, appendix, notes, bibliography, index, numerous illus. including one, p. (138), by R. Remington in text, pp. 150, 188 and 197.

897 Payne, L. W. et al. *Interesting Friends.* Rand McNally, Chicago etc., (1936), pic. cloth, pic. endsheets, 584 pp., index, numerous illus. including one, p. 329, by R.

898 ——— et al. *Good Companions.* Rand McNally, Chicago etc., (1936), pic. cloth, pic. endsheets, 584 pp., index, numerous illus. including one, p. 329, by R.

899 ——— et al. *Voices of America.* Rand McNally,

Chicago etc., (1936), pic. cloth, pic. endsheets, 700 pp., index, numerous illus. including five, pp. 87, 90, 91, 94 and 104, by R.

900 (Peckham.) *American Heritage*, Summer, 1951, one illus. by R. for Howard H. Peckham's "Detroit Besieged."

901 Pennell, Joseph. *Pen Drawings and Pen Draughtsmen*. Macmillan, London and N.Y., 1889, words "Printed by R. & R. Clark, Edinburgh" follow last line of text, cloth or boards, 318 pp., gilt top, preface, errata, introduction, index, 158 illus. including one, p. (212), by R. Much on Remington in text, pp. 184, 199-200, 210-214. Reissued by Macmillan in 1894 and 1920, and by T. Fisher Unwin, (London), in 1921.

902 ———. *Modern Illustration*. George Bell & Sons (Chiswick Press), London and N.Y., 1895, gilt lettered cloth, 146 pp., gilt top and other edges uncut, preface, introduction, index, numerous illus. including one, p. 128, by R., errata slip tipped-in following the title page stating "As the Index of Illustrations was prepared and sent to press with the latter part of the preface during the author's absence, he wishes it to be stated that he is in no way responsible for them." The frontis. in this first issue has this caption: "By Fred Walker. Process Block from an Original Study in the Possession of the Author."

903 ———. Same, the corrected edition, issued at Mr. Pennell's insistence. Caption under frontis. reads "By F. Walker. Kensington Museum," errata slip tipped-in following "Index of Illustrations." In addition to the trade edition in cloth there was a limited edition of 125 copies on Japanese vellum in printed wraps.

904 ———. *Die Modern Illustration*. Leipzig, n.d., a German edition of no. 902.

905 Pennoyer, A. Sheldon. (assembled and edited by). *This Was California*. Putnam's, N.Y., 1938, cloth, pic. endsheets, 224 pp., yellow top, preface, index, numerous illus. including one, the frontis., by R. Edition limited to 1250 copies signed by the author.

906 Peters, Joseph P. (with an introduction and appended compilation by). *Indian Battles and Skirmishes on the American Frontier, 1790–1898*. University Microfilms, Ann Arbor, 1966, pic. cloth, pp. 26, 112, 65 and 51, front cover illus. by R.

907 Peters, Quinton, ed. *Tulsa, I. T., 1907–1957*. Tulsa Chamber of Commerce, Tulsa, Okla., 1956,, colored pic. wraps, 56 pp., numerous illus. including one, p. (23), by R.

908 Peterson, Harold L. *The Treasury of the Gun*. Ridge Press Book, Golden Press, N.Y., (1962), cloth, brown endsheets, 249 (3) pp., acknowledgments, (preface), selected bibliography, index, numerous illus. (many in color) including three drawings, pp. 160, 180 and 216, and one color plate, p. 238, by R.

909 ———. *The Remington Historical Treasury of American Guns*. Thomas Nelson, N.Y. etc., (1966), fabricoid, 154 (5), pp., numerous illus. including one, p. 65, by R.

910 ——— and Elman, Robert. *The Great Guns*. A Ridge Press Book (Madison Square Press, Grosset and Dunlap), N.Y., (1971), cloth, blue endsheets, 252 pp., introduction, picture credits, bibliography, index, numerous (many in color) illus. including one, p. 229, by R.

911 *Photographic History of the War with Spain*. R. H. Woodward Co., Baltimore, 1899, fabricoid, unpaged, "introductory" by Major-General Joseph Wheeler, nearly 500 photos but with a frontispiece by R.

912 Pfluger, Mrs. Edward M. (Chairman, Catalogue Committee). *Winter Antiques Show*. East Side House, N.Y., 1959, colored pic. wraps, 144 pp., acknowledgment, indices, numerous illus. (some in color) including one, "Map in the Sand," p. 74, by R.

913 Place, Marian T. *Westward on the Oregon Trail*. American Heritage Pub. Co., 1962, words "First Edition" on title page, colored pic. cloth, pic. endsheets, 153 pp., "Foreword" by Earl Pomeroy (consultant), acknowledgments, "For Further Reading," index, numerous illus. including three, pp. 93, 99 and 134-5, by R. (Dunn)

914 Pitz, Henry C. *Illustrating Children Books*. Watson-Guptill, (1963), cloth, blue endsheets, 207 pp., preface, bibliography, index, numerous illus. including one, p. (77), by R. (Schoonover, Wyeth)

915 ——— (selected and with an introduction by) *Frederic Remington*. Dover Publications, N.Y., (1972), colored pic. wraps, unpaged, 173 drawings and illustrations.

916 Polley, Robert L., ed. *The Beauty of America in Great American Art*. Country Beautiful Foundation, Waukesha, Wisconsin, (1965), decor. cloth, grey endsheets, 162 pp., "Preface" by Eric F. Goldman, "Introduction" by Tracy Atkinson, indices, numerous illus. in color including four, pp. 78, (79), 81 and 90, by R. (Russell)

917 ——— (executive editor) et al. *America — This*

316   REMINGTON

Land of Ours. Country Beautiful Corporation, Waukesha, Wisconsin, (1970), cloth, 194 pp., numerous illus. including one in color, p. 134, by R. (Miller, Russell)

918 Pollock, J. M. *The Unvarnished West.* Simpkin, Marshall, Hamilton, Kent & Co., London, n.d. (1911?), cloth, 252 (1) pp., (1) of advs., preface, twenty illus. including two, pp. 42 and (92), by R.

919 Porter, C. Fayne. *Our Indian Heritage.* Chilton Books, Phila. and N.Y. (1964), words "First Edition" on copyright page, fabricoid, decor. endsheets, 228 (1) pp., acknowledgments, appendix, index, "C. Fayne Porter," illus. including one, between pp. 82–83, by R.

920 Pourade, Richard F. *The Glory Years.* Union-Tribune Pub. Co., (San Diego, Calif., 1964), cloth, 274 pp., credits, bibliography, index, numerous illus. including one, p. (36), by R. (Wyeth)

921 Powell, E. Alexander. *Gentlemen Rovers.* Scribner's, N.Y., 1913, words "Published, September, 1913" on copyright page, cloth, 245 pp., foreword, twelve illus. including one, facing p. 136, by R.

922 ———. *Some Forgotten Heroes.* Scribner's, N.Y., (1922), cloth, 178 pp., illustrated including one by R.

923 Powers, Alfred, ed. *Poems of the Covered Wagons.* Pacific Pub. House, Portland, Oregon, 1947, words "First Edition" on copyright page, cloth and pic. boards, 142 (2) pp., acknowledgments, illus. including one, p. (101), after R.

924 *The Prairie Scout* (volume one). The Kansas Corral of The Westerners, Abilene, Kansas, 1973, pic. cloth, 125 pp., introduction, index, includes "Frederic Remington in Kansas" by David Dary with six illus., pp. 81, 83, 85, 87, 89 and 93, by R. and two photos of him.

925 Pratt, Richard Henry. *Battlefield and Classroom.* Yale, New Haven & London, 1964, cloth, 358 pp., "Introduction" (and edited) by Robt. M. Utley, index, maps, illus. including one, following p. 337, by R.

926 Prentice, Ezra P. et al. (Programme Committee). *Programme Eleventh Annual Mounted Games, Squadron "A."* Robertson & Wallace, (N.Y.), Feb. 26, 1901, pic. wraps tied with silk cord, 44 pp., numerous illus. including four, front cover and pp. 22 and 24 (two), by R.

927 ——— et al. (Committee on Programme). *Programme Twelfth Annual Mounted Games, Squadron "A."* Roy Press, (N.Y.), March 2, 1902, colored pic. wraps tied with silk cord, 64 pp., numerous illus. including one, p. 36, by R.

928 Prentis, Noble A. *A History of Kansas.* E. P. Greer, Winfield, Kansas, 1899, decor. cloth, 379 pp., preface, appendix, illus. including one, p. 13, by R.

929 ———. Same, (edited and revised by Henrietta V. Race). Caroline Prentis, Topeka, 1909, decor. cloth, 403 pp., "Introduction" by Caroline Prentis, appendix, index, folding colored map, illus. including one, p. 18, by R.

930 (Price.) *The Vincent Price Treasury of American Art.* Country Beautiful Corporation, Waukesha, Wisconsin, (1972), cloth, tan endsheets, 320 pp., foreword, biographical index, glossary, numerous illus. including two, pp. 196 and 197 (in color), by R. (Hurd, Russell, Schreyvogel, Wyeth)

931 Quaife, Milo M., ed. *The Journals of Captain Meriwether Lewis and Sergeant John Ordway.* State Historical Society of Wisconsin, Madison, 1965, cover illus. by R., 444 pp.

932 Quebbeman, Frances A. *Medicine in Territorial Arizona.* Arizona Historical Foundation, Phoenix, 1966, cloth and boards, 424 pp., illus. including one, p. 3, by R.

933 Rachlis, Eugene. *Indians on the Plains.* American Heritage Pub. Co., N.Y., (1960), colored pic. cloth, pic. endsheets, 132 (1) pp., "Foreword" by John C. Ewers (consultant), acknowledgments, picture credits, bibliography, index, numerous illus. including three, front endsheet and pp. 52 and 92, by R. (Johnson Leigh, Schreyvogel)

934 Ralph, Julian. *On Canada's Frontier.* Harper, N.Y., 1892, decor. cloth, 325 pp., preface, numerous illus. including sixty-three by R. Issued in London the same year in a half-calf binding.

935 ———. *Our Great West.* Harper, N.Y., 1893, decor. cloth, 477 (1) pp., preface, maps, illus. including four, frontis. and pp. 75, 85 and 91, by R.

936 ———. *Dixie, or Southern Scenes and Sketches.* Harper, N.Y., 1896, decor. cloth, 411 (1) pp., author's note, illus. including ten, pp. 301, 305, 309, 313, 317, 321, 325, 327, 331 and 335, by R.

937 Ramsey, L. G. D., ed. *The Complete Encyclopedia of Antiques.* Hawthorn Books, N.Y. (but printed in Great Britain, 1962), words "First Ediiton 1962" on copyright page, cloth, 1472 pp., blue top, introduction, index, numerous illus. including one, p. 663, by R. (Russell)

938 Rathbone, Perry T. *Westward the Way*. City Art Museum of St. Louis, (Von Hoffmann Press, St. Louis, 1954), pic. cloth, introduction, acknowledgment, catalogue, biographies of the artists, 225 illus. including one, p. 126, by R.

939 Raymond, Dora Neill. *Captain Lee Hall of Texas*. Univ. of Okla. Press, Norman, 1940, words "First Edition" on copyright page, decor. cloth, 350 pp., tinted top, preface, index, seventeen full-page plates including four, facing pp. 150, 234, 290 and 322, by R., line drawings by Louis Linedean, maps.

939a *Readers' Digest Illustrated Guide to the Treasures of America*. The Readers' Digest Assn., Pleasantville, N.Y., (1974), fabricoid and decor. cloth, blue endsheets, 624 pp., index, numerous illus. including seven, pp. 62 (two), 63 (three), 408–9 and 542, by R. (Dunn, Miller, Russell)

940 Reed, Walt. *The Illustrator in America, 1900–1960's*. Reinhold, N.Y., (1966), cloth, pic. green endsheets, 271 (1) pp., "Is Illustration art" by Albert Dorne, bibliography, numerous illus. including four, pp. 32 (two, one in color) and 33 (two), by R. (Blumenschein, Crawford, Dunn, Dunton, Eggenhofer, Fischer, Fogarty, Goodwin, James, Keller, Koerner, Russell, Schoonover, Stoops, Von Schmidt, Wyeth, Zogbaum)

941 Rennert, Vincent Paul. *The Cowboy*. Crowell-Collier, N.Y., (1966), words "First Printing" on copyright page, cloth, 117 pp., "Lingo," bibliography, index, numerous illus. including nine, pp. (7), (11) two, (19), (25), (29) two, (49) and (63), by R. (Crawford)

942 ———. *Western Outlaws*. Crowell-Collier, N.Y., (1968), words "First Printing" on copyright page, pic. boards, 152 pp., introduction, bibliography, index, illustrations including one, p. (19), by R.

943 Rich, Daniel Cotton. *Half a Century of American Art*. Art Institute of Chicago, 1939, wraps, 61 pp., plus 78 plates, foreword, numerous illus. including one, plate XII, by R. (Blumenschein)

944 Rich, Lawson C. et al. *The Gridiron '82*. Beta Zeta Chapter of the Beta Theta Pi Fraternity, St. Lawrence Univ., (Ames & McIlvaine, Printers, N.Y.), (Canton, N.Y.), 1882, cloth and flexible boards, 90 pp., x of advs., numerous illus. including a page of sketches, seven in all, p. 84, and a tail piece, p. 90, by R.

945 Rich, Mabel Irene. *A Story of the Types of Literature*. Appleton-Century, N.Y., (1937), code number "(1)" follows last line of text, decor. cloth, pic. endsheets, 580 pp., preface, index, illus. including two, pp. 75 and 427, by R.

946 Richards, Irmagarde. *Our California Home*. Harr Wagner Pub. Co., S.F., (1930), pic. cloth, map endsheets, 436 pp., foreword, Little Spanish Dictionary, numerous illus. including one, p. 161, by R.

947 Risch, Erna. *Quartermaster Support of the Army, A History of the Corps, 1775–1939*. G.P.O., Washington, D.C., 1962, decor. buckram, 796 pp., "Foreword" by Major General Webster Anderson, preface, bibliographical note, index, charts, maps, numerous illus. including one, p. 482, by R.

948 Robbins, Charles L. *School History of the American People*. World Book Co., Yonkers-on-Hudson and Chicago, 1925, pic. cloth, 606 pp., "To the Teacher," acknowledgments, appendices, index, maps, numerous illus. including one, p. 401, by R. (Stoops)

949 (Robinett, Paul M. and Bortz, Abe.) *The United States Army*. G.P.O., Washington, D.C., 1963, illus. including one by R.

950 (Rockwell.) *The Norman Rockwell Album*. Doubleday, Garden City, N.Y., 1961, words "First Edition" on copyright page, full leather, green endsheets, 190 (1) pp., "Preface" by Kenneth Stuart, "Introduction" by S. Lane Faison, Jr., numerous illus. including one, p. 21, by R., boxed with one extra print. Also a trade edition in cloth.

951 Rockwell, Wilson, ed. *Memoirs of a Lawman*. Sage Books, Denver, 1962, cloth, 378 pp., preface, prologue, epilogue, thirty-six illus. including two, pp. (90) and (123), by R.

952 Rodney, George Brydges. *As a Cavalryman Remembers*. Caxton, Caldwell, Idaho, 1944, cloth, 297 pp., illus. including one, frontis., by R.

953 Roe, Frank Gilbert. *The Indian and the Horse*. Univ. of Okla. Press, Norman, 1955, words "First Edition" on copyright page, cloth, 434 pp., brown top, preface, introduction, appendices, bibliography, index, thirty-one illus. including one, between pp. 206 and 207, by R. (Leigh, Russell)

954 Roll, Charles. *Indiana, One Hundred and Fifty Years of American Development*. Lewis Pub. Co., Chicago & N.Y., 1931, pic. fabricoid, marbled endsheets, two volumes, 543 and 531 pp., all edges marbled, preface (I), index (I), illus. including one, p. (47–I), by R.

955 Rollinson, John K. *Wyoming Cattle Trails*. Caxton, Caldwell, Idaho, 1948, cloth, tinted endsheets, 366 pp., orange top, preface, appendices, bibliography, index, illus. including one, frontis. in color, by R. Numb., signed edition of 1000 copies.

956 Roosevelt, Theodore. *Ranch Life and the Hunting Trail*. Century, N.Y., (1888), tan cloth stamped in green and gold, 180 pp., all edges gilt, eighty-three illus. by R.

957 ———. Same, first British edition, T. Fisher Unwin, London, n.d. (1888), blue cloth with gilt decorations.

958 ———. Same, Century, N.Y., 1896, decor. cloth, 186 pp., ninety-four illus. by R. Reprinted in 1904 with the ninety-four illus.

959 ———. Same, Pemberton Press, Austin, 1966, pic. cloth, 186 (1) pp., "Roosevelt and the West" by J. P. Bryan, Jr., a facsimile reprint of the first edition but with a Remington illus. on the cover added.

960 ———. *Ranch Life in the Far West*. Northland, Flagstaff, 1968, cloth and marbled boards, 89 pp., "Preface" by Teri Card, numerous illus. by Remington. (First book printing of the articles as they appeared in *Century Magazine*.)

961 ———. *The Wilderness Hunter*. Putnam, N.Y. and London, (1893), gilt decor. cloth lettered in brown and gold, chapter headings in brown but without brown heading over the list of "Full-Page Illustrations," with a printed slip preceding the frontis. announcing a limited edition of 200 copies to be published "in the early autumn," 472 pp., preface, appendix, index, twenty-four full-page illus. including one, facing p. 242, by R.

962 ———. *Big Game Hunting in the Rockies and on the Great Plains*. Putnam, N.Y. and London, 1899, full tan buckram with morocco labels, pp. 323 and 476, gilt top and other edges uncut, foreword, addendum, indexes, fifty-five illus. including one, facing second p. 242, by R. Numb. and signed edition of 1000 copies.

963 ———. *The Rough Riders*. Scribner's, N.Y., 1899, decor. cloth, 298 pp., gilt top, appendices, numerous illus. including one, facing p. 132, by R. The presentation of the Remington bronze, "The Bronchobuster," by the regiment described, p. 226.

964 ———. *The Winning of the West*. Collier, N.Y., (1903), cloth, 4 vols., 380, 398, 407 and 493 pp., frontis. in each vol. by R. Executive Edition, *The Works of Theodore Roosevelt*, vols. 5, 6, 7 and 8, believed to be the first printing with Remington frontis.

965 ———. Same, Review of Reviews Co., N.Y., 1904, decor. cloth, Statesman Edition.

966 ———. Same, Premier Americana, Greenwich, Conn.,

(1964), colored pic. wraps, 320 pp., "Editor's Introduction" by Christopher Lasch, appendix, index, cover illus., in color, by R.

967 ———. *Good Hunting*. Harper, N.Y. and London, 1907, words "Published February, 1907" on copyright page, decor. cloth, with illus. in color mounted on front cover, 106 (1) pp., publisher's note, sixteen full-page plates, including five, frontis. and facing pp. 54, 96, 100 and 102, by R.

968 ———. *Stories of the Great West*. Century, N.Y., (1909), decor. cloth, 254 (1) pp., publisher's note, thirteen full-page plates and a tail piece by R.

969 Rorabacher, J. Albert. *The American Buffalo in Transition*. North Star Press, Saint Cloud, Minn., (1970), decor. fabricoid, pic. endsheets, 141 (5) pp., preface, appendices, bibliography, index, maps, numerous illus. including two, pp. (36) and 46, by R. (Miller, Russell)

970 Rossi, Paul A. (Director). *Run the Buffalo* (A Story of the Hide Hunters). Gilcrease Institute, Tulsa, Okla., 1969, colored pic. wraps, (20) pp., numerous illus. including one, photo of the bronze "The Buffalo Horse," by R. (Russell, Zogbaum)

971 ——— and Hunt, David C. *The Art of the Old West* (from the collection of the Gilcrease Institute — Knopf, N.Y., but printed in Italy, 1971), words "First Edition" on copyright page, pic. cloth, pic. brown endsheets, 335 (1) pp., preface, listing of artists and works, bibliography, numerous illus. including twenty-two, five in color, by R. (Blumenschein, Borein, James, Leigh, Miller, Russell, Schreyvogel, Wyeth)

972 Rugg, Harold. *A History of American Government and Culture*. Ginn & Co., Boston etc., (1931), decor. cloth, 635 pp., preface, appendix, index, maps, numerous illus. including one, p. 437, by R.

973 Rugoff, Milton, ed. et al. *The Britannica Encyclopedia of American Art*. N.Y. (but printed in Italy, 1973), cloth, 669 pp., bibliographies, numerous illus. including two in color, p. 469, by R. (Young)

974 Rush, N. Orwin. *Frederic Remington and Owen Wister*. Privately printed, Tallahassee, Florida, 1961, pic. wraps, 36 mimeographed pages, preface, several drawings by R.

975 Rush, Richard H. *Art as an Investment*. Prentice-Hall, Englewood Cliffs, N.J., (1961), decor. cloth, 418 pp., preface, index, numerous illus. including one, p. 205, by R.

976 Russell, Don, ed. *The Westerners Brand Book* (vol IX). The Westerners, Chicago, 1953, decor. cloth, 96 pp., index, illus. including one, p. 51, by R. Remington in text.

977———. *The Wild West* (A History of the Wild West Shows). (Amon Carter Museum, Fort Worth, 1970), three-tone pic. cloth, 150 (1) pp., "Introduction" by Director Mitchell A. Wilder, bibliography, index, numerous illus. including one in color, p. 49, by R.

978 Russell, Osborne. *Journal of a Trapper*. Oregon Historical Society, (Champoeg Press, Portland), 1955, decor. cloth, 179 (12) pp., "Editor's Preface," "Acknowledgments" and "Introduction" Notes" by Aubrey L. Haines (editor), preface notes, sources, index, maps, frontis. by R. Edition of 750 copies.

979 ———. Same, University of Nebraska Press, Lincoln, (1965), colored pic. wraps, 191 (11) pp., "Editor's Preface" by Aubrey L. Haines, acknowledgments, introduction, notes, sources, index, maps, illus. including one, the frontis., by R. Bison Book 316, a reprint of no. 978 with a front wrap illus. by Russell. (Russell)

980 Russell, R. H. (arranged by). *Star Gambol of the Lambs, May 1898*. R. H. Russell, N.Y., 1898, decor. wraps, (12) pp., illus. including one, "Elevating the Stage," by Lamb R.

981 Sandoz, Mari. *The Buffalo Hunters*. Hastings House, N.Y., (1954), cloth, map endsheets, 372 pp., foreword, bibliography, ten illus. including one, facing p. 181, by R.

982 Savelle, Max. *A Short History of American Civilization*. Dryden Press, (N.Y., 1957), cloth, tan endsheets, 665 pp., green top, preface, acknowledgments, appendix, index, numerous illus. including two, pp. 421 and 491, by R., maps.

983 Schmitt, Martin F. and Brown, Dee. *Fighting Indians of the West*. Scribner's, N.Y., 1948, code letter "A" on copyright page, pic. cloth, map endsheets, 362 pp., preface, introduction, bibliography, 270 illus. including eight, pp. (106), 108, 109, 191, 196, 198, 224 and 271, by R. (Dixon, Schreyvogel)

984 ———, eds. *The Cattle Drives of David Shirk*. Champoeg Press, (Portland, Oregon), 1956, decor. cloth, 148 pp., introduction, foreword, illus. with a frontis. by R. and a portrait of Shirk. Edition of 750 copies, printed by Lawton Kennedy.

985 Schomackers, Gunter. *Der Wilde Westen*. L. B. Ahnert — Verlag, West Germany, n.d., cloth, map endsheets, 217 (7) pp., *ein wort zuvor*, numerous illus. including twenty-eight, ten in color, by R. (Miller, Russell, Schreyvogel)

986 Scull, Penrose with Prescott C. Fuller. *From Peddlers to Merchant Princes*. Follett Pub. Co., Chicago, N.Y., 1967, words "First Printing" on copyright page, cloth, grey endsheets, 274 pp., "Foreword" by Robert E. Palmer, bibliography, index, numerous illus. including two, pp. 72 and 73, by R.

987 Seely, Howard. *The Jonah of Lucky Valley*. Harper, N.Y., April, 1892, blue wraps, 235 pp., (4) of advs., preface, thirteen illus. by R. Harper's Franklin Square Library no. 719, no. 719 is the last novel included in the list inside the front wrap.

988 Sell, Henry Blackman and Weybright, Victor. *Buffalo Bill and the Wild West*. Oxford University Press, N.Y., 1955, cloth and pic. boards, pic. endsheets, 278 pp., acknowledgments, bibliography, index, numerous illus. including two, pp. 65 and 241, by R. (Russell, Schreyvogel)

989 ———. Same, New American Library, (N.Y., 1959), words "First Printing, March, 1959" on copyright page, colored pic. wraps, 320 pp., all edges red, acknowledgments, bibliography, index, numerous illus. including two, pp. 83 and 279, by R. (Russell, Schreyvogel)

990 Serven, James E., ed. *Colt Dragoon Pistols*. Carl Metzer, Dallas, Texas, 1946, pic. wraps, 55 (1) pp., numerous illus. including two, front cover and p. 4, by R.

991 ———. *Colt Percussion Pistols*. Carl Metzer (Foundation Press, Santa Ana, Calif.), Dallas, Texas, 1947, pic. wraps, 59 (1) pp., numerous illus. including one, p. 3, by R.

992 ———. *Colt Firearms, 1836–1954*. Privately printed by the author, Santa Ana, Calif., 1954, fabricoid, green endsheets, 385 pp., acknowledgments, preface, indices, numerous illus. including three, pp. 36, 38 and 100, by R.

993 ———. *The Collecting of Guns*. Stackpole, Harrisburg, Pa., (1964), words "First Edition" on copyright page, pic. cloth, 272 pp., bibliography, numerous illus. including one, p. (46), by R.

994 ———. *Guns on the Arizona Frontier*. Arizona Pioneers' Historical Society, Tucson, Arizona, 1965, pic. wraps, 20 pp., "Introduction" by Sidney B. Brinckehoff, bibliography, illus. including three, pp. 17, 18 and 20, by R. Museum Monograph no. 2.

995 Severy, Merle, ed. et al. *America's Historylands*. National Geographic Society, (Lakeside Press, Chicago), Washington, D.C., (1962), words "First Printing" on copyright page, two-tone decor. cloth, pic. front endsheet, 576 pp., "Foreword" by Melville Bell Grosvenor, "Introduction" by Conrad L. Wirth, index for reference, 676 (463 in full color) illus. including four, pp. 359 (color), 489, 494-5 (color) and 514-5 (color), by R. (Leigh, Russell, Schreyvogel)

995a Seymour, Peter, ed. *The West That Was*. Hallmark Crown Editions, (Kansas City, Mo., 1973), fabricoid, 76 (1) pp., introduction, numerous illus. including seven, pp. (3), 29 (color), 34, 36 (color), 40–1 (color), 42–3 and 58–9, by R. (Leigh, Russell, Wyeth)

996 Shapiro, Irving. (adapted by). *The Golden Book of America*. Simon and Schuster, N.Y., 1957, words "First Printing" on copyright page, cloth and pic. boards, pic. endsheets, 216 pp., blue top, acknowledgments, "Foreword" by Bruce Catton, index, numerous illus. including six, pp. 92 (three), 93 (two) and 152-3, by R. (Russell, Schreyvogel)

997 ———. *America on Parade*. Guild Press, Poughkeepsie and N.Y., (1958), pic. boards, pic. endsheets, 92 (1) pp., "Foreword" by Bruce Catton, acknowledgments, numerous illus. including five, pp. (52, three) and 53 (two), by R. Item no. 996 adapted for young readers. (Russell)

998 Sharkey, Don et al. *America Today*. Sadlier, N.Y., Chicago, (1964), colored pic. cloth, 312 pp., introduction, appendix, index, maps, numerous illus. including one, p. (277), by R.

999 Shaw, Albert. *A Cartoon History of Roosevelt's Career*. Review of Reviews Co., N.Y., (1910), cloth, 253 pp., numerous illus. including two, p. (17), by R.

1000 Sheldon, George Wm. *Recent Ideals of American Art*. Appleton, N.Y., 1888, ¾ red morocco, 8 vols., 184 illus. including one, "Return of a Blackfoot War Party," by R. Edition of 500 numbered sets. A trade edition with 175 illus. was issued the same year.

1001 Shuffler, R. Henderson (Executive Director). *The Mexican Texans*. (Prepared by the staff), University of Texas, Institute of Texan Culture at San Antonio, (1971), pic. wraps, 32 pp., numerous illus. including one, p. 26, by R. (Lea)

1002 ———. *Los Mexicano Texanos*. University of Texas, Institute of Texan Cultures, (1971), pic. wraps, 32 pp., introduction, numerous illus. including one, p. 26, by R. (Cisneros, Lea)

1003 ———. *The Spanish Texans*. University of Texas, Institute of Texan Cultures, San Antonio, (1972), pic. wraps, 32 pp., numerous illus. including one, p. 15, by R. (Bugbee, Cisneros, Lea, Mead)

1004 ———. *The Italian Texans*. University of Texas, Institute of Texan Cultures, San Antonio, (1973), pic. wraps, 32 pp., numerous illus. including one, p. 3, by R. (Cisneros)

1005 Silber, Irwin (compiled and edited by). *Songs of the Great American West*. MacMillan, N.Y., (1967), words "First Printing" on copyright page, two-tone pic. cloth, tan endsheets, 334 pp., tan top, music annotated, edited and arranged by Earl Robinson, introduction, bibliography, discography, indices, numerous illustrations including front cover and nineteen in text by R. (De Yong, Eggenhofer, Russell)

1006 Silverman, Jerry. *Beginning the Folk Guitar*. Oak Publications, N.Y., (1964), pic. wraps, 96 pp., introduction, numerous illus. including nine, title page and pp. 7, 13, 15, 31, 45, 50, 68 and 78, by R.

1007 Singmaster, Elsie. *The Book of the United States*. Doran, N.Y., (1926), publisher's device on copyright page, cloth with illus. mounted on front cover, pic. endsheets, fifteen illus. including one, facing p. 257, by R.

1008 Sivell, Rhoda. *Voices from the Range*. T. Eaton Co., Toronto and Winnipeg, (1911), stiff wraps, with illus. mounted on front cover, decor. endsheets, 43 pp., six illus. including two, front cover and frontis. (same), by R. (Russell)

1009 ———. Same, T. Eaton Co,. Toronto and Winnipeg, (1911), pic. wraps, (or gilt on brown pic. cloth), 101 pp., six illus. including two, front cover and frontis. (same), by R. An expanded edition of no. 1008. An edition with 89 pp. is reported. (Russell)

1010 ———. Same, William Briggs, Toronto, 1912, pic. cloth, 102 pp., six illus. including two, front cover and frontis. (same), by R. A recent facsimile reprint, but not of any of the three editions described above, is reported. (Russell)

1011 Skinner, Constance Lindsay. *Adventurers of Oregon*. Yale, New Haven, (1920), decor. cloth, 290 pp., bibliographical note, index, frontis. by R. Text book edition, The Chronicles of America Series, vol. 22.

1012 Small, Joe Austell, ed. *The Best of the True West*. Messner, N.Y., (1964), words "First Edition" on copyright page, pic. cloth, 317 pp., foreword, illus. including one, p. 148, by R., and with the d/w illus. by R.

1013 Smith, F. Hopkinson, *American Illustrators*. Scribner's, N.Y., 1892, five parts, each in separate wraps, inserted in a decor. board folder with cloth back, 68 pp. plus 15 plates, including one "A Russian Cossack" in color, by R. Photo of Remington, p. 22, comments on his art, pp. 22-25 and one drawing, p. 23, by R. (Zogbaum)

1014 ———— et al. *The Year's Art*. Harry C. Jones, N.Y., 1893, decor. cloth, 328 pp., 678 illus. (by 302 artists) including fifteen by R.

1015 ———— et al. *Discussions on American Art and Artists*. American Art League, Boston etc., n.d., full cushioned leather, oblong quarto, 1100 illus. including two, pp. 178 and 181, by R. Photo of Remington, p. 250.

1016 Smith, Waddell F. *The Story of the Pony Express*. Hesperian House, S. F., (1960), words "Second Edition" on copyright page, decor. cloth, map endsheets, 195 pp., "Foreword" by A. R. Mortensen, "Historical Note" by Arthur E. Summerfield, introduction, "Heroic Effort-Tragic End" by Raymond W. Settle, bibliography, index, numerous illus. including one, facing p. 128, after R. While the brief Bradley account is reprinted, there is so much new material that to call this a "Second Edition" seems over-modest.

1017 Smithers, W. D. et al. *United States Cavalry*. Patton Museum of Cavalry and Armor, Fort Knox, Ky., (1966), colored pic. wraps, 52 pp., "Preface" by Colonel Edward M. Majors, numerous illus. including one, p. 22, by R. (Schreyvogel)

1018 Soby, James Thrall and Miller, Dorothy C. *Romantic Painting in America*. Museum of Modern Art, N.Y., (1943), cloth, 143 (1) pp., foreword and acknowledgment, "Preface" by Alfred H. Barr, Jr., index to plates, numerous illus. including one, p. 76, by R. Short Remington biography pp. 140-1.

1019 Spaeth, Eloise. *American Art Museums and Galleries*. Harper, N.Y., (1960), two-tone cloth, 282 pp., foreword, acknowledgments, bibliography, index, numerous illus. including one, p. (185), by R.

1020 Sprague, Marshall et al. *The Mountain States*. Life-Time Books, N.Y., (1967), colored pic. boards, map endsheets, 192 pp., "Introduction" by A. B. Guthrie, Jr., bibliography, index, maps, charts, numerous (many in color) illus. including one, p. 99, by R. (Russell)

1021 Spofford, A. R., ed. *The Library of Historic Events and Famous Events*. William Finley & Co., Phila.,

1896, leather, 10 vols., numerous illus. including one by R. Memorial Edition, numb. and signed.

1022 Squires, Henry C. *Catalogue of Sportmen's Supplies*. (Knickerbocker Press), N.Y., 1891, full leather, marbled endsheets, 204 pp., gilt top, preface, index, numerous illus. including five, pp. 5, 7, 38, 39 and 47, by R.

1023 Stammel, H. J. *Der Cowboy, Legende und Wirklichkeit von A-Z*. Bertlesmann Lexikon, West Germany, (1972), cloth, 416 pp., *vorwort*, numerous illus. incuding twenty-nine in color by R. plus d/w in color and Western-poster in color on four-fold d/w by him. (Russell)

1024 Stanley, Henry M. *Slavery and the Slave Trade in Africa*. Harper, N.Y., 1893, white cloth decor. and lettered in black, 86 pp., six illus., frontis. and facing pp. 28, 40, 50, 62 and 74, by R. Harper's "Black and White Series."

1025 Starbuck, Edwin Diller et al. *The High Trail*. World Book Co., Yonkers-on-Hudson, N.Y., (1936), decor. cloth, 340 pp., preface, "Biography and Life," "More Biography," glossary, illus. including one, p. (102), by R.

1026 Steadman, William E. et al. *The West and Walter Bimson*. The University of Arizona Museum of Art, Tucson, (1971), decor. cloth, pic. endsheets, 223 (2) pp., "Foreword" by President Richard A. Harvill, introduction, numerous illus. including fourteen, pp. 129 (color), 130 (color), 131 (six), 132 (color), 133 (color), 134, 135, 136 and 137, by R. (Beeler, Leigh, Russell, Schoonover, Wyeth)

1027 Steedman, Amy. *Boys and Girls Who Became Famous*. University Society, N.Y., (1955), fabricoid with illus. in color mounted on front cover, pic. endsheets, 401 pp., red top, introduction, general index, numerous illus. including one, p. 363, by R. The Bookshelf for Boys and Girls, vol. IX.

1028 Stevens, Montague. *Meet Mr. Grizzly*. Univ. of New Mexico Press, Albuquerque, 1943, cloth, 281 pp., preface, illus. including one, frontis., by R. Remington was a member of the General Miles party on a hunt with the author in 1893.

1029 ———— . Same, Robert Hale, (London, 1950), cloth, 286 pp., preface, twenty-one illus. including one, the frontis., by R. The first British edition of no. 1028.

1030 Stewart, John. *Frederic Remington, Artist of the Western Frontier*. Lothrop, N.Y., (1971), cloth, 128 pp., selected bibliography, index, map, twelve illus. by R. and photos of him.

COWBOY FUN by Remington from *Ranch Life and The Hunting Trail*

1031 Still, Bayrd, ed. *The West*. Capricorn Books, N.Y., (1961), decor. wraps, 279 (1) pp., introduction, acknowledgments, note on sources, six illus. including one, p. 132, by R., maps. Illus. at pp. 183 and 257 reversed .

1032 Stong, Phil. *Horses and Americans*. Stokes, N.Y., 1939, two-tone cloth, pic. endsheets, 333 pp., gilt top, acknowledgments, foreword, bibliography, index, numerous illus. including eight, facing pp. 12, 88, 185 (two) and 221 (four), by R. Author's Edition of 500 numb. signed copies, boxed. Also a trade edition in tan cloth with a title label mounted on front cover and brown top.

1033 Sullivan, Mark. *Our Times: The Turn of the Century, 1909–1914*. Scribner's, N.Y., London, 1932, code letter "A" on copyright page, cloth, 629 pp., index, numerous illus. including one, p. 522, by R.

1034 ———. *Our Times: The War Begins, 1909–1914*. Scribner's, N.Y., London, 1932, code letter "A" on copyright page, cloth, 629 pp., index, numerous illus. including one, p. 522, by R.

1035 ——— Items no. 1033 and 1034 became part of a six volume limited, signed edition of *Our Times*, issued in 1935.

1036 Summerhayes, Martha. *Vanished Arizona*. Salem, Press Co., Salem, Mass., (1911), words "Second Edition" on title page, cloth, 319 pp., preface, appendix, illus. including two small darwings, pp. 290 and 293, by R. A photo of Remington and Jack Summerhayes facing p. 288. Several letters from Remington quoted in full and much on him in text, Chapter 32. The first edition (1908) and the Lakeside Classic reprinted from it in 1939 barely mention Remington.

1037 Taft, Robert. *Photography and the American Scene*. Macmillan, N.Y., 1938, words "First Printing" on copyright page, cloth, 546 pp., introduction, appendix, bibliography and notes, index, numerous illus. including one, p. 415, by R. Remington in text, pp. 410 and 510.

1038 ———. *Remington in Kansas* (part V of The Pictorial Record of the Old West). Reprinted from *The Kansas Historical Quarterly*, Topeka, May, 1948, pic. wraps, (23) pp., six illus. by R., an 1883 photo of Remington.

1039 ———. *Artists and Illustrators of the Old West*. Scribner's, N.Y., 1953, code letter "A" on copyright page, cloth, map endsheets, 400 pp., preface and acknowledgments, sources and notes, index, 90 numb. illus. including three, nos. 73, 74 and 75, by R. (Blumenschein, Leigh, Schreyvogel)

1040 Tappan, Eva March. *Our Country's Story*. Houghton Mifflin, Boston etc., 1902, pic. cloth, advs. on back endsheet, 254 pp., preface, numerous illus. including four, pp. 36, 78, 115 and 185, by R. (Reissued with index, same Remington illus., 267 pp.)

1041 ———. *An Elementary History of Our Country*. A reissue of no. 1040 with a new title and the index, same Remington illus.

1042 ——— (selected and arranged by). *Adventurers and Achievements*. Houghton Mifflin, (Boston), 1907, cloth with paper label, 454 (1) pp., note, "To the Children," thirteen illus. including one, facing p. 16, by R. Vol. VIII of The Children's Hour, edition of 1000 numb. copies.

1043 ———. Same, trade edition in decor. red cloth, (Boston, 1907), same illus. by R.

1044 Taylor, J. Golden, ed. *Great Western Short Stories*. American West, Palo Alto, 1967, cloth, green endsheets, 572 pp., gilt top, editor's preface, "History, Myth, and the Western Writer" by Wallace Stegner, notes on authors and artists, nine illus. including five, pp. 69, 191, 225, 301 and 421, by R. Slipcase. (Russell)

1045 Tebbel, John and Jennison, Keith. *The American Indian Wars*. Harper, N.Y., (1960), cloth, map endsheets, 312 pp., bibliographical notes, index, numerous illus. including three, pp. 86, 285 and 292, by R. (Schreyvogel)

1046 Terrell, John Upton. *Traders of the Western Morning: Aboriginal Commerce in Precolumbian North America*. Southwest Museum, Los Angeles, 1967, wraps, frontis. by R.

1047 Thoburn, Joseph B. and Holcomb, Isaac M. *A History of Oklahoma*. Doud and Co., S. F., 1908, decor. cloth, 266 xiii pp., prefatory, acknowledgment, appendix, index, illus. including one, p. 14, after R.

1048 Thomas, Augustus. *Arizona*. R. H. Russell, N.Y., 1899, pic. cloth, 155 pp., illus. including one, front cover, by R.

1049 ———. *Souvenir of the 100th Performance of "Arizona" at the Grand Canyon Opera House, Chicago, Tuesday, Sept. 5, '99*. Blue boards with illus. by R.

1050 ———. *The Print of My Remembrance*. Scribner's, N.Y., London, 1922, cloth, 477 pp., appendix, index, illus. including three small drawings, facing pp. 326 and 424, by R. A caricature of Remington by Thomas, facing p. 326, and much on Remintgon in text.

1051 ——— et al. *Souvenir Book, The Lambs All Star*

Gambol, 1916. (N.Y., 1916), colored pic. wraps, (36) pp., numerous illus. including one by Lamb R. A Remington story by Thomas.

1052 Throop, George E. et al (Programme Committee). *Squadron "A" Games, Souvenir Programme, Feb. 18th, 1897.* (Richard K. Fox Press, N.Y.), colored pic. wraps, 39 (1) pp., numerous illus. including eight by R.

1053 Tibbles, Thomas Henry. *Buckskin and Blanket Days.* Doubleday, Garden City, N.Y., 1957, words "First Edition" on copyright page, colored pic. wraps, publisher's preface, front cover illus. by R. A pamphlet containing the first 32 pages of the book to be released Aug. 22, 1957.

1054 ———. Same, Bantam Books, N.Y., (1961), colored pic. wraps, 240 pp., (3) of advs., publisher's preface, front cover illus. by R.

1055 Tilford, Til et al. *King of the Plains.* Harper, N.Y. and London, 1910, words "Published October 1910" on copyright page, pic. cloth, 187 (1) pp., illus. including one, front cover, after R.

1056 Tinkle, Lon and Maxwell, Allen, eds. *The Cowboy Reader.* Longmans, Green, N.Y. etc., 1959, words "First Edition" on copyright page, cloth, 307 pp., editor's introduction, twenty-three illus. including three, p. 113, by R. (Bugbee, Lea, Russell)

1057 Todd, Col. Frederick (editor-in-chief). *Military Collector and Historian,* vol. VI, Spring, 1955. Company of Military Collectors and Historians, N.Y., pic. wraps, 30 (2) pp., numerous illus. including one, p. 16, by R.

1058 Todd, Lewis Paul et al. *Rise of the American Nation.* Harcourt Brace, N.Y., Burlingame, (1961), pic. cloth, 880 pp., index, maps in color, numerous illus. including one, p. 336, by R. (Miller)

1059 Twitchell, Ralph Emerson. *The Military Occupation of New Mexico, 1846–1851.* Smith-Brooks, Co., Denver, 1909, cloth with illus. in color mounted on front cover, 394 pp., introduction, numerous illus. including two, pp. (22) and (25), by R.

1060 ———. *The Conquest of Santa Fe.* Historical Society of New Mexico, (Santa Fe), n.d. (1923?), pic. wraps, 63 pp., illus. including one, p. 9, by R. Publication no. 24 of the Society.

1061 Underhill, Ruth M. *Red Man's Religion: Beliefs and Practices of the Indians North of Mexico.* Univ. of Chicago Press, 1965, cloth, 301 pp., illus. including two, following p. 132, by R.

1062 U.S. Information Service. *An Outline of American History.* (G.P.O., Washington, D.C., 1952), colored pic. boards, 148 pp., bibliography, numerous illus. including one, "Attack on Supply Train," facing p. 96, by R.

1063 *Grundiss der Geschichte der Vereinigten Staaten von Amerika.* (Bad Godesberg, West Germany, 1954), cloth and pic. boards, 159 (1) pp., *literaturverzeichnis,* numerous illus. including one in color, facing p. 64, by R. (German edition of no. 1062.)

1064 Utley, Robert M. *Fort Union National Monument.* National Park Service, Washington, D.C., 1962, colored pic. wraps, appendices, numerous illus. including five, title page and pp. 6, 44, 49 and back cover, by R. (Schreyvogel)

1065 ———. *Fort Davis National Historic Site.* (Handbook Series no. 38). National Park Service, Washington, D.C., 1965, decor. wraps, ten illus., pp. 8, (9), 19 (two), 22, (23 two), 29, 36 and 59, by R. (Zogbaum)

1066 ———. *Frontiersmen in Blue, 1848–1865.* Macmillan, N.Y., (1967), with words "First Printing" on copyright page, cloth, map endsheets, 384 pp., blue top, introduction, bibliography, index, maps, illus. including two, between pp. 176 and 177, by R. (Eggenhofer)

1066a ———. *Frontier Regulars, The United States Army and the Indian, 1866–1891.* Macmillan, N.Y., London, (1973), words "First Printing 1973" on copyright page, cloth, blue endsheets, 462 pp., introduction, bibliography, index, maps, illus. including eight, title page, six between pp. (142) and 143 and one between pp. 270 and 271, by R. (Russell, Schreyvogel)

1067 Van Brunt, Mrs. John (Chairman) et al. *The Story of a Great Highway.* Santa Fe Trail Committee, Kansas City Chapter, Daughters of the American Revolution, (Kansas City, n.d.), pic. wraps, 8 pp., two folding maps, three illus. including one, "Bicknell's Expedition Starting from Old Franklin in 1820," by R. The cover title is *The Old Santa Fe Trail.*

1068 Vanderbilt, Cornelius, Jr. *Ranches and Ranch Life in America.* Crown, N.Y., 1968, cloth, green endsheets, 280 pp., picture credit abbreviations, bibliography, numerous illus. including four, pp. 2, (7), 19 and 23, by R.

1069 Van Doren, Carl and Carmer, Carl. *American Scriptures.* Boni & Gaer, N.Y., 1946, cloth, 302 pp., blue top, foreword, 48 illus. including two, pp. 261 and 263, by R.

1070 Van Osdel, A. L. *Historic Landmarks in the Great Northwest.* Privately printed, (E. B. McIntyre, Book Binder, Yankton, S.D.), n.d. (1912?), pic. cloth, introduction, illus. including one, front cover, by R.

1071 Vaughan, John H. *History and Government of New Mexico.* Published by the author, (L. H. Jenkins, Richmond, Va.), State College, N.M., 1921, decor. cloth, 369 pp., (4) of advs., preface, index, illus. including four, pp. 102, 134, 177 and 181, by R.

1072 ———. Same, slightly enlarged edition of no. 1071 with 377 pages and same illus. by R.

1073 Vaughn, J. W. *The Reynolds Campaign on Powder River.* Univ. of Okla. Press, Norman, (1961), words "First Edition" on copyright page, cloth, 239 pp., introduction, appendices, bibliography, index, map, seventeen illus. including one, facing p. 144, by R. (Schreyvogel)

1074 ———. *The Battle of Platte Bridge.* Oklahoma, Norman, (1963), words "First edition" on copyright page, cloth, 132 pp., preface, bibliography, index, maps, seventeen illus. including one, facing p. 86, by R.

1075 Vorpahl, Ben Merchant. *My Dear Wister — The Frederic Remington - Owen Wister Letters.* American West, Palo Alto, (1972), cloth, tan sheets, 343 pp., "Foreword" by Wallace Stegner, introduction, notes, index, numerous illus. by R.

1076 Wade, Mason. *Francis Parkman, Heroic Historian.* Viking Press, N.Y., 1942, words "First Published in November 1942" on copyright page, cloth, map endsheets, 466 pp., blue top, preface, bibliographical note, index, eight illus. including one, facing p. 282, by R.

1077 Wainger, Bertrand M. and Oagley, Edith Brooks. *Exploring New York State.* Harcourt, Brace, N.Y. and Chicago, 1944, decor. cloth, map on front endsheet, index, illus. including one, p. 339, by R. Remington in text, p. 340.

1078 Walker, Henry Pickering. *The Wagonmasters.* Oklahoma, Norman, (1966), words "First edition" on copyright page, cloth, 347 pp., orange top, bibliography, index, 3 maps, 25 illus. including one, following p. 244, by R. (Russell)

1079 Wallace, Andrew. *The Image of Arizona, Pictures from the Past.* New Mexico, Albuquerque, (1971), words "First Edition" on copyright page, cloth, pic. endsheets, 224 pp., introduction, bibliography, index, numerous illus. including 48 by R. (Dixon, Zogbaum)

1080 Walworth, Jennette. *History of New York in Words of One Syllable.* Belford, Clarke & Co., Chicago etc., 1888, cloth and colored pic. boards, 186 pp., introduction, numerous illus. including one, p. 110, by R. (Deming)

1081 Ward, Mrs. A. B. et al. *The Luck of a Good for Nothing and other Turf Stories.* Outing Pub. Co., N.Y., (1895), wraps, 168 pp., illus. including five, pp. (76), 81, 83, 84 and (87), by R. Outing Library, vol. 1, no. 1, issued quarterly.

1082 ———. *The Luck of a Good-for-Nothing and Other Stories.* Outing Pub. Co., N.Y., (1895), cloth, 158 and 189 pp., (3) of advs., illus. including five, pp. (76), (81), 83, 84 and (87), by R. Nos. 1 and 2 of vol. 1 of Outing Library bound together with a cover title of *Short Stories from Outing.*

1083 Ward, Baldwin G., ed. *Year's Pictorial History of America.* (Year, Inc., L.A., 1954), cloth and boards, 415 (17) pp., "Foreword" by Allan Nevins, publisher's note, index, 2500 illus. including five, pp. 10, 15, 253, 254 and 273, by R. Fifty-five historical maps in color. (Leigh, Marchand, Russell)

1084 Ward, Don. *Cowboys and Cattle Country.* Heritage Pub. Co., N.Y., (1961), words "First Edition" on copyright page, colored pic. cloth, pic. endsheets, 153 pp., "Foreword" by Jeff C. Dykes (consultant), picture credits, index, numerous illus. including ten, pp. (42–43), 64–65, (78), (84–85), 96–97, (114 three), (115) and (120 one), by R. (Russell)

1085 Wardman, Ervin et al. (Programme Committee). *Squadron "A" Games, Souvenir Programme, 1898.* (Gilliss Bros., N.Y.), March 1, 1898, colored pic. wraps, pages unnumb., numerous illus. including one by R.

1086 Ware, Captain Eugene F. *The Indian War of 1864.* Univ. of Neb. Press, Lincoln, (1960), pic. wraps, 483 pp., "Introduction" (and notes) by Clyde C. Walton, appendices, abbreviated titles cited, notes, index, cover illus. by R. Bison Books edition.

1087 Warner, Charles Dudley. *Our Italy.* Harper, N.Y., 1891, decor. two-tone cloth, 226 pp., gilt top, appendix, index, numerous illus. including two small drawings, pp. 4 and 5, by R.

1088 ———. *The American Italy.* James R. Osgood, McIlvaine & Co., London, 1892. The first British edition of no. 1087.

1089 Watson, Douglas S(loane). *West Wind.* Privately printed (Johnck & Seeger) for his friends by Percy H. Booth, Los Angeles, 1934, morocco and boards, 109 (3) pp., preface, bibliography, six illus. including three, pp. (11), (27) and (69), by R., folding map. Edition limited to 175 copies. One of the Graphic Arts' Fifty Books of the Year.

1090 Webb, Victor I. et al. *The New World, Past and Present.* Scott, Foresman and Co., Chicago etc., (1938), preface, reference tables, index, numerous illus. including one, p. 319, by R. (Russell)

1091 Weber, David J. *The Taos Trappers* (The Fur Trade in the Far Southwest, 1540–1846). Oklahoma, Norman, (1971), words "First printing 1971" on copyright page, cloth, olive endsheets, 263 pp., preface, bibliography, index, maps, illus. including three, title page and two between pp. 144 and 145, by R.

1092 Weigley, Russell F. *History of the United States Army.* Macmillan, N.Y., 1967, cloth, 688 pp., illus. including one, following p. 304, by R.

1093 Westermeier, Clifford P. *Colorado's First Portrait: Scenes by Early Artists.* New Mexico, Albuquerque, 1970, words "First Edition" on copyright page, cloth, pic. endsheets, 206 pp., preface, numerous illus. including one, p. 39, by R. (Lungren, Zogbaum)

1094 Wetmore, Helen Cody. *Last of the Great Scouts.* Duluth Press Pub. Co., Chicago and Duluth, (1899), cloth, 296 pp., "Genealogy of Buffalo Bill," preface, seventeen illus. including two, frontis. and facing p. 243, by R. In the list of illustrations the plate facing p. 266 appears above the plate facing p. 243. (Deming)

1095 ———. Same, Partington Advg. Co., London, 1903, pic. boards, 296 pp., "Genealogy of Buffalo Bill," preface, twelve illus. including three, front cover and facing pp. 170 and 243, by R. Probably first British printing of no. 1094 — sold only at the Wild West Show in Europe. (Deming)

1096 ———. Same, Grossett and Dunlap, N.Y., (1918), pic. cloth and endsheets, 333 pp., green top, "Foreword" and one additional chapter by Zane Grey, frontis. and endsheet illus. by R.

1097 ———. Same, Univ. of Neb. Press, Lincoln, (1965), pic. wraps, 296 pp., "Introduction" by Donald F. Danker, preface, illus. including one, facing p. 243, by R. Bison Books edition. (Deming)

1098 ———. *Buffalo Bill.* Verlag von Englehorn, Stuttgart, 1902, cloth with illus. in color mounted on front cover, decor. endsheets, 304 pp., twelve illus. including two, facing pp. 200 and 243, by R. First German edition of no. 1094. (Deming)

1099 Wheeler, Major-General Joseph (introduction by). *Photographic History of the War with Spain.* R. H.

Woodward Co., Baltimore, 1899, fabricoid, unpaged, numerous illus. including one, "Famous Charge of the Rough Riders at El Caney," as the frontispiece, by R. (commissioned by the publisher for a $2000 fee). Publisher's subscription dummy.

1100 White, Anne Terry. *Indians and the Old West.* Simon and Schuster, N.Y., (1958), pic. boards, 56 pp., all edges red, numerous illus. including six, pp. (36), 43, 44, 45, 46–47 and 48, by R. (Lea, Leigh, Russell, Schreyvogel)

1101 Whitney, Caspar W. *A Sporting Pilgrimage.* Harper, N.Y., 1895, decor. cloth, 397 pp., preface, numerous illus. including six, frontis. and pp. 5, 8, 11, 15 and 19, by R.

1102 ———. *On Snow-Shoes to the Barren Grounds.* Harper, N.Y., 1896, pic. cloth, 324 pp., gilt top and other edges uncut, numerous illus. including fifteen full-page plates by R.

1103 ———. Same, Osgood, McIlvaine & Co., London, 1896, decor. morocco and marbled boards with all edges mottled. First British edition of no. 1102.

1104 Whittier, John Greenleaf. *The Works of,* vol. III. Houghton Mifflin, Boston and N.Y., (1892), parchment and red silk decor. with gilt, red endsheets, gilt top, nine illus. including two, facing pp. 176 and 372, by R. Artist's edition of 750 numbered sets.

1105 ———. *The Complete Poetical Works of.* Houghton Mifflin, Boston and N.Y., (1904), decor. cloth, 656 pp., publisher's note, biographical sketch, appendix, notes, index, illus. including two, pp. 371 and 470, by R.

1106 Wilcox, Harrison, ed. *Harper's History of the War in the Philippines.* Harper, N.Y. and London, 1900, decor. cloth, 471 (1) pp., appendix, index, numerous illus. including one, facing p. 324, by R.

1107 Wilder, Howard B. et al. *This is America's Story.* Houghton Mifflin, Boston, (1958), pic. cloth, 728 pp., appendix, indices, numerous illus. including two, pp. 355 and 417, by R. (Lea)

1108 Willard, John. *Adventure Trails in Montana.* Published by the author, but sponsored by Montana Historical Society, (State Pub. Co., Helena, 1964), cloth with illus. in color mounted on front cover (or wraps), colored pic. endsheets, 243 (7) pp., "Foreword" by Michael Kennedy, "Introduction" by Harold McCracken, index, numerous illus. including one, p. (4), by R. (Miller, Russell, Von Schmidt)

1108a ———. Same, new edition, Billings, (1971), with

added illus. in color (by Russell) on the back cover.

1109 Willets, Gilson et al. *Workers of the Nation.* Collier, N.Y., 1903, cloth with paper labels, 2 vols., 1104 pp. (continuous pagination), preface, 66 illus. including one, facing p. 1006, by R. (Leigh)

1110 Wilson, Everett B. *Early America at Work.* A. S. Barnes & Co., N.Y., (1963), cloth, 188 pp., introduction, numerous illus. including nine, pp. 16 (two), 18, (19), (20), 58, 127, 128 and 130, by R.

1111 Wilson, R. L. *Theodore Roosevelt — Outdoorsman.* Winchester, (N.Y., 1971), cloth, 278 pp., "Foreword" by Archibald B. Roosevelt, introduction, credits and references, index, numerous illus. including seven, pp. 43 (two), 63, 72, 74, 118 and 122, by R.

1112 Wilson, Woodrow. *A History of the American People.* Harper, N.Y. and London, 1902, 5 vols., white linen and boards, pp. 349 (1), 368 (1), 347 (1), 343 and 337 (1), appendices, index (v), numerous illus. including one, p. 314 (i), and one, p. 86 (ii), by R. Alumni edition of 350 sets, signed.

1113 ———— Same, trade edition of no. 1112 in gilt lettered red cloth.

1114 Winfrey, Dorman H. and Day, James M., eds. *The Indian Papers of Texas and the Southwest, 1825–1916.* Pemberton Press, Austin, 1966, five volumes, includes one illus. by R.

1115 Wirth, Conrad L. (Director). *Soldier and Brave.* National Park Service and Harper & Row, N.Y. etc., 1963, words "First Edition" on copyright page, cloth, map endsheets, 279 pp., "Introduction" by Ray Billington, "Foreword" by Wirth, index, numerous illus. including one, p. (64), by R., maps.

1116 ————. Same, new edition, U.S.D.I., National Park Service, (G.P.O.), Washington, D.C., 1971, cloth, 451 pp., "Foreword" by Rogers C. B. Morton (Secretary), "Preface" by George B. Hartzog, Jr., Director, National Park Service, suggested reading, index, maps, numerous illus. including three, pp. 10, 28, and 185, by R. (Eggenhofer, Leigh, Miller, Russell, Schreyvogel)

1117 Wissler, Clark et al. *Adventures in the Wilderness.* Yale, New Haven, 1925, leather and boards, 369 pp., numerous illus. including eight, pp. 51, 52, 142, 154, 306, 320 and 328 (two), by R. The Liberty Bell edition of The Pageant of America, 1500 numb. impressions.

1118 Wister, Fanny Kemble, ed. *Owen Wister Out West.* Univ. of Chicago Press, (Chicago, 1958), cloth and boards, 269 pp., brown top, preface, introduction, epilogue, "A Wister Bibliography," illus. with photos and with ten drawings, pp. (27), (41), (62), (87), (94), (131), (148), (162), (199) and 224, by R.

1119 Wister, Owen. *Red Men and White.* Harper, N.Y., 1896, decor. cloth, 280 pp., (4) of advs., preface, seventeen illus. by R.

1120 ————. Same, Macmillan, N.Y., 1928, decor. cloth, decor. endsheets, 345 pp., blue top, "Preface: Thirty-three Years After," "The Evolution of the Cow-Puncher," frontis., "There was no Flora McIvoy" (that did not appear in no. 1119), by R. The Writings of Owen Wister, vol. 1.

1121 ————. *Lin McLean.* Harper, N.Y. and London, 1898, decor. cloth, 277 pp., (2) of advs., nine illus. including two, spine and frontis., by R.

1122 ————. Same, but issued in 1907 with a "Preface" by the author, dated Nov. 12, 1907, commenting on his "scheme on construction" and the change to "chapters" in this reprint.

1123 ————. Same, Macmillan, N.Y., 1928, decor. cloth, and endsheets, 327 pp., blue top, "Preface: Thirty Years After," frontis., "A Sagebrush Pioneer," (that did not appear in no. 1121), by R. The Writings of Owen Wister, vol. 2.

1124 ————. *The Jimmyjohn Boss.* Harper, N.Y. and London, 1900, pic. cloth, 332 (1) pp., preface (in verse), twelve illus. including five, frontis. and facing pp. 4, 94, 98 and 210, by R.

1125 ————. *A Journey in Search of Christmas.* Harper, N.Y. and London, 1904, words "Published October, 1904" on copyright page, 92 (1) pp., gilt top, three illus., frontis. and facing pp. 52 and 90, by R.

1126 ————. Same, Musson Book Co., Toronto, (1904). First Canadian edition of no. 1125.

1127 ————. *The Virginian.* Macmillan, N.Y., 1911, words "Published October, 1911" on copyright page, parchment and boards, 506 pp., gilt top and other edges uncut, re-dedication and preface, "To the Reader," numerous illus. including ten full-page plates, facing pp. 50, 110, 154, 208, 240, 290, 328, 388, 410 and 468, by R. Edition limited to 100 numb., signed copies. (Russell)

1128 ————. Same, first trade edition of no. 1127, red cloth with illus. in color mounted on front cover, with (5) pp. of advs. added. (Russell)

1129 ————. Same, Macmillan, N.Y., 1928, decor. cloth and endsheets, 392 pp., blue top, "Preface — A Best

Seller," frontis., "The Last Cavalier," (that did not appear in no. 1127, by R. The Writings of Owen Wister, vol. 4.

1130 ———. Same, Grosset & Dunlap, N.Y., n.d. (1935?), cloth with pic. labels, pic. endsheets, 506 pp., green top, numerous illus. including four, frontis. and facing pp. 90, 202 and 354, by R. (Russell, Santee)

1131 ———. Same, a Macmillan reprint in 1944 of no. 1128 with ten Remington plates inserted at the end of the text.

1132 ———. Same, a Macmillan reprint with a drawing by Russell on the spine, 1949, numerous illus. including ten, facing pp. 42, 92, 130, 176, 204, 246, 280, 332, 352 and 400, by R. (Russell)

1133 ———. Hank's Woman. Macmillan, N.Y., 1928, decor. cloth, decor. endsheets, 328 pp., blue top, "Preface — Twenty-eight Years After," frontis. by R. The Writings of Owen Wister, vol. 3.

1134 ———. Members of the Family. Macmillan, N.Y., 1928, decor. cloth, decor. endsheets, 285 pp., blue top, "Preface — Thanking you in Advance," frontis. by R. The Writings of Owen Wister, vol. 5.

1135 ———. When West Was West. Macmillan, N.Y., 1928, decor. cloth, decor. endsheets, 499 pp., "Preface — Two Debts," frontis. by R. The Writings of Owen Wister, vol. 6.

1136 Woestemeyer, Ina Faye and Gambrill, J. Montgomery. The Westward Movement. Appleton-Century, N.Y., (1939), code number "(1)" follows last line of text, pic. cloth, 500 pp., illus. including three, one between pp. 36 and 37 and two between pp. 148 and 149, by R. (Deming)

1137 Wood, Dean Earl. The Old Santa Fe Trail from the Missouri River. E. L. Mendenhall, Kansas City, (1955), decor. cloth, 278 pp., introduction, illus. in four, frontis. and pp. (14), (248) and 268, by R., maps.

1138 Wood, William and Gabriel, Ralph Henry. The Winning of Freedom. Yale, New Haven, 1927, leather and boards, 366 pp., numerous illus. including two, pp. 94 and 111, by R. The Liberty Bell edition of "The Pageant of America," 1500 numb. impressions. (Deming)

1139 Woodburn, James Albert and Moran, Thomas Francis. Introduction to American History. Longmans, Green, N.Y., Chicago, 1916, decor. cloth, 308 pp., (4) of advs., preface, index, numerous illus. including two, pp. 107 and 247, by R., maps.

1140 Woodstrike, Frank H. Great Adventure. World Pub. Co., N.Y., (1937), fabricoid, 319 pp., "Introduction" by Jay Roderic de Spain, numerous illus. including two, pp. 281 and 285, by R. (Russell)

1141 Wright, Muriel H. The Story of Oklahoma. Webb Publishing Co., Oklahoma City, 1929, cloth, 342 pp., illus. including one, p. 52, by R.

1142 Wyer, Malcolm G. Western Historic Collection. Denver Public Library, June, 1950, wraps, (20) pp., four illus. including one by R. (Russell)

1143 Wyman, Walker D. and Ridge, Martin. The American Adventure. Lyons & Carnahan, Chicago etc., (1964), pic. cloth, 622 (1) pp., "To the Student" appendix, index, maps, charts and graphs, numerous illus. including three, title page (repeated on front cover) and pp. (240) and 317, by R. and a photo of him on the Famous Americans stamp, p. 328. (Zogbaum)

1144 Yellow Robe (Lacotawin), Rosebud. An Album of the American Indian. N.Y., (1969), pic. cloth, 86 (1) pp., introduction, glossary, numerous illus. including five, front cover (repeated on back cover), pp. (3), 22, (23) and 25, by R. (Schreyvogel)

1145 Zabriskie, George A. (President) et al. Annual Report of the New York Historical Society for the Year 1945. N.Y., 1946, wraps, 143 (1) pp., illus. including one, p. (18), by R. Remington in text, pp. 18 and 41.

1146 Zamonski, Stanley W. and Keller, Teddy. The Fifty-Niners. Sage Books, Denver, (1961), cloth, map endsheets, 281 pp., index, numerous illus. including one, p. 43, by R.

Photos of Remington Bronzes as Illustrations

1147 Barns, W. E. et al. Souvenir Program of the Thirteenth Annual Meeting of the Concatenated Order of Hoo-Hoo House of Hoo-Hoo, World's Fair, St. Louis, Sept. 9, 1904, pic. wraps, pages unnumb., numerous illus. including a photo of "Cowboys off the Trail" by R.

1148 Bates, Col. Charles Francis. Custer's Indian Battles. Privately printed, Bronxville, N.Y., (1936), pic. wraps, 36 (2) pp., acknowledgments, seventeen illus. including a photo of a bronze, p. 14, by R. (Schreyvogel)

1148a ———. Same, reprinted and bound with Custer's Last Battle by Charles Francis Roe with cover title Custer Engages the Hostiles. The Old Army Press, Fort Collins, Colo., (1973), decor. cloth, tan endsheets, 36 (2) and 40 (2) pp., numerous illus. including one, photo of the bronze "The Scalp," p. 14, by R. (Schreyvogel)

1149 Beck, James Montgomery et al. *Fairmount Park Art Assn. — Fiftieth Anniversary, 1871–1921.* Published by the Assn., Phila., 1922, cloth, blue endsheets, 279 pp., index, illus. including a photo, "Bronze Equestrian Statue of Cowboy," p. 169, by R. Portrait of Remington, p. 230 and biographical sketch, p. 231.

1150 Bradley, Lawson G. (compiled by). *Official Guide to the Lewis and Clark Centennial Exposition.* Portland, Ore., June 1–Oct. 15, 1905, colored pic. wraps, 62 pp., folding maps, two photos of "Hitting the Trail," pp. (5) and (13), by R.

1151 Cahill, Holger. *American Painting and Sculpture, 1862–1932.* Museum of Modern Art, W. W. Norton & Co., (Plandome Press), N.Y., (1932), cloth, 46 pp., plus (78) plates, including a photo of "Broncho Buster," no. 139, by R.

1152 ———— and Barr, Alfred H., Jr., eds. *Art in America in Modern Times.* Reynal Hitchcock, N.Y., (1934), wraps, 100 (8) pp., "Foreword" by F. A. Whiting, Pres. A. F. A., bibliography, numerous illus. including a photo of "Broncho Buster," p. 52, by R.

1153 Craven, Wayne. *Sculpture in America.* N.Y., (1968), cloth, red endsheets, 722 pp., red top, preface, selected bibliography, index, numerous illustrations including three photos, pp. (551-2), of Remington bronzes and much on Remington in text.

1154 Dawson, Glen (compiled by). *Frontier America.* Dawson's Book Shop, L. A., 1950, two-tone fabricoid, 184 pp., index, illus. including a photo of "The Cheyenne," between pp. 120 and 121, by R.

1155 Dodd, Loring Holmes. *The Golden Age of American Sculpture.* Chapman & Grimes, Boston, (1936), cloth, pic. endsheets, 108 pp., numerous illus. including a photo of "The Broncho Buster," p. (98), by R.

1156 Francis, David R. *The Universal Exposition of 1904,* vol. II. Louisiana Purchase Exposition Co., St. Louis, 1913, cloth, decor. endsheets, 427 pp., appendices, numerous illus. including a photo of "Cowboys," p. 227, by R.

1157 Gardner, Albert Ten Eyck. *American Sculpture.* Metropolitan Museum of Art, N.Y., (1965), cloth, tinted endsheets, 192 pp., intro., index, numerous illus. including photos of ten bronzes, pp. 70, 71 (two), 72, 73 (two), 74, 75 and 76 (two), by R.

1158 Garrett, Wendell D. et al. *The Arts in America — The Nineteenth Century.* Scribner's, N.Y., 1969, code letter "A" on copyright page, two-tone cloth, maroon endsheets, 412 pp., index, numerous illus. including a photo of one bronze, p. 279, by R.

1159 Good, Donnie D. *The Longhorn.* Gilcrease Institute, Tulsa, 1970, pic. wraps, unpaged, bibliography, illus. including a photo of the bronze "The Stampede" by R. (Borein, James)

1160 (Graham.) *James Graham and Sons* (advs. brochure). N.Y., (1944?), wraps, (8) pp., illus. including photos of two bronzes by R.

1161 Hagedorn, Hermann. *The Roosevelt Family of Sagamore Hill.* Macmillan, N.Y., 1954, words "First Edition" on copyright page, two-tone cloth, 435 pp., blue top, index, illus. including a photo showing "The Broncho Buster," p. 233, by R.

1162 Herner, Charles. *The Arizona Rough Riders.* Tucson, Arizona, (1970), cloth, map endsheets, 275 pp., prologue, appendices, notes, selected bibliography, index, maps, illus. with photos including one of the presentation of Remington's "Broncho Buster" to Theodore Roosevelt by the Rough Riders.

1163 Howe, Winifred E., ed. *Bulletin of the Metropolitan Museum of Art,* vol. XXXIV, no. 7. N.Y., July 1939, pic. wraps, pp. (166–187), illus. including a photo of "The Broncho Buster," p. 169, by R. Discussion of Remington sculpture, pp. 169–170.

1164 Lee, William H. *Glimpses of the Louisiana Exposition and the Famous Pike* (in color). Laird & Lee, Chicago, 1904, cloth, 32 colograph views and 168 copper plate scenes, including one, "Cowboys on Pike" ("Comin' Thru the Rye"), by R.

1165 McCann, Anabel Parker. "Decorative Sculpture at the Lewis and Clark Exposition," an article in *The Pacific Monthly,* July 1905, cloth, photos of "Shooting Up the Town," pp. 14 and 84, by R., comments, p. 87.

1166 McCracken, Harold (Director). *Buffalo Bill Historical Center.* Cody, Wyo., n.d., folder, five illus. including a photo, "Comin' Thru the Rye," by R.

1167 Masters, Hibbert B. et al. (Art Committee). *Exhibition of Bronzes.* Union League Club, (Brooklyn, N.Y.), 1905, wraps, 141 pp., photos of four bronzes by R.

1168 Myers, Jefferson (President). *Report of the Lewis and Clark Centennial Exposition Commission for the State of Oregon.* (J. R. Whitney, State Printer, Salem, 1906), wraps, 65 (1) pp., numerous illus. including two photos of "Hitting the Trail" by R.

1169 Pattison, James William. "The Sculpture Display at

the Louisiana Purchase Exposition," an article in *The World Today*, Sept., 1904, cloth, photo of "Cowboys" by R.

1170 Pierson, William H., Jr. and Davidson, Martha, eds. *Arts of the United States, A Pictorial Survey.* McGraw Hill, Chicago etc., (1960), cloth, 452 pp., "Preface" by Lamar Dodd, introduction, appendices, index, 4000 illus. including one, a photo of a bronze, p. 380, by R. (Young)

1171 ———. Same, reprinted by the University of Georgia Press in 1966.

1172 Proske, Beatrice Gilman. *Brookgreen Gardens Sculpture.* Printed by order of the Trustees, Brookgreen, S.C., 1943, 510 pp., "Foreword" by A. M. H., intro., numerous illus. including a photo of "The Broncho Buster," p. (62), by R. Chapter on Remington, pp. 61–65. (Deming)

1173 Reid, Robert Allan (Director of View Book Publications). *The Greatest of Expositions — Completely Illustrated* (official publication). Louisiana Purchase Exposition Co., (Sam'l F. Myerson Printing Co.), St. Louis, 1904, illus. including a photo of "Cowboys Shooting up a Western Town," a heroic plaster model of "Comin' Thru the Rye," by R.

1174 ———. *Souvenir View Book of the Lewis and Clark Centennial Exposition and Oriental Fair.* Robert A. Reid, (Bushong & Co.), Portland, 1905, wraps with colored illus. mounted on front cover, pages unnumb., numerous photos, including four showing "Hitting the Trail," heroic plaster model of "Comin' Thru the Rye," by R.

1175 ———. *Lewis and Clark Centennial Exhibition.* Official Photographic Co., Portland, 1905, album of mounted views including three showing "Hitting the Trail" by R. (The Albertype Co., Brooklyn, N.Y.)

1176 ———. *The Lewis and Clark Centennial Exposition Illustrated.* Robert A. Reid, Portland, 1905, wraps with colored illus. mounted on the front cover, album of views including two of "Hitting the Trail" by R.

1177 ———. *Sights and Scenes at the Lewis and Clark Centennial Exposition.* Bushong and Co., Portland, 1905, pic. wraps, pages unnumb., numerous photos including two of "Hitting the Trail" by R.

1178 Roosevelt, Theodore. *An Autobiography.* Macmillan, N.Y., 1913, words "Published November 1913" on copyright page, cloth with a small round illus. mounted on the front cover, 647 pp., advs., gilt top, foreword, appendices, index, illus. including a photo of "The Broncho Buster" by R.

1179 Saarinen, Aline B. *The Proud Possessors.* Random House, N.Y., (1958), words "First Printing" on copyright page, cloth, black endsheets, 423 (1) pp., yellow top, foreword, intro., sources and obligations, index, illus. including a photo of "Comin' Thru the Rye," between pp. 200 and 201, by R.

1180 Stock, Chester and Howard, Hildegarde. *The Ascent of Equus.* Los Angeles County Museum, Science Series no. 8, Paleontology Pub. no. 5, March 31, 1944, wraps, 38 pp., preface, reference list, illus. including a photo of a bronze by R.

1181 Wear, Bruce. *The Bronze World of Frederic Remington.* Gaylord, Tulsa, (1966), pic. cloth, 149 pp., preface, "Foreword" by C. Gregory Crampton, addendum, glossary, numerous photos of bronzes by R. and photos of him.

1182 *The World Almanac and Encyclopedia, 1904.* Press Pub. Co., N.Y., 1903, colored pic. wraps, xcvi, 592 pp., numerous illus. including a photo of "Off the Trail," p. lvi, by R.

The Remington Stamps

1183 Barclay, Lillian Elizabeth, as suggested by Ernest Dean Dorchester. *They Dreamed and Dared.* Steck Co., Austin, Texas, (1941), cloth, map endsheets, 612 pp., preface, index, illus. including two of stamps, pp. 483 and 501, by R.

1184 Brazer, Clarence W. *A Historical Catalog of U.S. Stamp Essays and Proofs — The Omaha Trans-Mississippi Issue, 1898.* Clarence W. Brazer, N.Y., (J. W. Stowell Printing Co., Federalsburg, Md.), 1939, wraps, 48 pp., numerous illus. including eight by R.

1185 ———. *Essays for U.S. Adhesive Postage Stamps.* Handbook Committee, American Philatelic Society, (J. W. Stowell, Chairman, Federalsburg, Md.), cloth, 1941, alphabetical index, numerical index, about 600 illus. including four by R.

1186 Burroughs, W. Dwight. *The Wonderland of Stamps.* Stokes, N.Y., (1910), cloth, 238 pp., preface, index, illus., Remington stamps in the Trans-Miss. series discussed, pp. 58–59.

1187 Clark, Hugh M., ed. *Catalogue of United States Stamps, Specialized, 1942.* Scott Publications, N.Y., (1941), (Twentieth edition, published annually), cloth, 488 pp., (7) of advs., numerous illus. including three of stamps, pp. 73 (two) and 142, by R. Other Scott catalogues also picture Remington stamps.

1188 *Famous American Series — United States Stamps.*

N.Y. Journal-American, (N.Y., 1940), wraps, pages unnumb., illus. including a photo of R. and a brief biographical sketch.

1189 Farley, James A. (Postmaster General). *A Description of U.S. Postage Stamps.* G.P.O., Wash., D.C., 1937, cloth wraps, 119 pp., "Foreword" by Farley, numerous illus. including photos of two stamps in the Trans-Miss. series, p. 31, by R. Other issues of this publication pictured Remington stamps.

1190 ————. Same, but junior edition. P. O. Dept., (1939), pic. wraps, 63 pp., letter from Pres. Roosevelt, same illus. by R.

1191 Felix, Erwin J. *How to Collect Stamps, Coins and Paper Money.* Winsor Press, (Chicago), 1954, colored pic. wraps, 160 pp., preface, acknowledgments, numerous illus. including a photo of a sheet of stamps, p. 60, by R.

1192 Gemming, Elizabeth and Klaus. *The World of Art, Learning Through Stamps, Volume I.* Barre Publishers, Barre, Mass., (1968), pic. cloth, 64 pp., numerous photos of stamps including "Smoke Signal," p. 55, by R.

1193 Hahn, George C. "Famous Americans Series," an article in *The American Philatelist,* Jan., 1949, with photos of the Remington stamp, his birthplace, the essay for the stamp, a first day cover and Remington.

1194 Kimble, Ralph A. *Commemorative Postage Stamps of the United States.* Grosset & Dunlap, N.Y., (1933), words "First Printing, May, 1933" on copyright page, fabricoid, 350 pp., red top, acknowledgments, intro., glossary of philatelic terms, index, illus., descriptions of the two Remington stamps in the Trans-Miss. Exposition issue, pp. 23 and 24.

1195 Logan, Milton B. (President). *Stamps of the United States and Possessions.* American Art Assn., Anderson Galleries, N.Y., 1939, wraps, 55 pp., illus. including a photo of the 50¢ stamp in the Trans-Miss. set, by R.

1196 Manley, Atwood. "Canton's Centennial Commemoration of Frederic Remington," an article in *Stamps,* Nov. 11, 1961.

1197 Marzulla, Elena, ed. et al. *United States Stamps and Stories.* U. S. Postal Service, (Washington, D.C.), 1972, colored pic. wraps, 224 pp., numerous reproductions of stamps in color including three, pp. 25 (two) and 57, by R. (Lea, Russell, Von Schmidt)

1198 Petersham, Maud and Miska. *America's Stamps.* Macmillan, N.Y., 1947, cloth, tinted endsheets, 144 pp., (preface), numerous illus. by the authors and from photos, including three, pp. 39 (two) and 109, by R.

1199 *Postage Stamps of the U. S., 1847–1949.* P. O. Dept., G. P. O., Washington, D.C., 1949, wraps, 185 pp., "Foreword" by Postmaster General Donaldson, numerous illus., three of stamps, pp. 31 (two) and 124, by R.

1200 Reinfeld, Fred. *Commemorative Stamps of the USA.* Crowell, N.Y., (1954), words "First Printing" on copyright page, cloth, 344 pp., blue top, author's note, sources of stamp designs, index, numerous illus. including photos of stamps, pp. 17, 19 and 184, by R. Biographical sketch, p. 184.

1201 Remington, Frederic. *8-Cent Stamp — Troops Guarding Train* (by R.). A dark lilac stamp in the Trans-Miss. "Omaha" Exposition issue of 1898. Two plates, 609 and 643, were used in printing 2,927,200.

1202 ————. *50-Cent Stamp — Western Mining Prospector* (by R.). An olive stamp in the Trans-Miss. "Omaha" Exposition issue of 1898. One plate, 603, was used in printing 540,000.

1203 ————. *10-Cent Stamp, Frederic Remington* (from a photo of R.). A brown stamp in the Famous American Series issued in 1940. First day sale at Canton, N.Y., Sept. 30, 1940. Two plates, 22599 and 22600, were used in the printing.

1204 ————. *4-Cent Stamp, Frederic Remington, Artist of the West, 1861–1891.* The illus. in color by R. Centennial of Remington's birth. First day sale at Washington, D.C., Oct. 4, 1961.

1205 Sloane, George B. et al. *The Stamp Specialist—Green Book.* (H. L. Linquist, N.Y., 1943), boards, 128 pp., numerous illus. including two, pp. 22 and 27, by R., and photos of three stamps, by R.

1206 Wierzbinski, Fryderyk. *Indianski Pioropusz.* Biuro Wydawnicze, Warszawa, Poland, 1971, wraps, numerous illus. including one, p. 1, of the Remington 4¢ stamp.

Dust Wrappers Illustrated by the Artist

1207 Altshuler, Constance Wynn. *Latest from Arizona: The Hesperian Letters, 1858–1861.* Arizona's Pioneers' Historical Society, Tucson, 1969, cloth, 293 pp., map.

1208 Azoy, A. C. M. *Charge! The Story of the Battle at San Juan Hill.* Longman, Green, N.Y. etc., 1961.

1209 Berthrong, Donald J. *The Southern Cheyennes*. Univ. of Okla. Press, Norman, 1963.

1210 Branch, Douglas. *The Cowboy and His Interpreters.* Cooper Square Publishers, N.Y., (1961). (James, Russell)

1211 Brown, Mark H. *The Plainsman of the Yellowstone.* Putnam's, N.Y., (1961).

1212 Coleman, Rufus A., ed. *The Golden West in Story and Verse.* Harper, N.Y. and London, (1932).

1213 Custer, Elizabeth B. *Boots and Saddles.* Univ. of Okla. Press, Norman, (1961).

1214 Farrell, Cliff. *Patch-Saddle Drive.* Doubleday, Garden City, N.Y., 1972, words "First Edition" on copyright page.

1215 Favour, Alpheus H. *Old Man Williams.* Univ. of Okla. Press, Norman, 1962.

1216 Finerty, John F. *Warpath and Bivouac.* Univ. of Okla. Press, Norman, 1961.

1217 Foner, Jack D. *The United States Soldier Between Two Wars 1865–1898* (Army Life and Reforms). Humanities Press, N.Y., 1970, cloth, 229 pp.

1218 Foote, Mary Hallock. *A Picked Company.* Houghton Mifflin, Boston and N.Y., 1912.

1219 Gordon, Charles Wm. *The Patrol of the Sundance Trail* by Ralph Gordon (pseud.). A. L. Burt Co., N.Y., n.d. (1914?).

1220 Gulick, Bill et al. *Holsters and Heroes.* Macmillan, N.Y., 1954.

1221 Hagen, Christopher S. *Rebellion der Rebellen.* Herder, Freiberg etc., West Germany, (1971), pic. cloth, 221 (3) pp., *bibliographie* (German text), Western poster on the reverse of the four-fold d/w by R.

1222 ———. *Whiskey Fur Goldfield.* Herder, Freiberg etc., West Germany, (1973), pic. cloth, 189 pp., (2) of advs., d/w illus. in color by R. (German text.) (Russell)

1223 Heckelman, Charles N. (edited and with an introduction by). *With Guidons Flying.* Doubleday, Garden City, N.Y., 1970, words "First Edition" on copyright page.

1224 Hooker, Forrestine C. *When Geronimo Rode.* Doubleday, Page, Garden City, N.Y., 1924.

1225 Knowles, Horace, ed. *Gentlemen, Scholars and Scoundrels* (A Treasury of the Best of *Harper's Magazine* from 1850 to the present). Harper, N.Y., 1959, cloth, 696 pp., small drawing on back of d/w by R.

1226 Lane, Jack C., ed. *Chasing Geronimo: The Journal of Leonard Wood, May-September, 1886.* New Mexico, Albuquerque, 1970.

1227 Laut, Agnes C. *The Conquest of Our Western Empire.* McBride, N.Y., 1932.

1228 (Lemmon.) *Boss Cowman, The Recollections of Ed Lemmon, 1857–1946.* University of Nebraska Press, Lincoln, 1969.

1229 Longstreet, Stephen. *War Cries on Horseback: The Story of the Indian Wars of the Great Plains.* Doubleday, Garden City, N.Y., 1970.

1230 Loomis, Noel M. (with a preface by). *Holsters and Heroes.* Macmillan, N.Y., 1954, words "First Printing" on copyright page.

1231 Mayhall, Mildred P. *The Kiowas.* Univ. of Okla. Press, Norman, 1962.

1232 Maule, Harry E., ed. *Great Tales of the American West.* Modern Library, N.Y., (1945).

1233 Parkhill, Forbes. *The Blazed Trail of Antoine Leroux.* Westernlore, Los Angeles, 1965.

1234 Patten, Lewis B. *Death Waited at Rialto Creek.* Doubleday, Garden City, 1966.

1235 Robertson, Frank C. *Fort Hall.* Hastings House, N.Y., 1963.

1236 Rohan, Jack. *Yankee Arms Maker — The Incredible Career of Samuel Colt.* Harper, N.Y. and London, 1935.

1237 Salomon, Julian Harris. *The Book of Indian Crafts and Indian Lore.* Harper, N.Y. and London, 1928.

1238 Schellie, Don. *Vast Domain of Blood.* Westernlore Press, Los Angeles, 1968.

1239 Smith, Helena Huntington. *The War on Powder River.* McGraw Hill, N.Y. etc., (1966).

1239a Stevens, Lt. Col. Phillip H. *Search Out the Land* (A History of American Military Scouts). Rand McNally, Chicago etc., (1969), words "First Printing, November 1969" on copyright page, cloth, 192 pp., illus. with photos.

1240 Tibbles, Thomas Henry. *Buckskin and Blanket Days.* Olbourne, London, (1958), words "First Published in Great Britain, 1958" on copyright page.

1241 Ward, Don, ed. *Branded West.* Houghton Mifflin, Boston, 1956.

1242 Wetmore, Helen Cody. *Last of the Great Scouts.* Grosset & Dunlap, N.Y., (1918).

1243 Wheeler, Col. Homer W. *Buffalo Days.* Bobbs-Merrill, Indianapolis, (1925).

1244 Wister, Owen. *When West Was West*. Macmillan, N.Y., 1928.

1245 Wormser, Richard. *The Yellowlegs* (The Story of the United States Cavalry). Doubleday, Garden City, N.Y., 1966.

1246 Wyckoff, James. *Lars*. Doubleday, Garden City, N.Y., 1965.

Ephemera Illustrated by the Artist

1247 The Albrecht Gallery, St. Joseph Art League, St. Joseph, Mo., n.d., folder invitation to the "St. Joseph to Sacramento" art exhibition with one illus. by R.

1248 Allred, B. W. (Bill). *Horses Need Good Grass*. Reprinted from *The Cattleman*, (Ft. Worth), Sept. 1948, folder, one illus. by R.

1249 *The American West*. Illus. folder announcing the new magazine with one illus. by R.

1250 Andrews, Byron. *The Facts About the Candidate* (Teddy Roosevelt). Sam Stone, Chicago, 1904, pic. wraps, size: approx. 1½" x 2", unpaged, illus. with drawings by A. J. Klapp including one of the presentation of Remington's "The Broncho Buster" in chapter 4. (In the D. J. M. Christlieb collection.)

1251 *The Art Institute of Chicago*. (Chicago), Summer 1969, folder, two illustrations, one a photo of the bronze, "The Rattlesnake," by R.

1252 *Artists of American Frontier*. Pennsylvania State University, University Park Pa., Feb. 21–March 31, 1965, folder, one illus. by R.

1253 *Artists of the Western Frontier* (Permanent Exhibition). Joslyn Art Museum, Ohaha, Nebraska, (1969), pic. folder, eight illus. including one, front cover, by R. (Russell)

1254 Bakker, Elna and Lillard, Richard. *The Great Southwest*. American West Pub Co., announcement of the book, (8) pp., numerous illus. including one by R.

1255 Bell, Lieut. Colonel Wm. Gardner. *"Old Bill" — Symbol of Mobile Warfare*. The United States Armor Assn., Washington, D.C., 1967, folder, one page text and one full-page drawing of "Old Bill" by R.

1256 Bruno, Guido, ed. *Bruno's Weekly*. N.Y., April 8th, 1916, pic. wraps, pp. (599)-614, includes a facsimile of a Remington letter illus. with one drawing.

1257 *Bulletin for the Months of May–June, 1953*. Childs Gallery, Boston, folder, one illus. by R.

1258 Burgess, Gelett and Hereford, Oliver. *Enfant Terrible*.

R. H. Russell, N.Y., April 1, 1898, folder, one illus. by R.

1259 *Century in the Saddle*. Colorado Cattlemen's Centennial Commission, Denver, (1966), advs. folder with four illus. including one by R.

1260 Comstock Editions (Ballantine Books). N.Y., Jan.–July 1972, double folder, illus. with one, front cover, by R.

1261 *Discover it for Yourself* (subscriber bonus offer for *The American West*). Folder, illus. including one by R.

1262 *Drawings by Remington, Copley, Homer*. Childs Gallery, Boston, (1948), folder, one illus. by R.

1263 *8th Annual Conference of the Western History Association* (Program). Tucson, Arizona, October 17–19, 1968, pic. wraps, (40) pp., four illus. including one by R.

1264 Estergreen, Marion. *Chapels on the Trail*. N.p. (Taos, N.M.), n.d., pic. wraps, 8 pp., map, drawings by T. M. Clark but two on the front cover are after R.

1265 *Explore the American West*. American Express, N.Y., 1968, colored pic. wraps, 15 pp., maps, ten illus. including three, pp. 4, 8 and back cover, by R. (Advs. booklet for "1968 Escorted Air Tours.")

1266 *Fifth U. S. Cavalry — 92nd Organization Day 1855–1947*. Camp McGill, Honshu (A.R.I. Ofuna), Japan, folder, battle honors, dinner menu, illus. on front cover by R.

1267 First General Insurance Co. Philadelphia, advs. flyer with one illus. in color by R.

1268 *Gift Shop Catalog*. Gilcrease Institute, Tulsa, n.d., pic. wraps, (16) pp., numerous illus. including twelve by R. (One of a series with varying numbers of Remington illustrations.) (Borein, Leigh, Russell)

1269 Hanson, Irvin W. *101 Frederic Remington Drawings of the Old West*. Color, Press, Willmar, Minn., 1968, advs. folder with two illus. by R.

1270 *The George H. Harding Museum*. Chicago, n.d., folder, four illus. including one, a drawing of the bronze "The Rattler," by R. States that "The Remington Room" contains 32 paintings and eight bronzes by R. Note on front "Closed for Relocation."

1271 *Harper's Book-Mark*. N.p., 1889, advs. folder, one illus. by R.

1272 *Harper's March 1895*. N.Y., advs. folder, one illus. by R.

1273 *Harper's May.* N.Y., 1898, advs. folder, one illus. by R.

1274 *Harper's July.* N.Y., 1898, advs. folder, one illus. by R.

1275 *Harper's Magazine for May.* N.Y., 1899, advs. folder, one illus. by R.

1276 Henderson, George. *The Frederic Remington—Owen Wister Letters.* Announcement of the book by the American West Pub. Co. with three illus. by R. and photos of Remington and Wister.

1277 Hetzel Union Gallery (The Pennsylvania State University, College of Arts and Architecture). *Artists of the American Frontier* (reception invitation). Feb. 21, 1965, folder with one illus. by R.

1278 *History Book Club Review.* Winter Special Issue, 1955, front cover illus. by R.

1279 Jackson, Harry. *Lost Wax Bronze Casting* (an announcement folder for the book). Northland Press, Flagstaff, n.d., nine illus. including one by R.

1280 Latendorf, E. Walter. *Remington Catalogue (No. 17) Circular.* Mannados Bookshop, N.Y., (1947), single sheets with two previously unpublished illus. by R.

1281 ———. *Mannados Bookshop.* N.Y., n.d. (June, 1951), (4) pp., three illus. by R.

1282 *Latest from Arizona!* Arizona Pioneers' Historical Society, Tucson, (1969), advs. folder, one illus. by R.

1283 The Leanin' Tree Ranch, Boulder, Colo. *Western Christmas Cards for 1968.* Colored pic. wraps, unpaged, numerous illus. in color including one by R.

1284 McCracken, Harold. *The Art Book of the Year—Frederic Remington.* (Lippincott, Phila. and N.Y., 1947), advs. leaflet for *"Frederic Remington, Artist of the Old West,"* portraits of Remington and the author, two illus., one in color, by R.

1285 ———. *Frederic Remington.* Remington Art Memorial, Ogdensburg, N.Y., n.d., folder, eight illus. by R.

1286 *The Magnificent Rockies.* Pictorial prospectus for the book by the American West Pub. Co., including one illus. in color by R.

1287 Mannados Bookshop, N.Y. *In Preparation Frederic Remington* (bibliographic check list). Broadside with two illus. by R.

1288 *The Albert K. Mitchell Collection of C. M. Russell and Frederic Remington Paintings.* National Cowboy Hall of Fame and Western Heritage Center, Okla-homa City, (1968), folder, photo of Mitchell and one illus., "The Sign of the Buffalo Scout," by R. (Russell)

1289 Monaghan, Jay (editor-in-chief). *The Book of the American West.* Advance announcement folder issued by Messner, with three illus. by R.

1290 ———. Same, advance announcement and prospectus, 16 pp., with sixteen illus. by R.

1291 National Cowboy Hall of Fame, Oklahoma City. *General Information.* 1965, folder with three illus. by R.

1292 *New York Graphic Society.* Greenwich, Conn., (1954), folder, (4) pp., numerous illus. including six by R.

1293 Pfeiffer, George, III. *The Custer Massacre.* Subscriber bonus opportunity (letter), folder, with one illus. by R.

1294 *Reinhold Presents a Magnificent Art "First."* Flyer advertising *The Illustrator in America* and *History of Watercolor Paintings in America,* double fold, illus. including one in color by R.

1295 *The Frederic Remington Book* (by Harold McCracken). Announcement folder, five illus. by R. (Russell)

1296 *The Remington Collection.* (Museum of Fine Arts of Houston, Houston, Texas, n.d.), 5 mimeographed sheets listing and commenting on the Remington paintings. (Available to the visitors at one time.)

1297 (Remington.) *The Frederic Remington Memorial.* (Republican-Journal), Ogdensburg, N.Y., 1925, pic. wraps, (5) pp., front cover illus. by R.

1298 ———. *The Remington Calendar, 1908.* Collier, N.Y., (1907), 4 sheets and a cover tied with a silk cord, five illus. in color by R.

1299 ———. *The Creek Indian Calendar, 1908.* Collier, N.Y., (1907), a single sheet and pad tied with silk cord, 14" x 18", one illus. in color by R.

1300 ———. *The Chieftain Calendar, 1908.* Collier, N.Y., (1907), a single sheet and pad tied with silk cord, 14" x 18", one illus. in color by R.

1301 ———. *The Unknown Explorers Calendar, 1908.* Collier, N.Y., (1907), a single sheet and pad tied with silk cord, 14" x 20", one illus. in color by R.

1302 ———. *Buffalo Hunt.* Jig of the Week Puzzle, no. 9, boxed. "Frederic" is misspelled with the added "k" on the box.

1303 ———. *Dismounted.* A Springbok Jigsaw Puzzle, Kansas City, Mo., over 500 pieces in color.

1304 ———. *Artistic Illustrations, Specimens of Magazine and Book Illustrations.* Engraving & Printing Co., N.Y., n.d., wraps, one illus. by R.

1305 ———. *Calendar, 1939.* Bankers Life Co., Des Moines, (1938), 11″ x 7½″, six illus. in color by R.

1306 ———. *Calendar, 1945.* Edward R. Bacon Grain Co., Chicago, (1944), 12½″ x 12½″, single sheet with one illus. in color by R.

1307 ———. *Calendar, 1945.* Hughes Tool Co., Houston, Texas, (1944), 11¾″ x 17¾″, 14 pp., thirteen illus. in color by R., biographical sketch of R.

1308 ———. *Poster.* 13″ x 16″, advs. for *The Century Magazine,* March, 1891, one illus., "A Bucking Broncho," in black and white, by R.

1309 ———. *Poster.* 9½″ x 13½″, advs. for Remington's *Pony Tracks,* Harper, N.Y., (1895).

1310 ———. *Poster.* 16½″ x 12″, advs. for Davis' *Cuba in War Time,* R. H. Russell, N.Y., (1897), one illus., "Regular Cavalryman — Spanish," in color, by R.

1311 ———. *Poster.* 16″ x 12½″, advs. for Remington's *Drawings,* R. H. Russell, N.Y., (1897), one illus., "Mounted Cowboy," in color, by R.

1312 ———. *Poster.* 17″ x 23½″, advs. for *Collier's,* (1898), one illus., "The Bugler — Cuban Soldier," in color by R.

1313 ———. *Poster.* 17″ x 23½″, advs. for *Collier's,* (1898), one illus., "A First Class Fighting Man," in color by R.

1314 ———. *Poster.* 13″ x 20″, advs. for *The Century Magazine,* Jan. 1902, one illus., "The Old Stage Coach of the Plains," in color by R.

1315 ———. *Poster.* 13″ x 19″, advs. for Lewis' *The Black Lion Inn,* R. H. Russell, N.Y., (1903), one illus., "Jim Britt," in black and white, by R.

1316 *Rendezvous for . . . Space.* (NASA, Goddard Space Flight Center, Greenbelt, Md.), n.d., pic. wraps, unpaged, numerous illus. including four by R.

1317 *The Rockwell Gallery of Western Art.* Corning, N.Y., n.d., pic. folder with nine illus. including three by R. (Eggenhofer, Russell)

1318 Smith, Harold S. (President). *Harold's Club's Fabulous Covered Wagon Room.* Reno, (1944?), advs. folder, numerous illus. including photos of four by R. that have been reproduced on illuminated glass.

1319 *St. Joseph to Sacramento* (exhibition of Western Art from the days of the Pony Express). The Albrecht

Gallery, St. Joseph Art League, St. Joseph, Missouri, opening July 6, (1969?), single folded sheet (invitation) with one illus. by R.

1320 *Taming a Frontier.* Reprinted from *Transmission Magazine* 17:1, (1968), folder with nine illus. including three (two in color) by R. (Russell, Wyeth, Young)

1321 Taylor, J. Golden. *Great Western Short Stories.* An Announcement of the book by the American West Pub. Co., with one illus. by R.

1322 *The "21" Club Gallery of Western Art (N.Y.) presents the sculpture of Frederic Remington re-created in a limited edition of fine silver art medals.* Double folder, with photos of ten bronzes by R.

1323 Wilder, Mitchell A. (Director). *Sid W. Richardson Exhibition.* Amon Carter Museum of Western Arts, Fort Worth, 1964, colored pic. folder, six illus. including three by R. (Hurd, Russell)

1324 *Wolfville Yarns of Alfred Henry Lewis.* The Kent State University Press, Kent, Ohio, 1968, advs. folder, three illus. by R.

1325 *Woolaroc Museum.* (Bartlesville, Okla., 1965), colored pic. folder with numerous illus. including one by R. (Leigh, Russell)

1326 Zoeller, L., Holden, S. and Gillham, A. *Days of Yesterday* (sheet music). Zipf Music Publishing Co., N.Y., 1923, wraps, with eight illus. by R.

Written by the Artist

1327 Becker, May Lambertson (selected by). *Golden Tales of the Far West.* Dodd, Mead, N.Y., 1935. Includes "When a Document is Official," pp. 95-105, by R,

1328 Burke, John M. et al. *Buffalo Bill's Wild West and Congress of Rough Riders of the World.* Cody and Salsbury (Fless and Ridge Printing Co.), N.Y., 1895, colored pic. wraps, 64 (32) pp., illus. includes a report on the show in London, pp. 48-49, by R.

1329 ———. Same, 1898, same report by R.

1330 ———. Same, 1899, same report by R.

1331 ———. Same, 1902, same report by R.

1332 Ellis, Edward S. *The Indian Wars of the United States.* P. D. Farrell & Co., Grand Rapids, Mich., (1892), decor. cloth and endsheets, 516 pp., intro., appendix, illus., Remington quoted, pp. 466-472.

1333 Guthrie, A. B., Jr. et al. *Der Mann der Zuviel Sprach.*

Nymphenberger Verlagshandlung, Munchen, (1963), cloth, 314 (1) pp., includes *"MacNeils Erlebnis"* (A Sketch by MacNeil) by R.

1334 Santee, Ross. *Apache Land.* Scribner's, N.Y., 1947, code letter "A" on copyright page, pic. cloth, 216 pp., foreword, numerous illus. by the author. A story, pp. 194-195, by R.

1335 Schaefer, Jack, ed. *Out West: An Anthology of Stories.* Houghton Mifflin, Boston, 1955, includes "A Sketch by MacNeil," pp. (223)-226, by R.

1336 ———— et al. *Der Mann der Zuviel Sprach (Die schonsten Geschichten aus dem Wilden Westen).* Nymphenburger Verlagshandlung, Munchen, (1965), cloth, 314 (1) pp., *biographische notizen, inhalt,* includes *"MacNeils Erlebnis"* by Frederic Remington and contributions by Charles M. Russell (two), Richter, Wister et al.

1337 Scobee, Barry. *Old Fort Davis.* Naylor, San Antonio, (1947), cloth, 101 pp., index, illus., tribute to Bullis, p. 60, by R.

1338 Targ, William. ed. *The American West.* World Pub. Co., Cleveland and N.Y., 1946, includes "When a Document is Official," pp. 199–206, by R.

1339 Vincent, George E., ed. *Theodore W. Miller — Rough Rider.* Privately printed (Werner Co.), Akron, Ohio, 1899, quotes a letter, p. 171, by R., Remington mentioned in text, pp. 89, 91, 125 and 142.

1340 Waldo, Edna La Moore. *Dakota.* Capital Pub. Co., Bismark, N.D., (1932), Remington quoted, pp. 146 and 147.

1341 Wanamaker, Rodman, honoring Col. Wm. F. Cody. *A Tribute to the North American Indian.* Speeches delivered at a dinner at Sherry's, N.Y., May 12, 1909, Phila., 1909, wraps, reproduces, in full, Remington's speech.

1342 Westermeir, Clifford P. *Trailing the Cowboy.* Caxton, Caldwell, Idaho, 1955, Remington quoted, p. 46.

1343 Wyman, Walker D. *The Wild Horse of the West.* Caxton, Caldwell, Idaho, 1945, Remington quoted, pp. 27, 98, 147 and 283.

The Artist and His Art

1344 Aderman, Ralph M., ed. *Historical Messenger* (of the Milwaukee County Historical Society) 29:1, Spring 1973, brief note about the Remington cover illus. and other mentions of him in the text.

1345 Allen, E. Douglas (compiled by). "Frederic Remington — Author and Illustrator — A List of his Contributions to American Periodicals," an article in the *Bulletin of the New York Public Library,* Dec. 1945.

1346 American Art Association, Anderson Galleries, N.Y., *An Unusual Collection of Autographs, Books, Manuscripts and Drawings,* sale no. 4037. Decor. wraps, 37 pp., offers twenty-two Remington items including a number of original drawings.

1347 *The Armed Forces of the United States as seen by the Contemporary Artist.* An exhibition at the Smithsonian Institution, Washington, D.C., 1968, pic. wraps, 64 (2) pp., illustrated, includes a brief biographical sketch of R. and lists one item, "General Leonard Wood and the Rough Riders," included in the exhibition.

1348 "Art Arises," an article in *Spur Magazine,* August 1939, Remington accepts General Miles' invitation to go West, with one illus. by R. and three other illus. in the Douthitt Gallery, advs. by R.

1349 Barnes, James. "Frederic Remington — Sculptor," an illus. article in *Collier's,* March 18, 1905, with four illus. by R.

1350 Bell, Col. William Gardner. "A Remington Painting is Restored," an article in *Corral Dust,* Fall 1966, Potomac Corral of The Westerners, one illus., "Mexican Cavalry," by R.

1351 Bigelow, Poultney. *Seventy Summers.* Longmans Green, N.Y., 1925, 2 vols., 332 and 290 pp., preface, index, frontis. in each volume. Bigelow and Remington were at Yale together and later were Harper associates, much on R.

1352 ————. Same, Edward Arnold & Co., London, 1925. The first British edition of item no. 1351.

1353 ————. "Frederic Remington: With Extracts from Unpublished Letters," an article in *Quarterly Journal,* N.Y. State Historical Society (Cooperstown, N.Y.), 1929.

1354 Birk, Eileen P. "Remington and the Old West," in the feature "Current and Coming" in *Antiques,* vol. XCII, no. 5, November, 1967, one photo of a Remington bronze. (Deming, Russell, Wyeth)

1355 Bolton, Theodore. *American Book Illustrators.* R. R. Bowker Co., N.Y., 1938, cloth, 238 pp., intro., index. The Remington list, pp. 154-168, includes 85 items. The edition consists of 1000 copies.

1356 ————. "Mannados Bookshop's Remington Catalog,"

an article in *Publisher's Weekly*, section two, May 17, 1947, self-wraps, pp. (B425-B448), illus. with four drawings by R.

1357 ———. A letter to *Publisher's Weekly*, August 17, 1946, commenting on *The Collector's Remington* by Helen L. (Teri) Card.

1358 *The Book Buyer*, September 1892, Charles Scribner's Sons, N.Y., pic. wraps, pp. 326–62, reviews *On Canada's Frontier* (no. 934), comments on Remington's art and with one illus. by. him.

1359 Same, May 1893, pic. wraps; pp. 142–84, notes reprint of *Tenting on the Plains* (no. 494) with brief comments on Remington's art and with one illus. by him.

1360 Same, September 1897, wraps, pp. 90–184, reviews *Wolfville* (no. 764), praises Remington's art and with one illus. by him.

1361 *Books by, and Books Illustrated by Frederic Remington.* The Scribner Book Store, N.Y. etc., n.d., four mimeographed page catalog offering twenty-six Remington items.

1362 Brininstool, E. A. *Trail Dust of a Maverick.* Dodd, Mead, N.Y., 1914, words "Published, March, 1914" on copyright page, cloth with illus. mounted on front cover, 249 pp., "Introduction" by Robt. J. Burdette, illus. with photos. Includes a poem, pp. 95-96, "Frederic Remington."

1363 Brown, Myra Lockwood and Taft, Robert. "Painter of the Rip-Roaring West," an article in *Country Gentleman*, Sept. 1947, with seven illus. in color by R.

1364 Bucklin, Clarissa, ed. *Nebraska Art and Artists.* School of Fine Arts, Univ. of Nebraska, Lincoln, (1932), pic. wraps, 82 pp., preface, index, illus., biographical sketch of R., p. 17.

1365 *Bulletin.* N.Y., July 1929, pic. wraps, pp. 166–187, much on Remington bronzes in the Metropolitan and with a photo of his "The Broncho Buster."

1365a Burnside, Wesley M. *Maynard Dixon, Artist of the West.* Brigham Young University Press, Provo, Utah, (1974), words "250 Limited Special Edition" on copyright page, imitation leather and cloth, orange top, 237 pp., preface, introduction, bibliography, index, numerous illus. by Dixon; includes "Frederic Remington Letters," pp. 213–17 (encouraging Dixon) and in the text pp. 5, 16, 23, 48, 135 and 145.

1366 Campbell, Walter S. *Sitting Bull Champion of the Sioux, A Biography* by Stanley Vestal (pseud.).

Houghton, Boston and N.Y., 1932, decor. cloth, 350 pp., preface, acknowledgments, bibliography, index, map, illustrated. Vestal criticizes Remington's painting of the meeting between Sitting Bull and General Miles as "unreal" — painted from heresay.

1367 Card, H(elen) L. *The Collector's Remington.* Privately printed, Woonsocket, R.I., (1946), wraps, 8 pp., "Notes on books by him (Remington); books illustrated by him and books which gossip about him."

1368 ———. *The Collector's Remington.* A series, II. Privately printed, Woonsocket, R.I., (1946), wraps, 10 pp., "The story of his bronzes, with a complete descriptive list." Limited to 100 copies and it is believed that only 100 copies of item no. 1367 were printed.

1369 ———. "Frederic Remington's Bronzes," an illus. article in *The American Scene* 5:4, 1964, with nine illus. by R. and one photo.

1370 *Catalogue of the Remington Collection.* Ogdensburg Public Library, Ogdensburg, N.Y., 1916, wraps, (16) pp., lists 322 items in the collection but is not illustrated.

1371 Caten, Emma Louise. *In Memoriam of Frederic Remington, 1861–1909 and Eva Adele Caten Remington, 1859–1918.* Privately printed, (1936), (35) pp. on one side of sheet only, plus photos of Frederic Remington, Eva A. Remington, L. (author) Caten (father of Eva and Emma). Full leather with raised bands and gilt decorations, silk endsheets, all edges gilt. Small edition (50?). Emma incorrectly gives date of Remington's birth as Oct. 1, 1861. Eva and Frederic married on Oct. 1, Fred was born on Oct. 4.

1372 City Book Auction, N.Y., Sales nos. 397 and 398, Jan. 17 and 24, 1948, decor. wraps, 63 pp., lists fourteen items illus. by R.

1373 ———. Sale no. 404, March 6, 1948, decor. wraps, 30 pp., lists seventeen items illus. by R.

1374 Cobham, George H. et al. *Loan Exhibition of Painting by Artists of the Old West.* N.Y., April 14–15, 1952, pic. wraps, 32 pp., lists eight items by Remington and there is much on him in Cobham's "Lest We Forget."

1375 Coffin, William A. "American Illustration of Today," an illus. article in *Scribner's Magazine*, March 1892, one drawing (first appearance) by R.

1376 ———. "The Broncho Buster," an article, pp. 318–319, in *Century Magazine*, vol. LII, May–October, 1896. Four photos of the bronze.

1377 Conrotto, Eugene L. "Two Artists; Two Impressions,"

an article in *Desert* (Magazine of the Outdoor Southwest), October, 1961, three illus. by R. and two by Delano.

1378 Cortissoz, Royal. "Frederic Remington: A Painter of American Life," an article in *Scribner's*, Feb., 1910, illus. by R.

1379 ———. *American Artists*. Scribner's, N.Y., London, 1923, words "Published November, 1923" on copyright page, cloth, 363 pp., preface, illus., includes a chapter, "Frederic Remington," pp. 225–244.

1380 Crocker, O. E. "Page from the Boyhood of Remington," an article in *Collier's* 45:28, September 17, 1919.

1381 Davis, Charles Belmont. "Remington — The Man and His Work," an article in *Collier's*, March 18, 1905.

1382 ———, ed. *Adventures and Letters of Richard Harding Davis*. Scribner's, N.Y., 1917, words "Published November, 1917" on copyright page, cloth, 417 pp., illus., Davis and Remington's adventures in the Spanish American War.

1383 ——— and Barnes, James. "Frederic Remington: Storyteller on Canvas and in Bronze," an illus. article in *The American Scene* 1:1, Spring 1958, with two illus. by R.

1384 DeKay, Charles. "A Painter of the West," an article in *Harper's Weekly* 54:14–15, January 8, 1910.

1384a De Marco, Mario A. "Frederic Remington, Western Artist Par Excellence," an article in *Real West* 17:130, September, 1974, with five illus. by R. and a composite by De Marco.

1384b Dippie, Brian W. "Brush, Palette and the Custer Battle — A Second Look," an article on the art of the Little Big Horn in *Montana* 24:1, Winter 1974, with two illus. by R. (Blumenschein, Dunton, Russell, Schreyvogel, Von Schmidt)

1385 Dodd, Loring M. An article on Remington in *Hobbies* (magazine), August, 1944.

1386 Dobie, J. Frank. "Tracks of Frederic Remington," an article in *Southwest Review*, Autumn 1961, photo of a Remington bronze on front cover.

1387 Du Plessix, Francine and Gray, Clive. "Thomas Gilcrease and Tulsa," an illus. article in *Art in America*, vol. 52, no. 3, June 1964, with one illus. in color and a photo of one bronze by R. Also includes "The Negro in American Art" by Marvin S. Sadik with one illus. by R.

1388 Dykes, Jeff C. "Frederic Remington — Western Historian," an article in *Corral Dust*, vol. III, no. 3, September 1958, Potomac Corral of the Westerners, Washington, D.C. (Also in *American Book Collector*, vol. IX, no. 8, April 1959, with five illus. by R.)

1389 ———. *High Spots in Western Illustrating*. (Kansas City Posse, The Westerners, Kansas City, 1964), cloth, 30 pp., intro., much on R. in "The Golden Age" and more than a dozen of the *High Spots* illus. by him. Edition limited to 250 numb., signed copies. An edition in wraps issued to members.

1390 Earle, Helen L. (compiler). *Biographical Sketches of American Artists*. Michigan State Library, Lansing, 1913, wraps, 245 pp., illus., Remington sketch, pp. 180–181.

1391 Edgerton, Giles. "Frederic Remington, Painter and Sculptor," an article in *The Craftsman*, March 1909, eleven illus. by R.

1392 Ellsworth, Wm. Webster. *A Golden Age of Authors*. Houghton Mifflin, Boston and N.Y., (1919), decor. cloth, 304 (1) pp., gilt top, illus., R., pp. 246–47.

1393 Fairbanks, C. M. "Artist Remington at Home and Afield," an article in *Metropolitan Magazine*, July 1896, with eight illus. by R. plus four photos.

1394 Garand, Rt. Rev. P. S. *The History of the City of Ogdensburg*. Privately printed, Ogdensburg, N.Y., 1927, cloth, 469 pp., preface, appendix, illus., includes a chapter on, pp. 327–39, and a picture of, the Remington Art Memorial.

1395 Garland, Hamlin. *Roadside Meeting*. Macmillan, N.Y., 1930, words "Pubished September, 1930" on copyright page, two-tone cloth, pic. endsheets, 474 pp., black top, decor. by Constance Garland. A meeting with Remington, pp. 394 and 395.

1396 Garrett, Charles H. "Remington and His Work," an article in *Success* (magazine), May 13, 1899, a portrait of, and illus. by, R.

1396a Hassrick, Peter. "Frederic Remington at the Amon Carter Museum," an article in *American Art Review* 1:1, September–October 1973, with five illus. (two in color) by R.

1397 Hoeber, Arthur. "Painters of Western Life," an article in *The Mentor* (magazine), June 15, 1915, illus. by R. (Leigh, Russell, Schreyvogel)

1398 Horan, James. *The Life and Art of Charles Schreyvogel*. Crown, N.Y., (1969), two-tone fabricoid, 62 pp. plus numerous plates including 39 in color; includes a chapter "The Other Remington" with much on the Remington attack on "Custer's Demand." One of 246 copies numbered and signed by the author and the artist's daughter, Ruth Schreyvogel Carothers.

1399 ———. Same, but first trade edition with 35 color plates.

1400 Hough, Emerson. "Wild West Faking," an article (critical of Remington) in *Collier's* (magazine), Dec. 19, 1908.

1401 Hough, Mrs. Nellie. "Remington at Twenty-Three," an article in *International Studio*, Feb., 1923, five illus. by R.

1402 Howes, Wright. *US-Iana*. R. R. Bowker Co., N.Y., 1954, cloth, 656 pp., foreword, abbreviations and symbols, lists six books by R. and many illus. by him.

1403 ———. Same, revised and enlarged. R. R. Bowker Co., N.Y., for the Newberry Library (Chicago), 1962, cloth, 652 pp., foreword, abbreviations and symbols, lists six books by R. and many illus. by him.

1404 Johnson, Merle. *American First Editions*. R. R. Bowker Co., N.Y., 1929, cloth with paper label on spine, 242 pp., gilt top, preface, R. list, nineteen items, pp. 182–183, years of birth and death under R.'s name both wrong: "1867–1907" should be "1861–1909." Edition consisted of 1000 copies.

1405 ———. *High Spots of American Literature*. Bennett Book Studio, N.Y., 1929, full morocco (or ¾ morocco and marbled boards), marbled endsheets, 114 pp., includes R.'s "The Way of an Indian," item no. 170, as a High Spot. Johnson comments, "Perhaps the only successful attempt to give the psychology of the Western Indian in his war and love-life." 750 numb. copies.

1406 Johnson, Robert Underwood. *Remembered Yesterdays*. Little, Brown, Boston, 1923, words "Published November, 1923" on copyright page, cloth, 624 pp., foreword, index, illus., a R. anecdote, pp. 499–501.

1407 Leeds, Morris A. "Remington and the Redman," an article in *Town & Country*, September 1965, with one illus. by R.

1408 Lichtenberger, Harley W. "Remington and Russell," biographical sketches in *The Westerners Brand Book, Chicago Corral*, May 1962.

1409 McCarrell, Joseph E. "Why I Collect and Enjoy the Work of Frederic Remington," an article in the *Quarterly Newsletter*, vol. XII, no. 3, The Book Club of California, S.F., Summer 1947.

1410 McCracken, Harold. "Historian of the Old West," an article in *Esquire*, January 1950, with six (four in color) illus. by R.

1411 ———. "Frederic Remington: Chronicler of the Old West," an illus. article in *Arizona Highways*, September 1950, with 21 illus. by R. plus one photo.

1412 ———. "Remington Rides Again," an article in *Antiquarian Bookman*, vol. VIII, no. 6, August 11, 1951, five illus. by R.

1413 ———. "Painter of the Wild West," an illus. article in *Modern Man* 5:3, November 1955, with five illus. by R. and a photo of him.

1414 ———. "Frederic Remington — Writer," an article in *The Westerners, New York Posse Brand Book*, vol. 3, no. 2, N.Y., 1956, portrait of R.

1415 ———. "Our Western Documentarians," an article in *American Artist*, vol. 24, no. 3, March 1960, five illus. by R. (Russell)

1416 ———. "He Documented the Old West," an article in *Corral Dust* (Potomac Corral, The Westerners), December 1961, on the occasion of the dedication of the Remington 4¢ stamp.

1417 ———. "Remington's Home and Studio," an illus. article in *The American Scene* 5:4, 1964, with nine illus. by R. and two photos.

1418 ———. "The Whitney Gallery of Western Art," an article in *Corral Dust* (Potomac Corral, The Westerners), Winter 1964, with one illus. by R.

1419 ———. "Frederic Remington's Studio," an article in *Southwestern Art*, Spring 1966, with photos of R. and his friends.

1420 ———. "Frederic Remington: Documentation of the Old West," a biographical sketch in *Smoke Signal* (Tucson Corral, The Westerners), Spring 1967.

1421 McKown, Robin. *Painter of the Wild West, Frederic Remington*. Julian Messner, N.Y., (1959), decor. cloth, 192 pp., acknowledgments, index, selected bibliography, a biography for young readers but not illustrated — what a pity!

1422 Marden, Orison Swett. *Little Visits with Great Americans*. Success Co., N.Y., 1905, decor. cloth and endsheets, 742 pp., preface, intro., index, illus., includes a chapter on R.

1423 Marshall, Edward. *The Story of the Rough Riders*. Dillingham, N.Y., 1899, pic. cloth, 320 pp., ("Tributes") by President McKinley, Sec. of War, General

Wood, and Col. Brodie, preface, roster, illus., presentation of Remington's "Broncho Buster" to Roosevelt, pp. 248-254.

1424 Maxwell, Perriton. "Frederic Remington — Most Typical of American Artists," an illus. article in *Pearson's Magazine*, October 1907, with nine illus. by R. plus one photo.

1425 Mellquist, Jerome. *The Emergence of an American Art.* Scribner's, N.Y., 1942, code letter "A" on copyright page, cloth, 421 pp., intro., appendix, index, illus., Remington, pp. 149, 153 and 222.

1426 Merrill, Arch. *Upstate Echoes.* (American Book Co., Knickerbocker Press, N.Y., 1950), boards, 152 pp., illus., Remington, pp. 10-14.

1427 Neuhas, Eugen. *The History and Ideals of American Art.* Stanford University Press, Stanford University, Calif., 1931, cloth with paper labels, 444 pp., tinted top, bibliography, index, illus., Remington, pp. 318-320 and 417-418.

1428 Paulding, Philip Rodney. "Illustrators and Illustrating," an article in *Munsey's Magazine*, May 1895, with a photo of R.

1429 Preyer, David C. *The Art of the Metropolitan Museum of New York.* Page, Boston, 1909, words "First Impression, November, 1909" on copyright page, gilt decor. red cloth, 419 pp., gilt top, preface, index, illus., appraisal of Remington's bronzes, pp. 67-68.

1430 Remington, Frederic. "Artist Wandering Among the Cheyennes," an illus. article in *Century Magazine*, August 1889, with eleven illus. by R.

1431 (Remington.) "Letter from Frederic Remington Regarding Percival G. Lowe's Book," in the *Journal of the U. S. Cavalry Association* 16:58, October 1905.

1432 (Remington.) "A Few Words from Mr. Remington (on his experiences in the West)," an article in *Collier's*, March 18, 1905, with one illus. by R.

1433 ———. Same, a reprint in *Collier's*, Jan. 8, 1910, but without the illustration.

1434 "Frederic Remington — A Painter of the Vanishing West," an article in *Current Literature*, November, 1907.

1435 "Frederic Remington, October 4, 1861-December 26, 1909," a pictorial tribute in *Collier's*, January 8, 1910, with twelve illus. by R. and with a photo of him.

1436 "The Remington Collection," an illus. article in *Spur Magazine*, September 1938, with four illus. by R. plus a Remington watercolor on the cover.

1437 "Frederic Remington," a pictorial feature in *Life*, Sept. 14, 1942, with a portrait of Remington, eight illus. in color and photos of six bronzes by R.

1438 "Frederic Remington — Was He an Impressionist at Heart," an illus. article in *The Link* 25:5, Sept.-Oct. 1960, with eight illus. by R.

1439 (Remington.) "The Painting of the Collection," an article in *The American Scene*, Summer 1961, with numerous illus. by R.

1440 "Frederic Remington," an illus. article in *Adirondack Life* 1:1, Winter 1970, six (three in color) illus. plus a page of sketches and two photos.

1441 Roosevelt, Theodore. "An Appreciation of the Art of Frederic Remington," an article in *Pearson's Magazine*, October 1907, a photo of the bronze "The Broncho Buster," front cover, by R.

1442 ———. "One Estimate," an appraisal of Remington's art in *Collier's*, January 8, 1910.

1443 Rush, N. Orwin. "Remington the Letter-Writer," an article in *The American Scene* 5:4, 1964, with six illus. by R.

1444 Russell, Don. "More on Custer Art," with comments on a Remington drawing in *The Westerners Brand Book, Chicago Corral*, July, 1948.

1445 Schuessler, Raymond. "The West of Frederic Remington's Cavalryman," an article in *Hoofs and Horns*, vol. 32, no. 2, August 1962, four illus. by R.

1445a ———. "Frederic Remington, Master Painter of the West," an article in *The Chronicle of the Horse* 36:43, October 26, 1973, with four (one on front cover) illus. by R.

1446 Shaw, Charles B. (compiled by). *American Painters.* North Carolina College for Women, Greensboro, July 1927, wraps, 75 pp., explanation, index, Remington list, p. 67.

1447 Sloane, Col. C. A. "Remington's Cavalryman," an article in *The Cavalryman's Journal*, Washington, D.C., 1943, also an article on Remington and one illus. by him. Remington's "Cavalryman" was used as the front cover illus. of the *Journal* for some years — this writer has a copy using it dated January, 1905 and it is believed that it was in use as early as 1902.

1448 Smith, Herbert L. "Saga of Frederic Remington," an illus. article in *Pen* (Federal Post Office Employees Assn., Denver), Nov. 1966, with three illus. by R.

1449 Smith, Thomas West. *The Story of a Cavalry Regi-*

ment, "Scott's 900," *Eleventh New York Cavalry.* Published by the Veterans Assn. of the Regiment (W. B. Conkey Co., Chicago, 1897), cloth, decor. endsheets, 344 (33) pp., preface, corrections, appendix, roster, illus., much on Major S. Pierre Remington, father of Frederic.

1450 Smith, Wm. H. (director of the book dept.). *The Famous Frederic Remington Collection formed by the late Merle Johnson,* etc. Kains Gallery, N.Y., 1937, wraps, 105 pp., auction sale no. 553.

1451 Spaulding, Edward S. *Santa Barbara Club.* (The Schauer Printing Studio, Santa Barbara, Calif.), 1954, wraps, pic. endsheets, 131 pp., members, illus., including four in color. Remington in text. Caballero edition, limited to 250 copies. (Borein)

1452 "The Story Behind the Painting: Remington's 'Pony Express,' " an article in *The American Scene* 1:3, Fall 1958, with one illus. by R.

1453 Swann Auction Galleries, N.Y. *Autographs and Original Manuscripts — Rare Books* (including a Remarkable Collection of Frederick [sic] Remington). Sale no. 336, Nov. 13, 1952, cloth, 33 pp., offers fifty items (some involving three or more volumes), illus. by R.

1454 ————. Sale no. 364, N.Y., Nov. 5, 1953, wraps, 33 pp., offers five Remington art items.

1455 Sydenham, Lieut. Alvin H. *The Journal of, 1889-1890* and *His Notes on Frederic Remington.* New York Public Library, N.Y., 1940, wraps, 29 pp.

1456 ————. "Frederic Remington," an article in the *Bulletin of the New York Public Library,* August 1940.

1457 Taft, Robert. "Frederic Remington, Artist of the Old West, by Harold McCracken," review in *Nebraska History,* vol. 29, no. 3, Sept. 1948.

1458 ————. Same, reprint of no. 1457, folder, (4) pp.

1459 Thomas, Augustus. "Recollections of Frederic Remington," an article in *Century Magazine,* July 1913, portrait of, and illus. by, R.

1460 Toole, K. Ross (editor-in-chief). *Probing The American West* (Papers from the Santa Fe Conference). Museum of New Mexico Press, Santa Fe, (1962), cloth, 216 (7) pp., "Introduction" by Ray A. Billington, notes, index, "Program Pamplet of the Conference on the History of Western America" with one illustration; includes "Frederic Remington and Owen Wister: The Story of a Friendship, 1893-1909" by N. Orwin Rush. (Perceval)

1461 "The Too Short Life of Frederic Remington," an article in *The English Westerners' Tally Sheet,* March-April 1969.

1462 Truettner, William H. "William T. Evans, Collector of American Paintings," an article in *The American Art Journal* 3:2, Fall 1971, with one illus. by R.

1463 Vail, R. W. G. "The Frederic Remington Collection," an article in the *Bulletin of the New York Public Library,* vol. 33, no. 2, February, 1929, three illus. by R. The collection announced as a part of the Spenser Collection of Illustrated Books in the Library.

1464 ————. *Frederic Remington, Chronicler of the Vanished West.* The N.Y. Public Library, N.Y., 1929, wraps, 7 pp., three illus., facing pp. 3, 6 and 7, by R. (First separate printing of the article "The Frederic Remington Collection" in the *Bulletin* February 1929.)

1465 Vaughan, Frank E. *The Spirit of Leadville in Verse.* Privately printed, Leadville, Colo., 1928, fabricoid, 155 pp., apology, preface, includes a long poem "Them Pictures Fred. Remington Makes."

1466 Vaughan, Malcolm. "Master Artist of the Wild West," an illus. article on Remington in *Reader's Digest,* September 1960 with two illus. (one in color) by R.

1467 ————. "Master Artist of the Wild West," an article in *Reader's Digest,* Jan. 1961, with two illus. by R.

1468 Vesey-Fitzgerald, Brian, ed. *The Book of the Horse.* Nicholson & Watson, London, Brussels, 1946, words "First Published in 1946" on copyright page, decor. fabricoid. pic. brown endsheets, 879 pp., foreword, indices, numerous illustrations, appraisal of Remington as a horse artist, p. 316.

1469 Walter, Jones S. An article in *Century* 85:959, April 1913, Remington on tiger-hunting.

1470 Wheeler, Edward J., ed. "Frederic Remington, A Painter of the Vanishing West," an article in *Current Literature,* vol. XLIII, no. 5, 1907, portrait of, and five illus. by R.

1471 Wheelwright, Joh. "Remington and Winslow Homer," an illus. essay in *Hound & Horn* 6:4, July-September 1933, with three illus. by R.

1472 White, G. Edward. *The Eastern Establishment and the Western Experience* (The West of Frederic Remington, Theodore Roosevelt and Owen Wister). Yale, New Haven, 1968, cloth, 238 pp., preface, introduction, references, index.

1473 Wildman, Edwin. "Frederic Remington, the Man," personal reminiscences of a friendship in *Outing Magazine*, March 1903, with one illus. by R. and with four photos.

1474 Wister, Owen. "Remington's Drawings," an article in *Current Literature*, December 1902.

1475 ———. *Members of the Family*. Macmillan, N.Y., 1911, words "Published May, 1911" on copyright page, decor. cloth, 317 pp., preface, illus. The preface includes an appreciation of Remington's art. (Dunn)

1476 ———. Same, but first British edition, issued in London by Macmillan and Co., Limited, in 1911.

1477 ———. "Remington — An Appreciation," an article following Remington's death in *Collier's*, Jan. 8, 1910.

1478 Wood, Leonard. "The Man We Knew," a tribute to Remington and his art in *Collier's*, January 8, 1910.

CARRYING FRESH MEAT TO CAMP by Remington from *Ranch Life in the Far West*

THE SHARP REPORT, AND THE GREAT LEAP OF THE COYOTE by Rowe from
Circle K

CLARENCE ROWE
1878–1930

Illustrated by the Artist

1 Burton, Frederick R. *Strongheart*. Dillingham, N.Y., (1908), cloth, 393 pp., four illus., frontis. and facing pp. 81, 204 and 373, by R.

2 Chisholm, A. M. *Precious Waters*. Doubleday, Page, Garden City, N.Y., 1913, pic. cloth and endsheets, 422 pp., six illus., front cover, endsheets, and four in color, frontis. and facing pp. 142, 254 and 356, by R.

3 Coppee, Francois (English version by Ruth Helen Davis). *The Guilty Man*. Dillingham, N.Y., (1911), cloth, 310 pp., "Introduction" by Marion Mills Miller, eight illus., frontis. and facing pp. 35, 132, 143, 221, 272, 298 and 303, by R.

4 DeLeon, T. C. *Crag-Nest*. Dillingham, N.Y., (1910), cloth, 220 pp., (8) of advs., five illus. including four, facing pp. 70, 108, 163 and 193, by R. (Hutchinson)

5 (Eberstadt.) *Americana*, Catalogue 138. Edward Eberstadt & Sons, N.Y., Dec. 1955, pic. wraps, 128 pp., forty illus. including one, facing p. 64, by R. (Johnson)

6 Freeland, George et al. *America's Building — The Makers of our Flag*. Scribner's N.Y. etc., (1937), code letter "A" on copyright page, pic. cloth, 425 pp., note, annotated list of readings, index, illus. including two, pp. 163 and 165, by R. (Fogarty, Thomason)

7 ———. Same, 1947 edition, with the same Rowe illus., pp. 163 and 165. (Fogarty, Thomason, Varian, Wyeth)

8 Hart, Albert Bushnell. *School History of United States*. American Book Co., N.Y., (1918), cloth, 505 pp., numerous illus. including one, p. 449, by R. (Keller, Varian)

9 Klein, Charles and Hornblow, Arthur. *The Third Degree*. Dillingham, N.Y., (1909), cloth, 356 pp., six illus., frontis. and facing pp. 142, 242, 302, 306 and 354, by R.

10 McCain, George Nox. *The Crimson Dice*. J. Murray Jordan, Phila., (1903), decor. cloth, 310 pp., four illus., frontis. and facing pp. 154, 192 and 242, by R.

11 Mabie, Hamilton Wright et al. *Book of Nature and Outdoor Life* (part 2). The University Society, N.Y., (1912), decor. cloth and endsheets, 416 pp., numerous illus. including one, p. 57, by R. to illustrate his own brief article "Out in the Big-game Country." (Lungren, Remington)

12 Marshall, Edward (based on a play by Olga Nethersale). *The Writing on the Wall*. Dillingham, N.Y., (1909), decor. cloth, 350 pp., introduction, six illus., frontis. and facing pp. 44, 96, 154, 286 and 330, by R.

13 ——— and Dazey, Chas. T. *In Old Kentucky*. Dillingham, N.Y., (1910), cloth, 352 pp., six illus., frontis. and facing pp. 64, 172, 287, 324 and 348, by R.

14 ———. *The Old Flute Player*. Dillingham, N.Y., (1910), cloth, 256 pp., four illus. including three, facing pp. 76, 173 and 208, by R.

15 Raine, William MacLeod. *Wyoming*. Dillingham, N.Y., (1908), red cloth with white lettering, words "issued July, 1908" on copyright page, 353 pp., four illus., frontis. and facing pp. 96, 208, and 334, by R.

16 ———. *Bucky O'Connor*. Dillingham, N.Y., (1910), red cloth with gilt lettering, 345 pp., four illus., frontis. and facing pp. 106, 274 and 330, by R.

17 ———. *A Texas Ranger*. Dillingham, N.Y., (1911), cloth, 337 pp., four illus. including three, facing pp. 64, 244 and 323, by R. (Dunton)

18 ———. *Brand Blotters*. Dillingham, N.Y., (1912), cloth, 348 pp., two illus., frontis. and facing p. 294, by R.

19 ———. *Mavericks*. Dillingham, N.Y., (1912), red

cloth with gilt lettering, 347 pp., (5) of advs., four illus., frontis. and facing pp. 116, 204 and 340, by R.

20 Riegel, Robert E. and Haugh, Helen. *United States of America*. Scribner's, N.Y. etc., (1949), code letter "A" on copyright page, buckram, 852 pp., preface, index, numerous illus. including one, p. 12, by R. (James, Leigh)

21 Sabin, Edwin L. *Range and Trail*. Thomas Y. Crowell, N.Y., (1910), pic. cloth, 445 pp., eight illus., frontis. and facing pp. 62, 104, 290, 360, 378, 410 and 430, by R.

22 ———. *Circle K*. Crowell, N.Y., (1911), pic. cloth, 305 pp., eight illus., frontis. and facing pp. 28, 52, 108, 180, 212, 270 and 284, by R.

23 ———. *Pluck on the Long Trail*. Crowell, N.Y., (1912), pic. cloth, 321 pp., four illus., frontis. and facing pp. 78, 178 and 214, by R.

24 ———. *Old Four-Toes*. Crowell, N.Y., (1912), pic. cloth, 350 pp., eight illus., frontis. and facing pp. 62, 74, 182, 198, 204, 322 and 332, by R.

25 ———. *Treasure Mountain*. Crowell, N.Y., (1913), pic. cloth, 294 pp., eight illus., frontis. and facing pp. 44, 102, 162, 198, 222, 256 and 280, by R.

26 ———. Same, first British edition, George G. Harrap, & Co., London etc., n.d., pic. cloth, 287 (1) pp., eight illus., frontis. and facing pp. 46, 102, 160, 194, 218, 252 and 276, by R.

27 ———. *Scarface Ranch*. Crowell, N.Y., (1914), pic. cloth, decor. endsheets, 297 pp., eight illus., frontis. (in color) and facing pp. 40, 86, 154, 218, 244, 264 and 288, by R. (The list of illustrations shows facing pp. 155 and 245 rather than pp. 154 and 244.)

28 Seltzer, Charles Alden. *The Range Riders*. Outing Publishing Co., N.Y., 1911, pic. cloth, 310 pp., twenty-one illus. by R.

29 ———. *The Triangle Cupid*. Outing, N.Y., 1912, pic.

cloth, 268 pp., illus. including six, pp. 164, 182, 185, 204, 211 and 227, by R.

30 Seton, Ernest Thompson. *The Preacher of Cedar Mountain*. Doubleday, Page, Garden City, N.Y., 1917, pic. cloth, 426 pp., preface, frontis. in color by R.

31 Sinclair, Bertrand. *Raw Gold*. Dillingham, N.Y., (1908), words "issued June, 1908" on copyright page, cloth, 311 pp., four illus., frontis. and facing pp. 161, 208 and 256, by R.

32 Sinclair-Cowan, Bertha M. *The Long Shadow* by B. M. Bower (pseud.). Dillingham, N.Y., 1909, pic. cloth, 302 pp., four illus. in color, frontis. and facing pp. 82, 156 and 305, by R.

33 Wister, Owen. *The Virginian*. Macmillan, N.Y., (1930), words "Revised edition with illustrations published April, 1930" on copyright page, cloth, 567 pp., "Introduction" (and edited) by James Fleming Hosic, revised by H. Y. Moffett, author's preface, twelve illus. by R.

The Artist and His Art

34 Fielding, Mantle. *Dictionary of American Painters, Sculptors and Engravers* (with an addendum compiled by James F. Carr). James F. Carr, N.Y., 1965, cloth, 529 pp., compiler's preface, author's preface, bibliography, partial bibliography. Brief biographical sketch of Rowe, p. 310.

35 Howard, Frances R., ed. *American Art Annual*. The American Federation of Arts, Washington, D.C., 1920, cloth, 680 pp., index, illustrated. Brief biographical sketch of Rowe.

36 Levy, Florence N., ed. *American Art Annual*. The American Federation of Arts, Washington, D.C., 1915, cloth, 566 pp., index, illustrated. Brief biographical sketch of Rowe.

CHARLEY POW-WOW'S WARNING by Rowe from *Treasure Mountain or The Young Prospectors*

ILLUSTRATION by Santee from *Apache Land*

Written and Illustrated by the Artist

1 *Men and Horses.* The Century Co., N.Y., (1926), pic. two-tone cloth, 268 pp., numerous illus.

2 *Cowboy.* Cosmopolitan Book Corp., N.Y., 1928, pic. cloth, 257 pp., numerous illus.

3 *Cowboy.* Pocket Books, N.Y., 1950, words "first printing (Pocket Book edition) October, 1950" on copyright page, colored pic. wraps, 184 pp., all edges red, illus.

4 *Cowboy.* Hastings House, N.Y., (1964), cloth, pic. endsheets, 257 pp., a reprint of the text of no. 2 but with new illus.

5 *Cowboy.* Ace Books, N.Y., (1965), colored pic. wraps, 160 pp., all edges yellow, "About the author," numerous illus. including the front cover in color. The illus. done for no. 4 are used in this reprint.

6 *The Pooch.* Cosmopolitan, N.Y., 1931, pic. cloth, 252 (1) pp., brown top, illus.

7 *Spike.* Grosset & Dunlap, N.Y., (1931), pic. cloth and endsheets, 252 (1) pp., red top, illus. A reprint with new title, of no. 6.

8 *The Bar X Golf Course.* Farrar & Rinehart, N.Y., (1933), publisher's emblem on copyright page, cloth, 159 pp., illus. Score card, with four small drawings by Santee, laid in.

9 *The Bar X Golf Course.* Northland Press, Flagstaff, (1971), pic. cloth, tan endsheets, 89 pp., thirteen illus.

10 *Sleepy Black.* Farrar & Rinehart, N.Y., (1933), publisher's emblem on copyright page, cloth, 250 pp., yellow top, numerous illus.

11 *Apache Land.* Scribner's, N.Y., 1947, code letter "A" on copyright page, pic. cloth, 216 pp., foreword, numerous illus.

12 *Apache Land.* Bantam Books, N.Y., (1956), colored pic. wraps, 242 pp., (2) of advs., foreword, illus.

13 *Apache Land.* Lincoln, Nebraska, (1971), words "First Bison Book printing May 1971" on copyright page, pic. wraps, 216 pp., foreword, numerous illus.

14 *The Bubbling Spring.* Scribner's, N.Y., London, 1949, code letter "A" on copyright page, cloth, 300 pp., numerous illus.

15 *The Bubbling Spring.* Manor Books, N.Y., (1972), colored pic. wraps, 300 pp., all edges yellow, numerous illus.

16 *Rusty.* Scribner's, (N.Y., 1950), code letter "A" on copyright page, pic. cloth, 240 pp., illus. (A special revised edition for the younger readers of no. 12.)

17 *Hard Rock and Silver Sage.* Scribner's, N.Y., London, 1951, code letter "A" on copyright page, pic. cloth, 224 (1) pp., numerous illus.

18 *Lost Pony Tracks.* Scribner's, N.Y., 1953, code letter "A" on copyright page, pic. cloth, 303 pp., brown top, twenty-six illus. (Russell in text.)

19 *Lost Pony Tracks.* Bantam Books, N.Y., (1956), words "Bantam edition published July 1956" on copyright page, colored pic. wraps, 245 pp., (3) of advs., all edges yellow, illus.

20 *Dog Days.* Scribner's, N.Y., 1955, code letter "A" on copyright page, decor. cloth, 244 pp., numerous illus.

21 *The Rummy Kid Goes Home and Other Stories of the Southwest.* Hastings House, N.Y., (1965), cloth, 160 pp., numerous illus.

Illustrated by the Artist

22 Abbott, E. C. ("Teddy Blue") and Smith, Helena Huntington. *We Pointed Them North.* Farrar & Rinehart, N.Y., Toronto, (1939), publisher's emblem on copyright page, cloth with illus. paper strip on covers,

281 pp., green top, "Introduction" by Mrs. Smith, maps, illus. with drawings by S. and with photos.

23 Ainsworth, Ed. *The Cowboy in Art*. World, N.Y. and Cleveland, (1968), words "First Printing 1968" on copyright page, full leather, orange endsheets, 242 pp., all edges gilt, "Foreword" by John Wayne, index, numerous illus. including fifteen drawings by S. Special edition of 1000 numbered copies, slipcase. (Beeler, Borein, Bugbee, De Yong, Dixon, Dunton, Eggenhofer, Ellsworth, Hurd, James, Johnson, Koerner, Mora, Perceval, Remington, Russell, Schreyvogel, Von Schmidt)

24 ———. Same, first trade edition in gilt lettered and illus. cloth, orange endsheets.

25 ———. Same, reprint by Bonanza Books, N.Y., in red lettered and illus. cloth, white endsheets.

26 Bennett, Russell H. *The Compleat Rancher*. Rinehart & Co., N.Y., Toronto, (1946), publisher's emblem on copyright page, cloth, 246 pp., introduction, bibliography, illus. by S.

27 Boyer, Mary G. (compiled by). *Arizona in Literature*. Clark, Glendale, 1934, cloth, 574 pp., preface, index, illus. including one drawing, p. 256, by S., reprints "The Punchers Tell a Few" by S.

28 Burt, Struthers. *The Diary of a Dude Wrangler*. Scribner's, N.Y., London, 1924, cloth, 331 pp., d/w illus. by S.

29 ———. *Powder River, Let'er Buck*. Farrar & Rinehart, N.Y., Toronto, (1938), publisher's emblem on copyright page, cloth, 389 (11) pp., red top, bibliography, index, "Rivers and American Folk" by Constance Lindsay Skinner, illus. by S.

30 Carlson, Raymond, ed. *Gallery of Western Painting*. McGraw-Hill, N.Y. etc., (1951), words "First Edition" on copyright page, cloth with illus. in color mounted on front cover, colored endsheets, 85 pp., foreword, 76 illus. including nineteen drawings by S. Biographical sketch of S. by Carlson. (Dixon, Leigh, Remington, Russell)

31 Carmer, Carl, ed. *Songs of the Rivers of America*. Farrar & Rinehart, N.Y., Toronto, (1942), publisher's emblem on copyright page, cloth, tinted endsheets, 196 pp., editor's foreword, "Introductory Notes about the Music" by Dr. Albert Sirmay, index, illus. including two, pp. 150 and 180, by S.

32 Coburn, Walt. *Mavericks*. Century, N.Y. and London, (1929), words "First Printing, August, 1929" on

copyright page, decor. cloth, 317 pp., small drawing on title page and two drawings on d/w by S.

33 ———. *Stirrup High*. Julian Messner, N.Y., (1957), cloth, 190 pp., "Foreword" by Fred Gipson, illus. by S.

34 Corle, Edwin. *The Gila*. Rinehart, N.Y., Toronto, (1951), publisher's emblem on copyright page, cloth, 402 pp., brown top, foreword, acknowledgments, bibliography, index, map, illus. by S.

35 ———. Same, Nebraska, Lincoln, (1964), pic. wraps, 402 pp., numerous illus. by S. Bison Book 305.

36 Cowan, Bud. *Range Rider*. Doubleday, Doran, Garden City, N.Y., 1930, words "First Edition" on copyright page, pic. cloth, 289 pp., orange top, "Introduction" by B. M. Bower (pseud.) (Bertha M. Sinclair-Cowan, Bud's wife), illus. by S.

37 ———. Same, a reprint by Sun Dial Press, N.Y., (1930).

38 Dalton, Emmett. *When the Daltons Rode*. Doubleday, Garden City, 1931, words "First Edition" on copyright page, pic. fabricoid, 313 pp., illus. with photos but illus. on back of d/w by S.

39 Dobie, J. Frank et al., eds. *Mustangs and Cowhorses*. Texas Folk-Lore Society, Austin, 1940, fabricoid, pic. endsheets, introduction, contributors, index, numerous illus. including two, pp. 56 and 351, by S. (Reprinted 1965 by the SMU Press in Dallas.) (Bugbee, James, Lea, Russell, Thomason)

40 ———. *Guide to Life and Literature of the Southwest*. The University of Texas Press, Austin, 1943, wraps, 111 pp., "A Declaration," 24 illus. including one, p. 76, by S. (Borein, Bugbee, Dunton, Lea, Russell, Thomason)

41 ———. Same, reprinted by the University Press in Dallas, in cloth, 1943.

42 *Hamley's Cowboy Catalog, No. 53*. Hamley & Co., Pendleton, Oregon, 1953, colored pic. wraps, 144 pp., "To Our Friends and Customers," index, numerous illus. including one by S. (James, Russell)

43 Hawthorne, Hildegarde. *The Mystery at Star-C Ranch*. Appleton, N.Y., London, 1929, code number "(1)" after last line of text, decor. cloth, 232 (1), pp., frontis. by S.

44 Hunt, Frazier. *Cap Mossman*. Hastings House, N.Y., (1951), pic. cloth and endsheets, 277 pp., sixteen illus. by S.

45 ———. *The Tragic Days of Billy the Kid*. Hastings

House, N.Y., (1956), pic. cloth, map endsheets, 316 pp., maps by R. N. (Bob) Mullin, front cover and d/w illus. by S.

46 Jeffers, Jo. *Ranch Wife.* Doubleday, Garden City, N.Y., 1964, words "First Edition" on copyright page, cloth, pic. endsheets, 273 pp., twelve illus. by S.

47 Larom, Henry V. *Mountain Pony.* McGraw-Hill, N.Y., London, (1946), pic. cloth, map endsheets, 240 pp., illus. by S.

48 ———. *Mountain Pony and Pinto Colt.* McGraw-Hill, N.Y., London, (1947), words "First Printing" on copyright page, pic. cloth, map endsheets, 202 pp., numerous illus. by S.

49 ———. *Mountain Pony and the Rodeo Mystery.* McGraw-Hill, N.Y. etc., (1949), pic. cloth, map endsheets, 228 pp., illus. by S.

50 ———. *Mountain Pony and the Elkhorn Mystery.* McGraw-Hill, N.Y. etc., (1950), pic. cloth, map endsheets, 222 pp., illus. by S.

51 Law, Frederick H., ed. *Stories of Today and Yesterday.* Century, N.Y., London, (1930), two-tone cloth, 439 pp., preface, introduction, eight illus. including one, facing p. 44, by S.

52 Lomax, John A. *Songs of the Cattle Trail and Cow Camp.* Duell, Sloan and Pearce, N.Y., (1950), cloth, pic. endsheets, 189 pp., red top, "Foreword" by Wm. Lyon Phelps, introduction, 78 illus. including four, pp. 23, (35), (75) and 141, by S. (Remington, Russell)

53 Mathews, Franklin K., ed. *The Boy Scouts Year-Book.* Appleton, N.Y., London, (1921), cloth with illus. in color on front cover, tan endsheets, 259 (1) pp., "Foreword" by James E. West (Chief Scout Executive), numerous illus. including two, pp. 190 and (191), by S.

54 Miller, Joseph (compiler). *Arizona Pictorial.* Peterson, Brooke, Steiner and Wist, Phoenix, 1944, fabricoid, unpaged, numerous (many in color) illus. including one drawing by S.

55 ———. *The Arizona Story.* Hastings House, N.Y., (1952), cloth, map endsheets, 345 pp., red top, "The Arizona Story," illus. by S.

56 ———. *Arizona: The Last Frontier.* Hastings House, N.Y., (1956), pic. cloth, map endsheets, 350 pp., foreword, index, numerous illus. by S.

57 ———, ed. *Arizona Cavalcade.* Hastings House, N.Y., (1962), cloth, 306 pp., preface, illus. by S.

58 Pace, Mildred Mastin et al. *Three Great Horse Stories.*

McGraw-Hill, N.Y. etc., (1957), pic. cloth, pp. 119, (3), 202, 180, 2, illus. including many by S.

59 Parkhill, Forbes. *Trooper's West.* Farrar & Rinehart, N.Y., Toronto, (1945), publisher's emblem on copyright page, pic. cloth, 249 pp., numerous illus. by S.

60 (Santee, Ross, State Director.) *Arizona.* Hastings House, N.Y., 1940, words "First Published in April 1940" on copyright page, cloth, map endsheets, 530 pp., "Foreword" by Thomas J. Tormey, preface, appendices, bibliography, index, maps, illus. with drawings by S. and with photos. (Ross Santee's name does not appear in this book except as an Arizona writer; he was the State Supervisor of the Federal Writers' Project and the editor-in-chief at the time it was issued. When the "brass" in Washington refused to let him include the names of the writers and researchers who compiled it, he refused to let his own name be used on it.)

61 *Southward to Sonora.* A separate from *Arizona Highways,* October 1940, colored pic. wraps, 20 pp., thirteen drawings by S.

62 Spring, Agnes W. (State Supervisor). *Wyoming.* Oxford University Press, N.Y., (1941), words "First Published in April, 1941", on copyright page, decor. cloth, map on front endsheet, 490 pp., (Foreword) by Governor Lester C. Hunt, preface, appendices, bibliography, index, maps, illus. with drawings, thirteen by S. and with photos. (Not only was Ross Santee loved by his "boys" — for example, Joe Miller and Jonreed Lauritzen — on the Arizona Project as an able administrator and helpful teacher and editor but the "brass" used him to help with some of the other State Guides — Mrs. Spring acknowledges the help of Ross and one of his men with the art work in *Wyoming* in her preface.)

62a Weaver, Paul E. (publisher). *Autumn 1972 Book List.* Northland Press, Flagstaff, pic. wraps, unpaged, numerous illus. including one by S. (Dixon, Perceval, Remington, Von Schmidt)

62b ———. *Autumn 1973 Book List.* Northland, colored pic. wraps, unpaged, numerous illus. including one by S. (Beeler, Blumenschein, Dixon, James, Perceval, Remington, Von Schmidt)

63 *Western Americana Books,* Hastings, N.Y., (1964), advs. folder with three drawings, front cover (two) and back cover, by S. (Eggenhofer, Russell)

64 White, Owen P. *Them Was the Days.* Minton, Balch & Co., N.Y., 1925, pic. cloth, 235 pp., tinted top, illus. by S.

65 ———. Same, Andrew Melrose, London, n.d.

66 ———. *Trigger Fingers*. Putnam's, N.Y., London, 1926, cloth, 323 pp., small drawing on title page and d/w illus. by S.

67 Wister, Owen. *The Virginian*. Grosset & Dunlap, N.Y., n.d., (1935), cloth with pic. paper labels, pic. endsheets, 506 pp., green top, rededication and preface, "To the Reader," 48 illus. including two, endsheets and title page, by S. (Remington, Russell)

68 ———. Same, Grosset & Dunlap, N.Y., (1947), words "Reprinted . . . May, 1947" on copyright page, boards, 506 pp., illus. including one, title page, by S. (Russell)

69 *World Series Rodeo, Seventh Annual*, Madison Square Garden, N.Y., October 14–30, 1932, colored pic. wraps, 48 pp., numerous illus. including one, p. 19, by S.; includes "A Brok's Own Story" by S.

70 Same, *Eighth Annual*, Madison Square Garden, N.Y., October 11–29, 1933, colored pic. wraps, 48 pp., numerous illus. including one, p. 18, by S. (James)

71 Same, *Eleventh Annual*, Madison Square Garden, N.Y., October 7–25, 1936, colored pic. wraps, 48 pp., numerous illus. including one, p. 29, by S.

Written by the Artist

72 Arnold, Oren. *Roundup*. Banks Upshaw & Co., Dallas, (1937), words "First Printing" on copyright page, pic. cloth and endsheets, 301 pp., preface, glossary, illus. Includes "Runaway" by S.

73 Autry, Gene (selected by). *Western Stories*. Dell Pub. Co., N.Y., (1947), colored pic. wraps, 191 pp., (1) of advs., all edges blue, "I Like Westerns." Includes "With Bated Breath" by S.

74 ———. *Gun Smoke Yarns*. Dell, N.Y., (1948), colored pic. wraps, 191 pp., (1) of advs., all edges blue, "Gun Smoke Aplenty." Includes "The Lower Trail" by S.

75 *Avon Western Reader, No. 4*. Avon Book Co., N.Y., (1947), colored pic. wraps, 126 pp. Includes "With Bated Breath" by S.

76 Baker, Ray Stannard (an anthology by). *Stories for Men* by David Grayson (pseud.). Little, Brown, Boston, 1936, cloth, 595 pp., "Explicit." Includes "With Bated Breath" by S.

77 Becker, May Lamberton (selected by). *Golden Tales of the Southwest*. Dodd, Mead, N.Y., 1939, cloth, pic. endsheets, 265 pp., tinted top, acknowledgments, foreword, illus. Includes "The Rummy Kid" by S., and brief appraisal of his writings and art.

78 *Chicago Rodeo*, November 16–24, 1929, colored pic. wraps, 48 pp., numerous illustrations. Includes "Western Riders Praise Rodeo" by Santee, Owen P. White et al.

79 De Grazia, Ted. *Padre Kino*. Southwest Museum, Los Angeles, 1962, wraps, 54 (1) pp., "Introduction" by Carl S. Dentzel, map, illus. by the author. Praise of De Grazia's work by Santee, et al.

80 Dennis, Wesley (edited and illus. by). *Palomino and Other Horses*. World Pub. Co., Cleveland and N.Y., (1950), code number "WPC 7-50" on copyright page, pic. cloth, 249 pp., brown top, introduction. Includes "A Fool About a Horse" by S.

81 Frederick, John T., ed. *Thirty-Four Present Day Stories*. Scribner's, N.Y. etc., (1941), code letter "A" on copyright page, cloth, 496 pp., preface. Includes "Water" by S.

82 ——— and Ward, Leo L. *Reading for Writing*. F. S. Crofts & Co., N.Y., 1941, words "Second edition, Fourth printing, January 1941" on copyright page, cloth, 463 pp., introduction, note on the second edition. Includes "I Didn't Want any Trouble" by S. (Maybe the first printing to include the Santee story.)

83 Gray, Charles Wright, ed. *"Hosses."* Henry Holt & Co., N.Y., (1927), words "Printed, September, 1927" on copyright page, cloth with small illus. in color mounted on front cover, pic. endsheets, "A Dedication: A Foreword." Includes "A Fool About a Horse" by S.

84 Hano, Arnold, ed. *Western Triggers*. Bantam Books, N.Y., (1948), words "Published February, 1948" on copyright page, colored pic. wraps, 181 pp., (3) of advs., all edges red. Includes "Shorty Buys a Hat" by S.

85 Hansen, Harry, ed. *O. Henry Memorial Award Prize Stories of 1935*. Garden City, N.Y., 1935. Includes "Water" by S., plus a brief biographical sketch, p. 104.

86 Harper, Wilhelmina (selected by). *Flying Hoofs*. Houghton Mifflin, Boston, 1939, pic. cloth, 292 pp., illus. including three in color. Includes "The Swede" by S.

87 (James.) *Will James' Book of Cowboy Stories*. Scribner's, N.Y., 1951, code letter "A" on copyright page, pic. cloth, 242 (1) pp., illus. by James. Includes "Will James" by S. as a foreword.

88 ———. Same, first British edition, Phoenix House, London, (1952), words "First published 1952" on

ILLUSTRATION by Santee from *The Bar X Golf Course*

copyright page, cloth, 242 (1) pp., "Will James" by S., illus. by James.

89 Perry, George Sessions, ed. *Roundup Time.* N.Y., London, (1943). Includes a story selected from *Sleepy Black* (no. 9) by S., plus a brief biographical sketch, p. 341.

90 Raine, Wm. MacLeod (selected by). *Western Stories.* Dell Pub. Co., N.Y., (1949), colored pic. wraps, 192 pp., all edges blue. Includes "Water" by S.

91 Sonnichsen, C. L. (compiled and edited by). *The Southwest in Life & Literature.* Devin-Adair, N.Y., 1962, decor. cloth, 554 pp., "The Fabulous Southwest, an Introduction," about the authors, small drawing on the title page. Includes "Mack Breaks His Last Bronc" by S., plus a brief biographical sketch, p. 552. (Russell)

92 Targ, William, ed. *Western Story Omnibus.* World, Cleveland and N.Y., (1945), words "First Printing, January 1945" on copyright page, cloth, 320 pp. Includes "The Rummy Kid" by S.

93 Tinkle, Lon and Maxwell, Allen, ed. *The Cowboy Reader.* Longmans, Green & Co., N.Y. etc., 1959, words "First Edition" on copyright page, cloth, 307 pp., editors' introduction, numerous illus. Includes "The Rough String" by S. (Bugbee, Lea, Remington, Russell)

94 Ward, Don, ed. *Pioneers West* (14 Stories of the Old Frontier). Dell, N.Y., (1966), words "First Dell printing — September, 1966" on copyright page, colored pic. wraps, 255 pp., (1) of advs., all edges green, introduction; reprints "Water" by S.

95 Webb, Walter Prescott. *The Great Plains.* Gim, (Boston etc., 1931), pic. cloth, 525 pp., illustrated; quotes Santee pp. 249 and 250.

Edited by the Artist

In addition to no. 50 above, Ross edited the following publications while serving as State Director of The Federal Writers' Project (after 1939, the Writers' Program) in Arizona:

96 *Arizona* (Recreation Series). Bacon & Wieck, Northport, N.Y., (1940), pic. wraps, 44 pp., map.

97 *Mission San Xavier Del Bac.* Hastings House, N.Y., 1940, words "First Published in March 1940" on copyright page, cloth, pic. endsheets, 57 pp., preface, bibliography, plan, illus. with photos.

98 *The Apache.* Arizona State Teachers College, Flag-

staff, August 1939, decor. wraps, 16 pp., "Foreword" by President Thomas J. Tormey, bibliography, one illus. A.S.T.C. Bulletin, vol. 20, no. 1.

99 *The Havasupai and Hualapai.* A.S.T.C., Flagstaff, Dec. 1940, decor. wraps, 35 (1) pp., "Foreword" by Pres. Tormey, bibliography, frontis. Bulletin, vol. 21, no. 5.

100 *The Hopi.* A.S.T.C., Flagstaff, September, 1937, wraps, 25 pp., "Foreword" by Pres. Tormey, introduction, bibliography, one illus. Bulletin, vol. 18, no. 2.

101 *The Navaho.* A.S.T.C., Flagstaff, November, 1937, wraps, 21 pp., "Foreword" by Ross Santee and Pres. Tormey, bibliography, one illus. Bulletin, vol. 18, no. 4.

102 *The Papago.* A.S.T.C., Flagstaff, October 1939, wraps, 16 pp., "Foreword" by Pres. Tormey, bibliography. Bulletin, vol. 20, no. 3.

The Artist and His Art

103 Adams, Ramon F. *The Rampaging Herd.* University of Oklahoma Press, 1959, words "First Edition" on the copyright page, cloth, 463 pp. Lists four books, item nos. 2007–10, by S. and several illus. by him.

104 Armstrong, Rolf. Cover portrait of a Cowboy, modeled by Santee, *Saturday Evening Post,* 1923.

105 Arnold, Oren. "He Did it for Fun," an illustrated article about Santee in *The Desert Magazine,* January 1944.

106 Bell, Col. William Gardner. "Ross Santee's last letter to the Editor" plus an obituary in *Corral Dust,* Summer 1965, letter in facsimile with one illus. by S.

107 ———. "Ross Santee," an article in *Corral Dust,* Potomac Corral, The Westerners, Washington, D.C., Fall 1965, Santee illus. on cover, the portrait of him by Armstrong and one photo of him.

108 Bolton, Theodore. *American Book Illustrators, Bibliographic Check Lists of 123 Artists.* R. R. Bowker Co., N.Y., 1938, cloth, 290 pp. Lists the Santee books published prior to 1938 plus nos. 28 and 52.

109 Brackett, Beryl. "Arizona's Cowboy Artist-Writer," an article in *Arizona Highways,* October 1936, drawing of Santee.

110 Carlson, Raymond. "Ross Santee, Artist-Author," an article in *Arizona Highways,* October 1956, with a photo of Santee.

111 ———. "So Long Ross," a tribute in *Arizona Highways,* September 1965.

112 Dobie, J. Frank. *Guide to Life and Literature of the Southwest* (Revised and Enlarged in Both Knowledge and Wisdom). Southern Methodist Univ. Press, Dallas, 1952, cloth, 222 pp. The second edition of no. 31 but the Santee drawing is omitted. Santee and his books praised, pp. 61, 118, 134, 135, 136 and 188.

113 Dykes, Jeff C. *High Spots in Western Illustrating.* (Kansas City Posse, The Westerners, 1964), cloth, 30 pp., introduction, two illus. No. 1 of this list is High Spot 47 and no. 10 is High Spot 71. Limited to 250 numbered and signed copies but an edition in wraps was issued to members.

114 Ford, Moselle Alden. *Ross Santee: Author and Artist of the Southwest.* Unpublished thesis, The University of Texas, El Paso, 1965.

115 Gerson, Rochelle. "Juvenile Authors: Some Bows and Encores," an article in *Saturday Review of Literature,* Nov. 11, 1950, includes a biographical sketch of Santee and a photo of him.

116 Houston, Neal B. *Ross Santee.* Steck-Vaughn Co., Austin, Texas, (1968), wraps, 44 pp., selected bibliography, four illus., pp. 19, 20, 21 and 22, by S.

117 Kirkpatrick, Nancy C. *Ross Santee, Arizona Writer and Illustrator, A Bibliography.* Library Science 400, n.p., May 1972, selfwraps, 28 Xeroxed pages, preface, three illus., pp. 11, 13 and 26, by S.

118 Kunitz, Stanley, ed. *Twentieth Century Authors, First Supplement.* H. W. Wilson Co., N.Y., 1955, includes a Santee bibliography and a portrait of him.

119 Miller, Joseph. *Arizona Indians.* Hastings House, N.Y., (1941), cloth, 59 pp., illus. Dedication "To Ross Santee and Eve."

120 Northland Press. *Spring 1972 Book List.* Flagstaff, Ariz., folder, nine illus. including one by S.

121 Past, Ray. *Illustrated by the Author: A Study of Six Western American Writers-Artists.* Unpublished doctoral dissertation, The University of Texas, Austin, 1950.

122 Powell, Lawrence Clark. *Heart of the Southwest.* Dawson's Book Shop, Los Angeles, 1955, cloth and boards, 42 pp., nos. 2, 12 and 14 above praised.

123 (Reynolds.) *The West of Ross Santee* (Catalogue 66). J. E. Reynolds, Van Nuys, California, Fall 1961, pic. wraps, unpaged, illus. with nine drawings by S. and with a photo of him. Includes "An Acknowledgment" by Reynolds; "The Art of Ross Santee" by Carl S. Dentzel; "Ross Santee — His 'Cowboy' " by J. Frank Dobie; "The Eve Santee Book Club" by J. C. (Jeff) Dykes; "Salud y Cartuchos" by W. H. Hutchinson; "The Man who Hazed Me In" by Jonreed Lauritzen, and it lists 103 items of Santee interest for sale.

124 Santee, Ellis M., M.D. (compiled and published by). *Genealogy of the Santee Family.* Cortland, N.Y., 1899, wraps, 127 pp., illus. Ross is listed and the year of his birth, as it is practically everywhere else, is given as 1889. In the copy owned by your compiler, Ross has corrected the date to 1888.

125 ———. Same, enlarged edition published by the author at Wilkes-Barre, Pennsylvania, 1927, cloth, 211 pp., editor's notes, directory, errata, illus. with photos.

126 Santee, Ross. "Advice is all right, if you don't take too much of it," an article in *The American Magazine,* June 1928. Primarily autobiographical — on his early struggles in getting an art education and in gaining acceptance of his art and writings. Seven drawings by S. plus a portrait of him by Rolf Armstrong.

127 ———. "The West I Remember," an article in *Arizona Highways,* October 1956. Autobiographical, illus. with four drawings and ten watercolors by S.

128 ———. *Drawings by Ross Santee.* A folder commenting on his art for distribution at an exhibition at the Phoenix Federal Art Center, Jan. 9–21 (no year given but while Ross was State Director, Federal Writers' Project, 1936–1941).

129 Swientochowski, John. "Sketch Book — Ross Santee," an article about Ross and his art in *Dateline Delaware,* vol. 2, no. 4, June 1961. Illus. by S.

130 Weadlock, Jack F. "A Dedication to the Memory of Ross Santee, 1889–1965," a brief lead article in *Arizona and the West,* vol. 7, no. 3, Autumn 1965. Illus. with a photo of S. Includes "A Selected List of the Works of Ross Santee Relating to the American West."

THE HEART OR HUTTON RANCH ON THE BIG LARAMIE RIVER by Schiwetz
from *Trans-Missouri Stock Raising*

EDWARD MUEGGE (BUCK) SCHIWETZ
Contemporary, 1898–

Catalogues of Art Exhibitions and Galleries

BAKER COLLECTOR GALLERY, LUBBOCK, TEXAS

1 *E. M. "Buck" Schiwetz*, April 26 to May 26, 1970, folder with seven illus. by S. and a photo of him.

DALLAS MUSEUM OF FINE ARTS

2 *A Century of Art and Life in Texas*, April 9–May 7, 1961, pic. wraps, unpaged, "Foreword" by Jerry Bywaters (Director), numerous illus. including one by S. (Dunton, Johnson, Lea, Remington)

HUMANITIES RESEARCH CENTER
THE UNIVERSITY OF TEXAS, AUSTIN

3 *Texana at the University of Texas*, March 1962, decor. wraps, 42 (2) pp., "Preface" by Walter Prescott Webb, introduction, bibliographies cited, illus. including one, p. (41), by S. (Crawford)

INSTITUTE OF TEXAN CULTURES, THE UNIVERSITY OF TEXAS, SAN ANTONIO

4 *Texas' Buck Schiwetz*, December 4, 1971–January 15, 1972, cloth and pic. boards, unpaged, "Texas' Buck Schiwetz" by R. Henderson Shuffler, numerous illus. by S. Limited edition of 200 numbered copies signed by Shuffler, Schiwtez and the designer William D. Wittliff, with six illus. that do not appear in the first trade edition, slipcase.

5 Same, first trade edition in pic. wraps, 1000 copies.

NATIONAL ACADEMY GALLERIES, NEW YORK

6 *Eighty-seventh Annual Exhibition, American Watercolor Society*, February 25–March 15, 1954, wraps, 64 pp., designed and edited by William Strosahl et al., numerous illus. including one, p. 19, by S. His entry "Souvenir of New Orleans" won the AWS Non-Members Award for 1954.

WITTE MEMORIAL MUSEUM, SAN ANTONIO

7 *Oils by Otis Dozier, Oils and Water Colors by Edward Schiwetz*, San Antonio Art League, February 15–29, 1948, folder with a catalog of the twenty-five works of art exhibited by S. and a brief biographical sketch of him.

Illustrated by the Artist

8 Adair, A. Garland and Coats, Ellen Bohlender. *Texas, Its History.* Philadelphia etc., (1954), decor. cloth, 395 pp., preface, index, maps, numerous illus. including two, pp. 29 and (57), by S.

9 *Announcing an Auction of Paintings by Twenty Noted Artists of the Southwest for the Benefit of the Dobie-Paisano Project.* Houston, May 11, (1966?), four-fold flyer, twenty-two illus. including one, "Fredericksburg Ensemble," by S. (Hurd, Lea)

10 Bradshaw, Mrs. Lillian Moore and Stone, Marvin. *Five Years Forward.* Dallas Public Library, Dallas, Texas, 1960, pic. wraps, 31 pp., "An Appreciation" by Paul Horgan, typography by Carl Hertzog, illus. by S.

11 Carroll, H. Bailey et al. *The Story of Texas.* Noble & Noble, N.Y., (1963), colored pic. cloth, 360 pp., preface, acknowledgments, numerous illus. including fourteen by S. (Lea, Wyeth)

12 Clark, Joseph L. and Linder, Dorothy A. *The Story of Texas.* D. C. Heath & Co., Boston, (1955), code no. "(5E4)" on copyright page, colored pic. cloth, 436 pp., acknowledgments, appendix, index, maps, numerous illus. including photos and many drawings by S. (Marchand, Remington)

13 ———. Same, 1963 edition.

14 *Cuero Gobbler.* Cuero (Texas) High School Annual, 1917, with illus. by S. Buck was the art editor.

15 Eads, Leila Reeves. *Defenders, A Confederate History of Henderson County, Texas.* (Henderson County Historical Survey Committee, 1969), colored pic. wraps, 42 pp., "Foreword" by Senator Ralph W. Yarborough, notes, bibliography, appendix, chronological events in Texas, numerous illus. including one, p. 16 (repeated on wraps), by S.

16 Elkins, J. A. (Senior Chairman of the Board) et al. *The New First City National Bank of Houston.* McCann-Erickson, Houston, 1961, stiff wraps, 16 pp., numerous illus. in color including one, the frontis., by S.

17 Fields, F. T. *Texas Sketch Book, Vol. I.* Humble Oil & Refining Co., (Houston, 1952), pic. wraps, 43 pp., foreword, numerous illus. by S.

18 ———. *Texas Sketch Book.* Humble Oil & Refining Co., Houston, (1955), colored pic. wraps, 92 pp., numerous illus. by S.

19 Fuerman, George. *Reluctant Empire.* Doubleday, Garden City, N.Y., 1957, words "First Edition" on copyright page, cloth, pic. endsheets, 284 pp., preface, index, twenty-eight illus. by S.

20 Gambrell, Herbert and Virginia. *A Pictorial History of Texas.* Dutton, N.Y., (1960), words "First Edition" on copyright page, cloth and decor. boards, brand illus. endsheets, 217 pp., acknowledgments, sources of illustrations, index, numerous illus. including nineteen by S. (James, Lea, Remington)

20a *The Garden Club of America — Forty-second Annual Meeting.* Houston, Texas, March 8–11, 1955, pic. wraps, spiral binder, 42 pp., map, illus. including six, pp. 3, 14, 28, 30, 36 and 41, by S.

21 Gavin, Marian. *Jailer, My Jailer.* Doubleday, Garden City, N.Y., 1964, words "First Edition" on copyright page, cloth, 280 pp., d/w illus. by S.

22 Hohn, Caesar (Dutch). *Dutchman on the Brazos.* Univ. of Texas Press, Austin, (1963), cloth, 194 pp., "Foreword" by Agnes Meyer, acknowledgments, index, illus. with nineteen drawings by S., and with photos.

23 Hunt, Lenoir. *Bluebonnets and Blood.* Texas Books, Houston, Texas, (1938), fabricoid, 433 pp. acknowledgments, foreword, afterword, bibliography, index, map, numerous illus. including nine, pp. (2), (18), (26), (38), (114), (144), (320), (366) and (376), by S.

24 Hutcheson, Edward C. *The Freedom Tree* (A Chapter from the Saga of Texas). Texian Press, Waco, 1970, pic. cloth, 178 pp., maps, illus. including one, the frontis. (repeated on the front cover), by S.

25 ———. Same, advs. folder, with one illus. by S. on the front cover.

26 Jenkins, John A. *A Catalogue of over 1400 County and Town Histories of Texas.* The Jenkins Co., Austin, Texas, (1964), pic. wraps, (77) (6) pp., "Somervell County" reprinted from *A History of Hood County,* two illus., front cover and p. (78), by S.

27 Kilman, Ed. *Cannibal Coast.* The Naylor Co., San Antonio, Texas, (1959), pic. cloth, map endsheets, 294 pp., "Introducing the Karankawas," bibliography, index, about the author, illus. with drawings by Tom Jones, d/w design in color by S.

28 Latham, Dr. Hiram. *Trans-Missouri Stock Raising.* Advertising brochure, Carl Hertzog of El Paso for the Old West Publishing Co., Denver, 1962, two illus. by S.

29 ———. *Trans-Missouri Stock Raising.* The Old West Publishing Co., Denver, Colorado, 1962, pic. cloth, facsimiles of original covers on orange endsheets, 94 pp., "Introduction," marginal annotations (in red) and brief biographical sketches of the letter writers by Jeff C. Dykes, two illus., frontis. and pp. viii and ix, by S., d/w and front cover illus. also by S. Designed and printed by Carl Hertzog in an edition of 999 copies.

30 Lomax, John A. *Will Hogg, Texan.* Univ. of Texas Press, Austin, 1956, cloth and boards, 51 pp., "foreword" by Robert L. Sutherland, four illus. including two, front and back endsheets, by S.

31 ———. Same, reissued for the dedication of the Will C. Hogg Building at the University of Texas, Austin, 1968.

32 *Longhorn.* Vol. XVII, published by the Senior Class, Texas A. & M. College, College Station, Texas, 1919, decor. cloth, marbled endsheets, 294 pp., "Foreword" (and edited) by John S. Stewart, Jr., numerous illus. including three, p. 43, facing p. 224 in color, and p. 270, by S. Photo of S. as member of the Architectural Club.

33 *The Longhorn.* Vol. XVIII, published by the Senior Class, Texas A. & M. College, College Station, Texas, 1920, simulated leather, marbled endsheets, 462 pp., "Foreword" (and edited) by K. J. Edwards, numerous illus. including eight, pp. 49, 251, (405) in color, 410,

OLD STONE FORT, NACOGDOCHES by Schiwetz from *Texas Sketchbook, rev. ed.*

413, 418, 419 and 425, by S. Photos of S. as a member of the Jr. Class, as asst. art editor of *The Longhorn*, as cartoonist for *The Battalion*, and as a member of the Architectural Club.

34 *The Longhorn*. Vol. XIX, published by the Senior Class, Texas A. & M. College, College Station, Texas, 1921, simulated leather, 459 pp., "Foreword" (and edited) by B. H. Barnes, numerous illus. including sixteen, three in color, by S. Photos of S. as a member of the Architectural Club, as President of the Trukey Trot Club, and as member of the Ross Volunteers. Buck was art editor of *The Longhorn* for 1921.

35 Mathews, Sallie Reynolds. *Interwoven*. Advertising brochure, eight sample pages from the new edition, Carl Hertzog, El Paso, 1958, map, three illus. by S.

36 ———. *Interwoven*. Carl Hertzog, El Paso, Texas, 1958, brands on two-tone decor. cloth, map on front endsheet, Reynolds-Mathews family trees on back endsheets, 226 (2) pp., "Introduction" by Robert Nail, foreword, addenda, index, illus. with drawings by S. and with the photos.

37 ———. Same, third edition, a facsimile reprint by the University of Texas Press in 1973 as number 13 in the M. K. Brown Range Life Series, with drawing on d/w by S.

38 *Matthews Memorial Presbyterian Church*. Albany, Texas, n.d., single sheet with a drawing of the church (from *Interwoven*) by S.

39 Morgan, Ruth. *Texas Looks to its Heritage*. First separate printing of an article in *Antiques*, June 1954, for the Texas Historical Foundation, Austin, folder with six illus. by S.

40 Moseley, J. A. R. (Bob). *The Excelsior Hotel, Jefferson, Texas*. Greeting from Bob Moseley, Christmas 1952, (Carl Hertzog, El Paso), folder, one full-page drawing by S.

41 Murray, Lois Smith. *Baylor at Independence*. Baylor University Press, Waco, Texas, 1972, decor. two-tone cloth, 421 pp., "Introduction" by Robert Crawford Cotner, bibliography, appendix, index, numerous illus. including three, between pp. 86–87, by S. (Lea)

42 Pool, William C. et al. *Texas, Wilderness to Space Age*. The Naylor Co., San Antonio, (1962), pic. cloth, pic. map endsheets, 512 pp., preface, appendix, selected bibliography, numerous illus. incuding twenty-seven by S. (Bugbee)

43 ———. Same, but 1963 with words "Second Edition,

revised and enlarged" on copyright page, numerous illus. including thirty-three by S.

44 Schiwetz, E. M. (Buck). *Houston Texas, Past and Present*. A portfolio of six drawings on stiff paper with a single sheet of text concerning the plates. Published by The Little Gallery, Houston, Texas, n.d. (1928?).

45 ———. *Buck Schiwetz' Texas*. Univ. of Texas Press, Austin, (1960), decor. cloth, 134 pp., acknowledgments, "Introducing Buck Schiwetz" by Walter Prescott Webb, profusely illus. including sixteen in color by S.

46 ———. *A Map of Historical Homes and Buildings throughout Texas*. Humble Oil & Refining Co. in cooperation with Texas Historic Foundation, Austin, Texas, n.d., with over forty illus. by S.

47 ———. *Farm Scenes*. A portfolio of twelve lithographic reproductions of a series of drawings on cotton farming in Texas by S. Southern Bagging Co. (Rein Printing Co.), Houston, Texas, 1940.

48 ———. *Industry in Texas*. A portfolio of fifty-two reproductions of drawings of Texas industrial scenes by S. Anderson, Clayton & Co., Houston, Texas, 1928. (This series ran weekly in the *Wall Street Journal* in 1927.)

49 ———. *Texas Landmarks*. A series of pencil drawings by S., reproduced on note paper by the Texas Fine Arts Association, Austin, Texas, n.d.

50 ———. *The Schiwetz Legacy, An Artist's Tribute to Texas, 1910–1971*. Texas, Austin and London, (1972), leather with illus. in gold on the front cover, tan endsheets, 144 pp., "Introduction" by R. Henderson Shuffler, illustrations selected by John H. Lindsey, notes by the artist with John Edward Weems, 96 (many in color) plates by S. Limited edition of 300 numbered copies signed by Schiwetz, slipcase.

51 ———. Same, first trade edition in cloth.

52 ———. Same, a special A&M Edition of 1000 copies bound in maroon and available through the Memorial Student Center.

53 ———. Same, announcement folder with three (two in color) illus. by S.

54 ——— et al. *Dow Diamond*. The Dow Chemical Co., Midland, Michigan, October, 1955, colored pic. wraps, 32 pp., numerous illus. including three, front cover (color), inside front cover, and pp. 2–3 (color), by S.

55 ———— et al. *Dow in Texas.* The Dow Chemical Co., Freeport, Texas, 1956, wraps, 12 pp., illus. including one by S.

56 ———— et al. *Welcome to the Dow Chemical Co.,* Freeport, Texas, 1957, colored pic. wraps, 18 pp., illus. including three, front cover (color) and pp. 2–3 and 5, by S. Re-issued in 1960 and in 1964.

57 ———— et al. *Seasons Greetings* (Christmas card). The Dow Chemical Co., Freeport, Texas, 1955, folder with two illus. by S.

58 ———— et al. Same, 1956, folder with two illus. by S.

59 ———— et al. Same, 1958, folder with one illus. by S.

59a *Season's Greetings 1959.* (Houston), calendar with thirteen illus. including eleven by S.

59b *Season's Greetings 1960.* Humble Oil & Refining Co., (Houston), calendar, opposite December 1959.

60 ———— et al. *A Look at Dow.* The Dow Chemical Co., Midland, Michigan, 1962, colored pic. wraps, 32 pp., numerous illus. including one, p. 12 (color), by S.

61 ———— et al. *Twelve from Texas.* Southern Methodist Univ. Press, Dallas, Texas, 1952. A portfolio of twelve lithographs including one, "The Bull Wheel," by S.

62 ———— et al. *Twice-Told Tales of Texas.* Humble Oil & Refining Co., (Houston, Texas, 1936), decor. wraps, 54 pp., illus. with photos of dioramas, and with four drawings, pp. 8, 19, 26 and 43, by S.

63 ————. *Six Spanish Missions in Texas.* University of Texas Press, Austin, (1968), portfolio, historical notes by Robert S. Weddle, six plates in color.

63a *The Texas Capitol* (Houston), n.d., colored pic. wraps, 8 pp., six illus. including front cover in color by S.

64 Turner, Martha Anne. *The Life and Times of Jane Long.* Texian Press, Waco, 1969, cloth, 210 pp., notes, index, twenty-four pages of illus. including eight by S.

65 *University of Texas Press* (Austin), *Fall and Winter 1972* (catalog). Austin and London, 1972, pic. wraps, 24 pp., illus. including two, front cover and inside front cover, by S.

65a *Western Americana.* University of Texas Press, Austin, (1974), pic. wraps, 37 (2) pp., order form, numer-

ous illus. including one, p. 24, by S. (Lea, Thomason)

66 Wolls, Tom Henderson. *Commodore Moore and the Texas Navy.* Univ. of Texas Press, Austin, (1960), decor. cloth, 218 pp., blue top, foreword, appendices, bibliography, index, illus., d/w illus. in color by S.

The Artist and His Art

67 Dykes, Jeff C. *High Spots in Western Illustrating.* (The Kansas City Posse, The Westerners, Kansas City, Mo., 1964), cloth, 30 pp., two illus. High Spots 90 is no. 36 in this check list and 97 is Buck's own *Texas* (no. 45). Edition limited to 250 numbered and signed copies but an edition of 500 copies in wraps was distributed to members.

68 Forrester-O'Brien, Esse. *Art and Artists of Texas.* Tardy Publishing Co., Dallas, (1935), cloth, blue end-sheets, 408 pp., "Preface" by Joseph Sartor, index, illus., biographical sketch of S., p. 189.

69 "Historic East Texas," an article in *The Lamp,* vol. 29, no. 2, March, 1947, Standard Oil Co. (New Jersey), N.Y., with five illus. in color by S. Brief biographical sketch and photo of S.

70 Kent, Norman (commentary by). A portfolio of "Drawings of Texas by Edward M. (Buck) Schiwetz," an article in *American Artist,* vol. 25, no. 10, December, 1961, with seven illus. by S. This issue also includes "Edward M. Schiwetz Discusses Mixed Techniques," with a photo of Buck and one illus. in color by him.

71 Lasswell, Mary. *I'll Take Texas.* Houghton Mifflin, Boston, 1958, cloth and boards, 376 pp., illus. by J. Alys Downs. Praises Buck's art, pp. 178–79.

72 Reid, Kenneth. "A Sketcher from Texas," an article in *Pencil Points,* February, 1929, illus. with sixteen drawings by S.

73 "Buck Schiwetz Show at ITC is 50-Year Review of Texas Scene," an article in *People* (Newsletter of the Institute of Texan Cultures at San Antonio) 1:6, November–December 1971, with two illus. by S. and a photo of him on the front cover.

74 Shuffler, Henderson. "Schiwetz Drawings Get Highest Acclaim," an article in *The Texas Aggie,* October, 1960, illus. with one drawing by S. and with a photo of him.

LITTLE TEBEAU WATCHED HIM FROM A DISTANCE by Schoonover from
Sled Trails and White Waters

FRANK E. SCHOONOVER
1877–1972

Catalogues of Art Exhibitions and Galleries

J. N. BARTFIELD ART GALLERIES, NEW YORK

1 *American Paintings and Sculpture, Historical – Western*, (number 100), 1969, colored pic. wraps, unpaged, 64 numbered illus. including no. 44 by S. (Johnson, Leigh, Remington, Russell, Wyeth)

THE BROOKLYN MUSEUM

2 *A Century of American Illustration*, March 22–May 14, 1972, colored pic. wraps, 155 pp., introduction, biographies, selected bibliographies, 119 numbered illus. including no. 67 by S. (Fogarty, Remington, Wyeth)

HELEN L. CARD, NEW YORK

3 *Hats Off to the American Illustrator!* Catalog No. Two, (Fall 1959), pic. wraps, 32 (2) pp., numerous illus. including two, pp. 18 and 19, by S. (Dixon, Goodwin, Remington)

4 *Hang On, Fellers! We're Out on a Limb*. Catalog No. Five, (1963), pic. wraps, 95 pp., numerous illus. including two, pp. 64 and 65, by S. (Deming, Eggenhofer, Leigh, Remington, Stoops, Wyeth)

THE COLONIAL ART COMPANY, OKLAHOMA CITY

5 *Western and Traditional American Paintings of the 19th and Early 20th Centuries*, auction at Senate Room, Lincoln Plaza Inn, June 10, 1973, pic. wraps, unpaged, 76 numbered illus. including nos. 43, 44, 45, 46, 47, 48, 49 and 50, by S. (Borein, Deming, Dixon, Eggenhofer, Elwell, Goodwin, Johnson, Koerner, Russell, Wyeth, Young)

DELAWARE ART MUSEUM, WILMINGTON

6 *The Golden Age of American Illustration 1880–1914*, September 14–October 15, 1972, pic. wraps, 67 (1) pp., numerous illus. including one, p. 63, by S. (Remington, Wyeth, Zogbaum)

7 *Frank E. Schoonover*, October 5–28, 1962, catalog of 61 items in the exhibition, folder with illus. on front cover by S.

DELAWARE ARTS SOCIETY, PARISH HOUSE OF CHRIST EPISCOPAL CHURCH, DOVER

8 *Frank E. Schoonover*, May 18 through June 1, 1969, catalog of the exhibition (folder) with an illus. on front cover by S.

GLENBOW-ALBERTA INSTITUTE, CALGARY, ALBERTA, CANADA

9 *Glenbow Collects an Exhibition*, art publication no. 1, 1970, colored pic. wraps, 61 pp., "Foreword" (and compiled) by Lorne E. Render, artist index, numerous illus. including one, p. 31, by S. (Borein, Remington, Russell)

INTERNATIONAL ART GALLERY, PITTSBURGH

10 *An Album of Brandywine Tradition Artists*, Great American Editions, N.Y., October 1971 for International and the other five galleries featuring the exhibition October 1971–October 1972, pic. wraps, 54 pp., "Howard Pyle and Late 19th Century American Illustration" by Rowland Elzea, numerous illus. including ten, pp. 2 (repeated on back fly), 14, 15, (16) in color, 17, 18 (two), 19 (two) and 20, by S. and photo of him. (Dunn, Wyeth)

KENNEDY GALLERIES, NEW YORK

11 *The Things that Were* (19th and 20th Century Paintings of the American West), June 1968, colored pic. wraps, pp. 52-123 (1), introduction, numerous illus. including two, p. 93, by S. (Blumenschein, Crawford, Leigh, Miller, Remington, Schreyvogel)

MUSEUM OF THE PLAINS INDIANS BROWNING, MONTANA

12 *Algonkian and Siouan Indians of the Far West* (an

art exhibition from the collections of the Glenbow Foundation, Calgary), June through September, 1962, pic. wraps, 19 mimeographed pages, foreword, describes Schoonover's "Dickering with the Factor," p. 6, and a brief biographical sketch of him, p. 18.

Illustrated by the Artist

13 Adams, Samuel Hopkins. *The Secret of Lonesome Cove*. Bobbs-Merrill, Indianapolis, (1912), cloth, 339 (1) pp., six illus., frontis. and facing pp. 8, 94, 146, 222 and 260, by S.

14 *Aesop's Fables*. Harper, N.Y. and London, 1927, cloth with an illus. in color mounted on front cover, 194 pp., illus. by Louis Rhead but with a frontis. in color (repeated on front cover) by S.

15 (Andersen.) *Hans Andersen's Fairy Tales*. Harper, N.Y. and London, 1921, cloth with illus. in color mounted on the front cover, 442 (1) pp., illus. by Louis Rhead but with a frontis. in color (repeated on front cover) by S.

16 Apgar, John F., Jr. *Frank E. Schoonover, Painter – Illustrator – A Bibliography*. Published by the author, n.p. (Morristown, N.J., 1969), pic. white cloth, unpaged, introduction, biographical sketch, 22 illus. by S. and several photos of him. Limited edition of 50 numbered copies signed by the author and Schoonover and with a photo of Schoonover.

17 ———. Same, trade edition of 500 copies in tan cloth.

18 *The Arabian Nights Entertainments*. Harper, N.Y. and London, 1921, cloth with illus. in color mounted on front cover, 430 pp., illus. by Louis Rhead but with a frontis. in color (repeated on front cover) by S.

19 Barron, Elwyn A. *Deeds of Heroism and Bravery*. Harper, N.Y. and London, 1920, cloth with illus. in color by S. mounted on the front cover, 402 pp.

20 Beach, Rex. *Pardners*. McClure, Phillips & Co., N.Y., 1905, decor. cloth, 278 pp., illus. including one, the frontis., by S.

21 Brady, Cyrus Townsend. *Colonial Fights and Fighters*. McClure, Phillips, N.Y., 1901, pic. cloth, 341 pp., prefatory note, index, six maps and plans, sixteen illus. including two, facing pp. 174 and 182, by S.

22 Braithwaite, W. S. *The Story of the Great War*. Frederick A. Stokes Co., N.Y., (1919), decor. cloth, 371 pp., twelve illus. in color including one, the frontis. by S.

23 *The Brandywine Heritage*. The Brandywine River Museum, Chadds Ford, Pa., (1971), cloth, 121 pp., "Foreword" by Richard McLanathan, numerous illus. including three, pp. 39 and 40 (two), by S. (Wyeth)

24 Brill, E. C. *South from Hudson Bay*. Macrae-Smith Co., Philadelphia, (1929), cloth, 319 pp., five illus. including one, the frontis. by S. Illus. on d/w in color by S.

25 Buchan, John. *The House of the Four Winds*. Houghton Mifflin, Boston, 1935, cloth, 309 pp., d/w illus. in color by S.

26 Burroughs, Edgar Rice. *A Princess of Mars*. A. C. McClurg & Co., Chicago, 1917, cloth, 326 (1) pp., four illus., frontis. and facing pp. 138, 178 and 226, by S.

27 ———. Reprint, Edgar Rice Burroughs Inc., Tarzana, Calif., 1939, frontis. and d/w (in color) by S.

28 ———. *The God of Mars*. McClurg, Chicago, 1918, cloth, 348 pp., frontis. by S.

29 ———. Reprint, Edgar Rice Burroughs Inc., Tarzana, Calif., 1940, frontis. and d/w (in color) by S.

30 ———. Reprint, Grosset & Dunlap, N.Y., n.d., frontis. by S.

31 Burt, Katharine Newlin. *Men of Moon Mountain*. Macrae-Smith, Philadelphia, 1938, words "First Printing" on copyright page, decor. cloth, 272 pp., orange top, d/w illus. in color by S.

32 Carter, Russell Gordon. *The Crimson Cutlass*. The Penn Publishing Co., Philadelphia, (1933), cloth, pic. endsheets, 302 pp., illus. with five full-page plates, frontis. in color and facing pp. 62, 162, 186 and 280, and with drawings by S.

33 Cauffman, Stanley Hart. *At the Sign of the Silver Ship*. Penn, Phila., 1925, decor. cloth, 333 pp., frontis. by S.

34 ———. *The Wolf, The Cat and the Nightingale*. Penn, Philadelphia, 1926, cloth, 312 pp., d/w illus. in color by S.

35 ———. *The Witch Finders*. Penn, Philadelphia, 1934, cloth, 347, pp., d/w in color by S.

36 Chambers, Robt. W. *Cardigan*. Harper, N.Y. and London, 1901, decor. red cloth, 512 (1) pp., illus. including five, frontis. and facing pp. 98, 314, 400 and 492, by S.

37 ———. *The Hidden Children*. Grosset & Dunlap, N.Y., 1930, cloth, 651 pp., d/w illus. in color by S.

38 Cheney, Warren. *His Wife*. Bobbs-Merrill, Indianapolis, (1907), cloth, 395 pp., frontis. in color by S.

39 Clemens, Samuel L. *Life on the Mississippi*, by Mark Twain (pseud.). Harper, N.Y., (1917), cloth with illus. in color mounted on the front cover, 528 (1) pp., illus. including one, the frontis., by S.

40 Collier, Virginia M. and Eaton, Jeanette. *Roland the Warrior*. Harcourt, Brace, N.Y., (1934), cloth, pic. endsheets, 237 pp., foreword, bibliography, illus. including fifteen full-page drawings and a double title page in color by S.

41 Cooper, Courtney Ryley. *Oklahoma*. Little, Brown, Boston, 1926, words "Published August 1926" on copyright page, cloth, 303 pp., d/w illus. in color by S.

42 Cooper, James Fenimore. *The Deer Slayer*. Harper, N.Y. and London, 1926, cloth, with an illus. in color mounted on front cover, 556 pp., illus. by Louis Rhead but with a frontis. in color (repeated on front cover) by S.

43 (Copley.) *The Copley Prints*. Curtis and Cameron, Boston, 1916, wraps, 104 pp., (8) of advs., numerous illus. including one, p. 76, by S. (Remington)

44 Cummings, Edward. *Marmaduke of Tennessee*. McClurg, Chicago, 1914, words "Published August, 1914," on copyright page, cloth, 371 pp., five illus. in color, frontis. and facing pp. 18, 180, 218 and 362, by S.

45 Curwood, James Oliver. *The Courage of Captain Plum*. Bobbs-Merrill, Indianapolis, (1908), cloth, 319 pp., illus. by S.

46 ———. Same, Grosset & Dunlap, N.Y., (1913).

47 Dawson, Bob (Americana Books). *The American West, Prints, Illustrated Books* (Catalog No. 20). Hazlet, N.J., n.d., pic. wraps, 24 pp., front cover illus. by S.

48 Defoe, Daniel. *Robinson Crusoe*. Harper, N.Y. and London, 1921, cloth with an illus. in color mounted on the front cover, 363 pp., illus. by Louis and Frederick Rhead but with a frontis. in color (repeated on the front cover) by S.

49 Department of the Army. *The Executive Corridor of the Secretary of the Army and Chief of Staff, U. S. Army*. GPO, Washington, D.C., 1966, wraps, the illus. include one by S. (Dunn)

50 Dodge, Mary Mapes. *Hans Brinker, or The Silver Skates*. Harper, N.Y. and London, 1924, cloth with an illus. in color mounted on the front cover, 341 pp., illus. by Louis Rhead but with a frontis. in color (repeated on front cover) by S.

51 Doyle, A. Conan. *The White Company*. Grosset and Dunlap, N.Y., 1927, pic. cloth, 391 pp., d/w illus. in color by S.

52 Dunn, Harvey et al. *The Howard Pyle Brandywine Edition, 1853–1933* (sample binding). Scribner's, N.Y., 1933, cloth with illus. in color mounted on front cover, sample, (25) pp., five illus. including one in color by S. (Dunn)

53 (Du Pont.) *Autobiography of an American Enterprise*. For E. I. Du Pont De Nemours & Co., Wilmington, Delaware by Scribner's, N.Y., 1952, two-tone cloth, map endsheets, by S., 138 pp., numerous illus.

54 Evans, Hubert. *Derry's Partner*. Dodd, Mead, N.Y., 1929, cloth, 258 pp., four illus. frontis. and facing pp. 136, 144 and 214, by S.

55 Fox, John, Jr. *Christmas Eve on Lonesome*. Scribner's, N.Y., 1904, words "Published, September, 1904" on copyright page, decor. cloth, 234 pp., eight illus. in color including one, the frontis., by S. (Keller)

56 Fraser, Georgia. *The White Captain*. Little, Brown, Boston, 1930, words "Published September, 1930" on copyright page, cloth, pic. endsheets, 319 pp., frontis. in color by S.

57 Fraser, W. A. *The Blood Lilies*. Scribner's, N.Y., 1903, words "Published September 1903" on copyright page, decor. cloth, 262 pp., six illus., frontis. and facing pp. 30, 118, 164, 192 and 236, by S.

58 Frith, Henry. *King Arthur and His Knights*. Garden City Publishing Co., Garden City, N.Y., 1932, cloth, 406 pp., four illus. in color, double title page and facing pp. 90, 266 and 346, by S.

59 Gerry, Margarita Spalding. *The Toy Shop* (A Romantic Story of Lincoln the Man). Harper, N.Y. and London, 1908, words "Published September, 1908" on copyright page, cloth with illus. in color mounted on front cover, 50 (1) pp., two illus. front cover and frontis., by S.

60 Glasgow, Ellen. *The Deliverance*. Doubleday, Page, N.Y., 1904, words "Published January, 1904" on copyright page, cloth, 543 pp., four illus. in color, frontis. and facing pp. 52, 168 and 342, by S.

61 Grey, Katherine. *Rolling Wheels*. Little, Brown, 1937, words "Published April, 1937" on copyright page, cloth with illus. in color mounted on front cover, pic. endsheets, 209 pp., six illus. in color, frontis. and facing pp. 76, 116, 150, 188 and 248, by S.

62 (Brothers Grimm.) *Grimm's Fairy Tales*. Harper, N.Y. and London, 1921, cloth with an illus. in color

mounted on the front cover, illus. by Louis Rhead but with a frontis. in color (repeated on front cover) by S.

63 Hall, John T. *Historic Delaware*. Longwood Open Air Theatre (Kennett Square, Pa.), June 20–21–22, colored pic. wraps, unpaged, illus. in color on front cover by S.

64 Harper, Wilhelmina. *The Girl of Tiptop*. Little, Brown, Boston, 1929, cloth, 332 pp., illus. including one, the frontis., by S.

65 Hart, A. B. and Bassett, J. S., eds. *The Great Explosion*. Harper, N.Y. and London, (1920), code letters "A–U" on copyright page, cloth, 400 pp., "Foreword" by Dr. Chas. W. Eliot, numerous illus. including one, the frontis., by S. Vol. 1 of Harper's *Pictorial Library of the World War*.

66 Hendryx, James B. *Connie Morgan in the Fur Country*. Putnam's, N.Y. and London, 1921, cloth with illus. mounted on front cover, 312 pp., eight illus., frontis. and facing pp. 54, 70, 80, 130, 156, 182 and 218, by S.

67 ———. *Connie Morgan in the Cattle Country*. Putnam's, N.Y. and London, 1923, cloth with illus. mounted on front cover, 307 pp., eight illus., frontis. and facing pp. 16, 32, 64, 96, 128, 164 and 196, by S.

68 Holland, Rupert Sargent. *Yankee Ships in Pirate Waters*. Macrae-Smith, Phila., (1931), pic. cloth and endsheets, 317 pp., foreword, decorations and five illus. in color, double title page and facing pp. 56, 106, 224 and 312, by S.

69 ———. Same, reprint by Garden City Publishing Co.

70 Horne, Charles C. *The Story of Our American People*. National Alumni, N.Y., n.d., decor. fabricoid, 465 pp., introduction, appendix, index, maps, numerous illus., eight in color including one, facing p. 420, by S. Vol. I of a two volume set. (Remington, Leigh)

71 Horton, R. J. *Rider O' the Stars*. Chelsea House, N.Y., (1924), cloth, 306 pp., (2) of advs., d/w illus. in color by S.

72 ———. *The Prairie Shrine*. A. L. Burt Co., N.Y., 1924, cloth, 320 pp., d/w illus. in color by S.

73 Housman, Lawrence (re-told by). *Stories from the Arabian Nights*. Garden City, Publishing Co., N.Y., 1932, cloth with illus in color mounted on front cover, 205 pp., illus. by Edmund Dulac but front cover illus. by S.

74 Hughes, Thomas. *Tom Brown's School-Days*. Harper, N.Y. and London, 1921, cloth with an illus. in color mounted on the front cover, 376 pp., illus. by Louis Rhead but with a frontis. in color (repeated on front cover) by S.

75 Johnston, Mary. *To Have and to Hold*. Houghton Mifflin, Boston and N.Y., 1931, cloth, 331 pp., illus. in color by S.

76 Jones, Evan. *Trappers and Mountain Men*. American Heritage Pub. Co., N.Y., (1961), words "First Edition" on copyright page, colored pic. cloth and endsheets, 153 pp., "Foreword" by Dale L. Morgan (consultant), picture credits, bibliography, index, numerous (many in color) illus. including one in color, p. (97), by S. (Remington, Russell)

77 Kauffman, Reginald Wright. *Barbary Bo*. Penn, Phila., 1929, cloth with illus. in color mounted on front cover, pic. endsheets, 261 pp., note, five illus., frontis. in color and facing pp. 34, 104, 138 and 190, by S.

78 Knowles, Sir James (compiled and arranged by). *King Arthur and His Knights*. Harper, N.Y. and London, 1923, cloth with illus. in color mounted on the front cover, 383 pp., illus. by Louis Rhead but with a frontis. in color (repeated on front cover) by S.

79 Lamb, Charles and Mary. *Tales from Shakespeare*. Harper, N.Y. and London, 1918, cloth with illus. in color mounted on front cover, 367 pp., illus. with drawings by Louis Rhead but with a frontis. in color (repeated on front cover) by S.

80 Latendorf, E. Walter. *Catalogue No. 26*. (Mannados Book Shop), N.Y., (1956), pic. wraps, 21 pp., "Fur Trapping in Canada" (Schoonover learns the ways of the North), eight illus. including five, pp. 1, 2 (two) and 3 (two), by S. (Eggenhofer, James)

81 Lee, Jeannette. *Happy Island*. Century, 1910, words "Published June 1910" on copyright page, cloth with illustration in color on front cover, 330 pp., frontis. in color (repeated on front cover and d/w) by S.

82 Longfellow, Henry Wadsworth. *The Children's Longfellow*. Houghton Mifflin, Boston and N.Y., 1908, cloth, with illus. in color mounted on the front cover, 334 pp., all edges green, Publishers Note, indices, eight illus. in color including one, facing p. 88, by S.

83 (McClurg.) *Monthly Bulletin of New Books*. A. C. McClurg & Co., Chicago, December, 1905, numerous illus. including one by S. (Dixon)

84 McIlwraith, Jean N. *The Curious Career of Roderick Campbell*. Houghton Mifflin, Boston and N.Y., 1901,

decor. cloth, 287 pp., four illus., frontis. and facing pp. 46, 224 and 274, by S.

85 Madison, Lucy Foster. *Joan of Arc.* Penn, Phila., 1918, cloth with illus. in color mounted on the front cover, 388 (1) pp., eight illus. in color, frontis. and facing pp. 20, 74, 80, 142, 156, 234 and 326, by S.

86 ———. *Lafayette.* Penn, Phila., 1921, cloth with illus. in color mounted on the front cover, 371 (1) pp., introduction, eight illus. in color, frontis. and facing pp. 18, 71, 133, 159, 184, 212 and 340, plus numerous line drawings, by S.

87 ———. *Washington.* Penn, Phila., 1925, cloth with illus. in color mounted on front cover, pic. endsheets, 399 pp., preface, decorations and eight illus. in color, frontis. and facing pp. 24, 38, 68, 84, 126, 300 and 390, by S.

88 ———. *Lincoln.* Penn, Phila., 1928, cloth with illus. in color mounted on front cover, 368 pp., numerous illus. including eight in color by S.

89 Marrayat, Captain. *Masterman Ready.* Harper, N.Y. and London, 1928, words "First Edition" on copyright page, cloth with an illus. in color mounted on front cover, 403 pp., illus. by John Rae but with a frontis. in color (repeated on front cover) by S.

90 Marsh, George. *Toilers of the Trail.* Penn, Phila., 1921, decor. cloth with illus. in color mounted on the front cover, 245 pp., nine illus., frontis. in color and facing pp. 80, 89, 109, 122, 139, 174, 221 and 228, by S.

91 ———. *The Whelps of the Wolf.* Penn, Phila., 1922, cloth, 303 pp., frontis. in color by S.

92 ———. *The Valley of Voices.* Penn, Phila., 1924, cloth, 352 pp., frontis. and d/w illus. in color by S.

93 ———. *Men Marooned.* Penn, Phila., 1925, pic. cloth, 314 pp., d/w illus. in color by S.

94 ———. *Under Frozen Stars.* Penn, Phila., 1928, cloth, 302 pp., d/w illus. in color by S.

95 ———. *Sled Trails and White Waters.* Penn, Phila., 1929, cloth with illus. in color mounted on front cover, 298 pp., numerous illus. including a frontis. in color, and nine other full-page plates by S.

96 ———. *The River of Skulls.* Penn, Philadelphia, 1936, cloth, 311 pp., frontis. and d/w illus. (in color) by S.

97 Miller (Mahony), Bertha E. and Whitney, Eleanor. *Five Years of Children's Books.* Doubleday, Garden City, N.Y., 1936, cloth, 599 pp., numerous illus. including one, p. 187, by S.

98 Mott, Lawrence. *Jules of the Great Heart.* Century, N.Y., 1905, cloth, 303 pp., frontis. in color, by S.

99 ———. *The White Darkness.* Outing, N.Y., 1907, pic. cloth, 308 pp., five illus. including three, frontis. and facing pp. 144 and 224, by S.

100 Mulford, Clarence Edward. *Bar – 20.* Outing, N.Y., 1907, pic. cloth, 382 pp., illus. including five, frontis. and facing pp. 8, 78, 118 and 182, by S.

101 ———. *The Man from Bar – 20.* McClurg, Chicago, 1918, words "Published May, 1918" on copyright page, cloth, 318 pp., four illus., frontis. and facing pp. 60, 166 and 280, by S.

102 ———. *The Bar – 20 Three.* McClurg, Chicago, 1921, words "Published April, 1921" on copyright page, cloth, 353 pp., frontis. by S.

103 Mulock, Dinah Maria. *The Fairy Book.* Harper, N.Y. and London, 1922, cloth with illus. in color mounted on the front cover, 404 pp., illus. by Louis Rhead but with a frontis. in color (repeated on front cover) by S.

104 Munroe, Kirk. *The Flamingo Feather.* Harper, N.Y. and London, (1915), cloth with illus. in color mounted on front cover, 222 pp., numerous illus. including ten in color by S.

105 Neihardt, John G. *The Lonesome Trail.* John Lane Co., N.Y., London, 1907, pic. cloth, 303 pp., frontis. by S.

106 Ogden, G. W. *The Rustler of Wind River.* McClurg, Chicago, 1917, cloth, 330 pp., frontis. by S.

107 Page, Thomas Nelson. *Under the Crust.* Scribner's, N.Y., 1907, words "Published November 1907" on copyright page, decor. cloth, 307 pp., eight illus. including one, facing p. 194, by S. (Marchand, Wyeth)

108 Paine, Ralph D. *Privateers of '76.* Penn, Phila., 1923, cloth with illus. in color mounted on front cover, 316 pp., line drawings and six full-page plates, frontis. in color and facing pp. 52, 108, 186, 224 and 260 by S.

109 ———. *Four Bells.* Houghton Mifflin, Boston and N.Y., 1924, cloth, 337 pp., frontis. by S.

110 ———. *Blackbeard Buccaneer.* Penn, Phila., 1922, cloth, 309 (1) pp., illus. including six full-page plates, frontis. in color and facing pp. 83, 120, 129, 164 and 224, by S.

111 Parker, Gilbert. *Northern Lights.* Harper, N.Y. and London, 1909, words "Published September, 1909"

on copyright page, pic. cloth, 351 (1) pp., note, sixteen illus. including one, facing p. 236, by S. (Crawford, Dunn, Wood)

112 ———. *The Lane That Had No Turning.* Doubleday, Page, N.Y., 1902, words "Published November, 1902" on copyright page, cloth with illus. mounted on front cover, pic. endsheets, 215 (2) pp., with numerous decor. and illus. including seven full-page plates, frontis. and pp. (35), (71), (87), (101), (139) and 203, by S.

113 Parrish, Randall. *The Maid of the Forest.* McClurg, Chicago, 1913, cloth, 427 (1) pp., five illus. in color, frontis. and facing pp. 98, 222, 326 and 386, by S.

114 ———. *Wolves of the Sea.* McClurg, Chicago, 1918, cloth, 355 pp., frontis. by S.

115 Pitz, Henry C. *Illustrating Children's Books.* Watson-Guptill Publications, (N.Y., 1963), cloth, blue endsheets, 207 pp., preface, bibliography, index, numerous illus. including one, p. 71, by S. (Remington, Wyeth)

115a ———. *The Bradywine Tradition.* Houghton Mifflin, Boston, 1969, words "First Printing" on copyright page, cloth, 252 pp., bibliography, preface, index, numerous illus. including two, one in color, between pp. 126 and 127 and one between pp. 222 and 223, by S. (Dunn, Hurd, Wyeth)

116 Pyle, Howard. *The Story of the Champions of the Round Table.* Scribner's, N.Y., 1933, cloth with illus. in color mounted on the front cover, 328 pp., illus. by the author, but with a frontis. in color by S. and with a tribute to Pyle by him. The Howard Pyle Brandywine edition, 1853–1933.

117 Reed, Walt. *The Illustrator in America.* Reinhold, N.Y., (1966), cloth, pic. green endsheets, 271 (1) pp., "Is Illustration Art?" by Albert Dorne, bibliography, numerous illus. including two, p. 69, by S. (Blumenschein, Crawford, Dunn, Dunton, Eggenhofer, Fischer, Fogarty, Goodwin, Keller, Koerner, Remington, Russell, Stoops, Wyeth)

118 Rhead, Louis. *Robin Hood.* Harper, N.Y. and London, 1921, cloth with illus. in color mounted on the front cover, 216 pp., illus. by the author but with a frontis. in color (repeated on front cover) by S.

119 Sabitini, Rafael. *The Carolinian.* Houghton Mifflin, Boston and N.Y., 1925, cloth, 485 pp., frontis. and d/w by S. Volume XV of the Definitive Edition of the Writings of Rafael Sabitini.

120 ———. Same, trade edition, 1925, without frontis. but with d/w illus. in color by S.

121 Schultz, James Willard. *Rising Wolf, the White Blackfoot.* Houghton Mifflin, Boston and N.Y., 1919, cloth, with illus. mounted on front cover, introduction, four illus. including three, frontis. and facing pp. 10 and 156, by S.

122 ———. *Seizer of Eagles.* Houghton Mifflin, Boston, 1922, decor. cloth, 229 pp., four illus., frontis. and facing pp. 70, 102 and 150, by S.

123 ———. *Plumed Snake Medicine.* Houghton Mifflin, Boston and N.Y., 1924, cloth with illus. in color mounted on front cover, 244 (1) pp., illus. including one, front cover, by S.

124 ———. *Questers of the Desert.* Houghton Mifflin, Boston and N.Y., 1925, cloth, 224 (1) pp., four illus. frontis. and facing pp. 126, 138 and 218, by S.

125 ———. *William Jackson, Indian Scout.* Houghton Mifflin, Boston and N.Y., 1926, decor. cloth, 200 (1) pp., four illus., frontis. and facing pp. 12, 84 and 182, by S.

126 ———. *Red Crow's Brother.* Houghton Mifflin, Boston and N.Y., 1927, cloth, map endsheets, 208 (1) pp., four illus., frontis. and facing pp. 22, 96 and 152, by S.

127 ———. *Skull Head, the Terrible.* Houghton Mifflin, Boston and N.Y., 1929, decor. cloth, map endsheets, 207 (1) pp., orange top, four illus., frontis. and facing pp. 72, 142 and 190, by S.

128 ———. *The White Buffalo Robe.* Houghton Mifflin, Boston and N.Y., 1936, decor. cloth, 220 (1) pp., eight illus., frontis. and facing pp. 16, 30, 40, 44, 106, 124 and 216, by S.

129 ———. *Stained Gold.* Houghton Mifflin, Boston and N.Y., 1937, cloth, 217 pp., eight illus., frontis. and pp. 4, 36, 48, 78, 104, 112 and 212 by S.

130 Scott, Sir Walter. *Ivanhoe.* Harper, N.Y. and London, 1922, cloth, pic. endsheets, numerous illus. including eleven in color by S.

131 Seltzer, Charles Alden. *The Range Boss.* McClurg, Chicago, 1916, words "Published Sept., 1916" on copyright page, cloth, 333 (1) pp., four illus., frontis. and facing pp. 66, 96 and 322, by S.

132 Serven, James E. *Colt Firearms 1836–1954.* Published by the author, Santa Ana, California, 1954, gilt decor. fabricoid, green endsheets, 385 pp., pref-

ace, indices, numerous illus. including one, p. 160, by S. (Remington)

133 Sinclair-Cowan, Bertha M. *Cabin Fever*, by B. M. Bower (pseud.). Little, Brown, 1918, cloth, 290 pp., frontis. by S.

134 Singmaster, Elsie. *Rifles for Washington*. Houghton Mifflin, Boston, 1938, pic. cloth, 321 pp., illus. including a double title page in color by S.

135 Skinner, Constance Lindsay. *Roselle of the North*. Macmillan, N.Y., 1927, cloth, 256 pp., illus. in color on title page by S.

136 Smith, Mary P. Wells. *The Boy Captive of Old Deerfield*. Little, Brown, Boston, 1929, cloth with illus. in color mounted on front cover, 295 pp., six illus. in color, frontis. and facing pp. 24, 58, 84, 194 and 238, by S.

137 Southard, Frank R. (selected by). *Portfolio of Prints, Pictures by Prominent Artists*. James J. and Fred F. McGuire, N.Y., 1921, seventy numbered plates including no. 61 by S.

138 Spruance, John S. *Delaware Stays in the Union — The Civil War Period: 1860–1865*. University of Delaware Press, Newark, Delaware, 1955, wraps with map on front cover, 34 pp., three illus., front cover, frontis. and p. 27, by S.

139 Spyri, Johanna. *Heidi*. Harper, N.Y. and London, 1924, cloth with an illus. in color mounted on front cover, 333 pp., illus. by Louis Rhead but with a frontis. in color (repeated on front cover) by S.

140 Stanley, H. A. *The Backwoodsman*. Doubleday, Page, N.Y., 1902, cloth with illus. mounted on front cover, 311 pp., front cover illus. by S.

141 Stevenson, Robert Louis. *Treasure Island*. Harper, N.Y. and London, 1921, cloth with illus. in color mounted on the front cover, 289 pp., illus. by Louis Rhead but with a frontis. in color (repeated on front cover) by S.

142 ———. *Kidnapped*. Harper, N.Y. and London, 1921, cloth with an illus. in color mounted on the front cover, 302 pp., illus by Louis Rhead but with a frontis. in color (repeated on front cover) by S.

143 ———. Same, reprint by Blue Ribbon Books, N.Y., n.d., with an added page of advs., for Rainbow Bindings (a new process to reproduce illus. in color on cloth) with a frontis. in color and repeated on the front cover by S.

144 Sublette, C. M. *The Scarlet Cockerel*. Little, Brown,

Boston, 1931, words "Published August 1931" on copyright page, cloth with illus. in color mounted on front cover, pic. endsheets, 293 pp., seven illus. in color by S.

145 Swan, Oliver G., ed. *Frontier Days*. Macrae-Smith, Phila., (1928), pic. cloth and endsheets, 512 pp., tinted top, preface, introduction, numerous illus., twelve in color, including three, frontis. and facing pp. 50 and 490, by S.

146 ———. Same, Grosset & Dunlap reprint, N.Y., (1928), cloth with illus. in color mounted on front cover, 250 pp., illus. by Charles Hargens et al. but with a frontis. in color by S.

147 ———. *Covered Wagon Days*. Grosset & Dunlap, N.Y., (1928), cloth with illus. mounted on front cover, pic. endsheets, 274 pp., eight plates in color including one, facing p. 254, by S. A partial reprint of no. 145 with a new title.

148 ———. *Deep Water Days*. Macrae-Smith, Phila., (1929), words "First Edition" on copyright page, decor. cloth, pic. endsheets, 506 pp., preface, acknowledgments, numerous illus., eleven in color, including two, facing pp. 48 and 240, by S. (Wyeth)

149 Swift, Jonathan. *Gulliver's Travels*. Harper, N.Y. and London, 1921, cloth with illus. in color mounted on the front cover, 350 pp., illus. by Louis Rhead but with a frontis. in color (repeated on front cover) by S.

150 Tappan, Eva March. *American Hero Stories*. Houghton Mifflin, Boston, 1926, cloth with illus. in color mounted on front cover, 301 pp., preface, five illus., front cover, frontis. and facing pp. 100, (154) and 188, by S., first with Schoonover illus.

151 Tomlinson, Everett T. *In the Hands of the Red Coats*. Houghton Mifflin, Boston and N.Y., 1900, pic. cloth, 370 pp., preface, four illus., frontis. and facing pp. 84, 292 and 320, by S.

152 ———. *A Jersey Boy in the Revolution*. Houghton Mifflin, Boston, 1899, cloth, 428 pp., four illus., frontis. and facing pp. 108, 146 and 250, by S. (The first book illus. by Schoonover.)

153 van Dyke, Henry. *Days Off and Other Digressions*. Scribner's, N.Y., 1907, words "Published, October, 1907" on copyright page, gilt decor. cloth, 322 p., gilt top, eight illus. in color including seven, frontis. and facing pp. 36, 88, 94, 206, 318 and 266, by S.

154 ———. Same, the Avalon Edition, Scribner's, N.Y.,

1920, gilt decor. cloth, 393 pp., gilt top, frontis. (sepia) by S.

155 ———. *The Broken Soldier and the Maid of France.* Harper, N.Y. and London, 1919, words "Published September, 1919" and code letters "H-T" on copyright page, gilt pic. cloth, 69 (1) pp., eight illus., d/w, front cover, two plates (frontis. and preceding p. 47) and four chapter headings by S.

156 Voss, Richard. *Sigurd Eckdel's Bride.* Little, Brown, Boston, 1900, cloth, 235 pp., translated by Mary J. Safford, four illus., frontis. and facing pp. 44, 100 and 212, by S.

157 Wallace, Dillon. *Bobby of the Labrador.* McClurg, Chicago, 1916, words "Published November, 1916" on copyright page, pic. cloth, 325 pp., five illus., frontis. and facing pp. 72, 114, 210 and 300, by S.

158 ———. *The Arctic Stowaways.* McClurg, Chicago, 1917, words "Published November, 1917" on copyright page, decor. cloth, 322 pp., five illus., frontis. and facing pp. 90, 148, 32 and 314, by S.

159 Ward, Christopher L. *The Delaware Tercentenary Almanack and Historical Respository.* (The Press of Kells, Neward, Delaware, 1937), words "First Edition" on the title page, cloth and boards, unpaged, numerous illus. including two drawings by S. (Wyeth)

160 Watson, Virginia. *With Cortes the Conqueror.* Penn, Phila., 1917, cloth with illus. in color mounted on front cover, pic. endsheets, 332 pp., introduction, illus. including eight in color, frontis. and facing pp. 16, 56, 106, 148, 206, 254 and 308, by S.

161 Weyman, Stanley J. *Count Hannibal.* Longman's Green, N.Y., 1901, pic. cloth, 404 pp., frontis. by S.

162 White, Stewart Edward et al. *Little Verses and Big Names.* George H. Doran Co., N.Y., 1915, cloth, 305 pp., (Message) by President Woodrow Wilson, "Nota Bene," "The Prayer and the Answer," Who's Who of contributors, fourteen illus. including one, facing p. 126, by S. Includes "The Snow Baby," a short Indian story, by S. This book compiled "For Sale for Supplying Milk to Sick Babies."

163 Wren, Percival Christopher. *Sinbad the Soldier.* Houghton Mifflin, Boston and N.Y., 1935, cloth, 329 pp., d/w illus. in color by S.

164 Wyss, David. *The Swiss Family Robinson.* Harper, N.Y. and London, 1921, cloth with illus. in color mounted on front cover, 602 pp., illus. by Louis Rhead but with a frontis. in color (repeated on front cover) by S.

The Artist and His Art

165 Abbott, Charles D. *Howard Pyle, A Chronicle.* Harper, N.Y. and London, 1925, words "First Edition" on copyright page, cloth and boards, 249 pp., "Introduction" by N. C. Wyeth, illus. by Pyle; Schoonover studied with Pyle and is mentioned a number of times.

166 (Bobbs-Merrill.) *1915 Publications of The Bobbs-Merrill Company.* Indianapolis, decor. wraps, 104 pp., lists books illus. by Schoonover pp. 1, 14 and 19.

167 Dykes, Jeff C. *High Spots in Western Illustrating.* (The Kansas City Possee, The Westerners, Kansas City, Mo., 1964), cloth, 30 pp., two illustrations. High Spot 51 is no. 145 of this check list. Limited to 250 numbered and signed copies but an edition in wraps issued to members.

168 Fielding, Mantle. *Dictionary of American Painters, Sculptors and Engravers.* N.Y., 1926, 433 pp., preface, bibliography. Brief biographical sketch of S., p. 322.

169 ———. *Same. but with an addendum.* James F. Carr, N.Y., 1965, cloth, 529 pp., compiler's preface, author's preface, bibliography, partial bibliography. Additional info. on S., p. 513.

170 Miller (Mahoney), Bertha E. and Whitney, Elinor. *Contemporary Illustrators of Children's Books.* The Bookshop for Boys and Girls, Boston, 1930, decor. cloth, 135 pp., numerous illus., biographical sketch of Schoonover, p. 64.

171 ——— et al. (compilers). *Illustrators of Children's Books.* The Horn Book, Boston, 1947, cloth and pic. boards, 527 pp., gilt top, preface, introduction, biographies, appendix, index, numerous illus., Schoonover in text, pp. 115 and 121, biographical sketch, pp. 355-356 and bibliographic list, p. 436 (only five books included).

172 Pitz, Henry C. "Frank E. Schoonover: An Exemplar of the Pyle Tradition," an article in *American Artist Magazine,* November 1964.

173 Schoonover, Frank E. "The Edge of the Wilderness," an article on personal experiences in *Scribner's Magazine,* April 1905, with nine illus. by S.

174 ———. "Breaking Trail," an article on personal ex-

periences in *Scribner's Magazine*, May 1905, with eight illus. by S. and a photo of him.

175 ———. "In the Haunts of Jean Lafitte," an article on personal experiences in *Harper's Monthly Magazine*, December 1911, eleven illus. (three in color) by S.

176 ———. "The Fur-Harvesters," an article on personal experiences in *Harper's Monthly Magazine*, October 1912, twelve illus. (two in color) by S.

177 ———. "At the Sign of the Yellow Birch Pole," an article with reminiscences in *Outdoor World & Recreation* 49:6 (New Series), December 1913.

178 ———. "Howard Pyle," an illus. article in *Art and Progress* 6:12, October 1915, a tribute to his teacher with some personal recollections.

179 *Frank E. Schoonover.* Wilmington Society of the Fine Arts, Wilmington, (1972), an invitation to his 95th birthday party at the Delaware Art Museum, with a brief statement concerning Schoonover's ties to the Society and the Museum. (He died a few days after the party.)

180 Schoonover, Frank E. et al. *Report of the Private View of the Exhibition of Works by Howard Pyle at the Art Alliance.* The Philadelphia Art Alliance, Jan. 2, 1923, wraps, limited to 25 numbered copies, no. 1 to 12 inclusive autographed by the speakers including Schoonover (on his teacher).

182 (Schoonover.) A biographical sketch in *Dateline Delaware Magazine*, September–October 1960 with numerous illus. by S.

CANADIAN TRAPPER by Schoonover from *The Brandywine Heritage*

NEARING THE FORT by Schreyvogel   *Collection of the National Cowboy Hall of Fame*

Catalogues of Art Exhibitions and Galleries

ARROWSMITH-FENN GALLERIES, SANTA FE

1 *Our Western Heritage*, (1973), folder with six illus. including two, front cover in color and back cover, by S. (Russell)

J. N. BARTFIELD ART GALLERIES, NEW YORK

2 *American Paintings and Sculpture, Historical-Western*, Catalogue Number 120, (1973), colored pic. wraps, unpaged but with 82 numbered illustrations including no. 79 by S. (Dixon, Leigh, Remington, Russell)

THE COLONIAL ART COMPANY, OKLAHOMA CITY

2a *Western and Traditional American Paintings of the 19th and Early 20th Centuries.* Auction Catalog, June 9, 1974, pic. wraps, unpaged, 111 numbered lots including no. 98, "The Indian Pottery Painter," by S. (Blumenschein, Borein, Deming, De Yong, Dixon, Dunton, Ellsworth, Johnson, Leigh, Remington, Zogbaum)

DENVER ART MUSEUM

3 *Building the West*, (Peerless Printing Co.), Denver, October 1955, wraps, 32 pp., (introduction), numerous illus. including one, p. 13, by S. (Remington)

4 *Colorado Collects Historical Western Art*, January 13 through April 15, 1973, brand decor. wraps, 72 pp., numerous illus. including one in color, p. 16. by S. (Johnson, Miller, Remington, Russell)

SAMUEL T. FREEMAN & CO., PHILADELPHIA

5 *The W. Hinkle Smith Collection*, 1971, pic. wraps, unpaged, numerous illus. including one by S., auction announcement. (Remington, Russell)

GALLERY WEST, DENVER

6 *Prospectives in Western Art*, 1972, pic. wraps, un-

paged, numerous illus. including one by S. (Borein, Deming, Dixon, Ellsworth, Remington, Russell)

GRAND CENTRAL ART GALLERIES, NEW YORK

7 *1955 Yearbook*, wraps with illus. in color mounted on front cover, 76 pp., numerous illus. including one, p. 15, by S. (Johnson, Leigh, Remington)

GREENFIELD GALLERIES, SEATTLE

8 *American Western Art Auction*, October 28, (1972), pic. wraps, 58 pp., numerous illus. including one, p. 19, by S. (Borein, Deming, Lungren, Remington, Russell)

THE GEORGE GUND MUSEUM OF WESTERN ART
NEW YORK

9 *The Gund Collection of Western Art, A Personal Narrative*, 1970, colored pic. wraps, 38 pp., nineteen illus. in color including one in color, p. 36, by S. (Johnson, Leigh, Remington, Russell)

10 Same, *A History and Pictorial Description of the American West*, 1973, pic. wraps, 62 pp., numerous illus. including two, pp. 37 and 39 (in color), by S. and a photo of him. (Johnson, Leigh, Miller, Remington, Russell)

HERITAGE INN, GREAT FALLS, MONTANA
(THE ADVERTISING CLUB OF GREAT FALLS)

10a *C. M. Russell Sixth Annual Auction of Original Western Art*, March 14–15, 1974, pic. wraps, unpaged, 165 numbered lots, numerous illus. including one, lot 121, by S. (Borein, Deming, Hurd, Russell)

KALAMAZOO INSTITUTE OF ARTS
KALAMAZOO, MICHIGAN

11 *Western Art*, February 17–March 19, 1967, pic. wraps, 17 (1) pp., numerous illus. including one, p.

9, by S. (Hurd, Johnson, Leigh, Miller, Remington, Russell)

KENDE GALLERIES (AT GIMBEL BROTHERS) NEW YORK

12 Sale No. 81, *Paintings*, 1943, wraps, 53 (1) pp., numerous illus., lists three items by S. (Remington)

13 Sale No. 85, *Paintings, Bronzes*, 1943, wraps, 31 pp., numerous illus. including two, p. 22 and a photo of a bronze, p. 18, by S. (Remington)

KENNEDY GALLERIES, NEW YORK

14 *Painters of the Old West*, October 1960, wraps with illus. mounted on front cover, pp. 102–147, numerous illus. including one, p. 136, by S. (Borein, Deming, Leigh, Remington, Russell)

15 *Recent Acquisitions in Important Western Paintings*, October 1961, pic. wraps, numerous illus. including one, front cover, by S. (Borein, Deming, Eggenhofer, Johnson, Remington, Russell)

16 *The Old West*, November 25–December 30, (1961), invitation card with one illus. by S.

17 *Recent Acquisitions in Important Western and Sporting Paintings and Sculptures*, October 1962, wraps, with illus. in color mounted on front cover, pp. 50–108, numerous illus. including one, p. 97, by S. (Borein, Johnson, Leigh, Marchand, Remington, Russell)

18 *Tradition and Change*, December 1963, colored pic. wraps, numerous illus. including one, p. 102, by S. (Koerner, Leigh, Lungren, Remington, Russell)

19 *Western Encounter: The Artists' Record*, October 1964, colored pic. wraps, 64 pp., numerous illus. including two, pp. 44 and 45, by S. (Johnson, Leigh, Marchand, Remington, Russell)

20 *Farewell to Adventure*, May 1965, colored pic. wraps, pp. 196–256, numerous illus. including one, p. 256, by S. (Remington, Russell)

21 *The Things That Were*, June 1968, colored pic. wraps, pp. 52–123, (1), numerous illus. including two, pp. 87 and 107 (color) by S. (Blumenschein, Crawford, Leigh, Miller, Remington, Schoonover)

22 *An Artists' Gazetteer: Beyond the Mississippi*, June 1971, colored pic. wraps, 64 pp., numerous illus. including one in color, p. 16, by S. (Borein, Marchand, Miller, Remington, Russell)

23 *Walking Westward: An American Journey*, March 1972, colored pic. wraps, pp. 196–256, numerous illus. including three, pp. 233, 237 and 239, by S. (Johnson, Lungren, Miller, Remington, Russell)

24 *The Great American West*, June 1973, colored pic. wraps, pp. 132–192, numerous illus. including one in color, p. 147, by S. (Blumenschein, Leigh, Miller, Remington, Russell)

E. WALTER LATENDORF, NEW YORK

25 *Young Spanish Officer*, 1952, folder, one illus. by S. (Lea, Remington, Young)

METROPOLITAN MUSEUM OF ART, NEW YORK

26 *Life in America: A Special Loan Exhibition of Paintings*, 1939, floral wraps, 230 pp., preface, "Introduction" by Harry B. Wehle, numerous illus. including one, p. 176, by S. (Remington)

MILLER SCHOOL (CHEYENNE CENTENNIAL COMMITTEE), CHEYENNE, WYOMING

27 *150 Years in Western Art*, July 1 through August 15, 1967, colored pic. wraps, 30 (2) pp., numerous illus. including one, p. 19, by S. (Koerner, Miller, Remington, Russell)

NATIONAL ACADEMY OF DESIGN, NEW YORK

28 *Illustrated Catalogue of 75th Annual Exhibition*, 1900, numerous illus. including one, "My Bunkie," by S. "My Bunkie" was awarded the Thomas B. Clarke Prize for 1900. (Remington)

29 Same, *77th*, 1902, numerous illus. including one, "Going for Reinforcements," by S.

30 Same, *79th*, 1904, numerous illus. including one, "Dead Sure," by S.

31 Same, *80th*, 1905, numerous illus. including one, "Attack at Dawn," by S.

THE NATIONAL ARCHIVES OF THE UNITED STATES WASHINGTON, D.C.

32 *Indians and the American West*, October 26, 1973–January 21, 1974, colored pic. wraps, unpaged, numerous illus. including no. 30 by S. (Blumenschein, Dunton)

PARKE-BERNET GALLERIES, NEW YORK

33 *Sale*, November 24, 1939, wraps, 42 pp., numerous illus. including one, p. 34, by S.

34 Sale No. 211, *Antique Furniture*, 1940, wraps,, 108 pp., illus. including photo of the bronze, "The Last Drop," by S. (The Bronze sold for $450.)

35 Sale No. 842, *Nineteenth Century American and*

European Painting, 1947, wraps, 92 pp., illuding two, pp. 21 and 76, by S.

36 Sale No. 2276, *American Paintings and Drawings*, 1964, wraps, 54 (2) pp., numerous illus. including two, pp. 35 and (39), by S. (Leigh, Remington, Russell)

PHOENIX ART GALLERY

37 *The West in Bronze*, May–July 1971, pic. wraps, unpaged, numbered plates including one by S. (Beeler, Remington, Russell)

THE UNIVERSITY OF TEXAS, AUSTIN

38 *Paintings from the C. R. Smith Collection*, Dec. 4, 1969–Jan. 15, 1970, wraps, unpaged, "Preface" by Donald B. Goodall and Marian B. Davis, numerous illus. including one by S. (Dixon, Eggenhofer, Johnson, Lea, Russell, Von Schmidt)

Illustrated by the Artist

39 Ainsworth, Ed. *The Cowboy in Art*. World, N.Y. and Cleveland, (1968), words "First Printing 1968" on copyright page, pic. leather, orange endsheets, all edges gilt, "Foreword" by John Wayne, index, numerous illus. including two, p. 49, by S. and a photo of him. DeLuxe edition of 1000 copies in slipcase. (Beeler, Borein, Bugbee, De Yong, Dixon, Dunton, Eggenhofer, Ellsworth, Hurd, James, Johnson, Koerner, Leigh, Mora, Perceval, Remington, Russell, Von Schmidt)

40 ———. Same, first trade edition in pic. cloth, orange endsheets.

41 ———. Same, reprint by Bonanza Books, N.Y., in pic. cloth, white endsheets.

42 Bancroft, Caroline. *Colorful Colorado*. Sage Books, Denver, (1959), cloth, map endsheets, 127 pp., "The Author" by Governor Stephen L. R. McNichols, acknowledgments, for further reading, index, numerous illus. including three, pp. 24, 25 and 68, by S. (Remington)

43 Bates, Col. Charles Francis. *Custer's Indian Fights*. Privately printed, Bronxville, N.Y., (1936), pic. wraps, 36 (2) pp., acknowledgments, maps, seventeen illus. including two, pp. (21) and 35, by S. (Remington)

44 ———. *Custer's Indian Battles*. 36 (2) pp., map, numerous illus. including two, pp. (21) and 33, by S. Bound with: *Custer's Last Battle* by General Charles Francis Roe, 40 (2) pp., maps, illus. with the cover title *Custer Engages the Hostiles*, decor. cloth and on the first binding "Roe" is spelled with a "w" on the spine, Old Army Press, Ft. Collins, (1973). (Remington)

44a Bennett, Ian. *A History of American Painting*. Hamlyn, London etc. (printed in Italy, 1973), cloth, black endsheets, 239 (1) pp., index, numerous illus. including one, p. 125, by S. (Miller, Remington, Russell)

45 Bennitt, Mark (editor-in-chief). *History of the Louisiana Purchase Exposition*. Universal Exposition Publishing Co., St. Louis, 1905, morocco and cloth, 800 pp., all edges marbled, "Introduction" by Walter B. Stevens, "Publisher's Preface" by Frank Parker Stockbridge, index to illustrations, numerous illus. including "Custer's Demand," p. 500, by S. (Remington)

46 Berthong, Donald J. *The Southern Cheyennes*. Oklahoma, Norman, 1963, words "First Edition" on copyright page, decor. cloth, 446 pp., red top, foreword, bibliography, index, illus. including one, between pp. 368 and 369, by S.

47 *Bison Book Catalog 1971–72*. Nebraska, Lincoln, (1971), pic. wraps, 48 pp., sixteen illus. including one, p. 6, by S. (Remington, Santee)

48 Brady, Cyrus Townsend. *Indian Fights and Fighters*. McClure, Phillips & Co., N.Y., 1904, words "Published December, 1904 N" on copyright page, pic. cloth, 423 pp., preface, bibliography, appendices, index, 13 maps and plans, 26 illus. including two, facing pp. 36 and 86, by S. (Blumenschein, Crawford, Deming, Elwell, Remington)

49 ———. Same, Nebraska, Lincoln, (1971), words First Bison Book printing: November 1971" on copyright page, with an "Introduction" by James T. King, colored pic. wraps, by S.

50 Brooks, Emerson M. *The Growth of a Nation*. Dutton, N.Y., 1956, words "First Edition" on copyright page, decor. cloth, map endsheets, 320 p., "Introduction" by Henry Bamford Parker, author's foreword, bibliography of selected references, index, maps, numerous illus. including one, p. 171, by S. (Russell, Young)

51 Brown, Dee. *Fort Phil Kearny: An American Saga*. G. P. Putnam's Sons, N.Y., (1962), two-tone cloth, 251 pp., bibliography, notes, index, illus. including one, between pp. 128 and 129, by S.

52 Davidson, Marshall B. et al. *The American Heritage History of the Artists' America*. American Heritage,

N.Y., (1973), cloth and boards, blue endsheets, 402 (14) p., introduction, index, numerous illus. including one in color, p. 278, by S. (Miller, Remington, Russell)

53 Downey, Fairfax. *Indian Fighting Army*. Scribner's, N.Y., 1941, code letter "A" on copyright page, cloth, 329 pp., illus. including two, facing pp. 47 and 92, by S. (Leigh, Remington)

54 Dykes, Jeff C., Allred, B. W. et al., eds. *Great Western Indian Fights*. Doubleday, Garden City, N.Y., 1960, words "First Edition" on copyright page, decor. cloth, pic. map endsheets, 336 pp., "The Writers," numerous illus. including two, between pp. 120 and 121, by S. (Dixon, Remington, Russell)

55 ———. Same, first Bison Books edition, Nebraska, Lincoln, (1966), colored pic. wraps,

56 (Eberstadt.) *Americana*. Catalog No. 136, Edward Eberstadt & Sons, N.Y., n.d., wraps, includes one illus. after Schreyvogel's "Custer's Demand" by W. A. Carson.

57 Edwards, G. P. *The Plains of Philippi*. Thomas Gilcrease Institute, Tulsa, 1968, pic. wraps, unpaged, seven illus. by S.

58 Emmett, Chris. *Fort Union and the Winning of the Southwest*. Univ. of Okla. Press, Norman, 1965, words "First Edition" on copyright page, cloth, 436 pp., yellow top, "Foreword" by W. S. Wallace, appendix, bibliography, index, illus., d/w drawing by S.

59 Ewers, John C. *Fact and Fiction in the Documentary Art of the American West*. Reprinted from *The Frontier Re-examined*, Univ. of Illinois Press, Urbana etc., 1967, wraps, pp. (79)-95, sixteen illus. including one, no. 11, between pp. 88 and 89, by S.

60 Ferris, Robert G. (series editor). *Soldier and Brave* (new edition). National Park Service, (G.P.O.), Washington, D.C., 1971, cloth, 451 pp., "Foreword" by Secretary Rogers C. B. Morton, "Preface" by Director George B. Hartzog, Jr., suggested reading, index, maps, numerous illus. including one, p. 29, by S. (Eggenhofer, Leigh, Miller, Remington, Russell, Zogbaum)

61 *Fine Art Reproductions of Old and Modern Masters*. N.Y. Graphic Society, Greenwich, Conn. etc., (1961), decor. cloth, 443 pp., introduction, numerous illus. including one in color, p. 317, by S. (Dixon, Hurd, Remington)

62 Same, (1965), decor. cloth, 540 pp., numerous illus. including one in color, p. 379, by S. (Hurd, Remington, Russell)

63 Fronval, George. *La Fantastique Epopee du Far West*. Darguad, Nevilly/s/ Seine, France, (1969), two volumes, colored pic. boards, pp. 126, (2), and 127, (1), numerous illus. including two, pp. (31) and 84, by S. (Koerner, Miller, Remington, Russell, Zogbaum)

63a ———. *La Veritable Histoire des Indiens Peaux-Rouges*. Fernand Nathan, Paris, France, (1973), cloth, pic. front endsheet, map back endsheet, 125 pp., numerous illus. including three in color, pp. (53), 89 and 90, by S. (Koerner, Leigh, Miller, Remington, Von Schmidt, Zogbaum)

64 Frost, Lawrence A. *The Custer Album*. Superior, Seattle, (1964), words "First Edition" on copyright page, cloth, pic. (facsimile) endsheets, 192 pp., author's preface, bibliography, index, maps, numerous illus. including seven, pp. (90) two, 91 (three), (104) and (117), by S.

65 ———. *The Phil Sheridan Album*. Superior, Seattle, (1968), words "First Edition" on copyright page, cloth, 173 (3) pp., preface, bibliography, index, numerous illus. including six, pp. (129), 130, (132) two and (133) two, by S.

66 Getlein, Frank et al. *The Lure of the Great West*. Country Beautiful, Waukesha, Wisconsin, (1973), boards, 352 pp., introuction, 375 illus. including thirteen (three in color) by S. (Blumenschein, Koerner, Leigh, Miller, Remington, Russell, Wyeth)

67 Heiderstadt, Dorothy. *Painters of America*. McDay, N.Y., (1970), cloth, red endsheets, 180 pp., introduction, bibliography, index, numerous illus. including one, p. (132), by S. and with a chapter "Charles Schreyvogel, Painter of Soldiers." (Miller, Remington, Russell)

68 Herr, Major General John K. and Wallace, Edward S. *The Story of the U.S. Cavalry, 1775–1942*. Little, Brown, Boston, (1953), words "First Edition" on copyright page, cloth, tinted endsheets, 275 pp., author's note and acknowledgments, "Foreword" by General Jonathan M. Wainwright, bibliography, numerous illus. including four, frontis. and pp. (182), (191) and (199), by S. (Remington)

69 Hester, George C. et al. *Texas, The Story of the Lone Star State*. Holt, (N.Y., 1948), decor. cloth, 472 pp., preface, appendices, proper names, index, references, maps, numerous illus. including one, p. 179, by S. (Remington)

70 Holme, Bryan (compiled and edited by). *Pictures to Live With*. Viking, N.Y., (1959), words "First Published in 1959" on copyright page, pic. cloth, 152 pp.,

index, numerous illus. including one, p. (71), by S. (Johnson, Leigh, Miller, Remington)

71 Horan, James D. *The Great American West*. Crown, Publishers, N.Y., (1959), cloth and boards, 288 pp., introduction, bibliography, picture credits, index, 650 illus. including one, p. 98, by S. (Eggenhofer, Hurd, Leigh, Marchand, Remington, Russell)

72 ———. *The Life and Art of Charles Schreyvogel*. Crown, N.Y., (1969), two-tone cloth, 62 pp., plus many plates, "Preface—Charles Schreyvogel, My Father" by Ruth Schreyvogel Carothers, foreword, sources, index, 160 illustrations including 36 in full color.

73 ———. Same, limited edition of 249 numbered copies signed by Horan and Mrs. Carothers with four additional color plates.

74 ———. Same, announcement folder with three illus. by S.

75 Kaegeben, Chas. F. *Souvenir Album of Paintings by Charles Schreyvogel*. Privately printed by the author (Graafmeyer Bros., Hoboken, N.J.), 1907, pic. wraps, (35) pp., photo of Schreyvogel and biographical sketch of him, twenty-nine illus. by S. Words "Presented with the compliments of Chas. F. Kaegeben upon the occasion of his 25th Annual Metzelsuppe, Hoboken, N.J., Oct. 24, 1907" on title page.

76 Latendorf, E. W. *Western Americana*. Catalog No. 24. Mannados Bookshop, N.Y., (1954), pic. wraps, 88 pp., 24 illus. including one, front cover, by S. (Borein, Dixon, Goodwin)

77 Loomis, Noel M. *Wells Fargo*. Clarkson N. Potter, N.Y., 1968, words "First Edition" on copyright page, cloth, tan endsheets, 340 (4) pp., notes, index, maps, numerous illus. including one, p. 174, by S.

78 McCracken, Harold. *Portrait of the Old West*. McGraw-Hill Book Co., N.Y. etc., (1952), words "First Edition" on copyright page, decor. cloth, 232 pp., special acknowledgment, preface, "Foreword" by R. W. G. Vail, "Biographical Check List of Western Artists," index, numerous illus. including many by S. (Remington, Russell)

79 McDermott, John Francis, ed. *The Frontier Re-Examined*. University of Illinois Press, Urbana, 1967, brick endsheets, cloth, 192 pp., foreword, contributors, index, maps, numerous illus. including one, between pp. 86 and 87, by S.

80 *Master Portfolio of Western Art*, Montana Historical Society, Helena, (1965), seventeen prints including two, "Going for Reinforcement" and "Cavalry," by S. (Johnson, Lea, Remington, Russell)

81 Millard, Joseph. *The Cheyenne Wars: The Dramatic Saga of the Greatest of All the Indian Tribes*. Monarch Books, Derby, Conn., (1964), colored pic. wraps, 144 pp., cover illus. by S.

82 Miller, Nyle H. et al. *Kansas: A Pictorial History*. The Kansas Centennial Commission and the State Historical Society, Topeka, 1961, cloth, map pic. endsheets, 319 pp., foreword, picture credits, index, numerous illus. including three, p. 58, by S. (Remington)

83 Monaghan, Jay (editor-in-chief). *The Book of the American West*. Julian Messner, N.Y., (1963), words "First Edition" on copyright page, pic. cloth, tan endsheets, 608 pp., introduction, suggestions for additional reading, index, about the editor-in-chief and authors, numerous illus. including one in color, p. 586, by S. (Borein, Johnson, Koerner, Leigh, Lungren, Remington, Russell)

84 Myrick, Herbert. *Cache La Poudre*. Orange Judd Co., N.Y., Chicago, Indian smoke-tanned buckskin, marbled endsheets, 302 pp., foreword, illus. including the cover design and frontis., by S. Edition of 500 numbered copies. Also a trade edition in pic. cloth. (Deming)

85 *The National Cowboy Hall of Fame and Winchester-Western Extend an Invitation . . . For You to Participate in a Program to Enrich Our Western Heritage through the Purchasing and Assembling of the Important Charles S. Schreyvogel Studio Collection and Major Work Memorial*. (Oklahoma City, 1970?), plain wraps, (12) pp., numerous illus. including a dozen by S. (The project involved selling 1000 memberships at $1000 — each contributor receiving a Winchester, the Model 1894.)

86 Neider, Charles, ed. *The Great West*. Coward-McCann, N.Y., 1958, cloth, map endsheets, 457 pp., brown top, a note on the selections, introduction, maps, numerous illus. including two, pp. 241 and 258, by S. (Miller, Remington)

87 (Price.) *The Vincent Price Treasury of American Art*. Country Beautiful Corporation, Waukesha, Wisconsin, (1972), cloth, tan endsheets, 320 pp., numerous illus. including two, pp. 188 (color) and 189, by S. (Hurd, Remington, Russell, Wyeth)

88 Rachlis, Eugene. *Indians on the Plains*. American Heritage, N.Y., (1960), pic. cloth and endsheets, 132 (1) pp., "Foreword" by John C. Ewers (consultant), acknowledgments, picture credits, bibliography, in-

dex, numerous illus. including one in color, p. (119), by S. (Johnson, Leigh, Remington)

89 Rossi, Paul A. and Hunt, David C. *The Art of the Old West*. (From the collection of the Gilcrease Institute — Knopf, N.Y., but printed in Italy, 1971), words "First Edition" on copyright page, pic. cloth, pic. brown endsheets, 335 (1) pp., preface, listing of artists and works, bibliography, numerous illus. including four, pp. (221) color, 222 color, 230 and 236, by S. (Blumenschein, Borein, James, Leigh, Miller, Remington, Russell, Wyeth)

90 *Santa Fe Village*. Santa Fe, (1971), folder with map and eight illus. including one by S.

91 Schmitt, Martin F. and Brown, Dee. *Fighting Indians of the West*. Scribner's, N.Y., 1948, code letter "A" on copyright page, colored pic. cloth, map endsheets, 362 pp., preface, introduction, bibliography, 270 illus. including five, pp. 32, 57, 75, 135 and 219, by S. (Dixon, Remington)

92 Schomaekers, Gunter. *Der Wilde Westen*. L. B. Ahnert-Verlag, West Germany, n.d., cloth, map endsheets, 217 (7) pp., *ein wort zu vor*, numerous illus. including ten, pp. (178), (179), (180), (193), 194, (201), (202), (204) two and 212, by S. (Miller, Remington, Russell)

93 Schreyvogel, Charles. *My Bunkie and Others*. Moffat, Yard & Co., N.Y., 1909, words "Published September 1909" on copyright page, decor. cloth and pic. boards, oblong folio, (5) pp., and 36 full-page plates by S., "Charles Schreyvogel and His Art."

94 Sell, Henry Blackman and Weybright, Victor. *Buffalo Bill and the Wild West*. Oxford Univ. Press, N.Y., 1955, cloth and pic. boards, pic. endsheets, 278 pp., acknowledgments, bibliography, index, numerous illus. including one, p. 66, by S. (Remington, Russell)

95 ———. Same, The New American Library, (N.Y., 1959), words "First Printing, March, 1959" on copyright page, colored pic. wraps, 320 pp., all edges red, acknowledgments, bibliography, index, numerous illus. including one, p. 84, by S. (Remington, Russell)

96 Severy, Merle, ed. et al. *America's History Lands*. National Geographic Society, Wash., D. C., (Lakeside Press, Chicago, 1962), words "First Printing" on copyright page, two-tone decor. cloth, pic. front endsheets, 576 pp., "Foreword" by Melville Bell Grosvenor (editor-in-chief), "Introduction" by Conrad L. Wirth, index, for references, 675 (463 in full color) illus. including one, p. 513, by S. (Leigh, Remington, Russell)

97 Shapiro, Irwin (adapted by). *The Golden Book of America*. Simon and Schuster, N.Y., (1957), words "First Printing" on copyright page, cloth, and pic. boards, pic. endsheets, 216 pp., blue top, acknowledgments, "Foreword" by Bruce Catton, index, numerous illus. including one, p. 91, by S. (Remington, Russell)

98 Smithers, W. D. et al. *United States Cavalry*. Pattou Museum of Cavalry and Armor, Fort Knox, Ky., (1966), colored pic. wraps, 52 pp., numerous illus. including one, p. 22, by S. (Remington)

99 Sparks, Colonel Ray G. *Reckoning at Summit Springs*. Lowell Press, Kansas City, 1969, pic. wraps, 5 pp., cover illus. by S.

100 Strate, David Kay. *Sentinel to the Cimarron: The Frontier Experience of Fort Dodge, Kansas*. Cultural Heritage and Arts Center, Dodge City, Kansas, (1970), cloth with illus. by Seltzer mounted on front cover, 147 (1) pp., preface, bibliography, index, maps, illus. including two, between pp. 62 and 63, by S. (Dixon)

101 Stroud, Harry A. *Conquest of the Prairies*. Texian Press, Waco, 1968, cloth, 281 pp., illus. including one, following p. 148, by S.

102 Stubbs, Mary Lee and Connor, Stanley Russell. *Armor-Cavalry: Regular Army and Army Reserve*. G.P.O., Washington, D.C., 1969, cloth, 477 pp., illus. including one, p. 21, by S.

103 ———. Same, *Part II: Army National Guard*. G.P.O., Washington, D.C., 1972, cloth, ???? pp., illus. including one by S.

104 Taft, Robert. *The End of a Century*. (The Pictorial Record of the Old West, XIII). Reprinted from *The Kansas Historical Quarterly*, Topeka, Kansas, August, 1951, pic. wraps, pp. 225-253, illus. including one, between pp. 240 and 241, by S. Photo of and much in text on S. (Blumenschein, Leigh)

105 ———. *Artists and Illustrators of the Old West*. Scribner's, N.Y., 1953, code letter "A" on copyright page, cloth, map endsheets, 399 pp., preface and acknowledgments, sources and notes, index, ninety illus. including two, plates nos. 80 and 81, by S. Much on Schreyvogel in text. (Blumenschein, Leigh, Remington)

106 Tebbel, John and Jennison, Keith. *The American Indian Wars*. Harper, N.Y., (1960), cloth, map endsheets, 312 pp., bibliographical notes, index, numerous illus. including one, p. 139, by S. (Remington)

107 Tilghman, Zoe A. *Oklahoma Stories*. Harlow Pub. Corp., Oklahoma City, 1956, pic. cloth, pic. endsheets, 230 pp., foreword, glossary, index (first issue has p. 230 appearing before p. 229), numerous illus. including one, p. 129, by S.

108 Tobis, Ernst. *Die Indianerschlact am Little Bighorn*. Verlag des Ministerium fur Nationale Verteidigung, by Patty Frank (pseud.), Berlin, 1957, pic. cloth, 143 (4) pp., "Forwort" by Eva Lips, folding maps, numerous illus. including two, between pp. 40 and 41, by S.

109 Utley, Robert M. *Fort Union National Monument*. National Park Service, Wash., D.C., 1962, colored pic. wraps, appendices, numerous illus. including one, p. 23, by S. (Remington)

110 Vaughan, J. W *The Reynolds Campaign on Powder River*. Univ. of Okla. Press, Norman, (1961), words "First Edition" on copyright page, cloth, 239 pp., introduction, appendices, bibliography, index, map, seventeen illus. including one, facing p. 145, by S. (Remington)

111 White, Anne Terry. *Indians and the Old West*. Simon and Schuster, N.Y., (1958), pic. boards, 56 pp., all edges red, numerous illus. including two, pp. 41 and 51, by S. (Lea, Leigh, Remington, Russell)

112 Yellow Robe (Lacotawin), Rosebud. *An Album of the American Indian*. Franklin Watts, N.Y., (1969), pic. cloth, 86 (1) pp., introduction, glossary, numerous illus. including one, p. (48), by S. (Remington)

The Artist and His Art

113 *American Art Annual*, vol. 10, 1913, Schreyvogel obit.

114 Boehm, Gustav. "A Painter of Western Realism," an article in *The Junior Munsey*, New York, vol. 8, June, 1900, five illus. by S.

115 Caffin, C. H., in an article in *Harper's Weekly*, vol. 44, Jan. 13, 1900, is critical of the choice of "My Bunkie" for the Clarke Prize.

116 Carothers, Archie D. "The Charles Schreyvogel Memorial Studio Collection," an article in *Persimmon Hill* 1:2, Fall 1970, with numerous illus. by S. and a biographical sketch of him.

116a Dippie, Brian W. "Brush, Palette and the Custer Battle — A Second Look," an article on the art of the Little Big Horn in *Montana* 24:1, Winter 1974, with one illus. by S. (Blumenschein, Dunton, Remington, Russell, Von Schmidt)

117 Dykes, Jeff C. *High Spots in Western Illustrating*. (Kansas City Posse, The Westerners, Kansas City, Mo., 1964), cloth, 30 pp., two illus. High Spots 33, 36, 63 and 80 each have one or more Schreyvogel illustrations and HS 38 is *My Bunkie* (no. 93 above). Edition limited to 250 numbered and signed copies, but an edition in wraps was distributed to the members.

118 Fielding, Mantle. *Dictionary of American Painters, Sculptors and Engravers*. N.Y., 1926, cloth, 433 pp., very brief biographical sketch of S.

119 ———. Same, reprinted by James F. Carr, N.Y., 1965 with an addendum of 95 pages but alas, nothing new on S.!

120 Forest, James Taylor (director). *The Artist in the American West, 1800–1900*. Fine Arts Museum of New Mexico, (Santa Fe), Oct. 8–Nov. 22, 1961, pic. wraps, 32 pp., numerous illus., brief biographical sketch of S. (Remington, Russell)

121 Hoeber, Arthur. "Painters of Western Life," an article in *Mentor Magazine*, June 15, 1915, with two illus. by S. and with a photo of him. (Blumenschein, Dunton, Leigh, Remington, Russell)

122 Horan, James D. "Charles Schreyvogel: Painter Historian of the Indian Fighting Army of the West," an article in *The Westerners Brand Book* 16:4, 1969, New York Posse, biography and one illus. by S.

123 Kobbe, Gustav. "A Painter of the Western Frontier," an article in *The Cosmopolitan*, vol. 31, no. 6, Irvington, N.Y., October, 1901, twelve illus. by S.

124 Levy, Florence Nightingale, ed. *American Art Annual*, vol. 3, 1900–1901, American Federation of Arts, Washington, D.C., includes brief biography of S.

125 Lidner, Clarence R. "The Romance of a Famous Painter," an article in *Leslie's Illustrated Weekly*, N.Y., vol. III, August 4, 1910, eleven illus. by S.

126 Lowell, Tex. "Schreyvogel — Artist on Horseback," an illus. article in *Southwest Heritage* 3:1, December 1968.

127 *Publishers' Weekly* 195:25, June 23, 1969, brief preview of Horan's *The Life and Art of Charles Schreyvogel* with one illus. by S. in the regular feature "Tips."

128 Schreyvogel, Charles. "Vital Pictures of Soldier Life in Western America," an article in *Woman's Home Companion*, May, 1905, also illus. by S.

THE HIRELING DEPUTIES PLUNGED INTO THE RIVER by Smith from
The Outlet

ELMER BOYD SMITH
1860–1943

Catalogues of Art Exhibitions and Galleries

GALLERY OF THE BOSTON ART CLUB

1 *Paint and Clay Club*, 1887, wraps with "A Leaf from the Sketch Book of E. Boyd Smith" with nine sketches and one drawing on another page.

Written and Illustrated by the Artist

2 *My Village*. Chas. Scribner's Sons, N.Y., 1896, pic. cloth, 325 pp., gilt top, pic. title page and numerous drawings in the text.

3 *The Story of Noah's Ark*. Houghton Mifflin, Boston and N.Y., 1905, words "Published November 1905" on copyright page, cloth and pic. boards, (56) pp., twenty-six color plates and illus. in color on title page.

4 *The Story of Pocahontas and Capt. John Smith*. Houghton Mifflin, Boston and N.Y., 1906, words "Published November, 1906" on copyright page, cloth and pic. boards, map endsheets, (56) pp., twenty-six color plates and illus. in color on title page.

5 *Santa Claus and All About Him*. Stokes, N.Y., 1908, cloth and boards, boxed, 62 pp., numerous illus. including sixteen in color.

6 *The Circus and All About It*. Stokes, N.Y., 1909, cloth and boards, 62 pp., numerous illus. including sixteen in color.

7 *The Farm Book*. Houghton Mifflin, Boston and N.Y., 1910, cloth and boards, unpaged, numerous illus.

8 *Chicken World*. Putnam's, N.Y., 1910, cloth and boards, (28) pp., numerous illus. in color.

9 *The Seashore Book*. Houghton Mifflin, Boston and N.Y., 1912, words "Published September 1912" on copyright page, cloth and pic. boards, pic. endsheets, (30) pp., numerous illus. including twelve color plates.

10 *The Railroad Book*. Houghton Mifflin, Boston and N.Y., 1913, cloth and pic. boards, pic. endsheets, (28) pp., numerous illus. including twelve color plates.

11 *The Early Life of Mr. Man Before Noah*. Houghton Mifflin, Boston and N.Y., 1914, cloth and pic. boards, pic. endsheets, (50) pp., twenty-three color plates and illus. in color on title page.

12 *In the Land of Make Believe*. Henry Holt, N.Y., (1916), words "Published August, 1916" on copyright page, cloth and pic. boards, pic. endsheets, (28) pp., numerous illus. including twelve color plates.

13 *After They Came Out of the Ark*. Putnam's, N.Y., London, (1918), cloth and pic. boards, pic. endsheets, 46 (1) pp., twenty-two color plates and illus. in color on title page.

14 *The Boyd Smith Mother Goose*. Putnam's, N.Y. and London, (1919), cloth, 223 pp., text collated and verified by Lawrence Elmendorf, numerous illus. including twenty in color by S.

15 *The Story of Our Country*. Putnam's, N.Y., London, 1920, cloth and pic. boards, map endsheets, 44 (1) pp., numerous illus. including twenty color plates.

16 *Fun in the Radio World*. Stokes, N.Y., 1923, cloth with illus. in color mounted on the front cover, pic. endsheets, (30) pp., numerous illus. including twelve in color.

17 *The Country Book*. Stokes, N.Y., 1924, cloth with illus. in color mounted on the front cover, pic. endsheets, (30) pp., numerous illus. including twelve in color.

18 ———. *Die Geschicte der Arche Noah*, erzahlt von Alice Berend. D. Reimer, Berlin, (1925), cloth and pic.

boards, pic. endsheets, (56) pp., illus. in color including twenty-six full page plates by S. (A translation in German of no. 3.)

19 *Lions 'n Elephants 'n Everything.* Putnam's, N.Y., London, (1929), cloth with illus. in color mounted on front cover, pic. endsheets, (32) pp., numerous illus. including twelve in color.

20 *So Long Ago.* Houghton Mifflin, Boston, 1944, cloth, 35 (1) pp., numerous illus. including sixteen color plates.

Illustrated by the Artist

21 Adams, Andy. *The Log of a Cowboy.* Houghton Mifflin, Boston and N.Y., 1903, words "Published May, 1903" on copyright page, pic. cloth, 387 pp., six illus., frontispiece and facing pp. 60, 138, 206, 236 and 292, by S.

22 ———. *A Texas Matchmaker.* Houghton Mifflin, 1904, words "Published May, 1904" on copyright page, pic. cloth, 355 pp., six illus., frontispiece and facing pp. 26, 40, 122, 190 and 308, by S.

23 ———. *The Outlet.* Houghton Mifflin, 1905, words "Published April 1905" on copyright page, pic. cloth, 371 pp., (4) of advs., preface, six illus., frontispiece and facing pp. 102, 224, 256, 320 and 366, by S.

24 ———. *Wells Brothers.* Houghton Mifflin, Boston and N.Y., 1911, words "Published March 1911" on copyright page, pic. cloth, 356 pp., illus. with photos by Erwin E. Smith and with drawings on the title page and front cover by S.

25 *Aesop's Fables.* Century, N.Y., 1911, words "Published, October, 1911" on copyright page, cloth, 172 pp., numerous drawings by S.

26 Anderson, Robert Gordon. *Seven O'Clock Stories.* Putnam's, N.Y. and London, (1920), cloth with illus. in color mounted on the front cover, pic. endsheets, 180 pp., twenty illus. in color by S.

27 Andrews, Mary Raymond Shipman. *The Enchanted Forest.* Dutton, N.Y., (1909), decor. cloth, 235 pp., six illus., frontis. (in color) and facing pp. 36, 61, 145, 185 and 210, by S.

28 Arbuthnot, May Hill. *Children and Books.* Scott, Foresman, Chicago etc., (1947), cloth, 626 pp., bibliography, numerous illus. including two, pp. 256 and 519, by S. (Wyeth)

29 Austin, Mary. *The Land of Little Rain.* Houghton Mifflin, Boston and N.Y., 1903, "Published October,

1903" on copyright page, pic. cloth, 280 (1) pp., four illus., frontis. and facing pp. 50, 98 and 276 plus drawings in the margins, by S.

30 ———. *The Flock.* Houghton Mifflin, Boston and N.Y., 1906, decor. cloth, 266 pp., frontis., chapter headpiece and drawings by S.

31 ———. Same, first British edition by Archibald Constable & Co., London, 1906.

32 ———. *The Ford.* Houghton Mifflin, Boston and N.Y., 1917, cloth, 440 pp., four tinted illus., frontis. and facing pp. 185, 377 and 439, by S.

33 ———. *The Lands of the Sun.* Houghton Mifflin, Boston and N.Y., 1927, words "Sierra Edition" on half title, decor. cloth, 214 pp., preface, eleven illus. including a tinted frontispiece by S.

34 (Bidpai.) *The Tortoise and the Geese and Other Fables of Bidpai,* retold by Maude Barrows Dutton. Houghton Mifflin, Boston and N.Y., 1908, cloth, 124 (2) pp., twelve illus. by S.

35 Brown, Abbie Farwell. *In the Days of Giants.* Houghton Mifflin, Boston etc., 1902, pic. cloth, 259 (2) pp., six illus., frontis. and facing pp. 62, 88, 122, 232 and 256, by S. (Reprinted in 1930.)

36 ———. *The Curious Book of Birds.* Houghton Mifflin, Boston and N.Y., 1903, words "Published October, 1903" on copyright page, pic. cloth, 191 pp., (introduction), eight full-page illus., frontis. and facing pp. 10, 16, 64, 106, 126, 148 and 160, by S.

37 ———. *John of the Woods.* Houghton Mifflin, Boston and N.Y., 1909, cloth, 189 (1) pp., fifteen illus. by S.

38 Cary, Mrs. M. (translator). *French Fairy Tales.* Thomas Y. Crowell, N.Y., 1919, illus. by S.

39 Cooper, James Fenimore. *Last of the Mohicans.* Holt, N.Y., (1910), cloth, 523 pp., chapter headings and eight illus. in color, frontis. and facing pp. 75, 154, 191, 272, 302, 403 and 458, by S.

40 Dana, Richard Henry, Jr. *Two Years before the Mast.* Houghton Mifflin, Boston and N.Y., 1911, two vols., large paper edition limited to 350 numbered sets, cloth and boards, 553 pp., "Introduction" by the author's son, Richard Henry Dana, numerous illus. from old prints, drawings and with a frontispiece in color — the chapter headings are by S.

41 ———. Same, trade edition in one volume, 1911, cloth with illus. in color mounted on front cover, map endsheets, 553 pp., illus. including seven in color by S.

SWIMMING THE PLATTE by Smith from *The Log Of A Cowboy*

42 Defoe, Daniel. *Robinson Crusoe.* Houghton Mifflin, Boston and N.Y., 1909, decor. cloth with illus. in color mounted on the front cover, 435 pp., forty-one illus. including twelve in color by S.

43 ———. *The Adventures of Robinson Crusoe.* Houghton Mifflin, Boston and N.Y., 1931, cloth, 336 (1) pp., four illus in color, frontis and facing pp. 100, 134 and 152, by S.

43a Dorson, Richard M. *America in Legend.* Pantheon Books (Random), N.Y., (1973), decor. cloth, orange endsheets, 336 pp., foreword, notes, bibliography, index, numerous illus. including two, pp. 130 and 149, by S. (Elwell)

44 Franklin, Ben. *Autobiography,* edited by Frank Woodworth Pine. Holt, N.Y., 1916, cloth, 346 pp., facsimiles and with illus. including ten in color by S.

45 Furlong, Rev. Philip J. *Pioneers and Patriots of America.* William H. Sadlier, N.Y., (1926), words "New York, April 26, 1926" on copyright page, pic. cloth, 422 pp., illus. including one, facing p. 161 (in color), by S. (Remington)

46 Harris, Joel Chandler. *Tales of the Home Folks in Peace and War.* Houghton Mifflin, Boston and N.Y,. 1898, decor. red cloth, 417 (1) pp., four illus. by S.

47 ———. *Planation Pageants.* Houghton Mifflin, Boston and N.Y., 1899, pic. cloth, slate endsheets, 247 pp., all edges tinted, twenty full page illus. by S.

48 Harte, Bret. *Tales of the Argonauts.* Houghton Mifflin, Boston and N.Y., (1896), cloth with paper label on spine, 410 pp., eight illus. including one, facing p. 82, by S. Vol. II of Autograph Edition, limited to 350 sets. An undetermined number of the 350 sets were bound in red morocco and marbled boards with matching marbled endsheets and gilt tops. One (or two) illustration in each volume is signed by the artist. This edition was followed by the Standard Library Edition, bound in red cloth with gilt tops in which the volume numbers, titles, contents and illustrations are the same as those in the Autograph Edition. (Remington)

49 ———. *The Story of a Mine and Other Tales.* Vol. III, 430 pp., eight illus. including one, facing p. 428, by S.

50 ———. *In the Carquinez Woods.* Vol. IV, 460 pp., six illus. including two, facing pp. 204 and 322, by S.

51 ———. *The Crusade of the Excelsior and Other Tales.* Vol. VI, 460 pp., six illus. including one, facing p. 420, by S.

52 ———. *Cressy and Other Tales.* Vol. VII, 488 pp., seven illus. including four, facing pp. 36, 90, 264 and 350, by S.

53 ———. *A First Family of Tasajara and Other Tales.* Vol. VIII, 483 pp., six illus. including two, facing pp. 10 and 116, by S.

54 ———. *A Treasure of the Redwoods and Other Tales.* Vol. XVIII, 363 pp., six illus. including two, facing pp. 120 and 330, by S. (Elwell, Fogarty)

55 Hinkel, John. *The Boomer.* (Book) List no. 11, Hinkel's Book Store, Stillwater, Oklahoma, (1954), pic. wraps, 20 pp., illus. on front cover by S.

56 ———. Same, no. 17, (1956), pic. wraps, 30 pp., illus. on front cover by S.

57 ———. Same, no. 23, (1958), pic. wraps, 35 pp., illus. on front cover by S.

58 ———. Same, no. 31, (1960), pic. wraps, 40 pp., illus. on front cover by S.

59 ———. Same, no. 43, (1963), pic. wraps, 35 pp., illus. on front cover by S.

60 ———. Same, no. 56, (1966), pic. wraps, 35 pp., illus. on front cover by S.

61 ———. Same, no. 69, (1970), pic. wraps, 29 pp., illus. on front cover by S.

62 Holbrook, Florence. *The Hiawatha Primer.* Houghton Mifflin, Boston etc., 1898, pic. cloth, 139, viii pp., (vocabulary), numerous illus. including six in color, frontis. and facing pp. 14, 74, 88, 102 and 126, by S.

63 ———. *The Book of Nature Myths.* Houghton Mifflin, Boston etc., (1902), words "Published November, 1902" on copyright page, cloth, 215 pp., illus by S.

64 Knibbs, Henry Herbert. *Songs of the Outlands.* Houghton Mifflin, Boston and N.Y., 1914, cloth and boards, drawings on half title, contents and pp. 1, 2 and 3, by S.

65 ———. *Overland Red.* Houghton Mifflin, Boston and N.Y., 1914, cloth, 348 (1) pp., illus. including several line drawings, one on the title page, by S. (Fischer)

66 ———. *Tang of Life.* Houghton Mifflin, Boston and N.Y., 1918, cloth, 393 (1) pp., four illus. in color, frontis. and facing pp. 192, 200 and 296, by S.

67 ———. *Jim Waring of Sonora-Town.* Grosset and Dunlap, N.Y., n.d., cloth, 393 (1) pp., (10) of advs., drawing on title page and four full-page plates,

frontis. and facing pp. 188, 220 and 300, by S. A reprint of *Tang of Life*, no. 66.

68 Marryat, Captain Frederick. *The Children of the New Forest*. Henry Holt, N.Y., (1911), cloth with illus. in color mounted on front cover, 397 pp., (8) of advs., chapter head drawings and nine plates in color, front cover, frontis. and facing pp. 40, 110, 146, 202, 268, 330 and 376, by S.

69 Meigs, Cornelia. *The Willow Whistle*. Macmillan, N.Y., 1931, cloth, 144 pp., illus. including a frontis. in color by S.

70 Merwin, Henry Childs. *The Life of Bret Harte*. Houghton Mifflin, Boston and N.Y., 1911, words "Published September 1911" on copyright page, cloth, 362 pp., gilt top, index, seventeen illus. including one, facing p. 166, by S. (Remington)

71 ———. Same, Chatto and Windus, London, 1912, cloth, 362 pp., index, seventeen illus. including one, facing p. 166, by S. First British edition. (Remington)

72 Miller (Mahoney), Bertha E. et al. *Illustrators of Children's Books, 1744–1945*. The Horn Book, Boston, 1947, cloth and pic. boards, 527 pp., gilt top, bibliographies, appendix, index, numerous illus. including one, p. 218, by S.

73 Oxley, J. MacDonald. *The Family on Wheels*. Thomas Y. Crowell, N.Y., (1905), pic. cloth, 219 pp., four illus., frontis. and facing pp. 60, 114 and 180, by S.

74 Schultz, James Willard. *Sinopah, the Indian Boy*. Houghton Mifflin, Boston and N.Y., 1913, words "Published March 1913" on copyright page, cloth with illus. mounted on front cover, 154 (1) pp., (2) of advs., four illus., frontis. and facing pp. 52, 96 and 124, by S.

75 Scott, Sir Walter. *Ivanhoe*. Houghton Mifflin, Boston & N.Y., 1913, pic. cloth, 676 pp., gilt top, notes, glossary, thirteen illus. in color by S.

76 Stevenson, Augusta. *Plays for the Home*. Houghton Mifflin, Boston and N.Y., 1913, pic. cloth, 181 pp., eleven illus. including the frontis in color by S.

77 Stoddard, Harriet et al. *Mary Hunter Austin, Centennial, 1868–1968*. (The Mary Austin Home, Independence, Calif., 1968), decor. wraps, 24 pp., Austin bibliography, numerous sketches (from *Land of Little Rain*) inside front and back wraps by S.

78 Tappan, Eva March (selected and arranged by). *Folk*

Stories and Fables. Houghton Mifflin, 1907, words "The First edition of The Children's Hour is limited to 1000 numbered copies (sets), of which this is No.———" on copyright page, buckram with morocco title label on spine, decorated title page, 519 (1) pp., sixteen illus. including one, facing p. (520), by S. Vol. I (of ten) of The Children's Hour. The first edition was followed by a trade edition in a considerably smaller format, bound in pic. red cloth, with decor. red endsheets and gilt tops. In the trade edition there is no date on the title page, but the frontis. is in color. (Keller)

79 ———. *Myths from Many Lands*. Vol. II, 509 (1) pp., eleven illus. including two, facing pp. 310 and 320, by S.

80 ———. *Poems and Rhymes*. Vol. IX, 514 (1) pp., fourteen illus. including one, facing p. 10, by S.

81 Tinlin, Christine (written by). *First Editions and Rare Books*. J & S Catalogue 7, Chicago, n.d., pic. wraps, 256 pp., numerous illus. including one, p. 1, by S.

82 Ward, (Phelps) Elizabeth Stuart. *The Supply at St. Agatha's*. Houghton Mifflin, Boston and N.Y., 1896, decor. cloth, 88 pp., (1) of advs., three illus. including two, frontis. and facing p. 36, by S.

The Artist and His Art

83 Burke, W. J. and Howe, Will D. *American Authors and Books, 1640–1940*. Gramercy Pub. Co., N.Y., (1943), cloth, 858 pp., a few lines on Smith, p. 696.

84 Fielding, Mantle. *Dictionary of American Painters, Sculptors and Engravers*. N.Y., 1926, 433 pp., preface, bibliography, two lines on Smith, p. 337.

85 Mechlin, Leila et al. *American Art Annual*. Vol. XVIII, Washington, D.C., 1921, cloth, 680 pp., illus., brief biographical sketch of Smith, p. 567.

86 Meigs, Cornelia et al. *A Critical History of Children's Literature*. Macmillan, N.Y., (1953), words "First Printing" on copyright page, decor. cloth, grey endsheets, 624 pp., "Introduction" by Dr. Henry Steele Commager, "Foreword" by Cornelia Meigs, index, Smith's own books praised, pp. 400–1.

87 Miller (Mahony), Bertha E. and Whitney, Elinor (compiled by). *Contemporary Illustrators of Children's Books*. The Bookshop for Boys and Girls, Boston, 1930, decor. cloth, 135 pp., illus., brief biographical sketch of Smith, p. 68.

THE LEADER OF THE MUSTANGS — A NATIVE AMERICAN by Stoops from
Mustangs of the Mesas

HERBERT MORTON STOOPS
1887–1948

Catalogues of Art Exhibitions and Galleries

HELEN L. CARD, NEW YORK

1 *Hang on Fellers! We're Out on a Limb*, Catalog no. 5, (1963), pic. wraps, 92 pp., numerous illus. including one, p. 50, by S. (Deming, Eggenhofer, Leigh, Remington, Schoonover, Wyeth)

NATIONAL ACADEMY OF DESIGN, NEW YORK

2 *Illustrated Catalogue of 114th Annual Exhibition*, 1940, wraps, numerous illus. including one, "Anno Domini," by S.

SOTHEBY PARKE BERNET, NEW YORK

3 *18th, 19th and Early 20th Century American Paintings, Watercolors and Sculpture*, Sept. 13, 1972, pic. wraps, 89 (4) pp., numerous illus. including two, pp. 17 and 20, by S. Auction sale no. 3399. (Dixon, Dunton, Johnson, Koerner)

Illustrated by the Artist

4 The Art Directors Club, N.Y. *Third Annual of Advertising Art in the U.S., 1924.* Cloth and boards, 165 pp., (20) of advs., (11) of indices, numerous illus. including nine, pp. 59, 63, 64, 78, 92 (four), and 92, by S.

5 ———. Same, *Fourth, 1925.* Cloth and boards, 128 pp., (25) of advs., (11) of indices, numerous illus. including three, pp. 65 and 72 (two), by S. (Fogarty)

6 ———. Same, *Fifth, 1926.* Cloth and boards, 136 pp., (22) of advs., (9) of indices, numerous illus. including one, p. 38, by S. (Dunn)

7 ———. Same, *Sixth, 1927.* Cloth, colored pic. map endsheets, 152 pp., (24) of advs., (11) of indices, numerous illus. including four, pp. 30, 34, 42 and 93, by S. (Dunn, Von Schmidt, Wyeth)

8 ———. Same, *Fourteenth, 1935.* Pic. cloth, 120 pp.,

(30) of advs., (4) of indices, numerous illus. including one, p. 28, by S. (Fogarty)

9 ———. Same, *Fifteenth, 1936.* Pic. cloth, numerous illustrations including one, p. 72, by S.

10 *The Artists Guild Annual for 1939.* The Committee for Guild Publicity, N.Y., 1939, decor. cloth, orange endsheets, 111 (8) pp., correction slip follows text, foreword, "Introduction" by Earnest Elmo Calkins, numerous illus. including six, facing p. 91, by S.

11 Brandt, Carl. *Bob Hazard, Dam Builder.* The Reilly & Britton Co., Chicago, (1916), decor. cloth, 272 pp., four illus., frontis. and facing pp. 70, 148 and 230, by S.

12 Brayer, Garnet M. and Herbert O. *American Cattle Trails, 1540–1900.* American Pioneer Trails Assn., Bayside, N.J., 1952, fabricoid, 128 pp., "Foreword" by Howard R. Driggs, maps, numerous illus. including six, pp. 23, 63, 82, 84, 94 and 103, by S. Special limited and numbered edition on text stock. (Borein)

13 ———. Same, trade edition in colored pic. wraps.

14 Clum, Woodworth. *Apache Agent.* Houghton Mifflin, Boston, 1936, pic. cloth, 296 (1) pp., cover illus. by S.

15 Coatsworth, Elizabeth (introduction by). *Story Parade (The Red Book Parade).* Winston, Philadelphia etc., 1937, cloth, colored pic. endsheets, 363 pp., introduction, classified index, numerous illus. including eleven by S.

16 Cobb, Irwin S. *Chivalry Peak.* Cosmopolitan, N.Y., 1927, cloth, 314 pp., illus. including frontis. and one double-page plate by S.

17 Cook, James B. and Driggs, H. R. *Longhorn Cowboy.* World Book Co., Yonkers, N.Y., 1927, cloth, pic. endsheets, 241 pp., brown top, numerous illus. by S.

18 Creel, George. *Sons of the Eagle* (Soaring Figures from America's Past). Bobbs-Merrill, Indianapolis, (1927), cloth, 321 (1) pp., eight illus., frontis. and facing pp. 88, 122, 132 (repeated on d/w), 142, 180, 192 and 262, by S.

19 Gates, Arthur I. et al. *We Grow Up*. Macmillan, n.p. (N.Y., 1939), words "Published February, 1939" on copyright page, colored pic. cloth, 248 pp. numerous illus. in color including 27 by S.

20 ——— and Minor, Lillian. *Beginning Days*. Macmillan, n.p. (N.Y., 1939), words "Published February, 1939" inside front cover, pic. wraps, 48 pp., numerous illus. in color by S. et al.

21 ——— et al. *Jim and Judy*. Macmillan, n.p. (N.Y., 1939), words "Published February, 1939" on the copyright page, colored pic. cloth, pic. endsheets, 154 pp., numerous illus. in color by S. et al.

22 ——— and Brown, Zeta I. *The Animal Parade*. Macmillan, n.p. (N.Y., 1939), words "Published September, 1939" inside front cover, pic. wraps, 48 pp., numerous illus. by S. et al.

23 ———. *Tony and Jo-Jo*. Macmillan, n.p. (N.Y., 1940), words "Published May, 1940" inside front cover, pic. wraps, 48 pp., numerous illus. by Stoops et al.

24 ——— and Mitchell, Frances. *The Sad Prince*. Macmillan, n.p. (N.Y., 1940), words "Published May, 1940" inside front cover, pic. wraps, 48 pp., numerous illus. by Stoops et al.

25 Gill, Richard Cochran. *Manga, an Amazon Jungle Indian*. Frederick A. Stokes, N.Y., 1937, cloth, map endsheets, 268 pp., illus. by S.

26 ———. *The Volcano of Gold*. Stokes, N.Y., 1938, cloth, map endsheets, 256 pp., numerous illus. by S.

27 Gillett, James H. and Driggs, H. R. *The Texas Ranger*. World Book Co., Yonkers, 1927, pic. cloth, 223 pp., "An Introduction" by Driggs, numerous illus. by S.

28 Goulart, Ron. *Cheap Thrills* (An Informal History of the Pulp Magazines). Arlington House, New Rochelle, N.Y., (1972), boards, 192 pp., preface, 16 pages of illus. including one, p. (105), by S.

29 Jackson, Helen Hunt. *Ramona*. Little, Brown, Boston, 1932, words "Published August, 1932" on copyright page, decor. cloth, pic. endsheets, 447 pp., numerous illus. including a frontis. in color by S.

30 Kyne, Peter B. *The Understanding Heart*. Cosmo-politan Book Corp., N.Y., 1926, cloth, 374 pp., four illus., frontis. and facing pp. 132, 292, and 366, by S.

31 Linderman, Frank B. *American*. The John Day Co., N.Y. (1930), cloth, 313 pp., numerous illus. by S.

32 ———. Same, but issued by World Book Company, Yonkers-on-Hudson, N.Y., (1930), pic. cloth, 324 pp., foreword, author's note, index, illus. with numerous drawings by S.

33 ———. *Old Man Coyote (Crow)*. John Day, N.Y., (1931), pic. cloth and endsheets, 254 pp., red top, illus. with drawings by S.

34 ———. *Red Mother*. John Day, N.Y., (1932), decor. cloth, pic. endsheets, 256 pp., foreword, illus. with drawings by S.

35 ———. *Stumpy*. John Day, N.Y., (1933), cloth, 147 (1) pp., illus. by S.

36 ———. *Plenty-Coups, Chief of the Crows*. University of Nebraska Press, Lincoln, 1962, colored pic. wraps, 324 pp., numerous illus. by S. Reprint of *American*, no. 31, Bison Book 128.

37 Longfellow, Henry Wadsworth. *Hiawatha's Childhood*. Garden City Pub. Co., Garden City, N.Y., (1941), cloth, colored pic. endsheets, (15) pp., illus., some in color, by S.

38 McConnell, Wm. J. *Frontier Law*. World, Yonkers, Chicago, 1924, pic. cloth, 233 pp., (10) of advs., numerous illus. by S.

39 Malkus, Alida Sims. *Stone Knife Boy*. Harcourt, N.Y., (1933), cloth, pic. endsheets, 270 pp., illus. by S.

40 Mallette, Gertrude E. *Chee-Cha-Ko*. Doubleday, Doran, N.Y., 1938, words "First Edition" on copyright page, cloth, pic. endsheets, 299 pp., blue top, frontis. in color by S.

41 ———. *No Vacancies*. Jr. Literary Guild and Doubleday, Doran, N.Y., (1939), fabricoid, pic. endsheets, 311 pp., blue top, frontis. by S.

42 Marshall, Edison. *Child of the Wild*. Cosmopolitan, N.Y., 1926, cloth, 297 pp., three illus., frontis., center spread and facing p. 274, by S.

43 Means, Florence Crannell. *Tangled Waters*. Houghton Mifflin, Boston, 1936, cloth, 212 pp., numerous illus. including the frontis. in color by S.

44 ———. *Adella Mary in Old Mexico*. Houghton Mifflin, Boston, 1939, pic. cloth, 226 (1) pp., illus. by S.

45 *Old Ranger's Yarns of Death Valley*. Pacific Coast

Borax Co., N.Y., (1932), colored pic. wraps, (12) pp., numerous illus. including three by S.

46 Phillips, Ethel Calvert. *Ride the Wind.* Houghton Mifflin, Boston, 1933, cloth, 190 pp., brown top, nine illus., frontis. and pp. 19, 35, 51, 57, 79, 139, 151 and 181, by S.

46a Reed, Walt. *The Illustrator in America 1900–1960's.* Reinhold, N.Y., (1966), cloth, pic. green endsheets, 271 (1) pp., "Is Illustration Art?" by Albert Dorne, bibliography, numerous illus. including two, p. (160), by S. (Blumenschein, Crawford, Dunn, Dunton, Eggenhofer, Fischer, Fogarty, Goodwin, James, Keller, Koerner, Remington, Russell, Schoonover, Wyeth)

47 Robbins, Charles L. *School History of the American People.* World, Yonkers, Chicago, 1925, pic. cloth, 606 pp., appendices, maps, numerous illus. including one, p. 333, by S. (Remington)

48 Rolt-Wheeler, Francis. *The Book of Cowboys.* Lothrop, Lee & Shepard Co., Boston, (1921), words "Published, April, 1921" on copyright page, pic. cloth, 394 pp., (4) of advs., thirty-three illus. including one, facing p. 268, by S. (Dixon, Russell)

49 Standing Bear, Chief. *Stories of the Sioux.* Houghton Mifflin, Boston and N.Y., 1934, decor. cloth, 79 pp., red top, preface, nine illus., frontis. and facing pp. 18, 24, 30, 34, 42, 48, 62 and 72, by S.

50 Starbuck, Edwin Diller and Staff (selected and edited by). *The High Trail.* World, Yonkers-on-Hudson, N.Y., (1936), decor. cloth, 340 pp., preface, glossary, illus. including one, p. 229, by S. (Remington)

51 ———. *Actions Speak.* World, Yonkers, (1936), decor. cloth, 340 pp., illus. including three drawings, pp. 11, 13 and 26, by S.

52 ———. *Lives That Guide.* World, Yonkers, 1939, decor. cloth, 319 pp., illus. including one drawing, p. 229, by S.

53 Steele, Rufus. *Scarneck.* Harper, N.Y. and London, 1930, cloth, pic. endsheets, 92 pp., illus. including the frontis. in brown, by S.

54 ———. *Mustangs of the Mesas.* Murray & Gee, Hollywood, Calif., (1941), cloth, 220 pp., illus. including two, facing pp. 13 and 214, by S. (Dixon)

55 Stoops, H. M. *Inked Memories of 1918.* Privately printed, 1924, (for the American Legion Posts by The Jell-O Co., Le Roy, N.Y.), cloth and boards with title label on front cover, unpaged, fifteen plates by S.

56 Stribling, T. S. *The Cruise of the Dry Dock.* Reilly and Britton, Chicago, (1917), cloth, 345 pp., four illus. in color, frontis. and facing pp. 48, 184 and 332, by S.

57 Stringer, Arthur. *Empty Hands.* Bobbs-Merrill, Indianapolis, (1924), decor. cloth, 360 pp., four illus., frontis. and facing pp. 12, 226 and 356, by S.

58 Van Dine, S. S. *The Bishop Murder Case.* Scribner's, N.Y., 1930, fabricoid, 349 pp., frontis. by S. The Philo Vance Series — the copies of the first edition (1929) examined did not include the Stoop frontispiece.

The Artist and His Art

58a Bolton, Theodore. *American Book Illustrators — Bibliographic Check Lists of 123 Artists.* R. R. Bowker Co., N.Y., 1938, cloth, 290 pp., introduction, index, lists eleven items illus. by S.

59 Mechlin, Leila et al. *American Art Annual.* Vol. XVIII, Washington, D.C., 1921, cloth, 680 pp., lists Stoops and his address, p. 577.

60 Merriam, Harold G. *Montana Adventure* (The Recollections of Frank B. Linderman). Nebraska, Lincoln, (1968), cloth, map endsheets, 224 pp., foreword, illustrated, Stoops as one of Linderman's favorite illustrators, pp. 192-195 and 214.

61 Stein, Harve (Director). *Herbert Morton Stoops, 1887–1948.* Stone Ledge Studio Art Galleries, Noank, Conn., n.d., single sheet with photo of Stoops. (Same biographical information, without photo, issued as single sheet by J. N. Bartfield, New York.)

THE ROYAL CHAPEL — CAPILLA RÉAL — MONTEREY by Suydam from
California's Missions

EDWARD HOWARD SUYDAM
1885–1940

Illustrated by the Artist

1 Beebe, Lucius. *Boston and the Boston Legend.* D. Appleton-Century Co., N.Y., London, 1935, code number "(1)" after last line of text, two-tone cloth with illus. mounted on front cover, pic. endsheets, 372 pp., numerous illus. including frontis. in color by S.

2 Bercovici, Konrad. *Nights Abroad.* The Century Co., N.Y., London, 1928, cloth, 315 pp., illus. by S.

3 Carr, Harry. *Los Angeles, City of Dreams.* Appleton-Century, N.Y., London, 1935, code number "(1)" after last line of text, two-tone, cloth with illus. mounted on front cover, pic. endsheets, 403 pp., numerous illus. including frontis. in color by S.

4 Dobie, Charles Caldwell. *San Francisco, a Pageant.* Appleton-Century, N.Y., London, 1933, code number "(1)" after last line of text, two-tone cloth with illus. mounted on front cover, pic. endsheets, 351 pp., numerous illus. including frontis. in color by S.

5 ———. *San Francisco's Chinatown.* Appleton-Century, N.Y., London, 1936, code number "(1)" after last line of text, cloth, pic. endsheets, 336, numerous illus. including frontis. in color by S.

6 Gessler, Clifford. *Hawaii: Isles of Enchantment.* Appleton-Century, N.Y., London, 1937, code number "(1)" after last line of text, decor. cloth, pic. endsheets, 382 pp., numerous illus. including frontis. in color by S.

7 ———. *Pattern of Mexico.* Appleton-Century, N.Y., London, 1941, code number "(1)" after last line of text, cloth, pic. endsheets, 441 (1) pp., numerous illus. by S.

8 Grafly, Dorothy. *A History of the Philadelphia Print Club.* (The Club), Philadelphia, 1929, cloth and boards with title label on front cover, 17 pp., five illus., frontis. and facing pp. 4, 8, 12 and 16, by S. Suydam in text.

9 Hawthorne, Hildegarde. *Romantic Cities of California.* Appleton-Century, N.Y., London, 1939, code number "(1)" after last line of text, cloth, pic. endsheets, 456 pp., numerous illus. including frontis. in color by S.

10 ———. *Williamsburg, Old and New.* Appleton-Century, N.Y., London, 1941, code number "(1)" after last line of text, cloth, pic. endsheets, 284 pp., numerous illus. by S.

11 ———. *California's Missions.* Appleton-Century, N.Y., 1942, code number "(1)" after last line of text, cloth, pic. endsheets, 237 pp., numerous illus. by S.

12 Irwin, Will. *Highlights of Manhattan.* Century, N.Y., London, (1927), words "First printing, October, 1927" on copyright page, cloth and boards with illus. mounted on front cover, 381 pp., numerous illus. including frontis. in color by S.

13 Jackson, Joseph Henry. *Anybody's Gold: The Story of California's Mining Towns.* Appleton-Century, N.Y., London, 1941, code number "(1)" after last line of text, cloth, map endsheets, 467 (1) pp., maps, numerous illus. by S.

14 Molloy, Robert. *Charleston, a Gracious Heritage.* Appleton-Century, N.Y., & London, (1947), code number "(1)" after last line of text, cloth, pic. endsheets, 311 pp., numerous illus. by S.

15 Moore, Charles. *Washington, Past and Present.* Century, N.Y., London, (1929), words "First Printing" on copyright page, two-tone green cloth with illus. mounted on front cover, pic. endsheets, 340 pp., numerous illus. including frontis. in color by S.

16 Morgan, Wallace and Suydam, E. H. (drawings by).

Abroad at Home. Cover title but with title pages for *Abroad at Home* (1914); *American Adventures* (1917); no. 26, *The Macadam Trial* (1931), and no. 24, *Chicago* (1931) bound in cloth, no text, numerous illus. including 41 by S.

17 Pound, Arthur. *Detroit, Dynamic City*. Appleton-Century, N.Y., London, 1940, code number "(1)" after last line of text, cloth, pic. endsheets, 397 (1) pp., numerous illus. including frontis. in color by S.

18 Rothery, Agnes. *Virginia: The New Dominion*. Appleton-Century, N.Y., London, 1940, code number "(1)" after last line of text, cloth, pic. endsheets 368 pp., numerous illus. including frontis. in color by S.

19 Salaman, Malcolm C., ed. (and The American Section by Helen Fagg). *Fine Prints of the Year* (An Annual Review of Contemporary Etching and Engraving). Holton & Truscott Smith, Ltd., London and Minton, Balch & Co., N.Y. (printed in Great Britain), 1930, words "October, 1930" on copyright page, cloth, 20, xx pp., xii of advs. plus 100 numbered plates including no. 91 by S.

20 Saxon, Lyle. *Fabulous New Orleans*. Century, N.Y., London, (1928), words "First printing, September, 1928" on copyright page, two-tone cloth with illus. mounted on front cover, pic. endsheets, 330 pp., numerous illus. including frontis. in color by S.

21 ———. Same, reprinted by R. L. Crager Co., New Orleans, 1952.

22 ———. *Old Louisiana*. Century, N.Y., London, (1929), words "First printing" on copyright page, two-tone cloth with illus. mounted on front cover, pic. endsheets, 388 pp., numerous illus. including frontis. in color by S.

23 ———. Same, reprinted by R. L. Crager Co., New Orleans, 1950.

24 ———. *Lafitte the Pirate*. Century, N.Y., London, (1930), words "First Printing" on copyright page, two-tone cloth with illus. mounted on front cover, pic. endsheets, 307 pp., numerous illus. including frontis. in color by S.

25 ———. *The Friends of Joe Gilmore*, and *Some Friends of Lyle Saxon* by Edward Dreyer. N.Y., (1948), two-tone decor. cloth, pic. endsheets, 182 pp., illus. with eight drawings, front endsheet, facing pp. 22, 39, 54, 71, 86, 103 and back endsheet, by S. and with photos. Suydam in text, pp. 46-47.

26 Simpson, John Thomas. *Hidden Treasure*. J. B. Lippincott Co., Phila., London, (1919), cloth, 303 pp., 17 illus. including two, frontis. and facing p. 70, by S.

27 Smith, Henry Justin. *Chicago, a Portrait*. Century, N.Y., London, (1931), words "First Printing" on copyright page, two-tone cloth with illus. mounted on front cover, pic. endsheets, 386 pp., numerous illus. including frontis. in color by S.

28 Suydam, Edward Howard et al. *Towers of Manhattan*. The N.Y. Edison Co., N.Y., 1928, vellum and boards, "Preface" but no other text, fifty full-page sketches including twenty-three by S.

29 Winn, Mary Day. *The Macadam Trail*. Alfred A. Knopf, N.Y., 1931, words "First Edition" on copyright page, decor. cloth, pic. endsheets, 319, xii pp., brown top, numerous illus. including frontis. in color by S. Much on Suydam in text.

The Artist and His Art

30 Bolton, Theodore. *American Book Illustrators: Bibliographic Check Lists of 123 Artists*. R. R. Bowker Co., N.Y., 1938, cloth, 290 pp. The list, pp. 192-193, includes eleven of the above items.

31 Blumann, Ethel and Thomas, Mable W., eds. *California Local History: A Centennial Bibliography*. Stanford University Press, Stanford, Calif., 1950, cloth, 576 pp. Lists four of the above items.

32 Burke, W. J. and Howe, Will D. *American Authors and Books, 1640–1940*. Gramercy Publishing Co., N.Y., (1943), cloth, 858 pp. Brief sketch, p. 734.

33 Fielding, Mantle. *Dictionary of American Painters, Sculptors and Engravers*. N.Y., 1926, cloth, 433 pp., preface, bibliography. Brief sketch, p. 357.

34 ———. Same, reprinted with addendum by James F. Carr, N.Y., 1965, cloth, 529 pp. No additional material on Suydam.

SITE OF LEESE HOUSE, GRANT AVENUE by Suydam from *San Francisco's Chinatown*

SAM HOUSTON by Thomason from *Gone To Texas*

JOHN WILLIAM THOMASON, JR.
1893–1944

Written and Illustrated by the Artist

1 *Fix Bayonets!* Charles Scribner's Sons, N.Y., 1926, cloth and pic. boards, 245 pp., numerous illus. including frontis. in color by T.

2 Same, 1970 reprint by Scribner with a new introduction by Robert Leckie.

3 *Red Pants and Other Stories.* Scribner's, N.Y., 1927, pic. cloth, 246 pp., numerous illus. by T.

4 *Marines and Others.* Scribner's, N.Y., 1929, pic. cloth, 290 pp., numerous illus. by T.

5 *Jeb Stuart.* Scribner's, N.Y., 1930, code letter "A" on copyright page, cloth, 512 pp., maps, numerous illus. by T.

6 *Salt Wind and Gobi Dust.* Scribner's, N.Y., 1934, code letter "A" on copyright page, cloth, 326 pp., numerous illus. by T.

7 *Gone to Texas.* Scribner's, N.Y., 1937, code letter "A" on copyright page, cloth, 274 pp., numerous illus. by T.

8 *Lone Star Preacher.* Scribner's, N.Y., 1941, code letter "A" on copyright page, cloth, 296 pp., numerous illus. by T.

9 *. . . . And a Few Marines.* Scribner's, N.Y., 1943, code letter "A" on copyright page, cloth, 667 pp., numerous illus. by T.

9a Same, reissued by Scribner's in 1958 with an added biographical sketch of Thomason by Colonel R. D. Heinl of the Marines.

10 *Stonewall Jackson and Praxitels Swan.* (Carl Hertzog, El Paso, Texas), Christmas, 1949, (greeting from Bob Mosley), folder, one full-page illus. by T.

11 Rosenfeld, Arnold. *A Thomason Sketchbook.* Texas, Austin and London, (1969), pic. cloth, 128 pp., "Foreword" (and edited) by Rosenfeld, "The Old Breed —

A Note on John W. Thomason, Jr." by John Graves, numerous illus. by T.

Illustrated by the Artist

12 Adams, James T. and Vannest, Charles G. *The Record of America.* Scribner's, N.Y., 1935, cloth, 941 pp., maps, numerous illus. including one in color, facing p. 258, by T. (Wyeth)

13 Blackford, Lieut.-Col. W. W., C.S.A. *War Years with Jeb Stuart.* Scribner's, N.Y., 1945, code letter "A" on copyright page, cloth, 322 pp., illus. including two, d/w and title page, by T.

14 Botkin, Ben A., ed. *A Treasure of Southern Folklore.* Crown Publishers, N.Y., (1949), pic. cloth, 776 pp., "Foreword" by Douglas Southall Freeman, design on front cover and small drawing on title page by T.

15 ———. Same, but Texas Edition, signed by Botkin.

16 Boyd, Thomas. *Through the Wheat.* Scribner's, N.Y., 1927, cloth, 260 pp., numerous illus. by T. (Reprint but first with Thomason's illustrations.)

17 Crockett, David. *The Adventures of Davy Crockett.* Scribner's, N.Y., 1934, code letter "A" on copyright page, cloth with illus. in color mounted on front cover, 259 pp., edited by Thomason and with numerous illus. by him.

18 ———. *Davy Crockett and His Adventures in Texas.* Scribner's, N.Y. etc., (1934), cloth with illus. in color mounted on front cover, 149 pp., edited and with an introduction by Thomason and with numerous illus. by him. (Generally ascribed to Richard Penn Smith.)

19 Dobie, J. Frank et al., eds. *Mustangs and Cowhorses.* Texas Folklore Society, Austin, 1940, fabricoid, pic. endsheets, 429 pp., numerous illus. including

one, p. 416, by T. (Bugbee, James, Lea, Leigh, Russell, Santee)

20 ———. Same, fascimile reprint by SMU Press, Dallas, 1965.

21 ———. *Guide to Life and Literature of the Southwest.* The University of Texas Press, Austin, Texas, 1943, wraps, 111 pp., twenty-four illus. including one, p. 43, by T. (Borein, Bugbee, Dunton, Hurd, James, Lea, Leigh, Russell)

22 ———. Same, but issued in pic. cloth by the University Press, Dallas, 1943.

23 ———. Same, Revised and Enlarged in both Knowledge and Wisdom. SMU Press, Dallas, 1952, decor. cloth, 222 pp., nineteen illus. including one, p. 57, by T. (Bugbee, Cisneros, Lea, Leigh, Russell)

24 Freeland, George et al. *America's Building — The Makers of Our Flag.* Scribner's, N.Y. etc., (1937), code letter "A" on copyright page, pic. cloth, 425 pp., note, annotated list of reading, index, illus. including one by T. (Fogarty, Rowe)

25 ———, Same, 1974 edition with one illus., p. 122, by T. (Fogarty, Rowe, Varian, Wyeth)

26 Henry, Robert Selph. *"First with the Most" Forest.* Bobbs-Merrill, Indianapolis, N.Y., (1944), words "First Edition" on copyright page, cloth, 558 pp., bibliography, illus. including one, the frontis., by T.

27 Hunt, Frazier. *Custer, the Last of the Cavaliers.* Cosmopolitan Book Corp., N.Y., 1928, cloth, 209 pp., tinted top, illus. with photos and with eight drawings by T.

28 ——— and Robert Hunt (as told to). *I Fought with Custer* (The Story of Sergeant Windolph). Scribner's, N.Y., London, 1947, code letter "A" on copyright page, cloth, 236 pp., preface, bibliography, index, maps, numerous illus. including one, facing p. 169, by T. (Remington)

29 Leckie, Robert. *The Story of World War I.* Random House, N.Y., (1965), pic. cloth, pic. endsheets, 189 pp., prologue, chronology, index, numerous illus. including six, pp. 154 (two — one in color) and 155 (four), by T. (Dunn)

30 Logan, Harlan. *Fiftieth Anniversary, Scribner's Magazine, 1887–1937.* Scribner's, N.Y., 1937, decor. wraps, 144 pp., numerous illus. including one, p. 102, by T. (Dunn, James, Remington)

31 Marbot, Jean Baptiste Antoine Marcelin, Baron de.

Adventures of General Marbot. Scribner's, N.Y., 1935, cloth with illus. in color mounted on front cover, 499 pp., edited by Thomason and with numerous illus. by him.

32 Marshall, General S. L. A. *World War I.* American Heritage Press, N.Y., 1971, cloth and boards, map endsheets, 497 (2) pp., numerous illus. including three drawings, p. 385, by T. (Dunn)

33 Meredith, Roy *The American Wars.* The World Pub. Co., Cleveland and N.Y., (1955), words "First Edition" on copyright page, pic. cloth, 348 (1) pp., red top, numerous illus. including seven, pp. 240, 246, 247, 249 and 255 (three), by T. (Deming, Dunn, Fischer, Remington)

34 Montross, Lynn. *The United States Marines — A Pictorial History.* Holt, Rinehart & Winston, N.Y., (1959), cloth and boards, 242 pp., "Introduction" by Senator Paul H. Douglas, credits, numerous illus. including two, pp. 129 and 137, by T.

35 ———. Same, reprint by Bramhall House, N.Y., with code letter "(C)" on copyright page.

36 Norwood, W. D., Jr. *John W. Thomason, Jr.* Steck-Vaughn Company, Austin, (1969), wraps, 44 pp., selected bibliography, four illus., pp. 19, 20, 21 and 22, by T. (Southwest Writers Series no. 25.)

37 Page, Thomas Nelson. *Two Little Confederates.* Scribner's, N.Y., 1932, cloth with illus. in color mounted on front cover, 189 (2) pp., numerous illus. by T.

38 Pitz, Henry C. *A Treasury of American Book Illustration.* Watson-Guptill Publications, N.Y., (1947), decor. cloth, 128 pp., numerous illus. including one, p. 38, by T. (James, Wyeth)

39 Rogers, John William, ed. *A Round-Up of the Most Interesting Texas Books of All Time.* The Dallas Times Herald, a reprint of "Book News," Oct. 7, 1945, self-wraps, 16 pp., illus. including one, p. 13, by T. (Bugbee, Hurd, Lea)

40 Roosevelt, Theodore, Jr. *Rank and File.* Scribner's, N.Y., London, 1928, cloth, 279 pp., ten illus. by T.

41 ——— and Rice, Grantland. *Taps.* Doubleday, Doran, Garden City, N.Y., 1932, cloth, 241 pp., numerous illus. by T.

42 *University of Texas Press.* (Catalog for) Spring and Summer, 1969, Austin, pic. wraps, 24 pp., announces publication of *A Thomason Sketchbook,* ten illus. including two, front cover and p. 2, by T.

A SPRINKLING OF OLD-TIME MARINES by Thomason from *Fix Bayonets!*

43 Carroll, Gordon, ed. *The Post Reader of Civil War Stories*. Doubleday, Garden City, N.Y., 1958, cloth, 331 pp., illus.; includes, pp. 266–315, three chapters from *Lone Star Preacher*, no. 7.

44 Cox, Mamie Wynne. *The Romantic Flags of Texas*. Banks Upshaw & Co., Dallas, (1936), fabricoid, 373 pp., illustrated, "Foreword" by T.

45 Greer, Hilton R., ed. *Best Short Stories from the Southwest*. Southwest Press, Dallas, Texas, (1928), cloth and decor. boards, 386 pp.; includes "The Conquest of Mike" by T.

46 Hemingway, Ernest et al. (edited and with an introduction by). *Men at War*. Crown, N.Y., (1942), cloth, 1072 pp.; includes, pp. 633–74, 998–99 and 1011–18, stories from *Lone Star Preacher*, no. 7 and pp. 843–60, "The Marines at Soissons" by T.

47 Karp, Marvin Allen, ed. *The Brave Ones*. Popular Library, N.Y., (1965), colored pic. wraps, 141 pp., (2) of advs., all edges red, includes "The Collaborator" by T.

48 Long, Ray (introduction by). *Literary Treasures of 1926*. Hearst's International-Cosmopolitan Magazine, (N.Y., 1927), gilt decor. morocco over flexible boards, brown endsheets, 316 pp., gilt top; includes "Red Pants" pp. 178–94, by T. (For private distribution only.)

49 Mason, F. Van Wyck, ed. *The Fighting American*. Reynal & Hitchcock, N.Y., (1943), decor. cloth, pic. endsheets, 747 pp., green top; includes "Gaines' Mill," pp. 454–71, by T.

50 McMillan, George. *The Old Breed, History of the First Marine Division in World War II*. Infantry Journal Press, Washington, (1949), words "First Edition" on copyright page, decor. cloth, map endsheets, 483 pp., maps, illustrated; quotes Thomason on "The Leathernecks, the old breed . . . ." (Lea)

51 Peery, William, ed. *21 Texas Short Stories*. University of Texas Press, Austin, 1954, cloth, 264 pp.; includes "A Preacher Goes to Texas," pp. 10–25, by T. Also biographical sketch, pp. 8–9, of T.

52 Perry, George Sessions. *Roundup Time: A Collection of Southwestern Writing*. Whittlesey House, N.Y., London, (1943), cloth, map endsheets, 384 pp., orange top; includes "A Name and a Flag," pp. 96–106, by T.

53 Sellars, David K. (edited for school use by). *Texas Tales*. Noble and Noble, Dallas and N.Y., (1955), pic. cloth, 274 pp., illus.; includes "A Name and a Flag," pp. 145–61, by T.

53a Shockley, Martin, ed. *Southwest Writers Anthology*. Steck-Vaughn Co., Austin, (1967), stiff wraps, 328 pp., introduction, index; includes "A Preacher goes to Texas" from *Lone Star Preacher* by T.

54 Sonnichsen, C. L. (compiled and edited by). *The Southwest in Life and Literature*. Devin-Adair, N.Y., 1962, decor. cloth, tan endsheets, 554 pp., orange top; includes "A Preacher Goes to Texas," pp. (121)–38, by T.

55 Stover, Elizabeth Matchett, ed. *Son of a Gun Stew*. University Press in Dallas, Southern Methodist University, 1945, cloth, 216 pp., "Foreword" by John William Rogers, "The Making of a Son-of-a-Gun Stew" by J. Frank Dobie (about the contributors), illus. by Bugbee; includes "Huntsville" by T.

56 Thomason, John W. et al. *O. Henry Prize Short Stories*. N.Y., 1931; includes "Born on an Iceberg," by T. It won the O. Henry Memorial Prize Award for Best Short Story of 1930.

57 ———. *Post Stories of 1935*. Little, Brown, Boston, 1936, words "First Edition" on copyright page, cloth, 476 pp.; includes pp. 56–78, "The Sergeant and the Spy," by T.

58 ———. *Post Stories of 1938*. Little, Brown, Boston, 1939, gilt decor. cloth, 424 pp.; includes "A Preacher Goes to Texas," by T.

59 ———. *The United States Army in The World War 1917–1919*, 17 volumes, Washington, D.C., 1948. Prepared for publication by the Historical Division of the Army. The monographs prepared by Thomason while on assignment to the Second Division Historical Section in the late twenties seem to have been largely ignored in this set — really a compilation of official papers.

60 Van Gelder, Robert and Dorothy (selected by). *American Legend*. Appleton-Century, N.Y. and London, (1946), code number "(1)" after last line of text, cloth, decor. endsheets, 535 pp.; includes "Gone to Texas," pp. 416–37, by T.

60a *Western Americana*. University of Texas Press, Austin, (1974), pic. wraps, 37 (2) pp., order form, numerous illus. including one, p. 23, by T. (Lea, Schwietz)

61 Woollcott, Alexander, ed. *As You Were*. Viking Press, N.Y., 1943, cloth, 655 pp., illustrated with facsimiles; includes "A Preacher Goes to War," pp.

173–99 and "The Confederate Army," pp. 540–45, by T.

The Artist and His Art

62 Barns, Florence E. *Texas Writers of Today.* Tardy Pub. Co., Dallas, (1935), cloth, tan endsheets, 513 (1) pp., folding map inside book cover. Brief biographical sketch and short quotation from *Huntsville*, p. 439.

63 Benet, William Rose. Eulogy in *The Saturday Review of Literature*, Spring 1944.

64 Bolton, Theodore. *American Book Illustrators, Bibliographic Check Lists of 123 Artists.* R. R. Bowker Co., N.Y., 1938, cloth, 290 pp., lists twelve of the above items, pp. 193–94, by T.

65 Burlingame, Roger. *Of Making Many Books.* Scribner's, N.Y., 1946, code letter "A" on copyright page, cloth, 347 pp., Thomason material pp. 56, 105, 126, 127 and 321–23.

66 Graves, John. "The Old Breed — A Note on John W. Thomason, Jr.," a critique in *Southwest Review* 54:1, Winter 1969, with two illus. by T.

67 Hunt, Frazier. "What a Fighter! What a Writer!" an article on Thomason in Hearst's *International and Cosmopolitan,* May, 1926.

68 Leisy, Ernest E. *The American Historical Novel.* University of Oklahoma Press, Norman, (1950), words "First Edition" on copyright page, cloth, 280 pp., blue top. Thomason's novels (nos. 6 and 7) discussed, pp. 175 and 186–87.

69 Mayfield, John S. "The Front Cover," a tribute to Thomason in *The Courier*, Syracuse University Library Associates, Summer 1970, with a front cover illus. (a first appearance) by T.

70 O'Brien, Esse Forester. *Art and Artists of Texas.* Tardy, Dallas, (1935), fabricoid, blue endsheets, 408 pp. Biographical sketch of Thomason, pp. 211–12.

71 Past, Ray. "John W. Thomason, Jr., Artist-Writer: An Exhibit," an article in *The Library Chronicle* of the University of Texas, vol. IV, no. 2, Summer 1951, two illus. by T.

72 Perkins, Maxwell E. *Editor to Author.* Scribner's, N.Y., London, 1950, cloth, 315 pp., note, frontis. photo of Perkins. Perkins was Thomason's editor and friend — several of his letters comment on Thomason's work.

73 *These Famous Authors Have Written New Books For You.* Scribner's, N.Y., (1932), advs. folder including an announcement of a new edition of Page's *Two Little Confederates* with thirty-five drawings by Thomason, three illus. including one by T.

74 Thomason, John W., Jr. "Huntsville," an article in *Southwest Review*, vol. 19, no. 1, Spring 1934. Autobiographical.

75 Turner, Martha Ann. "I Visit a Nonagenarian," an article in *Southwest Review*, vol. XLIX, no. 2, Spring 1964. The author visited Thomason's mother — the topics discussed were John, his books and his art.

76 "University Press Books: The Sixth Annual Show," a feature article in *Publishers' Weekly* 197:22, June 1, 1970, includes a description of *A Thomason Sketchbook* by the University of Texas Press and one illus. by T.

77 Willock, Colonel Roger. *Lone Star Marine.* Privately printed by the author, Princeton, N.J., (1961), cloth, 195 pp., illus. with photos. Primarily about Thomason as a Marine but with much on his books and art.

GENERAL O. O. HOWARD by Varian from *My Story of the Last Indian War in the Northwest*

GEORGE EDMUND VARIAN
1865–1923

Catalogues of Art Exhibitions and Galleries

HELEN L. CARD, NEW YORK

1 *Hang on, Fellers! We're Out on a Limb*, Catalog No. Five, (1963), pic. wraps, 92 pp., numerous illus. including one by V. (Deming, Eggenhofer, Leigh, Remington, Schoonover, Wyeth)

KENNEDY GALLERIES, NEW YORK

2 *A Plentiful Country*, An Exhibition of Important Paintings of the American West, June 1970, colored pic. wraps, 76 pp., introduction, index, numerous illus. including one, p. 63, by V. (Deming, Russell)

PHOENIX ART MUSEUM

2a *Western Art from The Eugene B. Adkins Collection*, November 1971–January 1972, colored pic. wraps, unpaged, "Preface" by R. D. A. Puckle, twenty illus. including one, "Death of Sitting Bull, December 1890," (no. 64), by V. (Dunton, Johnson, Leigh, Miller, Remington)

SOTHEBY PARKE BERNET, NEW YORK

3 *Important 18th, 19th and Early 20th Century American Paintings, Watercolors and Sculpture*, sale no. 3498, April 11, 1973, colored pic. wraps, unpaged but with over 70 numbered plates including one, no. 49, by V. (Blumenschein, Eggenhofer, James, Johnson, Leigh, Remington, Russell, Wyeth)

Illustrated by the Artist

4 Bacheller, Irving. *The Hand-Made Gentleman.* Harper, N.Y., 1909, words "Published April, 1909" on copyright page, pic. cloth, 331 (1) pp., double-page frontis. by V.

5 Baker, Ray Stannard. *Seen in Germany.* McClure, Phillips & Co., N.Y., 1901, words "October, 1901" on copyright page, cloth, 317 pp., numerous illus. including thirty-two by V.

6 Baldwin, James. *Fifty Famous Stories Retold.* American Books Co., N.Y., (1896), cloth, 172 pp., numerous illus. including six, pp. 52, 65, 80, 117, 146 and 152, by V.

7 ———. *Barnes's Elementary History of the United States* (told in biographies). American Book Co., N.Y., (1903), cloth, 360 pp., (8) of advs., numerous illus. including two, pp. 60 and 82, by V. (Keller)

8 ———. *Seventh Reader.* American Book Co., N.Y., (1911), cloth, numerous illus. including one, p. 176, by V.

9 Barstow, Charles L., ed. *The Progress of a United People.* The Century Co., (1912), words, "Published May, 1912" on copyright page, decor. cloth, 220 pp., index, numerous illus. including three, pp. 82, (89) and 90, by V. (Remington)

10 Bartlett, Frederick Orin. *The Forest Castaways.* Century, N.Y., 1911, cloth, 302 pp., illus. by V.

11 *Blatter and Bluten.* Band 27, St. Louis, wraps, 151 pp. including advs., one illus. by V.

12 Brooks, Stratton D. *Brooks Reader — Sixth Year.* American Book Co., N.Y., (1906), cloth, 448 pp., numerous illus. including three, pp. 35, 70 and 209, by V.

13 Carter, M. H., ed. *Panther Stories Retold from St. Nicholas.* Century, N.Y., 1904, pic. cloth, 189 pp., numerous illus. including two, facing pp. 43 and 47, by V. (Remington)

14 Cornyn, John Hubert. *Glooskap Stories.* Little, Brown, Boston, 1923, words "Published March, 1923" on copyright page, pic. cloth, 223 pp., six illus., frontis. and facing pp. 24, 88, 124, 158, and 194, by V.

15 Dimitry, John et al. *Indian Stories Retold from St. Nicholas.* Century, N.Y., 1905, pic. cloth, numerous illus. including two, pp. 145 and (151), by V. (Lungren, Remington)

16 Eastman, Charles Alexander. *Indian Child Life.* Little, Brown, Boston, 1918, cloth, 160 pp., illus. by V.

17 Elson, Henry W. *United States, Its Past and Present.* American Book Co., (1926), cloth, 550 pp., numerous illus. including one, p. 124, by V.

18 Fraser, W. Lewis et al. *The Year's Art as Recorded in The Quarterly Illustrator for 1894.* Harry C. Jones, N.Y., 1894, decor. cloth, 456 pp., 1400 illus. by 438 artists including one, p. 73, by V. (Crawford, Deming, Fogarty, Keller, Remington)

19 Freeland, George E. et al. *America's Building, The Makers of Our Flag.* Scribner's, N.Y., 1937, code letter "A" on copyright page, decor. cloth, 425 pp., numerous illus. including two, pp. 8 and 37, by V. (Fogarty, Rowe, Thomason, Wyeth)

20 Guerber, H. A. *The Story of the Thirteen Colonies* (Eclectic School Reading). American Book Co., N.Y. etc., (1898), decor. cloth, 342 pp., maps, numerous illus. including one, p. 212, by V. (Keller)

21 Halleck, Reuben. *History of American Literature.* American Book Co., N.Y., 1911, cloth, 431 pp., numerous illus. including one, pp. 117–8, by V.

22 Hammond, Captain Harold, U.S.A. *Further Fortunes of Pinkey Perkins.* Century, N.Y., (1906), words "Published October 1906" on copyright page, cloth, 391 pp., thirty-five illus. by V.

23 Hart, Albert Bushness. *School History of the United States.* American Book Co., N.Y., (1918), cloth, 505 pp., numerous illus. including ten, pp. 22, 48, 117, 127, 140, 161, 201, 220, 350 and 361, by V. (Keller)

24 Hawes, Charles Boardman. *The Mutineers.* The Atlantic Monthly Press, Boston, (1920), pic. cloth, map endsheets, 276 pp., five illus., frontis. and pp. 60, 66, 123 and 170, by V.

25 ———. *The Great Quest.* Atlantic Monthly Press, Boston, (1921), pic. cloth, map endsheets, 359 pp., illus. including five full-page plates, frontis. and facing pp. 78, 142, 220 and 258, by V.

26 Howard, Major General O. O. *Famous Indian Chiefs I Have Known.* Century, N.Y., 1908, words "Published September, 1908" on copyright page, pic. cloth, 364 pp., thirty-six illus. including seventeen by V. (Remington)

27 Judson, Harry Pratt and Bender, Ira C. *Graded Literature Readers, Fourth Book.* Maynard, Merrill & Co., N.Y., (1900), decor. cloth, 262 pp., numerous illus. including three, pp. 214, 227 and 236, by V. (Keller)

28 Kendall, Oswald. *The Romance of the Martin Connor.* Houghton Mifflin, Boston and N.Y., 1916, cloth, 312 pp., frontis. in color by Will Hammell and eight drawings, title page and facing pp. 46, 58, 74, 138, 192, 262 and 282, by V.

29 ———. *The Voyage of the Martin Connor.* Houghton Mifflin, Boston and N.Y., 1931, cloth with illus. in color mounted on front cover, 312 pp., illus. in color by Donald Teague but same illus. in black and white as in no. 28 by V. (A new edition of no. 28.)

30 Kennan, George. *The Tragedy of Pelee.* The Outlook Co., N.Y., 1902, words "Published November, 1902" on copyright page, cloth, 257 pp., maps, 18 illus. including seven facing pp. 84, 117, 132, 149, 164, 181 and 228, by V.

31 London, Jack. *Tales of the Fish Patrol.* Macmillan, N.Y., London, 1905, cloth, 243 pp., map, seven illus., frontis. and facing pp. 60, 86, 116, 158, 204 and 218, by V.

32 ———. Same, reprint for The Abercrombie & Fitch Library by Arno Press, N.Y., 1967, cloth and boards, green endsheets, with the added "A Note to the Reader" by C.A.P.

33 Lugard, Lady Flora Louisa (Shaw). *Castle Blair,* by Flora Louisa Shaw (pseud.). Little, Brown, Boston, 1923, pic. cloth, 341 pp., four illus., frontis. and facing pp. 70, 124 and 269, by V.

34 McMaster, John Bach. *A Primary History of the United States.* American Book Co., N.Y., (1901), cloth, 254 pp., numerous illus. including one, p. 207, by V.

35 Mabie, Hamilton W., ed. *Heroes and Patriots.* Volume 7, The After School Library, 1909, illus. including one by V.

36 Mabie, Hamilton Wright et al. *Book of Nature and Outdoor Life* (part 2). The University Society, N.Y., (1912), decor. cloth, pic. endsheets, 416 pp., numerous illus. including six, pp. 93, 206, 301, 302, 355 and 393, by V. Boys' and Girls' Bookshelf, vol. 5. (Lungren, Remington, Rowe)

37 Morgan, Thomas. *My Story of the Last Indian War in the Northwest.* Privately printed, Forest Grove, Ore,. (1954), pic. wraps, 29 pp., appendix, illus. with three photos and a full-page drawing, p. 14, by V.

SCATTERED A LINE OF IT ACROSS THE DARK TRAIL by Varian from
The Gold Cache

38 Musick, John R. *Stories of Missouri*. American Book Co., N.Y. etc., (1897), decor. cloth, 288 pp., preface, numerous illus. including 18 drawings by V. (Fogarty, Remington)

39 Pier, Arthur Stanwood. *Boys of St. Timothy's*. Scribner's, N.Y., 1904, words "Published September, 1904" on copyright page, cloth, 284 pp., six illus. including one, facing p. 240, by V. (Fogarty, Wyeth)

40 Powell, E. Alexander. *Gentlemen Rovers*. Scribner's, N.Y., 1913, words "Published September, 1913" on copyright page, decor. cloth, 245 pp., foreword, twelve illus. including one, facing p. 230, by V. (Remington)

41 Schultz, James Willard. *With the Indians in the Rockies*. Houghton Mifflin, Boston and N.Y., 1912, words "Published September, 1912" on copyright page, cloth with illus. mounted on front cover, 227 (1) pp., (2) of advs., six illus., frontis. and facing pp. 14, 76, 128, 200 and 210, by V.

42 ———. *The Quest of the Fish-Dog Skin*. Houghton Mifflin, Boston and N.Y., 1913, cloth with illus. mounted on front cover, 218 (1) pp., four illus., frontis. and facing pp. 20, 124 and 162, by V.

43 ———. *An Indian Winter*. Houghton Mifflin, Boston and N.Y., 1913, cloth, 227 (1) pp., frontis. by V.

44 ———. *On the Warpath*. Houghton Mifflin, Boston and N.Y., 1914, words "Published September 1914" on copyright page, cloth with illus. mounted on front cover, 244 (1) pp., four illus., frontis. and facing pp. 56, 106 and 176, by V.

45 ———. *The Gold Cache*. Houghton Mifflin, Boston and N.Y., 1917, words "Published September 1917" on copyright page, cloth with illus. mounted on front cover, 189 (1) pp., six illus., frontis. and facing pp. 68, 92, 126, 154 and 184, by V.

46 ———. *Lone Bull's Mistake*. Houghton Mifflin, Boston and N.Y., 1918, cloth with illus. mounted on front cover, 207 (1) pp., four illus., frontis. and facing pp. 68, 144 and 202, by V.

47 ———. *The War-Trail Fort*. Houghton Mifflin, Boston and N.Y., 1921, pic. cloth, 192 (1) pp., four illus., frontis. and facing pp. 40, 102 and 178, by V.

48 ———. *The Trail of the Spanish Horse*. Houghton Mifflin, Boston and N.Y., 1922, pic. cloth, 212 (1) pp., four illus., frontis. and facing pp. 46, 110 and 212, by V.

49 ———. *The Danger Trail*. Houghton Mifflin, Boston and N.Y., 1923, decor. cloth, 295 (1) pp., four illus., frontis. and facing pp. 70, 244 and 284, by V.

50 ———. *Plumed Snake Medicine*. Houghton Mifflin, Boston and N.Y., 1924, cloth, with illus. in color mounted on front cover, 244 (1) pp., four illus., frontis. and facing pp. 30, 68 and 162, by V. (Schoonover—front cover)

51 Slocum, Joshua. *Sailing Alone Around the World*. The Century Co., N.Y., 1900, cloth, 294 pp., maps, numerous illus. including six, pp. 47, 122, 173, (178), 183 and 197, by V. (Fogarty)

52 ———. Same, reprinted by Sheridan House, N.Y., (1954), with an "Introduction" by Walter Magnes Teller.

53 Smith, F. Hopkinson et al. *The Year's Art as Recorded in The Quarterly Illustrator*. Harry C. Jones, N.Y., 1893, decor. cloth, 328 pp., 678 illus. by 302 artists including two, pp. 4 and 106, by V. (Fogarty, Remington)

54 Stockton, Frank R. *Buccaneers and Pirates of Our Coast*. Macmillan, N.Y., London, 1898, cloth, 325 pp., illus. by B. West Clinedinst and V.

55 ———. *Stories of the Spanish Main*. Macmillan, N.Y., 1913, cloth, 232 pp., map, seven illus. including five, frontis. and pp. 81, 205, 221 and 227, by V. Everychild's Series — adapted from no. 54.

56 ———. *Stories of New Jersey*. American Book Co., N.Y. etc., 1896, gilt decor. cloth, decor. endsheets, 254 pp., preface, numerous illus. including one, p. 135, by V. (Keller)

57 Stoddard, William O. *Making Good in the Village*. Appleton, N.Y., 1916, cloth, 287 pp., four illus. in color, frontis. and facing pp. 32, 146 and 260, by V.

58 ———. *Making Good with an Invention*. Appleton, N.Y., 1916, cloth, 300 pp., four illus. in color, frontis. and facing pp. 24, 208 and 256, by V.

59 ———. *The Farm that Jack Built* (Making Good on the Farm). Appleton, N.Y., 1916, cloth, 311 pp., four illus. in color, frontis. and facing pp. 52, 114 and 174, by V.

60 Tappan, Eva March (selected and arranged by). *The Out-of-Door Book*. Houghton Mifflin, (Boston), 1907, buckram with morocco title label, 516 (1) pp., twelve illus. including one, facing p. 114, by V. Vol. 7 of the

first edition of The Children's Hour limited to 1000 numbered copies.

61 ———. Same, trade edition, pic. red cloth, decor. red endsheets, gilt top.

62 Turner, John Kenneth. *Barbarous Mexico.* Texas, Austin, 1969, cloth, 3221 pp., d/w illus. by V.

62a Woolley, Edward Mott. *Donald Kirk, The Morning Record Copy-Boy.* Little, Brown, Boston, 1912, words "published, September, 1912" on copyright page, cloth, 273 pp., four illus., frontis. and facing pp. 38, 96 and 186, by V.

62b ———. *Donald Kirk, The Morning Record Correspondent.* Little, Brown, Boston, 1913, words "Published, September, 1913" on copyright page, cloth, 269 pp., four illus., frontis. and facing pp. 80, 186 and 266, by V.

The Artist and His Art

63 Fielding, Mantle. *Dictionary of American Painters, Sculptors and Engravers.* N.Y., 1926, cloth, 433 pp., brief biographical sketch of V., p. 382.

64 ———. Same, facsimile reprint plus addendum, James F. Carr, N.Y., 1965, cloth, 529 pp., but no new material on V.

65 Howard, Francis R., ed. *The American Art Annual.* Vol. XVIII, The American Federation of Arts, Wash., D.C., 1921, cloth, 680 pp., index, brief biographical sketch of V., p. 593.

66 Miller (Mahony), Bertha E. et al. *Illustrators of Children's Books, 1744–1945.* The Horn Book, Boston, 1947, cloth and pic. boards, 527 pp., gilt top, illus., list of books illus. by V., p. 443.

IN SAN FRANCISCO, LIFE WAS GAY by Von Schmidt from
Harold Von Schmidt Draws and Paints the Old West

HAROLD VON SCHMIDT
Contemporary, 1893–

Catalogues of Art Exhibitions and Galleries

DEPARTMENT OF PARKS AND RECREATION
STATE OF CALIFORNIA, SACRAMENTO

1 *The Forty-Niners: An Exhibition of Paintings by Harold Von Schmidt*, 1949, wraps.

GOLDEN PALACE ROOM, INN OF SIX FLAGS
ARLINGTON, TEXAS

2 *A Convocation of Great American Artists*, November 16–18, 1973, McCulley Fine Arts Gallery, Dallas, wraps, unpaged, twenty illus. including one in color, "Cattle Guard," by VS. and with a biographical sketch and a photo of him.

HAMMER AND TONGS CLUB, SAN FRANCISCO

3 *Catalog*, June 16–30, 1919, wraps, lists three entries, "Grey's Quarry," "Daylight Saving" and "Bobby," by VS.

NEW ROCHELLE ART ASSOCIATION
NEW ROCHELLE, NEW YORK

4 *Exhibit Announcement*, March 9–April 15, 1941.

ST. FRANCIS HOTEL, SAN FRANCISCO

5 *Exhibit of California Paintings by California Artists*, June 5–17, 1922, wraps, lists "Navajo Land" by VS.

SOCIETY OF ILLUSTRATORS, NEW YORK

6 *Thirty-seventh Annual Exhibition*, 1939, wraps, one illus. by VS.

THE UNIVERSITY OF TEXAS AT AUSTIN

7 *Paintings from the C. R. Smith Collection*, December 4, 1969–January 15, 1970, wraps, 40 pp., numerous illus. including one, no. 26, by VS. and a biographical sketch of him. (Dixon, Eggenhofer, Johnson, Lea, Russell, Schreyvogel)

Illustrated by the Artist

8 Ainsworth, Ed. *The Cowboy in Art*. World, N.Y. and Cleveland, (1968), words "First Printing 1968" on copyright page, full leather, orange endsheets, 242 pp., all edges gilt, "Foreword" by John Wayne, index, numerous illus. including four, pp. 47, 93 and 95 (two) by VS. and a photo of him plus quotes and mention in the text. Special deluxe edition of 1000 copies, slipcase. (Beeler, Borein, Bugbee, De Yong, Dixon, Dunton, Eggenhofer, Ellsworth, Hurd, James, Johnson, Koerner, Mora, Perceval, Remington, Russell, Santee, Schreyvogel)

9 ———. Same, first trade edition in gilt lettered and decor. cloth, orange endsheets.

10 ———. Same, reprint by Bonanza Books, N.Y., in red lettered and decor. cloth, white endsheets.

11 *Annual of Advertising Art in the U.S., Sixth*. The Art Directors Club, N.Y., 1927, cloth, colored pic. map endsheets, 152 pp., (24) of advs., (1) of indices, numerous illus. including three, pp. 47, 64 and 111, by VS. (Dunn, Stoops, Wyeth)

12 Same, *Twenty-Second*. The Art Directors Club, N.Y., 1943, decor. cloth, black endsheets, 192 pp., (56) of advs., index, numerous illus. including two, pp. 85 and 89 (repeated p. 88), by VS.

13 Same, *Twenty-Third*. The Art Directors Club, N.Y., (1945), decor. cloth, pic. endsheets, 200 pp., (66) of advs., index, numerous illus. including two, pp. 61 and 135, by VS.

14 Same, *Twenty-Fourth*. The Art Directors Club, N.Y., (1945), cloth, decor. endsheets, unpaged, numerous illus.

15 Same, *Twenty-Seventh*. Art Directors Club of N.Y., 1948, decor. boards, colored endsheets, 353 pp.,

"Win, Place or Show" by President Paul Smith, numerous illus. including three, pp. 109, 111 and 115 (each repeated in a reduced size on the same page), by VS.

16 Arnstein, Flora J. et al., eds. *Oscar Weil, Letters and Papers*. The Book Club of California, San Francisco, 1923, buckram and boards with paper title labels, 119 (5) pp., decorative scroll on title page by VS. Edition of 400 copies.

17 Berry, Erick. *Homespun*. Lothrop Lee & Co., N.Y., Boston, 1937, cloth, 308 pp., five illus., frontis. and pp. 41, 95, 173 and 245, by VS.

18 ———. Same, Jr. Literary Guild, N.Y., 1937.

19 Blair, Arthur. *The World of Stamps and Stamp Collecting*. Hamlyn, London etc. (but printed in West Germany, 1972), cloth, 128 pp., appendix, index, numerous illus. including one in color, p. 67, "Pony Express" stamp, by VS.

20 Bloomgarden, Henry S. *American History Through Commemorative Stamps*. Arco, N.Y., (1969), cloth, 191 pp., "Introduction" by Carl Scheele, illus. with 68 full-page black and white reproductions of stamps including one, "Pony Express," p. 82, by VS. (Lea, Russell)

21 Cassidy, Sergeant Texas. *The Trials of a Recruit*. Privately published (San Francisco, 1920), pic. wraps, 36 pp., front cover illus. is a composite of two *Sunset* covers, one-half by VS.

22 Carroll, John M. *Von Schmidt, The Complete Illustrator*. The Old Army Press, (Fort Collins, Colo., 1973), cloth, 98 pp., "Introduction" by Norman Rockwell, preface to bibliography, bibliography, numerous illus. by VS. Limited 25 Author's Presentation Copies signed by the author, Norman Rockwell and Harold Von Schmidt, slipcase.

23 ———. Same, first trade edition, cloth and pic. d/w by VS.

24 Cather, Willa. *Death Comes for the Archbishop*. Knopf, N.Y., 1929, decor. flexible vellum, 343 pp., silver top, other edges uncut, numerous illus. by VS. Limited edition of 170 numbered large paper copies signed by the author, designed by Elmer Adler and printed on Rives cream plate paper, slipcase.

25 ———. Same, first trade of the illustrated edition, cloth.

26 ———. Same, first British printing of the illustrated edition, William Heinemann, London, cloth.

27 ———. *December Night* (a scene from *Death Comes for the Archbishop*). Knopf, 1933, words "First Edition in this format" inside front cover, boards, (14) pp., decorations and illustrations by VS.

28 Clark, Badger. *Spike*. Richard G. Badger, Boston, (1925), cloth, 215 pp., seven illus. including three, facing pp. 16, 40 and 192, by VS.

29 ———. Same, reissued in 1970.

30 *Early Days in the West*. Wells Fargo Nevada National Bank, n.p., 1923, pic. wraps, illus. including one, the front cover, by VS.

31 Fletcher, Robert H. *Free Grass to Fences*. University Publishers, Inc., N.Y., for the Historical Society of Montana, (1960), cloth and brand decor. boards, colored pic. endsheets, 233 (3) pp., orange top, "Speakof Cow People" by Michael Kennedy, numerous illus. including one, between pp. 68 and 69, by VS. (Elwell, Russell)

32 Gilpatric, Guyand and Raine, Norman Reilly. *Glencannon Meets Tugboat Annie*. Harper, N.Y., 1950, code letters "M-Z" on copyright page, cloth, 214 pp., d/w illus. by VS.

33 Guitar, Mary Anne. *22 Famous Painters and Illustrators Tell How They Work*. McKay, N.Y., 1964, cloth, yellow endsheets, 240 pp., "Introduction" by Albert Dorne, numerous illus. including five, pp. (216), 218, 220, 222 and 224, by VS. plus an interview and photo of him.

34 Glidden, Fred D. *High Vermillion* by Luke Short (pseud.). Houghton, Boston, 1947, cloth, 217 pp., d/w illus. by VS.

35 ———. *Ambush*. Houghton, Boston, 1949, cloth, 249 pp., d/w illus. in color by VS.

36 Halsey, Ashley, Jr. *Illustrating for the Saturday Evening Post*. Arlington House, N.Y., (1951), cloth, 160 pp., preface, "Foreword" by Kenneth Stuart, numerous illus. including one, p. 152, by VS. plus a biographical sketch and a photo of him (and son).

37 Harmsen, Dorothy. *Harmsen's Western Americana*. Northland Press, Flagstaff, (1971), morocco and cloth, blue endsheets, 213 pp., "Foreword" by Robert Rockwell, introduction, numerous illus. including one, p. (197), by VS. and with a biographical sketch of him. Author's edition of 150 numbered and signed copies, slipcase with morocco title label. (Beeler, Blumenschein, Borein, Dixon, Dunn, Dunton, Eggenhofer, Elwell, Hurd, Johnson, Leigh, Marchand, Miller, Russell, Wyeth)

38 ———. Same, first trade edition, two-tone cloth with red endsheets.

39 Hart, Charles Spencer. *General Washington's Son of Israel and Other Forgotten Heroes of History.* Lippincott, Philadelphia, London, (1937), cloth, pic. endsheets, 229 pp., ten illus., endsheets, frontis. (repeated in color on d/w) and facing pp. 32, 48, 98, 140, 152, 180 and 218, by VS.

40 Heyward, Du Bose. *Mamba's Daughter.* Doubleday, Garden City, N.Y., 1929, words "First Edition" on copyright page, cloth, pic. endsheets, 311 pp., endsheets illus. by VS.

41 Hornung, Otto. *The Illustrated Encyclopedia of Stamp Collecting.* Hamlyn, London etc. (but printed in Czechoslovakia, 1972), decor. cloth, 319 pp., "Foreword" by H. R. Holmes, introduction, index, numerous illus. from photos of stamps including one, p. 33, "Pony Express," by VS. (Remington)

42 Hubbard, Ralph. *Queer Person.* Doubleday, Garden City, N.Y., 1930, words "First Edition" on copyright page, decor. cloth, pic. endsheets, 336 pp., brown top, illus., d/w, endsheets, frontis. and several double-page drawings, between pp. 10–11, 90–91, 178–79, 202–03, 250–51, 282–83 and 314–15, by VS. (First use of double-page illustrations in the U.S.)

43 Huch, Ricarda (translated from the German by Catherine A. Phillips). *Defeat.* Knopf, N.Y., 1928, decor. cloth, 324 (2) pp., maps, d/w illus. by VS.

44 ——— (translated from the German by Catherine A. Phillips). *Victory.* Knopf, N.Y., 1929, decor. cloth, d/w illus. by VS.

45 Jastrow, Morris (translated by). *The Song of Songs* (being love lyrics from ancient Palestine). Grabhorn, San Francisco, 1922, parchment, unpaged, initials by Joseph Sinel, one illus. by VS. Edition of 310 copies for the Book Club of California.

46 Kapplow, Hal. *Laughing Historically.* Bernard Geis Associates, (N.Y., 1961), words "First Printing" on copyright page, pic. boards, 63 (1) pp., "Foreword" by the publishers, numerous illus. including one, p. 42, by VS. (Dunn, Wyeth)

47 Kennedy, Michael S., ed. *The Red Man's West* (True Stories of the Frontier Days). Hastings House, N.Y., (1965), pic. Indian-tanned deer-skin, colored pic. endsheets, 342 pp., introduction, index, numerous illus. including one, p. 115, by VS. Limited edition of 199 numbered copies, each with an original illus. by a contemporary western artist or a limited edition print, slipcase. (Koerner, Russell)

48 ———. Same, first trade edition in cloth, colored pic. d/w.

49 (Kodansha.) *Famous.* Kodansha Famous School, Tokyo, Japan, 1972, colored pic. wraps, 19 (1) pp., twenty-one (twelve in color) illus. by VS. and two photos of him. Text in Japanese.

50 Kyne, Peter B. *Outlaws of Eden.* Cosmopolitan Book Corp., N.Y., 1930, pic. cloth, 341 pp., six drawings, title page and pp. 126, 170, 218, 245 and 341, plus d/w and front cover, by VS.

51 ———. Same, reprint by Grosset & Dunlap, N.Y., n.d., also with d/w illus. by VS.

52 MacLean, Alistair. *H.M.S. Ulysses.* Doubleday, Garden City, N.Y., (1956), cloth, 316 pp., d/w illus. by VS.

53 Mack, Oren. *Indian Gold.* Knopf, N.Y., 1933, words "First Edition" on copyright page, pic. cloth, map endsheets, 243 (1) pp., orange top, foreword, illus. with thirty drawings by VS.

54 Marzulla, Elena, ed. et al. *United States Stamps and Stories.* Scott Pub. Co., Omaha, for the United States Postal Service, 1972, words "First Edition" on front cover, colored pic. wraps, 224 pp., numerous illus. from photos of stamps in color, including one, p. 89, "Pony Express," by VS. (Lea, Remington, Russell)

55 Miller (Mahony), Bertha E. and Whitney, Elinor. *Five Years of Children's Books.* Doubleday, Garden City, N.Y., 1936, words "First Edition" on copyright page, cloth, 599 pp., numerous illus. including one, p. 352, by VS. (Schoonover)

56 Moore, Anne Carroll. *The Three Owls, Third Book.* Coward-McCann, N.Y., 1931, cloth, pic. endsheets, 462 pp., blue top, "Distinctive Children's Books of a Decade," index, numerous illus. including one double-page drawing, pp. (204–5), by VS.

57 Morrell Packing Co. *1949 Calendar.* Ottumwa, Iowa, (1948), twelve illus. by VS. (two sizes — wall and desk with same illustrations).

58 The Old Army Press. *Catalog Number Five.* (Ft. Collins, Colo., 1973), colored pic. wraps, unpaged, illus. including two, one in color on the front cover, by VS. (Bjorklund, Cisneros, Eggenhofer)

59 Quillen, I. James and Krug, Edward. *Living in Our America: History for Young Citizens.* Scott, Foresman & Co., Chicago, (1951), cloth, 752 pp., appendix, in-

dex, maps, numerous illus. including one in color, p. 31, by VS. (attributed to Harold Schmitt).

60 Reed, Walt (compiled and edited by). *The Illustrator in America, 1900–1960's*. Reinhold Publishing Corp., Corp., N.Y., 1966, cloth, pic. endsheets, 262 pp., bibliography, 600 (32 in color) illus. including five (two in color), pp. 204 and 205, by VS. who also wrote the introductory commentary on the section "The Decade: 1900–1910." (Blumenschein, Crawford, Dunn, Dunton, Eggenhofer, Fischer, Fogarty, Goodwin, Keller, Koerner, Remington, Russell, Schoonover, Stoops, Wyeth)

61 ———. *Harold Von Schmidt Draws and Paints the Old West*. Northland Press, Flagstaff, (1972), words "First Edition" on copyright page, morocco and pic. cloth, slate endsheets, 230 pp., "Foreword" by Dean Krakel, "Introduction" by Harold McCracken, bibliography, numerous illus. by VS. and photos of him. Edition of 104 numbered copies signed by Reed and Von Schmidt, issued jointly with Von Schmidt's first sculpture, "The Startled Grizzly," slipcase with morocco title label. (Dixon, Dunn, James, Russell)

62 ———. Same, first trade edition in pic. cloth, d/w illus. in color by VS.

63 ———. Same, announcement folder with seven (three in color) illus. by VS. and photos of him and of author Walt Reed.

64 Ripley, Clements. *Gold is Where You Find It*. Grosset & Dunlap, N.Y., (1936), cloth, 331 pp., d/w illus. in color by VS.

65 Settle, Mary Lund and Raymond W. *Saddles and Spurs*. Stackpole, Harrisburg, Pa., 1955, pic. cloth, 217 pp., illus. including a detail from "Buffalo Bill and the Pony Express" by VS. on the title page, front cover and d/w.

66 Sperry, L. T. (President). *Mill on Mad River (150 Years of Craftsmanship in Metal)*. Scovill Mfg. Co., Waterbury, Conn., 1953, boards, unpaged, numerous illus. including one by VS.

67 Stewart, Edgar I., ed. et al. *George Armstrong Custer and his Seventh Cavalry at the Battle of the Little Big Horn, 1876*. Montana Historical Society, Helena, (1955), pic. wraps, 24 (1) pp., illus. including one, p. 17, by VS. (Montana Heritage Series, Number Seven.)

68 Stribling, T. S. *Backwater*. Doubleday, Garden City, N.Y., 1930, cloth, 308 pp., d/w illus. by VS.

69 Von Schmidt, Harold. *Famous Artists Advanced Pro-*

Program. Institute for Commercial Art, Westport, Conn., 1949.

70 ———. *How I Make a Picture*. Institute for Commercial Art, Westport, Conn., 1949–51, Lessons 1–8, eight parts, folio, illus.

71 Weaver, Paul E. (publisher). *Autumn 1972 Book List*. Northland Press, Flagstaff, Arizona, pic. wraps, unpaged, numerous illus. including two by VS. (Dixon, Perceval, Remington, Santee)

72 ———. *Autumn 1973 Book List*. Northland Press, Flagstaff, colored pic. wraps, unpaged, numerous illus. including one by VS. (Beeler, Blumenschein, Dixon, James, Perceval, Remington, Santee)

73 *West Virginia Inspirations for Printers: 1948, 1949*. West Virginia Pulp and Paper Co., n.p., decor. cloth, green endsheets, pp. (3359)–35557, numerous illus. including one in color, p. 3505, by VS.

74 Wierzbinski, Fryderyk. *Indianski Pioropusz*. Biuro Wydawnicze, Ruch, (Warszawa, 1972), pic. wraps, 82 (1) pp., numerous illus. including a photo of the "Pony Express" stamp, p. (50), by VS. (Lea, Remington, Russell)

75 Willard, John. *Adventure Trails in Montana*. Sponsored by the Montana Historical Society, (Helena, 1964), cloth with illus. in color mounted on front cover, 243 (7) pp., "Foreword" by Michael Kennedy, numerous illus. including one, p. 115, by VS. (Miller, Remington, Russell)

76 ———. Same, colored pic. wraps, (1964).

77 ———. Same, new edition, Billings, (1971), with added illus. in color (by Russell) on the back cover.

The Artist and His Art

78 *The Books of Northland Press*. Flagstaff, (1973), catalog folder with the announcement of the winning of the Western Heritage Award by *Harold Von Schmidt Draws and Paints the Old West*. It was selected as the Best Western Art Book of 1972 by the National Cowboy Hall of Fame.

79 *Cowboy Artists of America, Third Annual Exhibit*. National Cowboy Hall of Fame, Oklahoma City, Oklahoma, June 15 through September 2, 1968, pic. wraps, unpaged, numerous illus., Harold Von Schmidt was one of the judges — he was presented the Cowboy Hall of Fame "Gold Medal Award" for his lifelong contribution to the art of the Old West and there

is a photo of him receiving the award and one of Mrs. Von Schmidt cutting the ribbon to open the exhibit. (Beeler)

80 Dippie, Brian W. "Brush, Palette and the Custer Battle, A Second Look," an article commenting on the art of the Little Big Horn in *Montana* 24:1, Winter 1974, with one illus. by VS. (Blumenschein, Dunton, Remington, Russell, Schreyvogel)

81 Hinshaw, Merton E. (director). *Painters of the West.* Charles W. Bowers Memorial Museum, Santa Ana, 1972, pic. wraps, unpaged, illus., short biographical sketch of VS.

82 Holbrook, Stewart H. A brief article entitled "There Was a Man: Custer's Last Stand," with a full-color illus. by VS. in *Esquire*, September 1950.

83 Hydeman, Sid. *How to Illustrate for Money.* Harper, N.Y. and London, (1936), cloth and boards, 173 pp., "Foreword" by Edwin Balmer, index, illus. with photos, much on Dunn and Von Schmidt in text.

84 *An Introduction to American Artists Whose Paintings Appear in the Saturday Evening Post Art Exhibition.* Saturday Evening Post Co., (Philadelphia), n.d., wraps, includes a biographical sketch of VS.

85 Karolevitz, Robert F. *Where Your Heart Is* (The Story of Harvey Dunn, Artist). North Plains Press, Aberdeen, S.D., 1970, cloth, 208 pp., foreword, bibliography, index, numerous illus. by Dunn plus photos of him. Von Schmidt came east to study with Dunn and there is a photo of him and he is in the text pp. 88, 93, 119, 124 and 126.

86 Monthan, Doris. *Northland Press Quarterly* 2:4, December 1972, Flagstaff, much on Walt Reed's *Harold Von Schmidt Draws and Paints the Old West* with a photo of Reed and Von Schmidt.

87 Pratt Institute Art School. *Bulletin*, May 15, 1945.

88 Reed, Walt. "Harold Von Schmidt: Artist of the West," an article in *Westerner Magazine*, August 1971.

89 ———. "Harold Von Schmidt," an article in *Persimmon Hill* 3:1 (1972), with nine illus. including front and back covers by VS. and a photo of him. This issue also includes a review of Reed's *Harold Von Schmidt Draws and Paints the Old West* by Ingrid Morrison, Ed Muno and Dean Krakel.

90 Russell, Don. *Custer's Last* (or, The Battle of the Little Big Horn in Picturesque Perspective). (Amon Carter Museum of Western Art, Ft. Worth, Texas, 1968), cloth, 67 pp., "Preface" by Barbara Tyler, notes, bibliography, illus., comments on "There Was a Man: Custer's Last Stand," by VS., p. 51.

91 *Sat. Eve. Post New Letters* 1:37, April 13, 1945; 1:42, July 27, 1945; 2:5, January 19, 1946, and 5:6, January 29, 1949.

92 Society of Illustrators, N.Y. *Lecture Series, 1948.*

93 "Trustees' Gold Medal Award," a feature presentation in *Persimmon Hill* 3:3 (1973), prints the Harold Von Schmidt citation in full. Von was the first artist to receive the award from the National Cowboy Hall of Fame and there is a photo of him.

94 "Von" tells his own story in an article in *Famous Artists Magazine* 20:1, 1972, with five illus. by VS. and a photo of him in color on the front cover.

95 Same, in *North Light* 3:1, Winter 1971, with nine (two in color) illus. by VS. and three (one in color) photos of him.

96 Wolle, Muriel Sibell. "Harold Von Schmidt Draws and Paints the Old West," a review of the Walt Reed book in *The American West* 10:4, July 1973.

ILLUSTRATION by Von Schmidt from *Death Comes For The Archbishop*

ILLUSTRATION by Wood from *Curly*

STANLEY LLEWELLYN WOOD
1866–1928

Illustrated by the Artist

1 Allen, Grant. *Ivan Greet's Masterpiece*. Chatto & Windus, London, 1894, decor. cloth, decor. endsheets, 330 pp., 32 of advs., preface, frontis. by W.

2 Arnold, Edwin Lester. *The Constable of St. Nicholas*. Chatto & Windus, London, 1894, colored pic. cloth, decor. endsheets, 263 pp., 32 of advs., frontis. and front cover by W.

3 Baker, H. Barton. *Two Men from Kimberley*. Ward, Lock, London, 1904, cloth, 310 pp., frontis. by W.

4 Boothby, Guy. *A Bid for Fortune, or, Dr. Nikola's Vendetta*. Ward, Lock, London etc., 1895, decor. cloth, 334 pp., with numerous illus. by W.

5 ———. *The Marriage of Esther*. Ward, Lock, London etc., 1895, decor. cloth, 260 pp., 16 of advs., four illus., frontis. and facing pp. 157, 173 and 243, by W.

6 ———. *A Lost Endeavor*. Macmillan, N.Y., London, 1895, pic. cloth, 183 pp., four illus. frontis. and facing pp. 35, 127 and 179, by W.

7 ———. *Dr. Nikola*. Ward, Lock, London, 1896, cloth with illus. in color mounted on the front cover, 322 pp., (4) of advs., twenty-one illus. by W.

8 ———. *The Beautiful White Devil*. Ward, Lock, London, 1896, gilt pic. cloth, 289 pp., 6 of advs., six illus., frontis. and facing pp. 27, 89, 121, 223 and 230, by W.

9 ———. *In Strange Company*. Ward, Lock, London etc., 1896, pic. wraps, 80 pp., 8 of advs., six illus., front cover and facing pp. 16, 32, 48, 64 and 72, by W. Issued as a supplement to *The Windsor Magazine*, Christmas 1896.

10 ———. *The Fascination of the King*. Ward, Lock, London etc., 1897, cloth with illus. in color mounted on front cover, 286 pp., 16 of advs., preface, three illus., frontis. and facing pp. 112 and 190, by W.

11 ———. *The Phantom Stockman*. The Phono Co., Elgin and Dumferline, (1897), pic. wraps, 24 pp., in shorthand, preface, six illus., front cover, title page and pp. 8, 16, 19 and 24, by W. The Phono Novelette's no. 1.

12 ———. *The Lust of Hate*. Ward, Lock, London etc., 1898, pic. cloth, 283 pp., 12 of advs., four illus. frontis. and facing pp. 12, 248 and 266, by W.

13 ———. *The Kidnapped President*. Ward, Lock, London etc., 1902, decor. cloth, 308 pp., (12) of advs., three illus., frontis. and facing pp. 239 and 246, by W.

14 ———. *Sheilah McLeod*. Ward, Lock, London etc., n.d., cloth, 248 pp., (6) of advs., frontis. by W. (No. 117 of Ward, Lock's Seven Penny Net Novels — a reprint series?)

15 Boylan, Grace Duffie. *The Supplanter*. Lothrop, Lee & Shepard, Boston, (1913), words "Published, August, 1913" on copyright page, decor. cloth, 302 pp., (5) of advs., frontis. by W.

16 *The Boy's Own Annual*. The Boy's Own Paper, London, 1885, colored pic. cloth, 831 (1) pp., numerous illus. including one, front cover, by W.

17 Same, 1886, colored pic. cloth, 823 (1) pp., numerous illus. including one, front cover, by W.

18 Same, 1888, colored pic. cover, 840 pp., numerous illus. including one, front cover, by W.

19 Same, 1916, colored pic. cloth, 728 pp., numerous illus. including one, front cover, by W.

20 Same, 1919, colored pic. cloth, 664 pp., numerous illus., two in color, pp. 368 and 528 (repeated on front cover), by W.

21 Same, 1920–1921, colored pic. cloth, colored pic. endsheets, 664 pp., numerous illus. including one in color, facing p. 140, by W.

22 Same, 1924, colored pic. cloth, 848 pp., numerous illus. including one in color, facing p. 192, by W.

23 Same, 1925, colored pic. cloth, 856 pp., numerous illus. including one in color, facing p. 466, by W.

24 Same, 1926, colored pic. cloth, 765, iii pp., numerous illus. including one in color, facing p. 160, by W.

25 Brereton, Captain F. S. *With Shield and Assegai.* Blackie and Son, London etc., 1900, pic. cloth, six illus., frontis. and facing pp. 54, 138, 148, 208 and 304, by W.

26 ———. *In the King's Service* (A Tale of Cromwell's Invasion of Ireland). Blackie, London etc., 1901, pic. cloth, illus. by W.

27 ———. *One of the Fighting Scouts.* Blackie, London etc., 1903, pic. cloth, tinted endsheets, 352 pp., 32 of advs., all edges black, map, eight illus. frontis. and facing pp. 36, 134, 154, 196, 262, 296 and 336, by W.

28 ———. Same, Blackie reprint in colored pic. cloth, map, six illus., frontis. and facing pp. 32, 128, 264, 288 and 328, by W.

29 ———. *A Soldier of Japan.* Blackie, London etc., 1906, pic. cloth, grey endsheets, 350 pp., 32 of advs., all edges black, six illus., frontis. and facing pp. 68, 128, 190, 286 and 344, by W.

30 ———. *Roger the Bold.* Blackie, N.Y. etc., 1906, pic. cloth, black endsheets, 411 pp., (2) of advs., eight illus., frontis. and facing pp. 50, 94, 176, 256, 276, 316 and 404, by W.

31 ———. Same, but first British edition, Blackie, London etc., 1907 (actually printed in 1906 as a copy in your compiler's collection bears a Christmas 1906 inscription), pic. cloth, grey endsheets, 381 pp., 16 of advs., all edges gray, maps, eight illus., frontis. and facing pp. 48, 88, 162, 234, 292 and 374, by W.

32 ———. *Roughriders of the Pampas.* Blackie, London etc., (1908), pic. cloth, slate endsheets, 366 pp., (16) of advs., all edges black, six illus., frontis. and facing pp. 74, 124, 168, 210 and 276, by W.

33 ———. Same, H. M. Caldwell, N.Y. and Boston, (1908), pic. cloth, 358 pp., six illus., frontis. and facing pp. 68, 116, 158, 202 and 268, by W. (First American edition.)

34 ———. *A Hero of Sedan.* Blackie, London, 1910, colored pic. cloth, grey endsheets, 384 pp., 16 of advs., eight illus. in color, frontis. and facing pp. 48, 98, 130, 144, 247, 306 and 365, by W.

35 ———. *Scouts of the Baghdad Patrols.* Cassell and Company, London etc., n.d., colored pic. cloth, 305 (1) pp., four illus. in color, frontis. and facing pp. 52, 100 and 244, by W.

36 Bridges, T. C. et al. *The Lucky Boys' Budget.* Blackie, London etc., n.d., colored pic. boards, 96 pp., illus. incuding five, frontis. in color, title page and pp. (3), 4 and (9), by W.

37 Burton, Sir Richard F. (translator). *The Book of the Thousand Nights and A Night.* Press of the Carson-Harper Co., Denver, Colo., 1900–1901, sixteen volumes, buckram (or ¾ levant or ¾ morocco), 100 illus. by W. First reprint of the original unexpurgated edition, 1000 sets.

38 Chalmers, James. *Fighting the Matabele.* Blackie, London, 1898, colored pic. cloth, grey endsheets, 288 pp., six illus., frontis. and facing pp. 80, 156, 184, 202 and 224, by W.

39 Connell, F. Norreys. *How Soldiers Fight.* James Bowden, London, 1899, colored pic. cloth, 236 pp., (20) of advs., foreword, 24 illus. including six, frontis. and facing pp. 90, 129, 139, 173 and 214, by W. (Zogbaum)

40 Crellin, H. N. *Romances of the Old Seraglio.* Chatto & Windus, London, 1894, cloth, 248 pp., twenty-eight illus. by W.

41 Curwood, James Oliver. *The Treasure Hunters* (A Story of Life and Adventures in the Hudson Bay Wilds). Cassell, London etc., (1917), words "First published 1917" on copyright page, pic. cloth, 277 (1) pp., four illus. including one, the frontis. in color, by W.

42 Dewar, Sir Thomas Robert. *A Ramble Around the Globe.* Chatto & Windus, London, 1894, colored pic. cloth, decor. endsheets, 316 pp., 32 of advs., introduction, 220 illus. including fifteen by W.

43 Douglas, David. *On the Great Fur Trail.* "The Boy's Own Paper" Office, London, n.d., decor. cloth, 252 pp., frontis. by W.

44 Ellis, Edward S. *Astray in the Forest.* Cassell, London etc., 1898, pic. cloth, decor. endsheets, 154 pp., 16 of advs., six illus., frontis. and facing pp. 24, 44, 76, 124 and 148, by W.

45 ———. Same, 1903 reprint by Cassell, pic. cloth, with four illus., frontis. and facing pp. 44, 124 and 148, by W.

46 ———. *The Chieftain and the Scout.* Cassell, London

THE SNIPERS AT WORK by Wood from *One of the Fighting Scouts*

etc., n.d., pic. cloth, 296 pp., five illus. including one, the frontis. in color, by W.

47 ———. *The Pony Express.* Cassell, London etc., n.d. (1919?), colored pic. cloth, 311 (1) pp., blue top, four illus. including one, the frontis. in color, by W.

48 Fenn, Geo. Manville. *Old Gold; or, The Cruise of the "Jason" Brig.* Nister, London; Dutton, N.Y. (printed in Bavaria, 1900), pic. cloth, 416 pp., (8) of advs., gilt top, eight illus., frontis. and facing pp. 94, 126, 308, 356, 362, 380 and 390, by W.

49 ———. *The Lost Middy.* Nister, London (but printed in Bavaria, 1902), pic. cloth, 408 pp., 8 of advs., eight illus., frontis. and facing pp. 110, 118, 140, 236, 274, 306 and 354, by W.

50 Gibbon, Frederick P. *The Disputed V.C.* Blackie, London, 1904, pic. cloth, grey endsheets, 352 pp., all edges black, six illus., frontis. and facing pp. 42, 88, 214, 290 and 340, by W.

51 Gilson, Capt. Charles et al. *The Captain.* Newnes, London, 1909, colored pic. cloth, 576 pp., all edges gilt, numerous illus. including four, pp. (194), (195), 199 and 201, by W.

52 Glanville, Ernest. *A Fair Colonist.* Chatto & Windus, London, 1894, colored pic. cloth, decor. endsheets, 328 pp., 32 of advs., frontis. (repeated on front cover) by W.

53 Golding, Harry (general editor). *The Wonder Book of Daring Deeds.* Ward, Lock, London and Melbourne, n.d., cloth and colored pic. boards, pic. endsheets, 256 pp., numerous illus. including one drawing, p. 241, by W.

54 Grainger, Francis E. *Beacon Fires, War Stories of the Coast,* by Headon Hill (pseud.). Ward, Lock, London etc., 1897, pic. cloth, 304 pp., 8 of advs., frontis. by W.

55 ———. *The Divinations of Kala Persad.* Ward, Lock, London, 1895, decor. cloth, tinted endsheets, 246 pp., (2) of advs., two illus., frontis. and facing p. 138, by W.

56 Griffith, George. *Men Who Have Made the Empire.* C. Arthur Pearson, London, 1897, pic. cloth, 304 pp., (2) of advs., sixteen full-page plates by W.

57 ———. *The Virgin of the Sun.* Pearson, London, 1898, pic. cloth, 306 pp., introduction, frontis. by W.

58 Harrison, Frederick. *"1779," A Story of Old Shoreham.* Society for Promoting Christian Knowledge, London, n.d., pic. cloth, decor. endsheets, 312 pp.,

map, five illus., frontis. and facing pp. 63, 138, 379 and 510, by W.

59 Harte, Bret. *A Waif of the Plains.* Chatto & Windus, London, 1890, pic. cloth, decor. endsheets, 238 pp., 32 of advs., sixty illus. by W. (The "first" — issued before the Boston edition of 1890.) (Rare Book Collection of Library of Congress.)

60 ———. *A Protege of Jack Hamlin's.* Chatto & Windus, London, 1894, pic. cloth, decor. endsheets, 330 pp., 32 of advs., 26 illus. including one, the frontis., by W. (Rare Book Collection of L. C.)

61 ———. *A Ward of the Golden Gate.* Chatto & Windus, London, 1890, cloth, 302 (2) pp., fifty-nine illus. by W. (Rare Book Collection of L. C.)

62 Hawthorne, Julian, ed. *Classic Mystery and Detective Stories: Mediterranean.* Review of Reviews, N.Y., 1909, fabricoid and cloth, 150, 200 and 32 pp., frontis. by W. (The Lock & Key Library.)

63 Henty, G. A. *No Surrender.* Scribner's, N.Y., 1899, cloth, 345 pp., 32 of advs., preface, eight illus., frontis. and facing pp. 34, 50, 80, 94, 152, 206 and 334, by W.

64 ———. Same, Blackie, London, 1900, pic. cloth, grey endsheets, 352 pp., 32 of advs., all edges black, preface, eight illus., frontis. and facing pp. 44, 58, 88, 102, 162, 214 and 342, by W.

65 ———. *Rujub the Juggler.* Chatto & Windus, London, 1893, cloth, eight illus. by W.

66 ———. Same, Presentation Edition by Chatto & Windus, London, 1899, colored pic. cloth, green endsheets, 332 pp., 32 of advs., all edges gilt, eight illus, frontis. and facing pp. 10, 74, 170, 182, 220, 272 and 304, by W.

67 ———. Same, The Mershon Co., Rahway, N.J., N.Y., (1901), pic. cloth, 385 pp., (4) of advs., all edges green, publisher's introduction, four illus., frontis. and facing pp. 12, 197 and 257, by W. (First American edition?)

68 Herman, Henry. *Lady Turpin.* Ward, Lock, London, 1895, cloth, 170 pp., thirty illus. by W.

69 Hocking, Joseph. *Jabez Easterbrook.* Ward, Lock, London etc., n.d., decor. cloth, black endsheets, 362 pp., (14) of advs., gilt top, two illus., frontis. and facing p. 71, by W.

70 Hyne, Charles John Cutliffe Wright. *The Adventures of Captain Kettle.* Pearson, London, 1898, pic. cloth, 318, 15 pp., (1) of advs., thirty-three illus. by W.

71 ———. *Further Adventures of Captain Kettle*. Pearson, London, 1899, pic. cloth, 315 pp., (4) of advs., sixteen illus. by W.

72 ———. *The Little Red Captain*. Pearson, London, 1902, pic. cloth, 240 pp., (4) of advs., four illus., frontis. and facing pp. 42, 80 and 216, by W.

73 ———. *Captain Kettle, K. C. B.* Pearson, London, 1903, pic. cloth, 294 pp., (3) of advs., sixteen illus. by W.

74 ———. Same, (The Last Adventure). Pearson, London, (1928), words "Reprinted . . . 1928" on copyright page, cloth, 264 pp., d/w illus. in color by W.

75 ———. *Kate Meridith*. Cassell, London, 1907, cloth with illus. in color mounted on the front cover, 342 pp., eight illus. including seven, facing pp. 40, 84, 106, 136, 158, 298 and 324, by W.

76 Ironside, John. *Forged in Strong Fires*. Little, Brown, Boston, 1911, words "Published March, 1911" on copyright page, decor. cloth, 318 pp., (2) of advs., frontis. by W.

77 Johnson, Henry. *With Our Soldiers at the Front*. Religious Tract Society, London, (1900), cloth and boards, 192 pp., all edges stippled, fifteen illus. including two, facing pp. 81 and 151, by W.

78 Kelly, Florence Finch. *Emerson's Wife*. A. C. McClurg, Chicago, 1911, words "Published September, 1911" on copyright page, cloth, 334 (1) pp., four illus. in color, frontis. and facing pp. 86, 106 and 286, by W.

79 Ker, David. *Under the Flag of France*. Blackie, London etc., (1907), pic. cloth, slate endsheets, 344 pp., all edges black, preface, six illus., frontis. and facing pp. 8, 88, 162, 220 and 266, by W.

80 Kernahan, Coulson. *The Dumpling*. Cassell, London etc., (1906), cloth with illus. mounted on front cover, 339 pp., four illus., frontis. and facing pp. 126, 190 and 324, by W.

81 Knibbs, Henry Herbert. *The Ridin' Kid from Powder River*. Houghton Mifflin, Boston and N.Y., 1919, cloth, 457 pp., illus. including a frontis. in color by W.

82 Lange, Dietrich. *The Silver Island of the Chippewa*. Lothrop, Lee & Shepard, Boston, (1913), words "Published March, 1913" on copyright page, pic. cloth, 246 pp., (12) of advs., introduction, six illus., frontis. and facing pp. 84, 110, 138, 204 and 222, by W.

83 Mackenna, Stephen J. and O'Shea, John Augustus. *Brave Men in Action*. Chatto & Windus, London, 1899, colored pic. cloth, 586 pp., 32 of advs., all edges gilt, preface, eight illus., frontis. and facing pp. 26, 102, 134, 394, 406, 478 and 560, by W.

84 Marsh, Richard. *The Datchet Diamonds*. Ward, Lock, London etc., n.d., cloth, 302 pp., 12 of advs., two illus., frontis. and facing p. 82, by W.

85 Meigs, John. *The Cowboy in American Prints*. Swallow, Chicago, (1972), leather and cloth, pic. endsheets, 184 pp., introduction, numerous illus. including one, p. (67), by W. Limited to 300 numbered copies signed by the editor with an added manually signed lithograph by Peter Hurd, slipcase. (Beeler, Borein, Dixon, Hurd, Remington, Russell, Zogbaum)

86 ———. Same, trade edition in cloth.

87 Mitford, Bertram. *The Gun-Runner*. Chatto & Windus, London, 1893, pic. cloth, decor. endsheets, 359 pp., (32) of advs., frontis. by W.

88 ———. *The King's Assegai*. Chatto & Windus, London, 1894, pic. cloth, decor. endsheets, 248 pp., 32 of advs., six illus., frontis. and facing pp. 36, 130, 164, 226 and 243, by W. Reprinted in Seaside Library, Pocket Edition, no. 2168, Geo. Munro's Sons, N.Y., (1897).

89 ———. *Renshaw Fanning's Quest*. Chatto & Windus, London, 1894, colored pic. cloth, decor. endsheets, 307 pp., 4 and 32 of advs., conclusion, frontis. by W.

90 ———. *The Luck of Gerard Ridgeley*. Chatto & Windus, London, 1894, colored pic. cloth, decor. endsheets, 268 pp., 32 of advs., frontis. by W.

91 ———. *A Veldt Official: a Novel of Circumstance*. Ward, Lock, London etc., 1895, pic. cloth, decor. endsheets, 324 pp., (2) of advs., two illus., frontis. and facing p. 183, by W.

92 ———. *The Expiation of Wynne Palliser*. Ward, Lock & Bowden, London etc., 1896, pic. cloth, 343 pp., two illus., frontis. and facing p. 288, by W.

93 ———. *Fordham's Feud*. Ward, Lock, London, 1897, colored pic. cloth, 342 pp., four illus., frontis. and facing pp. 90, 188 and 322, by W.

94 ———. *The Curse of Clement Waynflete*. Ward, Lock, London etc., n.d., pic. cloth, 312 pp., prologue, four illus., frontis. and facing pp. 72, 240 and 267, by W.

95 Morrison, Arthur. *The Dorrington Deed Box*. Ward,

Lock, London etc., (1897?), cloth, 308 pp., 4 of advs., fifteen illus., including nine, frontis. and facing pp. 6, 30, 80, 83, 182, 195, 223 and 240, by W.

96 Muddock, J. E. *Maid Marian and Robin Hood: a Romance of Old Sherwood Forest.* Chatto & Windus, London, 1892, pic. cloth, decor. endsheets, 326 pp., 32 of advs., twelve illus. by W.

97 Newbolt, (Sir) Henry (John). *The Book of the Long Trail.* Longmans, Green, N.Y. etc., 1919, cloth, 312 pp., introduction, note, thirty-one illus. including a frontis. in color by W.

98 ———. *The Book of Good Hunting.* Longmans, Green, N.Y. etc., 1920, cloth, 272 pp., thirty-one illus. including a frontis. in color by W.

99 ———. *The Book of the Thin Red Line.* Longmans, Green, N.Y. etc., 1915, cloth, 308 pp., forty-six illus. including eight in color by W.

100 Oppenheim, E. Phillips. *A Millionaire of Yesterday.* Ward, Lock, London, (1900), cloth, 315 pp., (4) of advs., two illus., frontis. and facing p. 219, by W.

101 ———. *The Survivor.* Ward, Lock, London etc., 1904, colored pic. wraps, 123 pp., (4) of advs., two illus., frontis. and facing p. 32, by W.

102 ———. *As a Man Lives.* Ward, Lock, London etc., 1908, cloth, 304 pp., (4) of advs., four illus. including one, facing p. 88, by W.

103 Parker, Gilbert. *Northern Lights.* Harper & Bros., N.Y. and London, 1909, words "Published September, 1909" on copyright page, pic. cloth, 351 (1) pp., note, sixteen illus. including one, facing p. 56, by W. (Crawford, Dunn, Schoonover)

104 Payn, James. *A Trying Patient.* Chatto & Windus, London, 1893, decor. cloth, decor. endsheets, 285 pp., 32 of advs., frontis. by W.

105 Pemberton, Max. *The Garden of Swords.* Dodd, Mead, N.Y., 1899, decor. cloth, 329 pp., sixteen illus. by W.

106 Pocock, Roger. *Curly.* Little, Brown, Boston, (1905), words "Published May, 1905" on copyright page, pic. cloth, 320 pp., (4) of advs., frontis. by W.

107 Pratt, Ambrose. *Vigorous Daunt-Billionaire.* R. F. Fenno, N.Y., (1908), pic. cloth, 380 pp., illus. including eleven full-page plates by W.

108 Prichard, K. and Hesketh. *The Chronicles of Don Q.* J. B. Lippincott, Philadelphia; 1904, words "Published November, 1904" on copyright page, pic. cloth, 313 pp., (6) of advs., twelve illus. by W.

109 Raine, William MacLeod. *Mavericks.* Dillingham, N.Y., (1912), cloth, 347 pp., illus. by Clarence Rowe but d/w illus. in color by W.

110 Reid, Captain Mayne. *The Finger of Fate.* James Bowden, London, 1899, colored pic. cloth, 319 pp., (8) of advs., two illus., frontis. and facing p. 163, by W.

111 Roe, E. P. *Found Yet Lost.* Dodd Mead, N.Y., (1892), cloth, frontis. by W.

112 Ryan, Marah Ellis. *Told in the Hills.* Rand McNally, Chicago, N.Y., (1914), cloth, 362 pp., ten illus. in color, frontis. and facing pp. 22, 70, 114, 132, 143, 177, 269, 297 and 350, by W.

113 Scott, G. Firth. *The Last Lemurian: An Australian Story of Adventure.* Bowden, London, 1898, colored pic. cloth, 339 pp., 16 of advs., three illus., frontis. and facing pp. 225 and 280, by W.

114 Scott, Dr. Jonathan (text by). *Arabian Nights Entertainment.* The Aldine Edition, London, 1890(?), four volumes each with twenty-five illus. by W.

115 Shedd, George C. *The Incorrigible Dukane.* Small, Maynard, Boston, 1911, cloth, 359 pp., four illus., frontis. and facing pp. 108, 244 and 310, by W.

116 Shipp, E. Richard. *Intermountain Folk: Songs of Their Days and Ways.* The Casper Stationery Co., Casper, Wyo., 1922, pic. fabricoid, tan endsheets, 113 pp., gilt top, illus. (many in color) including two, p. (5) and facing p. 26 (both in color), by W.

117 Sinclair-Cowan, Bertha M. *Lonesome Land,* by B. M. Bower (pseud.). Little, Brown, Boston, 1912, words "Published February, 1912" on copyright page, pic. cloth, 322 pp., four illus., frontis. and facing pp. 50, 214 and 274, by W.

118 Smith, Ernest et al. *The Canadian Boys' Annual.* Cassell, London etc., n.d., cloth with illus. in color mounted on front cover, 232 pp., numerous illus., including one by W.

119 Stables, Dr. Gordon. *Roy Rob MacGregor, Highland Chief and Outlaw.* Nister, London; E. P. Dutton, N.Y., (1900?), pic. cloth, 304 pp., (8) of advs., eight illus., frontis. and facing pp. 20, 58, 86, 118, 172, 234 and 270, by W.

120 Titus, Harold. *Bruce of the Circle A.* Small, Maynard, Boston, (1918), decor. cloth, 294 pp., (10) of advs., illus. including two, facing pp. 148 and 224, by W.

121 Van Norman, Louis E., ed. *The Most Interesting Stories of All Nations: South Europe and Oriental.* Review of Reviews, N.Y., 1913, fabricoid and cloth,

decor. endsheets, 368 pp., frontis. by W. (The Lock & Key Library.)

122 Wason, Robert Alexander. *Friar Tuck.* Small, Maynard, Boston, (1912), words "Published September, 1912" on copyright page, cloth, four illus., frontis. and facing pp. 6, 106 and 172, by W.

123 Weston, James. *A Night in the Woods and Other Tales and Sketches.* London, n.d., colored pic. cloth, 96 pp., fifty illus. including eight in color. Stanley L. Wood listed as one of the illustrators and the tailpiece, p. 63, may be by him.

124 Whyte-Melville, G. J. *Tilbury Nogo.* Ward, Lock, London etc., n.d., decor. cloth, 352 pp., (8) of advs., preface, illus. including three, frontis. and facing pp. 115 and 187, by W.

125 ———. *Contraband.* Ward, Lock, London etc., n.d., decor. cloth, 300 pp., (16) of advs., four illus., frontis. and facing pp. 85, 101 and 152, by W.

126 Wood, Eric. *The Boy's Book of Redskins.* Funk and Wagnalls, N.Y., n.d., pic. cloth, 309 pp., preface, four illus., frontis. and facing pp. 70, 222 and 268, by W.

127 Wood, Field-Marshal Sir Evelyn, ed. *British Battles on Land and Sea.* Cassell, London, 1915, two volumes, cloth, 948 pp., over 500 illustrations including eighteen by W.

128 Wood, J. Claverdon. *Under the Serpent's Fang.* "The Boy's Own Paper" Office, London, n.d., pic. cloth, 264 pp., nine illus., frontis. in color and facing pp. 24, 56, 72, 104, 136, 168, 200 and 232, by W.

129 Wood, Stanley L. *One Hundred Illustrations to Captain Sir Richard Burton's Translation of The Arabian Nights.* Printed descriptions on protective tissues, loose in cloth portfolio with protective flaps, limited to 250 portfolios by Pickering and Chatto, London, n.d., (1890? — the drawings are dated 1888 and 1889 if at all).

The Artist and His Art

130 Blathwayt, Raymond. "The Real Captain Kettle," an article in *Pearson's Magazine* (1898?) with photos of C. J. Cutcliffe Hyne, the author of Captain Kettle stories, and of his illustrator, Stanley L. Wood, and based on interviews with Hyne and Wood.

131 Burton-Garbett, Arthur. "Letter" to the Editor concerning Wood in *Book Collecting & Library Monthly,* London, March 1969.

132 *Catalogue of Drawings.* Victoria and Allen Museum, London. Describes two drawings by Wood presented to the Museum by H. H. Harrod.

133 Doyle, Brian. *Who's Who of Boys' Writers and Illustrators.* Published by the author, London, 1964, wraps, 99 pp., introduction, brief biography of Wood, p. 99.

134 ———. "Letter" with information concerning Wood in *Book Collecting & Library Monthly,* London, April 1969.

135 Graves, Algernon. *A Dictionary of Artists Who Have Exhibited Works in the Principal London Exhibitions from 1760 to 1880.* Second edition, 1760–1893, lists Wood as a member of the Royal Academy and of the New Water-Color Society.

136 ———. *The Royal Academy of Arts: A Complete Dictionary of Contributors and Their Work from its Foundation in 1769 to 1904.* Eight volumes, 1905–06, volume VIII, 1906, lists five exhibitions, 1892, 1894, 1895, 1897 and 1903, showing work by W.

137 Hogarth, Paul. *Artists on Horseback* (The Old West in Illustrated Journalism, 1857–1900). Watson-Guptill, N.Y., (1972), words "First Printing, 1972" on copyright page, cloth, map endsheets, 288 pp., "Preface" by John C. Ewers, foreword, biographical notes including one of Wood, p. 284, index, numerous illus.

138 Mee, Arthur, ed. *I See All* (pictorial encyclopedia). Volume 5, p. 2989, Wood entry with a photo of him.

139 Starrett, Vincent. *Born in a Book Shop: Chapters from the Chicago Renascence.* University of Oklahoma Press, (1965), words "First edition" on copyright page, cloth, 325 pp., foreword, index, illus. with photos. Mentions exchanging visits — London and Chicago — with Stanley Wood. (Unfortunately space did not permit including Starrett's paise of Wood and Gordon Browne, his two favorite illustrators — he sent your compiler a copy of the part of his manuscript in which he says "Indeed, for my money, no better horse artist ever lived than Stanley L. Wood — there was more action in a Stanley Wood illustration than in the story itself.")

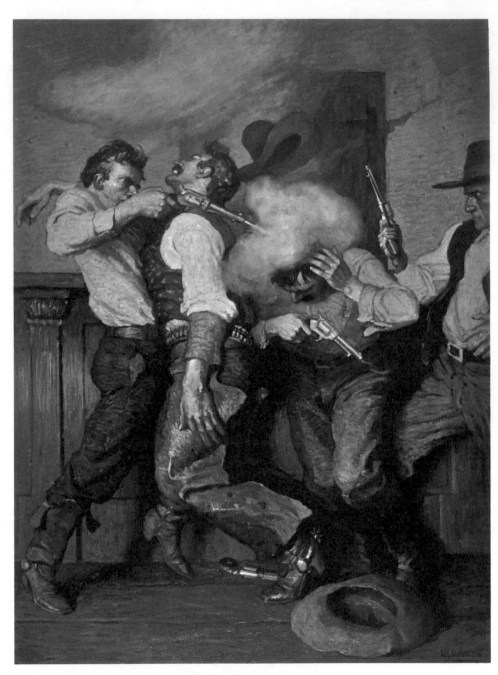

GUNFIGHT by Wyeth from *Nan of Music Mountain*

NEWELL CONVERS WYETH
1882–1945

Catalogues of Art Exhibitions and Galleries

AMERICAN LITHOGRAPHIC COMPANY GALLERIES
NEW YORK

1 *A Most Unusual Collection of Original Paintings Showing Some of the Recent Experiments of N. C. Wyeth*, July, but year not stated, folder with one illus. by W.

BAKER COLLECTOR GALLERY, LUBBOCK, TEXAS

2 *Spring, 1964* (catalogue), pic. wraps, (30) pp., foreword, numerous illus. including one, "In Penobscot Bay," by Wyeth. (Hurd, Remington, Russell)

3 *Winter, 1964* (catalogue), pic. wraps, (27) pp., foreword, numerous illus. including one by W. (Borein, Hurd)

4 Same, (Catalogue), n.d., pic. wraps, (28) pp., foreword, numerous illus. including one, "In Penobscot Bay," by W. (Ellsworth, Hurd, Johnson, Russell)

J. N. BARTFIELD ART GALLERIES, NEW YORK

5 *American Paintings and Sculpture, Historical, Western*, (number 100), 1969, colored pic. wraps, unpaged, 64 numbered illus. including four, nos. 52, 53, 54a and 54b, by W. (Johnson, Leigh, Remington, Russell, Schoonover)

BRANDYWINE RIVER MUSEUM
CHADDS FORD, PENNSYLVANIA

6 *The Brandywine Heritage*, May–September 1971, colored pic. wraps, 121 pp., "Foreword" by Richard McLanathan, numerous illus. including twenty-two, three in color, by W. (This exhibition catalog was issued in May 1971 — it was reissued in brown cloth for distribution by the New York Graphic Society, Greenwich, Conn., in September 1971.) (Schoonover)

6a *Opening Show*, Poster, June 19, 1971, 40 x 26 inches, one illus. by W.

6b *Prints*, n.d., wraps, unpaged, one illus. by W., seven by his son Andrew and one by his grandson James.

6c *N. C. Wyeth Exhibition*, May 20 to October 15, 1972, pic. folder with one illus. by W.

6d *N. C. Wyeth*, n.d., colored pic. wraps, unpaged, (Foreword) by Lincoln Kirstein, lists 137 items, with six prints in color in pocket inside back wrap.

7 *Wyeth, McCoy, Hurd — A Family Paints Itself*, (Spring 1973), folder with family portrait (1948) in Wyeth's studio with six of his paintings in view.

THE BROOKLYN MUSEUM

8 *A Century of American Illustrations*, March 22–May 14, 1972, colored pic. wraps, 155 pp., introduction, biographies, selected bibliographies, 119 numbered illus. including a detail in color from no. 50 by W. on the front cover. (Fogarty, Remington, Schoonover)

HELEN L. CARD, NEW YORK

9 *Hats Off to the American Illustrator!*, catalog no. two, (1959), pic. wraps, 32 pp., numerous illus. including one, inside back wraps, by W. (Dixon, Goodwin, Koerner, Schoonover)

10 *Hang On, Fellows! We're Out on a Limb*, catalog no. five, (1963), pic. wraps, 95 pp., numerous illus. including nine, pp. 73, 74, 79 (two), 80, 81 (two), 82 and 85, by W. (Deming, Eggenhofer, Leigh, Remington, Schoonover, Stoops)

CARNEGIE INSTITUTE, DEPT. OF FINE ARTS
PITTSBURGH, PENNSYLVANIA

11 *Directions in American Paintings*, 1941, numerous illus. including one, "Island Funeral," by W.

12 *Painting in the United States*, 1944, numerous illus. including one, "War Letter," by W.

13 *Painting in the United States, 1945*, numerous illus. including one, "Nightfall," by W.

CHICAGO ART INSTITUTE

14 *A Record of the Exhibition of Advertising Art*, sponsored by the Art Directors Club of Chicago, 1944, cloth, 258 pp., folio, numerous illus. including two, pp. 24 and 60–61 (each repeated reduced to final commercial form), by W.

CHRISTIE, MANSON & WOODS, HOUSTON, TEXAS

15 *Catalogue of Impressionist, American and Modern Paintings and Watercolors and a Group of Dorothy Doughty Birds*, The Warwick Hotel, April 6, 1970 (auction), colored pic. wraps, 94 pp., index, numerous illus. including two, one in color, by W.

THE COLONIAL ART COMPANY, OKLAHOMA CITY

16 *Western and Traditional American Paintings of the 19th and the Early 20th Centuries*, auction at Senate Room, Lincoln Plaza Inn, June 10, 1973, pic. wraps, unpaged, 76 numbered illus. including one, no. 40, by W. (Borein, Deming, Dixon, Eggenhofer, Elwell, Goodwin, Johnson, Koerner, Russell, Schoonover, Young)

CORCORAN GALLERY OF ART, WASHINGTON, D.C.

17 *Biennial Exhibition of Contemporary American Oil Paintings*, Twelfth, November 30, 1930 to January 11, 1931, numerous illus. including one, "Pennsylvania Barn," p. 29, by W.

18 Same, Thirteenth, December 4, 1932 to January 15, 1933, numerous illus. including one, "In a Dream I Meet General Washington," p. 79, by W.

19 Same, Fourteenth, March 24 to May 5, 1935, numerous illus. including one, "Three Fishermen," by W.

20 Same, Fifteenth, March 18 to May 9, 1937, numerous illus. including one, "The Letter," by W.

21 Same, Sixteenth, March 28 to May 7, 1939, numerous illus. including one, "Dark Harbor Lobsterman," p. 59, by W.

DELAWARE ART MUSEUM
THE WILMINGTON SOCIETY OF THE FINE ARTS

22 *Preserving a Priceless Heritage — Achieving a Community Art Center*, May 7, 1935, wraps, illus. including one, "Sailor's Fantasy," by W.

23 *N. C. Wyeth, N.A. 1882–1945, Memorial Exhibition*, January 7 to 27, 1946, wraps, (16) pp., biographical sketch of W., "Foreword" by Paul Horgan, photo of W. and three illus. by him.

24 *The Golden Age of American Illustration 1880–1914*, September 14–October 15, 1972, pic. wraps, 67 (1)

pp., numerous illus. including one, p. 67, by W. (Remington, Schoonover, Zogbaum)

25 *Bulletin No. 69*, February 1947, one illus., "The Spring House," by W.

26 *Pupils of Howard Pyle*, 1971, museum flier with one small illus. by W.

EDWARD EBERSTADT & SONS, NEW YORK

27 *A Distinguished Collection of Western Paintings*, catalogue 139, pic. wraps, iv pp., plus 131 numbered illus. including one, no. 126, by W. (Borein, Deming, Dixon, Johnson, Leigh, Remington, Russell, Zogbaum)

WILLIAM A. FARNSWORTH LIBRARY AND
ART MUSEUM, ROCKLAND, MAINE

28 *An Exhibition of Paintings from the World of N. C. Wyeth*, July 20–September 4, 1966, cloth, (34) pp., twenty-two illus. by W. and lists fifty-six other works in the exhibition.

GALLERIES OF CHARLES DANIEL FREY COMPANY
NEW YORK

29 *An Exhibition of Paintings by N. C. Wyeth*, Commencing August Seventeenth (but year not stated), folder with illus. on cover by W.

JAMES GRAHAM & SONS, NEW YORK

30 *N. C. Wyeth*, January 15–February 8, 1964, folder with three illus. by W.

GRAND CENTRAL ART GALLERIES, NEW YORK

31 *Exhibition of the Work of Prominent Illustrators*, October 31 through November 11, 1933, wraps, unpaged, illus. including one, "In a Dream I Meet General Washington," by W.

INTERNATIONAL ART GALLERY, PITTSBURGH

32 *An Album of Brandywine Artists*, Great American Editions, N.Y., October 1971 for International and the other five galleries featuring the exhibition October 1971–October 1972, pic. wraps, 54 pp., "Howard Pyle and Late 19th Century American Illustration" by Rowland Elzea, numerous illus. including four, pp. 23 (two) and 24 (two), by W. and a photo and biographical sketch of him. (Dunn, Schoonover)

IBM PERMANENT COLLECTION, NEW YORK

33 *Contemporary Art of the United States*, exhibited in the Gallery of Science and Art, IBM Building, World's Fair of 1940, N.Y., wraps, unpaged, numerous illus. including one, "Three Fishermen," by W. and with a photo and brief biographical sketch of him.

34 *Contemporary Art of the Western Hemisphere*, n.p., 1941, "Foreword" by Thomas J. Watson, numerous illus. including one, "Three Fishermen," by W. (Dixon)

KALAMAZOO INSTITUTE OF ARTS
KALAMAZOO, MICHIGAN

35 *Western Art*, February 17–March 19, 1967, pic. wraps, 17 (1) pp., numerous illus. including one, p. 16, by W. (Hurd, Johnson, Leigh, Miller, Remington, Russell, Schreyvogel)

KNOEDLER GALLERIES, NEW YORK

36 *Exhibition of Paintings by N. C. Wyeth, 1882–1945*, October 25–November 23, 1957, colored pic. wraps by W., (8) pp., biographical sketch and lists 110 works by W.

MACBETH GALLERY, NEW YORK

37 *In the Georges Islands, Paintings by N. C. Wyeth*, Dec. 5th–30th, 1939, folder, "Introduction" by Peter Hurd and with one illus. by W.

MAXWELL GALLERIES, SAN FRANCISCO

38 *American Art Since 1850*, August 2–October 31, 1968, pic. wraps, 84 pp., (Foreword) by Dr. F. M. Hinkhouse, numerous illus. including one, "The Scout," p. 35, by W. (Borein, Dixon, Johnson, Miller, Remington, Russell)

JOSEPH T. MENDOLA ART GALLERY

39 *The American Illustrator*, January 28th through February 1972, folder with one illus. by W.

NATIONAL ACADEMY OF DESIGN, NEW YORK

40 *Illustrated Catalog of Annual Exhibition*, 116th, 1942, numerous illus. including one, "Walden Pond Revisited," by W.

41 Same, 119th, 1945, numerous illus. including one, "In Penobscot Bay," by W.

NEEDHAM FREE PUBLIC LIBRARY
NEEDHAM, MASSACHUSETTS

42 *Dedication of the N. C. Wyeth Room, Needham Free Public Library*, October 27, 1968, folder with W. illus. on front cover, "N. C. Wyeth, 1882–1945" by his brother Stimson Wyeth, lists eighteen works of art by W.

NORTH CAROLINA MUSEUM OF ART, RALEIGH

43 *American Paintings Since 1900 from the Permanent Collection*, April 1–23, 1967, wraps, 46 pp., illus. including one, "Corn Harvest on the Brandywine," p. 44, by W.

PARKE-BERNET GALLERIES, NEW YORK

44 *American Paintings, Drawings, Sculpture*, March 16, 1967, wraps, 54 pp., numerous illus. including two, pp. 38 and 39, by W.

45 *18th–20th Century American Paintings, Drawings, Sculpture*, sale no. 2822, March 19–20, 1969, wraps, 158 pp., numerous illus. including one, p. 151, by W. (Johnson, Leigh, Remington, Russell)

46 *Nineteenth and Twentieth Century American Paintings and Sculpture*, sale no. 2914, October 22, 1969, wraps, 113 pp., numerous illus. including two, pp. 58 and 61, by W.

47 *American and Other Watercolors, Drawings and Sculpture*, sale no. 3079, September 24, 1970, wraps, 65 pp., numerous illus. including one by W.

THE PARRISH ART MUSEUM, SOUTHAMPTON, N.Y.

48 *Loan Exhibition of Paintings by the Wyeth Family*, July 30 to August 22, 1966, wraps, unpaged, illus. including one, "Self Portrait," by W.

THE PENNSYLVANIA ACADEMY OF THE FINE ARTS
PHILADELPHIA

49 *The Tenth Annual Philadelphia Water Color Exhibition*, November 10 to December 15, 1915, wraps, 56 pp., xvi of advs., illus. including one, "Captain Bones," p. 17, by W.

50 *Catalogue of the Twelfth Annual Philadelphia Water Color Exhibition and the Thirteenth Annual Exhibition of Miniatures*, November 8 to December 13, 1914, wraps, 102 pp., xii of advs., illus. including one, "The Black Dragon," p. 79, by W. and lists four other works exhibited by him.

51 *Catalogue of the Fifteenth Annual Philadelphia Water Color Exhibition and Sixteenth Annual Exhibition of Miniatures*, November 4 to December 9, 1917, wraps, 136 pp., xvi of advs., illus. including three, p. 49, by W. and lists three other works exhibited by him.

52 *Catalogue of the Eighteenth Annual Philadelphia Water Color Exhibition and the Nineteenth Annual Exhibition of Miniatures*, November 7 to December 12, 1920, wraps, 86 pp., xiv of advs., illus. including one, "The Captives," p. 63, by W. and lists four other works exhibited by him.

53 *Catalogue of the 115th Annual Exhibition*, February 8

to March 28, 1920, wraps, 112 pp., xvi of advs., illus. including one, "Buttonwood Farm," p. 21, by W.

54 *Catalogue of the 121st Annual Exhibition*, 1926, one illus., "Harbor of Herring Gut," by W.

55 *Catalogue of the 136th Annual Exhibition*, 1941, one illus., "John Teel, Fisherman," by W. (and others according to Mrs. Andrew Wyeth).

WILLIAM PENN MEMORIAL MUSEUM
HARRISBURG, PENNSYLVANIA

56 *N. C. Wyeth and the Brandywine Tradition*, Oct. 13– Nov. 28, 1965, wraps, purple endsheets, (40) pp., text by Henry C. Pitz, illus. with photos of W., his home, studio, etc., and with seven color plates by him.

PENNY HILL AUCTION CO., WILMINGTON

57 *How Old Man Plunkett Went On*, April 10, 1967, folder with one illus. by W.

PETERSEN GALLERIES, BEVERLY HILLS, CALIFORNIA

57a *Americana, Western and Sporting Art/Sculpture*, wraps, 25 pp., numerous illus. including one, p. 6, by W. (James, Johnson, Leigh, Remington, Russell, Zogbaum)

SOTHEBY PARKE BERNET, NEW YORK

57b *Important 18th, 19th and Early 20th Century American Paintings, Watercolors and Sculpture* (auction no. 3498), April 11, 1973, colored pic. wraps, unpaged but with over 70 plates including one by W. (Blumenschein, Eggenhofer, James, Johnson, Leigh, Remington, Russell, Varian)

STUDIO GUILD, NEW YORK

58. *Second Annual Art Display Week*, October 25–31, 1936, wraps, unpaged but plates numbered including no. 93, "The Red Pung," by W.

SWARTHMORE COLLEGE
SWARTHMORE, PENNSYLVANIA

59 *Three Generations of Wyeths*, March 1964, exhibition folder with cover illus. by W.

TUCSON ART CENTER

60 *Western Art in Arizona Collections*, February 18– March 18, 1973, pic. folder with ten prints laid in, one, "The Prospector," by W. (Remington, Russell)

UNIVERSITY OF ARIZONA ART GALLERY, TUCSON

61 *Our Western Heritage*, February 1–26, 1962, colored pic. wraps, unpaged, five illus. including one by W. (Remington, Russell)

WHITNEY GALLERY OF WESTERN ART
(BUFFALO BILL HISTORICAL CENTER)
CODY, WYOMING

62 *Special Exhibition Opening Season*, June 1 to October 1, 1969, pic. wraps, unpaged, ten illus. including one by W. (Koerner, Leigh)

WILMINGTON SAVINGS FUND SOCIETY

63 *Tribute to N. C. Wyeth* (photographic portrait of N. C. Wyeth, 1882–1945), October 21–November 1, 1968, colored pic. wraps, biography of Wyeth by Henry C. Pitz, cover illus., "The Apotheosis of the Famiy," by W. and lists thirty other works by him in the exhibition.

Illustrated by the Artist

64 Adams, James T. *The Record of America*. Scribner's, N.Y., 1922, cloth, numerous illus. including two, p. 97 and facing p. 580, by W. (Thomason)

65 ———. *History of the United States*, Federal Edition of four volumes in slipcase, Scribner's, N.Y., 1933, section of illus. follows text in each volume including one each in volumnes I, II and III by W. (Seven hundred and seventy sets — twenty for presentation.)

66 ———. Same, first trade edition, 1933, with same W. illus.

67 ——— and Vannest, Charles G. *The Record of America*. Scribner's, N.Y. etc., (1935), cloth, 941 pp., maps, numerous illus. including two, p. 97 and facing p. 580 (in color), by W. (Thomason)

68 (Alcott.) *Journals of Bronson Alcott*. Little, Brown, Boston, 1938, words "First Edition" on copyright page, cloth, 559 pp., "Preface" and selected (and edited) by Odell Shepard, introduction, index, nine illus. including one, the frontis. in color, by W.

69 Allen, Douglas and Douglas, Jr. *N. C. Wyeth* (The Collected Paintings, Illustrations and Murals). Crown, N.Y., (1972), cloth, blue endsheets, 335 pp., preface, "Foreword" by Paul Horgan, "Introduction" by Richard Layton, bibliography, notes, index, profusely (many in color) illus. by W. and with photos of him.

70 Allen, Hervey. *Anthony Adverse*. Farrar and Rinehart, N.Y., 1934, gilt stamped green cloth, two vols. in slipcase, 1224 pp. (continuous pagination), endsheets and frontis. in each vol. by W.

71 *The American Heritage Catalogue 1971–1972*. Marion, Ohio, (1971), colored pic. wraps, 32 pp., numer-

ous illus. in color including one, p. (12), by W. (Dunn, Russell)

72 Andress, J. Mace and Evans, W. A. *Health and Good Citizenship* (Book Two, The Practical Health Series). Ginn, Boston etc., (1933), pic. cloth, 419 pp., appendix, index, illus. including one, the frontis. in color, by W. (Revised Edition.)

73 Andrews, Mary Raymond Shipman. *The Militants.* Scribner's, N.Y., 1907, words "Published May, 1907" on copyright page, decor. cloth, 378 pp., (2) of advs., gilt top, eight illus. including two, frontis. and facing p. 214, by W. (Keller)

74 *First Annual of Advertising Art in the U.S.* The Art Directors Club, N.Y., 1921, cloth and boards, 118 pp., (12) of indices, numerous illus. including two, pp. 25 and 45, by W.

75 Same, *Second.* 1922, cloth and decor. boards, 171 pp., indices, numerous illus. incuding one, p. 51 (and repeated, p. 145), by W. (Blumenschein, Dunn, Keller)

76 Same, *Sixth.* 1927, cloth, colored pic. map endsheets, 152 pp., (24) of advs., indices, numerous illus. including one, p. 34 (and repeated p. 121), by W. (Dunn, Stoops, Von Schmidt)

77 Same, *Seventh.* 1928, cloth, colored pic. endsheets, 136 pp., (32) of advs., (9) of indices, numerous illus. including two, pp. 23 and 56–7 (in color), by W. (Dunn)

78 Same, *Eighth.* 1929, cloth, decor. endsheets, 134 pp., (36) of advs., (7) of indices, numerous illus. including one, pp. 52–3 in color, by W. (Dunn)

79 Same, *Twenty-Second.* 1943, cloth, 192 pp., numerous illus. including one, pp. 126–27, by W.

80 Same, *Twenty-Fourth.* 1945, cloth, 314 pp., numerous illus. including one, p. 22, by W.

81 Arbuthnot, May Hill. *Children and Books.* Scott, Foresman, Chicago, etc., (1947), cloth, 626 pp., preface, bibliography, index, numerous illus. including two, pp. 19 and 270, by W. (Smith)

82 (Arthurs.) *The American Historical Scene as Depicted by Stanley Arthurs and Interpreted by Fifty Authors.* University of Pennsylvania Press, Philadelphia, 1935, morocco and cloth, 151 pp., "Foreword" by A. Felix duPont, "Stanley Arthurs, a Record and a Tribute" by Christian Brinton, numerous illus. by Arthurs and one, a portrait of Arthurs in color, facing p. 2, by W. Wyeth was also one of the fifty authors — he wrote "Quiet Custom House." National Edition and quite limited. The Library of Congress copy is in the Rare Book Room.

83 Athearn, Robert C. *The Revolution* (volume 3 of 16, The American Heritage New Illustrated History of the United States). Dell, N.Y., 1963, pic. cloth, 269 pp., numerous illus. including one, p. 211, by W.

84 Atwood, Wallace W. *New Geography* (Book Two, Frye-Atwood Geographical Series). Ginn, Boston etc., (1920), pic. cloth, preface, appendix, index, maps, numerous illus. including two in color, frontis. and facing p. 180, by W.

85 ——— and Thomas, Helen Goss. *Home Life in Far-Away Lands.* Ginn, Boston etc., (1929), pic. cloth, 252 pp., index, maps, numerous illus. including one, the frontis. in color, by W.

86 Bacheller, Irving. *A Candle in the Wilderness.* Bobbs-Merrill, Indianapolis, (1930), words "First Edition" on copyright page, cloth, 318 pp., d/w illus. by W.

87 Baldwin, James (retold by). *The Sampo.* Scribner's, N.Y., 1912, words "Published October 1912" on copyright page, pic. cloth, 368 pp., poem, notes, four illus. in color, frontis. and facing pp. 16, 138 and 262, by W.

88 Ball, Bernice M. *Chester County and Its Day.* The Chester County Hospital, West Chester, Pa., (1970), one of 3000 copies signed by the author, decor. cloth, 225 pp., numerous illus. including one, p. 20, by W.

89 Barnard, Eunice Fuller and Tall, Lida Lee. *How the Old World Found the New.* Ginn, Boston etc., (1929), pic. cloth, 251 pp., numerous illus. including one, the frontis. in color, by W.

90 Bartlett, Frederic Orin. *The Guardian.* Small, Maynard, N.Y., 1912, cloth, 470 pp., frontis. in color by W.

91 Barton, Bruce. *The Man Nobody Knows.* Bobbs-Merrill, Indianapolis, (1925), cloth, 219 (1) pp., frontis. in color by W.

92 Beard, Charles A. and Mary R. *A Basic History of the United States.* Doubleday, Doran, N.Y., 1944, cloth, 554 pp., brown top, prefatory note, appendix, reading list, index, 64 illus. including two, between pp. 48–49 and 176–77, by W. (Dixon, Lea, Leigh)

93 Beith, John Hay. *David and Destiny* by Ian Hay (pseud.). Houghton Mifflin, Boston and N.Y., 1934, cloth, 317 pp., d/w, illus. by W.

94 Beitz, Les. *Treasury of Frontier Relics, a Collector's Guide.* Edwin House, N.Y., (1966), pic. cloth, 246 pp.,

"Foreword" by Fred Gipson, introduction, appendix, picture credits, index, numerous illus. including eleven, pp. (23), 35, 41, (83), (103), (121), (167), (203), (205), (207) and (209), by W. and a photo of him. (Remington)

95 Blanchard, Ferdinand Q. *How One Man Changed the World*. The Pilgrim Press, Boston, Chicago, 1935, pic. boards, 119 pp., frontis. by W.

96 Bonte, George Willard. *The Boys' Book of Battles*. Houghton Mifflin, Boston and N.Y., 1914, cloth with illus. in color by W. mounted on front cover, 410 pp., illus.

97 ———. *America Marches Past*. Appleton-Century, N.Y., London, 1936, decor. cloth, 196 pp., index, numerous illus. including one, p. 43, by W.

97a Bourne, Russell (project editor). *200 Years*. U. S. News & World Report, Washington, D.C., 1973, fabricoid and cloth, two volumes, numerous illus. including one, p. (48) (I), by W. (Dunn, Miller, Remington, Zogbaum)

98 Boyd, James. *Drums*. Scribner's, N.Y., (1928), orange cloth with pic. label, 409 pp., numerous illus. including fourteen full-page plates plus cover, endsheets and title page in color by W. Limited to 50 presentation copies boxed, signed by author and illustrator with facsimiles of letters between author and artist.

99 ———. Same, edition of 525 copies of which 500 were for sale.

100 ———. Same, first trade edition with all W. illus. but without author and artist letters.

101 Boyles, Kate and Virgil D. *Langford of the Three Bars*. A. C. McClurg, Chicago, 1907, words "Published April 15, 1907" on copyright page, colored pic. cloth, 277 (1) pp., (8) of advs., four illus. in color, frontis. and facing pp. 18, 146 and 258, by W.

102 Briggs, Thomas H. et al. *Junior High School English Book II* (For The Eighth Grade). Ginn, Boston etc., (1926), decor. cloth, 422 pp., preface, appendix, index, illus. including one, the frontis. in color, by W. (New Edition.)

103 ——— and McKinney, Isabel. *Ways to Better English*. Ginn, Boston etc., 1924, cloth, 416 pp., numerous illus. including one, the frontis. in color, by W.

104 Bronson, Edgar Beecher. *Reminiscences of a Ranchman*. Doran, N.Y., (1910), cloth with an illus. in color mounted on front cover, 370 pp., appendix, illus. in-cluding two, facing pp. 226 and 234, by W. (Dixon, Dunton)

105 ———. Same, but with the title *Cowboy Life on the Western Plains*.

106 Brotze, Emma Mae and Lehmberg, A. E. *The History of Texas*. Noble & Noble, Dallas, (1954), pic. cloth, 199 pp., appendix, index, numerous illus. including one, p. 83, by W. (Lea)

107 Buchan, John, Lord Tweedsmuir. *The Adventures of Richard Hannay*. Houghton Mifflin, Boston, 1915, d/w illus. in color by W.

108 ———. *The Thirty-Nine Steps*. Houghton Mifflin, Boston, d/w illus. in color by W.

109 ———. *Salute to Adventurers*. Houghton Mifflin, Boston and N.Y., (1930), cloth, 348 pp., d/w, illus. by W.

110 ———. *Man From the Norlands*. Houghton Mifflin, Boston, N.Y., 1936, cloth, 292 pp., d/w, illus. by W.

111 ———. *The Adventures of Richard Hannay*. Houghton Mifflin, Boston, 1939, cloth, 230 (1), 345 and 374 pp. (three novels in one), d/w illus. by W.

112 Bulfinch, Thomas. *Legends of Charlemagne*. Cosmopolitan Book Corp., N.Y., 1924, cloth with illus. in color mounted on front cover, colored pic. endsheets, 273 pp., eleven illus. in color, front cover, endsheets, title page and eight plates, by W.

113 Burdette, Robert J. *The Drums of the 47th*. Bobbs-Merrill, Indianapolis, (1914), cloth, 211 (1) pp., d/w, by W.

114 Burroughs, Edgar Rice. *The Return of Tarzan*. Burt, N.Y., (1915), cloth, 365 pp., (10) of advs., d/w illus. in color by W.

115 Burt, Maxwell Struthers. *Chance Encounters*. Scribner's, N.Y., 1921, cloth, 287 pp., frontis. by W.

116 Butterfield, Roger et al. (selected by). *The Saturday Evening Post Treasury*. Simon and Schuster, N.Y., (1954), cloth and pic. boards, maroon endsheets, 544 pp., maroon top, introduction, illus. including one, p. xv, by W.

117 Cadman, S. Parkes. *The Parables of Jesus*. McKay, Philadelphia, (1931), cloth, with illus. in color mounted on the front cover, 163 pp., foreword, nine illus., front cover, frontis., and facing pp. 34, 38, 42, 46, 76, 102 and 110, by W.

118 Canby, Henry Seidel. *Thoreau*. Houghton Mifflin, Boston, 1939, cloth, 508 pp., yellow top, illus. including one, facing p. 310, by W.

119 Carmer, Carl, ed. *Cavalcade of America*. Winston, Philadelphia etc., 1938, code no. "P-9-38" on copyright page, decor. cloth, 854 pp., preface, appendix, index, numerous illus. including one, p. 229, by W. Reprinted in 1942. (Dixon, Remington)

120 Carroll, H. Bailey et al. *The Story of Texas*. Noble & Noble, N.Y., (1963), colored pic. cloth, 360 pp., preface, appendix, index, numerous illus. including one, p. 119, by W. (Lea, Schiwetz)

121 *Chatterbox*. Harper, N.Y., 1929, numerous illus. including cover illus. by W.

122 Cheney, Warren. *The Challenge*. Bobbs-Merrill, Indianapolis, (1906), word "March" on copyright page, decor. cloth, 386 pp., (16) of advs., four illus., frontis. and facing pp. 108, 170 and 302, by W.

123 *A Christmas Bulletin of the Best Books of 1932*. The Baker and Taylor Co., N.Y., 1932, wraps with illus. in color by W. on front cover.

124 Clark, Marion G. *Westward to the Pacific*. Scribner's, N.Y. etc., (1932), code letter "A" on copyright page, cloth, 498 pp., (appendices), index, numerous illus. including one, p. 299, by W.

125 Clark, William H. *Farms and Farmers*. Page, Boston, (1945), words "First Impression, October, 1945" on copyright page, cloth, 346 pp., foreword, appendix, bibliography, index, illus. including one, the frontis., by W. (Cue, Remington)

126 Clemens, Samuel L. *The Mysterious Stranger*, by Mark Twain (pseud.). Harper, N.Y. and London, (1916), words "Published October 1916" on copyright page, cloth with illus. mounted on front cover, 150 (1) pp., gilt top, seven illus. in color, frontis. and facing pp. 20, 33, 60, 74, 108 and 148, by W.

127 ———. Same, but 1922 issue with a frontis. only by W.

128 ———. *The Adventures of Tom Sawyer*, by Mark Twain (pseud.). Winston, Philadelphia etc., (1931), cloth with illus. in color mounted on front cover, pic. endsheets, 264 pp., red top, preface, numerous illus. including the front cover and d/w by W. (Hurd)

129 Cody, Colonel William F. *The Great West that Was*. Reprinted from *Hearst's Magazine*, (1916), pic. wraps, 60 pp., with eleven illus. by W.

130 ———. *An Autobiography of Buffalo Bill*. Cosmopolitan, N.Y., 1920, pic. cloth, 328 pp., photo of Cody as frontis. and seven illus., facing pp. 55, 87, 125, 175, 209, 283 and 322, by W.

131 Connolly, James B. *The Crested Seas*. Scribner's, N.Y., 1907, words "Published September, 1907" on copyright page, pic. cloth, 311 pp., (4) of advs., gilt top, eight illus. including two, facing pp. 174 and 182, by W.

132 ———. *Wide Courses*. Scribner's, N.Y., 1912, pic. cloth, 336 pp., eight illus. including two, facing pp. 154 and 186, by W.

133 ———. *Head Winds*. Scribner's, N.Y., 1916, words "Published September, 1916" on copyright page, cloth, 299 pp., (4) of advs., five illus. including two, facing pp. 38 and 50, by W.

134 ———. *Running Free*. Scribner's, N.Y., 1917, words "Published September, 1917" on copyright page, cloth, 302 pp., (4) of advs., six illus. including two, frontis. and facing p. 242, by W.

135 ———. *Hiker Joy*. Scribner's, N.Y., 1920, words "Published May, 1920" on copyright page, cloth, 244 pp., four illus., frontis. and facing pp. 50, 116 and 240, by W.

136 ———. *Tide Rips*. Scribner's, N.Y., 1922, cloth, 246 pp., frontis. and one other illus. by W.

137 Cook, Fred. (adapted for young readers by). *The Golden Book of the American Revolution*. Golden Press, N.Y., (1959), colored pic. boards, pic. endsheets, 193 pp., "Introduction" by Bruce Catton, index, numerous illus. including one, p. 32, by W.

138 Cooper, James Fenimore. *The Last of the Mohicans*. Scribner's, N.Y., 1919, cloth with illus. in color mounted on front cover, colored pic. endsheets, 370 pp., seventeen illus. in color, endsheets, title page and fourteen color plates, by W. (Illustrated Classic.)

139 ———. *The Deerslayer*. Scribner's, N.Y., 1925, cloth with illus. in color mounted on front cover, colored pic. endsheets, 462 pp., twelve illus. in color, cover, endsheets, title page and nine plates, by W. (Illustrated Classic.)

140 *Cosmopolitan Publications Autumn of 1920*. Cosmopolitan Book Corp., N.Y., (1920), wraps, 10 pp., two illus., pp. 5 and 6, by W.

141 Creswick, Paul. *Robin Hood*. McKay, Philadelphia, 1917, cloth with illus. in color mounted on front cover, colored pic. endsheets, 362 pp., eleven illus. in color, cover, endsheets, title page and eight plates, by W.

142 ———. Same, but Scribner's, N.Y., 1957.

143 Curwood, James Oliver. *The Plains of Abraham*. Doubleday, Garden City, N.Y., 1928, words "First

Edition" on copyright page, decor. cloth, pic. endsheets, 316 pp., foreword, two illus., front and back endsheets, by W.

143a Davidson, Marshall B. et al. *The American Heritage History of the Writers' America.* American Heritage, N.Y., (1973), cloth and boards, blue endsheets, 403 (13) pp., introduction, index, numerous illus. including five, frontis. in color and pp. 113, (306) color and (307) two, by W. (Goodwin, Remington)

144 Davis, Charles Belmont. *The Lodger Overhead and Others.* Scribner's, N.Y., 1909, words "Published April 1909" on copyright page, decor. cloth, 370 pp., (1) of advs., illus. including two, facing pp. 134 and 138, by W. (Keller)

145 Defoe, Daniel. *Robinson Crusoe.* Cosmopolitan, N.Y., 1920, bright blue cloth with illus. on front cover, colored pic. endsheets, 368 pp., "Illustrator's Preface" by Wyeth, sixteen illus. in color, cover, endsheets, title page and thirteen plates, by W. (Trial binding?)

146 ———. Same, but in red cloth with a different illus. on the front cover. (Reprinted by McKay, Philadelphia, n.d., in black cloth with same illus. by W.)

147 Dodge, Mary Mapes. *Hans Brinker, or, The Silver Skates.* Garden City Publishing Co., (Garden City, N.Y.), 1932, cloth with W. illus. in color mounted on front cover, 305 pp., four illus. in color. (Hurd)

148 Dowdey, Clifford. *Where My Love Sleeps.* Atlantic — Little, Brown, Boston, 1945, words "First Edition" on copyright page, cloth, 298 pp., d/w, illus. by W.

149 Doyle, Arthur Conan. *The White Company.* McKay, Philadelphia, 1922, cloth with illus. in color on front cover, colored pic. endsheets, 363 pp., sixteen illus. in color, cover, endsheets, title page and thirteen plates, by W.

150 ———. *The Last Galley.* Doubleday, Page, Garden City, N.Y., 1911, cloth, 321 pp., frontis. in color by W.

151 (Eberstadt.) *Americana.* Catalogue 134, Edward Eberstadt & Sons, N.Y., 1954, pic. wraps, 111 pp., thirty-two illus. including one, facing p. 65, by W. (Dixon, Johnson, Miller)

152 ———. Same, catalogue 135, Edward Eberstadt & Sons, N.Y., 1955, wraps, 160 pp., illus. including one, back of back wrap, by W.

153 Elder, Donald et al. *The Goodhousekeeping Treasure.* Simon & Schuster, N.Y., 1960, cloth and boards, 638 pp., illus. including one, p. 29, by W.

154 Faris, John T. *Real Stories of the Geography Makers.*
Ginn, Boston, etc., (1925), pic. cloth, 332 pp., index, numerous illus. including one, p. 72, by W.

155 Fassett, James H. *The Corona Readers, Second Reader.* Ginn, Boston etc., (1920), pic. cloth, 224 pp., preface, illus. including one, the frontis. in color, by W.

156 Faul, Jane. *Books About Books, Illustrators Press Books.* J. & S. catalogue no. 10, Chicago, 1971, colored pic. wraps, 112 pp., illus. including one, p. 111, by W. (Remington, Russell)

157 Fielder, Mildred. *Wild Bill and Deadwood.* Superior Pub. Co., Seattle, (1965), words "First Edition" on copyright page, cloth, 160 pp., bbiliography, numerous illus. including one, p. 50 (also used in color on d/w), by W.

158 Fisher, Mrs. Dorothea Frances. *Home Fires of France*, by Dorothy Canfield (pseud.). Holt, N.Y., 1918, cloth, 306 pp., d/w illus. by W.

159 Flader, Louis (compiled and edited by). *Achievement in Photo-Engraving and Letter-Press.* American Photo-Engravers Assn., Chicago, (1927), decor. morocco, 488 pp. plus twelve lettered A–L (insert), numerous illus. including one in color, p. F, by W.

160 Forester, C. S. *Captain Horatio Hornblower.* Little, Brown, Boston, 1939, words "Published April 1939" on copyright page, decor. cloth, 662 pp., green top, five illus. including one, the frontis. in color, by W. (The four other illus. were drawn by Andrew Wyeth under his father's supervision.)

161 ———. Same, in three volumes, each with a frontis. drawn by Andrew Wyeth under his father's supervision (from number 160 above), slipcase.

162 ———. *Commodore Hornblower.* Little, Brown, Boston, 1945, cloth, 384 pp., d/w illus. in color by W.

163 ———. Same, 1946 reprint by Little, Brown with a frontis. by W.

164 Fox, John. *The Little Shepherd of Kingdom Come.* Scribner's, N.Y., 1931, vellum and figured cloth with gilt lettering, 322 pp., fourteen illus. in color on mounts by W. 512 numbered copies of which 12 were for presentation.

165 ———. Same, a boxed trade edition of no. 84 also issued in 1931. (Illustrated Classic.)

166 (Franklin.) *Pictorial Life of Ben Franklin* (In Commemoration of the 200th Anniversary of the Arrival of Franklin in Philadelphia). Dill & Collins, Philadelphia, 1923, cloth and boards, numerous illus. including one, the frontis., by W.

167 Freeland, George Earl et al. *America's Building, The Makers of Our Flag.* Scribner's, N.Y., (1937), pic. cloth, 425 pp., index, numerous illus. including eight, facing p. 84 in color, and pp. 81, 99 (two), 180, 184, 223 and 368, by W. (Fogarty, Rowe, Thomason, Varian)

168 French, Allen. *The Red Keep.* Houghton Mifflin, Boston, 1938, cloth, 309 (1) pp., illus. by Andrew Wyeth, but with a frontis. in color and d/w illus. by W.

169 Frye, Alexis Everett. *New Geography* (Book One, Frye-Atwood Geographical Series). Ginn, Boston etc., (1920), pic. cloth, 264, viii pp., preface, maps, numerous illus. including one, the frontis. in color, by W.

170 ———. *First Steps in Geography.* Ginn, Boston, 1927, pic. cloth, 189 pp., illus. including one, the frontis. in color, by W.

171 Gabriel, Ralph Henry. *The Lure of the Frontier.* Yale University Press, New Haven, 1929, morocco and boards, colored pic. endsheets, 327 pp., numerous illus. including one, the frontis. in color, by W. Vol. 2 of The Liberty Bell (first) Edition of "The Pageant of America," 1500 numbered copies. (There are two other editions.) (Deming, Dixon, Marchand, Remington, Russell)

172 Gates, Eleanor. *Cupid the Cowpunch.* McClure, N.Y., 1907, words "Published, November, 1907" on copyright page, cloth with illus. in color mounted on front cover, 316 pp., eight illus. incuding two, pp. 114 and 170, by W.

173 *Gems from Judge.* N.Y., 1922, cloth with illus. mounted on the front cover, frontis. in color by W.

174 Getlein, Frank et al. *The Lure of the Great West.* Country Beautiful, Waukesha, Wisconsin, (1973), boards, 352 pp., introduction, 375 illus. including two in color, pp. 299 and 300 (repeated on back of d/w), by W. (Blumenschein, Koerner, Leigh, Miller, Remington, Russell, Schreyvogel)

175 Glenn, Mabell et al., ed. *Song Programs for Youth: The World of Music.* Ginn, N.Y. etc., (1938), three vols., *Treasure* (1), *Adventure* (2), and *Discovery* (3), decor. cloth, tinted endsheets, 191 (1), 191 (1) and 191 (1) pp., illus. in color: six in vol. 1, frontis. and facing pp. 16, 49, 64, 113 and 128; four in vol. 2, frontis. and facing pp. 49, 113 and 128; and six in vol. 3, frontis. and facing pp. 16, 48, 64, 128 and 144, by W.

176 Goss, Madeleine. *Bethoven, Master Musician.* Doubleday, Garden City, N.Y., 1931, cloth, 290 pp., illus. including one, the frontis. in color, by W.

177 Grinnell, George Bird. *Blackfeet Indian Stories.* Scribner's, N.Y., 1913, words "Published September, 1913" on copyright page, cloth with illus. in color mounted on front cover, 214 pp., cover and frontis. in color, by W.

178 *A Guide to Washington Cathedral.* National Cathedral Assn., Washington, D.C., (1965), colored pic. wraps, 158 pp., numerous illus. including one in color, "The Chapel of The Holy Spirit Triptych," p. 48, by W.

179 Harding, Frank (compiled by). *A Livestock Heritage, Animals and People in Art.* Privately printed, (Geneva, Illinois, 1971), colored pic. wraps, unpaged, numerous illus. including one, "Indian Lance," by W. (Borein, Dunn, Eggenhofer, Koerner, Marchand, Remington, Russell)

180 Harmsen, Dorothy. *Harmsen's Western Americana.* Northland Press, Flagstaff, (1971), morocco and cloth, blue endsheets, 213 pp., "Foreword" by Robert Rockwell, introduction, numerous illus. including one, p. 204, by W. and with a biographical sketch of him. Author's edition of 150 numbered and signed copies, slipcase with morocco title label. (Beeler, Blumenschein, Borein, Dixon, Dunn, Dunton, Eggenhofer, Elwell, Hurd, Johnson, Leigh, Marchand, Miller, Russell, Von Schmidt)

181 ———. Same, first trade edition, two-tone cloth with red endsheets.

182 Hay, John. *The Pike County Ballads.* Houghton Mifflin, Boston and N.Y., (1912), words "Published October, 1912" on copyright page, cloth with illus. in color mounted on front cover, pic. endsheets, 45 (2) pp., brown top, 36 illus. including eight in color, cover, title page and pp. (8), (14), (20), (26), (32) and (40), by W.

183 Haydon, Harold (text by). *Great Art Treasures in America's Smaller Museums.* Putnam's in association with Country Beautiful Foundation, Waukesha, Wisconsin, (1967), words "First Edition" on copyright page, cloth, grey endsheets, 194 pp., introduction, index, numerous illus. including one, p. 27, by W. (Hurd, Miller, Remington, Russell)

184 ———. Same, but title changed to *Great Art Treasures in American Museums,* as published by Country Beautiful Corporation, Waukesha, Wisconsin.

185 *He Brought Adventure Into Our Lives.* Crown, (N.Y., 1972), folder announcing *N. C. Wyeth* by Douglas Allen and Douglas Allen, Jr., with eight (seven in color) illus. by W. and two photos of him.

186 Hewes, Agnes Danforth. *Glory of the Seas*. Knopf, N.Y., 1933, words "First Edition" on copyright page, cloth, 314 pp., title page and d/w illus. in color by W.

187 ———. Same, Junior Literary Guild edition, 1933, with frontis. in color by W.

188 Horwitt, Nathan George (written and arranged by). *A Book of Notable American Illustrators*. Walker Engraving Corp., N.Y., volume 2, 1927, cloth and boards, (31) pp., illus. including one, p. (17), by W. and a photo of him.

189 Hough, Emerson. *Heart's Desire*. Macmillan, N.Y., 1905, words "Published October, 1905" on copyright page, decor. cloth, 367 pp., (2) of advs., illus. including one ,facing p. 218, by W.

190 Hoyt, Charles B. *Heroes of the Argonne* (An Authentic History of the Thirty-fifth Division). Franklin Hudson Pub. Co., Kansas City, Mo., (1919), decor. cloth, 259 pp., foreword, maps, diagrams, illus. including frontis. in color by W.

191 Huneker, James. *The Steinway Collection of Paintings by American Artists*. Steinway & Sons, N.Y., 1919, vellum and boards, unpaged, twelve plates in color including two by W. An edition of five thousand for presentation. (Blumenschein, Dunn, Keller)

192 *An Invitation to Explore the National Geographic in its Home*. The National Geographic Society, Washington, 1933, boards with illus. mounted on the front cover, unpaged (32), seven illus. by W.

193 Irving, Washington. *Rip Van Winkle*. McKay, Philadelphia, (1921), cloth with illus. in color mounted on front cover, colored pic. endsheets, 86 pp., gilt top, numerous illus. including ten in color, cover, frontis., title page and facing pp. 10, 20, 32, 38, 44, 54 and 76, by W.

194 Jackson, Helen Hunt. *Ramona*. Little, Brown, Boston, 1939, decor. cloth, 424 pp., (Introduction) by May Lamberton Becker, four illus. in color, frontis. and facing pp. 44, 234 and 370, by W.

195 Janeway, Elizabeth et al. *Discovering Literature*. Houghton Mifflin, Boston, N.Y., 1968, pic. cloth, 626 pp., numerous illus. including one, p. 560, by W.

196 Johnson, Edna and Scott, Carrie E. (compiled by). *Anthology of Children's Literature*. Houghton Mifflin, Boston, 1940, cloth, colored pic. endsheets, 917 pp., seventeen illus. in color by W.

197 Johnston, Mary. *The Long Roll*. Houghton Mifflin Co., Boston and N.Y., 1911, words "First Edition" on paper label on spine, and with the words "Published May 1911" on copyright page, cloth, map endsheets, 683 pp., (6) of advs., four illus. in color, frontis. and facing pp. 220, 456 and 642, by W. Autograph Edition of 500 copies, uncut, signed by the author.

198 ———. Same, but first trade edition bound in decor. grey cloth and edges trimmed, with the words "Published May 1911" on copyright page.

199 ———. *Cease Firing*. Houghton Mifflin, Boston and N.Y., 1912, words "First Edition" on paper label on spine and words "Published November, 1912" on copyright page, cloth, 457 pp., four illus. in color, frontis. and facing pp. 128, 302 and 392, by W.

200 ———. Same, first trade edition in decor. grey cloth with the words "Published November, 1912" on copyright page.

201 ———. *The Witch*. Houghton Mifflin, Boston, 1914, words "Published October, 1914" on copyright page, cloth, 441 (1) pp., frontis. in color by W.

202 Kapplow, Hal. *Laughing Historically*. Bernard Geis Associates, (N.Y., 1961), words "First Printing" on copyright page, stiff pic. boards, "Foreword" by the publishers, numerous illus. including one, p. 8, by W. (Dunn)

202a Kelty, Mary G. and Sister Blanche Marie. *Modern American Life*. Ginn, Boston etc., (1943), pic. cloth, 444, xvi, (1) pp., index, numerous illus. including one, p. 98, by W. (Hurd, Fischer, Lea, Remington)

203 Kingsley, Charles. *Westward Ho!* Scribner's, N.Y., 1920, cloth with illus. in color mounted on front cover, colored pic. endsheets, 413 pp., seventeen illus. in color, cover, endsheets, title page and fourteen plates, by W.

204 Klemin, Diana. *The Illustrated Book: Its Art and Craft*. Clarkson N. Potter, N.Y., (1970), words "First Edition" on copyright page, cloth, 159 pp., introduction, bibliography, index, numerous illus. including one, p. 90, by W.

205 Koller, Larry, ed. *The American Gun* (vol. I, no. 2, Spring, 1961). Colored pic. boards, 96 pp., black endsheets, numerous illus., some in color, including one, (to illustrate the article "The Long, Long Rifle" by Herb Glass), p. (42), by W.

206 Kunitz, Stanley J. and Haycraft, Howard et al. *The Junior Book of Authors* (An Introduction to the Lives of Writers and Illustrators). H. W. Wilson Co., N.Y., 1934, pic. cloth, 430 pp., index, appendix, 260 illus. including one, a self-portrait, p. 387, by W.

ILLUSTRATION by Wyeth from *The Pike County Ballads*

207 Kupper, Winifred. *The Golden Hoof.* Knopf, N.Y., 1945, words "First Edition" on copyright page, cloth, 203 pp., (yellow paper) brown top, notes, frontis. by W.

208 Lancaster, Bruce (narrative by), with a chapter by J. H. Plumb. *The American Heritage Book of the Revolution.* American Heritage Pub. Co., N.Y., 1958, cloth and decor. boards, 384 pp., Richard M. Ketchum (editor in charge), "Introduction" by Bruce Catton, acknowledgments, index, numerous illus., many in color, including one, p. 129, by W. (Also issued in a deluxe edition in cloth with a matching slipcase.)

209 Landis, Frederick. *The Angel of Lonesome Hill.* Scribner's, N.Y., 1910, words "Published April, 1910" on copyright page, cloth and boards, 40 pp., frontis. by W.

210 Langdon, William Chauncy. *Everyday Things in American Life.* Scribner's, N.Y., London, 1937, code letter "A" on copyright page, cloth, pic. endsheets, 353 pp., blue top, numerous illus. including five, facing pp. 115, 118, 119, 121 and 214, by W.

211 Latendorf, E. Walter. *Rare Books, First Editions, Association Items.* Catalogue no. 13, Mannados Bookshop, N.Y., February 1941, pic. wraps, 56 pp., front cover illus. by W.

212 Law, Frederick Houk. *Modern Plays, Short and Long.* Century, N.Y., 1924, decor. cloth, 429 pp., illus. including one, facing p. 90, by W.

213 Lawler, Thomas Bonaventure. *Essentials of American History.* Ginn, Boston etc., (1918), cloth, 471 pp., preface to the revised edition, map, appendix, illus. including four in color, frontis. and facing pp. 182, 326 and 398, by W.

214 ———. *The Gateway to American History.* Ginn, Boston etc., 1924, cloth, 366 pp., introduction, index, numerous illus. including one, the frontis. in color, by W.

215 ———. *Standard History of America.* Ginn, Boston etc., 1933, decor. cloth, 625 pp., appendix, index, numerous illus., three in color, facing pp. 220, 378 and 460, by W.

216 ———. *Builders of America.* Ginn, Boston etc., 1936, decor. cloth, 371 pp., index, numerous illus. including one, p. 195, by W. (Revised.)

217 Lewis, Alfred Henry. *The Throwback.* Outing, N.Y., 1906, pic. cloth, 347 pp., four illus. in color, frontis. and facing pp. 78, 136 and 252, by W.

218 Lewis, John. *The Twentieth Century Book* (Its Illustration and Design). Reinhold, N.Y. (but printed in Great Britain, 1967), red balacron, 272 pp., preface, index, numerous illus. including six, pp. 204, 205, 206, 207, 212 and 213, by W. (Remington)

219 Lincoln, Joseph C. and Freeman. *Blair's Attic.* Coward McCann, N.Y., 1929, cloth, pic. endsheets, 369 pp., green top, end papers and d/w illus. by W.

220 Lodge, Henry Cabot et al. (selected by). *Prize Stories from Colliers.* Collier, N.Y., (1916), cloth, 381 pp., frontis. in color by W.

221 Long, Gabrielle Margaret Vere (Campbell). *Dark Rosaleen,* by Marjorie Bowen (pseud.). Houghton Mifflin, Boston and N.Y., 1933, cloth, 296 pp., d/w illus. by W.

222 Long, John Luther. *War, or What Happens When One Loves One's Enemy.* Bobbs-Merrill, Indianapolis, (1913), cloth, 370 (1) pp., four illus. in color, frontis. and facing pp. 44, 304 and 346, by W.

223 ———. Same, variant binding, boards with only a frontis. in color by W.

224 Long, William J. *America, A History of Our Country.* Ginn, Boston etc., (1923), decor. cloth, pp. 531, xxiii-xlvii, foreword, bibliography, index, maps, illus. including three in color, frontis. and facing pp. 336 and 410, by W.

225 Longfellow, Henry W. *The Children's Longfellow.* Houghton Mifflin, Boston and N.Y., 1908, cloth with illus. in color mounted on front cover, 344 pp., all edges green, illus. incuding one in color, facing p. 136 (also used on cover), by W. (Schoonover)

226 ———. *The Song of Hiawatha.* Houghton Mifflin, Boston and N.Y., 1916, cloth with illus. in color mounted on front cover, 242 pp., numerous illus. including one, the frontis. in color, by W. New Holiday Edition, boxed. (Remington)

227 ———. Same, (1929), a trade edition of no. 226.

228 ———. Same, first British edition, George C. Harrap, London, 1911, with frontis. in color by W. (Remington)

229 ———. *The Courtship of Miles Standish.* Houghton Mifflin, Boston and N.Y., 1920, cloth with illus. in color mounted on front cover, pic. endsheets, 147 (1) pp., twenty-six illus. including ten in color by W. Tercentenary Edition.

230 *McClure's — The Marketplace of the World.* N.Y., boards with illus. mounted on front cover, unpaged (28), frontis. in color by W.

231 McConathy, Osbourne et al., eds. *Music of Many Lands and Peoples*. Silver Burdette, N.Y., Boston etc., 1932, cloth, 268 pp., illus. including one (from the Steinway Collection, no. 97) by W.

232 ———. *Music Highways and Byways*. Silver Burdette, N.Y., Boston etc., (1936), cloth, 252 pp., illus. including one (from the Steinway Collection) by W.

232a McCracken, Harold. *The American Cowboy*. Double-day, Garden City, N.Y., 1973, words "Limited Edition" on copyright page, simulated leather, marbled endsheets, 196 pp., all edges gilt, references, index, numerous illus. including one, p. (123), by W. 300 numbered and signed copies, slipcase. (Borein, Cisneros, Eggenhofer, Johnson, Koerner, Lea, Leigh, Remington, Russell)

232b ———. Same, trade edition with words "First edition after the limited edition of 300 copies" on copyright page, cloth and colored pic. d/w.

233 Mackey, Margaret G. et al. *Your Country's Story: Pioneer, Builders, Leaders*. Ginn, Boston etc., (1961), colored pic. cloth, 560 pp., appendix, index, numerous illus. including five in color, pp. 23, 31, 54, 123 and 175 and one in black and white, p. 242, by W. (Hurd, Lea, Remington)

234 Malory, Sir Thomas. *The Boy's King Arthur*, edited for boys by Sidney Lanier. Scribner's, N.Y., 1917, cloth with illus. in color mounted on front cover, colored pic. endsheets, 320 (1) pp., seventeen illus. in color by W.

235 Marriott, Crittenden. *Sally Castleton, Southerner*. Lippincott, Philadelphia and London, 1913, words "Published January, 1913" on copyright page, cloth, 312 pp., (7) of advs., frontis. in color and five full page plates, facing pp. 103, 138, 204, 226 and 258, by W.

236 Matthews, Brander (chosen by). *Poem of American Patriotism*. Scribner's, N.Y., 1922, words "Published October, 1922" on copyright page, cloth with illus. in color mounted on front cover, colored pic. endsheets, 222 (1) pp., tinted top, seventeen illus. in color, cover, endsheets, title page and fourteen plates, by W.

237 Mellon, Gertrud A. and Wilder, Elizabeth F., eds. *Maine and Its Role in American Art*. Viking, N.Y., (1963), cloth and boards, 178 pp., index, illus. including one, p. 110, by W.

238 Merwin, Samuel. *Silk*. Houghton Mifflin, Boston, 1923, cloth, 266 (1) pp., frontis. in color by W.

239 Miller (Mahony), Bertha E. and Whitney, Elinor (compiled by). *Contemporary Illustrators of Children's Books*. The Bookshop For Boys and Girls, Boston, 1930, pic. cloth, 135 pp., appendix, illus. including two, facing p. 128 and endsheet, by W. and with Dudley Cammett Lunt's "The Brandywine Tradition — Howard Pyle and N. C. Wyeth."

240 Miller, Olive Beaupre, ed. *The Treasure Chest of My Bookhouse*. The Bookhouse for Children, Chicago, (1920), simulated green leather with illus. in color by W. mounted on the front cover, 448 pp., gilt top. Deluxe edition.

241 ———. Same, first trade edition in black cloth with illus. in color by W. mounted on front cover.

242 ———. *My Bookhouse* (volume 9, *The Treasure Chest)*. The Bookhouse for Children, Chicago, (1950), cloth with cover illus. by W.

243 Mulford, Clarence E. *Bar-20*. Outing, N.Y., 1907, pic. cloth, 382 pp., seven illus. including two, facing pp. 106 and 256, by W. (Schoonover)

244 Nevins, Allan and Commager, Henry Steele. *America, The Story of a Free People*. Little, Brown, Boston, 1942, words "First Edition" on copyright page, decor. cloth, 507 pp., preface, index, twenty-six illus. including one, facing p. 110, by W.

245 Nordoff, Charles and Hall, James Monroe. *The Hurricane*. Little, Brown, Boston, 1936, decor. cloth, 257 pp., d/w illus. in color by W.

246 ———. *The "Bounty" Trilogy*. Little, Brown, Boston, 1940, words "Published October, 1940" on copyright page, cloth, map endsheets, 903 pp., twelve plates and d/w, all in color, by W. Wyeth Edition.

247 ———. *Botany Bay*. Little, Brown, Boston, 1941, cloth, 374 pp., d/w illus. in color by W.

248 Packard, Leonard O. et al. *The Nations Today* (A Physical, Industrial and Commercial Geography). Macmillan, N.Y., 1939, pic. cloth, 727 pp., index, numerous illus. including one, p. 58, by W.

249 Page, Thomas Nelson. *Under the Crust*. Scribner's, N.Y., 1907, words "Published November, 1907" on copyright page, decor. cloth, 307 pp., gilt top, eight illus. including one, facing p. 132, by W. (Marchand, Schoonover)

250 ———. *The Land of the Spirit*. Scribner's, N.Y., 1913, words "Published April, 1913" on copyright page, cloth, 257 pp., six illus. including two, facing pp. 84 and 104, by W.

251 *Paintings in the Hotel duPont*. Wilmington, Dela-

ware, n.d., wraps, unpaged, illus. including one, "The Island Funeral," by W. and a biographical sketch of him.

252 Palmer, George Herbert (translated by). *The Odyssey of Homer.* Houghton Mifflin, Boston, 1924, gilt decor. cloth, 314 pp., fifteen mounted color plates by W.

253 ———. Same, autographed edition of 500 copies, signed by Palmer and Wyeth, 1929, cloth with pigskin back, slipcase and with an extra set of the color plates in an accompanying envelope.

254 ———. The Riverside Literature Series reprint, n.d., cloth, 402 pp., two illus., frontis. and facing p. xxxii, by W.

255 Parker, Sir Gilbert. *Northern Lights.* Harper, N.Y. and London, 1909, words "Published September, 1909" on copyright page, pic. cloth, 351 (1) pp., note, sixteen illus. including two, facing pp. 36 and 114, by W. (Crawford, Dunn, Schoonover, Wood)

256 Parkman, Francis. *The Oregon Trail.* Little, Brown, Boston, 1925, cloth and pic. boards, 364 pp., gilt top, publisher's preface, ten mounted plates including five in color, frontis. and facing pp. 14, 108, 226 and 312 plus d/w in color and cover illus. by W. The Wyeth-Remington Edition of 975 numbered copies of which 950 were for sale, slipcase. (Remington)

257 ———. Same, Beacon Hill Bookshelf edition, 1925, in black cloth with illus. mounted on front cover and only the Wyeth illustrations.

258 Parrish, Randall. *Beth Norvell.* McClurg, Chicago, 1907, decor. cloth, 341 pp., frontis. in color by W.

259 Parsons, Geoffrey. *The Stream of History.* Volume III, Scribner's, N.Y., 1929, cloth and boards with morocco title label on spine, 342 pp., illus. including one, frontis. in color, by W. Edition of 530 sets — 500 for sale.

260 ———. Same, first trade edition in blue cloth (simulated leather) in 1929.

261 ———. Same, but volume IV, cloth and boards with morocco title label on spine, 372 pp., index, illustrated including one, p. 251, by W. Edition of 530 sets — 500 for sale.

262 ———. Same, first trade edition in blue cloth (simulated leather) in 1929.

263 Phelps, Elizabeth Stuart. *The Story of Jesus Christ.* Houghton Mifflin, Boston and N.Y., 1926, cloth with illus. in color by W. mounted on the front cover, 413 pp., illustrated.

264 Phillips, Henry Wallace. *Mr. Scraggs.* The Grafton Press, N.Y., (1905), words "Published January, 1906" on copyright page, cloth with illus. mounted on front cover, 188 pp., eight illus. including one, facing p. 150, by W.

265 Pier, Arthur Stanwood. *Boys of St. Timothy's.* Scribner's, N.Y., 1904, words "Published September, 1904" on copyright page, cloth, 284 pp., six illus. including three, frontis. and facing pp. 58 and 214, by W. (Fogarty, Varian)

266 Pitz, Henry C. *A Treasury of American Book Illustration.* Watson-Guptill Publications, N.Y., 1947, decor. cloth, 128 pp., numerous illus. including one, p. 94, by W. (James, Thomason)

267 ———. *Illustrating Children's Books.* Watson-Guptill, N.Y., (1963), cloth, blue endsheets, 207 pp., bibliography, index, numerous illus. including one, p. 71, by W. (Remington, Schoonover)

268 ———. *The Brandywine Tradition.* Houghton Mifflin, Boston, 1969, words "First Printing" on copyright page, cloth, 252 pp., bibliography, preface, index, numerous illus. including two in color, between pp. 126 and 127, by W. and with a chapter on him and two photos of him. (Dunn, Hurd, Schoonover)

269 Porter, Jane. *The Scottish Chiefs.* Scribner's, N.Y., 1921, cloth with illus. in color mounted on front cover, colored pic. endsheets, 503 pp., seventeen illus. in color, cover, endsheets, title page and fourteen plates, by W.

270 Pourade, Richard F. *The Glory Years.* The Union-Tribune Pub. Co., (San Diego, Calif., 1964), cloth, 274 pp., bibliography, index, numerous illus. including one in color, p. 173, by W. (Remington)

271 (Price.) *The Vincent Price Treasury of American Art.* Country Beautiful Corporation, Waukesha, Wisconsin, (1972), cloth, tan endsheets, 320 pp., numerous illus. including two, pp. 200 and 201 (color), by W. (Hurd, Remington, Russell, Schreyvogel)

272 Pyle, Howard. *The Merry Adventures of Robin Hood.* Scribner's, N.Y., 1933, cloth with illus. in color mounted on front cover, 296 pp., "A Recollection" by Wyeth and a frontis. in color (also used on the cover) by him, other illus. by the author. A vol. in "The Howard Pyle Brandywine Edition, 1853–1933" set.

273 ———. *The Howard Pyle Brandywine Edition 1853–1933.* Scribner's, N.Y., n.d., colored pic. wraps, (8) pp., illus. by Pyle, front cover illus. in color by W. (Advertising booklet.)

274 ———. Same, salesman's dummy in cloth with illus. in color mounted on front cover, (24) pp., "A Recollection" by Wyeth, five illus. in color including one by W. (Dunn, Schoonover)

275 Quick, Herbert. *Vandemark's Folly.* Bobbs-Merrill, Indianapolis, 1922, gilt decor. cloth, 420 pp., introduction, eight illus., frontis. and facing pp. 31, 110, 152, 190, 246, 354 and 406, by W.

276 ———. *One Man's Life* (an Autobiography). Bobbs-Merrill, Indianapolis, (1925), cloth, 408 pp., illus. including three, pp. 76, 94 and facing p. 118, by W.

277 Raine, William MacLeod. *Roaring River.* Houghton Mifflin, Boston and N.Y., 1934, cloth, 297 pp., d/w illus. by W.

278 Rawlings, Marjorie Kinnan. *The Yearling.* Scribner's, N.Y., 1938, gilt decor. blue cloth, colored pic. endsheets, 400 pp., fourteen color plates and two line drawings by W. De Luxe Edition of 770 copies of which 750 were for sale, signed by Rawlings and Wyeth and with a facsimile of a letter from Wyeth, in slipcase. Pulitzer Prize Edition.

279 ———. Same, first trade edition with the Wyeth illus. in color but minus the two line drawings.

280 ———. Same, the Palmetto Edition, cloth, 428 pp., d/w in color by W.

281 ———. Same, condensation in *Reader's Digest Condensed Books* (volume 1), 1966, words "First Edition" on copyright page, cloth, 598 pp., *The Yearling* appears pp. 210–346, includes seven illus. in color, pp. (210–11), (225), (248), (261), (289), (299) and (327), by W.

282 Ray, Frederic (selections and commentary by). *O! Say Can You See.* Stackpole Books (A National Historical society book, Harrisburg, 1970), cloth, tan endsheets, 189 pp., numerous illus. including six in color, pp. (19), (25), (43), (69), (75) and (109), by W. plus a photo and a biographical sketch of him. (Dunn, Koerner, Remington, Russell)

283 Reed, Walt. *The Illustrator in America 1900–1960's.* Reinhold, N.Y., (1966), cloth, pic. green endsheets, 271 (1) pp., "Is Illustration Art?" by Albert Dorne, numerous illus. including four, pp. 72 (color) and 73 (three), by W. and with a brief biographical sketch of him. (Blumenschein, Crawford, Dunn, Dunton, Eggenhofer, Fischer, Fogarty, Goodwin, Keller, Koerner, Remington, Russell, Schoonover, Stoops, Von Schmidt)

284 Reynolds, Quentin. *The Fiction Factory* (The Story of 100 Years of Publishing at Street and Smith). Random House, N.Y., (1955), published in a limited edition of 50 copies, slipcase, morocco and pic. cloth, 283 pp., gilt top, index, numerous illus. including one in color, p. 100, by W.

285 ———. Same, words "First Printing" on copyright page, trade edition also issued in 1955, morocco and cloth.

286 Richmond, Leonard. *The Technique of the Poster.* Sir Isaac Pitman, London, 1933, cloth, 216 pp., index, illus. including one in color, plate xvii, by W.

287 Roberts, Kenneth. *Arundel.* Doubleday, Doran, Garden City, N.Y., 1930, words "First Edition" on copyright page, decor. cloth, decor. map endsheets, 618 pp., orange top, d/w illus. by W.

288 ———. *The Lively Lady.* Doubleday, Doran, Garden City, N.Y., 1931, words "First Edition" on copyright page, cloth, pic. endsheets, 374 pp., d/w illus. by W.

289 ———. *Rabble in Arms.* Doubleday, Page, Garden City, N.Y., 1933, words "First Edition" on copyright page, decor. cloth, map endsheets, 870 (2) pp., (2) of advs., "Kenneth Roberts" by Russell Doubleday inside back endsheet, d/w illus. by W.

290 ———. *Trending Into Maine.* Little, Brown, Boston, 1938, two-tone cloth, 394 pp., eighteen illus. including endsheets and fourteen plates in color by W. Arundel Edition of 1075 copies signed by Roberts and Wyeth, in slipcase with an extra set of the plates in four colors by the Tudor Press in an envelope.

291 ———. Same, first trade edition with d/w, also issued in 1938. Reissued in a revised edition by Doubleday, Doran in 1944, with fourteen illus. in color, by W.

292 Rollins, Philip Ashton. *The Cowboy.* Scribner's, N.Y., 1927, cloth, 353 pp., two illus., facing pp. 218 and 254, by W. (Russell)

293 ———. Same, revised and enlarged edition, 1936, pic. endsheets, 402 pp., (new) preface, appendix, index, map, illus. including one, facing p. 267, by W. (James)

294 ———. *Jinglebob.* Scribner's, N.Y., 1930, cloth with illus. in color mounted on front cover, pic. endsheets (different), 263 pp., seven illus., cover, endsheets (two), and in color facing pp. 32, 92, 162 and 218, by W.

295 Rossi, Paul A. and Hunt, David C. *The Art of the Old West* (from the collection of the Gilcrease Institute).

(Knopf, N.Y., but printed in Italy, 1971), words "First Edition" on copyright page, pic. cloth, pic. brown endsheets, 335 (1) pp., preface, listing of artists and works, bibliography, numerous illus. including one, "The James Gang," p. (258), by W. (Blumenschein, Borein, James, Leigh, Miller, Remington, Russell, Schreyvogel)

296 Russell, W. Clark. *The Wreck of the Grosvenor.* Grosset & Dunlap, N.Y., n.d., cloth, frontis. in color by W.

297 Sabatini, Rafael. *Captain Blood.* Houghton Mifflin, Boston, 1922, cloth, 355 pp., frontis. in color by W.

298 ———. Same, Riverside Bookshelf issue, 1927, cloth, 437 pp., illus. in color by Clyde O. De Land but end-paper illus. in color by W.

299 ———. *The King's Minion.* Houghton Mifflin, Boston and N.Y., 1930, cloth, 445 pp., d/w illus. by W.

300 ———. *Captain Blood Returns.* Houghton Mifflin, Boston and N.Y., 1931, cloth, 296 pp., d/w illus. by W.

301 ———. *The Black Swan.* Houghton Mifflin, Boston, 1932, cloth, 311 pp., d/w illus. by W.

302 ———. *The Stalking Horse.* Houghton Mifflin, Boston and N.Y., 1933, cloth, 304 pp., d/w illus. by W.

303 ———. *Venetian Masque.* Houghton Mifflin, Boston and N.Y., 1934, cloth, pic. endsheets, 323 pp., d/w illus. by W.

304 ———. *The Fortunes of Captain Blood.* Houghton Mifflin, Boston and N.Y., 1936, cloth, 240 pp., d/w illus. by W.

305 Seymour, Peter, ed. *The West That Was.* Hallmark Cards, Kansas City, Mo., (1973), fabricoid, pic. endsheets, 76 (1) pp., introduction, numerous illus. including one in color, p. 64, by W., boxed. (Remington, Russell)

306 Shuman, Eleanore Nolan. *The Trenton Story.* Mac-Crellish & Quigley, Trenton, N.J., (1958), cloth, 385 pp., appendix, numerous illus. including one, p. 72, by W.

307 *The Silver Burdett Story*, n.p., n.d., pic. cloth, illus. including one, p. 6, by W.

308 *The Solitude Series.* The Outing Publishing Co., N.Y., 1907, a portfolio of five prints in color, 16⅝" x 11½" mounted on boards 20" x 15", boxed.

309 Southhard, Frank R. (selected by). *Pictures by Prominent Artists.* Commercial Art Courses of the Extension Division, United Y.M.C.A. Schools, n.p., 1921, folio, seventy plates in black and white, 12¾" x 9¾", with two, no. 50 and no. 51, by W.

310 *Souvenir Guide to Missouri's Capitol.* (Jefferson City), n.d., colored pic. wraps, unpaged, numerous illus. including two by W.

311 Spearman, Frank H. *Whispering Smith.* Scribner's, N.Y., 1906, words "Published September, 1906" on copyright page, pic. cloth, 421 pp., four illus. in color, frontis. and facing pp. 26, 132 and 301, by W.

312 ———. *Nan of Music Mountain.* Scribner's, N.Y., 1916, words "Published April, 1916" on copyright page, cloth, 430 pp., (2) of advs., four illus in color, frontis. and facing pp. 134, 202 and 414, by W.

313 Steadman, William E. et al. *The West and Walter Bimson.* The University of Arizona Museum of Art, Tucson, (1971), decor. cloth, pic. endsheets, 223 (2) pp., "Foreword" by President Richard A. Harvill, introduction, numerous illus. including two in color, pp. 157 and 158, by W. with a brief biographical sketch of him. (Beeler, Leigh, Remington, Russell, Schoonover)

314 Stephenson, Nathaniel Wright and Tucker, Martha. *A School History of the United States.* Ginn, Boston etc., (1924), decor. cloth, 548, xil pp., numerous illus. including one, frontis. in color, by W.

315 Stevenson, Robert Louis. *Treasure Island.* Scribner's, N.Y., 1911, cloth with illus. in color on front cover, colored pic. endsheets, 273 pp., gilt top, seventeen plates by W. (Illustrated Classic.)

316 ———. *Inovla Thesavraria* (in Latin). Mount Hope Classics, volume V, E. Parmalee Prentice, N.Y., (1922), buckram, 361 pp., fourteen illus. in color by W.

317 ———. *Kidnapped.* Scribner's, N.Y., 1913, cloth with illus. in color on front cover, colored pic. endsheets, 289 pp., seventeen illus. in color, cover, endsheets, title page and fourteen plates, by W. (Illustrated Classic.)

318 ———. Same, Limited Edition Club, N.Y., 1938, cloth with illus. in color mounted on front cover, 289 pp., eleven illus. in color by W.

319 ———. *The Black Arrow.* Scribner's, N.Y., 1916, words "Published October, 1916" on copyright page, cloth with illus. in color mounted on front cover, colored pic. endsheets, 328 pp., gilt top, seventeen illus. in color, cover, endsheets, title page and fourteen plates, by W. (Illustrated Classic.)

AND HOW ARE YE, YE OULD DARLINT? by Wyeth from *The Riverman*

320 ———. Same, first Canadian printing with same Wyeth illus., issued in 1916 by the Copp Clark Co., Toronto.

321 ———. *David Balfour*. Scribner's, N.Y., 1924, cloth with illus. in color mounted on front cover, colored pic. endsheets, 356 pp., twelve illus. in color, cover, endsheets, title page and nine plates, by W. (Illustrated Classic.)

322 Stewart, Elinore Pruitt. *The Letters of a Woman Homesteader*. Houghton Mifflin, Boston, 1914, decor. cloth, 281 (1) pp., six illus. by W.

323 Swan, Oliver G., ed. *Deep Water Days*. Macrae-Smith, Philadelphia, (1929), words "First Edition" on copyright page, decor. cloth, pic. endsheets, 512 pp., tinted top, numerous illus. (twelve in color), including one in color, facing p. 160, by W. (Schoonover)

324 ———. *Anchors Aweigh!* Grosset & Dunlap, N.Y., (1929), pic. cloth, 235 pp., numerous illus. including one, the frontis., by W.

325 *Taming a Frontier*. Reprinted from *Transmission* (Magazine) 17:1, Northern Natural Gas Co., 1968, folder with nine illus. including one by W. (Remington, Russell, Young)

326 Thoreau, Henry David. *Men of Concord*. Houghton Mifflin, 1936, decor. cloth, colored pic. endsheets, 255 pp., edited by Francis H. Allen, thirty-three illus. including eleven in color by W.

327 Tobey, Walter L. *The Graphic Arts and Crafts Year Book*. Volume VI, Graphic Arts Press, Hamilton, Ohio, (1913), leather and cloth, numerous illus. including one, p. 100, by W.

328 Towne, Charles H., ed. *For France*. Doubleday, Page, Garden City, N.Y., 1917, cloth with illus. in color mounted on front cover, 412 pp., editor's note, "Foreword" by Theodore Roosevelt, front cover by W. (Contributions by a number of writers and artists to raise money for war relief.)

329 Turkington, Grace Alice. *My Country*. Ginn, Boston, (1918), cloth, 394 pp., map, illus. including one, the frontis. in color, by W. Reprinted in 1923, and 1932.

330 Tyron, Rolla M. and Lingley, Charles R. *The American People and Nation*. Ginn, Boston etc., (1927), pic. cloth, 654, xxxvii pp., numerous illus. including one in color, facing p. 2, by W.

331 ——— et al. *The American Nation, Yesterday and Today*. Ginn, Boston etc., (1930), pic. cloth, 625, xl

pp., appendix, index, numerous illus. including one in color by W.

332 Van Duyn Southworth, Gertrude and John. *The Story of Our America*. Iroquois Publishing Co., Syracuse, N.Y., (1955), pic. cloth, 868 pp., index, numerous illus. including six in color, pp. 2, 6, 100, 175, 264 and 324, by W.

333 Van Dyke, Henry. *The Lost Boy*. Harper, N.Y., 1914, code letters "G - O" on copyright page, decor. cloth, 43 (1) pp., three color plates, frontis. and facing pp. 4 and 24, by W.

334 ———. Same, smaller format in black morocco or green cloth, 69 pp., gilt top, also issued in 1914 and with code letters "G-O" on the copyright page.

335 ———. Same, second edition, 1914, code letter "L-O" on copyright page, decor. cloth, 68 (1) pp., three illus., frontis. and pp. 4 and 38, by W.

336 ———. *Little Rivers*. Scribner's, N.Y., 1920, autograph edition of 504 copies, The Works of Henry Van Dyke, volume I, Avalon Edition, morocco and cloth or cloth and boards, 290 pp., gilt top, frontis. by W. and signed by him in pencil.

337 ———. Same, first trade edition in blue cloth, 1920.

338 ———. *Fisherman's Luck*. Scribner's, N.Y., 1920, autograph edition of 504 copies, The Works of Henry Van Dyke, volume II, Avalon Edition, morocco and cloth or cloth and boards, 256 pp., gilt top, frontis. by W., signed by him in pencil.

339 ———. Same, first trade edition in blue cloth, 1920.

340 ———. *Even Unto Bethlehem*. Scribner's, N.Y., 1928, cloth, 103 pp., frontis. in color by W.

341 Verne, Jules. *The Mysterious Island*. Scribner's, N.Y., 1918, cloth with illus. in color mounted on front cover, colored pic. endsheets, 493 pp., sixty-eight illus. including seventeen in color by W. (Illustrated Classic.)

342 ———. Same, Grosset & Dunlap reprint, n.d., cloth, 500 pp., d/w in color by W.

343 ———. *Michael Strogoff*. Scribner's, N.Y., 1925, cloth with illus. in color mounted on front cover, colored pic. endsheets, 397 pp., twelve illus. in color, cover, endsheets, title page and nine plates, by W.

344 Vollintine, Grace. *The American People and Their Old World Ancestors*. Ginn, Boston etc., (1930), code number "230.1" on copyright page, pic. cloth, 576 pp., preface, book list, index, numerous illus. including two, facing pp. 4 and 240, by W. (Hurd)

345 Ward, Christopher L. *Dutch and Swedes on the Dela-ware.* University of Pennsylvania Press, Phialdelphia, 1930, cloth, map endsheets, 393 pp., index, frontis. in color by W.

346 ———. *Delaware Tercentenary Almanack and His-torical Repository, 1938.* (The Press of Kells, Newark, Dela., 1937), words "First Edition" on title page, cloth, (53) pp., numerous drawings by Arthurs, Schoonover, Andrew Wyeth, N. C. Wyeth, et al.

347 *Washington Cathedral.* National Cathedral Associa-tion, Washington, D.C., (1939), pic. wraps, 30 pp., illus. including two, pp. 5 and 14, by W.

548 Watson, Ernest W. *Forty Illustrators and How They Work.* Watson-Guptill Publications, N.Y., 1946, words "First Edition" on copyright page, cloth with paper title label, 318 pp., author's preface, numerous illus. including eight, pp. 311 (color), 313, 315 (two in color), 316 (three) and 317, by W. and two photos of him.

349 Wells, Henry Deskins et al. *A History of Collings-worth County and Other Stories.* Leader Publishing Co., Wellington, Texas, 1925, pic. wraps, 234 pp., foreword, frontis. by W. and other illus. from photos.

350 Wertenbacker, Thomas Jefferson and Smith, Donald E. *The United States of America.* Scribner's, N.Y., (1931), with code letter "A" on copyright page, cloth, 712 pp., index, maps, illus. including three in color, facing p. 114, 134 and 256, by W.

351 White, Stewart, Edward. *Arizona Nights.* McClure, N.Y., 1907, words "Published, October, 1907" on copyright page, cloth with illus. in color mounted on front cover, 351 pp., (4) of advs., seven illus. in color, frontis. and facing pp. 50, 54, 70, 84, 132 and 140, by W.

352 ———. Same, Doubleday, Page, Garden City, N.Y., 1916, (The Works of Stewart Edward White), pic. cloth, 351 pp., frontis. by W.

353 ———. Same, first Canadian edition.

354 ———. *Camp and Trail.* Outing, N.Y., 1907, pic. cloth, 236 pp., (1) of advs., preface, index, thirteen illus. including one, facing p. 16, by W. (Lungren)

355 ———. *The Riverman.* McClure, N.Y., 1908, cloth with illus. in color mounted on front cover, 368 pp., (4) of advs., fifteen illus. including thirteen, cover and twelve plates, by W.

356 ———. *The Westerners.* Doubleday, Page, Garden City, N.Y., 1913, (The Works of Stewart Edward White), pic. cloth, 344 pp., frontis. by W.

357 ———. *The Claim Jumpers.* Doubleday, Page, Gar-den City, N.Y., 1916, (The Works of Stewart Edward White), pic. cloth, 284 pp., frontis. by W.

358 Wiggin, Kate Douglas. *Susanna and Sue.* Houghton Mifflin, Boston and N.Y., 1909, words "Published October, 1909" on copyright page, decor. cloth with illus. in color mounted on front cover, decor. end-sheets, 225 pp., (4) of advs., seventeen illus. including thirteen drawings by W.

359 Wilder, Howard B. et al. *This is America's Story.* Houghton Mifflin, Boston, (1948), pic. cloth, 728 pp., appendix, index, numerous illus. including one, p. (322), by W. (Hurd, Lea, Remington)

360 Williams, Ben Ames. *All the Brothers Were Valiant.* Macmillan, 1919, cloth, 204 pp., d/w illus. by W.

361 ———. *Amateurs at War.* Houghton Mifflin, Boston, 1943, cloth, 498 pp., d/w in color by W.

362 Willis, Elizabeth Powers. *Lesby.* Scribner's, N.Y., 1931, code letter "A" on copyright page, red boards with cloth title label and spine gilt stamped, 177 (1) pp., red top, frontis. by W.

363 Wilson, Philip, ed., assisted by Alison Brand. *Art at Auction* (The Year· at Sotheby's and Parke-Bernet, 1966–67). American Heritage, N.Y., (1967), cloth, blue endsheets, 432 pp., indices, numerous illus. in-cluding one, p. (102), by W.

364 Wood, William and Gabriel, Ralph Henry. *In Defense of Liberty.* Yale, New Haven, 1928, morocco and boards, colored pic. endsheets, 370 pp., gilt top, fore-word, notes on pictures, index, numerous illus. in-cluding two, pp. 29 and 167, by W. Vol. 7, The Lib-erty Bell (first) Edition of "The Pageant of America," 1500 numbered copies. (Dunn, Keller, Thomason)

365 Woodward, W. E. *The Way Our People Lived* (An Intimate American History). Dutton, N.Y., 1944, cloth, tinted endsheets, 402 pp. plus an unpaged pic-torial supplement, bibliography, forty-two illus. in-cluding one by W. in the Supplement of Illustrations, following the text.

366 Wyeth, N. C. *The Wyeths* (The Intimate Correspond-ence of N.C. Wyeth 1901–1945). Gambit, Boston, 1971, words "First Printing" on copyright page, two-tone cloth, colored pic. endsheets, 858 pp., yellow top, edited and "The Setting" (Chapter I) by Betsy James Wyeth, genealogical chart, index, numerous illus. by and of W.

Written by the Artist

367 Abbott, Charles D. *Howard Pyle: a Chronicle.* Harper, N.Y. and London, 1925, words "First Edition" on copyright page, cloth and boards with paper title labels, 249 pp., tinted top, "Introduction" by N. C. Wyeth, illus.

368 (Arthurs.) *The American Historical Scene as Depicted by Stanley Arthurs and Interpreted by Fifty Authors.* First trade edition of no. 82, issued by Carlton House, N.Y., 1937, cloth, 153 pp., illus. by Arthurs but without the portrait in color by W. and the tribute by Brinton. It does include 'Quiet Custom House" written by W.

369 *Exhibition of Reproduction of Paintings by Old Masters and Modern American Painters and Illustrators.* N.p., n.d., wraps, 20 pp., "Introduction" by Wyeth, "Preface" by Edward W. Bok and J. H. Chapin, lists 171 works of art including seven by W.

370 Morse, Willard S. and Brinckle, Gertrude. *Howard Pyle: A Record of His Illustrations and Writings.* Privately printed, Wilmington, Dela., 1921, full leather, "Foreword" by N. C. Wyeth. Special Limited Edition of 12 copies signed by the bibliographers and by W.

371 ————. Same, first trade edition of 500 copies.

372 Wyeth, N.C., ed. *Marauders of the Sea.* Putnam's, N.Y., (1935), pic. cloth and endsheets, 319 pp. tinted top, "Introduction" (and edited) by W., illustrated. (Hurd)

373 ————, ed. *Great Stories of the Sea and Ships.* Mc-Kay, Philadelphia, (1940), pic. cloth and endsheets, 411 pp., green top, "Introduction" (and edited) by W., illustrated. (Hurd)

The Artist and His Art

374 Beitz, Les. "N. C. Wyeth, Painter of Western Men in Action," an illus. article in *True West* 15:2, November–December 1967, with five illus. by W. and two photos of him.

375 Bolton, Theodore. *American Book Illustrators: Bibliographic Check Lists of 123 Artists.* Bowker, N.Y., 1938, cloth, 290 pp., introduction, index, lists 46 items illus. by W.

376 Burke, W. J. and Howe, Will D. *American Authors and Books, 1640–1940.* Gramercy Pub. Co., N.Y., 1943, cloth, 858 pp., brief biographical sketch of W., p. 850.

377 Dykes, Jeff C. *High Spots of Western Illustrating.* Kansas City Posse, The Westerners, 1963, cloth, 30 pp., two illus., H. S. 46 is no. 256 above and H. S. 86 is no. 27 above. Limited to 250 numbered and signed copies. An edition of 500 copies in wraps was distributed to members.

378 Elzea, Rowland (acting director). *Howard Pyle, Diversity in Depth.* Delaware Art Museum, March 5–April 15, 1973, pic. wraps, 81 pp., numerous illus. by Pyle; includes "Notes from Howard Pyle's Monday Night Lectures," June–November 1904 as recorded by Ethel Pennewill Brown and Olive Rush with comments on Wyeth's "Indian and Moon Rising Out of Sea" (p. 19), "Indians in Canoes" (p. 21), "Pony Race and Indians" (p. 22) and "Indian and Panther" (p. 23).

379 Fielding, Mantle. *Dictionary of American Painters, Sculptors and Engravers.* N.Y., 1926, cloth, 433 pp., preface, bibliography, brief biographical sketch of W., p. 420.

380 ————. Same, but with addendum by James F. Carr and issued by him, N.Y., 1965, cloth, 529 pp., but no new material on W.

381 Fowler, Robert H., ed. *American History Illustrated.* May, 1966, brief biographical sketch of W., p. 3 and "The Call of the Wild" by him in color on front cover.

382 Hoopes, Isabel. "N. C. Wyeth," an article in *All-Arts Magazine* 1:4, September 1925, with three illus. by W.

383 Horgan, Paul. *Peter Hurd: A Portrait Sketch from Life.* University of Texas Press, Austin, 1965, cloth, 68 pp., illus. Much on W. who was Hurd's teacher and father-in-law.

384 Howard, Frances R., ed. *American Art Annual,* vol. 18. The American Federation of Arts, Washington, D.C., 1921, cloth, 680 pp., brief biographical sketch of W., p. 617. Repeated in other volumes of this annual.

385 *Illustrated Catalogue of the Post Exposition Exhibition in the Department of Fine Arts, Panama-Pacific International Exposition.* San Francisco Art Assn., January 1 to May 1, 1916, pic. wraps, 112 pp.; lists five works exhibited by W.

386 Kamp, Anton. "N. C. Wyeth Painter and Illustrator," an article in *The Artgum* 4:4, April 1926, with eleven illus. by W. and with two photos of him.

387 Logsdon, Gene. *Wyeth People* (A Portrait of Andrew Wyeth as he is seen by his Friends and Neighbors).

Doubleday, Garden City, N.Y., 1971, cloth, 159 pp., index, numerous references to W.

388 Lunt, Dudley. *N. C. Wyeth, Original Illustrations for Robinson Crusoe.* Wilmington Institute Free Library, Wilmington, Dela., (1965), folder, a page on W. and reprint of the "Illustrator's Preface" to *Robinson Crusoe* (no. 145 above) by W.

389 Meryman, Richard. "The Wyeths' Kind of Christmas Magic," an article in *Life*, Special Double Issue, Dec. 17, 1971, with three illus. in color by W.

390 Miller (Mahoney), Bertha E. et al. *Illustrators of Children's Books, 1744–1945.* The Horn Book, Boston, 1947, cloth and pic. boards, 527 pp., gilt top, preface, introduction, sources, indices, illus. Wyeth in text; list of 25 books he illustrated.

391 Moore, Anne Carroll. *The Three Owls: A Book About Children's Books.* Macmillan, N.Y., 1925, words "Published November, 1925" on copyright page, cloth, 376 pp., foreword, appendix, numerous illus.; discussion of Wyeth's illus. pp. 235, 236, 322, 323 and 324. (Moon)

392 *Official Catalogue of the Department of Fine Arts, Panama-Pacific International Exposition.* The Wahlgreen Co., San Francisco, 1915, wraps, 256 pp., W. wins the Gold Medal and lists six works by him.

393 "Our Cover," a brief statement, p. 3, *American History Illustrated* 1:9, January 1967, concerning "Sherman," the front cover illus. in color by W.

394 "Pa Wyeth and His Clan," an article in *Newsweek*, Dec. 18, 1939, illus. with photos of the family and a portrait of W. by daughter Henriette.

395 Pitz, Henry G. "N. C. Wyeth," a long article in *American Heritage*, October, 1965, family photos and numerous illus., many in color, including the front cover, by W.

396 *Report of the Department of Fine Arts.* Panama-Pacific International Exposition, San Francisco, 1915, wraps, 24 pp., the Gold Medal presented to W., p. 16.

397 Richardson, Dr. Edgar P. *Andrew Wyeth.* Pennsylvania Academy of Fine Arts, Philadelphia, 1966, colored pic. wraps, 111 pp., "Foreword" by Director Joseph T. Frazer, Jr., index, numerous illus. by Andrew Wyeth; much on N. C. Wyeth as his son's teacher in "The Preparation," pp. 10–11.

398 Smoth, Helen Huntington. "Long Ropes and Running Irons," an article in *True West*, January–February,

399 "The Stouthearted Heroes of a Beloved Painter" (Wyeth), a feature in *Life* (Magazine) 43:24, December 9, 1957, with nineteen in color by W. and a portrait of him by his daughter Henriette.

400 Watson, Ernest W. "N. C. Wyeth: Giant On A Hilltop," an article in *American Artist* 9:1, January 1945, with fifteen (three in color) illus. by W.

401 Wyeth, N. C. "A Day With the Round-Up," an article in *Scribner's Magazine* 39:3, March 1906, with seven (four in color) illus. by W.

402 ———. "A Sheep-Herder of the South-West," an article in *Scribner's Magazine* 45:1, January 1909, with four illus. by W.

403 ———. "The Illustrator and His Development," an article in *The American Art Student* 1:3 and 4, November–December 1916, with eight illus. by W.

404 ———. "For Better Illustration," an article in *Scribner's Magazine* 66:5, November 1919, with three illus. by W.

405 ———. "Howard Pyle as I Knew Him," an illus. tribute to his teacher in *The Mentor*, June 1927.

406 "N. C. Wyeth," in the Art Section, *Life* (Magazine) 20:24, June 17, 1946, with eight illus. in color by W.

407 "N. C. Wyeth — A Veteran Illustrator: In Memoriam," *Art News* 44:19, January 15–31, 1946, with two illus. by W. and a photo of him.

408 *Wyeth Family Show.* Lubbock Junior Welfare League at The Museum, Lubbock, Texas, April 15–May 13, 1951, folder, biographical sketch of W. and lists four works exhibited by him.

409 "Wyeths" by Wyeths, an article in *Town & Country* 100:4290, November 1946, with two illus. by W. and with a portrait of him by daughter and a drawing of him by son Andrew.

410 Young, Mahonri Sharp (director). *Exhibition of Paintings by Peter Hurd and Henriette Wyeth.* The Columbus Gallery of Fine Arts, (Columbus, Ohio, January 12–25, 1967), wraps, (23) pp., illus.; the "Introduction" by Mr. Young comments briefly on N. C. Wyeth (father of Henriette, Mrs. Peter Hurd, and father-in-law of Hurd), the teacher.

411 Young, William. *A Dictionary of American Artists, Sculptors and Engravers.* William Young and Co., n.p., (1968), decor. cloth, 515 pp.; a brief biography of W. and a list of the awards he earned.

SNAKE DANCER by Young from *The West, catalogue no. 25*

MAHONRI MACKINTOSH YOUNG
1877–1957

Catalogues of Art Exhibitions and Galleries

ADDISON GALLERY OF AMERICAN ART
(PHILLIPS ACADEMY), ANDOVER, MASSACHUSETTS

1 *Mahonri M. Young, Retrospective Exhibition*, 1940, wraps, 57 pp., "The Art of Mahonri" by Frank Jewett Mather, Jr., "Notes at the Beginning" by Young, self-portrait as the frontis. and forty-four (one in color) other illus by Y.

2 *The American Line: 100 Years of American Drawing*, (1959), oblong cloth, index, 100 drawings including one, no. 77, by Y. (Leigh)

ASSOCIATION OF AMERICAN ETCHERS, NEW YORK

3 *Yearbook American Etching, Annual Exhibition 1914*, (printed by John Lane Co., N.Y.), boards, unpaged, numerous illus. including three, "Tewa," "Fort Washington Point," and "Tewa," by Y.

BILTMORE GALLERIES, LOS ANGELES

3a *Catalog*, May 1969, colored pic. wraps, 54 pp., numerous illus. including two, p. 52, by Y. (Borein, Dixon, Dunton, Johnson, Koerner, Leigh, Miller, Remington)

THE BROOKLYN MUSEUM

4 *Catalogue of the Water Color Paintings, Pastels and Drawings in the Permanent Collections*, 1932, decor. wraps, 205 pp., index, numerous illus. including one, p. 149, by Y.

COLONIAL ART COMPANY, OKLAHOMA CITY
(SENATE ROOM, LINCOLN PLAZA INN)

4a *Western and Traditional American Paintings of the 19th and Early 20th Centuries* (auction catalog), June 10, 1973, pic. wraps, unpaged, 76 numbered illus. including one, no. 51, by Y. (Borein, Deming, Dixon, Eggenhofer, Elwell, Goodwin, Johnson, Koerner, Russell, Schoonover, Wyeth)

CORCORAN GALLERY OF ART, WASHINGTON, D.C.

5 *Commemorative Exhibition by Members of the National Academy of Design, 1825–1925*, October 17th to November 15th, 1915, decor. wraps, 160 pp., (20) of advs., list of works, numerous illus. including one, "The Rigger," p. 92, by Y. (Blumenschein)

THE GORHAM COMPANY NEW YORK

6 *Exhibition and Sales Catalogue, Famous Small Bronzes*, 1928, wraps, unpaged, illus. incuding one, "Elephant Bookends," by Y.

GRAND CENTRAL ART GALLERIES, NEW YORK

7 *Yearbook, 1936*, wraps with illus. in color mounted on the front cover, blue endsheets, 64 pp., "Memorial Meeting for Walter Clark" (founder) by Herbert Adams, numerous illus including one, p. 16, by Y. (Johnson)

B. F. LARSEN GALLERY, HARRIS FINE ARTS CENTER
BRIGHAM YOUNG UNIVERSITY, PROVO, UTAH

8 *An Exhibition of Sculpture, Paintings and Drawings of Mahonri M. Young* (from the Brigham Young University Art Collection), January 13 through February 3, 1969, pic. wraps, 12 pp., sixteen illus. by Y.— text by his son. (Also exhibited at M. Knoedler & Co., N.Y., March 11 through April 12, 1969.)

E. WALTER LATENDORF, NEW YORK
MANNADOS BOOKSHOP

9 *Young Spanish Officer* (by Remington), (1952), folder, illus. including one by Y. (Lea, Remington, Schreyvogel)

10 *On Neenah* (by Russell), on front cover, (April 1953), four page folder of bronzes for sale including photos of four by Y. (Russell)

LOS ANGELES MUSEUM

11 *Catalogue of Competition and Exhibition of Art, Xth Olympiad,* 1932, wraps, unpaged, illus. including one, photo of a bronze, "The Winner," by Y.

METROPOLITAN MUSEUM OF ART, NEW YORK

12 *The 75th Anniversary Exhibition of Painting and Sculpture by 75 Artists Associated with Art Students League of New York,* (March) 1951, wraps, tan endsheets, 75 numbered full-page plates with facing text including one, photo of a bronze, "The Knockdown," no. 38, by Y. (Remington)

13 *American Sculpture* (A Catalogue of the Collection of the Metropolaitan Museum of Art). Distributed by New York Graphic Society, Greenwich, Conn., (1965), words "First printing, April 1965, 3500 copies" on page following the text, cloth, tinted endsheets, 192 pp., text by Albert Ten Eyck Gardner (associate curator), introduction, index, numerous illus. including one, "Man with a Pick," p. 132, by Y. and a brief biography of him. (Remington)

READ MULLAN GALLERY OF WESTERN ART
PHOENIX, ARIZONA

14 *Catalog, Read Mullan Gallery of Western Art,* 1964, pic. wraps, unpaged, (12), (Foreword) by Read Mullan, numerous illus. including one, "Snake Dance," by Y. (Johnson, Leigh, Remington)

MUSEUM OF FINE ARTS, BOSTON

15 *Sport in American Art,* October 10 through December 10, 1944, wraps, 40 pp., "Pursuit of Pleasure" by Director G. H. Edgell, sixteen illus. including one, "Harness Races, Danbury Fair, Connecticut," p. 39, by Y.

15a *Sport in Art,* November 15–December 1955, wraps, unpaged, numerous illus. including one, "Beating Him to the Punch," by Y. Note: This exhibition was a joint presentation of The American Federation of Arts and *Sports Illustrated* and was shown in Washington, D.C., Louisville, Dallas, Denver, Los Angeles, San Francisco and Australia during 1956. (Hurd)

THE NATIONAL ART MUSEUM OF SPORT
NEW YORK (MADISON SQUARE GARDEN CENTER)

16 *The Artist and the Sportsman,* April 18–June 16, 1968, Renaissance Editions, N.Y., (1968), cloth, 95 pp., "Preface" by Winslow Ames, "From the Perspective of Sport" by Allison Danzig, "Introduction" by August Heckscher, notes on the artists, numerous illus. including a photo of a bronze, "Right to the Jaw," p. 81, by Y. (Remington)

SALT LAKE ART CENTER

17 *100 Years of Utah Painting,* October 22nd to November 23rd, 1965, cloth with an illus. in color mounted on the front cover, black endsheets, 62 pp., narrative and documentation by James L. Haseltine, biographies, bibliography, introduction, numerous illus. including three, p. 22 (two) and 61, by Y.

THE SCULPTORS' GALLERY, NEW YORK

18 *Sculpture, Drawings and Paintings by Mahonri Young,* 1918, text by Guy Pene DuBois, illus. by Y.

WOOLAROC MUSEUM (FRANK PHILLIPS FOUNDATION), BARTLESVILLE, OKLAHOMA

19 *Woolaroc Museum,* (1965), decor. boards, 64 pp., text by Ke Mo Ha (Patrick Patterson, Director), "Welcome to Woolaroc" by Paul Endacott et al., numerous illus. including a photo of a bronze, "Pioneer Woman," by Y. (Johnson, Leigh, Mora, Remington, Russell)

Illustrated by the Artist

20 Baur, John I. H. *Revolution and Tradition in Modern American Art.* Harvard, Cambridge, Mass., 1951, cloth, 170 pp., preface, notes, index, numerous illus. including one, a photo of the bronze "The Organ Grinder," between pp. 100 and 101, by Y. (Hurd)

21 ———. Same, reissued as a Praeger Paperback in 1967 with an added "Introduction to the Paperback Edition" by the author.

22 Brooks, Emerson M. *The Growth of a Nation.* Dutton, N.Y., 1956, words 'First Edition" on copyright page, decor. cloth, map endsheets, 320 pp., "Introduction" by Henry Bamford Parkes, author's foreword, bibliography, index, maps, numerous illus. including one, photo of the "Seagull Monument," p. 130, by Y. (Russell, Schreyvogel)

23 Brumme, C. Ludwig, ed. *Contemporary American Sculpture.* Crown, N.Y., (1948), decor. cloth, 156 pp., "Introduction" by William Zorach, preface and note on selection, biographical notes, 130 plates including one, plate 128, by Y.

24 Cahill, Holger and Barr, Alfred H., Jr., eds. *Art in America in Modern Times.* Reynal & Hitchcock, N.Y., (1934), cloth, 100 pp., (8) color plates, "Foreword" by F. A. Whiting (President, The American Federation of Arts), bibliography, numerous illus. including

one, a photo of the bronze "Chiseler," p. 59, by Y. (Remington)

25 Cox, William D., ed. *Boxing in Art and Literature.* Reynal Hitchcock, N.Y., 1955, cloth, 227 (2) pp., numerous illus. including three, pp. 193 (two) and 204, by Y.

26 Craven, Thomas, ed. *Treasury of American Prints.* Simon and Shuster, N.Y., 1939, portfolio, 8 pp. but 100 numbered prints including two, plates 98 and 99, by Y.

27 Cutright, Prudence et al. *Living Together in the Americas.* Macmillan, N.Y., (1953), pic. cloth, tinted endsheets, 502 pp., preface, index, maps, numerous illus. including one, p. 322, by Y.

28 Driggs, Howard R. *Mormon Trail.* American Pioneer Trails Assn., New York, n.d. (1947?), pic. cloth, 95 pp., "Foreword" by Horace M. Albright, maps, illus. including "This is the Place" by Y. outlined in gilt on the front cover.

29 ———. Same, but issued in wraps with an illus. in color on the front cover and a photo of "This is the Place" Monument on the back cover by Y.

30 *Encyclopaedia Britannica.* Wm. Benton, Publisher, Chicago. A biographical sketch of Y. appears in a number of editions — in the Fourteenth Edition the sketch appears in vol. 23, p. 904. In vol. 20 of the Fourteenth Edition (and perhaps others), photos of "Two Bantams" and a panel from the "Seagull Monument" appear facing p. 227 and Y. contributed to the long article on "Sculpture Technique."

31 Gallatin, Albert Eugene. *Art and the Great War.* Dutton, N.Y., 1919, cloth and boards, grey endsheets, 228 pp. plus 100 plates, bibliography, "One of the 'Buffaloes,'" a bronze by Y. (Dunn)

32 Gridley, Marion. *America's Indian Statues.* The Amerindian, Chicago, (1966), pic. wraps, 104 pp., illus. including one, photo of the bronze "Chief Washakie," p. 81, by Y.

33 Hayden, Senator Carl et al. *Acceptance of the Statue of Brigham Young* (presented by the State of Utah). G.P.O., Washington, D.C., 1950, cloth, pic. endsheets, 73 pp., five photos of the statue of Brigham Young placed in Statuary Hall in the Rotunda of the Capitol, frontis. and facing p. 19, 23, 44 and 64, sculpture by his grandson, Mahonri Mackintosh Young.

34 Hinckley, Gordon B. *What of the Mormons?* Church of Jesus Christ of Latter-day Saints, (Salt Lake City?), 1947, cloth, 230 pp., "The Question," indices, illus. including photos of two bronzes, pp. (174) and (179), by Y.

34a Hornaday, William T. *Thirty Years War for Wild Life.* Permanent Wild Life Protection Fund, Stamford, Conn., January 1931, cloth with illus. mounted on the front cover, 292 pp., (2) of advs., preface, appendix, index, numerous illus. including one, photo of "The Seagull Monument," p. viii, by Y.

35 Horne, Alice Merrill. *Devotees and Their Shrines* (A Hand Book of Utah Art). The Desert News, Salt Lake City, 1914, cloth, 158 (2) pp., foreword, introductory, includes a chapter on Mahonri M. Young with photos of bronzes by him, pp. 16, 84, 86, 87, 88, 89 and (159), plus a photo of him and a photo of the bronze of him by B. H. Roberts.

36 Humphreys, L. R. (compiled and edited by), with the editorial assistance of A. C. Matheson. *Utah: Resources and Activities.* Department of Public Instruction, Salt Lake City, 1933, fabricoid and boards, 458 pp., "Preface" by Charles H. Skidmore, State Superintendent, introduction, index, numerous (six in color) illus. including one, photo of the "Sea Gull Monument," p. 129, by Y.

37 Hunter, Milton R. *Utah: The Story of Her People, 1540–1947.* The Deseret News Press, Salt Lake City, 1946, fabricoid, 431 pp., preface, "Foreword" by Leland Hargrave Creer (University of Utah), index, maps, numerous (several in color) illus. including one, a photo of the "Sea Gull Monument," p. 143, by Y. Brief biographical sketch of Y., pp. 419–20.

38 ———. *The Utah Story.* Published by the author (Wheelwright Lithographing Co., Salt Lake City), 1960, words "First Edition, 1960" on copyright page, colored pic. cloth, 436 pp., preface, "Author of *The Utah Story*" by Dr. G. Homer Durham, list of illustrations, numerous illus. including photos of two bronzes, pp. 115 and 239, and of details of the "This is the Place" Monument, pp. 50, 67, 92, 94 and 96, by Y.

39 Karrer, Dr. H. L. *The Mormon Pioneer Memorial Bridge.* North Omaha Bridge Commission, 1953, colored pic. wraps, 13 (1) pp., map, illus. including one, a photo of "This is the Place" Monument, p. (12), by Y.

40 Keir, Malcolm. *The Epic of Industry.* Yale, New Haven, Conn., 1926, morocco and boards, gilt top, pic. endsheets, 329 pp., "The Epic of Industry" by Ralph H. Gabriel, notes on the pictures, index, nu-

merous illus. including one, photo of the bronze "The Stevedore," p. 311, by Y. Vol. 5, The Pageant of America, The Liberty Bell (or first) Edition, 1500 impressions. (Marchand)

41 Kent, Norman (selected and edited by). *Drawings by American Artists.* Watson-Guptill, N.Y., 1947, words "First Edition, 1947" on copyright page, cloth, 158 (1) pp., preface, numerous illus. including one, p. 158, by Y.

42 ———. Same, revised edition, Bonanza Books, N.Y., (1968), cloth, 126 (1) pp., preface, numerous illus. including one, p. (127), by Y.

43 Lambourne, Alfred. *A Play-House.* Privately printed by the author, Salt Lake City, illus. by Young et al.

44 ———. *A Book of Verse.* Salt Lake City, 1907, frontis., portrait of the author, an etching by Y.

45 Landgren, Marchal E. *Years of Art* (Story of the Art Students League of New York). McBride, N.Y., 1940, cloth, 267 pp., index, numerous illus. including one, a photo of a bronze, "The Pneumatic Drill," plate 67, by Y.

46 Larkin, Oliver W. *Art and Life in America.* Rinehart, N.Y., (1949), with the publisher's brand on the copyright page, cloth, 547 pp., author's foreword, bibliographical notes, index, numerous illus. incuding one, a photo of a bronze, "Boxer," p. 392, by Y. (Remington)

47 ———. Same, revised and enlarged edition, Holt, Rinehart, N.Y., (1960), cloth, 559 pp., illus. including a photo of a bronze, "The Digger," p. 393, by Y. (Remington)

48 Latendorf, E. W. *Western Americana* (catalogue no. 24). Mannados Bookshop, N.Y., n.d., pic. wraps, 88 pp., twenty-five illus. including three, pp. 87 and 88, by Y. (Borein, Dixon, Goodwin)

49 ———. *The West* (catalogue no. 25). Mannados Bookshop, N.Y., n.d., pic. wraps, numerous illus. including four, inside front cover, inside back cover (two) and back cover, by Y. (Remington, Russell)

50 ———. *Catalogue No. 27.* (Mannados Bookshop), N.Y., n.d., pic. wraps, 36 pp., numerous illus. including a photo of a bronze, p. 33, by Y. (De Yong, Eggenhofer, Goodwin, Lea, Lungren)

51 ———. *There Lies the Trail.* Mannados Bookshop, N.Y., n.d., pic. self-wraps, (8) pp., six illus. including photos of two bronzes, "There Lies the Trail" (front cover) and "Navajo Pony," by Y.

52 Mabey, Charles R. (Chairman, Historical Committee). *This is the Place, Utah Centennial 1847–1947.* (Utah Centennial Commission, Salt Lake City, 1947), colored pic. wraps, 25 (3) pp. illus. including two photos of details of "This is the Place" Monument, front cover and p. (2), by Y.

52a Mendelowitz, Daniel M. *A History of American Art.* Holt, Rinehart and Winston, N.Y., 1960, cloth, 662 pp., bibliography, index, numerous illus. including one, p. 626, by Y. (Miller, Remington)

53 Moore, Lamont. *The Sculptured Image.* Watts, N.Y., (1967), colored pic. cloth, 100 pp., introduction, numerous photos including one, "This is the Place" Monument, p. (63), by Y.

54 Morgan, Dale L. (State Supervisor). *Utah* (American Guide Series). Hastings, N.Y., 1941, words "First Published in 1941" on copyright page, cloth, map endsheets, 595 pp., "Foreword" by Gail Martin, preface, selected reading list, index, maps, numerous illus. including one, a photo of the "Seagull Monument," between pp. 314 and 315, by Y. and with text material on him, pp. 166, 167, 237, 240 and 256.

55 *Original Graphic Art* (catalog). Berlin Photographic Co., N.Y., 1915, wraps, unpaged, illus. including one, "The Sand Pit," by Y.

55a Pierson, William H., Jr. and Davidson, Martha, eds. *Arts of the United States, A Pictorial Survey.* McGraw Hill, Chicago etc., (1960), cloth, 452 pp., "Preface" by Lamar Dodd, introduction, appendices, index, including several by Y. (Remington)

55b ———. Same, reprinted by the University of Georgia Press in 1966 with 4156 numbered illustrations including five, no. 2054 (three), no. 3850 and no. 3851, by Y. (Hurd, Remington)

56 Proske, Beatrice Gilman. *Brookgreen Gardens Sculpture.* Brookgreen Gardens, Brookgreen, S.C., 1943, cloth, 510 pp., "Foreword" by A. M. H., introduction, index, plan with folding map, illus. with photos of numerous bronzes including one, "The Driller," p. (160), by Y. Brief biography of Y. in text, pp. 161–64. (Deming, Remington)

57 Roberts, Mike (Color Production). *Beautiful Salt Lake City and Vicinity in Glowing Natural Color.* (Intermountain Tourist Supply, Salt Lake City, n.d.), colored pic. wraps, unpaged, map, numerous illus. including photos of two bronzes by Y.

58 Roylance, Ward J., ed. *Utah Trails.* Volume 1 (fourth edition), Salt Lake City, 1968, colored pic. wraps, 47

trial proof no. 1   mahonri young

INDIAN GIRL by Young from *Fine Prints Of The Year 1926*

(1) pp., numerous illus. including one, a photo of "This is the Place" Monument by Y., p. 5.

58a Rugoff, Milton, ed. *The Britannica Encyclopaedia of American Art*. Encyclopaedia Britannica Educational Corp., (a Chanticleer Press Edition), Chicago, (1973), cloth, 669 pp., numerou illus. including one, p. 616, by Y. and a biographical sketch of him. (Remington)

59 Runyon, A. Milton and Bergane, Vilma F., eds. *Around the U.S.A. in 1000 Pictures*. Nelson Double-day, Garden City, N.Y., (1955), two-tone fabricoid, colored pic. wraps, 384 pp., "Foreword" by Paul J. C. Friedlander, maps, profusely illus. including photos of two bronzes, pp. 282 and 283, by Y.

60 Salaman, Malcolm C., ed. *Fine Prints of the Year 1926: An Annual Review of Contemporary Etching and Engraving*, vol. 4. Halton & Truscott Smith, London, Minton, Balch, N.Y. (printed in London, November, 1926), cloth, 17 pp., 100 plates, xxiv, directory of etchers and engravers, plate no. 100, "Indian Girl," an etching by Y. (Borein)

61 ———— and Fagg, Helen. Same, *1929*, vol. 7. Cloth, 20 pp., 100 plates, xxiv, one etching, "Apple Orchard," no. 100, by Y.

62 ———— and Hutchinson, Susan A. Same, *1932*. Tenth Annual Issue, cloth, 20 pp., 100 plates, xv, one etching, "Burro and the Juniper Tree," no. 100, by Y.

63 ————. Same, *1933*. Eleventh Annual Issue, cloth, 19 pp., 100 plates, xvi, one etching, "Pont Neuf," no. 100, by Y.

64 ————. Same, *1934*. Twelfth Annual Issue, cloth, 22 pp., 100 plates, xv, one etching, "Stampede," no. 100, by Y.

65 ————. Same, *1936*. Fourteenth Annual Issue, cloth, 41 pp., 100 plates, one etching, "Corrals at Polacca," no. 90, by Y. (Edited by Campbell Dodgson.)

66 Slatkin, Charles E. and Schoolman, Regina. *Treasury of American Drawings*. Oxford University Press, N.Y., 1947, cloth, numerous numbered plates including no. 160, "Boxer," by Y.

67 *Taming a Frontier*. Reprinted from *Transmission Magazine* 17:1 (1968), folder with nine illus. including one, a photo of a bronze, "Rolling His Own," front cover, by Y. (Remington, Russell, Wyeth)

68 Thornley, John D. et al. *Utah's Story*. Utah State Road Commission, Salt Lake City, (1942), colored pic. wraps, v, 90 pp., "Introduction" by John S. Evans, (chairman) et al., index, maps, numerous illus. in-cluding one, a photo of "The Seagull Monument," by Y.

68a Trask, John E. D. and Laurik, J. Nilsen, eds. *Catalogue De Luxe of the Department of Fine Arts, Panama-Pacific Exposition*. Paul Elder and Co., San Francisco, 1915, two volumes, vellum and boards, brown end-sheets, 482 (2) pp., gilt tops, introduction, numerous illus. including one, facing p. 434, by Y. Edition of 1100 copies. (Mora)

69 *Utah! Discovery Country*. Utah Travel Council, Salt Lake City, n.d., colored pic. wraps, 45, (1) pp., numerous illus. in color including one, a photo of "This is the Place" Monument, p. (32), by Y.

70 Zigrosser, Carl. *Six Centuries of Fine Prints*. Covici-Friedi, N.Y., (1937), cloth, 406 pp., index of plates, 488 numbered plates including one, no. 409, by Y.

71 ————. *The Artist in America*. Knopf, N.Y., 1942, cloth, 207 (1) pp., numerous illus. including three, between pp. 200–201, by Y. and a photo of him by Shipler.

72 ————. *The Book of Fine Prints*. Crown, N.Y., (1948), Revised Edition of no. 70, cloth, 499 pp., foreword, index of plates, 555 numbered plates including one, no. 393, by Y.

The Artist and His Art

73 "An art born in the west and epitomizing the west: illustrated from the work of Mahonri Young," an article in *The Touchstone* October, 1918. This issue also has an article, "Life as Mahonri Young Sees It."

74 *Biographical Sketches of American Artists*. Michigan State Library, Lansing, 1924, edition includes a biographical sketch of Young.

75 *Catalogue of the One Hundred and Eleventh Annual Exhibition of the Pennsylvania Academy of the Fine Arts, February 6–March 26, 1916*. Decor. wraps, 112, xvi pp., illustrated; Young, pp. 68 and 112.

76 Dougherty, Paul. " 'Rolling his own' — a new bronze by Mahonri Young," an article in *Vanity Fair*, May, 1925.

77 "The Drawings of Mahonri Young," an article in *Art Instruction*, June, 1939.

78 duBois, Guy Pene. "Mahonri Young — Sculptor," an article in *Arts and Decorations*, February, 1918.

79 *Encyclopaedia Americana*. Americana Corp., N.Y., a biographical sketch of Y. appears in a number of edi-

tions — in the current edition the sketch appears in vol. 29.

80 Fielding, Mantle. *Dictionary of American Painters, Sculptors and Engravers*. N.Y., 1926, cloth, 433 pp., brief biographical sketch, pp. 421–22, of Y.

81 ————. Same, but with an Addendum, compiled and published by James F. Carr, N.Y., 1965, cloth, pp. 529, additional information on Young, pp. 527–28.

82 Green, Samuel M. *American Art* (A Historical Survey). Ronald Press, N.Y., (1966), cloth, 706 pp., suggested reading, index, numerous illustrations; Young's sculpture praised, p. 630.

83 *Handbook* (no. 1). American Artist Group, (N.Y., 1935), Young sketch, pp. 75–76.

84 Heaton, Elsie S. et al. *Pioneers of Utah Art* (by Kaysville Art Club). Cloth, 137 pp., preface, illus. with photos of the artists; with a chapter on Y. and a photo of him, pp. 99–102.

85 Hind, Charles Lewis. "Mahonri Young's Drawings," an article in *The International Studio*, April, 1918.

86 Jackman, Rilla Evelyn. *American Arts*. Rand McNally, Chicago etc., (1928), cloth, 561 pp., illustrated; biographical sketch of Y., p. 416. (Blumenschein)

87 Lewine, J. Lester. "The Bronzes of Mahonri Young," an article in *The International Studio*, October, 1912.

88 "Life as Mahonri Young Sees It," an article in *The Touchstone*, vol. 4, October 1918.

89 "Mahonri Young's Artistic Search for the Rhythm of Labor," an article in *Current Opinion*, September, 1914.

90 "Mahonri Young's Sculpture Preserves his Mormon Past," an article in *Life*, February 17, 1941.

91 Myers, Jerome. *Artist in Manhattan*. American Artist Group, Inc., N.Y., (1940), cloth, 263 pp., publisher's note, index, illus. by the author; praise of Y. and his art, pp. 29 and 38.

92 "Prize Ring Sculptures by Mahonri Young," an article in *Vanity Fair*, September, 1928.

93 Roberts, B. H. *A Comprehensive History of the Church of Jesus Christ of Latter-day Saints*, volume III. Brigham Young University Press, Provo, 1965, fabricoid, 572 pp., map, frontis., much on "The Sea Gull Monument," pp. 354–6.

94 Rose, Josephine and Dougan, Terrill. *This is the Place, Salt Lake City*, (An Entertaining Guide). Privately printed, n.p., (March, 1972), decor. wraps, 199 (1) pp., illus. by Stephanie Churchill including a drawing of Young's "Seagull Monument" and a paragraph about him, p. 21.

95 Rugoff, Milton, ed. et al. *The Britannica Encyclopaedia of American Art*. N.Y. (but printed in Italy, 1973), cloth, 669 pp., bibliographies, biography of Y., p. 616.

96 Weitenkampf, Frank, "An Etching Sculptor: Mahonri Young," an article in *The American Magazine of Art*, April, 1922.

97 *Who's Who in America*. A. N. Marquis Co., Chicago, a biographical sketch of Young appears in a number of volumes (or editions) beginning with no. 13.

98 *Who Was Who in America*. A. N. Marquis Co., Chicago, 1960, volume 3, cloth, 959 pp.; the Y. biographical sketch appears p. 947.

99 Wier, Albert E. *Thesaurus of the Arts*. Putnam's, N.Y., (1943), cloth, red top, 690 pp., foreword, bibliography, brief biographical sketch, p. 658, of Y.

100 Wilson, James Patterson. "Art and Artists of the Golden West: A Sculptor and a Painter of Utah," an article in *Fine Arts Journal*, February, 1911.

HURRAH! THE WILD MISSOURI by Zogbaum from *Horse, Foot, and
Dragoons, Sketches of Army Life at Home and Abroad*

RUFUS FAIRCHILD ZOGBAUM
1849–1925

Catalogues of Art Exhibitions and Galleries

CORCORAN GALLERY OF ART, WASHINGTON, D.C.

1 *American Processional, the Story of Our Country*, July 8 through December 17, 1950, colored pic. wraps, 270 pp., "Washington: 1800–1950" by Edward Boykin, "Foreword" by Corcoran Thom, sources and permissions, index, numerous illus. including one, p. 226, by Z. (Miller, Remington)

DELAWARE ART MUSEUM, WILMINGTON

2 *The Golden Age of American Illustration, 1880–1914*, September 14–October 15, 1972, pic. wraps, 67 pp., numerous illus. including one, p. 47, by Z. (Remington, Schoonover, Wyeth)

EDWARD EBERSTADT & SONS, NEW YORK

3 *A Distinguished Collection of Western Paintings*, catalogue 139, (1965), pic. wraps, "Introduction" by Harold McCracken, unpaged but with 129 numbered illus. including number 128 by Z. (Borein, Deming, Dixon, Leigh, Miller, Remington, Russell, Wyeth)

FINE ARTS MUSEUM OF NEW MEXICO, SANTA FE

4 *The Artist in the American West, 1800–1900*, October 8 through November 22, 1961, pic. wraps, unpaged, "Introduction" by Director James Taylor Forrest, numerous illus. including one, plate no. 104, by Z. (Miller, Remington, Russell)

KENNEDY GALLERIES, NEW YORK

5 *Painters of the Old West*, October 1960, pic. wraps, pp. 102–147, introduction, numerous illus. including one, p. 146, by Z. (Borein, Deming, Leigh, Remington, Russell, Schreyvogel)

6 *Recent Acquisitions in Important Western Painting*, October 1961, pic. wraps, pp. 150–188, introduction, numerous illus. including two, pp. 188, by Z. (Borein, Deming, Eggenhofer, Johnson, Remington, Russell, Schreyvogel)

7 *The Eye of the Traveler*, November 1963, pic. wraps, 64 pp., introduction, numerous illus. including one, p. 53, by Z. (Russell)

METROPOLITAN MUSEUM OF ART, NEW YORK

8 *Life in America*, April 24 to October 29, 1939, decor. wraps, with paper label on front cover, 230 pp., "Preface" by William M. Ivins, Jr. (Acting Director), "Introduction" by Harry B. Wehle, index, numerous illus. including one, p. 201, by Z. (Remington, Schreyvogel)

PETERSEN GALLERIES, BEVERLY HILLS, CALIFORNIA

8a *Americana, Western and Sporting Art/Sculpture*, wraps, 25 pp., numerous illus. including one, p. 11, by Z. (James, Johnson, Leigh, Remington, Russell, Wyeth)

Illustrated by the Artist

9 Athearn, Robert G. *Union Pacific Country*. Rand McNally, Chicago etc., (1971), words "First Printing, April, 1971" on copyright page, cloth, 480 pp., introduction, bibliography, index, maps, numerous illus. including one, pp. (177–78), by Z.

9a Baird, Joseph A., Jr. (compiled by). *The West Remembered*. California Historical Society, San Francisco and San Marino, 1973, colored pic. wraps, 88 pp., "Foreword" by Mitchell A. Wilder, introduction, numerous illus. including one, p. 24, by Z. (Blumenschein, Borein, Dixon, James, Lungren, Marchand, Miller, Remington, Russell)

10 Barnes, James. *Ships and Sailors*. Stokes, N.Y., 1898, cloth, 124 pp., numerous illus. in color and black and white by Z. (Sailor's Songs.)

11 ———. *Yankee Ships and Yankee Sailors*. Macmillan, N.Y., London, 1897, cloth, 281 pp., numerous illus. by Chapman and Z.

12 Baur, John E. *Dogs on the Frontier*. Naylor, San Antonio, 1964, cloth, 238 pp., illus. including one by Z. (Remington)

13 Beebe, Lucius and Clegg, Charles. *The American West: The Pictorial Epic of a Continent*. Dutton, N.Y., 1955, words "First Edition" on copyright page, decor. cloth, pic. endsheets, 511 pp., foreword, bibliography, over 1000 illus. including eight, pp. (196), (232), (387) two, (406), (408), (419) and (486), by Z. (Eggenhofer, Remington)

14 Block, Eugene B. *Great Stagecoach Robbers of the West*. Doubleday, Garden City, N.Y., (1962), words "First Edition" on copyright page, cloth, pic. map endsheets, 262 pp., bibliography, eight pages of illus. with one drawing, "Hands Up," between pp. 192 and 193, by Z.

14a Bourne, Russell (project editor). *200 Years*. U.S. News & World Report, Washington, D.C., 1973, fabricoid and cloth, two vol., numerous illus. including one, p. 274 (II), by Z., slipcase. (Dunn, Miller, Remington, Russell, Wyeth)

15 Brady, Cyrus Townsend. *In the Wasp's Nest*. Scribner's, N.Y., 1902, words "Published, September, 1902" on copyright page, pic. cloth, 328 pp., preface, notes, eight illus., frontis. and facing pp. 24, 66, 96, 226, 254 and 310, by Z.

16 ———. *Indian Fights and Fighters*. McClure, Phillips, N.Y., 1904, words "Published December, 1904, N" on copyright page, pic. cloth, 423 pp., preface, appendices, index, numerous illus. including one, facing p. 116, by Z. (Blumenschein, Crawford, Deming, Elwell, Remington, Schreyvogel)

17 ———. Same, Nebraska, Lincoln, (1971), words "First Bison Book printing: November 1971" on copyright page, colored pic. wraps, 423 pp., "Introduction" by James T. King, numerous illus. including one, facing p. 116, by Z. (Blumenschein, Crawford, Deming, Elwell, Remington, Schreyvogel)

18 Brady, Jasper Ewing. *Tales of the Telegraph*. Doubleday & McClure Co., N.Y., 1899, decor. cloth, 272 pp., nine illus. including one, the frontis., by Z.

19 ———. Same, reprinted by Jamieson-Higgins Co., Chicago, 1900.

20 Brininstool, E. A. *Fighting Indian Warriors*. Stackpole, Harrisburg, 1953, decor. cloth, 353 pp., preface, numerous illus. including one, p. (99), by Z.

21 Brooks, Elbridge S. *The Century Book for Young Americans*. Century, N.Y., 1894, 249 pp., "Introduction" by Horace Porter, President-General, S.A.R., numerous illus. including a page of drawings, p. 117, by Z. (Lungren, Remington)

22 Brown, Dee and Schmitt, Martin F. *Trail Driving Days*. Scribner's, N.Y., London, 1952, code letter "A" on copyright page, decor. cloth, 264 pp., foreword, bibliography, numerous illus. including one, p. 241, by Z. (Remington, Russell)

22a Carleton, Will. *Rhymes of Our Planet*. Harper, N.Y., 1895, cloth, 195 pp., numerous illus. including one, p. (144), by Z.

23 Carley, Kenneth. *Minnesota in the Civil War*. Ross & Haines, Minneapolis, 1961, words "First Edition" on copyright page, cloth, red endsheets, 168 pp., chronology, roster, bibliography, index, illus. including six in color of which one double-page plate, "The Battle of Gettysburg," pp. (32–33), is by Z.

24 Carter, Lieutenant-Colonel W. H. *From Yorktown to Santiago*. The Lord Baltimore Press, Baltimore, 1900, pic. cloth, 317 pp., gilt top, preface, roster, thirteen illus. including one, facing p. 13, by Z. (Remington)

25 ———. General W. H. *Old Army Sketches*. The Lord Baltimore Press, Baltimore, 1906, gilt top, 203 pp., foreword, illus. including one, facing p. (85), by Z. (Remington)

26 Connell, F. Norreys. *How Soldiers Fight*. James Bowden, London, 1899, colored pic. cloth, 236 pp., (20) of advs., foreword, 24 illus. including one, facing p. 230, by Z. (Wood)

26a Cooper, James Fenimore. *The Spy*. Putnam, N.Y., (1896), decor. cloth, 430 pp., illus. by Z. (Mohawk Edition.)

26b ———. *Wing and Wing*. Putnam, N.Y., 1896, decor. cloth, 470 pp., illus. by Z. (Mohawk Edition.)

26c ———. *The Two Admirals*. Scribner's, N.Y., 1899, cloth, 421 pp., four illus., frontis. and facing pp. 40, 146 and 368, by Z. (Famous Novels of the Sea.)

27 Coy, Owen C. (compiled and edited by). *Pictorial History of California*. Univ. of Calif. Extension Division, Berkeley, (1925), buckram, grey endsheets, foreword of one page, 261 numbered plates including no. 197, by Z. (Remington)

28 Custer, Elizabeth B. *Following the Guidon*. Harper,

N.Y., 1890, decor. cloth, brown top, 341 pp., (2) of advs., preface, sixteen illus., including two, facing pp. 38 and 286, by Z. (Remington)

29 ———. Same, Oklahoma, Norman, (1966), words "First printing of the new edition" on copyright page, boards, 341 pp., "Introduction" by Jane R. Stewart, preface, illus. including two, facing pp. 38 and 286, by Z.

30 Davidson, Marshall B. *Life in America*. Houghton Mifflin, Boston, 1951, two vols. in cardboard slipcase, decor. cloth, 575 and 503 pp., "Foreword" by Francis Henry Taylor, Director, The Metropolitan Museum of Art (1), introduction (1), notes (2), acknowledgments (2), bibliography (2), list of artists (2), index (2), over 1200 illus. including two (vol. 1), pp. (287) and 289, by Z. (Miller, Remington)

31 Davis, Rebecca Harding. *Kent Hampden*. Scribner's, N.Y., 1892, pic. cloth, 152 pp., four illus., frontis. and facing pp. 40, 52 and 120, by Z.

32 Dickman, Major General J. T., ed. *The Santiago Campaign*. Society of Santiago de Cuba, (Williams Printing Co.), Richmond, Va., 1927, decor. cloth, 442 pp., "Foreword" by General Charles Dudley Rhodes, introduction, appendices, index, numerous illus. including two, facing pp. 80 and 104, by Z. (Remington)

33 Downey, Fairfax. *Indian-Fighting Army*. Scribner's, N.Y., 1941, code letter "A" on copyright page, cloth, 329 pp., acknowledgments, bibliography, index, numerous illus. including one, p. 101, by Z. (Leigh, Remington, Schreyvogel)

34 ———. Same, a new edition, especially revised by the author, Bantam Books, N.Y., (1963), words "Bantam Pathfinder edition published May 1963" on copyright page, colored pic. wraps, 275 (2) pp., acknowledgments, while the title page states "With drawings by Frederic Remington" the drawing, p. (89), is by Z. (Remington)

35 ———. Same, reprint by Old Army Press, Ft. Collins, Colorado, with a new "Introduction" by Mike Kowry, 1971, Z. illus., p. (101).

36 ———. *Fife, Drum and Bugle*. Old Army Press, Fort Collins, Colo., 1971, limited edition of 50 numbered copies signed by the author and E. L. Reedstrom, each copy with an original pen and ink drawing by Reedstrom, full leather, slipcase, "Introduction" by Harold L. Peterson, illus. including two by Z.

37 ———. Same, first trade edition in cloth.

37a Drake, F. S. *Indian History for Young Folks*. Harpers, N.Y., (1919), cloth, 454 pp., "Introduction" by F. J. Dowd, preface, index, maps, numerous illus. including four, facing pp. 312, 348, 476 and 482, by Z. (Remington)

38 (Eberstadt). *Americana*. Catalogue no. 136, Edward Eberstadt & Sons, N.Y., 1955, pic. wraps, illus. including one by Z. (Miller, Schreyvogel)

38a Eggleston, George C. *Southern Soldier Stories*. Macmillan, N.Y., 1898, cloth, 251 pp., (4) of advs., preface, six illus., frontis. and facing pp. 30, 56, 91, 119 and 224, by Z.

39 *Famous American Heroes*. Calendar for 1943, White & Wyckoff, Holyoke, Mass., one illus., "Admiral Dewey at Manila Bay, 1898" (part), by Z., over the calendar for April.

40 Ferris, Robert G. (series editor). *Soldier and Brave* (new edition). National Park Service (G.P.O.), Washington, D.C., 1971, cloth, pic. endsheets, 451 pp., "Foreword" by Secretary Rogers C. B. Morton, "Preface" by Director George B. Hartzog, Jr., suggested reading, index, maps, numerous illus. including one, rear endsheet, by Z. (Eggenhofer, Leigh, Miller, Remington, Russell, Schreyvogel)

41 Fielder, Mildred. *Wild Bill and Deadwood*. Superior, Seattle, (1965), words "First Edition" on copyright page, cloth, 160 pp., preface, bibliography, numerous illus. including one, p. (47), by Z. (Wyeth)

42 Fitzhugh, Percy Keese. *From Appomattox to Germany*. Harper, N.Y. and London, (1919), words "Published April, 1919" on copyright page, pic. cloth, 409 (1) pp., publisher's note, maps, numerous illus. including two, pp. (5) and (224), by Z. (Remington)

43 Forsyth, George A. (Brevet Brig.-Gen., Ret.). *Thrilling Days of Army Life*. Harper, N.Y. and London, 1900, colored pic. cloth, 196 (1) pp., (2) of advs., sixteen full-page plates by Z.

44 ———. *The Story of the Soldier*. Appleton, N.Y., 1900, decor. cloth, tan endsheets, 389 pp., editor's preface, author's preface, index, six illus. by Z.

45 ———. Same, but with the title *The Soldier*. The Brampton Society, N.Y., 1908, two vols., but with the same illus. by Z. (Builders of the Nation — National Edition.)

46 Fronval, George. *La Fantastique Epopee du Far West*. Dargaud, Nevilly/s/Seine, France, (1969), two vols., colored pic. boards, 126 (2) and 127 (1) pp., numer-

ous illus. including one, p. (29-II), by Z. (Koerner, Miller, Remington, Russell, Schreyvogel)

46a ———. *La Veritable Histoire Des Indiens Peaux-Rouges*. Fernand Nathan, Paris, France, (1973), cloth, pic. front endsheet, map back endsheets, 125 pp., numerous illus. including one, p. 89, by Z. (Koerner, Leigh, Miller, Remington, Schreyvogel, Von Schmidt)

47 Gabriel, Ralph Henry. *Toilers of Land and Sea*. Yale, New Haven, Conn., 1926, morocco and boards, gilt top, pic. endsheets, 340 pp., "The American Farmer," notes on the pictures, index, numerous illus. including one, p. 189, by Z. Vol. 3, The Pageant of America, The Liberty Bell (or first) Edition, 1500 impressions. (Dixon, Remington, Russell)

48 Goodman, David M. *Arizona Odyssey: Bibliographic Adventures in Nineteenth Century Magazines*. Arizona Historical Foundation, Tempe, 1969, words "First Edition" on copyright page, pic. cloth, orange endsheets, 360 pp., "Foreword" by Barry M. Goldwater, preface, illus. including one by Z. (Remington)

49 Hamm, William A. *From Colony to World Power*. D. C. Heath & Co., Boston, (1947), decor. cloth, 854 pp., preface, note on supplementary reading, appendix, index, maps, charts and diagrams, numerous illus. including one, p. (659), by Z. (Remington)

50 *Harpers Encyclopedia of United States History*. N.Y., 1901, ten vols., cloth, unpaged, vol. III includes one plate by Z. (Keller, Remington)

51 Havighurst, Walter, ed. *Land of the Long Horizons*. Coward-McCann, N.Y., (1960), decor. cloth, red top, red endsheets, 437 pp., introduction, acknowledgments, maps, numerous illus. including one, p. 95, by Z. (Deming, Remington)

52 Herr, Major General John K. and Wallace, Edward S. *The Story of the U.S. Cavalry, 1775–1942*. Little, Brown, Boston, (1953), words "First Edition" on copyright page, cloth, yellow endsheets, 275 pp., authors' notes and acknowledgments, "Foreword" by General Jonathan M. Wainwright, bibliography, numerous illus. including two, pp. (154) and 216, by Z. (Remington, Schreyvogel)

53 Hill, Francis. *The Outlaws of Horseshoe Hole* (A Tale of the Montana Vigilantes). Scribner's, N.Y., 1901, words "Published September, 1901" on copyright page, colored pic. cloth, 322 pp., (4) of advs., eight illus., frontis. and facing pp. 68, 116, 166, 186, 212, 232 and 279, by Z.

54 Hitchcock, Ripley, ed. *Decisive Battles of America*.

Harper, N.Y. and London, 1909, words "Published October, 1909" on copyright page, decor. pic. cloth, 396 (1) pp., introduction, index, maps, sixteen illus. including one, facing p. 340, by Z. (Remington)

55 Irving, Washington. *Astoria*. Putnam, N.Y. and London, 1897, morocco and marbled boards or decor. white buckram (with cloth dust wrappers), two vols. 389 and 391 pp., gilt tops, introduction (I), appendix (II), 28 illus. including three, frontis. (I and II) and facing p. 150 (I), by Z. (Tacoma Edition.)

56 Ivins, William M., Jr. (Acting Director). *Life in America*. The Metropolitan Museum of Art, N.Y., 1939, decor. wraps with paper title label on front cover, 230 pp., preface, "Introduction" by Harry B. Wehle, index, numerous illus. including one, p. 265, by Z. (Remington, Schreyvogel)

57 Jensen, Oliver (editor in charge). *The Nineties*. American Heritage, N.Y., (1967), colored pic. boards, 144 pp., editor's introduction, numerous illus. including one in color, p. 110, by Z.

58 King, Captain Charles. *A War-time Wooing*. Harper, N.Y., 1888, decor. cloth, 195 pp., eight illus. frontis. and facing pp. 8, 70, 90, (110), 136, 172 and 194, by Z.

59 ———. *Campaigning with Crook and Stories of Army Life*. Harper, N.Y., 1890, cloth, 295 pp., (8) of advs., preface, ten illus. including one, facing p. 180, by Z.

60 ———. Same, reprint by University Microfilms, Ann Arbor, (1966), with an added foreword.

61 ———. *Cadet Days: A Story of West Point*. Harper, N.Y., 1894, pic. cloth, 293 pp., twenty-four illus. by Z.

62 ———. Same, later printing with sixteen illus. by Z.

63 ———. General Charles. *The Iron Brigade: A Story of the Army of the Potomac*. Dillingham, N.Y., (1902), cloth, 379 pp., four illus., frontis. and facing pp. 66, 222 and 332, by Z.

64 Koury, Capt. Michael J. *Military Posts of Montana*. Old Army Press, Bellevue, Nebraska, 1970, limited edition of 50 copies, numbered and signed by the author, each with an original color illus. by Derek Fitz James, full leather, slipcase, illus. including five by Z.

65 ———. Same, first trade edition, bound in cloth or colored pic. wraps.

66 Kouwenhoven, John A. *Adventures of America*,

1857–1900. Harper, N.Y., 1938, cloth, pic. endsheets, unpaged but 255 numbered illus. including one, no. 249, by Z. (Remington)

67 Latendorf, E. Walter. *Frederic Remington and More Fact and Fiction of the Old West and the Wild West*. Catalogue no. 17, Mannados Bookshop, N.Y., (1947), pic. wraps, 72 pp., "Frederic Remington, an appreciation" by Harold McCracken, numerous illus. including one, inside back cover, by Z. (James, Remington)

68 Leckie, Robert. *Great American Battles*. Random House, N.Y., 1968, colored pic. boards, pic. endsheets, 177 pp., index, numerous illus. including one, p. 95, by Z. (Remington)

69 Marryat, Captain. *Mr. Midshipman Easy*. Putnam, N.Y., (1895), boards with illus. mounted on front cover, 412 pp. plus advs., seventeen illus. by Z.

70 Meigs, John, ed. *The Cowboy in American Prints*. Swallow Press, Chicago, (1972), leather and cloth, pic. endsheets, 184 pp., introduction, numerous illus. including one, p. (51), by Z. (Beeler, Borein, Dixon, Hurd, Remington, Russell, Wood)

71 ———. Same, trade edition in cloth.

72 Meredith, Roy. *The American Wars: A Pictorial History from Quebec to Korea*. World, Cleveland and N.Y., (1955), pic. buckram, red top, 349 pp., introduction, military artists of the American Wars, numerous illus. including one, p. 210, by Z. (Deming, Dunn, Fischer, Remington, Thomason)

73 Merritt, Brigadier-General Wesley et al. *The Armies of Today*. Harper, N.Y., 1893, decor. cloth, 438 pp., (2) of advs., numerous illus. including eight, frontis., pp. (3), (7), (11), (19), (27), (37) and 48, by Z. (Remington)

73a Miles, General Nelson A. (introduction by) et al. *Harper's Pictorial History of the War with Spain*. Harper, N.Y. and London, 1899, pic. cloth in 2 vols. (or in 32 parts in pic. wraps), 507 (1) pp., index, numerous illus. including nineteen (one in color), by Z. (Remington)

74 Monaghan, Jay (editor-in-chief), et al. *The Book of the American West*. Messner, N.Y., (1963), words "First Edition" on copyright page, decor. leather and endsheets, all edges gilt, 608 pp., introduction, suggestions for additional reading index, numerous illus. including two, pp. 223 and 229, by Z. De Luxe edition in slipcase. (Borein, Johnson, Koerner, Leigh, Miller, Remington, Russell, Schreyvogel)

75 ———. Same, first trade edition, in cloth.

75a Munroe, Kirk. *Brethren of the Coast*. Scribner's, N.Y., 1900, cloth, 303 pp., (4) of advs., eight illus., frontis. and facing pp. 30, 50, 84, 164, 230, 260 and 286, by Z.

75b ———. *Son of Satsuma or With Perry in Japan*. Scribner's, N.Y., 1901, words "Published October 1901" on copyright page, cloth, 306 pp., (4) of advs., eight illus., frontis. and facing pp. 6, 80, 102, 150, 174, 194 and 250, by Z.

76 Paine, Ralph D. *Roads of Adventure*. Houghton Mifflin, Boston and New York, 1922, pic. cloth, 452 pp., numerous illus. including one, the frontis., by Z.

77 Pelzer, Louis. *The Cattleman's Frontier*. Clark, Glendale, 1936, cloth, 351 pp., gilt top, preface, introduction, appendix, bibliography, index, illus. with numerous Wyoming brands and seven plates including two, frontis. and facing p. 203, by Z.

78 Porter, C. Fayne. *Our Indian Heritage*. Chilton, Philadelphia and N.Y., (1964), words "First Editon" on copyright page, fabricoid, decor. endsheets, 228 (1) pp., appendix, index, "C. Payne Porter," illus. including one, between pp. 82 and 83, by Z. (Remington)

79 Reed, Walt (compiled and edited by). *The Illustrator in America, 1900–1960's*. Reinhold, N.Y., (1966), cloth, pic. endsheets, 271 (1) pp., "Is Illustration Art?" by Alfred Dorne, bibliography, numerous illus. including one, p. 40, by Z. (Blumenschein, Crawford, Dunn, Dunton, Eggenhofer, Fischer, Fogarty, Goodwin, James, Keller, Koerner, Remington, Russell, Schoonover, Stoops, Von Schmidt, Wyeth)

80 Rodenbough, Theodore F. *The Catalogue of the Museum*. Military Service Institute of the United States, N.Y., 1884, wraps, 149 pp. plus advs., index to contributors, numerous illus. including four, pp. 22, 39, 40 and 109, by Z.

81 ———. *Uncle Sam's Medal of Honor*. Putnam, N.Y., 1886, cloth, 424 pp., (6) of advs., preface, appendix, illus. including one, the frontis., but repeated p. 248 with a different caption, by Z.

82 Rossi, Paul A. (Director). *Run the Buffalo (A Story of the Hide Hunters)*. Gilcrease Institute, Tulsa, Okla., 1969, colored pic. wraps, (20) pp., numerous illus. including one, inside back cover, by Z.

83 (Russell.) *Books and Artistic Publications*. The Holiday List of R. H. Russell, N.Y., 1899, 1900, decor. wraps, (48) pp., numerous illus. including one, "Manila Bay," by Z. (Remington)

83a Sears, Stephen W. *The American Heritage Century Collection of Civil War Art.* American Heritage, N.Y., 1974, cloth, "Foreword" by Bruce Catton, 30 maps, 724 illus. by some 50 artists including Z.

84 Sheehan, Donald H., ed. *This is America My Country.* Veterans' Historical Book Service, Inc., n.p., 1952, two vols., fabricoid, colored pic. endsheets, 1004 pp. (continuous pagination), foreword (I), index (I and II), numerous illus. including one, p. 606, by Z.

85 ———. Same, first Canadian edition, published simultaneously by Musson Book Co., (Toronto, 1952).

86 Shiflet, Kenneth. *The Convenient Coward.* Stackpole, Harrisburg, Pa., (1961), words "First Edition" on copyright page, boards, 308 pp., preface, bibliography, chapter headings illus. including two, pp. 98 and 118, by Z.

86a Smith, F. Hopkinson. *American Illustrators.* Scribner's, N.Y., 1892, five parts, each in separate wraps, insert in a decor. board folder with cloth back, 68 pp., plus 15 plates including "Napoleon at Waterloo" by Z. Photo of Z. and one drawing by him, p. 55, and comment on his art, p. 57. (Remington)

87 Smith, F. Hopkinson, et al. *The Year's Art as Recorded in the Quarterly Illustrator.* Harry C. Jones, N.Y., 1893, decor. cloth, 328 pp., 678 illus. (by 302 artists) including four, pp. (17), 202, 207 and (208), by Z. (Fogarty, Remington, Varian)

88 *Sport: or, Shooting and Fishing.* Bradless, Whidden Publishing Co., Boston, 1889, edited by A. C. Gould, cloth-bound portfolio containing the five separate parts, each in printed tan wraps, fifteen color plates, including one by Z. (Remington)

89 Taft, Robert. *The Pictorial Record of the Old West VIII. Graham and Zogbaum.* Reprinted from *The Kansas Historical Quarterly*, Topeka, Kansas, August, 1949, pic. wraps, pp. (209)-232, much on Zogbaum, photo of him and four full-page illus. between pp. 224 and 225, by him.

90 ———. *Artists and Illustrators of the Old West, 1850–1900.* Scribner's, N.Y., London, 1953, code letter "A" on copyright page, decor. cloth, map endsheets, 400 pp., preface, sources and notes, index, 90 numbered plates including four, nos. 69, 70, 71 and 72, by Z., and much on him in the text. (Blumenschein, Leigh, Remington, Schreyvogel)

91 Tebbel, John and Jennison, Keith. *The American Indian Wars.* Harper, N.Y., (1960), cloth, map end-

sheets, 312 pp., epilogue, bibliographical notes, index, maps, numerous illus., including one, p. (245), by Z. (Miller, Remington, Schreyogel)

92 Utley, Robert M. *Fort Davis National Historic Site* (Handbook Series no. 38). National Park Service, Washington, D.C., 1965, decor. wraps, 62 pp., illus. including two, pp. 42 and 44, by Z. (Remington)

92a Trumbull, Henry Clay. *War Memories of an Army Chaplain.* Scribner's, N.Y., 1898, cloth, 421 pp., illus. with photos and by Z.

93 Wallace, Andrew. *The Image of Arizona, Pictures from the Past.* New Mexico, Albuquerque, (1971), words "First Edition" on copyright page, cloth, pic. endsheets, 224 pp., introduction, bibliography, index, numerous illus. including two, pp. 134 and 141, by Z. (Dixon, Remington)

94 Westermeier, Clifford P. *Colorado's First Portrait: Scenes by Early Artists.* New Mexico, Albuquerque, 1970, words "First Edition" on copyright page, cloth, pic. endsheets, 206 pp., preface, numerous illus. including three, pp. 34 (two) and 35, by Z. (Remington)

95 Zogbaum, Rufus Fairchild. *Horse, Foot, and Dragoons, Sketches of Army Life at Home and Abroad.* Harper, N.Y., 1888, decor. cloth, gilt top, brown endsheets, 176 pp., 76 illus. including "The Company Guidon" on tissue, mounted as the frontis., by the author.

96 ———. *"All Hands," Pictures of Life in the United States Navy.* Harper, N.Y. and London, 1897, folio, 36 plates (6 double) by Z.

97 ———. *The Junior Officer of the Watch.* Appleton, N.Y., 1908, words "Published March, 1908," on copyright page and code number (1) on last page of text, decor. cloth, 311 pp., four illus., frontis. and facing pp. 140, 196 and 292, by Z.

The Artist and His Art

98 Alter, Judith MacBain. "Rufus Zogbaum and the Frontier West," an article in *Montana* (the Magazine of Western History) 23:4, October 1973, with fifteen illus. by Z.

99 Bell, Colonel William Gardner. "Rufus Fairchild Zogbaum," an article in *Corral Dust*, Spring 1965, with one illus. by Z. and a photo of him.

100 Burke, W. J. and Howe, Will D. *American Authors and Books, 1640–1940.* Gramercy Pub. Co., N.Y.,

(1943), cloth, 858 pp., lists two books written and illus. by Z. on p. 857.

101 Dykes, Jeff C. *High Spots of Western Illustrating.* The Kansas City Posse, The Westerners, Kansas City, Mo., 1963, cloth, 30 pp., two illus., item nos. 16, 22, 33 and 90 (above) are included in the High Spots. Limited and signed edition of 250 copies. An edition in wraps was distributed to members.

102 Fielding, Mantle. *Dictionary of American Painters, Sculptors and Engravers.* N.Y., 1926, cloth, 433 pp., brief biographical sketch, pp. 422–23, of Z.

103 ———. Same, but with an Addendum, compiled and published by James F. Carr, N.Y., 1965, cloth, 529 pp., but no additional information on Z.

104 Krakel, Dean and Hedgpeth, Don. "Short Grass, Stetson and Paint Brushes: A Survey of Cowboy Art," an article in *Persimmon Hill,* Summer 1971, with one illus. by Z. (Borein, James, Remington, Russell, Smith)

105 McCracken, Harold. *Portrait of the Old West.* Mc-Graw-Hill, N.Y. etc., (1952), words "First Edition" on copyright page, decor. cloth, 232 pp., preface, "Foreword" by R. W. G. Vail, biographical check list of Western artists, numerous illus., biographical sketch of Z. on p. 227. (Miller, Remington, Russell, Schreyvogel)

106 *Painters of the West.* Charles W. Bowers Memorial Museum, Santa Ana, Calif., March 5–30, 1972, pic. wraps, unpaged, fifteen illus., biographical sketch of Z. (Johnson, Koerner, Miller, Remington, Russell)

107 Pennell, Joseph. *Pen Drawing and Pendraughtsmen.* Macmillan, London and N.Y. (but printed in Edinburgh), 1889, boards, 318 pp., preface, introduction, index, errata, numerous illus., praises Z.'s art, p. 200, slipcase. (Lungren, Remington)

108 Russell, Don. *Custer's Last, or, The Battle of the Little Big Horn in Picturesque Perspective.* (Amon Carter Museum of Western Art, Ft. Worth, Texas, 1968), cloth, 67 pp., "Preface" by Barbara Tyler (Curator of History), bibliography, illus., brief discussion of Z.'s art, pp. 44–5. (Deming, Dunton, Russell)

109 Weintenkampf, F. *American Graphic Art.* Henry Holt, N.Y., 1912, words "Published October, 1912" on copyright page, cloth, gilt top, 372 pp., "A Word of Explanation," index, illus., comments on Z.'s art, p. 225. (Keller)

110 *Who's Who in America.* A. N. Marquis Co., Chicago, a number of volumes (or editions) include a biographical sketch of Z. beginning with no. 7.

111 Zogbaum, Rufus Fairchild. "War Pictures in Times of Peace," an article in *Harper's New Monthly Magazine* 67:399, August 1883, with eleven illus. by Z. (the artist accompanies the French troops on maneuvers, 1882).

112 ———. "A Day's 'Drive' with Montana Cow-boys," an article in *Harper's New Monthly Magazine,* July, 1885, (the artist seeks local color), three illus. by Z.

113 ———. "As an Artist Saw Western RR Travel," an article in *American History Illustrated,* November 1968, with one illus. by Z.

114 Zogbaum, Rufus Fairchild (Rear Admiral, U.S.N.). *From Sail to Saratoga: A Naval Autobiography.* Privately printed, Rome, n.d., cloth, 466 pp., frontis. portrait of the author, much on his father, also on Frederic Remington.

FIFTY GREAT WESTERN ILLUSTRATORS
WAS SET IN LINOTYPE ALDUS
WITH PALATINO DISPLAY
AND PRINTED ON NEKOOSA NATURAL TEXT
BOUND AT ROSWELL BOOKBINDING IN PHOENIX